About the Author

John W. Santrock received his Ph.D. from the College of Education and Human Development at the University of Minnesota. He taught at the University of Charleston and the University of Georgia before joining the faculty at the University of Texas at Dallas. He has worked as a school psychologist and currently teaches educational psychology at the undergraduate level. In 2006, John received the University of Texas at Dallas Excellence in teaching award. John's grandmother taught all grades in a one-room school for many years and his father was superintendent of a large school district. John's research has included publications in the *Journal of Educational Psychology* that focus on the contextual aspects of affectively toned cognition and children's self-regulatory behavior as well as teachers' perceptions of children from divorced families. He has been a member of

John Santrock, teaching in his undergraduate educational psychology class, in which he makes good use of small-group discussion.

the editorial boards of *Child Development* and *Developmental Psychology*. His publications include these leading McGraw-Hill texts: *Child Development* (11th ed.), *Adolescence* (11th ed.), *Life-Span Development* (11th ed.), and *Psychology* (7th ed.).

For the educators in my family:
My wife, Mary Jo, a teacher; my father,
John F. Santrock, Jr., a teacher,
principal, and superintendent of
schools; my mother, Ruth Smith
Santrock, an administrative
assistant; my grandmother, Della
Karnes Santrock, who taught
all grades in a one-room
school; and John F. Santrock,
Sr., a principal.

Brief Contents

Contents

CHAPTER 3

Social Contexts and Socioemotional Development   69

CHAPTER 4

Individual Variations   113

C H A P T E R   5

Sociocultural Diversity   143

CHAPTER 8

The Information-Processing Approach   262

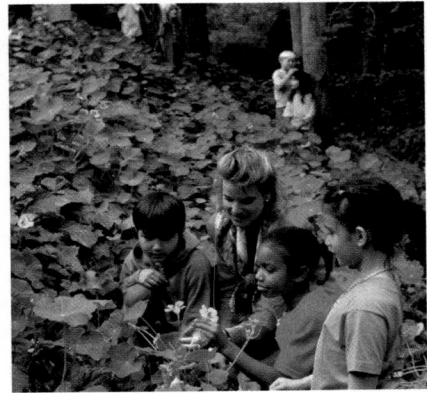

CHAPTER 11

Learning and Cognition in the Content Areas   364

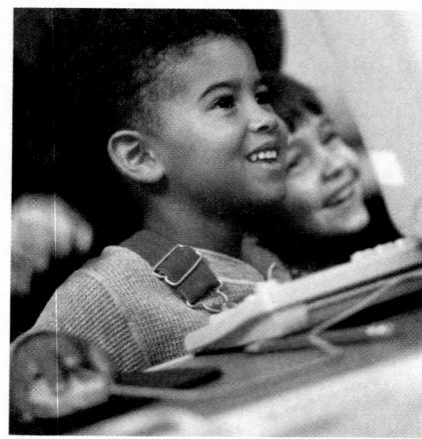

CHAPTER 12

Planning, Instruction, and Technology   405

CHAPTER 13

Motivation, Teaching, and Learning   449

C H A P T E R   1 4

Managing the Classroom   488

CHAPTER 15

Standardized Tests and Teaching   530

CHAPTER 16

Classroom Assessment   565

List of Features

SELF-ASSESSMENT

TECHNOLOGY AND EDUCATION

CRACK THE CASE

Expert Consultants for Educational Psychology, 3rd Ed.

Educational psychology has become an enormous, complex field and no single author, or even several authors, can possibly keep up with the rapidly changing content in the many different areas of the field. To solve this problem, author John Santrock sought the input of leading experts about content in many different areas of educational psychology. The experts provided detailed evaluations and recommendations for a chapter(s) or content in their area(s) of expertise. The biographies and photographs of the experts, who literally represent a who's who list in the field of educational psychology, follow.

Joyce Epstein

Joyce Epstein is Director of the Center on School, Family, and Community Partnerships and the National Network of Partnership Schools (NNPS), Principal Research Scientist, and Research Professor of Sociology at Johns Hopkins University. She has over one hundred publications. Her recent books include *School, Family, and Community Partnerships: Your Handbook for Action,* second edition; and *School, Family, and Community Partnerships: Preparing Educators and Improving Schools.* Dr. Epstein is known internationally for her research and development on family and community involvement. She serves on numerous editorial boards and advisory panels, and received the 2005 American Orthopsychiatric Association's Blanche F. Ittleson Award for scholarship and service to strengthen school and family connections. In all of her work, she has a passionate interest in connecting research, policy, and practice.

"The text is readable, informative, and up to date. Chapters provide a great deal of information, along with useful teaching strategies and opportunities to review and reflect on what is learned."

—JOYCE EPSTEIN

Dale Schunk

Dale Schunk is a leading expert on children's learning and motivation in educational settings. He is Dean of Education and Professor of Curriculum and Instruction at the University of North Carolina at Greensboro. He received his Ph.D. from Stanford University. Previously, he was a faculty member at the University of Houston, the University of North Carolina, and Purdue University (where he was head of the Department of Educational Studies). Dr. Schunk has published over 95 articles and chapters, is author of *Learning Theories: An Educational Perspective,* co-author with Paul Pintrich of *Motivation in Education: Theories, Research, and Applications,* and has edited several books on education and self-regulation. His awards include the Distinguished Service Award from Purdue University School of Education, the Early Contributions Award in Educational Psychology from the American Psychological Association, and the Albert J. Harris Research Award from the International Reading Association.

"Overall, this is one of the strongest educational psychology texts on the market. The author understands the material well and knows how to exemplify it for prospective teachers. In working with students, I find this to be a major problem—they understand the concepts but cannot think of ways to apply the ideas to teaching. John Santrock has done an excellent job in bridging the gap between theory/research and practice. . . . There are no real weaknesses of these chapters. . . . I will definitely recommend adoption of this text to my colleagues."

—DALE SCHUNK

James Kauffman

James Kauffman is a leading expert on children who are exceptional learners and special education. He is Professor Emeritus of Education at the University of Virginia. He is currently Director of Doctoral Study in Special Education at the University of Virginia and teaches a seminar in special education. Dr. Kauffman received his Ed.D. in special education from the University of Kansas and he is a past-president of the Council for Children with Behavioral Disorders (CCBD). He is also a former teacher in both general elementary and special education for students with emotional and behavioral disorders. Dr. Kauffman is author or co-author of numerous publications in special education, including the following books: *Characteristics of Emotional and Behavioral Disorders of Children and Youth; Learning Disabilities: Foundations, Characteristics, and Effective Teaching; Special Education: What It Is and Why We Need It;* and *Children and Youth with Emotional and Behavioral Disorders: A History of Their Education.*

> "I am amazed at John Santrock's current coverage. . . . As a text author, I'm aware of having to choose what to cover and what to say. If I were teaching this course, I think Santrock's book (at least based on this chapter—6) would be my choice."
>
> —JAMES KAUFFMAN

Barbara McCombs

Barbara McCombs is a leading expert on learner-centered psychological principles and school reform. She is a Senior Researcher at the University of Denver Research Institute located on the University of Denver's campus in Denver, Colorado. Dr. McCombs currently directs a new Human Motivation, Learning, and Development Center at the Denver Research Institute, which focuses on Professional Development of Educators, School Violence Prevention, Systemic Educational Reform, and Personal and Organizational Change. Her current research focuses on new models of teaching and learning, including transformational teacher development approaches and the use of technology as a primary tool for empowering youth. Dr. McCombs is the lead author on the highly acclaimed *Learner-Centered Psychological Principles: Guidelines for School Redesign and Reform,* which is disseminated by the American Psychological Association's Task Force on Psychology in Education. Dr. McCombs also has authored numerous journal articles and chapters in edited books. She has described a K–20 seamless professional development model in her book, *The Learner-Centered Classroom and School: Strategies for Enhancing Student Motivation and Achievement.* She also co-edits a series for the American Psychological Association, *Psychology in the Classroom,* and is currently working on a co-authored book, *Learner-Centered Practice and Assessments.*

> "I reviewed all 16 chapters in depth as well as took a detailed look at chapter 10. My overall assessment is that this is a very well done and comprehensive book in terms of coverage and organization. . . . John Santrock's text does a good job of covering constructivist and innovative programs."
>
> —BARBARA MCCOMBS

Richard Mayer

Richard Mayer is one of the leading experts on the application of cognitive psychology to children's education. Dr. Mayer is a Professor of Psychology at the University of California, Santa Barbara (UCSB), where he has served since 1975. He received a Ph.D. in psychology from the University of Michigan in 1973. His current research involves the intersection of cognition, instruction, and technology with a special focus on multimedia learning and problem solving. He is past-president of the Division of Educational Psychology of the American Psychological Association, former editor of the *Educational Psychologist,* and former co-editor of *Instructional Science,* former Chair of the UCSB Department of Psychology, and the year 2000 recipient of the E. L. Thorndike Award for career achievement in educational psychology. He was ranked #1 as the most productive educational psychologist for 1991–2001 (*Contemporary Educational Psychology*). Dr. Mayer is on the editorial boards of 11 journals, mainly in educational psychology, and has authored 18 books and more than 250 articles and chapters, including *The Promise of Educational Psychology: Vols. 1 and 2* (1999, 2002), *Multimedia Learning* (2001), *Learning and Instruction* (2003), *E-Learning and the Science of Instruction* (with R. Clark, 2003), and the *Cambridge Handbook of Multimedia Learning* (editor, 2005).

"Overall, this is a fine chapter (11) and I commend John Santrock for a job well done. . . . the chapter is written in a highly readable style, in which the author embeds the material within familiar teaching contexts. Many students will appreciate the friendly, hands-on, practical approach."

—RICHARD MAYER

Carolyn Evertson

Carolyn Evertson is a leading expert on classroom management and is Professor of Education Emerita at Peabody College, Vanderbilt University, where she is Director of *COMP: Creating Conditions for Learning,* a nationally disseminated program for helping teachers with classroom management, which has provided classroom management support for over 70,000 teachers. She received her Ph.D. from the University of Texas, Austin, and has published more than 100 articles and chapters on classroom management and supporting students' social and academic learning in school environments. She has authored or co-authored two texts, *Classroom Management for Elementary Teachers* and *Classroom Management for Middle and High School Teachers,* currently in their seventh editions and is co-editor (with Carol Weinstein) (2006) of the *Handbook of Classroom Management: Research, Practice and Contemporary Issues.*

". . . John Santrock's book is an excellent teaching tool combining a variety of media, reflection questions, problems, cases, assessments, and lists, to engage students. I would recommend it to my colleagues."

—CAROLYN EVERTSON

Carlos Díaz

Carlos Díaz is a leading expert on diversity and education. He is a Professor of Education at Florida Atlantic University in Boca Raton, where he received his Ed.D. in curriculum and instruction. Dr. Díaz is currently Project Director for the Master of Education in Cultural Foundations with E.S.O.L. endorsement program. He also has been a visiting professor at the University of Washington in Seattle. Dr. Díaz has authored a number of articles, chapters, and books, including these books: *Touch the Future: Teach!* (2006), *Multicultural Education in the 21st Century,* and *Global Perspectives for Educators.* He has received numerous awards, such as the Teaching Incentive Program Award, University Award for Excellence in Undergraduate Teaching, Professor of the Year, Notable America Men award, and recognition in *Who's Who Among Hispanic Americans, Rising Young Americans, and American Education.*

> "I feel that John Santrock's text does a better job of representing diversity issues than any educational psychology text I have read."
>
> —CARLOS DÍAZ

Karen Swan

Karen Swan is a leading expert on technology. She is Professor of Instructional Technology and RCET Professor in the Research Center for Educational Technology at Kent State University. Dr. Swan's research focuses mainly on technology and learning, an area in which she has published and presented widely. She has authored several hypermedia programs including *Set On Freedom: The American Civil Rights Movement,* co-edited books on *Social Learning from Broadcast Television* and *Ubiquitous Computing in Education,* and is currently working on a DVD on the latter topic. She served as a project director on several large scale grants including work for the U.S. Department of Education, the National Science Foundation, and the New York City Board of Education. Dr. Swan is an effective practices editor for the Sloan Consortium on Asynchronous Learning Networks, the special issues editor for the *Journal of Educational Computing Research,* and editor of the online, multimedia *Journal of the Research Center for Educational Technology.*

> "I think the real strength of John Santrock's text is the way it contextualizes educational psychology within a teaching context. Often it is hard to make teachers, or pre-service teachers see the relevance of learning principles, they think are too abstract. This text makes abstract theory more concrete and more relevant for teachers. Especially useful are application strategies and links to teaching portfolios and the PRAXIS™exam."
>
> —KAREN SWAN

James McMillan

James McMillan is a leading expert on assessment. He is Professor and Chair, Department of Foundations of Education at Virginia Commonwealth University in Richmond, Virginia, and Director of the Metropolitan Educational Research Consortium. He is author of *Classroom Assessment: Principles and Practice for Effective Instruction,* fourth edition, and *Essential Assessment Concepts for Teachers and Administrators,* and he also has authored books in educational psychology and educational research. Some of his publications include articles in *Educational Measurement, Educational Horizons, Educational and Psychological Measurement, Journal of Educational Psychology,* and the *American Educational Research Journal.* Dr. McMillan is currently investigating links between classroom assessment, grading practices, and student motivation. For the past several years, he has been active in Virginia's state testing and accountability program. Dr. McMillan also direts the Metropolitan Educational Research Consortium, a university/public school partnership that conducts and disseminates action research.

"John Santrock's material on NCLB is very well done and accurate . . . (and) overall these three chapters (1, 15, and 16) are very well done, accurate, with a friendly writing style."

—JAMES MCMILLAN

Gary Bitter

Gary Bitter is a leading expert on educational technology. He is a Professor of Educational Technology and Executive Director for Technology Based Learning and Research at Arizona State University. He earned his Ph.D. in mathematics and computer education at the University of Denver. Dr. Bitter's research and development of digital curricula and professional development materials are designed to transform pre-K–12 learning environments. Dr. Bitter has published more than 200 articles and books in the areas of educational technology, mathematics education, the professional development of teachers, and presented an estimated 1,200 talks to state, national, and international organizations. As the founding board member and first-elected president of the International Society for Technology in Education, he helped to redefine the boundaries of the pre-K–12 classrooms by forming a network of dedicated professionals sharing classroom-proven solutions to address the challenge of infusing technologies across the curriculum.

". . . I would definitely recommend course adoption of John Santrock's text to my colleagues. I like the layout and the ease of use. . . . Of course, a strength is the technology coverage."

—GARY BITTER

Preface

It is gratifying that the first two editions of *Educational Psychology* have been so well received. Preparing the third edition has been both highly rewarding and challenging: rewarding because I continue to learn more about educating students and because the feedback from students and instructors has been consistently enthusiastic; a challenge because of the need to continue meeting or exceeding instructors' expectations and keeping the material fresh and up to date.

One of my goals for each edition of *Educational Psychology* has been to write a book that students say this about:

> "I love this book."
>
> "I am using many of the ideas from my educational psychology text in my teaching and they are working great!"
>
> "I teach in the inner city, and my educational psychology text is a great resource for me. The focus on diversity and technology have been extremely useful. I am enriched by the book."

These comments come from Jennifer Holliman-McCarthy, Richard Harvell, and Greg Hill, who have used this text in their educational psychology course and gone on to become public school teachers.

Another goal I have had for each edition of *Educational Psychology* has been to write a book that instructors say this about:

> "I wasn't prepared to like this text. In general, ed psych texts are all too predictable. While people claim to be innovative, in the end they are not. In contrast, John Santrock's text is a big WOW! His book is different. It is written for the prospective teacher and not the future educational psychologist."
>
> "Those who are not using Santrock have not seen it. Please communicate my sincere enjoyment of this quality text to John Santrock."

These comments come from educational psychology instructors Randy Lennon, University of Northern Colorado, and Robert Brown, Florida Atlantic University–Boca Raton.

To continue to meet or exceed instructors' expectations and to keep the material fresh and up to date, I have made a number of key changes, which I describe next.

EMPHASIS ON PREPARING FOR PRACTICE AND PRAXIS™

In the second edition Classroom Update of *Educational Psychology*, I increased the number of opportunities for students to prepare for their practice as teachers and for the PRAXIS II™ *Principles of Learning and Teaching (PLT)* test. I greatly expanded this emphasis in this new third edition. Integrated into the third edition are many Best Practices that new teachers can adopt and numerous activities to help them do well on state standards-based tests, such as PRAXIS II™.

Best Practices. A number of times in each chapter students will read Best Practices: Strategies for . . . interludes that provide extensive, detailed recommendations that students can use when they become teachers. The format of this feature has been changed to provide better integration with comments from outstanding teachers. Thus, Through the Eyes of Teachers, which in the second edition was included as separate boxed inserts, is now integrated into the Best Practices interludes to provide a more seamless and linked presentation of strategies and examples for improving students' education. Further, a number of new Best Practices interludes have been created throughout the book and others expanded with new entries and more detailed descriptions of successful teaching strategies. Also, a number of new Through the Eyes of Teachers commentaries were obtained for the third edition of the book and have been embedded in the Best Practices interludes.

PRAXIS™ and State Standards–Based Tests. The use of external standards-based tests to assess the competence of both students and teachers is one of the most dramatic educational reforms in decades. The third edition of *Educational Psychology* gives considerably more attention to standards-based tests and No Child Left Behind legislation, beginning with an overview in chapter 1 and then further integration into other chapters where appropriate.

To give prospective teachers an opportunity to practice answering PRAXIS™-type items, a PRAXIS™ Practice section has been added to the Review and Reflect feature of the second edition and renamed Review, Reflect, and Practice in the third edition. This feature is aligned with the text's B-level (second-level) headings in each chapter in that students answer a PRAXIS™-type item for each of these headings. PRAXIS™-type items have also been added to many of the case studies at the end of each chapter.

The Practice and PRAXIS™ Package. Further integration of PRAXIS™ and state standards-based material into the package for *Educational Psychology,* third edition, involves an extensive array of media resources that will help students prepare for practice and a study guide for PRAXIS™. These are described further in the Ancillaries section of this Preface.

CONTENT AND CONTEMPORARY RESEARCH

Another important goal I have had for each edition of this text is to include solid content and research that is very up to date.

Recent Content and Research. The third edition of *Educational Psychology* presents the latest content and research, and includes more than 1,800 citations from the twenty-first century with more than 500 of these coming from 2005, 2006, and 2007. Later in the Preface I will highlight the main content and research additions on a chapter-by-chapter basis.

Expert Content and Research Consultants. Ten expert consultants provided author John Santrock with detailed content about the content of a chapter or chapters in their area(s) of expertise. The photographs and biographies of the experts appear on pp. xxi to xxv. The expert consultants for *Educational Psychology,* 3rd ed., were:

Joyce Epstein *The Johns Hopkins University*

Dale Schunk *University of North Carolina–Greensboro*

James Kauffman *University of Virginia*

Barbara McCombs *Denver Research Institute*

Richard Mayer *University of California–Santa Barbara*

Carolyn Evertson *Vanderbilt University*

Carlos Díaz *Florida Atlantic University*

Karen Swan *Kent State University*

James McMillan *Virginia Commonwealth University*

Gary Bitter *Arizona State University*

ACCESSIBILITY AND INTEREST

The new edition of this text should be accessible to students because of the extensive rewriting, organization, and learning system.

Writing and Organization. Every sentence, paragraph, section, and chapter of this book was carefully examined and when appropriate revised and rewritten. The result is a much clearer, better-organized presentation of material in this new edition.

The Learning System. I strongly believe that students should not only be challenged to study hard and think more deeply and productively about educational psychology, but should also be provided with an effective learning system. Instructors and students have commented about how student-friendly this book has become.

Now more than ever, students struggle to find the main ideas in their courses, especially in courses like educational psychology, which include so much material. The learning system centers on learning goals that, together with the main text headings, keep the key ideas in front of the reader from the beginning to the end of the chapter. Each chapter has no more than six main headings and corresponding learning goals, which are presented side-by-side in the chapter-opening spread. At the end of each main section of a chapter, the learning goal is repeated in a feature called Review, Reflect, and Practice, which prompts students to review the key topics in the section and poses a question to encourage them to think critically about what they have read. In addition, as indicated earlier, the Review and Reflect section also includes multiple-choice PRAXIS™-type items that give students an opportunity to practice answering the types of questions that are on state standards-based tests. At the end of the chapter, under the heading Reach Your Learning Goals, the learning goals summary guides students through a chapter review. In addition to the verbal tools just described, mini–chapter maps that link up with the learning goals are presented at the beginning of each major section in the chapter. A visual presentation of the learning system is presented later in the Preface in a section titled To the Student.

Other Learning Features. A number of other learning features help students to learn about educational psychology and ways to become an effective teacher. These include:

- *Best Practices Interludes* This very important feature highlights the emphasis on translating theory/research for effective teaching in the classroom. This feature appears a number of times in each chapter. New to this edition is the integration of Through the Eyes of Teachers, which provides descriptions of best practices by outstanding teachers, into the Best Practices interludes at appropriate places.
- *Teaching Stories* Each chapter opens with a high-interest story about one or more teachers related to the chapter's content.

- **Self-Assessments** These encourage students to examine their characteristics and skills related to the content of the chapter.
- **Diversity and Education Interludes** Diversity continues to be an important theme in the third edition. Chapter 5 is entirely devoted to sociocultural diversity, and each chapter has a Diversity and Education interlude, which is integrated into the text material, following immediately after material relevant to a diversity topic is presented.
- **Technology Boxes** In addition to the discussion of technology in the text of many chapters, each chapter has a Technology and Education box related to the chapter's content. A majority of the Technology and Education boxes are either new or have been significantly updated and expanded through the contributions of leading education technology expert, Karen Swan of Kent State University.
- **Case Studies** This full-page feature entitled Crack the Case presents high-interest case study descriptions followed by a number of questions, including multiple-choice PRAXIS™-type questions that are new in this edition.
- **Portfolio Activities** At the end of each chapter, four Portfolio Activities related to the chapter's content are presented. They are organized into three categories for instructors' ease of use: Independent Reflection, Collaborative Work, and Research/Field Experience. Each Portfolio Activity is coded to a specific INTASC standard.
- **Taking It to the Net** An extensive effort was made to create Internet activities that will provide meaningful learning experiences for students.
- **Through the Eyes of Students** These inserts that appear in most chapters give students an opportunity to see learning, teaching, and classroom experiences from the viewpoint of students.

CHAPTER-BY-CHAPTER CONTENT CHANGES

CHAPTER 1:
Educational Psychology: A Tool for Effective Teaching

- New section on engaging in developmentally appropriate teaching practices (Darling-Hammond & Bransford, 2005; Horowitz & others, 2005)
- New coverage of the importance of having high achievement expectations for students (Wigfield & others, 2006)

- Expanded and updated discussion of constructivist and direction instruction teaching practices with an emphasis on how many effective teachers use competent versions of both types of practices (Darling-Hammond & Bransford, 2005)
- New section on assessment skills under effective teaching, including new material on standards-based instruction (McMillan, 2007)
- New discussion of accountability, No Child Left Behind legislation, and the PRAXIS™ exam in the new section on assessment and the introduction to standardized tests (Essex, 2006; Phelps, 2005)
- Expanded coverage of Goal Setting and Instructional Planning section (Darling-Hammond & others, 2005)
- New section, Paying More Than Lip Service to Individual Variations, including coverage of the concept of differentiated instruction (Hallahan & Kauffman, 2006; Tomlinson, 2001; Winner, 2006)
- Expanded and updated coverage of issues and research on gender and ethnicity in educational psychology (Parke & Buriel, 2006; Wigfield & others, 2006)
- Update of percentage of students from low-income backgrounds that have computers in their homes
- Expanded and updated Technology and Education box on technology, schools, and communities (IBM, 2006; LISC, 2005; Zucker & McGhee, 2005)
- New Through the Eyes of Teachers insert, Paul August, "Finding Individuality in Diversity"
- At request of adopters and reviewers, considerably reduced length of research section to improve student motivation

CHAPTER 2:
Cognitive and Language Development

- Extensive rewriting of chapter for improved flow and student understanding
- New section, Developmental Issues, that focuses on nature-nurture, continuity-discontinuity, and early-later experience (Gottlieb, Wahlsten, & Lickliter, 2006; Kagan & Fox, 2006; Thelen & Smith, 2006)
- New section, Development and Education, that describes developmentally appropriate teaching practices and the concept of splintered development (Horowitz & others, 2005)
- Updated and expanded discussion of brain lateralization (Jabbour & others, 2005; Patararia & others, 2005)
- Much expanded coverage of changes in the brain, including intriguing recent research on the development of the amygdala and prefrontal cortex in

adolescence (Dahl, 2004; Nelson, 2005; Nelson, Thomas, & de Hahn, 2006)

- New section on plasticity in the brain (Bransford & others, 2005; Nelson, Thomas, & de Haan, 2006)
- Revised and expanded coverage of Piaget's concept of schemes.
- New Through the Eyes of Teachers insert, "Stimulating Students' Thinking and Discovery"
- Expanded and updated coverage of the zone of proximal development, including a new, extensive example of this concept
- Expanded discussion of scaffolding
- Expanded material on description of private speech with examples
- New Through the Eyes of Teachers insert, "Using Dialogue and Reframing Concepts to Find the Zone of Proximal Development"
- Added criticisms of Vygotsky's approach
- Significant updating and rewriting of the nature of language and its rule systems for improved understanding based on input from leading expert Jean Berko Gleason (2005)
- New coverage of metalinguistic awareness
- Description of recent study indicating the importance of vocabulary in second-grade students' reading comprehension (Berninger & Abbott, 2005)
- Expanded discussion of language development in adolescence
- New Best Practices interlude, "Strategies for Vocabulary Development"

CHAPTER 3:
Social Contexts and Socioemotional Development

- New Through the Eyes of Teachers insert on having students use classroom materials to construct a self-portrait as a means of exploring their identity
- New section on family management practices and students' academic and achievement behavior at school, including a recent research study with African American families (Taylor & Lopez, 2005)
- Updated and expanded coverage of Joyce Epstein's (2005; Sheldon & Epstein, 2005) ideas on school-family-community partnerships, including coverage of her overlapping spheres of influence theory and its ties to Bronfenbrenner's theory
- New discussion of ethnic variations in parenting styles and the adaptive styles of Asian American, African American, and Latino families (Chao, 2005; Harrision-Hale, McLoyd, & Smedley, 2004)

- New section on out-of-school care, including recent research studies on the importance of type of care (NICHD Early Child Care Research Network, 2004; The Wallace Foundation, 2004)
- Updated and expanded Technology and Education box that includes recent ideas about why there is a link between the amount of TV children watch and lower achievement in school (Comstock & Scharrer, 2006)
- Discussion of a recent successful intervention study to improve the social skills of rejected children (DeRosier & Marcus, 2005)
- New discussion of recent longitudinal research on the outcomes of not having a friend (Wentzel, Barry, & Caldwell, 2004)
- New discussion of controversy in early childhood education regarding academic emphasis
- Coverage of current consideration by the U.S. Congress of infusing Project Head Start with a stronger academic focus and commentary by early childhood experts about some concerns with this academic emphasis
- Revised and updated coverage of Turning Points recommendations for improving middle schools
- Inclusion of information from recent review of effective school dropout programs (Lehrer & others, 2003) and new discussion of gender differences in school dropout rates and revised estimates of the dropout rate for Native American youth
- Updated and expanded coverage of the "I Have a Dream" Program ("I Have a Dream" Foundation, 2005).
- Description of findings from the recent Indiana University High School Survey of Student Engagement (2004)
- Much expanded coverage of self-esteem, including discussion of recent concern that too many children grow up receiving empty praise as part of an effort to raise their self-esteem, which can harm their school achievement (Graham, 2005; Stipek, 2005), variation in self-esteem across domains, and increased differentiation of self-esteem in adolescence (Harter, 2006)
- Revised and updated coverage of culture, ethnicity, and identity
- New section on ethnic identity with a special focus on immigrant children's ethnic identity and recent research on ethnic identity, school engagement, and school success (Fuligni, Witkow, & Garcia, 2005; Lee, 2005)
- New section that describes the surge of interest in what constitutes a moral personality (Blasi, 2005; Lapsley & Narvaez, 2006)
- Expanded coverage of character education (Lapsley & Narvaez, 2006; Walker, 2002)

- New discussion of the controversy regarding Gilligan's care perspective
- Updated and expanded discussion of service learning (Benson & others, 2006)

CHAPTER 4:
Individual Variations

- Expanded coverage of Sternberg's triarchic theory of intelligence including discussion of his Triarchic Abilities Test
- New Through the Eyes of Teachers insert, "Giving Students a Choice of Which Type of Intelligence They Want to Use for a Project"
- Description of the recently developed Mayer-Salovey-Caruso Emotional Intelligence Test
- Expanded and updated evaluation of the controversy about whether intelligence is better conceptualized as general intelligence or multiple intelligences (Birney & others, 2005; Chiappi & MacDonald, 2005)
- Expanded and updated coverage of intervention programs for increasing intelligence (Ramey, Ramey, & Lanzi, 2006)
- New discussion of stereotype threat as a potential factor in cultural bias in intelligence testing (Sackett, Hardison, & Cullen, 2004; Steele & Aronson, 2004)
- New Through the Eyes of Teachers insert, "Paying Attention to the Details"
- Expanded and updated coverage of the key dimensions of temperament (Kagan, 2006; Rothbart & Bates, 2006)
- Expanded and updated discussion of teaching strategies involving students' temperament (Keogh, 2003)

CHAPTER 5:
Sociocultural Diversity

- New section on how adolescents in the United States, Europe, and East Asia spend their time (Larson & Verma, 1999; Larson & Wilson, 2004)
- Updated and expanded Technology and Education box, "Technology Connections with Students Around the World" (Swan & others, 2006)
- Much expanded and updated coverage of poverty and children's development, including information from a recent research review (Evans, 2004)
- New Through the Eyes of Teachers insert, "Daily After-School Reading Club for Students in a High-Poverty School"

- Coverage of recent study on parents' educational aspirations and adolescents' educational outcomes in low-income families (Schoon, Parsons, & Sacker, 2004)
- Significant updating and revision of bilingual education material based on a recent research review (Snow & Kang, 2006)
- Expansion of section on differences and diversity to include recent research on recognizing legitimate ethic differences and not being "color-blind" (Schofield, 2003)
- Discussion of two recent studies documenting that students in predominantly ethnic minority schools have far fewer resources than their counterparts in largely non-White schools (Oakes & Saunders, 2002; Shields & others, 2001)
- Coverage of Jonathan Kozol's (2005) recent book *The Shame of the Nation,* which portrays the continuing educational segregation and inequities of many minority students living in low-income circumstances
- Expansion of the Culturally Relevant Teaching section to include the "funds of knowledge approach" (Moll & Gonzáles, 2004)
- New discussion of how students from ethnic minority and low-income backgrounds benefit from a combination of rigorous academic programs combined with culturally relevant teaching and community connections, including a recent research study that documents the benefits of this combination in Latino students (Gandara, 2002)
- New coverage of James Banks' (2003, 2006) emphasis on the importance of future teachers writing a brief essay about a situation in which they had been marginalized from a group
- Updated and expanded description of James Comer's (2004, 2005) views in light of the recent emphasis on high standards and accountability
- Expanded and updated coverage of issues involved in teaching core values (Díaz, 2005)
- Much expanded and updated discussion of developmental changes in gender stereotyping (Miller & Ruble, 2005; Ruble, Martin, & Berenbaum, 2006; Trautner & others, 2005)
- Extensively revised and updated coverage of gender differences in communication, including a recent meta-analysis of gender and talk and criticism of Tannen's view (Leaper & Smith, 2004)
- New section on gender and emotion, including descriptions of developmental changes (Ruble, Martin, & Berenbaum, 2006)
- New section on gender differences in prosocial behavior
- New discussion of research on same-sex education (Warrington & Younger, 2003)

- Recent research on gender-role classification and academic self-efficacy (Choi, 2004)
- Updated discussion of the controversy regarding the extent of gender differences, including a recent meta-analysis by Janet Shibley Hyde (2005)
- Coverage of recent research on differences in the gender socialization of Latino and Latina adolescents in the United States (Raffaelli & Ontai, 2004)
- Expanded and updated discussion of gender differences in the brain (Lippa, 2005)
- New description of changes from elementary school to high school in the number of girls in gifted programs (Banks & others, 2005; U.S. Office of Education 1999)

CHAPTER 6:
Learners Who Are Exceptional

- Updating of percentage of students with different disabilities who receive special education services in the United States, including new figures (National Center for Education Statistics, 2006)
- Substantial reorganization and ordering of various disabilities with learning disabilities and attention deficit hyperactivity disorder now being discussed at the beginning of the chapter because of their prevalence
- Updated coverage of the identification of learning disabilities and new discussion of the causes of learning disabilities (Litt & others, 2005; McCrory & others, 2005)
- New discussion of Virginia Berninger's (2006) view that students with a learning disability in reading or writing need explicit instruction along many fronts including phonological, orthographic, and morphological awareness, as well as her view on changes needed in special education
- New section on the autism spectrum disorders, including new key term definitions for autism spectrum disorders, autistic disorder, and Asperger syndrome, as well as coverage of the roles of brain functioning and heredity in these disorders (Baron-Cohen, 2004)
- Reorganization of learning disabilities material for improved understanding and research updating
- New section on dyscalculia
- New Through the Eyes of Teachers insert that emphasizes a team approach for working with students who have a learning disability
- Updated coverage and recent research on attention deficit hyperactivity disorder, including new description of how Ritalin and Adderall work (Reeves & Schweitzer, 2004)

- Updated and expanded discussion of the link between fetal alcohol syndrome and mental retardation, including description of a recent longitudinal study (Bailey & others, 2004; O'Leary, 2004)
- New section on specific language impairment (Ratner, 2005; Simpson & Rice, 2005)
- New coverage of the 2004 reauthorization of the Individuals with Disabilities Act and its alignment with No Child Left Behind legislation (Hallahan & Kauffman, 2006)
- New discussion of James Kauffman and his colleagues' (Kauffman & Hallahan, 2005; Kauffman, McGee, & Brigham, 2004) views that in some cases full inclusion has gone too far and that too often children with disabilities are not challenged to reach their full potential
- Updated coverage of the percentage of the placements of students with disabilities in different settings
- Updated and expanded Technology and Education box, "Technology and Special Needs Students" (Hetzroni & Shrieber, 2004; Swan & others, 2005)
- New section, the Life Course of the Gifted, that describes the roles of heredity and environment (especially deliberate practice) in translating gifted status into successful achievements
- Expanded discussion of accelerating the education of children who are gifted and a new Best Practices interlude, "Strategies for Working with Children Who Are Gifted" (Colangelo, Assouline, & Gross, 2004)
- New coverage of Joseph Renzulli's Schoolwide Enrichment Model for improving outcomes for children who are gifted and children who are not gifted

CHAPTER 7:
Behavioral and Social Cognitive Approaches

- New chapter-opening Teaching Story on special education teacher Ruth Sidney Charney's strategies for noticing students' positive efforts (Charney, 2005)
- New description of the importance of not just knowing the basic principles of learning and cognition, but also being able to judiciously use them to meet diverse learning goals in contexts where students need differ (Bransford & others, 2005)
- Updated and expanded discussion of research and the use of physical punishment (Ateah, 2005; Regaldo & others, 2004; Slade & Wissow, 2004)
- Updated percentage of male college students who say they plan to become an elementary or secondary school teacher (Sax & others, 2004)

- Updated statistics on percentage of total classroom teachers in relation to ethnicity and gender
- Discussion of study illustrating the positive effects of watching *Sesame Street* (Cole & others, 2003)
- New Best Practices interlude, "Strategies for Encouraging Students to Be Self-Regulated Learners" (Alexander, 2006; Gutherie, Wigfield, & Perencevich, 2004)

CHAPTER 8:
The Information-Processing Approach

- New section, Cognitive Resources: Capacity and Speed of Processing Information
- New stand-alone section on attention, including description of three types of attention and how attention changes developmentally
- Expanded coverage of working memory including research comparing the working memory of children and adolescents
- New section on fuzzy trace theory (Brainerd & Reyna, 2004; Reyna, 2004)
- Much expanded and updated section on adaptive expertise, including numerous examples of how adaptive expertise is an important characteristic of competent teachers (Bransford & others, 2006; Hammerness & others, 2005; Schwartz, Bransford, & Sears, 2006, in press)
- New discussion of Patricia Alexander's acclimation stage of expertise
- New section on the child's theory of mind (Wellman, 2004)
- New section on the development of metacognition in adolescence (Kuhn & Franklin, 2006)
- Expanded discussion of the importance of self-monitoring in metacognition (Pressley & Hilden, 2006)
- New coverage of Pressley and his colleagues' observations of how extensively and intensely teachers in elementary and secondary school classrooms use strategy instruction (Pressley & others, 2001, 2003, 2004)
- Expanded Best Practices interlude on helping students develop better strategies, including the importance of connecting strategy instruction with students' knowledge (Pressley & Hilden, 2006)

CHAPTER 9:
Complex Cognitive Processes

- Much expanded and updated coverage of reasoning, including research on developmental changes in inductive and deductive reasoning (Kuhn, 2006, in press; Kuhn & Franklin, 2006)
- Updated coverage of critical thinking and the importance of encouraging students to discuss controversial topics (Winn, 2004)
- New Technology and Education box on using digital "mindtools" to stimulate students' critical thinking
- New section on critical thinking in adolescence
- New section on developmental changes in problem solving (Siegler, 2006; Siegler & Alibali, 2005: Zelazo & others, 2003)
- Expanded Best Practices interlude, "Strategies for Improving Students' Problem Solving"
- Updated coverage of decision making and new subsection on decision making in adolescence (Klaczynski, 2005; Kuhn & Franklin, 2006)
- Expanded discussion of creative thinking, including recent research on brainstorming, domain aspects of creativity, and school/classroom design
- New discussion of "teaching for transfer" and what this might entail (Bransford & others, 2005; Schwartz, Bransford, & Sears, 2006, in press)
- New Through the Eyes of Teachers insert, Chris Laster, "Bringing Science Alive and Connecting Students to the Community"

CHAPTER 10:
Social Constructivist Approaches

- Updated information about increased efforts to connect technology and collaborative learning (Rummel & Spada, 2005; van Drie & others, 2005)
- Expanded and updated discussion of mentoring (Karcher & others, 2005)
- New coverage of two peer tutoring programs: Reciprocal Peer Tutoring and Classwide Peer Tutoring (Ginsburg-Block, 2005; Struckman, 2005)
- Description of recent research on the use of PALS with Spanish-speaking English language learners (Saenz, Fuchs, & Fuchs, 2005)
- New section on evaluating cooperative learning, including strengths and potential drawbacks (Blumenfeld, Kompler, & Krajcik, 2006)
- Updating of the Valued Youth Program (Intercultural Development Research Assocation, 2004)
- Updated coverage of Fostering a Community of Learners based on a recent evaluation by leading science education experts Richard Lehrer and Laura Schauble (2006)

- Updated and expanded Technology and Education box, "Computer-Supported Intentional Learning Environments (Knowledge Forum)"
- New Through the Eyes of Teachers insert: Fraser Randolph, "Creating Opportunities that are social but structured"

CHAPTER 11:
Learning and Cognition in the Content Areas

- New chapter-opening teaching story on Wendy Nelson Kauffman, who teaches social studies
- Expanded and updated discussion of expert knowledge and pedagogical content knowledge (Grossman, Schoenfeld, & Lee, 2005)
- New coverage of Rich Mayer's (2004) view of the three key cognitive processes involved in learning to read
- New section, Language Rule Systems, that describes the importance of phonology, syntax, morphology, and semantics in reading
- New discussion of the importance of having a good vocabulary in reading comprehension (Berninger & Abbott, 2005; Paris & Paris, 2006; Snow & Kang, 2006)
- New section on cognitive processes in math, including a discussion of conceptual understanding, procedural fluency, effective organization of knowledge, and metacognitive strategies (National Research Council, 2005)
- Coverage of recent research that involved videotapes of math instruction in different countries and the implications of this research for U.S. math teachers (Hiebert & others, 2003)
- New Best Practices interlude, "Strategies for Teaching Mathematics"
- New section on Kathleen Metz's (2004) view that science education should focus on deep inquiry in a limited number of rich content domains
- New section, Inquiry and Science Content Knowledge (Lehrer & Schauble, 2006)
- New Best Practices interlude, "Strategies for Teaching Science"
- New commentary by a high school history teacher about what he has learned about how to teach history effectively and its application to other content areas as well (Bain, 2005)
- New Technology and Education box, "Content Area–Specific Technology Applications," with extensive Internet sites to improve student learning in various content areas

CHAPTER 12:
Planning, Instruction, and Technology

- Much expanded and updated coverage of planning based on the ideas of Linda Darling-Hammond and her colleagues (2005), including commentary about planning in light of the increase in state standards, backward mapping, and scope and sequence
- Discussion of recent interviews with experienced teachers and what they thought was missing from their planning in their early years of teaching (Kunzmann, 2003)
- Coverage of recent study on mothers' affect and students' motivation to do homework (Pomerantz, Yang, & Ng, 2005)
- Discussion of recent review of research on discovery learning versus guided discovery learning (Mayer, 2004)
- Updated and expanded conclusions about teacher-centered direct instruction and learner-centered constructivist instruction (Bain, 2005; Darling-Hammond & others, 2005; Donovan & Bransford, 2005)
- Extensive revision of the discussion of technology and education by leading expert Karen Swan
- New introduction to technology discussion that describes three ways that technology affects teacher planning and instruction (Darling-Hammond & others, 2005)
- Updated statistics on computers and Internet access in schools (National Center for Education Statistics, 2005)
- New description of how teachers can use technology to transform learning in the classroom (Wiske, Franz, & Breit, 2005)
- Coverage of recent study on Internet access at home by students from different ethnic groups (Rideout, Roberts, & Foehr, 2005) and a recent study on linking various aspects of computer use to higher academic achievement in young African American students (Judge, 2005)
- New section, Teaching, Learning, and Technology, that describes five strategies for more effectively using technology to improve students' understanding (Wiske, Franz, & Breit, 2005)
- Updated and expanded discussion of the future of technology in schools, including recent research on the benefits of ubiquitous computing (Swan & others, 2006)
- New Through the Eyes of Students insert, "Future Technology Chat" (Threshold/ISTE Forum, 2004)
- Expanded self-assessment, "Evaluating My Technology Skills and Attitudes"

- Updated description of the best Web sites for obtaining information about how to improve your use of technology in the classroom

CHAPTER 13:
Motivation, Teaching, and Learning

- Coverage of recent study on intrinsic/extrinsic motivation and academic outcomes in third- to eighth-grade students (Lepper, Corpus, & Iyengar, 2005)
- New Technology and Education box, "Technology Integration, Authentic Tasks, Curiosity, and Interest" (Zucker & McGhee, 2005)
- New section on interest in the discussion of intrinsic motivation (Wigfield & others, 2006)
- New section, Cognitive Engagement and Self-Responsibility (Blumenfeld & others, 2006)
- New conclusions section on intrinsic and extrinsic motivation that emphasizes how too often they have been pitted against each other as polar opposites when in the real world they both are operating (Wigfield & others, 2006)
- New discussion of NCLB in terms of its likely encouragement of a performance rather than a mastery orientation on the part of students (Meece, Anderman, & Anderman, 2006)
- New section, Expectations, with material on students' expectations and teachers' expectations (National Research Council, 2004; Wigfield & others, 2006)
- Discussion of recent research on parents' provision of specific activities at home and the extent to which this influences students' choice of courses and extracurricular activities consistent with these activities in adolescence (Simpkins & others, 2004)
- Expanded and updated description of the importance of the meaningfulness of academic work in influencing students' motivation (National Research Council, 2004)
- Much expanded and extensively revised main section, Students with Achievement Problems
- New section, Students Who Procrastinate, including a number of strategies teachers can use to help students reduce or eliminate their procrastinating tendencies (University of Buffalo Counseling Services, 2005)
- New section, Students Who Are Perfectionists, including strategies teachers can use to help students overcome their perfectionist tendencies

CHAPTER 14:
Managing the Classroom

- New Through the Eyes of Students insert, "Forensics Teacher Tommie Lindsey's Students," in which students from impoverished backgrounds talk about Lindsey, who was awarded a McArthur fellowship in 2005 for his efforts in helping them succeed at public speaking and debate
- Updated coverage of Gallup Poll (Gallup Organization, 2004) results for the American public's view of the main problems in U.S. public schools
- New Technology and Education box, "Automating Classroom Management with Student Response Systems" (Swan, Kratcoski, & Miller, 2006; Vahey, Roschell, & Tatar, 2006)
- Expanded and updated coverage of research on bullying and teaching strategy recommendations for reducing bullying (Evertson & Weinstein, 2006; Fekkes, Pijpers, & Verloove-Vanhorick, 2004; Hyman & others, 2006; Limber, 2004; Milsom & Gallo, 2006)
- New discussion of the Steps to Respect bullying intervention program, including information about a recent longitudinal study demonstrating its effectiveness (Frey & others, 2005)
- New coverage of the Good Behavior Game, a school-based behavior management program, that has shown good results in reducing disruptive behavior (Van Lier & others, 2004)

CHAPTER 15:
Standardized Tests and Teaching

- New coverage of the No Child Left Behind legislation, including its potential contributions as well as criticisms (Goldberg, 2005; Houston, 2005)
- New section, Standardized Tests of Teacher Candidates, which includes information about the three types of PRAXIS™ tests, individual state tests, criticisms of the current tests of teacher candidates, and the call for a national teacher test (Darling-Hammond & Baratz-Snowden, 2005)
- New Technology and Education box, "Standardized Testing, Data-Driven Decision Making, and Handheld Computers" (Hupert & Heinze, 2006, in press)
- Updating of the National Assessment of Educational Progress (NAEP) with reports of the 2005 results for reading, math, and science (NAEP, 2005)
- New discussion of a recent proposal by the prestigious National Academy of Education (Darling-Hammond &

Baratz-Snowden, 2005) for a national test for prospective teachers

- Updated and expanded coverage of international comparisons of U.S. students with other countries in math and science (Gonzales & others, 2004)
- New description of how state standards-based scores are based on standard scores that are unique to each state

CHAPTER 16:
Classroom Assessment

- Coverage of new trend in using more multiple-choice items to prepare students for high-stakes standards-based tests (McMillan, 2007)
- Description of how formative assessment has become a buzzword with its emphasis on assessment for learning rather than of learning (Stiggins, 2006)
- New coverage of the importance of informative feedback in formative assessment, including new figure 16.2 on the do's and don'ts of using praise when giving feedback
- New discussion of how many teachers say they write higher-order thinking items when in reality they write lower-level recall and recognition items (McMillan, 2007)
- New description of strategies for writing higher-level multiple-choice items (Center for Instructional Technology, 2006)
- New section on Web-based assessment, including information about three increasingly used Web-based assessments available to teachers
- New coverage of whether a missed assignment or paper should be given a zero (McMillan, 2007)
- New discussion of whether teachers should go strictly by the numbers in grading (McMillan, 2007)
- Updating of grade inflation discussion (College Board, 2004).

ACKNOWLEDGMENTS

I am deeply indebted to many people at McGraw-Hill who have provided outstanding guidance and support for this text. I especially thank David Patterson, editor, who has brought a wealth of publishing knowledge and vision to bear on this edition. I also thank Beth Mejia, publisher for education and psychology, for the superb guidance and support she has provided. Elaine Silverstein, the developmental editor for this edition of the book, has been terrific to work with and did an excellent job in improving the manuscript. Thanks also to Emily Pecora, developmental editor, for her terrific work in coordinating and monitoring many tasks and many people involved with this edition. Rick Hecker did an excellent job orchestrating the production of the book. I also appreciate the wonderful job of copyediting performed by Beatrice Sussman. Dr. Nancy DeFrates-Densch, Northern Illinois University, contributed enormously to the book by writing the case studies and the PRAXIS™ Practice items. I want to thank Deb Kalkman and Ronni Rowland for their outstanding work in writing the material for the book's extensive Ancillaries.

On pages xxi to xxv, the numerous expert content and research consultants for the book are profiled. As stated earlier, their feedback was invaluable in helping me to make the book's content superior to what I could have accomplished alone.

Peer Reviewers for the Third Edition. In planning the third edition, we asked educational psychology instructors what improvements in the text and accompanying ancillaries they would like to see to help their students to learn and them to teach. Their suggestions received were incredibly helpful. A special thanks to:

Bambi Bailey, *Midwestern State University*
Richard Benedict, *Madonna University*
Ronald Dugan, *The College of St. Rose*
Audrey Edwards, *Eastern Illinois University*
Nancy Knapp, *University of Georgia*
William Lan, *Texas Tech University*
Edward Levinson, *Indiana University*
Julie Matuga, *Bowling Green State University*
Ron Mulson, *Hudson Valley Community College*
David Oxendine, *University of North Carolina–Pembroke*
Barbara Powell, *Eastern Illinois University*
James Rodriquez, *San Diego State University*
Susan Sawyer, *Southeastern Louisiana University*
Alison Shook, *Albright College*
Jenny Singleton, *University of Illinois–Urban-Champaign*
Michael Steiff, *University of California–Davis*
David Tarver, *Angelo State University*
Libby Vesilind, *Bucknell University*
Ryan Wilke, *Florida State University*

Expert Consultants for the Second Edition. Beginning with the first edition, I have sought the input of leading experts in many different areas of educational psychology, who provided me with detailed evaluations and recommendations in their area of expertise. The expert consultants for *Educational Psychology,* 2e, were:

Albert Bandura, *Stanford University*
Gary Bitter, *Arizona State University*
Carlos Díaz, *Florida Atlantic University*
Eva Essa, *University of Nevada, Reno*
Carolyn Evertson, *Vanderbilt University*

Kenji Hakuta, *Stanford University*
Daniel Hallahan, *University of Virginia*
James McMillan, *Virginia Commonwealth University*
Valerie Pang, *San Diego State University*
Michael Pressley, *University of Notre Dame*
Dale Schunk, *University of North Carolina–Greensboro*
Robert Siegler, *Carnegie Mellon University*

Peer Reviewers for the Second Edition and Second Edition Classroom Update. An extensive number of educational psychology instructors gave me very detailed, helpful information about what they wanted in an ideal textbook for their course. Their ideas significantly influenced the content, organization, and pedagogy of the Second Edition and Classroom Update Edition of the book.

Eric Anderman, *University of Kentucky*
James M. Applefield, *University of North Carolina–Wilmington*
Jeffrey Baker, *Rochester Institute of Technology*
Dorothy A. Battle, *Georgia Southern University*
Douglas Beed, *University of Montana, Missoula*
Richard Benedict, *Madonna University*
John T. Binfet, *California State University–San Bernadino*
Joseph Braun, *California State University–Dominguez Hills*
Kathy Brown, *University of Central Oklahoma*
Robert G. Brown, *Florida Atlantic University*
Alison Bryant, *University of Missouri–Columbia*
Melva M. Burke, *East Carolina University*
Russell N. Carney, *Southwest Missouri State University*
Chuck Catania, *Miami University of Ohio*
John Newman Clark, *University of South Alabama*
Ellen Contopidis, *Keuka College*
Dorothy Valcarcel Craig, *Middle Tennessee University*
Rhoda Cummings, *University of Nevada–Reno*
Reagan Curtis, *Northwestern State University*
David Dalton, *Kent State University*
Nancy Defrates-Densch, *Northern Illinois University*
Gypsy Denzine, *Northern Arizona University*
Jesse Diaz, *Central Washington University*
Ronna Dillon, *Southern Illinois University–Carbondale*
Joseph DiMauro, *DeSales University*
Ruth Doyle, *Casper College*
Kenneth Durgans, *Xavier University*
Howard Epstein, *Miami University of Ohio*
Lena Ericksen, *Western Washington University*
Tsile Evers, *Miami University–Oxford*
Sheryl Feinstein, *Augusta College*
Aubrey Fine, *California Polytechnic University*
Diane Finley, *Prince George's Community College*
Ericka Fisher, *College of the Holy Cross*
William R. Fisk, *Clemson University*
M. Arthur Garmon, *Western Michigan University*

Alyssa Gonzalez, *Florida Atlantic University*
Caroline Gould, *Eastern Michigan University*
Charles R. Grah, *Austin Peay State University*
Kim Grilliot, *Bowling Green State University*
Lynne A. Hammann, *University of Akron*
Andrew Hanson, *California State University–Chico*
Walter Hapkiewicz, *Michigan State University*
Gregory Harper, *State University of New York–Fredonia*
Diane J. Harris, *San Francisco State University*
Jan Hayes, *Middle Tennessee State University*
William E. Herman, *State University of New York–Potsdam*
David Holliway, *Marshall University*
Sherri Horner, *University of Memphis*
Mara Huber, *State University of New York–Fredonia*
John H. Hummel, *Valdosta State University*
Judith Hughey, *Kansas State University*
Mona Ibrahim, *Concordia College*
Emilie Johnson, *Lindenwood University*
Steven Kaatz, *Bethel College*
Deborah Kalkman, *Northern Illinois University*
Susan Kelley, *Lycoming College*
Lee Kem, *Murray State University*
Elizabeth Kirk, *Miami University of Ohio*
Elaine Kisisel, *Calumet College of Saint Joseph*
Robert L. Kohn, *University of Kansas*
Becky Ladd, *Illinois State University*
Marvin Lee, *Shenandoah University*
Randy Lennon, *University of Northern Colorado*
Bernie Les, *Wayne State University*
Dov Liberman, *University of Houston*
Kim Loomis, *Kennesaw State University*
Catherine McCartney, *Bemidji State University*
John R. McClure, *Northern Arizona University*
Barbara F. Maestas, *Towson University*
P.Y. Mantzicopoulos, *Purdue University*
Julia M. Matuga, *Bowling Green State University*
Lisa Mehlig, *Northern Illinois University*
John K. Meis, *Flager College*
Dorothy D. Miles, *Saint Louis University*
Barbara Milligan, *Middle Tennessee State University*
Connie M. Moss, *Duquesne University*
Beverly Moore, *Auburn University*
Ronald Mulson, *Hudson Valley Community College*
Peter Myerson, *University of Wisconsin–Oshkosh*
Ernest Owen, *Western Kentucky University*
Joseph D. Nichols, *Indiana-Purdue University*
Nita A. Paris, *Kennesaw State University*
Jim Persinger, *Emporia State University*
Barbara M. Powell, *Eastern Illinois University*
Barbara L. Radigan, *Community College of Allegheny County*
Sandra Nagel Randall, *Saginaw Valley State University*
Marla Reese-Weber, *Illinois State University*

Robert Rice, *Western Oregon University*
Lynda Robinson, *University of the Ozarks*
Susan Rogers, *Columbus State Community College*
Lawrence R. Rogien, *Columbus State Community College*
Paul Rosenberg, *Muhlenberg College*
Deborah Salih, *University of Northern Iowa*
Jill Salisbury-Glennon, *Auburn University*
Ala Samarapungavan, *Purdue University*
Charles Jeff Sandoz, *University of Louisiana*
Rolando A. Santos, *California State University–Los Angeles*
Gayle Schou, *Grand Canyon University*
Marvin Seperson, *Nova Southeastern University*
Lisa Sethre-Hofstad, *Concordia College*
Patricia Slocum, *College of DuPage*
Brian G. Smith, *Moorhead State University*
Michael Smith, *Weber State University*
Daniel Stuempfig, *California State University–Chico*
Gabriele Sweidel, *Kutztown University of Pennsylvania*
David E. Tanner, *California State University, Fresno*
Sara Tannert, *Miami University of Ohio*
Karen Thierry, *Rutgers University*
Yuma I. Tomes, *Virginia Commonwealth University*
Donna Townsend, *Southwestern Assemblies of God University*
Julie Turner, *University of Notre Dame*
Atilano Valencia, *California State University–Fresno*
Eva G. Vandergiessen, *Fairmont State College*
David Vawter, *Winthrop University*
Linda Veronie, *Slippery Rock University*
Libby Vesilind, *Bucknell University*
Penny Warner, *Winona State University*
Linda Weeks, *Lamar University*
Earl F. Wellborn, Jr., *Missouri Valley College*
David Wendler, *Martin Luther College*
Glenda Wilkes, *University of Arizona*
Patricia Willems, *Florida Atlantic University*
Victor Willson, *Texas A&M University*
Steven R. Wininger, *Western Kentucky University*
Betsy Wisner, *State University of New York–Cortland*
Patricia Whang, *California State University–Monterey Bay*
Jina Yoon, *Wayne State University*
Michael Young, *University of Connecticutt*

Reviewers of the First Edition. I am also indebted to the many reviewers of the first edition of the text who did an outstanding job in helping me to create the foundation for the book. These instructors and expert research consultants provided this feedback:

Dr. Frank Adams, *Wayne State College*
Dr. Robert R. Ayres, *Western Oregon University*
Dr. James Applefield, *University of North Carolina–Wilmington*
Dr. Elizabeth C. Arch, *Pacific University*
Professor Roger Briscoe, *Indiana University of Pennsylvania*
Randy Brown, *University of Central Oklahoma*

Professor Kay Bull, *Oklahoma State University*
Dr. Mary D. Burbank, *University of Utah*
Dr. Sheryl Needle Cohn, *University of Central Florida*
Dr. Rayne Sperling Dennison, *Penn State*
Dr. Carlos F. Diaz, *Florida Atlantic University*
Professor Ronna Dillon, *Southern Illinois University*
Dr. Peter Doolittle, *Virginia Polytechnic University*
Dr. David Dungan, *Emporia State University*
Gordon Eisenmann, *Augusta State University*
Vicky Farrow, *Lamar University*
Dr. William L. Franzen, *University of Missouri–St. Louis*
Dr. Susan Goldman, *Vanderbilt University*
Dr. Algea Harrison, *Oakland University*
Dr. Jan Hayes, *Middle Tennessee State University*
Dr. Alice S. Honig, *Syracuse University*
Dr. Kathryn W. Linden, emeritus, *Purdue University*
Dr. Richard E. Mayer, *University of California–Santa Barbara*
Rita McKenzie, *Northern Arizona University*
Dr. James H. McMillan, *Virginia Commonwealth University*
Professor Sharon McNeely, *Northeastern Illinois University*
Ann Pace, *University of Missouri*
Dr. Karen Menke Paciorek, *Eastern Michigan University*
Dr. Peggy Perkins, *University of Nevada–Las Vegas*
Dr. Nan Bernstein Ratner, *University of Maryland–College Park*
Dr. Gilbert Sax, *University of Washington*
Dr. Dale Schunk, *University of North Carolina–Greensboro*
Judith Stechly, *West Liberty State University*
Dr. O. Suthern Sims, Jr., *Mercer University*
Dr. David Wendler, *Martin Luther College*
Dr. Allan Wigfield, *University of Maryland–College Park*
Dr. Tony L. Williams, *Marshall University*
Professor Ann K. Wilson, *Buena Vista University*
Dr. Peter Young, *Southern Oregon University*
Dr. Steven Yussen, *University of Minnesota*

Panel of Early Childhood, Elementary, Middle, and High School Teachers. A large panel of individuals who teach at the early childhood, elementary, middle, and high school levels provided me with material about special teaching moments that they have experienced. These moments appear in the Teaching Stories and Best Practices boxes throughout the text. I owe these teachers a great deal of thanks for sharing the real world of their teaching experiences:

Karen Abra, *School of the Scared Heart,* San Francisco, CA
Mrs. Lou Aronson, *Devils Lake High School,* Devils Lake, ND
Daniel Arnoux, *Lauderhill Middle Community School,* Broward, FL
Lynn Ayres, *East Middle School,* Ypsilanti, MI
Fay Bartley, *Bright Horizon Children Center,* Bronx, NY
Barbara M. Berry, *Ypsilanti High School,* Ypsilanti, MI
Kristen Blackenship, *Salem Church Elementary,* Midlothian, VA
Wendy Bucci, *Sugar Creek Elementary School,* Verona, WI

Stella Cohen, *Hackley School,* Tarrytown, NY
Connie Christy, *Aynor Elementary,* Aynor, SC
Julie Curry, *Hubbard Elementary School,* Forsyth, GA
Alina Durso, *PS 59–Beekman Hill International School,* New York, NY
Andrea Fenton, *Cortez High School,* Glendale Union, AZ
Mark Fodness, *Bemidji Middle School,* Bemidji, MN
Kathy Fuchser, *St. Francis High School,* Humphrey, NE
Lawren Giles, *Baechtel Grove Middle School,* Willits, CA
Jerri Hall, *Miller Magnet Middle School,* Bibb County, GA
Jenny Heiter, *Bremen High School,* Bremen, IN
Anita Marie Hitchcock, *Holley Navarre Primary,* Santa Rosa Schools, FL
Laura Johnson-Brickford, *Nordhoff High School,* Ojai, CA
Heidi Kaufman, *Associate Executive Director of Childcare, MetroWest YMCA,* Framingham, MA
Juanita Kerton, *Gramercy School/New York League for Early Learning,* New York, NY
Chaille Lazar, *Hedgcoxe Elementary,* Plano, TX
Margaret Longworth, *St. Lucie West Middle School,* St. Lucie, FL
Adriane Lonzarich, *Heartwood,* San Mateo, CA
RoseMary Moore, *Angelo State University,* Angelo, TX
Therese Olejniczak, *Central Middle School,* East Grand Forks, MN
Dennis Peterson, *Deer River High School,* Bemidji, MN
Chuck Rawls, *Appling Middle School,* Bibb County, GA
Verna Brown Rollins, *West Middle School,* Ypsilanti, MI
Donna L. Shelhorse, *Short Pump Middle School,* Henrico County, VA
Michele Siegal, *Brockton High School,* Brockton, MA
Jason Stanley, *Syracuse Dunbar Avoca,* Syracuse, NE
Vicky Stone, *Cammack Middle School,* Huntington, VA
Sandy Swanson, *Menomonee Falls High School,* Menomonee Falls, WI
Tamela Varney, *Central City Elementary,* Cabell County, WV
Marlene Wendler, *St. Paul's Lutheran School,* New Ulm, MN
William Willford, *Perry Middle School,* Perry, GA
Yvonne Wilson, *North Elementary School,* Deer River, MN
Susan Youngblood, *Weaver Middle School,* Bibb County, GA
Heather Zoldak, *Ridge Wood Elementary,* Northville, MI

Special Features and Ancillary Authors. I also benefited enormously from the efforts of this outstanding group of educational psychology instructors who wrote material for special features in the text and the ancillaries.

Nancy Defrates-Densch, *Northern Illinois University,* author of Crack the Cases, OLC case studies, *The Educational Psychology Guide to Preparing for the PRAXIS II™ Exam,* the Theory into Practice modules, and the Enter the Debate features.
Deborah Kalkman, *Northern Illinois University,* author of the instructor's manual and the PowerPoint presentations.

Veronica Rowland, *University of California–Irvine,* author of Taking It to the Net, the Student OLC, and *The Educational Psychology Guide to Preparing for the PRAXIS II™ Exam,* as well as revising author of the student study guide and test bank.
Karen Swan, *Kent State University,* technology expert consultant and reviser of Technology and Education modules.

ANCILLARIES

Supporting and Enriching Your Use of *Educational Psychology*

By now you may have noticed that this third edition of *Educational Psychology* is not accompanied by a student CD-ROM. Those materials—videos, case studies, everything—are now completely online.

Ancillaries for use with *Educational Psychology*

PrepCenter collects all the faculty support materials — case studies, online activities, video segments, PowerPoints, instructor's manual sections—and integrates them into a single, on-demand resource. This concept-based archive allows you to access every resource related to a single concept or theory, regardless of where this material appears in the textbook. A professor preparing for a lecture on "attribution" can search on the term and collect every case study, instructor's manual page, PowerPoint slide, and video segment related to the topic—all suitable for use as part of an in-class lecture, or for posting to a course website.

To use *PrepCenter,* just visit the instructor's side of the Online Learning Center at www.mhhe.com/santedu3e. If this is your first time using a McGraw-Hill text, you'll need to get an instructor username and password first, so contact your local McGraw-Hill sales representative to get started.

Student's Online Learning Center (www.mhhe.com/santedu3e)

The online learning center includes:

- The Study Guide, containing study resources including multiple choice, true/false, matching, short answer and essay quizzes.
- Two additional Crack the Case studies for each chapter of the text
- Self-assessment exercises
- Observation activities.
- The PRAXIS II study guide
- Bibliography Builder for easy and accurate citations and references
- A lesson planning tool

Instructor's Online Learning Center (www.mhhe.com/santedu3e)

All the material on the Online Learning Center can be sorted and downloaded through *PrepCenter,* or can be downloaded as complete documents. These include:

- The **Instructor's Manual,** a flexible planner with teaching suggestions, learning objectives, extended chapter outlines, lecture/discussion suggestions, video and film recommendations, classroom activity tips and handout forms.
- The **Test Bank,** with almost 1,000 questions specifically related to the main text, consisting of multiple-choice, stem questions, short-answer questions, critical thinking questions, essay questions and applied assessments.
- **PowerPoint Slides** for every chapter and concept presented in the text.

Print Supplements and Related Texts

PRAXIS II *Principles of Learning and Teaching Study Guide* Nancy Defrates-Densch, ISBN 0-07-298151-2

For students and instructors where the PRAXIS II *Principles of Learning and Teaching* exam is required, this study guide correlates all the textbook content to the test for easy review. It also offers an overview of the PRAXIS II exam, guidelines for analyzing case studies, a case study analysis practice activity, objective quizzes to confirm understanding of topics, and a practice test based on the PRAXIS II exam.

The study guide is available for download from the Online Learning Center and as a print guide that can be ordered as a free package item by instructors or purchased separately by students.

A Guide to Observation, Participation, and Reflection in the Classroom Arthea Reed and Verna Bergemann, ISBN 0-07-298553-4

This complete, hands-on guide to classroom observations provides detailed guides for observing the dynamics of the classroom, participating with the classroom teacher, and then reflecting on the experience. It also includes more than 50 practical blank forms that cover all aspects of observation, participation, and reflection, from the structured observation of a lesson to a checklist for determining teaching styles to reflections on small-group teaching.

Understanding Children: An Interview and Observation Guide for Educators Denise Daniels, Lorrie Beaumont, and Carol Doolin, ISBN 0-07-248185-4

This hands-on book is a guide for interviewing and observing children in educational settings. It includes practical tips for interviewing and observing children as a way to understand their behavior, learning, and development; makes connections to the work of major developmental theorists and educational researchers; and discusses the analysis of observational data and its uses for guiding educational practices (e.g., instruction, cooperative grouping, and parent conferences).

Teaching Portfolios: Presenting Your Professional Best Patricia Rieman and Jeanne Okrasinski, ISBN 0-07-287684-0

This portfolio handbook includes authentic, student-generated artifacts as well as insights from administrators, teachers, and parents. Issues of classroom management, diversity, communication, planning, standards-based education, and reflection are all addressed in the context of how to approach these important aspects within a teaching portfolio and during interviews. The materials are designed for continued use as the students become in-service educators.

Case Studies for Teacher Problem Solving Rita Silverman, William Welty, and Sally Lyon

Choose from an online menu of eighty cases addressing core curriculum areas in teacher education—development, classroom management, leadership, special education, diversity, teaching methods, educational psychology, and more. Visit *www.mhhe.com/primis* to preview the cases, then order a printed and bound copy for your consideration. If you like your case book, placing an order is easy. If you don't, make changes—there is no obligation.

Taking Sides and Annual Editions

Annual Editions: *Educational Psychology* 06/07, 21st Edition Kathleen M Cauley, James McMillan, and Gina Pannozzo ©2007, ISBN 0073516112

Taking Sides: *Clashing Views in Educational Psychology,* 4th Edition Leonard Abbeduto ©2006, ISBN 0073195103

Sources: *Notable Selections in Educational Psychology* Rhett Diessner and Stacy Simmons ©2000, ISBN 0072323345

To the Student

This book provides you with important study tools to help you more effectively learn about educational psychology. Especially important is the Learning Goals system that is integrated throughout each chapter. In the visual walk-through of features, pay special attention to how the Learning Goals system works.

ENCASING THE CHAPTER

The Learning Goals System

Using the Learning Goals system will help you to learn the material more easily. Key aspects of the Learning Goals system are the learning goals, mini-chapter maps, Review, Reflect, and Practice, Reach Your Learning Goals sections, which are all linked together.

At the beginning of each chapter, you will see a page that includes both a chapter outline and three to six learning goals that preview the chapter's main themes and underscore the most important ideas in the chapter. Then, at the beginning of each major section of a chapter,

you will see a mini-chapter map that provides you with a visual organization of the key topics you are about to read in the section. At the end of each section is Review, Reflect, and Practice in which the learning goal for the section is restated, a series of review questions related to the mini-chapter map are asked, a question that encourages you to think critically about a topic related to the section appears, and PRAXIS™ Practice items are presented. At the end of the chapter, you will come to a section titled Reach Your Learning Goals. This includes an overall chapter map that visually organizes all of the main headings, a restatement of the chapter's learning goals, and a summary of the chapter's content that is directly linked to the chapter outline at the beginning of the chapter and the questions asked in the Review part of Review, Reflect, and Practice within the chapter. The Reach Your Learning Goals summary essentially answers the questions asked in the within-chapter Review sections.

THE LEARNING GOALS SYSTEM

Chapter-Opening Outline and Learning Goals

This section previews the chapter's main themes and identifies the most important ideas. Each heading in the Outline appears later in the chapter as a mini chapter map.

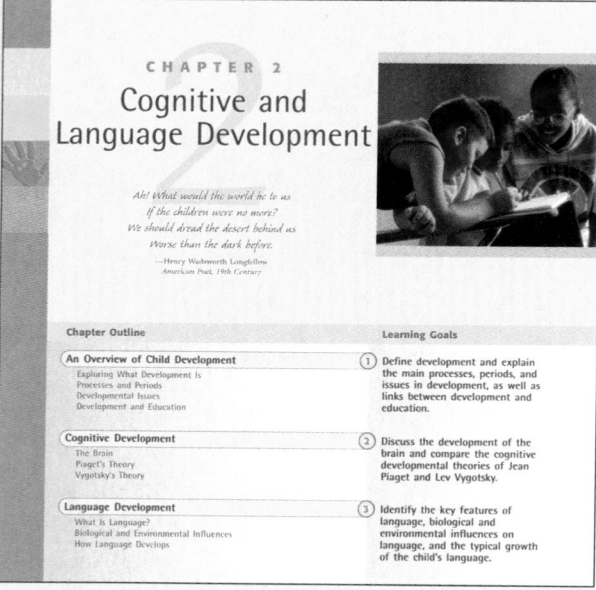

Mini–Chapter Map

Echoing the headings in the chapter-opening outline, these maps appear at the beginning of each major section in the chapter. The maps call your attention to the specific key topics that will be discussed in the upcoming text.

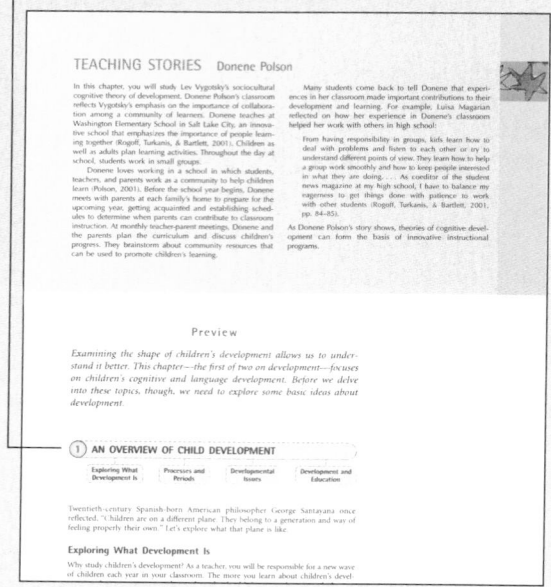

Review, Reflect, and Practice

These sections are paired with the mini-chapter maps to summarize the key topics from the preceeding text and help you think critically about them. The *Practice* questions let you apply your understanding of the reading to answer questions of the kind typically found on state standards-based tests.

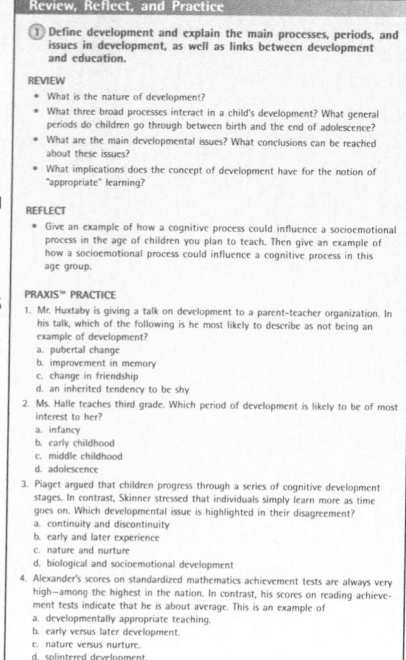

Reach Your Learning Goals

At the end of each chapter, this section presents the headings you saw in the chapter-opening outline. You will also find the *Learning Goals* restated in this section, along with a summary of the chapter content related to each goal.

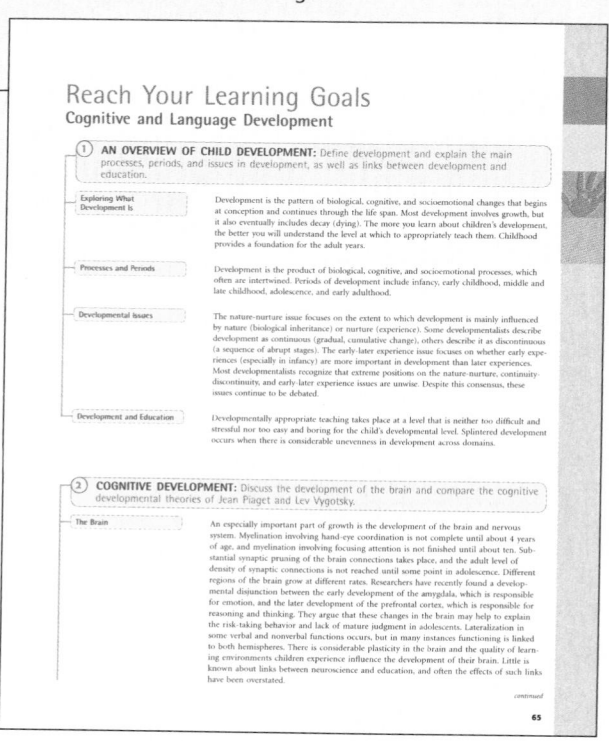

PRACTICE AND PRAXIS™

A number of learning features in the text will help you learn extensive strategies for becoming an effective teacher and preparing for state standards-based tests, such as PRAXIS™.

Teaching Stories

Each chapter opens with a high-interest teaching story that is linked to the chapter's content.

TEACHING STORIES Donene Polson

In this chapter, you will study Lev Vygotsky's sociocultural cognitive theory of development. Donene Polson's classroom reflects Vygotsky's emphasis on the importance of collaboration among a community of learners. Donene teaches at Washington Elementary School in Salt Lake City, an innovative school that emphasizes the importance of people learning together (Rogoff, Turkanis, & Bartlett, 2001). Children as well as adults plan learning activities. Throughout the day at school, students work in small groups.

Donene loves working in a school in which students, teachers, and parents work as a community to help children learn (Polson, 2001). Before the school year begins, Donene meets with parents at each family's home to prepare for the upcoming year, getting acquainted and establishing schedules to determine when parents can contribute to classroom instruction. At monthly teacher-parent meetings, Donene and the parents plan the curriculum and discuss children's progress. They brainstorm about community resources that can be used to promote children's learning.

Many students come back to tell Donene that experiences in her classroom made important contributions to their development and learning. For example, Luisa Magarian reflected on how her experience in Donene's classroom helped her work with others in high school:

From having responsibility in groups, kids learn how to deal with problems and listen to each other or try to understand different points of view. They learn how to help a group work smoothly and how to keep people interested in what they are doing. . . . As coeditor of the student news magazine at my high school, I have to balance my eagerness to get things done with patience to work with other students (Rogoff, Turkanis, & Bartlett, 2001, pp. 84–85).

As Donene Polson's story shows, theories of cognitive development can form the basis of innovative instructional programs.

Best Practices: Strategies for . . . Interlude

Numerous times in each chapter, this important feature provides recommendations for effective ways to educate students related to the content that has just been discussed. Also, embedded in many Best Practices interludes are Through the Eyes of Teachers inserts that present the strategies used by outstanding, in many cases, award-winning teachers.

Crack the Case

This presents a full-page case study related to the chapter's content after the last Review, Reflect, and Practice section and before the chapter's summary. The case study gives you an opportunity to apply what you have learned in the chapter to a real-world teaching issue or problem. At the end of the case study, you are asked a series of questions—in some cases, PRAXIS™-type multiple-choice items—to reflect on and think critically about the case.

CRACK THE CASE
The Case of the Book Report

Mr. Johnson assigned his high school senior American government students to read two books during the semester that had "something, anything to do with government or political systems" and to write a brief report about each of their chosen books.

One student in the class, Cindy, chose to read *1984* and *Animal Farm*, both by George Orwell. *1984* is a book about what could happen in "the future" year of 1984, given certain earlier political decisions. In essence, the world turns into a terrible place in which "Big Brother" monitors all of one's actions via two-way television-like screens. Infractions of minor rules are punished severely. *Animal Farm* is a brief novel about political systems in which the characters are portrayed as various farm animals such as pigs and dogs. Cindy enjoyed both books and completed them both before midterm. Her reports were insightful, reflecting on the symbolism contained in the novels and the implications for present-day government.

Cindy's friend, Lucy, had put off reading her first book until the last minute. She knew Cindy enjoyed reading about government and had finished her reports. Lucy asked Cindy if she knew of a "skinny book" she could read to fulfill the assignment. Cindy gladly shared her copy of *Animal Farm* with her friend, but as Lucy began reading the book she wondered why Cindy had given her this book. It didn't seem to fit the requirements of the assignment at all.

The day before the first reports were due, Mr. Johnson overheard the girls talking. Lucy complained to Cindy, "I don't get it. It's a story about pigs and dogs."

Cindy responded, "They aren't really supposed to be farm animals. It's a story about the promises of communism and what happened in the Soviet Union once the communists took over. It's a great story! Don't you see? The pigs symbolize the communist regime that overthrew the czars during the Russian Revolution. They made all kinds of promises about equality for everyone. The people went along with them because they were sick and tired of the rich and powerful

running everything while they starved. Once the czars were eliminated, the communists established a new government but didn't keep any of their promises, controlled everything. Remember in the book when the pigs moved into the house and started walking on two legs? That's supposed to be like when the communist leaders began acting just like the czars. They even created a secret police force—the dogs in the story. Remember how they bullied the other animals? Just like the secret police in the Soviet Union."

Cindy looked at her friend, dumbfounded. How could she *not* understand this book? It was so obvious.

1. Drawing on Piaget's theory, explain why Cindy understood the book.

2. Based on Piaget's theory, explain why Lucy didn't understand the book.

3. What could Mr. Johnson do to help Lucy understand?

4. How could Mr. Johnson have presented this assignment differently, so that Lucy did not need to rush through a book?

5. At which of Piaget's stages of cognitive development is Cindy operating?
   a. sensorimotor
   b. preoperational
   c. concrete operational
   d. formal operational
   Explain your choice.

6. At which of Piaget's stages of cognitive development is Lucy operating?
   a. sensorimotor
   b. preoperational
   c. concrete operational
   d. formal operational
   Explain your choice.

64

BEST PRACTICES
Strategies for Applying Vygotsky's Theory to Children's Education

Vygotsky's theory has been embraced by many teachers and has been successfully applied to education (Bearison & Dorvall, 2002; Budrova & Leong, 2007; Elkind, 2004; Rowe & Wertsch, 2004; Winsler & others, 2002). Here are some ways Vygotsky's theory can be incorporated in classrooms:

1. **Assess the child's ZPD.** Like Piaget, Vygotsky did not believe that formal, standardized tests are the best way to assess children's learning. Rather, Vygotsky argued that assessment should focus on determining the child's zone of proximal development (Camilleri, 2005; Meijer & Elshout, 2001). The skilled helper presents the child with tasks of varying difficulty to determine the best level at which to begin instruction.

2. **Use the child's zone of proximal development in teaching.** Teaching should begin toward the zone's upper limit, so that the child can reach the goal with help and move to a higher level of skill and knowledge. Offer just enough assistance. You might ask, "What can I do to help you?" Or simply observe the child's intentions and attempts and provide support when needed. When the child hesitates, offer encouragement. And encourage the child to practice the skill. You may watch and appreciate the child's practice or offer support when the child forgets what to do. Next, you can read about John Mahoney's teaching practices that reflect Vygotsky's emphasis on the importance of the zone of proximal development.

John Mahoney, teaching math.

THROUGH THE EYES OF TEACHERS
Using Dialogue and Reframing Concepts to Find the Zone of Proximal Development

John Mahoney teaches mathematics at a high school in Washington, D.C. In Mahoney's view, guiding students' success in math is both collaborative and individual. He encourages dialogue about math during which he reframes concepts that help students subsequently solve problems on their own. Mahoney also never gives students the answers to math problems. As one student commented, "He's going to make you think." His tests always include a problem that students have not seen but have enough knowledge to figure out the problem's solution. (Source: Briggs, 2005.)

3. **Use more-skilled peers as teachers.** Remember that it is not just adults that are important in helping children learn. Children also benefit from the support and guidance of more-skilled peers (John-Steiner & Mahn, 2003). For example, pair a child who is just beginning to read with one who is a more advanced reader.

4. **Monitor and encourage children's use of private speech.** Be aware of the developmental change from externally

talking to oneself when solving a problem during the preschool years to privately talking to oneself in the early elementary school years. In the elementary school years, encourage children to internalize and self-regulate their talk to themselves.

5. **Place instruction in a meaningful context.** Educators today are moving away from abstract presentations of material, instead providing students with opportunities to experience learning in real-world settings. For example, instead of just memorizing math formulas, students work on math problems with real-world implications.

6. **Transform the classroom with Vygotskian ideas.** Tools of the Mind is a curriculum that is grounded in Vygotsky's (1962) theory with special attention given to cultural tools and developing self-regulation, the zone of proximal development, scaffolding, private speech, shared activity, and play as important activity (Hyson, Copple, & Jones, 2006). The curriculum was created by Elena Bodrova and Deborah Leong (2007) and has been implemented in more than 200 classrooms. Most of the children in the Tools of the Mind programs are at-risk because of their living circumstances, which in many instances involve poverty and other difficult conditions such as being homeless and having parents with drug problems.

In a Tools of the Mind classroom, dramatic play has a central role. Teachers guide children in creating themes based on the children's interests, such as treasure hunt, store, hospital, and restaurant. Teachers also incorporate field trips, visitor presentations, videos, and books in the development of children's play. They also help children develop a play plan, which increases the maturity of their play. Play plans describe what the children expect to do in the play period, including the imaginary context, roles, and props to be used. The play plans increase the quality of their play and self-regulation.

PRAXIS™ PRACTICE

1. Mr. Huxtaby is giving a talk on development to a parent-teacher organization. In his talk, which of the following is he most likely to describe as not being an example of development?
   a. pubertal change
   b. improvement in memory
   c. change in friendship
   d. an inherited tendency to be shy

2. Ms. Halle teaches third grade. Which period of development is likely to be of most interest to her?
   a. infancy
   b. early childhood
   c. middle childhood
   d. adolescence

3. Piaget argued that children progress through a series of cognitive development stages. In contrast, Skinner stressed that individuals simply learn more as time goes on. Which developmental issue is highlighted in their disagreement?
   a. continuity and discontinuity
   b. early and later experience
   c. nature and nurture
   d. biological and socioemotional development

4. Alexander's scores on standardized mathematics achievement tests are always very high—among the highest in the nation. In contrast, his scores on reading achievement tests indicate that he is about average. This is an example of
   a. developmentally appropriate teaching.
   b. early versus later development.
   c. nature versus nurture.
   d. splintered development.

Please see the answer key at the end of the book.

PRAXIS™-Type Multiple-Choice Questions In Review and Reflect

At the end of each B-level head (second-level heading) in every chapter in the feature titled Review, Reflect, and Practice, you will get an opportunity to practice answering PRAXIS™-type multiple-choice questions related to the material you have just read.

Portfolio Items

Activities related to the chapter's content are presented at the end of the chapter. Depending on your instructor's requirements, you may be asked to write about these educational circumstances in a portfolio and/or discuss them with other students.

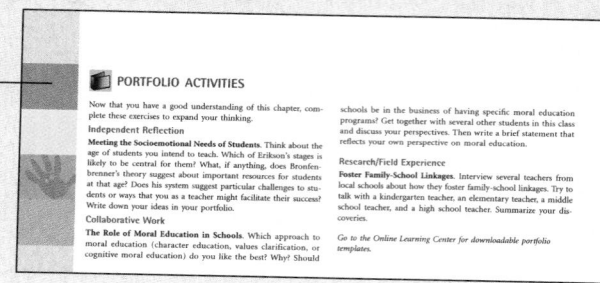

PORTFOLIO ACTIVITIES

Now that you have a good understanding of this chapter, complete these exercises to expand your thinking.

Independent Reflection

Meeting the Socioemotional Needs of Students. Think about the age of students you intend to teach. Which of Erikson's stages is likely to be central for them? What, if anything, does Bronfenbrenner's theory suggest about important resources for students at that age? Does his system suggest particular challenges to students or ways that you as a teacher might facilitate their success? Write down your ideas in your portfolio.

Collaborative Work

The Role of Moral Education in Schools. Which approach to moral education (character education, values clarification, or cognitive moral education) do you like the best? Why? Should

schools be in the business of having specific moral education programs? Get together with several other students in this class and discuss your perspectives. Then write a brief statement that reflects your own perspective on moral education.

Research/Field Experience

Foster Family-School Linkages. Interview several teachers from local schools about how they foster family-school linkages. Try to talk with a kindergarten teacher, an elementary teacher, a middle school teacher, and a high school teacher. Summarize your discoveries.

Go to the Online Learning Center for downloadable portfolio templates.

SELF-ASSESSMENT 2.1

Applying Piaget and Vygotsky in My Classroom

The grade level at which I plan to teach is _____

Piaget

The Piagetian stage of the majority of children in my classroom will likely be _____

The Piagetian concepts that I believe will help me the most in understanding and teaching children at this grade level are

Concept	Example
_____	_____
_____	_____
_____	_____

Vygotsky

The concepts in Vygotsky's theory that I believe will help me the most in understanding and teaching children at this grade level are

Concept	Example
_____	_____
_____	_____
_____	_____

Self-Assesment

This box appears one or more times in each chapter and is closely related to the content of the chapter. It is a powerful tool that helps you to evaluate and understand yourself in your efforts to become an outstanding teacher.

OTHER LEARNING FEATURES

Diversity and Education

These interludes appear once in each chapter, immediately following a related discussion of sociocultural diversity in the text. These interludes focus on important cultural, ethnic, and gender issues related to education.

TECHNOLOGY AND EDUCATION
Technology and Children's Vocabulary Development

Here are three ways to support children's vocabulary development using three types of technology (Miller, 2001).

Computers

CD-ROMs of stories, such as *Living Books*, can promote children's vocabulary development, especially when there is an online option for students to find the meaning of unfamiliar words. Using the computer for listening to and watching stories can be part of a student's reading center rotations, reading assignment, or an option during choice time. Learning new words can be enhanced if teachers plan a way for students to keep track of new words. For example, students can record new words in a portfolio for future reference.

An analysis of software products for children's vocabulary development offered the following guidelines (Wood, 2001):

1. *Relate the new to the known.* New vocabulary words are presented in a way that builds on students' previously acquired word knowledge; students are encouraged to map new word meanings onto their own experiences.

2. *Promote active, in-depth processing.* Students are motivated to construct the meanings of words rather than being taught through rote memorization of word meanings. This involves introducing a synonym for the new word or showing how it relates to a particular context; helping students apply their understanding of the word to a particular context; and challenging children to use the new word in a novel way to illustrate their understanding of its meaning.

3. *Encourage reading.* Reading promotes vocabulary development. It is important for software that promotes vocab-

ulary development to motivate students to extend their learning through reading.

Audiobooks

Teachers can create listening centers to support vocabulary development. Listening centers should include tape recorders, headphones, audiobooks, and corresponding literature. Audiobooks can be used to supplement printed materials, listen to dramatization of stories, and pique student interest. Audiobooks may especially benefit students with special needs (Casbergue & Harris, 1996). For example, students whose primary language is not English can use tapes to improve vocabulary development, reading, and pronunciation. Weak readers can use the tapes to contribute to literature discussions in class even though they may be reading less-complex materials.

Educational Television

Educational television can be used to help children learn the alphabet, to see people using vocabulary in different contexts, and to hear stories that will motivate children to read these stories later (Comstock & Scharrer, 2006; Lesser, 1989). One such program is *Reading Rainbow.* In one study, it was found that this program increases children's vocabulary and literacy (Wood & Duke, 1997). The show helps children to expand their vocabularies by introducing many potentially unfamiliar words per episode, linking the words by theme, creating rich contexts when using the words, clearly and directly explaining the meanings of new words, and linking new words in playful ways.

Metalinguistic awareness also improves considerably during the elementary school years. **Metalinguistic awareness** refers to knowledge of language, which allows children "to think about their language, understand what words are, and even define them" (Berko Gleason, 2005, p. 4). *Metacognition,* which we will discuss in more depth in chapter 8, "The Information-Processing Approach," is cognition about cognition, or knowing about knowing. Metalinguistic awareness is essentially cognition about language.

In elementary school, defining words becomes a regular part of classroom discourse and children increase their knowledge of syntax as they study and talk about the components of sentences, such as subjects and verbs (Ely, 2005). Children also make progress in understanding how to use language in culturally appropriate ways—pragmatics. By

metalinguistic awareness Knowledge of language.

61

DIVERSITY AND EDUCATION
African American Language Traditions and Poverty

Shirley Heath (1989) examined the language traditions of African Americans from low-income backgrounds. She traced some aspects of African American English to the time of slavery. Heath also examined how those speech patterns have carried over into African American English today. She found that agricultural areas in the southern United States have an especially rich oral tradition.

Specifically she found that adults do not simplify or edit their talk for children, in essence challenging the children to be highly active listeners. Also, adults ask only "real questions" of children—that is, questions for which the adult does not already know the answer. Adults also engage in a type of teasing with children, encouraging them to use their wits in communication. For example, a grandmother might pretend that she wants to take a child's hat. She then starts a lively exchange in which the child must understand many subtleties of argument, mood, and humor: Does Grandma really want my hat? Is she mad at me? Is she making a joke? Can I persuade her to give it back to me? Finally, there is an appreciation of wit and flexibility in how language is used, as well as an acknowledgment of individual differences—one person might be respected for recounting stories, another for negotiating and peacemaking skills.

Heath argues that the language tradition she describes is richly varied, cognitively demanding, and well suited to many real-life situations. She says that the oral and literary traditions among poor African Americans in the cities are well suited for many job situations. Years ago many inner-city jobs required only that a person follow directions in order to perform repetitious tasks. Today, many positions require continuous interactions involving considerable flexibility in language, such as the ability to persuade coworkers or to subtly express dissatisfaction.

Despite its utility in many job situations, the rich language tradition possessed by low-income African Americans does not meet with the educational priorities of our nation's schools. Too often schools stress rote memorization, minimizing group interaction and discouraging individual variations in communicative style. Also, the language tradition of African American culture is rapidly dying in the face of current life among poor African Americans, where the structure of low-income, frequently single-parent families often provides little verbal stimulation for children.

One mother agreed to let researcher Heath tape-record her interactions with her children over a 2-year period and to write notes about her activities with them. Within 500 hours of tape and more than a thousand lines of notes, the mother initiated talk with her three preschool children on only eighteen occasions (other than giving them a brief directive or asking a quick question). Few of the mother's conversations involved either planning or executing actions with or for her children.

Heath (1989) points out that the lack of family and community supports is widespread among urban housing projects, especially among African Americans. The deteriorating, impoverished conditions of these inner-city areas severely impede the ability of young children to develop the language skills they need to function competently.

Technology and Education

These boxes appear once in each chapter, highlighting key issues involving how technology can be used to improve education.

THROUGH THE EYES OF STUDENTS

"You Are the Coolest"

I just want to thank you for all the extra time you took to help me. You didn't have to do that but you did and I want to thank you for it. Thanks also for being straight up with me and not beating around the bush and for that you are the coolest. I'm sorry for the hard times I gave you. You take so much junk but through all that you stay calm and you are a great teacher.

Jessica, Seventh-Grade Student
Macon, Georgia
Letter to Chuck Rawls, Her Teacher, at the End of the School Year

Commitment and Motivation

Being an effective teacher also requires commitment and motivation. This includes having a good attitude and caring about students.

Beginning teachers often report that the investment of time and effort needed to be an effective teacher is huge. Some teachers, even experienced ones, say they have "no life" from September to June. Even putting in hours on evenings and weekends, in addition to all of the hours spent in the classroom, might still not be enough to get things done.

In the face of these demands, it is easy to become frustrated or to get into a rut and develop a negative attitude. Commitment and motivation help get effective teachers through the tough moments of teaching. Effective teachers have confidence in their own self-efficacy, don't let negative emotions diminish their motivation, and bring a positive attitude and enthusiasm to the classroom. These qualities are contagious and help make the classroom a place where students want to be.

So, what is likely to nurture your own positive attitudes and continued enthusiasm for teaching? As in all fields, success breeds success. It's important to become aware of times when you've made a difference in an individual student's life. Consider the words of one of the expert consultants for this book, Carlos Diaz (1997), now a professor of education at Florida Atlantic University, about Mrs. Oppel, his high school English teacher:

Through the Eyes of Students

This feature provides stimulating comments by students about their attitudes and feelings related to the chapter's content.

Key Terms

Key terms are boldfaced in the text and their definitions are provided in the margin next to where they are introduced in the text.

---

simple actions that can be performed on objects, such as sucking, looking, and grasping. Older children have schemas that include strategies and plans for solving problems. For example, a 6-year-old might have a schemas that involves the strategy of classifying objects by size, shape, or color. By the time we have reached adulthood, we have constructed an enormous number of diverse schemas, ranging from how to drive a car, to how to balance a budget, to the concept of fairness.

Assimilation and Accommodation To explain how children use and adapt their schemas, Piaget offered two concepts: assimilation and accommodation. **Assimilation** occurs when children incorporate new information into their existing schemas. **Accommodation** occurs when children adjust their schemas to fit new information and experiences.

Think about a young child who has learned the word *car* to identify the family's car. The child might call all vehicles that move on roads "cars," including motorcycles and trucks; the child has assimilated these objects to his or her existing schemas. But the child soon learns that motorcycles and trucks are not cars and fine-tunes the

schemas In Piaget's theory, actions or mental representations that organize knowledge.

assimilation Piagetian concept of the incorporation of new information into existing knowledge (schemas).

accommodation Piagetian concept of adjusting schemas to fit new information and experiences.

Glossary

All of the chapter's key terms are listed in the order in which they appear in the chapter, along with page numbers where they appeared. The key terms also are listed alphabetically, defined, and page-referenced in a Glossary at the end of the book.

KEY TERMS

development 28
nature-nurture issue 30
continuity-discontinuity issue 30
early-later experience issue 31
splintered development 32
lateralization 36
schemas 37
assimilation 37

accommodation 37
organization 38
equilibration 38
sensorimotor stage 38
preoperational stage 39
symbolic function substage 39
intuitive thought substage 40
centration 41
conservation 41

concrete operational stage 42
seriation 43
transitivity 43
formal operational stage 44
hypothetical-deductive reasoning 44
neo-Piagetians 47
zone of proximal development (ZPD) 49
scaffolding 49

social constructivist approach 50
language 54
phonology 55
morphology 55
syntax 55
semantics 56
pragmatics 56
metalinguistic awareness 61

Taking It to the Net

You are presented with questions related to the chapter that you can explore on the Internet. You will find links to the Web sites listed in the activities under Taking It to the Net on the Santrock *Educational Psychology*, third edition, Web site. These links will help you to think more deeply about the questions posed.

Educational Psychology, New York Version

TABLE OF CONTENTS

PART I: An Overview of Education in New York

NEW YORK STATE COUNTY MAP

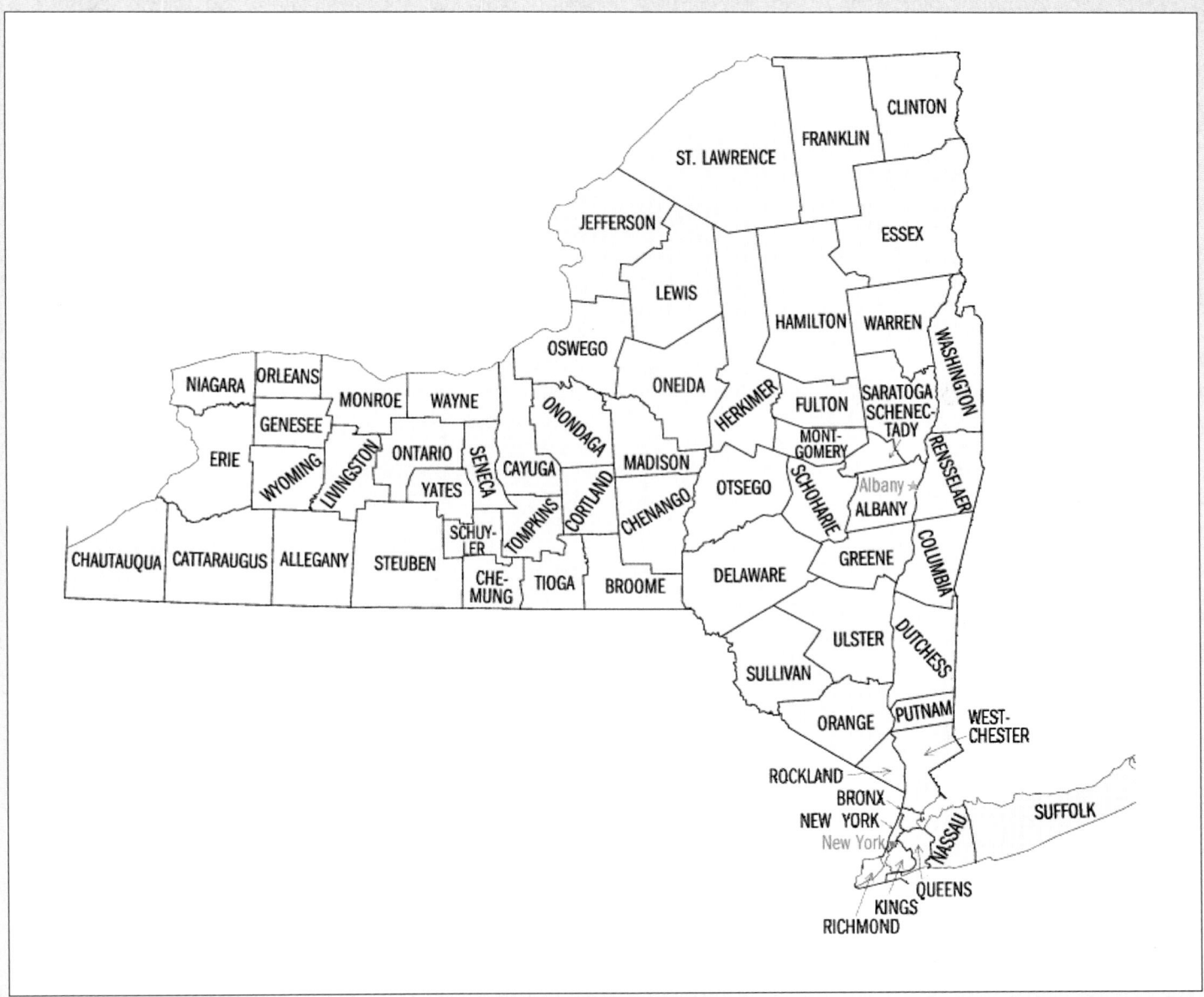

Source: US Census Bureau, State and County Quick Facts, http://quickfacts.census.gov

STUDENTS IN NEW YORK STATE

TABLE 1
Statistics for Public School Districts
July 2000 Report to the Governor and the Legislature

County	Enrollment						Dropouts and Youth at Risk							
	Total	% White	% Black	% Hisp	% Other	Annual Attendance Rate	Census Poverty Index	% Free/ Reduced Lunch	LEP Rate	Susp Rate	Dropout Rate	% to College 1997-98	Student/ Support Staff Ratio	Pupil Teacher Ratio
ALBANY	41256	76.9	17.5	2.6	3.0	94.4	11	37.3	1.36	6.27	2.11	84.8	152.49557	13.5
ALLEGANY	8763	98.0	0.8	0.3	0.9	95.4	18	49.4	.03	3.53	3.17	72.6	174.90758	12.4
BROOME	33463	90.9	4.9	1.6	2.6	94.9	11	42.2	1.86	3.89	3.02	84.5	153.30720	13.3
CATTARAUGUS	17466	91.3	1.9	0.7	6.1	95.0	16	48.5	.17	4.91	2.01	69.4	162.19325	13.4
CAYUGA	12797	94.8	3.5	0.7	1.0	94.5	12	32.6	.13	6.35	4.21	80.7	186.23145	14.7
CHAUTAUQUA	25243	90.6	2.5	5.2	1.6	94.9	18	43.4	1.84	3.92	2.73	75.5	156.81029	12.6
CHEMUNG	14011	89.3	8.6	1.0	1.0	95.2	15	42.6	.11	5.45	3.32	78.2	156.21072	14.7
CHENANGO	10207	98.0	1.1	0.5	0.5	95.1	15	45.0	.05	3.98	2.93	71.5	142.25912	12.2
CLINTON	13602	97.0	1.6	0.6	0.9	95.0	12	38.8	.07	3.65	3.25	73.3	139.66152	12.8
COLUMBIA	10131	88.6	7.5	2.6	1.3	94.0	11	38.9	1.06	7.72	3.9	78.0	173.43881	12.8
CORTLAND	7987	97.3	1.3	0.7	0.7	95.3	12	40.4	.53	4.56	3.24	70.1	151.84352	13.0
DELAWARE	7733	97.0	0.8	1.4	0.8	94.9	15	46.9	.56	3.11	1.89	73.2	136.48403	11.2
DUTCHESS	44764	80.5	11.9	4.9	2.7	94.0	06	26.0	1.39	6.17	2.26	86.1	169.62059	14.6
ERIE	144563	73.9	19.9	4.1	2.1	94.1	16	44.6	2.36	3.19	1.91	81.6	169.54660	14.1
ESSEX	5010	98.4	0.6	0.3	0.7	94.7	14	46.1	.1	3.61	2.21	73.4	140.94980	10.7
FRANKLIN	9116	89.7	0.7	0.4	9.3	95.0	16	51.5	.05	3.86	2.63	72.0	160.35853	13.0
FULTON	10012	96.9	1.4	0.9	0.8	94.3	16	45.4	.07	5.23	4.08	72.7	189.68882	12.9
GENESEE	11258	94.7	3.2	1.2	0.9	95.3	09	30.9	.15	3.9	2.08	80.6	165.57920	13.0
GREENE	7568	93.2	3.6	2.5	0.7	93.8	10	34.7	.46	7.54	2.62	73.0	163.06902	13.1
HAMILTON	713	99.2	0.1	0.1	0.6	95.9	09	32.0	0	.71	.44	84.0	89.28	7.0
HERKIMER	12101	98.1	0.8	0.6	0.5	95.0	16	46.3	.17	3.54	2.27	78.1	179.41101	13.1
JEFFERSON	19134	88.8	6.7	2.6	1.8	94.8	13	49.2	1.34	5.91	2.76	69.8	182.94160	14.1
LEWIS	5115	98.0	0.6	0.6	0.8	96.2	15	40.4	.06	2.51	1.81	68.2	193.21790	14.0
LIVINGSTON	10449	96.6	1.4	1.2	0.9	95.1	07	28.2	.21	4.8	2.79	74.1	149.20789	12.2
MADISON	12759	97.5	0.7	0.4	1.4	95.1	09	32.8	.09	4.39	2.08	77.0	169.37699	13.7
MONROE	123490	68.2	22.3	6.7	2.8	94.0	14	40.6	3.45	9.09	2.28	84.3	154.58668	13.5
MONTGOMERY	8098	87.8	1.3	10.2	0.7	94.0	16	43.9	2.17	5.88	4.18	77.8	155.19793	12.1
NASSAU	198341	69.6	13.6	10.6	6.2	95.3	04	17.9	4.74	3.71	.88	92.4	128.31027	13.2

TABLE 1 (Continued)
Statistics for Public School Districts
July 2000 Report to the Governor and the Legislature

| County | Enrollment | | | | | Dropouts and Youth at Risk | | | | | | | | |
	Total	% White	% Black	% Hisp	% Other	Annual Attendance Rate	Census Poverty Index	% Free/ Reduced Lunch	LEP Rate	Susp Rate	Dropout Rate	% to College 1997-98	Student/ Support Staff Ratio	Pupil Teacher Ratio
NIAGARA	36508	86.2	10.2	1.1	2.4	94.3	15	37.8	.66	7.96	1.41	79.2	157.85730	13.8
ONEIDA	38652	88.0	7.3	2.9	1.8	94.5	16	42.2	2.46	5.68	2.09	80.1	156.14282	13.8
ONONDAGA	79636	80.1	14.8	2.1	3.0	94.4	12	39.5	2.08	7.04	2.29	83.6	140.22675	13.7
ONTARIO	18304	93.7	3.1	2.0	1.2	95.5	09	25.1	1	3.16	2.4	83.3	173.31998	13.1
ORANGE	61291	75.1	11.3	11.8	1.9	94.0	09	31.8	3.3	6.92	2.87	80.2	166.12962	14.3
ORLEANS	8529	91.4	4.8	2.7	1.0	95.0	13	35.4	1.59	4.8	.93	71.5	163.66363	13.4
OSWEGO	25776	97.4	0.6	1.2	0.8	94.7	12	41.9	.5	5.06	4.04	70.7	179.91302	14.1
OTSEGO	10178	96.8	1.6	0.9	0.8	95.4	13	42.6	.26	3.11	2.32	77.6	150.53331	12.6
PUTNAM	15035	92.6	1.8	4.2	1.4	94.8	04	8.9	1.18	3.44	.98	89.4	184.23829	14.5
RENSSELAER	23569	89.7	6.7	2.0	1.5	94.4	13	35.0	.63	7.49	3.29	78.0	186.91104	13.7
ROCKLAND	40125	62.4	18.2	12.1	7.2	94.9	09	26.5	4.44	4.56	1.37	92.9	137.90010	13.2
ST. LAWRENCE	18858	97.5	0.5	0.3	1.6	94.9	18	46.1	.06	4.15	3.27	74.4	176.57825	13.4
SARATOGA	34825	96.2	1.7	0.7	1.4	95.2	06	18.5	.14	3.69	2.12	81.6	169.90585	14.2
SCHENECTADY	22082	81.6	11.6	3.8	3.0	94.1	11	38.6	1.4	9.51	3.54	79.0	138.74981	14.1
SCHOHARIE	5778	97.1	1.1	1.1	0.6	94.8	15	35.4	.22	3.18	2.84	71.5	145.65113	11.9
SCHUYLER	2373	98.3	0.9	0.4	0.4	95.4	15	34.1	.21	3.94	2.1	67.0	279.11079	14.2
SENECA	5429	96.7	1.1	0.9	1.2	95.6	12	38.6	.22	3.54	4.8	77.5	172.46916	12.4
STEUBEN	19500	96.7	1.7	0.6	1.0	95.2	16	46.3	.29	3.52	3.47	69.9	159.27725	13.2
SUFFOLK	238213	77.0	10.2	10.1	2.6	94.5	06	24.2	3.19	5.15	2.09	84.8	151.82809	13.9
SULLIVAN	11260	77.1	11.7	9.8	1.4	93.4	18	46.8	2.68	7.82	3.17	76.6	140.19535	11.9
TIOGA	9879	98.5	0.7	0.3	0.5	94.7	12	40.9	.19	4.3	2.65	72.1	198.77997	14.2
TOMPKINS	13496	88.5	5.3	1.8	4.4	95.1	13	32.7	2.27	3.19	1.51	84.3	118.95051	12.3
ULSTER	28682	86.4	7.0	5.1	1.5	93.9	09	35.1	1.43	6.64	2.49	73.1	152.25355	14.4
WARREN	11271	97.3	1.1	0.7	0.9	95.5	11	33.8	.18	3.58	2.4	76.3	157.85201	13.2
WASHINGTON	10863	98.1	0.8	0.6	0.6	95.5	11	37.2	.1	4.2	2.79	71.4	180.45137	13.4
WAYNE	18996	91.9	5.0	2.2	0.9	95.2	09	29.4	.68	5.62	2.49	76.0	131.31683	12.5
WESTCHESTER	137145	56.9	20.2	18.1	4.9	94.4	09	30.7	7.66	5.37	1.3	89.1	126.73524	13.0
WYOMING	6027	98.2	0.5	0.5	0.8	95.6	09	30.6	.07	2.39	2.23	66.3	162.74673	13.0
YATES	3235	97.7	1.0	0.7	0.5	95.9	20	39.9	.12	3.17	2.54	76.2	160.95477	13.2

TEACHERS IN NEW YORK STATE

TABLE 2
Statistics for Public School Districts
July 2000 Report to the Governor and the Legislature

Rank	Top 40	Average Class Size — Grade 8					Grade 10				% Minority	Annual Turnover %	Median Salary	Classroom Teachers Certification % Permanent	% Provisional	% Other	Median Years Exp.	% Master's +30 or Doctorate
		K	English	Math	Science	Social Studies	English	Math	Science	Social Studies								
1	SCARSDALE UFSD	21	19	20	20	21	23	19	18	23	2.4	7.7	84604	83.8	9.9	6.3	20	60.2
2	PORT JEFFERSON UFSD	23	22	18	22	22	14	22	21	15	0.0	6.5	82931	85.7	11.6	2.7	24	62.5
3	EAST WILLISTON UFSD	22	21	20	19	21	15	14	16	20	0.7	8.2	82210	84.2	4.6	11.2	19	44.7
4	BRONXVILLE UFSD	18	22	18	18	22	20	17	16	16	0.9	8.8	81939	82.6	5.2	12.2	19	62.6
5	RAMAPO CSD (SUFFERN)	19	21	17	23	21	18	18	22	19	3.0	7.3	81157	78.3	14.6	7.1	23	61.3
6	MAMARONECK UFSD	22	23	20	22	22	18	23	17	19	3.1	7.6	81048	84.4	10.7	4.9	21	59.5
7	EDGEMONT UFSD	20	21	21	21	20	18	18	14	17	2.3	7.2	80281	83.5	14.3	2.3	21	43.6
8	SACHEM CSD	21	23	21	26	25	24	16	22	25	1.3	5.2	80209	89.2	9.1	1.7	24	62.4
9	MANHASSET UFSD	17	24	16	23	22	18	16	18	21	5.8	7.2	79353	89.5	9.2	1.3	21	57.5
10	WHITE PLAINS CITY SD	19	20	22	24	21	22	26	25	20	21.2	5.0	79078	83.1	12.6	4.3	19	59.3
11	CONNETQUOT CSD	20	21	22	21	21	22	21	21	22	0.8	6.5	79017	85.9	10.5	3.6	24	53.2
12	GREAT NECK UFSD	18	20	21	23	21	23	20	23	23	2.8	6.7	78677	86.0	7.6	6.4	19	56.6
13	PORT WASHINGTON UFSD	18	22	20	18	21	16	20	20	16	4.4	9.3	78653	88.0	10.6	1.4	21	60.6
14	HARRISON CSD	22	23	21	21	22	16	17	16	16	0.7	6.9	78218	85.0	9.8	5.3	18	54.9
15	CARMEL CSD	21	22	21	21	21	19	24	18	19	1.3	12.1	78000	84.9	11.9	3.2	21	22.4
16	HAUPPAUGE UFSD	25	25	27	20	18	19	23	21	23	0.0	10.2	77607	76.8	18.1	5.1	21	51.4
17	NORTH SHORE CSD	19	24	24	24	24	22	21	17	21	1.8	10.8	77241	78.0	14.3	7.6	20	48.0
18	SHOREHAM-WADING RIVER CSD	21	25	19	21	20	22	21	20	23	0.5	8.3	77172	79.1	12.6	8.4	24	60.7
19	BLIND BROOK-RYE UFSD	24	22	18	22	23	21	17	17	22	1.1	4.6	77046	87.8	8.9	3.3	22	58.9
20	LONGWOOD CSD	25	27	25	28	27	25	25	22	25	4.9	5.6	76406	87.4	10.4	2.2	21	61.0
21	LONG BEACH CITY SD	24	24	23	27	26	22	21	21	22	9.6	6.4	76365	85.1	11.1	3.8	17	47.1
22	HERRICKS UFSD	19	21	20	23	22	22	20	22	22	4.1	13.2	76002	84.2	14.7	1.0	18	41.8
23	RYE CITY SD	18	18	16	18	18	22	18	19	20	2.7	9.7	75244	73.6	12.7	13.7	17	48.2
24	CHAPPAQUA CSD	18	23	23	23	22	0	23	22	24	2.1	7.0	75144	85.2	11.3	3.4	16	51.9
25	BROOKHAVEN-COMSEWOGUE	20	26	21	24	25	22	16	16	22	1.9	7.8	75000	77.3	21.9	0.8	22	55.8
26	SOUTHAMPTON UFSD	20	21	21	23	22	15	18	19	15	7.0	5.7	75000	84.1	9.0	6.9	19	46.9
27	HAVERSTRAW-STONY POINT CSD	19	24	23	24	24	19	21	19	22	10.3	4.8	74625	80.9	12.7	6.4	19	61.8
28	ROSLYN UFSD	19	19	21	20	20	21	20	18	24	4.8	9.6	74299	84.2	8.3	7.5	15	45.0
29	SAYVILLE UFSD	23	25	0	29	0	19	21	18	19	0.8	12.4	74083	79.7	17.3	3.0	20	49.2
30	PELHAM UFSD	18	22	22	22	22	19	21	18	19	5.1	10.0	74036	82.8	13.0	4.1	20	40.8
31	SOMERS CSD	18	24	23	22	23	21	18	7	20	1.4	6.6	73597	84.6	8.4	7.0	20	49.5
32	EAST ROCKAWAY UFSD	26	22	22	21	25	21	18	17	19	1.1	9.4	73113	85.3	12.6	2.1	16	44.2
33	UFSD - TARRYTOWNS	20	19	20	21	15	23	21	20	19	16.0	9.8	72922	78.0	13.2	8.8	18	50.5
34	THREE VILLAGE CSD	20	24	24	24	25	19	22	19	21	2.9	8.3	72916	80.9	14.8	4.3	22	58.2
35	SOUTH COUNTRY CSD	17	21	18	18	22	22	22	25	20	5.7	9.6	72871	82.4	13.4	4.3	19	53.7
36	SYOSSET CSD	20	19	22	24	22	20	20	20	22	1.2	11.8	72827	80.5	15.2	4.3	14	49.9
37	WEST HEMPSTEAD UFSD	21	24	24	24	24	19	21	17	19	2.4	7.7	72384	82.3	16.6	1.1	18	52.6
38	SOUTH ORANGETOWN CSD	20	21	20	23	22	19	21	20	20	1.7	9.2	72133	82.8	10.5	6.7	19	54.4
39	BALDWIN UFSD	22	21	20	22	21	18	22	20	23	7.1	9.0	72118	80.5	19.2	0.3	18	36.7
40	MT PLEASANT CSD	20	23	24	25	24	18	14	18	22	0.7	7.0	72099	81.9	9.4	8.7	20	37.0

TABLE 2 (Continued)
Statistics for Public School Districts
July 2000 Report to the Governor and the Legislature

| | | Average Class Size | | | | | | | | | | | | Classroom Teachers Certification | | | | |
| | | Grade 8 | | | | | Grade 10 | | | | | | | | | | | |
Rank	Bottom 40	K	English	Math	Social Studies	Science	English	Math	Science	Social Studies	% Minority	Annual Turnover %	Median Salary	% Permanent	% Provisional	% Other	Median Years Exp.	% Master's +30 or Doctorate
743	WHITNEY POINT CSD	18	22	23	23	22	22	17	22	18	0.0	8.9	37186	77.6	15.9	6.5	14	5.9
744	MORIAH CSD	19	23	22	24	24	22	9	19	24	0.0	8.6	37152	76.1	18.3	5.6	14	7.0
745	LITTLE VALLEY CSD	0	16	15	15	18	16	17	18	20	0.0	11.1	37127	86.5	10.8	2.7	10	10.8
746	ANDES CSD	13	9	9	9	16	10	8	10	13	4.2	4.8	37070	87.5	8.3	4.2	12	0.0
747	ST REGIS FALLS CSD	16	14	12	0	15	13	0	0	14	0.0	20.6	36950	71.9	21.9	6.3	10	9.4
748	MT MORRIS CSD	18	15	15	15	15	13	11	11	15	0.0	16.1	36912	75.4	19.7	4.9	15	6.6
749	CANASERAGA CSD	16	24	24	25	26	17	0	18	17	0.0	3.6	36760	69.0	24.1	6.9	18	6.9
750	GANANDA CSD	22	18	18	18	18	23	23	26	23	0.0	15.7	36677	73.9	14.8	11.4	14	3.4
751	WORCESTER CSD	23	35	35	22	38	0	18	0	17	0.0	13.5	36606	77.8	5.6	16.7	16	11.1
752	HAMILTON CSD	18	17	18	18	17	18	18	20	18	0.0	12.9	36455	80.3	14.1	5.6	15	9.9
753	SILVER CREEK CSD	17	21	21	19	0	29	17	0	0	0.9	5.5	36413	82.1	10.7	7.1	14	7.1
754	RED CREEK CSD	17	20	22	20	21	23	18	20	24	1.1	9.9	36292	84.0	10.6	5.3	15	10.6
755	BAINBRIDGE-GUILFORD CSD	15	20	16	20	21	25	17	19	25	0.0	10.9	36181	77.9	10.5	11.6	16	10.5
756	FRANKLINVILLE CSD	15	18	23	15	19	16	0	15	15	0.0	9.2	36090	79.0	16.0	4.9	13	11.1
757	AVOCA CSD	22	21	18	18	16	22	22	16	20	1.2	13.6	36006	75.9	17.2	6.9	9	6.9
758	CANDOR CSD	18	21	20	21	21	0	17	19	0	0.0	9.8	35964	74.4	16.3	9.3	17	3.5
759	MORRISVILLE-EATON CSD	14	24	24	24	24	20	7	17	16	0.0	13.0	35573	83.3	12.8	3.8	17	3.8
760	WALTON CSD	19	19	20	20	14	19	18	19	19	0.0	8.9	35572	80.6	9.7	9.7	16	10.7
761	CLYDE-SAVANNAH CSD	15	14	13	16	17	14	19	14	17	0.0	11.1	35521	68.0	25.2	6.8	12	5.8
762	CROWN POINT CSD	20	17	17	18	19	15	0	18	15	0.0	18.9	35517	78.4	16.2	5.4	15	8.1
763	GILBERTSVILLE-MOUNT UPTON	18	19	19	19	19	14	21	0	16	2.1	20.0	35452	76.9	19.2	3.8	14	11.5
764	OTEGO-UNADILLA CSD	18	24	19	25	24	19	17	19	21	1.7	5.6	35161	84.2	11.4	4.4	12	14.0
765	GENESEE VALLEY CSD	18	20	20	15	19	15	10	3	0	0.0	16.9	34846	67.5	22.1	10.4	12	10.4
766	GEORGETOWN-SOUTH OTSELIC	21	16	4	18	2	0	17	3	17	2.3	14.3	34639	71.4	26.5	2.0	13	2.0
767	EDMESTON CSD	21	24	24	24	24	19	21	13	19	2.1	6.4	34600	80.9	12.8	6.4	12	0.0
768	JEFFERSON CSD	0	39	19	19	39	21	13	11	19	0.0	21.4	34424	74.1	7.4	18.5	16	11.1
769	LAURENS CSD	15	36	12	34	19	17	0	19	15	2.6	22.5	34397	65.0	30.0	5.0	14	7.5
770	ALFRED-ALMOND CSD	13	23	16	23	19	17	14	15	15	0.0	15.2	34260	70.1	20.9	9.0	12	13.4
771	HANCOCK CSD	19	18	35	20	19	18	14	11	15	1.8	3.8	34198	72.4	13.8	13.8	13	10.3
772	REMSENBURG-SPEONK UFSD	23	0	0	0	0	0	17	0	0	0.0	13.6	34016	75.0	14.3	10.7	8	28.6
773	FRANKLIN CSD	12	0	22	20	20	25	0	23	26	0.0	18.9	33800	69.4	22.2	8.3	13	8.3
774	RAQUETTE LAKE UFSD	1	0	0	0	0	0	0	0	0	0.0	0.0	33794	0.0	0.0	100.0	12	0.0
775	OPPENHEIM-EPHRATAH CSD	17	14	11	21	14	19	11	25	0	0.0	16.7	33433	68.6	19.6	11.8	15	2.0
776	BROOKFIELD CSD	24	21	20	20	20	24	13	23	25	0.0	18.2	33349	56.5	21.7	21.7	11	0.0
777	GREENWOOD CSD	17	18	7	18	18	13	6	14	14	0.0	15.4	33318	82.6	4.3	13.0	12	13.0
778	CHARLOTTE VALLEY CSD	15	18	0	19	19	16	8	25	15	0.0	17.5	33240	76.2	19.0	4.8	12	9.5
779	BRADFORD CSD	29	21	21	21	21	12	0	12	12	0.0	11.1	33185	69.2	19.2	11.5	8	3.8
780	UNADILLA VALLEY CSD	14	20	21	22	22	16	0	0	17	0.0	9.0	30952	74.5	16.0	9.6	14	9.6
781	PUTNAM CSD	6	0	0	0	0	0	0	0	0	0.0	12.5	30688	62.5	37.5	0.0	5	37.5
782	NEW SUFFOLK COMN SD	0	0	0	0	0	0	0	0	0	0.0	0.0	27000	0.0	100.0	0.0	7	0.0
783	INLET COMN SD	6	0	0	0	0	0	0	0	0	0.0	0.0	24266	50.0	25.0	25.0	8	0.0

NEW YORK CITY SCHOOLS DISTRICT MAP

Source: New York City Dept. of Education, http://schools.nyc.gov

ENGLISH LANGUAGE LEARNERS IN NEW YORK CITY

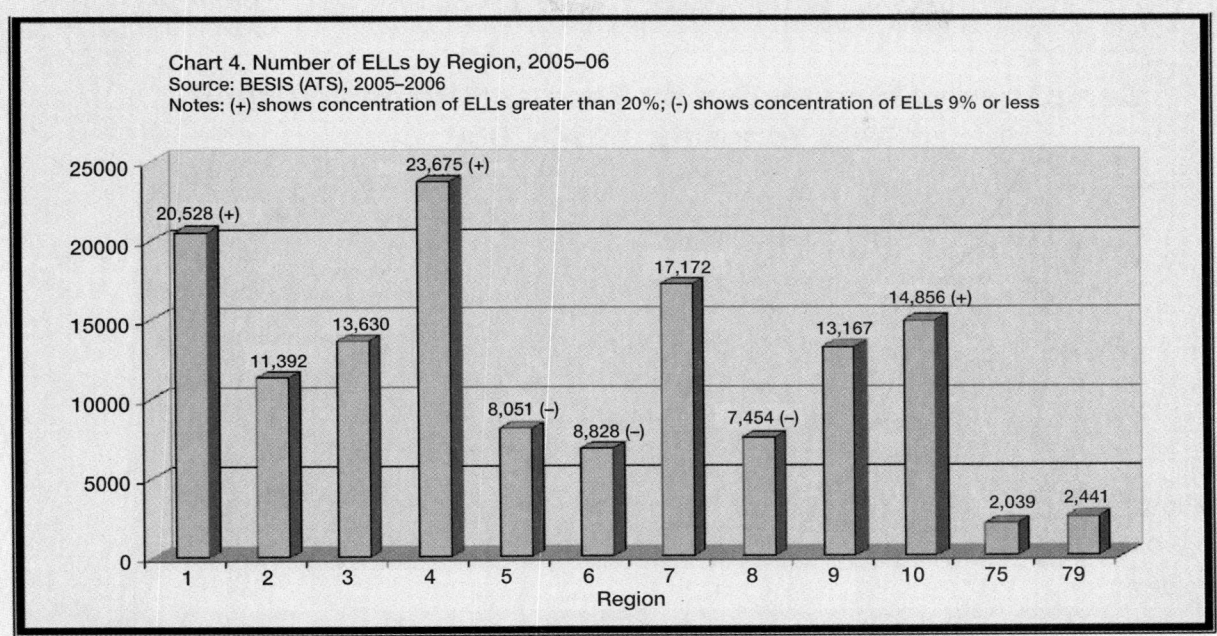

Chart 4. Number of ELLs by Region, 2005–06
Source: BESIS (ATS), 2005–2006
Notes: (+) shows concentration of ELLs greater than 20%; (-) shows concentration of ELLs 9% or less

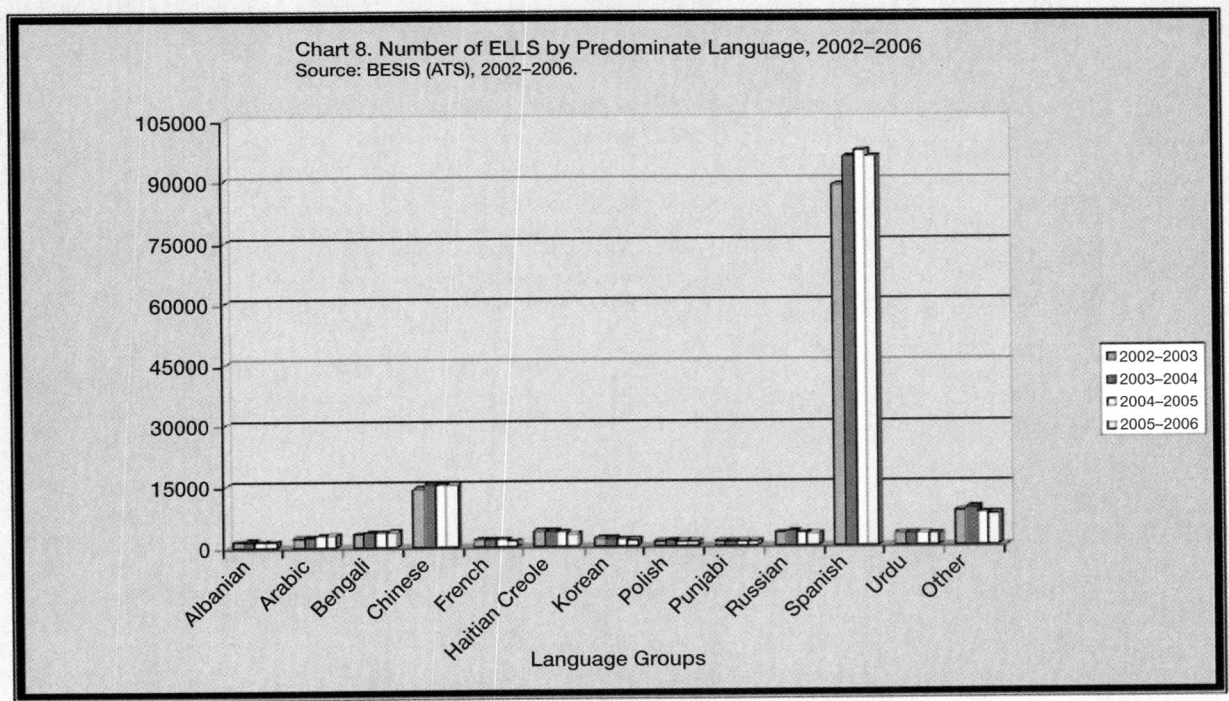

Chart 8. Number of ELLS by Predominate Language, 2002–2006
Source: BESIS (ATS), 2002–2006.

Source: http://schools.nyc.gov/Offices/SCA/Reports/projections05-14.htm

NEW YORK CITY DEMOGRAPHICS

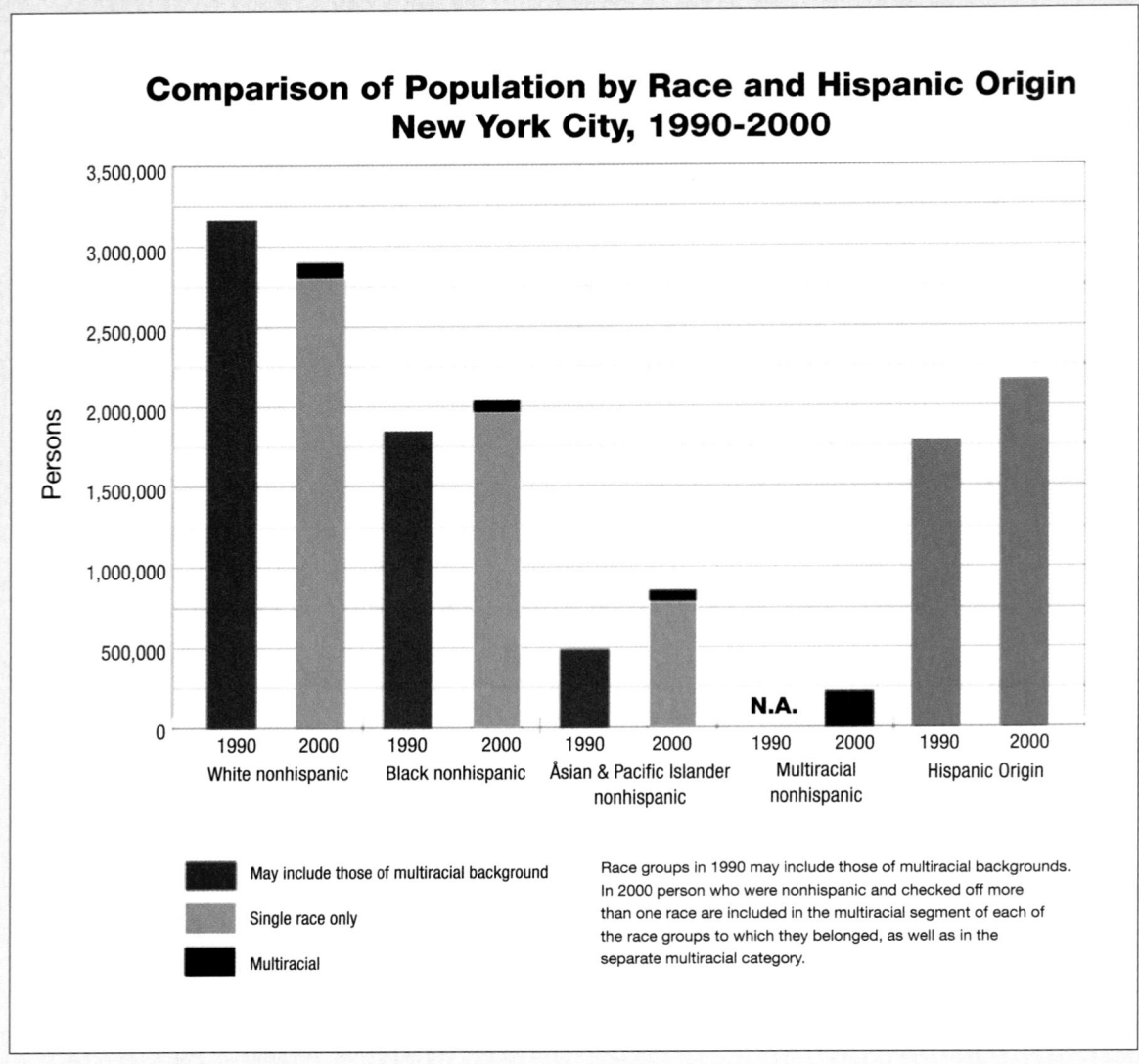

**Comparison of Population by Race and Hispanic Origin
New York City, 1990-2000**

Legend:
- May include those of multiracial background
- Single race only
- Multiracial

Race groups in 1990 may include those of multiracial backgrounds. In 2000 person who were nonhispanic and checked off more than one race are included in the multiracial segment of each of the race groups to which they belonged, as well as in the separate multiracial category.

Source: http://www.nyc.gov/

PART II: Becoming a Teacher in New York

CERTIFICATION REQUIREMENTS TO TEACH IN NEW YORK

Judith R. Levine, Farmingdale State University of New York

In order to be a classroom teacher in one of the public school systems in New York State, it is necessary to hold a teaching certificate. There are two different certificates which are earned sequentially.

1. An **Initial Certificate** is the entry level certificate for classroom teachers and is valid for five years. It is granted upon (a) completion of an accredited bachelor's level teacher preparation program in New York State or in a state that has a reciprocity agreement with New York, (b) the successful completion of the following three exams: Liberal Arts and Sciences Test (LAST), the Assessment of Teaching Skills-Written (ATS-W), and the appropriate Content Specialty Test(s) (CST), and (c) fingerprint clearance. The institution must recommend a candidate for certification upon his or her completion of a program in New York State. Candidates from programs in states with reciprocity must apply directly to the State Education Department of New York.

    Among the many requirements of certified programs are: (a) instruction in Child Abuse Identification, (b) instruction in School Violence Intervention and Prevention, and (c) student teaching.

    Several alternative paths to certification exist for those with other backgrounds. All must include teaching experience (student teaching, internship, or professional teaching) and workshops in Child Abuse Identification and in School Violence Intervention and Prevention. These other paths include, but are not limited to the following:

    - An individual who is a certified teacher in a state that has reciprocity with New York may become certified in New York by applying directly to the NYS Education Department Office of Teaching Initiatives and completing the other requirements described above.

    - An individual who is a certified teacher in a state that does not have a reciprocity agreement with New York must satisfy specific course and semester hour requirements while earning a bachelor's degree with a GPA of at least 2.5. Additionally, all other requirements described above must be met.

    - A recent college graduate in a field other than teaching may become certified by obtaining a master's degree from an accredited teacher education program and completing the other requirements described above.

    - An individual with a bachelor's degree in an academic major who wants to change careers and become a certified teacher can do so by enrolling in and completing an Alternative Teacher Certification Program and meeting the other requirements described above.

    - An individual who possesses certification from the National Board for Professional Teaching Standards may obtain certification in an equivalent New York State title by applying directly to the NYS Education Department Office of Teaching Initiatives.

2. A **Professional Certificate** grants permanent certification and is granted only to holders of an Initial Certificate in the same title. It requires a Master's degree or higher from an accredited program and one year of mentored teaching followed by two additional years of teaching experience. In order to maintain the professional certificate it is necessary to engage in 175 hours of professional development every five years. Activities that qualify include, but are not limited to, in-service training, formal course work, conference attendance/participation, research, and mentoring.

    The Initial and Professional certificates are issued in specific subject and/or grade titles, and a large number and variety of titles are offered. The basic grade titles are Early Childhood (birth - grade 2), Childhood (grades 1-6), Middle Childhood (grades 5-9), and Adolescence (grades 7-12). At the early childhood, childhood, and middle childhood levels certification is available as both a "generalist" and a "student with disabilities generalist".

    At the middle childhood level, certification is also available in specific subject areas and in a specific subject area for students with disabilities. At the adolescence (secondary) level certificates are again granted in specific subject areas or in a specific subject area for students with disabilities.

NEW YORK STATE TEACHER CERTIFICATE EXAMINATIONS

The series of tests that a candidate must pass in order to become certified as a teacher are designed to measure an individual's general knowledge and skills in the arts and sciences, knowledge of teaching theory and practice, and knowledge in the specific content area in which the candidate seeks certification.

1. **The Liberal Arts and Sciences Test (LAST)** consists of multiple choice questions and a written assignment. The test assesses the ability to apply conceptual and analytical skills, critical thinking and communications skill, and multicultural awareness to the following five areas:
   - Scientific, mathematical, and technological processes
   - Historical and social scientific awareness
   - Artistic expression and the humanities
   - Communication and research skill
   - Written analysis and expression

2. **The Assessment of Teaching Skills-Written (ATS-W)** consists of multiple choice questions and a written assignment. It measures professional and pedagogical knowledge. There are two different ATS-Ws. The Elementary ATS-W is for those who seek certification in Early Childhood or Childhood and the Secondary ATS-W is for those who seek certification in Middle Childhood or Adolescence.

3. **The Content Specialty Tests (CSTs)** consist of multiple choice questions and a written assignment. Each test measures knowledge and skills in the specific content area of certification (for example, biology or history). It should be noted that the CSTs for languages other than English include listening, speaking, and writing components.

For more information visit the New York State Education Department website at http://www.highered.nysed.gov/ or the New York State Teacher Certification Exam Website at http://www.nystce.nesinc.com.

NEW YORK STATE ASSESSMENT OF TEACHING SKILLS STANDARDS

Standard I.* The teacher designs instruction appropriate for all students that reflects an understanding of relevant content and is based on continuous and appropriate assessment.

Standard II.* The teacher creates a classroom environment of respect and rapport that fosters a positive climate for learning, equity, and excellence.

Standard III.* The teacher promotes student learning by providing responsive instruction that makes use of effective communication techniques, instructional strategies that actively engage students in the learning process, and timely, high-quality feedback.

Standard IV. The teacher fulfills professional roles and responsibilities and adheres to legal and ethical requirements of the profession.

* The developmental characteristics of students from early childhood to grade 12, including developmentally appropriate examples and instructional strategies, are defined in the corresponding assessment framework for PPR (EC-12), as well as in the standards for PPR at each of the other three certification levels (EC-Grade 4, Grades 4-8, and Grades 8-12).

STANDARD I. The teacher designs instruction appropriate for all students that reflects an understanding of relevant content and is based on continuous and appropriate assessment.

TEACHER KNOWLEDGE: WHAT TEACHERS KNOW
Teachers of Students in Grades EC–12

Students

The beginning teacher knows and understands:

1.1k the intellectual, social, physical, and emotional developmental characteristics of students in different age groups;

1.2k the implications of students' developmental characteristics for planning appropriate instruction;

1.3k characteristics and instructional needs of students with varied backgrounds, skills, interests, and learning needs;

1.4k different approaches to learning that students may exhibit and what motivates students to become active, engaged learners;

1.5k cultural and socioeconomic differences and the significance of these differences for instructional planning; and

1.6k appropriate strategies for instructing English language learners.

Content and Pedagogy

The beginning teacher knows and understands:

1.7k the importance of the state content and performance standards as outlined in the Texas Essential Knowledge and Skills (TEKS);

1.8k relevant content of the discipline being taught, including concepts, principles, relationships, methods of inquiry, and key issues;

APPLICATION: WHAT TEACHERS CAN DO
Teachers of Students in Grades EC–12

Students

The beginning teacher is able to:

1.1s plan lessons that reflect an understanding of students' developmental characteristics and needs;

1.2s adapt lessons to address students' varied backgrounds, skills, interests, and learning needs, including the needs of English language learners;

1.3s use effective approaches to address varied student learning needs and preferences;

1.4s plan instruction that motivates students to want to learn and achieve; and

1.5s acknowledge and respect cultural and socioeconomic differences among students when planning instruction.

Content and Pedagogy

The beginning teacher knows and understands:

1.6s use the Texas Essential Knowledge and Skills (TEKS) to plan instruction;

1.7s exhibit appropriate knowledge of a subject to promote student learning;

1.8s demonstrate awareness of common student misconceptions or likely sources of student error in relation to particular content;

STANDARD I. The teacher designs instruction appropriate for all students that reflects an understanding of relevant content and is based on continuous and appropriate assessment.

TEACHER KNOWLEDGE: WHAT TEACHERS KNOW
Teachers of Students in Grades EC–12 (continued)

Content and Pedagogy
The beginning teacher is able to:

1.9k the significance of the vertical alignment of content, including prerequisite knowledge and skills;

1.10k how lesson content and skills connect with other disciplines and within the discipline; and

1.11k current research on best pedagogical practices.

Selection of Instructional Goals and Objectives
The beginning teacher knows and understands:

1.12k the importance of developing instructional goals and objectives that are clear, relevant, meaningful, and age-appropriate;

1.13k the importance of developing instructional goals and objectives that can be assessed;

1.14k the importance of developing instructional goals and objectives that are suitable for students with varied learning needs; and

1.15k the importance of aligning instructional goals with campus and district goals.

1.16k the use of appropriate materials and resources for preparing instruction, presenting lessons, and assessing learning;

1.17k the importance of knowing when to integrate technology into instruction and assessment; and

1.18k the use of resources beyond the campus to help students meet academic and nonacademic needs.

Designing Coherent Instruction
The beginning teacher knows and understands:

1.19k the importance of designing instruction that reflects the TEKS;

1.20k features of instruction that maximize students' thinking skills;

1.21k the importance of planning lessons and structuring units so that activities progress in a logical sequence;

1.22k how materials, technology, and other resources may be used to support instructional goals and objectives and engage students in meaningful learning;

1.23k the benefits of designing instruction that integrates content across disciplines; and

1.24k the importance of engaging in continuous monitoring and self-assessment of instructional effectiveness.

APPLICATION: WHAT TEACHERS CAN DO
Teachers of Students in Grades EC–12 (continued)

Content and Pedagogy
The beginning teacher is able to:

1.9s plan instruction that reflects an understanding of important prerequisite relationships;

1.10s plan instruction that makes connections within the discipline and across disciplines; and

1.11s use a variety of pedagogical techniques to convey information and teach skills.

Selection of Instructional Goals and Objectives
The beginning teacher is able to:

1.12s develop instructional goals and objectives that are clear, relevant, meaningful, and age-appropriate;

1.13s develop instructional goals and objectives that are able to be assessed;

1.14s develop instructional goals and objectives that reflect students' age, developmental level, prior skills and knowledge, background, and interests; and

1.15s develop instructional goals and objectives that reflect different types of student learning and skills.

1.16s use various types of materials and other resources to aid in preparing and implementing instruction;

1.17s use technological tools to promote learning and expand instructional options; and

1.18s use resources available outside the school (e.g., museums, businesses, community members) to enhance students' learning opportunities.

Designing Coherent Instruction
The beginning teacher is able to:

1.19s plan instructional activities that progress sequentially and support stated instructional goals based on the TEKS;

1.20s select instructional resources that support instructional goals, enhance achievement, and engage students in learning;

1.21s use varied activities and instructional groupings to engage students in instructional content and meet instructional goals and objectives;

1.22s allocate time appropriately within lessons and units, including providing adequate opportunities for students to engage in reflection and closure; and

1.23s provide students with opportunities to explore content from many perspectives.

STANDARD I. The teacher designs instruction appropriate for all students that reflects an understanding of relevant content and is based on continuous and appropriate assessment.

TEACHER KNOWLEDGE: WHAT TEACHERS KNOW

Teachers of Students in Grades EC–12 (continued)

Assessment of Student Learning

The beginning teacher knows and understands:

1.25k the role of assessment in guiding instructional planning;

1.26k the importance of creating assessments that are congruent with instructional goals and objectives;

1.27k the characteristics, uses, advantages, and limitations of various assessment methods and strategies;

1.28k the role of technology in assessing student learning;

1.29k the benefits of and strategies for promoting student self-assessment;

1.30k the connection between the Texas statewide assessment program, the TEKS, and instruction; and

1.31k how to analyze data from local, state, and other assessments using common statistical measures.

APPLICATION: WHAT TEACHERS CAN DO

Teachers of Students in Grades EC–12 (continued)

Assessment of Student Learning

The beginning teacher is able to:

1.24s use a variety of assessment methods, including technology, that are appropriate for evaluating student achievement of instructional goals and objectives;

1.25s communicate assessment criteria and standards to students;

1.26s design assessments, where appropriate, that reflect real-world applications of knowledge and understanding;

1.27s promote students' use of self-monitoring and self-assessment;

1.28s analyze assessment results to aid in determining students' strengths and needs; and

1.29s use assessment results to help plan instruction for groups of students or individuals.

STANDARD II. The teacher creates a classroom environment of respect and rapport that fosters a positive climate for learning, equity, and excellence.

Creating an Environment of Respect and Rapport

The beginning teacher knows and understands:

2.1k the importance of creating a learning environment in which diversity and individual differences are respected;

2.2k the impact of teacher-student interactions and interactions among students on classroom climate and student learning and development; and

2.3k ways to establish a positive classroom climate that fosters active engagement in learning among students.

Establishing an Environment for Learning and Excellence

The beginning teacher knows and understands:

2.4k the importance of communicating enthusiasm for learning; and

2.5k the necessity of communicating teacher expectations for student learning.

Creating an Environment of Respect and Rapport

The beginning teacher is able to:

2.1s interact with students in ways that reflect support and show respect for all students;

2.2s use strategies to ensure that interactions among students are polite, respectful, and cooperative; and

2.3s use strategies to ensure that the classroom environment and interactions among individuals and groups within the classroom promote active engagement in learning.

Establishing an Environment for Learning and Excellence

The beginning teacher is able to:

2.4s communicate to all students the importance of instructional content and the expectation of high-quality work; and

2.5s ensure that instructional goals and objectives, activities, classroom interactions, assessments, and other elements of the classroom environment convey high expectations for student achievement.

STANDARD II. The teacher creates a classroom environment of respect and rapport that fosters a positive climate for learning, equity, and excellence.

TEACHER KNOWLEDGE: WHAT TEACHERS KNOW

Teachers of Students in Grades EC–12 (continued)

Managing Classroom Procedures

The beginning teacher knows and understands:

2.6k how classroom routines and procedures affect student learning and achievement;

2.7k how to organize student groups to facilitate cooperation and productivity;

2.8k the importance of time management for effective classroom functioning;

2.9k procedures for managing transitions;

2.10k routines and procedures for managing and using materials, supplies, and technology;

2.11k noninstructional duties (e.g., taking attendance) and procedures for performing these duties effectively; and

2.12k the classroom roles of paraprofessionals, volunteers, and other professionals, including substitute teachers, in accordance with district policies and procedures.

Managing Student Behavior

The beginning teacher knows and understands:

2.13k theories and techniques relating to managing and monitoring student behavior;

2.14k appropriate behavior standards and expectations for students at various developmental levels;

2.15k the significance of district policies and procedures for managing student behavior and ensuring ethical behavior in the classroom;

2.16k the importance of establishing classroom standards of student conduct and clear consequences for inappropriate behavior;

2.17k the value of encouraging students to work in an ethical manner and monitor their own behavior; and

2.18k appropriate responses to a variety of student behaviors and misbehaviors.

APPLICATION: WHAT TEACHERS CAN DO

Teachers of Students in Grades EC–12 (continued)

Managing Classroom Procedures

The beginning teacher is able to:

2.6s establish classroom rules and procedures to promote an organized and productive learning environment;

2.7s organize and manage groups to ensure that students work together cooperatively and productively;

2.8s schedule activities and manage class time in ways that maximize student learning;

2.9s manage transitions to maximize instructional time;

2.10s implement routines and procedures for the effective management of materials, supplies, and technology;

2.11s coordinate the performance of noninstructional duties with instructional activities;

2.12s monitor the performance of volunteers and paraprofessionals in the classroom in accordance with district policies and procedures; and

2.13s use volunteers and paraprofessionals to enhance and enrich instruction, and evaluate their effectiveness.

Managing Student Behavior

The beginning teacher is able to:

2.14s communicate high and realistic expectations for students' behavior and ensure that students understand behavior expectations and consequences for misbehavior;

2.15s consistently enforce standards and expectations for student behavior and ethical work habits;

2.16s encourage students to maintain ethical work standards and monitor their own behavior; and

2.17s use effective methods and procedures for monitoring and responding to positive and negative student behaviors.

STANDARD II. The teacher creates a classroom environment of respect and rapport that fosters a positive climate for learning, equity, and excellence.

TEACHER KNOWLEDGE: WHAT TEACHERS KNOW
Teachers of Students in Grades EC–12 (continued)

Maintaining a Physical and Emotional Environment that is Safe and Productive

The beginning teacher knows and understands:

2.19k features and characteristics of physical spaces that are safe and productive for learning;

2.20k the benefits and limitations of various arrangements of furniture in the classroom;

2.21k procedures for ensuring safety in the classroom;

2.22k physical accessibility as a potential issue in student learning; and

2.23k students' emotional needs and ways to address needs.

APPLICATION: WHAT TEACHERS CAN DO
Teachers of Students in Grades EC–12 (continued)

Maintaining a Physical and Emotional Environment that is Safe and Productive

The beginning teacher is able to:

2.18s organize the physical environment to facilitate learning;

2.19s create a safe and inclusive classroom environment;

2.20s use effective strategies for creating and maintaining a positive classroom environment; and

2.21s respect students' rights and dignity.

STANDARD III. The teacher promotes student learning by providing responsive instruction that makes use strategies that actively engage students in the learning process, and timely, high-quality feedback.

TEACHER KNOWLEDGE: WHAT TEACHERS KNOW
Teachers of Students in Grades EC–12

Communication

The beginning teacher knows and understands:

3.1k the importance of clear, accurate communication in the teaching and learning process;

3.2k principles and strategies for communicating effectively in varied teaching and learning contexts;

3.3k spoken and written language that is appropriate to students' ages, interests, and backgrounds; and

3.4k skills and strategies for engaging in skilled questioning and leading effective student discussions.

APPLICATION: WHAT TEACHERS CAN DO
Teachers of Students in Grades EC–12

Communication

The beginning teacher is able to:

3.1s communicate directions, explanations, and procedures clearly, accurately, and with an appropriate level of detail, both orally and in writing;

3.2s use effective interpersonal skills (including both verbal and nonverbal skills) to reach students and communicate the teacher's commitment to students;

3.3s use spoken and written language that is appropriate to students' ages, interests, and backgrounds;

3.4s use effective communication techniques, including questioning and discussion techniques, to foster active student inquiry, higher-order thinking, problem solving, and productive, supportive interactions;

3.5s use carefully framed questions to enable students to reflect on their understanding of content and to consider new possibilities; and

3.6s apply skills for leading discussions that engage all students in exploring important questions and that extend students' knowledge.

STANDARD III. The teacher promotes student learning by providing responsive instruction that makes use strategies that actively engage students in the learning process, and timely, high-quality feedback.

TEACHER KNOWLEDGE: WHAT TEACHERS KNOW	APPLICATION: WHAT TEACHERS CAN DO
Teachers of Students in Grades EC–12 (continued)	Teachers of Students in Grades EC–12 (continued)

Engaging Students in Learning

The beginning teacher knows and understands:

3.5k criteria for selecting appropriate instructional activities and assignments for students with varied characteristics and needs;

3.6k how to present content to students in relevant and meaningful ways;

3.7k the use of instructional materials, resources, and technologies that are appropriate and engaging for students in varied learning situations;

3.8k the importance of promoting students' intellectual involvement with content and their active development of understanding;

3.9k strategies and techniques for using instructional groupings to promote student learning;

3.10k different types of motivation, factors affecting student motivation, and effective motivational strategies in varied learning contexts; and

3.11k techniques for structuring and pacing lessons in ways that promote student engagement and learning.

Engaging Students in Learning

The beginning teacher is able to:

3.7s create lessons with a clearly defined structure around which activities are organized;

3.8s create activities and assignments that are appropriate for students and that actively engage them in the learning process;

3.9s select and use instructional materials, resources, and technologies that are suitable for instructional goals and that engage students cognitively;

3.10s represent content effectively and in ways that link with students' prior knowledge and experience;

3.11s use flexible grouping to promote productive student interactions and enhance learning;

3.12s pace lessons appropriately and flexibly in response to student needs;

3.13s engage students intellectually by teaching meaningful content in ways that promote all students' active and invested participation in the learning process; and

3.14s encourage students' self-motivation and active engagement in learning.

Providing Feedback to Students

The beginning teacher knows and understands:

3.12k characteristics of effective feedback for students;

3.13k the role of timely feedback in the learning process; and

3.14k how to use constructive feedback to guide each student's learning.

Providing Feedback to Students

The beginning teacher is able to:

3.15s use appropriate language and formats to provide each student with timely feedback that is accurate, constructive, substantive, and specific;

3.16s promote students' ability to use feedback to guide and enhance their learning; and

3.17s base feedback on high expectations for student learning.

Demonstrating Flexibility and Responsiveness

The beginning teacher knows and understands:

3.15k the significance of teacher flexibility and responsiveness in the teaching/learning process; and

3.16k situations in which teacher flexibility can enhance student learning.

Demonstrating Flexibility and Responsiveness

The beginning teacher is able to:

3.18s respond flexibly to various situations, such as lack of student engagement in a learning activity or the occurrence of an unanticipated learning opportunity;

3.19s adjust instruction based on ongoing assessment of student understanding; and

3.20s use alternative instructional approaches to ensure that all students learn and succeed.

STANDARD IV. The teacher fulfills professional roles and responsibilities and adheres to legal and ethical requirements of the profession.

TEACHER KNOWLEDGE: WHAT TEACHERS KNOW
Teachers of Students in Grades EC–12

Interacting and Communicating with Families
The beginning teacher knows and understands:

4.1k   the importance of families' involvement in their children's education; and

4.2k   appropriate ways for working and communicating effectively with families in varied contexts.

Interacting with Other Educators and Contributing to the School and District
The beginning teacher knows and understands:

4.3k   types of interactions among professionals in a school (e.g., vertical teaming, horizontal teaming, team teaching, mentoring) and the significance of these interactions;

4.4k   appropriate ways for working and communicating effectively with other professionals in varied educational contexts;

4.5k   the roles and responsibilities of specialists and other professionals at the building and district levels (e.g., department chairperson, principal, board of trustees, curriculum coordinator, special education professional);

4.6k   available educator support systems (e.g., mentors, service centers, state initiatives, universities);

4.7k   the various ways in which teachers may contribute to their school and district; and

4.8k   the value of participating in school activities.

APPLICATION: WHAT TEACHERS CAN DO
Teachers of Students in Grades EC–12

Interacting and Communicating with Families
The beginning teacher is able to:

4.1s   interact appropriately with families that have diverse characteristics, backgrounds, and needs;

4.2s   apply procedures for conducting effective parent-teacher conferences;

4.3s   communicate with families on a regular basis to share information about students' progress and respond appropriately to families' concerns; and

4.4s   engage families in their children's education and in various aspects of the instructional program.

Interacting with Other Educators and Contributing to the School and District
The beginning teacher is able to:

4.5s   maintain supportive and cooperative relationships with colleagues;

4.6s   engage in collaborative decision making and problem solving with other educators to support students' learning and well-being;

4.7s   work productively with supervisors and mentors to address issues and enhance professional skills and knowledge;

4.8s   communicate effectively and appropriately with other educators in varied contexts;

4.9s   collaborate professionally with other members of the school community to achieve school and district educational goals;

4.10s   participate in decision making, problem solving, and sharing ideas and expertise; and

4.11s   assume professional responsibilities and duties outside the classroom, as appropriate (e.g., serve on committees, volunteer to participate in events and projects).

STANDARD IV. The teacher fulfills professional roles and responsibilities and adheres to legal and ethical requirements of the profession.

Continuing Professional Development

The beginning teacher knows and understands:

4.9k the importance of participating in professional development activities to enhance content knowledge and pedagogical skill;

4.10k the importance of documenting self-assessments;

4.11k characteristics, goals, and procedures associated with teacher appraisal; and

4.12k the importance of using reflection and ongoing self-assessment to enhance teaching effectiveness.

**Legal and Ethical Requirements
and the Structure of Education in Texas**

The beginning teacher knows and understands:

4.13k legal requirements for educators (e.g., those related to special education, students' and families' rights, student discipline, equity, child abuse);

4.14k ethical guidelines for educators in Texas (e.g., in relation to confidentiality, interactions with students and others in the school community);

4.15k policies and procedures in compliance with Code of Ethics and Standards Practices for Texas Educators as adopted by the State Board for Educator Certification;

4.16k procedures and requirements for maintaining accurate student records;

4.17k the importance of adhering to required procedures for administering state-and district-mandated assessments; and

4.18k the structure of the education system in Texas, including relationships between campus, local, and state components.

Continuing Professional Development

The beginning teacher is able to:

4.12s participate in various types of professional development opportunities (e.g., conferences, workshops, work with mentors and other support systems);

4.13s enhance content and pedagogical knowledge through a variety of activities (e.g., reading journals, joining professional associations, attending conferences, engaging in coursework);

4.14s use evidence of self-assessment (e.g., portfolio) to identify strengths, challenges, and potential problems; improve teaching performance; and achieve instructional goals; and

4.15s use appropriate resources and support systems inside and outside the school to address professional development needs.

**Legal and Ethical Requirements
and the Structure of Education in Texas**

The beginning teacher is able to:

4.16s use knowledge of legal and ethical guidelines to guide behavior in educationrelated situations;

4.17s serve as an advocate for students and the profession;

4.18s maintain accurate records; and

4.19s use knowledge of the structure of state and local education systems to seek information and assistance in addressing issues.

INTERVIEWING FOR A TEACHING POSITION: Q AND A
Lynne A. Hammann

How should I prepare?

- Review professional program knowledge from your courses. Be sure to refresh your knowledge of (a) student characteristics and learning needs; (b) diverse students, special learning needs, inclusion, giftedness; (c) professional organization standards; (d) state standards for your area.
- Bring a professional portfolio, if you have one, with a table of contents, and section dividers, clearly labeled with your name, address, etc. Have representative samples available, including examples of student learning (papers, a website, class newspaper) as well as samples of your own professional knowledge.
- If you have an electronic portfolio (e.g., LiveText), bring a document containing your name, contact information, Visitor's Pass information, and brief directions on accessing the portfolio. Also bring hard copy samples.
- Learn about the district—size, administrators, educational policies, schools, test scores, money resources. Access district websites; get information from district offices; ask friends and colleagues.
- Learn what the district policies and concerns are about such "hot topics" as NCLB, diversity, technology, and continuing professional development.
- Apply for fingerprint clearance.

What questions might I be asked?

- What is your philosophy of education?
- How do you use technology in your classroom?
- Describe your experience/approach to collaboration.
- How do you assess students?
- Describe a lesson in _____ (daily/weekly).
- What is the role of effort (and/or motivation) in your classroom?
- What grade(s) do you want to teach and why? Refer to developmental characteristics of future learners, for example, "Eleventh-graders are beginning to discover who they are and construct their identities. They're in Erikson's Identity formation stage. In American literature, they have opportunities to ...."
- What makes your qualifications special? Prepare a short list of strengths, including content knowledge (refer to student teaching, other experiences) that you can state in a matter-of-fact way with examples.
- What experience do you have with inclusion? Cite specific examples from courses, field experiences, tutoring, student teaching, work experiences, volunteer organizations

- How would you include students with special learning needs in your class (or a lesson)? For example, if you had a child who had ADHD or Asperberger's Syndrome, explain how you would construct your lesson to meet his/her learning needs. Refer to your educational psychology classes, your methods classes, and diversity classes.
- Describe your approach to classroom management. Refer to methods classes and/or educational psychology classes. Include learners' developmental needs/characteristics. Have classroom management plan.
- What clubs or organizations would you volunteer for? Make sure you know what the school has available and explain why/how you are qualified for them.
- How will you communicate with parents? Use examples from field experiences, tutoring, student teaching, work experiences, and other organizations (such as church or scouts). Explain that you have some plans for your classroom, such as a Family Reading or Math or Science) night, or a class newsletter, emails, etc.

How can I find out what else I might be asked?

Talk to other teachers in the district/school.

What if I get a question I don't know the answer to?

It's ok to say, "That's an interesting question...let me reflect for a few moments..." and then answer professionally. You may need to "think on your feet" (as in a classroom) and say, "I'd have to give this some more thought, but I could say at this point..."

How should I dress?

Dress neatly, in clean clothes, with minimal (if any) cologne/after-shave. Dress professionally, even if school's teachers dress casually. Show interviewers your professional self—you are there to teach and guide children and be a role model for them.

- Women: professional dress, pant suit with blouse or blazer and dress pants, pale nail polish (if any) and conservative make up; no cleavage, nothing see-through, nothing too short
- Men: suit with dress shirt and tie, or dress pants with shirt and tie, blazer. Avoid displaying tattoos, multiple piercings, visible skin between pants/skirt and top. Wear professional shoes.

What questions should I prepare?

Refer to what you know about the district and ask for more information about a current topic (professional development opportunities, technology training opportunities, technology use, IEP procedures).

How can I feel more confident?

Anticipate possible questions. Ask a friend or teacher to do a mock interview. If you have an opportunity, record yourself and study it.

What should I do after the interview?

Shake hands. Thank interviewers for the opportunity to meet. Send a short professional letter within a day or two thanking district/interviewers for the opportunity to interview and restating a few positive points about the district. In the letter, say you're looking forward to hearing from them about the position.

PART III: The State of Education in New York

TEACHER CENTERS AND MENTORING PROGRAMS

Donna Lynn Ciampa, State University of New York—Suffolk

Teacher Centers in New York State originated in 1984. Established by the New York State Legislature, and supported by New York State United Teachers, they were originally defined as Teacher Resource and Computer Training Centers, meant to enhance the use of technology by the teacher within the classroom. Some teacher centers serve one school district; others serve a consortium of many districts. Every teacher center has a liaison in each building it serves. New teachers can inquire about the teacher center through this liaison or through their building union representative. Regardless of the size of the teacher center, the goal remains the same—to enable students to achieve high learning standards through teacher support in the following areas:

- strengthening teamwork among teachers across disciplines
- developing curriculum that connects to students' lives
- designing class activities that engage all students
- using technology as an instructional tool
- managing a classroom more effectively
- applying state standards in a meaningful way for students

(http://www.nyiteez.org/NYteachercenters/homepage.htm)

How do the teacher centers in New York State do this? First they provide professional development opportunities for educators. Each teacher center is governed by a policy board made up of at least 51% of teachers from the district(s) it serves. These teachers are appointed by the collective bargaining agent within their district. The remainder of the policy board consists of district administrators and representatives from the community, higher education, and business. This make-up ensures that the professional development offered is based on local district needs.

Professional development is provided by the teacher centers through a variety of venues. Graduate college credit is offered at a discounted rate. Seminars and workshops are sponsored, and consultants are often brought in to share the latest methods and trends in education. Collegial circles are supported and encouraged.

In addition to professional development opportunities, teacher centers fund mini grants which offer teachers financial support for innovative ideas that will help students to meet state standards. Other funds are available to parents

and parent teacher organizations (PTOs) to support student activities in collaboration with parents and community organizations. The grants often cover the costs of technological equipment, software, and various other materials to enhance student learning that may not be funded by the district due to budgetary constraints.

In the role of service center, teacher centers have extensive lending libraries for teachers and parents that offer videos, DVDs, books, and journals covering the most current approaches and research in education. Materials that are available for loan include educational DVDs and CDs for classroom use, digital cameras, digital video cameras, and audio equipment. These libraries are enhanced with specialized tools that include: button and poster makers, laminators, and dye cutters. Teachers have access to this equipment to use in enhancing lessons, for special projects, and to preserve the students' creative work

Beyond the materials and professional development, teacher centers offer new teacher training and support. The structure of the Mentor-Intern program ensures the assistance of all first year teachers in their transition into professional duties as of 2004. New teachers are paired with trained veteran classroom teachers who help them deal with complex topics such as classroom management and lesson planning, or issues as basic as student attendance and grade submission protocol. The mentor does this by:

- providing support and coaching to the new teacher
- opening his or her classroom to the new teacher for observation
- modeling teaching techniques and professional behaviors for the benefit of the new teacher
- sharing in goal setting for the new teacher
- making recommendations for further study by the new teacher
- working on lesson plans with the new teacher
- helping familiarize the new teacher with the school's floor plan and layout, staff, support services, and resources

New York State teacher centers are mostly funded by the State in the form of a competitive grant. However, the grant does not cover the full funding for the services provided. Teacher centers sometimes look for donations of money, equipment, or consultant fees from local businesses, the parent teacher associations (PTA), and grants from private foundations or corporations. The Local Education Agency (LEA), the district which is serviced by the teacher center, often provides the location, phone, custodial and/or secretarial support, and the administrative assistance needed to help the director run the teacher center effectively.

In the years since 1984, the bar for student achievement has been raised. New York State teacher centers have kept pace with the requirements. Through the support of its teachers and innovative use of current technology, they have enhanced the learning experience for thousands of children across the State.

TEACHER, PARENTS, STUDENTS: A TEAM
Donna Lynn Ciampa, State University of New York—Suffolk

Education is traditionally thought of as something that happens in schools when a teacher stands in front of a classroom, with the instruction flowing in one direction, from teacher to student. What is traditional, however, is not always accurate. Education is no longer the responsibility of the teacher alone, but has become an undertaking in which teacher, student and parent act as one unit. When parents are respected by the teacher as an integral part of the student's learning process, they are more supportive of both the teacher and the student. Students also need to know that they are equal players. Too often students perceive that they are not active participants in their learning, and that they don't have choices or responsibilities in regard to what, how, and with whom they learn. Given the opportunity, students will rise to the occasion and become active learners. All three members of this team—teachers, parents, and students—are necessary for the success of the student.

How do educators establish this sense of teamwork and what can they do to make sure each parent, student and teacher considers him or herself a party of the team?

From the first day, teachers should make it clear that they are eager to hear what parents and students have to say—that family input counts. Teachers should insure that parents know they have a role in their children's education and that students recognize their responsibilities and opportunities as well. Teachers must keep parents informed. Notes home do not have to indicate that there is a problem. For example, small postcards to celebrate a student's success can go a long way toward supporting student learning and instilling a sense of pride in accomplishment. These kinds of communication also open the door between the parent and the student.

Newsletters can also serve many purposes. A weekly newsletter keeps parents current on what is being learned by the students. It can be a great place to highlight student or class accomplishments as they pertain to character education and good citizenship. Reminders of special due dates can be included as well. Regardless of the grade level—whether kindergartners or seniors in high school—newsletters are a wonderful way to connect with the families and encourage delight in education.

The agenda book is a perfect device to communicate with parents quickly and easily. Short notes regarding student progress and/or needs can be recorded next to the student's homework assignments. The parent's initials on the page or a return note can be used to track parental attention. This method is recommended for communications where a more formal correspondence or meeting may not be necessary.

Students also need to be kept informed. A great way to do this is through daily news announcements. Much like the newsletters to the parents, daily news announcements can be used to announce upcoming events, spotlight student successes and community involvement, and give a preview of upcoming lessons. Students should also be kept up to date on their academic progress. This can be done by giving personalized periodic progress reports or holding student conferences. If a student knows where she stands academically and what needs to be done to succeed, the student will be more likely to respond positively.

When communicating with parents—whether in person, via telephone, or email—teachers should strive to use positive language. The choice of words can make the difference between a productive relationship and a contentious, adversarial one. For example, rather than bluntly telling a parent that a student is "failing this quarter," it is much more effective for the teacher to include both the teacher and student in the conversation and ask "how can we make sure that you (the student) have a better learning experience next quarter?" If the parent and student have no immediate suggestions, a well-thought out plan should be offered and the parent and student be given an opportunity to give feedback. Teachers need to remember to use the word we. The teacher, parent and student are a team, and there is no 'I' in the word team.

Parents should be involved in classroom activities and field trips. Parents often have hidden talents that students are proud to show off and that can provide the entire class with a new learning experience. Teachers shouldn't limit their spectrum to the talents of the parents, however. Remember that talented parents produce talented children; students may surprise everyone by what they know. Including parents and students in the planning of events, lessons, and even field trips is important. Having the entire team involved makes the learning experience much more memorable.

Education is a team project. Getting the parents and students involved with the teacher in and out of the classroom can only enhance the experience of a student as he or she moves through her education and into the world of adulthood.

PART IV: Web Resources for New York's Future Teachers

GENERAL RESOURCES

The University of the State of New York/ The New York State Education Department

http://www.nysed.gov/

The University of the State of New York is an integrated educational system comprised of thousands of public and private elementary and secondary schools, colleges and universities, and numerous other educational professionals, institutions, and services. It is broken up into five main branches: Elementary, Middle, Secondary, and Continuing Education (EMSC), Higher Education (OHE), Office of Cultural Education (OCE), Office of the Professions (OP), and Vocational and Educational Services for Individuals with Disabilities (VESID). The site is a hub for a vast amount of information on topics such as grants and finance, laws and regulation, licensing and certification, reports and statistics, individual schools, curriculum and instruction, and much more.

The New York Times: Education News

http://www.nytimes.com/pages/education/index.html

This site features the latest news and feature stories about education in New York and around the country.

NewYork.Teachers.Net

http://newyork.teachers.net/

This resource includes a chat room, classified ads, a searchable database of lesson plans, job listings, and more.

CERTIFICATION AND TEACHING CAREERS

New York State Education Department: Office of Teaching Initiatives

http://www.highered.nysed.gov/tcert/

This site includes information on demographics, job banks, certification, mentoring, employment guidelines, and fingerprinting.

TEACH Online

http://www.highered.nysed.gov/tcert/news/news5162006.htm

TEACH Online is a certification and fingerprint clearance web portal where you can apply for certification, track your application, pay fees, search certification requirements, and apply for fingerprint clearance.

New York State Teacher Certification Examinations

http://www.nystce.nesinc.com/

This site provides test registration information and materials, test frameworks, preparation guides, score reporting, and more.

NYSUT: Teacher Certification in New York State

http://www.nysut.org/research/bulletins/ teachercertification.html

This site explains the New York state teacher certification process and how it has changed in the last several years. The site includes information on different types of teaching certificates including conditional provisional certificates, transitional certificates, modified temporary licenses for uncertified teachers, and limited certificates, and also addresses substitute teachers and fingerprinting.

RESOURCES FOR NEW TEACHERS

The New York State Mentor Teacher-Internship Program

http://www.nysut.org/research/bulletins/20060504 mentorinternship.html

This bulletin describes the program and its requirements.

The New Teacher Center: Understanding New York City's Groundbreaking Induction Initiative

http://www.newteachercenter.org/pdfs/NYCPolicy Paper.pdf

This New Teacher Center policy paper explains how New York City's mentoring program was conceived and implemented and assesses its effectiveness.

PROFESSIONAL ASSOCIATIONS

NYSUT

http://www.nysut.org/

On September 1, 2006, the New York State NEA joined the New York State United Teachers to form the largest union in New York State. Their site includes resources for media communications, legislative action, member services, professional development, special reports, news, links, and numerous additional resources.

The New York State Association for the Education of Young Children

http://www.nysaeyc.org/

The NYSAEYC site includes information about mini grants, NYSAEYC chapters, professional development, credentials, and public policy, as well as a calendar and links.

Association of Mathematics Teachers of New York State

http://www.amtnys.org/

The AMTNYS site includes information on meetings, association publications, membership, and links as well as email discussions and the association journal.

New York State Alliance for Arts Education

http://www.nysaae.org/

The NYSAAE site offers information news and information about alliance projects, funding, and advocacy, as well as membership information, an arts teaching toolkit, and links.

New York State Art Teachers Association

http://www.nysata.org/

This site includes information about NYSATA regions, the association conference, advocacy, programs, job postings, publications, online galleries, and membership.

The New York State Technology Education Association

http://www.nystea.com/

This site provides information on NYSTEA districts and regions, the association conference, middle-level reform, job openings, and membership, as well as news, the association journal, an events calendar, documents and forms, an FAQ, and links.

New York State Association for Computers and Technologies in Education

http://www.nyscate.org/

This site includes online assessments, strategies, rubrics, and tutorials, a newsletter, association news, podcasts, an events calendar, and information about the association conference, grants and awards, membership, and advocacy.

New York State Association for Bilingual Education

http://www.nysabe.org/

The NYSABE website offers news, links, and information about membership, conferences, events, and more.

New York State Outdoor Education Association

http://www.nysoea.org/welcome.htm

The NYSOEA website includes news and information about membership, conferences, and events.

The New York State Theater Education Association

http://www.nystea.org/

The NYSTEA site provides information on conferences, regional chapters, jobs, and membership, and includes links.

PROFESSIONAL DEVELOPMENT

New York State Education Department: Maintaining Your Certificate

http://www.highered.nysed.gov/tcert/certificate/maintaincert.htm

This site provides information about professional development requirements, necessary recordkeeping, and approved activities for different types of certification.

ACCOUNTABILITY

New York State School Report Card

http://www.emsc.nysed.gov/irts/reportcard/

This site includes links to New York State school report cards for each academic year beginning with the 1998-1999 school year.

New York State Department of Education–The 655 Report

http://www.emsc.nysed.gov/irts/655report/home.shtml

This site includes the full texts—over 500 pages each in total—of the Chapter 655 Report for the years 1999-2005, detailing progress in New York schools as measured through statistical data and achievement records.

New York State Department of Education–No Child Left Behind Act

http://www.emsc.nysed.gov/deputy/nclb/nclbhome.htm

This site details the No Child Left Behind Act and New York State's compliance with it. It includes NCLB requirements for teachers and professionals, accountability rules, status of schools and districts in need of improvement, information on supplemental educational services and state testing in grades 3-8, fund allocations, the full text of the law, and more.

NYSUT: No Child Left Behind

http://www.nysut.org/research/bulletins/2002 nochildleftbehind.html

The NYSUT site includes fact sheets, lists of approved supplemental educational services providers, and news and updates about grants, regulations, testing, and much more.

STATE STANDARDS

New York State Learning Standards
http://usny.nysed.gov/teachers/nyslearningstandards.html

This site includes New York State core subject area learning standards and standards and alternate performance indicators for students with severe disabilities.

New York State Academy for Teaching and Learning: New York State Learning Standards
http://www.emsc.nysed.gov/nysatl/standards.html

At this site, you can search for learning standards, performance indicators, and learning experiences by content area and level.

CURRICULUM PLANNING

New York State Education Department: Virtual Learning System
http://eservices.nysed.gov/vls/welcome.do

This site offers web-based, standards-aligned resources for preK-12 teaching, all organized by subject area. Resources are searchable and include sample tasks and numerous lesson plans. News, information, a toolkit with publications and links, and assessment materials are included for each subject area.

The New York Times Lesson Plan Archive
http://www.nytimes.com/learning/teachers/lessons/archive.html

This searchable archive includes hundreds of free lesson plans across a broad range of subjects for grades 6-12. Lesson plans can be searched by key word, grade range, or subject. Subjects include American history, civics, current events, economics, fine arts, geography, health, journalism, language arts, mathematics, science, social studies, technology, and more.

NYSATA Visual Arts Curriculum Companion
http://www.nysata.org/curriculumcompanion.php

At this site, you can order NYSATA's standards-based core visual arts curriculum for grades PreK-Commencement.

ProTeacher! New York Lesson Plans
http://www.proteacher.com/090134.shtml

This site includes maps, facts, activity sheets, a puzzle, and other materials for use in teaching about New York.

The New York State Library: Resources and Services for Teachers
http://www.nysl.nysed.gov/teachers.htm

New York state teachers may obtain a fourth grade curriculum guide for the Dutch in Colonial America and an instructional packet on labor history in New York at this site.

ASSESSMENT AND TESTING

New York State Regents Exams
http://www.nysedregents.org/

Past exams, scoring keys and rating guides, teacher dictations copy, and conversion charts, all arranged by subject, can be found here.

New York State Alternate Assessment
http://www.vesid.nysed.gov/specialed/alterassessment/

This site provides news and information about the New York State Alternate Assessment, including scoring dates, new requirements, age criteria, and more.

New York Performance Standards Consortium
http://performanceassessment.org/

The New York Performance Standards Consortium is a coalition of high schools that focus on active learning and performance assessments. Their site describes the consortium, its participants and partners, components of performance assessments and rubrics, legislation and activism opportunities, and research, reports, and data.

EDUCATIONAL TECHNOLOGY

NYSERNet
http://www.nysernet.org/

NYSERNet is a private non-profit corporation that provides network and internet services to educational institutions throughout New York State. Their site provides information about their projects and services, as well as news and job postings.

New York State Department of Education: Office of Technology Policy
http://www.emsc.nysed.gov/technology/

This site includes news and information about state and federal technology grants, technology frameworks, NCLB implementation, program assessment, and more.

New York State Department of Education: Technology Education
http://www.emsc.nysed.gov/ciai/mst/tech.html

This site includes news, assessment materials, publications, and information on standards and frameworks, learning experiences, and professional development.

LEGISLATIVE ISSUES

New York State Department of Education: Laws and Regulations
http://usny.nysed.gov/lawsregs/

This site includes general education department, state, and federal legal resources, and information about policies affecting higher education, professionals, public and private schools, and special education.

Advocates for Children of New York
http://www.advocatesforchildren.org/index.php

AFC works to ensure quality and equal educational services for New York's most impoverished children. Their site includes information about the AFC and its funding, a description of their projects, services, and ongoing legislative efforts, resources for parents and professionals, publications, and more.

Making the Pendulum Swing: Challenging Bad Education Policy in New York State
http://www.essentialschools.org/cs/resources/view/ces_res/380

This article discusses the advocacy strategies that teachers, parents, and students used to speak out against over-dependence on standardized testing in New York State.

EXCEPTIONAL STUDENTS

New York State Department of Education: Vocational and Educational Services for Individuals with Disabilities
http://www.vesid.nysed.gov/specialed/

This site includes legal information as well as information related to behavioral interventions, quality assurance, transitions, autism, alternate assessment, data and research, and funding, as well as lists of approved schools, parent resources, and much more.

The New York Institute for Special Education
http://www.nyise.org/

The New York Institute for Special Education is a private, non-profit educational facility located in Bronx, New York.

The school provides programs for individuals who are blind or visually impaired, have emotional or learning disabilities, or who are experiencing developmental delays. The school also runs a summer camp for children who are blind or visually impaired. This site includes information about their programs, a link to the wealth of information available at the Blindness Resource Center, and more.

NYSUT Special Education Guide
http://www.nysut.org/specialed/

This NYSUT guide provides general information, questions and answers, resources, a glossary of acronyms, a parent-teacher checklist, and more.

The Center for Autism and Related Disabilities
http://www.albany.edu/psy/autism/autism.html

CARD is a State University of New York at Albany-based resource center that engages in research and provides training and support to families and professionals. Services are provided at no cost to individuals in a ten-country area surrounding Albany. The CARD site features fact sheets, newsletters, information on workshops and training, distance education, sibling and summer programs, and much more.

BILINGUAL EDUCATION

New York State Bilingual and ESL Network
http://www.emsc.nysed.gov/biling/nysben.html

The Bilingual and ESL Network page provides news and information on laws and regulations, NCLB, professional organizations, data, assessment, standards, publications, and many other resources.

NEW YORK EMPLOYMENT RESOURCES

Employment Opportunities with the New York State Education Department
http://oms32.nysed.gov/hr/

This site lists education department job openings, their locations, and application deadlines, and includes an application form.

NY Education Jobs
http://www.nyeducationjobs.com/

This site offers a select number of job postings free to visitors. Full job postings are available to members for a small fee. Members can search online postings or listings in New York newspapers.

NY EdJobs.org

http://www.nyedjobs.org/

This site features a calendar, news, and resources, and allows users to search for currently available education jobs by region.

The New York Times Job Market: Education Jobs

http://jobmarket.nytimes.com/jobs/category/education-jobs

This site includes listings for jobs in higher education, teaching, and administration.

NYC Teaching Fellows

http://www.nyctf.org/about/fellowship.html

NYC Teaching Fellows is a program that recruits recent graduates and professionals to teach in high-need areas in NYC. The program subsidizes fellows' work toward a master's degree and fellows receive a regular teacher's salary and benefits. The NYCTF website provides information and statistics, details about particular programs and benefits, certification requirements, and application materials.

NATIONAL EMPLOYMENT RESOURCES

Teachers Support Network

http://www.teacherssupportnetwork.com/

At this site, you can search for jobs by level, subject area, and state.

EDinformatics

http://www.edinformatics.com/education/employment.htm

This site provides links to sites listing jobs in different specializations and areas around the country.

EducationAmerica.net

http://www.educationamerica.net

At this site, you can search for teaching, administrative, and support jobs by state or region. The site also includes information on state certification, teacher salaries, and resume writing.

National Teacher Recruitment Clearinghouse

http://www.recruitingteachers.org/channels/clearinghouse/

This clearinghouse site offers numerous resources for job seekers, including information for new and current teachers, career changers, paraprofessionals, and college students, as well as a job bank and licensing information.

National Educators Employment Network

http://www.teachersatwork.com/find_job.cfm

At this site, you can search for jobs by subject area.

Teachers.Net Job Center

http://jobs.teachers.net/Teachers/SearchJobs/tabid/63/Default.aspx

At Teachers.Net you can search jobs by position type, grade level, key word, and location.

TeachersOnline.com

http://67.104.186.98/teachers

The TeachersOnline.com nationwide teacher recruitment site allows you to search jobs by keyword, level, state, position type, and salary requirements.

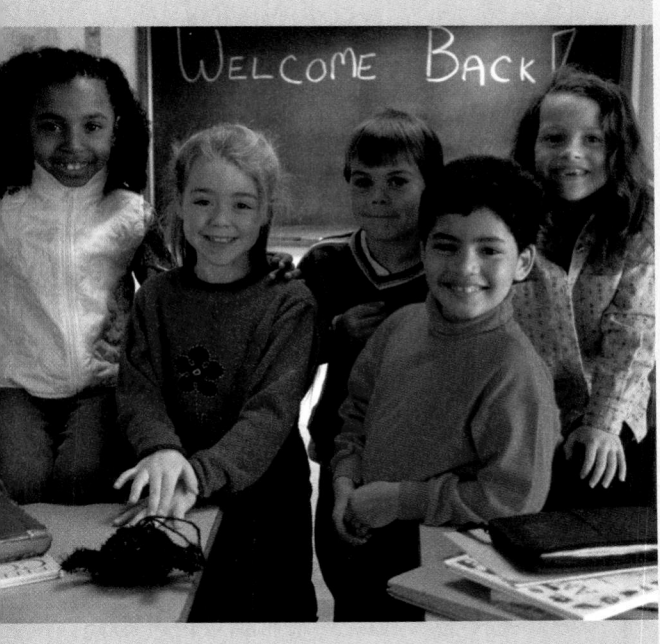

CHAPTER 1

Educational Psychology: A Tool for Effective Teaching

I touch the future. I teach.

—Christa McAuliffe
American Educator and Astronaut, 20th Century

Chapter Outline

Exploring Educational Psychology
Historical Background
Teaching: Art and Science

Effective Teaching
Professional Knowledge and Skills
Commitment and Motivation

Research in Educational Psychology
Why Research Is Important
Research Methods
Program Evaluation Research, Action Research,
  and the Teacher-as-Researcher

Learning Goals

1 Describe some basic ideas about the field of educational psychology.

2 Identify the attitudes and skills of an effective teacher.

3 Discuss why research is important to effective teaching and how educational psychologists and teachers can conduct and evaluate research.

TEACHING STORIES Margaret Metzger

Effective teachers know that principles of educational psychology and educational research will help them guide students' learning. Margaret Metzger has been an English teacher at Brookline High School, in Massachusetts, for more than 25 years. Here is some advice she gave to a student teacher she was supervising that incorporates her understanding of basic principles of educational psychology, such as teaching how to learn and the need to apply educational research to teaching practice:

> Emphasize *how* to learn, rather than *what* to learn. Students may never know a particular fact, but they always will need to know how to learn. Teach students how to read with a genuine comprehension, how to shape an idea, how to master difficult material, how to use writing to clarify thinking. A former student, Anastasia Korniaris, wrote to me, "Your class was like a hardware store. All the tools were there. Years later I'm still using that hardware store that's in my head. . . ."
>
> Include students in the process of teaching and learning. Every day ask such basic questions as, "What did you think of this homework? Did it help you learn the material? Was the assignment too long or too short? How can we make the next assignment more interesting? What should the criteria for assessment be?" Remember that we want students to take ownership of their learning. . . .
>
> Useful research has been conducted lately on learning styles and frames of intelligence. Read that research. The basic idea to keep in mind is that students should think for themselves. Your job is to teach them how to think and to give them the necessary tools. Your students will be endlessly amazed at how intelligent they are. You don't need to show them how intelligent you are. . . .
>
> In the early years of teaching you must expect to put in hours and hours of time. You would invest similarly long hours if you were an intern in medical school or an associate in a law firm. Like other professionals, teachers work much longer hours than outsiders know. . . .
>
> You have the potential to be an excellent teacher. My only concern is that you not exhaust yourself before you begin. Naturally, you will want to work very hard as you learn the craft. (Source: Metzger, 1996, pp. 346–351.)

Preview

In the quotation that opens this chapter, twentieth-century teacher and astronaut Christa McAuliffe commented that when she touched the future, she taught. As a teacher, you will touch the future because children are the future of any society. In this chapter, we explore what the field of educational psychology is all about and how it can help you positively contribute to children's futures.

1 EXPLORING EDUCATIONAL PSYCHOLOGY

| Historical Background | Teaching: Art and Science |

Psychology is the scientific study of behavior and mental processes. **Educational psychology** is the branch of psychology that specializes in understanding teaching and learning in educational settings. Educational psychology is a vast landscape that will take us an entire book to describe.

Historical Background

The field of educational psychology was founded by several pioneers in psychology in the late nineteenth century just before the start of the twentieth century. Three pioneers—William James, John Dewey, and E. L. Thorndike—stand out in the early history of educational psychology.

 William James   Soon after launching the first psychology textbook, *Principles of Psychology* (1890), William James (1842–1910) gave a series of lectures called "Talks to

educational psychology The branch of psychology that specializes in understanding teaching and learning in educational settings.

2

Teachers" (James, 1899/1993) in which he discussed the applications of psychology to educating children. James argued that laboratory psychology experiments often can't tell us how to effectively teach children. He emphasized the importance of observing teaching and learning in classrooms for improving education. One of his recommendations was to start lessons at a point just beyond the child's level of knowledge and understanding to stretch the child's mind.

John Dewey   A second major figure in shaping the field of educational psychology was John Dewey (1859–1952), who became a driving force in the practical application of psychology. Dewey established the first major educational psychology laboratory in the United States, at the University of Chicago in 1894. Later, at Columbia University, he continued his innovative work. We owe many important ideas to John Dewey (Berliner, 2006; Glassman, 2001). First, we owe to him the view of the child as an active learner. Before Dewey, it was believed that children should sit quietly in their seats and passively learn in a rote manner. In contrast, Dewey argued that children learn best by doing. Second, we owe to Dewey the idea that education should focus on the whole child and emphasize the child's adaptation to the environment. Dewey reasoned that children should not be just narrowly educated in academic topics but should learn how to think and adapt to a world outside school. He especially thought that children should learn how to be reflective problem solvers (Dewey, 1933). Third, we owe to Dewey the belief that all children deserve to have a competent education. This democratic ideal was not in place at the beginning of Dewey's career in the latter part of the nineteenth century, when quality education was reserved for a small portion of children, especially boys from wealthy families. Dewey pushed for a competent education for all children—girls and boys—as well as children from different socioeconomic and ethnic groups.

E. L. Thorndike   A third pioneer was E. L. Thorndike (1874–1949), who focused on assessment and measurement and promoted the scientific underpinnings of learning. Thorndike argued that one of schooling's most important tasks is to hone children's reasoning skills, and he excelled at doing exacting scientific studies of teaching and learning (Beatty, 1998). Thorndike especially promoted the idea that educational psychology must have a scientific base and should focus strongly on measurement (O'Donnell & Levin, 2001).

Diversity and Early Educational Psychology   The most prominent figures in the early history of educational psychology, as in most disciplines, were mainly White males, such as James, Dewey, and Thorndike. Prior to changes in civil rights laws and policies in the 1960s, only a few dedicated non-White individuals obtained the necessary degrees and broke through racial exclusion barriers to take up research in the field (Banks, 2006; Cushner, 2006).

Two pioneering African American psychologists, Mamie and Kenneth Clark, conducted research on African American children's self-conceptions and identity (Clark & Clark, 1939). In 1971, Kenneth Clark became the first African American president of the American Psychological Association. In 1932, Latino psychologist George Sanchez conducted research showing that intelligence tests were culturally biased against ethnic minority children.

Like ethnic minorities, women also faced barriers in higher education and so have only gradually become prominent contributors to psychological research. One often overlooked person in the history of educational psychology is Leta Hollingworth. She was the first individual to use the term *gifted* to describe children who scored exceptionally high on intelligence tests (Hollingworth, 1916).

The Behavioral Approach   Thorndike's approach to the study of learning guided educational psychology through the first half of the twentieth century. In American psychology, B. F. Skinner's (1938) view, which built on Thorndike's ideas, strongly influenced educational psychology in the middle of the century. Skinner's behavioral approach, which is described in detail in chapter 7, involved attempts to precisely determine the best conditions for learning. Skinner argued that the mental processes

William James

John Dewey

E. L. Thorndike

James, Dewey, and Thorndike created and shaped the field of educational psychology. *What were their ideas about educational psychology?*

George Sanchez

Mamie and Kenneth Clark

Leta Hollingworth

Like other disciplines, educational psychology had few ethnic minority individuals and women involved in its early history. These individuals were among the few people from such backgrounds to overcome barriers and contribute to the field.

proposed by psychologists such as James and Dewey were not observable and therefore could not be appropriate subject matter for a scientific study of psychology, which he defined as the science of observable behavior and its controlling conditions. In the 1950s, Skinner (1954) developed the concept of *programmed learning*, which involved reinforcing the student after each of a series of steps until the student reached a learning goal. In an early technological effort, he created a teaching machine to serve as a tutor and reinforce students for correct answers (Skinner, 1958).

The Cognitive Revolution However, the objectives spelled out in the behavioral approach to learning did not address many of the actual goals and needs of classroom educators (Hilgard, 1996). In reaction, as early as the 1950s, Benjamin Bloom created a taxonomy of cognitive skills that included remembering, comprehending, synthesizing, and evaluating, which he believed teachers should help students use and develop (Bloom & Krathwohl, 1956). A review chapter in the *Annual Review of Psychology* (Wittrock & Lumsdaine, 1977) stated, "A cognitive perspective implies that a behavioral analysis of instruction is often inadequate to explain the effects of instruction on learning." The cognitive revolution in psychology began to take hold by the 1980s and ushered in a great deal of enthusiasm for applying the concepts of cognitive psychology—memory, thinking, reasoning, and so on—to helping students learn. Thus, toward the latter part of the twentieth century, many educational psychologists returned to an emphasis on the cognitive aspects of learning advocated by James and Dewey at the beginning of the century (Pressley & Hilden, 2006).

Both cognitive and behavioral approaches continue to be a part of educational psychology today (Bransford, 2006; Pressley & Harris, 2006). We have much more to say about these approaches in chapters 7 through 11.

More recently, educational psychologists have increasingly focused on the socioemotional aspects of students' lives. For example, they are analyzing the school as a social context and examining the role of culture in education (Diaz, Pelletier, & Provenzo, 2006; Kress & Elias, 2006; Okagaki, 2006). We explore the socioemotional aspects of teaching and learning in many chapters of the book.

Teaching: Art and Science

How scientific can teachers be in their approach to teaching? Both science and the art of skillful, experienced practice play important roles in a teacher's success (Oakes & Lipton, 2007; Morrison, 2006).

Educational psychology draws much of its knowledge from broader theory and research in psychology. For example, the theories of Jean Piaget and Lev Vygotsky were not created in an effort to inform teachers about ways to educate children, yet in chapter 2, "Cognitive and Language Development," you will see that both of these theories have many applications that can guide your teaching. The field also draws from theory and research more directly created and conducted by educational psychologists, and from teachers' practical experiences. For example, in chapter 13, "Motivation, Teaching, and Learning," you will read about Dale Schunk's (2004; Schunk & Meece, 2006) classroom-oriented research on self-efficacy (the belief that one can master a situation and produce positive outcomes). Educational psychologists also recognize that teaching sometimes must depart from scientific recipes, requiring improvisation and spontaneity (Gage, 1978).

As a science, educational psychology's aim is to provide you with research knowledge that you can effectively apply to teaching situations. But your teaching will still remain an art. In addition to what you can learn from research, you will also continually make important judgments in the classroom based on your personal skills and experiences, as well as the accumulated wisdom of other teachers.

Review, Reflect, and Practice

1 Describe some basic ideas about the field of educational psychology.

REVIEW
- How is educational psychology defined? Who were some key thinkers in the history of educational psychology and what were their ideas?
- How would you describe the roles of art and science in the practice of teaching?

REFLECT
- John Dewey argued that children should not sit quietly in their seats and learn in a rote manner. Do you agree with Dewey? Why or why not?

PRAXIS™ PRACTICE
1. Mr. Smith believes that all children are entitled to an education and that this education should focus on the whole child. His views are most consistent with those of
   a. Benjamin Bloom
   b. John Dewey
   c. B. F. Skinner
   d. E. L. Thorndike
2. Four teachers are discussing influences on being an effective teacher. Which of the following four statements they make is likely to be most accurate?
   a. Applying information from scientific research is the most important factor in being an effective teacher.
   b. You can't beat a teacher's own personal experiences for becoming an effective teacher.
   c. Being an effective teacher is influenced by scientific research knowledge, teaching skills, and personal experiences.
   d. A teacher's innate skills trump all other factors in being an effective teacher.

Please see the answer key at the end of the book.

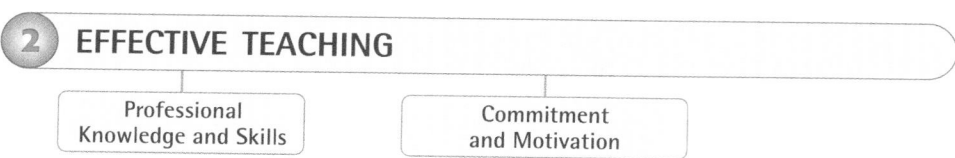

2   EFFECTIVE TEACHING

| Professional Knowledge and Skills | Commitment and Motivation |

Because of the complexity of teaching and individual variation among students, effective teaching is not "one size fits all" (Diaz, 1997). Teachers must master a variety of perspectives and strategies and be flexible in their application. This requires two key ingredients: (1) professional knowledge and skills and (2) commitment and motivation.

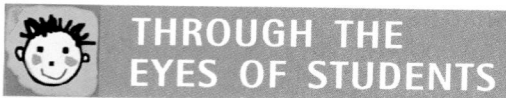

THROUGH THE EYES OF STUDENTS

A Good Teacher

Mike, Grade 2:

A good teacher is a teacher that does stuff that catches your interest. Sometimes you start learning and you don't even realize it. A good teacher is a teacher that does stuff that makes you think. (Nikola-Lisa & Burnaford, 1994)

Professional Knowledge and Skills

Effective teachers have good command of their subject matter and a solid core of teaching skills. They have excellent instructional strategies supported by methods of goal setting, instructional planning, and classroom management. They know how to motivate, communicate, and work effectively with students who have different levels of skills and come from culturally diverse backgrounds. Effective teachers also understand how to use appropriate levels of technology in the classroom.

Subject Matter Competence   In their wish lists of teacher characteristics, secondary school students increasingly have mentioned "teacher knowledge of their subjects" (NASSP, 1997). Having a thoughtful, flexible, conceptual understanding of subject matter is indispensable for being an effective teacher. Of course, knowledge of subject matter includes more than just facts, terms, and general concepts. It also includes knowledge about organizing ideas, connections among ideas, ways of thinking and arguing, patterns of change within a discipline, beliefs about a discipline, and the ability to carry ideas from one discipline to another. Clearly, having a deep understanding of the subject matter is an important aspect of being a competent teacher (Ellis, 2007; Peters & Stout, 2006; Van de Walle, 2007).

Instructional Strategies   At a broad level, two major approaches characterize how teachers teach: constructivist and direct instruction. The constructivist approach was at the center of William James' and John Dewey's philosophies of education. The direct instruction approach has more in common with E. L. Thorndike's view.

The **constructivist approach** is a learner-centered approach that emphasizes the importance of individuals actively constructing their knowledge and understanding with guidance from the teacher. In the constructivist view, teachers should not attempt to simply pour information into children's minds. Rather, children should be encouraged to explore their world, discover knowledge, reflect, and think critically with careful monitoring and meaningful guidance from the teacher (Eby, Herrell, & Jordan, 2006; Halpern, 2006; Kafai, 2006). Constructivists argue that for too long children have been required to sit still, be passive learners, and rotely memorize irrelevant as well as relevant information (Henson, 2004; Silberman, 2006).

Today, constructivism may include an emphasis on *collaboration*—children working with each other in their efforts to know and understand (Bodrova & Leong, 2007; Hyson, Copple, & Jones, 2006). A teacher with a constructivist instructional philosophy would not have children memorize information rotely but would give them opportunities to meaningfully construct knowledge and understand the material while guiding their learning (Ornstein, Lasley, & Mindes, 2005).

By contrast, the **direct instruction approach** is a structured, teacher-centered approach characterized by teacher direction and control, high teacher expectations for students' progress, maximum time spent by students on academic tasks, and efforts by the teacher to keep negative affect to a minimum. An important goal in the direct instruction approach is maximizing student learning time (Stevenson, 2000).

constructivist approach A learner-centered approach to learning that emphasizes the importance of individuals actively constructing knowledge and understanding with guidance from the teacher.

direct instruction approach A structured, teacher-centered approach characterized by teacher direction and control, high teacher expectations for students' progress, maximum time spent by students on academic tasks, and efforts by the teacher to keep negative affect to a minimum.

Some experts in educational psychology emphasize that many effective teachers use both a constructivist *and* a direct instruction approach rather than either exclusively (Darling-Hammond & Bransford, 2005; Schwartz & others, 1999). Further, some circumstances may call more for a constructivist approach, others for a direct instruction approach. For example, experts increasingly recommend an explicit, intellectually engaging direct instruction approach when teaching students with a reading or a writing disability (Berninger, 2006). Whether you teach more from a constructivist approach or more from a direct instruction approach, you can be an effective teacher.

What characterizes constructivist and direct instruction approaches to educating students?

Goal Setting and Instructional Planning Skills   Whether constructivist or more traditional, effective teachers set high goals for their teaching and organize plans for reaching those goals (Blumenfeld, Mark, & Harris, 2006; Meece, Anderman, & Anderman, 2006). They also develop specific criteria for success, spending considerable time in instructional planning, organizing their lessons to maximize students' learning (Posner & Rudnitsky, 2006). As they plan, effective teachers reflect and think about how they can make learning both challenging and interesting. Good planning

> requires consideration of the kinds of information, demonstrations, models, inquiry opportunities, discussion, and practice students need over time to understand particular concepts and develop particular skills. Although research has found that all of these features can support learning, the process of instructional design requires that teachers figure out which things students should do when, in what order, and how (Darling-Hammond & others, 2005, p. 186).

Developmentally Appropriate Teaching Practices   Competent teachers have a good understanding of children's development and know how to create instruction materials appropriate for their developmental levels (Darling-Hammond & Bransford, 2005; Horowitz & others, 2005). U.S. schools are organized by grade and to some degree by age, but these are not always good predictors of children's development.

At any grade level, there is usually a two- or three-year span of ages with an even wider span of skills, abilities, and developmental stages. Understanding developmental pathways and progressions is extremely important for teaching in ways that are optimal for each child (Horowitz & others, 2005, p. 93).

Throughout this text we call attention to developmental aspects of educating children and provide examples of teaching and learning that take into account a child's developmental level. Chapter 2, "Cognitive and Language Development," and chapter 3, Social Contexts and Socioemotional Development, are devoted exclusively to development.

Classroom Management Skills   An important aspect of being an effective teacher is keeping the class as a whole working together and oriented toward classroom tasks. Effective teachers establish and maintain an environment in which learning can occur. To create this optimal learning environment, teachers need a repertoire of strategies for establishing rules and procedures, organizing groups, monitoring and pacing classroom activities, and handling misbehavior (Evertson, Emmer, & Worsham, 2006; Kaufmann & others, 2006).

Motivational Skills   Effective teachers have good strategies for helping students become self-motivated and take responsibility for their learning (Anderman & Wolters, 2006; Blumenfeld, Krajcik, & Kempler, 2006; Wigfield, Byrnes, and Eccles, 2006; Wigfield & others, 2006). Educational psychologists increasingly stress that this is best accomplished by providing real-world learning opportunities of optimal difficulty and novelty for each

"My mom told me to tell you that I am the educational challenge you were told about in college."

Reprinted by permission of Heiser Zedonek.

student (Brophy, 2004). Students are motivated when they can make choices in line with their personal interests. Effective teachers give them the opportunity to think creatively and deeply about projects (Blumenfeld, Kempler, & Krajcik, 2006; Starko, 2005).

In addition to guiding students to become self-motivated learners, the importance of establishing high expectations for students' achievement is increasingly being recognized (Wigfield & others, 2006). High expectations for children's achievements needs to come from teachers and parents. Too often children are rewarded for inferior or mediocre performance with the result that they do not reach their full potential. When high expectations are created, a key aspect of education is to provide children—especially low-achieving children—effective instruction and support to meet these expectations. Chapter 13 covers the topic of motivation in detail.

Communication Skills   Also indispensable to teaching are skills in speaking, listening, overcoming barriers to verbal communication, tuning in to students' nonverbal communication, and constructively resolving conflicts. Communication skills are critical not only in teaching but also in interacting with parents. Effective teachers use good communication skills when they talk "with" rather than "to" students, parents, administrators, and others; keep criticism at a minimum; and have an assertive rather than aggressive, manipulative, or passive communication style (Alberti & Emmons, 2001; Evertson, Emmer, & Worsham, 2006). Effective teachers work to improve students' communication skills as well (Powell & Caseau, 2004). This is especially important because communication skills have been rated as the skills most sought after by today's employers (Collins, 1996).

Paying More Than Lip Service to Individual Variations   Virtually every teacher knows that it is important to take individual variations into account when teaching, but this is not always easy to do. Your students will have varying levels of intelligence, use different thinking and learning styles, and have different temperaments and personality traits. You also are likely to have some gifted students and others with different types of disabilities (Hallahan & Kauffman, 2006; Winner, 2006).

Effectively teaching a class of students with such diverse characteristics requires much thought and effort. **Differentiated instruction** involves recognizing individual variations in students' knowledge, readiness, interests, and other characteristics, and taking these differences into account in planning curriculum and engaging in instruction (Tomlinson, 2001). Differentiated instruction emphasizes tailoring assignments to meet students' needs and abilities. It is unlikely that a teacher can generate 20 to 30 different lesson plans to address the needs of each student in a classroom. However, differentiated instruction advocates discovering "zones" or "ballparks" in which students in a classroom cluster, thus providing three or four types/levels of instruction rather than 20 to 30. In chapter 4, "Individual Variations," and chapter 6, "Learners Who Are Exceptional," we provide strategies to help you guide students with different levels of skills and different characteristics to learn effectively.

Working Effectively with Students from Culturally Diverse Backgrounds   Today, one of every five children in the United States is from an immigrant family, and by 2040 one of every three U.S. children is projected to fit this description (Suarez-Orozco, 2002). Nearly 80 percent of the new immigrants are people of color from Latin America, Asia, and the Caribbean. Approximately 75 percent of the new immigrants are of Spanish-speaking origin, although children speaking more than 100 different languages are entering U.S. schools (OBEMLA, 2000).

In today's world of increasing intercultural contact, effective teachers are knowledgeable about people from different cultural backgrounds and are sensitive to their needs (Bennett, 2007; Diaz, Pelletier, & Provenzo, 2006; Okagaki, 2006; Spring, 2006, 2007). Effective teachers encourage students to have positive personal contact with diverse students and think of ways to create such settings. They guide students in thinking critically about cultural and ethnic issues, forestall or reduce

differentiated instruction Involves recognizing individual variations in students' knowledge, readiness, interests, and other characteristics, and taking these differences into account when planning curriculum and engaging in instruction.

What are some strategies effective teachers use to help students become motivated?

What are some strategies effective teachers use regarding diversity issues?

bias, cultivate acceptance, and serve as cultural mediators (Banks, 2001, 2006; Cushner, 2006; Redman, 2007; Spencer, 2006). An effective teacher also needs to be a broker, or middle person, between the culture of the school and the culture of certain students, especially those who are unsuccessful academically (Diaz, 1997; Diaz, Pelletier, & Provenzo, 2006).

Here are cultural questions that competent teachers are sensitive to include (Pang, 2005):

- Do I recognize the power and complexity of cultural influences on students?
- Are my expectations for my students culturally based or biased?
- Am I doing a good job of seeing life from the perspective of my students who come from different cultures than mine?
- Am I teaching the skills students may need to talk in class if their culture is one in which they have little opportunity to practice "public" talking?

We explore diversity issues throughout the book and in Diversity and Education interludes. The one on page 10 further explores the cultural aspects of schools.

Assessment Skills   Competent teachers also have good assessment skills. There are many aspects to effectively using assessment in the classroom (Gronlund, 2006; McMillan, 2007; Nitko & Brookhart, 2007; Reynolds, Livingston, & Willson, 2006). You will need to decide what type of tests you want to use to document your students' performance after instruction. You also will need to use assessment effectively before and during instruction (McMillan, 2007). For example, before teaching a unit on plate tectonics, you might decide to assess whether your students are familiar with terms like *continent, earthquake,* and *volcano.*

During instruction, you might want to use ongoing observation and monitoring to determine whether your instruction is at a level that challenges students and to detect which students need your individual attention (Ercikan, 2006). You will need to develop a grading system that communicates meaningful information about your students' performance.

Other aspects of assessment you will be involved with include state-mandated tests to assess students' achievement and teachers' knowledge and skills (Reynolds, Livingston, & Willson, 2006). The federal government's No Child Left Behind (NCLB) legislation requires states to test students annually in mathematics, English/language arts, and science and holds states accountable for the success and failure of their students.

DIVERSITY AND EDUCATION
The Cultural School

Valerie Pang (2005), an expert on cultural issues in schools, believes that many teachers don't adequately take into account the cultural context of the school and cultural backgrounds students bring to the classroom. Teachers may not share their students' cultural experiences because they live in neighborhoods far from the school in which they teach. The teachers and students also may have grown up in very different cultures. Pang (2005) says teachers should become more familiar with the neighborhood in which the school is located if they live outside of it. They might shop at neighborhood stores, get to know the community leaders, and read community newspapers. In this way, teachers can become more in tune with their students' rhythm and culture. Pang also recommends that teachers bring examples from the children's lives into their teaching.

An example of bringing local, cultural meaning to students involves a San Diego high school social studies class whose teacher invited Dr. Dorothy Smith—an African American college professor, community leader, and former chair of the San Diego School Board—to speak to her class. Dr. Smith talked about issues the students and parents were dealing with as citizens. She brought up many issues: What does it mean to be an African American? How important is it to go to college? How can I make a contribution to my neighborhood?

In preparation, the students developed interview questions to ask Dr. Smith. Also, one group of students videotaped her discussion so that the interview could be shown to other classes. Another group took notes and wrote an article about her talk for the student newspaper.

When students are given the opportunity to meet people like Dr. Smith, they are provided not only with important cultural role models but also with connections to the culture of their own neighborhood.

Because of NCLB, the extent to which instruction should be tied to standards, or what is called *standards-based instruction,* has become a major issue in educational psychology and U.S. classrooms. This issue is all about standards of excellence and what it takes to get students to pass external, large-scale tests. Many educational psychologists stress that the challenge is to teach creatively within the structure imposed by NCLB (McMillan, 2007). Much more information about No Child Left Behind is provided in chapter 15, "Standardized Tests and Teaching."

Before you become a teacher, your subject matter knowledge and teaching skills are also likely to be assessed by the state in which you plan to teach (Tittle, 2006). A large majority of states now use the PRAXIS™ test to determine whether prospective teachers are qualified to teach. Because of the increasing use of the PRAXIS™ test, this text includes a number of resources to help you prepare for this test.

Technological Skills   Technology itself does not necessarily improve students' ability to learn. Other conditions are also necessary to create supportive learning environments (Bereiter & Scardamalia, 2006,a,b; Berson & others, 2007; Bitter & Legacy, 2006). These conditions include vision and support from educational leaders; teachers skilled in using technology for learning; content standards and curriculum resources; assessment of effectiveness of technology for learning; and an emphasis on the child as an active, constructive learner (International Society for Technology in Education, 2001).

Effective teachers develop their technological skills and integrate computers appropriately into classroom learning (Cruz & Duplass, 2007; Sawyer, 2006). This integration should match up with students' learning needs, including the need to

TECHNOLOGY AND EDUCATION

Schools and Communities

Not only is technology helping children learn more effectively in school, but it is also increasingly opening up schools to communities (Dick, Carey, & Carey, 2005). In many districts, students and parents can communicate with teachers and administrators through e-mail. Teachers can post students' work on Web pages. Some schools provide students with laptop computers they can take home (Pea & Maldonado, 2006; Silvernail & Lane, 2004; Zucker & McGhee, 2005).

Better communication between parents and teachers was one goal of a state-funded Indiana program called the Buddy System (Rockman & Mayer, 1994). In this program, computers and modems were placed in the homes of 7,000 elementary school students, most of them in grades 4 and 5, for 1 or 2 years. The students' parents, many of whom had never been to their children's schools, had to go there to pick up the computer equipment and get training. Many of the parents and teachers report that the computer connection has resulted in increased communication with each other.

A special concern is to enable students from low-income backgrounds to have adequate access to computers. The Foshay Learning Center, a K–12 public school in Los Angeles, has created eight satellite learning centers in low-income apartment complexes. Without leaving their buildings, students in this school can use the computers to get help with

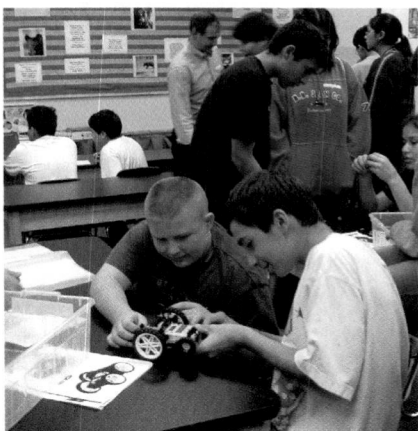

Cherokee Middle School students tackle LEGO robotic kit.

homework, learn about technology, and participate in active learning experiences. Such programs are especially important because, according to one survey, Americans earning less than $30,000 a year comprise only 18 percent of Internet users, despite comprising 28 percent of the population. Low-income youth are especially vulnerable, being eight times less likely to use computers at home as children in families earning $75,000 or more (Local Initiatives Support Corporation [LISC], 2005).

IBM recently created a Team Tech Volunteer program that will provide technology services to more than 2,500 health and human service agencies. The Team Tech program gives students opportunities to become volunteers in their community and provides technological services that can improve the education and learning of students. Another project was created by Steve Scott, an IBM employee in North Carolina, who recruited five IBM peers to hold a technology cap for 28 eighth-grade Native American students at Cherokee Middle School (IBM, 2006). The IBM employees discussed career opportunities and presented technical information in interesting, easy to understand ways. One project involves having teams of students work on LEGO robotic kits.

Do a thorough assessment of the businesses in your community. Like IBM, some might be willing to provide technological services and expertise for your classroom.

prepare for tomorrow's jobs, many of which will require technological expertise and computer-based skills. In addition, effective teachers are knowledgeable about various assistive devices to support the learning of students with disabilities (Provenzo, 2005).

National Educational Technology Standards (NETS) have been established by the International Society for Technology in Education (ISTE) (2000, 2001). The NETS standards include:

- Technology foundation standards for students, which describe what students should know about technology and be able to do with technology;
- Standards for using technology in learning and teaching, which describe how technology should be used throughout the curriculum for teaching, learning, and instructional management;
- Educational technology support standards, which describe systems, access, staff development, and support services needed to provide effective use of technology; and
- Standards for student assessment and evaluation of technology use, which describe various means of assessing student progress and evaluating the use of technology in learning and teaching.

To think further about schools, communities, and technology, see the Technology and Education box.

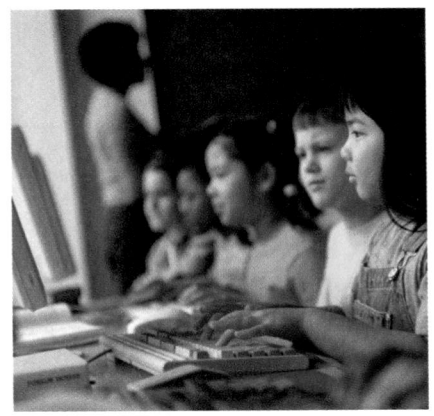

What are some important aspects of incorporating technology in the classroom?

THROUGH THE EYES OF STUDENTS

"You Are the Coolest"

I just want to thank you for all the extra time you took to help me. You didn't have to do that but you did and I want to thank you for it. Thanks also for being straight up with me and not beating around the bush and for that you are the coolest. I'm sorry for the hard times I gave you. You take so much junk but through all that you stay calm and you are a great teacher.

Jessica, Seventh-Grade Student
Macon, Georgia
Letter to Chuck Rawls, Her Teacher, at the End of the School Year

Commitment and Motivation

Being an effective teacher also requires commitment and motivation. This includes having a good attitude and caring about students.

Beginning teachers often report that the investment of time and effort needed to be an effective teacher is huge. Some teachers, even experienced ones, say they have "no life" from September to June. Even putting in hours on evenings and weekends, in addition to all of the hours spent in the classroom, might still not be enough to get things done.

In the face of these demands, it is easy to become frustrated or to get into a rut and develop a negative attitude. Commitment and motivation help get effective teachers through the tough moments of teaching. Effective teachers have confidence in their own self-efficacy, don't let negative emotions diminish their motivation, and bring a positive attitude and enthusiasm to the classroom. These qualities are contagious and help make the classroom a place where students want to be.

So, what is likely to nurture your own positive attitudes and continued enthusiasm for teaching? As in all fields, success breeds success. It's important to become aware of times when you've made a difference in an individual student's life. Consider the words of one of the expert consultants for this book, Carlos Diaz (1997), now a professor of education at Florida Atlantic University, about Mrs. Oppel, his high school English teacher:

> To this day, whenever I see certain words *(dearth, slake)* I recognize them fondly as some of Mrs. Oppel's vocabulary words. As a teacher, she was very calm and focused. She also was passionate about the power of language and the beauty of literature. I credit her, at least partially, for my determination to try to master the English language and become a professor and writer. I wish I could bottle these characteristics and implant them in all of my students.

The better teacher you become, the more rewarding your work will be. And the more respect and success you achieve in the eyes of your students, the better you will feel about your commitment to teaching.

With that in mind, stop for a moment and think about the images you have of your own former teachers. Some of your teachers likely were outstanding and left you with a very positive image. In a national survey of almost a thousand students 13 to 17 years of age, having a good sense of humor, making the class interesting, and having knowledge of the subject matter were the characteristics students listed as the most important for teachers to have (NASSP, 1997). Characteristics secondary school students most frequently attributed to their worst teachers were having a boring class, not explaining things clearly, and showing favoritism. These characteristics and others that reflect students' images of their best and worst teachers are shown in figure 1.1.

Think about the roles that a good sense of humor and your own genuine enthusiasm are likely to play in your long-term commitment as a teacher. Also, notice other characteristics in figure 1.1 that relate to the caring nature of outstanding teachers. Effective teachers care for their students, often referring to them as "my students." They really want to be with the students and are dedicated to helping them learn. At the same time, they keep their role as a teacher distinct from student roles. Beyond their own caring, effective teachers also look for ways to help their students consider others' feelings and care about each other.

To think about the best and worst characteristics of the teachers you have had, complete Self-Assessment 1.1. Use the self-assessment to further explore the attitudes behind your commitment to become a teacher.

SELF-ASSESSMENT 1.1
The Best and Worst Characteristics of My Teachers

When you studied figure 1.1, were you surprised by any of the characteristics listed by students to describe their best and worst teachers? Which of the top five characteristics students listed for the best teachers surprised you the most? Which of the top five characteristics of the worst teachers surprised you the most?

Now think about the top five characteristics of the best teachers you have had. Then think about the main five characteristics of the worst teachers you have had. In generating your lists, don't be constrained by the characteristics described in figure 1.1. Also, after you have listed each characteristic, write down one or more examples of situations that reflected the characteristic.

Five Characteristics of the Best Teachers I Have Had

Characteristics	Examples of Situations That Reflected the Characteristic
1. _____	_____
2. _____	_____
3. _____	_____
4. _____	_____
5. _____	_____

Five Characteristics of the Worst Teachers I Have Had

Characteristics	Examples of Situations That Reflected the Characteristic
1. _____	_____
2. _____	_____
3. _____	_____
4. _____	_____
5. _____	_____

Characteristics of best teachers	% Total		Characteristics of worst teachers	% Total
1. Have a sense of humor	79.2		1. Are dull/have a boring class	79.6
2. Make the class interesting	73.7		2. Don't explain things clearly	63.2
3. Have knowledge of their subjects	70.1		3. Show favoritism toward students	52.7
4. Explain things clearly	66.2		4. Have a poor attitude	49.8
5. Spend time to help students	65.8		5. Expect too much from students	49.1
6. Are fair to their students	61.8		6. Don't relate to students	46.2
7. Treat students like adults	54.4		7. Give too much homework	44.2
8. Relate well to students	54.2		8. Are too strict	40.6
9. Are considerate of students' feelings	51.9		9. Don't give help/individual attention	40.5
10. Don't show favoritism toward students	46.6		10. Lack control	39.9

FIGURE 1.1 Student's Images of Their Best and Worst Teachers

BEST PRACTICES
Strategies for Becoming an Effective Teacher

1. *Effective teaching requires teachers to wear many different hats.* It's easy to fall into the trap of thinking that if you have good subject matter knowledge, excellent teaching will follow. Being an effective teacher requires many diverse skills. Next, you can read about how Susan Bradburn, who teaches fourth and sixth grades at West Marian Elementary School in North Carolina, brings many different skills to create effective lessons.

THROUGH THE EYES OF TEACHERS
The Turtle Lady

Susan created a school museum in which students conduct research and create exhibitions. She has put her school museum concept "on wheels" by having students take carts to other classes and into the community, and she has used the award money to spread the use of mobile museums to other North Carolina schools. Nick-named "the turtle lady" because of her interest in turtles and other animals, Susan takes students on 3-day field trips to Edisto Island, South Carolina, to search for fossils and study coastal

Susan Bradburn (left) with several students at West Marian Elementary School.

ecology. Her students sell calendars that contain their original poetry and art, and they use the proceeds to buy portions of a rain forest so it won't be destroyed.

2. *Engage in perspective taking.* You want to be the very best teacher you can possibly be. Think about what your students need from you to improve their academic and life skills. Put your heart and mind into helping them construct these skills. Also think about how you perceive your students and how they perceive you. Here is how

one teacher benefited from reflecting about how his perceptions of students' diversity was too stereotypical.

THROUGH THE EYES OF TEACHERS
Finding Individuality in Diversity

Paul August taught for 6 years in an integrated school but says that experience did not adequately prepare him, a non-Latino White, for teaching in an all African American school. Initially, he perceived the African American students as looking alike. At the end of the school year, however, he realized how ridiculous this was, and individuality had bloomed in his classroom both on his part and his students. He no longer was seen by his students as a White guy but as a teacher.

Later, when Paul was transferred to teach in a predominantly Asian American school, he says that he regressed into the "they all look alike" stereotype. Once again, though, over time individuality trumped nationality and he "could see the differences in faces, names, and cultures of Chinese, Vietnamese, Cambodians, Laotions, Japanese, and Mien" (August, 2002, p. A29).

3. *Keep the list of characteristics of effective teachers we have discussed in this chapter with you through your teaching career.* Looking at the list and thinking about the different areas of effective teaching can benefit you as you go through your student teaching, your days as a beginning teacher, and even your years as an experienced teacher. By consulting it from time to time, you might realize that you have let one or two areas slip and need to spend time improving yourself.

Review, Reflect, and Practice

(2) Identify the attitudes and skills of an effective teacher.

REVIEW
- What professional knowledge and skills are required to be an effective teacher?
- Why is it important for teachers to be committed and motivated?

REFLECT
- What is most likely to make teaching rewarding for you in the long run?

PRAXIS™ PRACTICE

1. Suzanne spends a considerable amount of time writing lesson plans, developing criteria for student success, and organizing materials. Which professional skill is she demonstrating?
   a. classroom management
   b. communication
   c. developmentally appropriate teaching practices
   d. goal setting and instructional management
2. Mr. Marcinello, who is midway through his first year of teaching, feels frustrated with his job. He is developing a negative attitude, and it is carrying over in his teaching. Which of the following areas does Mr. Marincello need to work on the most at this point to become an effective teacher?
   a. classroom management and communication
   b. commitment and motivation
   c. technology and diversity
   d. subject matter competence and individual variations

Please see the answer key at the end of the book.

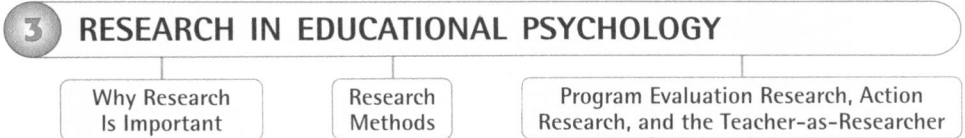

3 RESEARCH IN EDUCATIONAL PSYCHOLOGY

| Why Research Is Important | Research Methods | Program Evaluation Research, Action Research, and the Teacher-as-Researcher |

Research can be a valuable source of information about teaching. We will explore why research is important and how it is done, including how you can be a teacher-researcher.

Why Research Is Important

It sometimes is said that experience is the best teacher. Your own experiences and experiences that other teachers, administrators, and experts share with you will make you a better teacher. However, by providing you with valid information about the best ways to teach children, research also can make you a better teacher (Fraenkel & Wallen, 2005, Gall, Gall, & Borg, 2007).

We all get a great deal of knowledge from personal experience. We generalize from what we observe and frequently turn memorable encounters into lifetime "truths." But how valid are these conclusions? Sometimes we err in making these personal observations or misinterpret what we see and hear. Chances are, you can think of many situations in which you thought other people read you the wrong way, just as they might have felt that you misread them. When we base information only on personal experiences, we also aren't always totally objective because we sometimes make judgments that protect our ego and self-esteem (McMillan, 2004; McMillan & Schumacher, 2006).

We get information not only from personal experiences but also from authorities or experts. In your teaching career, you will hear many authorities and experts spell out a "best way" to educate students. The authorities and experts, however, don't always agree, do they? You might hear one expert one week tell you about a reading method that is absolutely the best, yet the next week hear another expert tout a

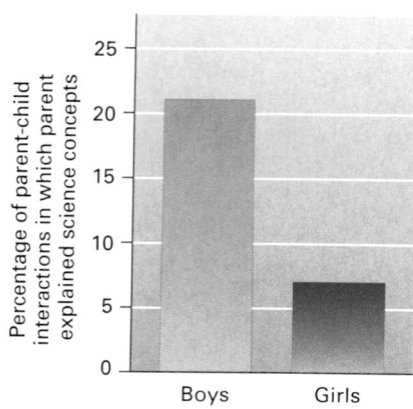

FIGURE 1.2 Parents' Explanations of Science to Sons and Daughters at a Science Museum

In a naturalistic observation study at a children's science museum, parents were three times more likely to explain science to boys than girls (Crowley & others, 2001). The gender difference occurred regardless of whether the father, the mother, or both parents were with the child, although the gender difference was greatest for fathers' science explanations to sons and daughters.

different method. One experienced teacher might tell you to do one thing with your students, while another experienced teacher tells you to do the opposite. How can you tell which one to believe? One way to clarify the situation is to look closely at research on the topic.

Research Methods

Collecting information (or data) is an important aspect of research. When educational psychology researchers want to find out, for example, whether regularly playing video games detracts from student learning, eating a nutritious breakfast improves alertness in class, or getting more recess time decreases absenteeism, they can choose from many methods of gathering research information.

The three basic methods used to gather information in educational psychology are descriptive, correlational, and experimental.

Descriptive Research Descriptive research has the purpose of observing and recording behavior. For example, an educational psychologist might observe the extent to which children are aggressive in a classroom or interview teachers about their attitudes toward a particular type of teaching strategy. By itself, descriptive research cannot prove what causes some phenomenon, but it can reveal important information about people's behavior and attitudes (Lammers & Badia, 2005; Leary, 2004).

Observation We look at things all the time. Casually watching two students interacting, however, is not the same as the type of observation used in scientific studies. Scientific observation is highly systematic. It requires knowing what you are looking for, conducting observations in an unbiased manner, accurately recording and categorizing what you see, and effectively communicating your observations (Best & Kahn, 2006; McBurney & White, 2007).

A common way to record observations is to write them down, often using shorthand or symbols. In addition, tape recorders, video cameras, special coding sheets, one-way mirrors, and computers increasingly are being used to make observation more accurate, reliable, and efficient.

Observations can be made in laboratories or in naturalistic settings. A **laboratory** is a controlled setting from which many of the complex factors of the real world have been removed (Gall, Gall, & Borg, 2007). Some educational psychologists conduct research in laboratories at the colleges or universities where they work and teach. Although laboratories often help researchers gain more control in their studies, they have been criticized as being artificial (Beins, 2004).

In **naturalistic observation,** behavior is observed out in the real world. Educational psychologists conduct naturalistic observations of children in classrooms, at museums, on playgrounds, in homes, in neighborhoods, and in other settings (Brophy, 2006). Naturalistic observation was used in one study that focused on conversations in a children's science museum (Crowley & others, 2001). Parents were three times as likely to engage boys as girls in explanatory talk while visiting different exhibits at the science museum (see figure 1.2). In another study, Mexican American parents who had completed high school used more explanations with their children as they were observed at a science museum than Mexican American parents who had not completed high school (Tennebaum & others, 2002).

Participant observation occurs when the observer-researcher is actively involved as a participant in the activity or setting (McMillan, 2004). The participant observer will often participate in a context and observe awhile, then take notes on what he or she has viewed. The observer usually makes these observations and writes down notes over a period of days, weeks, or months and looks for patterns in the observations (Glesne, 2007). For example, to study a student who is doing poorly in the class without apparent reason, the teacher might develop a plan to observe the student from

laboratory A controlled setting from which many of the complex factors of the real world have been removed.

naturalistic observation Observation outside of a laboratory in the real world.

participant observation Observation conducted at the same time the teacher-researcher is actively involved as a participant in the activity or setting.

time to time and record observations of the student's behavior and what is going on in the classroom at the time.

Interviews and Questionnaires   Sometimes the quickest and best way to get information about students and teachers is to ask them for it. Educational psychologists use interviews and questionnaires (surveys) to find out about children's and teachers' experiences, beliefs, and feelings. Most interviews take place face-to-face, although they can be done in other ways, such as over the phone or the Internet. Questionnaires usually are given to individuals in written form. They, too, can be transmitted in many ways, such as directly by hand, by mail, or via the Internet.

Good interviews and surveys involve concrete, specific, and unambiguous questions and some means of checking the authenticity of the respondents' replies (Rosnow & Rosenthal, 2005). Interviews and surveys, however, are not without problems. One crucial limitation is that many individuals give socially desirable answers, responding in a way they think is most socially acceptable and desirable rather than how they truly think or feel (Babbie, 2005). Skilled interviewing techniques and questions that increase forthright responses are crucial to obtaining accurate information (Navdi, 2006). Another problem with interviews and surveys is that the respondents sometimes simply lie.

Standardized Tests   **Standardized tests** have uniform procedures for administration and scoring. They assess students' aptitudes or skills in different domains. Many standardized tests allow a student's performance to be compared with the performance of other students at the same age or grade level, in many cases on a national basis (Gregory, 2007). Students might take a number of standardized tests, including tests that assess their intelligence, achievement, personality, career interests, and other skills. These tests can provide outcome measures for research studies, information that helps psychologists and educators make decisions about an individual student, and comparisons of students' performance across schools, states, and countries.

Standardized tests also play an important role in a major contemporary educational psychology issue—*accountability,* which involves holding teachers and students responsible for student performance (McNergney & McNergney, 2007). As we indicated earlier, both students and teachers increasingly are being given standardized tests in the accountability effort. The U.S. government's No Child Left Behind Act is at the centerpiece of accountability; it mandated that in 2005 every state had to give standardized tests to students in grades 3 through 8 in language arts and math, with testing for science achievement added in 2007 (Essex, 2006).

Case Studies   A **case study** is an in-depth look at an individual. Case studies often are used when unique circumstances in a person's life cannot be duplicated, for either practical or ethical reasons. For example, consider the case study of Brandi Binder (Nash, 1997). She developed such severe epilepsy that surgeons had to remove the right side of her brain's cerebral cortex when she was 6 years old. Brandi lost virtually all control over muscles on the left side of her body, the side controlled by the right side of her brain. At age 17, however, after years of therapy ranging from leg lifts to mathematics and music training, Brandi is an *A* student. She loves music and art, which usually are associated with the right side of the brain. Her recuperation is not 100 percent—for example, she has not regained the use of her left arm—but her case study shows that if there is a way to compensate, the human brain will find it. Brandi's remarkable recovery also provides evidence against the stereotype that the left side (hemisphere) of the brain is solely the source of logical thinking and the right hemisphere exclusively the source of creativity. Brains are not that neatly split in terms of most functioning, as Brandi's case illustrates.

Although case studies provide dramatic, in-depth portrayals of people's lives, we need to exercise caution when interpreting them (Bogdon & Biklin, 2007; Leary,

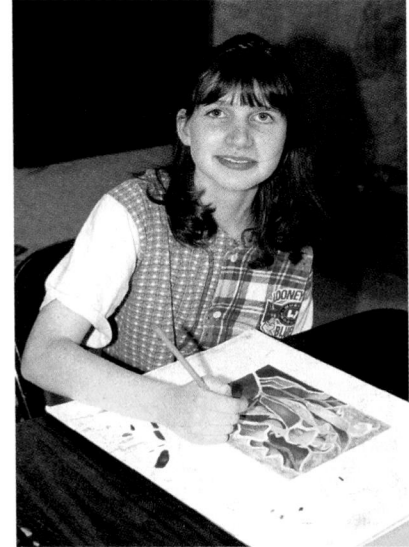

Brandi Binder is evidence of the brain's hemispheric flexibility and resilience. Despite having the right side of her cortex removed because of a severe case of epilepsy, Brandi engages in many activities often portrayed as only "right-brain" activities. She loves music and art and is shown here working on one of her paintings.

standardized tests Tests with uniform procedures for administration and scoring. They assess students' performance in different domains and allow a student's performance to be compared with the performance of other students at the same age or grade level on a national basis.

case study An in-depth look at an individual.

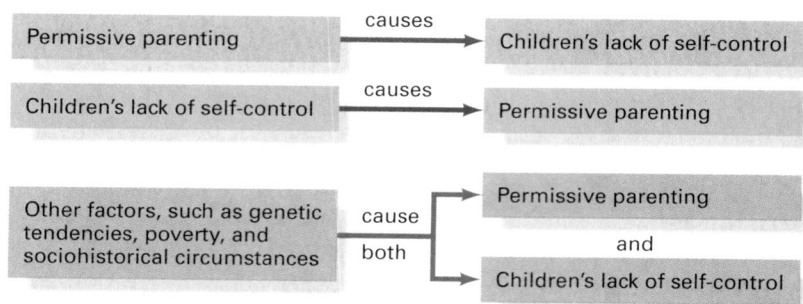

FIGURE 1.3 Possible Explanations for Correctional Data

An observed correlation between two events cannot be used to conclude that one event caused the other. Some possibilities are that the second event caused the first event or that a third, unknown event caused the correlation between the first two events.

2004). The subject of a case study is unique, with a genetic makeup and set of experiences that no one else shares. For these reasons, the findings often do not lend themselves to statistical analysis and may not generalize to other people.

Ethnographic Studies An **ethnographic study** consists of in-depth description and interpretation of behavior in an ethnic or a cultural group that includes direct involvement with the participants (Berg, 2007; McMillan & Wergin, 2002). This type of study might include observations in naturalistic settings as well as interviews. Many ethnographic studies are long-term projects.

In one ethnographic study, the purpose was to examine the extent to which schools were enacting educational reforms for language minority students (U.S. Office of Education, 1998). In-depth observations and interviews were conducted in a number of schools to determine if they were establishing high standards and restructuring the way education was being delivered. Several schools were selected for intensive evaluation, including Las Palmas Elementary School in San Clemente, California. The study concluded that this school, at least, was making the necessary reforms for improving the education of language minority students.

Correlational Research In **correlational research,** the goal is to describe the strength of the relation between two or more events or characteristics. Correlational research is useful because the more strongly two events are correlated (related or associated), the more effectively we can predict one from the other (Sprinthall, 2007). For example, if researchers find that low-involved, permissive teaching is correlated with a student's lack of self-control, it suggests that low-involved, permissive teaching might be one source of the lack of self-control.

Correlation by itself, however, does not equal causation (Vogt, 2007). The correlational finding just mentioned does not mean that permissive teaching necessarily causes low student self-control. It could mean that, but it also could mean that the student's lack of self-control caused the teachers to throw up their arms in despair and give up trying to control the out-of-control class. It also could be that other factors, such as heredity, poverty, or inadequate parenting, caused the correlation between permissive teaching and low student self-control. Figure 1.3 illustrates these possible interpretations of correlational data.

Experimental Research **Experimental research** allows educational psychologists to determine the causes of behavior. Educational psychologists accomplish this task by performing an *experiment*, a carefully regulated procedure in which one or more of

ethnographic study In-depth description and interpretation of behavior in an ethnic or a cultural group that includes direct involvement with the participants.

correlational research Research that describes the strength of the relation between two or more events or characteristics.

experimental research Research that allows the determination of the causes of behavior; involves conducting an experiment, which is a carefully regulated procedure in which one or more of the factors believed to influence the behavior being studied is manipulated and all others are held constant.

the factors believed to influence the behavior being studied is manipulated and all other factors are held constant. If the behavior under study changes when a factor is manipulated, we say that the manipulated factor causes the behavior to change. *Cause* is the event that is being manipulated. *Effect* is the behavior that changes because of the manipulation. Experimental research is the only truly reliable method of establishing cause and effect. Because correlational research does not involve manipulation of factors, it is not a dependable way to isolate cause (Mitchell & Jolley, 2007).

Experiments involve at least one independent variable and one dependent variable. The **independent variable** is the manipulated, influential, experimental factor. The label *independent* indicates that this variable can be changed independently of any other factors. For example, suppose we want to design an experiment to study the effects of peer tutoring on student achievement. In this example, the amount and type of peer tutoring could be an independent variable.

The **dependent variable** is the factor that is measured in an experiment. It can change as the independent variable is manipulated. The label *dependent* is used because the values of this variable depend on what happens to the participants in the experiment as the independent variable is manipulated. In the peer tutoring study, achievement is the dependent variable. This might be assessed in a number of ways. Let's say in this study it is measured by scores on a nationally standardized achievement test.

In experiments, the independent variable consists of differing experiences given to one or more experimental groups and one or more control groups. An **experimental group** is a group whose experience is manipulated. A **control group** is a comparison group that is treated in every way like the experimental group except for the manipulated factor. The control group serves as the baseline against which the effects of the manipulated condition can be compared. In the peer tutoring study, we need to have one group of students who get peer tutoring (experimental group) and one group of students who don't (control group).

Another important principle of experimental research is **random assignment:** Researchers assign participants to experimental and control groups by chance. This practice reduces the likelihood that the experiment's results will be due to any preexisting differences between the groups (Kantowitz, Roediger, & Elmes, 2005). In our study of peer tutoring, random assignment greatly reduces the probability that the two groups will differ on such factors as age, family status, initial achievement, intelligence, personality, health, and alertness.

To summarize the experimental study of peer tutoring and student achievement, each student is randomly assigned to one of two groups. One group (the experimental group) is given peer tutoring; the other (the control group) is not. The independent variable consists of the differing experiences (tutoring or no tutoring) that the experimental and control groups receive. After the peer tutoring is completed, the students are given a nationally standardized achievement test (dependent variable). Figure 1.4 illustrates the experimental research method applied to time management and students' grades.

Program Evaluation Research, Action Research, and the Teacher-as-Researcher

In discussing research methods so far, we have referred mainly to methods used to improve our knowledge and understanding of general educational practices. The same methods also can be applied to research whose aim is more specific, such as determining how well a particular educational strategy or program is working (Best & Kahn, 2006; Gall, Gall, & Borg, 2007). This more narrowly targeted work often includes program evaluation research, action research, and the teacher-as-researcher.

Independent variable

Dependent variable

FIGURE 1.4 The Experimental Research Strategy Applied to a Study of the Effects of Time Management on Students' Grades

independent variable The manipulated, influential, experimental factor in an experiment.

dependent variable The factor that is measured in an experiment.

experimental group The group whose experience is manipulated in an experiment.

control group In an experiment, a group whose experience is treated in every way like the experimental group except for the manipulated factor.

random assignment In experimental research, the assignment of participants to experimental and control groups by chance.

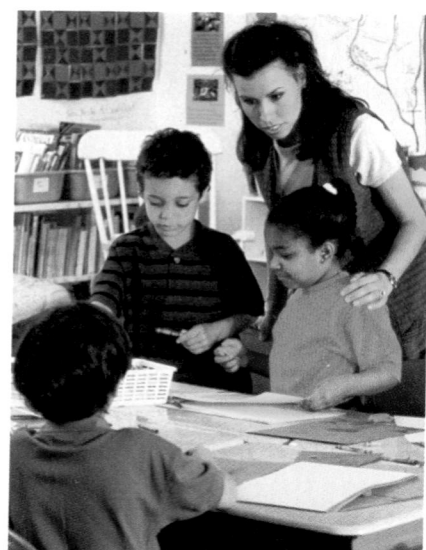

What methods can a teacher-as-researcher use to obtain information about students?

Program Evaluation Research   **Program evaluation research** is research designed to make decisions about the effectiveness of a particular program (Felner, 2006; Fitzpatrick, Sanders & Worthen, 2004; McMillan, 2004). It often focuses on a specific location or type of program. Because program evaluation research often is directed at answering a question about a specific school or school system, its results are not intended to be generalized to other settings (Mertler & Charles, 2005). A program evaluation researcher might ask questions like these:

- Has a gifted program started 2 years ago had positive effects on students' creative thinking and academic achievement?
- Has a technology program in place for 1 year improved students' attitudes toward school?
- Which of two reading programs being used in this school system has improved students' reading skills the most?

Action Research   **Action research** is used to solve a specific classroom or school problem, improve teaching and other educational strategies, or make a decision at a specific location (Berg, 2007; Hendricks, 2006). The goal of action research is to improve educational practices immediately in one or two classrooms, at one school, or at several schools. Action research is carried out by teachers and administrators rather than educational psychology researchers. The practitioners, however, might follow many of the guidelines of scientific research described earlier, such as trying to make the research and observations as systematic as possible to avoid bias and misinterpretation. Action research can be carried out schoolwide or in more limited settings by a smaller group of teachers and administrators; it can even be accomplished in a single classroom by an individual teacher (Bogdan & Biklin, 2007).

Teacher-as-Researcher   The concept of **teacher-as-researcher** (also called "teacher-researcher") is the idea that classroom teachers can conduct their own studies to improve their teaching practices (Creswell, 2005). This is an important outgrowth of action research. Some educational experts believe that the increasing emphasis on the teacher-as-researcher reinvents the teacher's role, fuels school renewal, and improves teaching and learning (Flake & others, 1995; Gill, 1997). The most effective teachers routinely ask questions and monitor problems to be solved, then collect data, interpret them, and share their conclusions with other teachers (Cochran-Smith, 1995).

To obtain information, the teacher-researcher uses methods such as participant observation, interviews, and case studies (Glesne, 2007). One good, widely used technique is the clinical interview, in which the teacher makes the student feel comfortable, shares beliefs and expectations, and asks questions in a nonthreatening manner. Before conducting a clinical interview with a student, the teacher usually will put together a targeted set of questions to ask. Clinical interviews not only can help you obtain information about a particular issue or problem but also can provide you with a sense of how children think and feel.

In addition to participant observation, the teacher might conduct several clinical interviews with a student, discuss the student's situation with the child's parents, and consult with a school psychologist about the student's behavior. Based on this work as teacher-researcher, the teacher may be able to create an intervention strategy that improves the student's behavior.

Thus, learning about educational research methods not only can help you understand the research that educational psychologists conduct but also has another practical benefit. The more knowledge you have about research in educational psychology, the more effective you will be in the increasingly popular teacher-researcher role (Thomas, 2005b).

program evaluation research Research designed to make decisions about the effectiveness of a particular program.

action research Research used to solve a specific classroom or school problem, improve teaching and other educational strategies, or make a decision at a specific level.

teacher-as-researcher Also called teacher-researcher, this concept involves classroom teachers conducting their own studies to improve their teaching practice.

BEST PRACTICES
Strategies for Becoming an Effective Teacher-Researcher

1. *As you plan each week's lessons, think about your students and which ones might benefit from your role as a teacher-researcher.* As you reflect on the past week's classes, you might notice that one student seemed to be sliding downhill in her performance and that another student seemed to be especially depressed. As you think about such students, you might consider using your observer participation and/or clinical interview skills in the following week in an effort to find out why they are having problems.

2. *Take a course in educational research methods.* This can improve your understanding of how research is conducted.

3. *Use the library or Internet resources to learn more about teacher-researcher skills.* This might include locating information about how to be a skilled clinical interviewer and a systematic, unbiased observer. A good book on improving your observation skills is *A Guide to Observation and Participation in the Classroom* (Reed, Bergemann, & Olson, 2001).

4. *Ask someone else (such as another teacher) to observe your class and help you develop some strategies for the particular research problem that you want to solve.*

Review, Reflect, and Practice

(3) **Discuss why research is important to effective teaching and how educational psychologists and teachers can conduct and evaluate research.**

REVIEW

- Why is research important in educational psychology?
- What are some types of research? What is the difference between correlational and experimental research?
- What are some kinds of research that relate very directly to effective classroom practices? What tools might a teacher use to do classroom research?

REFLECT

- In your own K–12 education, can you remember a time when one of your teachers might have benefited from conducting action research regarding the effectiveness of his or her own teaching methods? What action research questions and methods might have been useful to the teacher?

PRAXIS™ PRACTICE

1. Which of the following is more scientific?
   a. systematic observation
   b. personal experience
   c. a person's opinion
   d. a book written by a journalist

2. Mr. McMahon wants to know how much time his students spend off-task each day. To determine this, he carefully watches the students in class, keeping a record of off-task behavior. Which research approach has he used?
   a. case study
   b. experiment
   c. laboratory experiment
   d. naturalistic observation

continued on page 22

3. Ms. Simon has been hired to determine how effective a school's health education program has been in reducing adolescent pregnancies. Which type of research will she conduct?
   a. action research
   b. experimental research
   c. program evaluation
   d. teacher-as-researcher

Please see the answer key at the end of the book.

CRACK THE CASE
The Case of the Curriculum Decision

Mrs. Jefferson is frustrated with the social studies curriculum that her school district has used for the past 8 years. The manner in which the material is presented bothers her. The books are not very exciting and don't hold students' interest. The print is small and there are few pictures, charts, maps, or graphs. The material itself also bothers her because it is ethnocentric and says little about the accomplishments of women. In addition, the teachers' guide doesn't offer much besides worksheets and test items. The district has a policy of replacing curriculum materials every 10 years. "This is the year to start looking," she thinks. "I really want some input into this decision."

She talks to her principal, who tells her that a committee of five teachers and one administrator is being established to examine various social studies curricula that cover the entire grade span of the school. Mrs. Jefferson asks to be a part of the committee. "That's great," replies the principal. "Now we'll have a representative from each grade level and special education. I know you'll be a valuable part of the committee."

At the first committee meeting, Mrs. Jefferson is a bit overwhelmed by what some of the other teachers are saying. One sees no point in developing a new curriculum "because, after all, history doesn't change, and we can always supplement with current events material." Another teacher wants a curriculum that has no actual textbooks, only guidelines for several projects students can complete. This teacher had read an article in a popular magazine touting this type of curriculum. Yet another teacher wants to implement a new version of the curriculum they have been using—because if they develop something entirely different, she would have to revamp her teaching, which she says would be "an incredible task." The administrator tells the rest of the committee that they have 1 year to make their decision: "That way all the materials can

be ordered, and each teacher will have some time to become familiar with the material before implementing it."

The committee calls various publishers of social studies curricular materials and asks for preview copies of their materials. In response, they receive a veritable cornucopia of textbooks and ancillary materials including reading lists, workbooks, instructor's guides, test banks, and CD-ROMs. Wading through all the materials to make a decision that will impact students for a decade seems like a momentous task. However, Mrs. Jefferson and her colleagues are determined to choose the right curriculum for their students. To do this, they decide to engage in considerable research. "It's a good thing we have a year to do this," thinks Mrs. Jefferson.

1. How would you go about engaging in the research necessary to make a good decision regarding what curriculum to implement?

2. What issues need to be considered? Why?

3. What type of research would be most appropriate?
   a. case study
   b. correlational research
   c. experimental research
   d. naturalistic observation
   Explain your choice.

4. If Mrs. Jefferson and her colleagues decide to conduct an experimental study in which they compare the influence of two different curricula on student achievement, what would the independent variable be?
   a. student achievement
   b. observation
   c. correlated factors
   d. which curriculum is used

Reach Your Learning Goals
Educational Psychology: A Tool for Effective Teaching

(1) EXPLORING EDUCATIONAL PSYCHOLOGY: Describe some basic ideas about the field of educational psychology.

Historical Background

Educational psychology is the branch of psychology that specializes in understanding teaching and learning in educational settings. William James and John Dewey were important pioneers in educational psychology, as was E. L. Thorndike. Among the important ideas in educational psychology that we owe to Dewey are these: the child as an active learner, education of the whole child, emphasis on the child's adaptation to the environment, and the democratic ideal that all children deserve a competent education. There were few individuals from ethnic minority groups and few women in the early history of educational psychology because of ethnic and gender barriers. Further historical developments included Skinner's behaviorism in the mid-twentieth century and the cognitive revolution that had taken hold by the 1980s. Also in recent years, there has been expanded interest in the socioemotional aspects of children's lives, including cultural contexts.

Teaching: Art and Science

Teaching is linked to both science and art. In terms of art, skillful, experienced practice contributes to effective teaching. In terms of science, information from psychological research can provide valuable ideas.

(2) EFFECTIVE TEACHING: Identify the attitudes and skills of an effective teacher.

Professional Knowledge and Skills

Effective teachers have subject matter competence, use effective instructional strategies, pay more than lip service to individual variations, work with diverse ethnic and cultural groups, and have skills in the following areas: goal setting and planning, developmentally appropriate teaching practices, classroom management, motivation, communication, assessment, and technology.

Commitment and Motivation

Being an effective teacher also requires commitment and motivation. This includes having a good attitude and caring about students. It is easy for teachers to get into a rut and develop a negative attitude, but students pick up on this and it can harm their learning.

(3) RESEARCH IN EDUCATIONAL PSYCHOLOGY: Discuss why research is important to effective teaching and how educational psychologists and teachers can conduct and evaluate research.

Why Research Is Important

Personal experiences and information from experts can help you become an effective teacher. The information you obtain from research also is extremely important. It will help you sort through various strategies and determine which are most and least effective. Research helps to eliminate errors in judgment that are based only on personal experiences.

Research Methods

Numerous methods can be used to obtain information about various aspects of educational psychology. Research data-gathering methods can be classified as descriptive, correlational, and experimental. Descriptive methods include observation, interviews, questionnaires, standardized tests, ethnographic studies, and case studies. In correlational research, the goal

continued

is to describe the strength of the relation between two or more events or characteristics. An important research principle is that correlation does not equal causation. Experimental research is the only kind of research that can discover behavior's causes. Conducting an experiment involves examining the influence of at least one independent variable (the manipulated, influential, experimental factor) on one or more dependent variables (the measured factor). Experiments involve the random assignment of participants to one or more experimental groups (the groups whose experience is being manipulated) and one or more control groups (comparison groups treated in every way like the experimental group except for the manipulated factor).

Program Evaluation Research, Action Research, and Teacher-as-Researcher

Program evaluation research is research designed to make decisions about the effectiveness of a particular program. Action research is used to solve a specific classroom or social problem, improve teaching strategies, or make a decision about a specific location. The teacher-as-researcher (teacher-researcher) conducts classroom studies to improve his or her educational practices.

KEY TERMS

educational psychology 2
constructivist approach 6
direct instruction approach 6
differentiated instruction 8
laboratory 16
naturalistic observation 16

participant observation 16
standardized tests 17
case study 17
ethnographic study 18
correlational research 18
experimental research 18

independent variable 19
dependent variable 19
experimental group 19
control group 19
random assignment 19

program evaluation
research 20
action research 20
teacher-as-researcher 20

PORTFOLIO ACTIVITIES

Now that you have a good understanding of this chapter, complete these exercises to expand your thinking.

Independent Reflection

1. After some thinking, write a personal statement about the following. What kind of teacher do you want to become? What strengths do you want to have? What kinds of potential weaknesses might you need to overcome? Either place the statement in your portfolio or seal it in an envelope that you will open after your first month or two of teaching.

2. At the beginning of the chapter, you read teacher-astronaut Christa McAuliffe's quote: "I touch the future. I teach." Don your creative thinking hat and come up with one or more brief quotes that describe positive aspects of teaching.

3. Think about the grade level you are planning to teach. Consider at least one way your classroom at that grade level is

likely to be challenging. Write about how you will cope with this.

Research/Field Experience

4. Information about educational psychology appears in research journals and in magazines and newspapers. Find an article in a research or professional journal (such as *Contemporary Educational Psychologist, Educational Psychologist, Educational Psychology Review, Journal of Educational Psychology,* or *Phi Delta Kappan*) and an article in a newspaper or magazine on the same topic. How does the research/professional article differ from the newspaper or magazine account? What can you learn from this comparison? Write down your conclusions and keep copies of the articles.

Go to the Online Learning Center for downloadable portfolio templates.

TAKING IT TO THE NET

- Begin building your network of support by subscribing to an education-related mailing list. Joining an e-mail list will keep you informed about the latest news in education and provide you with helpful instructional resources. Describe the mailing list you selected and what you hope to gain from it. **www.educationworld.com/maillist.shtml**
- The World Wide Web offers educators unlimited resources for increasing their effectiveness in the classroom. Examine a Web site for educators. How could the available resources contribute to your effectiveness in the classroom? **www.educationworld.com/**

- Teachers can use student surveys in the classroom to improve their teaching practices? Select one of your ideas, and formulate a brief (eight to ten questions) sample survey that you could use for future classroom research. **www.educationworld.com/a_curr/curr364.shtml**

Connect to the Online Learning Center to explore possible answers.

 ## STUDY, PRACTICE, AND SUCCEED

Visit **www.mhhe.com/santedu3e** to review the chapter with self-grading quizzes and Self-Assessments, to apply the chapter material to two more Crack the Case studies, and for suggested activities to develop your teaching portfolio.

CHAPTER 2

Cognitive and Language Development

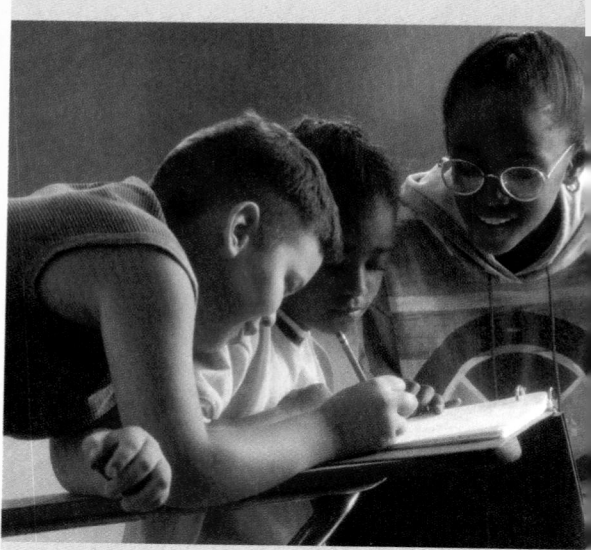

Ah! What would the world be to us
If the children were no more?
We should dread the desert behind us
Worse than the dark before.

—Henry Wadsworth Longfellow
American Poet, 19th Century

Learning Goals

1 Define development and explain the main processes, periods, and issues in development, as well as links between development and education.

2 Discuss the development of the brain and compare the cognitive developmental theories of Jean Piaget and Lev Vygotsky.

3 Identify the key features of language, biological and environmental influences on language, and the typical growth of the child's language.

TEACHING STORIES   Donene Polson

In this chapter, you will study Lev Vygotsky's sociocultural cognitive theory of development. Donene Polson's classroom reflects Vygotsky's emphasis on the importance of collaboration among a community of learners. Donene teaches at Washington Elementary School in Salt Lake City, an innovative school that emphasizes the importance of people learning together (Rogoff, Turkanis, & Bartlett, 2001). Children as well as adults plan learning activities. Throughout the day at school, students work in small groups.

Donene loves working in a school in which students, teachers, and parents work as a community to help children learn (Polson, 2001). Before the school year begins, Donene meets with parents at each family's home to prepare for the upcoming year, getting acquainted and establishing schedules to determine when parents can contribute to classroom instruction. At monthly teacher-parent meetings, Donene and the parents plan the curriculum and discuss children's progress. They brainstorm about community resources that can be used to promote children's learning.

Many students come back to tell Donene that experiences in her classroom made important contributions to their development and learning. For example, Luisa Magarian reflected on how her experience in Donene's classroom helped her work with others in high school:

> From having responsibility in groups, kids learn how to deal with problems and listen to each other or try to understand different points of view. They learn how to help a group work smoothly and how to keep people interested in what they are doing. . . . As coeditor of the student news magazine at my high school, I have to balance my eagerness to get things done with patience to work with other students (Rogoff, Turkanis, & Bartlett, 2001, pp. 84–85).

As Donene Polson's story shows, theories of cognitive development can form the basis of innovative instructional programs.

Preview

Examining the shape of children's development allows us to understand it better. This chapter—the first of two on development—focuses on children's cognitive and language development. Before we delve into these topics, though, we need to explore some basic ideas about development.

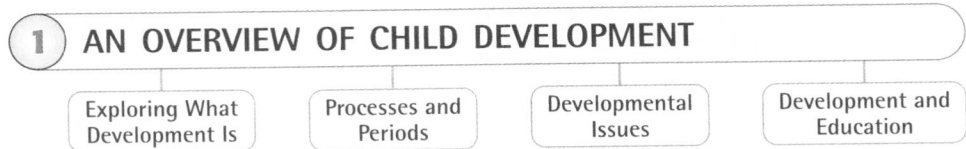

1 AN OVERVIEW OF CHILD DEVELOPMENT

| Exploring What Development Is | Processes and Periods | Developmental Issues | Development and Education |

Twentieth-century Spanish-born American philosopher George Santayana once reflected, "Children are on a different plane. They belong to a generation and way of feeling properly their own." Let's explore what that plane is like.

Exploring What Development Is

Why study children's development? As a teacher, you will be responsible for a new wave of children each year in your classroom. The more you learn about children's development, the more you can understand at what level it is appropriate to teach them.

Childhood has become such a distinct phase of the human life span, it is hard to imagine that it was not always thought of in that way. In medieval times, however, laws generally did not distinguish between child and adult offenses, and children often were treated like miniature adults.

Today, we view children quite differently than in medieval times. Childhood is seen as an eventful, unique time of life that lays an important foundation for the adult years and is highly differentiated from them. We identify distinct periods within childhood during which children master special skills and confront new life tasks. We protect our children from the excesses of adult work through tough child labor laws, treat their most serious transgressions under a special system of juvenile justice, and have government provisions to help children when family support systems fail or when a family seriously threatens a child's well-being (Benson & others, 2006; Ramey, Ramey, & Lanzi, 2006). We value childhood as a special time of growth and change, and we invest great resources in caring for and educating our children.

Each child develops partly like all other children, partly like some other children, and partly like no other children. We often direct our attention to a child's uniqueness. But psychologists who study development often are drawn to children's shared characteristics—as are teachers who must manage and educate groups of same- or similar-age children. As humans, every person travels some common paths—Leonardo da Vinci, Joan of Arc, Martin Luther King, Jr., Madonna, and most likely you—all walked at about 1 year, engaged in fantasy play as a child, developed an expanded vocabulary in the elementary school years, and became more independent as a youth.

Just what do psychologists mean when they speak of a person's "development"? **Development** is the pattern of biological, cognitive, and socioemotional changes that begins at conception and continues through the life span. Most development involves growth, although it also eventually involves decay (dying).

Processes and Periods

The pattern of child development is complex because it is the product of several processes: biological, cognitive, and socioemotional. Development also can be described in terms of periods.

Biological, Cognitive, and Socioemotional Processes *Biological processes* produce changes in the child's body and underlie brain development, height and weight gains, motor skills, and puberty's hormonal changes. Genetic inheritance plays a large part.

Cognitive processes involve changes in the child's thinking, intelligence, and language. Cognitive developmental processes enable a growing child to memorize a poem, imagine how to solve a math problem, come up with a creative strategy, or speak meaningfully connected sentences.

Socioemotional processes involve changes in the child's relationships with other people, changes in emotion, and changes in personality. Parents' nurturance toward their child, a boy's aggressive attack on a peer, a girl's development of assertiveness, and an adolescent's feelings of joy after getting good grades all reflect socioemotional processes in development.

Periods of Development For the purposes of organization and understanding, we commonly describe development in terms of periods. In the most widely used system of classification, the developmental periods are infancy, early childhood, middle and late childhood, adolescence, early adulthood, middle adulthood, and late adulthood.

Infancy extends from birth to 18 to 24 months. It is a time of extreme dependence on adults. Many activities are just beginning, such as language development, symbolic thought, sensorimotor coordination, and social learning.

development The pattern of biological, cognitive, and socioemotional processes that begins at conception and continues through the life span. Most development involves growth, although it also eventually involves decay (dying).

Early childhood (sometimes called the "preschool years") extends from the end of infancy to about 5 years. During this period, children become more self-sufficient, develop school readiness skills (such as learning to follow instructions and identify letters), and spend many hours with peers. First grade typically marks the end of early childhood.

Middle and late childhood (sometimes called the "elementary school years") extends from about 6 to 11 years of age. Children master the fundamental skills of reading, writing, and math, achievement becomes a more central theme, and self-control increases. In this period, children interact more with the wider social world beyond their family.

Adolescence involves the transition from childhood to adulthood. It begins around ages 10 to 12 and ends around 18 to 21. Adolescence starts with rapid physical changes, including height and weight gains and development of sexual functions. Adolescents intensely pursue independence and seek their own identity. Their thought becomes more abstract, logical, and idealistic.

Early adulthood begins in the early twenties and stretches into the thirties. It is a time when work and love become main themes in life. Individuals make important career decisions and usually seek an intimate relationship through marriage or a relationship with a significant other. Other developmental periods have been described for older adults, but we will confine our discussion to the periods most relevant for children's education.

Several periods of human development are shown in figure 2.1 along with the processes of development (biological, cognitive, and socioemotional). The interplay of these processes produces the periods of human development.

Periods of Development

| Infancy
(Birth to 18–24
months) | Early childhood
(2–5 years) | Middle and
late childhood
(6–11 years) | Adolescence
(10–12 to
18–21 years) | Early adulthood
(20s and 30s) |

Biological
processes

Cognitive
processes

Socioemotional
processes

Processes of Development

FIGURE 2.1 Periods and Processes of Development

Development moves through the infancy, early childhood, middle and late childhood, adolescence, and early adulthood periods. These periods of development are the result of biological, cognitive, and socioemotional processes.

Developmental Issues

Many questions about children's development remain unanswered. For example, what drives the biological, cognitive, and socioemotional processes of development, and how does what happens in infancy influence middle childhood or adolescence? Despite all of the knowledge that developmentalists have acquired, debate continues about the relative importance of factors that influence the developmental processes and about how the periods of development are related. The most important issues in the study of children's development include nature and nurture, continuity and discontinuity, and early and later experience.

FIGURE 2.2 Continuity and Discontinuity in Development

Is our development like that of a seedling gradually growing into a giant oak? Or is it more like that of a caterpillar suddenly becoming a butterfly?

Nature and Nurture   The **nature-nurture issue** involves the debate about whether development is primarily influenced by nature or by nurture (Bjorklund, 2006; Shiraev & Levy, 2007). *Nature* refers to an organism's biological inheritance, *nurture* to its environmental experiences. Almost no one today argues that development can be explained by nature or nurture alone. But some ("nature" proponents) claim that the most important influence on development is biological inheritance, and others ("nurture" proponents) claim that environmental experiences are the most important influence.

According to the nature proponents, just as a sunflower grows in an orderly way—unless it is defeated by an unfriendly environment—so does a person. The range of environments can be vast, but a genetic blueprint produces commonalities in growth and development. We walk before we talk, speak one word before two words, grow rapidly in infancy and less so in early childhood, and experience a rush of sexual hormones in puberty. Extreme environments—those that are psychologically barren or hostile—can stunt development, but nature proponents emphasize the influence of tendencies that are genetically wired into humans.

By contrast, other psychologists emphasize the importance of nurture, or environmental experiences, to development (Bronfenbrenner & Morris, 2006; Trask & Hamon, 2007). Experiences run the gamut from the individual's biological environment (nutrition, medical care, drugs, and physical accidents) to the social environment (family, peers, schools, community, media, and culture). For example, a child's diet can affect how tall the child grows and even how effectively the child can think and solve problems. Despite their genetic wiring, a child born and raised in a poor village in Bangladesh and a child in the suburbs of Denver are likely to have different skills, different ways of thinking about the world, and different ways of relating to people.

Continuity and Discontinuity   Think about your own development for a moment. Did you become the person you are gradually, like the seedling that slowly, cumulatively grows into a giant oak? Or did you experience sudden, distinct changes, like the caterpillar that changes into a butterfly (see figure 2.2)?

The **continuity-discontinuity issue** focuses on the extent to which development involves gradual, cumulative change (continuity) or distinct stages (discontinuity). For the most part, developmentalists who emphasize nurture usually describe development as a gradual, continuous process, like the seedling's growth into an oak. Those who emphasize nature often describe development as a series of distinct stages, like the change from caterpillar to butterfly.

Consider continuity first. As the oak grows from seedling to giant oak, its development is continuous. It becomes more of an oak, not a different kind of organism. Similarly, a child's first word, though seemingly an abrupt, discontinuous event, is actually the result of weeks and months of growth and practice. Puberty, another seemingly abrupt, discontinuous occurrence, is actually a gradual process occurring over several years.

Viewed in terms of discontinuity, each person is described as passing through a sequence of stages in which change is qualitatively rather than quantitatively different. As the caterpillar changes to a butterfly, it becomes a different kind of organism,

nature–nurture issue Nature refers to an organism's biological inheritance, nurture to environmental influences. The "nature" proponents claim biological inheritance is the most important influence on development; the "nurture" proponents claim environmental experiences are the most important.

continuity–discontinuity issue The issue regarding whether development involves gradual, cumulative change (continuity) or distinct stages (discontinuity).

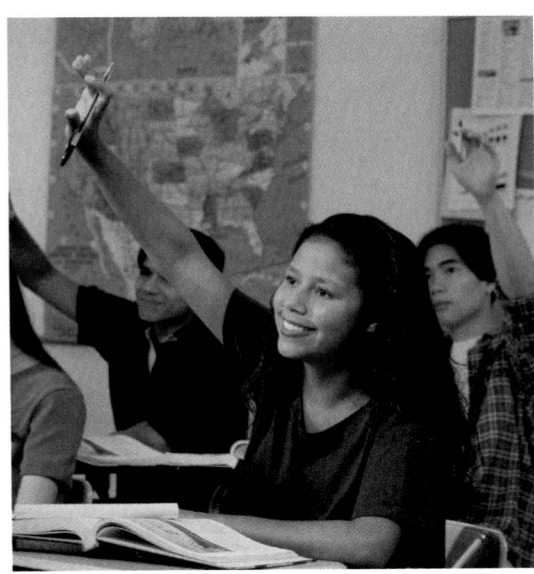

To what extent are early experiences, such as those involving relationships with parents, likely to be linked to later development, such as success in school?

not more of a caterpillar—its development is discontinuous. Similarly, a child moves at some point from not being able to think abstractly about the world to being able to. This is a qualitative, discontinuous change in development, not a quantitative, continuous change.

Early and Later Experience   The **early-later experience issue** focuses on the degree to which early experiences (especially in infancy) or later experiences are the key determinants of the child's development. That is, if infants experience harmful circumstances, can those experiences be overcome by later, positive ones? Or are the early experiences so critical—possibly because they are the infant's first, prototypical experiences—that they cannot be overridden by a later, better environment? To those who emphasize early experiences, life is an unbroken trail on which a psychological quality can be traced back to its origin (Kagan, 1992, 2003; Kagan & Fox, 2006). In contrast, to those who emphasize later experiences, development is like a river, continually ebbing and flowing.

The early-later experience issue has a long history and continues to be hotly debated among developmentalists (Gottlieb, Wahlsten, & Lickliter, 2006; Thompson, 2006). Plato was sure that infants who were rocked frequently become better athletes. Nineteenth-century New England ministers told parents in Sunday afternoon sermons that the way they handled their infants would determine their children's later character. Some developmentalists argue that, unless infants experience warm, nurturing care during the first year or so of life, their development will never quite be optimal (Carlson, Sroufe, & Egeland, 2004; Keller, 2007; Sroufe & others, 2005a,b).

In contrast, later-experience advocates argue that children are malleable throughout development, and that later sensitive caregiving is just as important as earlier sensitive caregiving. A number of life-span developmentalists (developmentalists who focus on the entire life span) stress that too little attention has been given to later experiences in development (Baltes, 2003; Baltes, Lindenberger, & Staudinger, 2006; Elder & Shanahan, 2006). They accept that early experiences are important contributors to development, but no more important than later experiences. Jerome Kagan (2003) points out that even children who show the qualities of an inhibited temperament, which is linked to heredity, have the capacity to change their behavior.

early-later experience issue The issue of the degree to which early experiences (especially infancy) or later experiences are the key determinants of the child's development.

People in Western cultures, especially those influenced by Freudian theory, tend to support the idea that early experiences are more important than later experiences (Chan, 1963; Lamb & Sternberg, 1992). The majority of people in the world do not share this belief. For example, people in many Asian countries believe that experiences occurring after about 6 or 7 years of age are more important to development than are earlier experiences. This view stems from the long-standing Eastern belief that children's reasoning skills begin to develop in important ways during middle childhood.

Evaluating the Developmental Issues Most developmentalists recognize that it is unwise to take an extreme position on the issues of nature and nurture, continuity and discontinuity, and early and later experiences. Development is not all nature or all nurture, not all continuity or all discontinuity, and not all early or later experiences (Gottlieb, Wahlsten, & Lickliter, 2006; Thelen & Smith, 2006). Nature and nurture, continuity and discontinuity, and early and later experiences all play a part in development through the human life span. Along with this consensus, there is still spirited debate about how strongly development is influenced by each of these factors (Sroufe & others, 2005a,b). Are girls less likely to do well in math mostly because of inherited characteristics or because of a combination of society's expectations and early experience? Can enriched experiences during adolescence remove deficits resulting from poverty, neglect, and poor schooling during childhood? The answers also have a bearing on social policy decisions about children and adolescents, and consequently on each of our lives.

Development and Education

In chapter 1, we briefly described the importance of engaging in developmentally appropriate teaching practices (Horowitz & others, 2005; Hyson, Copple, & Jones, 2006). Here we expand on this important topic and discuss the concept of splintered development.

Developmentally appropriate teaching takes place at a level that is neither too difficult and stressful nor too easy and boring for the child's developmental level. One of the challenges of developmentally appropriate teaching is that you likely will have children with an age range of several years and a range of abilities and skills in the classes you teach (Horowitz & others, 2005). Competent teachers are aware of these developmental differences. Rather than characterizing students as "advanced," "average," and "slow," they recognize that their development and ability are complex, and children often do not display the same competence across different skills.

Splintered development refers to the circumstances in which development is uneven across domains (Horowitz & others, 2005). One student may have excellent math skills but poor writing skills. Within the area of language, another student may have excellent verbal language skills but not have good reading and writing skills. Yet another student may do well in science but lack social skills.

A special challenge is the cognitively advanced student whose socioemotional development is at a level expected for a much younger child. For example, a student may excel at science, math, and language but be immature emotionally. Such a child may not have any friends and be neglected or rejected by peers. This student will benefit considerably from having a teacher who helps him or her learn how to manage emotions and behave in more socially appropriate ways.

As we discuss development in this chapter and the next, keep in mind how the developmental changes we describe can help you understand the optimal level for teaching and learning. For example, it is not a good strategy to try to push children to read before they are developmentally ready—but when they are ready, reading materials should be presented at the appropriate level.

splintered development The circumstances in which development is uneven across domains.

Review, Reflect, and Practice

1 Define development and explain the main processes, periods, and issues in development, as well as links between development and education.

REVIEW

- What is the nature of development?
- What three broad processes interact in a child's development? What general periods do children go through between birth and the end of adolescence?
- What are the main developmental issues? What conclusions can be reached about these issues?
- What implications does the concept of development have for the notion of "appropriate" learning?

REFLECT

- Give an example of how a cognitive process could influence a socioemotional process in the age of children you plan to teach. Then give an example of how a socioemotional process could influence a cognitive process in this age group.

PRAXIS™ PRACTICE

1. Mr. Huxtaby is giving a talk on development to a parent-teacher organization. In his talk, which of the following is he most likely to describe as not being an example of development?
   a. pubertal change
   b. improvement in memory
   c. change in friendship
   d. an inherited tendency to be shy

2. Ms. Halle teaches third grade. Which period of development is likely to be of most interest to her?
   a. infancy
   b. early childhood
   c. middle childhood
   d. adolescence

3. Piaget argued that children progress through a series of cognitive development stages. In contrast, Skinner stressed that individuals simply learn more as time goes on. Which developmental issue is highlighted in their disagreement?
   a. continuity and discontinuity
   b. early and later experience
   c. nature and nurture
   d. biological and socioemotional development

4. Alexander's scores on standardized mathematics achievement tests are always very high—among the highest in the nation. In contrast, his scores on reading achievement tests indicate that he is about average. This is an example of
   a. developmentally appropriate teaching.
   b. early versus later development.
   c. nature versus nurture.
   d. splintered development.

Please see the answer key at the end of the book.

Now that we have discussed some basic ideas about the nature of development, we will examine cognitive development at greater length. In examining different processes of development—biological, cognitive, and socioemotional—we indicated that these processes interact. In keeping with this theme, in our exploration of cognitive development, we will describe the physical development of the brain.

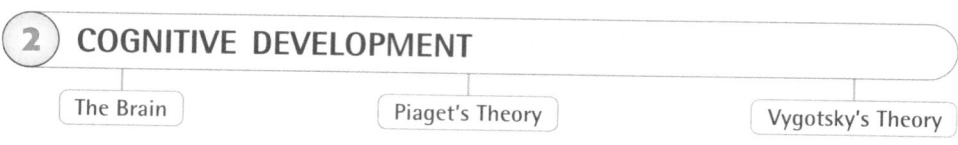

Twentieth-century American poet Marianne Moore said that the mind is "an enchanting thing." How this enchanting thing develops has intrigued many psychologists. First, we explore the development of the brain and then turn to two major cognitive theories of development—Piaget's and Vygotsky's.

The Brain

Until recently, little was known for certain about how the brain changes as children develop. Not long ago, scientists thought that genes determined how children's brains were "wired" and that unlike most cells, the cells in the brain responsible for processing information stopped dividing early in childhood. Whatever brain children's heredity dealt them, they were essentially stuck with it. This view, however, turned out to be wrong. Instead, the brain has considerable *plasticity,* or the ability to change, and its development depends on experience (Nelson, Thomas, and de Haan, 2006; Stettler & others, 2006). What children do can change the development of their brain.

The old view of the brain in part reflected the fact that scientists did not have the technology to detect and map sensitive changes in the brain as it develops. Today, sophisticated brain-scanning techniques allow better detection of these changes. Considerable progress is being made in charting developmental changes in the brain, although much is still unknown, and connections to children's education are difficult to make (Nelson, Thomas, & de Haan, 2006).

Brain Cells and Regions   The number and size of the brain's nerve endings continue to grow at least until adolescence. Some of the brain's increase in size also is due to *myelination,* the process of encasing many cells in the brain with a myelin sheath. This increases the speed at which information travels through the nervous system. Myelination in the areas of the brain related to hand-eye coordination is not complete until about 4 years of age. Myelination in brain areas important in focusing attention is not complete until about 10 years of age (Tanner, 1978). The implications for teaching are that children will have difficulty focusing their attention and maintaining it for very long in early childhood, but their attention will improve as they move through the elementary school years. The most extensive increase in myelination in the brain's frontal lobes, where reasoning and thinking occur, takes place during adolescence (Nelson, Thomas, & de Haan, 2006).

Another important aspect of the brain's development at the cellular level is the dramatic increase in connections between neurons (nerve cells). *Synapses* are tiny gaps between neurons where connections between neurons are made. Researchers have discovered an interesting aspect of synaptic connections. Nearly twice as many of these connections are made than ever will be used (Huttenlocher & Dabholkar, 1997; Huttenlocher & others, 1991). The connections that are used become strengthened and will survive, whereas the unused ones will be replaced by other pathways or

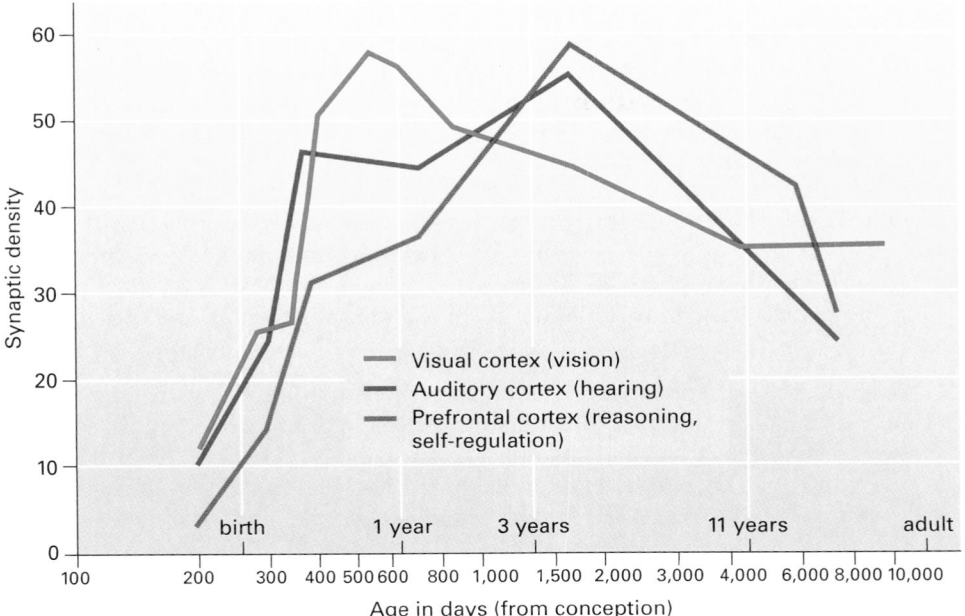

The graph shows the dramatic increase and then pruning is synaptic density for three regions of the brain: visual cortex, auditory cortex, and prefrontal cortex. Synaptic density is believed to be an important indication of the extent of connectivity between neurons.

disappear. That is, in the language of neuroscience, these connections will be "pruned." Figure 2.3 vividly shows the dramatic growth and later pruning of synapses in the visual, auditory, and prefrontal cortex areas of the brain. These areas are critical for higher-order cognitive functioning such as learning, memory, and reasoning. Notice that in the prefrontal cortex (where higher-level thinking and self-regulation take place) the peak of overproduction occurs at about 1 year of age. Notice also that it is not until middle to late adolescence that the adult density of the synapses is achieved.

In a study that used sophisticated brain-scanning techniques, children's brains were shown to undergo substantial anatomical changes between the ages of 3 and 15 (Thompson & others, 2000). By repeatedly obtaining brain scans of the same children for up to 4 years, researchers found that children's brains experience rapid, distinct growth spurts. The amount of brain material in some areas can nearly double within a year, followed by a drastic loss of tissue as unneeded cells are purged and the brain continues to reorganize itself. In this study, the overall size of the brain did not change from 3 to 15 years of age. However, rapid growth in the frontal lobes, especially areas related to attention, occurred from 3 to 6 years of age. Figure 2.4 shows the location of the brain's four lobes. Rapid growth in the temporal lobes (language processing) and parietal lobes (spatial location) occurred from age 6 through puberty.

Until recently, little research has been conducted on developmental changes in the brain during adolescence. While research in this area is still in its infancy, an increasing number of studies are under way (Dick & others, 2006; Toga, Thompson, & Sowell, 2006). Scientists now say that the adolescent's brain is different from the child's brain and the adult's brain, and that the adolescent's brain is still growing (Keating, 2004; Nelson, Thomas, & de Haan, 2006).

One of the most fascinating recent discoveries about the adolescent's brain focuses on developmental changes in areas involving emotion and higher-level cognitive functioning (Blakemore & Choudhury, 2006; Keating, 2004; Kuhn & Franklin, 2005; Price, 2005; Steinberg, 2005, 2006). The *amygdala* is a region of the brain that handles information processing about emotion; the prefrontal cortex is especially important in higher-level cognitive functioning. The amygdala matures earlier than the prefrontal cortex (see figure 2.5). This means that the brain region for putting the brakes on risky, impulsive behavior is still under construction during adolescence (Giedd, 2004; Giedd & others, 2006). Or consider this interpretation of the development

FIGURE 2.4 The Brain's Four Lobes

Shown here are the locations of the brain's four lobes: frontal, occipital, temporal, and parietal.

Prefrontal cortex
Involved in higher-order cognitive functioning, such as decision making

Amygdala
Involved in processing information about emotion

FIGURE 2.5 Developmental Changes in the Adolescent's Brain

The amygdala, which is responsible for processing information about emotion, matures earlier than the prefrontal cortex, which is responsible for making decisions and other higher-order cognitive functions. *What are some possible implications of these developmental changes in the brain for adolescents' behavior?*

FIGURE 2.6 The Human Brain's Hemispheres

The two halves (hemispheres) of the human brain are clearly seen in this photograph.

lateralization The specialization of functions in each hemisphere of the brain.

of emotion and cognition in adolescence: "early activation of strong 'turbo-charged' feelings with a relatively unskilled set of 'driving skills' or cognitive abilities to modulate strong emotions and motivations" (Dahl, 2004, p. 18). This developmental disjunction may account for increased risk taking and other problems in adolescence. "Some things just take time to develop and mature judgment is probably one of them" (Steinberg, 2004, p. 56).

Lateralization   The cerebral cortex (the highest level of the brain) is divided into two halves, or hemispheres (see figure 2.6). **Lateralization** is the specialization of functions in each hemisphere of the brain.

In individuals with an intact brain, there is a specialization of function in some areas:

1. *Verbal processing.* The most extensive research on the brain's two hemispheres involves language. In most individuals, speech and grammar are localized to the left hemisphere (Jabbour & others, 2005; Lohman & others, 2005; Wilke & others, 2005). This does not mean, however, that all language processing is carried out in the brain's left hemisphere. For example, understanding such aspects of language as appropriate use of language in different contexts, evaluation of the emotional expressiveness of language, metaphor, and much of humor involves the right hemisphere (Gegeshidze & Tsaqareli, 2004). Also, when children lose much of their left hemisphere because of an accident, surgery for epilepsy, or other reasons, the right hemisphere in many cases can reconfigure itself for increased language processing (Pataraia & others, 2005).

2. *Nonverbal processing.* The right hemisphere is usually more dominant in processing nonverbal information such as spatial perception, visual recognition, and emotion (Demaree & others, 2005; Floel & others, 2004). For example, for most individuals, the right hemisphere is mainly at work when they process information about people's faces (O'Toole, 2005; Sergerie, Lepage, & Armony, 2005). The right hemisphere also may be more involved when people express emotions or recognize others' emotions.

Because of the differences in functioning of the brain's two hemispheres, people commonly use the phrases "left-brained" and "right-brained" to say which hemisphere is dominant. Unfortunately, much of this talk is seriously exaggerated. For example, lay-people and the media commonly exaggerate hemispheric specialization by claiming that the left brain is logical and the right brain is creative. However, most complex functioning—such as logical and creative thinking—in normal people involves communication between both sides of the brain (Smith & Bulman-Fleming, 2005). Scientists who study the brain are typically very cautious with terms such as *left-brained* and *right-brained* because the brain is more complex than those terms suggest (Knect & others, 2001).

Plasticity   As we have seen, the brain has plasticity, and its development depends on context (Giedd & others, 2006; Nelson, Thomas, & de Haan, 2006; Whitford & others, 2006). What children do can change the development of their brain.

In a classic experiment, researcher Mark Rosenzweig (1969) was curious about whether experiences change the brain's development. He conducted experiments with rats and other animals to investigate this possibility. Animals were randomly assigned to grow up in different environments. Animals in an enriched environment lived in cages with stimulating features, such as wheels to rotate, steps to climb, levers to press, and toys to manipulate. In contrast, other animals had the early experience of growing up in standard cages or in barren, isolated conditions.

The results were stunning. The brains of the animals growing up in the enriched environment developed better than the brains of the animals reared in standard or isolated conditions. The brains of the "enriched" animals weighed more, had thicker layers, had more neuronal connections, and had higher levels of neurochemical activity. Similar findings occurred with older animals living in vastly different environments, although the results were not as strong as for the younger animals.

Experts on learning argue that just as an enriched environment led to more advanced brain development in rats and other animals, so too can enriched environments produce improvements in brain functioning and learning (Blakemore & Frith, 2005; Bransford & others, 2005). By engaging students in optimal learning environments, you can stimulate the development of their brain (Ansari, 2005; Howard-Jones, 2005).

The Brain and Children's Education   What types of environments are the best for stimulating children's brains, and how much change can be expected? What do the new findings in "brain science" tell us? Unfortunately, statements about the implications of brain science for children's education are speculative at best and often far removed from what neuroscientists know about the brain (Blakemore & Frith, 2005; Bransford & others, 2005; Breur, 1999; Goswami, 2005). We don't have to look any further than the hype about "left-brained" individuals being more logical and "right-brained" individuals being more creative to see that links between neuroscience and brain education are incorrectly made (Sousa, 1995).

Another commonly promoted link between neuroscience and brain education is that there is a critical or sensitive period—a biological window of opportunity—when learning is easy, effective, and easily retained. However, there is no neuroscientific evidence to support this belief (Blakemore & Frith, 2005; Breur, 1999). One leading neuroscientist even told educators that although children's brains acquire a great deal of information during the early years, most learning likely takes place after synaptic formation stabilizes, which is after the age of 10 (Goldman-Rakic, 1996).

Piaget's Theory

Poet Noah Perry once asked, "Who knows the thoughts of a child?" More than anyone, the famous Swiss psychologist Jean Piaget (1896–1980) knew.

Cognitive Processes   What processes do children use as they construct their knowledge of the world? Piaget believed that these processes are especially important in this regard: schemas, assimilation and accommodation, organization, and equilibration.

Schemas   Piaget (1954) said that as the child seeks to construct an understanding of the world, the developing brain creates **schemas.** These are actions or mental representations that organize knowledge. In Piaget's theory, behavioral schemas (physical activities) characterize infancy and mental schemas (cognitive activities) develop in childhood (Lamb, Bornstein, & Teti, 2002). A baby's schemas are structured by simple actions that can be performed on objects, such as sucking, looking, and grasping. Older children have schemas that include strategies and plans for solving problems. For example, a 6-year-old might have a schemas that involves the strategy of classifying objects by size, shape, or color. By the time we have reached adulthood, we have constructed an enormous number of diverse schemas, ranging from how to drive a car, to how to balance a budget, to the concept of fairness.

Assimilation and Accommodation   To explain how children use and adapt their schemas, Piaget offered two concepts: assimilation and accommodation. **Assimilation** occurs when children incorporate new information into their existing schemas. **Accommodation** occurs when children adjust their schemas to fit new information and experiences.

Think about a young child who has learned the word *car* to identify the family's car. The child might call all vehicles that move on roads "cars," including motorcycles and trucks; the child has assimilated these objects to his or her existing schemas. But the child soon learns that motorcycles and trucks are not cars and fine-tunes the

schemas In Piaget's theory, actions or mental representations that organize knowledge.

assimilation Piagetian concept of the incorporation of new information into existing knowledge (schemas).

accommodation Piagetian concept of adjusting schemas to fit new information and experiences.

Assimilation occurs when people incorporate new information into their existing schematic knowledge. *How might this eight-year-old girl first attempt to use the hammer and nail, based on her preexisting schematic knowledge about these objects?*

FIGURE 2.7 Assimilation and Accommodation

Accommodation occurs when people adjust their knowledge schemas to new information. *How might the girl adjust her schemas regarding hammers and nails during her successful effort to hang the picture?*

category to exclude motorcycles and trucks, accommodating the scheme.

Consider an 8-year-old girl who is given a hammer and nail to hang a picture on the wall. She has never used a hammer, but from observing others do this she realizes that a hammer is an object to be held, that it is swung by the handle to hit the nail, and that it usually is swung a number of times. Recognizing each of these things, she fits her behavior into this scheme she already has (assimilation). But the hammer is heavy, so she holds it near the top. She swings too hard and the nail bends, so she adjusts the pressure of her strikes. These adjustments reflect her ability to slightly alter her conception of the world (accommodation). Just as both assimilation and accommodation are required in this example, so are they required in many of the child's thinking challenges (see figure 2.7).

Organization To make sense out of their world, said Piaget, children cognitively organize their experiences. **Organization** in Piaget's theory is the grouping of isolated behaviors and thoughts into a higher-order system. Continual refinement of this organization is an inherent part of development. A boy with only a vague idea about how to use a hammer also may have a vague idea about how to use other tools. After learning how to use each one, he relates these uses, organizing his knowledge.

Equilibration and Stages of Development **Equilibration** is a mechanism that Piaget proposed to explain how children shift from one stage of thought to the next. The shift occurs as children experience cognitive conflict, or disequilibrium, in trying to understand the world. Eventually, they resolve the conflict and reach a balance, or equilibrium, of thought. Piaget believed there is considerable movement between states of cognitive equilibrium and disequilibrium as assimilation and accommodation work in concert to produce cognitive change. For example, if a child believes that the amount of a liquid changes simply because the liquid is poured into a container with a different shape—for instance, from a container that is short and wide into a container that is tall and narrow—she might be puzzled by such issues as where the "extra" liquid came from and whether there is actually more liquid to drink. The child will eventually resolve these puzzles as her thought becomes more advanced. In the everyday world, the child is constantly faced with such counterexamples and inconsistencies.

Assimilation and accommodation always take the child to a higher ground. For Piaget, the motivation for change is an internal search for equilibrium. As old schemas are adjusted and new schemas are developed, the child organizes and reorganizes the old and new schemas. Eventually, the organization is fundamentally different from the old organization; it is a new way of thinking.

Thus, the result of these processes, according to Piaget, is that individuals go through four stages of development. A different way of understanding the world makes one stage more advanced than another. Cognition is *qualitatively* different in one stage compared with another. In other words, the way children reason at one stage is different from the way they reason at another stage.

Piagetian Stages Each of Piaget's stages is age-related and consists of distinct ways of thinking. Piaget proposed four stages of cognitive development: sensorimotor, preoperational, concrete operational, and formal operational (see figure 2.8).

The Sensorimotor Stage The **sensorimotor stage**, which lasts from birth to about 2 years of age, is the first Piagetian stage. In this stage, infants construct an understanding

organization Piaget's concept of grouping isolated behaviors into a higher-order, more smoothly functioning cognitive system; the grouping or arranging of items into categories.

equilibration A mechanism that Piaget proposed to explain how children shift from one stage of thought to the next. The shift occurs as children experience cognitive conflict or disequilibrium in trying to understand the world. Eventually, they resolve the conflict and reach a balance or equilibrium of thought.

sensorimotor stage The first Piagetian stage, lasting from birth to about 2 years of age, in which infants construct an understanding of the world by coordinating sensory experiences with motor actions.

Sensorimotor Stage	Preoperational Stage	Concrete Operational Stage	Formal Operational Stage
The infant constructs an understanding of the world by coordinating sensory experiences with physical actions. An infant progresses from reflexive, instinctual action at birth to the beginning of symbolic thought toward the end of the stage.	The child begins to represent the world with words and images. These words and images reflect increased symbolic thinking and go beyond the connection of sensory information and physical action.	The child can now reason logically about concrete events and classify objects into different sets.	The adolescent reasons in more abstract, idealistic, and logical ways.
Birth to 2 Years of Age	*2 to 7 Years of Age*	*7 to 11 Years of Age*	*11 to 15 Years of Age Through Adulthood*

FIGURE 2.8 Piaget's Four Stages of Cognitive Development

of the world by coordinating their sensory experiences (such as seeing and hearing) with their motor actions (reaching, touching)—hence the term *sensorimotor*. At the beginning of this stage, infants show little more than reflexive patterns to adapt to the world. By the end of the stage, they display far more complex sensorimotor patterns.

Piaget argued that an especially important cognitive accomplishment in infancy is object permanence. This involves understanding that objects and events continue to exist even when they cannot be seen, heard, or touched. A second accomplishment is the gradual realization that there is a difference or boundary between oneself and the surrounding environment. Imagine what your thought would be like if you could not distinguish between yourself and your world. Your thought would be chaotic, disorganized, and unpredictable. This is what the mental life of a newborn is like, according to Piaget. The young infant does not differentiate between self and world and has no sense of object permanence. By the end of the sensorimotor period, the child differentiates between the self and the world and is aware that objects continue to exist over time.

The Preoperational Stage   The **preoperational stage** is the second Piagetian stage. Lasting approximately from 2 to 7 years of age, it is more symbolic than sensorimotor thought but does not involve operational thought. However, it is egocentric and intuitive rather than logical.

Preoperational thought can be subdivided into two substages: symbolic function and intuitive thought. The **symbolic function substage** occurs roughly between 2 and 4 years of age. In this substage, the young child gains the ability to represent mentally an object that is not present. This stretches the child's mental world to new dimensions. Expanded use of language and the emergence of pretend play are other examples of an increase in symbolic thought during this early childhood substage. Young children begin to use scribbled designs to represent people, houses, cars, clouds, and many other aspects of the world. Possibly because young children are not very concerned about reality, their drawings are fanciful and inventive (Winner, 1986). Suns are blue, skies are green, and cars float on clouds in their imaginative world. The symbolism is simple but strong, not unlike abstractions found in some modern art. As the famous twentieth-century Spanish artist Pablo Picasso once remarked, "I used to draw like Raphael but it has taken me a lifetime to draw like young children." One 3½-year-old looked at the scribble he had just drawn and described it as a pelican kissing a seal (see figure 2.9a). In the elementary school years, children's drawings become more realistic, neat, and precise (see figure 2.9b). Suns are yellow, skies are blue, and cars travel on roads.

preoperational stage The second Piagetian stage, lasting from about 2 to 7 years of age; symbolic thought increases but operational thought is not yet present.

symbolic function substage The first substage of preoperational thought, occurring between about 2 to 4 years of age; the ability to represent an object not present develops and symbolic thinking increases; egocentrism and animism occur.

(a)

(b)

FIGURE 2.9 Developmental Changes in Children's Drawings

(*a*) A 3½-year-old's symbolic drawing. Halfway into this drawing, the 3½-year-old artist said it was "a pelican kissing a seal." (*b*) This 11-year-old's drawing is neater and more realistic but also less inventive.

intuitive thought substage The second substage of preoperational thought, lasting from about 4 to 7 years of age. Children begin to use primitive reasoning and want to know the answer to all sorts of questions. They seem so sure about their knowledge in this substage but are unaware of how they know what they know.

Even though young children make distinctive progress in this substage, their preoperational thought still has two important limitations: egocentrism and animism. *Egocentrism* is the inability to distinguish between one's own perspective and someone else's perspective. The following telephone interaction between 4-year-old Mary, who is at home, and her father, who is at work, typifies egocentric thought:

Father: Mary, is Mommy there?
Mary: (Silently nods)
Father: Mary, can I speak to Mommy?
Mary: (Nods again silently)

Mary's response is egocentric in that she fails to consider her father's perspective; she does not realize that he cannot see her nod.

Piaget and Barbel Inhelder (1969) initially studied young children's egocentrism by devising the three mountains task (see figure 2.10). The child walks around the model of the mountains and becomes familiar with what the mountains look like from different perspectives. The child also can see that there are different objects on the mountains. The child then is seated on one side of the table on which the mountains are placed. The experimenter moves a doll to different locations around the table. At each location the child is asked to select from a series of photos the one that most accurately reflects the view the doll is seeing. Children in the preoperational stage often pick the view that reflects where they are sitting rather than the doll's view.

Animism also characterizes preoperational thought. It is the belief that inanimate objects have "lifelike" qualities and are capable of action. A young child might show animism by saying, "That tree pushed the leaf off and it fell down" or "The sidewalk made me mad. It made me fall down."

What further cognitive changes take place in the preoperational stage? The **intuitive thought substage** is the second substage of preoperational thought, starting at about 4 years of age and lasting until about 7 years of age. At this substage, children begin to use primitive reasoning and want to know the answers to all sorts of questions. Piaget called this substage "intuitive" because the children seem so sure about their knowledge and understanding yet are unaware of how they know what they know. That is, they say they know something but know it without the use of rational thinking.

An example of young children's limitation in reasoning ability is the difficulty they have putting things into correct categories. Look at the collection of objects in figure 2.11a. You would probably respond to the direction "Put the things together that you believe belong together" by grouping the objects by size and shape. Your sorting might look something like that shown in figure 2.11b. Faced with a similar collection of

View 1   View 2

FIGURE 2.10 The Three Mountains Task

View 1 shows the child's perspective from where he or she is sitting. View 2 is an example of the photograph the child would be shown, mixed in with others from different perspectives. To correctly identify this view, the child has to take the perspective of a person sitting at spot *b*. Invariably, a perschool child who thinks in a preoperational way cannot perform this task. When asked what a view of the mountains looks like from position *b*, the child selects a photograph taken from location *a*, the child's view at the time.

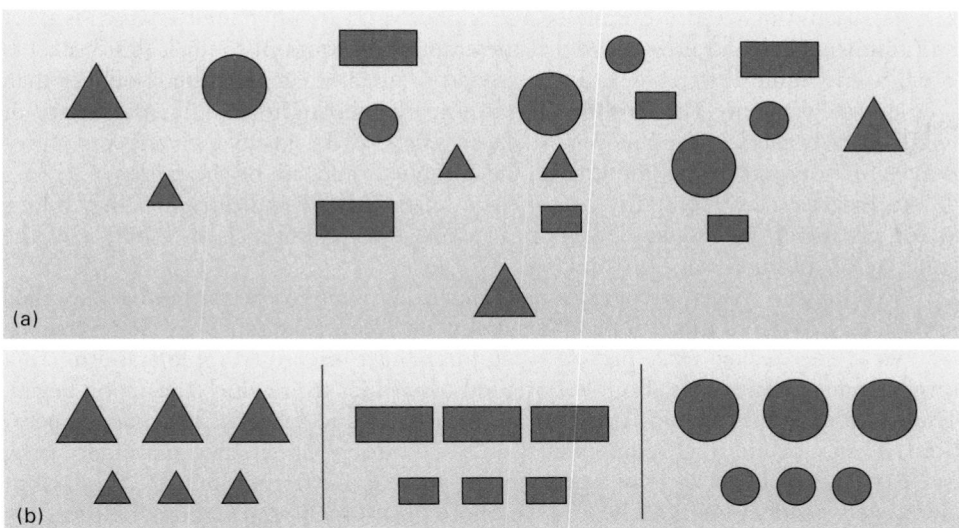

FIGURE 2.11 Arrays
(*a*) A random array of objects. (*b*) An ordered array of objects.

objects that can be sorted on the basis of two or more properties, preoperational children seldom are capable of using these properties consistently to sort the objects into appropriate groupings. In the social realm, if a 4-year-old girl is given the task of dividing her peers into groups according to whether they are friends and whether they are boys or girls, she is unlikely to arrive at a classification of friendly boys, friendly girls, unfriendly boys, unfriendly girls.

Many of these preoperational examples show a characteristic of thought called **centration,** which involves focusing (or centering) attention on one characteristic to the exclusion of all others. Centration is most clearly present in preoperational children's lack of **conservation,** the idea that some characteristic of an object stays the same even though the object might change in appearance. For example, to adults it is obvious that a certain amount of liquid stays the same regardless of a container's shape. But this is not obvious at all to young children. Rather, they are struck by the height of the liquid in the container. In this type of conservation task (Piaget's most famous), a child is presented with two identical beakers, each filled to the same level with liquid (see figure 2.12). The child is asked if the beakers have the same amount of liquid. The child usually

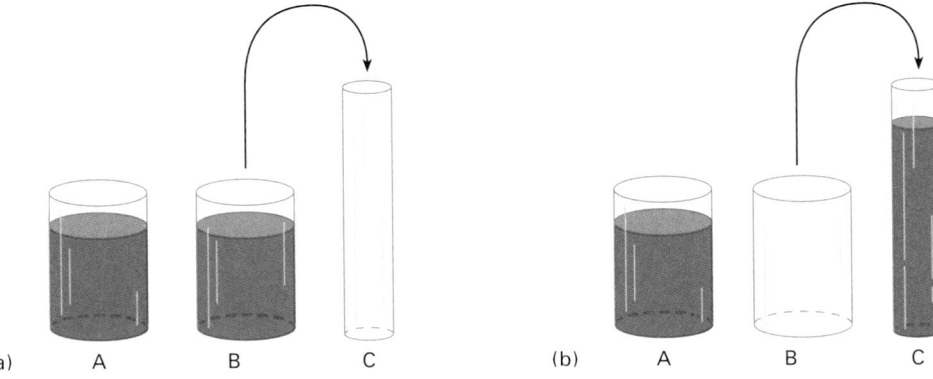

FIGURE 2.12 Piaget's Conservation Task

The beaker test is a well-known Piagetian test to determine whether a child can think operationally—that is, can mentally reverse actions and show conservation of the substance. (*a*) Two identical beakers are presented to the child. Then, the liquid is poured from B into C, which is taller and thinner than A or B. (*b*) The child is asked if these beakers (A and C) have the same amount of liquid. The preoperational child says no. When asked to point to the beaker that has more liquid, the preoperational child points to the tall, thin beaker.

centration Focusing, or centering, attention on one characteristic to the exclusion of all others; characteristic of preoperational thinking.

conservation The idea that some characteristic of an object stays the same even though the object might change in appearance; a cognitive ability that develops in the concrete operational stage, according to Piaget.

"I still don't have all the answers, but I'm beginning to ask the right questions."

says yes. Then the liquid from one beaker is poured into a third beaker, which is taller and thinner. The child now is asked if the amount of liquid in the tall, thin beaker is equal to the liquid that remains in the second original beaker. Children younger than 7 or 8 usually say no. They justify their answer by referring to the differing height or width of the beakers. Older children usually answer yes. They justify their answers appropriately: If you poured the liquid back, the amount would still be the same.

In Piaget's view, failing the conservation of liquid task indicates that the child is at the preoperational stage of thinking. Passing the test suggests the child is at the concrete operational stage of thinking.

According to Piaget, preoperational children also cannot perform what he called *operations*. In Piaget's theory, operations are mental representations that are reversible.

As in the beaker task, preschool children have difficulty understanding that reversing an action brings about the original conditions from which the action began. These two examples should further help you understand Piaget's concepts of operations. A young child might know that 4 + 2 = 6 but not understand that the reverse, 6 − 2 = 4, is true. Or let's say a preschooler walks to his friend's house each day but always gets a ride home. If asked to walk home from his friend's house, he probably would reply that he didn't know the way because he never had walked home before.

Some developmentalists do not believe Piaget was entirely correct in his estimate of when conservation skills emerge. For example, Rochel Gelman (1969) trained preschool children to attend to relevant aspects of the conservation task. This improved their conservation skills. Gelman also has shown that attentional training on one type of conservation task, such as number, improves young children's performance on another type of conservation task, such as mass. She argues that young children develop conservation skills earlier than Piaget envisioned and that such skills can be improved with attentional training.

Further, children show considerable variation in attaining conservation skills. Researchers have found that 50 percent of children develop conservation of mass at 6 to 9 years of age, 50 percent demonstrate conservation of length at 4 to 9 years of age, 50 percent show conservation of area at 7 to 9 years of age, and 50 percent of children don't attain conservation of weight until 8 to 10 years of age (Horowitz & others, 2005; Sroufe & others, 1992).

Yet another characteristic of preoperational children is that they ask a lot of questions. The barrage begins around age 3. By about 5, they have just about exhausted the adults around them with "Why?" "Why" questions signal the emergence of the child's interest in figuring out why things are the way they are. Following is a sampling of 4- to 6-year-olds' questions (Elkind, 1976):

> "What makes you grow up?"
> "What makes you stop growing?"
> "Who was the mother when everybody was a baby?"
> "Why do leaves fall?"
> "Why does the sun shine?"

The Concrete Operational Stage The **concrete operational stage,** the third Piagetian stage of cognitive development, lasts from about 7 to about 11 years of age. Concrete operational thought involves using operations. Logical reasoning replaces intuitive reasoning, but only in concrete situations. Classification skills are present, but abstract problems go unsolved.

A concrete operation is a reversible mental action pertaining to real, concrete objects. Concrete operations allow the child to coordinate several characteristics rather than focus on a single property of an object. At the concrete operational level, children can do mentally what they previously could do only physically, and they can reverse concrete operations. For example, to test conservation of matter, the child is presented with two identical balls of clay. The experimenter rolls one ball into a long, thin shape. The child is asked if there is more clay in the ball or in the long, thin

concrete operational stage Piaget's third cognitive developmental stage, occurring between about 7 to 11 years of age. At this stage, the child thinks operationally and logical reasoning replaces intuitive thought but only in concrete situations; classification skills are present but abstract problems present difficulties.

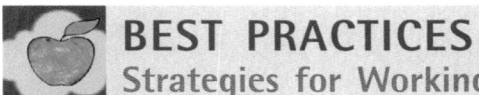

BEST PRACTICES
Strategies for Working with Preoperational Thinkers

1. *To reduce egocentrism, involve children in social interactions.*

2. *Ask children to make comparisons.* These might involve such concepts as bigger, taller, wider, heavier, and longer.

3. *Give children experience in ordering operations.* For example, have children line up in rows from tall to short and vice versa. Bring in various examples of animal and plant life cycles, such as several photographs of butterfly development or the sprouting of beans or kernels of corn. Examples of these natural stages help children's ordering ability.

4. *Have children draw scenes with perspective.* Encourage them to make the objects in their drawings appear to be at the same location as in the scene they are viewing.

For example, if they see a horse at the end of a field, they should place the horse in the same location in the drawing.

5. *Construct an inclined plane or a hill.* Let children roll marbles of various sizes down the plane. Ask them to compare how quickly the different-size marbles reach the bottom. This should help them understand the concept of speed.

6. *Ask children to justify their answers when they draw conclusions.* For example, when they say that pouring a liquid from a short, wide container into a tall, thin container makes the liquid change in volume, ask, "Why do you think so?" or "How could you prove this to one of your friends?"

---

piece of clay. By the time children are seven or eight years old, most answer that the amount of clay is the same. To answer this problem correctly, children have to imagine that the clay ball can be rolled out into a long, thin strip and then returned to its original round shape. In this example, the preoperational child would have focused either on height or length. The concrete operational child coordinates information about both dimensions.

An important concrete operation is classifying or dividing things into different sets or subsets and considering their interrelationships. Reasoning about a family tree of four generations reveals a child's concrete operational skills (Furth & Wachs, 1975). The family tree shown in figure 2.13 suggests that the grandfather (A) has three children (B, C, and D), each of whom has two children (E through J), and one of these children (J) has three children (K, L, and M). Concrete operational thinkers understand the classification. For example, they can reason that person J can at the same time be father, brother, and grandson. A preoperational thinker cannot.

Some Piagetian tasks require children to reason about relations between classes. One such task is **seriation,** the concrete operation that involves ordering stimuli along some quantitative dimension (such as length). To see if students can serialize, a teacher might place eight sticks of different lengths in a haphazard way on a table. The teacher then asks the student to order the sticks by length. Many young children end up with two or three small groups of "big" sticks or "little" sticks rather than a correct ordering of all eight sticks. Another mistaken strategy they use is to evenly line up the tops of the sticks but ignore the bottoms. The concrete operational thinker simultaneously understands that each stick must be longer than the one that precedes it and shorter than the one that follows it.

Transitivity involves the ability to reason about and logically combine relationships. If a relation holds between a first object and a second object, and also holds between the second object and a third object, then it also holds between the first and third objects. For example, consider three sticks (A, B, and C) of differing lengths. A is the longest, B is intermediate in length, and C is the shortest. Does the child understand that if A is longer than B, and B is longer than C, then A is

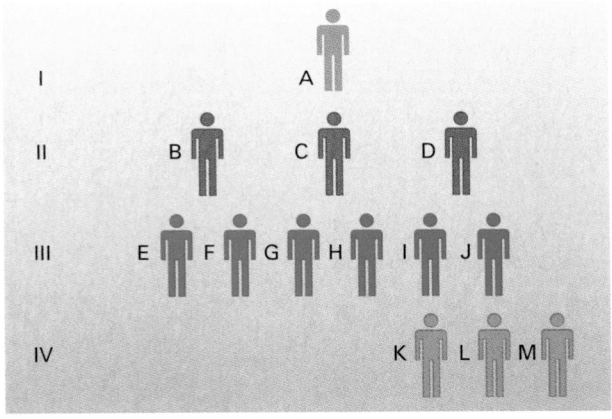

FIGURE 2.13 Classification

Classification is an important ability in concrete operational thought. When shown a family tree of four generations (I to IV), the preoperational child has trouble classifying the members of the four generations; the concrete operational child can classify the members vertically, horizontally, and obliquely (up and down and across).

seriation A concrete operation that involves ordering stimuli along some quantitative dimension.

transitivity The ability to reason and logically combine relationships.

BEST PRACTICES
Strategies for Working with Concrete Operational Thinkers

1. *Encourage students to discover concepts and principles.* Ask relevant questions about what is being studied to help them focus on some aspect of their learning. Refrain from telling students the answers to their questions outright. Try to get them to reach the answers through their own thinking.

2. *Involve children in operational tasks.* These include adding, subtracting, multiplying, dividing, ordering, seriating, and reversing. Use concrete materials for these tasks, possibly introducing math symbols later.

3. *Plan activities in which students practice the concept of ascending and descending classification hierarchies.* Have students list the following in order of size (such as largest to smallest): city of Atlanta, state of Georgia, country of United States, Western Hemisphere, and planet Earth.

4. *Include activities that require conservation of area, weight, and displaced volume.* Realize that there is considerable variation in children's attainment of conservation across different domains.

5. *Create activities in which children order and reverse order.* Many third-graders have difficulty in reversing

order, such as going from tall to short rather than short to tall. They also have trouble, after listing the cities they will pass through in taking a trip, reversing the order for coming home.

6. *Continue to ask students to justify their answers when they solve problems.* Help them to check the validity and accuracy of their conclusions.

7. *Encourage children to work in groups and exchange thoughts with each other.* For example, ask a group of children to create a play, sharing their viewpoints with each other.

8. *When trying to teach anything complex, create props and visual aids.* For example, in teaching a social science lesson on what a democracy is, show a video that illustrates the concept. Encourage students to manipulate and experiment in science, use concrete materials in mathematics, create and act out in language arts, and discuss their perspectives with each other and take field trips in social studies.

longer than C? In Piaget's theory, concrete operational thinkers do; preoperational thinkers do not.

The Formal Operational Stage   The **formal operational stage,** which emerges at about 11 to 15 years of age, is Piaget's fourth and final cognitive stage. At this stage, individuals move beyond reasoning only about concrete experiences and think in more abstract, idealistic, and logical ways.

The abstract quality of formal operational thinking is evident in verbal problem solving. The concrete operational thinker needs to see the concrete elements A, B, and C to make the logical inference that if A = B and B = C, then A = C. In contrast, the formal operational thinker can solve this problem when it is verbally presented.

Accompanying the abstract nature of formal operational thought are the abilities to idealize and imagine possibilities. At this stage, adolescents engage in extended speculation about the ideal qualities they desire in themselves and others. These idealistic thoughts can merge into fantasy. Many adolescents become impatient with their newfound ideals and the problems of how to live them out.

At the same time as adolescents are thinking more abstractly and idealistically, they also are beginning to think more logically. As formal operational thinkers, they think more like scientists. They devise plans to solve problems and systematically test solutions. Piaget's term **hypothetical-deductive reasoning** embodies the concept that adolescents can develop hypotheses (best hunches) about ways to solve problems and systematically reach a conclusion.

formal operational stage Piaget's fourth cognitive developmental stage, which emerges between about 11 and 15 years of age; thought is more abstract, idealistic, and logical in this stage.

hypothetical–deductive reasoning Piaget's formal operational concept that adolescents can develop hypotheses to solve problems and systematically reach (deduce) a conclusion.

One example of hypothetical-deductive reasoning involves a modification of the familiar game "Twenty Questions." Individuals are shown a set of 42 color pictures displayed in a rectangular array (six rows of seven pictures each) and asked to determine which picture the experimenter has in mind (that is, which is "correct"). The subjects are only allowed to ask questions to which the experimenter can answer yes or no. The object of the game is to select the correct picture by asking as few questions as possible.

Adolescents who are deductive hypothesis testers formulate a plan and test a series of hypotheses, which considerably narrows the field of choices. The most effective plan is a "halving" strategy (*Q:* Is the picture in the right half of the array? *A:* No. *Q:* OK. Is it in the top half? And so on). A correct halving strategy guarantees the answer in seven questions or

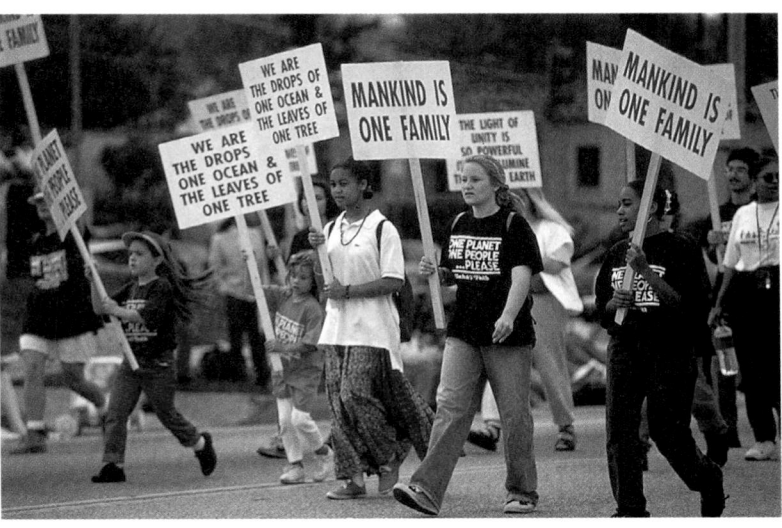

Might adolescents' ability to reason hypothetically and to evaluate what is ideal versus what is real lead them to engage in demonstrations, such as this protest related to better ethnic relations? What other causes might be attractive to adolescents' newfound cognitive abilities of hypothetical-deductive reasoning and idealistic thinking?

less. In contrast, the concrete operational thinker might persist with questions that continue to test some of the same possibilities that previous questions could have eliminated. For example, they might ask whether the correct picture is in row 1 and are told that it is not. Later, they ask whether the picture is *X*, which is in row 1.

Thus, formal operational thinkers test their hypotheses with judiciously chosen questions and tests. In contrast, concrete operational thinkers often fail to understand the relation between a hypothesis and a well-chosen test of it, stubbornly clinging to ideas that already have been discounted.

A form of egocentrism also emerges in adolescence (Elkind, 1978). *Adolescent egocentrism* is the heightened self-consciousness reflected in adolescents' beliefs that others are as interested in them as they themselves are. Adolescent egocentrism also includes a sense of personal uniqueness. It involves the desire to be noticed, visible, and "on stage." Consider 12-year-old Tracy, who says, "Oh my gosh! I can't believe it. Help! I can't stand it!" Her mother asks, "What is the matter?" Tracy responds, "Everyone in here is looking at me." The mother queries, "Why?" Tracy says, "This one hair won't stay in place," as she rushes to the rest room to plaster it with hairspray. Perceived uniqueness also is evident in 16-year-old Margaret's feelings after her boyfriend has broken up with her. She tells her mother, "You have no idea how I feel. You have never experienced this kind of pain."

Egocentrism is a normal adolescent occurrence, more common in the middle school than in high school years. However, for some individuals, adolescent egocentrism can contribute to reckless behavior, including suicidal thoughts, drug use, and failure to use contraceptives during sexual intercourse. Egocentricity leads some adolescents to think that they are invulnerable.

Evaluating Piaget's Theory   What were Piaget's main contributions? Has his theory withstood the test of time?

Contributions   Piaget is a giant in the field of developmental psychology. We owe to him the present field of children's cognitive development. We owe to him a long list of masterful concepts including assimilation and accommodation, object permanence, egocentrism, conservation, and hypothetical-deductive reasoning. Along with William James and John Dewey, we also owe Piaget the current vision of children as active, constructive thinkers. And we owe to him the current belief that concepts do not emerge all of a sudden, full-blown, but instead emerge through a series of partial accomplishments that lead to increasingly comprehensive understanding (Haith & Benson, 1998).

Many adolescent girls spend long hours in front of the mirror, depleting cans of hairspray, tubes of lipstick, and jars of cosmetics. *How might this behavior be related to changes in adolescent cognitive and physical development?*

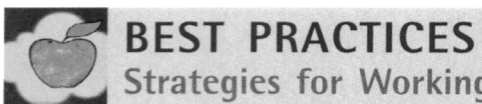

BEST PRACTICES
Strategies for Working with Formal Operational Thinkers

1. *Realize that many adolescents are not full-fledged formal operational thinkers.* Although Piaget believed formal operational thought emerges between 11 and 15 years of age, many students in this age range actually are concrete operational thinkers or are just beginning to use formal operational thought. Thus, many of the teaching strategies discussed earlier regarding the education of concrete operational thinkers still apply to many young adolescents. As discussed next, Jerri Hall, a math teacher at Miller Magnet High School, in Georgia, emphasizes that when a curriculum is too formal and too abstract it will go over students' heads.

THROUGH THE EYES OF TEACHERS
Piaget as a Guide

I use Piaget's developmental theory as a guide in helping children learn math. In the sixth, seventh, and eighth grades, children are moving from the concrete to the abstract stage in their cognitive processes; therefore, when I teach, I try to use different methods to aid my students to understand a concept. For example, I use fraction circles to help students understand how to add, subtract, multiply, and divide fractions, and the students are allowed to use these until they become proficient with the algorithms. I try to incorporate hands-on experiences in which students discover the rules themselves, rather than just teaching the methods and having the students practice them with drill. It is extremely important for students to understand the why behind a mathematical rule so they can better understand the concept.

2. *Propose a problem and invite students to form hypotheses about how to solve it.* For example, a teacher might say, "Imagine that a girl has no friends. What should she do?"

3. *Present a problem and suggest several ways it might be approached.* Then ask questions that stimulate students to evaluate the approaches. For example, describe several ways to investigate a robbery and ask students to evaluate which is best.

4. *Select a particular problem that is familiar to the class and ask questions related to it.* For example, the teacher asks, "What factors should be considered if we are going to be able to get the economy back on track?"

5. *Ask students to discuss their prior conclusions.* For example, ask, "What steps did you go through in solving this problem?"

6. *Develop projects and investigations for students to carry out.* Periodically ask them how they are going about collecting and interpreting the data.

7. *Encourage students to create hierarchical outlines when you ask them to write papers.* Make sure they understand how to organize their writing in terms of general and specific points. The abstractness of formal operational thinking also means that teachers with students at this level can encourage them to use metaphors.

8. *Recognize that adolescents are more likely to use formal operational thinking in the areas in which they have the most expertise and experience.* For example, a student who loves English and reads and writes a lot might use formal operational thinking in that area. The same student, however, might not like math and might show concrete operational thinking in that area.

Piaget also was a genius when it came to observing children. His careful observations showed us inventive ways to discover how children act on and adapt to their world (Vidal, 2000). Piaget showed us some important things to look for in cognitive development, such as the shift from preoperational to concrete operational thinking. He also showed us how children need to make their experiences fit their schemas (cognitive frameworks) yet simultaneously adapt their schemas to experience. Piaget also revealed how cognitive growth is likely to occur if the context is structured to allow gradual movement to the next higher level.

Criticisms Piaget's theory has not gone unchallenged. Questions have been raised in the following areas:

- *Estimates of children's competence.* Some cognitive abilities emerge earlier than Piaget thought (Bornstein, Arterberry, & Mash, 2005; Cohen & Cashon, 2006). For example, some aspects of object permanence emerge earlier than he believed. Even 2-year-olds are nonegocentric in some contexts. When they real- ize that another person will not see an object, they investigate whether the per- son is blindfolded or looking in a different direction. Conservation of number has been demonstrated as early as age 3, although Piaget did not think it emerged until 7. Young children are not as uniformly "pre-" this and "pre-" that (precausal, preoperational) as Piaget thought (Flavell, Miller, & Miller, 2002).

- Other cognitive abilities can emerge later than Piaget thought. Many adoles- cents still think in concrete operational ways or are just beginning to master formal operations. Even many adults are not formal operational thinkers. In sum, recent theoretical revisions highlight more cognitive competencies of infants and young children and more cognitive shortcomings of adolescents and adults (Bauer, 2006; Keating, 2004).

- *Stages.* Piaget conceived of stages as unitary structures of thought. Thus, his theory assumes developmental synchrony—that is, various aspects of a stage should emerge at the same time. Some concrete operational concepts, however, do not appear in synchrony. For example, children do not learn to conserve at the same time as they learn to cross-classify. Thus, most contemporary devel- opmentalists agree that children's cognitive development is not as stagelike as Piaget thought (Bjorklund, 2005; Garton, 2004; Horowitz & others, 2005; Kuhn & Franklin, 2006; Siegler, 2006).

- *Training children to reason at a higher level.* Some children who are at one cog- nitive stage (such as preoperational) can be trained to reason at a higher cog- nitive stage (such as concrete operational). This poses a problem for Piaget. He argued that such training is only superficial and ineffective, unless the child is at a maturational transition point between the stages (Gelman & Opfer, 2004; Gelman & Williams, 1998).

- *Culture and education.* Culture and education exert stronger influences on chil- dren's development than Piaget believed (Greenfield, Suzuki, & Rothstein- Fisch, 2006). The age at which children acquire conservation skills is related to the extent to which their culture provides relevant practice (Cole, 2005, 2006). For example, an outstanding teacher can guide students' learning experiences that will help them move to a higher cognitive stage.

Still, some developmental psychologists believe we should not throw out Piaget altogether (Smith, 2004). These **neo-Piagetians** argue that Piaget got some things right but that his theory needs considerable revision. In their revision of Piaget, neo- Piagetians emphasize how children process information through attention, memory, and strategies (Case, 2000). They especially believe that a more accurate vision of children's thinking requires more knowledge of strategies, how fast and how auto- matically children process information, the particular cognitive task involved, and the division of cognitive problems into smaller, more precise steps.

Despite such criticisms, Piaget's theory is a very important one, and as we already have seen, information about his stages of development can be applied to teaching children. Here are some more ideas for applying Piaget's theory to chil- dren's education.

Vygotsky's Theory

According to Vygotsky, mental functions have external, or social, connections. Vygotsky argued that children develop more systematic, logical, and rational concepts as a result of *dialogue* with a skilled helper. Thus, in Vygotsky's theory, other people and language play key roles in a child's cognitive development (Bodrova & Leong, 2007; Fidalgo & Pereira, 2005; Hyson, Copple, & Jones, 2006; Stetsenko & Arievitch, 2004).

The Zone of Proximal Development   Vygotsky's belief in the importance of social influences, especially instruction, on children's cognitive development is reflected in

Piaget is shown here with his family. Piaget's careful observations of his three children—Lucienne, Laurent, and Jacqueline—contributed to the develop- ment of his cognitive theory.

An outstanding teacher and education in the logic of science and mathematics are important cultural experiences that promote the development of operational thought. *Might Piaget have underesti- mated the roles of culture and schooling in children's cognitive development?*

neo-Piagetians Developmental psy- chologists who believe that Piaget got some things right but that his theory needs considerable revision; emphasize how to process information through attention, memory, and strategies.

BEST PRACTICES
Strategies for Applying Piaget's Theory to Children's Education

1. *Take a constructivist approach.* In a constructivist vein, Piaget emphasized that children learn best when they are active and seek solutions for themselves. Piaget opposed teaching methods that treat children as passive receptacles. The educational implication of Piaget's view is that in all subjects students learn best by making discoveries, reflecting on them, and discussing them, rather than blindly imitating the teacher or doing things by rote.

2. *Facilitate rather than direct learning.* Effective teachers design situations that allow students to learn by doing. These situations promote students' thinking and discovery. Teachers listen, watch, and question students to help them gain better understanding. They ask relevant questions to stimulate students' thinking and ask them to explain their answers. As you will see next, Suzanne Ransleben creates imaginative classroom situations to facilitate students' learning.

Suzanne Ransleben, teaching English.

THROUGH THE EYES OF TEACHERS
Stimulating Students' Thinking and Discovery

Suzanne Ransleben teaches ninth- and tenth-grade English in Corpus Christi, Texas. She designs classroom situations that stimulate students' reflective thinking and discovery. Suzanne created Grammar Football to make diagramming sentences more interesting for students and has students decipher song lyrics to help them better understand how to write poetry. When students first encounter Shakespeare "They paint interpretations of their favorite line from *Romeo and Juliet*." (Source: Briggs, 2004, p. 7D.)

3. *Consider the child's knowledge and level of thinking.* Students do not come to class with empty heads. They have many ideas about the physical and natural world including concepts of space, time, quantity, and causality. These ideas differ from the ideas of adults. Teachers need to interpret what a student is saying and respond with discourse close to the student's level.

4. *Use ongoing assessment.* Individually constructed meanings cannot be measured by standardized tests. Math and language portfolios (which contain work in progress as well as finished products), individual conferences in which students discuss their thinking strategies, and written and verbal explanations by students of their reasoning can be used to evaluate progress.

5. *Promote the student's intellectual health.* When Piaget came to lecture in the United States, he was asked, "What

can I do to get my child to a higher cognitive stage sooner?" He was asked this question so often here compared with other countries that he called it the American question. For Piaget, children's learning should occur naturally. Children should not be pushed and pressured into achieving too much too early in their development, before they are maturationally ready. Some parents spend long hours every day holding up large flash cards with words on them to improve their baby's vocabulary. In the Piagetian view, this is not the best way for infants to learn. It places too much emphasis on speeding up intellectual development, involves passive learning, and will not work.

6. *Turn the classroom into a setting of exploration and discovery.* What do actual classrooms look like when the teachers adopt Piaget's views? Several first- and second-grade math classrooms provide some good examples (Kamii, 1985, 1989). The teachers emphasize students' own exploration and discovery. The classrooms are less structured than what we think of as a typical classroom. Workbooks and predetermined assignments are not used. Rather, the teachers observe the students' interests and natural participation in activities to determine what the course of learning will be. For example, a math lesson might be constructed around counting the day's lunch money or dividing supplies among students. Often games are prominently used in the classroom to stimulate mathematical thinking. For example, a version of dominoes teaches children about even-numbered combinations. A variation on tic-tac-toe involves replacing *X*s and *O*s with numbers. Teachers encourage peer interaction during the lessons and games because students' different viewpoints can contribute to advances in thinking.

his concept of the zone of proximal development. **Zone of proximal development (ZPD)** is Vygotsky's term for the range of tasks that are too difficult for the child to master alone but that can be learned with guidance and assistance of adults or more-skilled children. Thus, the lower limit of the ZPD is the level of skill reached by the child working independently. The upper limit is the level of additional responsibility the child can accept with the assistance of an able instructor (see figure 2.14). The ZPD captures the child's cognitive skills that are in the process of maturing and can be accomplished only with the assistance of a more-skilled person (Gray & Feldman, 2004; Kinginger, 2002; Kulczewski, 2005). Vygotsky (1962) called these the "buds" or "flowers" of development, to distinguish them from the "fruits" of development, which the child already can accomplish independently.

Teaching in the zone of proximal development reflects the concept of developmentally appropriate teaching we described earlier in the chapter. It involves being aware of "where students are in the process of their development and taking advantage of their readiness. It is also about teaching to enable developmental readiness, not just waiting for students to be ready" (Horowitz & others, 2005, p. 105).

Let's consider an example that reflects the zone of proximal development (Frede, 1995, p. 125):

> A 5-year-old child is pushing a small shopping cart through the house area of his preschool. His teacher notices that he is putting fruit in the small basket and all other groceries in the larger section of the cart. She has watched him sort objects over the past few weeks and thinks that he may now be able to classify along two dimensions at the same time, with some help from her. She goes to the cash register to pretend to be the cashier and says, "We need to be careful how we divide your groceries into bags. We want to use one bag for things that go in the refrigerator, and other bags for things that will go in the cabinet." Together they devise a system with one bag for each of the following categories: food in cartons that will go into the refrigerator, loose vegetables and fruit for the refrigerator, food cartons that go in the cabinet, and food cans for the cabinet. In this example, the child's unassisted level of classification was fairly gross—fruit versus non-fruit. With the teacher's help, he was able to apply a more sophisticated form of classification.

Scaffolding   Closely linked to the idea of the ZPD is the concept of scaffolding. **Scaffolding** means changing the level of support. Over the course of a teaching session, a more skilled person (a teacher or advanced peer) adjusts the amount of guidance to fit the child's current performance (Collins, 2006; de Vries, 2005; John-Steiner & Mahn, 2003; Quintana & others, 2006; Sawyer, 2006). When the student is learning a new task, the skilled person may use direct instruction. As the student's competence increases, less guidance is given. Scaffolding is often used to help students attain the upper limits of their zone of proximal development (Horowitz & others, 2005).

Dialogue is an important tool of scaffolding in the zone of proximal development (Tappan, 1998). Vygotsky viewed children as having rich but unsystematic, disorganized, and spontaneous concepts. In a dialogue, these concepts meet with the skilled helper's more systematic, logical, and rational concepts. As a result, the child's concepts become more systematic, logical, and rational. For example, a dialogue might take place between a teacher and a child when the teacher uses scaffolding to help a child understand a concept like "transportation."

Asking probing questions is an excellent way to scaffold students' learning and help them to develop more sophisticated thinking skills. A teacher might ask a student such questions as "What would an example of that be?" "Why do you think that is so?" "Now, what's the next thing you need to do?" and "How can you connect those?" Over time, students should begin internalizing these kinds of probes and improve monitoring their own work (Horowitz & others, 2005).

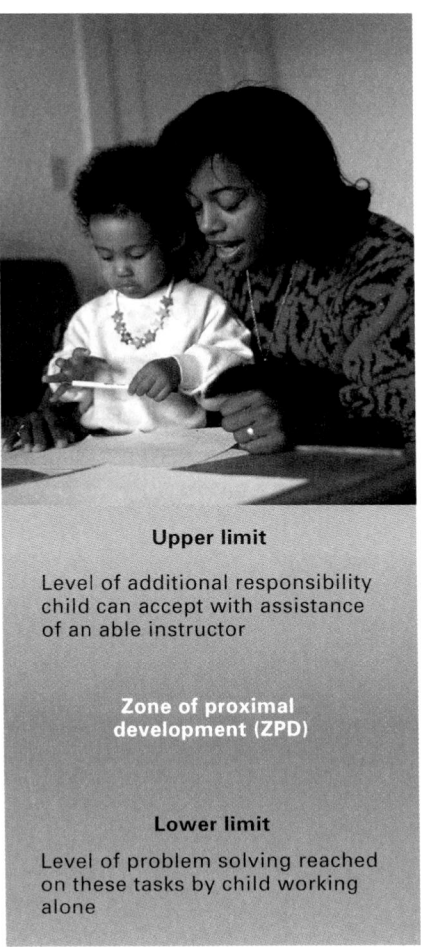

Upper limit

Level of additional responsibility child can accept with assistance of an able instructor

Zone of proximal development (ZPD)

Lower limit

Level of problem solving reached on these tasks by child working alone

FIGURE 2.14 Vygotsky's Zone of Proximal Development

Vygotsky's zone of proximal development has a lower limit and an upper limit. Tasks in the ZPD are too difficult for the child to perform alone. They require assistance from an adult or a skilled child. As children experience the verbal instruction or demonstration, they organize the information in their existing mental structures, so they can eventually perform the skill or task alone.

zone of proximal development (ZPD) Vygotsky's term for the range of tasks that are too difficult for children to master alone but that can be mastered with guidance and assistance from adults or more-skilled children.

scaffolding A technique that involves changing the level of support for learning. A teacher or more-advanced peer adjusts the amount of guidance to fit the student's current performance.

Many teachers who successfully use scaffolding circulate around the classroom, giving "just-in-time" assistance to individuals, or detecting a class-wide misconception and then leading a discussion to correct problem. They also give "children time to grapple with problems" and guide them when they observe that the child can no longer make progress (Horowitz & others, 2005, pp. 106–107).

Language and Thought The use of dialogue as a tool for scaffolding is only one example of the important role of language in a child's development. According to Vygotsky, children use speech not only for social communication, but also to help them solve tasks. Vygotsky (1962) further believed that young children use language to plan, guide, and monitor their behavior. This use of language for self-regulation is called *private speech*. For example, young children talk aloud to themselves about such things as their toys and the tasks they are trying to complete. Thus, when working on a puzzle, a child might say, "This piece doesn't go; maybe I'll try that one." A few minutes later she utters, "This is hard." For Piaget private speech is egocentric and immature, but for Vygotsky it is an important tool of thought during the early childhood years.

Vygotsky said that language and thought initially develop independently of each other and then merge. He emphasized that all mental functions have external, or social, origins. Children must use language to communicate with others before they can focus inward on their own thoughts. Children also must communicate externally and use language for a long period of time before they can make the transition from external to internal speech. This transition period occurs between 3 and 7 years of age and involves talking to oneself. After a while, the self-talk becomes second nature to children, and they can act without verbalizing. When this occurs, children have internalized their egocentric speech in the form of *inner speech,* which becomes their thoughts.

Vygotsky argued that children who use private speech are more socially competent than those who don't (Santiago-Delefosse & Delefosse, 2002). He argued that private speech represents an early transition in becoming more socially communicative. For Vygotsky, when young children talk to themselves, they are using language to govern their behavior and guide themselves.

Piaget held that self-talk is egocentric and reflects immaturity. However, researchers have found support for Vygotsky's view that private speech plays a positive role in children's development (Winsler, Diaz, & Montero, 1997; Winsler, Carlton, & Barry, 2000). Researchers have found that children use private speech more when tasks are difficult, after they make mistakes, and when they are not sure how to proceed (Berk, 1994). They also have revealed that children who use private speech are more attentive and improve their performance more than children who do not use private speech (Berk & Spuhl, 1995).

We have discussed a number of ideas about both Piaget's and Vygotsky's theories and how the theories can be applied to children's education. To reflect on how you might apply their theories to your own classroom, complete Self-Assessment 2.1 on page 52.

Evaluating Vygotsky's Theory How does Vygotsky's theory compare with Piaget's? Although both theories are constructivist, Vygotsky's is a **social constructivist approach,** which emphasizes the social contexts of learning and the construction of knowledge through social interaction.

In moving from Piaget to Vygotsky, the conceptual shift is from the individual to collaboration, social interaction, and sociocultural activity (Rogoff, 2003). The endpoint of cognitive development for Piaget is formal operational thought. For Vygotsky, the endpoint can differ, depending on which skills are considered to be the most important in a particular culture. For Piaget, children construct knowledge by transforming, organizing, and reorganizing previous knowledge. For Vygotsky, children construct knowledge through social interaction (Stetsenko & Arievitch, 2004). The implication of Piaget's theory for teaching is that children need support to

social constructivist approach
Emphasizes the social contexts of learning and that knowledge is mutually built and constructed; Vygotsky's theory exemplifies this approach.

BEST PRACTICES
Strategies for Applying Vygotsky's Theory to Children's Education

Vygotsky's theory has been embraced by many teachers and has been successfully applied to education (Bearison & Dorvall, 2002; Budrova & Leong, 2007; Elkind, 2004; Rowe & Wertsch, 2004; Winsler & others, 2002). Here are some ways Vygotsky's theory can be incorporated in classrooms:

1. *Assess the child's ZPD.* Like Piaget, Vygotsky did not believe that formal, standardized tests are the best way to assess children's learning. Rather, Vygotsky argued that assessment should focus on determining the child's zone of proximal development (Camilleri, 2005; Meijer & Elshout, 2001). The skilled helper presents the child with tasks of varying difficulty to determine the best level at which to begin instruction.

2. *Use the child's zone of proximal development in teaching.* Teaching should begin toward the zone's upper limit, so that the child can reach the goal with help and move to a higher level of skill and knowledge. Offer just enough assistance. You might ask, "What can I do to help you?" Or simply observe the child's intentions and attempts and provide support when needed. When the child hesitates, offer encouragement. And encourage the child to practice the skill. You may watch and appreciate the child's practice or offer support when the child forgets what to do. Next, you can read about John Mahoney's teaching practices that reflect Vygotsky's emphasis on the importance of the zone of proximal development.

THROUGH THE EYES OF TEACHERS
Using Dialogue and Reframing Concepts to Find the Zone of Proximal Development

John Mahoney teaches mathematics at a high school in Washington, D.C. In Mahoney's view, guiding students' success in math is both collaborative and individual. He encourages dialogue about math during which he reframes concepts that help students subsequently solve problems on their own. Mahoney also never gives students the answers to math problems. As one student commented, "He's going to make you think." His tests always include a problem that students have not seen but have enough knowledge to figure out the problem's solution. (Source: Briggs, 2005.)

3. *Use more-skilled peers as teachers.* Remember that it is not just adults that are important in helping children learn. Children also benefit from the support and guidance of more-skilled children (John-Steiner & Mahn, 2003). For example, pair a child who is just beginning to read with one who is a more advanced reader.

4. *Monitor and encourage children's use of private speech.* Be aware of the developmental change from externally

John Mahoney, teaching math.

talking to oneself when solving a problem during the preschool years to privately talking to oneself in the early elementary school years. In the elementary school years, encourage children to internalize and self-regulate their talk to themselves.

5. *Place instruction in a meaningful context.* Educators today are moving away from abstract presentations of material, instead providing students with opportunities to experience learning in real-world settings. For example, instead of just memorizing math formulas, students work on math problems with real-world implications.

6. *Transform the classroom with Vygotskian ideas.* Tools of the Mind is a curriculum that is grounded in Vygotsky's (1962) theory with special attention given to cultural tools and developing self-regulation, the zone of proximal development, scaffolding, private speech, shared activity, and play as important activity (Hyson, Copple, & Jones, 2006). The curriculum was created by Elena Bodrova and Deborah Leong (2007) and has been implemented in more than 200 classrooms. Most of the children in the Tools of the Mind programs are at-risk because of their living circumstances, which in many instances involve poverty and other difficult conditions such as being homeless and having parents with drug problems.

   In a Tools of the Mind classroom, dramatic play has a central role. Teachers guide children in creating themes based on the children's interests, such as treasure hunt, store, hospital, and restaurant. Teachers also incorporate field trips, visitor presentations, videos, and books in the development of children's play. They also help children develop a play plan, which increases the maturity of their play. Play plans describe what the children expect to do in the play period, including the imaginary context, roles, and props to be used. The play plans increase the quality of their play and self-regulation.

SELF–ASSESSMENT 2.1

Applying Piaget and Vygotsky in My Classroom

The grade level at which I plan to teach is _____

Piaget

The Piagetian stage of the majority of children in my classroom will likely be

_____

The Piagetian concepts that I believe will help me the most in understanding and teaching children at this grade level are

Concept	Example
_____	_____
_____	_____
_____	_____

Vygotsky

The concepts in Vygotsky's theory that I believe will help me the most in understanding and teaching children at this grade level are

Concept	Example
_____	_____
_____	_____
_____	_____

explore their world and discover knowledge. The main implication of Vygotsky's theory for teaching is that students need many opportunities to learn with the teacher and more-skilled peers. In both Piaget's and Vygotsky's theories, teachers serve as facilitators and guides, rather than as directors and molders of learning. Figure 2.15 compares Vygotsky's and Piaget's theories.

Even though their theories were proposed at about the same time, most of the world learned about Vygotsky's theory later than they learned about Piaget's theory, so Vygotsky's theory has not yet been evaluated as thoroughly. Vygotsky's view of the importance of sociocultural influences on children's development fits with the current belief that it is important to evaluate the contextual factors in learning (Budrova & Leong, 2007; Goos, 2004; Rowe & Wertsch, 2004).

Some critics say Vygotsky overemphasized the role of language in thinking. Also, his emphasis on collaboration and guidance has potential pitfalls. Might facilitators be too helpful in some cases, as when a parent becomes too overbearing and controlling? Further, some children might become lazy and expect help when they might have done something on their own.

In our coverage of cognitive development, we have focused on the views of two giants in the field: Piaget and Vygotsky. However, information processing also has emerged as an important perspective in understanding children's cognitive development (Munakata, 2006; Siegler, 2006; Siegler & Alibali, 2005). It emphasizes how information enters the mind, how it is stored and transformed, and how it is retrieved to perform mental activities such as problem solving and reasoning. It also focuses on how automatically and quickly children process information. Because information processing will be covered extensively in chapters 8 and 9, we mention it only briefly here.

Topic	Vygotsky	Piaget
Sociocultural Context	Strong Emphasis	Little Emphasis
Constructivism	Social constructivist	Cognitive constructivist
Stages	No general stages of development proposed	Strong emphasis on stages (sensorimotor, preoperational, concrete operational, and formal operational)
Key Processes	Zone of proximal development, language, dialogue, tools of the culture	Schema, assimilation, accommodation, operations, conservation, classification, hypothetical-deductive reasoning
Role of Language	A major role; language plays a powerful role in shaping thought	Language has a minimal role; cognition primarily directs language
View on Education	Education plays a central role, helping children learn the tools of the culture	Education merely refines the child's cognitive skills that have already emerged
Teaching Implications	The teacher is a facilitator and guide, not a director; establish many opportunities for children to learn with the teacher and more-skilled peers	Also views the teacher as a facilitator and guide, not a director; provide support for children to explore their world and discover knowledge

FIGURE 2.15 Comparison of Vygotsky's and Piaget's Theories

Review, Reflect, and Practice

(2) Discuss the development of the brain and compare the cognitive developmental theories of Jean Piaget and Lev Vygotsky.

REVIEW

- How does the brain develop and what implications does this development have for children's education?
- What four main ideas did Piaget use to describe cognitive processes? What stages did he identify in children's cognitive development? What are some criticisms of his view?
- What is the nature of Vygotsky's theory? How can Vygotsky's theory be applied to education and his theory compared to Piaget's? What is a criticism of Vygotsky's theory?

REFLECT

- Do you consider yourself to be a formal operational thinker? Do you still sometimes feel like a concrete operational thinker? Give examples.

continued on page 54

> ### Review, Reflect, and Practice *continued*
>
> #### PRAXIS™ PRACTICE
> 1. Sander is a 16-year-old boy who takes many risks, such as driving fast, drinking and driving, and having unprotected sex. Recent research on the brain indicates that a likely reason for this risk-taking behavior is that Sander's
>   a. hippocampus is damaged.
>   b. prefrontal cortex is still developing.
>   c. brain lateralization is incomplete.
>   d. myelination is complete.
> 2. Mrs. Gonzales teaches first grade. Which of her following strategies would a Piagetian approach be most likely to endorse?
>   a. Demonstrating how to perform a math operation and having students imitate her
>   b. Creating flash cards to teach vocabulary
>   c. Using a standardized test to assess students' reading skills
>   d. Designing contexts that promote student's thinking and discovery
> 3. Mr. Gould's fourth-grade students are learning about the relations among percentages, decimals, and fractions. Mr. Gould distributes an assignment requiring students to convert fractions to decimals and then to percentages. Christopher can do this assignment without help from Mr. Gould or his classmates. What would Vygotsky say about this task for Christopher?
>   a. This task is appropriate for Christopher because it is within his zone of proximal development.
>   b. This task is inappropriate for Christopher because it is above his zone of proximal development.
>   c. This task is inappropriate for Christopher because it is below his zone of proximal development.
>   d. This task is inappropriate for Christopher because it is within his zone of proximal development.
>
> *Please see the answer key at the end of the book.*

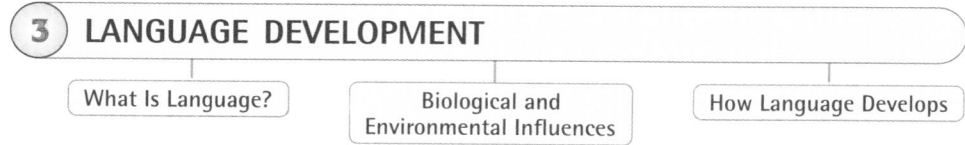

3 LANGUAGE DEVELOPMENT

What Is Language?   Biological and Environmental Influences   How Language Develops

Think how important language is in children's everyday lives. They need language to speak with others, listen to others, read, and write. Their language enables them to describe past events in detail and to plan for the future. Language lets us pass down information from one generation to the next and create a rich cultural heritage. As you learned earlier, in Vygotsky's view, language plays a key role in children's cognitive development.

What Is Language?

language A form of communication, whether spoken, written, or signed, that is based on a system of symbols.

Language is a form of communication—whether spoken, written, or signed—that is based on a system of symbols. Language consists of the words used by a community (vocabulary) and the rules for varying and combining them (grammar and syntax).

All human languages have some common characteristics (Waxman & Lidz, 2006). These include infinite generativity and organizational rules. *Infinite generativity* is the ability to produce an endless number of meaningful sentences using a finite set of words and rules.

When we say "rules," we mean that language is orderly and that rules describe the way language works (Berko Gleason, 2004, 2005). Language involves five systems of rules: phonology, morphology, syntax, semantics, and pragmatics.

Phonology   Every language is made up of basic sounds. **Phonology** is the sound system of a language, including the sounds used and how they may be combined (Menn & Stoel-Gammon, 2005). For example, English has the sounds *sp, ba,* and *ar,* but the sound sequences *zx* and *qp* do not occur.

A *phoneme* is the basic unit of sound in a language; it is the smallest unit of sound that affects meaning. A good example of a phoneme in English is /k/, the sound represented by the letter *k* in the word *ski* and the letter *c* in the word *cat*. The /k/ sound is slightly different in these two words, and in some languages such as Arabic these two sounds are separate phonemes.

Morphology   **Morphology** refers to the units of meaning involved in word formation. A *morpheme* is a minimal unit of meaning; it is a word or a part of a word that cannot be broken into smaller meaningful parts. Every word in the English language is made up of one or more morphemes. Some words consist of a single morpheme (for example, *help*), whereas others are made up of more than one morpheme (for example, *helper,* which has two morphemes, *help + er,* with the morpheme *-er* meaning "one who," in this case "one who helps"). Thus, not all morphemes are words by themselves; for example, *pre-, -tion,* and *-ing* are morphemes.

Just as the rules that govern phonology describe the sound sequences that can occur in a language, the rules of morphology describe the way meaningful units (morphemes) can be combined in words (Tager-Flusberg, 2005). Morphemes have many jobs in grammar, such as marking tense (for example, *she walks* versus *she walked*) and number (*she walks* versus *they walk*).

Syntax   **Syntax** involves the way words are combined to form acceptable phrases and sentences. If someone says to you, "Bob slugged Tom" or "Bob was slugged by Tom," you know who did the slugging and who was slugged in each case because you have a syntactic understanding of these sentence structures. You also understand that the sentence "You didn't stay, did you?" is a grammatical sentence but that "You didn't stay, didn't you?" is unacceptable and ambiguous.

If you learn another language, English syntax will not get you very far. For example, in English an adjective usually precedes a noun (as in *blue sky*), whereas in Spanish the adjective usually follows the noun *(cielo azul)*. Despite the differences in

FRANK & ERNEST © Thaves/Dist. by Newspaper Enterprise Association, Inc.

phonology A language's sound system.

morphology Refers to the units of meaning involved in word formation.

syntax The ways that words must be combined to form acceptable phrases and sentences.

their syntactic structures, however, the world's languages have much in common. For example, consider the following short sentences:

The cat killed the mouse.
The mouse ate the cheese.
The farmer chased the cat.

In many languages, it is possible to combine these sentences into more complex sentences. For example:

The farmer chased the cat that killed the mouse.
The mouse the cat killed ate the cheese.

However, no language we know of permits sentences like the following one:

The mouse the cat the farmer chased killed ate the cheese.

Can you make sense of this sentence? If you can, you probably can do it only after wrestling with it for several minutes. You likely could not understand it at all if someone uttered it during a conversation. It appears that language users cannot process subjects and objects arranged in too complex a fashion in a sentence. That is good news for language learners, because it means that all syntactic systems have some common ground. Such findings are also considered important by researchers interested in the universal properties of syntax (Chang, Dell, & Bock, 2006; Tager-Flusberg, 2005).

Semantics **Semantics** refers to the meaning of words and sentences. Every word has a set of semantic features, or required attributes related to meaning. *Girl* and *women,* for example, share many semantic features but they differ semantically in regard to age.

Words have semantic restrictions on how they can be used in sentences (Pan, 2005). The sentence *The bicycle talked the boy into buying a candy bar* is syntactically correct but semantically incorrect. The sentence violates our semantic knowledge that bicycles don't talk.

Pragmatics A final set of language rules involves **pragmatics,** the appropriate use of language in different contexts. Pragmatics covers a lot of territory. When you take turns speaking in a discussion or use a question to convey a command ("Why is it so noisy in here? What is this, Grand Central Station?"), you are demonstrating knowledge of pragmatics. You also apply the pragmatics of English when you use polite language in appropriate situations (for example, when talking to a teacher) or tell stories that are interesting, jokes that are funny, and lies that convince. In each of these cases, you are demonstrating that you understand the rules of your culture for adjusting language to suit the context.

Pragmatic rules can be complex, and they differ from one culture to another (Bryant, 2005). If you were to study the Japanese language, you would come face-to-face with countless pragmatic rules about conversing with individuals of various social levels and with various relationships to you. Some of these pragmatic rules concern the ways of saying "thank you." Indeed, the pragmatics of saying "thank you" are complex even in our own culture. Preschoolers' use of the phrase *thank you* varies with sex, socioeconomic status, and the age of the individual they are addressing.

At this point, we have discussed five important rule systems involved in language. An overview of these rule systems is presented in figure 2.16.

Biological and Environmental Influences

semantics The meaning of words and sentences.

pragmatics The use of appropriate use of language in different contexts.

Famous linguist Noam Chomsky (1957) argued that humans are prewired to learn language at a certain time and in a certain way. Some language scholars view the remarkable similarities in how children acquire language all over the world, despite the vast variation in language input they receive, as strong evidence that language has a biological basis.

Rule System	Description	Examples
Phonology	The sound system of a language. A phoneme is the smallest sound unit in a language.	The word *chat* has three phonemes or sounds: /ch/ /a/ /t/. An example of phonological rule in the English language is while the phoneme /r/ can follow the phonemes /t/ or /d/ in an English consonant cluster (such as *track* or *drab*), the phoneme /l/ cannot follow these letters.
Morphology	The system of meaningful units involved in word formation.	The smallest sound units that have a meaning are called morphemes, or meaning units. The word *girl* is one morpheme, or meaning unit; it cannot be broken down any further and still have meaning. When the suffix *s* is added, the word becomes *girls* and has two morphemes because the *s* changed the meaning of the word, indicating that there is more than one girl.
Syntax	The system that involves the way words are combined to form acceptable phrases and sentences.	Word order is very important in determining meaning in the English language. For example, the sentence "Sebastian pushed the bike" has a different meaning than "The bike pushed Sebastian."
Semantics	The system that involves the meaning of words and sentences.	Knowing the meaning of individual words—that is, vocabulary. For example, semantics includes knowing the meaning of such words as *orange*, *transportation*, and *intelligent*.
Pragmatics	The system of using appropriate conversation and knowledge of how to effectively use language in context.	An example is using polite language in appropriate situations, such as being mannerly when talking with one's teacher. Taking turns in a conversation involves pragmatics.

FIGURE 2.16 The Rule Systems of Language

Children also vary in their acquisition of language in ways that cannot be explained by environmental input alone. For example, pioneering language researcher Roger Brown (1973) searched for evidence that parents reinforce their children for speaking grammatically. He found that they sometimes smiled and praised their children for grammatical sentences, but they also reinforced sentences that were ungrammatical. From these observations, Brown concluded that processes operating within the child were overriding the environmental input of reinforcement.

As we said earlier, some language scholars view the similarities in children's language acquisition all over the world as strong evidence that language has a biological foundation. However, other language experts, argue that the child's experiences, the particular language to be learned, and the context in which learning takes place can strongly influence language acquisition (Goorhuis-Brouwer & others, 2004; Hoff, 2006; Tomasello, 2006).

Children clearly do not learn language in a social vacuum (Anderson, Moffatt, & Shapiro, 2006; Snow & Kang, 2006; Waxman & Lidz, 2006). Enough variation occurs in language development when children's caregivers differ substantially in input styles to show that the environment plays a significant role in language development, especially in the acquisition of vocabulary (Nagy, 2005; Tamis-LeMonda, Bornstein, & Baumwell, 2001). For example, in one study, by the time they were 3 years old, children living in poverty conditions showed vocabulary deficits, compared with their counterparts in middle-income families, and the deficits continued to be present when they entered school at 6 years of age (Farkas, 2001).

In sum, children are neither exclusively biological linguists nor exclusively social architects of language (Berko Gleason, 2005; Dick & others, 2005). No matter how long you converse with a dog, it won't learn to talk, because it doesn't have the human child's biological capacity for language. Unfortunately, though, some children fail to develop good language skills even in the presence of very good role models and interaction. An interactionist view emphasizes the contributions of both biology and experience in language development. That is, children are biologically prepared to learn language as they and their caregivers interact.

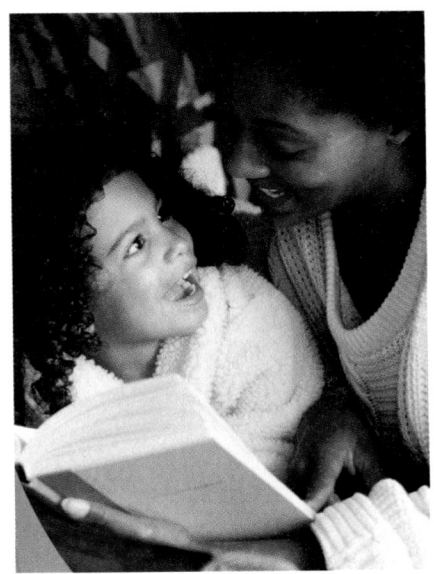

Both biological and environmental influences play important roles in children's language development.

DIVERSITY AND EDUCATION
African American Language Traditions and Poverty

Shirley Heath (1989) examined the language traditions of African Americans from low-income backgrounds. She traced some aspects of African American English to the time of slavery. Heath also examined how those speech patterns have carried over into African American English today. She found that agricultural areas in the southern United States have an especially rich oral tradition.

Specifically she found that adults do not simplify or edit their talk for children, in essence challenging the children to be highly active listeners. Also, adults ask only "real questions" of children—that is, questions for which the adult does not already know the answer. Adults also engage in a type of teasing with children, encouraging them to use their wits in communication. For example, a grandmother might pretend that she wants to take a child's hat. She then starts a lively exchange in which the child must understand many subtleties of argument, mood, and humor: Does Grandma really want my hat? Is she mad at me? Is she making a joke? Can I persuade her to give it back to me? Finally, there is an appreciation of wit and flexibility in how language is used, as well as an acknowledgment of individual differences—one person might be respected for recounting stories, another for negotiating and peacemaking skills.

Heath argues that the language tradition she describes is richly varied, cognitively demanding, and well suited to many real-life situations. She says that the oral and literary traditions among poor African Americans in the cities are well suited for many job situations. Years ago many inner-city jobs required only that a person follow directions in order to perform repetitive tasks. Today, many positions require continuous interactions involving considerable flexibility in language, such as the ability to persuade coworkers or to subtly express dissatisfaction.

Despite its utility in many job situations, the rich language tradition possessed by low-income African Americans does not meet with the educational priorities of our nation's schools. Too often schools stress rote memorization, minimizing group interaction and discouraging individual variations in communicative style. Also, the language tradition of African American culture is rapidly dying in the face of current life among poor African Americans, where the structure of low-income, frequently single-parent families often provides little verbal stimulation for children.

One mother agreed to let researcher Heath tape-record her interactions with her children over a 2-year period and to write notes about her activities with them. Within 500 hours of tape and more than a thousand lines of notes, the mother initiated talk with her three preschool children on only eighteen occasions (other than giving them a brief directive or asking a quick question). Few of the mother's conversations involved either planning or executing actions with or for her children.

Heath (1989) points out that the lack of family and community supports is widespread among urban housing projects, especially among African Americans. The deteriorating, impoverished conditions of these inner-city areas severely impede the ability of young children to develop the language skills they need to function competently.

In or out of school, encouragement of language development, not drill and practice, is the key (Hiebert & Kamil, 2005; Oates & Grayson, 2004). Language development is not simply a matter of being rewarded for saying things correctly and imitating a speaker. Children benefit when their parents and teachers actively engage them in conversation, ask them questions, and emphasize interactive rather than directive language. You can read about how urban poverty conditions can restrict the language development of African American children in the Diversity and Education interlude.

How Language Develops

What are some of the key developmental milestones in language development? We will examine these milestones in infancy, early childhood, middle and late childhood, and adolescence.

Infancy Language acquisition advances past a number of milestones in infancy (Edwards, 2004; Waxman & Lidz, 2006). Because the main focus of this text is on children and adolescents rather than infants, we will only describe several of the many language milestones in infancy. Babbling begins at about 3 to 6 months. Infants usually utter their first word at about 10 to 13 months. By 18 to 24 months, infants usually have begun to string two words together. In this two-word stage, they quickly grasp the importance of language in communication, creating phrases such as "Book there," "My candy," "Mama walk," and "Give Papa."

Early Childhood As children leave the two-word stage, they move rather quickly into three-, four-, and five-word combinations. The transition from simple sentences expressing a single proposition to complex sentences begins between 2 and 3 years of age and continues into the elementary school years (Bloom, 1998).

Young children's understanding sometimes gets way ahead of their speech. One 3-year-old, laughing with delight as an abrupt summer breeze stirred his hair and tickled his skin, commented, "I got breezed!" Many of the oddities of young children's language sound like mistakes to adult listeners. From the children's point of view, however, they are not mistakes. They represent the way young children perceive and understand their world at that point in their development.

Let's explore the changes in the five rules systems we described earlier—phonology, morphology, syntax, semantics, and pragmatics—during early childhood. In terms of phonology, most preschool children gradually become sensitive to the sounds of spoken words (National Research Council, 1999). They notice rhymes, enjoy poems, make up silly names for things by substituting one sound for another (such as *bubblegum, bubblebum, bubbleyum*), and clap along with each syllable in a phrase.

As they move beyond two-word utterances, there is clear evidence that children know morphological rules. Children begin using the plural and possessive forms of nouns (*dogs* and *dog's*); putting appropriate endings on verbs (*-s* when the subject is third-person singular, *-ed* for the past tense, and *-ing* for the present progressive tense); and using prepositions (*in* and *on*), articles (*a* and *the*), and various forms of the verb *to be* ("I *was going* to the store"). In fact, they *overgeneralize* these rules, applying them to words that do not follow the rules. For example, a preschool child might say "foots" instead of "feet" or "goed" instead of "went."

Children's understanding of morphological rules was the subject of a classic experiment by children's language researcher Jean Berko (1958). Berko presented preschool and first-grade children with cards like the one shown in figure 2.17. Children were asked to look at the card while the experimenter read the words on it aloud. Then the children were asked to supply the missing word. This might sound easy, but Berko was interested not just in the children's ability to recall the right word but also in their ability to say it "correctly" with the ending that was dictated by morphological rules. *Wugs* is the correct response for the card in figure 2.17. Although the children were not perfectly accurate, they were much better than chance would dictate. Moreover, they demonstrated their knowledge of morphological rules not only with the plural forms of nouns ("There are two wugs") but also with the possessive forms of nouns and with the third-person singular and past-tense forms of verbs.

What makes Berko's study impressive is that all of the words were *fictional;* they were created especially for the experiment. Thus, the children could not base their responses on remembering past instances of hearing the words. Instead, they were forced to rely on *rules*. Berko's study demonstrated not only that the children relied on rules, but also that they had *abstracted* the rules from what they had heard and could apply them to novel situations.

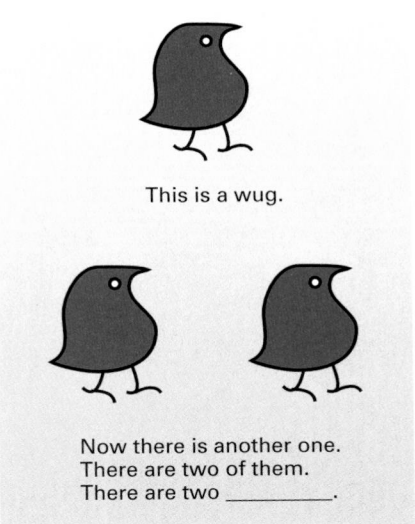

This is a wug.

Now there is another one.
There are two of them.
There are two _____.

FIGURE 2.17 Stimuli in Berko's Study of Young Children's Understanding of Morphological Rules

In Jean Berko's (1958) study, young children were presented cards such as this one with a "wug" on it. Then the children were asked to supply the missing word and say it correctly. "Wugs" is the correct response here.

Preschool children also learn and apply rules of syntax (Marchman & Thal, 2005; Tomasello, 2006). After advancing beyond two-word utterances, the child shows a growing mastery of complex rules for how words should be ordered. Consider *wh*-questions, such as "Where is Daddy going?" or "What is that boy doing?" To ask these questions properly, the child must know two important differences between *wh*- questions and affirmative statements (for instance, "Daddy is going to work" and "That boy is waiting on the school bus"). First, a *wh*- word must be added at the beginning of the sentence. Second, the auxiliary verb must be inverted—that is, exchanged with the subject of the sentence. Young children learn quite early where to put the *wh*-word, but they take much longer to learn the auxiliary-inversion rule. Thus, preschool children might ask, "Where daddy is going?" and "What that boy is doing?"

Children's knowledge of semantics or meanings also rapidly advances in early childhood (Hiebert & Kamil, 2005). The speaking vocabulary of a 6-year-old child ranges from 8,000 to 14,000 words. Assuming that word learning began when the child was 12 months old, this translates into a rate of 5 to 8 new word meanings a day between the ages of 1 and 6. To read about strategies for using technology to support children's vocabulary, see the Technology and Education box.

Substantial changes in pragmatics also occur during early childhood. A 6-year-old is simply a much better conversationalist than a 2-year-old. What are some of the changes in pragmatics that are made in the preschool years? At about 3 years of age, children improve in their ability to talk about things that are not physically present. That is, they improve their command of the characteristic of language known as *displacement*. Children become increasingly removed from the "here and now" and are able to talk about things not physically present, as well as things that happened in the past or may happen in the future. Preschoolers can tell you what they want for lunch tomorrow, something that would not have been possible at the two-word stage in infancy. Preschool children also become increasingly able to talk in different ways to different people.

Middle and Late Childhood   The advances in language that take place in early childhood lay the foundation for later development in the elementary school years. As they enter school, children gain new skills that make it possible for them to learn to read and write: These include increasingly using language in a displaced way, learning what a word is, and learning how to recognize and talk about sounds (Berko Gleason, 2004). They have to learn the alphabetic principle, that the alphabet letters represent sounds of the language. As children develop during middle and late childhood, changes in their vocabulary and grammar also take place.

Vocabulary development continues at a breathtaking pace for most children during the elementary school years. After 5 years of word learning, the 6-year-old child does not slow down. According to some estimates, elementary school children in the United States are moving along at the awe-inspiring rate of 22 words a day! The average U.S. 12-year-old has developed a speaking vocabulary of approximately 50,000 words.

Further changes in semantics occur in the elementary school years. Preschool children typically respond with a word that often follows the stimulus word in a sentence. For example, when asked to respond to *dog,* the young child may say *barks;* to the word *eat, lunch.* But at about 7 years of age, children may begin to respond with a word that is the same part of speech as the stimulus word. For example, a child may now respond to the word *dog* with *cat* or *horse.* To *eat,* the 7-year-old might say *drink.* This is evidence that children now have begun to categorize their vocabulary by parts of speech (Berko Gleason, 2004).

During the elementary school years, children become increasingly able to understand and use complex grammar—for example, stating sentences such as *The boy kissed his mother who wore a hat.* They also learn to use language in a more connected way. Now they can produce connected discourse, relating sentences to one another and producing descriptions, definitions, and narratives that hang together and make sense. Children must be able to do these things orally before they can be expected to do them in written assignments.

TECHNOLOGY AND EDUCATION

Technology and Children's Vocabulary Development

Here are three ways to support children's vocabulary development using three types of technology (Miller, 2001).

Computers

CD-ROMs of stories, such as *Living Books,* can promote children's vocabulary development, especially when there is an online option for students to find the meaning of unfamiliar words. Using the computer for listening to and watching stories can be part of a student's reading center rotations, reading assignment, or an option during choice time. Learning new words can be enhanced if teachers plan a way for students to keep track of new words. For example, students can record new words in a portfolio for future reference.

An analysis of software products for children's vocabulary development offered the following guidelines (Wood, 2001):

1. *Relate the new to the known.* New vocabulary words are presented in a way that builds on students' previously acquired word knowledge; students are encouraged to map new word meanings onto their own experiences.

2. *Promote active, in-depth processing.* Students are motivated to construct the meanings of words rather than being taught through rote memorization of word meanings. This involves introducing a synonym for the new word or showing how it relates to a particular context; helping students apply their understanding of the word to a particular context; and challenging children to use the new word in a novel way to illustrate their understanding of its meaning.

3. *Encourage reading.* Reading promotes vocabulary development. It is important for software that promotes vocabulary development to motivate students to extend their learning through reading.

Audiobooks

Teachers can create listening centers to support vocabulary development. Listening centers should include tape recorders, headphones, audiobooks, and corresponding literature. Audiobooks can be used to supplement printed materials, listen to dramatization of stories, and pique student interest. Audiobooks may especially benefit students with special needs (Casbergue & Harris, 1996). For example, students whose primary language is not English can use tapes to improve vocabulary development, reading, and pronunciation. Weak readers can use the tapes to contribute to literature discussions in class even though they may be reading less-complex materials.

Educational Television

Educational television can be used to help children learn the alphabet, to see people using vocabulary in different contexts, and to hear stories that will motivate children to read these stories later (Comstock & Scharrer, 2006; Lesser, 1989). One such program is *Reading Rainbow.* In one study, it was found that this program increases children's vocabulary and literacy (Wood & Duke, 1997). The show helps children to expand their vocabularies by introducing many potentially unfamiliar words per episode, linking the words by theme, creating rich contexts when using the words, clearly and directly explaining the meanings of new words, and linking new words in playful ways.

Metalinguistic awareness also improves considerably during the elementary school years. **Metalinguistic awareness** refers to knowledge of language, which allows children "to think about their language, understand what words are, and even define them" (Berko Gleason, 2005, p. 4). *Metacognition,* which we will discuss in more depth in chapter 8, "The Information-Processing Approach," is cognition about cognition, or knowing about knowing. Metalinguistic awareness is essentially cognition about language.

In elementary school, defining words becomes a regular part of classroom discourse and children increase their knowledge of syntax as they study and talk about the components of sentences, such as subjects and verbs (Ely, 2005). Children also make progress in understanding how to use language in culturally appropriate ways—pragmatics. By

metalinguistic awareness Knowledge of language.

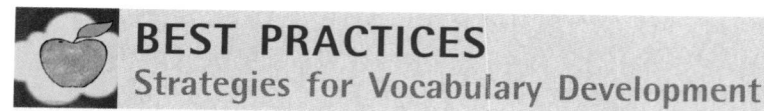

BEST PRACTICES
Strategies for Vocabulary Development

In the discussion of semantic development, we described the impressive gains in vocabulary that many children make as they go through the early childhood, middle and late childhood, and adolescent years. However, there are significant individual variations in children's vocabulary, and a good vocabulary contributes in important ways to school success. For example, a recent study found that vocabulary development was an important contributor to reading comprehension in second-grade students (Berninger & Abbott, 2005). Other research studies have also found that vocabulary plays an important role in reading comprehension and success in school (Paris & Paris, 2006; Snow & Kang, 2006). In addition to those described in the Technology and Education box, here are some further strategies for improving students' vocabularies:

Preschool and Kindergarten

1. *Explain new vocabulary in books that you read to young children.*

2. *Name and describe all of things in the classroom.*

3. *In everyday conversation with children, introduce and elaborate on words that children are unlikely to know about.* This activity can also be used at higher grade levels.

Elementary, Middle, and High School

1. *If students have severe deficits in vocabulary knowledge, provide intense vocabulary instruction.*

2. *As a rule, don't introduce more than 10 words at a time.*

3. *Give students an opportunity to use words in a variety of contexts.* These contexts might include read-aloud, fill-in-the-blank sentences, and read-and-respond activities (students read short, information articles about a topic that includes targeted vocabulary words and then respond to questions about the articles).

4. *Writing can help students process word meanings actively.* For example, assign students a topic to write about using assigned vocabulary words. (Sources: Curtis & Longo, 2001; U.S. Department of Education, 2006.)

the time they enter adolescence, most children know the rules for the use of language in everyday contexts—that is, what is appropriate or is inappropriate to say.

Adolescence   Language development during adolescence includes increased sophistication in the use of words. As they develop abstract thinking, adolescents become much better than children at analyzing the function a word plays in a sentence.

Adolescents also develop more subtle abilities with words. They make strides in understanding *metaphor*, which is an implied comparison between unlike things. For example, individuals "draw a line in the sand" to indicate a nonnegotiable position; a political campaign is said to be a marathon, not a sprint. And adolescents become better able to understand and to use *satire*, which is the use of irony, derision, or wit to expose folly or wickedness. Caricatures are an example of satire. More advanced logical thinking also allows adolescents, from about 15 to 20 years of age, to understand complex literary works.

Most adolescents are also much better writers than children are. They are better at organizing ideas before they write, at distinguishing between general and specific points as they write, at stringing together sentences that make sense, and at organizing their writing into an introduction, body, and concluding remarks.

Everyday speech changes during adolescence "and part of being a successful teenager is being able to talk like one" (Berko Gleason, 2005, p. 9). Young adolescents often speak a dialect with their peers that is characterized by jargon and slang (Cave, 2002). A *dialect* is a variety of language distinguished by its vocabulary, grammar, or pronunciation. Nicknames that are satirical and derisive ("stilt," "refrigerator," "spaz") are part of the dialect of many young adolescents. They might use such labels to show that they belong to the group and to reduce the seriousness of a situation (Cave, 2002).

Review, Reflect, and Practice

(3) Identify the key features of language, biological and environmental influences on language, and the typical growth of the child's language.

REVIEW
- What is language? Describe these five features of spoken language: phonology, morphology, syntax, semantics, and pragmatics.
- What evidence supports the idea that humans are "prewired" for learning language? What evidence supports the importance of environmental factors?
- What milestones does a child go through in the course of learning language and what are the typical ages of these milestones?

REFLECT
- How have teachers encouraged or discouraged your own mastery of language? What experiences have done the most to expand your language skills?

PRAXIS™ PRACTICE
1. Josh has developed a large vocabulary. Which of the following language systems does this reflect?
   a. semantics
   b. pragmatics
   c. syntax
   d. morphology
2. Children raised in isolation from human contact often show extreme, long-lasting language deficits that are rarely entirely overcome by later exposure to language. This evidence supports which aspect of language development?
   a. biological
   b. environmental
   c. interactionist
   d. pragmatic
3. Tamara is discussing the birds she saw flying over her neighborhood. She says, "We saw a flock of gooses." If Tamara's language development is normal for her age, how old is Tamara likely to be?
   a. 2 years old
   b. 4 years old
   c. 6 years old
   d. 8 years old

Please see the answer key at the end of the book.

CRACK THE CASE
The Case of the Book Report

Mr. Johnson assigned his high school senior American government students to read two books during the semester that had "something, anything to do with government or political systems" and to write a brief report about each of their chosen books.

One student in the class, Cindy, chose to read *1984* and *Animal Farm*, both by George Orwell. *1984* is a book about what could happen in "the future" year of 1984, given certain earlier political decisions. In essence, the world turns into a terrible place in which "Big Brother" monitors all of one's actions via two-way television-like screens. Infractions of minor rules are punished severely. *Animal Farm* is a brief novel about political systems in which the characters are portrayed as various farm animals such as pigs and dogs. Cindy enjoyed both books and completed them both before midterm. Her reports were insightful, reflecting on the symbolism contained in the novels and the implications for present-day government.

Cindy's friend, Lucy, had put off reading her first book until the last minute. She knew Cindy enjoyed reading about government and had finished her reports. Lucy asked Cindy if she knew of a "skinny book" she could read to fulfill the assignment. Cindy gladly shared her copy of *Animal Farm* with her friend, but as Lucy began reading the book she wondered why Cindy had given her this book. It didn't seem to fit the requirements of the assignment at all.

The day before the first reports were due, Mr. Johnson overheard the girls talking. Lucy complained to Cindy, "I don't get it. It's a story about pigs and dogs."

Cindy responded, "They aren't really supposed to be farm animals. It's a story about the promises of communism and what happened in the Soviet Union once the communists took over. It's a great story! Don't you see? The pigs symbolize the communist regime that overthrew the czars during the Russian Revolution. They made all kinds of promises about equality for everyone. The people went along with them because they were sick and tired of the rich and powerful running everything while they starved. Once the czars were eliminated, the communists established a new government but didn't keep any of their promises, controlled everything. Remember in the book when the pigs moved into the house and started walking on two legs? That's supposed to be like when the communist leaders began acting just like the czars. They even created a secret police force—the dogs in the story. Remember how they bullied the other animals? Just like the secret police in the Soviet Union."

Lucy commented, "I still don't get it. How can a pig or a dog be a communist or a cop? They're just animals."

Cindy looked at her friend, dumbfounded. How could she *not* understand this book? It was so obvious.

1. Drawing on Piaget's theory, explain why Cindy understood the book.
2. Based on Piaget's theory, explain why Lucy didn't understand the book.
3. What could Mr. Johnson do to help Lucy understand?
4. How could Mr. Johnson have presented this assignment differently, so that Lucy did not need to rush through a book?
5. At which of Piaget's stages of cognitive development is Cindy operating?
   a. sensorimotor
   b. preoperational
   c. concrete operational
   d. formal operational
   Explain your choice.
6. At which of Piaget's stages of cognitive development is Lucy operating?
   a. sensorimotor
   b. preoperational
   c. concrete operational
   d. formal operational
   Explain your choice.

Reach Your Learning Goals
Cognitive and Language Development

(1) AN OVERVIEW OF CHILD DEVELOPMENT: Define development and explain the main processes, periods, and issues in development, as well as links between development and education.

Exploring What Development Is

Development is the pattern of biological, cognitive, and socioemotional changes that begins at conception and continues through the life span. Most development involves growth, but it also eventually includes decay (dying). The more you learn about children's development, the better you will understand the level at which to appropriately teach them. Childhood provides a foundation for the adult years.

Processes and Periods

Development is the product of biological, cognitive, and socioemotional processes, which often are intertwined. Periods of development include infancy, early childhood, middle and late childhood, adolescence, and early adulthood.

Developmental Issues

The nature-nurture issue focuses on the extent to which development is mainly influenced by nature (biological inheritance) or nurture (experience). Some developmentalists describe development as continuous (gradual, cumulative change), others describe it as discontinuous (a sequence of abrupt stages). The early-later experience issue focuses on whether early experiences (especially in infancy) are more important in development than later experiences. Most developmentalists recognize that extreme positions on the nature-nurture, continuity-discontinuity, and early-later experience issues are unwise. Despite this consensus, these issues continue to be debated.

Development and Education

Developmentally appropriate teaching takes place at a level that is neither too difficult and stressful nor too easy and boring for the child's developmental level. Splintered development occurs when there is considerable unevenness in development across domains.

(2) COGNITIVE DEVELOPMENT: Discuss the development of the brain and compare the cognitive developmental theories of Jean Piaget and Lev Vygotsky.

The Brain

An especially important part of growth is the development of the brain and nervous system. Myelination involving hand-eye coordination is not complete until about 4 years of age, and myelination involving focusing attention is not finished until about ten. Substantial synaptic pruning of the brain connections takes place, and the adult level of density of synaptic connections is not reached until some point in adolescence. Different regions of the brain grow at different rates. Researchers have recently found a developmental disjunction between the early development of the amygdala, which is responsible for emotion, and the later development of the prefrontal cortex, which is responsible for reasoning and thinking. They argue that these changes in the brain may help to explain the risk-taking behavior and lack of mature judgment in adolescents. Lateralization in some verbal and nonverbal functions occurs, but in many instances functioning is linked to both hemispheres. There is considerable plasticity in the brain and the quality of learning environments children experience influence the development of their brain. Little is known about links between neuroscience and education, and often the effects of such links have been overstated.

continued

Piaget's Theory

Jean Piaget proposed a major theory of children's cognitive development that involves these important processes: schemas, assimilation and accommodation, organization, and equilibration. In his theory, cognitive development unfolds in a sequence of four stages: sensorimotor (birth to about age 2), preoperational (from about ages 2 to 7), concrete operational (from about ages 7 to 11), and formal operational (from about ages 11 to 15). Each stage is a qualitative advance. In the sensorimotor stage, infants construct an understanding of the world by coordinating sensory experiences with motor actions and accomplish object permanence. Thought is more symbolic at the preoperational stage, although the child has not yet mastered some important mental operations. Preoperational thought includes symbolic function and intuitive thought substages. Egocentrism, animism, and centration are constraints. At the concrete operational stage, children can perform operations, and logical thought replaces intuitive thought when reasoning can be applied to specific or concrete examples. Classification, seriation, and transitivity are important concrete operational skills. At the formal operational stage, thinking is more abstract, idealistic, and logical. Hypothetical-deductive reasoning becomes important. Adolescent egocentrism characterizes many young adolescents. We owe to Piaget a long list of masterful concepts as well as the current vision of the child as an active, constructivist thinker. Criticisms of his view focus on estimates of children's competence, stages, the training of children to reason at a higher cognitive level, and the neo-Piagetian criticism of not being precise enough about how children learn.

Vygotsky's Theory

Lev Vygotsky proposed another major theory of cognitive development. Vygotsky's view emphasizes that cognitive skills need to be interpreted developmentally, are mediated by language, and have their origins in social relations and culture. Zone of proximal development (ZPD) is Vygotsky's term for the range of tasks that are too difficult for children to master alone but that can be learned with the guidance and assistance of adults and more-skilled children. Scaffolding and dialogue are important concepts in Vygotsky's theory. He also believed that language plays a key role in guiding cognition. Applications of Vygotsky's ideas to education include using the child's zone of proximal development and scaffolding, using skilled peers as teachers, monitoring and encouraging children's use of private speech, and accurately assessing the zone of proximal development. These practices can transform the classroom and establish a meaningful context for instruction. Like Piaget, Vygotsky emphasized that children actively construct their understanding of the world. Unlike Piaget, he did not propose stages of cognitive development, and he emphasized that children construct knowledge through social interaction. In Vygotsky's theory, children depend on tools provided by the culture, which determines which skills they will develop. Some critics say that Vygotsky overemphasized the role of language.

(3) LANGUAGE DEVELOPMENT: Identify the key features of language, biological and environmental influences on language, and the typical growth of the child's language.

What Is Language?

Language is a form of communication, whether spoken, written, or signed, that is based on a system of symbols. Human languages are infinitely generative. All human languages also have organizational rules of phonology, morphology, syntax, semantics, and pragmatics. Phonology is the sound system of a language; morphology refers to the units of meaning involved in word formation; syntax involves the ways that words must be combined to form acceptable phrases and sentences; semantics refers to the meaning of words and sentences; and pragmatics describes the appropriate use of language in different contexts.

Biological and Environmental Influences

Children are biologically prepared to learn language as they and their caregivers interact. Some language scholars argue that the strongest evidence for the biological basis of language is that children all over the world reach language milestones at about the same age despite vast differences in their environmental experiences. However, children do not learn language in a social vacuum. Children benefit when parents and teachers actively engage them in conversation, ask them questions, and talk with, not just to, them. In sum, biology and experience interact to produce language development.

How Language Develops

Language acquisition advances through stages. Babbling occurs at about 3 to 6 months, the first word at 10 to 13 months, and two-word utterances at 18 to 24 months. As children move beyond two-word utterances, they can demonstrate that they know some morphological rules, as documented in Berko Gleason's study. Children also make advances in phonology, syntax, semantics, and pragmatics. Vocabulary development increases dramatically during the elementary schools years, and by the end of elementary school most children can apply appropriate rules of grammar. Metalinguistic awareness also advances in the elementary school years. In adolescence, language changes include more effective use of words; improvements in the ability to understand metaphor, satire, and adult literary works; and writing.

 # KEY TERMS

development 28
nature-nurture
  issue 30
continuity-discontinuity
  issue 30
early-later experience
  issue 31
splintered development 32
lateralization 36
schemas 37
assimilation 37

accommodation 37
organization 38
equilibration 38
sensorimotor stage 38
preoperational stage 39
symbolic function
  substage 39
intuitive thought
  substage 40
centration 41
conservation 41

concrete operational
  stage 42
seriation 43
transitivity 43
formal operational stage 44
hypothetical-deductive
  reasoning 44
neo-Piagetians 47
zone of proximal
  development (ZPD) 49
scaffolding 49

social constructivist
  approach 50
language 54
phonology 55
morphology 55
syntax 55
semantics 56
pragmatics 56
metalinguistic
  awareness 61

 # PORTFOLIO ACTIVITIES

Now that you have a good understanding of this chapter, complete these exercises to expand your thinking.

Independent Reflection

1. Select the general age of the child you expect to teach one day. Make a list of that child's characteristic ways of thinking according to Piaget's theory of cognitive development. List other related characteristics of the child based on your own childhood. Then make a second list of your own current ways of thinking. Compare the lists. In what important cognitive ways do you and the child differ? What adjustments in thinking will you need to make when you set out to communicate with the child? Summarize your thoughts in a brief essay.

2. How might thinking in formal operational ways rather than concrete operational ways help students develop better study skills?

3. What is the most useful idea related to children's language development that you read about in this chapter? Write the idea down in your portfolio and explain how you will implement this idea in your classroom.

Research/Field Experience

4. Find an education article in a magazine or on the Internet that promotes "left-brained" and "right-brained" activities for learning. In a brief report, criticize the article based on what you read in this chapter about neuroscience and brain education.

Go to the Online Learning Center for downloadable portfolio templates.

TAKING IT TO THE NET

- Reflect on Vygotsky's concepts of "scaffolding" and "zone of proximal development" (ZPD). How do teachers identify what is within a child's ZPD? How do teachers determine the type of assistance to give, how much to give, and when a child can work independently? Provide an example of each of these concepts. **naecs.crc.uiuc.edu/newsletter/volume3/number4.html**
- Experts argue that enriched classroom and home environments produce improvements in brain functioning and learning. Describe an enriched school environment, including both physical (classroom arrangement) and non-physical (instructional techniques) attributes. How could this environment contribute to healthy brain development? **www.atozteacherstuff.com/pages/1814.shtml**
- Vocabulary is a critical component of reading comprehension; however, low-income students are exposed to far less written and oral language than their more affluent counterparts. Locate vocabulary games and activities on the Web and devise a strategy for sharing these activities with parents to maximize students' contact with language. **www.childdevelopmentinfo.com/learning/vocabulary.shtml**

Connect to the Online Learning Center to explore possible answers.

 STUDY, PRACTICE, AND SUCCEED

Visit **www.mhhe.com/santedu3e** to review the chapter with self-grading quizzes and Self-Assessments, to apply the chapter material to two more Crack the Case studies, and for suggested activities to develop your teaching portfolio.

CHAPTER 3

Social Contexts and Socioemotional Development

In the end, the power behind development is life.

—Erik Erikson
European-Born American Psychotherapist, 20th Century

Chapter Outline	Learning Goals
Contemporary Theories	**1** Describe two contemporary perspectives on socioemotional development: Bronfenbrenner's ecological theory and Erikson's life-span development theory.
Bronfenbrenner's Ecological Theory	
Erikson's Life-Span Development Theory	
Social Contexts of Development	**2** Discuss how the social contexts of families, peers, and schools are linked with socioemotional development.
Families	
Peers	
Schools	
Socioemotional Development	**3** Explain these aspects of children's socioemotional development: self-esteem, identity, and moral development.
The Self	
Moral Development	

TEACHING STORIES   Keren Abra

The socioemotional contexts of children's lives influence their ability to learn. Keren Abra teaches fifth grade in San Francisco. A student in her class, Julie, was very quiet, so quiet that in classroom discussions she whispered her responses. Her parents, who had gone through a bitter divorce, agreed that Julie needed a good therapist.

Julie was significantly underachieving, doing minimal work and scoring low on tests. A crisis of low grades and incomplete work brought her mother to school one evening, and her father the next morning, to talk with Keren. Later that week, Keren spoke with Julie, who looked terrified. Following are Keren's comments about her talk with Julie:

> I kept some objectives in mind. This child needed to know that she was a good student, that she was loved, that adults could be consistent and responsible, and that she didn't have to hide and keep secrets . . . I told her that her parents

had come in because we all were concerned about her and knew we needed to help her. I told her that her parents loved her very much and asked if she knew this (she and I agreed that nobody's perfect, least of all adults with their own problems). I explained that a tutor was going to help her with her work . . . I talked with Julie about how much I liked her and about coming forward more in class.

Change did not happen overnight with Julie, but she did begin to increasingly look me in the eye with a more confident smile. She spoke out more in class, and improved her writing efforts. Her best months were when she was seeing both a therapist and a tutor, although her grades remained a roller coaster. At the end of the school year, she commented that she and her mother both noticed that her best work was when she felt supported and confident. For an 11-year-old, that is a valuable insight.

Preview

Divorce is just one of the many aspects of children's social contexts that can have profound effects on their performance in school. Later in the chapter, we examine the topic of divorce and provide further teaching strategies for helping students cope with the divorce of their parents. In this chapter, we explore how parents cradle children's lives, as well as how children's development is influenced by successive waves of peers, friends, and teachers. Children's small world widens as they become students and develop relationships with many new people. In this second chapter on development, we study these social worlds and examine children's socioemotional development.

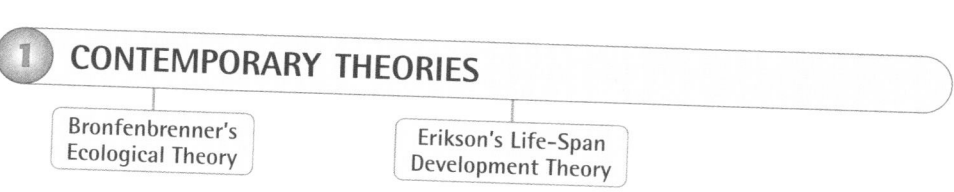

A number of theories address children's socioemotional development. In this chapter, we focus on two main theories: Bronfenbrenner's ecological theory and Erikson's life-span development theory. These two theories were chosen for the comprehensive way they address the social contexts in which children develop (Bronfenbrenner) and major changes in children's socioemotional development (Erikson). In chapter 7, we discuss other theories—behavioral and social cognitive—that also are relevant to socioemotional development.

Bronfenbrenner's Ecological Theory

The ecological theory developed by Urie Bronfenbrenner (1917–2005) primarily focuses on the social contexts in which children live and the people who influence their development.

Five Environmental Systems Bronfenbrenner's (1995, 2000, 2004; Bronfenbrenner & Morris, 1998, 2006) **ecological theory** consists of five environmental systems that range from close interpersonal interactions to broad-based influences of culture. The five systems are the microsystem, mesosystem, exosystem, macrosystem, and chronosystem (see figure 3.1).

A *microsystem* is a setting in which the individual spends considerable time, such as the student's family, peers, school, and neighborhood. Within these microsystems, the individual has direct interactions with parents, teachers, peers, and others. For Bronfenbrenner, the student is not a passive recipient of experiences but is someone who reciprocally interacts with others and helps to construct the microsystem.

The *mesosystem* involves linkages between microsystems. Examples are the connections between family experiences and school experiences and between family and peers. For example, consider one important mesosystem, the connection between schools and families. In one study of a thousand eighth-graders, the joint impact of family and classroom experiences on students' attitudes and achievement was examined as the students made the transition from the last year of middle school to the first year of high school (Epstein, 1983). Students who were given greater opportunities for communication and decision making, whether at home or in the classroom, showed more initiative and earned better grades.

In another mesosystem study, which targeted Latino and African American students in low-income areas, middle school and high school students participated in a program designed to connect their families, peers, schools, and parents' work (Cooper, 1995). The students commented that the outreach program helped them to bridge the gaps across their different social worlds. Many of the students saw their schools and neighborhoods as contexts in which people expected them to fail, become pregnant and leave school, or behave delinquently. The outreach program provided students with expectations and moral goals to do "something good for your people," such as working in the community and encouraging siblings to go to college.

The *exosystem* is at work when experiences in another setting (in which the student does not have an active role) influence what students and teachers experience in the immediate context. For example, consider the school and park supervisory boards in a community. They have strong roles in determining the quality of schools, parks, recreation facilities, and libraries. Their decisions can help or hinder a child's development.

The *macrosystem* involves the broader culture. *Culture* is a very broad term that includes the roles of ethnicity and socioeconomic factors in children's development. It's the most encompassing context in which students and teachers live, including the society's values and customs (Cole, 2006; Greenfield, Suzuki, & Rothstein-Finsch, 2006; Shweder & others, 2006). For example, some cultures (such as those of Islamic countries—for example, Egypt or Iran) emphasize traditional gender roles. Other cultures (such as found in the United States) accept more varied gender roles. In most Islamic countries, educational systems promote male dominance. In the United States, schools increasingly have endorsed the value of equal opportunities for females and males.

Socioeconomic status, an important aspect of culture, can have important effects on students' school performance. For example, poverty can overwhelm children's development and impair their ability to learn, although some children in impoverished circumstances are remarkably resilient (McLoyd, 2005; McLoyd, Aikens, &

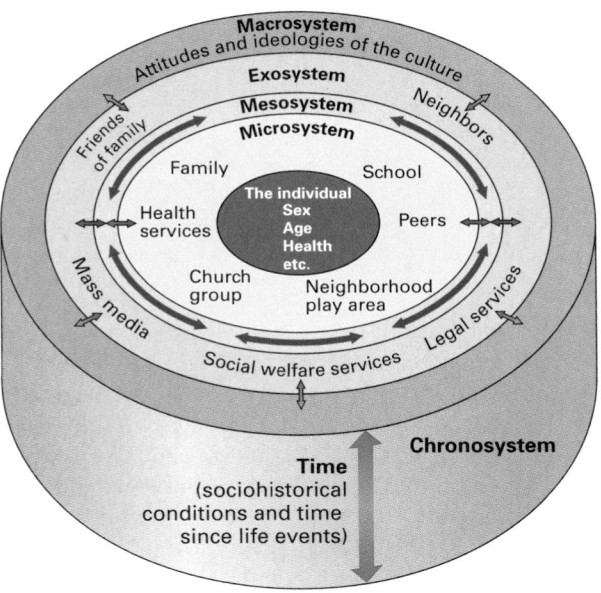

FIGURE 3.1 Bronfenbrenner's Ecological Theory of Development
Bronfenbrenner's ecological theory consists of five environmental systems: microsystem, mesosystem, exosystem, macrosystem, and chronosystem.

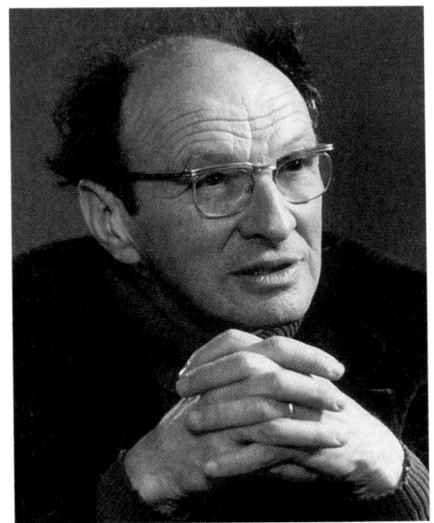

Urie Bronfenbrenner developed ecological theory, a perspective that is receiving increased attention. *What is the nature of ecological theory?*

ecological theory Bronfenbrenner's theory that consists of five environmental systems: microsystem, mesosystem, exosystem, macrosystem, and chronosystem.

BEST PRACTICES
Strategies for Educating Children Based on Bronfenbrenner's Theory

Think about the child as embedded in a number of environmental systems and influences. These include schools and teachers, parents and siblings, the community and neighborhood, peers and friends, the media, religion, and culture.

1. *Pay attention to the connection between schools and families.* Build these connections through formal and informal outreach.

2. *Recognize the importance of the community, socioeconomic status, and culture in the child's development.* These broader social contexts can have powerful influences on the child's development (Greenfield, Suzuki, & Rothstein-Fisch, 2006; Shweder & others, 2006; Shriaev & Levy, 2007). Next, Juanita Kirton, an assistant principal at the Gramercy School in New York City, describes the community's value for her students.

THROUGH THE EYES OF TEACHERS

The Community Is Full of Learning Opportunities and Supports for Students

Use of community supports is very important, and New York City is full of opportunities. For example, I have worked closely with the Disabled Library in our neighborhood. They have been great at supplying audiobooks for the children and lending the school special equipment. Also, the local fire department has been visited during numerous field trips—the firefighters have been especially attentive to the students because of their various disabilities. The fire department has also come to the school, which was very exciting for the children. It was amazing to see how patient the firefighters were with the students.

Many colleges and universities have contributed items and sent student teachers to visit the school. Donations from the Hasbro toy company during the holidays have made a big difference in in the way some students and families spent their holiday vacation. Our students are very visible in the New York City community, where we are located. This helps our neighbors get to know the staff and children and creates a safer environment.

Burton, 2006; Ryan, Fauth, & Brooks-Gunn, 2006). We will say much more about poverty and education in chapter 5, "Sociocultural Diversity."

The *chronosystem* includes the sociohistorical conditions of students' development. For example, the lives of children today are different in many ways from when their parents and grandparents were children. Today's children are more likely to be in child care, use computers, live in a divorced or remarried family, have less contact with relatives outside their immediate family, and grow up in new kinds of dispersed, deconcentrated cities that are not quite urban, rural, or suburban.

Evaluating Bronfenbrenner's Theory Bronfenbrenner's theory has gained popularity in recent years. It provides one of the few theoretical frameworks for systematically examining social contexts on both micro and macro levels, bridging the gap between behavioral theories that focus on small settings and anthropological theories that analyze larger settings. His theory has been instrumental in showing how different contexts of children's lives are interconnected. As we have just discussed, teachers often need to consider not just what goes on in the classroom but also what happens in students' families, neighborhoods, and peer groups.

Critics of Bronfenbrenner's theory say that it gives too little attention to biological and cognitive factors in children's development. They also point out that the theory does not address the step-by-step developmental changes that are the focus of theories such as Piaget's and Erikson's.

Erikson's Life-Span Development Theory

Complementing Bronfenbrenner's analysis of the social contexts in which children develop and the people who are important in their lives, the theory of Erik Erikson (1902–1994) presents a developmental view of people's lives in stages. Let's take Erikson's journey through the human life span.

Eight Stages of Human Development In Erikson's (1968) theory, eight stages of development unfold as people go through the human life span (see figure 3.2). Each stage consists of a developmental task that confronts individuals with a crisis. For Erikson, each crisis is not catastrophic but a turning point of increased vulnerability and enhanced potential. The more successfully an individual resolves each crisis, the more psychologically healthy the individual will be. Each stage has both positive and negative sides.

Trust versus mistrust is Erikson's first psychosocial stage. It occurs in the first year of life. The development of trust requires warm, nurturing caregiving. The positive outcome is a feeling of comfort and minimal fear. Mistrust develops when infants are treated too negatively or are ignored.

Autonomy versus shame and doubt is Erikson's second psychosocial stage. It occurs in late infancy and the toddler years. After gaining trust in their caregivers, infants begin to discover that their behavior is their own. They assert their independence and realize their will. If infants are restrained too much or punished too harshly, they develop a sense of shame and doubt.

Initiative versus guilt is Erikson's third psychosocial stage. It corresponds to early childhood, about 3 to 5 years of age. As young children experience a widening social world, they are challenged more than they were as infants. To cope with these challenges, they need to engage in active, purposeful behavior. In this stage, adults expect children to become more responsible and require them to assume some responsibilities for taking care of their bodies and belongings. Developing a sense of responsibility increases initiative. Children develop uncomfortable guilt feelings if they are irresponsible or are made to feel too anxious.

Industry versus inferiority is Erikson's fourth psychosocial stage. It corresponds approximately with the elementary school years, from 6 years of age until puberty or early adolescence. Children's initiative brings them into contact with a wealth of new experiences. As they move into the elementary school years, they direct their energy toward mastering knowledge and intellectual skills. At no time are children more enthusiastic about learning than at the end of early childhood, when their imagination is expansive. The danger in the elementary school years is developing a sense of inferiority, unproductiveness, and incompetence.

Identity versus identity confusion is Erikson's fifth psychosocial stage. It corresponds to the adolescent years. Adolescents try to find out who they are, what they are all about, and where they are going in life. They are confronted with many new roles and adult statuses (such as vocational and romantic). Adolescents need to be allowed to explore different paths to attain a healthy identity. If adolescents do not adequately explore different roles and don't carve out a positive future path, they can remain confused about their identity.

Intimacy versus isolation is Erikson's sixth psychosocial stage. It corresponds to the early adult years, the twenties and thirties. The developmental task is to form positive close relationships with others. Erikson describes intimacy as finding oneself but losing oneself in another person. The hazard of this stage is that one will fail to form an intimate relationship with a romantic partner or friend and become socially isolated. For such individuals, loneliness can become a dark cloud over their lives.

Generativity versus stagnation is Erikson's seventh psychosocial stage. It corresponds to the middle adulthood years, the forties and fifties. Generativity means transmitting something positive to the next generation. This can involve such roles as parenting and teaching, through which adults assist the next generation in developing useful lives. Erikson described stagnation as the feeling of having done nothing to help the next generation.

Integrity versus despair is Erikson's eighth and final psychosocial stage. It corresponds to the late adulthood years, the sixties until death. Older adults review their lives, reflecting on what they have done. If the retrospective evaluations are positive, they develop a sense of integrity. That is, they view their life as positively integrated and worth living. In contrast, older adults become despairing if their backward glances are mainly negative.

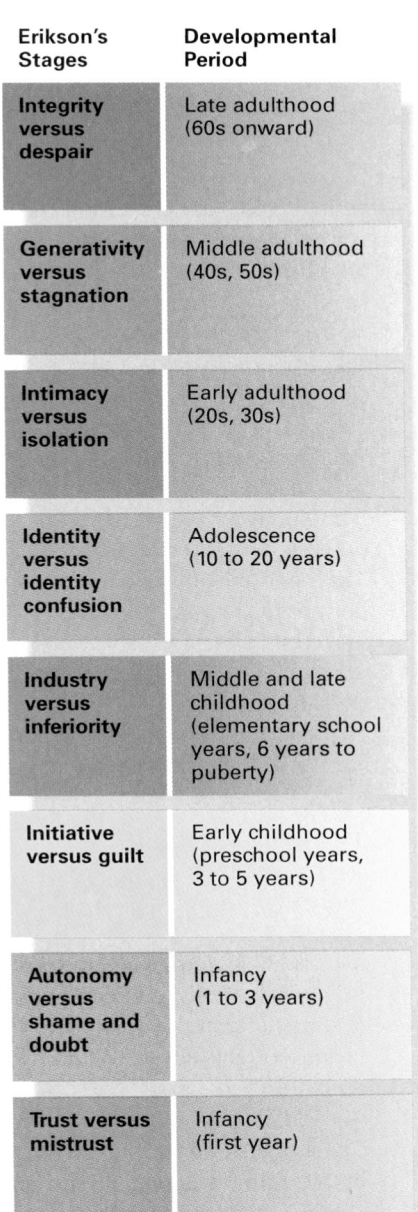

Erikson's Stages	Developmental Period
Integrity versus despair	Late adulthood (60s onward)
Generativity versus stagnation	Middle adulthood (40s, 50s)
Intimacy versus isolation	Early adulthood (20s, 30s)
Identity versus identity confusion	Adolescence (10 to 20 years)
Industry versus inferiority	Middle and late childhood (elementary school years, 6 years to puberty)
Initiative versus guilt	Early childhood (preschool years, 3 to 5 years)
Autonomy versus shame and doubt	Infancy (1 to 3 years)
Trust versus mistrust	Infancy (first year)

FIGURE 3.2 Erikson's Eight Life–Span Stages

BEST PRACTICES
Strategies for Educating Children Based on Erikson's Theory

1. *Encourage initiative in young children.* Children in pre-school and early childhood education programs should be given a great deal of freedom to explore their world. They should be allowed to choose some of the activities they engage in and given exciting materials to stimulate their imagination. Children at this stage love to play. It not only benefits their socioemotional development but also is an important medium for their cognitive growth. Especially encourage social play with peers and fantasy play. Help children assume responsibility for putting toys and materials back in place after they have used them. Children can be given a plant or flower to care for and be assisted in caring for it. Criticism should be kept to a minimum so that children will not develop high levels of guilt and anxiety. Young children are going to make lots of mistakes and have lots of spills. They need good models far more than harsh critics. Structure their activities and environment for successes rather than failures by giving them developmentally appropriate tasks. For example, don't frustrate young children by having them sit for long periods of time doing academic paper-and-pencil tasks.

2. *Promote industry in elementary school children.* Teachers have a special responsibility for children's development of industry. It was Erikson's hope that teachers could provide an atmosphere in which children become passionate about learning. In Erikson's words, teachers should mildly but firmly coerce children into the adventure of finding out that they can learn to accomplish things they never thought they could do. In elementary school, children thirst to know. Most arrive at elementary school steeped in curiosity and a motivation to master tasks. Challenge students, but don't overwhelm them. Be firm in requiring students to be productive, but don't be overly critical. Especially be tolerant of honest mistakes and make sure that every student has opportunities for many successes.

3. *Stimulate identity exploration in adolescence.* Recognize that the student's identity is multidimensional. Aspects include vocational goals; intellectual achievement; and interests in hobbies, sports, music, and other areas. Ask adolescents to write essays about such dimensions, exploring who they are and what they want to do with their lives. Encourage adolescents to think independently and to freely express their views. This stimulates self-exploration. Also encourage adolescents to listen to debates on religious, political, and ideolog-ical issues. This will stimulate them to examine different perspectives.

Encourage adolescents to talk with a school counselor about career options as well as other aspects of their identity. Have people from different careers come and talk with your students about their work regardless of the grade you teach. Next, Therese Olejniczak, a teacher at Central Middle School in East Grand Forks, Minnesota, describes how she encourages students to think about their identity on the first day of school.

THROUGH THE EYES OF TEACHERS
Using Art to Explore Adolescents' Identities

My seventh-grade art students come to class the first day to read a list of classroom rules. I surprise them by passing out sheets of art paper, old magazines, and glue with the verbal directions to tell me about themselves—build a self-portrait—with torn paper. The students are inventive, enthusiastic, and excited to focus on their identities, and waste no time beginning. . . . After the opening project, my students are at ease knowing their creative expression is allowed and encouraged, and I am better able to understand their many changing attitudes and need to express them.

4. *Examine your life as a teacher through the lens of Erikson's eight stages* (Gratz & Bouton, 1996). For example, you might be at the age at which Erikson says the most important issue is identity versus identity confusion or intimacy versus isolation. An important aspect of development for young adults is to have positive, close relationships with others. Your identity will benefit from having a positive relationship with a partner and with one or more friends. Erikson stressed that one of identity's most important dimensions is vocational. Your successful career as a teacher could be key in your overall identity. Many teachers develop strong camaraderie with other teachers or their mentors, which can be very rewarding.

5. *Benefit from the characteristics of some of Erikson's other stages.* Competent teachers trust, show initiative, are industrious and model a sense of mastery, and are motivated to contribute something meaningful to the next generation. In your role as a teacher, you will actively meet the criteria for Erikson's concept of generativity.

Evaluating Erikson's Theory   Erikson's theory captures some of life's key socio-emotional tasks and places them in a developmental framework. His concept of identity is especially helpful in understanding older adolescents and college students (Cote, 2006; Kroger, 2007). His overall theory was a critical force in forging our current view of human development as lifelong rather than being restricted only to childhood.

Erikson's theory is not without criticism. Some experts believe that his stages are too rigid. Bernice Neugarten (1988) says that identity, intimacy, independence, and many other aspects of socioemotional development are not like beads on a string that appear in neatly packaged age intervals. Rather, they are important issues throughout most of our lives. Although much research has been done on some of Erikson's stages (such as identity), the overall scope of his theory (such as whether the eight stages always occur in the order he proposed) has not been scientifically documented. For example, for some individuals (especially females), intimacy concerns precede identity or develop simultaneously.

Erik Erikson with his wife, Joan, an artist. Erikson generated one of the most important developmental theories of the twentieth century. *Which stage of Erikson's theory are you in? Does Erikson's description of this stage characterize you?*

Review, Reflect, and Practice

① **Describe two contemporary perspectives on socioemotional development: Bronfenbrenner's ecological theory and Erikson's life-span development theory.**

REVIEW

- What are Bronfenbrenner's five environmental systems?
- What Eriksonian stages does a person pass through between birth and the end of adolescence?

REFLECT

- How well do you think your own socioemotional development can be described using Erikson's theory?

PRAXIS™ PRACTICE

1. Which of the following is the best example of the mesosystem?
   a. Ike's parents monitor his behavior closely. They know where he is and with whom at all times.
   b. Ike's parents express concern about his grades. They attend parent-teacher conferences and belong to the PTA, as does John's teacher. They chaperone field trips.
   c. Ike attends church regularly, attends religious school each week, and is preparing for his confirmation.
   d. Ike is quite adept with technology. His parents often ask him to program their electronic devices, because of their lack of experience with these things when they were children.
2. Ms. Koslowsky teaches fourth grade. Understanding that it is important for her students to do well on the state-mandated achievement tests, she has high expectations for their daily work. Often her lessons frustrate some of her students because they don't understand the material. Rather than helping them to understand, she forges ahead. She is then frustrated by their performance on homework, often making caustic remarks on their papers. How would Ms. Koslowsky's teaching style be described from Erikson's perspective?
   a. Ms. Koslowsky's teaching style is closely aligned with the need to promote industry in elementary school children. Her high expectations will motivate the children to succeed.
   b. Ms. Koslowsky's teaching style is closely aligned with elementary-school-age children's need to discover who they are and establish an identity.

continued on page 76

c. Ms. Koslowsky's teaching style is unlikely to promote industry in elementary-school-age children. Instead, it is likely to make them feel inferior.

d. Ms. Koslowsky's teaching style is likely to increase students' initiative. They will respond to her high expectations by taking initiative in their work.

Please see the answer key at the end of the book.

2 SOCIAL CONTEXTS OF DEVELOPMENT

| Families | Peers | Schools |

In Bronfenbrenner's theory, the social contexts in which children live are important influences on their development. Let's explore three of the contexts in which children spend much of their time: families, peers, and schools.

Families

Children grow up in diverse families. Some parents nurture and support their children. Others treat them harshly or ignore them. Some children have experienced their parents' divorce. Others live their entire childhood in a never-divorced family. Others live in a stepfamily. Some children's mothers and fathers work full-time and place them in after-school programs; others have parents present when they come home from school. Some children grow up in an ethnically uniform neighborhood, others in a neighborhood that is more mixed. Some children's families live in poverty; others are economically advantaged. Some children have siblings; others don't. These varying circumstances affect children's development and influence students in and beyond the classroom (Luster & Okagaki, 2005; Parke & Buriel, 2006; Thompson, 2006).

Parenting Styles Is there a best way to parent? Diana Baumrind (1971, 1996), a leading authority on parenting, thinks so. She argues that parents should be neither punitive nor aloof. Rather, they should develop rules for children, while being supportive and nurturing. Hundreds of research studies, including her own, support her view (Collins & Steinberg, 2006). Baumrind says that parenting styles come in four main forms:

- **Authoritarian parenting** is restrictive and punitive. Authoritarian parents exhort children to follow their directions and respect them. They place firm limits and controls on their children and allow little verbal exchange. For example, an authoritarian parent might say, "Do it my way or else. There will be no discussion!" Children of authoritarian parents often behave in socially incompetent ways. They tend to be anxious about social comparison, fail to initiate activity, and have poor communication skills.

- **Authoritative parenting** encourages children to be independent but still places limits and controls on their actions. Extensive verbal give-and-take is allowed and parents are nurturant and supportive. An authoritative parent might put his or her arm on the child's shoulder in a comforting way and say, "You know you should not have done that. Let's talk about how you can handle the situation differently the next time." Children whose parents are authoritative often behave in socially competent ways. They tend to be self-reliant, delay gratification, get along with their peers, and show high self-esteem. Because of these positive outcomes, Baumrind strongly endorses authoritative parenting.

authoritarian parenting A restrictive and punitive parenting style in which there is little verbal exchange between parents and children; associated with children's social incompetence.

authoritative parenting A positive parenting style that encourages children to be independent but still places limits and controls on their actions; extensive verbal give-and-take is allowed; associated with children's social competence.

How does Ruth Chao describe the parenting style of Asian American parents?

- **Neglectful parenting** is a parenting style in which parents are uninvolved in their children's lives. When their offspring are adolescents or perhaps even young children, these parents cannot answer the question "It is 10 P.M. Do you know where your child is?" Children of neglectful parents develop the sense that other aspects of their parents' lives are more important than they are. Children of neglectful parents often behave in socially incompetent ways. They tend to have poor self-control, don't handle independence well, and aren't achievement motivated.

- **Indulgent parenting** is a parenting style in which parents are highly involved with their children but place few limits or restrictions on their behaviors. These parents often let their children do what they want and get their way because they believe the combination of nurturant support and lack of restraints will produce a creative, confident child. The result is that these children usually don't learn to control their own behavior. These parents do not take into account the development of the whole child.

Do the benefits of authoritative parenting transcend the boundaries of ethnicity, socioeconomic status, and household composition? Although some exceptions have been found, evidence links authoritative parenting with competence on the part of the child in research across a wide range of ethnic groups, social strata, cultures, and family structures (Collins & Steinberg, 2006; Steinberg, Blatt-Eisengart, & Cauffman, 2006).

Nonetheless, researchers have found that in some ethnic groups, aspects of the authoritarian style may be associated with more positive child outcomes than Baumrind predicts. Elements of the authoritarian style may take on different meanings and have different effects depending on the context.

For example, Asian American parents often continue aspects of traditional Asian child-rearing practices sometimes described as authoritarian. Many Asian American parents exert considerable control over their children's lives. However, Ruth Chao (2001, 2005; Chao & Tseng, 2002) argues that the style of parenting used by many Asian American parents is distinct from the domineering control of the authoritarian style. Instead, Chao argues that the control reflects concern and involvement in children's lives and is best conceptualized as a type of training. The high academic achievement of Asian American children may be a consequence of the "training" provided by their parents (Stevenson & Zusho, 2002).

neglectful parenting A parenting style of uninvolvement in which parents spend little time with their children; associated with children's social incompetence.

indulgent parenting A parenting style of involvement but few limits or restrictions on children's behavior; linked with children's social incompetence.

FIGURE 3.3 Single-Parent Families in Various Countries

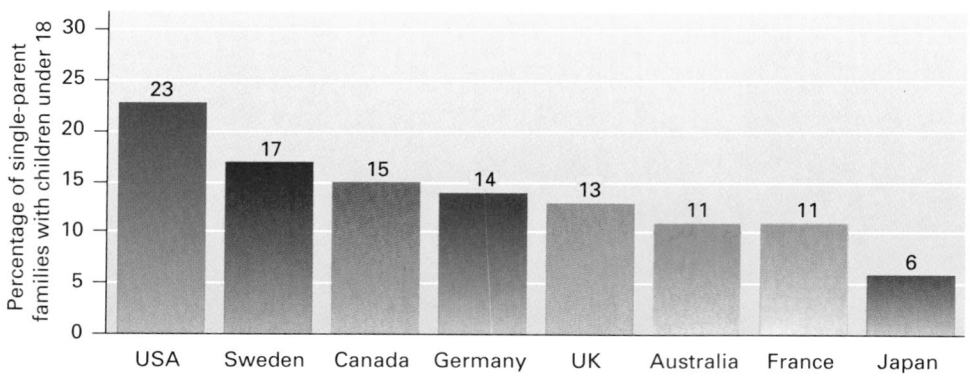

An emphasis on requiring respect and obedience is also associated with the authoritarian style. However, in many African American and Latino families, especially in low-income, dangerous neighborhoods, this type of child rearing may have positive outcomes. In these contexts, requiring obedience to parental authority may be an adaptive strategy to keep children from engaging in antisocial behavior that can have serious consequences for the victim or the perpetrator (Harrison-Hale, McLoyd, & Smedley, 2004; McLoyd, Aikens, & Burton, 2006).

The Changing Family in a Changing Society Increasing numbers of children are being raised in divorced families, stepparent families, and families in which both parents work outside the home. As divorce has become epidemic, a staggering number of children have been growing up in single-parent families. The United States has a higher percentage of single-parent families than virtually any other industrialized country (see figure 3.3). Today, about one in every four children in the United States have lived a portion of their lives in a stepfamily by age 18. Also, more than two of every three mothers with a child from 6 to 17 years of age are in the labor force.

Children of Divorce The effects of divorce on children are complex, depending on such factors as the child's age, the child's strengths and weaknesses at the time of the divorce, the type of custody, socioeconomic status, and postdivorce family functioning (Lansford & others, 2006). The use of support systems (relatives, friends, housekeepers), an ongoing positive relationship between the custodial parent and the ex-spouse, the ability to meet financial needs, and quality schooling help children adjust to the stressful circumstances of divorce (Huurre, Junkkari, & Aro, 2006).

E. Mavis Hetherington's (1995, 2000, 2005; Hetherington & Kelly, 2002; Hetherington & Stanley-Hagan, 2002) research documents the importance of schools when children grow up in a divorced family. Throughout elementary school, children in divorced families had the highest achievement and fewest problems when both the parenting environment and the school environment were authoritative (according to Baumrind's categorization). In the divorced families, when only one parent was authoritative, an authoritative school improved the child's adjustment. The most negative parenting environment occurred when neither parent was authoritative. The most negative school environment was chaotic and neglecting.

In response to the high divorce rate, the state of Florida passed a law requiring that all high school students be taught marital and relationship skills (Peterson, 1998). Many schools teach some form of family life course, but marriage and family experts believe such courses need upgrading to include the latest research on communication skills, the factors most likely to cause divorce, strategies for conflict resolution, and family problem-solving techniques (Gottman, 1996).

Let's look at a child in the midst of a family situation in which parents are getting divorced (Brodkin & Coleman, 1995). Maggie is a 10-year-old fifth-grader who had been a happy child and had done well in school, but all of that changed when her parents recently separated. Her father moved out and Maggie's mother became depressed. Maggie began to not show up for school. Now, although she is at school regularly, she has trouble concentrating on her schoolwork.

How might you as a teacher help Maggie? Some strategies follow:

1. *Reach out to the parents.* Call Maggie's mother instead of waiting to see if things get better on their own.

2. *Recommend professional help.* Tell the parent(s) that many people going through a divorce—including parents and children—benefit from professional counseling. In some school districts, there are regular meetings for children of divorce or divorced parents, led by a mental health professional or a teacher with special training.

3. *Support the child.* The daily caring you give children like Maggie can make a difference in their ability to cope with the divorce and concentrate on their schoolwork.

4. *Recommend a good book related to divorce.* Here are three excellent books on divorce (Norcross & others, 2003):
   - For children 3 to about 8 years old: Brown and Brown (1988), *Dinosaurs Divorce*
   - For older children and adolescents: Gardner (1985), *The Boys and Girls Book About Divorce*
   - For parents: Hetherington and Kelly (2002), *Divorce Reconsidered,* and Kalter (1990), *Growing Up with Divorce*

Ethnic and Socioeconomic Variations in Families   Earlier, we described variations in parenting styles of African American, Latino, and Asian American families. Families in different ethnic groups also vary in their size, structure, and composition; their reliance on kinship networks; and their levels of income and education (Parke & Buriel, 2006; Ramsay, 2006; Trask & Hamon, 2007). Large and extended families are more common among some minority groups than among the general population (McAdoo, 2002). For example, 19 percent of Latino families have three or more children, compared with 14 percent of African American and 10 percent of non-Latino White families. African American and Latino children interact more with grandparents, aunts, uncles, cousins, and more-distant relatives than do non-Latino White children (Gonzales & others, 2004).

Single-parent families are more common among African Americans and Latinos than among non-Latino White Americans. Single parents often have less time, money, and energy than do two-parent households. Ethnic minority parents are less educated and more likely to be low-income than their White counterparts (Harwood & others, 2002). Still, many impoverished ethnic minority families manage to find ways to raise competent children (McLoyd, Aikens, & Burton, 2006; Tucker, Subramanian, & James, 2004).

Some aspects of home life can help to protect ethnic minority children from injustice. The community and the family can filter out destructive racist messages, and parents can present alternative frames of reference to counter negative messages. The extended family also can serve as an important buffer to stress.

In the United States and most other Western cultures, child-rearing practices differ among different socioeconomic status (SES) groups (*SES* refers to a grouping of people with similar occupational, educational, and economic characteristics). Low-income parents often place a high value on external characteristics such as obedience and neatness. In contrast, middle-SES families frequently place a high value on internal characteristics such as self-control and delay of gratification. Middle-SES parents are more likely to explain, praise, accompany their discipline with reasoning, and ask their children questions. Low-income parents are more likely to use physical punishment and criticize their children (McLoyd, Aikens, & Burton, 2006).

There also are socioeconomic differences in the way that parents think about education (Hoff, Laursen, & Tardif, 2002). Middle-SES parents more often think of

DIVERSITY AND EDUCATION
Are America's Schools Leaving Latinas Behind?

The high school graduation rate of Latinas is lower than for girls in any other ethnic group, and they are the least likely to go to college (National Center for Education Statistics, 2001). Findings like these prompted a recent report by the American Association of University Women, which concluded that U.S. schools are not meeting Latinas' educational needs (Ginorio & Huston, 2000). The report found that although Latinas bring many strengths and personal resources to school, for them to be successful schools need to view bilingualism and other values as assets rather than liabilities.

What educational challenges do Latinas face?

Despite the importance of education to the Latino community, family needs and peer pressure often clash with Latinas' school expectations. For example, many Latinas face pressure about going to college from boyfriends and fiancés who expect their girlfriends or future wives to not be "too educated."

Contrary to stereotypes about Latino communities, most Latino parents hope that their children will excel in school. However, many Latino families face economic and social problems that defer the realization of those dreams for their children (Rodriguez-Galindo, 2006).

Latino girls and boys face similar educational challenges and experience stereotyping and other obstacles that discourage their success in school. Some obstacles, though, are different for Latinas than Latinos (DeMirjyn, 2006; Lara, 2006). Latinas are three times as likely to fear for their personal safety in schools as other girls, and too often Latinos are assumed to be gang members by teachers and counselors simply because they speak Spanish (Ginorio & Huston, 2000).

Recommendations for improving the education of Latinas and Latinos include the following:

- *All adults need to encourage academic success.* Latinas and Latinos need to hear from all the adults in their lives that college and professional careers are rewarding options and ones that they can achieve.
- *Involve the whole family in the process of college preparation.* Teachers and counselors need to work with Latino families to demystify college requirements and the long-term benefits of college.
- *Deal meaningfully with stereotypes and challenges such as adolescent pregnancy that impact school performance.* This includes offering child care and alternative scheduling and recognizing that being a young mother and completing one's education are not incompatible.

education as something that should be mutually encouraged by parents and teachers. Low-income parents are more likely to view education as the teacher's job.

In the Diversity and Education interlude, we will explore educational concerns about America's fastest-growing female minority population—Latinas.

School–Family Linkages In Bronfenbrenner's theory, linkages between the family and the school are an important mesosystem (Fiese, Eckert, & Spagnola, 2006). Also, in Hetherington's study, which we just discussed, an authoritative school environment benefited children from divorced families. Two aspects of family/school linkages are family management and parental involvement, which we discuss next.

Family Management   Researchers have found that family management practices are positively related to students' grades and self-responsibility, and negatively to school-related problems (Taylor, 1996). One of the most important practices in this regard is maintaining a structured and organized family environment, such as establishing routines for homework, chores, bedtime, and so on. Creating a family environment in which high expectations for achievement are present is also important (Jeynes, 2003).

One recent study focused on African American families, examining links between mothers' reports of family management practices, including routine and achievement expectations, and adolescents' school-related behavior (Taylor & Lopez, 2005). Family routine (well managed and organized) was positively related to adolescents' school achievement, paying attention in class, and attendance, and negatively linked to school-related problems. Compared with the students whose mothers had low expectations for achievement, students whose mothers had high expectations made better grades and had more consistent school attendance.

Parental Involvement and School-Family-Community Connections   Experienced teachers know the importance of getting parents involved in children's education. In one survey, teachers listed parental involvement as the number one priority in improving education (Chira, 1993). However, schools often don't set goals or implement effective programs to make that involvement occur (Epstein, 2001).

All parents, even those with considerable education, need yearly guidance from teachers in how to remain productively involved in their children's education. For one thing, education expert Joyce Epstein (2001, 2005; Epstein & Sheldon, 2006) explains that almost all parents want their children to succeed in school, but need clear and useful information from their children's teachers and from other school and district leaders in order to help their children develop their full potential. For example, sometimes parents ask their child, "How was school today?" We know that may end with the child responding, "Fine" or "Okay" and not much more. Parents should be guided, instead, to ask their child, "Would you read to me something you wrote today?" or "Could you show me something you learned in math today?" or similar direct questions about work and projects in other content areas. Conversations or homework assignments that enable students to share ideas and celebrate successes are likely to promote positive school-related parent-child interactions.

A low level of parental involvement concerns educators because it is linked with students' low achievement (Anguiano, 2004; Myers-Walls & Frias, 2007). By contrast, in a study of more than 16,000 students, the students were more likely to get *A*s and less likely to repeat a grade or be expelled if both parents were highly involved in their schooling (National Center for Education Statistics, 1997). In this study, high involvement was defined as the parent participating in three or four of the following: school meetings, a teacher conference, a class meeting, or volunteering. Other studies have found that students' grades and academic achievement are linked to parental involvement (Carpenter-Aeby & Aeby, 2001; Epstein, 2005; Sheldon & Epstein, 2005; Simon, 2004).

One problem that can interfere with building partnerships between school and family is negative perceptions of families (Workman & Gage, 1997). Some children come to school poorly clothed, on drugs, with knives or guns, and without their homework. They might not be motivated to learn and might show little respect for the teacher. In such circumstances, it can be hard to get past blaming parents for the problems that children present to the teacher. However, to get parents more positively involved in their children's education, you have to get past the blaming. Think of parents as having potential strengths that, if tapped, can help you educate the child more effectively (Hiatt-Michael, 2001).

Consider the following example of a successful partnership between schools and families. In Lima, Ohio, the goal is for each school to establish a personal relationship with every parent. At an initial parent-teacher conference, parents are given a packet

TECHNOLOGY AND EDUCATION
Communicating with Parents about Television and Children's Development

Many children spend more time in front of the television set than they do with their parents. U.S. 8- to 14-year-olds average more than 21 hours a week watching television (Comstock & Scharrer, 2006; Roberts, Henriksen, & Foehr, 2004). Amazingly, the 20,000 hours of television, on average, that children watch by the time they graduate from high school represents more hours than they have spent in the classroom!

The more children watch TV, the lower their school achievement (Comstock & Scharrer, 2006). Why might watching TV be negatively related to children's achievement? Three possibilities are interference, displacement, and self-defeating tastes/preferences. In terms of interference, having a TV on can distract children while they are doing cognitive tasks such as homework. In terms of displacement, TV can take time away from engaging in achievement-related tasks, such as homework, reading, writing, and mathematics. Researchers have found that children's reading achievement is negatively linked to the amount of time they watch TV (Comstock & Scharrer, 2006). In terms of self-defeating tastes and preferences, TV attracts children to entertainment, sports, commercials, and other activities that capture their interest more than school achievement. Children who are heavy TV watchers tend to view books as dull and boring (Comstock & Scharrer, 2006).

Here are some recommendations that you can communicate to parents about reducing TV's negative impact and increasing its positive impact on their children's development (Singer & Singer, 1987):

- Monitor children's viewing habits and plan what they will watch, instead of letting them view TV randomly. Be active with young children between planned programs.
- Look for children's programs that feature children in the child's age group.
- Make sure that television is not a substitute for other activities.
- Develop discussions about sensitive television themes with children. Give them the opportunity to ask questions about the programs.
- Balance reading and television activities. Children can "follow up" on interesting television programs by checking out the library books from which some programs have been adapted and by pursuing additional stories by the authors of those books.
- Point out positive examples of females performing competently both in professions and at home, and positive examples that show how various ethnic and cultural groups contribute to a better society.

that discusses how they can participate in the child's learning activities at home. Conferences, regular phone calls, and home visits strengthen the school-family connection. These make other kinds of communication (such as progress reports, report cards, activity calendars, or discussion of problems that arise during the year) more welcome and successful. For more about effective communication with parents, see the Technology and Education box.

For ways to develop effective school-family-community partnerships and programs, see the Web site of the National Network of Partnership Schools at Johns Hopkins University (NNPS): www.partnershipschool.org Especially look at the section titled "In the Spotlight."

Out-of-School Care   In addition to actively participating in their children's schooling, children benefit when parents arrange and monitor out-of-school care (Coley, Morris, & Hernandez, 2004). The increase in single-parent families and families in which both parents work outside the home has made out-of-school child care a more important aspect of children's development.

Too many U.S. children are largely unsupervised for 2 to 4 hours a day during each school week. During the summer months, they might be unsupervised for entire days, five days a week. These children easily can find their way into trouble, possibly stealing, vandalizing, or abusing a sibling. In one study of children in the after-school hours, unsupervised peer contact, lack of neighborhood safety, and low monitoring were linked with externalizing problems such as acting out problems and delinquency (Pettit & others, 1999).

One study examined whether out-of-school care was linked with children's academic achievement toward the end of the first grade. Five types of out-of-school care were studied: before- and after-school programs, extracurricular activities, father care,

BEST PRACTICES
Strategies for Forging School–Family–Community Linkages

Joan Epstein (2001, 2005; Epstein & Sheldon, 2006) developed an integrated theory of school, family, and community partnerships that helps to explain children's learning and development. Drawing on Bronfenbrenner's theory, her *overlapping spheres of influence theory* helps educators zero in on the three main contexts that influence students' school success—home, school, and community. Epstein describes interactions that include both macro school-level actions (such as a Back-to-School Night for all educators and families) and micro individual actions (such as parent-teacher conferences for one parent and teacher).

Epstein (1996, 2001, 2005; Epstein & Sanders, 2002; Epstein & Sheldon, 2006; Epstein & others, 2002) has developed six types of involvement that can be implemented to develop comprehensive school, family, and community partnerships in any elementary, middle, or high school. These goal-oriented and age-appropriate activities include the following:

1. *Provide assistance to families.* Assist schools in understanding families' backgrounds, cultures, and goals for children. Schools can provide parents with information about child-rearing skills, the importance of family support, child and adolescent development, and home contexts that enhance learning at each grade level. Teachers are an important contact point between schools and families and can become aware of whether the family is meeting the child's basic physical and health needs. Next, Juanita Kirton, who earlier described the importance of involving the community in children's education, talks about the importance of involving parents in children's schooling.

THROUGH THE EYES OF TEACHERS
Connecting with Parents

Parents are the primary ingredient of the classroom team at the Gramercy School. Many parents of preschool children have no idea as to how or if their child will develop. It becomes the job of educators and other professionals to assist parents in their child's development. We then become partners. We have ongoing parent training groups, support groups, and parents can spend time in school with a therapist at any time. Gramercy School has an open-door policy. . . . When a family faces a very challenging situation, I might meet with them or I might call in the psychologist to assist with specific issues. We have on occasion asked parents to assist other parents or to be a resource for others. This is powerful and gives support to families.

2. *Communicate effectively with families about school programs and their child's progress.* This involves both school-to-home and home-to-school communication. Encourage parents to attend parent-teacher conferences and other school functions. Their attendance conveys to their children that they are interested in their school performance. Set up times for parent meetings that are convenient for them to attend. Most parents cannot come to meetings during the school day because of other obligations. One option is "work nights" for parents and children to come to school and work on various projects to improve the school's physical appearance, mount artwork, and so on. Also, work on developing activities in which parents can get to know each other, not just know the teacher.

Here are some specific strategies for improving communication (Rosenthal & Sawyers, 1997):

- Invite parents to meet you before the school year begins at an orientation, or invite parents to a potluck dinner.
- Send home children's work each week accompanied by a note or a letter written in the parents' primary language. The letter might review the week's activities and include suggestions for helping children with their homework.
- In schools with computerized telephone systems, record messages about study units and homework assignments so that parents can call at their convenience. In McAllen, Texas, the school district has developed a community partnership with local radio stations. The district sponsors "Discusiones Escolares," a weekly program in Spanish that encourages parents to become more involved in their children's education. Parents can check out copies of the script or a cassette tape of each program from the parent coordinators at their schools.
- Use PTA/PTO meetings effectively. Sometimes the parent-teacher conference is the only contact teachers have with parents. Schedule the first conference in the first two weeks of school so that parents can raise concerns, ask questions, and make suggestions. This can avoid potential problems from the outset. At this first meeting, try to find out about the family's structure (intact, divorced, stepfamily), rules, roles, and learning style. Practice active listening skills and say something positive about their child to establish yourself as someone who can be approached.
- Another way of making a school family-friendly is to create a parent room or parent center at the school (Johnson, 1994). Here parents can help each other, help the school, and receive information or assistance from the school or community.

continued on page 84

BEST PRACTICES *continued*
Strategies for Forging School–Family–Community Linkages

3. *Encourage parents to be volunteers.* Improve training, work, and schedules to involve parents as volunteers at school and to increase attendance at school meetings. Try to match the skills of volunteers to classroom needs. Remember from the opening teaching story in chapter 2 that in some schools parents are extensively involved in educational planning and assisting teachers. Parents have different talents and abilities, just like children, which is reflected in the following comments by Heather Zoldak, a teacher at Ridge Wood Elementary School in Michigan.

THROUGH THE EYES OF TEACHERS
Encouraging Parent Involvement

Understanding that parents come with different levels of comfort with the school environment is important when encouraging parent support for the classroom. Prepare a variety of opportunities for parents to become involved both inside the classroom and to support the classroom in other ways. Due to busy schedules, work restrictions, or comfort level based on their own experiences with school, some parents may be more involved if they can help outside the classroom on field trips or even prepare items at home for an upcoming project. Taking steps to build the comfort level and relationship with parents is a key factor in encouraging parents to be volunteers.

4. *Involve families with their children in learning activities at home.* This includes homework and other curriculum-linked activities and decisions. Parents want to know how to help their children at home and guide them in becoming motivated to do their best work. Epstein (1998) coined the term *interactive homework* and designed a program that encourages students to go to their parents for help. In one elementary school that uses Epstein's approach, a weekly teacher's letter informs parents about the objective of each

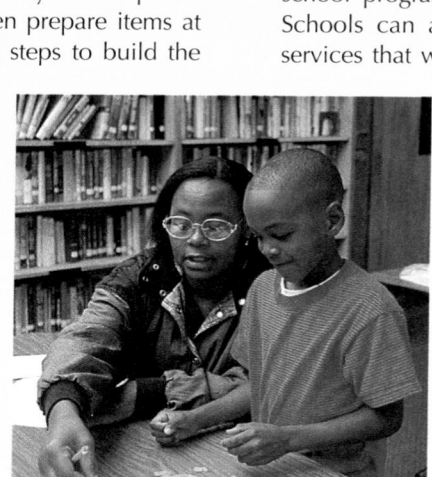

This mother is working with her son at a Saturday math workshop in Oakland, California, sponsored by Family Math.

assignment, gives directions, and asks for comments. One interactive homework assignment in language arts encourages students to interview a parent about hairstyles popular when the parent was the student's age. After the interview, the student draws a picture of what the hairstyle looked like and writes a paragraph on "Hairstyles Then and Now." You can see this and other examples of interactive homework in language arts, math, and science on the Web site www.partnershipschool.org in the section on Teachers Involve Parents in Schoolwork (TIPS).

5. *Include families as participants in school decisions.* Parents can be invited to be on PTA/PTO boards, various committees, councils, and other parent organizations. At Antwa Elementary School in a rural area of Wisconsin, potluck supper parent-teacher organization meetings involve discussions with parents about school and district educational goals, age-appropriate learning, child discipline, and testing performance.

6. *Coordinate community collaboration.* Help interconnect the work and resources of community businesses, agencies, colleges and universities, and other groups to strengthen school programs, family practices, and student learning. Schools can alert families to community programs and services that will benefit them.

Enable students, staff, and families to contribute their service to the community. An example of coordinating community collaboration is First Thursdays at the Baltimore Museum of Art and Lockerman-Bundy Elementary School in Baltimore. On one First Thursday, the school provided a hot dog dinner for 247 students and their families before boarding buses to the museum for an evening that focused on "Portraits in Paris."

According to Epstein (2005), schools can choose from hundreds of practices to represent the six types of involvement. Family and community activities can be designed and implemented for each type of involvement to help students reach specific school goals.

and nonadult care—usually an older sibling (NICHD Early Child Care Research Network, 2004). "Children who consistently participated in extracurricular activities during kindergarten and first grade obtained higher standardized math test scores than children who did not consistently participate in these activities. . . . Participation in other types of out-of-school care was not related to child functioning in the first grade" (p. 280). Note, though, that these results may reflect the influence of other factors. For example, parents who enroll their children in extracurricular activities may be more achievement-oriented and have higher achievement expectations for their children than parents who don't place their children in these activities.

After-school programs can make a difference in children's lives (Barnett & Gareis, 2006; Morris & Kalil, 2006. A recent study found that low-income parents were especially dissatisfied with the quality of options available in after-school programs (The Wallace Foundation, 2004). Researchers and policymakers recommend that after-school programs have warm and supportive staff, a flexible and relaxed schedule, multiple activities, and opportunities for positive interactions with staff and peers (Vandell & Pierce, 2002).

Children spend considerable time with peers and friends. *What peer statuses can children have? How do peer relations change developmentally?*

Peers

In addition to families and teachers, peers also play powerful roles in children's development. Just what are peers?

In the context of child development, *peers* are children of about the same age or maturity level. Same-age peer interaction plays a unique role in children's socioemotional development. One of the most important functions of the peer group is to provide a source of information and comparison about the world outside of the family.

Good peer relations might be necessary for normal development (Howes & Tonyan, 2000; Rubin, Bukowski, & Parker, 2006). Social isolation, or the inability to "plug in" to a social network, is linked with many problems and disorders, ranging from delinquency and problem drinking to depression (Kupersmidt & Coie, 1990). In one study, poor peer relations in childhood were associated with dropping out of school and delinquent behavior in adolescence (Roff, Sells, & Golden, 1972). In another study, harmonious peer relations in adolescence were related to positive mental health at midlife (Hightower, 1990).

Peer relations may influence whether children and adolescents develop problems. (Bukowski & Adams, 2005; Collins & Steinberg, 2006; Ladd, Herald, & Andrews, 2006; Masten, 2005). In one study of more than 3,000 eleventh-grade students, peer pressure was strongly linked to alcohol use (Borden, Donnermeyer, & Scheer, 2001). In another study, associating with certain crowds in the tenth grade ("jocks" and "criminals") was linked with being in a substance-abuse program in the early twenties (Barber, Eccles, & Stone, 2001).

Peer Statuses   Developmentalists have pinpointed five types of peer status: popular children, average children, neglected children, rejected children, and controversial children (Rubin, Bukowski, & Parker, 2006; Wentzel & Battle, 2001).

Many children worry about whether or not they are popular. *Popular children* are frequently nominated as a best friend and are rarely disliked by their peers. Popular children give out reinforcements, listen carefully, maintain open lines of communication with peers, are happy, act like themselves, show enthusiasm and concern for others, and are self-confident without being conceited (Hartup, 1983).

Neglected children are infrequently nominated as a best friend but are not disliked by their peers. *Rejected children* are infrequently nominated as someone's best friend and are often actively disliked by their peers. *Controversial children* are frequently nominated both as someone's best friend and as being disliked.

Rejected children often have more serious adjustment problems than do neglected children (Coie, 2004; Ladd, Buhs, & Troop, 2004). In one study, more than a hundred fifth-grade boys were evaluated over a period of 7 years until the end of high school (Kupersmidt & Coie, 1990). The most important factor in predicting whether rejected children would engage in delinquent behavior or drop out of secondary school was aggression toward peers in elementary school. Aggression, impulsiveness, and disruptiveness characterize the majority of rejected children, although 10 to 20 percent of rejected children are actually shy. One recent social-skills intervention program was successful in increasing social acceptance and self-esteem and decreasing depression and anxiety in peer-rejected children (DeRosier, & Marcus, 2005). Students participated in the program once a week (50 to 60 minutes) for 8 weeks. The program included instruction in how to manage emotions, how to improve prosocial skills, how to become better communicators, and how to compromise and negotiate.

A special peer relations problem involves bullying. We will discuss bullying in chapter 14, "Managing the Classroom," where we will provide strategies for dealing with bullies.

Friendship The importance of friendship was recently underscored in a 2-year longitudinal study (Wentzel, Bary, & Caldwell, 2004). Sixth-grade students who did not have a friend engaged in less prosocial behavior (cooperation, sharing, helping others), had lower grades, and were more emotionally distressed (depression, low well-being) than their counterparts with one or more friends. Two years later, in the eighth grade, the students who did not have a friend in the sixth grade were still more emotionally distressed. Why are friendships so significant?

Friendships contribute to peer status and provide other benefits (Parker & Asher, 1987:

- *Companionship.* Friendship gives children a familiar partner, someone who is willing to spend time with them and join in collaborative activities.
- *Physical support.* Friendship provides resources and assistance in times of need.
- *Ego support.* Friendship helps children feel they are competent, worthy individuals. Especially important in this regard is social approval from friends.
- *Intimacy/affection.* Friendship provides children with a warm, trusting, close relationship with others. In this relationship, children often feel comfortable about disclosing private, personal information.

Having friends can be a developmental advantage, but keep in mind that friendships are not all alike (Gest, Graham-Bermann, & Hartup, 2001; Rubin, Bukowski, & Parker, 2006). Having friends who are socially skilled and supportive is a developmental advantage. However, it is not developmentally advantageous to have coercive and conflict-ridden friendships. And it sometimes is disadvantageous to a child or an adolescent to be friends with someone who is several years older. Students with older friends engage in more deviant behaviors than their counterparts who have same-age friends (Berndt, 1999). Early-maturing adolescents are especially vulnerable in this regard (Magnusson, 1988).

Developmental Changes in Peer Relations During the elementary school years, children's peer groups increasingly consist of same-sex peers (Maccoby, 1998,

THROUGH THE EYES OF STUDENTS

We Defined Each Other with Adjectives

"I was funky. Dana was sophisticated. Liz was crazy. We walked to school together, went for bike rides, cut school, got stoned, talked on the phone, smoked cigarettes, slept over, discussed boys and sex, went to church together, and got angry at each other. We defined each other with adjectives and each other's presence. As high school friends, we simultaneously resisted and anticipated adulthood and womanhood. . . .

"What was possible when I was 15 and 16? We still had to tell out parents where we were going! We wanted to do excitedly forbidden activities like going out to dance clubs and drinking whiskey sours. Liz, Dana, and I wanted to do these forbidden things in order to feel: to have intense emotional and sensual experiences that removed us from the suburban sameness we shared with each other and everyone else we knew. We were tired of the repetitive experiences that our town, our siblings, our parents, and our school offered to us. . . .

"The friendship between Dana, Liz, and myself was born out of another emotional need: the need for trust. The three of us had reached a point in our lives when we realized how unstable relationships can be, and we all craved safety and acceptance. Friendships all around us were often uncertain. We wanted and needed to be able to like and trust each other." (Garrod & others, 1992, pp. 199–200)

BEST PRACTICES
Strategies for Improving Children's Social Skills

In every class you teach, some children will likely have weak social skills. One or two might be rejected children. Several others might be neglected. Are there things you can do to help these children improve their social skills? As you think about this, keep in mind that improving social skills is easier when children are 10 years of age or younger (Malik & Furman, 1993). In adolescence, peer reputations become more fixed as crowds and peer groups take on more importance. Here are some good strategies for improving children's social skills:

1. *Help rejected children learn to listen to peers and "hear what they say" instead of trying to dominate peers.* In one study, socially rejected young adolescents were coached on the importance of showing behaviors (such as having better empathy, listening carefully, and improving communication skills) that would improve their chance of being liked by others (Murphy & Schneider, 1994). The intervention helped the rejected youth develop better friendships.

2. *Help neglected children attract attention from peers in positive ways and hold their attention.* They can do this by asking questions, listening in a warm and friendly way, and saying things about themselves that relate to the peers' interests. Also work with neglected children on entering groups more effectively.

3. *Provide children low in social skills with knowledge about how to improve these skills.* In one study of sixth- and seventh-graders, knowledge of both appropriate and inappropriate strategies for making friends was related positively to peer acceptance (Wentzel & Erdley, 1993). Knowledge of appropriate strategies included knowing:
   - How to initiate interaction, such as asking someone about his or her favorite activities and asking the other child to do things together
   - That it is important to be nice, kind, and considerate
   - That it is necessary to show respect for others by being courteous and listening to what others have to say

   Knowledge of inappropriate strategies includes knowing:
   - That it is not a good idea to be aggressive, show disrespect, be inconsiderate, hurt others' feelings, gossip, spread rumors, embarrass others, or criticize others
   - Not to present yourself negatively, be self-centered, care only about yourself, or be jealous, grouchy, or angry all the time
   - Not to engage in antisocial behavior, such as fighting, yelling at others, picking on others, making fun of others, being dishonest, breaking school rules, or taking drugs

4. *Read and discuss appropriate books on peer relations with students and devise supportive games and activities.* Include these as thematic units in your curriculum for young children. Make books on peer relations and friendship available to older children and adolescents.

2002; Rubin, Bukowski, & Parker, 2006). After extensive observations of elementary school playgrounds, two researchers characterized the settings as "gender school" (Luria & Herzog, 1985). They said that boys teach one another the required masculine behavior and strictly reinforce it, and girls often pass on the female culture and mainly congregate with each other.

In early adolescence, participation in mixed-sex groups increases. Also in adolescence, many students become members of crowds, and allegiance to the crowd can exert a powerful influence over their lives (Brown, 2004). Group identity with the crowd can override the adolescent's personal identity. In any secondary school, there often are three to six well-formed crowds. Some typical crowds are jocks, populars, brains, druggies, and toughs. Although many adolescents want to be in a crowd, some are fiercely independent and have no desire to be in one.

Friendship likely plays a more important developmental role in secondary school than in elementary school (Sullivan, 1953). Adolescents disclose more personal information to their friends than younger children do (Buhrmester & Furman, 1987). And adolescents say that they depend more on their friends than on their parents to satisfy their needs for companionship, reassurance of worth, and intimacy (Furman & Buhrmester, 1992).

Schools

In school, children spend many years as members of a small society that exerts a tremendous influence on their socioemotional development. How does this social world change as children develop?

Schools' Changing Social Developmental Contexts   Social contexts vary through the early childhood, elementary school, and adolescent years (Minuchin & Shapiro, 1983). The early childhood setting is a protected environment whose boundary is the classroom. In this limited social setting, young children interact with one or two teachers, usually female, who are powerful figures in their lives. Young children also interact with peers in dyads or small groups.

The classroom still is the main context in elementary school, although it is more likely to be experienced as a social unit than is the early childhood classroom. The teacher symbolizes authority, which establishes the climate of the classroom, the conditions of social interaction, and the nature of group functioning. Peer groups are more important now, and students have an increased interest in friendship.

As children move into middle and junior high school, the school environment increases in scope and complexity (Wigfield & others, 2006). The social field is now the whole school rather than the classroom. Adolescents interact with teachers and peers from a broader range of cultural backgrounds on a broader range of interests. More of the teachers are male. Adolescents' social behavior becomes weighted more strongly toward peers, extracurricular activities, clubs, and the community. Secondary school students are more aware of the school as a social system and might be motivated to conform to it or challenge it.

Early Childhood Education   There are many variations in how young children are educated. However, an increasing number of education experts advocate that this education be developmentally appropriate (Slentz & Krogh, 2001).

Developmentally Appropriate Education   In chapters 1 and 2, we described the importance of engaging in developmentally appropriate teaching practices. Here we expand on this topic in our discussion of developmentally appropriate education for children from birth to 8 years of age. **Developmentally appropriate education** is based on knowledge of the typical development of children within an age span (age appropriateness) as well as the uniqueness of the child (individual appropriateness). Developmentally appropriate education contrasts with developmentally inappropriate practice, which ignores concrete, hands-on methods in the teaching of young children. Direct teaching, largely through abstract paper-and-pencil tasks presented to large groups of young children, is believed to be developmentally inappropriate. Although we are discussing developmentally appropriate education in this chapter on

developmentally appropriate education Education based on knowledge of the typical development of children within an age span (age appropriateness) as well as the uniqueness of the child (individual appropriateness).

socioemotional development, the concept applies to children's physical and cognitive development as well.

Here are some of the themes of developmentally appropriate education (Brede-kamp & Copple, 1997):

- *Domains of children's development—physical, cognitive, and socioemotional—are closely linked and development in one domain can influence and be influenced by development in other domains.* Recognition of the connections across domains can be used to plan children's learning experiences.

- *Development occurs in a relatively orderly sequence with later abilities, skills, and knowledge building on those already acquired.* Knowledge of typical development within the age range served by the program provides a general framework to guide teachers in preparing the learning environment.

- *Individual variation characterizes children's development.* Each child is a unique individual and all children have their own strengths, needs, and interests. Recognizing this individual variation is a key aspect of being a competent teacher.

- *Development is influenced by multiple social and cultural contexts.* Early child-hood teachers need to understand how sociocultural contexts—such as poverty and ethnicity—affect children's development. Teachers should learn about the culture of the majority of the children they serve if the culture differs from their own.

- *Children are active learners and should be encouraged to construct an understand-ing of the world around them.* Children contribute to their own learning as they strive to make meaning out of their daily experiences.

- *Development advances when children have opportunities to practice newly acquired skills as well as when they experience a challenge just beyond their present level of mastery.* In tasks that are just beyond the child's independent reach, the adult and more-competent peers can provide scaffolding that allows the child to learn.

- *Children develop best in the context of a community where they are safe and valued, their physical needs are met, and they feel psychologically secure.* Children benefit from having caring teachers who genuinely want to help them learn and develop in positive ways.

Figure 3.4 contrasts developmentally appropriate and developmentally inappropriate practices in constructing curriculum goals, teaching strategies, and creating a caring community of learners (Bredekamp & Copple, 1997).

Do developmentally appropriate educational practices improve young children's development? Yes. Young children in developmentally appropriate classrooms are likely to have less stress, be more motivated, be more skilled socially, have better work habits, be more creative, have better language skills, and demonstrate better math skills than children in developmentally inappropriate classrooms (Hart & others, 1996, 2003; Sherman & Mueller, 1996; Stipek & others, 1995).

How common are programs that use developmentally appropriate practice? As few as one-third to one-fifth of early childhood programs follow this educational strategy. Even fewer elementary schools do. Child-initiated activities and small-group instruction are the exception rather than the rule (Dunn & Kontos, 1997).

An increasingly popular approach to young children's education in the United States is the developmentally appropriate education practiced in Reggio Emilia, a small town in northern Italy (Stegelin, 2003). There children are encouraged to learn by investigating and exploring topics that interest them. A wide range of stimulating media and materials are available for children to use as they learn. Children often explore topics in a group. Two co-teachers serve as guides. The Reggio Emilia teach-ers view a project as an adventure. The project might start from a teacher's suggestion,

Component	Appropriate Practice	Inappropriate Practice
Creating a caring community of learners	• To promote a positive climate for learning, teachers help children learn how to develop positive relationships with other children and adults. • Teachers foster group cohesiveness and create activities that meet children's individual needs. • Teachers bring each child's home culture and language into the shared culture of the school. • Teachers recognize the importance of having children work and play collaboratively.	• Little or no effort is made to build a sense of community. • The curriculum and environment are essentially the same for each group of children that comes through the program without considering the interests and identities of the children. • Cultural and other individual differences are ignored. • Teachers don't help children develop feelings of caring and empathy for each other.
Teaching to enhance development and learning	• Teachers plan and prepare a learning environment that fosters children's initiative, active exploration of material, and sustained engagement with other children, adults, and activities. • In selecting materials, teachers consider children's developmental levels and cultural backgrounds. • Teachers maintain a safe, healthy environment and carefully supervise children. • Teachers give children opportunities to plan and select many of their program activities from a variety of learning areas and projects. • Teachers encourage children's language and communication skills. • Teaching strategies involve observing and interacting with children to determine what each child is capable of doing. • Teachers support children's play and child-chosen activities. They also provide many opportunities for children to plan, think about, reflect on, and discuss their own experiences. • Activities are interesting and at the right level to challenge children and encourage their intrinsic motivation. • Teachers facilitate the development of social skills and self-control by providing positive guidance strategies.	• The environment is disorderly with little structure. • The organization of the environment limits children's interaction with other children. • Teachers don't adequately monitor children. • Learning materials are mainly drill-and-practice, workbook-type activities rather than interesting and engaging activities. • The program provides few or no opportunities for children to make choices. • Children spend too much time sitting and being quiet. • Children do a lot of paper-and-pencil seatwork. • Teachers don't provide adequate time for children to develop concepts and skills. • Too many activities are uninteresting and unchallenging, or so difficult, that they diminish children's intrinsic motivation to learn. • Teachers spend too much time providing negative feedback and punishment.
Constructing appropriate curriculum	• Curriculum goals assess learning in all developmental areas—physical, social, emotional, language, aesthetic, and intellectual. • Curriculum content from various disciplines, such as math, science, or social studies, is integrated through themes, projects, play, and other learning experiences. • The curriculum plan is designed to help children explore key ideas in disciplines appropriate for their age. • Culturally diverse and nonsexist materials are provided. • Teachers use a variety of approaches and daily opportunities to develop children's language and literacy skills through meaningful experiences. • Children have daily opportunities for aesthetic expression through art and music, as well as daily opportunities to develop gross- and fine-motor skills.	• Curriculum goals are narrowly focused. • The curriculum is too trivial and follows a rigid plan that doesn't take into account children's interests. • In some programs, the curriculum is not adequately planned. • Curriculum expectations are not well matched to children's intellectual capacities and developmental characteristics. • Children's cultural and linguistic backgrounds are ignored. • Reading and writing instruction is too rigid. • Instruction focuses on isolated skill development through rote memorization. • Little effort is made to provide children with opportunities to engage in aesthetic activities. • Little time is spent in gross- or fine-motor activities.

FIGURE 3.4 Examples of NAEYC Guidelines for Appropriate and Inappropriate Practices for 3- through 5-Year-Olds

a child's idea, or an event such as a snowfall or something else unexpected. Children are given ample time to think about and plan the project. Cooperation is a major theme in the Reggio Emilia approach (Firlik, 1996). Reggio Emilia reflects the constructivist approach to education that initially was described in chapters 1 and 2 and will be explored in greater depth in later chapters, especially chapter 10, "Social Constructivist Approaches."

Controversy in Early Childhood Education   Currently there is controversy about what the curriculum of U.S. early childhood education should be (Cress, 2004). On one side are those who advocate a child-centered, constructivist approach much like that emphasized by the National Association for the Education of Young Children (NAEYC) along the lines of developmentally appropriate practice. On the other side are those who advocate an academic, direct instruction approach.

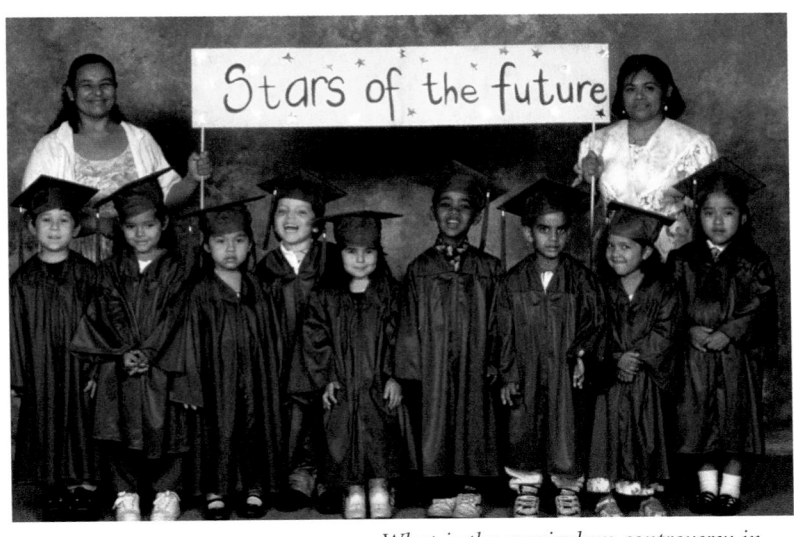

What is the curriculum controversy in early childhood education?

In reality, many high-quality early childhood education programs include both academic and constructivist approaches. Many education experts such as Lilian Katz (1999) worry about academic approaches that place too much pressure on young children to achieve and don't provide any opportunities to actively construct knowledge. Competent early childhood programs also should focus on cognitive development *and* socioemotional development, not exclusively on cognitive development (Anderson & others, 2003; Jacobson, 2004; Kagan & Scott-Little, 2004; NAEYC, 2002). Early childhood education should encourage adequate preparation for learning, varied learning activities, trusting relationships between adults and children, and increased parental involvement (Hildebrand, Phenice, & Hines, 2000). Too many young children go to substandard early childhood programs. According to a report by the Carnegie Corporation (1996), four out of five early childhood programs did not meet quality standards.

Early Childhood Education for Children from Low-Income Families   For many years, many children from low-income families did not receive any education before they entered first grade. In the 1960s, an effort was made to break the cycle of poverty and inadequate education for young children in the United States. *Project Head Start* was designed to provide young children from low-income families opportunities to acquire the skills and experiences that are important for success in school. Funded by the federal government, Project Head Start began in 1965 and continues to serve disadvantaged children today.

In high-quality Head Start programs, parents and communities are involved in positive ways (Thurgood, 2001). The teachers are knowledgeable about children's development and use developmentally appropriate practices. Researchers have found that when young children from low-income families experience a quality Head Start program, there are substantial long-term benefits. These include being less likely to drop out of school, to be in a special education class, or to be on welfare than their low-income counterparts who did not attend a Head Start program (Lazar & others, 1982; Schweinhart, 1999). However, Head Start programs are not all created equal (McCarty, Abbott-Shim, & Lambert, 2001). One estimate is that 40 percent of the 1,400 Head Start programs are inadequate (Zigler & Finn-Stevenson, 1999). More attention needs to be given to developing high-quality Head Start programs (Raver & Zigler, 1997; Zigler & Styco, 2004).

The U.S. Congress is considering changes that would infuse Head Start programs with a stronger academic focus. Although early childhood experts clearly hope that the overall quality of Head Start programs will improve, some worry that the emphasis on academic skills will come at the expense of reduced health services and decreased emphasis on socioemotional skills.

The Transition to Elementary School   As children make the transition to elementary school, they interact and develop relationships with new and significant others. School provides them with a rich source of ideas to shape their sense of self.

A special concern about early elementary school classrooms is that they not proceed primarily on the basis of negative feedback. I (your author) vividly remember my first-grade teacher. Unfortunately, she never smiled; she was a dictator in the classroom, and learning (or lack of learning) progressed more on the basis of fear than of enjoyment and passion. Fortunately, I experienced some warmer, more student-friendly teachers later on.

Children's self-esteem is higher when they begin elementary school than when they complete it (Blumenfeld & others, 1981). Is that because they experienced so much negative feedback and were criticized so much along the way? We will say more about the roles of reinforcement and punishment in children's learning in chapter 7 and about managing the classroom in chapter 14.

For now, though, consider the following two elementary school classrooms and what effect they might have on children's learning and self-esteem (Katz & Chard, 1989). In one, students spend the entire morning making identical pictures of traffic lights as they sit glued to their chairs. The teacher seems uninterested in their work, except when she occasionally comes around and informs them of their mistakes. The teacher makes no attempt to get the students to relate the pictures to anything else the class is doing.

In the other class, students are investigating a school bus. They write to the district's school superintendent and ask if they can have a bus parked at their school for a few days. They study the bus, discover how it functions, and discuss traffic rules. Then, in the classroom, they build their own bus out of cardboard. The students are having fun, but they also are practicing writing, reading, and even some arithmetic. When the class has parents' night, the teacher is ready to report on how each child is doing. But the main thing the parents want to do is to see the bus, because their children have been coming home and talking about the bus for weeks. Which class would you say reflects developmentally appropriate education?

The Schooling of Adolescents   Three special concerns about adolescent schooling are (1) the transition to middle or junior high school, (2) effective schooling for young adolescents, and (3) the quality of high schools. How might the transition to middle or junior high school be difficult for many students?

The Transition to Middle or Junior High School   This transition can be stressful because it coincides with many other developmental changes (Conti, 2001; Eccles, 2004; Wigfield, Byrenes, & Eccles, 2006; Wigfield & others, 2006). Students are beginning puberty and have increased concerns about their body image. The hormonal changes of puberty stimulate increased interest in sexual matters. Students are becoming more independent from their parents and want to spend more time with peers. They must make the change from a smaller, more personalized classroom to a larger, more impersonal school. Achievement becomes more serious business and getting good grades becomes more competitive.

As students move from elementary to middle or junior high school, they experience the *top-dog phenomenon*. This refers to moving from the top position (in elementary school, being the oldest, biggest, and most powerful students in the school) to the lowest position (in middle or junior high school, being the youngest, smallest, and least powerful students in the school). Schools that provide more support, less anonymity, more stability, and less complexity improve student adjustment during this transition (Fenzel, Blyth, & Simmons, 1991). Also, one study found that when parents were attuned to their young adolescents' developmental needs and supported their autonomy in decision making, the students were better adjusted during the school transition (Eccles, Lord, & Buchanan, 1996).

Effective Schools for Young Adolescents   Some critics argue that today's middle and junior high schools have become watered-down versions of high schools. Instead of offering curricular and extracurricular activities geared to the biological and psychological development of young adolescents, say the critics, middle and junior high schools mimic the curricular and extracurricular schedules of high schools.

In a 1989 report, "Turning Points: Preparing American Youth for the 21st Century," the Carnegie Foundation concluded that most young adolescents in the United States attend massive, impersonal schools; learn from seemingly irrelevant curricula; trust few adults in school; and lack access to health care and counseling. The Carnegie Foundation (1989) report recommended the following:

- Develop smaller "communities" or "houses" to lessen the impersonal nature of large middle schools.
- Lower student-to-counselor ratios from several hundred-to-1 to 10-to-1.
- Involve parents and community leaders in schools.
- Develop curricula that produce students who are literate, understand the sciences, and have a sense of health, ethics, and citizenship.
- Have teachers team teach in more flexibly designed curriculum blocks that integrate several disciplines, instead of presenting students with disconnected, rigidly separated 50-minute segments.
- Boost students' health and fitness with more in-school programs, and help students who need public health care to get it.

In *Turning Points 2000,* there was continued emphasis on the earlier Turning Points recommendations (Jackson & Davis, 2000). Some of the new emphases in the 2000 recommendations focused on teaching a curriculum grounded in rigorous academic standards, using instructional methods designed to prepare all students to achieve higher standards, provide a safe and healthy school environment, and involve parents and communities in supporting student learning and healthy development. In sum, middle schools throughout the nation need a major redesign if they are to be effective in educating adolescents for becoming competent adults in the twenty-first century.

Improving America's High Schools   Just as there are concerns about U.S. middle school education, so are there concerns about U.S. high school education (Kaufman, 2001). Many students graduate from high school with inadequate reading, writing, and mathematical skills, including many who go on to college and have to enroll in remediation classes there. Other students drop out of high school and do not have skills that will allow them to advance in the work world (Christensen & Thurlow, 2004; Lehr & others, 2003).

In the last half of the twentieth century, high school dropout rates declined overall (*Child Trends,* 2006). For example, in the 1940s, more than half of U.S. 16- to 24-year-olds had dropped out of school; in 2003, only 10 percent had dropped out. Figure 3.5 shows the trends in high school dropout rates from 1972 through 2004. Notice that the dropout rate of Latino adolescents remains high (24 percent of 16- to 24-year-old Latino adolescents had dropped out of school in 2004). Although statistics on Native American youth have not been adequately obtained, some estimates indicate that they likely have the highest dropout rate in the United States with only about 50 to 70 percent completing their high school education.

Gender differences characterize U.S. dropout rates with males more likely to drop out than females (12 versus 9 percent) (*Child Trends,* 2006). The gender gap in

FIGURE 3.5 Trends in High School Dropout Rates

From 1972 through 2004, the school dropout rate for Latinos remained very high (24 percent of 16- to-24-year-olds in 2004). The African American dropout rate was still higher (12 percent) than the White non-Latino rate (7 percent) in 2004. The overall dropout rate declined considerably from the 1940s through the 1960s but has declined only slightly since 1972.

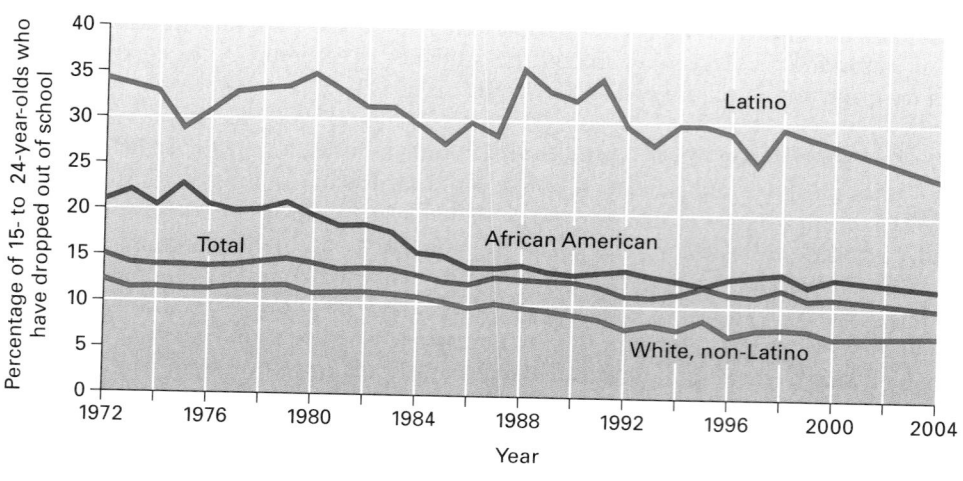

dropout rates is especially large for Latino adolescents (27 versus 20 percent) and African American adolescents (12.5 versus 9.5 percent) (data for 2003).

Students drop out of schools for many reasons (Christensen & Thurlow, 2004). In one study, almost 50 percent of the dropouts cited school-related reasons for leaving school, such as not liking school or being expelled or suspended (Rumberger, 1995). Twenty percent of the dropouts (but 40 percent of the Latino students) cited economic reasons for leaving school. One-third of the female students dropped out for personal reasons, such as pregnancy or marriage.

A recent review of school-based dropout programs found that the most effective programs provided early reading programs, tutoring, counseling, and mentoring (Lehrer & others, 2003). They also emphasized the importance of creating caring environments and relationships, and offered community-service opportunities.

"I Have a Dream" (IHAD) is an innovative comprehensive, long-term dropout prevention program administered by the National IHAD Foundation in New York. Since the National IHAD Foundation was created in 1986, it has grown to number over 180 projects in 64 cities and 27 states, serving more than 12,000 children ("I Have a Dream" Foundation, 2005). Local IHAD projects around the country "adopt" entire grades (usually the third or fourth) from public elementary schools, or corresponding age cohorts from public housing developments. These children—"Dreamers"—are then provided with a program of academic, social, cultural, and recreational activities throughout their elementary, middle school, and high school years. An important part of this program is that it is personal rather than institutional: IHAD sponsors and staff develop close long-term relationships with the children. When participants complete high school, IHAD provides the tuition assistance necessary for them to attend a state or local college or vocational school.

The IHAD Program was created in 1981, when philanthropist Eugene Lang made an impromptu offer of college tuition to a class of graduating sixth-graders at P.S. 121 in East Harlem. Statistically, 75 percent of the students should have dropped out of school; instead, 90 percent graduated and 60 percent went on to college. Other evaluations of IHAD programs have found dramatic improvements in grades, test scores, and school attendance, as well as a reduction of behavioral problems of Dreamers. For example, in Portland, Oregon, twice as many Dreamers as control-group students had reached a math standard, and the Dreamers were less likely to be referred to the juvenile justice system (Davis, Hyatt, & Arrasmith, 1998).

Even when students graduate from high school, many not only are poorly prepared for college, but they also are poorly prepared for the demands of the modern,

These adolescents participate in the "I Have a Dream" (IHAD) Program, a comprehensive, long-term dropout prevention program that has been very successful.

high-performance workplace. A review of hiring practices at major companies indicated that many companies now have sets of basic skills they want new hires to have. These include the ability to read at relatively high levels, do at least elementary algebra, use personal computers for straightforward tasks such as word processing, solve semistructured problems in which hypotheses must be formed and tested, communicate effectively (orally and in writing), and work effectively in groups with persons of various backgrounds (Murnane & Levy, 1996).

An increasing number of educators argue that the nation's high schools need a new mission for the twenty-first century, one which addresses these problems (National Commission on the High School Senior Year, 2001):

1. More support is needed to enable all students to graduate from high school with the knowledge and skills to succeed in postsecondary education and careers. Many parents and students, especially those in low-income and minority communities, are unaware of the knowledge and level of skills required to succeed in postsecondary education.

2. High schools need to have higher expectations for student achievement. A special concern is the senior year of high school, which has become too much of a party-time rather than a time to prepare for one of life's most important transitions. Some students who have been accepted to college routinely ignore the academic demands of their senior year. One recent survey of 90,000 high school students in 26 states found that almost 20 percent of college-track seniors did not take a math course in their final year of high school (Indiana University High School Survey of Student Engagement, 2004). In this survey, 55 percent of the students studied less than 3 hours a week, yet approximately two-thirds of those students said they mainly got As and Bs. Thus, many students are getting high grades without studying much.

3. U.S. high school students spend too much time working in low-level service jobs. Researchers have found that when tenth-graders work more than 14 hours a week their grades drop, and when eleventh-graders work 20 or more hours a week their grades decline (Greenberger & Steinberg, 1986). At the same time, shorter, higher-quality work experiences, including community service and internships, have been shown to benefit high school students.

Review, Reflect, and Practice

② Discuss how the social contexts of families, peers, and schools are linked with socioemotional development.

REVIEW
- What four parenting styles did Baumrind propose and which is likely to be the most effective? How do aspects of families such as divorce and ethnicity/socioeconomic status affect children's development and education? In what ways can school-family linkages be fostered?
- What are peers and the five peer statuses? What differences can positive or negative peer relations make in a child's and an adolescent's development and education? What risks are attached to certain peer statuses? How do friendships matter?
- What is meant by developmentally appropriate education? What transitional problems do students face as they move through different levels of schooling?

continued on page 96

Review, Reflect, and Practice *continued*

REFLECT

- What parenting style(s) have you witnessed and experienced? What effects did they have?

PRAXIS™ PRACTICE

1. Which of the following teachers is most likely to encourage appropriate parental involvement in their children's education?
   a. Mr. Bastian sends home weekly progress notes to the parents who request them. He invites each parent to a conference at the end of the first grading period, and contacts parents if a child is in serious trouble at school.
   b. Ms. Washington contacts parents before the school year begins. She holds a meeting for parents to discuss her expectations for both children and parents and to answer questions. She requests volunteers to help in the classroom and chaperone field trips. She sends home weekly progress reports that include academic and social information.
   c. Ms. Jefferson tells parents that their children need to develop independence, which won't happen if they hover around at school and interfere with the educational process.
   d. Ms. Hernandez holds two parent-teacher conferences each year and e-mails parents if children fall behind in their work or present any problems in class. She occasionally e-mails a parent when a child has made marked improvement or accomplished something special.

2. Samuel is in fourth grade. He is large for his age, but not very mature. He is extremely sensitive to any kind of criticism—constructive or not. He cries when somebody teases him, which is often. Samuel often elicits teasing from his peers by engaging in it himself. Which peer status is most likely for Samuel?
   a. controversial
   b. neglected
   c. popular
   d. rejected

3. Which of the following is the best example of a developmentally appropriate unit on pioneer life for fourth-graders?
   a. Mr. Johnson's class has read about the daily lives of pioneers and are now constructing log cabins that demonstrate their understanding of the typical cabin of the period. Mr. Johnson moves around the room, giving help when needed, asking students why they are including certain features, and ensuring that all stay on task.
   b. In Ms. Lincoln's class, each student has read a different book about pioneer life and is now writing a book report. The students work quietly at their desks on their reports. She occasionally chastises students for talking or for daydreaming.
   c. Mr. Roosevelt's class is taking turns reading aloud a book about pioneer life. Each student reads a paragraph of the book in turn. When they are finished with the book, they will be tested on the content.
   d. Ms. Silver is lecturing to her students about pioneer life. She has gone over reasons for the westward migration, modes of transportation, and clearing the land and building a cabin. She will give them a test about pioneer life on Friday.

Please see the answer key at the end of the book.

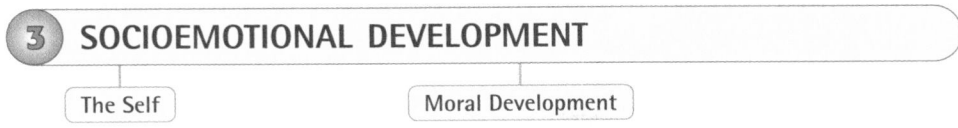

③ SOCIOEMOTIONAL DEVELOPMENT

| The Self | | Moral Development |

So far we have discussed three important social contexts that influence students' socioemotional development: families, peers, and schools. In this section, we focus more on the individual students themselves, as we explore the development of the self and morality.

The Self

According to twentieth-century Italian playwright Ugo Betti, when children say "I," they mean something unique, not to be confused with any other. Psychologists often refer to that "I" as the self. Two important aspects of the self are self-esteem and identity.

Self-Esteem **Self-esteem** refers to an individual's overall view of himself or herself. Self-esteem also is referred to as *self-worth* or *self-image*. For example, a child with high self-esteem might perceive that she is not just a person but a *good* person.

Interest in self-esteem arose from the work of psychotherapist Carl Rogers (1961). Rogers said that the main reason individuals have low self-esteem is that they have not been given adequate emotional support and social approval. He especially thought that as children grow up, they get told, "You didn't do that right," "Don't do that," "You should have done that better," or "How could you be so dumb?"

For many students, periods of low self-esteem come and go. But for some students, persistent low self-esteem translates into other, more serious problems. Persistent low self-esteem is linked with low achievement, depression, eating disorders, and delinquency (Harter, 1999, 2006). The seriousness of the problem depends not only on the nature of the student's low self-esteem but on other conditions as well. When low self-esteem is compounded by difficult school transitions (such as the transition to middle school) or family problems (such as divorce), the student's problems can intensify.

Researchers have found that self-esteem changes as children develop (Galambos, Barker, & Krahn, 2006). In one recent study, both boys and girls had high self-esteem in childhood but their self-esteem dropped considerably in early adolescence (Robins & others, 2002). The self-esteem of girls dropped about twice as much as that of boys during adolescence (see figure 3.6). Other researchers have found that the self-esteem of girls drops more than that of boys during adolescence (Kling & others, 1999; Major & others, 1999). Among the reasons given for the self-esteem decline in both boys and girls are the upheaval in physical changes of puberty, increased achievement demands and expectations, and inadequate support from schools and parents. Among the reasons given for the gender disparity in the decline of self-esteem are the high expectations for physical attractiveness in girls, which becomes more pronounced with pubertal change, and motivation for social relationships that is not rewarded by society (Crawford & Unger, 2004). However, note in figure 3.6 that despite the drop in self-esteem among adolescent girls, their average self-esteem score (3.3) was still higher than the neutral point on the scale (3.0).

Variations in self-esteem have been linked with many aspects of development (Harter, 2006). For example, one recent study found that adolescents who had low self-esteem had lower levels of mental health, physical health, and economic prospects as adults than adolescents with high self-esteem (Trzesniewski & others, 2006). However, much of the research on self-esteem is *correlational* rather than *experimental*. Recall from chapter 1 that correlation does not equal causation. Thus,

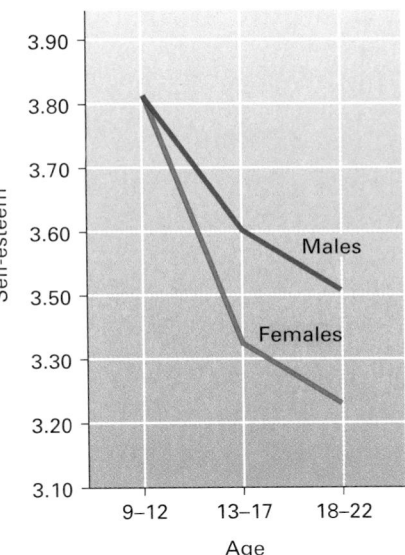

FIGURE 3.6 The Decline of Self-Esteem in Adolescence

In one study, the self-esteem of both boys and girls declined during adolescence, but it declined considerably more for girls than boys (Robins & others, 2002). The self-esteem scores represent the mean self-esteem scores on a 5-point scale, with higher scores reflecting higher self-esteem.

self-esteem Also called self-image and self-worth, the individual's overall conception of himself or herself.

if a correlational study finds an association between children's low self-esteem and low academic achievement, low academic achievement could cause the low self-esteem as much as low self-esteem causes low academic achievement (Bowles, 1999).

In fact, there are only moderate correlations between school performance and self-esteem, and these correlations do not suggest that high self-esteem produces better school performance (Baumeister & others, 2003). Efforts to increase students' self-esteem have not always led to improved school performance (Davies & Brember, 1999; Hansford & Hattie, 1982).

Children with high self-esteem show greater initiative, but this can produce positive or negative outcomes (Baumeister & others, 2003). High self-esteem children are prone to both prosocial and antisocial actions. For example, they are more likely than children with low self-esteem to defend victims against bullies, but they are also more likely to be bullies.

Researchers have also found strong links between self-esteem and happiness (Baumeister & others, 2003). For example, the two were strongly related in an international study of 13,000 college students from 49 universities in 31 countries (Diener & Diener, 1995). It seems likely that high self-esteem increases happiness (Baumeister & others, 2003).

Many studies have found that individuals with low self-esteem report that they feel more depressed than individuals with high self-esteem (Arndt & Greenberg, 2002; Baumeister & others, 2003; Fox & others, 2004). Low self-esteem has also been linked to suicide attempts and to anorexia nervosa (Fenzel, 1994; Osvath, Voros, & Fekete, 2004).

Students' self-esteem often varies across different domains, such as academic, athletic, physical appearance, social skills, and so on (Harter, 1999, 2006). Thus, a student might have high self-esteem in regard to his or her school work but have low self-esteem in the areas of athletic skills, physical appearance, and social skills. Even within the academic domain, a student might have high esteem in some subjects (math, for example) and low self-esteem in others (English, for example).

Also, as students age their self-esteem becomes more differentiated (Harter, 2006; Horowitz & others, 2005). For example, Susan Harter (1989) added three new self-perception domains in her assessment of adolescents' self-perceptions (close friendship, romantic appeal, and job competence) to the five she assesses with children (scholastic competence, athletic competence, social acceptance, physical appearance, and behavioral conduct).

Identity Development   Another important aspect of the self is identity. Earlier in the chapter we indicated that Erik Erikson (1968) argued that the most important issue in adolescence involves identity development—searching for answers to questions like these: Who am I? What am I all about? What am I going to do with my life? Not usually considered during childhood, these questions become nearly universal concerns during the high school and college years (Kroger, 2007; Pals, 2006).

Identity Statuses   Canadian researcher James Marcia (1980, 1998) analyzed Erikson's concept of identity and concluded that it is important to distinguish between exploration and commitment. *Exploration* involves examining meaningful alternative identities. *Commitment* means showing a personal investment in an identity and staying with whatever that identity implies.

The extent of an individual's exploration and commitment is used to classify him or her according to one of four identity statuses (see figure 3.7).

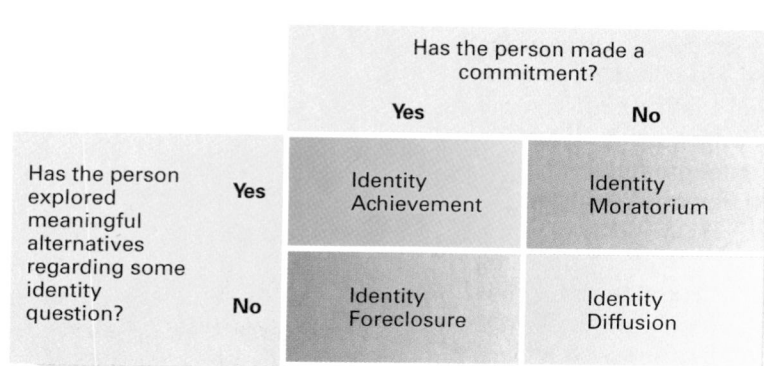

FIGURE 3.7 Marcia's Four Identity Statuses

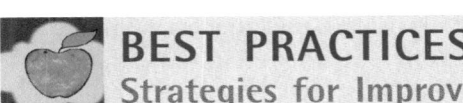
BEST PRACTICES
Strategies for Improving Children's Self-Esteem

A current concern is that too many of today's children and adolescents grow up receiving empty praise and as a consequence have inflated self-esteem (Graham, 2005; Stipek, 2005). Too often they are given praise for mediocre or even poor performance. They may have difficulty handling competition and criticism. The title of a book, *Dumbing Down Our Kids: Why American Children Feel Good About Themselves But Can't Read, Write, or Add* (Sykes, 1995) vividly captures the theme that many U.S. children's, adolescents', and college students' academic problems stem from unmerited praise as part of an effort to prop up their self-esteem. Instead, it is possible to raise children's self-esteem through four strategies (Bednar, Wells, & Peterson, 1995; Harter, 1999, 2006):

1. *Identify the causes of low self-esteem and the areas of competence important to the self.* This is critical. Is the child's low self-esteem due to poor school achievement? family conflict? weak social skills? Students have the highest self-esteem when they perform competently in areas that they themselves feel are important. Thus, find out from students with low self-esteem what areas of competence they value.

2. *Provide emotional support and social approval.* Virtually every class has children who have received too many negative evaluations. These children might come from an abusive and demeaning family that constantly puts them down, or they might have been in prior classrooms that delivered too much negative feedback. Your emotional support and social approval can make a big difference in helping them value themselves more. A school counselor also likely will benefit these children. The following comments by Judy Logan, a middle school teacher in San Francisco, underscore the importance of providing emotional support.

THROUGH THE EYES OF TEACHERS
Listening, Explaining, and Supporting

I believe that a good teacher should passionately be on the side of her students. That does not mean I support them in everything I do. It means I demand the best of them and am willing to help them be their best selves. It means I listen, explain, support, and allow without judgment, sarcasm, or the need to impose the truth from the outside. The passage from childhood to adulthood we call adolescence is a very vulnerable journey. It is often a difficult time for students and for their families. It is an adolescent's "job" to rebel at times and to question the family environment that was such a comfortable cocoon during childhood. No matter how wonderful the parents, how loving the family, each adolescent needs to have other adults in whom to confide. . . .

3. *Help children achieve.* Achieving can improve children's self-esteem. Straightforward teaching of real academic skills often improves children's achievement, and subsequently their self-esteem. Often it is not enough to tell children they can achieve something; you also have to help them develop their academic skills.

4. *Develop children's coping skills.* When children face a problem and cope with it rather than avoid it, their self-esteem often improves. Students who cope rather than avoid are likely to face problems realistically, honestly, and nondefensively. This produces in them favorable thoughts about themselves that raise their self-esteem. On the other hand, for students with low self-esteem, their unfavorable self-evaluations trigger denial, deception, and avoidance. This type of self-generated disapproval makes a student feel personally inadequate.

- **Identity diffusion** occurs when individuals have not yet experienced a crisis (that is, they have not yet explored meaningful alternatives) or made any commitments. Not only are they undecided about occupational and ideological choices, but they are also likely to show little interest in such matters.
- **Identity foreclosure** occurs when individuals have made a commitment but have not yet experienced a crisis. This occurs most often when parents hand down commitments to their adolescents, more often than not in an authoritarian manner. In these circumstances, adolescents have not had adequate opportunities to explore different approaches, ideologies, and vocations on their own.
- **Identity moratorium** occurs when individuals are in the midst of a crisis but their commitments are either absent or only vaguely defined.

identity diffusion The identity status in which individuals have neither explored meaningful alternatives nor made a commitment.

identity foreclosure The identity status in which individuals have made a commitment but have not explored meaningful alternatives.

identity moratorium The identity status in which individuals are in the midst of exploring alternatives but have not yet made a commitment.

- **Identity achievement** occurs when individuals have undergone a crisis and have made a commitment.

Let's explore some examples of Marcia's identity statuses. A 13-year-old adolescent has neither begun to explore her identity in any meaningful way nor made an identity commitment, so she is *identity diffused*. An 18-year-old boy's parents want him to be a medical doctor, so he is planning on majoring in premedicine in college and really has not adequately explored any other options; he is *identity foreclosed*. Nineteen-year-old Sasha is not quite sure what life paths she wants to follow, but she recently went to the counseling center at her college to find out about different careers, so she is in *identity moratorium* status. Twenty-one-year-old Marcelo extensively explored a number of different career options in college, eventually getting his degree in science education, and is looking forward to his first year of teaching high school students, so he is *identity achieved*. Our examples of identity statuses have focused on the career dimension, but remember that other dimensions are also important. Adolescents can explore alternative identities in numerous areas, such as vocational, religious, intellectual, political, sexual, gender, ethnic, and interests. An adolescent can be farther along the path to identity in some of these areas than in others. While many high school students are exploring different areas of their identity, some will be identity diffused and others will be foreclosed because of the authoritarian ways of their parents.

To further consider identity, complete Self-Assessment 3.1. There you will be able to apply Marcia's identity statuses to a number of different areas of identity in your own life.

Ethnic Identity *Ethnic identity* is an enduring aspect of the self that includes a sense of membership in an ethnic group, along with the attitudes and feelings related to that membership (Phinney, 1996). The indicators of identity often differ for each succeeding generation of immigrants (Phinney, 2003, 2006; Phinney & others, 2006). First-generation immigrants are likely to be secure in their identities and unlikely to change much; they may or may not develop a new identity. The degree to which they begin to feel "American" appears to be related to whether or not they learn English, develop social networks beyond their ethnic group, and become culturally competent in their new country. Second-generation immigrants are more likely to think of themselves as "American" possibly because citizenship is granted at birth. For second-generation immigrants, ethnic identity is likely to be linked to retention of their ethnic language and social networks. In the third and later generations, the issues become more complex. Broad social factors may affect the extent to which members of this generation retain their ethnic identities. For example, media images may either discourage or encourage members of an ethnic group from identifying with their group or retaining parts of its culture. Discrimination may force people to see themselves as cut off from the majority group and encourage them to seek the support of their own ethnic culture.

The immediate contexts in which ethnic minority youth live also influence their identity development (Spencer, 2006; Spencer & others, 2001). In the United States, many ethnic minority youth live in pockets of poverty, are exposed to drugs, gangs, and crime, and interact with youth and adults who have dropped out of school or are unemployed. Support for developing a positive identity is scarce. In such settings, programs for youth can make an important contribution to identity development.

THROUGH THE EYES OF STUDENTS

Identity Exploring

Parents do not understand that teenagers need to find out who they are, which means a lot of experimenting, a lot of mood swings, a lot of emotions and awkwardness. Like any teenager, I am facing an identity crisis. I am still trying to figure out whether I am a Chinese American or an American with Asian eyes.

Michelle Chin, age 16

identity achievement The identity status in which individuals have explored meaningful alternatives and made a commitment.

SELF–ASSESSMENT 3.1

Where Are You Now? Exploring Your Identity

Your identity is made up of many different parts, and so too will your students' identities be comprised of many different dimensions. By completing this checklist, you should gain a better sense of your own identity and the different aspects of your future students' identities. For each component, check your identity status as diffused, foreclosed, in a moratorium, or achieved.

Identity Component	Identity Status			
	Diffused	Foreclosed	Moratorium	Achieved
Vocational identity				
Religious identity				
Achievement/intellectual identity				
Political identity				
Sexual identity				
Gender identity				
Relationship identity				
Lifestyle identity				
Ethnic and cultural identity				
Personality characteristics				
Interests				

If you checked "Diffused" or "Foreclosed" for any areas, take some time to think about what you need to do to move into a "Moratorium" identity status in those areas and write about this in your portfolio.

Researchers are also increasingly finding that a positive ethnic identity is related to positive outcomes for ethnic minority adolescents (Lee, 2005; Riekmann, Wadsworth, & Deyhle, 2004; Umana-Taylor, 2004, 2006). For example, one recent study revealed that ethnic identity was linked with higher school engagement and lower aggression (Van Buren & Graham, 2003). Another study with ninth-grade students found that the strength of adolescents' ethnic identification was a better predictor of their academic success than the specific ethnic labels they used to describe themselves (Fuligni, Witkow, & Garcia, 2005).

Shirley Heath and Milbrey McLaughlin (1993) studied 60 youth organizations that involved 24,000 adolescents over a period of 5 years. They found that these organizations were especially good at building a sense of ethnic pride in inner-city youth. Heath and McLaughlin stress that many inner-city youth have too much time on their hands, too little to do, and too few places to go. Organizations that perceive youth as fearful, vulnerable, and lonely but also as capable, worthy, and eager to have a healthy and productive life contribute in positive ways to the identity development of ethnic minority youth.

Moral Development

As children develop a sense of self and an identity, they also develop a sense of morality. Moral development has important implications in the classroom. For example, a strong moral sense may increase the likelihood that students will consider others' feelings or not cheat on a test. In one recent survey of 8,600 U.S. high school students, 70 percent admitted that they had cheated on at least one school exam in the current school year, up from 60 percent in 1990 (*Upfront,* 2000). In this survey, almost 80 percent said they had lied to a teacher at least once.

Domains of Moral Development **Moral development** concerns rules and conventions about just interactions between people. These rules can be studied in three domains: cognitive, behavioral, and emotional.

In the cognitive domain, the key issue is how students reason or think about rules for ethical conduct. In the behavioral domain, the focus is on how students actually behave rather than on the morality of their thinking. In the emotional domain, the emphasis is on how students morally feel. For instance, do they associate strong enough guilt feelings with an immoral action to resist performing that action? Do they show empathy toward others?

Piaget's Theory Piaget (1932) stimulated interest in how students think about moral issues. He extensively observed and interviewed 4- to 12-year-old children. He watched them play marbles, seeking to learn how they used and thought about the game's rules. He also asked children about ethical rules, quizzing them about theft, lies, punishment, and justice. From this he derived a stage theory of moral development.

Heteronomous morality is Piaget's first stage of moral development. It lasts from approximately 4 to 7 years of age. At this stage, justice and rules are conceived of as unchangeable properties of the world, removed from the control of people. **Autonomous morality** is Piaget's second stage of moral development, reached at about 10 years of age or older. At this point, the child becomes aware that rules and laws are created by people and that, in judging an action, the actor's intentions as well as the consequences should be considered. Children 7 to 10 years of age are in a transition between the two stages, showing some features of both.

The heteronomous thinker also believes in immanent justice, the concept that if a rule is broken, punishment will be meted out immediately. Young children believe that a violation is in some way automatically connected to punishment. They often look around in a worried fashion after committing a transgression, expecting inevitable punishment. Older children, being moral autonomists, recognize that punishment is socially mediated and occurs only if a relevant person witnesses the wrongdoing and that, even then, punishment is not inevitable.

Piaget said that moral development is mainly advanced through the mutual give-and-take of peer relations. In the peer group, where all members have similar power and status, children negotiate rules and discuss and settle disagreements. In Piaget's view, parents play a less important role in children's moral development because they have so much more power than children and hand down rules in an authoritarian way.

Kohlberg's Theory Lawrence Kohlberg (1976, 1986), like Piaget, stressed that moral development primarily involves moral reasoning and occurs in stages. Kohlberg arrived at his theory after interviewing children, adolescents, and adults (primarily

moral development Development with respect to the rules and conventions of just interactions between people.

heteronomous morality In Piaget's theory, the first stage of moral development (about 4 to 7 years of age), in which justice and rules are conceived of as unchangeable properties of the world, beyond the control of people.

autonomous morality In Piaget's theory, the second stage of moral development (entered at about 10 years of age), in which children become aware that rules and laws are created by people and that in judging action, the actor's intentions as well as consequences need to be considered.

males) about their views on a series of moral dilemmas. Here is an example of the type of dilemma he presented:

> A woman is near death and is suffering from a special kind of cancer. There is only one drug that doctors think might save her. It was recently discovered by a druggist living in the same town as the woman. The drug was expensive to make, but the druggist is charging 10 times what the drug cost him to make. The sick woman's husband, Heinz, tries to borrow the money to buy the drug from every place he can think of but he can't raise enough money. He tells the druggist that his wife is dying and asks him to sell it to him cheaper or let him pay later. But the druggist says, "No, I discovered it and I deserve to make money from it." Later, Heinz gets desperate, breaks into the druggist's store, and steals the drug for his wife.

After reading the story (or, in the case of young children, hearing it read to them), individuals are asked a series of questions, such as these: Was Heinz right to steal the drug? Is it a husband's duty to steal the drug? Would a good husband steal? Did the druggist have the right to charge so much for the drug? Why or why not?

Kohlberg's Levels and Stages of Moral Development   Based on the reasons individuals gave in response to the dilemma just discussed and 10 others like it, Kohlberg constructed a theory of moral development that has three main levels with two stages at each of the levels. A key concept in understanding Kohlberg's theory is *internalization,* which refers to the developmental change from externally controlled behavior to internally controlled behavior.

Preconventional reasoning is the lowest level of moral development in Kohlberg's theory. At this level, the child shows no internalization of moral values. Moral reasoning is controlled by external rewards and punishment.

Conventional reasoning is the second, or intermediate, level in Kohlberg's theory. At this level, the child's internalization is intermediate. The child abides internally by certain standards, but they are essentially the standards imposed by other people, such as parents, or by society's laws.

Postconventional reasoning is the highest level in Kohlberg's theory. At this level, morality is completely internalized and not based on external standards. The student recognizes alternative moral courses, explores options, and then decides on the moral code that is best for him or her. A summary of Kohlberg's three levels and six stages, along with examples of each of the stages, is presented in figure 3.8.

In studies of Kohlberg's theory, longitudinal data show a relation of the stages to age, although few people ever attain the two highest stages, especially stage 6 (Colby & others, 1983). Before age 9, most children reason about moral dilemmas at a preconventional level. By early adolescence, they are more likely to reason at the conventional level.

Kohlberg stressed that underlying changes in cognitive development promote more advanced moral thinking. He also said that children construct their moral thoughts as they pass through the stages—that they do not just passively accept a cultural norm for morality. Kohlberg argued that a child's moral thinking can be advanced through discussions with others who reason at the next higher stage. Like Piaget, Kohlberg thought that the mutual give-and-take of peer relations promotes more advanced moral thinking because of the role-taking opportunities they provide children.

Kohlberg's Critics   Kohlberg's provocative theory has not gone unchallenged (Gibbs, 2003; Lapsley, 2006; Lapsley & Narvaez, 2006; Nucci, 2004; Shweder & others, 2006; Turiel, 2006). One powerful criticism centers on the idea that moral thoughts don't always predict moral behavior. The criticism is that Kohlberg's theory places too much emphasis on moral thinking and not enough on moral behavior. Moral reasons sometimes can be a shelter for immoral behavior. Bank embezzlers and U.S. presidents endorse the loftiest of moral virtues, but their own behavior can prove to be immoral. No one wants a nation of stage-6 Kohlberg thinkers who know what is right yet do what is wrong.

Lawrence Kohlberg, the architect of a provocative cognitive developmental theory of moral development.

preconventional reasoning In Kohlberg's theory, the lowest level of moral development; at this level, the child shows no internalization of moral values and moral reasoning is controlled by external rewards and punishments.

conventional reasoning In Kohlberg's theory, the middle level of moral development; at this level, internalization is intermediate in the sense that individuals abide by certain standards (internal) but these essentially are the standards of others (external).

postconventional reasoning In Kohlberg's theory, the highest level of moral development; at this level, moral development is internalized and moral reasoning is self-generated.

LEVEL 1 Preconventional Level No Internalization	LEVEL 2 Conventional Level Intermediate Internalization	LEVEL 3 Postconventional Level Full Internalization
Stage 1 Heteronomous Morality *Children obey because adults tell them to obey. People base their moral decisions on fear of punishment.*	**Stage 3** Mutual Interpersonal Expectations, Relationships, and Interpersonal Conformity *Individuals value trust, caring, and loyalty to others as a basis for moral judgments.*	**Stage 5** Social Contract or Utility and Individual Rights *Individuals reason that values, rights, and principles undergird or transcend the law.*
Stage 2 Individualism, Purpose, and Exchange *Individuals pursue their own interests but let others do the same. What is right involves equal exchange.*	**Stage 4** Social Systems Morality *Moral judgments are based on understanding of the social order, law, justice, and duty.*	**Stage 6** Universal Ethical Principles *The person has developed moral judgments that are based on universal human rights. When faced with a dilemma between law and conscience, a personal, individualized conscience is followed.*

FIGURE 3.8 Kohlberg's Three Levels and Six Stages of Moral Development

Carol Gilligan says that girls experience life differently than boys do; in Gilligan's words, girls have a "different voice." She argues that relationships are central to every aspect of a female's life.

justice perspective A moral perspective that focuses on the rights of the individual; Kohlberg's theory is a justice perspective.

care perspective A moral perspective that focuses on connectedness and relationships among people; Gilligan's approach reflects a care perspective.

Another line of criticism is that Kohlberg's theory is too individualistic. Carol Gilligan (1982, 1998) distinguishes between the justice perspective and the care perspective. Kohlberg's is a **justice perspective** that focuses on the rights of the individual, who stands alone and makes moral decisions. The **care perspective** views people in terms of their connectedness. Emphasis is placed on relationships and concern for others. According to Gilligan, Kohlberg greatly underplayed the care perspective—possibly because he was a male, most of his research was on males, and he lived in a male-dominant society.

In extensive interviews with girls from 6 to 18 years of age, Gilligan found that they consistently interpret moral dilemmas in terms of human relationships, not in terms of individual rights. Gilligan (1996) also has argued that girls reach a critical juncture in their development in early adolescence. At about 11 or 12 years of age, they become aware of how much they prize relationships yet come to realize this interest is not shared by the male-dominant society. The solution, says Gilligan, is to give relationships and concern for others a higher priority in our society. Gilligan does not recommend totally throwing out Kohlberg's theory. She argues the highest level of moral development occurs when individuals combine the care and justice perspectives in positive ways.

Controversy exists over whether the gender difference in moral judgment is as strong as Gilligan says (Hyde, 2005, 2007; Walker, 2005). For example, a *meta-analysis* (a statistical analysis that combines the results of many different studies) cast doubt on Gilligan's claim of substantial gender differences in moral judgment (Jaffee & Hyde, 2000). Overall, this analysis found only a small gender difference in care-based reasoning. However, some researchers have found differences in how boys and girls interpret moral situations with girls giving more prosocial, helping responses (Eisenberg, Fabes, & Spinrad, 2006; Eisenberg & Morris, 2004).

Moral Personality Recently there has been a surge of interest in what might constitute a *moral personality*. The interest has focused on three areas: moral identity, moral character, and moral exemplars:

- *Moral identity.* Individuals have a moral identity when moral notions and commitments are central to their lives (Blasi, 2005). In this view, if students behave in a manner that violates their moral commitment, it places the integrity of their self at risk (Lapsley & Narvaez, 2006).

- *Moral character.* An emphasis on moral character suggests that if students don't have a moral character, they will wilt under pressure or fatigue, fail to follow through, become distracted and discouraged, and fail to behave morally. The moral character approach emphasizes the importance of having certain moral virtues, such as "honesty, truthfulness, and trustworthiness, as well as those of care, compassion, thoughtfulness, and considerateness. Other salient traits revolve around virtues of dependability, loyalty, and conscientiousness" (Walker, 2002, p. 74).

- *Moral exemplars.* Moral exemplars are people who have lived exemplary moral lives. Then have a moral personality, identity, character, and set of virtues that reflect moral excellence and commitment. Students may benefit when teachers invite moral exemplars to talk with them about their lives and experiences.

Moral Education   Is there a best way to educate students so they will develop better moral values? Moral education is hotly debated in educational circles. We will study one of the earliest analyses of moral education, then turn to some contemporary views.

The Hidden Curriculum   Recall from chapter 1 that John Dewey was one of educational psychology's pioneers. Dewey (1933) recognized that even when schools do not have specific programs in moral education, they provide moral education through a "hidden curriculum." The **hidden curriculum**—conveyed by the moral atmosphere that is a part of every school—is created by school and classroom rules, the moral orientation of teachers and school administrators, and text materials. Teachers serve as models of ethical or unethical behavior. Classroom rules and peer relations at school transmit attitudes about cheating, lying, stealing, and consideration for others. Through its rules and regulations, the school administration infuses the school with a value system.

Character Education   **Character education** is a direct approach to moral education that involves teaching students basic moral literacy to prevent them from engaging in immoral behavior and doing harm to themselves or others. The argument is that behaviors such as lying, stealing, and cheating are wrong and that students should be taught this throughout their education (Lapsley & Narvaez, 2006; Nucci, 2004). According to the character education approach, every school should have an explicit moral code that is clearly communicated to students. Any violations of the code should be met with sanctions (Bennett, 1993). Instruction in moral concepts with respect to specific behaviors, such as cheating, can take the form of example and definition, class discussions and role-playing, or rewards to students for proper behavior.

Some character education movements are the Character Education Partnership, the Character Education Network, the Aspen Declaration on Character Education, and the publicity campaign "Character Counts." Among the books that promote character education are William Bennett's (1993) *The Book of Virtues* and William Damon's (1995) *Greater Expectations*. Critics argue that some character education programs encourage students to be too passive and noncritical.

Values Clarification   **Values clarification** means helping people to clarify what their lives are for and what is worth working for. In this approach, students are encouraged to define their own values and to understand others' values. Values clarification differs from character education in not telling students what their values should be.

In values clarification exercises, there are no right or wrong answers. The clarification of values is left up to the individual student. Advocates of values clarification

hidden curriculum Dewey's concept that every school has a pervasive moral atmosphere even if it does not have a program of moral education.

character education A direct approach to moral education that involves teaching students basic moral literacy to prevent them from engaging in immoral behavior and doing harm to themselves or others.

values clarification An approach to moral education that emphasizes helping people clarify what their lives are for and what is worth working for; students are encouraged to define their own values and understand the values of others.

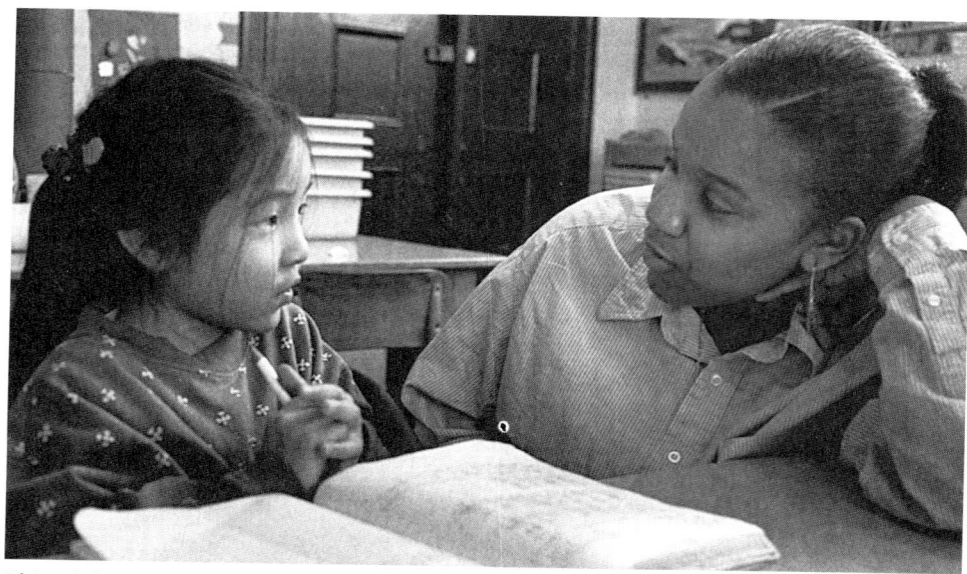

This adolescent volunteered to work in the National Helpers Network, which gives students an opportunity to participate in service learning. Among the service provided are helping with environmental concerns, improving neighborhoods, and tutoring. Students also participate in weekly seminars that encourage them to reflect on their active involvement in the community.

say it is value-free. Critics, however, argue that its controversial content offends community standards. They also say that because of its relativistic nature, values clarification undermines accepted values and fails to stress right behavior.

Character education should involve more than a listing of moral virtues on a classroom wall (Walker, 2002). Instead, children and adolescents need to participate in critical discussions of values—to discuss and reflect on how to incorporate virtues into their daily lives. Exposing children to moral exemplars worthy of emulating and getting them to participate in community service are also strategies important in character education.

Cognitive Moral Education **Cognitive moral education** is an approach based on the belief that students should learn to value ideals such as democracy and justice as their moral reasoning develops. Kohlberg's theory has been the basis for a number of cognitive moral education programs. In a typical program, high school students meet in a semester-long course to discuss a number of moral issues. The instructor acts as a facilitator rather than as a director of the class. The hope is that students will develop more advanced notions of such concepts as cooperation, trust, responsibility, and community. Toward the end of his career, Kohlberg (1986) recognized that the school's moral atmosphere is more important than he initially envisioned. For example, in one study, a semester-long moral education class based on Kohlberg's theory was successful in advancing moral thinking in three democratic schools but not in three authoritarian schools (Higgins, Power, & Kohlberg, 1983).

Service Learning Another approach to moral education—service learning—takes education out into the community (Benson & others, 2006; Hart, 2006; Metz & Youniss, 2005; Reinders & Youniss, 2006; Youniss, 2006). **Service learning** is a form of education that promotes social responsibility and service to the community. In service learning, students engage in activities such as tutoring, helping older adults, working in a hospital, assisting at a child-care center, or cleaning up a vacant lot to make

cognitive moral education An approach to moral education based on the belief that students should value things such as democracy and justice as their moral reasoning develops; Kohlberg's theory has served as the foundation for many cognitive moral education efforts.

service learning A form of education that promotes social responsibility and service to the community.

BEST PRACTICES
Strategies for Improving Children's Prosocial Behavior

Prosocial behavior involves the positive side of moral development (in contrast to antisocial behavior such as cheating, lying, and stealing). Prosocial behavior is behavior that is regarded as being altruistic, fair, sharing, or generally empathetic (Eisenberg, Fabes, & Spinrad, 2006). Here are some strategies that teachers can adopt to improve students' prosocial behavior (Wittmer & Honig, 1994, pp. 5–10):

1. *"Value and emphasize consideration of others' needs."* This encourages students to engage in more helping activities. Nel Noddings (2001) explains the morality of caring as one of teaching students to feel for others, which leads to empathy and concern.

2. *"Model prosocial behaviors."* Students imitate what teachers do. For example, a teacher who comforts a student in times of stress is likely to observe students imitating her comforting behavior.

3. *"Label and identify prosocial and antisocial behaviors."* Often go beyond just saying, "That's good" or "That's nice" to a student. Be specific in identifying prosocial behaviors. Say, "You are being helpful" or "You gave him a tissue; he really needed it to wipe his nose." Or regarding antisocial behavior, to a young child you might say something like "That's not being nice. How would you feel if he messed up your papers like that?"

4. *"Attribute positive social behaviors to each child."* Attribute positive intentions to a positive act, such as "You shared because you like to help others."

5. *"Notice and positively encourage prosocial behaviors, but do not overuse external rewards."* Commenting on positive behaviors and attributing positive characteristics to students rather than using external rewards helps students to internalize prosocial attitudes.

6. *"Facilitate perspective taking and understanding others' feelings."* Helping students notice and respond to others' feelings can increase their consideration of others.

7. *"Use positive discipline strategies."* Reason with students when they do something wrong. If a student is too aggressive and harms another student, point out the consequences of the student's behavior for the victim. Avoid harsh, punitive behavior with students.

8. *"Develop class and school projects that foster altruism."* Let children come up with examples of projects they can engage in that will help others. These projects might include cleaning up the schoolyard, writing as pen pals to children in troubled lands, collecting toys or food for individuals in need, and making friends with older adults during visits to a nursing home.

a play area. Thus, service learning takes education out into the community (Reinders & Youniss, 2006; Youniss, 2006).

One goal of service learning is to help students to become less self-centered and more strongly motivated to help others (Pritchard & Whitehead, 2004). One eleventh-grade student worked as a reading tutor for students from low-income homes with reading skills well below their grade levels. She commented that until she did the tutoring she didn't realize how many students had not experienced the same opportunities that she had had when she was growing up. An especially rewarding moment was when one young girl told her, "I want to learn to read like you do so I can go to college when I grow up." A key feature of service learning is that it benefits both the student volunteers and the recipients of their help (Hamilton & Hamilton, 2004).

Students who engage in service learning tend to share certain characteristics, such as being extraverted, having a high level of self-understanding, and showing a commitment to others (Eisenberg & Morris, 2004). Also, females are more likely to volunteer to engage in community service than males (Eisenberg & Morris, 2004).

Researchers have found that service learning benefit students in a number of ways:

- Their grades improve, they become more motivated, and set more goals (Johnson & others, 1998; Search Institute, 1995).
- Their self-esteem improves (Hamburg, 1997; Johnson & others, 1998).
- They have an improved sense of being able to make a difference for others (Search Institute, 1995).

- They become less alienated (Calabrase & Schumer, 1986).
- They increasingly reflect on society's political organization and moral order (Yates, 1995; Youniss, 2006).

Recent figures indicate that 26 percent of U.S. public high schools require students to participate in service learning (Metz & Youniss, 2005). One recent study found that participating in the required 40 hours of community service improved the civic attitudes and behaviors of 12th grade students who had never before participated in a service learning program (Metz & Youniss, 2005). The benefits of service learning, both for the volunteer and for the recipient, suggest that more students should be required to participate in service learning programs (Benson & others, 2006).

Review, Reflect, and Practice

(3) Explain these aspects of children's socioemotional development: self-esteem, identity, and moral development.

REVIEW

- What is self-esteem and what are some ways to increase students' self-esteem? What is the nature of identity development and what are the four statuses of identity?
- What is moral development and what stages of moral development were described by Piaget? What levels were identified by Kohlberg and what are two criticisms of his theory? Contrast the justice and care perspectives. What are some forms of moral education?

REFLECT

- What is the level of moral development likely to be among the children you intend to teach? How might this affect your approach to how you manage students' relations with others in class?

PRAXIS™ PRACTICE

1. Teachers can have the most positive impact on students' self-esteem and achievement by
   a. making academic tasks easy.
   b. having children who often receive negative feedback from peers work in groups with these peers to foster social approval.
   c. helping children succeed by teaching them appropriate learning strategies.
   d. intervening in children's problems so that they don't get frustrated.
2. Marika sees Jamal take Yosuke's snack. Soon afterward, she sees Yosuke retaliate by taking Jamal's favorite pen. Marika does not report these incidents to the teacher, because they involve equal exchanges. According to Kohlberg, which stage of moral development has Marika reached?
   a. stage 1
   b. stage 2
   c. stage 3
   d. stage 4

Please see the answer key at the end of the book.

In chapters 2 and 3 we have examined how students develop, focusing mainly on the general pattern. In chapter 4, we will explore how individual students vary with regard to intelligence and other personal characteristics.

CRACK THE CASE
The Case of the Fight

Many schools, including the one in which Miss Mahoney teaches, emphasize character education as a strategy for preventing violence. The basic idea is to promote empathy among students and to disallow behaviors such as teasing, name-calling, and threats of any kind. Miss Mahoney has included character education in the curriculum of her fifth-grade class. However, many of her students, especially the boys, continue to display the very behaviors she is trying to eliminate.

Two students in Miss Mahoney's class, Santana and Luke, are on the same club soccer team and often get into verbal conflicts with each other, although they appreciate each other's talents on the field. Tuesday night at practice, in violation of the team's rules, Santana told Luke that he "sucks." Luke decides to let it go. He doesn't want Santana to suffer a one-game suspension, recognizing Santana's value to the team in light of facing a tough opponent that weekend.

Thursday in class, Luke accuses Santana of stealing the cards he was using to organize a project. Luke is very angry. Santana also gets infuriated, claiming he did not steal them. He then finds them on the floor and hands them to Luke. "Here's your dumb cards, Luke," he says. "See, I didn't steal them."

In anger, Luke says, "Fine. Then how come they're all crinkled? You know, I could beat you up and maybe I just will."

"Yeah, right. You and who else?" asks Santana with a sneer.

Two other boys working nearby overheard the altercation and begin contributing their perspectives.

"Yeah, Santana, Luke would kick your rear," says Grant.

"I think Santana would win," chimes in Peter.

"Meet me at the park tomorrow after school and let's just see!" demands Santana.

"No problem," retorts Luke.

Thursday evening, they are both at soccer practice. Nothing is said about the fight that was to take place the next day after school.

Friday morning Santana's mother calls Miss Mahoney to tell her that Santana is afraid to come to school because Luke has threatened to beat him up. Obviously, Miss Mahoney is concerned and realizes she must address the situation. Luke's mother also talks to the principal about the situation. However, all Santana's mother told either of them is that Luke had threatened to beat up her son. She didn't know why and did not think the reason mattered in the least. She wanted her son protected and the other boy punished.

That morning Luke's mother was in the school for another purpose. The principal stopped her to talk about the situation, telling her that Santana had told his mother he was afraid to come to school because Luke was going to beat him up. Luke's mother asked for more information. On hearing Santana's side of the story, which was simply that Luke had threatened him, she told the principal that this didn't sound right—that Luke was impulsive enough that if he'd wanted to beat up Santana, he probably would have just hit him, not planned a fight for a later date. She wanted to talk to Luke before she jumped to any conclusions and asked that Miss Mahoney and the principal talk to both of the boys and any other children involved.

Both Miss Mahoney and the principal did as Luke's mother asked. The story that came out is the one you read. They decided that Luke should serve an in-school suspension the following day and miss recess all week "because it is the third 'incident' we've had with him this year." Santana received no punishment and walked away from the meeting, grinning.

- What are the issues in this case?
- At what stage of moral development would you expect these boys to be, based on the information you have? What predictions can you make regarding each boy's sense of self and emotional development?
- What can you say about the boys' mothers?
- What do you think about the punishment that Luke received? How would you have handled this situation?
- What impact do you think this will have on the boys' future relationship? What impact on their attitudes toward school?

Reach Your Learning Goals
Social Contexts and Socioemotional Development

① CONTEMPORARY THEORIES: Describe two contemporary perspectives on socioemotional development: Bronfenbrenner's ecological theory and Erikson's life-span development theory.

Bronfenbrenner's Ecological Theory

Bronfenbrenner's ecological theory seeks to explain how environmental systems influence children's development. Bronfenbrenner described five environmental systems that include both micro and macro inputs: microsystem, mesosystem, exosystem, macrosystem, and chronosystem. Bronfenbrenner's theory is one of the few systematic analyses that includes both micro and macro environments. Critics say the theory lacks attention to biological and cognitive factors. They also point out that it does not address step-by-step developmental changes.

Erikson's Life-Span Development Theory

Erikson's life-span development theory proposes eight stages, each centering on a particular type of challenge or dilemma: trust versus mistrust, autonomy versus shame and doubt, initiative versus guilt, industry versus inferiority, identity versus identity confusion, intimacy versus isolation, generativity versus stagnation, and integrity versus despair. Erikson's theory has made important contributions to understanding socioemotional development, although some critics say the stages are too rigid and that their sequencing lacks research support.

② SOCIAL CONTEXTS OF DEVELOPMENT: Discuss how the social contexts of families, peers, and schools are linked with socioemotional development.

Families

Baumrind proposed four parenting styles: authoritarian, authoritative, neglectful, and indulgent. Authoritative parenting is associated with children's social competence. Greater numbers of children are growing up in diverse family structures than at any other point in history. A special concern is the number of children of divorce. When both the parenting and school environment are authoritative, children in divorced families benefit. Other special concerns are ethnic and socioeconomic variations in families. Middle-income families are more likely to use discipline that encourages internalization; low-income families are more likely to use discipline that focuses on external characteristics. Two important aspects of school-family linkages are family management and parental involvement. Fostering school-family partnerships involves providing assistance to families, communicating effectively with families about school programs and student progress, encouraging parents to be volunteers, involving families with their children in learning activities at home, including families in school decisions, and coordinating community collaboration. Another important aspect of parenting involves structuring and monitoring out-of-school care.

Peers

Peers are children of about the same age or maturity level. Social isolation, or the inability to "plug in" to a social network, is linked with many problems. Children can have one of five peer statuses: popular, average, rejected, neglected, or controversial. Rejected children often have more serious adjustment problems than neglected children. Friendship is an important aspect of students' social relations. Peer relations begin to consume more of children's time in elementary and secondary schools. Same-sex peer groups predominate in elementary school. In early adolescence, participation in mixed-sex groups increases and being a member of a crowd becomes more important.

Schools

Schools involve changing social developmental contexts from preschool through high school. The early childhood setting is a protected environment with one or two teachers, usually female. Peer groups are more important in elementary school. In middle school, the social field enlarges to include the whole school, and the social system becomes more complex.

Controversy characterizes early childhood education curricula. On the one side are the developmentally appropriate, child-centered, constructivist advocates; on the other are those who advocate an instructivist, academic approach. Head Start has provided early childhood education for children from low-income families. High-quality Head Start programs are effective educational interventions, but up to 40 percent of these programs may be ineffective. A special concern is that many early elementary school classrooms rely mainly on negative feedback. The transition to middle or junior high is stressful for many students because it coincides with so many physical, cognitive, and socioemotional changes. It involves going from the top-dog position to the lowest position in a school hierarchy. Effective schools for young adolescents adapt to individual variations in students, take seriously what is known about the development of young adolescents, and give as much emphasis to socioemotional as to cognitive development. An increasing number of educational experts also believe that substantial changes need to be made in U.S. high school education.

(3) SOCIOEMOTIONAL DEVELOPMENT: Explain these aspects of children's socioemotional development: self-esteem, identity, and moral development.

The Self

Self-esteem, also referred to as self-worth or self-image, is the individual's overall conception of himself or herself. Self-esteem often varies across domains and becomes more differentiated in adolescence. Four keys to increasing students' self-esteem are to (1) identify the causes of low self-esteem and the domains of competence important to the student, (2) provide emotional support and social approval, (3) help students achieve, and (4) develop students' coping skills. Marcia proposed that adolescents have one of four identity statuses (based on the extent to which they have explored or are exploring alternative paths and whether they have made a commitment): identity diffusion, identity foreclosure, identity moratorium, identity achievement.

Moral Development

Moral development concerns rules and conventions about just interactions between people. These rules can be studied in three domains: cognitive, behavioral, and emotional. Piaget proposed two stages of moral thought: heteronomous morality (ages 4 to 7 years) and autonomous morality (10 years and older). Piaget argued that the mutual give-and-take of peer relations advances moral development. Kohlberg, like Piaget, stressed that the key to understanding moral development is moral reasoning and that it unfolds in stages. Kohlberg identified three levels of moral development (preconventional, conventional, and postconventional), with two stages at each level. As individuals go through the three levels, their moral thinking becomes more internalized. Two main criticisms of Kohlberg's theory are (1) Kohlberg did not give enough attention to moral behavior, and (2) Kohlberg's theory gave too much power to the individual and not enough to relationships with others. In this regard, Gilligan argued that Kohlberg's theory is a male-oriented justice perspective. She believes that what is needed in moral development is a female-oriented care perspective. Recently there has been a surge of interest in what constitutes a moral personality. Three aspects of moral personality are identity, character, and exemplars. The hidden curriculum is the moral atmosphere that every school has. Three types of moral education are character education, values clarification, and cognitive moral education. Service learning is becoming increasingly important in schools.

 KEY TERMS

PORTFOLIO ACTIVITIES

Now that you have a good understanding of this chapter, complete these exercises to expand your thinking.

Independent Reflection

Meeting the Socioemotional Needs of Students. Think about the age of students you intend to teach. Which of Erikson's stages is likely to be central for them? What, if anything, does Bronfenbrenner's theory suggest about important resources for students at that age? Does his system suggest particular challenges to students or ways that you as a teacher might facilitate their success? Write down your ideas in your portfolio.

Collaborative Work

The Role of Moral Education in Schools. Which approach to moral education (character education, values clarification, or cognitive moral education) do you like the best? Why? Should schools be in the business of having specific moral education programs? Get together with several other students in this class and discuss your perspectives. Then write a brief statement that reflects your own perspective on moral education.

Research/Field Experience

Foster Family-School Linkages. Interview several teachers from local schools about how they foster family-school linkages. Try to talk with a kindergarten teacher, an elementary teacher, a middle school teacher, and a high school teacher. Summarize your discoveries.

Go to the Online Learning Center for downloadable portfolio templates.

 TAKING IT TO THE NET

- How can teachers help children and youth successfully resolve the challenges of the different stages of psychosocial development? Describe a teaching strategy that could be used to foster independence, confidence, and risk-taking in students. **www.extension.umn.edu/distribution/youthdevelopment/DA6715.html**

- Research shows that family involvement greatly influences student attitudes, attendance, and academic achievement. Develop an action plan for involving families in your classroom in a variety of ways. What are some of the challenges to involving families, and how do you plan to overcome these? **www.ncrel.org/sdrs/areas/issues/envrnmnt/famncomm/pa300.htm**

- Do you believe that helping students develop good character is just as important as teaching reading, writing, and math? Or should families solely be in control of character and moral instruction? Why? In what ways do teachers inherently impact students' character development through their daily interactions? **chiron.valdosta.edu/whuitt/col/morchr/morchr.html**

Connect to the Online Learning Center to explore possible answers.

 STUDY, PRACTICE, AND SUCCEED

Visit **www.mhhe.com/santedu3e** to review the chapter with self-grading quizzes and Self-Assessments, to apply the chapter material to two more Crack the Case studies, and for suggested activities to develop your teaching portfolio.

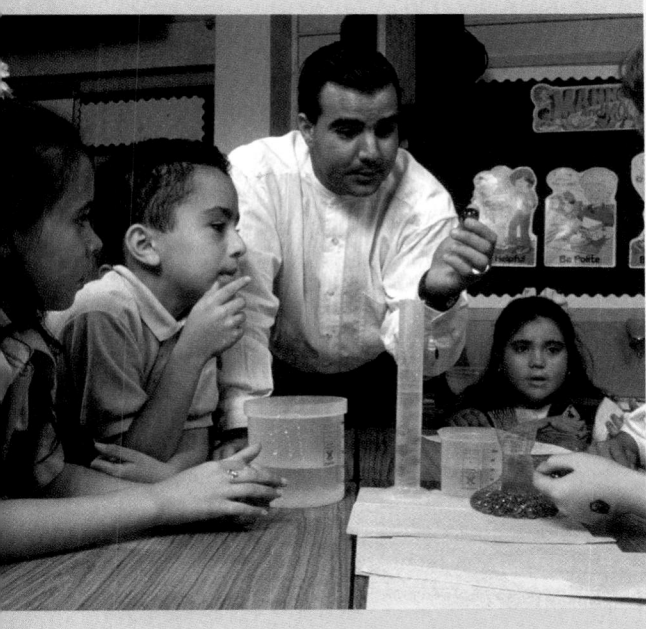

CHAPTER 4

Individual Variations

Individuals play out their lives in different ways.

—Thomas Huxley
English Biologist, 19th Century

Learning Goals

1 Discuss the concept of intelligence, how it is measured, and some controversies about its use by educators.

2 Describe learning and thinking styles.

3 Define personality, identify the "big five" factors of personality, and discuss person-situation interaction. Also, define temperament, identify three types of children's temperament, and evaluate teaching strategies linked to children's temperament.

TEACHING STORIES Shiffy Landa

Shiffy Landa, a first-grade teacher at H. F. Epstein Hebrew Academy in St. Louis, Missouri, uses the multiple-intelligences approach of Howard Gardner (1983, 1993) in her classroom. Gardner argues that there is not just one general type of intelligence but at least eight specific types.

Landa (2000, pp. 6–8) believes that the multiple-intelligences approach is the best way to reach children because they have many different kinds of abilities. In Landa's words, "My role as a teacher is quite different from the way it was just a few years ago. No longer do I stand in front of the room and lecture to my students. I consider my role to be one of a facilitator rather than a frontal teacher. The desks in my room are not all neatly lined up in straight rows . . . students are busily working in centers in cooperative learning groups, which gives them the opportunity to develop their interpersonal intelligences."

Students use their "body-kinesthetic intelligence to form the shapes of the letters as they learn to write. . . . They also use this intelligence to move the sounds of the vowels that they are learning, blending them together with letters, as they begin to read."

Landa says that "intrapersonal intelligence is an intelligence that often is neglected in the traditional classroom." In her classroom, students "complete their own evaluation sheets after they have concluded their work at the centers. They evaluate their work and create their own portfolios," in which they keep their work so they can see their progress.

As she was implementing the multiple-intelligences approach in her classroom, Landa recognized that she needed to educate parents about it. She created "a parent education class called The Parent-Teacher Connection," which meets periodically to view videos, talk about multiple intelligences, and discuss how they are being introduced in the classroom. She also sends a weekly newsletter to parents, informing them about the week's multiple-intelligences activities and students' progress.

Preview

Shiffy Landa's classroom techniques build on Howard Gardner's multiple-intelligence theory, one of theories of intelligence that we explore in this chapter. You will see that there is spirited debate about whether people have a general intelligence or a number of specific intelligences. We also examine learning and thinking styles, as well as personality and temperament. For each of these topics, an important theme is students' individual variations and the best strategies for teachers to use related to these variations.

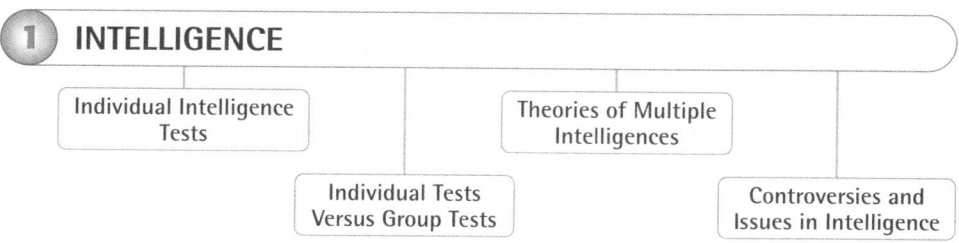

The concept of intelligence generates controversy and heated debate (Birney & others, 2005; Sternberg, 2006). Does each person have a general mental capacity that can be measured and quantified? Are intelligence tests useful and fair? Should these tests be used to place students in special classes or tracks? Do individuals have a general mental capacity or a number of specific mental capacities? If people have various mental capacities, what are they? How many do they have?

Twentieth-century English novelist Aldous Huxley said that children are remarkable for their curiosity and intelligence. What did Huxley mean when he used the word *intelligence*? Intelligence is one of our most prized possessions, yet even the most intelligent people have not been able to agree on what intelligence is. Unlike height, weight, and age, intelligence cannot be directly measured. You can't peer into a student's head and observe the intelligence going on inside. We only can evaluate a student's intelligence indirectly by studying the student's intelligent acts. For the most part, we have relied on written intelligence tests to provide an estimate of a student's intelligence.

Some experts describe intelligence as problem-solving skills. Others describe it as the ability to adapt to and learn from life's everyday experiences. Combining these ideas, we can arrive at a fairly traditional definition of **intelligence:** problem-solving skills and the ability to adapt to and learn from life's everyday experiences. But even this broad definition doesn't satisfy everyone. As you will see shortly, some theorists propose that musical skills should be considered part of intelligence. Also, a definition of intelligence based on a theory such as Vygotsky's would have to include the ability to use the tools of the culture with help from more-skilled individuals. Because intelligence is such an abstract, broad concept, it is not surprising that there are so many different ways to define it.

Not only are there many ways to define intelligence, there are many ways to measure it. In the next two sections, we will describe the main individual and group tests of intelligence. Then we will examine two major theories of multiple intelligence, those of Robert J. Sternberg and Howard Gardner.

Individual Intelligence Tests

Psychologist Robert J. Sternberg recalls being terrified of taking IQ tests as a child. He says that he literally froze when the time came to take such tests. Even as an adult, Sternberg remembers the humiliation of being in the sixth grade and taking an IQ test with fifth-graders. Sternberg eventually overcame his anxieties about IQ tests. Not only did he begin to perform better on them, but at age 13 he devised his own IQ test and began using it to assess classmates—until the school principal found out and scolded him. Sternberg became so fascinated by intelligence that he made its study one of his lifelong pursuits. Later in the chapter we will discuss his theory of intelligence. To begin, though, let's go back in time to examine the first valid intelligence test.

The Binet Tests   In 1904 the French Ministry of Education asked psychologist Alfred Binet to devise a method of identifying children who were unable to learn in school. School officials wanted to reduce crowding by placing in special schools students who did not benefit from regular classroom teaching. Binet and his student Theophile Simon developed an intelligence test to meet this request. The test is called the 1905 Scale. It consisted of 30 questions, ranging from the ability to touch one's ear to the abilities to draw designs from memory and define abstract concepts.

Binet developed the concept of **mental age (MA),** an individual's level of mental development relative to others. In 1912, William Stern created the concept of **intelligence quotient (IQ),** which refers to a person's mental age divided by chronological age (CA), multiplied by 100. That is, $IQ = MA/CA \times 100$.

If mental age is the same as chronological age, then the person's IQ is 100. If mental age is above chronological age, then IQ is more than 100. For example, a 6-year-old with a mental age of 8 would have an IQ of 133. If mental age is below chronological age, then IQ is less than 100. For example, a 6-year-old with a mental age of 5 would have an IQ of 83.

The Binet test has been revised many times to incorporate advances in the understanding of intelligence and intelligence testing. These revisions are called the *Stanford-Binet tests* (because the revisions were made at Stanford University). By administering the test to large numbers of people of different ages from different backgrounds, researchers have found that scores on a Stanford-Binet test approximate a normal distribution (see figure 4.1). As described more fully in chapter 15, "Standardized Tests and Teaching," a **normal distribution** is symmetrical, with a

intelligence Problem-solving skills and the ability to adapt to and learn from life's everyday experiences.

mental age (MA) An individual's level of mental development relative to others.

intelligence quotient (IQ) A person's mental age (MA) divided by chronological age (CA), multiplied by 100.

normal distribution A symmetrical distribution, with a majority of scores falling in the middle of the possible range of scores and few scores appearing toward the extremes of the range.

FIGURE 4.1 The Normal Curve and Standard-Binet IQ Scores

The distribution of IQ scores approximates a normal curve. Most of the population falls in the middle range of scores. Notice that extremely high and extremely low scores are very rare. Slightly more than two-thirds of the scores fall between 84 and 116. Only about 1 in 50 individuals has an IQ of more than 132, and only about 1 in 50 individuals has an IQ of less than 68.

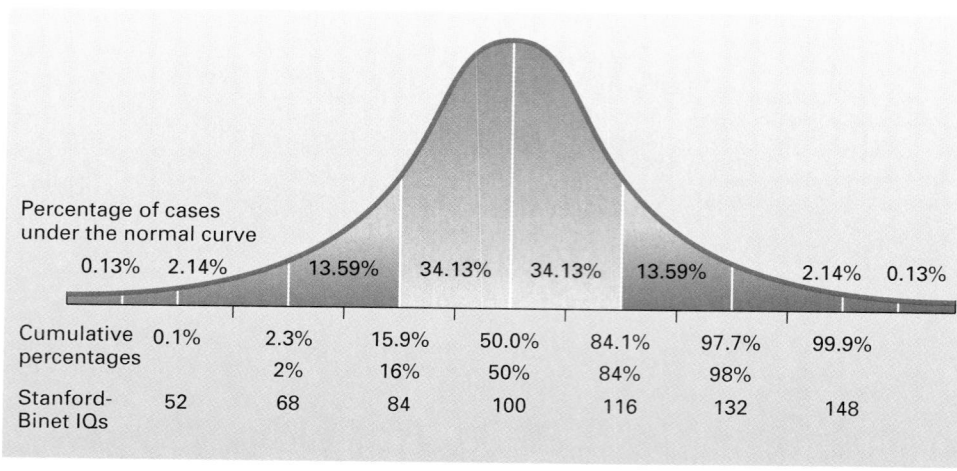

majority of the scores falling in the middle of the possible range of scores and few scores appearing toward the extremes of the range.

The current Stanford-Binet test is administered individually to people aged 2 through adult. It includes a variety of items, some of which require verbal responses, others nonverbal responses. For example, items that reflect a typical 6-year-old's level of performance on the test include the verbal ability to define at least six words, such as *orange* and *envelope,* as well as the nonverbal ability to trace a path through a maze. Items that reflect an average adult's level of performance include defining such words as *disproportionate* and *regard,* explaining a proverb, and comparing idleness and laziness.

The fourth edition of the Stanford-Binet was published in 1985. One important addition to this version was the analysis of the individual's responses in terms of four functions: verbal reasoning, quantitative reasoning, abstract visual reasoning, and short-term memory. A general composite score is still obtained to reflect overall intelligence. The Stanford-Binet continues to be one of the most widely used tests to assess students' intelligence (Aiken, 2006).

The Wechsler Scales   Another set of tests widely used to assess students' intelligence is called the *Wechsler scales,* developed by psychologist David Wechsler. They include the Wechsler Preschool and Primary Scale of Intelligence–III (WPPSI-III) to test children 4 to 6½ years of age; the Wechsler Intelligence Scale for Children–IV Integrated (WISC-IV Integrated) for children and adolescents 6 to 16 years of age; and the Wechsler Adult Intelligence Scale (WAIS-III).

In addition to an overall IQ, the Wechsler scales also yield a verbal IQ and a performance IQ (based on items that don't require verbal responses). Verbal IQ is based on six verbal subscales, performance IQ on five performance subscales. This allows the examiner to quickly see patterns of strengths and weaknesses in different areas of the student's intelligence (Woolger, 2001). Examples of items used on two different Wechsler subscales are shown in figure 4.2.

Individual Tests Versus Group Tests

Intelligence tests such as the Stanford-Binet and Wechsler are given on an individual basis. A psychologist approaches an individual assessment of intelligence as a structured interaction between the examiner and the student. This provides the psychologist with an opportunity to sample the student's behavior. During the testing, the examiner observes the ease with which rapport is established, the student's enthusiasm and interest, whether anxiety interferes with the student's performance, and the student's degree of tolerance for frustration.

Verbal Subscales

Similarities

A child must think logically and abstractly to answer a number of questions about how things might be similar.

Example: "In what way are a lion and a tiger alike?"

Comprehension

This subscale is designed to measure an individual's judgment and common sense.

Example: "What is the advantage of keeping money in a bank?"

Nonverbal Subscales

Block Design

An child must assemble a set of multicolored blocks to match designs that the examiner shows. Visual-motor coordination, perceptual organization, and the ability to visualize spatially are assessed.

Example: "Use the four blocks on the left to make the pattern on the right."

FIGURE 4.2 Sample Subscales of the Wechsler Intelligence Scale for Children (WISC–IV)

The Wechsler includes 11 subscales, 6 verbal and 5 nonverbal. Three of the subscales are shown here.

Simulated items similar to those found in the *Wechsler Intelligence Scale for Children—Fourth Edition.* Copyright © 2003 by Harcourt Assessment, Inc. Reproduced with permission. All rights reserved.

Students also may be given an intelligence test in a group (Drummond, 2000). Group intelligence tests include the Lorge-Thorndike Intelligence Tests, the Kuhlman-Anderson Intelligence Tests, and the Otis-Lennon School Mental Abilities Tests. Group intelligence tests are more convenient and economical than individual tests, but they do have their drawbacks. When a test is given to a large group, the examiner cannot establish rapport, determine the student's level of anxiety, and so on. In a large-group testing situation, students might not understand the instructions or might be distracted by other students.

Because of such limitations, when important decisions are made about students, a group intelligence test should always be supplemented with other information about the student's abilities. For that matter, the same strategy holds for an individual intelligence test, although it usually is wise to have less confidence in the accuracy of group intelligence test scores. Many students take tests in large groups at school, but a decision to place a student in a class for students who have mental retardation, a special education class, or a class for students who are gifted should not be based on a group test alone. In such instances, an extensive amount of relevant information about the student's abilities should be obtained outside the testing situation (Domino, 2000).

Theories of Multiple Intelligences

Is it more appropriate to think of a student's intelligence as a general ability or as a number of specific abilities? Psychologists have thought about this question since early in the twentieth century.

Early Views   Binet and Stern both focused on a concept of general intelligence, which Stern called IQ. Wechsler believed it is possible and important to describe both a person's general intelligence and more specific verbal and performance intelligences. He was building on the ideas of Charles Spearman (1927), who said that people have both a general intelligence, which he called *g*, and specific types of intelligence, which he called *s*. Whether such a thing as *g* really exists is an ongoing controversy that we will explore in greater depth later in the chapter.

BEST PRACTICES
Strategies for Interpreting Intelligence Test Scores

Psychological tests are tools (Anastasi & Urbino, 1997). Like all tools, their effectiveness depends on the user's knowledge, skill, and integrity. A hammer can be used to build a beautiful kitchen cabinet or to break down a door. Similarly, psychological tests can be well used or badly abused. Here are some cautions about IQ that can help teachers avoid using information about a student's intelligence in negative ways:

1. *Avoid unwarranted stereotypes and negative expectations about students based on IQ scores.* Too often, sweeping generalizations are made on the basis of an IQ score. Imagine that you are in the teachers' lounge on the second day of school in the fall. You mention one of your students, and another teacher remarks that she had him in her class last year. She says that he was a real dunce and that he scored 83 on an IQ test. How hard is it to ignore this information as you go about teaching your class? Probably difficult. But it is important that you not develop the expectation that because Johnny scored low on an IQ test, it is useless to spend much time teaching him. An IQ test should always be considered a measure of current performance. It is not a measure of fixed potential. Maturational changes and enriched environmental experiences can advance a student's intelligence.

2. *Don't use IQ tests as the main or sole characteristic of competence.* A high IQ is not the ultimate human value. Teachers need to consider not only students' intellectual competence in areas such as verbal skills but also their creative and practical skills.

3. *Especially be cautious in interpreting the meaningfulness of an overall IQ score.* It is wiser to think of intelligence as consisting of a number of domains. Many educational psychologists stress that it is important to consider the student's strengths and weaknesses in different areas of intelligence. Intelligence tests such as the Wechsler scales can provide information about those strengths and weaknesses.

Robert J. Sternberg, who developed the triarchic theory of intelligence.

triarchic theory of intelligence
Sternberg's view that intelligence comes in three main forms: analytical, creative, and practical.

As early as the 1930s, L. L. Thurstone (1938) said people have seven specific intellectual abilities, which he called primary abilities: verbal comprehension, number ability, word fluency, spatial visualization, associative memory, reasoning, and perceptual speed. More recently, the search for specific types of intelligence has heated up (Gregory, R. J. (2007). *Psychological Testing* (5th Ed.). Boston: Allyn & Bacon).

Sternberg's Triarchic Theory According to Robert J. Sternberg's (1986, 2004, 2006) **triarchic theory of intelligence,** intelligence comes in three forms: analytical, creative, and practical. Analytical intelligence involves the ability to analyze, judge, evaluate, compare, and contrast. Creative intelligence consists of the ability to create, design, invent, originate, and imagine. Practical intelligence focuses on the ability to use, apply, implement, and put into practice.

To understand what analytical, creative, and practical intelligence mean, let's look at examples of people who reflect these three types of intelligence:

- Consider Latisha, who scores high on traditional intelligence tests such as the Stanford-Binet and is a star analytical thinker. Latisha's *analytical intelligence* approximates what has traditionally been called intelligence and what is commonly assessed by intelligence tests. In Sternberg's view, analytical intelligence consists of several components: the ability to acquire or store information; to retain or retrieve information; to transfer information; to plan, make decisions, and solve problems; and to translate thoughts into performance.

- Todd does not have the best test scores but has an insightful and creative mind. Sternberg calls the type of thinking at which Todd excels *creative intelligence.* According to Sternberg, creative people have the ability to solve new problems quickly, but they also learn how to solve familiar problems in an automatic way so their minds are free to handle other problems that require insight and creativity.

- Finally, consider Emanuel, a person whose scores on traditional IQ tests are low but who quickly grasps real-life problems. He easily picks up knowledge about how the world works. Emanuel's "street smarts" and practical know-how are what Sternberg calls *practical intelligence.* Practical intelligence includes the ability to get out of trouble and a knack for getting along with people. Sternberg describes practical intelligence as all of the important information about getting along in the world that you are not taught in school.

"You're wise, but you lack tree smarts."

Sternberg (2002) says that students with different triarchic patterns look different in school. Students with high analytic ability tend to be favored in conventional schools. They often do well in classes in which the teacher lectures and gives objective tests. These students typically get good grades, do well on traditional IQ tests and the SAT, and later gain admission to competitive colleges.

Students high in creative intelligence often are not in the top rung of their class. Creatively intelligent students might not conform to teachers' expectations about how assignments should be done. They give unique answers, for which they might get reprimanded or marked down.

Like students high in creative intelligence, students who are practically intelligent often do not relate well to the demands of school. However, these students frequently do well outside the classroom's walls. Their social skills and common sense may allow them to become successful managers or entrepreneurs, despite undistinguished school records.

Sternberg (2004) stresses that few tasks are purely analytic, creative, or practical. Most tasks require some combination of these skills. For example, when students write a book report, they might analyze the book's main themes, generate new ideas about how the book could have been written better, and think about how the book's themes can be applied to people's lives. Sternberg argues that it is important for classroom instruction to give students opportunities to learn through all three types of intelligence.

Sternberg (1993; Sternberg & others, 2001) developed the Sternberg Triarchic Abilities Test (STAT) to assess analytical, creative, and practical intelligence. The three kinds of abilities are examined through verbal items and essays, quantitative items, and drawings with multiple-choice items. The goal is to obtain a more complete assessment of intelligence than is possible with a conventional test.

The analytical section of STAT is much like a conventional test, with individuals required to provide the meanings of words, complete number series, and complete matrices. The creative and practical sections are different from conventional tests. For example, in the creative section, individuals write an essay on designing an ideal school. The practical section has individuals solve practical everyday problems such as planning routes and purchasing tickets to an event.

An increasing number of studies are investigating the effectives of the STAT in predicting such important aspects of life as success in school. For example, in one recent study of 800 college students, scores on the STAT were effective in predicting college grade-point average (Sternberg & others, 2001). More research, however, is needed to determine the validity and reliability of the STAT.

Howard Gardner, here working with a young child, developed the view that intelligence comes in the forms of these eight kinds of skills: verbal, mathematical, spatial, bodily-kinesthetic, musical, intrapersonal, interpersonal, and naturalist.

Gardner's Eight Frames of Mind As we indicated in the Teaching Stories introduction to this chapter, Howard Gardner (1983, 1993, 2002) says there are many specific types of intelligence, or frames of mind. They are described here along with examples of the occupations in which they are reflected as strengths (Campbell, Campbell, & Dickinson, 2004):

- *Verbal skills:* the ability to think in words and to use language to express meaning (authors, journalists, speakers)
- *Mathematical skills:* the ability to carry out mathematical operations (scientists, engineers, accountants)
- *Spatial skills:* the ability to think three-dimensionally (architects, artists, sailors)
- *Bodily-kinesthetic skills:* the ability to manipulate objects and be physically adept (surgeons, craftspeople, dancers, athletes)
- *Musical skills:* a sensitivity to pitch, melody, rhythm, and tone (composers, musicians, and music therapists)
- *Intrapersonal skills:* the ability to understand oneself and effectively direct one's life (theologians, psychologists)
- *Interpersonal skills:* the ability to understand and effectively interact with others (successful teachers, mental health professionals)
- *Naturalist skills:* the ability to observe patterns in nature and understand natural and human-made systems (farmers, botanists, ecologists, landscapers)

Gardner argues that each form of intelligence can be destroyed by a different pattern of brain damage, that each involves unique cognitive skills, and that each shows up in unique ways in both the gifted and idiot savants (individuals who have mental retardation but have an exceptional talent in a particular domain, such as drawing, music, or numerical computation).

Although Gardner has endorsed the application of his model to education, he has also witnessed some misuses of the approach. Here are some cautions he gives about using it (Gardner, 1998):

- There is no reason to assume that every subject can be effectively taught in eight different ways to correspond to the eight intelligences, and attempting to do this is a waste of effort.
- Don't assume that it is enough just to apply a certain type of intelligence. For example, in terms of bodily-kinesthetic skills, random muscle movements have nothing to do with cultivating cognitive skills.
- There is no reason to believe that it is helpful to use one type of intelligence as a background activity while children are working on an activity related to a different type of intelligence. For example, Gardner believes that playing music in the background while students solve math problems is a misapplication of his theory.

Project Spectrum Project Spectrum is an innovative attempt by Gardner (1993; Gardner, Feldman, & Krechevsky, 1998) to examine the proposed eight intelligences in young children. Project Spectrum begins with the basic idea that every student has the potential to develop strengths in one or more areas. It provides a context in which to see more clearly the strengths and weaknesses of individual children.

What is a Spectrum classroom like? The classroom has rich and engaging materials that can stimulate the range of intelligences. However, teachers do not try to evoke an intelligence directly by homogeneously grouping activity materials that are labeled "spatial," "verbal," and so on. Rather, they use materials that relate to a combination of intelligence domains. For example, a naturalist corner houses biological specimens that students can explore and compare, eliciting not only students' sensory capacities but also their logical analytical skills. In a story-telling area, students create imaginative tales with stimulating props and design their own storyboards, thus using their linguistic, dramatic, and imaginative skills. In a building corner, students can construct a model of their classroom and arrange small-scale photographs of the students and teachers in their class. This area stimulates the use of both spatial and personal skills. In all, the Spectrum classroom has twelve such areas, which are designed to elicit and improve students' multiple intelligences.

The Spectrum classroom can identify skills that are typically missed in a regular classroom. In one first-grade Spectrum classroom was a boy who was the product of a highly conflicted home and had been at risk for school failure. When Project Spectrum was introduced, the boy was identified as being the best student in the class at taking apart and putting together common objects, such as a food grinder or a doorknob. His teacher became encouraged when she found that he possessed this skill, and his overall school performance began to improve.

These children attend the Key School, which has "pods" where they can pursue activities of special interest to them. Every day, each child can choose from activities that draw on Gardner's eight frames of mind. The school's pods include gardening, architecture, gliding, and dancing.

In addition to identifying unexpected strengths in students, Project Spectrum also can locate undetected weaknesses. Gregory was doing very well in first grade, especially in skills in math computation and conceptual knowledge. However, he performed poorly in a number of other Spectrum areas. He did well only in the areas in which he needed to give the correct answer and a person in authority gave it to him. As a result of the Spectrum program, Gregory's teacher began to search for ways to encourage him to take risks on more open-ended tasks, to try things out in innovative ways, and to realize that it's okay to make mistakes.

The Key School   The Key School, a K–6 elementary school in Indianapolis, immerses students in activities that involve a range of skills that closely correlate with Gardner's eight frames of mind (Goleman, Kaufman, & Ray, 1993). Each day every student is exposed to materials designed to stimulate a range of human abilities, including art, music, language skills, math skills, and physical games. In addition, students devote attention to understanding themselves and others.

The Key School's goal is to allow students to discover their natural curiosity and talent, then let them explore these domains. Gardner underscores that if teachers give students the opportunities to use their bodies, imaginations, and different senses, almost every student finds that he or she is good at something. Even students who are not outstanding in any single area will still find that they have relative strengths.

For 9-week time periods, the school emphasizes different themes, such as the Renaissance in sixteenth-century Italy and "Renaissance Now" in Indianapolis. Students develop projects related to the theme. The projects are not graded. Instead, students present them to their classmates, explain them, and answer questions. Collaboration and teamwork are emphasized in the theme projects and in all areas of learning.

The Technology and Education box on page 122 describes how technology can be used in Gardner's eight types of intelligence.

We have discussed a number of ideas about Gardner's eight types of intelligence. To evaluate your strengths and weaknesses in these areas, complete Self-Assessment 4.1.

Emotional Intelligence   Both Gardner's and Sternberg's theories include one or more categories related to the ability to understand one's self and others and to get along in the world. In Gardner's theory, the categories are interpersonal intelligence and intrapersonal intelligence; in Sternberg's theory, practical intelligence. Other theorists who emphasize interpersonal, intrapersonal, and practical aspects of intelligence focus on what is called *emotional intelligence*, which was popularized by Daniel Goleman (1995) in his book *Emotional Intelligence*.

The concept of emotional intelligence was initially developed by Peter Salovey and John Mayer (1990). They conceptualize **emotional intelligence** as the ability to perceive and express emotion accurately and adaptively (such as taking the perspective of

emotional intelligence The ability to monitor one's own and others' emotions and feelings, to discriminate among them, and to use this information to guide one's thinking and action.

TECHNOLOGY AND EDUCATION
Technology and Multiple Intelligences

Technology can be used to facilitate learning in each area of intelligence:

Verbal Skills. Computers encourage students to revise and rewrite compositions; this should help them to produce more competent papers. "Learning keyboarding is as important today as learning to write with a pencil, and learning to use a word processor is as important as learning to type."

Logical/Mathematical Skills. "Students of every ability can learn effectively through interesting software programs that provide immediate feedback and go far beyond drill-and-practice exercises." These programs challenge students to use their thinking skills to solve math problems.

Spatial Skills. Computers allow students to see and manipulate material. They can create many different forms before they make final copies of a written project. Virtual-reality technology can provide students with opportunities to exercise their visual-spatial skills.

Bodily-Kinesthetic Skills. "Computers rely mostly on eye-hand coordination for their operation—keyboarding and the use of a mouse or touch-screen. This kinesthetic activity . . . makes the student an active participant in the learning."

Musical Skills. "The development of musical intelligence can be enhanced by technology in the same way that verbal fluency is enhanced by word processors . . . The Musical Instrument Digital Interface (MIDI) makes it possible to compose for and orchestrate many different instruments through the computer."

Interpersonal Skills. "When students use computers in pairs or small groups, their comprehension and learning are facilitated and accelerated. Positive learning experiences can result as students share discoveries, support each other in solving problems, and work collaboratively on projects."

Intrapersonal Skills. "Technology offers the means to explore a line of thought in great depth" and to have extensive access to a range of personal interests. "The opportunity for students to make such choices is at the heart of giving them control over their own learning and intellectual development."

Naturalist Skills. Electronic technologies can "facilitate scientific investigation, exploration, and other naturalist activities. Telecommunications technologies help students to understand the world beyond their own environments." For example, National Geographic Online allows students to go on expeditions with famed explorers and photographers. (Source: Dickinson, 1998, 1–3.)

---

others), to understand emotion and emotional knowledge (such as understanding the roles that emotions play in friendship and marriage), to use feelings to facilitate thought (such as being in a positive mood, which is linked to creative thinking), and to manage emotions in oneself and others (such as being able to control one's anger).

The Mayer-Salovey-Caruso Emotional Intelligence Test (MSCEIT) measures the four aspects of emotional intelligence just described: perceiving emotions, understanding emotions, facilitating thought, and managing emotions (Mayer, Salovey, & Caruso, 2002, 2004, 2006). The test consists of 141 items, can be given to individuals 17 years of age and older, and takes about 30 to 45 minutes to administer. Because the MSCEIT has only been available since 2001, few studies have been conducted to examine its ability to predict outcomes (Salovey & Pizarro, 2003). One recent study that used the MSCEIT found that youths with higher emotional intelligence were less likely to have smoked cigarettes or to have used alcohol (Trinidad & Johnson, 2002).

Do Children Have One Intelligence or Many Intelligences? Figure 4.3 provides a comparison of Gardner's, Sternberg's, and Salovey/Mayer's views. Notice that Gardner includes a number of types of intelligence not addressed by the other views, and that Sternberg is unique in emphasizing creative intelligence. These theories of multiple intelligence have much to offer. They have stimulated us to think more broadly about what makes up people's intelligence and competence (Kornhaber, Fierros, & Veeneba, 2005; Moran & Gardner, 2006; Weber, 2005). And they have motivated educators to develop programs that instruct students in different domains (Winner, 2006).

FIGURE 4.3 Comparing Gardner's, Sternberg's, and Salovey/Mayer's Intelligences

Gardner	Sternberg	Salovey/Mayer
Verbal Mathematical	Analytical	
Spatial Movement Musical	Creative	
Interpersonal Intrapersonal	Practical	Emotional
Naturalistic		

BEST PRACTICES
Strategies for Implementing Each of Gardner's Multiple Intelligences

Applications of Gardner's theory of multiple intelligences to children's education continue to be made (Hirch, 2004; Kornhaber, Fierros, & Veenema, 2004; Weber, 2005). Following are some strategies that teachers can use related to Gardner's eight types of intelligence (Campbell, Campbell, & Dickinson, 2004):

1. *Verbal Skills*
   - Read to children and let them read to you.
   - Visit libraries and bookstores with children.
   - Have children summarize and retell a story they have read.

2. *Mathematical Skills*
   - Play games of logic with children.
   - Be on the lookout for situations that can inspire children to think about and construct an understanding of numbers.
   - Take children on field trips to computer labs, science museums, and electronics exhibits.

3. *Spatial Skills*
   - Have a variety of creative materials for children to use.
   - Take children to art museums and hands-on children's museums.
   - Go on walks with children. When they get back, ask them to visualize where they have been and then draw a map of their experiences.

4. *Bodily-Kinesthetic Skills*
   - Provide children with opportunities for physical activity and encourage them to participate.
   - Provide areas where children can play indoors and outdoors. If this is not possible, take them to a park.
   - Encourage children to participate in dance activities.

5. *Musical Skills*
   - Give children an opportunity to play musical instruments.
   - Create opportunities for children to make music and rhythms together using voices and instruments.
   - Take children to concerts.

6. *Intrapersonal Skills*
   - Encourage children to have hobbies and interests.
   - Listen to children's feelings and give them sensitive feedback.
   - Have children keep a journal or scrapbook of their ideas and experiences.

7. *Interpersonal Skills*
   - Encourage children to work in groups.
   - Help children to develop communication skills.
   - Provide group games for children to play.

8. *Naturalist Skills*
   - Create a naturalist learning center in the classroom.
   - Engage children in outdoor naturalist activities, such as taking a nature walk or adopting a tree.
   - Have children make collections of flora or fauna and classify them.

Next, Joanna Smith, a high school English teacher, describes how she implements Gardner's multiple intelligences into her classroom.

THROUGH THE EYES OF TEACHERS
Giving Students a Choice of Which Type of Intelligence They Want to Use for a Project

I try to draw on Gardner's eight frames of mind throughout the year by giving a variety of assignments. My students sometimes have a choice about which "type of intelligence" to use, depending on their project. For example, at the end of the first semester, students do an outside reading project based on a self-selected book. They create a project based on the book's themes and characters. For example, students might give a monologue from a character's perspective, create a family tree, make a CD of thematic songs, or give a "tour" of the book's setting live or on tape. This type of project is always successful because it allows students to choose in what mode, in what frame of mind, they will present their knowledge.

Theories of multiple intelligences also have many critics. They conclude that the research base to support these theories has not yet developed. In particular, some argue that Gardner's classification seems arbitrary. For example, if musical skills represent a type of intelligence, why don't we also refer to chess intelligence, prizefighter intelligence, and so on?

SELF-ASSESSMENT 4.1
Evaluating Myself on Gardner's Eight Types of Intelligence

Read these items and rate yourself on a 4-point scale. Each rating corresponds to how well a statement describes you: 1 = not like me at all, 2 = somewhat unlike me, 3 = somewhat like me, and 4 = a lot like me.

	1	2	3	4

Verbal Thinking
1. I do well on verbal tests, such as the verbal part of the SAT.
2. I am a skilled reader and read prolifically.
3. I love the challenge of solving verbal problems.

Logical/Mathematical Thinking
4. I am a very logical thinker.
5. I like to think like a scientist.
6. Math is one of my favorite subjects.

Spatial Skills
7. I am good at visualizing objects and layouts from different angles.
8. I have the ability to create maps of spaces and locations in my mind.
9. If I had wanted to be, I think I could have been an architect.

Bodily–Kinesthetic Skills
10. I have great hand-eye coordination.
11. I excel at sports.
12. I am good at using my body to carry out an expression, as in dance.

Musical Skills
13. I play one or more musical instruments well.
14. I have a good "ear" for music.
15. I am good at making up songs.

Insightful Skills for Self-Understanding
16. I know myself well and have a positive view of myself.
17. I am in tune with my thoughts and feelings.
18. I have good coping skills.

Insightful Skills for Analyzing Others
19. I am very good at "reading" people.
20. I am good at collaborating with other people.
21. I am a good listener.

Naturalist Skills
22. I am good at observing patterns in nature.
23. I excel at identifying and classifying objects in the natural environment.
24. I understand natural and human-made systems.

Scoring and Interpretation

Total your scores for each of the eight types of intelligence and place the totals in the blank that follows the label for each kind of intelligence. Which areas of intelligence are your strengths? In which are you the least proficient? It is highly unlikely that you will be strong in all eight areas or weak in all eight areas. By being aware of your strengths and weaknesses in different areas of intelligence, you can get a sense of which areas of teaching students will be the easiest and most difficult for you. If I (your author) had to teach musical skills, I would be in big trouble because I just don't have the talent. However, I do have reasonably good movement skills and spent part of my younger life playing and coaching tennis. If you are not proficient in some of Gardner's areas and you have to teach students in those areas, consider getting volunteers from the community to help you. For example, Gardner says that schools need to do a better job of calling on retired people, most of whom likely would be delighted to help students improve their skills in the domain or domains in which they are competent. This strategy also helps to link communities and schools with a sort of "intergenerational glue."

Gardner (1998) has himself criticized the emotional intelligence advocates as going too far in including emotions in the concept of intelligence. He also stresses that creativity should not be included in the concept of intelligence. Although he maintains that understanding emotions and being creative are important aspects of human competence and functioning, Gardner says that emotional understanding and creativity are different from intelligence.

A number of psychologists still support Spearman's concept of *g* (general intelligence) (Bouchard, 2004; Johnson & others, 2004). For example, one expert on intelligence, Nathan Brody (2000, 2006), argues that people who excel at one type of intellectual task are likely to excel at other intellectual tasks. Thus, individuals who do well at memorizing lists of digits are also likely to be good at solving verbal problems and spatial layout problems. This general intelligence includes abstract reasoning or thinking, the capacity to acquire knowledge, and problem-solving ability (Brody, 2000; Carroll, 1993).

Advocates of the concept of general intelligence point to its success in predicting academic and work performance. For example, scores on what are claimed to be tests of general intelligence are substantially correlated with academic achievement and moderately correlated with work performance (Lubinski, 2000). Individuals with higher scores on tests designed to measure general intelligence tend to get higher-paying, more prestigious jobs (Wagner, 1997). However, general IQ tests predict only about one-fourth of the variation in job success, with most variation being attributable to other factors such as motivation and education (Wagner & Sternberg, 1986). Further, the correlations between IQ and achievement decrease the longer people work at a job, presumably because as they gain more job experience they perform better (Hunt, 1995).

Some experts who argue for the existence of general intelligence believe that individuals also have specific intellectual abilities (Brody, 2000; Chiappe & MacDonald, 2005). In one study, John Carroll (1993) conducted an extensive examination of intellectual abilities. He concluded that all intellectual abilities are related to each other, which supports the concept of general intelligence, but that there are many specialized abilities as well. Some of these specialized abilities, such as spatial abilities and mechanical abilities, are not adequately reflected in the curriculum of most schools. In sum, controversy still characterizes whether it is more accurate to conceptualize intelligence as a general ability, specific abilities, or both (Birney & others, 2005; Horn, 2006).

Controversies and Issues in Intelligence

The topic of intelligence is surrounded by controversy. Is nature or nurture more important in determining intelligence? Are intelligence tests culturally biased? Should IQ tests be used to place children in particular schooling tracks?

Nature and Nurture   The **nature-nurture issue** involves the debate about whether development is primarily influenced by nature or by nurture. *Nature* refers to a child's biological inheritance, *nurture* to environmental experiences.

"Nature" proponents believe that intelligence is primarily inherited and that environmental experiences play only a minimal role in its manifestation (Detterman, 2000; Herrnstein & Murray, 1994; Jensen, 1969). The emerging view of the nature-nurture issue is that many complicated qualities, such as intelligence, probably have some genetic loading that gives them a propensity for a particular developmental trajectory, such as low, average, or high intelligence. The actual development of intelligence, however, requires more than just heredity.

Most experts today agree that the environment also plays an important role in intelligence (Campbell, 2006; Comer, 2006; Sternberg & Grigorenko, 2004; Sternberg, Grigorenko, & Kidd, 2005). This means that improving children's environments can raise their intelligence (Ramey, Ramey, & Lanzi, 2006). It also means that enriching children's environments can improve their school achievement and the acquisition

nature-nurture issue *Nature* refers to an organism's biological inheritance, *nurture* to environmental influences. The "nature" proponents claim biological inheritance is the most important influence on development; the "nurture" proponents claim that environmental experiences are the most important.

FIGURE 4.4 The Increase In IQ Scores from 1932 to 1997

As measured by the Stanford-Binet intelligence test, American children seem to be getting smarter. Scores of a group tested in 1932 fell along a bell-shaped curve with half below 100 and half above. Studies show that if children took that same test today, half would score above 120 on the 1932 scale. Very few of them would score in the "intellectually deficient" end, on the left side, and about one-fourth would rank in the "very superior" range.

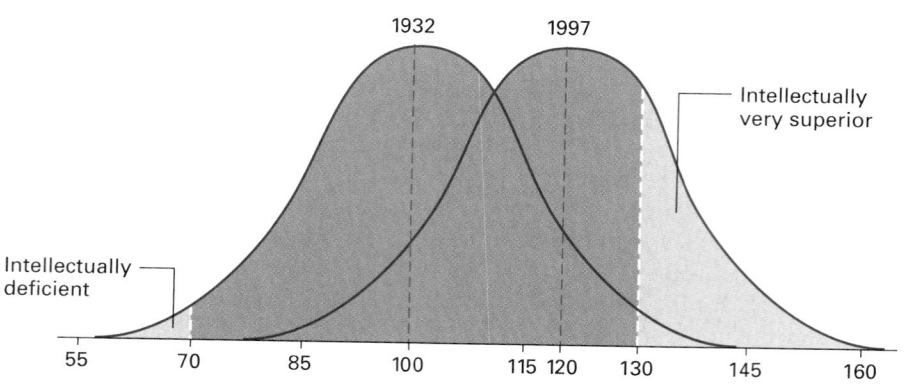

of skills needed for employment. Craig Ramey and his associates (1988) found that high-quality early educational child care (through 5 years of age) significantly raised the tested intelligence of young children from impoverished backgrounds. Positive effects of this early intervention were still evident in the intelligence and achievement of these students when they were 13 and 21 years of age (Campell, 2006; Campbell & Ramey, 1994; Campbell & others, 2001; Ramey, Ramey, & Lanzi, 2001, 2006).

Another argument for the importance of environment in intelligence involves the increasing scores on IQ tests around the world. Scores on these tests have been increasing so fast that a high percentage of people regarded as having average intelligence in the early 1900s would be considered below average in intelligence today (Flynn, 1999, 2006) (see figure 4.4). If a representative sample of today's children took the Stanford-Binet test used in 1932, about one-fourth would be defined as very superior, a label usually accorded to fewer than 3 percent of the population. Because the increase has taken place in a relatively short period of time, it can't be due to heredity but, rather, might result from such environmental factors as the explosion in information people are exposed to and the much higher percentage of the population receiving education. This worldwide increase in intelligence test scores over a short time frame is called the *Flynn effect*, after the researcher who discovered it—James Flynn (1999, 2006).

Studies of schooling also reveal effects on intelligence (Ceci & Gilstrap, 2000; Christian, Bachnan, & Morrison, 2001). The biggest effects occurred when large groups of children were deprived of formal education for an extended period, resulting in lower intelligence. In one study, the intellectual functioning of ethnic Indian children in South Africa, whose schooling was delayed by 4 years because of the unavailability of teachers, was investigated (Ramphal, 1962). Compared with children in nearby villages who had teachers, the Indian children whose entry into school was delayed by 4 years experienced a drop of 5 IQ points for each year of delay.

One analysis of studies on schooling and intelligence concluded that schooling and intelligence influence each other (Ceci & Williams, 1997). For example, individuals who finish high school are more intelligent than those who drop out of school. This might be because brighter individuals stay in school longer, or because the environmental influence of schooling contributes to their intelligence.

Further, intelligence test scores tend to rise during the school year and decline during the summer months (Ceci & Gilstrap, 2000). Also, children whose birthdays just make the cutoff point for school entrance temporarily have higher intelligence scores than those born just slightly later, who are a year behind them in school (Ceci & Gilstrap, 2000).

Researchers increasingly are interested in manipulating the early environment of children who are at risk for impoverished intelligence (Campbell, 2006; Ramey, Ramey, & Lanzi, 2006; Sternberg & Grigorenko, 2004). The emphasis is on prevention rather than remediation. Many low-income parents have difficulty providing an intellectually stimulating environment for their children. Programs that educate parents to be more sensitive caregivers and better teachers, as well as support services such as quality child-care programs, can make a difference in a child's intellectual development.

A recent review of the research on early interventions concluded that (Brooks-Gunn & others, 2003):

- High-quality center-based interventions are associated with increases in children's intelligence and school achievement.
- The interventions are most successful with poor children and children whose parents have little education.
- The positive benefits continue through adolescence but are not as strong as in early childhood or the beginning of elementary school. The programs continued into middle and late childhood have the best long-term results.

It is extremely difficult to tease apart the effects of nature or nurture, so much so that psychologist William Greenough (1997, 2000) says that asking which is more important is like asking what's more important to a rectangle, its length or its width. We still do not know what, if any, specific genes actually promote or restrict a general level of intelligence. If such genes exist, they certainly are found both in children whose families and environments appear to promote the development of children's abilities and in children whose families and environments do not appear to be as supportive. Regardless of one's genetic background, growing up "with all the advantages" does not guarantee high intelligence or success, especially if those advantages are taken for granted. Nor does the absence of such advantages guarantee low intelligence or failure, especially if the family and child can make the most of whatever opportunities are accessible to them.

Ethnicity and Culture   Are there ethnic differences in intelligence? Are conventional tests of intelligence biased, and if so, can we develop culture-fair tests?

Ethnic Comparisons   In the United States, children from African American and Latino families score below children from White families on standardized intelligence tests. On the average, African American schoolchildren score 10 to 15 points lower on standardized intelligence tests than White American schoolchildren do (Brody, 2000; Lynn, 1996). These are *average scores,* however. About 15 to 25 percent of African American schoolchildren score higher than half of White schoolchildren do, and many Whites score lower than most African Americans. The reason is that the distribution of scores for African Americans and Whites overlap.

As African Americans have gained social, economic, and educational opportunities, the gap between African Americans and Whites on standardized intelligence tests has begun to narrow (Ogbu & Stern, 2001; Onwuegbuzi & Daley, 2001). This gap especially narrows in college, where African American and White students often experience more similar environments than in the elementary and high school years (Myerson & others, 1998). Also, when children from disadvantaged African American families are adopted into more-advantaged middle-socioeconomic-status families, their scores on intelligence tests more closely resemble national averages for middle-socioeconomic-status children than for lower-socioeconomic-status children (Scarr & Weinberg, 1983).

Cultural Bias and Culture-Fair Tests   Many of the early tests of intelligence were culturally biased, favoring urban children over rural children, children from middle-income families over children from low-income families, and White children over minority children (Miller-Jones, 1989). The standards for the early tests were almost

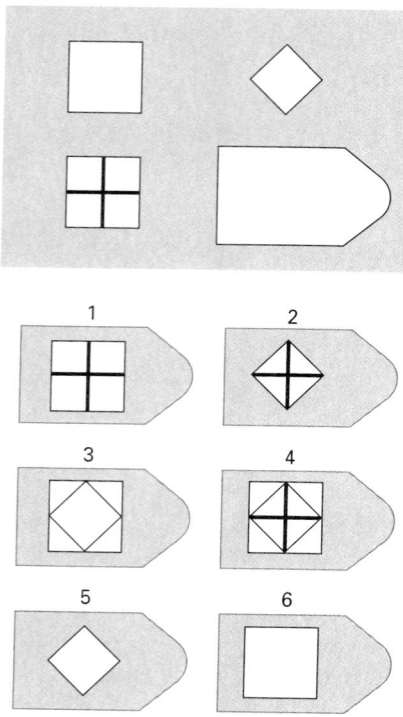

FIGURE 4.5 Sample Item from the Raven Progressive Matrices Test

Individuals are presented with a matrix arrangement of symbols, such as the one at the top of this figure, and must then complete the matrix by selecting the appropriate missing symbol from a group of symbols, such as the ones at the bottom.

Simulated items similar to those found in the *Raven's Progressive Matrices*. Copyright © 1976, 1958, 1938 by Harcourt Assessment, Inc. Reproduced with permission. All rights reserved.

stereotype threat The anxiety that one's behavior might confirm a negative stereotype about one's group.

culture-fair tests Tests of intelligence that are intended to be free of cultural bias.

exclusively based on White, middle-socioeconomic-status children. Also, some of the items were obviously culturally biased. For example, one item on an early test asked what you should do if you find a 3-year-old in the street. The "correct" answer was "Call the police." However, children from impoverished inner-city families might not choose this answer if they have had bad experiences with the police, and children living in rural areas might not have police nearby. Contemporary intelligence tests attempt to reduce such cultural bias (Merenda, 2004).

One potential influence on intelligence test performance is **stereotype threat,** the anxiety that one's behavior might confirm a negative stereotype about one's group (Max & Stapel, 2006; Steele & Aronson, 2004). For example, when African Americans take an intelligence test, they may experience anxiety about confirming the old stereotype that Blacks are "intellectually inferior." In one study, the verbal part of the Graduate Record Examination was given individually to African American and White students at Stanford University (Steele & Aronson, 1995). Half the students of each ethnic group were told that the researchers were interested in assessing their intellectual ability. The other half were told that the researchers were developing a new test, and that the test they were taking might not be reliable and valid (therefore, it would not mean anything in relation to their intellectual ability). The White students did equally well on the test in both conditions. However, the African American students did more poorly when they thought the test was assessing their intellectual ability; when they thought the test was just in the development stage and might not be reliable or valid, they performed as well as the White students.

Other studies have confirmed the existence of stereotype threat (Brown & Day, 2006; Cohen & Sherman, 2005; Helms, 2005; Rosenthal & Crisp, 2006; Steele & Aronson, 2004). African American students do more poorly on standardized tests if they believe they are being evaluated. If they believe the test doesn't count, they perform as well as White students (Aronson, 2002). However, some critics believe the extent to which stereotype threat explains the testing gap has been exaggerated (Cullen, Hardison, & Sackett, 2004; Sackett, Hardison, & Cullen, 2004, 2005).

The Diversity and Education interlude further explores possible IQ test bias.

Culture-fair tests are intelligence tests that aim to avoid cultural bias. Two types of culture-fair tests have been developed. The first includes questions familiar to people from all socioeconomic and ethnic backgrounds. For example, a child might be asked how a bird and a dog are different, on the assumption that virtually all children are familiar with birds and dogs. The second type of culture-fair test contains no verbal questions. Figure 4.5 shows a sample question from the Raven's Progressive Matrices Test. Even though tests such as the Raven's Progressive Matrices are designed to be culture-fair, people with more education still score higher than those with less education do (Shiraev & Levy, 2007).

Why is it so hard to create culture-fair tests? Most tests tend to reflect what the dominant culture thinks is important (Gregory, 2007; Merenda, 2004). If tests have time limits, that will bias the test against groups not concerned with time. If languages differ, the same words might have different meanings for different language groups. Even pictures can produce bias because some cultures have less experience with drawings and photographs (Anastasi & Urbina, 1997). Within the same culture, different groups could have different attitudes, values, and motivation, and this could affect their performance on intelligence tests. Items that ask why buildings should be made of brick are biased against children with little or no experience with brick houses. Questions about railroads, furnaces, seasons of the year, distances between cities, and so on can be biased against groups who have less experience than others with these contexts.

Ability Grouping and Tracking   Another controversial issue is whether it is beneficial to use students' scores on an intelligence test to place them in ability groups. Two types of ability grouping have been used in education: between-class and within-class.

DIVERSITY AND EDUCATION
The Controversy over Cultural Bias in IQ Tests

Larry P. is African American and poor. When he was 6 years old, he was placed in a class for the "educable mentally retarded" (EMR), which is supposed to mean that Larry learns much more slowly than average students. The primary reason Larry was placed in the EMR class was his very low score of 64 on an intelligence test.

Is there a possibility that the intelligence test Larry took was culturally biased? This question continues to be debated. The controversy has been the target of various lawsuits challenging the use of standardized IQ tests to place African American students in EMR classes. The initial lawsuit, filed on Larry P.'s behalf in California, claimed that the IQ test underestimated his true learning ability. His lawyers argued that IQ tests place too much emphasis on verbal skills and fail to account for the backgrounds of African American students from low-income families, and that Larry P. was incorrectly labeled as mentally retarded and might be burdened with that stigma forever.

As part of the lengthy court battle involving Larry P., six African American EMR students were independently retested by psychologists. The psychologists made sure that they established good rapport with the students and made special efforts to overcome the students' defeatism and distraction. For example, items were reworded in terms more consistent with the students' social background, and recognition was given to nonstandard answers that showed a logical, intelligent approach to problems. This modified testing approach produced scores of 79 to 104—17 to 38 points higher than the students received when initially tested. In every case, the scores were above the ceiling for placement in an EMR class.

In Larry's case, the judge ruled that IQ tests are culturally biased and should not be used in decisions about placing students in EMR classes. However, in subsequent rulings, such as *Pase* v. *Hannon* in Illinois, judges have ruled that IQ tests are not culturally biased. Also, a task force established by the American Psychological Association concluded that IQ tests are not culturally biased (Neisser & others, 1996). The controversy continues.

Between-Class Ability Grouping (Tracking) **Between-class ability grouping (tracking)** consists of grouping students based on their ability or achievement. Tracking has long been used in schools as a way to organize students, especially at the secondary level (Gustafson, 2006; Slavin, 1990, 1995). The positive view of tracking is that it narrows the range of skill in a group of students, making it easier to teach them. Tracking is said to prevent less-able students from "holding back" more talented students.

A typical between-class grouping involves dividing students into a college preparatory track and a general track. Within the two tracks, further ability groupings might be made, such as two levels of math instruction for college preparatory students. Another form of tracking takes place when a student's abilities in different subject areas are taken into account. For example, the same student might be in a high-track math class and a middle-track English class.

Critics of tracking argue that it stigmatizes students who are consigned to low-track classes (Banks & others, 2005; Smith-Maddox & Wheelock, 1995). For example, students can get labeled as "low-track" or "the dummy group." Critics also say that low-track classrooms often have less-experienced teachers, fewer resources, and lower expectations (Wheelock, 1992). Further, critics stress that tracking is used to segregate students according to ethnicity and socioeconomic status because higher

between–class ability grouping (tracking) Grouping students based on their ability or achievement.

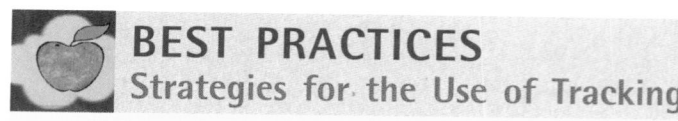

BEST PRACTICES
Strategies for the Use of Tracking

1. *Use other measures of student knowledge and potential in particular subject areas to place students in ability groups rather than a group-administered IQ test.*

2. *Avoid labeling groups as "low," "middle," and "high."* Also avoid comparisons of groups.

3. *Don't form more than two or three ability groups.* You won't be able to give a larger number of groups adequate attention and instruction.

4. *Consider the students' placements in various ability groups as subject to review and change.* Carefully monitor students' performance, and if a low-track student progresses adequately, move the student to a higher group. If a high-track student is doing poorly, evaluate whether the high track is the right one for the student and decide what supports the student might need to improve performance.

5. *Especially consider alternatives to tracking for low-achieving students.* Throughout this book we will describe instructional strategies and support services for low-achieving students, such as those being used in the AVID program.

tracks have fewer students from ethnic minority and impoverished backgrounds (Banks, 2006; Banks & others, 2005). In this way, tracking can actually replay segregation within schools. The detractors also argue that average and above-average students do not get substantial benefits from being grouped together.

Does research support the critics' contention that tracking is harmful to students? Researchers have found that tracking harms the achievement of low-track students (Brewer, Rees, & Argys, 1995; Hallinan, 2003; Slavin, 1990). However, tracking seems to benefit high-track students (such as those in a gifted program). Also, researchers have found that "students who are 'tracked-up' or who are exposed to a more rigorous curriculum learn more than the same ability students who are 'tracked-down' or offered a less challenging course of study (Gamoran, 1990; Hallinan, 2003) . . ." (Banks & others, 2005, p. 239).

One variation of between-class ability grouping is the **nongraded (cross-age) program,** in which students are grouped by their ability in particular subjects regardless of their age or grade level (Fogarty, 1993). This type of program is used far more in elementary than in secondary schools, especially in the first three grades. For example, a math class might be composed of first-, second-, and third-graders grouped together because of their similar math ability. The **Joplin plan** is a standard nongraded program for instruction in reading. In the Joplin plan, students from second, third, and fourth grade might be placed together because of their similar reading level.

We mentioned that tracking has negative effects on low-track students. When tracks are present, it is especially important to give low-achieving students an opportunity to improve their academic performance and thus change tracks. In the San Diego County Public Schools, the Achieving Via Individual Determination (AVID) program provides support for underachieving students. Instead of being placed in a low track, they are enrolled in rigorous courses but are not left to achieve on their own. A comprehensive system of support services helps them succeed. For example, a critical aspect of the program is a series of workshops that teach students notetaking skills, question-asking skills, thinking skills, and communication skills. The students also are clustered into study groups and urged to help each other clarify questions about assignments. College students, many of them AVID graduates, serve as role models, coaches, and motivators for the students. At each AVID school, a lead teacher

nongraded (cross-age) program A variation of between-class ability grouping in which students are grouped by their ability in particular subjects, regardless of their age or grade level.

Joplin plan A standard nongraded program for instruction in reading.

oversees a team of school counselors and teachers from every academic discipline. In recent years, the dropout rate in AVID schools has declined by more than one-third, and an amazing 99 percent of the AVID graduates have enrolled in college.

In sum, tracking is a controversial issue especially because of the restrictions it places on low-track students. Too often, scores on a single-group IQ test are used to place students in a particular track. Researchers have found that group IQ tests are not good predictors of how well students will do in a particular subject area (Garmon & others, 1995).

Within-Class Ability Grouping **Within-class ability grouping** involves placing students in two or three groups within a class to take into account differences in students' abilities. A typical within-class ability grouping occurs when elementary school teachers place students in several reading groups based on their reading skills. A second-grade teacher might have one group using a third-grade, first-semester reading program; another using a second-grade, first-semester program; and a third group using a first-grade, second-semester program. Such within-class grouping is far more common in elementary than in secondary schools. The subject area most often involved is reading, followed by math. Although many elementary school teachers use some form of within-class ability grouping, there is no clear research support for this strategy.

Review, Reflect, and Practice

1 **Discuss the concept of intelligence, how it is measured, and some controversies about its use by educators.**

REVIEW

- Precisely what do the concepts of intelligence and IQ mean? What did Binet and Wechsler contribute to the field of intelligence?
- What are some pros and cons of individual versus group tests of intelligence?
- What is Sternberg's triarchic theory of intelligence? What is Gardner's system of "frames of mind"? What is Mayer, Salovey, and Goleman's concept of emotional intelligence? How is each theory relevant to education? What are some aspects of the controversy about whether intelligence is better conceptualized as general intelligence or multiple intelligences?
- What are three controversies related to intelligence?

REFLECT

- Suppose that you were about to teach a particular group of children for the first time and were handed intelligence test scores for every child in the class. Would you hesitate to look at the scores? Why or why not?

PRAXIS™ PRACTICE

1. If Alex has an IQ of 135, what can we say about him?
   a. His score indicates that he is far below average in intelligence, and he is likely to need substantial help with even simple daily tasks.
   b. His score suggests that he is below average in intelligence and is likely to struggle with school.
   c. His score indicates he has slightly above average intelligence with his mental and chronological age about the same.
   d. His score indicates that he is far above average in intelligence with his mental age considerably above his chronological age.

continued on page 132

within-class ability grouping Placing students in two or three groups within a class to take into account differences in students' abilities.

Review, Reflect, and Practice *continued*

2. Susan took the Otis-Lennon School Mental Abilities Tests to determine if she qualified for her school's gifted program. Based on her score of 125, she did not qualify for the program. Which of the following is a valid statement regarding this screening procedure?
   a. Because this was an individual test, the psychologist was able to ensure that rapport had been established and that anxiety did not interfere with her performance. Thus, the decision should stand.
   b. Because this was a group test, the psychologist was unable to ensure that rapport had been established and anxiety did not interfere with her performance. Thus, the decision should not stand. More information is needed.
   c. Because her score was well above average, she should be included in the gifted program.
   d. Because her score is just average, she should not be included in the gifted program.

3. Which of these students best exemplifies Sternberg's practical intelligence?
   a. Jamal, who writes wonderful science fiction stories
   b. Chandra, who is able to understand *The Great Gatsby's* symbolism at a complex level
   c. Mark, who is the most talented athlete in the school
   d. Susan, who gets along well with others and is good at "reading" others' emotions

4. Which of these statements is most consistent with current research on the nature-nurture issue in intelligence?
   a. Because intelligence in mainly inherited, there is little room to improve students' intelligence.
   b. Because intelligence is influenced by both heredity and environment, providing students with an enriched classroom environment might have a positive influence on their intelligence.
   c. Students who delay schooling tend to score higher on intelligence tests than those who do not, which suggests that environment is more important for intelligence than heredity.
   d. Recent steep increases in intelligence indicate that intelligence is mainly determined by heredity.

Please see the answer key at the end of the book.

② LEARNING AND THINKING STYLES

| Impulsive/Reflective Styles | Deep/Surface Styles |

learning and thinking styles
Individuals' preferences in how they use their abilities.

Intelligence refers to ability. **Learning and thinking styles** are not abilities but, rather, preferred ways of using one's abilities (Sternberg, 1997). In fact, teachers will tell you that children approach learning and thinking in an amazing variety of ways. Teachers themselves also vary in their styles of learning and thinking. None of us has just a single learning and thinking style; each of us has a profile of many styles. Individuals vary so much that literally hundreds of learning and thinking styles have been proposed by educators and psychologists. Our coverage of learning and thinking styles is not meant to be exhaustive but introduces two widely discussed sets of styles: impulsive/reflective and deep/surface.

BEST PRACTICES
Strategies for Working with Impulsive Children

1. *Monitor students in the class to determine which ones are impulsive.*

2. *Talk with them about taking their time to think through an answer before they respond.*

3. *Encourage them to label new information as they work with it.*

4. *Model the reflective style as a teacher.*

5. *Help students set high standards for their performance.*

6. *Recognize when impulsive students start to take more time to reflect. Compliment them on their improvement.*

7. *Guide students in creating their own plan to reduce impulsivity.*

Impulsive/Reflective Styles

Impulsive/reflective styles, also referred to as conceptual tempo, involve a student's tendency either to act quickly and impulsively or to take more time to respond and reflect on the accuracy of an answer (Kagan, 1965). Impulsive students often make more mistakes than reflective students.

Research on impulsivity/reflection shows that reflective students are more likely than impulsive students to do well at these tasks (Jonassen & Grabowski, 1993):

- Remembering structured information
- Reading comprehension and text interpretation
- Problem solving and decision making

Reflective students also are more likely than impulsive students to set their own learning goals and concentrate on relevant information. Reflective students usually have higher standards for performance. The evidence is strong that reflective students learn more effectively and do better in school than impulsive students.

In thinking about impulsive and reflective styles, keep in mind that although most children learn better when they are reflective rather than impulsive, some children are simply fast, accurate learners and decision makers. Reacting quickly is a bad strategy only if you come up with wrong answers. Also, some reflective children ruminate forever about problems and have difficulty finishing tasks. Teachers can encourage these children to retain their reflective orientation but arrive at more timely solutions. In chapter 7, "Behavioral and Social Cognitive Approaches," we will discuss a number of other strategies for helping students self-regulate their behavior.

Deep/Surface Styles

Deep/surface styles involve how students approach learning materials. Do they do this in a way that helps them understand the meaning of the materials (deep style) or as simply what needs to be learned (surface style) (Marton, Hounsell, & Entwistle, 1984)? Students who approach learning with a surface style fail to tie what they are learning into a larger conceptual framework. They tend to learn in a passive way, often rotely memorizing information. Deep learners are more likely to actively construct what they learn and give meaning to what they need to remember. Thus, deep learners take a constructivist approach to learning. Deep learners also are more likely to be self-motivated to learn, whereas surface learners are more likely to be motivated to learn because of external rewards, such as grades and positive feedback from the teacher (Snow, Corno, & Jackson, 1996).

impulsive/reflective styles Also referred to as conceptual tempo, they involve a student's tendency either to act quickly and impulsively or to take more time to respond and reflect on the accuracy of the answer.

deep/surface styles Involve the extent to which students approach learning materials in a way that helps them understand the meaning of the materials (deep style) or as simply what needs to be learned (surface style).

BEST PRACTICES
Strategies for Helping Surface Learners Think More Deeply

1. *Monitor students to determine which ones are surface learners.*

2. *Discuss with students the importance of not just rotely memorizing material.* Encourage them to connect what they are learning now with what they have learned in the past.

3. *Ask questions and give assignments that require students to fit information into a larger framework.* For example, instead of just asking students to name the capital of a particular state, ask them if they have visited the capital and what their experiences were, what other cities are located in that section of the United States, or how large or small the city is.

4. *Be a model who processes information deeply rather than just scratching the surface.* Explore topics in depth and talk about how the information you are discussing fits within a larger network of ideas.

5. *Avoid using questions that require pat answers.* Instead, ask questions that require students to deeply process information. Connect lessons more effectively with children's existing interests.

Next, East Grand Forks, Minnesota, middle school teacher, Therese Olejniczak, describes how she gets

students to slow down so they won't gloss over important material.

THROUGH THE EYES OF TEACHERS
Paying Attention to the Details

Seventh-graders are in a hurry, no matter which intelligences they favor or use. I often teach study skills to students to help them slow down and gather details they might miss in their haste to complete assignments.

One method I use is to have the entire class silently read an article on a topic I've selected with their interests in mind. Then I ask the students to list details of the article on the blackboard. I call on students one at a time as they raise their hands enthusiastically, and each student—in his or her adolescent need to belong—participates by contributing details to the list.

Afterward, the students and I review the details, marveling at the depth of information they have found. Unplanned peer-tutoring occurs when students discover obscure items that others have skimmed past, revealing to one another their need to slow down. Small groups then create final reports that include a written summary and illustration.

Review, Reflect, and Practice

(2) Describe learning and thinking styles.

REVIEW
- What is meant by learning and thinking styles? Describe impulsive/reflective styles.
- How can deep/surface styles be characterized?

REFLECT
- Describe yourself or someone else you know well in terms of the learning and thinking styles presented in this section.

PRAXIS™ PRACTICE
1. Ms. Garcia has her students read passages from a novel and then gives them 30 minutes to describe the gist of what they have read. Which students are likely to do well on this task?
   a. Students with an impulsive style of thinking.
   b. Students with a reflective style of thinking.
   c. Students with practical intelligence.
   d. Students with average intelligence.

2. Which question encourages a deep style of thinking?
   a. What is the inverse of one-half?
   b. What is the lowest prime number?
   c. How much flour would you use to make half of the cookie recipe?
   d. What does it mean to say that addition is the opposite of subtraction?

   Please see the answer key at the end of the book.

3 PERSONALITY AND TEMPERAMENT

> Personality   Temperament

We have seen that it is important to be aware of individual variations in children's cognition. It also is important to understand individual variations in their personality and temperament.

Personality

We make statements about personality all the time and prefer to be around people with certain types of personality. Let's examine just what the term *personality* means.

Personality refers to distinctive thoughts, emotions, and behaviors that characterize the way an individual adapts to the world. Think about yourself for a moment. What is your personality like? Are you outgoing or shy? considerate or caring? friendly or hostile? These are some of the characteristics involved in personality. As we see next, one view stresses that five main factors make up personality.

The "Big Five" Personality Factors As with intelligence, psychologists are interested in identifying the main dimensions of personality (Feist & Feist, 2006; Maddi, 2005; Robins, 2005). Some personality researchers believe they have identified the **"big five" factors of personality,** the "supertraits" thought to describe personality's main dimensions: openness, conscientiousness, extraversion, agreeableness, and neuroticism (emotional stability) (see figure 4.6). (Notice that if you create an acronym from these trait names, you get the word *OCEAN*.) A number of research studies point toward these factors as important dimensions of personality (De Raad, 2005; Lee, Ashton, & Shin, 2005; McRae & Costa, 2003, 2006).

The "big five" factors can give you a framework for thinking about your students' personalities. Your students will differ in their emotional stability, how extraverted or introverted they are, how open to experience, how agreeable, and how conscientious they are. However, some experts contend that the "big five" factors do not capture all of personality. They argue that the range of personality also should include such factors as how positive (joyous, happy) or negative (angry, sad) students are, as well as how self-assertive they are.

Person–Situation Interaction In discussing learning and thinking styles, we indicated that a student's style can vary according to the subject matter the student is learning or thinking about. The same is true for personality characteristics. According to the concept of **person-situation interaction,** the best way to characterize an individual's personality is not in terms of personal traits or characteristics alone but also in terms of the situation involved. Researchers have found that students choose to be in some situations and avoid others (Ickes, Snyder, & Garcia, 1997).

Suppose you have an extravert and an introvert in your class. According to the theory of person-situation interaction, you can't predict which one will show the best adaptation unless you consider the situation they are in. The theory of person-situation

personality Distinctive thoughts, emotions, and behaviors that characterize the way an individual adapts to the world.

"big five" factors of personality Emotional stability, extraversion, openness to experience, agreeableness, and conscientiousness.

person–situation interaction The view that the best way to conceptualize personality is not in terms of personal traits or characteristics alone but also in terms of the situation involved.

Openness	**C**onscientiousness	**E**xtraversion	**A**greeableness	**N**euroticism (emotional stability)
• Imaginative or practical	• Organized or disorganized	• Sociable or retiring	• Softhearted or ruthless	• Calm or anxious
• Interested in variety or routine	• Careful or careless	• Fun-loving or somber	• Trusting or suspicious	• Secure or insecure
• Independent or conforming	• Disciplined or impulsive	• Affectionate or reserved	• Helpful or uncooperative	• Self-satisfied or self-pitying

FIGURE 4.6 The "Big Five" Factors of Personality

Each column represents a broad "super-trait" that encompasses more narrow traits and characteristics. Using the acronym OCEAN can help you to remember the big five personality factors (Openness, Conscientiousness, and so on).

interaction predicts that the extravert will adapt best when asked to collaborate with others and that the introvert will adapt best when asked to carry out tasks independently. Similarly, the extravert likely will be happier when socializing with lots of people at a party, the introvert when in a more private setting alone or with a friend.

In sum, don't think of personality traits as always dooming a student to behave in a particular way across all situations. The context or situation matters (Kamrath, Mendoza-Denton, & Mischel, 2005; Mathews, Zeidner, & Roberts, 2006; Mroczek & Little, 2006). Monitor situations in which students with varying personality characteristics seem to feel most comfortable and provide them with opportunities to learn in those situations. If a particular personality trait is detrimental to the student's school performance (perhaps one student is so introverted that he or she fears working in a group), think of ways you can support the student's efforts to change.

Temperament

Temperament is closely related to personality and to learning and thinking styles. **Temperament** is a person's behavioral style and characteristic ways of responding. Some students are active; others are calm. Some respond warmly to people; others fuss and fret. Such descriptions involve variations in temperament.

Scientists who study temperament seek to find the best ways to classify temperaments (Saucier & Simonds, 2006; Shiner, 2006). The most well-known classification was proposed by Alexander Chess and Stella Thomas (Chess & Thomas, 1977; Thomas & Chess, 1991). They believe that there are three basic styles, or clusters, of temperament:

- An **easy child** is generally in a positive mood, quickly establishes regular routines in infancy, and adapts easily to new experiences.
- A **difficult child** reacts negatively and cries frequently, engages in irregular daily routines, and is slow to accept change.
- A **slow-to-warm-up child** has a low activity level, is somewhat negative, and displays a low intensity of mood.

temperament A person's behavioral style and characteristic ways of responding.

easy child A temperament style in which the child is generally in a positive mood, quickly establishes regular routines, and easily adapts to new experiences.

difficult child A temperament style in which the child tends to react negatively, has aggressive tendencies, lacks self-control, and is slow to accept new experiences.

slow-to-warm-up child A temperament style in which the child has a low activity level, is somewhat negative, shows low adaptability, and displays a low intensity of mood.

In their longitudinal investigation, Chess and Thomas found that 40 percent of the children they studied could be classified as easy, 10 percent as difficult, and 15 percent as slow to warm up. Notice that 35 percent did not fit any of the three patterns. Researchers have found that these three basic clusters of temperament are moderately stable across the childhood years.

A difficult temperament, or a temperament that reflects a lack of control, can place a student at risk for problems. In one study, adolescents with a difficult temperament had unusually high incidences of drug abuse and stressful events (Tubman & Windle, 1995). In another study, a temperament factor labeled "out of control" (being irritable and distractible) assessed when children were 3 to 5 years of age was related to acting out and behavioral problems at 13 to 15 years of age (Caspi & others, 1995). Across the same age span, a temperament factor labeled "approach" (friendliness, eagerness to explore new situations) was associated with a low incidence of anxiety and depression.

Another way of classifying temperament focuses on the differences between a shy, subdued, timid child and a sociable, extraverted, bold child. Jerome Kagan (2002,

BEST PRACTICES
Strategies for Teaching Children with Different Temperaments

These are some teaching strategies related to students' temperaments (Keogh, 2003; Sanson & Rothbart, 1995):

1. *Show attention to and respect for individuality* (Sanson & Rothbart, 1995). Teachers need to be sensitive to the student's signals and needs. The goal of good teaching might be accomplished in one way with one student, in another way with another student, depending on the students' temperaments.

2. *Consider the structure of the students' environment* (Sanson & Rothbart, 1995). Crowded, noisy classrooms often pose greater problems for a "difficult" child than for an "easy" child. Fearful, withdrawn students often benefit from slower entry into new contexts.

3. *Be aware of problems that can emerge by labeling a child "difficult" and packaged programs for "difficult children"* (Sanson & Rothbart, 1995). Some books and programs for parents and teachers focus specifically on the child's temperament (Cameron, Hansen, & Rosen, 1989). Most of these focus on the difficult child. Acknowledging that some children are harder to teach than others often is helpful. Advice on how to handle a particular temperament also can be useful. However, whether a particular characteristic is truly "difficult" depends on its fit with the environment, so the problem does not necessarily rest with the child. As with labeling a child as more or less intelligent, labeling the child as "difficult" has the danger of becoming a self-fulfilling prophecy. Also keep in mind that temperament can be modified to some degree (Sanson & Rothbart, 2002).

Here are some effective strategies for dealing with difficult children in the classroom (Keogh, 2003):

- Try to avoid confrontations and power struggles by anticipating problem situations for the student; if the student engages in disruptive behavior, intervene at the first instance of the disruption.

- Evaluate the physical context of the classroom, such as where the difficult child sits, who sits near him or her, and so on for clues about reducing disruptive behavior.

- Minimize delay times between activities and standing in line, which gives a difficult child less time to be disruptive.

4. *Use effective strategies with shy and slow-to-warm-up students.* Keep in mind that it is easy to overlook shy, slow-to-warm-up children because they are unlikely to cause problems in the classroom. Following are some strategies for helping these children (Keogh, 2003):

- Don't place this type of student immediately into group activities, and let the student become involved in groups at his or her own pace initially. If over time, shy students are still reluctant to actively participate in groups, encourage them but don't push them.

- Assign students' work partners with their temperaments in mind; for example, don't pair an intense difficult child with a shy, slow-to-warm-up child.

- Help shy, slow-to-warm-up students get started on activities that they appear hesitant about beginning, and be available to provide help during these activities.

6. *Help children with problems controlling their emotions to regulate their behavior.* In this regard, you can:

- Control your emotions when interacting with students. By observing how you handle difficult situations, students may model your calm behavior.

- Recognize that you are an important person in being able to guide children to regulate their emotions. Instruct children to talk to themselves in ways that may help to reduce their frustration and arousal. For example, if children have difficulty controlling their anger, they can learn to distract themselves from arousing events or stop and take a series of deep breaths.

2006; Kagan & Snidman, 1991) regards shyness with strangers (peers or adults) as one feature of a broad temperament category called *inhibition to the unfamiliar.*

Mary Rothbart and John Bates (1998, 2006) emphasize that three broad dimensions best represent what researchers have found to characterize the structure of temperament. Here are their descriptions of the three temperament dimensions (Rothbart, 2004, p. 495):

- *Extraversion/surgency,* which includes "positive anticipation, impulsivity, activity level, and sensation seeking." Kagan's uninhibited children fit into this category.

- *Negative affectivity,* which includes "fear, frustration, sadness, and discomfort." These children are easily distressed; they may fret and cry often. Kagan's inhibited children fit this category.

- *Effortful control (self-regulation),* which includes "attentional focusing and shifting, inhibitory control, perceptual sensitivity, and low-intensity pleasure." Infants high on effortful control show an ability to keep their arousal from getting too high and have strategies for soothing themselves. By contrast, children low on effortful control are often unable to control their arousal; they become easily agitated and intensely emotional.

In Rothbart's view, "Early theoretical models of temperament stressed the way we are moved by our positive and negative emotions or level of arousal, with our actions driven by these tendencies" (2004, p. 497). The more recent emphasis on effortful control, however, advocates that individuals can engage in a more cognitive, flexible approach to stressful circumstances.

This chapter has been about individual variations. Because individual variations are so important in effectively teaching children, we will address them throughout the book. For example, in chapter 6, we will focus on teaching exceptional students, including those with a learning disability and those who are gifted. Also, in chapter 5, we will explore individual variations in students' culture, ethnicity, socioeconomic status, and gender.

Review, Reflect, and Practice

(3) Define personality, identify the "big five" factors of personality, and discuss person-situation interaction. Also, define temperament, identify three types of children's temperament, and evaluate teaching strategies linked to children's temperament.

REVIEW

- What is meant by the concept of personality? What are the "big five" factors of personality? What does the idea of person-situation interaction suggest about personality?
- How is temperament different from personality? Describe an easy child, a difficult child, and a slow-to-warm-up child. What are other categorizations of temperament? What are some good teaching strategies related to children's temperament?

REFLECT

- Describe yourself in terms of the "big five" personality factors. In your K–12 education, how aware do you think your teachers were of your personality strengths and weaknesses? Might things have been different if they had known you better?

PRAXIS™ PRACTICE

1. Maria is an outgoing, agreeable, fun-loving child. According to the concept of person-situation interaction, which of the following is likely to characterize Maria?
   a. Maria enjoys working independently on detail-oriented tasks.
   b. Maria likes to work on tasks that involve interaction with other students.
   c. Maria prefers to read by herself in a corner.
   d. Maria needs to be taught to control her impulses.
2. Stanton has been a challenging student. His frustration tolerance is low, and when he gets frustrated he often disrupts the class with angry outbursts. His teacher has difficulty handling him. What advise is most likely to help her deal with Stanton?
   a. She should show her frustration in dealing with him because once he realizes the impact of his behavior on others, he will learn to control his behavior.
   b. She should be calm with Stanton so he can observe a more adaptive response to frustration.
   c. She should send him out of the classroom every time he gets angry.
   d. She should separate him from his classmates and make him do his classwork by himself so that they don't imitate his behavior.

Please see the answer key at the end of the book.

CRACK THE CASE
The Case of the Workshops

Mr. Washington and his colleague, Ms. Rosario, had just attended a workshop on adapting instruction to children's learning styles. Ms. Jacobson and her colleague, Mr. Hassan, had just attended a workshop on adapting instruction to cover multiple intelligences. The four met in the teachers' workroom and were discussing what they had learned.

"Well," said Mr. Washington, "this certainly explains why some students seem to want to sit and listen to me talk, while others like to be more actively involved. Joe's obviously an executive type. He likes lectures. Martha, on the other hand, must be legislative. She just loves to work on projects and can't stand it when I tell her how to do things."

"No, I don't think so," Ms. Jacobson replies. "I think Joe's high in verbal intelligence. That's why he can make sense out of your lectures. He writes well, too. Martha likes to do things with her hands. She's higher in spatial and bodily-kinesthetic intelligence."

Mr. Washington responds, "No, no, no. Learning styles explain their differences much better. Here look at this."

At that point, Mr. Washington shows Ms. Jacobson the handouts from the workshop he and Ms. Rosario had attended. Mr. Hassan gets out the handouts from the workshop he and Ms. Jacobson had attended as well. They begin comparing notes. They all recognize students in each of the schemes in the handouts. In fact, they can recognize the same student in both sets of handouts.

At this point, two other teachers—Mrs. Peterson and Mrs. Darby—walk into the room. They are very excited about a graduate class they are taking at a nearby university.

Mrs. Peterson says, "You know, I never thought about personality when considering teaching methods. It's no wonder Martha doesn't behave terribly well in my class. She's just too impulsive for the kind of structure I have."

Ms. Jacobson is dismayed. "You mean they're telling you we have to adapt our classrooms to the students' personalities now, too?" she asks.

Mr. Hassan is also upset. "Gee," he says, "just when I thought I had it all figured out. Used to be we just had to consider IQ. Now all this. We have 25 kids in our classes. How can we possibly adapt to all these differences? What are we supposed to do, have 25 different lesson plans? Maybe we should do some kind of profile on them and then group them by profile. What do you think, guys?"

1. What are the issues in this case?
2. To what extent should teachers adapt their instruction to the strengths, learning styles, and personalities of their students? Why?
3. What will you do in your classroom to accommodate individual differences such as students' strengths, learning styles, and personalities?
4. What other individual differences do you think you might have to accommodate? How will you do this?
5. On which theory is Ms. Jacobson basing her comments regarding Joe and Martha?
   a. Gardner's eight frames of mind
   b. general intelligence
   c. Sternberg's triarchic theory of intelligence
   d. Vygotsky's sociocultural theory
6. What type of grouping is Mr. Adams most likely discussing?
   a. between-class ability grouping
   b. Joplin plan
   c. nongraded program
   d. within-class ability grouping

Reach Your Learning Goals
Individual Variations

(1) INTELLIGENCE: Discuss the concept of intelligence, how it is measured, and some controversies about its use by educators.

Individual Intelligence Tests

Intelligence consists of problem-solving skills and the ability to adapt to and learn from life's everyday experiences. Interest in intelligence often focuses on individual differences and assessment. Binet and Simon developed the first intelligence test. Binet developed the concept of mental age, and Stern created the concept of IQ as MA/CA × 100. The Stanford-Binet score distribution approximates a normal curve. The Wechsler scales also are widely used to assess intelligence. They yield an overall IQ, as well as verbal and performance IQs.

Individual Tests Versus Group Tests

Group tests are more convenient and economical, but they have a number of drawbacks (lack of opportunities to establish rapport, distraction from other students). A group intelligence test should always be supplemented with other relevant information when decisions are made about students. This also holds for an individual intelligence test.

Theories of Multiple Intelligences

According to Sternberg's triarchic theory of intelligence, intelligence comes in three forms: analytical, creative, and practical. Gardner argues there are eight types of intelligence, or frames of mind: verbal, mathematical, spatial, bodily-kinesthetic, musical, insight about others, insight about self, and naturalist. Project Spectrum and the Key School involve educational applications of Gardner's theory of multiple intelligences. Mayer, Salovey, and Goleman stress emotional intelligence is an important aspect of being a competent person. These approaches have much to offer, stimulating teachers to think more broadly about what makes up a student's competencies. However, they have been criticized along the lines of including some skills that should not be classified under intelligence and for the lack of a research base to support the approaches. Also, advocates of the general concept of intelligence argue that intelligence is a reasonably good predictor of school and work performance.

Controversies and Issues in Intelligence

Three controversies and issues related to intelligence are (1) the nature-nurture question of how heredity and environment interact to produce intelligence, (2) how fairly intelligence testing applies across cultural and ethnic groups, and (3) whether students should be grouped according to ability (tracking). It is especially important to recognize that intelligence tests are an indicator of current performance, not fixed potential.

(2) LEARNING AND THINKING STYLES: Describe learning and thinking styles.

Impulsive/Reflective Styles

Styles are not abilities but, rather, preferred ways of using abilities. Each individual has a number of learning and thinking styles. Impulsive/reflective styles also are referred to as conceptual tempo. This dichotomy involves a student's tendency to act quickly and impulsively or to take more time to respond and reflect on the accuracy of an answer. Impulsive students typically make more mistakes than reflective students.

Deep/Surface Styles

Deep/surface styles involve the extent to which students approach learning in a way that helps them understand the meaning of materials (deep style) or as simply what needs to be learned (surface style).

(3) PERSONALITY AND TEMPERAMENT: Define personality, identify the "big five" factors of personality, and discuss person-situation interaction. Also, define temperament, identify three types of children's temperament, and evaluate teaching strategies linked to children's temperament.

| Personality |

Personality refers to distinctive thoughts, emotions, and behaviors that characterize the way an individual adapts to the world. Psychologists have identified the "big five" personality factors: emotional stability, extraversion, openness to experience, agreeableness, and conscientiousness. The "big five" factors give teachers a framework for thinking about a student's personality characteristics. The concept of person-situation interaction states that the best way to characterize an individual's personality is not in terms of traits alone but also in terms of both the traits and the situations involved.

| Temperament |

Temperament refers to a person's behavioral style and characteristic way of responding. Chess and Thomas believe there are three basic temperament styles, or clusters: easy (generally in a positive mood), difficult (reacts negatively and cries easily), and slow to warm up (low activity level, somewhat negative). A difficult temperament places a child at risk for problems. Other temperament categorizations have been proposed by Kagan (inhibition to the unfamiliar) and Rothbart and Bates (extraversion/surgency, negative affectivity, and effortful control [self-regulation]). In education involving students' temperaments, teachers can show attention to, and respect for, individuality; consider the structure of a student's environment; be aware of the problems involved when labeling a student as "difficult"; and use effective classroom strategies with difficult children, shy, slow-to-warm up children, and children who have difficulty regulating their emotions.

 ## KEY TERMS

intelligence 115
mental age (MA) 115
intelligence quotient (IQ) 115
normal distribution 115
triarchic theory of
    intelligence 118
emotional intelligence 121
nature-nurture issue 125
stereotype threat 128

culture-fair tests 128
between-class ability
    grouping (tracking) 129
nongraded (cross-age)
    program 130
Joplin plan 130
within-class ability
    grouping 131

learning and thinking
    styles 132
impulsive/reflective styles 133
deep/surface styles 133
personality 135
"big five" factors of
    personality 135

person-situation
    interaction 135
temperament 136
easy child 136
difficult child 136
slow-to-warm-up child 136

 ## PORTFOLIO ACTIVITIES

Now that you have a good understanding of this chapter, complete these exercises to expand your thinking.

Independent Reflection

Your Multiple Intelligences. Evaluate your own intelligence profile according to Gardner. In what frames of mind do you come out strongest? In which of Sternberg's three areas do you feel you are the strongest? Write about your self-evaluation. (INTASC: Principles *2, 3*)

Collaborative Work

Personality Profiles. Form a group of five or six students from your class, and have one person identify his or her personality and temperament traits. Have other members do the same, in turn. After all have presented, discuss how the individuals in your group

are similar or different. How will your personalities and temperaments translate into teaching styles? Write about this experience. (INTASC: Principles *2, 3*)

Research/Field Experience

Learning Styles in the Classroom. Interview several teachers about students' different learning and thinking styles. Ask them what teaching strategies they use to accommodate these differences in students. Write a synopsis of your interviews. (INTASC: Principles *2, 3, 4, 9*)

Go to the Online Learning Center for downloadable portfolio templates.

TAKING IT TO THE NET

- How could you conduct a lesson about Howard Gardner's theory of multiple intelligences in your classroom? Why do you think it is important for students to be aware of this theory and its implications for education and society? How could you involve students in planning lessons and projects that utilize many learning styles? **school.discovery.com/lessonplans/programs/multipleintelligences/index.html**

- What is your learning style? Take an online test to discover if you are more active or reflective? visual or verbal? sequential or global? In what ways do you think your learning style will impact your teaching style in the classroom? **www.engr.ncsu.edu/learningstyles/ilsweb.html**

- Reflect on what it means to be emotionally intelligent. How can a teacher's emotional intelligence impact the classroom? How can a student's emotional intelligence impact his or her academic performance and social relationships? Describe a classroom activity or routine that can help students increase their capacity for emotional intelligence and for "knowing themselves, choosing themselves, and giving themselves." **www.6seconds.org/modules.php?name=News&file=article&sid=2**

Connect to the Online Learning Center to explore possible answers.

 ## STUDY, PRACTICE, AND SUCCEED

Visit **www.mhhe.com/santedu3e** to review the chapter with self-grading quizzes and self-assessments, to apply the chapter material to two more Crack the Case studies, and for suggested activities to develop your teaching portfolio.

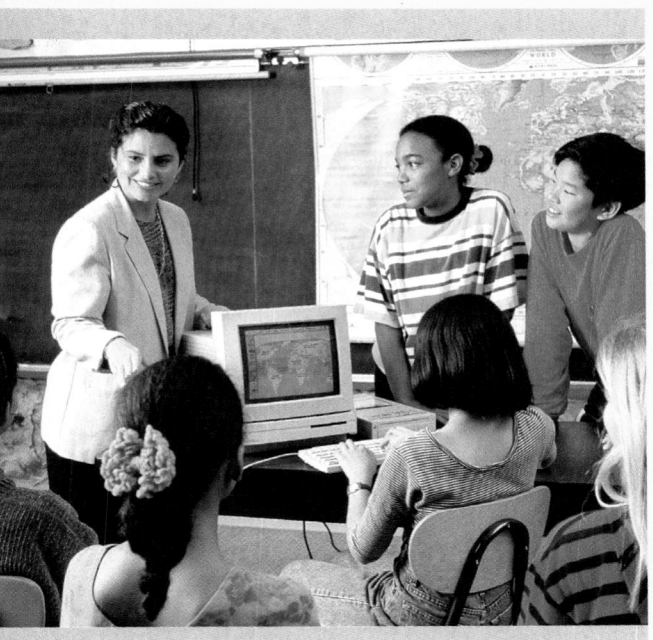

Sociocultural Diversity

We need every human gift and cannot afford
to neglect any gift because of artificial barriers
of sex or race or class or national origin.

—Margaret Mead
American Anthropologist, 20th Century

Chapter Outline

Learning Goals

Culture and Ethnicity

Culture
Socioeconomic Status
Ethnicity
Bilingualism

1 Discuss how variations in culture, socioeconomic status, and ethnic background might raise special classroom needs.

Multicultural Education

Empowering Students
Culturally Relevant Teaching
Issues-Centered Education
Improving Relationships Among Children from Different Ethnic Groups
The Issue of Whether a Core of "White" Values Should Be Taught

2 Describe some ways to promote multicultural education.

Gender

Views on Gender Development
Gender Stereotyping, Similarities, and Differences
Gender-Role Classification
Gender in Context
Eliminating Gender Bias

3 Explain the various facets of gender, including similarities and differences in boys and girls; discuss gender issues in teaching.

TEACHING STORIES   Margaret Longworth

Margaret Longworth taught high school for many years and was a Teacher of the Year. She recently moved to the middle school level and currently teaches language arts at West Middle School in St. Lucie, Florida. When considering sociocultural diversity, she believes it is important for teachers to make schools "user-friendly" for parents. In her words:

> Many parents—especially ethnic minority parents of color—are very intimidated by schools. They think teachers know everything. Principals know everything. And God forbid that they ever would need to approach the school board. To combat this intimidation, I became user-friendly. Many students and parents center their lives around the church in my community. So, to break the barriers between school and home, my Haitian paraprofessional began setting up meetings for me at the Haitian churches. The churches gave me their Sunday evening services. After they completed their preliminaries, they turned the service over to me. Through the assistance of an interpreter, I presented opportunities to help parents develop academic and life skills

through education. I talked with them about special education classes, gifted classes, language programs, and scholarships, and encouraged them to keep their children in school. In turn, they felt confident enough to ask me about different happenings at school. Because of the parent-school-church connections that I was able to build up, I rarely had a discipline problem. If I did have to call parents, they would leave work or whatever they were doing and show up in my classroom. Many of these parents developed a relationship with the principal and guidance counselor and felt free to talk with school officials.

Margaret Longworth believes that in the classroom the key to improving children's interethnic relations is understanding. She comments:

> Understanding others' points of view requires spending time with them and getting to know them—how they think and feel. As students talk with each other and begin to appreciate each other, they soon learn that in many ways they aren't that different after all.

Preview

Ours is a multicultural world of diverse backgrounds, customs, and values. Margaret Longworth's Teaching Story shows how teachers can improve students' lives and educational orientation by building bridges to their community. In this chapter we explore many ways teachers have found to educate children from diverse cultural, socioeconomic, and ethnic backgrounds, including ways to make the classroom relevant for these children. We also examine gender in schools, including ways in which teachers interact differently with boys and girls.

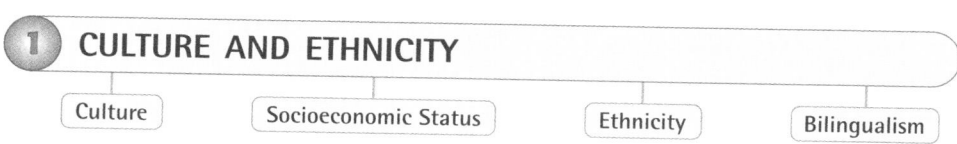

1 CULTURE AND ETHNICITY

| Culture | Socioeconomic Status | Ethnicity | Bilingualism |

The students in the schools of Fairfax County, Virginia, near Washington, D.C., come from 182 countries and speak more than a hundred languages. Although the Fairfax County schools are a somewhat extreme example, they are harbingers of what is coming to America's schools. By the year 2025, 50 percent of all public school students are predicted to be from backgrounds that are currently classified as "minority." This challenges current definitions of the term. It also points to an important educational goal of helping students develop respect for people from different cultural and ethnic backgrounds (Banks, 2006; Nieto, 2004; Okagki, 2006; Sheets, 2005).

In this section, we will explore diversity in terms of cultures, socioeconomic status, and ethnicity. We'll also examine language issues, including the debate about bilingual education.

Culture

Culture refers to the behavior patterns, beliefs, and all other products of a particular group of people that are passed on from generation to generation. These products result from the interactions among groups of people and their environments over many years (Chun, Organista, & Marin, 2002; Shiraev & Levy, 2007). A cultural group can be as large as the United States or as small as an isolated Amazon tribe. Whatever its size, the group's culture influences the behavior of its members (Berry & others, 2006; Matsumoto, 2004; Sam & Berry, 2006).

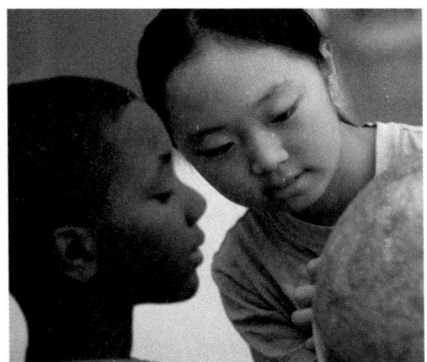

What are some differences in individualist and collectivist cultures? What are some teaching strategies for working with students from these cultures?

Psychologist Donald Campbell and his colleagues (Brewer & Campbell, 1976; Campbell & LeVine, 1968) found that people in all cultures tend to

- believe that what happens in their culture is "natural" and "correct" and what happens in other cultures is "unnatural" and "incorrect,"
- perceive their cultural customs as universally valid,
- behave in ways that favor their cultural group,
- feel proud of their cultural group, and
- feel hostile toward other cultural groups.

Psychologists and educators who study culture often are interested in comparing what happens in one culture with what happens in one or more other cultures (Roopnarine & Metindogan, 2006). **Cross-cultural studies** involve such comparisons, providing information about the degree to which people are similar and to what degree certain behaviors are specific to certain cultures.

Individualist and Collectivist Cultures   Comparisons of American students with Chinese, Japanese, and Taiwanese students revealed that American students tend to go about their work more independently, whereas Asian students are more likely to work in groups (Stevenson & Hofer, 1999). These differences in cultures have been described with two terms: *individualism* and *collectivism* (Shiraev & Levy, 2007; Triandis, 2001). **Individualism** refers to a set of values that give priority to personal goals rather than to group goals. Individualist values include feeling good, personal distinction, and independence. **Collectivism** consists of a set of values that support the group. Personal goals are subordinated to preserve group integrity, interdependence of the group's members, and harmonious relationships. Many Western cultures such as those of the United States, Canada, Great Britain, and the Netherlands are described as individualist. Many Eastern cultures such as those of China, Japan, India, and Thailand are labeled collectivist. Mexican culture also has stronger collectivist characteristics than U.S. culture. However, the United States has many collectivist subcultures, such as Chinese American and Mexican American.

Humans always have lived in groups, whether large or small. They always have needed one another for survival. Critics argue that the Western emphasis on individualism undermines the human species' need for relatedness (Kagiticibasi, 1996). Some social scientists believe that many problems in Western cultures have intensified because of the cultural emphasis on individualism. Compared with collectivist cultures, individualist cultures tend to have higher rates of suicide, drug abuse, crime, adolescent pregnancy, divorce, child abuse, and mental disorders (Triandis, 2001). However, regardless of their cultural background, people need a positive sense of self and connectedness to others to develop fully as human beings (Brown & Kysilka, 2002; Shiraev & Levy, 2007).

culture The behavior patterns, beliefs, and all other products of a particular group of people that are passed on from generation to generation.

cross-cultural studies Studies that compare what happens in one culture with what happens in one or more other cultures; they provide information about the degree to which people are similar and to what degree behaviors are specific to certain cultures.

individualism A set of values that give priority to personal rather than to group goals.

collectivism A set of values that support the group.

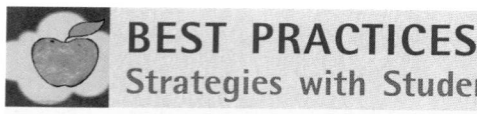

BEST PRACTICES
Strategies with Students from Individualist and Collectivist Backgrounds

You come from a cultural background with individualist or collectivist leanings, or in some cases possibly both. As a teacher, you will need to interact effectively with students, parents, teachers, and school personnel who come from individualist and collectivist backgrounds.

If you are an individualist, these strategies will help you interact more effectively with students, parents, and school personnel from collectivist cultures (Triandis, Brislin, & Hui, 1988):

1. *Place more emphasis on cooperation than on competition.*

2. *If you have to criticize, do so carefully and only in private.* Criticizing people from a collectivist culture in public places causes them to "lose face."

3. *Cultivate long-term relationships.* Be patient. People in collectivist cultures like dealing with "old friends."

If you are a collectivist, these strategies will help you interact more effectively with students, parents, and school personnel from individualist cultures (Triandis, Brislin, & Hui, 1988):

1. *Compliment the person more than you are used to doing in your culture.*

2. *Avoid feeling threatened if the individualist acts competitively.*

3. *It is okay to talk about your accomplishments and be less modest than you are used to being, but don't boast.*

Cross-Cultural Comparisons of Adolescents' Time Use In addition to examining whether cultures are individualist or collectivist, another important cross-cultural comparison involves how children and adolescents spend their time. Reed Larson and Suman Verma (Larson, 2001; Larson & Verma, 1999) examined how adolescents in the United States, Europe, and East Asia spend their time in work, play, and developmental activities such as school (see figure 5.1). U.S. adolescents spent about 60 percent as much time on schoolwork as East Asian adolescents did, mainly because U.S. adolescents did less homework. U.S. adolescents also spent more time in paid work than their counterparts in most developed countries. And what U.S. adolescents had more of than adolescents in other industrialized countries was free time. About 40 to 50 percent of U.S. adolescents' waking hours (not counting summer vacations) was spent in discretionary activities, compared with 25 to 35 percent in East Asia and 35 to 45 percent in Europe. Whether this additional discretionary time is a liability or an asset for U.S. adolescents, of course, depends on how they use it.

FIGURE 5.1 Average Daily Time Use of Adolescents in Different Regions of the World

Activity	Postindustrial, schooled populations		
	United States	Europe	East Asia
Household labor	20 to 40 minutes	20 to 40 minutes	10 to 20 minutes
Paid labor	40 to 60 minutes	10 to 20 minutes	0 to 10 minutes
Schoolwork	3.0 to 4.5 hours	4.0 to 5.5 hours	5.5 to 7.5 hours
Total work time	4 to 6 hours	4.5 to 6.5 hours	6 to 8 hours
TV viewing	1.5 to 2.5 hours	1.5 to 2.5 hours	1.5 to 2.5 hours
Talking	2 to 3 hours	*insufficient data*	45 to 60 minutes
Sports	30 to 60 minutes	20 to 80 minutes	0 to 20 minutes
Structured voluntary activities	10 to 20 minutes	10 to 20 minutes	0 to 10 minutes
Total free time	6.5 to 8.0 hours	5.5 to 7.5 hours	4.0 to 5.5 hours

The largest amounts of U.S. adolescents' free time were spent using the media and engaging in unstructured leisure activities, often with friends. We will further explore adolescents' media use later in the chapter. U.S. adolescents spent more time in voluntary structured activities—such as sports, hobbies, and organizations—than East Asian adolescents.

According to Reed Larson (2001; Larson & Wilson, 2004), U.S. adolescents may have too much unstructured time for optimal development. When adolescents are allowed to choose what they do with their time, they typically engage in unchallenging activities such as hanging out and watching TV. Although relaxation and social interaction are important aspects of adolescence, it seems unlikely that spending large numbers of hours per week in unchallenging activities fosters development. Structured voluntary activities may provide more promise for adolescent development than unstructured time, especially if adults give responsibility to adolescents, challenge them, and provide competent guidance in these activities (Larson & Wilson, 2004).

Socioeconomic Status

Most countries have many subcultures. One of the most common ways of categorizing subcultures involves socioeconomic status. **Socioeconomic status (SES)** refers to the categorization of people according to their economic, educational, and occupational characteristics. In the United States, SES has important implications for education. Low-SES individuals often have less education, less power to influence a community's institutions (such as schools), and fewer economic resources.

The Extent of Poverty in America   In a report on the state of America's children, the Children's Defense Fund (1992) described what life is like for all too many children. When sixth-graders in a poverty-stricken area of St. Louis were asked to describe a perfect day, one boy said that he would erase the world, then sit and think. Asked if he wouldn't rather go outside and play, the boy responded, "Are you kidding, out there?"

In 2004, 17.8 percent of children were living in families below the poverty line, a slight increase from 2001 (16.2 percent) but down from a peak of 22.7 percent in 1993 (U.S. Census Bureau, 2005). The most recent U.S. figure of 17.8 percent is still much higher than those from other industrialized nations. For example, Canada has a child poverty rate of 9 percent and Sweden has a rate of 2 percent.

The U.S. child poverty rate is especially high for children who live in female-headed families—just short of 50 percent. More than 40 percent of African American and almost 40 percent of Latino children currently live below the poverty line. Compared with non-Latino White children, children of color are more likely to experience persistent poverty over many years (McLoyd, Aikens, & Burton, 2006). Nonetheless, in terms of actual numbers, there are more non-Latino White children (almost 9 million) living below the poverty line than African American children (almost 4 million) or Latino children (also almost 4 million) living in poverty, because there are far more non-Latino White children overall in the United States.

Educating Students from Low-SES Backgrounds   Children in poverty often face problems at home and at school that compromise their learning (Blumenfeld & others, 2005; McLoyd, Aikens, & Burton, 2006; Ryan, Fauth, & Brooks-Gunn, 2006). A recent review of the environment of childhood poverty concluded that compared with their economically more-advantaged counterparts, poor children experience these adversities (Evans, 2004, p. 77):

- Exposure "to more family turmoil, violence, separation from their families, instability, and chaotic households" (Emery & Laumann-Billings, 1998).
- "Less social support, and their parents are less responsive and more authoritarian" (Bo, 1994; Cochran & others, 1990).

socioeconomic status (SES) The categorization of people according to their economic, educational, and occupational characteristics.

a.

b.

FIGURE 5.2 Language Input in Professional and Welfare Families and Young Children's Vocabulary Development

(*a*) Parents from professional families talked with their young children more than parents from welfare families. (*b*) Children from professional families developed vocabularies that were twice as large as those from welfare families. Thus, by the time children went to preschool, they already had experienced considerable differences in language input in their families and had developed different levels of vocabulary depending on the socioeconomic context in which they had lived.

- "Read to relatively infrequently, watch more TV, and have less access to books and computers" (Bradley & others, 2001; Hart & Risley, 1995).
- Schools and child-care facilities that are inferior and parents who "are less involved in their children's school activities" (Benveniste, Carnoy, & Rothstein, 2003; U.S. Department of Health and Human Services, 1999).
- Air and water that are more polluted and homes that "are more crowded, more noisy, and of lower quality" (Myers, Baer, & Choi, 1996).
- More dangerous and physically deteriorating neighborhoods with less adequate municipal services (Brody & others, 2001; Sampson, Raudenbush, & Earls, 1997).

The following two studies illustrate how poverty can negatively impact learning and development:

- One study compared the home language environments of 3-year-old children from professional and welfare families (Hart & Risley, 1995). All of the children developed normally in terms of learning to talk and acquiring all of the forms of English and basic vocabulary. However, there were enormous differences in the sheer amount of language to which the children were exposed and the level of language development the children eventually attained. As can be seen in figure 5.2, professional parents talked much more to their young children than did welfare parents, and this difference was linked with the children's vocabulary development.
- Another study of more than 1,200 adolescents 12 to 14 years of age examined the role of poverty in math and reading achievement (Eamon, 2002). Poverty was related to lower math and reading scores through its association with less cognitively stimulating and supportive home environments. The study also found that poverty was related to behavior problems at school.

The schools that children from impoverished backgrounds attend often have fewer resources than schools in higher-income neighborhoods (Banks & others, 2005; McLoyd, Aikens, & Burton, 2006; Ryan, Fauth, & Brooks-Gunn, 2006). In low-income areas, students tend to have lower achievement test scores, lower graduation rates, and lower rates of college attendance. School buildings and classrooms are often old, crumbling, and poorly maintained. They are also more likely to be staffed by young teachers with less experience than schools in higher-income neighborhoods. Schools in low-income areas also are more likely to encourage rote learning, whereas schools in higher-income areas are more likely to work with children to improve their thinking skills (Spring, 2006). In sum, far too many schools in low-income neighborhoods provide students with environments that are not conducive to effective learning.

In *Savage Inequalities,* Jonathan Kozol (1991) vividly described some of the problems that children of poverty face in their neighborhood and at school. Here are some of Kozol's observations in one inner-city area. East St. Louis, Illinois, which is 98 percent African American, has no obstetric services, no regular trash collection, and few jobs. Blocks upon blocks of housing consist of dilapidated, skeletal buildings. Residents breathe the chemical pollution of nearby Monsanto Chemical Company. Raw sewage repeatedly backs up into homes. Child malnutrition is common. Fear of violence is real. The problems of the streets spill over into the schools, where sewage also backs up from time to time. Classrooms and hallways are old and unattractive, athletic facilities inadequate. Teachers run out of chalk and paper and the science labs are 30 to 50 years out of date. Kozol says that anyone who visits places like East St. Louis, even for a brief time, comes away profoundly shaken.

DIVERSITY AND EDUCATION
The Quantum Opportunities Program

A downward trajectory is not inevitable for students living in poverty. One potential path for these students is to become involved with a caring mentor. The Quantum Opportunities Program, funded by the Ford Foundation, was a 4-year, year-round mentoring effort (Carnegie Council on Adolescent Development, 1995). The ninth-grade students in the program were from poor minority families. Each day for 4 years, mentors provided sustained support, guidance, and concrete assistance to the students.

The Quantum program required students to participate in these kinds of activities:

- Academic-related activities outside school hours, including reading, writing, math, science, social studies, peer tutoring, and computer skills training
- Community service projects, including tutoring elementary school students, cleaning up the neighborhood, and volunteering in hospitals, nursing homes, and libraries
- Cultural enrichment and personal development activities, including life skills training and planning for college or a job

In exchange for their commitment to the program, students were offered financial incentives that encouraged their participation, completion, and long-range planning. A stipend of $1.33 was given to students for each hour they participated in these activities. For every 100 hours of education, service, or development activities completed, a student received a $100 bonus. The average cost per participant was $10,600 for all 4 years, which was half the cost of only 1 year in prison.

An evaluation of the Quantum project compared the mentored students with a nonmentored control group. Follow-up studies found that 63 percent of the mentored students graduated from high school, but only 42 percent of the control group did; 42 percent of the mentored students were enrolled in college, but only 16 percent of the control group were; and compared with the mentored group, the control group students were twice as likely to receive food stamps or welfare and had more arrests.

Another message from Kozol's observations is that although children in low-income neighborhoods and schools experience many inequities, these children and their families also have many strengths, including courage. Parents in such impoverished circumstances may intensely pursue ways to get more effective teachers and better opportunities for their children.

One trend in antipoverty programs is two-generational intervention (McLoyd, 1998, 2000; McLoyd, Aikens, & Burton, 2006). This involves providing both services for children (such as educational child care or preschool education) and services for parents (such as adult education, literacy training, and job skills training). Recent evaluations of the two-generation programs suggest that they have more positive effects on parents than they do on children (St. Pierre, Layzer, & Barnes, 1996). Also discouraging for the education of these children is that when the two-generational programs show benefits, they are more likely to be health benefits than cognitive gains. To learn about one effective program for intervening in the lives of children living in poverty, read the Diversity and Education interlude.

In his book *Savage Inequalities,* Jonathan Kozol vividly portrayed the problems that children of poverty face in their neighborhood and at school. *What are some of these problems?*

BEST PRACTICES
Strategies for Working with Children in Poverty

1. *Improve thinking and language skills.* If you teach in a school in a low-income neighborhood, adopt the goal of helping children improve their thinking and language skills. As described next, this is an important goal in the classroom of Jill Nakamura, a first-grade teacher in Fresno, California.

THROUGH THE EYES OF TEACHERS

Daily After-School Reading Club for Students in a High-Poverty School

Jill Nakamura teaches in a school located in a high-poverty area. She visits students at home early in the school year in a effort to connect with them and develop a partnership with their parents. "She holds daily after-school reading club for students reading below grade level . . . ; those who don't want to attend must call parents to tell them. In a recent school year (2004), she "raised the percent of students reading at or above grade level from 29 percent to 76 percent" (Wong, 2004, p. 6D).

2. *Don't overdiscipline.* Where poverty and other factors make it difficult to maintain safety and discipline, recognize the right, workable tradeoff between discipline and children's freedom. We will say more about classroom discipline in chapter 14, "Managing the Classroom."

3. *Make student motivation a high priority.* Because many children from low-income backgrounds might come to your class not having experienced high parental standards for achievement and thus might lack the motivation to learn, pay special attention to motivating these children to learn. We will address this topic further in chapter 13, "Motivation, Teaching, and Learning."

4. *Think about ways to help parents.* Recognize that many parents in poor areas are not able to provide much academic supervision or assistance to their children. Look for ways to support the parents who can be trained and helped to do so. One recent study found that when low-

Jill Nakamura, teaching in her first-grade classroom.

income parents had high educational aspirations, it was linked to more positive educational outcomes in youth (Schoon, Parsons, & Sacker, 2004).

5. *Look for ways to involve talented people from impoverished communities.* Recognize that parents in poor areas can be quite talented, caring, responsive people in ways that teachers might not expect. Most impoverished communities have people whose wisdom and experience defy stereotypes. Find these people and ask them to volunteer their services to help support children's learning in your classroom, accompany children on field trips, and make the school more attractive.

6. *Observe the strengths of children from low-income backgrounds.* Many children from these circumstances come to school with considerable untapped knowledge, and teachers can access such richness (Pang, 2005). For example, these children may have substantial knowledge about how to use mass transit, while richer children are simply transported in cars.

Ethnicity

The word *ethnic* comes from the Greek word that means "nation." **Ethnicity** refers to a shared pattern of characteristics such as cultural heritage, nationality, race, religion, and language. Everyone is a member of one or more ethnic groups, and relations between people from different ethnic backgrounds, not just in the United States but in virtually every corner of the world, are often charged with bias and conflict.

How does ethnicity differ from race? The term *race*, now discredited as a biological concept, refers to the classification of people or other living things according

ethnicity A shared pattern of characteristics such as cultural heritage, nationality, race, religion, and language.

to specific physiological characteristics. The term has never worked well in describing people in any scientific sense because humans are so diverse that they don't fit into neatly packaged racial categories. Thus, race no longer is recognized as an authentic scientific concept. Popularly, the word *race* has loosely been used to refer to everything from a person's mannerisms to religion to skin color. Social psychologist James Jones (1994, 1997) points out that thinking in racial terms has become embedded in most cultures. He says that people often stereotype others because of their supposed race and inappropriately classify them as being more or less intelligent, competent, responsible, or socially acceptable on this basis. Although the term *race* is still embedded in the American vocabulary, we will mainly use the term *ethnicity* in this book.

Nowhere is the changing tapestry of American culture more apparent than in the changing ethnic balances among America's citizens (Banks, 2006; Spring, 2006; Wiese & Garcia, 2006). At the onset of the twenty-first century, one-third of all school-age children fell into the category now loosely referred to as "children of color" (principally African Americans, Latinos, Asian Americans, and Native Americans). By the year 2025 that portion will reach one-half. This changing demographic promises not only the richness that diversity produces but also difficult challenges in extending the American dream to individuals of all ethnic groups (Okagki, 2006). Historically, people of color have found themselves at the bottom of the American economic and social order. They have been disproportionately represented among the poor and the inadequately educated (McLoyd, Aikens, & Burton, 2006).

An important point about any ethnic group is that it is diverse (Pang, 2005). There are many ready examples: Mexican Americans and Cuban Americans are Latinos, but they had different reasons for migrating to the United States, come from varying socioeconomic backgrounds, and experience different rates and types of employment in the United States. Individuals born in Puerto Rico are distinguished from Latino individuals who have immigrated to the United States in that they are born U.S. citizens and are therefore not immigrants, regardless of where they live in the United States. The U.S. government currently recognizes 511 different Native American tribes, each having a unique ancestral background with differing values and characteristics. Asian Americans include individuals of Chinese, Japanese, Filipino, Korean, and Southeast Asian origin, each group having distinct ancestries and languages. The diversity of Asian Americans is reflected in their educational attainment. Some achieve a high level of education; many others have little education. For example, 90 percent of Korean American males graduate from high school, but only 71 percent of Vietnamese males do.

Ethnicity and Schools   Educational segregation is still a reality for children of color in the United States (Buck, 2002). Almost one-third of African American and Latino students attend schools in which 90 percent or more of the students are from minority groups, typically their own minority group. The school experiences of students from different ethnic groups also depart in other ways (Okagki, 2006; Yeakey & Henderson, 2002). For example, African American and Latino students are much less likely than non-Latino White or Asian American students to be enrolled in academic, college preparatory programs and much more likely to be enrolled in remedial and special education programs. Asian American students are far more likely than students from other ethnic minority groups to take advanced math and science courses in high school. African American students are twice as likely as Latinos, Native Americans, or Whites to be suspended from school. Ethnic minorities of color constitute the majority in 23 of the 25 largest school districts in the United States, a trend that is increasing (Banks, 1995). However, 90 percent of the teachers in America's schools are non-Latino White, and the percentage of minority teachers is projected to be even lower in coming years.

Further, just as the schools of students from low-income backgrounds have fewer resources than those of students from higher-income backgrounds, so too do

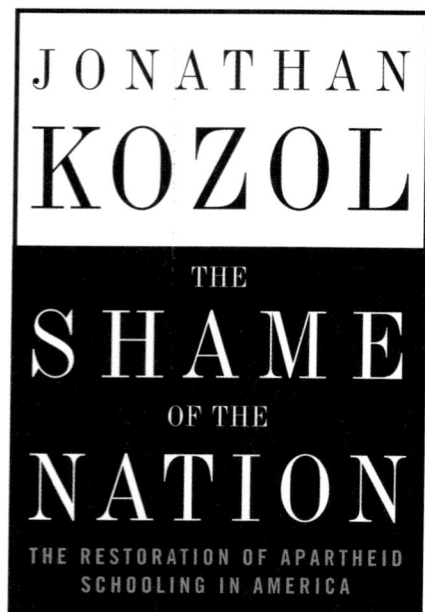

What is the nature of Jonathan Kozol's (2005) book, The Shame of the Nation?

the schools of students from ethnic minority backgrounds have fewer resources than the schools of their counterparts from largely non-Latino White backgrounds (Banks & others, 2005; McLoyd, Aikens, & Burton, 2006; Oakes & Lipton, 2007). For example, recent studies found that students in California's predominantly minority schools had less access to every instructional resource surveyed, including textbooks, supplies, and computers, and were five times more likely to have uncertified teachers than students in predominantly non-Latino White schools (Oakes & Saunders, 2002; Shields & others, 2001).

In a recent book, *The Shame of the Nation,* Jonathan Kozol (2005) described his visits to 60 U.S. schools in low-income areas of cities 11 states. He saw many schools in which the minority population was 80 to 90 percent, concluding that school segregation is still present for many poor minority students. Kozol saw many of the inequities just summarized—unkempt classrooms, hallways, and restrooms; inadequate textbooks and supplies; and lack of resources. He also saw teachers mainly instructing students to rotely memorize material, especially as preparation for mandated tests, rather than engage in higher-level thinking. Kozol also frequently observed teachers using threatening disciplinary tactics to control the classroom.

Prejudice, Discrimination, and Bias **Prejudice** is an unjustified negative attitude toward an individual because of the individual's membership in a group. The group toward which the prejudice is directed might be defined by ethnicity, sex, age, or virtually any other detectable difference (Monteith, 2000). Our focus here is prejudice against ethnic groups of color.

People who oppose prejudice and discrimination often have contrasting views. Some value and praise the strides made in civil rights in recent years. Others criticize American schools and other institutions because they believe that many forms of discrimination and prejudice still exist there (Jackson, 1997; Murrell, 2000).

American anthropologist John Ogbu (1989; Ogbu & Stern, 2001) asserts that ethnic minority students are placed in a position of subordination and exploitation in the American educational system. He argues that students of color, especially African American and Latino students, have inferior educational opportunities, are exposed to teachers and school administrators who have low academic expectations for them, and encounter negative stereotypes of ethnic minority groups.

Like Ogbu, educational psychologist Margaret Beale Spencer (Spencer, 2006; Spencer & Dornbusch, 1990) argues that institutional racism permeates many American schools. That is, well-meaning teachers, acting out of misguided liberalism, fail to challenge children of color to achieve. Such teachers prematurely accept a low level of performance from these children, substituting warmth and affection for high standards of academic success.

Diversity and Differences Historical, economic, and social experiences produce both prejudicial and legitimate differences among various ethnic groups. Individuals who live in a particular ethnic or cultural group adapt to that culture's values, attitudes, and stresses. Their behavior might be different from one's own yet be functional for them. Recognizing and respecting these differences is an important aspect of getting along in a diverse, multicultural world (Spencer, 2000, 2006). One recent study revealed that when teachers were "color-blind" (that is, they did not recognize ethnic differences in students), they suspended African American male students at a disproportionately high rate and did not integrate multicultural education into their classrooms (Schofield, 2003). "A well-meaning statement such as 'I don't see color' fails to legitimize" ethnic "identifications that often define the experiences of people of color" (Banks & others, 2005, p. 267).

Unfortunately, when differences between ethnic minority groups and the White majority were emphasized, it was damaging to ethnic minority individuals. For too long, virtually all differences were thought of as deficits or inferior characteristics on the part of the ethnic minority group (Meece & Kurtz-Costes, 2001).

prejudice An unjustified negative attitude toward an individual because of the individual's membership in a group.

Another important dimension of every ethnic group is its diversity (Banks, 2006; Spring, 2006). Not only is U.S. culture diverse—so is every ethnic group within the U.S. culture.

Bilingualism

Throughout the world many children speak more than one language (Anderson, Moffatt, & Shapiro, 2006). *Bilingualism*—the ability to speak two languages—has a positive effect on children's cognitive development. Children fluent in two languages perform better than their single-language counterparts on tests of control of attention, concept formation, analytical reasoning, cognitive flexibility, and cognitive complexity (Bialystok, 1999, 2001). They also are more conscious of the structure of spoken and written language and better at noticing errors of grammar and meaning, skills that benefit their reading ability (Bialystok, 1997).

Learning a Second Language   U.S. students are far behind their counterparts in many developed countries in learning a second language. For example, in Russia, schools have 10 grades, called *forms,* which roughly correspond to the 12 grades in American schools. Children begin school at age 7 in Russia and begin learning English in the third form. Because of this emphasis on teaching English, most Russian citizens under the age of 40 today are able to speak at least some English.

Learning a second language is easier for children than for adolescents or adults. Adults make faster initial progress, but their eventual success in the second language is not as great as children's. For example, in one study, Chinese and Korean adults who immigrated to the United States at different ages were given a test of grammatical knowledge (Johnston & Newport, 1991). Those who began learning English when they were 3 to 7 years old scored as well as native speakers on the test, but those who arrived in the United States (and started learning English) in later childhood or adolescence had lower test scores (see figure 5.3). Children's ability to pronounce a second language with the correct accent also decreases with age, with an especially sharp drop occurring after the age of about 10 to 12 (Asher & Garcia, 1969). In sum, researchers have found that early exposure to two languages is best (Petitto, Kovelman, & Harasymowycz, 2003).

Bilingual Education   A current controversy related to bilingualism involves the millions of U.S. children who come from homes in which English is not the primary language (Buyd-Batstone, 2006; Echevarria & Graves, 2007). What is the best way to teach these children?

Bilingual education teaches academic subjects to immigrant children in their native language while slowly teaching English (Gonzales, Yawkey, & Minaya-Rowe, 2006; Padilla, 2006). Advocates of bilingual education argue that if children who do not know English are taught only in English, they will fall behind in academic subjects. How, they ask, can 7-year-olds learn arithmetic or history taught only in English when they do not speak the language? Critics of bilingual programs use two arguments: that the programs are counterproductive, or that existing programs are too brief.

Those who oppose bilingual education argue that programs are not successful in teaching English to the children of immigrants. California, Arizona, and Massachusetts have significantly reduced access to bilingual education programs. Some states continue to endorse bilingual education, but the requirement that test scores be reported separately for English-language learners (students whose main language is

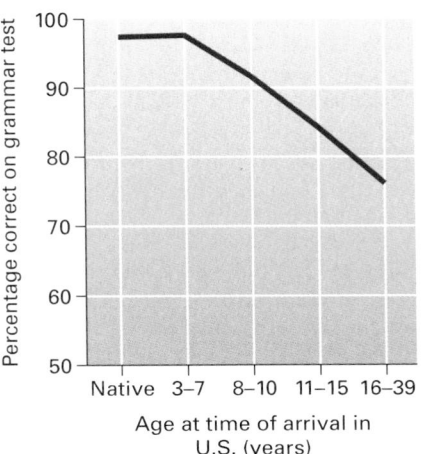

FIGURE 5.3 Grammar Proficiency and Age at Arrival in the United States

In one study, 10 years after arriving in the United States, individuals from China and Korea took a grammar test (Johnson & Newport, 1991). People who arrived before the age of 8 had a better grasp of grammar than those who arrived later.

A first- and second-grade bilingual English-Cantonese teacher instructing students in Chinese in Oakland, California. *What is the nature of bilingual education?*

bilingual education Teaching academic subjects to immigrant children in their native language while slowly teaching English.

BEST PRACTICES
Strategies for Working with Linguistically and Culturally Diverse Children

Here are some classroom recommendations for working with linguistically and culturally diverse children:

1. *"Recognize that all children are cognitively, linguistically, and emotionally connected to the language and culture of their home."*

2. *"Acknowledge that children can demonstrate their knowledge and capacity in many ways.* Whatever language children speak, they should be able to show their capabilities and feel appreciated and valued."* Next, Verna Rollins, a middle-school language-arts teacher in Ypsilanti, Michigan, describes her experience with a Romanian student.

THROUGH THE EYES OF TEACHERS
Helping a 12-Year-Old Romanian Student to Become Proficient in English

Christina, a 12-year-old Romanian student, has been in America for about 15 months and is developing proficiency in English. Knowing she needs to learn to speak, read, and write standard English to be a successful, contributing member of American society, I looked for strengths that she brought to our community. Christina attended school in Romania and was able to read and write in her first language at an age-appropriate level. To take into account the context of language learning, I've altered many assignments I've given to Christina, and I've used gestures and my knowledge of other Romance languages to help her understand writing tasks. I've also encouraged Christina to accompany her writing with drawings that were unhampered by language deficiencies.

3. *"Understand that without comprehensible input, second-language learning can be difficult.* It takes time to be linguistically competent in any language."*

4. *"Model appropriate use of English, and provide the child with opportunities to use newly acquired vocabulary and language."* Learn at least a few words in the child's first language to demonstrate respect for the child's culture.

5. *"Actively involve parents and families in the early learning program and setting."* Encourage and assist parents in becoming knowledgeable about the value for children of knowing more than one language. Provide parents with strategies to support and maintain home language learning.

6. *"Recognize that children can and will acquire the use of English even when their home language is used and respected."* Next, Daniel Arnoux, a middle-school English teacher in Broward, Florida, describes how he seeks to make a difference in the lives of students whose natural first language is not English.

THROUGH THE EYES OF TEACHERS
Giving Students a Sense of Pride

For the past 7 years I have been teaching ESOL (English for speakers of other languages) in addition to other middle school subjects. I believe that I've made a difference in my students' lives by giving them a sense of pride in their heritage and by providing a learning environment in which they can grow.

To achieve equality, the educational system must recognize students' ethnic background and gender. The student's home culture isn't to be discarded but instead used as a teaching tool. What works best in improving children's interethnic problems is to confront the problem head-on. I create lessons that teach empathy and tolerance toward others. I've used my free time to talk to classes about human rights and prejudice toward students of different nationalities and cultures—in particular Haitian students who are continually harassed and sometimes beaten in school.

Try always to know your students as human beings, and they will surely open up to you and learn. Tell them that you believe in them. If you believe they can achieve, they will.

7. *"Collaborate with other teachers to learn more about working with linguistically and culturally diverse children"* (source: National Association for the Education of Young Children, 1996, pp. 7–11).

not English) in the federally mandated No Child Left Behind state assessments has shifted attention to literacy in English (Snow & Kang, 2006).

Drawing general conclusions about the effectiveness of bilingual education is difficult—programs vary considerably in the number of years they are in effect, type of instruction, qualities of schooling other than bilingual education, teachers, school population, and other factors. Further, no effectively conducted experiments comparing bilingual to English-only education in the United States have been performed (Snow & Kang, 2006). Some experts argue that the quality of instruction is more important in determining outcomes than the language in which it is delivered (Lesaux & Siegel, 2003).

Some researchers have reported support for bilingual education in that children have difficulty learning a subject when it is taught in a language they do not understand, and when both languages are integrated in the classroom, children learn the second language more readily and participate more actively (Hakuta, 2000, 2001, 2005; Pérez, 2004; Pérez & others, 2004; Soltero, 2004). Many of the research results, however, report only modest rather than strong support for bilingual education, and some bilingual education advocates now acknowledge that competent English-only instruction can produce positive outcomes for English-language learners (Lesaux & Siegel, 2003).

Some critics of current programs argue that too often immigrant children receive only 1 year of bilingual education, whereas it takes them approximately 3 to 5 years to develop speaking proficiency and 7 years to develop reading proficiency in English (Hakuta, Butler, & Witt, 2000). Immigrant children vary in their ability to learn English (Ariza, 2006; Herrera & Murray, 2005; Lessow-Hurley, 2005). Children from lower socioeconomic backgrounds have more difficulty than those from higher socioeconomic backgrounds (Hakuta, 2001; Rueda & Yaden, 2006). Thus, especially for low-SES immigrant children, more years of bilingual education may be needed than they currently receive.

Review, Reflect, and Practice

(1) Discuss how variations in culture, socioeconomic status, and ethnic background might raise special classroom needs.

REVIEW
- What is culture? How do individualistic and collectivistic cultures differ?
- What is socioeconomic status? In what ways are children from impoverished backgrounds likely to have difficulty in school?
- How is ethnicity involved in children's schooling?
- What is the nature of second language learning? What characterizes bilingual education?

REFLECT
- In the context of education, are all ethnic differences negative? Come up with some differences that might be positive in U.S. classrooms.

PRAXIS™ PRACTICE
1. Mr. Austin, who grew up in the midwestern United States, teaches math in a high school with students who have immigrated from Mexico, Korea, Vietnam, India, Pakistan, Poland, and the Czech Republic. He often uses competitive games as class activities, many of which involve individual races to solve problems on the white board at the front of the classroom. Some of his students seem to immensely enjoy the games, but some students get upset because they are unable to solve a problem. They become even more upset when Mr. Austin constructively criticizes them during the game. The most plausible explanation is that students who do *not* enjoy the games
   a. are not good athletes.
   b. have low self-esteem.
   c. grew up in a collectivist culture.
   d. grew up in an individualist culture.

continued on page 156

Review, Reflect, and Practice *continued*

2. Sally is a third-grade student at an economically diverse school. Sally lives in poverty, as do about one-fourth of her class. Another one-fourth of the class come from upper-middle-income families and another half come from middle-income families. Sally's teacher, Ms. Roberts, has assigned a diorama (a scenic representation with sculpted figures and lifelike objects) project in lieu of a standard book report on *Charlotte's Web*.

   Kanesha, one of the more affluent children in the class, has created an elaborate diorama in a large shoe box. She placed plastic animals and small dolls in the diorama. The inside of her box is paneled with craft sticks to look like barn siding, and she used fine fishing line to create a web.

   Although Sally read, understood, and enjoyed the book, her diorama does not compare favorably to Kanesha's. First, she did not have a shoe box to use, so she used an old shoe box she found at a grocery store. She made her animals out of paper because she could not afford plastic animals. She made her web out of an old shoe-lace.

   When Sally looked at her diorama next to Kanesha's she almost cried. She did cry when Ms. Roberts gushed over how lovely Kanesha's diorama looked. What should Ms. Roberts done differently?
   a. She should have explained the income differences to the students before they began their project.
   b. She should have had the students write traditional book reports.
   c. She should have provided the materials and then had the students create the dioramas.
   d. She should have praised Sally's diorama more than Kanesha's.

3. Robert teaches at an ethnically diverse elementary school. Since he decided to become a teacher, his goal has been to teach in a school like this one because he wants to help ethnic minority children. In his class, he makes considerable effort to ensure that all of his students are successful and feel part of the larger group. He is warm and caring toward his students, sometimes even providing lunch for those who forget to bring one or don't have enough money for the cafeteria. He often praises minority students for work that he would find only average from his majority students. What is Robert doing wrong?
   a. He is substituting nurturance for academic standards.
   b. He should provide a more nurturing environment for all students.
   c. He should provide lunch for all of his students or none of them.
   d. He is setting standards for minority students that are too high.

4. Mr. Williams teaches first grade and thinks his students will benefit from learning a second language, so he labels many of the items in his classroom in both English and Spanish. He chose Spanish because that is the second most common language in the area in which he teaches. What research supports Mr. Williams' approach?
   a. First-graders are the right age to learn to read a second language but aren't too old to learn to speak a second language.
   b. Because students in most countries do not learn to read a second language, Mr. Williams is giving his students an important advantage.
   c. Children learn a second language better and more easily at this age than they will when they get older.
   d. Mr. Williams should select a second language that is unfamiliar to most of his class.

Please see the answer key at the end of the book.

In 1963, President John Kennedy said, "Peace is a daily, a weekly, a monthly process, of gradually changing opinions, slowly eroding old barriers, quietly building new structures." Cultural and ethnic tensions regularly threaten this fragile peace. The hope is that multicultural education can contribute to making our nation more like what the late civil rights leader Martin Luther King, Jr., dreamed of: a nation where children will be judged not by the color of their skin but by the quality of their character.

Multicultural education is education that values diversity and includes the perspectives of a variety of cultural groups on a regular basis. Its enthusiasts believe that children of color should be empowered and that multicultural education benefits all students. An important goal of multicultural education is equal educational opportunity for all students. This includes closing the gap in academic achievement between mainstream students and students from underrepresented groups (Bennett, 2007; Pang, 2005; Redman, 2007; Spring, 2006, 2007).

Multicultural education grew out of the civil rights movement of the 1960s and the call for equality and social justice for women and people of color (Spring, 2007). As a field, multicultural education includes issues related to socioeconomic status, ethnicity, and gender. Because social justice is one of the foundational values of the field, prejudice reduction and equity pedagogy are core components (Aldridge & Goldman, 2007; Banks, 2006). *Prejudice reduction* refers to activities teachers can implement in the classroom to eliminate negative and stereotypical views of others. *Equity pedagogy* refers to the modification of the teaching process to incorporate materials and learning strategies appropriate to both boys and girls and to various ethnic groups.

You and your students will benefit if you take a course or have some type of preparation involving multicultural education. For example, a recent study of math and science teachers revealed that their students' achievement was enhanced when their "teachers had a degree in the field in which they were teaching *and* had had preparation regarding multicultural education, special education, and English language development (Wenglinksy, 2002)" (Banks & others, 2005, p. 233).

Empowering Students

The term **empowerment** refers to providing people with the intellectual and coping skills to succeed and make this a more just world. In the 1960s to 1980s, multicultural education was concerned with empowering students and better representing minority and cultural groups in curricula and textbooks. Empowerment continues to be an important theme of multicultural education today (McLaren, 2007; Schmidt, 2001). In this view, schools should give students the opportunity to learn about the experiences, struggles, and visions of many different ethnic and cultural groups (Banks, 2003, 2006; Bennett, 2007). The hope is that this will raise minority students' self-esteem, reduce prejudice, and provide more-equal educational opportunities. The hope also is that it will help White students become more tolerant toward minority groups and that both White students and students of color will develop multiple perspectives within their curricula.

multicultural education Education that values diversity and includes the perspectives of a variety of cultural groups on a regular basis.

empowerment Providing people with intellectual and coping skills to succeed and make this a more just world.

Banks (2003, 2006) suggests that future teachers can benefit from writing a brief essay about a situation in which they felt marginalized (being excluded) by another group. Virtually everyone, whether from a minority or majority group, has experienced this type of situation at some point in their life. Banks emphasizes that you should be in a better position to understand the issues of sociocultural diversity after writing such an essay.

Sonia Nieto (1992, 2003, 2005), a Puerto Rican who grew up in New York City, believes that her education made her feel that her cultural background was somehow deficient. She provides these recommendations:

- The school curriculum should be openly antiracist and antidiscriminatory. Students should feel free to discuss issues of ethnicity and discrimination.
- Multicultural education should be a part of every student's education. This includes having all students become bilingual and study different cultural perspectives. Multicultural education should be reflected everywhere in the school, including bulletin boards, lunch rooms, and assemblies.
- Students should be trained to be more conscious of culture. This involves getting students to be more skillful at analyzing culture and more aware of the historical, political, and social factors that shape their views of culture and ethnicity. The hope is that such critical examination will motivate students to work for political and economic justice.

Culturally Relevant Teaching

Culturally relevant teaching is an important aspect of multicultural education (Farr, 2005; Spring, 2006). It seeks to make connections with the learner's cultural background (Pang, 2005).

Multicultural education experts believe that good teachers are aware of and integrate culturally relevant teaching into the curriculum because it makes teaching more effective (Diaz, 2001; Diaz, Pelletier, & Provenzo, 2006). Some researchers have found that students from some ethnic groups behave in ways that may make some educational tasks more difficult than others. For example Jackie Irvine (1990) and Janice Hale-Benson (1982) observed that African American students are often expressive and high in energy. They recommended that, when students behave in this way, giving them opportunities to make presentations rather than always being required to perform on a written exam might be a good strategy. Other researchers have found that many Asian American students prefer visual learning more than their European American peers (Litton, 1999; Park, 1997). Thus, with these students teachers might want to use more three-dimensional models, graphic organizers, photographs, charts, and writing on the board.

Going into the community where your students live and their parents work can improve your understanding of their ethnic and cultural backgrounds (Banks & others, 2005). The *funds of knowledge approach* emphasizes that teachers should visit students' households to develop social relationships with their students' family members to learn more about their cultural and ethnic background so that they can incorporate this knowledge into their teaching (Moll & Gonzáles, 2004). Through this approach, teachers can learn more about the occupations, interests, and community characteristics of their students' families. Examples of the funds of knowledge approach include guiding students to understand how their parents' carpentry skills relate to geometry and how the type of language students encounter outside of the classroom might help teachers in teaching students in English classes in school. Researchers have found that when the funds of knowledge approach is used Latino students' academic performance improves (Gonzáles, Moll, & Amanti, 2005). The funds of knowledge approach acts as a bridge between the student's school and community.

Teachers need to have high achievement expectations for students from ethnic minority and low-income backgrounds and engage them in rigorous academic programs. When high achievement expectations and rigorous academic programs are combined with culturally relevant teaching and community connections, students from ethnic minority and low-income backgrounds benefit enormously. In one recent study of California students, a 4-year evaluation found that Latino students who participated in a rigorous academic program that included community-based writing and study, academic advising, and time with community leaders were almost twice as likely to apply to and attend universities than their counterparts who did not participate in the program (Gandara, 2002).

Issues-Centered Education

Issues-centered education also is an important aspect of multicultural education. In this approach, students are taught to systematically examine issues that involve equity and social justice. They not only clarify their values but also examine alternatives and consequences if they take a particular stance on an issue. Issues-centered education is closely related to moral education, which we discussed in chapter 3, "Social Contexts and Socioemotional Development."

Consider the circumstance when some students were concerned with the lunch policy at a high school (Pang, 2005). The students who were on federally subsidized programs were forced to use a specific line in the cafeteria, which "labeled" them poor. Many of these low-income students felt humiliated and embarrassed to the point that they went without lunch. The students alerted teachers to what had happened to them, and together, the students and teachers developed a plan of action. They presented the plan to the school district, which revised its lunch line policy at the ten high schools affected by it.

Improving Relations among Children from Different Ethnic Groups

A number of strategies and programs are available to improve relationships among children from different ethnic groups. To begin, we will discuss one of the most powerful strategies.

The Jigsaw Classroom When social psychologist Eliot Aronson was a professor at the University of Texas at Austin, the school system contacted him for ideas to reduce the increasing racial tension in classrooms. Aronson (1986) developed the concept of the **jigsaw classroom,** which involves having students from different cultural backgrounds cooperate by doing different parts of a project to reach a common goal. Aronson used the term *jigsaw* because he saw the technique as much like a group of students cooperating to put different pieces together to complete a jigsaw puzzle.

How might this work? Consider a class of students, some White, some African American, some Latino, some Native American, and some Asian American. The lesson concerns the life of Joseph Pulitzer. The class might be broken up into groups of six students each, with the groups being as equally mixed as possible in terms of ethnic composition and achievement level. The lesson about Pulitzer's life is divided into six parts, and one part is assigned to each member of each six-person group. The parts might be passages from Pulitzer's biography, such as how the Pulitzer family came to the United States, Pulitzer's childhood, his early work, and so on. All students in each group are given an allotted time to study their parts. Then the groups meet, and each member works to teach his or her part to the group. Learning depends on the students' interdependence and cooperation in reaching the same goal.

Sometimes the jigsaw classroom strategy is described as creating a superordinate goal or common task for students. Team sports, drama productions, and music performances are additional examples of contexts in which students cooperatively and often very enthusiastically participate to reach a superordinate goal.

Positive Personal Contact with Others from Different Cultural Backgrounds
Contact by itself does not always improve relationships. For example, busing ethnic minority students to predominantly White schools, or vice versa, has not reduced prejudice or improved interethnic relations (Minuchin & Shapiro, 1983). What

jigsaw classroom A classroom in which students from different cultural backgrounds cooperate by doing different parts of a project to reach a common goal.

Positive personal contact that involves sharing doubts, hopes, ambitions, and much more is one way to improve interethnic relations.

matters is what happens after students arrive at a school. In one comprehensive study of more than 5,000 fifth-graders and 4,000 tenth-graders, multiethnic curricula projects that focused on ethnic issues, mixed work groups, and supportive teachers and principals all helped improve students' interethnic relations (Forehand, Ragosta, & Rock, 1976).

Relations improve when students talk with each other about their personal worries, successes, failures, coping strategies, interests, and so on. When students reveal personal information about themselves, they are more likely to be perceived as individuals than simply as members of a group. Sharing personal information frequently produces this discovery: People from different backgrounds share many of the same hopes, worries, and feelings. Sharing personal information can help break down in-group/out-group and we/they barriers.

Perspective Taking Exercises and activities that help students see other people's perspectives can improve interethnic relations. In one exercise, students learn certain proper behaviors of two distinct cultural groups (Shirts, 1997). Subsequently, the two groups interact with each other in accordance with those behaviors. As a result, they experience feelings of anxiety and apprehension. The exercise is designed to help students understand the culture shock that comes from being in a cultural setting with people who behave in ways that are very different from what one is used to. Students also can be encouraged to write stories or act out plays that involve prejudice or discrimination. In this way, students "step into the shoes" of students who are culturally different from themselves and feel what it is like to not be treated as an equal (Cushner, 2006).

Studying people from different parts of the world also encourages students to understand different perspectives (Mazurek, Winzer, & Majorek, 2000). In social studies, students can be asked why people in certain cultures have customs different from their own. Teachers can also encourage students to read books on many different cultures. To read further about bringing the global community into American students' classrooms, see the Technology and Education box.

Critical Thinking and Emotional Intelligence Students who learn to think deeply and critically about interethnic relations are likely to decrease their prejudice and stereotyping of others. Students who think in narrow ways are often prejudiced. However, when students learn to ask questions, think first about issues rather than respond automatically, and delay judgment until more complete information is available, they become less prejudiced.

Emotional intelligence benefits interethnic relations. Recall from chapter 4 that being emotionally intelligent means having emotional self-awareness, managing your emotions, reading emotions, and handling relationships. Consider how the following emotionally intelligent skills can help students to improve their relations with diverse others: understanding the causes of one's feelings, being good at managing one's own anger, being good at listening to what other people are saying, and being motivated to share and cooperate.

Reducing Bias Louise Derman-Sparks and the Anti-Bias Curriculum Task Force (1989) created a number of tools to help young children reduce, handle, or even eliminate their biases. The antibias curriculum argues that although differences are good, discriminating against someone is not. It encourages teachers to confront troublesome bias issues rather than covering them up.

These are some of the antibias strategies recommended for teachers:

- Display images of children from a variety of ethnic and cultural groups. Select books for students that also reflect this diversity.

- Choose play materials and activities that encourage ethnic and cultural understanding. Use dramatic play to illustrate nonstereotypic roles and families from diverse backgrounds.

TECHNOLOGY AND EDUCATION
Technology Connections with Students Around the World

Traditionally, students have learned within the walls of their classroom and interacted with their teacher and other students in the class. With advances in telecommunications, students can learn with and from teachers and students around the world.

For example, in the Global Laboratory Project, an international, telecommunication-based project, students investigated local and global environments (Schrum & Berenfeld, 1997). After sharing their findings, students collaboratively identified various aspects of environments, discussed research plans, and conducted distributed studies using the same methods and procedures. Students from such diverse locations as Moscow, Russia; Warsaw, Poland; Kenosha, Wisconsin; San Antonio, Texas; Pueblo, Colorado; and Aiken, South Carolina participated. As their data collection and evaluation evolved, students continued to communicate with their peers worldwide and to learn more, not only about science, but also about the global community.

New advances in telecommunication make it possible for students around the world to communicate through videoconferencing over the Internet. For example, at the Research Center for Educational Technology (RCET) at Kent State University, Ohio elementary students and their teachers are collaborating with their peers at the Instituto Thomas Jefferson in Mexico City on a variety of projects including studies of plant biology, climate, and biography using both Internet-based videoconferencing and e-mail (Swan & others, 2006). RCET researchers have found that projects that share common understandings but highlight local differences are especially productive.

An increasing number of schools are also using Internet-based videoconferencing for foreign language instruction. Instead of simulating a French cafe in a typical French

Students in Research Center for Educational Technology's AT&T classroom at Kent State University studying plant biology with students at the Instituto Thomas Jefferson in Mexico City.

language class, American students might talk with French students in a real cafe in France.

Such global technology projects can go a long way toward reducing American students' ethnocentric beliefs. The active building of connections around the world through telecommunications gives students the opportunity to experience others' perspectives, better understand other cultures, and reduce prejudice.

- Talk with students about stereotyping and discriminating against others. Make it a firm rule that no child is allowed to be teased or excluded because of their ethnicity or race.
- Engage parents in discussions of how children develop prejudice and inform parents about your efforts to reduce ethnic bias in your classroom.

Increasing Tolerance The "Teaching Tolerance Project" provides schools with resources and materials to improve intercultural understanding and relationships between White children and children of color (Heller & Hawkins, 1994). The biannual magazine *Teaching Tolerance* is distributed to every public and private school in the United States (you can obtain a free copy by contacting Teaching Tolerance through www.tolerance.org). The magazine's purpose is to share views on and provide resources for teaching tolerance. For elementary school teachers, the "Different and Same" videos and materials (available through www.fci.org) can help children become more tolerant.

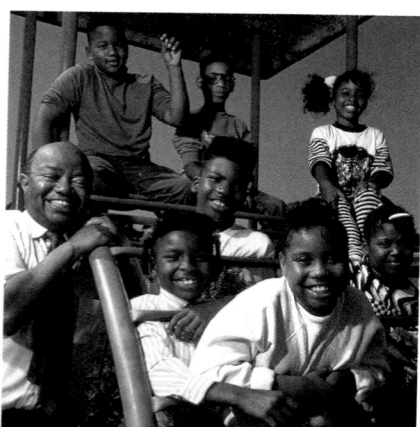

James Comer (*left*) is shown with some inner-city African American students who attend a school where Comer has implemented his community team approach.

The School and Community as a Team Yale psychiatrist James Comer (1988, 2004, 2005, 2006; Comer & others, 1996) stresses that a community team approach is the best way to educate children. Three important aspects of the Comer Project for Change are (1) a governance and management team that develops a comprehensive school plan, assessment strategy, and staff development program; (2) a mental health or school support team; and (3) a parents' program. The Comer program emphasizes no-fault (the focus should be on solving problems, not blaming), no decisions except by consensus, and no paralysis (that is, no naysayer can stand in the way of a strong majority decision). Comer says the entire school community should have a cooperative rather than an adversarial attitude. The Comer program is currently operating in more than 600 schools in 82 school districts in 26 states.

One of the first schools to implement the Comer approach was the Martin Luther King, Jr., Elementary School in New Haven, Connecticut. When the Comer program began there, its students were an average of 19 months below grade level in language arts and 18 months below grade level in math. After 10 years of the Comer program, the students' national achievement test scores were at grade level, and after 15 years they were 12 months above grade level. Even though no socioeconomic changes had taken place in this predominantly African American, low-income, inner-city area over this period, school absenteeism dropped dramatically, serious behavior problems decreased, parent participation increased substantially, and staff turnover was almost nil.

In his latest book, *Leave No Child Behind,* Comer (2004) agrees with the increased emphasis on higher standards and accountability in U.S. schools but argues that the emphasis on test scores and curriculum alone is inadequate. Comer says that children's socioemotional development and relationships with caregivers also need to be improved if educational reform is to be successful.

The Issue of Whether a Core of "White" Values Should Be Taught

Some educators have opposed the emphasis on including information about diverse ethnic groups in the curriculum. They also have opposed ethnocentric education that emphasizes any particular non-White minority group. In one proposal, Arthur Schlesinger (1991) argued that all students should be taught a set of core values that, he claimed, are derived from the White Anglo-Protestant tradition. These core values include mutual respect, individual rights, and tolerance of differences. Critics of Schlesinger's view point out that these are not peculiarly White Anglo-Protestant values but values that most ethnic and religious groups in American endorse. Indeed, multicultural education includes the Western tradition.

In another proposal, E. D. Hirsch (1987) stressed that all students should be taught a common core of cultural knowledge to ensure that they become "culturally literate." He listed a number of names, phrases, dates, and concepts that he believes students at different grade levels should know. Hirsch claims that a program of cultural literacy based on his terms and concepts will help students from impoverished backgrounds and immigrants adapt to mainstream American culture. Although Hirsch's early presentation of his ideas did not address cultural differences or social injustice, he recently updated his work to make it more multicultural.

Thus, multicultural education has its critics who argue that all children should be taught a common core of cultural values, especially White Anglo-Protestant values. However, advocates of multicultural education don't oppose teaching a core of such values as long as it does not make up the entire curriculum. They argue that U.S. core values should include elements from all segments of the nation's population and that mainstream White students can benefit from learning about "core values" derived from other groups. In the view of diversity expert Carlos Diaz (2005), the evolving issue is not about "core values" per se but rather about who defines "core values" in a heterogeneous society. Historically, people/scholars of color have not been at that table.

BEST PRACTICES
Strategies for Multicultural Education

We already have discussed many ideas that will benefit children's relations with people from different ethnic and cultural backgrounds. Further guidelines for multicultural teaching include these recommendations from leading multicultural education expert James Banks (2001):

1. *Be sensitive to racist content in materials and classroom interactions.* A good source for learning more about racism is Paul Kivel's (1995) book *Uprooting Racism.*

2. *Learn more about different ethnic groups.* According to diversity expert Carlos Diaz (2005), only when you consider yourself "multiculturally literate" will you likely encourage students to think deeply and critically about diversity. Otherwise, says Diaz, teachers tend to see diversity as a "can of worms" that they don't want to open because they lack the background to explain it. To increase your multicultural literacy, read at least one major book on the history and culture of American ethnic groups. Two of Banks' books that includes historical descriptions of these groups are *Cultural Diversity and Education* (2006) and *Teaching Strategies for Ethnic Studies* (2003).

3. *Be aware of students' ethnic attitudes.* Respond to students' cultural views in sensitive ways. Kathy Fucher, a high school teacher in Humphrey, Nebraska, addresses students' feelings in the following way.

THROUGH THE EYES OF TEACHERS
Seeking to Reduce Prejudice Toward Latino Students in Nebraska

The meatpacking industry in Nebraska has brought many Latinos to our area. I find my students have a definite negative attitude toward them, usually as a result of their parents' influence. My effort to help them realize their prejudice is to teach David Gutterson's *Snow Falling on Cedars* to senior-level students. Though the fictional novel takes place off Puget Sound and deals with Japanese immigrants during World War II, I take students through discussion questions that provide striking similarity to their prejudice against Latinos. I have no way to measure the degree of prejudice, but I feel that education and awareness are key steps in decreasing the problem.

4. *Use trade books, films, videotapes, and recordings to portray ethnic perspectives.* Banks' (2003) book *Teaching*

Strategies for Ethnic Studies describes a number of these. Next, Marlene Wendler, a fourth-grade teacher in New Ulm, Minnesota, describes her teaching strategies in this regard.

THROUGH THE EYES OF TEACHERS
Using Literature to Show How Minorities Have Been Treated

I use literature to help students understand other people and how they have sometimes been treated unfairly. During January I focus on the southeastern United States in our social studies class and integrate language arts by having the whole class read *Meet Addy* and *Mississippi Bridge.* On Martin Luther King Day we read his biography. We get a little overview of how the Jews were treated in World War II through *Number the Stars.* We also get interested in learning more about Anne Frank. When the children read how these minorities were treated, they understand more fully that all people are more similar to them than different.

5. *Take into account your students' developmental status when you select various cultural materials.* In early childhood and elementary school classrooms, make the learning experience specific and concrete. Banks stresses that fiction and biographies are especially good choices for introducing cultural concepts to these students. Banks recommends that students at these levels can study such concepts as similarities, differences, prejudice, and discrimination but are not developmentally ready to study concepts such as racism.

6. *Perceive all students in positive ways and have high expectations for them regardless of their ethnicity.* All students learn best when their teachers have high achievement expectations for them and support their learning efforts.

7. *Recognize that most parents, regardless of their ethnicity, are interested in their children's education and want them to succeed in school.* However, understand that many parents of color have mixed feelings about schools because of their own experiences with discrimination. Think of positive ways to get parents of color more involved in their children's education and view them as partners in their children's learning.

Review, Reflect, and Practice

② **Describe some ways to promote multicultural education.**

REVIEW

- What is multicultural education? What is the aim of "empowering" students?
- What is culturally relevant teaching?
- What is issues-centered education? Give an example of it.
- How can teachers improve relationships among children from different ethnic groups?
- Why do some teachers think we should still teach a core of "White Anglo-Protestant values"?

REFLECT

- In terms of multicultural education, what do you hope to do differently as a teacher than what your former teachers did?

PRAXIS™ PRACTICE

1. According to Sonia Nieto, which of these is the best educational practice for empowering students?
   a. avoiding discussion of prejudice and discrimination
   b. teaching a second language to all White students
   c. having separate weekly classes on multicultural topics
   d. encouraging all students to study culture critically

2. Which teacher's practice best exemplifies the concept of multicultural education?
   a. Mr. Lincoln, who does not allow any discussion of race or ethnicity in his class, deeming it irrelevant to his students' education
   b. Mr. Peters, who has differing expectations of his students based on gender, ethnicity, and SES
   c. Mr. Welch, who displays favoritism to members of ethnic minority groups
   d. Mr. Patterson, who integrates issues related to ethnicity, SES, and gender into the curriculum and expects high achievement from all students

3. Middlesborough High School is an ethnically diverse school with considerable racial tension and conflict. When possible, the students self-select single-ethnicity groups. When forced to work in ethnically diverse groups, the students often argue and fail to cooperate. Several racially motivated violent episodes have occurred during this school year. Based on information in the text, which of these practices is most likely to improve relationships among the students from different ethnic groups?
   a. Assign the students to read books about various ethnic groups' history and contributions and discuss them in class in mixed ethnic groups.
   b. Keep putting students of mixed ethnicity together in classes and project groups so that they get to know each other and the conflict will decrease.
   c. Allow the students to stay in single-ethnicity groups, because they are old enough to make these choices for themselves.
   d. Ignore ethnicity altogether so that students gradually become less aware of ethnic differences.

4. E. D. Hirsch advocates teaching a core set of knowledge, comprising cultural literacy, so that
   a. multicultural topics will take up less of the curriculum.
   b. all students learn to adapt to mainstream culture.
   c. all students see the superiority of Anglo-Saxon culture.
   d. students become more sensitive to racist content.

Please see the answer key at the end of the book.

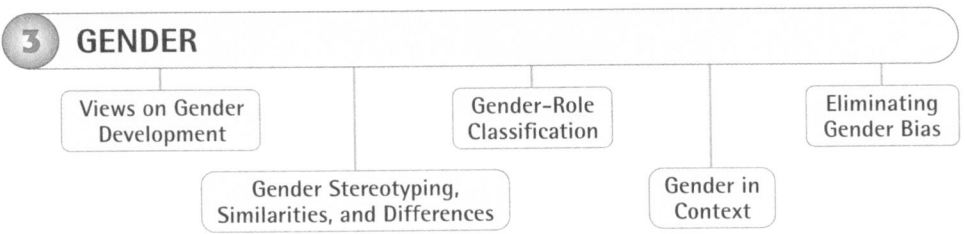

Gender refers to the sociocultural and psychological dimensions of being female or male. Gender is distinguished from *sex,* which involves the biological dimensions of being female or male. **Gender roles** are the social expectations that prescribe how males and females should think, act, and feel.

Views on Gender Development

There are various ways to view gender development. Some stress biological factors in the behavior of males and females; others emphasize social or cognitive factors (Lippa, 2005).

Biological Views   In humans the 23rd pair of chromosomes (the sex chromosomes) determine whether the fetus is a female (XX) or a male (XY). No one denies the presence of genetic, biochemical, and anatomical differences between the sexes. Even gender experts with a strong environmental orientation acknowledge that girls and boys are treated differently because of their physical differences and their different roles in reproduction. What is at issue is the directness or indirectness of biological and environmental influences. For example, androgen is the predominant sex hormone in males. If a high androgen level directly influences brain functioning, which in turn increases some behavior such as aggression or activity level, then the biological effect is direct. If a child's high androgen level produces strong muscle development, which in turn causes others to expect the child to be a good athlete and, in turn, leads the child to participate in sports, then the biological effect on behavior is more indirect.

Some biological approaches address differences in the brains of females and males (Lippa, 2005). One approach focuses on differences between females and males in the corpus callosum, the massive band of fibers that connects the brain's two hemispheres (LeDoux, 1996, 2002). The corpus collosum is larger in females than in males, and this may explain why females are more aware than are males of their own and others' emotions. This might occur because the right hemisphere is able to pass more information about emotions to the left hemisphere. The areas of the brain involved in emotional expression show more metabolic activity in females than males (Gur & others, 1995). Also, an area of the parietal lobe that functions in visuospatial skills is larger in males than females (Frederikse & others, 2000).

However, the brains of females and males are far more similar than they are different. We also know that the brain has considerable plasticity and that experiences can modify its growth. In sum, biology is not destiny when gender attitudes and behavior are at issue. Children's socialization experiences matter a great deal (Lippa, 2005).

Socialization Views   Both psychoanalytic and social cognitive theories describe social experiences that influence children's gender development:

- The **psychoanalytic theory of gender** stems from Freud's view that the preschool child develops a sexual attraction to the opposite-sex parent. At 5 or 6 years of age, the child renounces this attraction because of anxious feelings. Subsequently, the child identifies with the same-sex parent, unconsciously adopting the same-sex parent's characteristics. However, today many child

gender The sociocultural and psychological dimensions of gender.

gender roles The social expectations that prescribe how males and females should think, act, and feel.

psychoanalytic theory of gender A theory that stems from Freud's view that the preschool child develops a sexual attraction to the opposite-sex parent, then by about 5 or 6 years of age renounces the attraction because of anxious feelings. Subsequently, the child identifies with the same-sex parent, unconsciously adopting the same-sex parent's characteristics.

developmentalists do not believe gender development proceeds on the basis of identification, at least not in terms of Freud's emphasis on childhood sexual attraction (Callan, 2001). Children become gender-typed much earlier than 5 or 6 years of age, and they become masculine or feminine even when the same-sex parent is not present in the family.

- The **social cognitive theory of gender** emphasizes that children's gender development occurs through observation and imitation of gender behavior, and through the rewards and punishments children experience for gender-appropriate and gender-inappropriate behavior. Unlike identification theory, social cognitive theory argues that sexual attraction to parents is not involved in gender development. Parents often use rewards and punishments to teach their daughters to be feminine ("Karen, you are being a good girl when you play gently with your doll") and their sons to be masculine ("Keith, a boy as big as you is not supposed to cry"). Peers also extensively reward and punish gender behavior (Lott & Maluso, 2001; Rubin, Bukowski, & Parker, 2006). And, by observing adults and peers at home, at school, in the neighborhood, and on television, children are widely exposed to a myriad of models who display masculine and feminine behavior. Critics of the social cognitive view argue that gender development is not as passively acquired as it indicates. Later, we will discuss the cognitive views of gender development, which stress that children actively construct their gender world.

Many parents encourage boys and girls to engage in different types of play and activities (Bronstein, 2006; Lott & Maluso, 2001). Girls are more likely to be given dolls and, when old enough, are more likely to be assigned baby-sitting duties. Girls are encouraged to be more nurturant than boys. Fathers are more likely to engage in aggressive play with their sons than with their daughters. Parents allow their adolescent sons to have more freedom than their adolescent daughters.

Peers also extensively reward and punish gender-related behavior (Rubin, Bukowski, & Parker, 2006). After extensive observations of elementary school classrooms, two researchers characterized the play settings as "gender school" (Luria & Herzog, 1985). In elementary school, boys usually hang out with boys and girls with girls. It is easier for "tomboy" girls to join boys' groups than for "feminine" boys to join girls' groups, because of our society's greater sex-typing pressure on boys. Developmental psychologist Eleanor Maccoby (1998, 2002), who has studied gender for a number of decades, believes that peers play an especially important gender-socializing role, teaching each other what is acceptable and unacceptable gender behavior.

Television also has a gender-socializing role, portraying females and males in particular gender roles (Comstock & Scharrer, 2006; Ward, 2003). Even with the onset of more diverse programming in recent years, researchers still find that television presents males as more competent than females (Pacheco & Hurtado, 2001). In one analysis of rap videos on TV, teenage girls were primarily shown as concerned with dating, shopping, and their appearance (Campbell, 1988). They were rarely depicted as interested in school or career plans. Attractive girls were mainly pictured as "airheads," unattractive girls as intelligent. Schools and teachers also have gender-socializing influences on boys and girls.

The Cognitive View Observation, imitation, rewards and punishment—these are the mechanisms by which gender develops, according to social cognitive theory. Interactions between the child and the social environment are the main keys to gender development in this view. Some critics argue that this explanation pays too little attention to the child's own mind and understanding and portrays the child as passively acquiring gender roles (Martin, Ruble, & Szkrybalo, 2002).

Gender schema theory, currently the most widely accepted cognitive theory of gender, states that gender typing emerges as children gradually develop gender schemas of what is gender-appropriate and gender-inappropriate in their culture. A

social cognitive theory of gender A theory that children's gender development occurs through observation and imitation of gender behavior, as well as reinforcement and punishment of gender behavior.

gender schema theory States that gender typing emerges as children gradually develop gender schemas of what is gender-appropriate and gender-inappropriate in their culture.

schema is a cognitive structure, a network of associations that guides an individual's perceptions. A *gender schema* organizes the world in terms of female and male. Children are internally motivated to perceive the world and to act in accordance with their developing schemas.

Gender schema theory states that gender typing occurs when children are ready to encode and organize information along the lines of what is considered appropriate for females and males in their society (Martin & Dinella, 2001; Martin & Halverson, 1981; Ruble, Martin, & Berenbaum, 2006). Bit by bit, children pick up what is gender-appropriate and gender-inappropriate in their culture, and develop gender schemas that shape how they perceive the world and what they remember. Children are motivated to act in ways that conform with these gender schemas.

The playground in elementary school is like going to "gender school," as boys prefer to interact with boys and girls choose to interact with girls.

Gender Stereotyping, Similarities, and Differences

What are the real differences between boys and girls? Before attempting to answer that question, let's consider the problem of gender stereotypes.

Gender Stereotypes   **Gender stereotypes** are broad categories that reflect impressions and beliefs about what behavior is appropriate for females and males. All stereotypes—whether they relate to gender, ethnicity, or other categories—refer to an image of what the typical member of a category is like. Many stereotypes are so general that they become ambiguous. Consider the categories of "masculine" and "feminine." Diverse behaviors can be assigned to each category, such as scoring a touchdown or growing facial hair for "masculine," playing with dolls or wearing lipstick for "feminine." But the behaviors that make up a category can be modified by cultural change. At one point in history, muscular development might be thought of as masculine; at another time a more lithe, slender physique might be the ideal masculine body. Likewise, at some points in history, the "ideal" feminine body has been voluptuous and round. Today, it is thinner and athletic. Earlier in the twentieth century, being dependent was thought to be an important dimension of femininity, whereas today a much greater emphasis is placed on females' sensitivity to others in relationships. Which behaviors are popularly held to reflect a category also can fluctuate according to socioeconomic circumstances. For example, more low-income than middle-class individuals have a rough-and-tough image of masculinity.

Stereotyping students as "masculine" or "feminine" can have significant consequences (Halpern, 2006; Kite, 2001; Smith, 2007). Labeling a male "feminine" or a female "masculine" can diminish his or her social status and acceptance in groups.

Gender stereotyping changes developmentally (Ruble, Martin, & Berenbaum, 2006). By the time children enter elementary school, they have considerable knowledge about which activities are linked with being male or female. Until about 7 to 8 years of age, gender stereotyping is extensive probably because young children don't recognize individual variations in masculinity and femininity. By 5 years of age, both boys and girls stereotype boys as powerful and in more negative terms, such as mean, and girls in more positive terms, such as nice (Miller & Ruble, 2005). Across the elementary school years, children become more flexible in their gender attitudes (Trautner & others, 2005). In early adolescence, gender stereotyping might increase again. As their bodies change dramatically during puberty, boys and girls are often confused and concerned about what is happening to them. The safe strategy for boys is to become the very best male possible (that is, "masculine"), and the safe strategy for girls is to become the very best female possible (that is, "feminine"). Thus, gender intensification created by pubertal change may produce greater stereotyping in young adolescents, although whether this happens is still debated (Galambos, 2004; Liben & Bigler, 2002). In high school, flexibility in gender attitudes often increases, especially in U.S. adolescents.

gender stereotypes Broad categories that reflect impressions and beliefs about what behavior is appropriate for females and males.

FIGURE 5.4 National Science Scores for Boys and Girls

In the National Assessment of Educational Progress, data collected in 2005 indicated that boys had slightly higher scores than girls in the fourth, eighth, and twelfth grades (Grigg, Lauko, & Brockway, 2006). The science scores could range from 0 to 300.

Stereotypes are often negative and can be wrapped in prejudice and discrimination. **Sexism** is prejudice and discrimination against an individual because of the person's sex. A person who says that women cannot be competent engineers is expressing sexism. So is a person who says that men cannot be competent early childhood teachers. Later in this chapter, when we discuss gender in the schools, we will describe some strategies for creating a nonsexist classroom.

Gender Similarities and Differences in Academically Relevant Domains Many aspects of students' lives can be examined to determine how similar or different girls and boys are (Crawford & Unger, 2004).

Physical Performance Because physical education is an integral part of U.S. educational systems, it is important to address gender similarities and differences in physical performance (Eisenberg, Martin, & Fabes, 1996). In general, boys outperform girls in athletic skills such as running, throwing, and jumping. In the elementary school years the differences often are not large; they become more dramatic in the middle school years (Smoll & Schutz, 1990). The hormonal changes of puberty result in increased muscle mass for boys and increased body fat for girls. This leads to an advantage for boys in activities related to strength, size, and power. Nonetheless, environmental factors are involved in physical performance even after puberty. Girls are less likely to participate in activities that promote the motor skills necessary to do well in sports (Thomas & Thomas, 1988).

Activity level is another area of physical performance in which gender differences occur. From very early in life, boys are more active than girls are in terms of gross motor movements (Ruble, Martin, & Berenbaum, 2006). In the classroom, this means that boys are more likely than girls to fidget and move around the room, and they are less likely to pay attention. In physical education classes, boys expend more energy through movement than girls do.

Math and Science Skills Mixed findings have been reported regarding math skills. In some analyses, boys perform better at math, and this has long been a source of concern (Eisenberg, Martin, & Fabes, 1996). For example, in the National Assessment of Educational Progress in the United States, fourth- and eighth-grade males continued to outperform females in math through 2005 (The Nation's Report Card, 2005). However, not all recent studies have shown differences. For example, in one national study, no differences in boys' and girls' math performance were found in the fourth, eighth, and twelfth grades (Coley, 2001).

Overall, when they do exist, gender differences in math skills tend to be small (Hyde, 2005, 2007). Statements such as "Males outperform females in math" should not be read as a claim that all males outperform all females in math. Rather, such statements refer to averages (Hyde & Plant, 1995). In addition, when gender differences in math do appear, they are not uniform across contexts. Boys do better at math related to measurement, science, and sports; girls do better at math that involves such traditional female tasks as cooking and sewing (Linn & Hyde, 1989).

One area of math that has been examined for possible gender differences is visuospatial skills, which include being able to rotate objects mentally and determine what they would look like when rotated. These types of skills are important in courses such as plane and solid geometry and geography. Researchers have found that males have better visuospatial skills than females (Blakemore, Berenbaum, & Liben, 2005; Ruble, Martin, & Berenbaum, 2006). Despite equal participation in the National Geography Bee, in most years all 10 finalists are boys (Liben, 1995). However, some experts argue that the gender difference in visuospatial skills is small (Hyde, 2007).

What about science? Are there gender differences? In one recent national study of science achievement, boys did slightly better in science than girls in the fourth, eighth, and twelfth grades (National Assessment of Educational Progress, 2005) (see figure 5.4). In another study focused on eighth- and tenth-graders, boys scored higher than girls

sexism Prejudice and discrimination against an individual because of the person's sex; of being female or male.

on science tests, especially among average- and high-ability students (Burkham, Lee, & Smerdon, 1997). In science classes that emphasized hands-on lab activities, girls' science test scores improved considerably. This suggests the importance of active involvement of students in science classrooms, which may promote gender equity.

Many gender experts believe the gender differences in math and science that do exist are due to the experiences that boys and girls have (Meece & Scantlebury, 2006; Wigfield & others, 2006). There are far more male than female math and science models in the culture. Boys take more math and science courses than girls do. For example, in one recent national survey males were overwhelmingly more likely to take computer science and physics courses (Coley, 2001). Also, parents have higher expectations for boys' math and science skills. In one study of 1,500 families, parents bought more math and science books and games for their sons than for their daughters, said that boys have more math talent than girls, and commented that boys are better suited to a career in math (Eccles & others, 1991).

Verbal Skills   A major review of gender similarities and differences conducted in the 1970s concluded that girls have better verbal skills than boys do (Maccoby & Jacklin, 1974). However, more recent analyses suggest that in some instances there may be little or no differences in girls' and boys' verbal skills. For example, today males score as high as females on the verbal portion of the SAT test (Educational Testing Service, 2002).

During the elementary and secondary school years, however, there is strong evidence that females outperform males in reading and writing. In recent national studies, females had higher reading achievement than males in grades 4, 8, and 12, with the gap widening as students progressed through school (Coley, 2001; National Assessment of Educational Progress, 2005). Figure 5.5 shows the gender gap in reading in a national assessment of reading in the fourth grade (National Assessment of Educational Progress, 2005); females also have performed better than males in grades 4, 8, and 12 in writing skills (National Assessment of Educational Progress, 2002).

Educational Attainment   Males are more likely to drop out of school than females, although the difference is small (15 percent versus 13 percent) (National Center for Education Statistics, 2001). Females (90 percent) are more likely than males (87 percent) to complete high school in the United States.

Evidence suggests that boys predominate in the academic bottom half of high school classes (DeZolt & Hull, 2001). That is, although many boys perform at the average or advanced level, the bottom 50 percent academically is made up mainly of boys. The percentage of males in college during the 1950s was almost 60 percent. Today, the percentage of males enrolled in college classes has dropped to approximately 45 percent (DeZolt & Hull, 2001). Females are more likely to be engaged with academic material, be attentive in class, put forth more academic effort, and participate more in class than boys are (DeZolt & Hull, 2001). However, even when girls outperform boys in academic achievement, they tend to play down their achievement (Ruble, Martin, & Berenbaum, 2006; Wiafield, Byrnes, & Eccles, 2006).

Relationship Skills   Sociolinguist Deborah Tannen (1990) says that boys and girls grow up in different worlds of talk—parents, siblings, peers, teachers, and others talk to boys and girls differently. In describing this talk, Tannen distinguishes between rapport talk and report talk:

- **Rapport talk** is the language of conversation and a way of establishing connections and negotiating relationships. Females enjoy rapport talk and conversation that is relationship-oriented more than boys do.
- **Report talk** is talk that gives information. Public speaking is an example of report talk. Males hold center stage through report talk with such verbal performances as storytelling, joking, and lecturing with information.

FIGURE 5.5 National Reading Scores for Boys and Girls

In the National Assessment of Educational Progress, data collected in 2005 indicated that girls did better in reading in the fourth and eighth grades (National Assessment of Educational Progress, 2005). The data for the fourth grade are shown above. An earlier assessment found that the gender difference in reading favoring girls also occurs in the twelfth grade (National Assessment of Educational Progress, 1998).

"So according to the stereotype, you can put two and two together, but I can read the handwriting on the wall."

Joel Pett, *The Lexington Herald-Leader,* CartoonArts International/CWS.

rapport talk The language of conversation and a way of establishing connections and negotiating relationships; more characteristic of females than males.

report talk Talk that gives information; more characteristic of males than females.

Some researchers criticize Tannen's ideas as being overly simplified and view communication between males and females as more complex (Edwards & Hamilton, 2004; Hyde, 2005, 2007; MacGeorge, 2004). For example, in a recent meta-analysis of gender differences in talkativeness (general communicative competence), affiliative speech (language used to establish or maintain connections with others, such as showing support or expanding on a person's prior remarks), and self-assertive speech (language used to influence others, such as directive statements or disagreements) (Leaper & Smith, 2004). (A *meta-analysis* is a statistical analysis that combines the results of many different studies.) The review confirmed the criticism that Tannen overemphasizes the size of gender differences in communication. Gender differences did occur, but they were small with girls only slightly more talkative and engaging in more affiliative speech than boys, and boys being more likely to use self-assertive speech. Perhaps the most important message from this review is that gender differences in communication often depended on the context:

- *Group size.* The gender difference in talkativeness (girls being more competent in communicating) occurred more in large groups than in *dyads*.
- *Speaking with peers or adults.* No average differences in talk with peers occurred, but girls talked more with adults than boys did.
- *Familiarity.* The gender difference in self-assertive speech (boys using it more) was more likely to occur when talking with strangers than with familiar individuals.
- *Age.* The gender difference in affiliative speech was largest in adolescence. This may be due to adolescent girls' increased interest in socioemotional behavior traditionally prescribed for females.

Prosocial Behavior   Are there gender differences in prosocial behavior (positive moral behavior)? Females view themselves as more prosocial and empathetic, and they engage in more prosocial behavior than do males (Eisenberg, Fabes, & Spinrad, 2006; Eisenberg & Morris, 2004). For example, a review of research found that across childhood and adolescence, females engaged in more prosocial behavior (Eisenberg & Fabes, 1998). The biggest gender difference occurred for kind and considerate behavior, with a smaller difference in sharing.

Aggression   One of the most consistent gender differences is that boys are more physically aggressive than girls (Dodge, Coie, & Lynam, 2006; Ruble, Martin, & Berenbaum, 2006). The difference is especially pronounced when children are provoked—this difference occurs across all cultures and appears very early in children's development (Ostrov, Keating, & Ostrov, 2004). Both biological and environmental factors have been proposed to account for gender differences in physical aggression. Biological factors include heredity and hormones; environmental factors include cultural expectations, adult and peer models, and the rewarding of physical aggression in boys.

Although boys are consistently more physically aggressive than girls, might girls show as much or more verbal aggression, such as yelling, than boys? When verbal aggression is examined, gender differences typically either disappear or are sometimes even more pronounced in girls (Eagly & Steffen, 1986). Recently, increased interest has been shown in *relational aggression,* which involves harming someone by manipulating a relationship (Crick, Ostrov, & Werner, 2006; Young, Boye, & Nelson, 2006). Researchers have found mixed results regarding gender and relational aggression with some studies showing girls engaging in more relational aggression and others revealing no differences between boys and girls (Young, Boye, & Nelson, 2006).

Emotion and Its Regulation   Beginning in the elementary school years, boys are more likely to hide their negative emotions such as sadness, and girls are less likely to express emotions such as disappointment that might hurt others' feelings (Eisenberg, 1986). Beginning in early adolescence, girls say they experience more sadness, shame, and guilt, and report more intense emotions; boys are more likely to deny that they experience these emotions (Ruble, Martin, & Berenbaum, 2006). An important skill is to be able to regulate and control one's emotions and behavior. Boys usually show less self-regulation than girls (Eisenberg, Spinrad, & Smith, 2004). This low self-control can translate into behavior problems. In one study, children's low self-regulation was linked with greater aggression, teasing of others, overreaction to frustration, low cooperation, and inability to delay gratification (Block & Block, 1980).

Gender Controversy   The previous sections revealed some substantial differences in physical abilities, reading and writing skills, aggression, and self-regulation, but small or nonexistent differences in communication, math, and science. Controversy swirls about such similarities and differences. Evolutionary psychologists such as David Buss (2004) argue that gender differences are extensive and caused by the adaptive problems faced across evolutionary history. Alice Eagly (2001) also concludes that gender differences are substantial but reaches a very different conclusion about their cause. She emphasizes that gender differences are due to social conditions that have resulted in women having less power and controlling fewer resources than men.

By contrast, Janet Shibley Hyde (1986, 2005, 2007) concludes that gender differences have been greatly exaggerated, especially fueled by popular books such as John Gray's (1992) *Men Are from Mars, Women Are from Venus* and Deborah Tannen's (1990) *You Just Don't Understand*. She argues that the research shows that females and males are similar on most psychological factors. In a recent review, Hyde (2005) summarized the results of 44 meta-analyses of gender differences and similarities. In most areas, including math ability, communication, and aggression, gender differences were either nonexistent or small. The largest difference occurred on motor skills (favoring males), followed by sexuality (males masturbate more and are more likely to endorse sex in a casual, uncommitted relationship) and physical aggression (males are more physically aggressive than females).

Hyde's recent summary of meta-analyses is still not likely to quiet the controversy about gender differences and similarities, but further research should continue to provide a basis for more accurate judgments about this controversy.

Gender–Role Classification

Gender-role classification involves evaluating boys and girls in terms of groups of personality traits. In the past, a well-adjusted boy was supposed to be independent, aggressive, and powerful. A well-adjusted female was supposed to be dependent, nurturant, and uninterested in power. At the same time, overall, masculine characteristics were considered to be healthy and good by society, while feminine characteristics were considered undesirable.

In the 1970s, as more females and males began to express open dissatisfaction with the burdens imposed by rigid gender expectations, alternatives to femininity and masculinity were proposed. Instead of restricting masculinity to male competency and femininity to female competency, it was proposed that individuals could have both "masculine" and "feminine" traits. This thinking led to the development of the concept of **androgyny,** which refers to the presence of desirable masculine and feminine characteristics in the same person (Bem, 1977; Spence & Helmreich, 1978). The androgynous boy might be assertive ("masculine") and nurturant ("feminine"). The androgynous girl might be powerful ("masculine") and sensitive to others' feelings ("feminine").

Measures have been developed to assess androgyny. One of the most widely used measures is the Bem Sex-Role Inventory. To see whether your gender-role classification is masculine, feminine, or androgynous, complete Self-Assessment 5.1.

Gender experts such as Sandra Bem argue that androgynous individuals are more flexible, competent, and mentally healthy than their masculine or feminine counterparts. For example, a recent study found that masculine and androgynous individuals had higher expectations for being able to control the outcomes of their academic

androgyny The presence of desirable masculine and feminine characteristics in the same individual.

SELF-ASSESSMENT 5.1

What Gender-Role Orientation Will I Present to My Students?

The items below inquire about what kind of person you think you are. Place a check mark in the column that best describes you for each item: 1 = Not like me at all, 2 = Somewhat unlike me, 3 = Somewhat like me, and 4 = Very much like me.

Item	1	2	3	4
1. I'm independent.	___	___	___	___
2. My emotional life is important to me.	___	___	___	___
3. I provide social support to others.	___	___	___	___
4. I'm competitive.	___	___	___	___
5. I'm a kind person.	___	___	___	___
6. I'm sensitive to others' feelings.	___	___	___	___
7. I'm self-confident.	___	___	___	___
8. I'm self-reflective.	___	___	___	___
9. I'm patient.	___	___	___	___
10. I'm self-assertive.	___	___	___	___
11. I'm aggressive.	___	___	___	___
12. I'm willing to take risks.	___	___	___	___
13. I like to tell secrets to my friends.	___	___	___	___
14. I like to feel powerful.	___	___	___	___

Scoring and Interpretation

Items 1, 4, 7, 10, 11, 12, and 14 are masculine items. Items 2, 3, 5, 6, 8, 9, and 13 are feminine items. Look at the pattern of your responses. If you mainly checked 3 and 4 for the masculine items and mainly 1 and 2 for the feminine items, you likely are characterized by masculinity. If you mainly checked 3 and 4 for the feminine items and 1 and 2 for the masculine items, you likely are characterized by femininity. If you mainly checked 3 and 4 for both the masculine items and the feminine items, you likely are characterized by androgyny. If you mainly checked 1 and 2 for both the masculine and feminine items, your gender-role classification is likely undifferentiated.

efforts than feminine or undifferentiated (not masculine, feminine, or androgynous) individuals (Choi, 2004).

To some degree, though, which gender-role classification is "best" depends on the context. For example, feminine orientations might be more desirable in close relationships because of the expressive nature of close relationships, and masculine orientations might be more desirable in traditional academic and work settings because of the achievement demands in these contexts.

Of special concern are adolescent boys who adopt a strong masculine role. Researchers have found that high-masculinity adolescent boys often engage in problem behaviors, such as delinquency, drug abuse, and unprotected sexual intercourse (Pleck, 1995). They present themselves as virile, macho, and aggressive and often do poorly in school.

Androgyny and Education   Can and should androgyny be taught to students? In general, it is easier to teach androgyny to girls than to boys, and it is easier to teach it before the middle school grades. For example, in one study a gender curriculum was put in place for one year in the kindergarten, fifth, and ninth grades (Guttentag & Bray, 1976). It involved books, discussion materials, and classroom exercises with an androgynous bent. The program was most successful with fifth-graders, least successful with ninth-graders. The ninth-graders, especially the boys, showed a boomerang effect—more traditional gender-role attitudes after the year of androgynous instruction than before it.

Despite such mixed findings, the advocates of androgyny programs believe that traditional sex typing is harmful for all students and especially has prevented many girls from experiencing equal opportunity. The detractors argue that androgyny programs are too value-laden and ignore the diversity of gender roles in our society.

Gender-Role Transcendence   Some critics of androgyny say that enough is enough and that there is too much talk about gender. They argue that androgyny is less of a panacea than originally envisioned (Paludi, 2002; Woodhill & Samuels, 2004). An alternative is **gender-role transcendence,** the view that people's competence should be conceptualized in terms of them as persons rather than in terms of their masculinity, femininity, or androgyny (Pleck, 1983).

Parents should rear their children to be competent individuals, not masculine, feminine, or androgynous, say the gender-role critics. They believe such gender-role classification leads to too much stereotyping.

Gender in Context

Earlier we said that the concept of gender-role classification involves categorizing people in terms of personality traits. However, recall from our discussion of personality in chapter 4, "Individual Variations," that it is beneficial to think of personality in terms of person-situation interaction rather than personality traits alone. Let's now further explore gender in context.

Helping Behavior and Emotion   The stereotype is that females are better than males at helping. But it depends on the situation (Ruble, Martin, & Berenbaum, 2006). Females are more likely than males to volunteer their time to help children with personal problems and engage in caregiving behavior. However, in situations where males feel a sense of competence or that involve danger, males are more likely to help (Eagly & Crowley, 1986). For example, a male is more likely than a female to stop and help a person stranded by the roadside with a flat tire.

She is emotional; he is not. That's the master emotional stereotype. However, like helping behavior, emotional differences in males and females depend on the particular emotion involved and the context in which it is displayed (Shields, 1991). Males are more likely to show anger toward strangers, especially male strangers, when they feel they have been challenged. Males also are more likely to turn their anger into aggressive action. Emotional differences between females and males often show up in contexts that highlight social roles and relationships. For example, females are more likely to discuss emotions in terms of relationships. They also are more likely to express fear and sadness.

Culture   The importance of considering gender in context is most apparent when examining what is culturally prescribed behavior for females and males in different countries around the world (Best, 2001). In the United States there is now more acceptance of androgyny and similarities in male and female behavior, but in many other countries roles have remained gender-specific. For example, in many Middle Eastern countries the division of labor between males and females is dramatic. In Iraq and Iran males are socialized and schooled to work in the public sphere; females are socialized to remain in the private world of home and child rearing. Any deviations from this

gender-role transcendence View that people's competence should be conceptualized in terms of them as persons rather than in terms of whether they are masculine, feminine, or androgynous.

traditional masculine and feminine behavior is severely disapproved of. Likewise, in China, although women have made some strides, the male role is still dominant.

Cultural and ethnic backgrounds also influence how boys and girls will be socialized in the United States. A recent study indicated that Latino and Latina adolescents were socialized differently as they were growing up (Raffaelli & Ontai, 2004). Latinas experienced far greater restrictions than Latinos in curfews, interacting with members of the other sex, getting a driver's license, getting a job, and involvement in after-school activities.

Eliminating Gender Bias

How gendered are social interactions between teachers and students? What can teachers do to reduce or eliminate gender bias in their classrooms?

Teacher–Student Interaction   Teachers interact more with boys and girls at all levels of schooling (Ruble, Martin, & Berenbaum, 2006). What evidence is there that this interaction is biased against boys? Here are some factors to consider (DeZolt & Hull, 2001):

- Complying, following rules, and being neat and orderly are valued and reinforced in many classrooms. These are behaviors that are typically associated with girls rather than boys.
- A large majority of teachers are females, especially in the elementary school. This may make it more difficult for boys than girls to identify with their teachers and model their teachers' behavior.
- Boys are more likely than girls to be identified as having learning problems.
- Boys are more likely than girls to be criticized.
- School personnel tend to ignore that many boys are clearly having academic problems, especially in the language arts.
- School personnel tend to stereotype boys' behavior as problematic.

What evidence is there that the classroom is biased against girls? Consider the following factors (Sadker & Sadker, 1994, 2005):

- In a typical classroom, girls are more compliant, boys more rambunctious. Boys demand more attention; girls are more likely to quietly wait their turn. Educators worry that girls' tendency to be compliant and quiet comes at a cost: diminished assertiveness.
- In many classrooms, teachers spend more time watching and interacting with boys, while girls work and play quietly on their own. Most teachers don't intentionally favor boys by spending more time with them, yet somehow the classroom frequently ends up with this type of gendered profile.
- Boys get more instruction than girls and more help when they have trouble with a question. Teachers often give boys more time to answer a question, more hints at the correct answer, and further tries if they give the wrong answer.
- Girls and boys enter first grade with roughly equal levels of self-esteem, yet by the middle school years, girls' self-esteem is significantly lower than boys' (Robins & others, 2002).
- Although girls are identified for gifted programs more than boys in elementary school, by high school there are more boys than girls in gifted programs (U.S. Office of Education, 1999). There especially is a low number of African American and Latino girls in gifted programs (Banks & others, 2005).

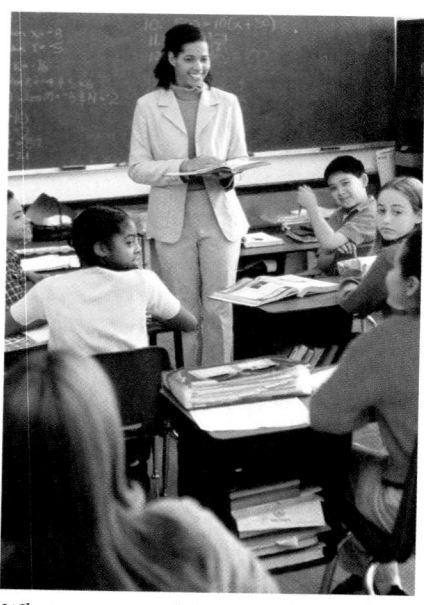

What are some of the ways that teachers interact with students on the basis of gender?

Thus, there is evidence of gender bias against both males and females in schools (DeZolt & Hull, 2001; Halpern, 2006; Thornton & Goldstein, 2006). Many school personnel are not aware of their gender-biased attitudes. These attitudes are deeply entrenched in, and supported by, the general culture. Increasing awareness of gender bias in schools is clearly an important strategy in reducing such bias.

Might same-sex education be better for children than co-ed education? The research evidence related to this question is mixed (Ruble, Martin, & Berenbaum, 2006). Some research indicates that same-sex education has positive outcomes for girls' achievement; other research does not show any improvements in achievement for girls or boys in same-sex education (Mael, 1998; Warrington & Younger, 2003).

Curriculum Content and Athletics Content   Schools have made considerable progress in reducing sexism and sex stereotyping in books and curriculum materials largely in response to Title IX of the Educational Amendment Act of 1972, which states that schools must treat females and males equally (Eisenberg, Martin, & Fabes, 1996). As a result, today's textbooks and class materials are more gender-neutral. Also, schools now offer girls far more opportunities to take vocational educational courses and participate in athletics than was the case when their parents and grandparents went to school (Gill, 2001). In 1972, 7 percent of high school athletes were girls. Today, that figure has risen to nearly 40 percent. In addition, schools no longer can expel, or eliminate services for, pregnant adolescents.

Nonetheless, bias still remains at the curricular level. For example, school text adoptions occur infrequently, and therefore many students still are studying outdated, gender-biased books.

Sexual Harassment   Sexual harassment occurs in many schools (Fitzgerald, Collinsworth, & Harned, 2001; Huerta & others, 2006; White & Frabutt, 2006). In a study of eighth- to eleventh-graders by the American Association of University Women (1993), 83 percent of the girls and 60 percent of the boys said that they had been sexually harassed. Girls reported being more severely harassed than boys. Sixteen percent of the students said they had been sexually harassed by a teacher. Examples of harassment by students and teachers in this study included

- sexual comments, jokes, gestures, or looks;
- sexual messages about a student on bathroom walls and other places or sexual rumors spread about the student;
- spying on a student who was dressing or showering at school;
- flashing or mooning;
- comments that a student was gay or lesbian;
- touching, grabbing, or pinching in a sexual manner;
- intentionally brushing up against a student in a sexual way; and
- pulling a student's clothing off or down.

The Office for Civil Rights of the U.S. Department of Education has published a 40-page policy guide on sexual harassment. In this guide, a distinction is made between quid pro quo and hostile environment sexual harassment. **Quid pro quo sexual harassment** occurs when a school employee threatens to base an educational decision (such as a grade) on a student's submission to unwelcome sexual conduct. For example, a teacher gives a student an *A* for allowing the teacher's sexual advances or an *F* for resisting the teacher's approaches. **Hostile environment sexual harassment** occurs when students are subjected to unwelcome sexual conduct that is so severe, persistent, or pervasive that it limits the students' ability to benefit from their education. Such a hostile environment is usually created by a series of incidents, such as repeated sexual overtures.

Sexual harassment is a form of power and dominance of one person over another, which can result in harmful consequences for the victim. Sexual harassment can be especially damaging when the perpetrators are teachers and other adults who have considerable power and authority over students (Sears & others, 2006). As a society, we need to be less tolerant of sexual harassment (Hock, 2007).

quid pro quo sexual harassment
Threats by a school employee to base an educational decision (such as a grade) on a student's submission to unwelcome sexual conduct.

hostile environment sexual harassment   Subjection of students to unwelcome sexual conduct that is so severe, persistent, or pervasive that it limits the students' ability to benefit from their education.

Every student, female or male, deserves an education free of gender bias. Here are some strategies for attaining this desirable educational climate (Derman-Sparks & the Anti-Bias Curriculum Task Force, 1989; Sadker & Sadker, 1994):

1. *If you are given textbooks that are gender-biased, discuss this with your students.* By talking with your students about stereotyping and bias in the texts, you can help them think critically about such important social issues. If these textbooks are not gender-fair, supplement them with other materials that are. Many schools, libraries, and colleges have gender-fair materials that you can use.

2. *Make sure that school activities and exercises are not gender-biased.* Assign students projects in which they find articles about nonstereotypical males and females, such as a female engineer or a male early childhood education teacher. Invite people from the community who have nonstereotypical jobs (such as a male flight attendant or a female construction worker) to come to your class and talk with your students. Next, Judy Logan, who has taught language arts and social studies for many years in San Francisco, describes one way that she helps students understand the contributions of females.

THROUGH THE EYES OF TEACHERS
The Inclusive Quilt

In my 25 years of teaching middle school, one of my goals has been for my classroom to be a blend of some of the things I know and some of the things my students know. The quilt experience serves as an example. . . . My idea was to have the students feel connected not only to the women in the fields of science, politics, art, social reform, music, sports, literature, journalism, space, law, civil rights, education, humor, etc., but also to the women in their own families.

I put a big piece of butcher paper on the blackboard, with the word *inclusive* at the top and asked the students to develop a list of what was needed to make our quilt truly inclusive. Hands popped up, and students volunteered categories first. We should have women in medicine. Sports. Civil Rights. The list grew.

What else? How else can we make this quilt inclusive? What else do we know about diversity? Hands popped up again to create a second list. We should have Native American women. European American women. Latino women. Asian American women. Lesbian women. Again, our list grew. . . . We began to brainstorm a third list of individual women who were potential subjects

Judy Logan, in front of the inclusive quilt in her classroom.

for quilt squares. We created a long list of possibilities like Nancy Reagan, Jackie Kennedy, and Martha Washington, who did not end up on the final quilt itself, because the students decided they didn't want to have a lot of presidents' wives on the quilt. They ended up honoring Eleanor Roosevelt and Abigail Adams, who fit other categories on our list, such as social reform. . . .

I give some thought to whom I want to honor on my patch. I decide to honor Brenda Collins, who is also named Eagle Woman. She is a member of the Bird Clan of the Cherokee Nation. She is a medicine woman, the first woman of her clan to get a Ph.D. and a teacher at Santa Rosa Junior College. She is also a friend and mentor. I have heard her speak several times, and I remember her saying that to be an educated Indian woman is like having a foot in each of two canoes, in rapid waters, always balancing two cultures. I decide to put two canoes and rapid water on her patch, with an eagle's wing by one canoe, and her doctoral degree by the other canoe. . . .

The finished quilt is colorful and diverse. No two patches are the same. I have provided the outline, the framework for the assignment, but each participant has created something uniquely their own. . . . (Logan, 1997, pp. 1–23).

3. *Be a nonsexist role model as a teacher.* Help students learn new skills and share tasks in a nonsexist manner.

4. *Analyze the seating chart in your classroom and determine whether there are pockets of gender segregation.* When your students work in groups, monitor whether the groups are balanced by gender.

5. *Enlist someone to track your questioning and reinforcement patterns with boys and girls.* Do this on several occasions to ensure that you are giving equal attention and support to girls and boys.

6. *Use nonbiased language.* Don't use the pronoun *he* to refer to inanimate objects or unspecified persons. Replace words such as *fireman, policeman,* and *mailman* with words such as *firefighter, police officer,* and *letter carrier*. To improve your use of nonsexist language, consult *The Nonsexist Word Finder: A Dictionary of Gender-Free Usage* (Maggio, 1987). Also ask students to suggest fair terminology (Wellhousen, 1996).

7. *Keep up-to-date on sex equity in education.* Read professional journals on this topic. Be aware of your own rights as a female or male and don't stand for sexual inequity and discrimination.

8. *Be aware of sexual harassment in schools and don't let it happen.*

Review, Reflect, and Practice

(3) **Explain the various facets of gender, including similarities and differences in boys and girls; discuss gender issues in teaching.**

REVIEW

- What is gender and what are gender roles? How have psychologists attempted to explain gender from biological, socialization, and cognitive perspectives?
- What problems are created by gender stereotypes? How are boys and girls similar and different?
- How can gender roles be classified?
- How might looking at behaviors in context reduce gender stereotyping?
- What evidence is there of gender bias in the classroom? What progress have schools made in reducing bias?

REFLECT

- From your own K–12 education, come up with at least one instance in which your school or teacher favored either boys or girls. As a teacher, how would you try to correct that gender bias?

PRAXIS™ PRACTICE

1. In Jack's family, the person who does the cooking does not do the dishes. Since Jack's mother generally cooks, his father generally does the dishes. One day in the "housekeeping" area of his kindergarten class, Jack was pretending to be the father of the family. His "wife" Emily pretended to cook dinner on the toy stove. After the family ate, Emily started to pretend to wash the dishes. Jack gasped and cried, "Hey, I'm the dad!"
   This example best supports which theory of gender development?
   a. biological
   b. cognitive developmental
   c. social cognitive
   d. psychoanalytic

2. Which teacher's opinion about gender differences is best supported by current research?
   a. Mr. Kain, who believes that girls are more talkative than boys
   b. Ms. Nash, who believes that boys are better at math than girls
   c. Ms. Kim, who believes that boys are more physically aggressive than girls
   d. Ms. Walter, who believes that boys are generally fairer and more law-abiding than girls

3. Which student would best be described as androgynous?
   a. Alex, who is sensitive to others' feelings, shares secrets with friends, and provides social support to others
   b. Chris, who is independent, competitive, patient, self-reflective, and provides social support to others
   c. Pat, who is kind, sensitive, self-reflective, and likes to tell secrets to friends
   d. Terry, who is independent, competitive, self-confident, aggressive, and willing to take risks

4. A male is most likely to display helping behavior in which situation?
   a. A friend's car battery has died and needs a jump.
   b. A small child needs help with writing a poem for language arts class.
   c. A family member is ill and needs someone to provide care.
   d. A friend needs advice about a personal problem.

continued on page 178

5. Ms. Vandt teaches fifth grade. Her class is comprised of approximately equal numbers of boys and girls. She often wonders why the boys can't behave more like the girls. The girls sit quietly, follow rules, and work well together. The boys have problems sitting still. They are rowdy and loud. Ms. Vandt tries to treat all of her students the same, but she often needs to reprimand the boys. What should she do?
   a. Allow the children time and space to move around and blow off steam. This will help the boys to attend better in class and the girls to socialize.
   b. Continue to reprimand the boys when they behave inappropriately. They will learn to sit quietly and be compliant.
   c. Divide the children into gender-specific groups so that the boys don't interfere with the girls' work.
   d. Point out the girls' compliant behavior as a model for the boys, so that they will understand what is expected of them.

Please see the answer key at the end of the book.

CRACK THE CASE
The Case of These Boys

Imagine that Larry is a 9-year-old boy in the fourth-grade class in which you are student teaching. You have heard him and a number of other students complaining about gender bias on the part of their teacher, Mrs. Jones. One day you overhear Larry being reprimanded by Mrs. Jones for an altercation he had with Annie, a female classmate.

"It isn't fair, Mrs. Jones," Larry says. "Annie took my homework and ripped it, and I get in trouble for taking it back."

"Now, Larry," admonishes Mrs. Jones. "You know Annie would never do that. You go apologize to her. I'll see you after school."

Larry walks away with a very angry look on his face, muttering, "The girls *never* get in trouble. It's always the boys."

You have heard this from students of Mrs. Jones in the past but have never really believed it. Over the course of the next three weeks you pay much closer attention to Mrs. Jones' behavior with a special sensitivity to gender bias. You notice that girls receive higher grades than do boys, except in math. Boys are required to stay after school several times, girls not at all. When Mrs. Jones is on recess duty and there are altercations between boys and girls on the playground, the boys end up standing against the wall, while the girls walk away, smiling. In class, the girls are used as models of behaviors *much* more frequently than the boys. Their work receives more praise

as well. You examine what students have been reading over the course of the year. Their required reading thus far consists of *Little House on the Prairie, Charlotte's Web,* and *Little Women.*

The only thing you notice that appears to favor the boys is that they receive more of Mrs. Jones' attention. On further examination, however, you see that much of the attention is disciplinary in nature.

At one point, you overhear Mrs. Jones as she is walking down the hall, saying to a colleague, "These boys, I just don't know what I am going to do with them."

1. What are the issues in this case?
2. Based on the ideas and information presented in your text to this point, discuss what you believe to be happening in this classroom and the possible influences on Mrs. Jones' ideas of gender. Cite research and theories of gender development.
3. What influence do you believe Mrs. Jones' behavior will have on her students? Why?
4. What should Mrs. Jones do at this point? Why? What sort of outside assistance might help her?
5. If you were a student teacher in this classroom, what, if anything, would you do? Why?
6. What will you do in your own classroom to minimize gender bias?

Reach Your Learning Goals
Sociocultural Diversity

(1) CULTURE AND ETHNICITY: Discuss how variations in culture, socioeconomic status, and ethnic background might raise special classroom needs.

Culture

Culture refers to the behavior patterns, beliefs, and all other products of a particular group of people that are passed on from generation to generation. The products result from the interaction among groups of people and their environment over many years. Cultures have been classified as individualistic (having a set of values that give priority to personal goals rather than group goals) and collectivistic (having a set of values that support the group). Many Western cultures are individualistic, many Eastern cultures collectivistic. U.S. adolescents spend less time in school and doing homework, more time in paid work, and have more discretionary time than their counterparts in Europe and East Asia. Concern is evidenced about what U.S. adolescents do with all of the discretionary time many of them have.

Socioeconomic Status

Socioeconomic status (SES) is the categorization of people according to economic, educational, and occupational characteristics. The most emphasis is given to distinctions between individuals with low and middle socioeconomic status. Low-SES individuals usually have less education, less power to influence schools and other community institutions, and fewer economic resources than higher-SES individuals. Currently more than 20 percent of America's children live in poverty. Children in poverty face problems at home and at school that present barriers to their learning. Schools in low-income neighborhoods often have fewer resources and less-experienced teachers, and they are more likely to encourage rote learning rather than thinking skills.

Ethnicity

The school population increasingly consists of children of color, predicted to reach 50 percent by 2025. School segregation is still a factor in the education of children of color. African American and Latino students are less likely than non-Latino White and Asian American students to be enrolled in college preparatory courses. Historical, economic, and social experiences produce legitimate differences among ethnic groups, and it is important to recognize these differences. However, too often the differences are viewed as deficits on the part of the minority group when compared with the mainstream non-Latino White group. It is important to recognize the extensive diversity that exists within each cultural group.

Bilingualism

Researchers have found that bilingualism does not interfere with performance in either language. Success in learning a second language is greater in childhood than in adolescence. Bilingual education aims to teach academic subjects to immigrant children in their native languages while gradually adding English instruction. Bilingual education is complex and controversial.

(2) MULTICULTURAL EDUCATION: Describe some ways to promote multicultural education.

Empowering Students

Multicultural education is education that values diversity and includes the perspectives of a variety of cultural groups on a regular basis. Empowerment, which consists of providing people with the intellectual and coping skills to succeed and make this a more just world, is an important aspect of multicultural education today. It involves giving students the opportunity to learn about the experiences, struggles, and visions of many different ethnic and cultural groups. The hope is that empowerment will raise minority students' self esteem, reduce prejudice, and provide more-equal educational opportunities.

Culturally Relevant Teaching

Culturally relevant teaching is an important aspect of multicultural education. It seeks to make connections with the learner's cultural background.

continued

Issues-centered education also is an important aspect of multicultural education. In this approach, students are taught to systematically examine issues that involve equity and social justice.

Among the strategies/related ideas for improving relationships between children from different ethnic groups are these: the jigsaw classroom (having students from different cultural backgrounds cooperate by doing different parts of a project to reach a common goal), positive personal contact, perspective taking, critical thinking and emotional intelligence, reduced bias, increased tolerance, and development of the school and community as a team.

Proponents of teaching a core of White Anglo-Protestant values argue that such values as mutual respect, individual rights, and tolerance of differences should be taught to all children. Critics argue that these are not peculiarly White Anglo-Protestant values but simply Western tradition. Hirsch argues that students should be taught a common core of cultural knowledge to ensure that they become "culturally literate." Diversity critics argue that White students can benefit from learning about "core values" derived from other cultural groups. An evolving issue involves who defines "core values" in a heterogeneous society.

---

(3) GENDER: Explain the various facets of gender, including similarities and differences in boys and girls; discuss gender issues in teaching.

Gender refers to the sociocultural dimension of being female or male, as distinguished from sex, which is the biological dimension of being female or male. Gender roles are expectations that prescribe how males and females should think, feel, and act. In terms of biological views on gender development, the 23rd pair of chromosomes (the sex chromosomes) determines whether a fetus is female (XX) or male (XY). At issue is the directness or indirectness of biological effects. The brains of females and males are far more similar than different. When students' gender behavior is at issue, biology is not destiny. Two social views of gender are psychoanalytic theory and social cognitive theory. Peers especially play a powerful role in rewarding gender-appropriate behavior and punishing gender-inappropriate behavior. The most widely accepted current cognitive view of gender is gender schema theory.

Gender stereotypes are broad categories that reflect impressions and beliefs about what behavior is appropriate for females and males. All stereotypes involve an image of what the typical member of a category is like. Some gender stereotypes can be harmful for children, especially those that involve sexism (prejudice and discrimination against a person because of the person's sex). Psychologists have studied gender similarities and differences in physical performance, math and science skills, verbal skills, school attainment, relationship skills (rapport talk and report talk), and aggression/self-regulation. In some cases, gender differences are substantial (as in physical performance, reading and writing skills, school attainment, and physical aggression); in others they are small or nonexistent (as in relationship communication and many math skills). Today, controversy still swirls about how common or rare such differences really are.

Gender-role classification focuses on how masculine, feminine, or androgynous an individual is. In the past, competent males were supposed to be masculine (powerful, for example), females feminine (nurturant, for example). The 1970s brought the concept of androgyny, the idea that the most competent individuals have both masculine and feminine positive characteristics. A special concern involves adolescents who adopt a strong masculine role. Programs that have tried to teach androgyny to students have had mixed results. Some experts believe too much attention is given to gender in our society and that we should instead pursue gender-role transcendence.

| Gender in Context | Evaluation of gender-role categories and gender similarities and differences in areas such as helping behavior and emotion suggest that the best way to think about gender is not in terms of personality traits but instead in terms of person-situation interaction (gender in context). Although androgyny and multiple gender roles are often available for American children to choose from, many countries around the world still are male-dominant. |

| Eliminating Gender Bias | There is gender bias in schools against boys and girls. Many school personnel are unaware of these biases. An important teaching strategy is to attempt to eliminate gender bias. Schools have made considerable progress in reducing sexism and sex stereotyping in books and curriculum materials, but some bias still exists. Sexual harassment is a special concern in schools and is more pervasive than once believed. Recently, a distinction has been made between quid pro quo sexual harassment and hostile environment sexual harassment. |

 ## KEY TERMS

culture 145
cross-cultural studies 145
individualism 145
collectivism 145
socioeconomic status
    (SES) 147
ethnicity 150
prejudice 152

bilingual education 153
multicultural education 157
empowerment 157
jigsaw classroom 159
gender 165
gender roles 165
psychoanalytic theory
    of gender 165

social cognitive theory
    of gender 166
gender schema theory 166
gender stereotypes 167
sexism 168
rapport talk 169
report talk 169
androgyny 171

gender-role
    transcendence 173
quid pro quo sexual
    harassment 175
hostile environment sexual
    harassment 175

 ## PORTFOLIO ACTIVITIES

Now that you have a good understanding of this chapter, complete these exercises to expand your thinking.

Independent Reflection

Fostering Cultural Understanding in the Classroom. Imagine that you are teaching a social studies lesson about the westward movement in U.S. history and a student makes a racist, stereotyped statement about Native Americans, such as "The Indians were hot-tempered and showed their hostility toward the White settlers." How would you handle this situation? (Banks, 1997). Describe the strategy you would adopt. (INTASC: Principles *1, 2, 4, 6, 7*)

Collaborative Work

Planning for Diversity. With three or four other students in the class, come up with a list of specific diversity goals for your future classrooms. Also brainstorm and come up with some innovative activities to help students gain positive diversity experiences, such as the inclusive quilt discussed in this chapter. Summarize the diversity goals and activities. (INTASC: Principles *3, 4, 5, 6*)

Research/Field Experience

Equity in Action. Observe lessons being taught in several classrooms that include boys and girls and students from different ethnic groups. Did the teachers interact with females and males differently? If so, how? Did the teachers interact with students from different ethnic groups in different ways? If so, how? Describe your observations. (INTASC: Principles *3, 6, 9*)

Go to the Online Learning Center for downloadable portfolio templates.

 ## TAKING IT TO THE NET

- How does your state measure up in the area of children's socioeconomic status and school resources? Offer some evidence as to why you think your state ranks low/average/high compared with other states. How can conditions be improved? **www.aecf.org/kidscount/sld/databook.jsp**

- What is your position on the debate about multicultural education? Do you believe that multicultural perspectives should be integrated into academic subjects? Or do you think that multicultural education dilutes the rigor of "regular" curriculum and that many subjects do not lend themselves well to this approach? Why? http://www.tolerance.org/teach/magazine/features.jsp?p=0&is=17&ar=174

- Analyze a curriculum activity at the Teaching Tolerance Web site. Discuss how conducting this kind of lesson could help reduce gender, racial, or cultural bias in the classroom. www.tolerance.org/teach/index.jsp

Connect to the Online Learning Center to explore possible answers.

 ## STUDY, PRACTICE, AND SUCCEED

Visit www.mhhe.com/santedu3e to review the chapter with self-grading quizzes and self-assessments, to apply the chapter material to two more Crack the Case studies, and for suggested activities to develop your teaching portfolio.

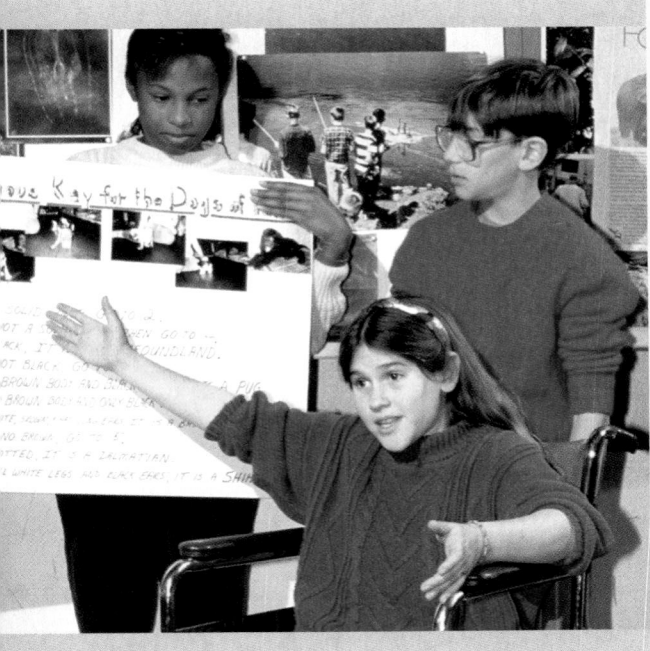

CHAPTER 6

Learners Who Are Exceptional

Only the educated are free.

—Epicurus
Greek Philosopher, 4th Century B.C.

Chapter Learning Goals

1 Describe the various types of disabilities and disorders.

2 Explain the legal framework, as well as placements and supports for children with disabilities.

3 Define what gifted means and discuss some approaches to teaching children who are gifted.

TEACHING STORIES   Verna Rollins

Verna Rollins teaches language arts at West Middle School in Ypsilanti, Michigan, and has developed a reputation for effectively dealing with so-called hard to teach, or difficult, students. She has found that the best strategy to use with these students is to find out what they need, decide how to provide it, provide it, and constantly evaluate whether it is working. She tells the story of one such student who was taught in her regular education classroom at the insistence of his mother but against the wishes of the special education staff. Here is Verna Rollins' description of how this went:

> Jack was in a special education classroom for children with physical disabilities. He has twisted legs, cerebral palsy, seizures, and some other brain damage from birth. He also has a comparatively short attention span. Since he drools, speaks in a loud monotone, stutters when he is excited, and has so little motor control that his penmanship is unreadable, people often think he is mentally retarded. He was not challenged to read or to write in his special classroom,

essentially being made to think that he couldn't really do well at either one. Actually, he is quite bright.

> My strategies included making sure that he had all the equipment he needed to succeed. I gave him tissues for the drooling and mutually agreed-upon reminders to wipe his mouth. I found that he could speak softly and without stuttering if he calmed down. We developed a signaling plan in which I would clear my throat when he talked too loudly and I would prompt him with the phrase "slow speech" when he was too excited to speak in a smooth voice.

> He used a computer to take quizzes and needed a little more time to complete any task, but he was so excited about being "out in the real world" that his attention span improved, as did his self-worth. In fact, his mother wrote a letter to me expressing her gratitude for the "most positive influence you have been on him! You have reinstilled and greatly increased his love of reading and writing. You have given my child a wonderful gift."

Preview

Verna Rollins was challenged to find the best way to teach a child with multiple disabilities in her classroom. Jack and his classmates benefited when she rose to that challenge. Like Verna Rollins, when you teach you will work with children with disabilities. In the past, public school did little to educate these children. Today, however, children with disabilities must have a free, appropriate education and increasingly they are educated in regular classrooms. In this chapter, we study children with many different types of disabilities, as well as another group of children who are exceptional, those who are gifted.

1 WHO ARE CHILDREN WITH DISABILITIES?

Approximately 13 percent of all children from 3 to 21 years of age in the United States receive special education or related services (National Center for Education Statistics, 2003). Figure 6.1 shows the approximate percentages of children with various disabilities who receive special education services (National Center for Education Statistics, 2006). Within this group, 44.4 percent have a learning disability.

Who Are Children with Disabilities?

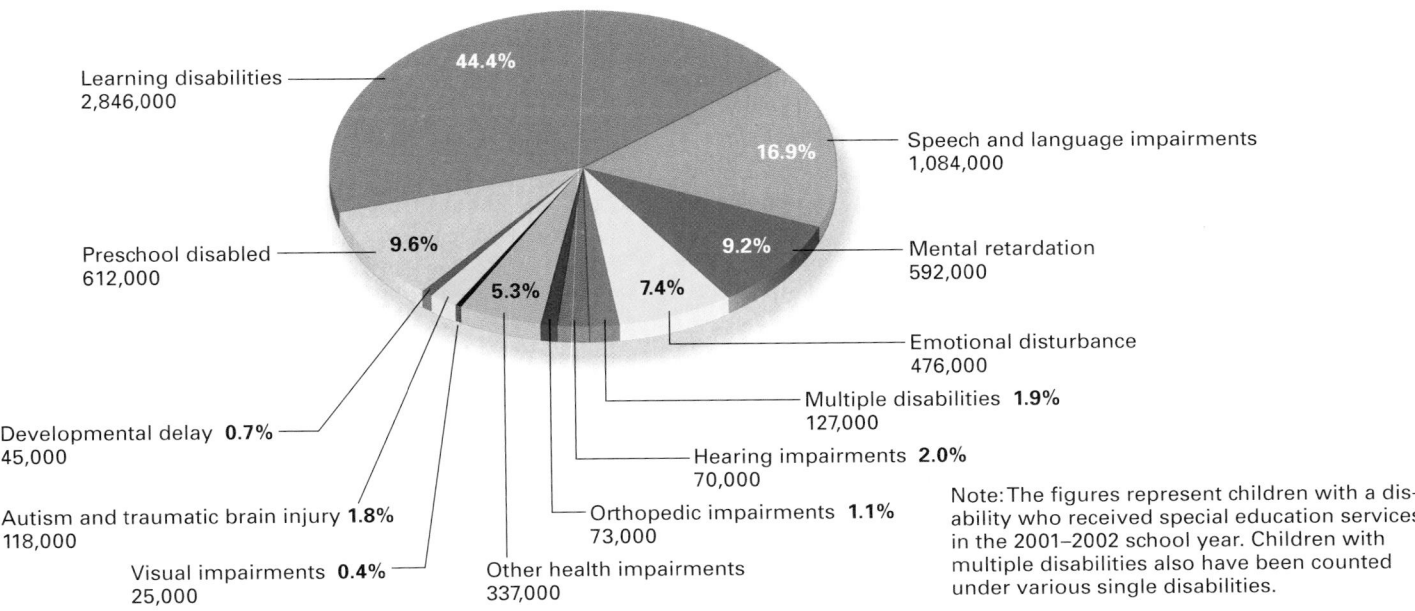

Learning disabilities
2,846,000

44.4%

16.9% — Speech and language impairments
1,084,000

Preschool disabled
612,000

9.6%

5.3%

7.4%

9.2% — Mental retardation
592,000

— Emotional disturbance
476,000

Multiple disabilities **1.9%**
127,000

Developmental delay 0.7%
45,000

Hearing impairments **2.0%**
70,000

Autism and traumatic brain injury 1.8%
118,000

Orthopedic impairments **1.1%**
73,000

Visual impairments 0.4%
25,000

Other health impairments
337,000

Note: The figures represent children with a disability who received special education services in the 2001–2002 school year. Children with multiple disabilities also have been counted under various single disabilities.

FIGURE 6.1 The Diversity of Children Who Have a Disability

Substantial percentages of students also have speech or language impairments (16.9 percent of those with disabilities), mental retardation (9.2 percent), or serious emotional disturbance (7.4 percent). Figure 6.2 shows the three largest groups of students with a disability who were served by federal programs in 2001–2002 (National Center for Education Statistics, 2006.)

At one time the terms *disability* and *handicap* were used interchangeably, but today a distinction is made between them. A **disability** involves a limitation on a person's functioning that restricts the individual's abilities. A **handicap** is a condition imposed on a person who has a disability. This condition could be imposed by society, the physical environment, or the person's own attitudes (Lewis, 2002).

Educators increasingly speak of "children with disabilities" rather than "disabled children" to emphasize the person, not the disability. Also, children with disabilities are no longer referred to as "handicapped," although the term *handicapping conditions* is still used to describe the impediments to the learning and functioning of individuals with a disability that have been imposed by society. For example, when children who use a wheelchair do not have adequate access to a bathroom, transportation, and so on, this is referred to as a handicapping condition.

Disability	Percentage Served
Specific Learning Disabilities	6.0
Speech or Language Impairments	2.3
Mental Retardation	1.3

FIGURE 6.2 The Three Highest Percentages of Students with a Disability Served by a Federal Program in 2001–2002 as a Percentage of Total School Enrollment

Learning Disabilities

Bobby's second-grade teacher complains that his spelling is awful. Eight-year-old Tim says reading is really hard for him, and a lot of times the words don't make much sense. Alisha has good oral language skills but has considerable difficulty in computing correct answers to arithmetic problems. Each of these students has a learning disability.

Characteristics After examining the research on learning disabilities, leading expert Linda Siegel (2003) recently concluded that a diagnosis of **learning disabilities** should be given only when the child (1) has an IQ above the retarded range; (2) has a significant difficulty in a school-related area (especially reading or mathematics); and (3) does not display certain severe emotional disorders, experience difficulties as a result of using English as a second language, have sensory disabilities, or have specific neurological deficits.

disability A personal limitation that restricts an individual's functioning.

handicap A condition imposed on a person who has a disability.

learning disability A disability in which children (1) have an IQ above the retarded range; (2) have significant difficulty in an academic area; and (3) have no other diagnosed problem or disorder, such as sensory disabilities or severe emotional disorders, causing the difficulty.

A recent national survey found that 8 percent of U.S. children have a learning disability (Bloom & Dey, 2006). About three times as many boys as girls are classified as having a learning disability (U.S. Department of Education, 1996). Among the explanations for this gender difference are a greater biological vulnerability among boys and *referral bias* (that is, boys are more likely to be referred by teachers for treatment because of their behavior) (Liederman, Kantrowitz, & Flannery, 2005).

About 5 percent of all school-age children in the United States receive special education or related services because of a learning disability. In the federal classification of children receiving special education and related services, attention deficit hyperactivity disorder (ADHD) is included in the learning disabilities category. Because of the significant interest in ADHD today, we will discuss it by itself following learning disabilities.

In the past three decades, the percentage of children classified as having a learning disability has increased substantially—from less than 30 percent of all children receiving special education and related services in 1977 to a slightly less than 45 percent today. Some experts say that the dramatic increase reflects poor diagnostic practices and overidentification. They argue that teachers sometimes are too quick to label children with the slightest learning problem as having a learning disability, instead of recognizing that the problem may rest in their ineffective teaching. Other experts say the increase in the number of children being labeled with a "learning disability" is justified (Hallahan & Kaufmann, 2006).

Most learning disabilities are lifelong. Compared with children without a learning disability, children with a learning disability are more likely to show poor academic performance, high dropout rates, and poor employment and postsecondary education records (Berninger, 2006; Wagner & Blackorby, 1996). Children with a learning disability who are taught in the regular classroom without extensive support rarely achieve the level of competence of even children who are low-achieving and do not have a disability (Hocutt, 1996). Still, despite the problems they encounter, many children with a learning disability grow up to lead normal lives and engage in productive work (Mercer & Pullen, 2005; Pueschel & others, 1995).

Identification Diagnosing whether a child has a learning disability is often a difficult task (Berninger, 2006). One identification procedure requires a significant discrepancy between actual achievement and expected achievement, the latter being estimated by an individually administered intelligence test. However, many educators question the adequacy of this approach (Francis & others, 2005). Another identification strategy that has recently been proposed is *response-to-intervention*, or *response-to-treatment*, which involves students not learning effectively in response to effective instruction (Fuchs & others, 2003). Whether this approach can be effectively implemented, however, is still being debated (Kavale, Holdnack, & Mostert, 2005).

Initial identification of a possible learning disability usually is made by the classroom teacher. If a learning disability is suspected, the teacher calls on specialists. An interdisciplinary team of professionals is best suited to verify whether a student has a learning disability. Individual psychological evaluations (of intelligence) and educational assessments (such as current level of achievement) are required (Mercer & Pullen, 2005). In addition, tests of visual-motor skills, language, and memory may be used.

In the early childhood years, disabilities often are identified in receptive and expressive language. Input from parents and teachers is considered before making a final diagnosis. For many school systems, the trigger for assessing students with learning disabilities is a two-grade-level lag in reading (Purcell-Gates, 1997). This can be a major impediment to identifying disabilities at the age when help can be the most effective—during the first 2 years of elementary school. If the two-grade lag is rigidly interpreted, many children can't get early help even if they are showing clear signs of a learning disability.

"Your feelings of insecurity seem to have started when Mary Lou Gumblatt said, 'Maybe I don't have a learning disability—maybe you have a teaching disability.'"

Tony Saltzman, from *Phi Delta Kappan* (1975). Reprinted by permission of Tony Saltzman.

Current classification of learning disabilities involves an "either/or" determination: A child either has a learning disability or does not. Yet in reality, learning disabilities vary in their intensity (Reschly, 1996; Terman & others, 1996). Severe learning disabilities, such as dyslexia, have been recognized for more than a century and are relatively easy to diagnose. However, most children with a learning disability have a milder form, which often makes them hard to distinguish from children without a learning disability. In the absence of nationally accepted criteria for classification, identifying students with a learning disability varies from one state to the next and even one teacher to the next (Lyon, 1996).

Reading, Writing, and Math Difficulties The most common academic areas in which children with a learning disability have problems are reading, writing, and math (Hallahan & others, 2005).

Dyslexia The most common problem that characterizes children with a learning disability involves reading (Moats, 2004). Such children have difficulty with phonological skills, which involve being able to understand how sounds and letters match up to make words. **Dyslexia** is a category reserved for individuals with a severe impairment in their ability to read and spell (Ramus, 2004; Spafford & Grosser, 2005).

Dysgraphia **Dysgraphia** is a learning disability that involves a difficulty in expressing thoughts in writing composition (Hammil, 2004; Vellutino & others, 2004). In general, the term *dysgraphia* has been used to describe extremely poor handwriting. Children with dysgraphia may write very slowly, their writing products may be virtually illegible, and they may make numerous spelling errors because of their inability to match up sounds and letters.

Dyscalculia **Dyscalculia**, also known as developmental arithmetic disorder, is a learning disability that involves difficulty in math computation. It is estimated to characterize 2 to 6 percent of U.S. elementary school children (National Center for Learning Disabilities, 2006). Researchers have found that children with difficulties in math computation often have cognitive and neuropsychological deficits, including poor performance in working memory, visual perception, and visuospatial abilities (Kaufman, 2003; Shalev, 2004). A child may have both a reading and a math disability, and there are cognitive deficits that characterize both types of disabilities, such as poor working memory (Siegel, 2003). One recent study found that dyscalculia is an enduring learning disability in many children; more than half of these children still performed very poorly in math when they reached the fifth grade (Shalev, Manor, & Gross-Tsur, 2005).

Causes and Intervention Strategies The precise causes of learning disabilities have not yet been determined. However, some possible causes have been proposed. Learning disabilities tend to run in families with one parent having a disability such as dyslexia or dyscalculia, although the specific genetic transmission of learning disabilities is not known (McCrory & others, 2005; Monuteaux & others, 2005; Petrill & others, 2006). Researchers have recently used brain-imaging techniques, such as magnetic resonance imaging, to reveal specific regions of the brain that might be involved in learning disabilities (Berninger, 2006; Vinckenbosch, Robichon, & Eliez, 2005). This research indicates that learning disabilities likely do not involve a single, specific brain location but rather are due to problems in integrating information from multiple brain regions or subtle difficulties in brain structures and functions. Another possibility is that some learning disabilities are caused by problems during prenatal development or delivery. A number of studies have found that learning disabilities are more prevalent in low-birth-weight infants (Litt & others, 2005).

Many interventions have focused on improving the child's reading ability (Berninger, 2006; Vukovic & Siegel, 2006). For example, in one study, instruction in

dyslexia A severe impairment in the ability to read and spell.

dysgraphia A learning disability that involves difficulty in expressing thoughts in writing composition. In general, the term dysgraphia is used to describe extremely poor handwriting.

dyscalculia Also known as developmental arithmetic disorder, this learning disability involves difficulty in math computation.

phonological awareness at the kindergarten level had positive effects on reading development when the children reached the first grade (Blachman & others, 1994).

Unfortunately, not all children who have a learning disability that involves reading problems have the benefit of appropriate early intervention. Most children whose reading disability is not diagnosed until the third grade or later and who receive standard interventions fail to show noticeable improvement (Lyon, 1996). However, intensive instruction over a period of time by a competent teacher can help many children (Berninger, 2006; Bost & Vaughn, 2002).

Children with severe phonological deficits that lead to poor decoding and word recognition skills respond to intervention more slowly than do children with mild to moderate reading problems (Torgesen, 1995). Also, the success of even the best-designed reading intervention depends on the teacher's training and skills.

Recently, Virginia Berninger (2006) proposed a new model for helping students who have a learning disability. She argues that schools need to make greater use of the *language arts block*, a daily time period when language arts are taught at the same time in all classes in the same grade or across grades. Berninger also argues that for students with a learning disability, direct instruction usually works better than a constructivist approach. Therefore, she recommends that during the language arts block "at least one class or section at the elementary and middle school level" offer "explicit, intellectually engaging reading and writing instruction" that focuses on:

- Phonological, orthographic, and morphological awareness. *Phonological awareness* involves being able to identify the sounds of words and word parts (such as syllables). *Orthographic awareness* is the ability to visually perceive the sequences and patterns of individually printed letters within words. For example, students need to visually distinguish between *b* and *d* when they are trying to decode text. *Morphological awareness* involves helping students understand the meaning of words through their spelling. This approach follows from the brain scan research showing how such training can make important changes in the brain related to reading-related processes (Richards & others, 2006).
- A set of skills that include the alphabetic principle (involves the ability to associate sounds with letters and use these sounds to form words); word families (a group of words that share a common sound, such as *farm* and *harm*); oral and silent reading fluency; automatic writing of letters; compositional fluency (number of words written in a minute); note taking; study skills; and test taking.

Berninger stresses that not all students need direct, explicit instruction in these areas but that students with dyslexia, dysgraphia, and language learning disability do. She also concludes that "one reason for the relative ineffectiveness of special education is that special education teachers are not given much preservice training in the psychology of teaching reading or taught instructional practices that cover all reading and writing skills . . . in a grade-appropriate manner from K–12" (Berninger, 2006).

Attention Deficit Hyperactivity Disorder

Matthew has attention deficit hyperactivity disorder, and the outward signs are fairly typical. He has trouble attending to the teacher's instructions and is easily distracted. He can't sit still for more than a few minutes at a time, and his handwriting is messy. His mother describes him as very fidgety.

attention deficit hyperactivity disorder (ADHD) A disability in which children consistently show one or more of the following characteristics over a period of time: (1) inattention, (2) hyperactivity, and (3) impulsivity.

Characteristics **Attention deficit hyperactivity disorder (ADHD)** is a disability in which children consistently show one or more of these characteristics over a period of time: (1) inattention, (2) hyperactivity, and (3) impulsivity. Inattentive children have difficulty focusing on any one thing and may get bored with a task after only a few minutes. One recent study found that problems in sustaining attention were the most common type of attentional problem in children with ADHD (Tsal, Shalev, & Mevorach, 2005). Hyperactive children show high levels of physical activity, almost

BEST PRACTICES
Strategies for Working with Children Who Have Learning Disabilities

1. *Take the needs of the child with a learning disability into account during instructional time.* Clearly state the objective of each lesson. Present it visually on the board or with an overhead projector as well. Be sure directions are explicit. Explain them orally. Use concrete examples to illustrate abstract concepts.

2. *Provide accommodations for testing and assignments.* This refers to changing the academic environment so that these children can demonstrate what they know. An accommodation usually does not involve altering the amount of learning the child has to demonstrate. Common accommodations include reading instructions to children, highlighting important words (such as *underline,* or *answer two of the three questions*), using/giving untimed tests, and extra time on assignments.

3. *Make modifications.* This strategy changes the work itself, making it different from other children's work in an effort to encourage children's confidence and success. Asking a child with dyslexia to give an oral report while other children give written reports is an example of a modification. Next, you can read about the modifications that Kristin Blankenship, a third-grade teacher in Salem, Virginia, made.

THROUGH THE EYES OF TEACHERS
Classroom Modifications to Improve the Reading Skills of Students with a Learning Disability

Throughout the last several years, up to half of the 24 students in my third-grade class have been diagnosed with learning disabilities. The majority of these students have difficulties with reading; therefore, modifications are often made in the other subject areas where reading is involved. For example, in math, I often have my students pair up to work on word problems. They take turns reading the problems and thinking through the solutions together. Both students seem to benefit from each other in these situations.

In social studies and science, I often have teams work on discussing related problems, such as planning a fundraiser as a part of an economics unit. Within the team, leaders and recorders are assigned to read the directions and write the answers for their team, which takes some pressure off of having to spell and read independently. Tests and quizzes are also read aloud in these subject areas. Another helpful strategy is to give directions in short pieces, often demonstrating what you want the students to do.

These children especially seem to benefit from hands-on experiences as well as art activities. After making salt dough maps one year, my students developed an understanding of the landforms and three regions of Virginia. They may not have been able to grasp these concepts just from reading the textbook and listening to discussions. Many strategies useful when teaching students with learning disabilities actually benefit the whole class.

4. *Improve organizational and study skills.* Many children with a learning disability do not have good organizational skills. Teachers and parents can encourage them to keep long-term and short-term calendars and create "to-do" lists each day. Projects should be broken down into their elements, with steps and due dates for each part (Strichart & Mangrum, 2002).

5. *Work with reading and writing skills.* As we indicated earlier, the most common type of learning disability involves reading problems. Make sure that an expert diagnosis of the child's reading problems has been made, including the particular deficits in the reading skills involved. Children with a reading problem often read slowly, so they need more advance notice of outside reading assignments and more time for in-class reading. Many children with a learning disability that involves writing deficits find that a word processor helps them compose their writing projects more quickly and competently. Compensatory tools that can be used include handheld talking electronic dictionaries (such as the Franklin Language Master, which gives students alternate spellings for phonetic attempts—*nummonia* for *pneumonia*, for example—where spellcheckers might fail them, and provides definitions for easily confused words, such as *there* and *their*), talking word processors that give valuable auditory feedback, and taped books. Some agencies will record textbooks for students for a minimal fee. Next, you can read about how two teachers improved the classroom experiences of students with a learning disability.

THROUGH THE EYES OF TEACHERS
Creating a Character Named Uey Long and Using a Team Approach

Nancy Downing, a second-grade teacher at McDermott Elementary School in Little Rock, Arkansas, takes a multisensory approach to education, which she developed while working with her own child, who has

continued on page 190

BEST PRACTICES *continued*
Strategies for Working with Children Who Have Learning Disabilities

learning difficulties. She created Downfeld Phonics using phonics, sign language, and lively jingles to make learning fun for students. She developed the character Uey Long (a uey is the sign over a short vowel) to demonstrate vowel rules.

Julie Curry, who teaches in Macon, Georgia, emphasizes the importance of a team approach. In her view, learning to read and reading to learn is hard work for students with a learning disability as well as hard work for teachers and parents involved in the child's life. A reading disability cannot be successfully remediated within a resource or inclusion classroom alone. To teach and implement strategies for the child's success requires a team approach. Strategies, technology, structuring the environment and collaboration need to be consistent from the school to the home and even down to the football field.

Nancy Downing, teaching in her classroom in Little Rock, Arkansas.

6. *Challenge children with a learning disability to become independent and reach their full potential.* It is not only important to provide support and services for children with a learning disability but to also guide them toward becoming responsible and independent (Kauffman, McGee, & Brigham, 2004). Teachers need to challenge children with a learning disability to become all they can be. We will have more to say about the importance of challenging children with disabilities to reach their potential later in the chapter.

7. *Remember that learning disabilities do not end with elementary school.* In the following description, Gayle Venable, a language arts, special education teacher/consultant in San Francisco, provides some tips for working with older children and adolescents.

THROUGH THE EYES OF TEACHERS

Learning Disabilities in Older Children and Adolescents

For some children, it's not until third or fourth grade that teachers become aware that children are having problems with reading. This may occur because the number of words that children are called upon to read expands at such a phenomenal rate. Children can't just learn them by sight anymore. Most children begin to infer the relationships between sounds and symbols by fourth grade or earlier; by fourth grade they have made those inferences even if they haven't explicitly been taught to them. By contrast, children with learning disabilities often don't figure out those links for themselves or during the course of normal classroom learning. Thus, they need to be explicitly taught about them to a greater degree than other students.

Later, students start having more trouble with the complex vocabulary that is being introduced to them, and they may not be able to remember as many words. As the pace of learning accelerates in later grades, more and more information has to be gained through reading. In the earlier grades, students get a lot of information orally; they are not expected to get all or even most of their information from reading. When the switch takes place from learning-to-read to reading-to-learn, children with learning disabilities may have trouble because they don't read competently. What also shows up in elementary school is that many children with learning disabilities have difficulty with spelling.

Using these seven main teaching strategies we have described is not meant to give children with a learning disability an unfair advantage, just an equal chance to learn. Balancing the needs of children with learning disabilities and those of other children is a challenging task.

always seeming to be in motion. Impulsive children have difficulty curbing their reactions and don't do a good job of thinking before they act. Depending on the characteristics that children with ADHD display, they can be diagnosed as (1) ADHD with predominantly inattention, (2) ADHD with predominantly hyperactivity/impulsivity, or (3) ADHD with both inattention and hyperactivity/ impulsivity.

Diagnosis and Developmental Status The number of children diagnosed and treated for ADHD has increased substantially, by some estimates doubling in the 1990s (Stein, 2004). A recent national survey found that 7 percent of U.S. children

3 to 17 years of age had ADHD (Bloom & Dey, 2006). The disorder occurs as much as four to nine times more in boys than in girls. There is controversy about the increased diagnosis of ADHD (Daley, 2006; Zentall, 2006), however. Some experts attribute the increase mainly to heightened awareness of the disorder. Others are concerned that many children are being diagnosed without undergoing extensive professional evaluation based on input from multiple sources.

Signs of ADHD may be present in the preschool years. Parents and preschool or kindergarten teachers may notice that the child has an extremely high activity level and a limited attention span. They may say the child is "always on the go," "can't sit still even for a second," or "never seems to listen." Many children with ADHD are difficult to discipline, have a low frustration tolerance, and have problems in peer relations. Other common characteristics of children with ADHD include general immaturity and clumsiness.

Although signs of ADHD are often present in the preschool years, children with ADHD are not usually classified until the elementary school years (Stein & Perrin, 2003; Zentall, 2006). The increased academic and social demands of formal schooling, as well as stricter standards for behavioral control, often illuminate the problems of the child with ADHD (Daley, 2006). Elementary school teachers typically report that this type of child has difficulty in working independently, completing seat work, and organizing work. Restlessness and distractibility also are often noted. These problems are more likely to be observed in repetitive or difficult tasks, or tasks the child perceives to be boring (such as completing worksheets or doing homework).

It used to be thought that children with ADHD improved during adolescence, but now it is believed that this often is not the case. Estimates suggest symptoms of ADHD decrease in only about one-third of adolescents. Increasingly, it is being recognized that these problems may continue into adulthood (Faraone, Biederman, & Mick, 2006; Seidman, 2006).

Causes and Treatment   Definitive causes of ADHD have not been found. However, a number of causes have been proposed, such as heredity, low levels of certain neurotransmitters (chemical messengers in the brain), prenatal and postnatal abnormalities, and environmental toxins, such as lead (Biederman & Faraone, 2003; Waldman & Gizer, 2006). Thirty to 50 percent of children with ADHD have a sibling or parent who has the disorder (Heiser & others, 2004).

About 85 to 90 percent of children with ADHD take stimulant medication such as Ritalin or Adderall (which has fewer side effects than Ritalin) to control their behavior (Denney, 2001). Ritalin and Adderall are stimulants, and for most individuals, they speed up the nervous system and behavior (Raphaelson, 2004). However, in many children with ADHD, the drug speeds up underactive areas of the prefrontal cortex that controls attention, impulsivity, and planning. This enhanced ability to focus their attention results in what *appears* to be a "slowing down" of behavior in these children (Reeves & Schweitzer, 2004). Researchers have found that a combination of medication (such as Ritalin) and behavior management improves the behavior of children with ADHD better than medication alone or behavior management alone (Chronis & others, 2004). Some critics argue that many physicians are too quick to prescribe stimulants for children with milder forms of ADHD (Marcovitch, 2004).

Stimulant medication has been found to be effective in improving the attention of many children with ADHD, but it usually does not improve their attention to the same level as that of children who do not have ADHD (Barbaresi & others, 2006; Tucha & others, 2006).

However, not all children with ADHD respond positively to prescription stimulants. In one study, Ritalin was less effective with children who have a high anxiety level, children who are older, and children who have less severe symptoms (Gray & Kagan, 2000). Further, in 2006, the U.S. government issued a warning about the cardiovascular risks of stimulant medications used to treat ADHD.

Recent studies also are focusing on the possibility that exercise might reduce ADHD (Tantillo & others, 2002). For example, researchers have found that exercise

Many children with ADHD show impulsive behavior, such as this child who is jumping out of his seat and throwing a paper airplane at other children. *How would you handle this situation if you were a teacher and this were to happen in your classroom?*

BEST PRACTICES
Strategies for Working with Children Who Have ADHD

1. *Monitor whether the child's stimulant medication is working effectively.*

2. *Repeat and simplify instructions about in-class and homework assignments.*

3. *Supplement verbal instructions with visual instructions.*

4. *Modify testing if necessary.*

5. *Involve a special education resource teacher.*

6. *State clear expectations and give the child immediate feedback.*

7. *Use behavior management strategies, especially providing positive feedback for progress.* We will discuss these approaches in considerable detail in chapter 7, "Behavioral and Social Cognitive Approaches."

8. *Provide structure and teacher-direction.* In many instances, a structured learning environment benefits children with ADHD. Next, Joanna Smith, a high school English teacher, describes how she arranges her classroom to accommodate students with ADHD.

THROUGH THE EYES OF TEACHERS
Structuring the Classroom to Benefit Students with ADHD

I have found success with these students when I seat them in the front row, make instructions explicit, break down larger tasks into smaller ones, write necessary information on the board and point out exactly where it is, allow extra time on tests (as specified on his or her plan), and check in with the students frequently. This frequent contact allows me to know how the student is doing, how much he understands, and gives him a welcomed opportunity to chat.

9. *Connect learning to real-life experiences.*

10. *Use computer instruction, especially learning that involves a gamelike format.*

11. *Provide opportunities for students to get up and move around.*

12. *Break assignments into shorter segments.*

increases the levels of two neurotransmitters—dopamine and norepinephrine—that improve concentration (Ferrando-Lucas, 2006; Rebollo & Montiel, 2006). Some mental health professionals are recommending that children and youth with ADHD exercise several times a day (Ratey, 2006). They also speculate that the increase in rates of ADHD have coincided with the decrease in exercise that children are getting.

Mental Retardation

Increasingly, children with mental retardation are being taught in the regular classroom (Friend & Bursuck, 2006; Hodapp & Dykens, 2006; Vaughn, Bos, & Schumm, 2006). The most distinctive feature of mental retardation is inadequate intellectual functioning (Zigler, 2002). Long before formal tests were developed to assess intelligence, individuals with mental retardation were identified by a lack of age-appropriate skills in learning and in caring for themselves. Once intelligence tests were created, numbers were assigned to indicate how mild or severe the retardation was. A child might be only mildly retarded and able to learn in the regular classroom or severely retarded and unable to learn in that setting.

In addition to low intelligence, deficits in adaptive behavior and early onset also are included in the definition of mental retardation. Adaptive skills include skills needed for self-care and social responsibility such as dressing, toileting, feeding, self-control, and peer interaction. By definition, **mental retardation** is a condition with an onset before age 18 that involves low intelligence (usually below 70 on a traditional individually administered intelligence test) and difficulty in adapting to everyday life. For an individual to be given a diagnosis of mental retardation, the low IQ and low adaptiveness should be evident in childhood, not following a long period of normal functioning that is interrupted by an accident or other type of assault on the brain.

mental retardation A condition with an onset before age 18 that involves low intelligence (usually below 70 on a traditional individually administered intelligence test) and difficulty in adapting to everyday life.

Classification and Types of Mental Retardation   As indicated in figure 6.3, mental retardation is classified as mild, moderate, severe, or profound. Approximately 89 percent of students with mental retardation fall into the mild category. By late adolescence, individuals with mild mental retardation can be expected to develop academic skills at approximately the sixth-grade level (Terman & others, 1996). In their adult years, many can hold jobs and live on their own with some supportive supervision or in group homes. Individuals with more severe mental retardation require more support.

If you have a student with mental retardation in your classroom, the degree of retardation is likely to be mild. Children with severe mental retardation are more likely to also show signs of other neurological complications, such as cerebral palsy, epilepsy, hearing impairment, visual impairment, or other metabolic birth defects that affect the central nervous system (Terman & others, 1996).

Most school systems still use the classifications mild, moderate, severe, and profound. However, because these categorizations based on IQ ranges aren't perfect predictors of functioning, the American Association on Mental Retardation (1992) developed a new classification system based on the degree of support children require to function at their highest level (Hallahan & Kauffman, 2006). As shown in figure 6.4, the categories used are intermittent, limited, extensive, and pervasive.

Causes   Mental retardation is caused by genetic factors and brain damage. Let's explore genetic causes first.

Genetic Factors   The most commonly identified form of mental retardation is **Down syndrome,** which is genetically transmitted. Children with Down syndrome have an extra (47th) chromosome. They have a round face, a flattened skull, an extra fold of skin over the eyelids, a protruding tongue, short limbs, and retardation of motor and mental abilities. It is not known why the extra chromosome is present, but the health of the male sperm or female ovum might be involved (MacLean, 2000; Nokelainen & Flint, 2002). Women between the ages of 18 and 38 are far less likely than younger or older women to give birth to a child with Down syndrome. Down syndrome appears in about 1 in every 700 live births. African American children are rarely born with Down syndrome.

With early intervention and extensive support from the child's family and professionals, many children with Down syndrome can grow into independent adults (Boyles & Contadino, 1997; Taylor, Brady, & Richards, 2005). Children with Down syndrome can fall into the mild to severe retardation categories (Terman & others, 1996).

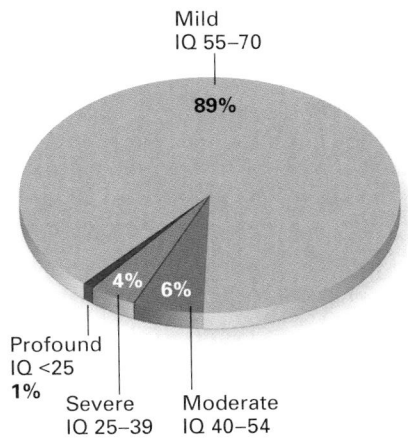

FIGURE 6.3 Classification of Mental Retardation Based on IQ

A child with Down syndrome. *What causes a child to develop Down syndrome?*

Intermittent	Supports are provided "as needed." The individual may need episodic or short-term support during life-span transitions (such as job loss or acute medical crisis). Intermittent supports may be low- or high-intensity when provided.
Limited	Supports are intense and relatively consistent over time. They are time-limited but not intermittent. They require fewer staff members and cost less than more-intense supports. These supports likely will be needed for adaptation to the changes involved in the school-to-adult period.
Extensive	Supports are characterized by regular involvement (for example, daily) in at least some setting (such as home or work) and are not time-limited (for example, extended home-living support).
Pervasive	Supports are constant, very intense, and are provided across settings. They may be of a life-sustaining nature. These supports typically involve more staff members and intrusiveness than the other support categories.

FIGURE 6.4 Classification of Mental Retardation Based on Levels of Support

Down syndrome A genetically transmitted form of mental retardation due to an extra (47th) chromosome.

BEST PRACTICES
Strategies for Working with Children Who Are Mentally Retarded

During the school years, the main goals often are to teach children with mental retardation basic educational skills such as reading and mathematics, as well as vocational skills (Boyles & Contadino, 1997). Here are some positive teaching strategies for interacting with children who have mental retardation:

1. *Help children who are mentally retarded to practice making personal choices and to engage in self-determination when possible* (Westling & Fox, 2000).

2. *Always keep in mind the child's level of mental functioning.* Children who have mental retardation will be at a considerably lower level of mental functioning than most other students in your class. If you start at one level of instruction, and the child is not responding effectively, move to a lower level.

3. *Individualize your instruction to meet the child's needs.*

4. *As with other children with a disability, make sure that you give concrete examples of concepts.* Make your instructions clear and simple.

5. *Give these children opportunities to practice what they have learned.* Have them repeat steps a number of times and overlearn a concept to retain it.

6. *Be sensitive to the child's self-esteem.* Especially avoid comparisons with children who do not have mental retardation.

7. *Have positive expectations for the child's learning.* It is easy to fall into the trap of thinking that the child with mental retardation cannot achieve academically. Set a goal to maximize his or her learning.

8. *Recognize that many children with mental retardation not only have academic needs but also require help in improving their self-maintenance and social skills.*

9. *Look for resource support.* Use teacher aides and recruit volunteers such as sensitive retirees to help you educate children with mental retardation. They can assist you in increasing the amount of one-on-one instruction the child receives.

10. *Consider using applied behavior analysis strategies.* Some teachers report that these strategies improve children's self-maintenance, social, and academic skills. If you are interested in using these strategies, consult a resource such as *Applied Behavior Analysis for Teachers,* by Paul Alberto and Anne Troutman (2006). The precise steps involved in applied behavior analysis can especially help you use positive reinforcement effectively with children who have mental retardation.

11. *If you teach in a secondary school, evaluate the vocational skills students with mental retardation will need in order to obtain a job* (Rogan, Luecking, & Held, 2001).

12. *Involve parents as equal partners in the child's education.*

Fragile X syndrome is the second most commonly identified form of mental retardation. It is genetically transmitted by an abnormality on the X chromosome, resulting in mild to severe mental retardation (Roberts & others, 2005). In general, the level is more severe in males than in females. Characteristics of fragile X children include an elongated face, prominent jaws, elongated ears, a flattened bridge of the nose, and poor coordination. About 7 percent of mild mental retardation in females is a result of fragile X syndrome.

Brain Damage   Brain damage can result from many different infections and environmental hazards (Das, 2000; Hodapp & Dykens, 2006). Infections in the pregnant mother-to-be, such as rubella (German measles), syphilis, herpes, and AIDS, can cause retardation in the child. Meningitis and encephalitis are infections that can develop in childhood. They cause inflammation in the brain and can produce mental retardation.

Environmental hazards that can result in mental retardation include blows to the head, malnutrition, poisoning, birth injury, and alcoholism or heavy drinking on the part of the pregnant woman (Berine-Smith, Patton, & Kim, 2006). **Fetal alcohol syndrome (FAS)** is a cluster of abnormalities that appears in the offspring of mothers who drink alcohol heavily during pregnancy. The abnormalities include facial

fragile X syndrome A genetically transmitted form of mental retardation due to an abnormality on the X chromosome.

fetal alcohol syndrome (FAS) A cluster of abnormalities, including mental retardation and facial abnormalities, that appear in the offspring of mothers who drink alcohol heavily during pregnancy.

deformities and defective limbs, face, and heart. Most of these children have below average intelligence, and some are mentally retarded (Bookstein & others, 2002; O'Leary, 2004). One recent study found that prenatal exposure to binge drinking was linked to a greater likelihood of having IQ scores in the mentally retarded range and a higher incidence of acting-out behavior at 7 years of age (Bailey & others, 2004). Although many mothers of FAS infants are heavy drinkers, many mothers who are heavy drinkers do not have children with FAS or have one child with FAS and other children who do not have it.

Physical Disorders

Physical disorders in children include orthopedic impairments, such as cerebral palsy, and seizure disorders. Many children with physical disorders require special education and related services, such as transportation, physical therapy, school health services, and psychological services (Best, Heller, & Bigge, 2005).

Orthopedic Impairments   **Orthopedic impairments** involve restricted movement or lack of control over movement due to muscle, bone, or joint problems. The severity of problems ranges widely. Orthopedic impairments can be caused by prenatal or perinatal problems, or they can be due to disease or accident during the childhood years. With the help of adaptive devices and medical technology, many children with orthopedic impairments function well in the classroom (Boyles & Contadino, 1997).

   Cerebral palsy is a disorder that involves a lack of muscular coordination, shaking, or unclear speech. The most common cause of cerebral palsy is lack of oxygen at birth. In the most common type of cerebral palsy, which is called *spastic*, children's muscles are stiff and difficult to move (Meberg & Broch, 2004). The rigid muscles often pull the limbs into contorted positions (Russman & Ashwal, 2004). In a less common type, *ataxia*, the child's muscles are rigid one moment and floppy the next moment, making movements clumsy and jerky.

   Computers especially can help children with cerebral palsy to learn (Best, Heller, & Bigge, 2005; Ullman, 2005). If they have the coordination to use the keyboard, they can do their written work on the computer. A pen with a light can be added to a computer and used by the student as a pointer. Many children with cerebral palsy have unclear speech. For these children, speech and voice synthesizers, communication boards, talking notes, and page turners can improve their communication.

Seizure Disorders   The most common seizure disorder is **epilepsy,** a neurological disorder characterized by recurring sensorimotor attacks or movement convulsions. Epilepsy comes in different forms (Barr, 2000). In one common form called *absence seizures,* a child's seizures are brief in duration (often less than 30 seconds) and occur anywhere from several to a hundred times a day. Often they occur as brief staring

THROUGH THE EYES OF STUDENTS

It's Okay to Be Different

Why me? I often ask myself, why did I have to be the one? Why did I get picked to be different? It took more than ten years for me to find answers and to realize that I'm not *more* different than anyone else. My twin sister was born with no birth defects but I was born with cerebral palsy.

   People thought I was stupid because it was hard for me to write my own name. So when I was the only one in the class to use a typewriter, I began to feel I was different. It got worse when the third-graders moved on to the fourth grade and I had to stay behind. I got held back because the teachers thought I'd be unable to type fast enough to keep up. Kids told me that was a lie and the reason I got held back was because I was a retard. It really hurt to be teased by those I thought were my friends. . . .

   I have learned that no one was to blame for my disability. I realize that I can do things and that I can do them very well. Some things I can't do, like taking my own notes in class or running in a race, but I will have to live with that. . . .

   There are times when I wish I had not been born with cerebral palsy, but crying isn't going to do me any good. I can only live once, so I want to live the best I can. . . . Nobody else can be the Angela Marie Erickson who is writing this. I could never be, or ever want to be, anyone else.

Angie Erickson
Ninth-Grade Student
Wayzata, Minnesota

orthopedic impairments Restricted movements or lack of control of movements, due to muscle, bone, or joint problems.

cerebral palsy A disorder that involves a lack of muscle coordination, shaking, or unclear speech.

epilepsy A neurological disorder characterized by recurring sensorimotor attacks or movement convulsions.

Eyes Closed

In kindergarten, children truly begin to appreciate, not fear or think strange, each other's differences. A few years ago a child in my kindergarten class was walking down the hall with his eyes closed and ran into the wall. When I asked him what he was doing, he said, "I was just trying to do like Darrick. How come he does it so much better?" Darrick is his classmate who is legally blind. He wanted to experience what it was like to be blind. In this case, imitation truly was the greatest form of flattery.

Anita Marie Hitchcock
Kindergarten Teacher
Holle Navarre Primary
Santa Rosa County, Florida

spells, sometimes accompanied by motor movements such as twitching of the eyelids. In another common form of epilepsy, labeled *tonic-clonic*, the child loses consciousness and becomes rigid, shakes, and moves jerkily. The most severe portion of a tonic-clonic seizure lasts for about 3 to 4 minutes. Children who experience seizures are usually treated with one or more anticonvulsant medications, which often are effective in reducing the seizures but do not always eliminate them. When they are not having a seizure, students with epilepsy show normal behavior.

If you have a child in your class who has a seizure disorder, become well acquainted with the procedures for monitoring and helping the child during a seizure. Also, if a child seems to space out in your class, especially under stress, it might be worthwhile to explore whether the problem is boredom, drugs, or potentially a neurological condition.

Sensory Disorders

Sensory disorders include visual and hearing impairments. Visual impairments include the need for corrective lenses, low vision, and being educationally blind. Children who are hearing impaired can be born deaf or experience a loss in hearing as they develop.

Visual Impairments Some students have mild vision problems that have not been corrected. If you notice students squinting a lot, holding books close to their faces to read them, rubbing their eyes frequently, and complaining that things appear blurred or that words move about on the page, refer them to the appropriate school professionals to have their vision checked (Boyles & Contadino, 1997). Many will only need corrective lenses. However, a small portion of students (about 1 in every 1,000 students) have more serious visual problems and are classified as visually impaired. This includes students who have low vision and students who are blind.

Children with *low vision* have a visual acuity of between 20/70 and 20/200 (on the familiar Snellen scale, in which 20/20 vision is normal) with corrective lenses. Children with low vision can read large-print books or regular books with the aid of a magnifying glass. Children who are *educationally blind* cannot use their vision in learning and must rely on their hearing and touch to learn. Approximately 1 in every 3,000 children is educationally blind. Almost half of these children were born blind, and another one-third lost their vision in the first year of life. Many children who are educationally blind have normal intelligence and function very well academically with appropriate supports and learning aids. However, multiple disabilities are not uncommon in educationally blind students. Students who have multiple disabilities often require a range of support services to meet their educational needs.

An important task in working with a child who has visual impairments is to determine the modality (such as touch or hearing) through which the child learns best. Seating in the front of the class often benefits the child with a visual impairment.

For half a century, recorded textbooks from Recording for the Blind & Dyslexic have contributed to the educational progress of students with visual, perceptual, or other disabilities. More than 90,000 volumes of these audio and computerized books are available at no charge (phone: 1-866-732-3585). One issue in the education of students who are blind involves the underusage of Braille and the low rates of Braille proficiency among teachers who instruct blind students (Hallahan & Kauffman, 2006).

Hearing Impairments A hearing impairment can make learning very difficult for children (Anderson & Shames, 2006; Goldberg & Richburg, 2004). Children who are born deaf or experience a significant hearing loss in the first several years of life usually do not develop normal speech and language. You also might have some children in

BEST PRACTICES
Strategies for Working with Children Who Have a Hearing Impairment

1. *Be patient.*

2. *Speak normally (not too slowly or too fast).*

3. *Don't shout, because this doesn't help.* Speaking distinctly is more helpful.

4. *Reduce distractions and background noises.*

5. *Face the student to whom you are speaking, because the student needs to read your lips and see your gestures.*

your class who have hearing impairments that have not yet been detected (Wake & Poulakis, 2004). If you have students who turn one ear toward a speaker, frequently ask to have something repeated, don't follow directions, or frequently complain of earaches, colds, and allergies, consider having the student's hearing evaluated by a specialist, such as an audiologist.

Many children with hearing impairments receive supplementary instruction beyond the regular classroom. Educational approaches to help students with hearing impairments learn fall into two categories: oral and manual. *Oral approaches* include using lip reading, speech reading (a reliance on visual cues to teach reading), and whatever hearing the student has. *Manual approaches* involve sign language and finger spelling. Sign language is a system of hand movements that symbolize words. Finger spelling consists of "spelling out" each word by signing each letter of a word. Oral and manual approaches are increasingly used together for students who are hearing impaired (Hallahan & Kauffman, 2006).

The following medical and technological advances also have improved the learning of children with hearing impairments (Boyles & Contadino, 1997):

- Cochlear implants (a surgical procedure). This is controversial because many people in the deaf community are opposed to them, viewing them as intrusive and antagonistic to the deaf culture. Others argue that cochlear implants have substantially improved the lives of many children who are hearing impaired (Hallahan & Kauffman, 2006).
- Tubes in the ears (a surgical procedure for middle-ear dysfunction). This is not a permanent procedure.
- Hearing aids and amplification systems.
- Telecommunication devices, the teletypewriter-telephone, and RadioMail (using the Internet).

Speech and Language Disorders

Speech and language disorders include a number of speech problems (such as articulation disorders, voice disorders, and fluency disorders) and language problems (difficulties in receiving information and expressing language) (Hulit & Howard, 2006; Justice, 2006; Reed, 2005). As you saw in figure 6.1, approximately 17 percent of all children who receive special education services have a speech or language impairment (National Center for Education Statistics, 2006).

speech and language disorders A number of speech problems (such as articulation disorders, voice disorders, and fluency disorders) and language problems (difficulties in receiving information and expressing language).

Articulation Disorders   **Articulation disorders** are problems in pronouncing sounds correctly. A child's articulation at 6 or 7 years is still not always error-free, but it should be by age 8. A child with an articulation problem might find communication with peers and the teacher difficult or embarrassing. As a result, the child might avoid asking questions, participating in discussions, or communicating with peers. Articulation problems can usually be improved or resolved with speech therapy, though it might take months or years (Hulit & Howard, 2006).

articulation disorders Problems in pronouncing sounds correctly.

Voice Disorders **Voice disorders** are reflected in speech that is hoarse, harsh, too loud, too high-pitched, or too low-pitched. Children with cleft palate often have a voice disorder that makes their speech difficult to understand. If a child speaks in a way that is consistently difficult to understand, refer the child to a speech therapist.

Fluency Disorders **Fluency disorders** often involve what is commonly called "stuttering." Stuttering occurs when a child's speech has a spasmodic hesitation, prolongation, or repetition (Ratner, 2005). The anxiety many children feel because they stutter often just makes their stuttering worse. Speech therapy is recommended.

Language Disorders **Language disorders** include a significant impairment in a child's receptive or expressive language. Language disorders can result in significant learning problems (Anderson & Shame, 2006; Ratner, 2005). Treatment by a language therapist generally produces improvement in the child with a language disorder, but the problem usually is not eradicated. Language disorders include difficulties in these areas:

- Phrasing questions properly to get the desired information
- Following oral directions
- Following conversation, especially when it is rapid and complex
- Understanding and using words correctly in sentences

These difficulties involve both receptive and expressive language.
Receptive language involves the reception and understanding of language. Children with a receptive language disorder have a glitch in the way they receive information. Information comes in, but the child's brain has difficulty processing it effectively, which can cause the child to appear disinterested or aloof.

Once a message is received and interpreted, the brain needs to form a response. **Expressive language** involves the ability to use language to express one's thoughts and communicate with others. Some children can easily understand what is said to them, but they have difficulties when they try to form a response and express themselves. A problem in speaking is a common expressive language disorder. There are several observable characteristics of children who have an oral expressive language disorder (Boyles & Contadino, 1997, pp. 189–190):

- They might appear "shy and withdrawn" and have problems "interacting socially."
- They might "give delayed responses to questions."
- They might have a problem "finding the correct words."
- Their thoughts might be "disorganized and disjointed," frustrating the listener.
- They might "omit integral parts of the sentence or information needed for understanding."

Specific Language Impairment **Specific language impairment (SLI)** involves "problems in language development accompanied by no other obvious physical, sensory, or emotional difficulties" (Berko Gleason, 2005, p. 7). In some cases, the disorder is referred to as *developmental language disorder* (Simpson & Rice, 2005). One large-scale study found that more than 7 percent of U.S. 5-year-olds could have specific language impairment (Tomblin, 1996).

Children with SLI have problems in understanding and using words in sentences so both receptive and expressive language are involved. One indicator of SLI in 5-year-old children is their incomplete understanding of verbs (Simpson & Rice, 2005). They typically drop the –s from verb tenses (such as "She walk to the store" instead of "She walks to the store") and ask questions without "be" or "do" verbs (rather than saying "Does he live there?" the child will say "He live there?"). These characteristics

voice disorders Disorders producing speech that is hoarse, harsh, too loud, too high-pitched, or too low-pitched.

fluency disorders Disorders that often involve what is commonly referred to as "stuttering."

language disorders Significant impairments in a child's receptive or expressive language.

receptive language The reception and understanding of language.

expressive language The ability to use language to express one's thoughts and communicate with others.

specific language impairment (SLI) Involves problems in language development that are not accompanied by other obvious physical, sensory, or emotional problems; in some cases, the disorder is called developmental language disorder.

BEST PRACTICES
Strategies for Children with Receptive or Oral Expressive Language Disorder

Here are some strategies to support students with a receptive language disorder:

1. *Use a multisensory approach to learning rather than an oral approach alone. Supplement oral information with written materials or directions.*

2. *Monitor the speed with which you present information. Slow down or go back and check with the children for understanding.*

3. *Give the child some time to respond, as much as 10 to 15 seconds.*

4. *Provide concrete, specific examples of abstract concepts.*

Here are some strategies to support a child with an oral expressive language disorder:

1. *Give the child plenty of time to respond.*

2. *Recognize that the child has trouble responding orally, so consider asking the child to do written work rather than an oral report.*

3. *Provide choices or give the child the initial sound in word-finding problems.*

4. *Let the child know ahead of time what question might be asked so that the child can prepare an answer and thus appear more competent among peers.*

make children with specific language impairment sound like children who are approximately 2 years younger than they are.

SLI may have a genetic basis and it tends to run in families, although some children with SLI come from families with no history of the condition. Early identification of SLI is important and can usually be accurately accomplished by 5 years of age and in some cases earlier. Intervention includes modeling correct utterances, rephrasing the child's incorrect utterances during conversation, and other language instruction (Ratner, 2005). Parents may also wish to send a child with SRI to a speech or language pathologist in private practice. In many cases, these interventions are effective in improving the child's language development.

Autism Spectrum Disorders

Autism spectrum disorders (ASD), also called pervasive developmental disorders, range from the severe disorder labeled *autistic disorder* to the milder disorder called *Asperger syndrome*. Autism spectrum disorders are characterized by problems in social interaction, problems in verbal and nonverbal communication, and repetitive behaviors. Children with these disorders may also show atypical responses to sensory experiences (National Institute of Mental Health, 2006). Autism spectrum disorders can often be detected in children as early as 1 to 3 years of age. By this age, parents may notice unusual behaviors occurring. In some cases, parents report that their child was different from birth, being unresponsive to people or staring at one object for a very long time. In other cases, parents report that their child developed normally for a year or two but suddenly became withdrawn or indifferent to people.

Autistic disorder is a severe developmental autism spectrum disorder that has its onset in the first 3 years of life and includes deficiencies in social relationships, abnormalities in communication, and restricted, repetitive, and stereotyped patterns of behavior. Estimates indicate that approximately two to five of every 10,000 young children in the United States have autistic disorder. Boys are about four times more likely to have an autistic disorder than girls.

Asperger syndrome is a relatively mild autism spectrum disorder in which the child has relatively good verbal language, milder nonverbal language problems, and a restricted range of interests and relationships. Children with Asperger syndrome often engage in obsessive repetitive routines and preoccupations with a particular

autism spectrum disorders (ASD) Also called pervasive developmental disorders, they range from the severe disorder labeled autistic disorder to the milder disorder called Asperger syndrome. Children with these disorders are characterized by problems in social interaction, verbal and nonverbal communication, and repetitive behaviors.

autistic disorder A severe developmental autism spectrum disorder that has its onset in the first 3 years of life and includes deficiencies in social relationships, abnormalities in communication, and restricted, repetitive, and stereotyped patterns of behavior.

Asperger syndrome A relatively mild autism spectrum disorder in which the child has relatively good language, milder nonverbal language problems, a restricted range of interests and relationships, and often engages in repetitive routines.

subject (South, Ozofnoff, & McMahon, 2005). For example, a child may be obsessed with baseball scores or railroad timetables.

What causes the autism spectrum disorders? The current consensus is that autism is a brain dysfunction with abnormalities in brain structure (including the cerebellum and cerebral cortex—frontal and temporal lobes), and abnormalities in neurotransmitters such as serotonin and dopamine (Lainhart, 2006; Penn, 2006). Genetic factors may play a role in the development of the autism spectrum disorders (Baron-Cohen, 2004; Cohen & others, 2005). One recent study found that approximately 50 percent of boys with Asperger syndrome had a paternal family history of autism spectrum disorders (Gillberg & Cederlund, 2005). There is no evidence that family socialization causes autism (Rutter & Schopler, 1987). Mental retardation is present in some children with autism; others show average or above-average intelligence (Sigman & McGovern, 2005).

Children with autism benefit from a well-structured classroom, individualized instruction, and small-group instruction (Pueschel & others, 1995). As with children who are mentally retarded, behavior modification techniques are sometimes effective in helping autistic children learn (Alberto & Troutman, 2006; Volkmar & others, 2004).

Emotional and Behavioral Disorders

Most children have emotional problems sometime during their school years. A small percentage has problems so serious and persistent that they are classified as having an emotional or a behavioral disorder (Lane, Greshman, & O'Shaughnessy, 2002). **Emotional and behavioral disorders** consist of serious, persistent problems that involve relationships, aggression, depression, fears associated with personal or school matters, and other inappropriate socioemotional characteristics (Kauffman, 2005; Keenan & others, 2004). Approximately 7 percent of children who have a disability and require an individualized education plan fall into this classification. Boys are three times as likely as girls to have these disorders (U.S. Department of Education, 2003).

Various terms have been used to describe emotional and behavioral disorders, including *emotional disturbances, behavior disorders,* and *maladjusted children* (Coleman & Webber, 2002). The term *emotional disturbance (ED)* recently has been used to describe children with these types of problems for whom it has been necessary to create individualized learning plans. However, critics argue that this category has not been clearly defined (Council for Exceptional Children, 1998).

Aggressive, Out-of-Control Behaviors Some children who are classified as having a serious emotional disturbance and engage in disruptive, aggressive, defiant, or dangerous behaviors are removed from the classroom (Terman & others, 1996). These children are much more likely to be boys than girls and more likely to come from low-income than from middle- or high-income families (Achenbach & others, 1991; Dodge, Coie, & Lynam, 2006). Children with a serious emotional disturbance are more likely than any other children with a disability to initially be classified as having a disability-related problem during their secondary school years. However, the majority of these children began to show signs of their emotional problem in the elementary school years (Wagner, 1995).

When these children are returned to the regular classroom, both the regular classroom teacher and a special education teacher or consultant must spend a great deal of time helping them adapt and learn effectively. This means devoting several hours per week for several weeks for one or two students to help them make an effective transition back into the classroom. The more severe the problem, the less likely it is that a return to the classroom will work (Wagner, 1995).

In chapter 3, we discussed rejected students and improving students' social skills (Rubin, Bukowski, & Parker, 2006). Many of the comments and recommendations we made there apply to children with a serious emotional disturbance. In chapter 7,

emotional and behavioral disorders
Serious, persistent problems that involve relationships, aggression, depression, fears associated with personal or school matters, and other inappropriate socioemotional characteristics.

What are some characteristics of students who show aggressive, out-of-control behaviors?

What are some characteristics of students who are depressed?

"Behavioral and Social Cognitive Approaches", and chapter 14, "Managing the Class-room", we will discuss more strategies and plans for effectively dealing with children who show emotional and behavioral problems.

Depression, Anxiety, and Fears   Some children turn their emotional problems inward. Their depression, anxiety, or fears become so intense and persistent that their ability to learn is significantly compromised (Jensen, 2005; Kauffman, 2005). All children feel depressed from time to time, but most get over their despondent, down mood in a few hours or a few days. For some children, however, the negative mood is more serious and longer lasting. *Depression* is a type of mood disorder in which the individual feels worthless, believes that things are not likely to get better, and behaves lethargically for a prolonged period of time. When children show these signs for 2 weeks or longer, they likely are experiencing depression. Having a poor appetite and not being able to sleep well also can be associated with depression.

Depression is much more likely to appear in adolescence than in childhood and has a much higher incidence in girls than in boys (Culbertson, 1997). Experts on depression say that this gender difference is likely due to a number of factors. Females tend to ruminate on their depressed mood and amplify it, whereas males tend to distract themselves from the negative mood; girls' self-images are often more negative than those of boys during adolescence; and societal bias against female achievement might be involved (Nolen-Hoeksema, 2007).

Be vigilant in recognizing the signs of depression in children. Because it is turned inward, depression is far more likely to go unnoticed than aggressive, acting-out behaviors. If you think that a child has become depressed, have the child meet with the school counselor. Cognitive therapy has been especially effective in helping individuals become less depressed, as have some drug therapies (Beckham, 2000).

Anxiety involves a vague, highly unpleasant feeling of fear and apprehension (Kowalski, 2000). It is normal for children to be concerned or worried when they face life's challenges, but some children have such intense and prolonged anxiety that it substantially impairs their school performance. Some children also have personal or school-related fears that interfere with their learning. If a child shows marked or

SELF–ASSESSMENT 6.1

Evaluating My Experiences with People Who Have Various Disabilities and Disorders

Read each of these statements and place a checkmark next to the ones that apply to you.

1. Learning Disabilities

_____ I know someone who has a learning disability and have talked with him or her about the disability.
_____ I have observed students with learning disabilities in the classroom and talked with teachers about their strategies for educating them.

2. Attention Deficit Hyperactivity Disorder

_____ I know someone with ADHD and have talked with him or her about the disability.
_____ I have observed students with ADHD in the classroom and talked with teachers about their strategies for educating them.

3. Mental Retardation

_____ I know someone who has mental retardation and have talked with his or her parents about their child's disability.
_____ I have observed students with mental retardation in the classroom and talked with their teachers about their strategies for educating them.

4. Physical Disorders

_____ I know someone with a physical disorder and have talked with him or her about the disability.
_____ I have observed students with physical disorders in the classroom and talked with their teachers about strategies for educating them.

5. Sensory Disorders

_____ I know someone with a sensory disorder and have talked with him or her about the disability.
_____ I have observed students with sensory disorders in the classroom and talked with their teachers about their strategies for educating them.

6. Speech and Language Disorders

_____ I know someone with a speech and language disorder and have talked with him or her about the disability.
_____ I have observed students with a speech and language disorder in the classroom and talked with their teacher about strategies for educating them.

7. Autism Spectrum Disorders

_____ I know someone with an autism spectrum disorder.
_____ I have observed students with an autism spectrum disorder in the classroom and talked with their teachers about the best strategies for educating them.

8. Emotional and Behavioral Disorders

_____ I know someone with an emotional and behavioral disorder and have talked with him or her about the disorder.
_____ I have observed students with emotional and behavioral disorders and talked with their teachers about strategies for educating them.

For those disabilities that you did not place a checkmark beside, make it a point to get to know and talk with someone who has the disability and observe students with the disability in the classroom. Then talk with their teachers about their strategies for educating them.

substantial fears that persist, have the child see the school counselor. Some behavioral therapies have been especially effective in reducing inappropriate anxiety and fear (Davidson & Neale, 2007). More information about anxiety appears in chapter 13, "Motivation, Teaching, and Learning."

At this point we have explored many different disabilities and disorders. To evaluate your experiences with people who have these disabilities and disorders, complete Self-Assessment 6.1.

Review, Reflect, and Practice

(1) Describe the various types of disabilities and disorders.

REVIEW

- What is the definition of a learning disability? What are some common learning disabilities? How are they identified? How are they best treated?
- What are some important aspects of attention deficit hyperactivity disorder for teachers to know?
- What is the nature of mental retardation?
- What types of physical disabilities in children are teachers likely to see?
- What are some common visual and hearing sensory disorders in children?
- What are the differences among articulation, voice, fluency, and language disorders?
- What characterizes autism spectrum disorders?
- What are the main types of emotional and behavioral disorders?

REFLECT

- Considering the age group of children and the subject that you plan to teach, which of the disabilities that we have discussed do you think will present the most difficulty for your teaching? Where should you focus your attention in learning more about this disability?

PRAXIS™ PRACTICE

1. Marty is in the fourth grade. Intelligence tests indicate that he is of average to above-average intelligence. However, his grades in reading, social studies, spelling, and science are very low. His math grades, on the other hand, are quite high and his writing skills are adequate. Achievement tests indicate that he reads at the first-grade level. When he reads aloud, it is apparent that he has difficulty matching sounds and letters. Marty most likely has
   a. ADHD
   b. dyscalculia
   c. dyslexia
   d. dysgraphia
2. Which of the following classroom environments is most likely to help students with ADHD achieve?
   a. Ms. Caster's class, which is very loosely structured so that students will only have to attend to something for a short period of time.
   b. Ms. Dodge's class, which is tightly structured and has explicit expectations. Student learning is often supplemented with computer games and physical activity.
   c. Ms. Ebert's class, in which students are expected to sit still for extended periods of time, working independently on seatwork.
   d. Ms. Fish's class, in which students work at their own pace on self-selected tasks and receive sporadic feedback regarding their progress and behavior.

continued on page 204

Review, Reflect, and Practice *continued*

3. Marci is a White non-Latino with mild mental retardation. In addition to cognitive deficits, she has poor motor skills. Her legs and arms are shorter than average. She has a round face, with an extra fold of skin over her eyelids. Her tongue protrudes. What is most likely the cause of Marci's mental retardation?
   a. Down syndrome
   b. fetal alcohol syndrome
   c. fragile X syndrome
   d. maternal illness during pregnancy

4. Mark is a middle school student in Ms. Walsh's language arts class. She observes that Mark often stares out the window. Sometimes calling his name redirects his attention to her; at times he continues to stare out the window for several seconds and appears oblivious to Ms. Walsh's reprimands. Mark's grades are suffering as a result of his inattention. What is the most likely explanation for Mark's inattention?
   a. ADHD
   b. absence seizure disorder
   c. tonic-clonic epilepsy
   d. cerebral palsy

5. Amiel's first-grade teacher notices that he squints a lot and holds books close to his face. Amiel most likely has which of the following disorders?
   a. physical disorder
   b. speech and language disorder
   c. sensory disorder
   d. autism spectrum disorder

6. Carrie's third-grade teacher, Ms. Brown, often gets frustrated when Carrie tries to answer questions in class. Carrie takes a long time to answer. Her sentence structure is not as good as that of other students in her class, and she often presents ideas in what sounds like a random manner. Ms. Brown should suspect that Carrie has
   a. articulation disorder.
   b. expressive language disorder.
   c. receptive language disorder.
   d. specific language impairment.

7. Mike is a seventh-grade boy of above-average intelligence. He has good language skills but does not interact well with other young adolescents. He has one friend and responds well to his mother and to the aide who works with him, although he shies away from contact with other people. He does fairly well in school, as long as his routine is not disrupted. He especially enjoys math and anything to do with numbers. He has memorized the batting averages of the starting line-up of all major league baseball teams. Mike most likely has
   a. autistic disorder.
   b. Asperger syndrome.
   c. behavioral disorder.
   d. specific language disorder.

8. Which middle school student is at greatest risk of developing a serious emotional disturbance?
   a. Jill, the most popular girl in the seventh grade, who sometimes says demeaning things to less popular girls
   b. Kevin, an eighth-grader who gets good grades in most subjects, has difficulty interacting with classmates, and has memorized all of Shakespeare's sonnets
   c. Harriet, a sixth-grade girl whose ADHD symptoms are controlled well by medication
   d. Mark, a seventh-grade boy who gets poor grades in many classes and frequently acts out in angry, violent ways

Please see the answer key at the end of the book.

② EDUCATIONAL ISSUES INVOLVING CHILDREN WITH DISABILITIES

| Legal Aspects | Placements, Services, and Parents as Educational Partners | Technology |

Public schools are legally required to serve all children with disabilities in the least restrictive environment possible. We will explore the legal aspects of working with children who have a disability, profile the placements and services available to these children, and examine the roles of parents and technology in educating children with a disability.

Legal Aspects

Beginning in the mid-1960s to mid-1970s, legislatures, the federal courts, and the U.S. Congress laid down special educational rights for children with disabilities. Prior to that time, most children with disabilities were either refused enrollment or inadequately served by schools. In 1975, Congress enacted **Public Law 94-142,** the Education for All Handicapped Children Act, which required that all students with disabilities be given a free, appropriate public education and which provided the funding to help implement this education.

Individuals with Disabilities Education Act (IDEA)   In 1990, Public Law 94-142 was recast as the **Individuals with Disabilities Education Act (IDEA).** IDEA was amended in 1997 and then reauthorized in 2004 and renamed the Individuals with Disabilities Education Improvement Act. IDEA spells out broad mandates for services to all children with disabilities (Hallahan & Kauffman, 2006; Hardman, Drew, & Egan, 2006; Smith, 2007). These include evaluation and eligibility determination, appropriate education and an individualized education plan (IEP), and education in the least restrictive environment (LRE).

Children who are thought to have a disability are evaluated to determine their eligibility for services under IDEA. Schools are prohibited from planning special education programs in advance and offering them on a space-available basis. In other words, schools must provide appropriate education services to all children who are determined to need to them.

Children must be evaluated before a school can begin providing special services (Friend, 2006; Werts, Culatta, & Tompkins, 2007). Parents must be invited to participate in the evaluation process. Reevaluation is required at least every 3 years (sometimes every year), when requested by parents, or when conditions suggest a reevaluation is needed. A parent who disagrees with the school's evaluation can obtain an independent evaluation, which the school is required to consider in providing special education services. If the evaluation finds that child has a disability and requires special services, the school must provide the child with appropriate services.

IDEA requires that students with disabilities have an **individualized education plan (IEP).** An IEP is a written statement that spells out a program specifically tailored for the student with a disability. In general, the IEP should be (1) related to the child's learning capacity, (2) specially constructed to meet the child's individual needs and not merely copy what is offered to other children, and (3) designed to provide educational benefits.

IDEA has many other specific provisions that relate to the parents of a child with a disability (Heward, 2006; Lewis & Doorlag, 2006). These include requirements that schools send notices to parents of proposed actions, that parents be allowed to attend meetings regarding the child's placement or individualized education plan, and that

Public Law 94-142 The Education for All Handicapped Children Act, which required that all students with disabilities be given a free, appropriate public education and which provided the funding to help implement this education.

Individuals with Disabilities Education Act (IDEA) This act spells out broad mandates for services to all children with disabilities, including evaluation and determination of eligibility, appropriate education and an individualized education plan (IEP), and education in the least restrictive environment (LRE).

individualized education plan (IEP) A written statement that spells out a program specifically tailored for the student with a disability.

Increasingly, children with disabilities are being taught in the regular classroom, as is this child with mild mental retardation.

parents have the right to appeal school decisions to an impartial evaluator.

Amendments were made to IDEA in 1997. Two of these involve positive behavioral support and functional behavioral assessment.

Positive behavioral support focuses on culturally appropriate application of positive behavioral interventions to attain important behavior changes in children (Wheeler & Richey, 2005). "Culturally appropriate" refers to considering the unique and individualized learning histories of children (social, community, historical, gender, and so on). Positive behavioral support especially emphasizes supporting desirable behaviors rather than punishing undesirable behaviors in working with children with a disability or disorder.

Functional behavioral assessment involves determining the consequences (what purpose the behavior serves), antecedents (what triggers the behavior), and setting events (in which contexts the behavior occurs) (Alberto & Troutman, 2006; Chandler & Dahlquist, 2005). Functional behavioral assessment emphasizes understanding behavior in the context in which it is observed and guiding positive behavioral interventions that are relevant and effective.

A major aspect of the 2004 reauthorization of IDEA involved aligning it with the government's No Child Left Behind (NCLB) legislation, which was designed to improve the educational achievement of all students, including those with disabilities. Both IDEA and NCLB mandate that most students with disabilities be included in general assessments of educational progress. This alignment includes requiring most students with disabilities "to take standard tests of academic achievement and to achieve at a level equal to that of students without disabilities. Whether this expectation is reasonable is an open question" (Hallahan & Kauffman, 2006, pp. 28–29). Alternative assessments for students with disabilities and funding to help states improve instruction, assessment, and accountability for educating students with disabilities are included in the 2004 reauthorization of IDEA.

Least Restrictive Environment (LRE) Under IDEA, the child with a disability must be educated in the **least restrictive environment (LRE).** This means a setting as similar as possible to the one in which children who do not have a disability are educated. And schools must make an effort to educate children with a disability in the regular classroom. Educating children with a disability in the regular classroom used to be called *mainstreaming.* That term, however, has been replaced by the term **inclusion,** which means educating a child with special educational needs full-time in the regular classroom (Mastropieri & Scruggs, 2007; Wood, 2006). One recent study found that the academic achievement of students with learning disabilities benefited from inclusion (Rea, McLaughlin, & Walther-Thomas, 2002).

Not long ago it was considered appropriate to educate children with disabilities outside the regular classroom. Today, however, schools must make every effort to provide inclusion for children with disabilities (Friend, 2006; Lewis & Doorlag, 2006). These efforts can be very costly financially and very time consuming in terms of faculty effort.

The principle of "least restrictive environment" compels schools to examine possible modifications of the regular classroom before moving the child with a disability to a more restrictive placement. Also, regular classroom teachers often need specialized training to help some children with disabilities, and state educational agencies are required to provide such training (Heward, 2006; Vaughn, Bos, Schumm, 2007).

least restrictive environment (LRE) A setting that is as similar as possible to the one in which children who do not have a disability are educated.

inclusion Educating children with special education needs full-time in the regular classroom.

What is least restrictive likely depends to some degree on the child's disability (Hallahan & Kauffman, 2006; Turnbull, Turnbull & Tompkins, 2007). Most children with a learning disability or a speech impairment can be educated in the regular classroom, but children with severe hearing or vision impairments may need to be educated in separate classes or schools.

Many legal changes regarding children with disabilities have been extremely positive. Compared with several decades ago, far more children today are receiving competent, specialized services. For many children, inclusion in the regular classroom, with modifications or supplemental services, is appropriate (Friend, 2006). However, some leading experts on special education argue that the effort to use inclusion to educate children with disabilities has become too extreme in some cases. For example, James Kauffman and his colleagues (Kauffman & Hallahan, 2005; Kauffman, McGee, and Brigham, 2004) state that inclusion too often has meant making accommodations in the regular classroom that do not always benefit children with disabilities. They advocate a more individualized approach that does not always involve full inclusion but rather allows for options such as special education outside the regular classroom. Kauffman and his colleagues (2004, p. 620) acknowledge that children with disabilities "*do* need the services of specially trained professionals to achieve their full potential. They *do* sometimes need altered curricula or adaptations to make their learning possible." However, "we sell students with disabilities short when we pretend that they are not different from typical students. We make the same error when we pretend that they must *not* be expected to put forth extra effort if they are to learn to do some things—or learn to do something in a different way." Like general education, an important aspect of special education should be to challenge students with disabilities "to become all they can be."

Research on outcomes for inclusion suggest these conclusions (Hocutt, 1996):

- *Children's academic and social success.* These outcomes are affected more by the quality of the instruction given than by where the child is placed (such as regular classroom, resource room, or special education classroom). When inclusion is used, it works best when regular classroom teachers are given lengthy, often multiyear training, planning time, administrative support, and sometimes additional instructional staff.

- *Children with severe emotional disturbance.* In secondary school, adolescents with this disorder are more likely to succeed if they participate in vocational education and are integrated into the school through activities such as sports. However, adolescents with a long history of course failures are more likely to drop out of school if they are placed in the regular classroom.

- *Children with hearing impairments.* Children with these disorders gain some academic advantages but have lower self-esteem when they are in the regular classroom.

- *Children with educable mental retardation (usually defined as having an IQ from 50 to 70 along with adaptive behavior problems in the same range).* A supportive teacher, competent instruction, and supportive classmates seem to have an even greater impact on these children than on children without disabilities.

- *Children who do not have a disability.* They do not appear to be negatively affected by the inclusion of children with a disability in the regular classroom as long as supportive services are provided (Cole, Waldron, & Majid, 2004). This research finding is especially important—many parents of students who are not disabled worry that teachers will not have adequate time to help their child learn because they will be spending so much time with children who have disabilities. When the inclusion program brings a lower overall teacher-child ratio, children who do not have a disability actually are likely to benefit academically from inclusion.

DIVERSITY AND EDUCATION
Minority Students in Special Education

The U.S. Department of Education (2000) has three concerns about the over-representation of minority students in special education programs and classes: (1) students may be unserved or receive services that do not meet their needs; (2) students may be misclassified or inappropriately labeled, and (3) placement in special education classes may be a form of discrimination.

African American students are overrepresented in special education—15 percent of the U.S. student population is African American, but 20 percent of special education students are African American. In some disabilities, the discrepancies are even greater. For example, African American students represent 32 percent of the students in programs for mild mental retardation, 29 percent in programs for moderate mental retardation, and 24 percent in programs for serious emotional disturbance.

However, it is not just a simple matter of overrepresentation of certain minority groups in special education. Latino children may be underidentified in the categories of mental retardation and emotional disturbance.

More appropriate inclusion of minority students in special education is a complex problem and requires the creation of a successful school experience for all students. Recommendations for reducing disproportionate representation in special education include the following (Burnette, 1998):

- Reviewing school practices to identify and address factors that might contribute to school difficulties
- Forming policy-making groups that include community members and promote partnerships with service agencies and cultural organizations
- Helping families get social, medical, mental health, and other support services
- Training more teachers from minority backgrounds and providing all teachers with more extensive course work and training in educating children with disabilities and diversity issues

One concern about special education involves disproportionate representation of students from minority backgrounds in special education programs and classes (Artilies & others, 2005). The Diversity and Education interlude addresses this issue.

Placements, Services, and Parents as Educational Partners

Children with disabilities can be placed in a variety of settings, and a range of services can be used to improve their education (Kauffman & Hallahan, 2005; Sailor & Roger, 2005).

Placements   Today in the United States only a small percentage of students with disabilities are being educated outside of regular schools, although the percentage of students with disabilities educated in the regular classroom varies from state to state (Hallahan & Kauffman, 2006). In the 2003–2004 school year, almost 50 percent of U.S. students with disabilities spent 80 percent of the school day in a regular classroom (National Center for Education Statistics, 2005). This represents a 5 percent increase since 1994. Approximately 4 percent of U.S. students with disabilities are educated in separate schools. Let's now explore the types of services that are available to students with disabilities.

BEST PRACTICES
Strategies for Working with Children with Disabilities as a Regular Teacher

1. *Carry out each child's individualized education plan (IEP).* Haille Lazar, a special education teacher in Plano, Texas, describes the importance of the IEP.

THROUGH THE EYES OF TEACHERS
Follow Each Child's IEP

General education teachers must take responsibility for students with special needs. These children are part of their classroom. Teachers should not think of their classroom roster as twenty students plus the child in the wheelchair. Always make sure that children with special needs are not left behind. This happens more than you think. The class may go to the library with the teacher leading the line. The students follow in a single file, but no one thinks to push the child sitting in the wheelchair into the line. And special education teachers and assistants may not always be around to perform routine tasks; they service many children throughout the school.

Read and review the individualized education plan (IEP) for each child in your class and preferably your entire grade level to ensure that all goals and objectives as well as any classroom modifications are being met. Is the child supposed to be seated near the teacher? Is the student hearing impaired and should not sit near a fan or air-conditioning unit? Is the student supposed to take tests in small groups, one-on-one, or read aloud? Don't presume the special education teacher will tell you everything in a child's IEP.

---

2. *Encourage your school to provide increased support and training in how to teach children with disabilities.* Next, Michelle Evans, a sixth-grade teacher, describes her relationship with resource personnel and some strategies that worked for her students.

THROUGH THE EYES OF TEACHERS
Strategies for Working with Children Who Have a Disability

Support and resource personnel are invaluable. Communication with parents, student, and with anyone involved is essential. Make certain that you communicate with your entire class, too. . . . Because I want each student to feel successful, I create different levels of mastery or participation in learning objectives.

One student with cerebral palsy had difficulty standing, mental impairments, and other problems. She had little and often no short-term memory. As we sat together

and talked, I found that her strength was that she loved to copy words, stories, and other things. Her hands were weak, but writing helped them. Her parents wanted her to do anything she could. By capitalizing on her fondness for copying and writing, she eventually learned math facts and spelling words. I assigned a poem about having a positive attitude as a memorization for everyone in the class. A few kids complained that the poem would be too hard to memorize when I presented it. She copied that poem so many times that three days after the assignment she stood and delivered it flawlessly to the class. I could see the complainers melt away as we all realized that she was the first to recite the poem. Her parents came to witness her accomplishment. There wasn't a dry eye in the room by the time she finished. She taught us a great deal.

---

3. *Use the support that is available and seek other support.* Many well-educated, conscientious people in the community might be willing to volunteer some of their time to help you provide more individualized instruction for students with disabilities. This in turn provides a lower teacher-student ratio that benefits all of your students.

4. *Become more knowledgeable about the types of children with disabilities in your classroom.* Read education journals, such as *Exceptional Children, Teaching Exceptional Children,* and *Journal of Learning Disabilities,* to keep up-to-date on the latest information about these children. Look into taking a class at a college or university or a continuing education course on topics such as exceptional children, mental retardation, learning disabilities, and emotional and behavioral disorders.

5. *Be cautious about labeling children with a disability.* It is easy to fall into the trap of using the label as an explanation of the child's learning difficulties. For example, a teacher might say, "Well, Larry has trouble with reading because he has a learning disability," when, in fact, the teacher really knows only that for some unknown reason Larry is having trouble with reading. Also, labels have a way of remaining after the child has improved considerably. Remember that terms such as *mental retardation* and *learning disability* are descriptive labels for disorders. Always think of children with disabilities in terms of what the best conditions are for improving their learning and how they can be helped to make progress rather than in terms of unchanging labels.

6. *Remember that children with disabilities benefit from many of the same teaching strategies that benefit*

continued on page 210

BEST PRACTICES *continued*
Strategies for Working with Children with Disabilities as a Regular Teacher

children without disabilities. These include being caring, accepting, and patient; having positive expectations for learning; helping children with their social and communication skills as well as academic skills; and challenging children with disabilities to reach their full potential.

7. *Help children without a disability to understand and accept children with a disability.* Provide children without a disability information about children with a disability and create opportunities for them to interact with each

other in positive ways. Peer tutoring and cooperative learning activities can be used to encourage positive interaction between children without a disability and children with a disability (Fuchs, Fuchs, & Burish, 2000). We will discuss these activities further in chapter 10, "Social Constructivist Approaches."

8. *Keep up-to-date on technology available for educating children with a disability* (Ullman, 2005). We will discuss this topic shortly.

Services Services for children can be provided by the regular classroom teacher, a resource teacher, a special education teacher, a collaborative consultant, other professionals, or an interactive team (Dettmer, Dyck, & Thurston, 2002).

The Regular Classroom Teacher With the increase in inclusion, the regular classroom teacher is responsible for providing more of the education of children with disabilities than in the past (Smith & others, 2006; Vaughn, Bos, & Schumm, 2007). The Best Practices interlude can help you provide a more effective education for these children.

The Resource Teacher A resource teacher can provide valuable services for many children who have a disability. Many children with disabilities spend most of their school day in a regular classroom and a small portion of their day in a resource room where a resource teacher works with them. In a typical arrangement, a child might spend 1 or 2 hours a day in the resource room and the remainder of time in the regular classroom. In many situations, resource teachers work with these children to improve their reading, writing, or mathematical skills.

The regular classroom teacher and the resource teacher should collaborate and coordinate their efforts. In some cases, the resource teacher will work with the child in the regular classroom setting rather than seeing the child in a resource room.

The Special Education Teacher Some teachers have extensive training in special education and teach children with disabilities in a separate "special education classroom." Some children will spend time with the special education teacher part of the school day and the rest of the day in the regular classroom, as happens with a resource teacher. However, the special education teacher typically assumes greater responsibility for the child's overall program than the resource teacher, who usually works in support of the regular classroom teacher. A child might learn reading, writing, mathematics, or science with the special education teacher and be in the regular classroom for physical education, art, or music. The most frequent area in which the special education teacher works with the child who has a disability is reading, and the most frequent classification of a special education teacher is as a teacher of children who have specific learning disabilities (U.S. Department of Education, 2000).

In some school systems, if more than a set percentage (say, 60 percent) of the child's time is spent with a special education teacher, the child's program is called *self-contained special education.* Self-contained special education also is in effect when children are educated in separate schools for children with disabilities.

Related Services In addition to regular classroom teachers, resource teachers, and special education teachers, a number of other special education personnel provide

BEST PRACTICES
Strategies for Communicating with Parents of Children with Disabilities

1. *Let parents know that you understand and appreciate their child's individuality.* Make it a point to talk about their child's strengths rather than focusing only on their child's problems. Especially focus on positive aspects of their child at the beginning and the end of the conversation.

2. *Place yourself in the shoes of parents of a child with a disability.* Many parents with a child who has a disability often feel frustrated. They may be struggling with a new diagnosis of their child or be confronting the complexities of an education plan for their child for the first time. Relay a diagnosis with compassion and an appropriate degree of hope for the child.

3. *Provide parents with information about their child's disability.* Once a child has been diagnosed with a disability, teachers should engage parents in an ongoing conversation about what this diagnosis means for the child. Teachers and parents need to work cooperatively in establishing and meeting realistic learning goals for the child. Know what resources can be used to help the child and discuss these with parents.

4. *Talk with parents, not to them.* View each meeting with the child's parents as an opportunity to learn more about the child. It is easy to fall into the trap of acting like an authority and talking "to" rather than "with" parents. View parents as being an equal partner with you and other professionals in educating the child with a disability. Encourage parents to ask questions and express their emotions. If you don't know the answer to a parent's question, tell them that you will try to find out the information for them.

5. *Avoid stereotyping children.* Educate yourself about children's diversity and the range of backgrounds they come from. Avoid making stereotypical judgments about children and their parents based on their socioeconomic status, ethnicity, family structure, religion, or gender. Good relationships and effective communication are undermined by biased assumptions.

6. *Reach out to parents to establish and maintain effective communication with them.* Tell them how important they are in helping you and other school professionals to understand and educate their child. Be sure to support their attendance at individualized education plan (IEP) meetings.

7. *Talk with parents about how the media can provide erroneous portrayals of children with disabilities.* Popular magazines, newspapers, movies, television, and radio at times provide inaccurate information about children with disabilities. Caution parents about this, and tell them that they are always welcome to discuss anything they read about or hear pertaining to their child's disability with you or other school personnel.

services for children with disabilities (U.S. Department of Education, 2000). These include teacher aides, psychologists, counselors, school social workers, nurses, physicians, occupational therapists, and physical therapists, as well as speech and hearing specialists such as audiologists (Lacey, 2001). In addition, transportation services also might be provided if needed by the children.

Teacher aides especially can help the regular classroom teacher provide individualized instruction for children with disabilities (Hardman, Drew, & Egan, 2006). Some teacher aides are certified to work with children who have disabilities. Psychologists might be involved in assessing whether a child has a disability and might be part of the team that creates the IEP. They and counselors might also work with some children who have a disability. My (your author's) first job was as a school psychologist assigned to a reading clinic to evaluate the cognitive and socioemotional skills of children with reading problems. School psychologists might make recommendations to teachers about ways that children with a disability can learn more effectively. School social workers often help to coordinate family and community services for children with a disability. Nurses and physicians might conduct medical assessments and/or prescribe medication for children with disabilities. Physical therapists and occupational therapists might be involved in helping children recover from remediable physical or cognitive impairments. Speech and hearing specialists may be included when their skills will help improve children's skills in their area of expertise.

Collaborative Consultation and Interactive Teaming In the last two decades, collaborative consultation has been increasingly advocated in educating children with disabilities (Hallahan & Kauffman, 2006). In collaborative consultation, people with diverse expertise interact to provide services for children. Researchers have found that collaborative consultation often results in gains for children, as well as improved skills and attitudes for teachers (Idol, Nevin, & Paolucci-Whitcomb, 1994).

Ideally, collaborative consultation encourages shared responsibility in planning and decision making. It also enables educators with diverse expertise to construct effective alternatives to traditional educational approaches. When collaborative consultation is used, many children remain in the regular classroom, and the regular classroom teacher is actively involved in planning the child's education (Bryant & Bryant, 1998).

Increasingly, the term *interactive teaming* is being used (Thomas, Correa, & Morsink, 1995). Interactive team members are professionals and parents who collaborate to provide direct or indirect services to children (Coben & others, 1997). They share knowledge and skills, teaching other members their expertise when appropriate. Actual team sizes vary, and teams change in composition depending on the complexity of the child's needs. Persons involved can include educational, medical, administrative, vocational, and allied health specialists; social services personnel; and parents.

Parents as Educational Partners Educators and researchers increasingly recognize how important it is for teachers and parents to jointly guide the learning of children with disabilities (Friend, 2006; Hallahan & Kauffman, 2006; Hardman, Drew, & Egan, 2006). The Individuals with Disabilities Education Act (IDEA) mandates parent participation in developing educational programs for all children with disabilities.

Technology

The Individuals with Disabilities Education Act (IDEA), including its 1997 amendments, requires that technology devices and services be provided to students with disabilities if they are necessary to ensure a free, appropriate education (Male, 2003; Ulman, 2005).

Two types of technology that can be used to improve the education of students with disabilities are instructional technology and assistance technology (Blackhurst, 1997). *Instructional technology* includes various types of hardware and software, combined with innovative teaching methods, to accommodate students' learning needs in the classroom. Examples include videotapes, computer-assisted instruction, and complex hypermedia programs in which computers are used to control the display of audio and visual images stored on videodisc.

Assistive technology consists of various services and devices to help students with disabilities function within their environment. Examples include communication aids, alternative computer keyboards, and adaptive switches. To locate such services, educators can use computer databases such as the Device Locator System (Academic Software, 1996).

Teams of educators and other professionals often combine these technologies to improve the learning of students with disabilities (Ulman, 2005). For example, students unable to use their hands to operate a computer keyboard might use a voice-operated computer (assistive technology) that provides instruction from a software program that was designed to provide spelling instruction (instructional technology). To read further about instructional and assistive technologies, see the Technology and Education box.

TECHNOLOGY AND EDUCATION

Technology and Special Needs Students

Technology can be used to help students with special needs. The following distinguish between assistive and instructive technologies serve these purposes (Roblyer, Edwards & Havrileck (1997):

Assistive Technologies

Assistive technologies are software and hardware designed specifically to help students with special needs. For example, software and special hardware such as closed-circuit television can enlarge computer images and text for children with a visual impairment. Printers can produce large print or Braille. Tactile devices that scan a page and translate the text into vibrating, tactile displays also can be used with children who are visually impaired. Captioned video provides subtitles for television and other videopresentations so that children who are hearing impaired can read what others are saying.

Telecommunication technologies for the deaf allow children with hearing impairments to communicate with people over the phone. The Internet gives children with a disability who are homebound access to educational opportunities. Many children with physical disabilities (such as cerebral palsy) cannot use traditional devices such as a keyboard and a mouse. Touch screens, touch tablets, optical pointers, alternative keyboards, and voice-controlled devices are alternatives that allow them to use a computer.

Instructional Applications

Software and hardware designed for use with traditional students are also being used with considerable success with students who have special needs, especially in inclusion classes.

Traditional applications involve the use of computer-based tutorials, drill and practice, and games. Applications such as these have been used to improve the decoding and vocabulary skills of children. Game-type software is often used to motivate children with a disability.

Constructivist applications focus on students' understanding and thinking skills. Among the constructivist applications that can be used effectively with children with disabilities are cognitive organizers such as *IdeaFisher* and *Inspiration*. Both can be used with children who have a learning disability. Word prediction software can be used to help children with physical disabilities write on a computer.

Word processing has helped many children with disabilities make progress in their written language skills (Hetzroni & Shrieber, 2004; Holberg, 1995). Talking word processors such as *Write: Outloud, Intellitalk, KidsWorks 2,* and *The Amazing Writing Machine* can be especially helpful in the education of children with speech problems. On request, these programs read text aloud.

Mobile computers also hold great promise for use with special needs students. Preliminary research provides evidence that the use of mobile computing devices in inclusive classes can improve the engagement of special needs students and help lessen the achievement gap between special needs and regular students (Swan & others, 2005).

(a)

(b)

These special input devices can help students with physical disabilities use computers more effectively. (a) A student uses a special input device attached to the student's head to send signals to the computer. (b) Many students with physical disabilities such as cerebral palsy cannot use a conventional keyboard and mouse. Many can use alternative keyboards effectively.

Review, Reflect, and Practice

(2) **Explain the legal framework, as well as placements and supports for children with disabilities.**

REVIEW

- What is IDEA? How is it related to IEPs and LREs? What is the current thinking about inclusion?
- What different types of placement and services are possible? Who carries them out? How can teachers best communicate with parents as educational partners?
- What is the difference between instructional and assistive technology?

REFLECT

- What do you think will present the greatest challenges to you in teaching children with a disability?

PRAXIS™ PRACTICE

1. Jenny has a moderate learning disability. She is educated in the special education classroom of her school, as she has been for the past 2 years. She and her classmates eat lunch in the resource room as well. Each of the students in the resource room works on different things, due to their very different abilities and disabilities. This placement was made because the regular education teachers in Jenny's school do not have the necessary skills to teach Jenny. Therefore, she was placed in the resource room with the school's sole special educator. What is the legal issue with this placement?
   a. Jenny's IEP does not specify a diagnosis.
   b. Jenny is not being educated in the least restrictive environment.
   c. Jenny's placement needs to be reconsidered at least every 6 months.
   d. The functional behavior assessment did not consider the use of technology.

2. Marc has a mild learning disability. His reading skills lag behind grade level by 2 years. As a result, he struggles in coursework that involves extensive reading, such as English, social studies, and science. He does much better in math. What type of services would be most appropriate for Marc?
   a. Marc should be taught by a special educator in a class comprised only of students with special education needs.
   b. Marc should be taught in a regular education classroom, by a regular education teacher, with no modifications.
   c. Marc should be taught in a regular classroom, with some modifications made to his curriculum, and perhaps with the help of an aide or occasional resource room services.
   d. Marc should either be homeschooled or taught in a separate school for students with disabilities.

3. Azel has cerebral palsy. His teacher has found an alternative computer keyboard to facilitate his learning. What type of technology is the teacher using?
   a. instructional technology
   b. computer-assisted instruction
   c. assistive technology
   d. complex hypermedia

Please see the answer key at the end of the book.

③ CHILDREN WHO ARE GIFTED

| Characteristics | Life Course of the Gifted | Educating Children Who Are Gifted |

The final type of exceptionality we will discuss is quite different from the disabilities and disorders that we have described so far. **Children who are gifted** have above-average intelligence (usually defined as an IQ of 130 or higher) and/or superior talent in some domain such as art, music, or mathematics. Admissions standards for children who are gifted in schools are typically based on intelligence and academic aptitude, although there is increasing call to widen the criteria to include such factors as creativity and commitment (Renzulli & Reis, 1997). Some critics argue that too many children in "gifted programs" aren't really gifted in a particular area but are just somewhat bright, usually cooperative, and, usually, non-Latino White (Castellano & Diaz, 2002). They believe the mantle of brilliance is cast on many children who are not that far from simply being "smart normal." Although general intelligence as defined by an overall IQ score still remains as a key criterion in many states' decision of whether a child should be placed in a gifted program, changing conceptions of intelligence increasingly include ideas such as Gardner's multiple intelligences, and placement criteria are likely to move away from an IQ criterion in the future (Davidson, 2000; Davis & Rimm, 2004; Winner, 2006).

Characteristics

Ellen Winner (1996), an expert on creativity and giftedness, described three criteria that characterize children who are gifted:

1. *Precocity.* Children who are gifted are precocious when given the opportunity to use their gift or talent. They begin to master an area earlier than their peers. Learning in their domain is more effortless for them than for children who are not gifted. In most instances, children who are gifted are precocious because they have an inborn high ability in a particular domain or domains, although this inborn precocity has to be identified and nourished.

2. *Marching to their own drummer.* Children who are gifted learn in a qualitatively different way than children who are not gifted. One way they march to a different drummer is that they require less support, or scaffolding (discussed in chapter 2), from adults to learn than their nongifted peers do. Often they resist explicit instruction. They also often make discoveries on their own and solve problems in unique ways within their area of giftedness. They can be normal or below normal in other areas.

3. *A passion to master.* Children who are gifted are driven to understand the domain in which they have high ability. They display an intense, obsessive interest and an ability to focus. They are not children who need to be pushed by their parents. They frequently have a high degree of internal motivation.

A fourth area in which children who are gifted excel involves information-processing skills. Researchers have found that children who are gifted learn at a faster pace, process information more rapidly, are better at reasoning, use better strategies, and monitor their understanding better than their nongifted counterparts (Davidson & Davidson, 2004; Sternberg & Clinkenbeard, 1995).

Life Course of the Gifted

Is giftedness a product of heredity or environment? Likely both. Individuals who are gifted recall that they had signs of high ability in a particular area at a very young age, prior to or at the beginning of formal training (Howe & others, 1995). This

At 2 years of age, art prodigy Alexandra Nechita colored in coloring books for hours and took up pen and ink. She had no interest in dolls or friends. By age 5 she was using watercolors. Once she started school, she would start painting as soon as the got home. At the age of 8, in 1994, she saw the first public exhibit of her work. In succeeding years, working quickly and impulsively on canvases as large as 5 feet by 9 feet, she has completed hundreds of paintings, some of which sell for close to $100,000 apiece. As a teenager, she continues to paint—relentlessly and passionately. It is, she says, what she loves to do. *What are some characteristics of children who are gifted?*

children who are gifted Children with above-average intelligence (usually defined as an IQ of 130 or higher) and/or superior talent in some domain such as art, music, or mathematics.

suggests the importance of innate ability in giftedness. However, researchers also have found that individuals with world-class status in the arts, mathematics, science, and sports all report strong family support and years of training and practice (Bloom, 1985). Deliberate practice is an important characteristic of individuals who become experts in a particular domain. *Deliberate practice* is practice that occurs at an appropriate level of difficulty for the individual, provides corrective feedback, and allows opportunities for repetition (Ericsson, 1996). In one study, the best musicians engaged in twice as much deliberate practice over their lives as the least successful ones did (Ericsson, Krampe, & Tesch, 1993).

Do children who are gifted become gifted and highly creative adults? In Terman's research on children with superior IQs, the children typically became experts in a well-established domain, such as medicine, law, or business. However, most did not become major creators (Winner, 2000). That is, they did not create a new domain or revolutionize an old domain.

One reason that some children who are gifted do not become gifted adults is that they have been pushed too hard by overzealous parents and teachers. As a result, they lose their intrinsic (internal) motivation (Winner, 1996, 2006). As adolescents, they may ask themselves, "Who am I doing this for?" If the answer is not for one's self, they may not want to do it anymore.

Educating Children Who Are Gifted

Increasingly, experts argue that the education of children who are gifted in the United States requires a significant overhaul, as reflected in the titles of recent books and reports: *Genius Denied: How to Stop Wasting Our Brightest Young Minds* (Davidson & Davidson, 2004) and *A Nation Deceived: How Schools Hold Back America's Brightest Students* (Colangelo, Assouline, & Gross, 2004).

Underchallenged children who are gifted can become disruptive, skip classes, and lose interest in achieving. Sometimes these children just disappear into the woodwork, becoming passive and apathetic toward school (Rosselli, 1996). Teachers must challenge children who are gifted to reach high expectations (Hargrove, 2005; Tassell-Baska & Stambaugh, 2006; Winner, 2006).

Four program options for children who are gifted follow (Hertzog, 1998):

- *Special classes.* Historically, this has been the common way to educate children who are gifted. The special classes during the regular school day are called "pullout" programs. Some special classes also are held after school, on Saturdays, or in the summer.

- *Acceleration and enrichment in the regular classroom setting.* This could include early admission to kindergarten, grade skipping (also known as double promotion), telescoping (completing two grades in one year), advanced placement, subject-matter acceleration, and self-paced instruction (Colangelo, Assoline, & Gross, 2004; Johnsen, 2005). Curriculum compacting is a variation of acceleration in which teachers skip over aspects of the curriculum that they believe children who are gifted do not need.

- *Mentor and apprenticeship programs.* Some experts stress these are important, underutilized ways to

THROUGH THE EYES OF STUDENTS

Children Who Are Gifted Speak

James Delisle (1987) interviewed hundreds of elementary school children who are gifted. Here are some of their comments.

In response to: Describe Your Typical School Day.

> Oh what a bore to sit and listen,
> To stuff we already know.
> Do everything we've done and done again,
> But we must still sit and listen.
> Over and over read one more page
> Oh bore, oh bore, oh bore.
>
> 9-year-old girl, New York

> I sit there pretending to be reading along when I'm really six pages ahead. When I understand something and half the class doesn't, I have to sit there and listen.
>
> 11-year-old girl, New York

In response to: What Makes a Teacher a Gifted Teacher?

> Will challenge you and let the sky be your limit.
>
> 11-year-old boy, Michigan

> Opens your mind to help you with your life.
>
> 11-year-old boy, New Jersey

BEST PRACTICES
Strategies for Working with Children Who Are Gifted

Here are some recommended strategies for working with children who are gifted (Colangelo, Assouline, & Gross, 2004, pp. 49–50):

1. *Recognize that the child is academically advanced.*

2. *Guide the child to new challenges and ensure that school is a positive experience.*

3. *Monitor the accurate evaluation of the child's readiness to be accelerated.*

4. *Discuss with parents ways to appropriately challenge the child.*

5. *Learn about and use resources for children who are gifted.* Among these are National Research Center on Gifted and Talented Education at the University of Connecticut and the Belin-Blank Center at the University of Iowa; *Gifted Child Quarterly* and *Gifted Child Today* journals; books on children who are gifted: *Genius Denied* by Davidson and Davidson (2004); *A Nation Deceived* by Colangelo, Assouline, and Gross (2004); and *Handbook of Gifted Education* (3rd ed.) by Colangelo and Davis (2003).

This concludes our coverage of children who are exceptional learners. From time to time in this chapter, we described some behavioral strategies for changing children's behavior. For example, we indicated that children who are mentally retarded often benefit from the use of precise steps in using positive reinforcement to change their behavior. In chapter 7, we will explore many aspects of positive reinforcement and other learning strategies.

motivate, challenge, and effectively educate children who are gifted (Pleiss & Feldhusen, 1995).
- *Work/study and/or community service programs*

Educational reform has brought into the regular classroom many strategies that once were the domain of separate gifted programs. These include an emphasis on problem-based learning, having children do projects, creating portfolios, and critical thinking. Combined with the increasing emphasis on educating all children in the regular classroom, many schools now try to challenge and motivate children who are gifted in the regular classroom (Hertzog, 1998). Some schools also include after-school or Saturday programs or develop mentor apprenticeship, work/study, or community service programs. Thus, an array of in-school and out-of-school opportunities is provided.

The Schoolwide Enrichment Model (SEM), developed by Joseph Renzulli (1998), is a program for children who are gifted that focuses on total school improvement. Renzulli says that when enrichment has a school-wide emphasis, positive outcomes are likely to occur, not only for children who are gifted but also for children who are not gifted and for classroom and resource teachers. When school-wide enrichment is emphasized, "us" versus "them" barriers often decrease, and classroom teachers are more willing to use curriculum compacting with their children who are most gifted. Instead of feeling isolated, resource teachers begin to feel more like members of a team, especially when they work with regular classroom teachers on enriching the entire classroom. Thus, important goals of SEM are to improve outcomes for both students who are gifted and those who are not gifted and to improve the contributions and relationships of classroom and resource teachers.

Research evaluation of acceleration and enrichment programs has not revealed which approach is best (Winner, 1997). Some researchers have found support for acceleration programs (Kulik, 1992), although critics say a potential problem of grade skipping is that it places children with others who are physically more advanced and socioemotionally different. Other researchers have found support for enrichment programs (Renzulli & Reis, 1997).

Ellen Winner (1997, 2006) argues that too often children who are gifted are socially isolated and underchallenged in the classroom. It is not unusual for them to be ostracized and labeled "nerds" or "geeks" (Silverman, 1993). A child who is gifted who is the only such child in the classroom does not have the opportunity to learn with students of like ability. Many eminent adults report that school was a negative experience for them, that they were bored and sometimes knew more than their teachers (Bloom, 1985). Winner believes that American education will benefit when standards are raised for all children. When some children are still underchallenged, she recommends that they be allowed to attend advanced classes in their domain of exceptional ability. For example, some especially precocious middle school students are allowed to take college classes in their area of expertise.

Review, Reflect, and Practice

(3) **Define what gifted means and discuss some approaches to teaching children who are gifted.**

REVIEW

- What is the definition of being gifted? What characteristics does Winner ascribe to children who are gifted?
- How can the life course of the gifted be described?
- What are some options for educating students who are gifted?

REFLECT

- Suppose that you had several students in your class who were strikingly gifted. Might this lead to problems? Explain. What might you do to prevent such problems from developing?

PRAXIS™ PRACTICE

1. Ms. Larson has a student in her kindergarten class who continuously surprises her. He requested that she allow him to play with a puzzle of the United States that no children had played with in years. She observed him expertly put each state in place, saying its name as he did so. Soon he was teaching the other students in the class each state's name, its capitol, and where it belonged in the puzzle. On a recent trip to the school learning center, he asked to check out a book of international flags that was written at an eighth-grade level. Her first instinct was to deny his request, but instead she asked him about the book. He told her "I know I can't read *all* of it, but I can read the names of the countries, and I want to learn more flags. See how many I already know?" He then flipped through the book, correctly identifying most of the flags. Which characteristics of giftedness is this student showing?
   a. numerical ability, highly developed social skills, and precocity
   b. verbal ability, intensity, and a passion to master
   c. high reading level, marching to his own drummer, and stubbornness
   d. precocity, marching to his own drummer, and a passion to master

2. Research suggests that the best way to encourage children who are gifted to succeed in school is to
   a. promote a love of learning for its own sake.
   b. remind them of their parents' high expectations.
   c. promote a spirit of competition for rewards.
   d. employ them as peer teachers as much as possible.

3. The kindergarten student in Ms. Larson's class (item 1) continued to progress in school. In fourth grade, he finished third in his K–8 school's geography bee. He finished first in the next 2 years. In seventh grade, he finally took his first course in geography. He received C's. He often complained to his parents that he already knew the material being taught, that he wanted to learn "new stuff, not just listen to the same old junk." His teacher put a great deal of emphasis on completing map worksheets, which he completed very quickly and sloppily. He often became disruptive in class. How should the geography teacher handle this situation?
   a. The teacher should punish the student for disrupting class. The student should continue to do the same assignments as the other students, because he needs to understand that not all work is fun.
   b. The teacher should consider curriculum compacting, because he has already mastered the course content. Once challenged, his disruptive behavior is likely to diminish.
   c. The teacher should ask this student to become a co-teacher.
   d. The teacher should use the students' sloppy work as a negative example to the rest of the class.

Please see the answer key at the end of the book.

CRACK THE CASE?
The Case of Now What?

Before the school year starts, Ms. Inez always holds a "get acquainted meeting" with the parents of her incoming kindergartners. She does this so that she can explain what the children will be doing in kindergarten, her educational philosophy and expectations, the procedure for dropping students off at school the first day, and of course, to allow parents to ask any questions and share any concerns they might have. Inevitably, parents do have concerns and questions they would like addressed.

Here are some typical things she hears from parents:

"Joey still naps in the afternoon; can we have him changed to the morning class?"

"Ashley has severe asthma. She will need to have her nebulizer close in case she has an asthma attack. Do you know how to use one?"

"I just know that Steve won't be able to sit still for very long. Do you let the kids move a lot?"

"I hope you give the kids lots of active time. Bill won't be able to sit still for long either."

"Alex is very advanced for his age. What can you do to challenge him?"

"Amanda is advanced, too."

"So is my Timmy."

"Well, Peter seems to be behind. He doesn't speak very well."

Ms. Inez listens respectfully to each concern or question and assures the parents, "I'll do everything I can to ensure your children have a good year in my class. All children are different and learn at different rates, so don't be too worried about your child being a little bit behind or ahead. I think we'll all do fine together." As she is leaving for the evening, she chuckles at the number of parents who think their children are very advanced. It's the same every year—about a third of the parents are convinced that their child is the next Einstein.

The school year begins uneventfully. Ms. Inez uses the children's free-play time to observe them. Although there are obvious differences between the children, she doesn't notice that any of the children are truly exceptional, except perhaps for Harman and Rowan. Their lack of attention and inability to sit still during story time is beginning to be a bit disruptive. Ms. Inez makes a note to herself to talk to their parents about the possibility that they might have ADHD and recommend testing. Some other students might be candidates for this as well, including Alex. Although Ms. Inez has learned how to use Ashley's nebulizer, she hasn't needed to use it thus far.

Each day at the beginning of class, Ms. Inez marks off the day of the month on the calendar with a large X. She then writes a statement on the blackboard, describing the day's weather. On the tenth day of school she writes on the board, "Today is sunny and hot." She then reads the statement to the students so that they can begin to make word associations. "Today is sunny and warm." Alex shouts out, "That isn't what you wrote. You wrote today is sunny and hot." Ms. Inez is astounded. Later, during free-play time she asks Alex to sit with her. Alex looks longingly at the puzzles, but grudgingly complies. "Alex, will you read this book to me?"

"Sure," replies Alex, and he does so flawlessly.

Ms. Inez queries, "Do you have this book at home?"

Alex: "Yep. Lots of others, too."

Ms. Inez: "How about this one? Do you have it?"

Alex: "Nope."

Ms. Inez: "Well then, suppose you try to read this one to me."

Alex: "OK, but then can I go play with the puzzles?"

Ms. Inez: "Certainly."

Alex reads the book to Ms. Inez, missing only a few words, and then rushes off to play with the puzzles, build towers of blocks and knock them down, and play with trucks. The next day during calendar time Ms. Inez asks the class, "If today is the fifteenth day of the month and there are 30 days in the month, how could we find out how many days are left?"

The children call out, "We could count the days that don't have X's on them."

"Very good," replies Ms. Inez.

Alex looks puzzled. "What's wrong, Alex?" asks Ms. Inez. "Why don't we just subtract?" he asks.

1. What are the issues in this case?

2. Why do you suppose Ms. Inez makes light of parents' perceptions of their children's strengths?

3. How should Ms. Inez approach the parents of the students she thinks might have ADHD?

4. Is it appropriate for her to recommend testing of any of the children? Why or why not? Would it be appropriate for her to recommend a particular doctor for this testing? Why or why not?

5. If Alex can already read and subtract, are there other skills he has likely mastered? If so, what might they be? How might this impact his experiences in kindergarten?

6. How should Ms. Inez address this?

7. Which of the following is most likely true about Alex?
   a. Alex has a fluency disorder.
   b. Alex has a learning disability.
   e. Alex has ADHD.
   d. Alex is gifted.

Reach Your Learning Goals
Learners Who Are Exceptional

1 **WHO ARE CHILDREN WITH DISABILITIES?** Describe the various types of disabilities and disorders.

Learning Disabilities

Children with a learning disability have an IQ above the retarded range; they have significant difficulty in an academic area; and their difficulty is not attributable to some other diagnosed problem or disorder, such as sensory disabilities or severe emotional disorders. An estimated 13 percent of U.S. children between 3 and 21 years of age receive special education or related services. Slightly less than 45 percent of these students are classified as having a learning disability (in the federal classification, this includes attention deficit hyperactivity disorder [ADHD]). Substantial percentages of children with a disability have mental retardation, speech and language disorders, or a serious emotional disturbance. The term children with disabilities is now used rather than disabled children, and children with disabilities are no longer referred to as handicapped children. Diagnosing whether a child has a learning disability is difficult. About three times as many boys as girls have a learning disability. The most common academic problem for children with a learning disability is reading. Dyslexia is a severe impairment in the ability to read and spell. Dysgraphia is a learning disability that involves having difficulty in expressing thoughts in writing composition. Dyscalculia is a learning disability that involves difficulties in math computation. Controversy surrounds the "learning disability" category; some critics believe it is overdiagnosed; others argue that it is not. Diagnosis is difficult, especially for mild forms. Initial identification of children with a possible learning disability often is made by the classroom teacher, who then asks specialists to evaluate the child. Various causes of learning disabilities have been proposed. Many interventions targeted for learning disabilities focus on reading ability and include such strategies as improving decoding skills. The success of even the best-designed interventions depends on the training and skills of the teacher.

Attention Deficit Hyperactivity Disorder

Attention deficit hyperactivity disorder (ADHD) is a disability in which children consistently show problems in one or more of these areas: inattention, hyperactivity, and impulsivity. Although signs of ADHD may be present in early childhood, diagnosis of ADHD often doesn't occur until the elementary school years. Many experts recommend a combination of academic, behavioral, and medical interventions to help students with ADHD learn and adapt.

Mental Retardation

Mental retardation is a condition with an onset before age 18 that involves low intelligence (usually below 70 on an individually administered intelligence test) and difficulty in adapting to everyday life. Mental retardation has been classified in terms of four categories based mainly on IQ scores: mild, moderate, severe, and profound. More recently, a classification system based on degree of support required has been advocated. Causes of mental retardation include genetic factors (as in Down syndrome and fragile X syndrome), brain damage (which can result from many different infections, such as AIDS), and environmental hazards.

Physical Disorders

Among the physical disorders that students might have are orthopedic impairments (such as cerebral palsy) and seizure disorders (such as epilepsy).

Sensory Disorders

Sensory disorders include visual and hearing impairments. Visual impairments include having low vision and being educationally blind. An important task is to determine which modality (such as touch or hearing) the student who is visually impaired learns best in. A number of technological devices help these students learn. Educational strategies for students with hearing impairments fall into two main categories: oral and manual. Increasingly, both approaches are used with the same student in a total-communication approach.

continued

| Speech and Language Disorders |

Speech and language disorders include a number of speech problems (such as articulation disorders, voice disorders, and fluency disorders) and language problems (difficulties in receiving and expressing language). Articulation disorders are problems in pronouncing words correctly. Voice disorders are reflected in speech that is too hoarse, loud, high-pitched, or low-pitched. Children with cleft palate often have a voice disorder. Fluency disorders often involve what we commonly call "stuttering." Language disorders involve significant impairments in children's receptive or expressive language. Receptive language involves the reception and understanding of language. Expressive language involves using language for expressing one's thoughts and communicating with others. Specific language impairment (SLI) is another type of speech and language disorder that children may have.

| Austism Spectrum Disorders |

Autism is a severe disorder with an onset in the first 3 years of life, and it involves abnormalities in social relationships and communications. It also is characterized by repetitive behaviors. The current consensus is that autism involves an organic brain dysfunction. Autism spectrum disorder (ASD) is an increasingly popular term that refers to a broad range of autism disorders including the classical, severe form of autism, as well as Asperger syndrome.

| Emotional and Behavioral Disorders |

Emotional and behavioral disorders consist of serious, persistent problems that involve relationships, aggression, depression, fears associated with personal or school matters, and other inappropriate socioemotional characteristics. The term emotional disturbance (ED) recently has been used to describe this category of disorders, although it is not without criticism. In severe instances of aggressive, out-of-control behaviors, students are removed from the classroom. The problems are far more characteristic of boys than of girls. Problems involving depression, anxiety, and fear, involving turning problems inward are much more likely to appear in girls than in boys.

---

(2) **EDUCATIONAL ISSUES INVOLVING CHILDREN WITH DISABILITIES:** Explain the legal framework, as well as placements and supports for children with disabilities.

| Legal Aspects |

The educational rights for children with disabilities were laid down in the mid-1960s. In 1975, Congress enacted Public Law 94-142, the Education for All Handicapped Children Act, which mandated that all children be given a free, appropriate public education. Public Law 94-142 was recast in 1990 as the Individuals with Disabilities Education Act (IDEA), which spells out broad requirements for services to all children with disabilities. Children who are thought to have a disability are evaluated to determine their eligibility for services. The IDEA has many provisions that relate to the parents of children with disabilities. IDEA was amended in 1997 and then reauthorized in 2004 and renamed the Individuals with Disabilities Improvement Act. The 2004 version especially focuses on its alignment with No Child Left Behind legislation, which has raised questions about whether students with disabilities can be expected to meet the same general education standards and achievement as students without disabilities. The IEP is a written plan of the program specifically tailored for the child with a disability. The plan should (1) relate to the child's learning capacity, (2) be individualized and not a copy of a plan that is offered to other children, and (3) be designed to provide educational benefits. The concept of least restrictive environment (LRE) is contained in the IDEA. It states that children with disabilities must be educated in a setting that is as similar as possible to the one in which children without disabilities are educated. This provision of IDEA has given a legal basis to making an effort to educate children with disabilities in the regular classroom. The term inclusion means educating children with disabilities full-time in the regular classroom. The trend is toward using inclusion more. Children's academic and social success is affected more by the quality of instruction they receive than by where they are placed.

Placements, Services, and Parents as Educational Partners	The range of placements include regular classroom with supplementary instructional support provided in the regular classroom; part of the time spent in a resource room; full-time placement in a special education class; special schools; homebound instruction; and instruction in a hospital or another institution. Services include those provided by the classroom teacher in the regular classroom, those provided by a resource teacher (either in a separate resource room or in the regular classroom), those provided by a special education teacher, and other services provided by teacher aides, psychologists, collaborative consultants, and interactive teams. Some good communication strategies include letting parents know that you understand and appreciate their child's individuality; placing yourself in the parents' shoes; providing them with information about their child's disability; talking with, not to, parents; avoiding stereotypes; reaching out to establish and maintain contact with parents; and talking with parents about how the media sometimes erroneously portray children with disabilities.
Technology	Instructional technology includes various types of hardware and software, combined with innovative teaching methods, to accommodate children's needs in the classroom. Assistive technology consists of various services and devices to help children with disabilities function within their environment.

(3) **CHILDREN WHO ARE GIFTED:** Define what gifted means and discuss some approaches to teaching children who are gifted.

Characteristics	Children who are gifted have above-average intelligence (usually defined as an IQ of 130 or higher) and/or superior talent in some domain, such as art, music, or mathematics. Some critics argue that gifted programs include too many children who are just somewhat bright, usually cooperative, and, usually, non-Latino White. Winner described children who are gifted as having three main characteristics: precocity, marching to the tune of a different drummer, and a passion to master.
Life Course of the Gifted	Giftedness likely involves a combination of heredity and environment. Deliberate practice is often important in the achievement of the gifted. In Terman's study, many gifted children became successful achievers in adulthood, but most did not become major creators.
Educating Children Who Are Gifted	Educational programs available for children who are gifted include special classes ("pullout" programs), acceleration, enrichment, mentor and apprenticeship programs, as well as work/study or community service programs. Debate focuses on whether acceleration or enrichment programs most benefit children who are gifted. Children who are gifted increasingly are being educated in the regular classroom. Some experts recommend that increasing the standards in the regular classroom will help children who are gifted, although programs such as mentoring and additional instruction might be needed for children who are still underchallenged.

 KEY TERMS

disability 185
handicap 185
learning disability 185
dyslexia 187
dysgraphia 187
dyscalculia 187
attention deficit hyperactivity disorder (ADHD) 188
mental retardation 192
Down syndrome 193
fragile X syndrome 194

fetal alcohol syndrome (FAS) 194
orthopedic impairments 195
cerebral palsy 195
epilepsy 195
speech and language disorders 197
articulation disorders 197
voice disorders 198
fluency disorders 198
language disorders 198

receptive language 198
expressive language 198
specific language impairment (SLI) 198
autism spectrum disorders (ASD) 199
autistic disorder 199
Asperger syndrome 199
emotional and behavioral disorders 200
Public Law 94-142 205

Individuals with Disabilities Education Act (IDEA) 205
individualized education plan (IEP) 205
least restrictive environment (LRE) 206
inclusion 206
children who are gifted 215

PORTFOLIO ACTIVITIES

Now that you have a good understanding of this chapter, complete these exercises to expand your thinking.

Independent Reflection

Fostering Positive School-Home Linkages for Children with Disabilities. Place yourself in the role of a parent. Imagine that the school has just notified you that your child has a learning disability. Write down answers to these questions: (1) What feelings are you likely to be having as a parent? (2) As a parent, what questions do you want to ask the teacher? (3) Now put yourself in the role of the teacher. How would you respond to these questions? (INTASC: Principles *3, 10*)

Collaborative Work

Technology Resources for Gifted Students. Together with three or four other students in your class, come up with a list and description of software programs that you think would benefit gifted children. One good source of information on such software is the *Journal of Electronic Learning*. Write down the list and descriptions. (INTASC: Principles *3, 4, 9*)

Research/Field Experience

Inclusion in Action. Interview elementary school, middle school, and high school teachers about their impressions of inclusion and other aspects of educating children with disabilities. Ask them what their most successful strategies are in working with children who have disabilities. Also ask what the biggest challenges are. Write a summary of the interviews. (INTASC: Principle *9*)

Go to the Online Learning Center for downloadable portfolio templates.

 TAKING IT TO THE NET

- Teachers who work with special needs children typically develop an individualized education plan (IEP) for each child. What is an IEP? Review sample IEPs online, and discuss how all students could benefit from receiving the type of feedback present in an IEP. How could you use an IEP as a model for tailoring your instruction to the special needs of all students? **www.bced.gov.bc.ca/specialed/iepssn/**

- You recommend that a student be assessed for possible entry into your school's gifted program, but the school psychologist informs you that the child is a *C* student. Is it possible to be a "gifted underachiever"? Explain. **ericec.org/digests/darchives/e478.html**

- Imagine that you have two students in your classroom who have been diagnosed with ADHD. What are some strategies for helping these children succeed in the classroom? Why is family support so important, and what specific actions will you take to maintain ongoing communication with them? **www.ldonline.org/ld_indepth/add_adhd/tec_home_school_collab.html**

Connect to the Online Learning Center to explore possible answers.

 STUDY, PRACTICE, AND SUCCEED

Visit **www.mhhe.com/santedu3e** to review the chapter with self-grading quizzes and self-assessments, to apply the chapter material to two more Crack the Case studies, and for suggested activities to develop your teaching portfolio.

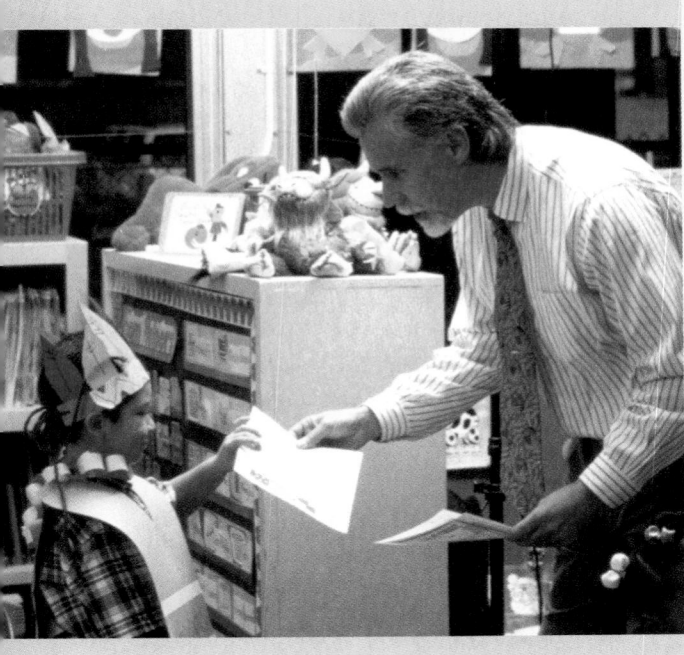

CHAPTER 7

Behavioral and Social Cognitive Approaches

To learn is a natural pleasure.

—Aristotle
Greek Philosopher, 4th Century B.C.

TEACHING STORIES   Ruth Sidney Charney

Ruth Sidney Charney has been a teacher for more than 35 years. She has developed the responsive classroom approach to teaching and learning, a method that emphasizes positive reinforcement of students' good behavior. Following are some of her thoughts about reinforcing students' learning (Charney, 2005, pp. 1–2):

> We reinforce children when we notice. We notice the personal detail our children bring to school and we notice their efforts to behave and learn. . . . We applaud the five correct answers on the math paper (when last week there were only two), the extra sentence in writing, the crisp adjectives, the ten minutes of fair play in a game. . . .
>
> We reinforce by noticing the positive attempts children make to follow the rules and meet class expectations. We reinforce when children are practicing new skills or when they demonstrate behaviors recently modeled. . . .
>
> Examples of noticing and reinforcing students include:

- "Today's the day, isn't it?" the teacher whispers to Hector. He smiles at her and they share a quick high-five salute, acknowledging Hector's impending solo performance in the church choir.
- "Snazzy new boots?" the teacher asks Leila as she struts into class. . . .
- "Thanks for helping Tessa with her spelling. I notice you gave her good hints so she could spell some of the words herself."
- "I noticed it took much less time today to get in line. What did you notice . . . ?"
- "I noticed you got your math done this morning with no interruption. That took lots of concentration. . . ."
- "Thank you for your very efficient clean-up today. I noticed caps back on markers, pencils with points down in cans, paper off the floor . . . ."
- "You really found an interesting way to solve the problem and complete the project together."

Preview

Virtually everyone agrees that helping students learn is an important function of schools. However, not everyone agrees on the best way to learn. We begin this chapter by examining just what learning involves, then turn to the main behavioral approaches to learning. Next we explore how behavioral principles are applied to educating students. In the final section, we will discuss the social cognitive approaches to learning.

1   WHAT IS LEARNING?

What Learning Is and Is Not   Approaches to Learning

Learning is a central focus of educational psychology. When people are asked what schools are for, a common reply is "To help children learn."

What Learning Is and Is Not

When children learn how to use a computer, they might make some mistakes along the way, but at a certain point they will get the knack of the behaviors required to use the computer effectively. The children will change from being individuals who cannot operate a computer into being individuals who can. Once they have learned how, they don't lose those skills. It's like learning to drive a car. Once you have learned how, you don't have to learn all over again. Thus, **learning** can be defined as a relatively permanent influence on behavior, knowledge, and thinking skills, which comes about through experience.

Not everything we know is learned. We inherit some capacities—they are inborn or innate, not learned. For example, we don't have to be taught to swallow, to flinch at loud noises, or to blink when an object comes too close to our eyes. Most human behaviors, however, do not involve heredity alone. When children use a computer in a new way, work harder at solving problems, ask better questions, explain an answer in a more logical way, or listen more attentively, the experience of learning is at work.

The scope of learning is broad (Chance, 2006; Domjan, 2006; Martin & Pear, 2007; Watson & Tharp, 2007). It involves academic behaviors and nonacademic behaviors. It occurs in schools and everywhere else that children experience their world.

Approaches to Learning

A number of approaches to learning have been proposed. Next we explore behavioral and cognitive approaches to learning.

Behavioral   The learning approaches that we discuss in the first part of this chapter are called *behavioral*. **Behaviorism** is the view that behavior should be explained by observable experiences, not by mental processes. For the behaviorist, behavior is everything that we do, both verbal and nonverbal, that can be directly observed: a child creating a poster, a teacher explaining something to a child, one student picking on another student, and so on. **Mental processes** are defined by psychologists as the thoughts, feelings, and motives that each of us experiences but that cannot be observed by others. Although we cannot directly see thoughts, feelings, and motives, they are no less real. Mental processes include children thinking about ways to create the best poster, a teacher feeling good about children's efforts, and children's inner motivation to control their behavior.

For the behaviorist, these thoughts, feelings, and motives are not appropriate subject matter for a science of behavior because they cannot be directly observed (Terry, 2006). Classical conditioning and operant conditioning, two behavioral views that we will discuss shortly, adopt this stance. Both of these views emphasize **associative learning,** which consists of learning that two events are connected or associated. For example, associative learning occurs when a student associates a pleasant event with learning something in school, such as the teacher smiling when the student asks a good question.

Cognitive   Cognition means "thought," and psychology became more cognitive or began focusing more on thought in the last part of the twentieth century. The cognitive emphasis continues today and is the basis for numerous approaches to learning (Bransford & others, 2005, Goldstein, 2006; Sawyer, 2006; Sternberg, 2006). We discuss four main cognitive approaches to learning in this book: social cognitive; cognitive information-processing; cognitive constructivist; and social constructivist. The *social cognitive* approaches, which emphasize how behavior, environment, and person (cognitive) factors interact to influence learning, will be covered later in this chapter (Bandura, 2005, 2006). The second set of approaches, *information-processing,* focuses on how children process information through attention, memory, thinking, and other cognitive processes (Munakata, 2006; Siegler, 2006). The third set of approaches, *cognitive constructivist,* emphasizes the child's cognitive construction of knowledge and understanding. The fourth set of cognitive approaches, *social constructivist,* focuses on collaboration with others to produce knowledge and understanding.

learning A relatively permanent influence on behavior, knowledge, and thinking skills, which comes about through experience.

behaviorism The view that behavior should be explained by observable experiences.

mental processes Thoughts, feelings, and motives that cannot be observed by others.

associative learning Learning that two events are connected (associated).

FIGURE 7.1 Approaches to Learning

Adding these four cognitive approaches to the behavioral approaches, we arrive at five main approaches to learning that we discuss in this book: behavioral, social cognitive, cognitive information-processing, cognitive constructivist, and social constructivist. All contribute to our understanding of how children learn. A summary of the five approaches is presented in figure 7.1.

As you read chapters 7 through 11 on learning and cognition, keep in mind that students are more likely to learn in optimal ways in appropriate learning environments. Students learn best when learning environments are "tailored to specific learning goals, to the students' backgrounds and prior knowledge, and to the contexts in which learning will occur. Thus teachers not only need to understand the basic principles of learning but must also know how, to use them judiciously to meet diverse learning goals in contexts where students' needs differ" (Bransford & others, 2005, p. 78).

Review, Reflect, and Practice

(1) Define learning and describe five approaches to studying it.

REVIEW

- Are there any behaviors that don't reflect learning? What is learning?
- What essentially is behaviorism? What are four main cognitive approaches to learning?

REFLECT

- How do you learn? Think of a behavior you engage in and describe how you learned it.

PRAXIS™ PRACTICE

1. According to the psychological definition of learning, all of the following are examples of learning *except*
   a. writing.
   b. sneezing.
   c. swimming.
   d. washing dishes.

2. Mr. Zeller does not believe his students have learned anything unless they demonstrate it to him. This demonstration could be through assignments they turn in to him, answering questions in class, or the way they behave. Which approach to learning is most consistent with Mr. Zeller's ideas?
   a. cognitive
   b. behavioral
   c. social cognitive
   d. conditioning

Please see the answer key at the end of the book.

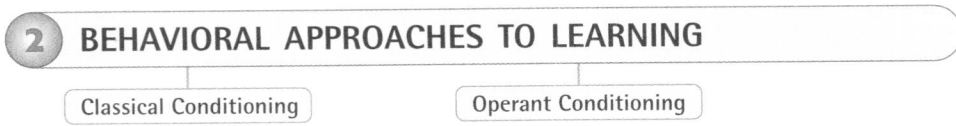

② BEHAVIORAL APPROACHES TO LEARNING

| Classical Conditioning | Operant Conditioning |

The behavioral approaches emphasize the importance of children making connections between experiences and behavior. The first behavioral approach we will examine is classical conditioning.

Classical Conditioning

In the early 1900s, Russian physiologist Ivan Pavlov was interested in the way the body digests food. In his experiments, he routinely placed meat powder in a dog's mouth, causing the dog to salivate. The dog salivated in response to a number of stimuli associated with the food, such as the sight of the food dish, the sight of the individual who brought the food into the room, and the sound of the door closing when the food arrived. Pavlov recognized that the dog's association of these sights and sounds with the food was an important type of learning, which came to be called *classical conditioning.* If a dog runs into the kitchen at the sound of the can opener, this is an example of classical conditioning.

Classical conditioning is a type of learning in which an organism learns to connect, or associate, stimuli. In classical conditioning, a neutral stimulus (such as the sight of a person) becomes associated with a meaningful stimulus (such as food) and acquires the capacity to elicit a similar response. To fully understand Pavlov's (1927) theory of classical conditioning we need to understand two types of stimuli and two types of responses: unconditioned stimulus (UCS), unconditioned response (UCR), conditioned stimulus (CS), and conditioned response (CR).

Figure 7.2 summarizes the way classical conditioning works. An *unconditioned stimulus (UCS)* is a stimulus that automatically produces a response without any prior learning. Food was the UCS in Pavlov's experiments. An *unconditioned response (UCR)* is an unlearned response that is automatically elicited by the UCS. In Pavlov's experiments, the dog's salivation in response to food was the UCR. A *conditioned stimulus (CS)* is a previously neutral stimulus that eventually elicits a conditioned response after being associated with the UCS. Among the conditioned stimuli in Pavlov's experiments were various sights and sounds that occurred prior to the dog's actually eating the food, such as the sound of the door closing before the food was placed in the dog's dish. A *conditioned response (CR)* is a learned response to the conditioned stimulus that occurs after UCS-CS pairing.

Classical conditioning can be involved in both positive and negative experiences of children in the classroom. Among the things in the child's schooling that produce

Ivan Pavlov (1849–1936), the Russian physiologist who developed the concept of classical conditioning.

classical conditioning A form of associative learning in which a neutral stimulus becomes associated with a meaningful stimulus and acquires the capacity to elicit a similar response.

FIGURE 7.2 Pavlov's Classical Conditioning

In one experiment, Pavlov presented a neutral stimulus (bell) just before an unconditioned stimulus (food). The neutral stimulus became a conditioned stimulus by being paired with the unconditioned stimulus. Subsequently, the conditioned stimulus (bell) by itself was able to elicit the dog's salivation.

FIGURE 7.3 Classical Conditioning Involved in Teachers' Criticism of Children and Tests

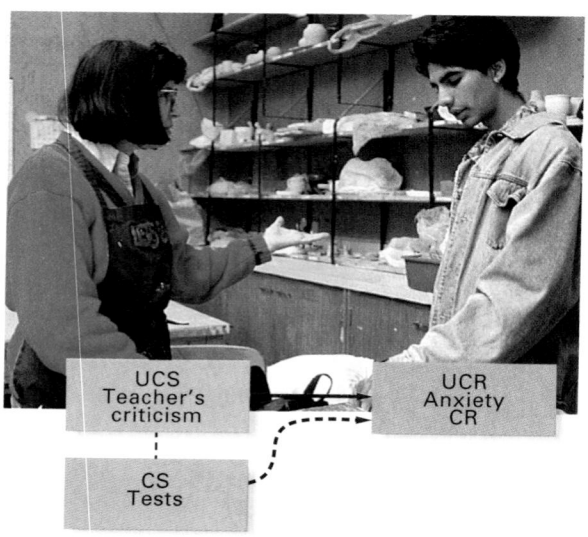

pleasure because they have become classically conditioned are a favorite song, feelings that the classroom is a safe and fun place to be, and a teacher's warmth and nurturing. For example, a song could be neutral for the child until the child joins in with other classmates to sing it with accompanying positive feelings.

Children can develop fear of the classroom if they associate the classroom with criticism, so the criticism becomes a CS for fear. Classical conditioning also can be involved in test anxiety. For example, a child fails and is criticized, which produces anxiety; thereafter, the child associates tests with anxiety, so they then can become a CS for anxiety (see figure 7.3).

Some children's health problems also might involve classical conditioning. Certain physical complaints—asthma, headaches, and high blood pressure—might be partly due to classical conditioning. We usually say that such health problems are caused by stress. Often what happens, though, is that certain stimuli, such as a parent's or teacher's heavy criticism, are conditioned stimuli for physiological responses. Over time, the frequency of the physiological responses can produce a health problem. A teacher's persistent criticism of a student can cause the student to develop headaches, muscle tension, and so on. Anything associated with the teacher, such as classroom learning exercises and homework, might trigger the student's stress and subsequently be linked with headaches or other physiological responses.

Generalization, Discrimination, and Extinction   In studying a dog's responses to various stimuli, Pavlov rang a bell before giving meat powder to the dog. By being paired with the UCS (meat), the bell became a CS and elicited the dog's salivation. After a time, Pavlov found that the dog also responded to other sounds, such as a whistle. The more bell-like the noise, the stronger the dog's response. *Generalization* in classical conditioning involves the tendency of a new stimulus similar to the original conditioned stimulus to produce a similar response. Let's consider a classroom example. A student is criticized for poor performance on a biology test. When the student begins to prepare for a chemistry test, she also becomes very nervous because these two subjects are closely related in the sciences. Thus, the student's anxiety generalizes from taking a test in one subject to taking a test in another.

Discrimination in classical conditioning occurs when the organism responds to certain stimuli but not others (Murphy, Baker, & Fouguet, 2001). To produce discrimination, Pavlov gave food to the dog only after ringing the bell, not after any other sounds. Subsequently, the dog responded only to the bell. In the case of the student taking tests in different classes, she doesn't become nearly as nervous about taking an English test or a history test because they are very different subject areas.

Extinction in classical conditioning involves the weakening of the conditioned response (CR) in the absence of the unconditioned stimulus (UCS). In one session, Pavlov rang the bell repeatedly but did not give the dog any food. Eventually the dog stopped salivating at the sound of the bell. Similarly, if the student who gets nervous while taking tests begins to do much better on tests, her anxiety will fade.

Systematic Desensitization   Sometimes the anxiety and stress associated with negative events can be eliminated by classical conditioning (Powell & Symbaluk, 2002). **Systematic desensitization** is a method based on classical conditioning that reduces anxiety by getting the individual to associate deep relaxation with successive visualizations of increasingly anxiety-producing situations. Imagine that you have a student in your class who is extremely nervous about talking in front of the class. The goal of systematic desensitization is to get the student to associate public speaking with relaxation, such as walking on a quiet beach, rather than anxiety. Using successive visualizations, the student might practice systematic desensitization two weeks before the talk, then a week before, four days before, two days before, the day before, the morning of the talk, on entering the room where the talk is to be given, on the way to the podium, and during the talk.

Desensitization involves a type of counterconditioning (McNeil, 2000). The relaxing feelings that the student imagines (UCS) produce relaxation (UCR). The student then associates anxiety-producing cues (CS) with the relaxing feelings. Such relaxation is incompatible with anxiety. By initially pairing a weak anxiety-producing cue with relaxation and gradually working up the hierarchy (from two weeks before the talk to walking up to the podium to give the talk), all of the anxiety-producing cues should generate relaxation (CR).

Chances are you will have students who fear speaking in front of the class or have other anxieties, and there may be circumstances in your own life where you might benefit from replacing anxiety with relaxation. For example, it is not unusual for some teachers to feel comfortable when talking in front of their students but to get very nervous if asked to give a presentation at a teaching conference. Counselors and mental health professionals have been very successful at getting individuals to overcome their fear of public speaking using systematic desensitization. Should you be interested in adopting this strategy, do it with the help of a school psychologist rather than on your own.

Evaluating Classical Conditioning   Classical conditioning helps us understand some aspects of learning better than others. It excels in explaining how neutral stimuli become associated with unlearned, involuntary responses (LoLordo, 2000; Miller, 2006). It is especially helpful in understanding students' anxieties and fears. However,

systematic desensitization A method based on classical conditioning that reduces anxiety by getting the individual to associate deep relaxation with successive visualizations of increasingly anxiety-provoking situations.

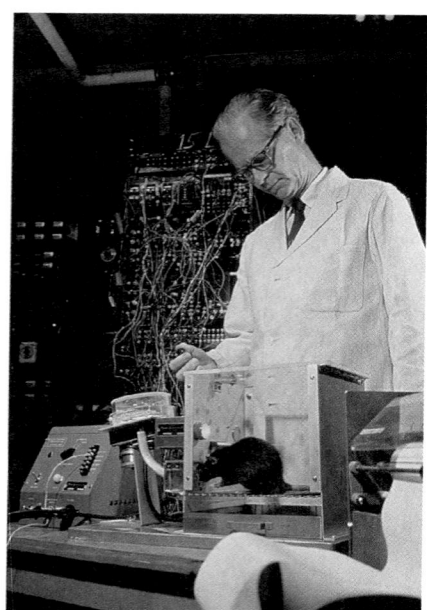

B. F. Skinner conducting an operant conditioning study in his behavioral laboratory. The rat being studied is in a Skinner box.

operant conditioning Also called instrumental conditioning, this is a form of learning in which the consequences of behavior produce changes in the probability that the behavior will occur.

law of effect The principle that behaviors followed by positive outcomes are strengthened and that behaviors followed by negative outcomes are weakened.

reinforcement (reward) A consequence that increases the probability that a behavior will occur.

punishment A consequence that decreases the probability that a behavior will occur.

positive reinforcement reinforcement based on the principle that the frequency of a response increases because it is followed by a rewarding stimulus.

negative reinforcement Reinforcement based on the principle that the frequency of a response increases because an aversive (unpleasant) stimulus is removed.

it is not as effective in explaining voluntary behaviors, such as why a student studies hard for a test or likes history better than geography. For these areas, operant conditioning is more relevant.

Operant Conditioning

Our examination of operant conditioning begins with a general definition, then turns to the views of Thorndike and Skinner.

Operant conditioning (also called *instrumental conditioning*) is a form of learning in which the consequences of behavior produce changes in the probability that the behavior will occur. Operant conditioning's main architect was B. F. Skinner, whose views built on the connectionist views of E. L. Thorndike.

Thorndike's Law of Effect   At about the same time that Ivan Pavlov was conducting classical conditioning experiments with dogs, American psychologist E. L. Thorndike (1906) was studying cats in puzzle boxes. Thorndike placed a hungry cat inside a box and put a piece of fish outside. To escape from the box, the cat had to learn how to open the latch inside the box. At first the cat made a number of ineffective responses. It clawed or bit at the bars and thrust its paw through the openings. Eventually the cat accidentally stepped on the treadle that released the door bolt. When the cat was returned to the box, it went through the same random activity until it stepped on the treadle once more. On subsequent trials, the cat made fewer and fewer random movements, until it immediately clawed the treadle to open the door. Thorndike's **law of effect** states that behaviors followed by positive outcomes are strengthened and that behaviors followed by negative outcomes are weakened.

The key question for Thorndike was how the correct stimulus-response (S-R) bond strengthens and eventually dominates incorrect stimulus-response bonds. According to Thorndike, the correct S-R association is strengthened, and the incorrect association is weakened, because of the consequences of the organism's actions. Thorndike's view is called *S-R theory* because the organism's behavior is due to a connection between a stimulus and a response. As we see next, Skinner's approach significantly expanded on Thorndike's basic ideas.

Skinner's Operant Conditioning   Operant conditioning, in which the consequences of behavior lead to changes in the probability that the behavior will occur, is at the heart of B. F. Skinner's (1938) behaviorism. Consequences—rewards or punishments—are contingent on the organism's behavior.

Reinforcement and Punishment   **Reinforcement (reward)** is a consequence that increases the probability that a behavior will occur. In contrast, **punishment** is a consequence that decreases the probability a behavior will occur. For example, you might tell one of your students, "Congratulations. I'm really proud of the story that you wrote." If the student works harder and writes an even better story the next time, your positive comments are said to reinforce, or reward, the student's writing behavior. If you frown at a student for talking in class and the student's talking decreases, your frown is said to punish the student's talking.

To reinforce behavior means to strengthen the behavior. Two forms of reinforcement are positive reinforcement and negative reinforcement. In **positive reinforcement,** the frequency of a response increases because it is followed by a rewarding stimulus, as in the example in which the teacher's positive comments increased the student's writing behavior. Similarly, complimenting parents on being at a parent-teacher conference might encourage them to come back again.

Conversely, in **negative reinforcement,** the frequency of a response increases because it is followed by the removal of an aversive (unpleasant) stimulus (Frieman, 2002). For example, a father nags at his son to do his homework. He keeps nagging. Finally, the son gets tired of hearing the nagging and does his homework. The son's response (doing his homework) removed the unpleasant stimulus (nagging).

Positive Reinforcement	**Negative Reinforcement**	**Punishment**
BEHAVIOR		
Student asks a good question	Student turns homework in on time	Student interrupts teacher
CONSEQUENCE		
Teacher praises student	Teacher stops criticizing student	Teacher verbally reprimands student
FUTURE BEHAVIOR		
Student asks more good questions	Student increasingly turns homework in on time	Student stops interrupting teacher

Remember that reinforcement comes in positive and negative forms. In both forms, the consequences increase behavior. In punishment, behavior is decreased.

FIGURE 7.4 Reinforcement and Punishment

One way to remember the distinction between positive and negative reinforcement is that in positive reinforcement something is added. In negative reinforcement, something is subtracted, or removed. It is easy to confuse negative reinforcement and punishment. To keep these terms straight, remember that negative reinforcement *increases* the probability a response will occur, while punishment *decreases* the probability it will occur. Figure 7.4 summarizes and presents examples of the concepts of positive reinforcement, negative reinforcement, and punishment.

Generalization, Discrimination, and Extinction   In our coverage of classical conditioning, we discussed generalization, discrimination, and extinction. These processes also are important dimensions of operant conditioning (Hergenhan & Olson, 2001; Martin & Pear, 2007). Remember that in classical conditioning, generalization is the tendency of a stimulus similar to the conditioned stimulus to produce a response similar to the conditioned response. *Generalization* in operant conditioning means giving the same response to similar stimuli. Especially of interest is the extent to which behavior generalizes from one situation to another. For example, if a teacher praises the student for asking good questions related to English, will this generalize to harder work in history, math, and other subjects?

Remember that in classical conditioning, discrimination means responding to certain stimuli but not others. *Discrimination* in operant conditioning involves differentiating among stimuli or environmental events. For example, a student knows that the tray on the teacher's desk labeled "Math" is where she is supposed to place today's math work, while another tray labeled "English" is where today's English assignments are to be put. This might sound overly simple, but it is important because students' worlds are filled with such discriminative stimuli. Around school these discriminative stimuli might include signs that say "Stay Out," "Form a Line Here," and so on.

In operant conditioning, *extinction* occurs when a previously reinforced response is no longer reinforced and the response decreases. In the classroom, the most common use of extinction is for the teacher to withdraw attention from a behavior that the attention is maintaining. For example, in some cases a teacher's attention inadvertently reinforces a student's disruptive behavior, as when a student pinches another student and the teacher immediately talks with the perpetrator. If this happens on a regular basis, the student might learn that pinching other students is a good way to get the teacher's attention. If the teacher withdraws his attention, the pinching might extinguish.

Review, Reflect, and Practice

② **Compare classical conditioning and operant conditioning.**

REVIEW

- What is classical conditioning? Create your own example to illustrate the relationship among UCS, UCR, CS, and CR. In the context of classical conditioning, what is generalization, discrimination, extinction, and desensitization?
- How is operant conditioning related to Thorndike's law of effect? Explain the different types of reinforcement and punishment. In the context of operant conditioning, what is generalization, discrimination, and extinction?

REFLECT

- Do you think that your emotions are the result of classical conditioning, operant conditioning, or both? Explain.

PRAXIS™ PRACTICE

1. Sylvia is participating in a class spelling bee. The teacher asks her to spell the word *mortgage*. "Don't forget the *t*, don't forget the *t*," Sylvia says to herself. "M-O-R-T-A-G-E," says Sylvia. "I'm sorry, that's incorrect, Sylvia," says her teacher. One of the students in the back of the class snickers and comments, "Gee, about time Miss Smarty-pants got one wrong. See she's not so smart." Some other students join in the laughter. Sylvia begins to cry and runs out of the room. After that, Sylvia becomes very anxious about spelling bees. According to classical conditioning theory, what is the conditioned stimulus in this scenario?
   a. the teacher telling her she is incorrect
   b. the other students' laughter
   c. the word *mortgage*
   d. spelling bees

2. Tyler is a fourth-grade student. He loves to crack jokes, often at his teacher's expense. One day he called his teacher, Ms. Bart, "Ms. Fart." Ms. Bart quickly admonished him for his behavior and told him that name-calling was unacceptable. She made him stay after school to discuss his behavior. The other students in the class thought Tyler's nickname for Ms. Bart was hilarious, laughing along with Tyler and later telling him what a good name that was for Ms. Bart. The next day, Tyler again called Ms. Bart by the insulting nickname. According to operant conditioning theory, Tyler continued to use this name in spite of having to stay after school the day before because
   a. the behavior had continued for a lengthy period of time.
   b. he was positively reinforced by his classmates for the behavior.
   c. he was negatively reinforced by his teacher for his behavior.
   d. he was punished by his teacher for his behavior.

Please see the answer key at the end of the book.

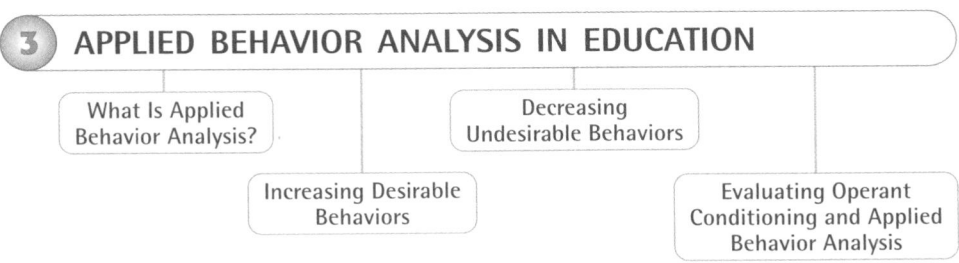

3 APPLIED BEHAVIOR ANALYSIS IN EDUCATION

- What Is Applied Behavior Analysis?
- Increasing Desirable Behaviors
- Decreasing Undesirable Behaviors
- Evaluating Operant Conditioning and Applied Behavior Analysis

Many applications of operant conditioning have been made outside of research laboratories in the wider worlds of classrooms, homes, business settings, hospitals, and other real-world settings (Heward & others, 2005; Lutzker & Whitaker, 2005; Miller, 2006; Umbreit & others, 2007). This section describes how teachers can use applied behavior analysis to improve students' behavior and learning.

What Is Applied Behavior Analysis?

Applied behavior analysis involves applying the principles of operant conditioning to change human behavior. Three uses of applied behavior analysis are especially important in education: increasing desirable behavior, using prompts and shaping, and decreasing undesirable behavior (Alberto & Troutman, 2006). Applications of applied behavior analysis often use a series of steps (Hazel & Gredler, 2005; Miller, 2006; Zirpoli, 2005). These often begin with some general observations and then turn to determining the specific target behavior that needs to be changed, as well as observing its antecedent conditions. Behavioral goals are then set, particular reinforcers or punishers are selected, a behavior management program is carried out, and the success or failure of the program is evaluated (Kerr & Nelson, 2006).

Increasing Desirable Behaviors

Six operant conditioning strategies can be used to increase a child's desirable behaviors: choose effective reinforcers; make reinforcers contingent and timely; select the best schedule of reinforcement; consider contracting; use negative reinforcement effectively; and use prompts and shaping.

Choose Effective Reinforcers   Not all reinforcers are the same for every child. Applied behavior analysts recommend that teachers find out what reinforcers work best with which children—that is, individualize the use of particular reinforcers. For one student it might be praise, for another it might be getting to spend more time participating in a favorite activity, for another it might involve being a hall monitor for a week, and for yet another it could be getting to surf the Internet. To find out the most effective reinforcers for a child, you can examine what has motivated the child in the past (reinforcement history), what the student wants but can't easily or frequently get, and the child's perception of the reinforcer's value. Some applied behavior analysts recommend asking children which reinforcers they like best (Raschke, 1981). Another recommendation is to consider novel reinforcers to reduce the child's boredom. Natural reinforcers such as praise and privileges are generally recommended over material rewards such as candy, stars, and money.

Activities are some of the most common reinforcers that teachers use. Named after psychologist David Premack, the **Premack principle** states that a high-probability

applied behavior analysis Application of the principles of operant conditioning to change human behavior.

Premack principle The principle that a high-probability activity can serve as a reinforcer for a low-probability activity.

"Once it became clear to me that, by responding correctly to certain stimuli, I could get all the bananas I wanted, getting this job was a pushover."

activity can serve as a reinforcer for a low-probability activity. The Premack principle is at work when an elementary school teacher tells a child, "When you complete your writing assignment, you can play a game on the computer" (but only effective if playing games on a computer is more desirable for the student than writing). The Premack principle also can be used with the entire class. A teacher might tell the class, "If all of the class gets their homework done by Friday, we will take a field trip next week."

Make Reinforcers Contingent and Timely   For a reinforcer to be effective, the teacher must give it only after the child performs the particular behavior. Applied behavior analysts often recommend that teachers make "If . . . then" statements to children—for example, "Tony, if you finish ten math problems, then you can go out to play." This makes it clear to Tony what he has to do to get the reinforcer. Applied behavior analysts say that it is important to make the reinforcer contingent on the child's behavior. That is, the child has to perform the behavior to get the reward. If Tony does not complete ten math problems and the teacher still lets him go out to play, the contingency has not been established.

Reinforcers are more effective when they are given in a timely way, as soon as possible after the child performs the target behavior (Umbreit & others, 2007). This helps children see the contingency connection between the reward and their behavior. If the child completes the target behavior (such as doing ten math problems by midmorning) and the teacher doesn't give the child playtime until late afternoon, the child might have trouble making the contingency connection.

Select the Best Schedule of Reinforcement   Most of the examples given so far assume continuous reinforcement—that is, the child is reinforced every time he or she makes a response. In continuous reinforcement, children learn very rapidly, but when the reinforcement stops (the teacher stops praising), extinction also occurs rapidly. In the classroom, continuous reinforcement is rare. A teacher with a classroom of twenty-five or thirty students can't praise a child every time she makes an appropriate response.

Partial reinforcement involves reinforcing a response only part of the time. Skinner (1957) developed the concept of **schedules of reinforcement,** which are partial reinforcement timetables that determine when a response will be reinforced. The four main schedules of reinforcement are fixed-ratio, variable-ratio, fixed-interval, and variable-interval.

On a *fixed-ratio schedule,* a behavior is reinforced after a set number of responses. For example, a teacher might praise the child only after every fourth correct response, not after every response. On a *variable-ratio schedule,* a behavior is reinforced after an average number of times, but on an unpredictable basis. For example, a teacher's praise might average out to being given every fifth response but be given after the second correct response, after eight more correct responses, after the next seven correct responses, and after the next three correct responses.

Interval schedules are determined by the amount of time elapsed since the last behavior was reinforced. On a *fixed-interval schedule,* the first appropriate response after a fixed amount of time is reinforced. For example, a teacher might praise a child for the first good question the child asks after two minutes have elapsed or give a quiz every week. On a *variable-interval schedule,* a response is reinforced after a variable amount of time has elapsed. On this schedule, the teacher might praise the child's question-asking after three minutes have gone by, then after fifteen minutes have gone by, after seven minutes have gone by, and so on. Giving a pop quiz at uneven intervals is another example of a variable-interval schedule.

What is the effect of using these schedules of reinforcement with children?

- Initial learning is usually faster with continuous rather than partial reinforcement. In other words, when students are first learning a behavior, continuous reinforcement works better. However, partial reinforcement produces greater

schedules of reinforcement Partial reinforcement timetables that determine when a response will be reinforced.

persistence and greater resistance to extinction than continuous reinforcement does. Thus, once children master a response, partial reinforcement works better than continuous reinforcement.

- Children on fixed schedules show less persistence and faster response extinction than children on variable schedules. Children show the most persistence on a variable-interval schedule. This schedule produces slow, steady responding because children don't know when the reward will come. As we mentioned earlier, giving pop quizzes at uneven intervals is a good example of the variable-interval schedule. If the teacher starts making the quizzes more predictable (for example, once a week on Fridays), children will begin to show the stop-start work pattern that characterizes the fixed-interval schedule. That is, they won't work hard for most of the week; then toward the end of the week they will start cramming for the quiz. Thus, if your goal as a teacher is to increase children's persistence after the behavior has been established, variable schedules work best, especially the variable-interval schedule. Figure 7.5 shows the different response patterns associated with the different schedules of reinforcement.

FIGURE 7.5 Schedules of Reinforcement and Different Patterns of Responding

In this figure, each hash mark indicates the delivery of reinforcement. Notice that ratio schedules (reinforcement is linked with number of responses) produce higher rates of responding than interval schedules (reinforcement is linked with the amount of time elapsed). The predictability of a reward also is important in that a predictable (fixed) schedule produces a higher response rate than an unpredictable (variable) schedule.

Consider Contracting   **Contracting** involves putting reinforcement contingencies in writing. If problems arise and children don't uphold their end of the bargain, the teacher can refer the children to the contract they agreed to. Applied behavior analysts suggest that a classroom contract should be the result of input from both the teacher and the student. Classroom contracts have "If . . . then" statements and are signed by the teacher and child, then dated. A teacher and child might agree on a contract that states that the child agrees to be a good citizen by doing _____, _____, and _____. As part of the contract, the teacher agrees to _____ if the student behaves in this manner. In some instances, the teacher asks another child to sign the contract as a witness to the agreement.

Use Negative Reinforcement Effectively   Remember that in *negative reinforcement,* the frequency of response increases because the response removes an aversive (unpleasant) stimulus (Alberto & Troutman, 2006). A teacher who says, "Thomas, you have to stay in your seat and finish writing your story before you join the other students in making a poster," is using negative reinforcement. The negative condition of being left in his seat while the other children are doing something enjoyable will be removed if Thomas finishes the story he should have completed earlier.

Using negative reinforcement has some drawbacks. Sometimes when teachers try to use this behavioral strategy, children throw a tantrum, run out of the room, or destroy materials. These negative outcomes happen most often when children don't have the skills or capabilities to do what the teacher asks of them.

Use Prompts and Shaping   Earlier in our discussion of operant conditioning, we indicated that discrimination involves differentiating among stimuli or environmental events. Students can learn to discriminate among stimuli or events through differential reinforcement. Two differential reinforcement strategies available to teachers are prompts and shaping (Alberto & Troutman, 2006).

Prompts   A **prompt** is an added stimulus or cue that is given just before a response that increases the likelihood that the response will occur. A reading teacher who holds up a card with the letters *w-e-r-e* and says, "Not was, but . . ." is using a verbal prompt.

contracting Putting reinforcement contingencies into writing.

prompt An added stimulus or cue that is given just before a response and increases the likelihood the response will occur.

An art teacher who places the label *watercolors* on one group of paints and *oils* on another also is using prompts. Prompts help get behavior going. Once the students consistently show the correct responses, the prompts are no longer needed.

Instructions can be used as prompts (Alberto & Troutman, 2006). For example, as the art period is drawing to a close, the teacher says, "Let's get started on reading." If the students keep doing art, the teacher adds the prompt, "Okay, put away your art materials and come with me over to the reading area." Some prompts come in the form of hints, as when the teacher tells students to line up "quietly." Bulletin boards are common locations for prompts, frequently displaying reminders of class rules, due dates for projects, the location of a meeting, and so on. Some prompts are presented visually, as when the teacher places her hand on her ear when a student is not speaking loudly enough.

Shaping   When teachers use prompts, they assume that students can perform the desired behaviors. But sometimes students do not have the ability to perform them. In this case, shaping is required. **Shaping** involves teaching new behaviors by reinforcing successive approximations to a specified target behavior. Initially, you reinforce any response that in some way resembles the target behavior. Subsequently, you reinforce a response that more closely resembles the target, and so on until the student performs the target behavior, and then you reinforce it (Chance, 2006).

Suppose you have a student who has never completed 50 percent or more of her math assignments. You set the target behavior at 100 percent, but you reinforce her for successive approximations to the target. You initially might provide a reinforcer (some type of privilege, for example) when she completes 60 percent, then the next time only when she completes 70 percent, then 80, then 90, and finally 100 percent.

Shaping can be an important tool for the classroom teacher because most students need reinforcement along the way to reaching a learning goal. Shaping can be especially helpful for learning tasks that require time and persistence to complete. However, when using shaping, remember to implement it only if the other types of positive reinforcement and prompts are not working. Also remember to be patient. Shaping can require the reinforcement of a number of small steps en route to a target behavior, and these might take place only over an extended period of time.

Decreasing Undesirable Behaviors

When teachers want to decrease children's undesirable behaviors (such as teasing, hogging a class discussion, or smarting off to the teacher), what are their options? Applied behavior analysts Paul Alberto and Anne Troutman (2006) recommend using these steps in this order:

1. Use differential reinforcement.
2. Terminate reinforcement (extinction).
3. Remove desirable stimuli.
4. Present aversive stimuli (punishment).

Thus, the teacher's first option should be differential reinforcement. Punishment should be used only as a last resort and always in conjunction with providing the child information about appropriate behavior.

Use Differential Reinforcement   In *differential reinforcement*, the teacher reinforces behavior that is more appropriate or that is incompatible with what the child is doing. For example, the teacher might reinforce a child for doing learning activities on a computer rather than playing games with it, for being courteous rather than

shaping Teaching new behaviors by reinforcing successive approximations to a specified target behavior.

BEST PRACTICES
Strategies for Using Time-Out

In using time-out, you have several options:

1. *Keep the student in the classroom, but deny the student access to positive reinforcement.* This strategy is most often used when a student does something minor. The teacher might ask the student to put his head down on the desk for a few minutes or might move the student to the periphery of an activity so the student can still observe other students experiencing positive reinforcement. Next, kindergarten teacher Rosemary Moore describes an innovative use of time-out.

THROUGH THE EYES OF TEACHERS
The Peace Place

Resolving conflicts is always difficult for children. When my kindergartners engaged in power struggles, they often turned to me to referee. I thought it would be much more beneficial if they could arrive at their own compromise. Ownership of the plan would make it more acceptable to all parties. To accomplish this, I put two small chairs in a corner of the room. Above the chairs was a sign that said, "Peace Place." Then when I heard a struggle begin, I would send the parties to this corner. There they sat facing each other with their knees almost touching. Their task was to negotiate a "peace plan." When the plan was agreed upon, they were to come to me. I would listen to their plan and either approve it or send them back for another try. Initially, this took some time, but as the children began to realize that the time they spent arguing was time away from the activity they

were arguing about, they arrived at their plan much more quickly. It was a pleasure to watch them grow in their negotiating abilities.

---

2. *For time-out to be effective, the setting from which the student is removed has to be positively reinforcing, and the setting in which the student is placed has to not be positively reinforcing.* For example, if you seat a student in the hall outside your classroom and students from other classes come down the hall and talk with the student, the time-out is clearly not going to serve its intended purpose.

3. *If you use time-out, be sure to identify the student's behaviors that resulted in time-out.* For example, say to the student, "You tore up Corey's paper, so go to time-out right now for five minutes." Don't get into an argument with the student or accept lame excuses as to why the student should not get a time-out. If necessary, take the student to the time-out location. If the misbehavior occurs again, reidentify it and place the student in a time-out again. If the student starts yelling, knocking over furniture, and so on when you assess time-out, add time to time-out. Be sure to let the student out of time-out when the designated time away from positive reinforcement is up. Don't comment on how well the student behaved during time-out; just return the student to the prior activity.

4. *Keep records of each time-out session, especially if a time-out room is used.* This will help you monitor effective and ethical use of time-outs.

---

interrupting, for being seated rather than running around the classroom, or for doing homework on time rather than late.

Terminate Reinforcement (Extinction) The strategy of terminating reinforcement involves withdrawing positive reinforcement from a child's inappropriate behavior. Many inappropriate behaviors are inadvertently maintained by positive reinforcement, especially the teacher's attention. Applied behavior analysts point out that this can occur even when the teacher gives attention to an inappropriate behavior by criticizing, threatening, or yelling at the student. Many teachers find it difficult to determine whether they are giving too much attention to inappropriate behavior. A good strategy is to get someone to observe your classroom on several occasions and chart the patterns of reinforcement you use with your students (Alberto & Troutman, 2006). If you become aware that you are giving too much attention to a student's inappropriate behavior, ignore that behavior and give attention to the student's appropriate behavior. Always combine taking attention away from inappropriate behavior with giving attention to appropriate behavior. For

This second-grade student has been placed in "time-out" for misbehaving. *What is the nature of time out?*

Country	Mean score (5 point scale)
Canada	3.14
United States	3.13
South Korea	3.00
Malaysia	2.90
Great Britian	2.68
Finland	2.34
Greece	2.26
Germany	2.13
Spain	2.05
Argentina	1.96
Sweden	1.35

FIGURE 7.6 Attitudes about Corporal Punishment in Different Countries

A 5-point scale was used to assess attitudes toward corporal punishment, with scores closer to 1 indicating an attitude against its use and scores closer to 5 suggesting an attitude for its use.

time-out Removing an individual from positive reinforcement.

response cost Taking a positive reinforcer away from an individual.

instance, when a student stops monopolizing the conversation in a group discussion after you withdraw your attention, compliment the student on the improved behavior.

Remove Desirable Stimuli Suppose you have tried the first two options, and they haven't worked. A third option is to remove desirable stimuli from the student. Two strategies for accomplishing this are "time-out" and "response cost."

Time-Out The most widely used strategy that teachers use to remove desirable stimuli is **time-out.** In other words, take the student away from positive reinforcement.

Response Cost A second strategy for removing desirable stimuli involves **response cost,** which refers to taking a positive reinforcer away from a student, as when the student loses certain privileges. For example, after a student misbehaves, the teacher might take away 10 minutes of recess time or the privilege of being a class monitor. Response cost typically involves some type of penalty or fine. As with the time-out, response cost should always be used in conjunction with strategies for increasing the student's positive behaviors.

Present Aversive Stimuli (Punishment) Most people associate the presentation of aversive (unpleasant) stimuli with punishment, as when a teacher yells at a student or a parent spanks a child. However, in accordance with the definition of punishment given earlier in the chapter, an aversive stimulus is punishment only if it decreases the undesirable behavior (Branch, 2000; Mazur, 2002). All too often, though, aversive stimuli are not effective punishments, in that they do not decrease the unwanted behavior and indeed sometimes increase the unwanted behavior over time. One recent study found that when parents used spanking to discipline 4- to 5-year-old children, the problem behavior increased over time (McLoyd & Smith, 2002). Another recent longitudinal study found that spanking before age 2 was related to behavioral problems in middle and late childhood (Slade & Wissow, 2004).

The most common types of aversive stimuli that teachers use are verbal reprimands. These are more effectively used when the teacher is near the student rather than across the room and when used together with a nonverbal reprimand such as a frown or eye contact (Van Houten & others, 1982). Reprimands are more effective when they are given immediately after unwanted behavior and when they are short and to the point. Such reprimands do not have to involve yelling and shouting, which often just raise the noise level of the classroom and present the teacher as an uncontrolled model for students. Instead, a firmly stated "stop doing that" with eye contact is often sufficient to stop unwanted behavior. Another strategy is to take the student aside and reprimand the student in private rather than in front of the entire class.

Many countries, such as Sweden, have banned the physical punishment of schoolchildren (which usually involves school paddling) by principals and teachers. However, in 2003, 23 U.S. states still allowed it with the greatest prevalence in southern states. One recent study of college students in 11 countries found that the United States and Canada have more favorable attitudes toward corporal punishment than many other countries (Curran & others, 2001; Hyman & others, 2001) (see figure 7.6). Use of corporal punishment by parents is legal in every state in America, and it is estimated that 70 to 90 percent of American parents have spanked their children (Straus, 1991). A recent national survey of U.S. parents with 3- and 4-year-old children found that 26 percent of parents reported spanking their children frequently, and 67 percent of the parents reported yelling at their children frequently (Regaldo & others, 2004).

In U.S. schools, male minority students from low-income backgrounds are the most frequent recipients of physical punishment. Most psychologists and educators argue that physical punishment of students should not be used in any circumstance.

Physical or otherwise, numerous problems are associated with using aversive stimuli as intended punishment (Hyman, 1997; Hyman & Snook, 1999):

- Especially when you use intense punishment such as yelling or screaming, you are presenting students with an out-of-control model for handling stressful situations (Sim & Ong, 2005).
- Punishment can instill fear, rage, or avoidance in students. Skinner's biggest concern was this: What punishment teaches is how to avoid something. For example, a student who experiences a punitive teacher might show a dislike for the teacher and not want to come to school.
- When students are punished, they might become so aroused and anxious that they can't concentrate clearly on their work for a long time after the punishment has been given.
- Punishment tells students what not to do rather than what to do. If you make a punishing statement, such as "No, that's not right," always accompany it with positive feedback, such as "but why don't you try this."
- What is intended as punishment can turn out to be reinforcing. A student might learn that misbehaving will not only get the teacher's attention but put the student in the limelight with classmates as well.
- Punishment can be abusive. When parents discipline their children, they might not intend to be abusive but they might become so aroused when they are punishing the child that they become abusive (Ateah, 2005; Baumrind, Larzelere, & Cowan, 2002).

A final lesson in all of this is to spend a lot more class time monitoring what students do right rather than what they do wrong (Maag, 2001). Too often disruptive behavior, not competent behavior, grabs a teacher's attention. Every day make it a point to scan your classroom for positive student behaviors that you ordinarily would not notice and give students attention for them.

Evaluating Operant Conditioning and Applied Behavior Analysis

Operant conditioning and applied behavior analysis have made contributions to teaching practice (Kazdin, 2001; Martin & Pear, 2007; Purdy & others, 2001). Reinforcing and punishing consequences are part of teachers' and students' lives. Teachers give grades, praise and reprimand, smile and frown. Learning about how such consequences affect students' behavior improves your capabilities as a teacher. Used effectively, behavioral techniques can help you manage your classroom. Reinforcing certain behaviors can improve some students' conduct and—used in conjunction with the time-out—can increase desired behaviors in some incorrigible students (Charles, 2005; Kauffman & others, 2005).

Critics of operant conditioning and applied behavior analysis argue that the whole approach places too much emphasis on external control of students' behavior—a better strategy is to help students learn to control their own behavior and become internally motivated. Some critics argue that it is not the reward or punishment that changes behavior but, rather, the belief or expectation that certain actions will be rewarded or punished (Schunk, 2004). In other words, the behavioral theories do not give adequate attention to cognitive processes involved in learning. Critics also point to potential ethical problems when operant conditioning is used inappropriately, as when a teacher immediately resorts to punishing students instead of first considering reinforcement strategies, or punishes a student without also giving the student information about appropriate behavior. Another criticism is that when teachers spend a lot of time using applied behavior analysis, they might focus too much on student conduct and not enough on academic learning. We will have much more to say about student conduct in chapter 14, "Managing the Classroom."

Review, Reflect, and Practice

(3) **Apply behavior analysis to education.**

REVIEW

- What is applied behavior analysis?
- What are six ways to increase desirable behaviors?
- What are four ways to decrease undesirable behaviors?
- What are some effective and ineffective uses of operant conditioning and applied behavior analysis?

REFLECT

- Come up with your own example in an educational setting for each of the six ways to increase desirable behavior.

PRAXIS™ PRACTICE

1. The uses of applied behavior analysis in education include all of the following *except*
   a. punishing students for undesirable behavior.
   b. increasing desirable behavior.
   c. using prompts and shaping.
   d. decreasing undesirable behavior.

2. Ms. Sanders wants her students to be quiet and ready to learn as soon as possible after coming in from recess. Sometimes the children are so excited that they have difficulty quieting down. To help remind them that it is time to be quiet and listen, Ms. Sanders flicks the light switch on and off several times. The children immediately quiet and listen to her instructions. According to applied behavioral analysis, what is Ms. Sanders doing when she turns the lights on and off?
   a. prompting
   b. punishing
   c. coercing
   d. shaping

3. Sid is a real handful in class. He talks when he should be working quietly. He gets out of his seat without permission. He often disrupts class. His third-grade teacher, Ms. Marin, sends him out into the hall when he misbehaves as a form of time-out. However, Sid continues to misbehave. At one point, Ms. Marin checks on Sid in the hall and finds him quietly tossing a ball back and forth with a child from another class.
   Why has time-out been ineffective with Sid?
   a. Ms. Marin did not present an aversive enough stimulus to Sid.
   b. Ms. Marin did not use differential reinforcement effectively.
   c. Sid finds being in class to be reinforcing.
   d. Sid finds being in the hallway to be reinforcing.

4. Critics of applied behavior analysis techniques often point out that when these techniques are used in the classroom they
   a. lead to physical abuse of students.
   b. do not work effectively.
   c. take time away from academics.
   d. emphasize external control of behavior.

Please see the answer key at the end of the book.

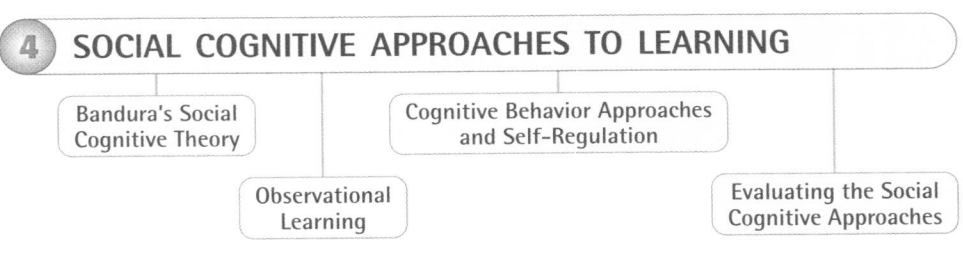

SOCIAL COGNITIVE APPROACHES TO LEARNING

Because students' thoughts affect their behavior and learning, a number of cognitive approaches to learning have been proposed. In this section, we will explore several social cognitive approaches, beginning with social cognitive theory. This theory evolved out of behavioral theories but has become increasingly more cognitive (Schunk, 2004; Schunk & Zimmerman, 2006).

Bandura's Social Cognitive Theory

Social cognitive theory states that social and cognitive factors, as well as behavior, play important roles in learning. Cognitive factors might involve the student's expectations for success; social factors might include students' observing their parents' achievement behavior. Social cognitive theory is an increasingly important source of classroom applications (Choi, 2005; Petosa & others, 2005).

Albert Bandura (1986, 1997, 2001, 2004, 2005, 2006) is the main architect of social cognitive theory. He says that when students learn, they can cognitively represent or transform their experiences. Recall that in operant conditioning, connections occur only between environmental experiences and behavior.

Bandura developed a *reciprocal determinism model* that consists of three main factors: behavior, person/cognitive, and environment. As shown in figure 7.7, these factors can interact to influence learning: Environmental factors influence behavior, behavior affects the environment, person (cognitive) factors influence behavior, and so on. Bandura uses the term *person,* but I have modified it to *person/cognitive* because so many of the person factors he describes are cognitive. The person factors Bandura describes that do not have a cognitive bent are mainly personality traits and temperament. Recall from chapter 4, "Individual Variations," that such factors might include being introverted or extraverted, active or inactive, calm or anxious, and friendly or hostile. Cognitive factors include expectations, beliefs, attitudes, strategies, thinking, and intelligence.

Consider how Bandura's model might work in the case of the achievement behavior of a high school student we will call Sondra:

- *Cognition influences behavior.* Sondra develops cognitive strategies to think more deeply and logically about how to solve problems. The cognitive strategies improve her achievement behavior.
- *Behavior influences cognition.* Sondra's studying (behavior) has led her to achieve good grades, which in turn produce positive expectancies about her abilities and give her self-confidence (cognition).
- *Environment influences behavior.* The school Sondra attends recently developed a pilot study-skills program to help students learn how to take notes, manage their time, and take tests more effectively. The study-skills program improves Sondra's achievement behavior.
- *Behavior influences environment.* The study-skills program is successful in improving the achievement behavior of many students in Sondra's class. The students' improved achievement behavior stimulates the school to expand the program so that all students in the high school participate in it.
- *Cognition influences environment.* The expectations and planning of the school's principal and teachers made the study-skills program possible in the first place.

Albert Bandura *(above)* and Walter Mischel are the architects of contemporary social cognitive theory.

Behavior

Person/
Cognitive   Environment

FIGURE 7.7 Bandura's Social Cognitive Theory

Bandura's social cognitive theory emphasizes reciprocal influences of behavior, environment, and person/cognitive factors.

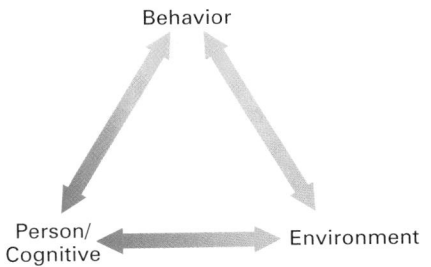

social cognitive theory Bandura's theory that social and cognitive factors, as well as behavior, play important roles in learning.

FIGURE 7.8 Bandura's Classic Bobo Doll Study: The Effects of Observational Learning on Children's Aggression

In the top frame, an adult model aggressively attacks the Bobo doll. In the bottom frame, a kindergarten-age girl who has observed the model's aggressive actions follows suit. In Bandura's experiment, under what conditions did the children reproduce the model's aggressive actions?

self-efficacy The belief that one can master a situation and produce positive outcomes.

observational learning Learning that involves acquiring skills, strategies, and beliefs by observing others.

• *Environment influences cognition.* The school establishes a resource center where students and parents can go to check out books and materials on improving study skills. The resource center also makes study-skills tutoring services available to students. Sondra and her parents take advantage of the center's resources and tutoring. These resources and services improve Sondra's thinking skills.

In Bandura's learning model, person/cognitive factors play important roles. The person/cognitive factor that Bandura (1997, 2004, 2005, 2006) has emphasized the most in recent years is **self-efficacy,** the belief that one can master a situation and produce positive outcomes. Bandura says that self-efficacy has a powerful influence over behavior. For example, a student who has low self-efficacy might not even try to study for a test because he doesn't believe it will do him any good. We will have much more to say about self-efficacy in chapter 13, "Motivation, Teaching, and Learning."

Next, we discuss the important learning process of observational learning, which is another of Bandura's main contributions. As you read about observational learning, note how person/cognitive factors are involved.

Observational Learning

Observational learning is learning that involves acquiring skills, strategies, and beliefs by observing others. Observational learning involves imitation but is not limited to it. What is learned typically is not an exact copy of what is modeled but rather a general form or strategy that observers often apply in creative ways. The capacity to learn behavior patterns by observation eliminates tedious trial-and-error learning. In many instances, observational learning takes less time than operant conditioning.

The Classic Bobo Doll Study A classic experiment by Bandura (1965) illustrates how observational learning can occur even when a student watches a model who is not reinforced or punished. The experiment also illustrates a distinction between learning and performance.

Equal numbers of kindergarten children were randomly assigned to watch one of three films in which a person (the model) beat up an adult-size plastic toy called a Bobo doll (see figure 7.8). In the first film, the aggressor was rewarded with candy, soft drinks, and praise for aggressive behavior. In the second film, the aggressor was criticized and spanked for the aggressive behavior. And in the third film, there were no consequences for the aggressor's behavior.

Subsequently, each child was left alone in a room filled with toys, including a Bobo doll. The child's behavior was observed through a one-way mirror. Children who watched the films in which the aggressor's behavior either was reinforced or went unpunished imitated the aggressor's behavior more than did the children who saw the aggressor get punished. As you might expect, boys were more aggressive than girls. An important point in this study, however, is that observational learning occurred just as extensively when modeled aggressive behavior was *not* reinforced as when it was reinforced.

A second important point in this study focuses on the distinction between learning and performance. Just because students don't perform a response doesn't mean they didn't learn it. In Bandura's study, when children were given an incentive (stickers or fruit juice) to imitate the model, differences in the children's imitative behavior in the three conditions were eliminated. Bandura believes that when a child observes behavior but makes no observable response, the child may still have acquired the modeled response in cognitive form.

Bandura's Contemporary Model of Observational Learning Since his early experiments, Bandura (1986) has focused on exploring specific processes that are involved in observational learning. These include attention, retention, production, and motivation (see figure 7.9):

- *Attention.* Before students can imitate a model's actions, they must attend to what the model is doing or saying. Attention to the model is influenced by a host of characteristics. For example, warm, powerful, atypical people command more attention than do cold, weak, typical people. Students are more likely to be attentive to high-status models than to low-status models. In most cases, teachers are high-status models for students.

- *Retention.* To reproduce a model's actions, students must code the information and keep it in memory so that they retrieve it. A simple verbal description or a vivid image of what the model did assists students' retention. For example, the teacher might say, "I'm showing the correct way to do this. You have to do this step first, this step second, and this step third," as she models how to solve a math problem. A video with a colorful character demonstrating the importance of considering other students' feelings might be remembered better than if the teacher just tells the students to do this. Such colorful characters are at the heart of the popularity of *Sesame Street* with children. Students' retention will be improved when teachers give vivid, logical, and clear demonstrations.

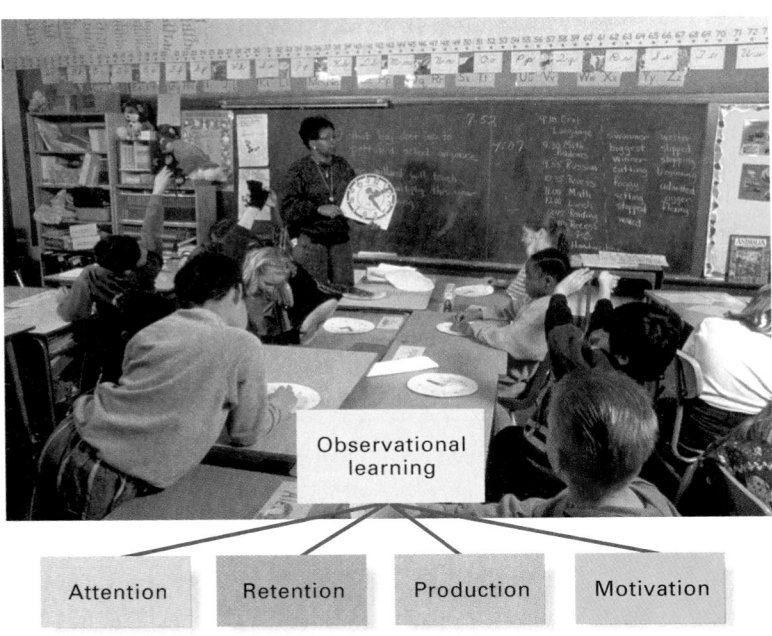

FIGURE 7.9 Bandura's Model of Observational Learning

In Bandura's model of observational learning, four processes need to be considered: attention, retention, production, and motivation. *How might these processes be involved in this classroom situation in which a teacher is demonstrating how to tell time?*

- *Production.* Children might attend to a model and code in memory what they have seen—but, because of limitations in their motor ability, not be able to reproduce the model's behavior. A 13-year-old might watch basketball player Lebron James and golfer Michelle Wie execute their athletic skills to perfection, or observe a famous pianist or artist, but not be able to reproduce their motor actions. Teaching, coaching, and practice can help children improve their motor performances.

- *Motivation.* Often children attend to what a model says or does, retain the information in memory, and possess the motor skills to perform the action but are not motivated to perform the modeled behavior. This was demonstrated in Bandura's classic Bobo doll study when children who saw the model being punished did not reproduce the punished model's aggressive actions. However, when they subsequently were given a reinforcement or incentive (stickers or fruit juice), they did imitate the model's behavior.

Bandura argues that reinforcement is not always necessary for observational learning to take place. But if the child does not reproduce the desired behaviors, four types of reinforcement can help do the trick: (1) reward the model; (2) reward the child; (3) instruct the child to make self-reinforcing statements such as "Good, I did it!" or "Okay, I've done a good job of getting most of this right; now if I keep trying I will get the rest"; or (4) show how the behavior leads to reinforcing outcomes.

As you can see, you will be an important model in students' lives, and you have many options for providing students with an array of competent models. To evaluate the roles that models and mentors have played in your own life and can play in your students' lives, complete Self-Assessment 7.1. To explore the lack of male and minority role models and mentors in children's education, read the Diversity and Education interlude on page 247.

SELF-ASSESSMENT 7.1

Models and Mentors in My Life and My Students' Lives

Having positive role models and mentors can make an important difference in whether individuals develop optimally and reach their full potential. First, evaluate the role models and mentors who have played an important part in your life. Second, think about the type of role model you want to be for your students. Third, give some thought to how you will incorporate other models and mentors into your students' lives. Fourth, explore who your education mentor might be.

My Models and Mentors

List the most important role models and mentors in your life. Then describe what their positive modeling and mentoring have meant to your development.

Role Models and Mentors	Their Contributions
1. _____	_____
2. _____	_____
3. _____	_____
4. _____	_____
5. _____	_____

The Type of Role Model I Want to Be for My Students

Describe which characteristics and behaviors you believe are the most important for you to model for your students.

1. _____

2. _____

3. _____

4. _____

5. _____

How I Will Incorporate Models and Mentors in My Classroom

Describe a systematic plan for bringing models and mentors into your students' lives in one or more domain(s) you plan to teach, such as math, English, science, and music.

_____

_____

_____

_____

Who Will Be My Education Mentor? What Would My Ideal Education Mentor Be Like?

Do you have someone in mind who might serve as an education mentor when you become a teacher? If so, describe the person.

_____

_____

What would your ideal education mentor be like?

_____

_____

_____

_____

DIVERSITY AND EDUCATION
Male and Minority Role Models and Mentors

As students in U.S. schools have become more ethnically diverse in recent decades, their teachers are overwhelmingly non-Latino White females. In 2000, approximately 17 percent of U.S. public school students were African American, but less than 8 percent of their teachers were African American (National Center for Education Statistics, 2002). Only a small percentage of the African American teachers were males. In the same year, Latinos made up about 16 percent of U.S. public school students, but less than 6 percent of their teachers were Latino. In 2000, 38 percent of U.S. public schools did not have a single ethnic minority teacher.

Men comprise about 10 percent of elementary school teachers but nearly half of middle and high school teachers (many of whom are lured by additional incentives for coaching athletic teams). The situation is likely to get worse. In a recent national survey of college students, only 1.1 percent of males said their probable career would be as an elementary school teacher or administrator, and only 4.7 percent indicated that a similar career in secondary education was likely to be in their future (Pryor & others, 2005).

The education program at Livingstone College in Salisbury, North Carolina, is trying to do something about the shortage of male teachers of color. They developed a special program to recruit men of color into the teaching profession. One of the program's graduates, Nakia Douglas, teaches kindergarten. He says he wants to eliminate negative stereotypes about African American males—that they are poor role models, aren't responsible, and shouldn't be teaching young children. Another graduate, Mistor Williams, teaches history to eighth-graders in a school with a large percentage of ethnic minority students. He says that he feels the responsibility to provide a role model and support for ethnic minority students.

If you are a White female, think about ways you can bring women and men of color into your classroom to talk with students and demonstrate their work skills. This is especially important when you have a number of students of color in your class.

Regardless of your ethnic background, look around the community for possible mentors for students, especially students who come from low-income backgrounds and who lack positive role models (Johnson, 2006). For example, the aim of the 3-to-1 mentoring program is to surround each ethnic minority male student with three positive ethnic minority role models. The program began when several African American men were challenged by a sermon delivered by Zach Holmes at the St. Luke's Methodist Church in Dallas. In the sermon, Reverend Holmes urged his congregation to become more involved with children, both their own and children in the community who don't have good role models. The 3-to-1 mentoring program has signed up more than 200 men and 100 boys (ages 4 to 18). That's far short of the goal of three mentors for each boy, but the men are working on increasing the number of mentors in the program. Some of the men in the mentoring program have their own children, like Dr. Leonard Berry, a physician, who has two sons and a daughter. He heeded the minister's challenge and regularly participates in the mentoring program, which involves academic tutoring as well as outings to activities such as sporting and cultural events. The mentors also take the students to visit the Johnson Space Center in Houston.

As a teacher you do not have to wait for someone in the community to bring mentors to your students. Look around the community in which you teach and evaluate who would be good candidates for mentoring your students or starting a mentoring program. Contact them and get the program started. Clearly, mentoring programs can benefit all students, male or female, of any ethnic background.

In the present educational climate that emphasizes reflection and critical thinking, it is easy to overlook the power of observational learning in educating children (Schunk, 2004), yet observational learning remains one of the most common and effective means of learning. The Best Practices interlude can help you to use this powerful form of learning in your classroom.

Dr. Leonard Berry is a mentor in the 3-to-1 program in Dallas. He is shown here with Brandon Scarbough, 13 (*front*), and his own son, Leonard, 12 (*back*). Brandon not only has benefited from Dr. Berry's mentoring but also has become friends with his son.

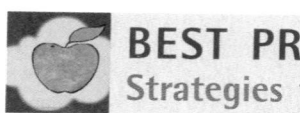

BEST PRACTICES
Strategies for Effectively Using Observational Learning

1. *Think about what type of model you will present to students.* Every day, hour after hour, students will watch and listen to what you say and do. Just by being around you, students will absorb a great deal of information. They will pick up your good or bad habits, your expectations for their high or low achievement, your enthusiastic or bored attitude, your controlled or uncontrolled manner of dealing with stress, your learning style, your gender attitudes, and many other aspects of your behavior.

2. *Demonstrate and teach new behaviors.* Demonstrating means that you, the teacher, are a model for your students' observational learning. Demonstrating how to do something, such as solve a math problem, read, write, think, control anger, and perform physical skills, is a common teacher behavior in classrooms. For example, a teacher might model how to diagram a sentence, develop a strategy for solving algebraic equations, or shoot a basketball. When demonstrating how to do something, you need to call students' attention to the relevant details of the learning situation. Your demonstrations also should be clear and follow a logical sequence.

3. *Think about ways to use peers as effective models.* The teacher is not the only model in the classroom. As with teachers, children can pick up their peers' good and bad habits, high or low achievement orientations, and so on through observational learning. Remember that students are often motivated to imitate high-status models. Older peers usually have higher status than same-age peers. Thus, a good strategy is to have older peers from a higher-grade model how to engage in the behaviors you want your students to perform. For students with low abilities or who are not performing well, a low-achieving student who struggles but puts considerable effort into learning and ultimately performs the behaviors can be a good model. More will be said in chapter 10, "Social Constructivist Approaches," about peer collaboration and peers as tutors.

4. *Think about ways that mentors can be used as models.* Students and teachers benefit from having a mentor— someone they look up to and respect, someone who serves as a competent model, someone who is willing to work with them and help them achieve their goals. As a teacher, a potential mentor for you is a more experienced teacher, possibly someone who teaches down the hall and has had a number of years of experience in dealing with some of the same problems and issues you will have to cope with.

   In the Quantum Opportunities program, students from low-income backgrounds significantly benefited from meeting with a mentor over a 4-year period (Carnegie Council on Adolescent Development, 1995). These mentors modeled appropriate behavior and strategies, gave sustained support, and provided guidance. Just spending a few hours a week with a mentor can make a difference in a student's life, especially if the student's parents have not been good role models.

5. *Evaluate which classroom guests will provide good models for students.* Who else would be beneficial models for your students? To change the pace of classroom life for you and your students, invite guests who have something meaningful to talk about or demonstrate. Recall what we said in chapter 4 about Gardner's theory of multiple intelligences: There likely are some domains (physical, musical, artistic, or other) in which you don't have the skills to serve as a competent model for your students. When you need to have such skills demonstrated to your students, spend some time locating competent models in the community. Invite them to come to your classroom to demonstrate and discuss their skills. If this can't be arranged, set up field trips in which you take students to see them where they are working or performing. Next, fourth-grade teacher Marlene Wendler describes a positive role model her school brings to teachers' classrooms.

THROUGH THE EYES OF TEACHERS
Here Comes the Judge

Our local judge has taken a proactive role in trying to eliminate teen behavioral problems. With a half dozen adults from the community, he comes to the fourth-grade classrooms in our areas and puts on skits about bullying. They show the whole group picking on a student in a bus situation. Then they do the skit again with someone in the group stopping the bullying. The students then role-play bullying situations, learning what to do if they are bullied and how to help someone who is bullied. Having the judge come to our school has made a lasting impression on our students.

---

6. *Consider the models children observe on television, videos, and computers.* Students observe models when they watch television programs, videos, films, or computer screens in your classroom (Kirsh, 2006). The principles of observational learning we described earlier apply to these media. For example, the extent to which the students perceive the media models as high or low in status, intriguing or boring, and so on will influence the extent of their observational learning. And as we indicated in chapter 3, "Social Contexts and Socioemotional Development," it is important to monitor children's TV watching to ensure that they are not being exposed to too many negative models, especially violent ones.

   To read about applications of observational learning in the popular children's television show *Sesame Street*, see the Technology and Education box.

TECHNOLOGY AND EDUCATION

Educational Lessons from Sesame Street

One of television's major programming attempts to educate young children is *Sesame Street,* which is designed to teach both cognitive and social skills (Bryant, 2006; Fisch, 2004, 2006; Linebarger & Dale, 2005; Truglio & Kotler, 2006). The program began in 1969 and is still going strong. A fundamental message of *Sesame Street* is that education and entertainment work well together (Lesser, 1972). On *Sesame Street,* learning is exciting and entertaining. One recent study found that preschool children who watched *Sesame Street* were more likely to positively resolve conflicts, make positive comments about others, and engage in less stereotyping than their counterparts who did not watch the TV show (Cole & others, 2003).

What educational lessons can be learned from Sesame Street?

Sesame Street also illustrates the point that teaching can be done in both direct and indirect ways. Using the direct way, a teacher tells children exactly what they are going to be taught and then actually teaches it to them. This method is often used on *Sesame Street* to teach cognitive skills. But social skills usually are communicated in indirect ways on the show. Thus, rather than telling children "You should cooperate with people," a sequence of events is shown to help children figure out what it means to be cooperative and what the advantages are.

Should the world be shown to children as it is, or as it ought to be? The *Sesame Street* advisory board of educators and psychologists decided that the real world should be shown—but with an emphasis on what the world would be like if everyone treated each other with decency and kindness. To show the world as it really is, the program might show an adult doing something unjustifiably inconsiderate to another adult, with alternative ways of coping with this acted out. Finally, the program would portray the happy outcomes when people stop acting inconsiderately.

Some of the attentional techniques used on *Sesame Street* are worthwhile to consider in the classroom. These involve first *catching* the child's attention, then *directing* it, and finally *sustaining* it. Music and sound are very effective in eliciting children's attention. For example, in teaching children to discriminate sounds, an automobile horn might be sounded or a computer's keyboard repeatedly pressed. Music is especially useful because it leads children to become actively involved in what they are watching or listening. It is not unusual for children watching *Sesame Street* to get up out of their seats and start dancing and singing along with the jingles. Once the child's attention has been captured, it should be directed to something. Surprise and novelty are especially helpful in this regard. They make children work hard to figure out what is going to happen. Their attention is directed because they begin to anticipate what is going to happen next.

Once attention is directed, it then needs to be maintained. *Sesame Street* especially uses humor to accomplish this. Humor is judiciously placed: Ernie outsmarts Bert; the Cookie Monster annoyingly interrupts a lecture given by Kermit the Frog. For young children, physical gags often are funnier than verbal ones, and much of the humor that is effective involves physical acts that are surprising and incongruous.

Cognitive Behavior Approaches and Self-Regulation

Operant conditioning spawned applications and other real-world settings, and the interest in cognitive behavior approaches has also produced such applications. In the fifth century B.C., the Chinese philosopher Confucius said, "If you give a man a fish, you feed him for a day. If you teach a man to fish, you feed him for a lifetime." As you read about the cognitive behavior approaches and self-regulation, you will discover that they reflect Confucius' simple expression.

Cognitive Behavior Approaches In the **cognitive behavior approaches**, the emphasis is on getting students to monitor, manage, and regulate their own behavior rather than letting it be controlled by external factors. In some circles, this has been called *cognitive behavior modification*. Cognitive behavior approaches stem from

cognitive behavior approaches
Changing behavior by getting individuals to monitor, manage, and regulate their own behavior rather than letting it be controlled by external factors.

Poster 1
While listening

1. Does this make sense?
2. Am I getting this?
3. I need to ask a question before I forget.
4. Pay attention.
5. Can I do what the teacher is saying to do?

Poster 2
While planning

1. Do I have everything together?
2. Do I have my friends tuned out so I can get this done?
3. I need to get organized first.
4. What order can I do this in?
5. I know this stuff.

Poster 3
While working

1. Am I working fast enough?
2. Stop staring at my girlfriend (boyfriend) and get back to work.
3. How much time is left?
4. Do I need to stop and start all over?
5. This is hard for me but I can manage it.

Poster 4
While checking

1. Did I finish everything?
2. What do I need to recheck?
3. Am I proud of this work?
4. Did I write all of the words?
5. I think I'm finished. I organized myself. Did I daydream too much, though?

FIGURE 7.10 Some Posters Developed by a Fifth–Grade Class to Help Them Remember How to Effectively Talk to Themselves

Source: From Brenda H. Manning and Beverly D. Payne, *Self-Talk for Teachers and Students: Metacognitive Strategies for Personal and Classroom Use.* Published by Allyn and Bacon, Boston, MA. Copyright © 1996 by Pearson Education. Reprinted by permission of the publisher.

both cognitive psychology, with its emphasis on the effects of thoughts on behavior, and behaviorism, with its emphasis on techniques for changing behavior. Cognitive behavior approaches try to change students' misconceptions, strengthen their coping skills, increase their self-control, and encourage constructive self-reflection (Meichenbaum, 1993; Molina, Dulmus, & Sowers, 2005; Watson & Tharp, 2007).

Self-instructional methods are cognitive behavior techniques aimed at teaching individuals to modify their own behavior. Self-instructional methods help people alter what they say to themselves.

Imagine a situation in which a high school student is extremely nervous about taking standardized tests, such as the SAT. The student can be encouraged to talk to himself in positive ways. Following are some self-talk strategies that students and teachers can use to cope more effectively with such stressful situations (Meichenbaum, Turk, & Burstein, 1975):

- Prepare for anxiety or stress.
  "What do I have to do?"
  "I'm going to develop a plan to deal with it."
  "I'll just think about what I have to do."
  "I won't worry. Worry doesn't help anything."
  "I have a lot of different strategies I can use."
- Confront and handle the anxiety or stress.
  "I can meet the challenge."
  "I'll keep on taking just one step at a time."
  "I can handle it. I'll just relax, breathe deeply, and use one of the strategies."
  "I won't think about my stress. I'll just think about what I have to do."
- Cope with feelings at critical moments.
  "What is it I have to do?"
  "I knew my anxiety might increase. I just have to keep myself in control."
  "When the anxiety comes, I'll just pause and keep focusing on what I have to do."
- Use reinforcing self-statements.
  "Good, I did it."
  "I handled it well."
  "I knew I could do it."
  "Wait until I tell other people how I did it!"

In many instances, the strategy is to replace negative self-statements with positive ones. For example, a student might say to herself, "I'll never get this work done by tomorrow." This can be replaced with positive self-statements such as these: "This is going to be tough but I think I can do it." "I'm going to look at this as a challenge rather than a stressor." "If I work really hard, I might be able to get it done." Or in having to participate in a class discussion, a student might replace the negative thought "Everyone else knows more than I do, so what's the use of saying anything" with positive self-statements such as these: "I have as much to say as anyone else." "My ideas may be different, but they are still good." "It's okay to be a little nervous; I'll relax and start talking." Figure 7.10 shows posters that students in one fifth-grade class developed to help them remember how to talk to themselves while listening, planning, working, and checking.

Talking positively to oneself can help teachers and students reach their full potential (Watson & Tharp, 2007). Uncountered negative thinking has a way of becoming a self-fulfilling prophecy. You think you can't do it, and so you don't. If negative self-talk is a problem for you, at random times during the day ask yourself, "What am I saying to myself right now?" Moments that you expect will be potentially stressful are excellent times to examine your self-talk. Also monitor your students' self-talk. If you hear students saying, "I can't do this" or "I'm so slow I'll never get this done," spend some time getting them to replace their negative self-talk with positive self-talk.

Cognitive behaviorists recommend that students improve their performance by monitoring their own behavior (Rock, 2005; Watson & Tharp, 2007). This can involve getting students to keep charts or records of their behavior. When I (your author) wrote this book, I had a chart on my wall with each of the chapters listed. I planned how long it would take me to do each of the chapters, and then as I completed each one I checked it off and wrote down the date of completion. Teachers can get students to do some similar monitoring of their own progress by getting them to keep records of how many assignments they have finished, how many books they have read, how many homework papers they have turned in on time, how many days in a row they have not interrupted the teacher, and so on. In some cases, teachers place these self-monitoring charts on the walls of the classroom. Alternatively, if the teacher thinks that negative social comparison with other students will be highly stressful for some students, then a better strategy might be to have students keep private records (in a notebook, for example) that are periodically checked by the teacher.

Self-monitoring is an excellent strategy for improving learning, and one that you can help students learn to do effectively (Watson & Tharp, 2007). By completing Self-Assessment 7.2 on the next page, you should get a sense of the benefits of self-monitoring for your students.

Self-Regulatory Learning   Educational psychologists increasingly advocate the importance of self-regulatory learning (Alexander, 2006; Boekaerts & Corno, 2005; Cooper, Horn, & Strahan, 2005; Schunk & Zimmerman, 2006; Wigfield & others, 2006). **Self-regulatory learning** consists of the self-generation and self-monitoring of thoughts, feelings, and behaviors in order to reach a goal. These goals might be academic (improving comprehension while reading, becoming a more organized writer, learning how to do multiplication, asking relevant questions) or they might be socioemotional (controlling one's anger, getting along better with peers). What are some of the characteristics of self-regulated learners? Self-regulatory learners (Winne, 1995, 1997, 2001, 2005)

FIGURE 7.11 A Model of Self-Regulatory Learning

- set goals for extending their knowledge and sustaining their motivation,
- are aware of their emotional makeup and have strategies for managing their emotions,
- periodically monitor their progress toward a goal,
- fine-tune or revise their strategies based on the progress they are making, and
- evaluate obstacles that may arise and make the necessary adaptations.

Researchers have found that high-achieving students are often self-regulatory learners (Alexander, 2006; Boekaerts, 2006; Schunk & Zimmerman, 2006; Wigfield & others, 2006). For example, compared with low-achieving students, high-achieving students set more specific learning goals, use more strategies to learn, self-monitor their learning more, and more systematically evaluate their progress toward a goal.

Teachers, tutors, mentors, counselors, and parents can help students become self-regulatory learners (Boekaerts, 2006; Schunk & Zimmerman, 2006). Barry Zimmerman, Sebastian Bonner, and Robert Kovach (1996) developed a model for turning low-self-regulatory students into students who engage in these multistep strategies: (1) self-evaluation and monitoring, (2) goal setting and strategic planning, (3) putting a plan into action and monitoring it, and (4) monitoring outcomes and refining strategies (see figure 7.11).

Zimmerman and colleagues describe a seventh-grade student who is doing poorly in history and apply their self-regulatory model to her situation. In step 1, she

self-instructional methods Cognitive behavior techniques aimed at teaching individuals to modify their own behavior.

self-regulatory learning The self-generation and self-monitoring of thoughts, feelings, and behaviors in order to reach a goal.

SELF–ASSESSMENT 7.2

Self–Monitoring

Self-monitoring can benefit you as well as your students. Many successful learners regularly self-monitor their progress to see how they are doing in their effort to complete a project, develop a skill, or perform well on a test or other assessment. For the next month, self-monitor your study time for this course you are taking in educational psychology. To achieve high grades, most instructors recommend that students spend two or three hours out of class studying, doing homework, and working on projects for every hour they are in class in college (Santrock & Halonen, 2006). The experience of self-monitoring your own study time should give you a sense of how important such skills are for your students to develop. You might adapt this form for students' homework, for example. Remember from our discussion of Bandura's cognitive social learning theory that self-efficacy involves your belief that you can master a situation and produce positive outcomes. One way to evaluate self-efficacy is your expectancy for attaining a particular score on an upcoming quiz or test. Determine what score or grade you want to achieve on your next quiz or test. Then each day you study, rate your self-efficacy for achieving the score you desire on a 3-point scale: 1 = not very confident, 2 = moderately confident, and 3 = very confident.

Form for Self-Monitoring Study Time

Date	Assignment	Time Started	Time Finished	Study Context			Self-Efficacy
				Where?	With Whom?	Distractions	

self-evaluates her studying and test preparation by keeping a detailed record of them. The teacher gives her some guidelines for keeping these records. After several weeks, the student turns the records in and traces her poor test performance to low comprehension of difficult reading material.

In step 2, the student sets a goal, in this case of improving reading comprehension, and plans how to achieve the goal. The teacher assists her in breaking the goal into components, such as locating main ideas and setting specific goals for understanding a series of paragraphs in her textbook. The teacher also provides the student with strategies, such as focusing initially on the first sentence of each paragraph and then scanning the others as a means of identifying main ideas. Another support the teacher might offer the student is adult or peer tutoring in reading comprehension if it is available.

In step 3, the student puts the plan into action and begins to monitor her progress. Initially, she may need help from the teacher or tutor in identifying main ideas in the reading. This feedback can help her monitor her reading comprehension more effectively on her own.

In step 4, the student monitors her improvement in reading comprehension by evaluating whether it has had any impact on her learning outcomes. Most importantly, has her improvement in reading comprehension led to better performance on history tests?

Self-evaluations reveal that the strategy of finding main ideas has only partly improved her comprehension, and only when the first sentence contained the paragraph's main idea, so the teacher recommends further strategies. Figure 7.12 describes how teachers can apply the self-regulatory model to homework.

FIGURE 7.12 Applying the Self-Regulatory Model to Homework

1. Self-Evaluation and monitoring

- The teacher distributes forms so that students can monitor specific aspects of their studying.
- The teacher gives students daily assignments to develop their self-monitoring skills and a weekly quiz to assess how well they have learned the methods.
- After several days, the teacher begins to have students exchange their homework with their peers. The peers are asked to evaluate the accuracy of the homework and how effectively the student engaged in self-monitoring. Then the teacher collects the homework for grading and reviews the peers' suggestions.

2. Goal setting and strategic planning

- After a week of monitoring and the first graded exercise, the teacher asks students to give their perceptions of the strengths and weaknesses of their study strategies. The teacher emphasizes the link between learning strategies and learning outcomes.
- The teacher and peers recommend specific strategies that students might use to improve their learning. Students may use the recommendations or devise new ones. The teacher asks students to set specific goals at this point.

3. Putting a plan into action and monitoring it

- The students monitor the extent to which they actually enact the new strategies.
- The teacher's role is to make sure that the new learning strategies are openly discussed.

4. Monitoring outcomes and refining strategies

- The teacher continues to give students opportunities to gauge how effectively they are using their new strategies.
- The teacher helps students summarize their self-regulatory methods by reviewing each step of the self-regulatory learning cycle. She also discusses with students the hurdles the students had to overcome and the self-confidence they have achieved.

Chapter 7 Behavioral and Social Cognitive Approaches

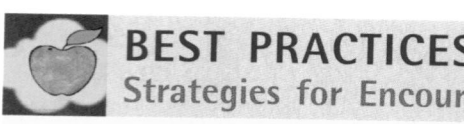

BEST PRACTICES
Strategies for Encouraging Students to Be Self-Regulated Learners

Following are some effective strategies for guiding students to engage in self-regulated learning:

1. *Gradually guide students to become self-regulated learners.* It is not a good strategy to just assume that you can all of a sudden give students the independence to self-regulate their learning (Alexander, 2006). Helping students become self-regulated learners takes time and requires considerable monitoring, guidance, and encouragement on your part (Cooper, Horn, & Strahan, 2005).

2. *Make the classroom learning experience challenging and interesting for students.* When students are bored and uninterested in learning, they are less likely to become self-regulated learners. Instead of just giving students a particular book to read, providing students with a variety of interesting books is likely to encourage their motivation to read (Gutherie, Wigfield, & Perencevich, 2004; Gutherie & others, 2004). Giving students choices increases students' personal investment in their learning and increases their self-regulation (Alexander, 2006; Blumenfeld, Kempler & Krajcik, 2006).

3. *Provide tips about thoughts and actions that will help students engage in self-regulation.* These might include giving specific guidelines as needed, such as "Planning for 30 minutes will help you . . ." and "Every day stop and monitor where you are in what you want to accomplish." Other suggestions include encouraging students to reflect on their strengths and weaknesses in a learning situation and encouraging them to search for help and ways to use help effectively (All Kinds of Minds, 2005).

4. *Give students opportunities to experience the type of activities recommended by Zimmerman and his colleagues* (1996). That is, create projects for students in which they self-evaluate their current learning, set a goal to improve their learning and plan how to reach the goal, put the plan into action and monitor their progress toward the goal, and monitor the outcome and refine their strategies. Monitor students' progress through these steps and encourage their ability to engage in these learning activities independently.

5. *Especially pay attention to low-achieving students.* High-achieving students are more likely to already be self-regulated learners than low-achieving students. All students can benefit from practicing their self-regulated learning skills, but recognize that low-achieving students will need more instruction and time to develop these skills.

6. *Model self-regulated learning.* Verbalize effective self-regulation strategies for students, and tell students how you use self-regulation in your learning (Randi, 2004).

The development of self-regulation is influenced by many factors, among them modeling and self-efficacy (Pintrich & Schunk, 2002; Schunk & Zimmerman, 2006; Zimmerman & Schunk, 2004). Models are important sources for conveying self-regulatory skills. Among the self-regulatory skills that models can engage in are planning and managing time effectively, attending to and concentrating, organizing and coding information strategically, establishing a productive work environment, and using social resources. For example, students might observe a teacher engage in an effective time management strategy and verbalize appropriate principles. By observing such models, students can come to believe that they also can plan and manage time effectively, which creates a sense of self-efficacy for academic self-regulation and motivates students to engage in those activities.

Self-efficacy can influence a student's choice of tasks, effort expended, persistence, and achievement (Bandura, 1997, 2005, 2006; Bandura & Locke, 2003; Schunk & Zimmerman, 2006). Compared with students who doubt their learning capabilities, those with high self-efficacy for acquiring a skill or performing a task participate more readily, work harder, persist longer in the face of difficulty, and achieve at a higher level. Self-efficacy can have a strong effect on achievement, but it is not the only influence. High self-efficacy will not result in competent performance when requisite knowledge and skills are lacking. We will further explore self-efficacy, goal setting, planning, and self-regulation in chapter 13, "Motivation, Teaching, and Learning."

Teachers who encourage students to be self-regulatory learners convey the message that students are responsible for their own behavior, for becoming educated, and for becoming contributing citizens to society (Lajoie & Azevedo, 2006). Another message conveyed by self-regulatory learning is that learning is a personal experience that requires active and dedicated participation by the student (Zimmerman, Bonner, & Kovach, 1996).

Evaluating the Social Cognitive Approaches

The social cognitive approaches have made important contributions to educating children. While keeping the behaviorists' scientific flavor and emphasis on careful observation, they significantly expanded the emphasis of learning to include social and cognitive factors. Considerable learning occurs through watching and listening to competent models and then imitating what they do. The emphasis in the cognitive behavior approach on self-instruction, self-talk, and self-regulatory learning provides an important shift from learning controlled by others to responsibility for one's own learning (Watson & Tharp, 2007). These self-enacted strategies can significantly improve students' learning.

Critics of the social cognitive approaches come from several camps. Some cognitive theorists believe the approaches still focus too much on overt behavior and external factors and not enough on the details of how cognitive processes such as thinking, memory, and problem solving actually take place. Some developmentalists criticize them for being nondevelopmental, in the sense that they don't specify age-related, sequential changes in learning. It is true that social cognitive theory does not address development in great depth because it is mainly a theory of learning and social behavior. But labeling it as nondevelopment is not accurate. Also, humanistic theorists fault them for not placing enough attention on self-esteem and caring, supportive relationships. All of these criticisms also can be, and have been, leveled at the behavioral approaches, such as Skinner's operant conditioning, discussed earlier in the chapter.

Review, Reflect, and Practice

 Summarize social cognitive approaches to learning.

REVIEW
- How does figure 7.7 help to summarize Bandura's social cognitive theory? What does he mean by self-efficacy?
- What did the Bobo doll study demonstrate? What is Bandura's model of observational learning?
- What is the focus of self-instructional methods? What does self-regulatory learning involve?
- What are some contributions and criticisms of the cognitive and social learning approaches?

REFLECT
- Give some examples of how you use self-instructional and self-regulatory methods in your personal life. How effective are these methods? Should you use them more than you do? Explain.

continued on page 256

Review, Reflect, and Practice *continued*

PRAXIS™ PRACTICE

1. Macy sits staring at her math homework. She has not attempted a single problem. "What's the use?" she sighs, "I'll never get it right." According to Bandura's social cognitive theory, what is the most plausible explanation for Macy's response?
   a. Macy does not have the requisite language skills to do her homework.
   b. Macy has low self-efficacy.
   c. Macy has too much math anxiety.
   d. Macy's teacher has not provided enough negative feedback about her math homework.

2. Matt is the star of his high school's basketball team. The team is doing very well this year, in large part because of Matt's performance. This makes him a very popular student. About halfway through basketball season, Matt decides to shave his head. Soon other members of the basketball team shave their heads. Then the trend spreads to the rest of the school. By the end of February, 30% of the male students in the school have shaved heads. According to Bandura's social cognitive theory, what is the most plausible explanation for the students' behavior?
   a. Matt is a high-status role model.
   b. Matt was not punished.
   c. Matt was positively reinforced.
   d. Matt's self-efficacy was raised.

3. Marsha, a junior in high school, has debilitating test anxiety. She is particularly anxious about high-stakes tests, such as final exams. She often becomes so anxious that she "blanks out" and forgets everything that she has studied. What would a teacher using a cognitive behavior modification approach do to help her with her test anxiety?
   a. Guide Marsha in learning to engage in positive self-talk.
   b. Give her a study-skills book to read.
   c. Encourage her to think more about the consequences if she does do better on the tests.
   d. Tell Marsha to study until she has overlearned the material.

4. An important way in which social cognitive theory builds on behavioral theory is its emphasis on
   a. personality.
   b. self-efficacy.
   c. attitudes.
   d. careful observation.

Please see the answer key at the end of the book.

CRACK THE CASE
The Case of Consequences

Adam, a student in Mr. Potter's fourth-grade class, is disruptive from time to time, although he is very bright. One day during language arts, Adam began talking loudly to other students in his area. He was also laughing and telling jokes. Mr. Potter chose to ignore Adam's behavior, hoping he would stop on his own. But Adam didn't stop. Instead, his behavior became more raucous. Still Mr. Potter ignored it. Soon Adam was making enough noise that Mr. Potter was afraid that students in the neighboring classrooms would be disturbed, so he verbally reprimanded Adam.

Adam was a bit quieter for the next few minutes. After that, however, he once again became loud and disruptive. Again Mr. Potter verbally reprimanded him. This time he also told Adam that if he continued with his disruptive behavior, he would have to go to the office. Adam's behavior became even more disruptive, so Mr. Potter sent him to the office. When Adam arrived at the office it was full of people—teachers getting their mail and making copies, volunteers signing in, students who were ill, students sent on errands, and other students who had been sent for disciplinary reasons. The school secretary told Adam to have a seat, which he did. He conversed with every person who entered the office as well as those who were there when he arrived. Half an hour after his arrival, he was sent back to class. He behaved quite well for the rest of the day, to Mr. Potter's relief.

The next day when students were assigned to write a paragraph, Adam once again became disruptive. He loudly told jokes to his classmates, laughed until tears were streaming down his face, and threw a paper airplane across the room. Mr. Potter reprimanded him and asked him to stop. When Adam didn't comply, Mr. Potter sent him to the office, which was once again bustling with activity.

Over the course of the next two weeks, Adam was sent to the office for disrupting class each day, always during a writing assignment. Mr. Potter was perplexed. Even more perplexing was that within three school days other children were becoming disruptive as well, requiring that they too be sent to the office.

1. What are the issues in this case?

Answer the following questions using principles of behavioral learning theories and correct terminology:

2. Why did Adam continue to disrupt class despite the consequences?

3. What has Adam learned?

4. Why did the other students join Adam in his disruptive behavior?

5. What should Mr. Potter do now?

6. What was Mr. Potter most likely trying to do when he initially ignored Adam's disruptive behavior?
   a. He was trying to extinguish the behavior by not reinforcing it.
   b. He was trying to negatively reinforce the behavior.
   c. He was trying to positively reinforce the behavior.
   d. He was trying to punish the behavior.

7. If Adam's goal was to escape writing assignments, which of the following best explains the consequences in operant conditioning terms?
   a. Adam was negatively reinforced for his behavior. An aversive stimulus was removed.
   b. Adam was positively reinforced for his behavior. A pleasant stimulus was presented.
   c. Adam was punished for his behavior. A pleasant stimulus was removed.
   d. Adam was punished for his behavior. An aversive stimulus was presented.

Reach Your Learning Goals
Behavioral and Social Cognitive Approaches

① **WHAT IS LEARNING?** Define learning and describe five approaches to studying it.

What Learning Is and Is Not

Learning is not involved in inborn, innate behaviors. Learning is a relatively permanent change in behavior, knowledge, and cognitive skills that occurs through experience. Experience is a great teacher.

Approaches to Learning

Behaviorism is the view that behavior should be explained by experiences that can be directly observed, not by mental processes. Classical conditioning and operant conditioning are behavioral views that emphasize associative learning. Psychology became more cognitive in the last part of the twentieth century, and the cognitive emphasis continues today. This is reflected in four cognitive approaches to learning we discuss in this book. Social cognitive approaches emphasize the interaction of behavior, environment, and person (cognition) in explaining learning. Information-processing approaches focus on how children process information through attention, memory, thinking, and other cognitive processes. Cognitive constructivist approaches emphasize the child's construction of knowledge and understanding. Social constructivist approaches focus on collaboration with others to produce knowledge and understanding.

② **BEHAVIORAL APPROACHES TO LEARNING:** Compare classical conditioning and operant conditioning.

Classical Conditioning

In classical conditioning, the organism learns to connect, or associate, stimuli. A neutral stimulus (such as the sight of a person) becomes associated with a meaningful stimulus (such as food) and acquires the capacity to elicit a similar response. Classical conditioning involves these factors: unconditioned stimulus (UCS), conditioned stimulus (CS), unconditioned response (UCR), and conditioned response (CR). Classical conditioning also involves generalization, discrimination, and extinction. Generalization is the tendency of a new stimulus similar to the original conditioned stimulus to produce a similar response. Discrimination occurs when the organism responds to certain stimuli and not to others. Extinction involves the weakening of the CR in the absence of the UCS. Systematic desensitization is a method based on classical conditioning that reduces anxiety by getting the individual to associate deep relaxation with successive visualizations of increasingly anxiety-producing situations. Classical conditioning is better at explaining involuntary behavior than voluntary behavior.

Operant Conditioning

In operant conditioning (also called instrumental conditioning), the consequences of behavior produce changes in the probability that the behavior will occur. Operant conditioning's main architect was B. F. Skinner, who built on the connectionist view of E. L. Thorndike. Thorndike's law of effect states that behaviors followed by positive outcomes are strengthened; those followed by negative behaviors are weakened. His view was called S-R theory. Skinner greatly expanded on Thorndike's ideas. Reinforcement (reward) is a consequence (either positive or negative) that increases the probability that a behavior will occur; punishment is a consequence that decreases the probability that a behavior will occur. In positive reinforcement, a behavior increases because it is followed by a rewarding stimulus (such as praise). In negative reinforcement, a behavior increases because the response removes an aversive (unpleasant) stimulus. Generalization, discrimination, and extinction also are involved in operant conditioning. Generalization means giving the same response to similar stimuli. Discrimination is differentiating among stimuli or environmental events. Extinction occurs when a previously reinforced response is no longer reinforced and the response decreases.

(3) APPLIED BEHAVIOR ANALYSIS IN EDUCATION: Apply behavior analysis to education.

What Is Applied Behavior Analysis?

Applied behavior analysis involves applying the principles of operant conditioning to change human behavior.

Increasing Desirable Behaviors

Find out which reinforcers work best with which students. The Premack principle states that a high-probability activity can be used to reinforce a low-probability activity. "If . . . then" statements can be used to make it clear to students what they have to do to get a reward. Applied behavior analysts recommend that a reinforcement be contingent—that is, be given in a timely manner and only if the student performs the behavior. Skinner described a number of schedules of reinforcement. Most reinforcement in the classroom is partial. Skinner described four schedules of partial reinforcement: fixed-ratio, variable-ratio, fixed-interval, and variable-interval. Contracting involves putting reinforcement contingencies in writing. Although negative reinforcement can increase some students' desirable behavior, exercise caution with students who don't have good self-regulatory skills. A prompt is an added stimulus or cue that increases the likelihood that a discriminative stimulus will produce a desired response. Shaping involves teaching new behaviors by reinforcing successive approximations to a specified target behavior.

Decreasing Undesirable Behaviors

Strategies for decreasing undesirable behaviors include using differential reinforcement, terminating reinforcement, removing desirable stimuli, and presenting aversive stimuli. In differential reinforcement, the teacher might reinforce behavior that is more appropriate or that is incompatible with what the student is doing. Terminating reinforcement (extinction) involves taking reinforcement away from a behavior. Many inappropriate behaviors are maintained by teacher attention, so taking away the attention can decrease the behavior. The most widely used strategy for removing desirable stimuli is time-out. A second strategy is response cost, which occurs when a positive reinforcer, such as a privilege, is taken away from the student. An aversive stimulus becomes a punisher only when it decreases behavior. The most common forms of punisher in the classroom are verbal reprimands. Punishment should be used only as the last option and in conjunction with reinforcement of desired responses. Physical punishment should not be used in the classroom.

Evaluating Operant Conditioning and Applied Behavior Analysis

Used effectively, behavioral techniques can help you manage your classroom. Critics say that these approaches place too much emphasis on external control and not enough on internal control. They also argue that ignoring cognitive factors leaves out much of the richness of students' lives. Critics warn about potential ethical problems when operant conditioning is used inappropriately. And some critics say that teachers who focus too much on managing the classroom with operant techniques may place too much emphasis on conduct and not enough on academic learning.

(4) SOCIAL COGNITIVE APPROACHES TO LEARNING: Summarize social cognitive approaches to learning.

Bandura's Social Cognitive Theory

Albert Bandura is the main architect of social cognitive theory. His reciprocal determinism model of learning includes three main factors: person/cognition, behavior, and environment. The person (cognitive) factor given the most emphasis by Bandura in recent years is self-efficacy, the belief that one can master a situation and produce positive outcomes.

Observational Learning

Observational learning is learning that involves acquiring skills, strategies, and beliefs by observing others. In the Bobo doll experiment, Bandura illustrated how observational learning can occur even by watching a model who is not reinforced or punished. The experiment also demonstrates a distinction between learning and performance. Since his early experiments, Bandura has focused on the specific processes that are involved in observational learning. These include attention, retention, production, and motivation.

continued

Cognitive Behavior Approaches and Self-Regulation

Self-instructional methods are cognitive behavior techniques aimed at teaching individuals to modify their own behavior. In many cases, it is recommended that students replace negative self-statements with positive ones. Cognitive behaviorists believe that students can improve their performance by monitoring their behavior. Self-regulatory learning consists of the self-generation and self-monitoring of thoughts, feelings, and behaviors to reach a goal. High-achieving students are often self-regulatory learners. One model of self-regulatory learning involves these components: self-evaluation and monitoring, goal setting and strategic planning, putting a plan into action, and monitoring outcomes and refining strategies. Self-regulatory learning gives students responsibility for their learning.

Evaluating the Social Cognitive Approaches

The social cognitive approaches have significantly expanded the scope of learning to include cognitive and social factors, in addition to behavior. The concept of observational learning is an important one, and a considerable amount of learning in classrooms takes place in this manner. The cognitive behavior emphasis on self-instruction, self-talk, and self-regulatory learning provides an important shift from learning controlled by others to self-management of learning. Critics of the cognitive and social learning approaches say that they still place too much emphasis on behavior and external factors and not enough on the details of cognitive processes. They also are criticized for being nondevelopmental (although social cognitive advocates argue this label is not justified) and not giving enough attention to self-esteem and warmth.

KEY TERMS

learning 227
behaviorism 227
mental processes 227
associative learning 227
classical conditioning 229
systematic desensitization 231
operant conditioning 232

law of effect 232
reinforcement (reward) 232
punishment 232
positive reinforcement 232
negative reinforcement 232
applied behavior analysis 235
Premack principle 235

schedules of reinforcement 236
contracting 237
prompt 237
shaping 238
time-out 240
response cost 240
social cognitive theory 243

self-efficacy 244
observational learning 244
cognitive behavior
approaches 249
self-instructional methods 251
self-regulatory learning 251

PORTFOLIO ACTIVITIES

Now that you have a good understanding of this chapter, complete these exercises to expand your thinking.

Independent Reflection

Design a Self-Regulation Plan. Letitia is a high school student who doesn't have adequate self-regulatory skills, and this is causing her to have serious academic problems. She doesn't plan or organize, has poor study strategies, and uses ineffective time management. Using Zimmerman's four-step strategy, design an effective self-regulation program for Letitia. (INTASC: Principle 5)

Collaborative Work

Decreasing Undesirable Behaviors. Together with three or four other students in your class, consider the following students' undesirable behaviors. You want to decrease the behaviors. What is the best strategy for each? Discuss and compare your strategies with the group. (1) Andrew, who likes to utter profanities every now and then; (2) Sandy, who tells you to quit bugging her when you ask her questions; (3) Matt, who likes to mess up other students' papers; and (4) Rebecca, who frequently talks with other students around her while you are explaining or demonstrating something. (INTASC: Principles 2, 5)

Research/Field Experience

Sesame Street and Social Cognitive Learning. *Sesame Street* uses many effective techniques to increase children's attention and help them learn. Watch an episode. Analyze the show. How were these techniques used on the show you watched? Describe any additional techniques you observed that you might be able to use in your classroom. (INTASC: Principles 2, 7, 9)

Go to the Online Learning Center for downloadable portfolio templates.

TAKING IT TO THE NET

- Make a list of specific classroom activities that foster student self-regulation. Which of the activities would be most effective in helping students become more responsible for their learning and developing metacognitive skills? Explain why. Develop a brief action plan for implementing your chosen activity. **www.ncrel.org/sdrs/areas/issues/students/learning/lr200.htm**

- An important principle of Bandura's social cognitive theory is that exposure to positive role models can alter students' attitudes. How do you think a teacher's behavior and attitude in the classroom influences students' behaviors and attitudes? What kind of student behavior would you expect to find in a classroom with an authoritarian teacher? Authoritative teacher?

Permissive teacher? **chiron.valdosta.edu/whuitt/col/soccog/soclrn.html**

- Develop a system of classroom rewards/consequences for a particular age/grade level. Does your system utilize intrinsic motivators, extrinsic motivators, or a combination of both? Provide examples of student rewards and explain why you selected those specific items. Discuss the benefits and challenges of implementing your rewards system. **www.education-world.com/a_curr/curr301.shtml**

Connect to the Online Learning Center to explore possible answers.

STUDY, PRACTICE, AND SUCCEED

Visit **www.mhhe.com/santedu3e** to review the chapter with self-grading quizzes and self-assessments, to apply the chapter material to two more Crack the Case studies, and for suggested activities to develop your teaching portfolio.

CHAPTER 8

The Information-Processing Approach

The mind is an enchanting thing.

—Marianne Moore,
American Poet, 20th Century

Chapter Outline		Learning Goals
The Nature of the Information-Processing Approach Information, Memory, and Thinking Cognitive Resources: Capacity and Speed of Processing Information Mechanisms of Change	①	Describe the information-processing approach.
Attention What Is Attention? Developmental Changes	②	Characterize attention and summarize how it changes during development.
Memory What Is Memory? Encoding Storage Retrieval and Forgetting	③	Discuss memory in terms of encoding, storage, and retrieval.
Expertise Expertise and Learning Acquiring Expertise Expertise and Teaching	④	Draw some lessons about learning from the way experts think.
Metacognition Developmental Changes The Good Information-Processing Model Strategies and Metacognitive Regulation	⑤	Explain the concept of metacognition and identify some ways to improve children's metacognition.

TEACHING STORIES   Laura Bickford

Laura Bickford chairs the English Department at Nordoff High School in Ojai, California. She recently spoke about how she encourages students to think:

> I believe the call to teach is a call to teach students how to think. In encouraging critical thinking, literature itself does a good bit of work for us, but we still have to be guides. We have to ask good questions. We have to show students the value in asking their own questions, in having discussions and conversations. In addition to reading and discussing literature, the best way to move students to think critically is to have them write. We write all the time in a variety of modes: journals, formal essays, letters, factual reports, news articles, speeches, or other formal oral presentations. We have to show students where they merely scratch the surface in their thinking and writing. I call these moments "hits and runs." When I see this "hit and run" effort, I draw a window on the paper. I tell them it is a "window of opportunity" to go deeper, elaborate, and clarify. Many students don't do this kind of thinking until they are prodded to do so.
>
> I also use metacognitive strategies all the time—that is, helping students know about knowing. These include: asking students to comment on their learning after we have finished particular pieces of projects and asking them to discuss in advance what we might be seeking to learn as we begin a new project or activity. I also ask them to keep reading logs so they can observe their own thinking as it happens. For example, they might copy a passage from a reading selection and comment on it. Studying a passage from J. D. Salinger's *The Catcher in the Rye*, a student might write: "I've never thought about life the way that Holden Caulfield does. Maybe I see the world differently than he does. He always is so depressed. I'm not depressed. Salinger is good at showing us someone who is usually depressed. How does he manage to do that?" In addition, I ask students to comment on their own learning by way of grading themselves. This year a student gave me one of the most insightful lines about her growth as a reader that I have ever seen from a student. She wrote, "I no longer think in a monotone when I'm reading." I don't know if she grasps the magnitude of that thought or how it came to be that she made that change. It is magic when students see themselves growing like this.

Preview

In the opening story, teacher Laura Bickford tells how she uses metacognitive strategies, one of the important aspects of cognitive learning and a major topic of this chapter. In addition to metacognition, we'll explore what it means to take an information-processing approach in teaching and examine three important aspects of cognition: attention, memory, and expertise.

① THE NATURE OF THE INFORMATION-PROCESSING APPROACH

Information, Memory, and Thinking	Cognitive Resources: Capacity and Speed of Processing Information	Mechanisms of Change

How capable are children? Proponents of the information-processing approach to learning believe they are highly capable. Children attend to information being presented and tinker with it. They develop strategies for remembering. They form concepts. They reason and solve problems. These important skills are the topics of this section.

Information, Memory, and Thinking

The **information-processing approach** emphasizes that children manipulate information, monitor it, and strategize about it. Central to this approach are the processes of memory and thinking. According to the information-processing approach, children develop a gradually increasing capacity for processing information, which allows them to acquire increasingly complex knowledge and skills (Keil, 2006; Munakata, 2006).

Behaviorism and its associative model of learning was a dominant force in psychology until the 1950s and 1960s, when many psychologists began to acknowledge that they could not explain children's learning without referring to mental processes such as memory and thinking (Gardner, 1985). The term *cognitive psychology* became a label for approaches that sought to explain behavior by examining mental processes. Although a number of factors stimulated the growth of cognitive psychology, none was more important than the development of computers. The first modern computer, developed by John von Neumann in the late 1940s, showed that inanimate machines could perform logical operations. This suggested that some mental operations might be carried out by computers, possibly telling us something about the way human cognition works. Cognitive psychologists often draw analogies to computers to help explain the relation between cognition and the brain (Anderson, 2005). The physical brain is compared to the computer's hardware, cognition to its software. Although computers and software aren't perfect analogies for brains and cognitive activities, nonetheless, the comparison contributed to our thinking about the child's mind as an active information-processing system.

Cognitive Resources: Capacity and Speed of Processing Information

As children grow and mature, and as they experience the world, their information-processing abilities increase. These changes are likely influenced by increases in both capacity and speed of processing (Frye, 2004). These two characteristics are often referred to as *cognitive resources*, which are proposed to have an important influence on memory and problem solving.

Both biology and experience contribute to growth in cognitive resources. Think about how much faster you can process information in your native language than a second language. The changes in the brain we described in chapter 2 provide a biological foundation for increased cognitive resources. As children grow and mature, important biological developments occur both in brain structures, such as changes in the frontal lobes, and at the level of neurons, such as the blooming and pruning of connections between neurons that produces fewer but stronger connections (Kuhn & Franklin, 2006; Nelson, Thomas, & de Haan, 2006). Also, as we discussed in chapter 2, myelination (the process that covers the axon with a myelin sheath) increases the speed of electrical impulses in the brain. Myelination continues through childhood and adolescence.

Most information-processing psychologists argue that an increase in capacity also improves processing of information (Case, 2000; Halford, 2004). For example, as children's information-processing capacity increases, they likely can hold in mind several dimensions of a topic or problem simultaneously, whereas younger children are more prone to focus on only one dimension. Adolescents can discuss how the varied experiences of the Founding Fathers influenced the Declaration of Independence and Constitution. Elementary-age children are more likely to focus on simple facts about the founders' lives.

What is the role of processing speed? How fast children process information often influences what they can do with that information. If an adolescent is trying to add up mentally the cost of items he is buying at the grocery store, he needs to be able to compute the sum before he has forgotten the price of the individual items. Children's speed in processing information is linked with their competence in

information–processing approach A cognitive approach in which children manipulate information, monitor it, and strategize about it. Central to this approach are the cognitive processes of memory and thinking.

thinking (Bjorklund, 2005). For example, how fast children can articulate a series of words affects how many words they can store and remember. Generally, fast processing is linked with good performance on cognitive tasks. However, some compensation for slower processing speed can be achieved through effective strategies.

Researchers have devised a number of ways for assessing processing speed. For example, it can be assessed through a *reaction-time task* in which individuals are asked to push a button as soon as they see a stimulus such as a light. Or individuals might be asked to match letters or numbers with symbols on a computer screen.

There is abundant evidence that the speed with which individuals complete such tasks improves dramatically across the childhood years (Kail, 2000). Processing speed continues to improve in early adolescence (Kuhn & Franklin, 2006; Luna & others, 2004). Think how much faster you could process the answer to a simple arithmetic problem as an adolescent than as a child. In one study, 10-year-olds were approximately 1.8 times slower at processing information than young adults on such tasks as reaction time, letter matching, mental rotation, and abstract matching (Hale, 1990). Twelve-year-olds were approximately 1.5 times slower than young adults, but 15-year-olds processed information on the tasks as fast as the young adults.

How does speed of processing information change during childhood and adolescent years?

Mechanisms of Change

According to Robert Siegler (1998), three mechanisms work together to create changes in children's cognitive skills: encoding, automaticity, and strategy construction.

Encoding is the process by which information gets stored in memory. Changes in children's cognitive skills depend on increased skill at encoding relevant information and ignoring irrelevant information. For example, to a 4-year-old, an *s* in cursive writing is a shape very different from an *s* that is printed. But a 10-year-old has learned to encode the relevant fact that both are the letter *s* and to ignore the irrelevant differences in their shape.

Automaticity refers to the ability to process information with little or no effort. Practice allows children to encode increasing amounts of information automatically. For example, once children have learned to read well, they do not think about each letter in a word as a letter; instead, they encode whole words. Once a task is automatic, it does not require conscious effort. As a result, as information processing becomes more automatic, we can complete tasks more quickly and handle more than one task at a time (Mayer & Wittrock, 2006; Schraw, 2006). Imagine how long it would take you to read this page if you did not encode words automatically but instead focused your attention on each letter in each word.

Strategy construction is the creation of new procedures for processing information. For example, children's reading benefits when they develop the strategy of stopping periodically to take stock of what they have read so far. Developing an effective repertoire of strategies and selecting the best one to use on a learning task is a critical aspect of becoming an effective learner (Pressley & Harris, 2006; Pressley & Hilden, 2006).

In addition to these mechanisms of change, children's information processing is characterized by *self-modification* (Siegler, 1998, 2004, 2006; Siegler & Alibali, 2005). That is, children learn to use what they have learned in previous circumstances to adapt their responses to a new situation. For example, a child who is familiar with dogs and cats goes to the zoo and sees lions and tigers for the first time. She then modifies her concept of "animal" to include her new knowledge. Part of this self-modification draws on **metacognition,** which means knowing about knowing (Flavell, 2004; Flavell, Miller, & Miller, 2002; Kuhn & Franklin, 2006). One example of metacognition is what children know about the best ways to remember what they have read. Do they know that they will remember what they have read better if they can relate it to their own lives in some way? Thus, in Siegler's application of the information processing to development, children play an active role in their cognitive development when they develop metacognitive strategies.

encoding The mechanism by which information gets into memory.

automaticity The ability to process information with little or no effort.

strategy construction Discovering a new procedure for processing information.

metacognition Cognition about cognition, or "knowing about knowing."

Review, Reflect, and Practice

(1) Describe the information-processing approach.

REVIEW

- What view does the information-processing approach take of children as learners?
- What are two important cognitive resources and how do they contribute to developmental changes in children's information processing?
- What are some key mechanisms of change in the information-processing approach?

REFLECT

- In terms of your ability to learn, are there ways that you wish you were more like a computer? Or are you better than any computer in all aspects of processing information? Explain.

PRAXIS™ PRACTICE

1. Information processing is most closely aligned with
   a. behaviorism
   b. cognitive psychology
   c. social cognitive theory
   d. ecological theory

2. According to the information-processing approach, a 15-year-old can compute faster than a 10-year-old because the
   a. 15-year-old's brain has had more time to develop, and the 15-year-old has had more experience working with numbers.
   b. 15-year-old has had more experiences of both positive and negative reinforcement.
   c. 15-year-old's brain has lost many of its original connections and undergone demyelinization.
   d. 15-year-old has had much more time to develop rote memory skills.

3. Ms. Parks wants her students to know their basic math facts without having to stop to think about them. Therefore, Ms. Parks plays many math games with her second-grade students, such as addition and subtraction bingo, math bees, and card games. What is Ms. Parks' goal in playing these games with her students?
   a. to help her students to develop automaticity in knowing their math facts
   b. to encourage strategy construction
   c. to foster encoding skills
   d. to improve metacognitive skills, such as self-awareness

Please see the answer key at the end of the book.

(2) ATTENTION

> What Is Attention?   Developmental Changes

The world holds a lot of information that we need to perceive. What is attention and what effect does it have? How does it change developmentally?

What Is Attention?

Attention is the focusing of mental resources. Attention improves cognitive processing for many tasks, from grabbing a toy to hitting a baseball or adding numbers. At any one time, though, children, like adults, can pay attention to only a limited amount of information. They allocate their attention in different ways. Psychologists have labeled these types of allocation as sustained attention, selective attention, and divided attention.

- **Sustained attention** is the ability to maintain attention to a selected stimulus for a prolonged period of time. Sustained attention is also called *vigilance*. Recall from our discussion in chapter 6 that in one recent study difficulties in sustaining attention were the most common type of attentional problem characterizing children with ADHD (Tsal, Shavel, & Mevorach, 2005).

- **Selective attention** is focusing on a specific aspect of experience that is relevant while ignoring others that are irrelevant. Focusing on one voice among many in a crowded room or a noisy restaurant is an example of selective attention.

- **Divided attention** involves concentrating on more than one activity at the same time. If you are listening to music while you are reading this, you are engaging in divided attention.

What are some developmental changes in attention?

Developmental Changes

Some important changes in attention occur during childhood. Much of the research on attention has focused on selective attention. One recent study of 5- to 7-year-old children found that the older children and more socially advantaged children in a sample resisted the interference of competing demands and focused their attention better than the younger children and more socially disadvantaged children (Mezzacappa, 2004).

The length of time children can pay attention increases as they get older. The toddler wanders around, shifts attention from one activity to another, and seems to spend little time focused on any one object or event. In contrast, the preschool child might watch television for half an hour at a time (Giavecchio, 2001). One study that observed 99 families in their homes for 4,672 hours found that visual attention to television dramatically increased in the preschool years (Anderson & others, 1985).

Researchers have found that preschool children's attention is related to their achievement-related and social skills (Ruff & Rothbart, 1996). In regard to achievement-related skills, one recent study of more than 1,000 children found that their sustained attention at 54 months of age was linked to their school readiness (which included achievement and language skills) (NICHD Early Child Care Research Network, 2003). In regard to social skills, young children who have difficulty regulating their attention are more likely than other children to experience peer rejection and engage in aggressive behavior (Eisenberg & others, 2000).

Control over attention shows important changes during childhood (Ruff & Capozzoli, 2003). External stimuli are likely to determine the target of the preschooler's attention; what is *salient*, or obvious, grabs the preschooler's attention. For example, suppose a flashy, attractive clown presents the directions for solving a problem. Preschool children are likely to pay attention to the clown and ignore the directions, because they are influenced strongly by the salient features of the environment. After the age of 6 or 7, children pay more attention to features relevant to performing a task or solving a problem, such as the directions. This change reflects a shift to *cognitive control* of attention, so that children act less impulsively and reflect more. Instead of being controlled by the most striking

attention Concentrating and focusing mental resources.

sustained attention The ability to maintain attention to a selected stimulus for a prolonged period of time; also called vigilance.

selective attention Focusing on a specific aspect of experience that is relevant while ignoring others that are irrelevant.

divided attention Concentrating on more than one activity at a time.

BEST PRACTICES
Strategies for Helping Students Pay Attention

1. *Encourage students to pay close attention and minimize distraction.* Talk with children about how important it is to pay attention when they need to remember something. Give them exercises with opportunities to give their undivided attention to something.

2. *Use cues or gestures to signal that something is important.* This might involve raising your voice, repeating something with emphasis, and writing the concept on the board or on a transparency.

3. *Help students generate their own cue or catch phrase for when they need to pay attention.* Possibly vary this from month to month. Give them a menu of options to select from, such as "Alert," "Focus," or "Zero in." Teach them to say their word or pet phrase quietly but firmly to themselves when they catch their minds wandering.

4. *Make learning interesting.* Boredom can set in quickly for students, and when it does their attention wanes. Relating ideas to students' interests increases their attention. So does infusing the classroom with novel, unusual, or surprising exercises. Just starting off a biology exercise on heredity and aging with a question such as "Can you live to be 100?" or "Might someone be able to live to be even 400 some day?" is sure to capture students' attention. Think of dramatic questions such as these to introduce various topics.

5. *Use media and technology effectively as part of your effort to vary the pace of the classroom.* Video and television programs have built-in attention-getting formats, such as zooming in on an image; flashing a vivid, colorful image on the screen; and switching from one setting to another. Look for relevant videos and television programs that can help you vary the classroom's pace and increase students' attention. Unfortunately, too many teachers show videos only to keep students quiet, which does not promote learning. Also, if the curriculum is dull, it doesn't matter what kinds of "tricks" or "splashes" the teacher uses—students will not learn effectively. Make sure that the media and technology you use captures students' attention in meaningful ways that promote effective learning (Goldman, 1998).

6. *Focus on active learning to make learning enjoyable.* A different exercise, a guest, a field trip, and many other activities can be used to make learning more enjoyable, reduce student boredom, and increase attention. Next, middle school English and drama teacher Lynn Ayres describes how games can add interest at all grade levels.

THROUGH THE EYES OF TEACHERS
Turning Boring Exercises into Active Learning Games

I have found that the most boring exercises (such as the kind you find on worksheets and textbooks) can be turned into an active learning game. One favorite game in my seventh-grade English class was "sit-set, rise-raise." I'd put two students in chairs next to tables and place a book on each table. If I said "rise" they were to stand. If I said "raise" they were to raise the book. They were to seat themselves if I said "sit" and they were to place the book on the table if I said "set." If I said "rise" and one of them stood up and the other student lifted the book, the student with the book held up was out and was replaced by a teammate. Or if they both stood up, the one who stood up first stayed, and the other student was replaced by a teammate. The students loved that game, and they really learned the difference between those two commonly confused pairs of verbs in the process.

That game taught me the effectiveness of getting students physically involved. I developed dozens of other games involving bells and timers and teams that had students running around the room, ringing bells, trying to beat a member of the opposing team in telling me if a word was a noun or an adjective. Almost any workbook or textbook exercise can be turned into a physical activity game if you put some thought into it, and middle school students learn so much more from doing an exercise that is both physical and mental.

7. *Don't overload students with too much information.* We live in an information society where sometimes the tendency is to feel like you have to get students to learn everything. But students who are given too much information too fast might not attend to anything.

8. *Be aware of individual differences in students' attentional skills.* Some students have severe problems in paying attention. You will need to take this into account when presenting material. Before you begin an exercise, look around the room for potential distractions, such as an open window to a playground where students are being noisy. Close the window and draw the shade to eliminate the distraction.

stimuli in their environment, older children can direct their attention to more important stimuli.

Attention to relevant information increases steadily through the elementary and secondary school years (Davidson, 1996). Processing of irrelevant information decreases in adolescence.

As children grow up, their abilities both to direct selective attention and to divided attention also improve. Older children and adolescents are better than younger children at tasks that require shifts of attention. For example, writing a good story requires shifting attention among many competing tasks—spelling the words, composing grammar, structuring paragraphs, and conveying the story as a whole. Children also improve in their ability to do two things at once. For example, in one investigation, 12-year-olds were markedly better than 8-year-olds and slightly worse than 20-year-olds at allocating their attention in a situation involving two tasks (divided attention) (Manis, Keating, & Morrison, 1980). These improvements in divided attention might be due to an increase in cognitive resources (through increased processing speed or capacity), automaticity, or increased skill at directing resources.

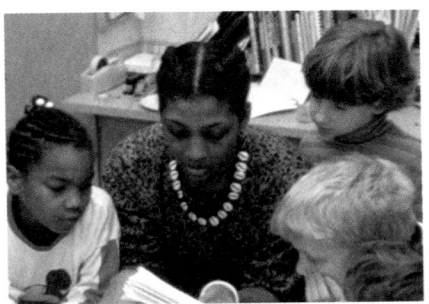

What are some good strategies teachers can use to get students' attention?

Review, Reflect, and Practice

2 Characterize attention and summarize how it changes during development.

REVIEW

- What is attention? What are three ways attention can be allocated?
- How does attention develop in childhood and adolescence?

REFLECT

- Imagine that you are an elementary school teacher and a child is having difficulty sustaining attention on a learning task. What strategies would you try to use to help the child sustain attention?

PRAXIS™ PRACTICE

1. Ms. Samson teaches first grade. Often while she is working with one group of children, she must monitor the behavior of the rest of the class, occasionally intervening in some manner. Sometimes she has three or four students at her desk, each needing something different from her. This does not seem to faze her in the least. She can talk to one student while tying another's shoes and monitoring the behavior of the rest with no problem. What skill has Ms. Samson mastered?
   a. divided attention
   b. selective attention
   c. sustained attention
   d. personal attention

2. Mark shifts his attention very quickly from one thing to another. The more colorful and noisy the thing, the more likely it is to draw his attention. He rarely attends to any one thing for more than a few minutes. From this description, Mark is most likely to be a
   a. toddler.
   b. preschooler.
   c. elementary-school-age child.
   d. adolescent.

Please see the answer key at the end of the book.

③ MEMORY

| What Is Memory? | Encoding | Storage | Retrieval and Forgetting |

Twentieth-century playwright Tennessee Williams once commented that life is all memory except for that one present moment that goes by so quickly that you can hardly catch it going. But just what is memory?

What Is Memory?

Memory is the retention of information over time. Educational psychologists study how information is initially placed or encoded into memory, how it is retained or stored after being encoded, and how it is found or retrieved for a certain purpose later. Memory anchors the self in continuity. Without memory you would not be able to connect what happened to you yesterday with what is going on in your life today. Today, educational psychologists emphasize that it is important not to view memory in terms of how children add something to it but, rather, to underscore how children actively construct their memory (Schacter, 2001).

The main body of our discussion of memory will focus on encoding, storage, and retrieval. Thinking about memory in terms of these processes should help you to understand it better (see figure 8.1). For memory to work, children have to take information in, store it or represent it, and then retrieve it for some purpose later.

As you learned earlier, *encoding* is the process by which information gets into memory. *Storage* is the retention of information over time. *Retrieval* means taking information out of storage. Let's now explore each of these three important memory activities in greater detail.

FIGURE 8.1 Processing Information in Memory

As you read about the many aspects of memory in this chapter, think about the organization of memory in terms of these three main activities.

Encoding

In everyday language, encoding has much in common with attention and learning. When a student is listening to a teacher, watching a movie, listening to music, or talking with a friend, he or she is encoding information into memory. In addition to attention, which we just discussed, encoding consists of a number of processes: rehearsal, deep processing, elaboration, constructing images, and organization.

Rehearsal   **Rehearsal** is the conscious repetition of information over time to increase the length of time information stays in memory. For example, when you make a date to meet your best friend for lunch, you are likely to repeat, or rehearse, the date and time: "OK—Wednesday at 1:30." Rehearsal works best when you need to encode and remember a list of items for a brief period of time. When you must retain information over long periods of time, as when you are studying for a test you won't take until next week, other strategies usually work better than rehearsal. Rehearsal does not work well for retaining information over the long term because it often involves just rote repetition of information without imparting any meaning to it. When you construct your memory in meaningful ways, you remember better. As we will see next, you also remember better when you process material deeply and elaborate it.

Deep Processing   Following the discovery that rehearsal is not an efficient way to encode information for long-term memory, Fergus Craik and Robert Lockhart (1972) proposed that we can process information at a variety of levels. Their theory,

memory The retention of information over time, which involves encoding, storage, and retrieval.

rehearsal The conscious repetition of information over time to increase the length of time information stays in memory.

levels of processing theory, states that the processing of memory occurs on a continuum from shallow to deep, with deeper processing producing better memory. Shallow processing means analyzing a stimuli's sensory, or physical, features at a shallow level. This might involve detecting the lines, angles, and contours of a printed word's letters or a spoken word's frequency, duration, and loudness. At an intermediate level of processing, you recognize the stimulus and give it a label. For example, you identify a four-legged, barking object as a dog. Then, at the deepest level, you process information semantically, in terms of its meaning. For example, if a child sees the word *boat*, at the shallow level she might notice the shapes of the letters, at the intermediate level she might think of the characteristics of the word (for instance, that it rhymes with *coat*), and at the deepest level she might think about the last time she went fishing with her dad on a boat and the kind of boat it was. Researchers have found that individuals remember information better when they process it at a deep level (Otten, Henson, & Rugg, 2001).

Elaboration   Cognitive psychologists soon recognized, however, that there is more to good encoding than just depth of processing. They discovered that when individuals use elaboration in their encoding of information, their memory benefits (Terry, 2006). **Elaboration** is the extensiveness of information processing involved in encoding. Thus, when you present the concept of democracy to students, they likely will remember it better if they come up with good examples of it. Thinking of examples is a good way to elaborate information. For instance, self-reference is an effective way to elaborate information. If you are trying to get students to remember the concept of fairness, the more they can generate personal examples of inequities and equities they have personally experienced, the more likely they are to remember the concept.

The use of elaboration changes developmentally (Nelson, 2006; Schneider, 2004; Schneider & Pressley, 1997). Adolescents are more likely to use elaboration spontaneously than children are. Elementary school children can be taught to use elaboration strategies on a learning task, but they are less likely than adolescents to use the strategies on other learning tasks in the future. Nonetheless, verbal elaboration can be an effective memory strategy even with young elementary school children. In one study, the experimenter told second- and fifth-grade children to construct a meaningful sentence for a keyword (such as "The postman carried a letter in his cart" for the keyword *cart*). As shown in figure 8.2, both second- and fifth-grade children remembered the keywords better when they constructed a meaningful sentence containing the word than when the keyword and its definition were told to the child (Pressley, Levin, & McCormick, 1980).

One reason elaboration works so well in encoding is that it adds to the distinctiveness of memory code (Ellis, 1987; Hunt & Ellis, 2004). To remember a piece of information, such as a name, an experience, or a fact about geography, students need to search for the code that contains this information among the mass of codes in their long-term memory. The search process is easier if the memory code is unique (Hunt & Kelly, 1996). The situation is not unlike searching for a friend at a crowded airport—if your friend is 6 feet 3 inches tall and has flaming red hair, it will be easier to find him in the crowd than if he has more common features. Also, as a person elaborates information, more information is stored. And as more information is

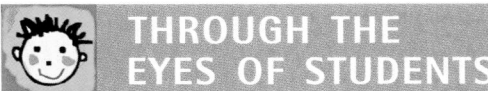
THROUGH THE EYES OF STUDENTS

The Cobwebs of Memory

I think the point of having memories is to share them, especially with close friends or family. If you don't share them, they are just sitting inside your brain getting cobwebs. If you have a great memory of Christmas and no one to share it with, what's the point of memories?

Seventh-Grade Student
West Middle School
Ypsilanti, Michigan

levels of processing theory The theory that processing of memory occurs on a continuum from shallow to deep, with deeper processing producing better memory.

elaboration The extensiveness of information processing involved in encoding.

FIGURE 8.2 Verbal Elaboration and Memory

Both second- and fifth-grade children remembered words better when they constructed a meaningful sentence for the word (verbal elaboration group) than when they merely heard the word and its definition (control group). The verbal elaboration worked better for the fifth-graders than the second-graders.

stored, it becomes easier to differentiate the memory from others. For example, if a student witnesses another student being hit by a car that speeds away, the student's memory of the car will be far better if she deliberately encodes her observations that the car is a red 1995 Pontiac with tinted windows and spinners on the wheels than if she observes only that it is a red car.

Constructing Images When we construct an image of something, we are elaborating the information. For example, how many windows are there in the apartment or house where your family has lived for a substantial part of your life? Few of us ever memorize this information, but you probably can come up with a good answer, especially if you reconstruct a mental image of each room.

Allan Paivio (1971, 1986) argues that memories are stored in one of two ways: as verbal codes or as image codes. For example, you can remember a picture by a label (*The Last Supper*, a verbal code) or by a mental image. Paivio says that the more detailed and distinctive the image code, the better your memory of the information will be.

Researchers have found that encouraging children to use imagery to remember verbal information works better for older children than for younger children (Schneider, 2004). In one study, experimenters presented twenty sentences to first- through sixth-grade children to remember (such as "The angry bird shouted at the white dog" and "The policeman painted the circus tent on a windy day") (Pressley & others, 1987). Children were randomly assigned to an imagery condition (make a picture in your head for each sentence) and a control condition (children were told just to try hard). Figure 8.3 shows that the imagery instructions improved memory more for the older children (grades 4 through 6) than for the younger children (grades 1 through 3). Researchers have found that young elementary school children can use imagery to remember pictures better than they can verbal materials, such as sentences (Schneider & Pressley, 1997).

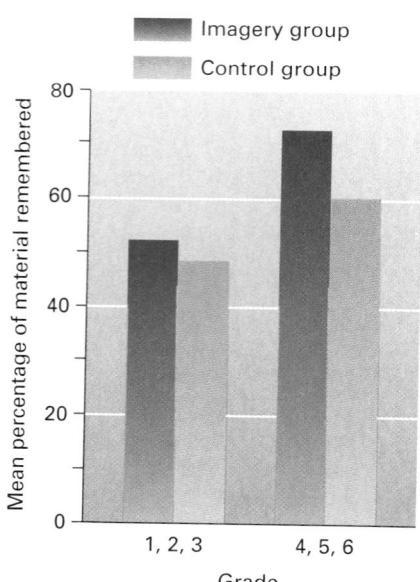

FIGURE 8.3 Imagery and Memory of Verbal Information

Imagery improved older elementary school children's memory for sentences more than younger elementary school children's memory for sentences.

Organization If students organize information when they are encoding it, their memory benefits. To understand the importance of organization in encoding, complete the following exercise: Recall the 12 months of the year as quickly as you can. How long did it take you? What was the order of your recall? Your answers are probably a few seconds and in natural order (January, February, March, and so on). Now try to remember the months in alphabetical order. Did you make any errors? How long did it take you? There is a clear distinction between recalling the months in natural order and recalling alphabetically. This exercise is a good one to use with your students to help them understand the importance of organizing their memories in meaningful ways.

The more you present information in an organized way, the easier your students will remember it. This is especially true if you organize information hierarchically or outline it. Also, if you simply encourage students to organize information, they often

FRANK & ERNEST © Thaves/Dist. by Newspaper Enterprise Association, Inc.

will remember it better than if you give them no instructions about organizing (Mandler, 1980).

Chunking is a beneficial organizational memory strategy that involves grouping, or "packing," information into "higher-order" units that can be remembered as single units. Chunking works by making large amounts of information more manageable and more meaningful. For example, consider this simple list of words: *hot, city, book, forget, tomorrow, smile.* Try to hold these in memory for a moment; then write them down. If you recalled all six words, you succeeded in holding 30 letters in your memory. But it would have been much more difficult to try to remember those 30 letters. Chunking them into words made them meaningful.

Storage

After children encode information, they need to retain, or store, the information. Memory storage involves three types of memory with different time frames: sensory memory, working (or short-term) memory, and long-term memory.

"*Can we hurry up and get to the test? My short-term memory is better than my long-term memory.*"

© 2006; reprinted courtesy of Bunny Hoest and *Parade.*

Memory's Time Frames   Children remember some information for less than a second, some for about half a minute, and other information for minutes, hours, years, even a lifetime. The three types of memory, which correspond to these different time frames, are *sensory memory* (which lasts a fraction of a second to several seconds); *short-term memory* (also called *working memory;* lasts about 30 seconds), and *long-term memory* (which lasts up to a lifetime).

Sensory Memory   **Sensory memory** holds information from the world in its original sensory form for only an instant, not much longer than the brief time a student is exposed to the visual, auditory, and other sensations.

Students have a sensory memory for sounds for up to several seconds, sort of like a brief echo. However, their sensory memory for visual images lasts only for about one-fourth of a second. Because sensory information lasts for only a fleeting moment, an important task for the student is to attend to the sensory information that is important for learning quickly, before it fades.

Short-Term Memory   **Short-term memory** is a limited-capacity memory system in which information is retained for as long as 30 seconds, unless the information is rehearsed or otherwise processed further, in which case it can be retained longer. Compared with sensory memory, short-term memory is limited in capacity but relatively longer in duration. Its limited capacity intrigued George Miller (1956), who described this in a paper with a catchy title: "The Magical Number Seven, Plus or Minus Two." Miller pointed out that on many tasks, students are limited in how much information they can keep track of without external aids. Usually the limit is in the range of 7 $\pm$ 2 items.

The most widely cited example of the 7 $\pm$ 2 phenomenon involves **memory span,** the number of digits an individual can report back without error from a single presentation. How many digits individuals can report back depends on how old they are. In one study, memory span increased from two digits in 2-year-olds, to five digits in 7-year-olds, to six to seven digits in 12-year-olds (Dempster, 1981) (see figure 8.4). Many college students can handle lists of eight or nine digits. Keep in mind that these are averages and that individuals differ. For example, many 7-year-olds have a memory span of fewer than six or seven digits; others have a memory span of eight or more digits.

Related to short-term memory, British psychologist Alan Baddeley (1993, 1998, 2000, 2001) proposed that **working memory** is a three-part system that temporarily holds information as people perform tasks. Working memory is a kind of mental "workbench" where information is manipulated and assembled to help us make decisions, solve problems, and comprehend written and spoken language. Notice that

chunking Grouping, or "packing," information into "higher-order" units that can be remembered as single units.

sensory memory Memory that holds information from the world in its original form for only an instant.

short-term memory A limited-capacity memory system in which information is retained for as long as 30 seconds, unless the information is rehearsed, in which case it can be retained longer.

memory span The number of digits an individual can report back without error in a single presentation.

working memory A kind of "mental workbench" that lets individuals manipulate, assemble, and construct information when they make decisions, solve problems, and comprehend written and spoken language.

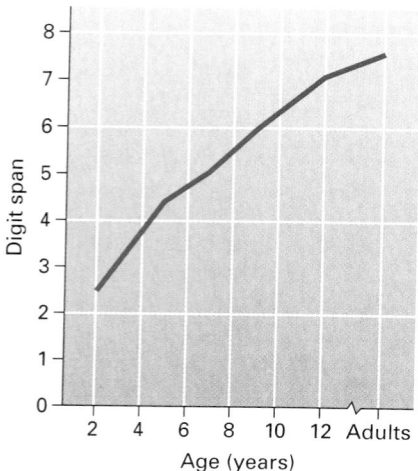

FIGURE 8.4 Developmental Changes in Memory Span

In one study, memory span increased about 3 digits from 2 years of age to 5 digits at 7 years of age (Dempster, 1981). By 12 years of age, memory span had increased on average another 1½ digits.

working memory is not like a passive storehouse with shelves to store information until it moves to long-term memory. Rather, it is a very active memory system (Hitch, 2006; Kane & others, 2004; Schraw, 2006).

Figure 8.5 shows Baddeley's view of working memory and its three components: phonological loop, visuospatial memory, and central executive. Think of them as an executive (central executive) with two assistants (phonological loop and visuospatial working memory) to help do your work.

- The *phonological loop* is specialized to briefly store speech-based information about the sounds of language. The phonological loop contains two separate components: an acoustic code, which decays in a few seconds, and rehearsal, which allows individuals to repeat the words in the phonological store.
- *Visuospatial working memory* stores visual and spatial information, including visual imagery. Like the phonological loop, visuospatial working memory has a limited capacity. The phonological loop and visuospatial working memory function independently. You could rehearse numbers in the phonological loop while making spatial arrangements of letters in visuospatial working memory.
- The *central executive* integrates information not only from the phonological loop and visuospatial working memory but also from long-term memory. In Baddeley's view, the central executive plays important roles in attention, planning, and organizing behavior. The central executive acts much like a supervisor who monitors which information and issues deserve attention and which should be ignored. It also selects which strategies to use to process information and solve problems. As with the other two components of working memory—the phonological loop and visuospatial working memory—the central executive has a limited capacity.

Let's examine an aspect of life in which working memory is involved. In one study, verbal working memory was impaired by negative emotion (Gray, 2001). In other words, when people are feeling bad about something, their working memory may become less efficient. In another study, college students who wrote about a negative emotional event showed sizeable improvement in working memory, compared with students who wrote about a positive emotional event and those in a control group who wrote about their daily schedule (Klein & Boals, 2001). The writing effect on working memory was associated with higher grade-point averages. This study demonstrated that working memory is malleable and can be affected by an experience such as writing about one's emotional experiences (Miyake, 2001). For example, students with math anxiety often experience deficiencies in working memory when doing math problems because of intrusive thoughts and worries about math (Ashcraft & Kirk, 2001). Such students might benefit from writing about their math anxiety.

Is the working memory of adolescents better than the working memory of children? One study found that it was (Swanson, 1999). Investigators examined the performances of children and adolescents on both verbal and visuospatial working memory tasks. The two verbal tasks were auditory digit sequence (the ability to remember numerical information embedded in a short sentence, such as "Now suppose somebody wanted to go to the supermarket at 8651 Elm Street") and semantic association (the ability to organize words into abstract categories) (Swanson, 1999, p. 988). In the semantic association task, the participant was presented with a series of words (such as *shirt, saw, pants, hammer, shoes,* and *nails*) and then asked to remember how they go together. The two visuospatial tasks involved mapping/directions and a visual matrix. In the mapping/directions task, the participant was shown a street map indicating the route a bicycle would take. After briefly looking at the map, participants were asked to redraw the route on a blank map. In the visual matrix task, participants were asked to study a matrix showing a series of dots. After looking at the matrix for five seconds, they were asked to answer questions about the location of the dots. As shown in figure 8.6, working memory increased substantially from 8 through 24 years of age no matter what the task. Thus, the adolescent years are likely to be an important developmental period for improvement in working memory.

Long-Term Memory   **Long-term memory** is a type of memory that holds enormous amounts of information for a long period of time in a relatively permanent fashion. A typical human's long-term memory capacity is staggering and the efficiency with which individuals can retrieve information is impressive. It often takes only a moment to search through this vast storehouse to find the information we want. Think about your own long-term memory. Who wrote the Gettysburg Address? Who was your first-grade teacher? You can answer thousands of such questions instantly. Of course, not all information is retrieved so easily from long-term memory.

A Model of the Three Memory Stores   This three-stage concept of memory we have been describing was developed by Richard Atkinson and Richard Shiffrin (1968). According to the **Atkinson-Shiffrin model,** memory involves a sequence of sensory memory, short-term memory, and long-term memory stages (see figure 8.7). As we have seen, much information makes it no further than the sensory memories of sounds and sights. This information is retained only for a brief instant. However, some information, especially that to which we pay attention, is transferred to short-term memory, where it can be retained for about 30 seconds (or longer with the aid of rehearsal). Atkinson and Shiffrin claimed that the longer information is retained in short-term memory through the use of rehearsal, the greater its chance is of getting into long-term memory. Notice in figure 8.7 that information in long-term memory also can be retrieved back into short-term memory.

Some contemporary experts on memory believe that the Atkinson-Shiffrin model is too simple (Bartlett, 2005). They argue that memory doesn't always work in a neatly packaged three-stage sequence, as Atkinson and Shiffrin proposed. For example, these contemporary experts stress that *working memory* uses long-term memory's contents in more flexible ways than simply retrieving information from it. Despite these problems, the model is useful in providing an overview of some components of memory.

FIGURE 8.5 Working Memory

In Baddeley's working memory model, working memory is like a mental workbench where a great deal of information processing is carried out. Working memory consists of three main components: The phonological loop and visuospatial working memory serve as assistants, helping the central executive do its work. Input from sensory memory goes to the phonological loop, where information about speech is stored and rehearsal takes place, and visuospatial working memory, where visual and spatial information, including imagery, are stored. Working memory is a limited-capacity system, and information is stored there for only a brief time. Working memory interacts with long-term memory, using information from long-term memory in its work and transmitting information to long-term memory for longer storage.

FIGURE 8.6 Developmental Changes in Working Memory

Note: The scores shown here are the means for each age group and the age also represents a mean age. Higher scores reflect superior working memory performance.

long-term memory A type of memory that holds enormous amounts of information for a long period of time in a relatively permanent fashion.

Atkinson–Shiffrin model A model of memory that involves a sequence of three stages: sensory memory, short-term memory, and long-term memory.

FIGURE 8.7 Atkinson and Shiffrin's Theory of Memory

In this model, sensory input goes into sensory memory. Through the process of attention, information moves into short-term memory, where it remains for 30 seconds or less, unless it is rehearsed. When the information goes into long-term memory storage, it can be retrieved over the lifetime.

Long-Term Memory's Contents Just as different types of memory can be distinguished by how long they last, memory can be differentiated on the basis of its contents (Schraw, 2006). For long-term memory, many contemporary psychologists accept the hierarchy of contents described in figure 8.8 (Bartlett, 2005; Squire, 1987). In this hierarchy, long-term memory is divided into the subtypes of declarative and procedural memory. Declarative memory is subdivided into episodic memory and semantic memory.

Declarative and Procedural Memory **Declarative memory** is the conscious recollection of information, such as specific facts or events that can be verbally communicated. Declarative memory has been called "knowing that" and more recently has been labeled "explicit memory." Demonstrations of students' declarative memory could include recounting an event they have witnessed or describing a basic principle of math. However, students do not need to be talking to be using declarative memory. If students simply sit and reflect on an experience, their declarative memory is involved.

Procedural memory is nondeclarative knowledge in the form of skills and cognitive operations. Procedural memory cannot be consciously recollected, at least not in the form of specific events or facts. This makes procedural memory difficult, if not impossible, to communicate verbally. Procedural memory is sometimes called "knowing how," and recently it also has been described as "implicit memory" (Schacter, 2000). When students apply their abilities to perform a dance, ride a bicycle, or type on a computer keyboard, their procedural memory is at work. It also is at work when they speak grammatically correct sentences without having to think about how to do it.

declarative memory The conscious recollection of information, such as specific facts or events that can be verbally communicated.

procedural memory Knowledge in the form of skills and cognitive operations. Procedural memory cannot be consciously recollected, at least not in the form of specific events or facts.

FIGURE 8.8 Classification of Long-Term Memory's Contents

Episodic and Semantic Memory   Cognitive psychologist Endel Tulving (1972, 2000) distinguishes between two subtypes of declarative memory: episodic and semantic. **Episodic memory** is the retention of information about the where and when of life's happenings. Students' memories of the first day of school, whom they had lunch with, or the guest who came to talk with their class last week are all episodic.

Semantic memory is a student's general knowledge about the world. It includes

- knowledge of the sort learned in school (such as knowledge of geometry);
- knowledge in different fields of expertise (such as knowledge of chess, for a skilled 15-year-old chess player); and
- "everyday" knowledge about meanings of words, famous people, important places, and common things (such as what the word *pertinacious* means or who Nelson Mandela is).

Semantic memory is independent of the person's identity with the past. For example, students might access a fact—such as "Lima is the capital of Peru"—and not have the foggiest idea when and where they learned it.

Representing Information in Memory   How do students represent information in their memory? Three main theories have addressed this question: network, schema, and fuzzy trace.

Network Theories   **Network theories** describe how information in memory is organized and connected. They emphasize nodes in the memory network. The nodes stand for labels or concepts. Consider the concept "bird." One of the earliest network theories described memory representation as hierarchically arranged, with more-concrete concepts ("canary," for example) nestled under more abstract concepts (such as "bird"). However, it soon became clear that such hierarchical networks are too neat to accurately portray how memory representation really works. For example, students take longer to answer the question "Is an ostrich a bird?" than to answer the question "Is a canary a bird?" Thus, today memory researchers envision the memory network as more irregular and distorted (Schraw, 2006). A typical bird, such as a canary, is closer to the node, or center, of the category "bird" than is the atypical ostrich.

Schema Theories   Long-term memory has been compared to a library of books. The idea is that our memory stores information just as a library stores books. In this analogy, the way students retrieve information is said to be similar to the process they use to locate and check out a book. The process of retrieving information from long-term memory, however, is not as precise as the library analogy suggests. When we search through our long-term memory storehouse, we don't always find the exact "book" we want, or we might find the "book" we want but discover that only "several pages" are intact—we have to reconstruct the rest.

Schema theories state that when we reconstruct information, we fit it into information that already exists in our mind. A **schema** is information—concepts, knowledge, information about events—that already exists in a person's mind. Unlike network theories, which assume that retrieval involves specific facts, schema theory claims that long-term memory searches are not very exact. We often don't find precisely what we want, and we have to reconstruct the rest. Often when asked to retrieve information, we fill in the gaps between our fragmented memories with a variety of accuracies and inaccuracies.

We have schemas for all sorts of information. If you tell virtually any story to your class and then ask the students to write down what the story was about, you likely will get many different versions. That is, your students won't remember every detail of the story you told and will reconstruct the story with their own particular stamp on it. Suppose you tell your class a story about two men and two women who were involved in a train crash in France. One student might reconstruct the story by saying the characters died in a plane crash, another might describe three men and three women,

episodic memory The retention of information about the where and when of life's happenings.

semantic memory A student's general knowledge about the world.

network theories Theories that describe how information in memory is organized and connected; they emphasize nodes in the memory network.

schema theories Theories that when we construct information, we fit it into information that already exists in our mind.

schema Information—concepts, knowledge, information about events—that already exists in a person's mind.

another might say the crash was in Germany, and so on. The reconstruction and distortion of memory is nowhere more apparent than in the memories given by courtroom witnesses. In criminal court trials such as that of O. J. Simpson and Scott Peterson the variations in people's memories of what happened underscores how we reconstruct the past rather than take an exact photograph of it.

In sum, schema theory accurately predicts that people don't always coldly store and retrieve bits of data in a computer-like fashion (Chen & Mo, 2004; Schacter, 2001; Schraw, 2006). The mind can distort an event as it encodes and stores impressions of reality.

A **script** is a schema for an event. Scripts often have information about physical features, people, and typical occurrences. This kind of information is helpful when teachers and students need to figure out what is happening around them. In a script for an art activity, students likely will remember that you will instruct them on what to draw, that they are supposed to put on smocks over their clothes, that they must get the art paper and paints from the cupboard, that they are to clean the brushes when they are finished, and so on. For example, a student who comes in late to the art activity likely knows much of what to do because he has an art activity script.

Fuzzy Trace Theory   Another variation of how individuals reconstruct their memories is **fuzzy trace theory** which states that when individuals encode information it creates two types of memory representations: (1) a *verbatim memory trace*, which consists of precise details, and (2) a *fuzzy trace*, or *gist*, which is the central idea of the information (Brainerd & Reyna, 2004; Reyna, 2004; Reyna & Brainerd, 1995). For example, consider a child who is presented with information about a pet store that has 10 birds, 6 cats, 8 dogs, and 7 rabbits. Then the child is asked two different types of questions: (1) verbatim questions, such as: "How many cats are in the pet store, 6 or 8?" and (2) gist questions, such as: "Are there more cats or more dogs in the pet store?" Researchers have found that preschool children tend to remember verbatim information better than gist information, but elementary-school-aged children are more likely to remember gist information (Brainerd & Gordon, 1994). According to Brainerd and Reyna, the increased use of gist information by elementary-school-aged children accounts for their improved memory, because fuzzy traces are less likely to be forgotten than verbatim traces.

Retrieval and Forgetting

After students have encoded information and then represented it in memory, they might be able to retrieve some of it but might also forget some of it. What factors influence whether students can retrieve information?

Retrieval   When we retrieve something from our mental "data bank," we search our store of memory to find the relevant information. Just as with encoding, this search can be automatic or it can require effort. For example, if you ask your students what month it is, the answer will immediately spring to their lips. That is, the retrieval will be automatic. But if you ask your students to name the guest speaker who came to the class 2 months earlier, the retrieval process likely will require more effort.

An item's position on a list also affects how easy or difficult it will be to remember it (Pressley & Harris, 2006). In the **serial position effect,** recall is better for items at the beginning and end of a list than for items in the middle. Suppose that when you give a student directions about where to go to get tutoring help, you say, "Left on Mockingbird, right on Central, left on Balboa, left on Sandstone, and right on Parkside." The student likely will remember "Left on Mockingbird" and "Right on Parkside" better than "Left on Balboa." The *primacy effect* is that items at the beginning of a list tend to be remembered. The *recency effect* is that items at the end of the list also tend to be remembered.

Figure 8.9 shows a typical serial position effect with a slightly stronger recency effect than primacy effect. The serial position effect applies not only to lists but also to events. If you spread out a history lesson over a week and then ask students about it the following Monday, they likely will have the best memory for what you told them on Friday of last week and the worst memory for what you told them on Wednesday of last week.

script A schema for an event.

fuzzy trace theory States that memory is best understood by considering two types of memory representations: (1) verbatim memory trace and (2) gist. In this theory, older children's better memory is attributed to the fuzzy traces created by extracting the gist of information.

serial position effect The principle that recall is better for items at the beginning and the end of a list than for items in the middle.

Another factor that affects retrieval is the nature of the cues people use to prompt their memory (Allan & others, 2001). Students can learn to create effective cues. For example, if a student has a "block" about remembering the name of the guest who came to class 2 months ago, she might go through the alphabet, generating names with each letter. If she manages to stumble across the right name, she likely will recognize it.

Another consideration in understanding retrieval is the **encoding specificity principle:** that associations formed at the time of encoding or learning tend to be effective retrieval cues. For example, imagine that a 13-year-old child has encoded this information about Mother Teresa: She was born in Albania, lived most of her life in India, became a Roman Catholic nun, was saddened by seeing people sick and dying in Calcutta's streets, and won a Nobel Prize for her humanitarian efforts to help the poor and suffering. Later, when the child tries to remember details about Mother Teresa, she can use words such as *Nobel Prize, Calcutta,* and *humanitarian* as retrieval cues. The concept of encoding specificity is compatible with our earlier discussion of elaboration: The more elaboration children use in encoding information, the better their memory of the information will be. Encoding specificity and elaboration reveal how interdependent encoding and retrieval are.

Yet another aspect of retrieval is the nature of the retrieval task itself. *Recall* is a memory task in which individuals must retrieve previously learned information, as students must do for fill-in-the-blank or essay questions. *Recognition* is a memory task in which individuals only have to identify ("recognize") learned information, as is often the case on multiple-choice tests. Many students prefer multiple-choice items because they provide good retrieval cues, which fill-in-the-blank and essay items don't do.

Forgetting   One form of forgetting involves the cues we just discussed. **Cue-dependent forgetting** is retrieval failure caused by a lack of effective retrieval cues. The notion of cue-dependent forgetting can explain why a student might fail to retrieve a needed fact for an exam even when he is sure he "knows" the information. For example, if you are studying for a test in this course and are asked a question about a distinction between recall and recognition in retrieval, you likely will remember the distinction better if you possess the cues "fill-in-the-blank" and "multiple-choice," respectively.

The principle of cue-dependent forgetting is consistent with **interference theory,** which states that we forget not because we actually lose memories from storage but, rather, because other information gets in the way of what we are trying to remember. For a student who studies for a biology test, then studies for a history test, and then takes the biology test, the information about history will interfere with remembering the information about biology. Thus, interference theory implies that, if you have more than one test to study for, you should study last what you are going to be tested on next. That is, the student taking the biology test would have benefited from studying history first and studying biology afterward. This strategy also fits with the recency effect we described earlier.

Another source of forgetting is memory decay. According to **decay theory,** new learning involves the creation of a neurochemical "memory trace," which will eventually disintegrate. Thus, decay theory suggests that the passage of time is responsible for forgetting. Leading memory researcher Daniel Schacter (2001) now refers to forgetting that occurs with the passage of time as *transience.*

Memories decay at different speeds. Some memories are vivid and last for long periods of time, especially when they have emotional ties. We can often remember these "flashbulb" memories with considerable accuracy and vivid imagery. For example, consider a car accident you were in or witnessed, the night of your high school graduation, an early romantic experience, and where you were when you heard about the destruction of the World Trade Center towers. Chances are, you will be able to retrieve this information many years after the event occurred.

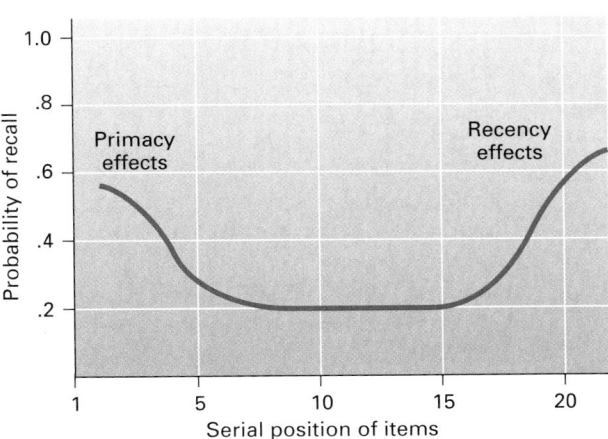

FIGURE 8.9 The Serial Position Effect When a person is asked to memorize a list of words, the words memorized last usually are recalled best, those at the beginning next best, and those in the middle least efficiently.

encoding specificity principle The principle that associations formed at the time of encoding or learning tend to be effective retrieval cues.

cue-dependent forgetting Retrieval failure caused by a lack of effective retrieval cues.

interference theory The theory that we forget not because we actually lose memories from storage but because other information gets in the way of what we are trying to remember.

decay theory The theory that new learning involves the creation of a neurochemical "memory trace," which will eventually disintegrate. Thus, decay theory suggests that the passage of time is responsible for forgetting.

BEST PRACTICES
Strategies for Helping Students Improve Their Memory

1. *Motivate children to remember material by understanding it rather than by memorizing it.* Children will remember information better over the long term if they understand the information rather than just rehearse and memorize it. Rehearsal works well for encoding information into short-term memory, but when children need to retrieve the information from long-term memory it is much less efficient. For most information, encourage children to understand it, give it meaning, elaborate on it, and personalize it. Give children concepts and ideas to remember and then ask them how they can relate the concepts and ideas to their own personal experiences and meanings. Give them practice on elaborating a concept so they will process the information more deeply.

2. *Assist students in organizing what they put into their memory.* Children will remember information better if they organize it hierarchically. Give them some practice arranging and reworking material that requires some structuring.

3. *Teach mnemonic strategies.* Mnemonics are memory aids for remembering information. Mnemonic strategies can involve imagery and words. Here are some different types of mnemonics:

   • *Method of loci.* In the *method of loci,* children develop images of items to be remembered and mentally store them in familiar locations. Rooms of a house and stores on a street are common locations used in this memory strategy. For example, if children need to remember a list of concepts, they can mentally place them in the rooms of their house, such as entry foyer, living room, dining room, and kitchen. Then when they need to retrieve the information, they can imagine the house, mentally go through the rooms, and retrieve the concepts. Next, teacher Rosemary Moore describes a similar idea for teaching spelling words.

THROUGH THE EYES OF TEACHERS

Seeing Words in the Mind's Eye

Many children memorize spelling words quite easily, but a few struggle with this. I wanted to help these students as much as I could, so I would write the spelling words on

index cards and place them in random order and various positions (vertical, diagonal, upside down) across the front of the room. As we did spelling assignments, exercises, and games throughout the week the words were there for the students to refer to if they got "stuck." The index cards were taken down before the test on Friday, but as I called out each of the spelling words I would notice students turning their eyes to the place where that particular word had been displayed. I believe they were seeing the word in their "mind's eye." My students' spelling scores improved dramatically.

• *Rhymes.* Examples of mnemonic rhymes are the spelling rule "*i* before *e* except after *c,*" the month rule "Thirty days hath September, April, June, and November," the bolt-turning rule "Right is tight, left is loose," and the alphabet song.

• *Acronyms.* This strategy involves creating a word from the first letters of items to be remembered. For example, *HOMES* can be used as a cue for remembering the five original Great Lakes: *Huron, Ontario, Michigan, Erie,* and *Superior.*

• *Keyword method.* Another mnemonic strategy that involves imagery is the *keyword method,* in which vivid imagery is attached to important words. This method has been used to practical advantage in teaching students how to rapidly master new information such as foreign vocabulary words, the states and capitals of the United States, and the names of U.S. presidents. For example, in teaching children that Annapolis is the capital of Maryland, you could ask them to connect vivid images of Annapolis and Maryland, such as two apples getting married (Levin, 1980) (see figure 8.10).

FIGURE 8.10 The Keyword Method
To help children remember the state capitals, the keyword method was used. A special component of the keyword method is the use of mental imagery, which was stimulated by presenting the children with a vivid visual image, such as two apples being married. The strategy is to help the children associate *apple* with Annapolis and *marry* with Maryland.

Some educators argue against teaching children to use mnemonics because they involve rote memorization. Clearly, as we said earlier, remembering for understanding is preferred over rote memorization. However, if children need to learn lists of concepts, mnemonic devices can do the trick. Think of mnemonic devices as a way for children to learn some specific facts that they might need to know to solve problems.

DIVERSITY AND EDUCATION
Culture, Gender, and Memory

A culture sensitizes its members to certain objects, events, and strategies, which in turn can influence the nature of memory (Cole, 2006; Greenfield & others, 2006; Nasir & others, 2006). Cross-cultural studies find cultural differences in the use of organizational strategies (Schneider & Bjorklund, 1998). Failure to use appropriate organizational strategies to remember information is often related to a lack of appropriate schooling (Cole, 2006). Children who have experienced schooling are more likely to cluster items together in meaningful ways, which helps them to remember the items. Schooling presents children with specialized information-processing tasks—such as committing large amounts of information to memory in a short time and using logical reasoning—that may generate specialized memory strategies. There is no evidence that schooling increases memory capacity per se; rather, it influences the strategies for remembering (Cole, 2006; Cole, Cole, & Lightfoot, 2005).

Gender is another aspect of sociocultural diversity that has been given little attention in memory research until recently (Burton & others, 2004; Halpern, 2006). Researchers have found these gender differences in memory:

- Females more quickly access and retrieve phonological, semantic, and episodic information in long-term memory (Halpern, 2006). Episodic memory is memory for personal events that include the time and place the event occurred. Females also appear to be better than males in emotionally linked memory, such as memory for an emotional film (Cahill & others, 2001).

- Males are better than females on tasks that require transformations in visuospatial working memory (Halpern, 2006). These tasks include mental rotation, which involves the imagined motion of stationary objects (such as what a shape would look like if it were rotated in space).

On many memory tasks, though, researchers do not find gender differences, or when differences occur they are small (Hyde, 2005, 2007).

Students in a classroom in Nairobi, Kenya. *How might schooling influence memory?*

In their study of memory, researchers have not extensively examined the roles that sociocultural factors such as culture and gender might play in memory. In the Diversity and Education interlude, we will explore these topics.

Review, Reflect, and Practice

(3) Discuss memory in terms of encoding, storage, and retrieval.

REVIEW

- What is memory? What is necessary for it to work?
- How are these five processes—rehearsal, deep processing, elaboration, constructing images, and organization—involved in encoding?
- What are the three time frames of memory? How are long-term memory's contents described? What are three theories about how they might they be represented in memory?
- What makes a memory easier or harder to retrieve? What are some theories about why we forget?

REFLECT

- Which principles and strategies in our discussion of memory are likely to be useful for the subjects and grade levels at which you plan to teach?

PRAXIS™ PRACTICE

1. Natalie is playing a game called "memory" at a birthday party. A covered tray with 15 objects is brought into the room. The cover is removed and the children have 30 seconds to memorize the objects. They will then write down the objects they remember. The child who correctly remembers the most objects wins the game. Natalie notices that five of the objects are hair-related items—a comb, a brush, shampoo, a barrette, and a ponytail holder. She notices that another five objects are school supplies—a pencil, a pen, a ruler, a marker, and a glue stick. The final five objects appear to be random. Natalie has no problem remembering the items that she was able to group by type. She only remembers two of the other items. What memory strategy is Natalie using?
   a. chunking
   b. constructing images
   c. elaboration
   d. rehearsal

2. To test his students' memory skills, Mr. Watkins reads lists of nonsense words to them and asks them to recall as many as they can. Veronica can recall five words. If she performs as is expected for age, how old is Veronica most likely to be?
   a. 4
   b. 7
   c. 12
   d. 17

3. When asked to describe in detail how to make a peanut-butter-and-jelly sandwich, Maria skips several steps. When asked to make a sandwich, Maria does so flawlessly. Why is it that although Maria knows how to make a sandwich, she is unable to describe the process in detail?
   a. It is difficult to translate procedural memory into words.
   b. Maria has not encoded the process into long-term memory.
   c. It is difficult to translate episodic memory into semantic memory.
   d. Maria's episodic memory is faulty.

4. Mr. Madison wants his students to know the names of all of the states in the United States. To help them, he teaches them a song in which each state name is sung in alphabetical order. Most of his students learn the song with relative ease. They even sing the song to themselves when he gives them a quiz that requires them to write down the name of each state. However, when he gives them blank U.S. maps to fill in with state names, his students cannot complete them successfully. Why were they able to remember the names of the states, but not their locations?
    a. Mnemonic devices, such as the song Mr. Madison taught his students, are not effective for memorizing material.
    b. Mnemonic devices, such as the song Mr. Madison taught his students, increase the likelihood of cue-dependent forgetting.
    c. Mnemonic devices, such as the song Mr. Madison taught his students, increase the serial position effect.
    d. Mnemonic devices, such as the song that Mr. Madison taught his students, involve rote memorization and do not generalize to other memory tasks.

Please see the answer key at the end of the book.

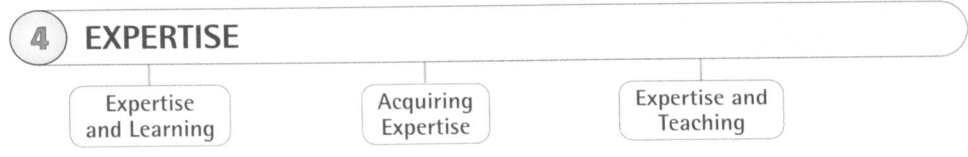

In the last section we considered various aspects of memory. Our ability to remember new information about a subject depends considerably on what we already know about it (Carver & Klahr, 2001; Ericsson & others, 2006; Keil, 2006). For example, a student's ability to recount what she saw when she was at the library is largely governed by what she already knows about libraries, such as where books on certain topics are likely to be and how to check books out. If she knew little about libraries, the student would have a much harder time recounting what was there.

The contribution of prior content knowledge to our ability to remember new material is especially evident when we compare the memories of experts and novices in a particular knowledge domain (Donovan & Bransford, 2005). An expert is the opposite of a novice (someone who is just beginning to learn a content area). Experts demonstrate especially impressive memory in their areas of expertise. One reason that children remember less than adults is that they are far less expert in most areas.

Expertise and Learning

Studying the behavior and mental processes of experts can give us insights into how to guide students in becoming more effective learners. What is it, exactly, that experts do? According to the National Research Council (1999), they are better than novices at

1. detecting features and meaningful patterns of information;
2. accumulating more content knowledge and organizing it in a manner that shows an understanding of the topic;
3. retrieving important aspects of knowledge with little effort;
4. adapting an approach to new situations; and
5. using effective strategies.

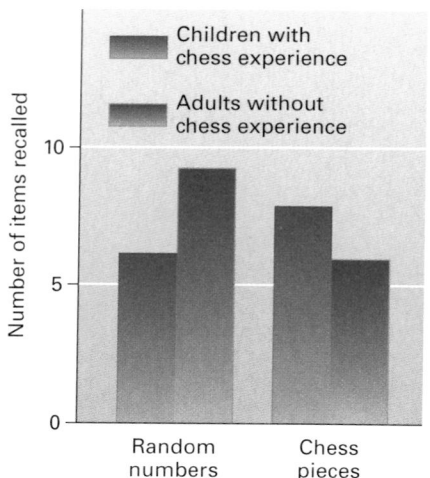

FIGURE 8.11 Memory for Numbers and Chess Pieces

In this section we will consider various ways that you can help your students learn and remember these skills that experts use so effortlessly.

Detecting Features and Meaningful Patterns of Organization Experts are better at noticing important features of problems and contexts that novices may ignore (Bransford & others, 2006). Thus, the attentional advantage of experts starts them off at a more advantageous level than novices in a learning context. Experts also have superior recall of information in their area of expertise. The process of chunking, which we discussed earlier, is one way they accomplish this superior recall. For example, "Chess masters perceive chunks of meaningful information, which affects their memory of what they see. . . . Lacking a hierarchical, highly organized structure for the domain, novices cannot use this chunking strategy" (National Research Council, 1999, p. 21).

In areas where children are experts, their memory is often extremely good. In fact, it often exceeds that of adults who are novices in that content area. This was documented in a study of 10-year-old chess experts (Chi, 1978). These children were excellent chess players but not especially brilliant in other ways. As with most 10-year-olds, their memory spans for digits were shorter than an adult's. However, they remembered the configurations of chess pieces on chessboards far better than did the adults who were novices at chess (see figure 8.11).

Expert teachers recognize features and patterns that are not noticed by novice teachers (National Research Council, 1999, pp. 21, 25). For example, in one study, expert and novice teachers had a very different understanding of the events in a videotaped classroom lesson, in which three screens showed simultaneous events taking place throughout the classroom (left, center, and right areas) (Sabers, Cushing, & Berliner, 1991). One expert teacher said, "On the left monitor, the students' note taking indicates that they have seen sheets like this before; it's fairly efficient at this point because they're used to the format they are using." One novice teacher sparsely responded, "It's a lot to watch."

Organization and Depth of Knowledge Experts' knowledge is organized around important ideas or concepts more than novices' knowledge is (National Research Council, 1999). This provides experts with a much deeper understanding of knowledge than novices have (Bransford & others, 2006; Simon, 2001; Voss & others, 1984).

Experts in a particular area usually have far more elaborate networks of information about that area than novices do (see figure 8.12). The information they represent in memory has more nodes, more interconnections, and better hierarchical organization.

The implications for teaching are that too often a curriculum is designed in a way that makes it difficult for students to organize knowledge in meaningful ways. This especially occurs when there is only superficial coverage of facts before moving on to the next topic. In this context, students have little time to explore the topic in depth and get a sense of what the important, organizing ideas are. This type of shallow presentation can occur in any subject area but is common in history and science texts that emphasize facts (National Research Council, 1999).

Fluent Retrieval Retrieval of relevant information can range from taking a lot of effort to being fluent and almost effortless (National Research Council, 1999). Experts retrieve information in an almost effortless, automatic manner, while novices expend a great deal of effort in retrieving information.

Effortless retrieval places fewer demands on conscious attention. Since the amount of information a student can attend to at one time is limited, ease of processing information in some aspects of a task frees up capacity to attend to other aspects of a task.

Consider expert and novice readers. Expert readers can quickly scan the words of a sentence and paragraph, which allows them to devote attention to understanding

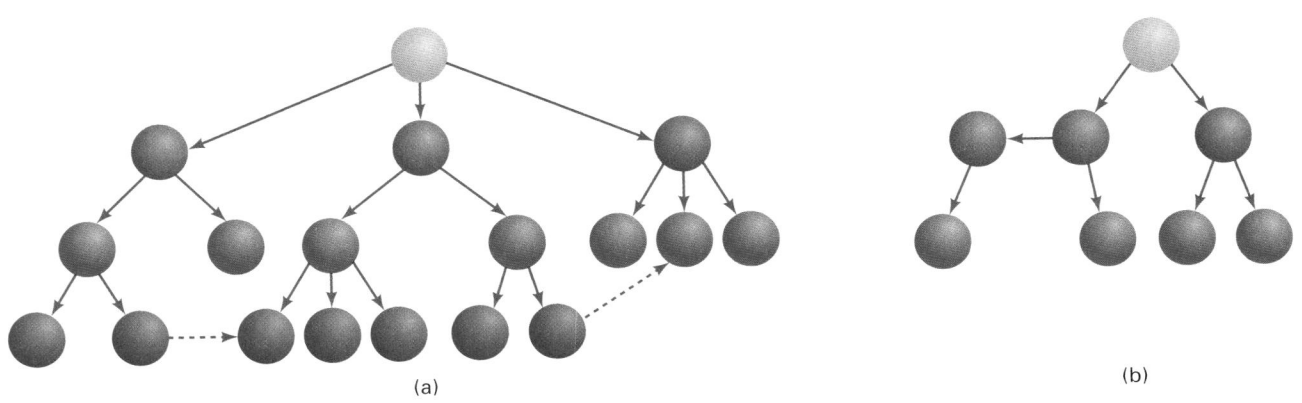

FIGURE 8.12 An Example of How Information Is Organized in the Mind of an Expert and a Novice

(a) An expert's knowledge is based on years of experience in which small bits of information have been linked with many other small pieces, which together are placed in a more general category. This category is in turn placed in an even more general category of knowledge. The dotted lines are used as pointers, associations between specific elements of knowledge that connect the lower branches and provide mental shortcuts in the expert's mind. *(b)* The novice's knowledge shows far fewer connections, shortcuts, and levels than an expert's knowledge.

what they are reading. However, novice readers' ability to decode words is not yet fluent, so they have to allocate considerable attention and time to this task, which restricts the time they can give to understanding a passage. An important aspect of teaching is to help students develop the fluency they need to competently perform cognitive tasks (Beck & others, 1991).

Adaptive Expertise   An important aspect of expertise "is whether some ways of organizing knowledge are better" than others for helping people to be "flexible and adaptive to new situations than others" (National Research Council, 1999, p. 33). Adaptive experts are able to approach new situations flexibly rather than always responding in a rigid, fixed routine (Bransford & others, 2006; Hatano, 1990; Hatano & Oura, 2003). An important theme in a recent book, *Preparing Teachers for a Changing World* (Darling-Hammond & Bransford, 2005, p. 3), was to "help teachers become 'adaptive experts' who are prepared for effective lifelong learning that allows them to continually add to their knowledge and skills." Thus, teachers characterized by adaptive expertise are flexible and open to rethinking important ideas and practices to improve their students' learning (Hammerness & others, 2005).

Indeed, innovation *and* efficiency are the two main dimensions of one model of adaptive expertise (Bransford & others, 2006; Schwartz, Bransford, & Sears, 2006, in press). Experts characterized by *efficiency* can quickly retrieve and apply information in skillful ways to explain something or solve a problem. Experts characterized by *innovation* involves moving away from efficiency, at least on a short-term basis, and unlearning previous routines. Innovation occurs when individuals "let go" and rethink their routine way of doing something.

In this model, adaptive experts possess a balance of efficiency and innovation (Bransford & others, 2006; Schwartz, Bransford, & Sears, 2006). For example, efficiency is at work when a teacher teaches students to speedily complete math computations, but this efficiency may limit the students' competence when they face new math problems. When this efficiency-oriented teacher adapts and adds teaching for understanding and application, innovation is taking place. The new skills she teaches are likely to increase the students' competence when they encounter new math problems.

What are some characteristics of teachers who are adaptive experts?

Adaptive experts are motivated to learn from others (Hammerness & others, 2005). This may not be that difficult when the learning involves making a teacher's existing routines and practices more efficient. However, as we just indicated, adaptive expertise also includes innovation that requires sometimes replacing or transforming prior routines and practices, which is often not easy to do. Your teaching likely will benefit if you seek feedback from other competent teachers, even if their approaches are different than yours. This might occur when you watch a videotape of your teaching with other teachers who provide feedback about your teaching or invite a colleague to come to your classroom to observe your teaching.

Strategies   Experts use effective strategies in understanding the information in their area of expertise and in advancing it (Ornstein, Haden, & Elischberger, 2006; Pressley & Hilden, 2006). Earlier in the chapter we described a number of strategies that students can use to remember information. Let's now explore some effective strategies that students can develop to become experts at learning and studying.

Patricia Alexander (2003) uses the label *acclimation* to describe the initial stage of expertise in a particular domain (such as English, biology, or mathematics). At this stage, students have limited and fragmented knowledge that restricts their ability to detect the difference between accurate and inaccurate and relevant and tangential information. To help students move beyond the acclimation stage, teachers need to guide students in determining what content is central and what is peripheral, as well as what is accurate and well supported and what is inaccurate and unsupported. In Alexander's (2003) view, students don't come to the classroom equipped with the strategies they need to move beyond the acclimation stage. Teachers must help students learn effective strategies and practice them in relevant situations before students can experience their value. Students also need to be encouraged to change and combine strategies to solve the problem at hand.

Spreading Out and Consolidating Learning   Students' learning benefits when teachers talk with them about the importance of regularly reviewing what they learn. Children who have to prepare for a test will benefit from distributing their learning over a longer period rather than cramming for the test at the last minute. Cramming tends to produce short-term memory that is processed in a shallow rather than deep manner. A final, concentrated tune-up before the test is better than trying to learn everything at the last minute.

Asking Themselves Questions   When children ask themselves questions about what they have read or about an activity, they expand the number of associations with the information they need to retrieve. At least as early as the middle of elementary school, the self-questioning strategy can help children to remember. For example, as children read, they can be encouraged to stop periodically and ask themselves questions such as "What is the meaning of what I just read?" "Why is this important?" and "What is an example of the concept I just read?" Students can use the same self-questioning strategy when they listen to you conduct a lesson, hear a guest give a talk, or watch a video. If you periodically remind children to generate questions about their experiences, they are more likely to remember the experiences.

Taking Good Notes   Taking good notes from either a lecture or a text benefits learning. When children are left to take notes without being given any strategies, they tend to take notes that are brief and disorganized. When they do write something down, it often is a verbatim record of what they have just heard. Give children some practice in taking notes and then evaluate their note taking. Encourage children not to write down everything they hear when they take notes. It is impossible to do this,

What are some good study strategies?

anyway, and it can prevent them from getting the big picture of what the speaker is saying. Here are some good note-taking strategies:

- *Summarizing.* Have the children listen for a few minutes and then write down the main idea that a speaker is trying to get across in that time frame. Then have the child listen for several more minutes and write down another idea, and so on.
- *Outlining.* Show the children how to outline what a speaker is saying, using first-level heads as the main topics, second-level heads as subtopics under the first-level heads, and third-level heads under the second-level heads.
- *Concept maps.* Help the children practice drawing concept maps, which are similar to outlines but visually portray information in a more spiderlike format (see chapter 9).

All three note-taking strategies described so far—summarizing, outlining, and concept maps—help children evaluate which ideas are the most important to remember. Outlining and concept maps also help children arrange the material hierarchically, which underscores an important theme of learning: It works best when it is organized.

Using a Study System   Various systems have been developed to help people to remember information that they are studying from a book. One of the earliest systems was called *SQ3R*, which stands for *Survey, Question, Read, Recite,* and *Review.* A more recently developed system is called *PQ4R*, which stands for *Preview, Question, Read, Reflect, Recite,* and *Review.* Thus, the PQ4R system adds an additional step, "Reflect," to the SQ3R system. From the later elementary school years on, students will benefit from practicing the PQ4R system (Adams, Carnine, & Gersten, 1982). The system benefits students by getting them to meaningfully organize information, ask questions about it, reflect on it, and review it. Here are more details about the steps in the PQ4R system:

- *Preview.* Tell your students to briefly survey the material to get a sense of the overall organization of ideas—to look at the headings to see the main topics and subtopics that will be covered.
- *Question.* Encourage the children to ask themselves questions about the material as they read it.
- *Read.* Now tell the children to read the material. Encourage your students to be active readers—to immerse themselves in what they are reading and strive to understand what the author is saying. This helps students to avoid being empty readers whose eyes just track the lines of text but whose minds fail to register anything important.
- *Reflect.* By occasionally stopping and reflecting on the material, students increase its meaningfulness. Encourage the children to be analytic at this point in studying. After they have read something, challenge them to break open the ideas and scratch beneath their surface. This is a good time for them to think out applications and interpretations of the information, as well as connecting it with other information already in their long-term memory.
- *Recite.* This involves children self-testing themselves to see if they can remember the material and reconstruct it. At this point, encourage the children to make up a series of questions about the material and then try to answer them.
- *Review.* Tell your students to go over the material and evaluate what they know and don't know. At this point they should reread and study the material they don't remember or understand well.

We will further explore strategies later in the chapter in our discussion of metacognition. To evaluate the extent to which you use good memory and study strategies, complete Self-Assessment 8.1.

SELF-ASSESSMENT 8.1

How Effective Are My Memory and Study Strategies?

Teachers who themselves practice using good memory and study strategies are more likely to model and communicate these to their students than teachers who don't use such strategies. Candidly respond to these items about your own memory and study strategies. Rate yourself on this scale: 1 = never, 2 = some, 3 = moderate, 4 = almost always, or 5 = always. Then total your points.

1. I'm a good time manager and planner.
2. I'm good at focusing my attention and minimizing distractions.
3. I try to understand material rather than rotely memorizing it.
4. I ask myself questions about what I have read or about class activities.
5. I take good notes in class and from textbooks.
6. I regularly review my notes.
7. I use mnemonic strategies.
8. I'm very organized in the way I encode information.
9. I spread out my studying to consolidate my learning.
10. I use good retrieval cues.
11. I use the PQ4R method or a similar study method.

1	2	3	4	5

Total

Scoring and Interpretation

If you scored 50–55 total points, you likely use good memory and study strategies. If you scored 45–49 points, you likely have some reasonably good memory and study strategies. If you scored below 45, spend some time working on improving your memory and study strategies.

If you would like to learn more about effective memory and study strategies, one resource is a book called *Your Guide to College Success* (Santrock & Halonen, 2002). Also, to gain more experience in developing good memory and study strategies, contact the study skills center at your college or university; specialists there likely will be able to help you.

Acquiring Expertise

What determines whether or not someone becomes an expert? Can motivation and practice get someone to expert status? Or does expertise also require a great deal of talent (Sternberg & Ben-Zeev, 2001)?

Practice and Motivation   One perspective is that a particular kind of practice—*deliberate practice*—is required to become an expert (Hatano & Oura, 2003; Schraw, 2006). Deliberate practice involves practice that is at an appropriate level of difficulty for the individual, provides corrective feedback, and allows opportunities for repetition (Ericsson, 1996, 2006).

In one study of violinists at a music academy, the extent to which children engaged in deliberate practice distinguished novices and experts (Ericsson, Krampe, & Tesch-Romer, 1993). The top violinists averaged 7,500 hours of deliberate practice by age 18, the good violinists only 5,300 hours. Many individuals give up on becoming an expert because they won't put forth the effort it takes to engage in extensive deliberate practice over a number of years.

TECHNOLOGY AND EDUCATION

Experts and Technology

As described by the National Research Council (1999), experts in many fields are using new technologies to represent information in new ways. For example, three-dimensional models of the surface of Venus or of a molecular structure can be electronically created and viewed from any angle.

One of the characteristics of expertise we have discussed involves organizing knowledge meaningfully around important ideas. The Belvedere computer technology system is designed to help students who lack a deep understanding of many areas of science, have difficulty zeroing in on the key issues in a scientific debate, and have trouble recognizing connections of ideas in scientific theories (Suthers & others, 1995). Belvedere uses graphics with specialized boxes to represent connections of ideas in an effort to support students' reasoning about scientific issues. An online advisor gives students hints to help them improve their understanding and reasoning.

The Belvedere system can also help students in nonscientific studies such as analyzing social policies. This system helps students by (1) giving arguments a concrete, diagram-like form and providing tools for focusing on particular problems encountered in the construction and evaluation of complex arguments; (2) providing access to online information resources; and (3) supporting students working in small groups to construct documents to be shared with others.

Such extensive practice requires considerable motivation. Students who are not motivated to practice long hours are unlikely to become experts in a particular area. Thus, a student who complains about all of the work, doesn't persevere, and doesn't extensively practice solving math problems over a number years is not going to become an expert in math.

Talent   A number of psychologists who study expertise believe that it requires not only deliberate practice and motivation but also talent (Bloom, 1985; Hunt, 2006; Schraw 2006; Shiffrin, 1996; Sternberg & Ben-Zeev, 2001).

A number of abilities—music and athletic, for example—seem to have a heritable component (Plomin, 1997). For example, is it likely that Mozart could have become such an outstanding musical composer just because he practiced long hours? Is it likely that Tiger Woods became such a fantastic golfer just because he was motivated to do so? Many talented individuals have attempted to become as great as Mozart or Woods but have given up trying after only mediocre performances. Clearly, heredity matters. Nonetheless, Mozart and Woods would not have developed expertise in their fields without being highly motivated and engaging in extensive deliberate practice. Talent alone does not make an expert (Hunt, 2006; Winner, 2006).

Expertise and Teaching

Being an expert in a particular domain—such as physics, history, or math—does not mean that the expert is good at helping others learn it (Bransford & others, 2005, 2006). Indeed, "expertise can sometimes hurt teaching because many experts forget what is easy and what is difficult for students" (National Research Council, 1999, p. 32).

Some educators have distinguished between the content knowledge required for expertise and the pedagogical content knowledge necessary to effectively teach it (Shulman, 1987). *Pedagogical content knowledge* includes ideas about common difficulties that students have as they try to learn a content area; typical paths students must take to understand the area; and strategies for helping students overcome the difficulties they experience.

Expert teachers are good at monitoring students' learning and assessing students' progress. They also know what types of difficulties students are likely to encounter, are aware of students' existing knowledge, and use this awareness to teach at the right level and to make new information meaningful. Some educational psychologists argue that in the absence of expert pedagogical awareness of their own students, inexpert teachers simply rely on textbook publishers' materials, which, of course, contain no information about the particular pedagogical needs of students in the teacher's classroom (Brophy, 2004). To read further about expertise, see the Technology and Education box.

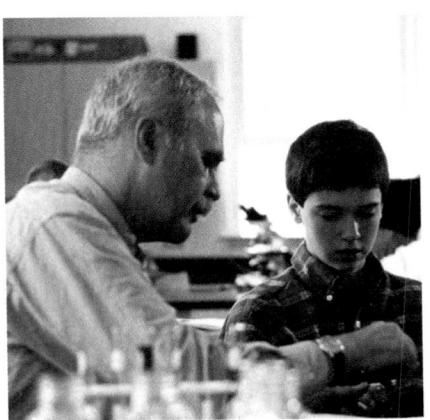

An expert teacher monitoring a student's learning. *What are some characteristics of expert teachers?*

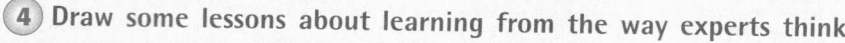

Review, Reflect, and Practice

4 **Draw some lessons about learning from the way experts think.**

REVIEW

- What do experts do that novices often don't do in the process of learning?
- What does it take to become an expert?
- Is subject experience enough to make a good teacher? What else is needed?

REFLECT

- Choose an area in which you feel at least somewhat of an expert. Compare your ability to learn in that field with the ability of a novice.

PRAXIS™ PRACTICE

1. The case studies in this text are designed to help educational psychology students learn the material and begin to develop expertise. The first question of each case study asks students to identify the issues in the case. The author most likely included this question for each case because he understood that
   a. it is important for students to consolidate their learning.
   b. it is important for students to learn to determine what content is central and what is peripheral.
   c. in learning, it is important to strike a balance between efficiency and innovation.
   d. students need a great deal of help in developing fluid retrieval skills.

2. Ryan is the best player on his soccer team. His coach thinks of him as a coach's dream player because he works so hard. It is rare for Ryan to perform a skill better than his teammates when it is initially introduced, but by the time the next practice comes, he will have mastered the skill. At one point, Ryan decided that he wanted to be able to score from a corner kick. He gathered up all the soccer balls he could find and kicked them one after another from the corner, trying to curl them into the goal. When he had finished, he gathered the balls and did it again. He continued this for an entire afternoon, and thereafter for at least an hour after school each day. His coach was very happily surprised when, in the next game, Ryan scored a goal from a corner kick. Why has Ryan developed expertise in soccer?
   a. He engages in extensive deliberative practice.
   b. He is relying on an inborn talent.
   c. He has an excellent teacher in his coach.
   d. He uses the PQ4R method 3.

3. Mr. Williams is a former college history professor who is now teaching high school American history. He discusses his research and writing with his students and tries to make history come alive by telling them about how historians find out about the past. After a month of teaching, he finds that his students seem confused during class discussions and perform poorly on tests of factual knowledge. The most likely explanation is that Mr. Williams lacks
   a. content expertise.
   b. pedagogical content knowledge.
   c. metacognition.
   d. cue-dependent knowledge.

Please see the answer key at the end of the book.

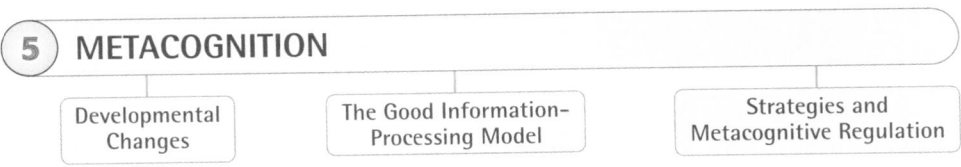

So far in this chapter, we have examined a number of ways that you help students improve their ability to process information as they learn, including how to improve their attention and memory, as well as strategies that can increase the likelihood that they will make the transition from being a novice to being an expert. Another way that you can help children process information more effectively is by encouraging them to examine what they know about how their mind processes information. As you read at the beginning of this chapter, this involves metacognition, which involves cognition about cognition, or "knowing about knowing" (Flavell, 1999, 2004; Flavell, Miller, & Miller, 2002). A distinction can be made between metacognitive knowledge and metacognitive activity. *Metacognitive knowledge* involves monitoring and reflecting on one's current or recent thoughts. This includes both factual knowledge, such as knowledge about the task, one's goals, or oneself, and strategic knowledge, such as how and when to use specific procedures to solve problems. *Metacognitive activity* occurs when students consciously adapt and manage their thinking strategies during problem solving and purposeful thinking (Ferrari & Sternberg, 1998; Kuhn & others, 1995).

Metacognitive skills have been taught to students to help them solve math problems (Cardelle-Elawar, 1992). In each of thirty daily lessons involving math story problems, a teacher guided low-achieving students in learning to recognize when they did not know the meaning of a word, did not have all of the information necessary to solve a problem, did not know how to subdivide the problem into specific steps, or did not know how to carry out a computation. After the thirty daily lessons, the students who were given this metacognitive training had better math achievement and better attitudes toward math.

One expert on children's thinking, Deanna Kuhn (1999; Kuhn & Franklin, 2006), argues that metacognition should be a stronger focus of efforts to help children become better critical thinkers, especially at the middle school and high school levels. She distinguishes between first-order cognitive skills, which enable children to know about the world (and have been the main focus of critical thinking programs), and second-order cognitive skills—meta-knowing skills—which involve knowing about one's own (and others') knowing.

Developmental Changes

How does metacognition change in childhood? Are there further changes in metacognition during adolescence?

Childhood Many studies have focused on children's metamemory, or knowledge of how memory works. In the last several decades, there has been extensive interest in children's theories about how the human mind works.

Metamemory By 5 or 6 years of age, children usually know that familiar items are easier to learn than unfamiliar ones, that short lists are easier than long ones, that recognition is easier than recall, and that forgetting becomes more likely over time (Lyon & Flavell, 1993). In other ways, however, young children's metamemory is limited. They don't understand that related items are easier to remember than unrelated ones or that remembering the gist of a story is easier than remembering information verbatim (Kreutzer & Flavell, 1975). By fifth grade, students understand that gist recall is easier than verbatim recall.

Preschool children also have an inflated opinion of their memory abilities. For example, in one study, a majority of preschool children predicted that they would be

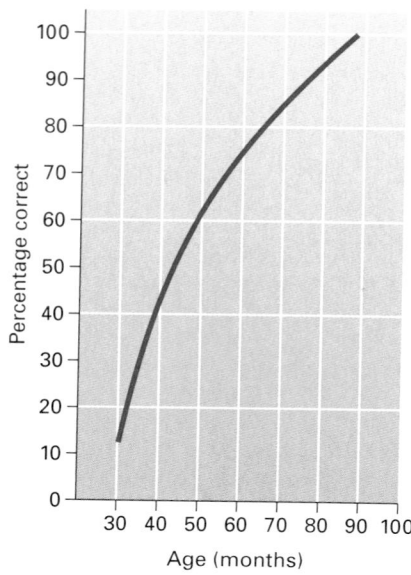

FIGURE 8.13 Developmental Changes in False-Belief Performance

False-belief performance dramatically increases from 2½ years of age through the middle of the elementary school years. In a summary of the results of many studies, 2½-year-olds gave incorrect responses about 80 percent of the time (Wellman, Cross, & Watson, 2001). At 3 years, 8 months, they were correct about 50 percent of the time, and after that, gave increasingly correct responses.

able to recall all ten items of a list of ten items. When tested, none of the young children managed this feat (Flavell, Friedrichs, & Hoyt, 1970). As they move through the elementary school years, children give more realistic evaluations of their memory skills (Schneider & Pressley, 1997).

Preschool children also have little appreciation for the importance of memory cues, such as "It helps when you can think of an example of it." By 7 or 8 years of age, children better appreciate the importance of cueing for memory. In general, children's understanding of their memory abilities and their skill in evaluating their performance on memory tasks is relatively poor at the beginning of the elementary school years but improves considerably by age 11 or 12 (Bjorklund & Rosenblum, 2000).

Theory of Mind   **Theory of mind** refers to awareness of one's own mental processes and the mental processes of others. Even young children are curious about the nature of the human mind (Flavell, 1999, 2004; Wellman, 1997, 2000, 2004). Their theory of mind changes as they go through the childhood years (Flavell, Miller, & Miller, 2002; Harris, 2006; Wellman, 2004):

- *Two to Three Years of Age.* Children begin to understand three mental states: (1) *perceptions*—children realize that other people see what is in front of their eyes and not necessarily in front of the children's eyes; (2) *desires*—children understand that if someone wants something, he or she will try to get it; and (3) *emotions*—children can distinguish between positive (for example, "happy") and negative (for example, "sad") emotions. Despite these advances, children who are 2 to 3 years of age have only a minimal understanding of how mental life can be linked to behavior. They think that people are at the mercy of their desires and don't understand how beliefs influence behavior.

- *Four to Five Years of Age.* Children begin to understand that the mind can represent objects and events accurately or inaccurately. Most children realize that people have *false beliefs*—beliefs that are not true—by the time they are 5 years old (Wellman, Cross, & Watson, 2001) (see figure 8.13). For example, in one study children were shown a Band-Aid box and asked what was inside (Jenkins & Astington, 1996). To the children's surprise, the box contained pencils. When asked what a child who had never seen the box would think was inside, 3-year-olds typically responded "pencils." The 4- and 5-year-olds, grinning in anticipation of other children's false beliefs, were more likely to say "Band-Aids."

- *Middle and Late Childhood.* It is only beyond the early childhood years that children have a deepening appreciation of the mind itself rather than just an understanding of mental states (Wellman, 2004). Not until middle and late childhood do children see the mind as an active constructor of knowledge or processing center (Flavell, Green, & Flavell, 1998). In middle and late childhood, children move from understanding that beliefs can be false to an understanding of beliefs and mind as "interpretive," exemplified in an awareness that the same event can be open to multiple interpretations (Carpendale & Chandler, 1996).

Adolescence   In addition to the metacognition changes in memory and theory of mind that occur in childhood, important changes in metacognition take place during adolescence (Kuhn & Franklin, 2006). Compared with children, adolescents have an increased capacity to monitor and manage cognitive resources to effectively meet the demands of a learning task. This increased metacognitive ability results in more effective cognitive functioning and learning.

An important aspect of cognitive functioning and learning is determining how much attention will be allocated to available resources. Evidence is accumulating that adolescents have a better understanding of how to effectively deploy their attention to different aspects of a task than children have (Kuhn & Franklin, 2006). In one investigation, 12-year-olds were markedly better than 8-year-olds, and slightly worse than 20-year-olds, at allocating their attention between two tasks (Manis, Keating, & Morrison,

theory of mind Awareness of one's own mental processes and the mental processes of others.

1980). Adolescents may have more resources available to them than children (through increased processing speed, capacity, and automaticity), or they may be more skilled at directing the resources. Further, adolescents have a better meta-level understanding of strategies—that is, knowing the best strategy to use and when to use it in performing a learning task.

Keep in mind, though, that there is considerable individual variation in adolescents' metacognition. Indeed, some experts argue that individual variation in metacognition become much more pronounced in adolescence than in childhood (Kuhn & Franklin, 2006). Thus, some adolescents are quite good at using metacognition to improve their learning, others far less effective.

What are some changes in metacognition during adolescence?

The Good Information-Processing Model

Michael Pressley and his colleagues (Pressley, Borkowski, & Schneider, 1989; Pressley & Harris, 2006; Schneider & Pressley, 1997) have developed a metacognitive model called the Good Information-Processing model. It emphasizes that competent cognition results from a number of interacting factors. These include strategies, content knowledge, motivation, and metacognition. They believe that children become good at cognition in three main steps:

1. *Children are taught by parents or teachers to use a particular strategy.* With practice, they learn about its characteristics and advantages for learning *specific knowledge.* The more intellectually stimulating children's homes and schools are, the more specific strategies they will encounter and learn to use.

2. *Teachers may demonstrate similarities and differences in multiple strategies in a particular domain, such as math, which motivates students to see shared features of different strategies.* This leads to better *relational knowledge.*

3. *At this point, students recognize the general benefits of using strategies, which produces general strategy knowledge.* They learn to attribute successful learning outcomes to the efforts they make in evaluating, selecting, and monitoring strategy use *(metacognitive knowledge and activity).*

Strategies and Metacognitive Regulation

In Pressley's (McCormick & Pressley, 1997; Pressley, 1983; Pressley & Harris, 2006; Pressley & Hilden, 2006) view, the key to education is helping students learn a rich repertoire of strategies that results in solutions of problems. Good thinkers routinely use strategies and effective planning to solve problems. Good thinkers also know when and where to use strategies (metacognitive knowledge about strategies). Understanding when and where to use strategies often results from the learner's monitoring of the learning situation.

Pressley argues that when students are given instruction about effective strategies, they often can apply strategies that they previously have not used on their own. He emphasizes that students benefit when the teacher models the appropriate strategy and overtly verbalizes its steps. Then, students subsequently practice the strategy, guided and supported by the teacher's feedback until the students can use it autonomously. When instructing students about employing a strategy, it also is a good idea to explain to them how using the strategy will benefit them. However, there are some developmental limitations to this approach. For instance, young children often cannot use mental imagery competently.

Just having students practice the new strategy is usually not enough for them to continue to use the strategy and transfer it to new situations. For effective maintenance and transfer, encourage students to monitor the effectiveness of the new strategy relative to their use of old strategies by comparing their performance on tests and other assessments (Graham, 2006). Pressley says that it is not enough to say, "Try it, you will like it"; you need to say, "Try it and compare."

BEST PRACTICES
Strategies for Helping Students Use Strategies

The following strategies are based on the recommendations of Michael Pressley and his colleagues (Pressley & Hilden, 2006; Pressley & McCormick, 1995):

1. *Recognize that strategies are a key aspect of solving problems.* Monitor students' knowledge and awareness of strategies for effective learning outcomes. Many students do not use good strategies and are unaware that strategies can help them learn.

2. *Model effective strategies for students.*

3. *Give students many opportunities to practice the strategies.* As students practice the strategies, provide guidance and support to the students. Give them feedback until they can use the strategies independently. As part of your feedback, inform them about where and when the strategies are most useful.

4. *Encourage students to monitor the effectiveness of their new strategy in comparison to the effectiveness of old strategies.*

5. *Remember that it takes students a considerable amount of time to learn how to use an effective strategy.* Be patient and give students continued support during this tedious learning experience. Keep encouraging students to use the strategy over and over again until they can use it automatically.

6. *Understand that students need to be motivated to use the strategies.* Students are not always going to be motivated to use the strategies. Especially important to students' motivation is their expectations that the strategies will lead to successful learning outcomes. It can also help if students set goals for learning effective strategies. And when students attribute their learning outcomes to the effort they put forth, their learning benefits.

7. *Encourage children to use multiple strategies.* Most children benefit from experimenting with multiple strategies, finding out what works well, when, and where.

8. *Read more about strategy instruction.* A good place to start is the recent chapter by Michael Pressley and Katherine Hilden (2006), which includes extensive ideas about how to improve children's use of strategies.

9. *Ask questions that help to guide students' thinking in various content areas.* These might include, "How can proofreading help me in writing a paper?" "Why is it important periodically to stop when I'm reading and try to understand what is being said so far?" and "What is the purpose of learning this formula?"

An important aspect of metacognition is monitoring how well one is performing on a task (Pressley & Harris, 2006; Pressley & Hilden, 2006). This might involve becoming aware that one has not studied enough for a test or needs to reread a particular section of a chapter to understand it better. Mismonitoring is common. For example, elementary school students often think they are better prepared for a test than they actually are and think they understand text material better than they do. One strategy is to encourage students who mismonitor to create practice tests and questions to assess how complete their understanding is.

Learning how to use strategies effectively often takes time. Initially, it takes time to learn to execute the strategies, and it requires guidance and support from the teacher. With practice, students learn to execute strategies faster and more competently. *Practice* means that students use the effective strategy over and over again until they perform it automatically. To execute the strategies effectively, they need to have the strategies in long-term memory, and extensive practice makes this possible. Learners also need to be motivated to use the strategies. Thus, an important implication for helping students develop strategies such as organization is that once a strategy is learned, students usually need more time before they can use them efficiently (Schneider, 2004). Further, it is important for teachers to be aware that students may drop an effective strategy or continue to use a strategy that does not help them (Miller, 2000).

Do children use one strategy or multiple strategies in memory and problem solving? They often use more than one strategy (Schneider & Bjorklund, 1998; Siegler & Alibali, 2005). Most children benefit from generating a variety of alternative strategies and experimenting with different approaches to a problem and discovering what works well, when, and where (Schneider & Bjorklund, 1998). This is especially true for children from the middle elementary school grades on, although some cognitive psychologists believe that even young children should be encouraged to practice varying strategies (Siegler & Alibali, 2005).

Pressley and his colleagues (Pressley & Hilden, 2006; Pressley & others, 2001, 2003, 2004) have spent considerable time in recent years observing the use of strategy instruction by teachers and strategy use by students in elementary and secondary school classrooms. They conclude that teachers use of strategy instruction is far less complete and intense than what is needed for students to learn how to use strategies effectively. They argue that education needs to be restructured so that students are provided with more opportunities to become competent strategic learners.

A final point about strategies is that many strategies depend on prior knowledge (Pressley & Harris, 2006; Pressley & Hilden, 2006). For example, students can't apply organizational strategies to a list of items unless they know the correct categories into which the items fall. The point about the importance of prior knowledge in strategy use coincides with the emphasis in our discussion earlier in the chapter of how experts use more effective strategies than novices.

Review, Reflect, and Practice

5 Explain the concept of metacognition and identify some ways to improve children's metacognition.

REVIEW

- How do young children compare with older children in their metacognitive abilities?
- According to Pressley and colleagues' Good Information-Processing model, competent cognition results from what interacting factors?
- How can children be helped to learn metacognitive strategies and self-regulation?

REFLECT

- How might the three steps in the Good Information-Processing model be part of teaching a topic to children? Select a topic that you might teach one day and try working through it as an example.

PRAXIS™ PRACTICE

1. Sharmala's uncle has just played a trick on her. He presented her with a can that looked like a can of peanuts. However, when she opened the can, a cloth snake sprang out at her. Sharmala thought the trick was very funny and can hardly wait to play it on her brother. When her uncle asked her what she thought her brother would expect to be in the can, she giggled and responded, "Peanuts, but won't he be surprised." This is an example of Sharmala's development of
   a. the ability to allocate attention to different aspects of a problem.
   b. problem-solving expertise.
   c. metamemory skills.
   d. theory of mind.

continued on page 296

Review, Reflect, and Practice *continued*

2. Marvel has learned to use strategies to solve math problems but does not use them to study for history exams or spelling quizzes. According to the Good Information-Processing model, the next step for Marvel's metacognitive development would most likely be to
   a. ask his teacher for specific strategies for studying history.
   b. ask his parents about the benefits of using strategies for math.
   c. understand shared features of many different strategies.
   d. learn to attribute successful learning to use of strategies.

3. Mr. Quinton has taught his students the PQ4R strategy for reading textbooks, in hopes that it will help them on their next history test. The majority of his class improves their scores. Mr. Quinton is disappointed when in spite of improved performance, many of his students don't continue using the PQ4R strategy. What is the most plausible explanation for the students' behavior?
   a. They did not compare the results of using the PQ4R with their prior strategies.
   b. They don't have the requisite background knowledge to use the PQ4R strategy effectively.
   c. They have not had enough practice to use the strategy effectively.
   d. They have not yet developed expertise in using the strategy.

Please see the answer key at the end of the book.

CRACK THE CASE
The Case of the Test

George has a test next week in his eighth-grade history class. He is having considerable difficulty remembering terms, names, and facts. On his last test, he identified General Sherman as a Vietnam War hero and Saigon as the capital of Japan. Historical dates are so confusing to him that he does not even try to remember them. In addition, George has difficulty spelling.

The test will consist of fifty objective test items (multiple-choice, true/false, and fill-in-the-blank) and two essay items. In general, George does better on essay items. He purposely leaves out any names about which he is uncertain and always omits dates. Sometimes he mixes up his facts, though, and often loses points for misspelled words. On objective items he has real problems. Usually, more than one answer will appear to be correct to him. Often he is "sure" he is correct, only to discover later that he was mistaken.

Before the last test, George tried to design some mnemonic devices to help him understand. He used

acronyms, such as *HOMES* (for *H*uron, *O*ntario, *M*ichigan, *E*rie, and *S*uperior). While he remembered his acronyms quite well, he could not recall what each letter stood for. The result was a test paper filled with acronyms. Another time a classmate suggested that George try using concept maps. This classmate lent George the concept maps she had designed for her own use. George looked at them and found them to be very busy and confusing—he couldn't figure out what they even meant. They were not at all useful to him.

George has decided he is in need of some serious help if he is to pass this class. He has sought you out for his help.

1. What are the issues in this case?
2. With what type of learning is George having difficulty?
3. What type of learning is easier for George?
4. Design a study-skills program for George drawing on principles of the cognitive information-processing approach.

Reach Your Learning Goals
Information Processing

---

(1) THE NATURE OF THE INFORMATION-PROCESSING APPROACH: Describe the information-processing approach.

Information, Memory, and Thinking	The information-processing approach emphasizes that children manipulate information, monitor it, and strategize about it. Central to this approach are the processes of memory and thinking. The development of computers stimulated interest in cognitive psychology.
Cognitive Resources: Capacity and Speed of Processing Information	Capacity and speed of processing speed, often referred to as cognitive resources, increase across childhood and adolescence. Changes in the brain serve as biological foundations for developmental changes in cognitive resources. In terms of capacity, the increase is reflected in older children being able to hold in mind several dimensions of a topic simultaneously. A reaction-time task has often been used to assess speed of processing. Processing speed continues to improve in early adolescence.
Mechanisms of Change	According to Siegler, three important mechanisms of change are encoding (how information gets into memory), automaticity (ability to process information with little or no effort), and strategy construction (creation of new procedures for processing information). Children's information processing is characterized by self-modification, and an important aspect of this self-modification involves metacognition—that is, knowing about knowing.

---

(2) ATTENTION: Characterize attention and summarize how it changes during development.

What Is Attention?	Attention is focusing mental resources. Three ways that people can allocate their attention are sustained attention (the ability to maintain attention to a selected stimulus for a prolonged period of time; also referred to as vigilance), selective attention (focusing on a specific aspect of experience that is relevant while ignoring others that are irrelevant), and divided attention (concentrating on more than one activity at the same time).
Developmental Changes	Salient stimuli tend to capture the attention of the preschooler. After 6 or 7 years of age, there is a shift to more cognitive control of attention. Selective attention improves through childhood and adolescence.

---

(3) MEMORY: Discuss memory in terms of encoding, storage, and retrieval.

What Is Memory?	Memory is the retention of information over time and involves encoding, storage, and retrieval.
Encoding	In everyday language, encoding has much to do with attention and learning. Rehearsal, deep processing, elaboration, constructing images, and organization are processes involved in encoding, which is the mechanism by which information gets into memory. Rehearsal increases the length of time that information stays in memory. In deep processing, information is processed semantically, in terms of its meaning. Elaboration involves the extensiveness of information processing. Constructing images helps to elaborate the information, and the more information is presented in an organized way, the easier it is to remember.

continued

Storage

One way that memory varies involves its time frames: sensory memory, short-term memory, and long-term memory. There is increasing interest in working memory, a kind of mental workbench. The Atkinson-Shiffrin model states that memory involves a sequence of three stages: sensory, short-term, and long-term memory. Long-term memory includes different types of content. Many cognitive psychologists accept this hierarchy of long-term memory's contents: division into declarative and procedural memory subtypes, with declarative memory further subdivided into episodic and semantic memory. Declarative memory (explicit memory) is the conscious recollection of information, such as specific facts or events. Procedural memory (implicit memory) is knowledge of skills and cognitive operations about how to do something; it is hard to communicate verbally. Episodic memory is the retention of information about the where and when of life's happenings; semantic memory is a general knowledge about the world.

Three major approaches to how information is represented are network theories (which focus on how information is organized and connected, with emphasis on nodes in the memory network) schema theories (which stress that students often reconstruct information and fit it into an existing schema), and fuzzy trace theory (which states that memory is best understood by considering two types of memory representation: (1) verbatim memory trace and (2) gist. In this theory, older children's better memory is attributed to the fuzzy traces created by extracting the gist of information). A script is a schema for an event.

Retrieval and Forgetting

Retrieval is influenced by the serial position effect (memory is better for items at the beginning and end of a list than for items in the middle), the effectiveness retrieval cues, encoding specificity, and the memory task (such as recall versus recognition). Forgetting can be explained in terms of cue-dependent forgetting (failure to use effective retrieval cues), interference theory (because information gets in the way of what we are trying to remember), and decay (losing information over time).

4 EXPERTISE: Draw some lessons about learning from the way experts think.

Expertise and Learning

Five important characteristics of experts are that they (1) notice features and meaningful patterns of information that novices don't, (2) have acquired a great deal of content knowledge that is organized in a manner that reflects deep understanding of the subject, (3) can retrieve important aspects of their knowledge with little effort, (4) are adaptive in their approach to new situations, and (5) use effective strategies.

Acquiring Expertise

Becoming an expert usually requires deliberate practice, motivation, and talent.

Expertise and Teaching

Being an expert in a particular area does not mean that the expert is good at helping others learn it. Pedagogical content knowledge is required to effectively teach a subject.

5 METACOGNITION: Explain the concept of metacognition and identify some ways to improve children's metacognition.

Developmental Changes

Children's metamemory improves considerably through the elementary school years. At 5 years of age, children understand that people can have false beliefs, and in middle and late childhood they understand that people actively construct knowledge. Adolescents have an increased capacity to monitor and manage resources to effectively meet the demands of a learning task, although there is considerable individual variation in metacognition during adolescence.

| The Good Information Processing Model | The Good Information-Processing model stresses that competent cognition results from several interacting factors including strategies, content knowledge, motivation, and metacognition. |

| Strategies and Metacognitive Regulation | In Pressley's view, the key to education is helping students learn a rich repertoire of strategies that result in solutions to problems. Most children benefit from using multiple strategies and exploring which ones work well, when, and where. For example, teachers can model strategies for students and ask questions that help guide students' thinking in various content areas. |

 KEY TERMS

information-processing
    approach 264
encoding 265
automaticity 265
strategy construction 265
metacognition 265
attention 267
sustained attention 267
selective attention 267
divided attention 267

memory 270
rehearsal 270
levels of processing
    theory 271
elaboration 271
chunking 273
sensory memory 273
short-term memory 273
memory span 273
working memory 273

long-term memory 275
Atkinson-Shiffrin model 275
declarative memory 276
procedural memory 276
episodic memory 277
semantic memory 277
network theories 277
schema theories 277
schema 277
script 278

fuzzy trace theory 278
serial position effect 278
encoding specificity
    principle 279
cue-dependent
    forgetting 279
interference theory 279
decay theory 279
theory of mind 292

 PORTFOLIO ACTIVITIES

Now that you have a good understanding of this chapter, complete these exercises to expand your thinking.

Independent Reflection

Developing Expert Knowledge. Think about the experts you know. Are your parents or instructors considered experts in their fields? How do you think they came to become experts and how long did it take? Based on what you know about how experts process information, which strategies do you think these experts use to organize, remember, and utilize their knowledge and skills? (INTASC: Principles **2**, 4, 9)

Collaborative Work

Strategies to Enhance Memory. Get together with three or four other students in the class and brainstorm about the best ways to guide students in developing better memory and study strategies. Discuss how you might do this differently for children and adolescents at different grade levels. For example, at what age should students start learning effective note-taking strategies? For children too young to be taking elaborate notes, are there gamelike activities that might help them begin to learn the concept and value of taking notes or keeping running records of some event? Write your conclusions. (INTASC: Principles **2**, 4)

Research/Field Experience

Capturing Students' Attention. Observe a kindergarten, elementary, middle school, and high school classroom and focus on how the teacher maintains students' attention. How effective are each teacher's strategies? Would you do things differently to capture the students' attention? (INTASC: Principles **2**, 9)

Go to the Online Learning Center for downloadable portfolio templates.

 TAKING IT TO THE NET

- Information-processing theorists emphasize that learning results from interaction between the environment and the learner's prior knowledge. Describe teaching techniques that help students connect new information with previous experiences and learning. Why are these connections so critical for learning to occur? www.ncrel.org/sdrs/areas/issues/students/learning/lr100.htm

- Take a moment to reflect upon your own study strategies, and describe your typical study routine. In relation to memory research, how could you improve your study techniques? Design a classroom activity that you could use to help students develop effective study skills. www.mtsu.edu/~studskl/mem.html

- Plan a classroom project for a particular grade level and subject area. First, describe the strategies you will use to capture student attention. Then outline how you intend to maintain student attention throughout the project. Explain how your strategies are appropriate for your students' age group based on what you've learned about brain development. **www.teachers.ab.ca/ Quick+Links/Publications/Other+Publications/Teaching+ Students+with+Learning+Disabilities/c.htm**

Connect to the Online Learning Center to explore possible answers.

 ## STUDY, PRACTICE, AND SUCCEED

Visit **www.mhhe.com/santedu3e** to review the chapter with self-grading quizzes and self-assessments, to apply the chapter material to two more Crack the Case studies, and for suggested activities to develop your teaching portfolio.

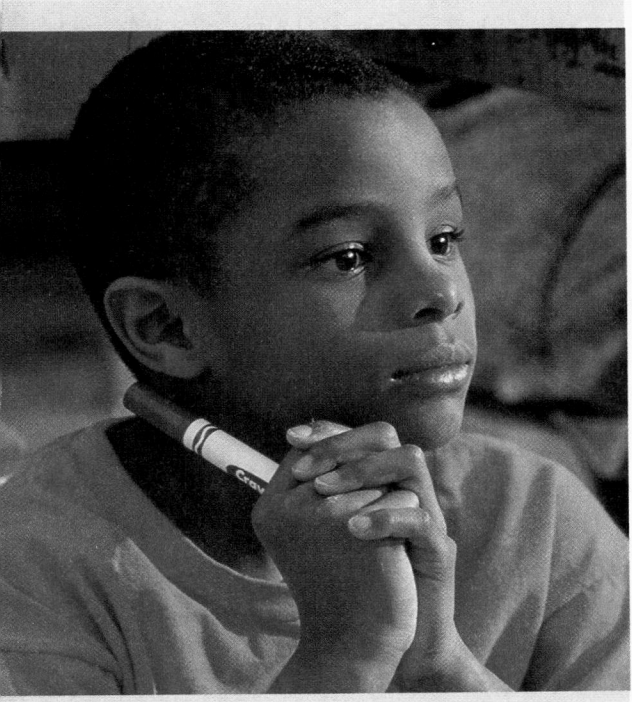

CHAPTER 9

Complex Cognitive Processes

I think, therefore I am.

—René Descartes
French Philosopher and Mathematician, 17th Century

Learning Goals

1 Discuss conceptual understanding and strategies for teaching concepts.

2 Describe several types of thinking and ways that teachers can foster them.

3 Take a systematic approach to problem solving.

4 Define transfer and explain how to enhance it as a teacher.

TEACHING STORIES   Marilyn Whirry

Marilyn Whirry is a twelfth-grade English teacher at Mira Costa High School in Manhattan Beach, California. In 1999, she was named Teacher of the Year in the United States and honored at a White House Reception. The following description of Marilyn's teaching appeared in a report by the Council of Chief State School Officers (2005, pp. 1–3).

> Marilyn's enthusiasm for life carries over into the classroom. Marilyn says about her life: "It is a canvas with swirling brush strokes that depict the motifs of my experience." According to Marilyn, teachers may never know how many students' lives they changed for the better because of their sense of responsibility and excitement for life.
>
> "Marilyn's teaching philosophy centers around embracing and celebrating the act of learning. She says that teachers need to help students become motivated to search for

knowledge and to discover answers to questions of why and how. One of Marilyn's most important goals as a teacher is to get students to think deeply as they read and write." ... Her teaching strategies include getting students to become aware of writing techniques in literary works that "promote dialogue and debate in group discussions."

> One of Marilyn's former students, Mary-Anna Rae, said that Marilyn's "intellectual engagement and her passion for life make her a powerful role model for students. In everything she does, she makes it clear that she is listening, attending to the students' deepest thinking." Mary-Anna, who now teaches herself, adds that Marilyn "enriched and expanded her world." Mary-Anna also says that Marilyn helped her to "grow more confident in what I had to say, finding my writer's voice and discovering that I could give my life purpose."

Preview

One of Marilyn Whirry's major goals is to get her students to think deeply, an important emphasis in this chapter. In addition to exploring many aspects of thinking, we examine how teachers can guide students to engage in these other complex cognitive processes: understanding concepts, solving problems, and transfering what they learn to other settings.

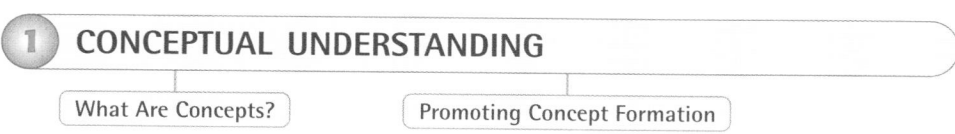

1 CONCEPTUAL UNDERSTANDING

| What Are Concepts? | Promoting Concept Formation |

Conceptual understanding is a key aspect of learning (Brophy, 2006; Murphy & Mason, 2006). An important teaching goal is to help students understand the main concepts in a subject rather than just memorize isolated facts. In many cases, conceptual understanding is enhanced when teachers explore a topic in depth and give appropriate, interesting examples of the concepts involved. As you will see, concepts are the building blocks of thinking.

What Are Concepts?

Concepts are categories that group objects, events, and characteristics on the basis of common properties. Concepts are elements of cognition that help us to simplify and summarize information (Hahn & Ramscar, 2001; Klausmeier, 2004; Mandler, 2004). Imagine a world in which we had no concepts: We would see each object as unique and would not be able to make any generalizations. If we had no concepts, we would find the most trivial problems difficult to formulate and even impossible to solve. Consider the concept of book. If a student were not aware that a book is made of sheets of paper of uniform size, all bound together along one edge, and full of printed words and pictures in some meaningful order, each time the student encountered a

concepts Categories used to group objects, events, and characteristics on the basis of common properties.

new book she would have to figure out what it was. In a way, then, concepts keep us from "reinventing the wheel" each time we come across a new piece of information.

Concepts also aid the process of remembering, making it more efficient. When students group objects to form a concept, they can remember the concept, then retrieve the concept's characteristics. Thus, when you assign math homework, you probably won't have to go through the details of what math is or what homework is. Students will have embedded in their memory a number of appropriate associations. In ways such as this, concepts not only help to jog memory but also make communication more efficient. If you say, "It's time for art," students know what you mean. You don't have to go into a lengthy explanation of what art is. Thus, concepts help students to simplify and summarize information, as well as improve the efficiency of their memory, communication, and use of time.

Students form concepts through direct experiences with objects and events in their world. For example, in constructing a sophisticated concept of cartoons, children might initially experience TV cartoon shows, then read comic strips, and eventually look at some political caricatures. Students also form concepts through experience with symbols (things that stand for, or represent, something else). For example, words are symbols. So are math formulas, graphs, and pictures.

Some concepts are relatively simple, clear, and concrete, whereas others are more complex, fuzzy, and abstract (Barsalou, 2000). The former are easier to agree on. For example, most people can agree on the meaning of "baby." But we have a harder time agreeing on what is meant by "young" or "old." We agree on whether something is an apple more readily than on whether something is a fruit. Some concepts are especially complex, fuzzy, and abstract, like the concepts involved in theories of economic collapse or string theory in physics.

Promoting Concept Formation

In a number of ways, teachers can guide students to recognize and form effective concepts. The process begins with becoming aware of the features of a given concept.

Learning about the Features of Concepts   An important aspect of concept formation is learning the key features, attributes, or characteristics of the concept. These are the defining elements of a concept, the dimensions that make it different from another concept. For example, in our earlier example of the concept of "book," the key features include sheets of paper, being bound together along one edge, and being full of printed words and pictures in some meaningful order. Other characteristics such as size, color, and length are not key features that define the concept of "book." Consider also these critical features of the concept of "dinosaur": extinct and reptilian. Thus, in the case of the concept of "dinosaur," the feature "extinct" is important.

Defining Concepts and Providing Examples   An important aspect of teaching concepts is to clearly define them and give carefully chosen examples. The *rule-example strategy* is an effective way to do this (Tennyson & Cocchiarella, 1986). The strategy consists of four steps:

1. *Define the concept.* As part of defining it, link it to a superordinate concept and identify its key features or characteristics. A *superordinate* concept is a larger class into which it fits. Thus, in specifying the key features of the concept of dinosaur, you might want to mention the larger class into which it fits: reptiles.

2. *Clarify terms in the definition.* Make sure that the key features or characteristics are well understood. Thus, in describing the key features of the concept of dinosaur, it is important for students to know what a reptile is—usually an egg-laying vertebrate with an external covering of scales or horny plates that breathes by means of lungs.

3. *Give examples to illustrate the key features or characteristics.* With regard to dinosaurs, one might give examples and descriptions of different types of

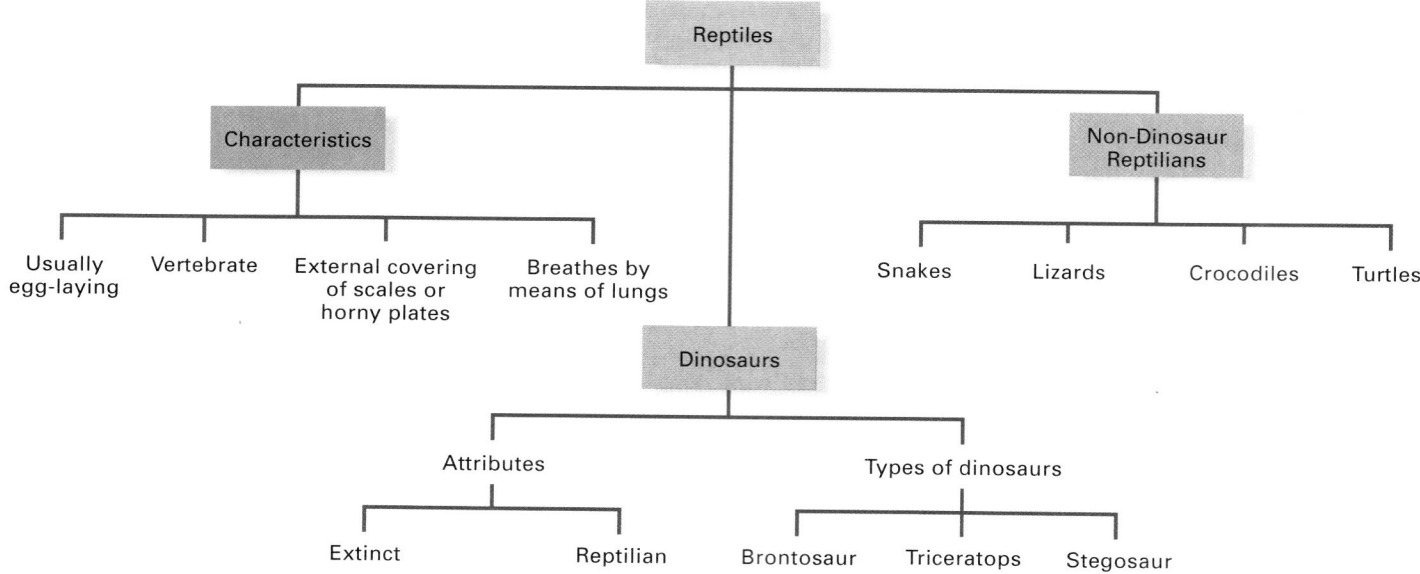

FIGURE 9.1 Example of a Concept Map for the Concept of Reptile

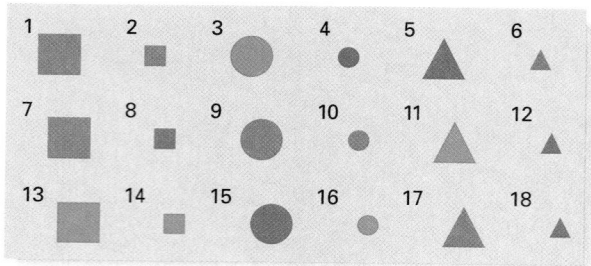

FIGURE 9.2 Getting Students to Generate Hypotheses about a Concept

You can use arrangements like the one shown here to help students generate hypotheses about what concept you have in mind. This encourages students to develop the most efficient strategies for understanding what a concept is. For example, you might select the concept "squares and purple triangles" or "purple triangles and purple squares" and ask students to figure out what concept you're thinking of. You also can let students take turns selecting the concept.

concept map A visual presentation of a concept's connections and hierarchical organization.

dinosaurs, such as *triceratops, brontosaur,* and *stegosaur.* The concept can be further clarified by giving examples of other reptiles that are not dinosaurs, such as snakes, lizards, crocodiles, and turtles. Indeed, giving nonexamples of a concept as well as examples is often a good strategy for teaching concept formation. More examples are required when you teach complex concepts and when you work with less-sophisticated learners (Moore, 1998).

4. *Provide additional examples.* Ask students to categorize concepts, explain their categorization, or have them generate their own examples of the concept. Give examples of other dinosaurs, such as pterodactyl, *Ornitholestes,* and *Dimetrodon,* or ask students to find more examples themselves. Also ask them to think up other nonexamples of dinosaurs, such as dogs, cats, and whales.

Concept Maps A **concept map** is a visual presentation of a concept's connections and hierarchical organization. Getting students to create a map of a concept's features or characteristics can help them to learn the concept (Kinchin, Hay, & Adams, 2000; Nesbit & Hadwin, 2006; Nicoll, 2001). The concept map also might embed the concept in a superordinate category and include examples and nonexamples of the concept. The visual aspects of the concept map relate to our chapter 8 discussion of the use of imagery in memory. You might create a concept map with students' help, or let them try to develop it individually or in small groups. Figure 9.1 shows an example of a concept map for the concept of reptile.

Hypothesis Testing *Hypotheses* are specific assumptions and predictions that can be tested to determine their accuracy. Students benefit from the practice of developing hypotheses about what a concept is and is not. One way to develop a hypothesis is to come up with a rule about why some objects fall within a concept and others do not. Here is an example of how you can give your students practice in developing such hypotheses: Present your students with the picture of geometric forms shown in figure 9.2. Then silently select the concept of one of those geometric forms (such as "circle" or "green circle") and ask your students to develop hypotheses about what concept you have selected. They zero in on your concept by asking you questions related to the geometric forms and eliminating nonexamples.

BEST PRACTICES
Strategies for Helping Students Form Concepts

1. *Use the rule-example strategy.* Remember that this involves four steps: (a) Define the concept; (b) clarify the terms in the definition; (c) give examples to illustrate the key features or characteristics; and (d) provide additional examples and ask students to categorize these and explain their categorization, or have students generate their own examples of the concepts.

2. *Help students learn not only what a concept is but also what it is not.* Let's return to the concept "cartoon." Students can learn that even though they are humorous, jokes, clowns, and funny poems are not cartoons. If you are teaching the concept of "triangle," ask students to list the characteristics of "triangle" such as "three-sided," "geometric shape," "can be of any size," "can be of any color," "sides can vary in length," "angles can be different," and so on; also ask them to list examples of things that are not triangles, such as circles, squares, and rectangles.

3. *Make concepts as clear as possible and give concrete examples.* Spend some time thinking about the best way to present a new concept, especially an abstract one. Make it as clear as possible. If you want students to understand the concept "vehicle," ask them to come up with examples of it. They probably will say "car" and maybe "truck" or "bus." Show them photographs of other vehicles, such as a sled and a boat, to illustrate the breadth of the concept.

4. *Help students relate new concepts to concepts they already know.* In chapter 8, we discussed the strategy of outlining for taking notes. Once students have learned this procedure, it is easier for them to learn how to construct concept maps, because you can show them how concept maps are linked with outlining in terms of hierarchical organization. As another example of helping students to relate a new concept to concepts they already know, they might know what gold and silver are but not be aware of what platinum and plutonium are. In this case, build on their knowledge of gold and silver to teach the concepts of platinum and plutonium.

5. *Encourage students to create concept maps.* Getting students to visually map out the hierarchical organization of a concept can help them learn it. The hierarchical arranging can help students understand the concept's characteristics from more general to more specific. Hierarchical organization benefits memory.

6. *Ask students to generate hypotheses about a concept.* Generating hypotheses encourages students to think and develop strategies. Work with students on developing the most efficient strategies for determining what a concept is.

7. *Give students experience in prototype matching.* Think of different concepts and then ask students what the prototypes of the concepts are. Then ask them for nonprototypical examples of the concept.

8. *Check for students' understanding of a concept and motivate them to apply the concept to other contexts.* Make sure that students don't just rotely memorize a concept. Ask students how the concept can be applied in different contexts. For example, in learning the concept of fairness, ask students how fairness can make life smoother, not only at school but also at play, at home, and at work.

You might also let the students take turns selecting a concept and answering questions from the other students. Work with your students on developing the most efficient strategies for identifying the correct concept.

Prototype Matching   In **prototype matching,** individuals decide whether an item is a member of a category by comparing it with the most typical item(s) of the category (Rosch, 1973). The more similar the item is to the prototype, the more likely it is that the individual will say the item belongs to the category; the less similar, the more likely the person will judge that it doesn't belong in the category. For example, a student's concept of a football player might include being big and muscular like an offensive lineman. But some football players, such as many field goal kickers, are not so big and muscular. An offensive lineman is a more prototypical example of a football player than a field goal kicker. When students consider whether someone belongs in the category "football player," they are more likely to think of someone who looks like an offensive lineman than to think of someone who looks like a field goal kicker. Similarly, robins are viewed as being more typical birds than ostriches or penguins. Nonetheless, members of a category can vary greatly and still have qualities that make them a member of that category.

prototype matching A process in which individuals decide whether an item is a member of a category by comparing it with the most typical item(s) of the category.

Review, Reflect, and Practice

(1) Discuss conceptual understanding and strategies for teaching concepts.

REVIEW

- What are concepts and why are they indispensable to thinking?
- What are some ways that students can be guided to construct effective concepts?

REFLECT

- What might the concept "art" mean to a 3-year-old? to a 10-year-old? to a 16-year-old? to a professional artist? How do such changes come about?

PRAXIS™ PRACTICE

1. Which of the following is the best example of a superordinate concept?
   a. collie
   b. dog
   c. german shepherd
   d. poodle
2. Ms. Peloti wants her students to learn about the concept "bird." She discusses the characteristics of birds with her students, including a defining characteristic: feathers. She then discusses irrelevant characteristics, such as flying—insects and bats fly too, but they are not birds. Finally, the class discusses what a typical bird looks like. They finally agree that the most typical bird is a robin. Ms. Peloti then gives the children a list of animals and asks them to determine if they are birds by comparing them to the robin. What strategy of concept formation does this task represent?
   a. concept mapping
   b. hypothesis testing
   c. prototype matching
   d. relating concepts

Please see the answer key at the end of the book.

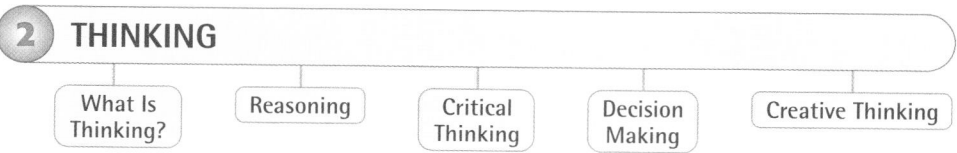

(2) THINKING

What Is Thinking? | Reasoning | Critical Thinking | Decision Making | Creative Thinking

What does it mean to think? How can teachers help students to become better thinkers? In this section, we will attempt to answer these important questions.

What Is Thinking?

Thinking involves manipulating and transforming information in memory. We think to form concepts, reason, think critically, make decisions, think creatively, and solve problems. Students can think about the concrete, such as a vacation at the beach or how to win at a video game. They can also think about more abstract subjects, such as the meaning of freedom or identity. They can think about the past (such as what happened to them last month) and the future (what their life will be like in the year 2020). They can think about reality (such as how to do better on the next test) and fantasy (what it would be like to meet Elvis Presley or land a spacecraft on Mars).

thinking Manipulating and transforming information in memory, which often is done to form concepts, reason, think critically, make decisions, think creatively, and solve problems.

Reasoning

Reasoning is logical thinking that uses induction and deduction to reach a conclusion. We begin by focusing on inductive reasoning.

Inductive Reasoning   **Inductive reasoning** involves reasoning from the specific to the general. That is, it consists of drawing conclusions (forming concepts) about all members of a category based on observing only some of its members (Kuhn, 2006; Markman & Gentner, 2001). For example, when a student in English class reads only a few Emily Dickinson poems and is asked to draw conclusions from them about the general nature of Dickinson's poems, inductive reasoning is being requested. When a student is asked whether a concept in a math class applies to other contexts, such as business or science, again, inductive reasoning is being called for. Educational psychology research is inductive when it studies a sample of participants to draw conclusions about the population from which the sample is drawn. It is also inductive in that scientists rarely take a single study as strong evidence to reach a conclusion about a topic, instead requiring a number of studies on the same topic to have more confidence in a conclusion.

Indeed, an important aspect of inductive reasoning is repeated observation. Through repeated observation, information about similar experiences accumulates to the point that a repetitive pattern can be detected and a more accurate conclusion drawn about it. To study this aspect of inductive reasoning, researchers have examined whether inductive inferences are justified based on evidence about a single instance of two co-occurring events (Kuhn, Katz, & Dean, 2004). When two events occur together in time and space, we often conclude that one has caused the other, despite the possibility that other factors are involved. For example, a parent might conclude, "Harry is a bad influence on my daughter; Sharon didn't drink before she met him." The boy might be the cause, but the event may have been a coincidence. Of course, if there is repeated evidence (for example, every girl Harry has ever gone out with develops a drinking problem), then the argument becomes more persuasive.

Consider also a child who observes a black snake and concludes "All snakes are black." The child's cousin sends him an e-mail about a pet snake she recently bought, and the child concludes that the pet snake must be black. However, the child clearly has not observed all of the snakes in the world—actually only one in this case—so he only has seen a small sample of the world's snake population. Of course, he would be forced to change his mind if he saw a gray snake or a white snake. The conclusions drawn as a result of inductive reasoning are never finally certain, only more or less probable. But induction can provide conclusive *negative* results—for example, seeing a yellow snake proves that the assertion "All snakes are black" is *false*.

Notice that inductive conclusions are never entirely certain—that is, they may be inconclusive. An inductive conclusion may be very likely, but there always is a chance that it is wrong, just as a sample does not perfectly represent its population (Johnson-Laird, 2000; Kuhn, 2006, in press). Teachers can help students improve their inductive reasoning by encouraging them to consider that the conclusion they reach depends on the quality and the quantity of the information available. Students often overstate a conclusion, making it more definitive than the evidence indicates.

Let's now consider another aspect of inductive reasoning: It is basic to analogies (Goswami, 2004). An **analogy** is a correspondence between otherwise dissimilar things. Analogies can be used to improve students' understanding of new concepts by comparing them with already learned concepts.

One type of analogy involves formal reasoning and has four parts, with the relation between the first two parts being the same as, or very similar to, the relation between the last two. For example, solve this analogy: Beethoven is to music as Picasso is to _____. To answer correctly ("art"), you had to induce the relation

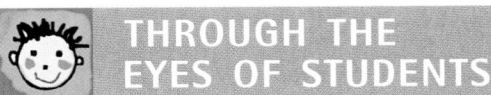

THROUGH THE EYES OF STUDENTS

The Thinking Room

I recently talked with my granddaughter, Jordan Bowles, who is just beginning the second grade in Apex, North Carolina. I asked her what her classes were like this year.

She responded, "The usual stuff. Well, there is this one new class that I go to once a week. It's in the thinking room."

I then asked her what she was supposed to learn there.

Jordan said, "They are going to teach me not to jump to conclusions and my mom is happy about that."

inductive reasoning Reasoning from the specific to the general.

analogy A correspondence in some respects between otherwise dissimilar things.

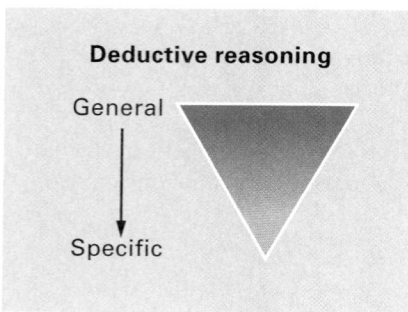

FIGURE 9.3 Inductive and Deductive Reasoning

The pyramid at the top (right side up) represents inductive reasoning—going from specific to general. The pyramid or triangle at the bottom (upside down) represents deductive reasoning—going from general to specific.

between Beethoven and music (the former created the latter) and apply this relationship to Picasso (what did he create?).

How good are children and adolescents at inductive reasoning? Adolescents are better at many aspects of inductive reasoning than are children, including analogies and false inclusion when generalizing from a single event, but not as good as young adults (Kuhn & Franklin, 2006).

Deductive Reasoning In contrast to inductive reasoning, **deductive reasoning** is reasoning from the general to the specific. Figure 9.3 provides a visual representation of the difference between inductive and deductive reasoning.

When you solve puzzles or riddles, you are engaging in deductive reasoning. When you learn about a general rule and then understand how it applies in some situations but not others, you are engaging in deductive reasoning (Kuhn & Franklin, 2006). Deductive reasoning is always certain in the sense that if the initial rules or assumptions are true, then the conclusion will be correct. When psychologists use theories and intuitions to make predictions, then evaluate these predictions by making further observations, they are using deductive reasoning.

Many aspects of deductive reasoning have been studied, including the occasions when knowledge and reasoning conflict (Kuhn & Franklin, 2006; Wigfield, Byrnes, & Eccles, 2006). During adolescence, individuals are increasingly able to reason deductively even when the premises being reasoned about are false. Consider this deductive inference problem:

All basketball players are motorcycle drivers.
All motorcycle drivers are women.

Assuming that these two statements are true, decide if the following statement is true or false:

All basketball players are women.

Children rarely conclude that such conclusions are valid deductions from the premises. From early adolescence through early adulthood, individuals improve in their ability to make accurate conclusions when knowledge and reasoning conflict. That is, they can "reason independently of the truth status of the premises" (Kuhn & Franklin, 2006).

Critical Thinking

Currently, there is considerable interest in critical thinking among psychologists and educators, although it is not an entirely new idea (Halpern, 2007; Moseley & others, 2006; Sternberg, 2007; Sternberg, Ruediger & Halpern, 2007). The famous educator John Dewey (1933) proposed a similar idea when he talked about the importance of getting students to think reflectively. The well-known psychologist Max Wertheimer (1945) talked about the importance of thinking productively rather than just guessing at a correct answer. **Critical thinking** involves thinking reflectively and productively and evaluating the evidence. Many of the "Reflect" questions that appear in every section of this book call for critical thinking.

Critical Thinking in Schools Here are some ways teachers can consciously build critical thinking into their lesson plans:

- Ask not only what happened but also "how" and "why."
- Examine supposed "facts" to determine whether there is evidence to support them.
- Argue in a reasoned way rather than through emotions.
- Recognize that there is sometimes more than one good answer or explanation.
- Compare various answers to a question and judge which is really the best answer.
- Evaluate and possibly question what other people say rather than immediately accept it as the truth.
- Ask questions and speculate beyond what we already know to create new ideas and new information.

deductive reasoning Reasoning from the general to the specific.

critical thinking Thinking reflectively and productively and evaluating the evidence.

Jacqueline and Martin Brooks (1993, 2001) lament that few schools really teach students to think critically. In their view, schools spend too much time on getting students to give a single correct answer in an imitative way rather than encouraging students to expand their thinking by coming up with new ideas and rethinking earlier conclusions. They believe that too often teachers ask students to recite, define, describe, state, and list rather than to analyze, infer, connect, synthesize, criticize, create, evaluate, think, and rethink.

One way to encourage students to think critically is to present them with controversial topics or articles that present both sides of an issue to discuss. Some teachers shy away from having students engage in these types of critical thinking debates or discussions because it is not "polite" or "nice" (Winn, 2004). However, critical thinking is promoted when students encounter conflicting accounts of arguments and debates, which can motivate them to delve more deeply into a topic and attempt to resolve an issue (Andriessen, 2006; Gong, 2005; Van Gelder, 2005). In these circumstances, students often benefit when teachers refrain from stating their own views, allowing students to more freely explore different sides of issues and multiple perspectives on topics.

Getting students to think critically is not always an easy task (Black, 2004; Mayer & Wittrock, 2006). Many students come into a class with a history of passive learning, having been encouraged to recite the correct answer to a question, rather than put forth the intellectual effort to think in more complex ways. By using more assignments that require students to focus on an issue, a question, or a problem, rather than just reciting facts, teachers stimulate students' ability to think critically. To read about ways to use technology to stimulate students' critical thinking, see the Technology and Education box.

Critical Thinking in Adolescence If a solid basis of fundamental skills (such as literacy and math skills) is not developed during childhood, critical-thinking skills are unlikely to mature in adolescence. For those adolescents who lack fundamental skills, potential gains in adolescent thinking are not likely. For other adolescents, this time is an important transitional period in the development of critical thinking (Keating, 1990, 2004). Several cognitive changes occur during adolescence that allow improved critical thinking, including the following (Keating, 1990):

- Increased speed, automaticity, and capacity of information processing, which frees cognitive resources for other purposes (see chapter 8)
- More knowledge in a variety of domains
- An increased ability to construct new combinations of knowledge
- A greater range and more spontaneous use of strategies or procedures such as planning, considering alternatives, and cognitive monitoring

In one study of fifth-, eighth-, and eleventh-graders, critical thinking increased with age but still occurred in only 43 percent of the eleventh-graders (Klaczynski & Narasimham, 1998). Many adolescents showed self-serving biases in their reasoning.

Decision Making

Think of all the decisions you have to make in your life. Which grade level and subject should I teach? Should I go to graduate school right after college or get a job first? Should I establish myself in a career before settling down to have a family? Should I buy a house or rent? **Decision making** involves thinking in which individuals evaluate alternatives and make choices among them.

In deductive reasoning, people use clear-cut rules to draw conclusions. When we make decisions, the rules are seldom clear-cut and we may have limited knowledge about the consequences of the decisions (Gigerenzer & Selton, 2001; Tversky & Fox, 1995). In addition, important information might be missing, and we might not trust all of the information we have (Matlin, 2005).

In one type of decision-making research, investigators have studied how people weigh the costs and benefits of various outcomes (Redelmeier, 2005). They have

"For God's sake, think! Why is he being so nice to you?"

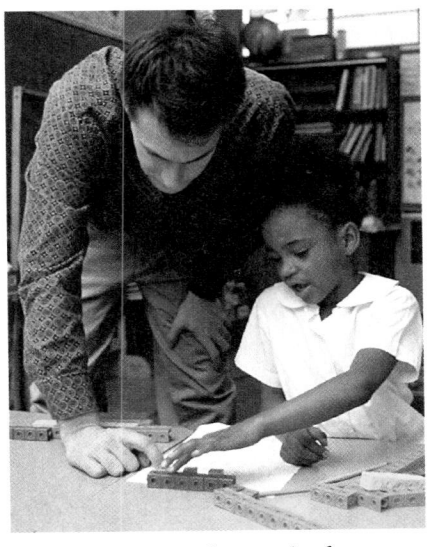

What are some good strategies for nurturing children's critical thinking?

decision making Evaluating alternatives and making choices among them.

TECHNOLOGY AND EDUCATION
Digital Mindtools

David Jonassen (1996) argues that one of the best uses of technology in education involves computer applications that encourage students to think critically about the content they are studying. He calls such applications "mindtools," and sees them as constructivist tools that scaffold student creation of knowledge and reasoning about subject content. Jonassen distinguishes several categories of mindtools, including semantic organization tools, dynamic modeling tools, information interpretation tools, and conversation and collaboration tools.

Semantic organization tools, such as concept mapping tools, help students organize, analyze, and visualize information they are studying. For example, students studying climate can query global databases to test their hypotheses concerning links between climate and population.

Dynamic modeling tools help students explore connections between concepts. These include spreadsheets, expert systems, systems modeling tools, and microworlds. For example, spreadsheets have been used in mathematics classes to help students explore mathematical relations between numbers. Microworlds stimulate real-world phenomena, such as genetic combinations.

Information interpretation tools help learners access and interpret information. For example, visualization tools create visual models of complex phenomena that make them more comprehensible. Knowledge construction tools, such as hypermedia, video editing or web design programs, scaffold student construction of knowledge in various forms.

Finally, a variety of digital *conversation and collaboration tools,* such as e-mail, online discussion, chat, videoconferencing, and blogs, make it possible for students to interact and collaborate with experts and other students around the world. For example, students studying foreign languages can converse with native speakers using computer-mediated communication.

The photographs in this Technology and Education box portray educational settings designed to stimulate students to think critically.

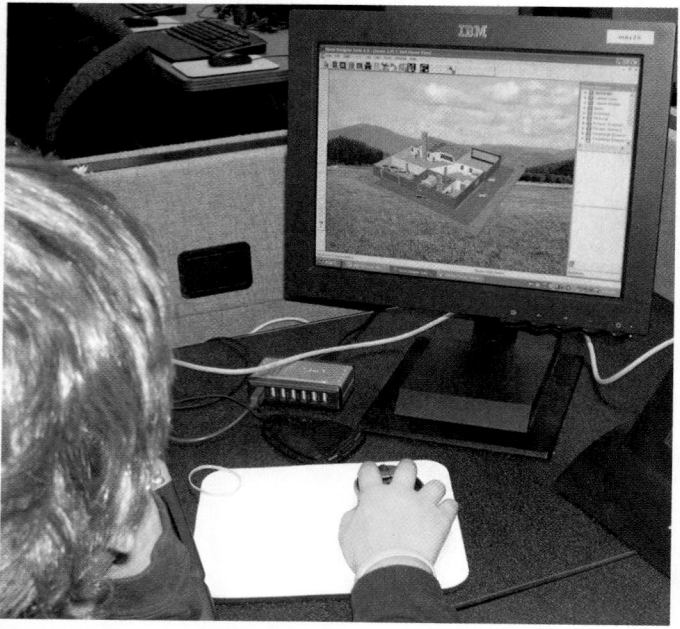

Students in the Research Center for Educational Technology's AT&T classroom at Kent State University studying energy by designing an energy-efficient home using *Better Homes & Garden Home Designer* software.

Kindergarten students in the Research Center for Educational Technology's AT&T classroom at Kent State University exploring patterns by programming the Logo Robotic Turtle.

found that people choose the outcome with the highest expected value (Smyth & others, 1994). For example, in choosing a college, a high school student might list the pluses and minuses of going to different colleges (related to such factors as cost, quality of education, and social life), then make a decision based on how the colleges fared on these criteria. In making a decision, the student might have weighed some of these factors more heavily than others (such as cost three points, quality of education two points, and social life one point).

BEST PRACTICES
Strategies for Improving Children's Thinking

Twentieth-century German dictator Adolph Hitler once remarked that it was such good fortune for people in power that most people do not think. Education should help students become better thinkers. Every teacher would agree with that goal, but the means for reaching it are not always in place in schools. Here are some guidelines for helping students to become better thinkers.

1. *Be a guide in helping students to construct their own thinking.* You can't and shouldn't do students' thinking for them. However, you can and should be an effective guide in helping students construct their own thinking. Teachers who help students construct their own thinking (Brooks & Brooks, 1993, 2001)

Do

- Highly value students' questions.
- View students as thinkers with emerging theories about the world.
- Seek students' points of view.
- Seek elaboration of students' initial responses.
- Nurture students' intellectual curiosity.

Don't

- View students' minds as empty or see their role as a teacher as simply pouring information into students' minds.
- Rely too heavily on textbooks and workbooks.
- Simply seek the correct answer to validate student learning.

2. *Use thinking-based questions.* One way to analyze your teaching strategies is to see whether you use a lecture-based approach, fact-based questioning, or thinking-based questioning (Sternberg & Spear-Swirling, 1996). In the lecture-based approach, the teacher presents information in the form of a lecture. This is a helpful approach for quickly presenting a body of information, such as factors that led to the French Revolution. In fact-based questioning, the teacher asks questions primarily designed to get students to describe factual information. This is best used for reinforcing newly acquired information or testing students' content knowledge. For example, the teacher might ask, "When did the French Revolution

Alan Haskvitz with middle school students Simon Alarcon and Tracy Blozis, examining bones and trying to figure out where in the animal kingdom they belong.

occur? Who were the king and queen of France at that time?" In thinking-based questioning, the teacher asks questions that stimulate thinking and discussion. For example, the teacher might ask, "Compare the French and American revolutions. How were they similar? How were they different?"

Make a point to include thinking-based questions in your teaching. They will help your students construct a deeper understanding of a topic. Next, two teachers describe how they get students to think more productively and the importance of having high expectations for higher-level thinking.

THROUGH THE EYES OF TEACHERS
Challenging Students to Be Intellectual Risk-Takers

Alan Haskvitz, who teaches social studies at Suzanne Middle School in Walnut, California, believes in learning by doing and the importance of motivating students to improve the community. His students have rewritten voting instructions adopted by Los Angeles County, lobbied for a law requiring state government buildings to have rough-resistant landscaping, and created measures to reduce the city's graffiti. Alan has compiled thousands of teacher resources on this Web site: **www.reacheverychild.com.** He challenges students to be independent thinkers and intellectual risk-takers. He has students create an ideal island and discuss what everything from government to geography would be like on the island. (Sources: Briggs, 1999; Educational Cyber Playground, 2006).

THROUGH THE EYES OF TEACHERS
Use the Word Explain *Often and Have High Expectations*

Donna Shelhorse, a teacher at Short Pump Middle School in Virginia, says: "I use the word *explain* a lot. I do not accept an answer without asking the student to explain. This gets the students to think about their answers and provide support for their answers."

De Tonack, a high school math teacher, recommends having high expectations for students to engage in higher-level learning. She especially advocates getting students to do independent research projects. In her words, "What better educational challenge and potential for growth than doing a primary research, not just a

continued on page 312

BEST PRACTICES *continued*
Strategies for Improving Children's Thinking

report on someone's findings. This is a struggle. Students are conditioned to do reports, not research. Encourage visiting the state historical society, museums, doing interviews, conducting surveys, doing experiments. The hardest challenge is probably coming up with a question to investigate, but perhaps that is what an educated person must know how to do. Students in our program have investigated local light pollution; the development of Omaha's Boystown; the North Platte, Nebraska, World War II canteen; the orphan train through the Midwest."

3. *Provide positive role models for thinking.* Look around your community for positive role models who can demonstrate effective thinking, and invite them to come to your classroom and talk with your students. Also think about contexts in the community, such as museums, colleges and universities, hospitals, and businesses, where

you can take students and they can observe and interact with competent thinkers.

4. *Be a thinking role model for students as a teacher.* Have an active and inquiring mind yourself. Examine what we have said about thinking in this chapter. Work on being a positive thinking model for students by practicing these strategies.

5. *Keep up-to-date on the latest developments in thinking.* Continue to learn actively about new developments in teaching students to become more effective thinkers after you have become a teacher. Over the next decade there will especially be new technology programs through which you can improve students' thinking skills. Go to libraries now and then to read educational journals, and attend professional conferences that include information about thinking.

*"You take all the time you need, Larry—
this certainly is a big decision."*

confirmation bias The tendency to search for and use information that supports our ideas rather than refutes them.

belief perseverance The tendency to hold on to a belief in the face of contradictory evidence.

Another fruitful subject of decision-making research is the biases and flawed heuristics (rules of thumb) that affect the quality of decisions. In many cases, our decision-making strategies are well adapted to deal with a variety of problems (Nisbett & Ross, 1980). However, we are prone to certain flaws in our thinking (Stanovich, 2004). Common flaws involve confirmation bias, belief perseverance, overconfidence bias, hindsight bias, and the availability and representativeness heuristics. Decision making is improved when we become aware of these potential flaws.

Confirmation Bias **Confirmation bias** is the tendency to search for and use information that supports our ideas rather than refutes them (Betch & others, 2001; Gavetti & Rivkin, 2005). Thus, in making a decision, a student might have an initial belief that a certain approach is going to work. He tests out the approach and finds out that it does work some of the time. He concludes that his approach is right rather than further exploring the fact that in a number of cases it doesn't work.

We tend to seek out and listen to people whose views confirm our own rather than listen to dissenting views. Thus, you might have a particular teaching style, such as lecturing, that you like to use. If so, you probably have a tendency to seek advice from other teachers who use that style rather than from teachers who prefer other styles, such as collaborative problem solving by students.

In one study, Deanna Kuhn and her colleagues (1994) had participants listen to an audiotaped reenactment of an actual murder trial. Then, they were asked what their verdict would be and why. Rather than considering and weighing possibilities drawing on all the evidence, many participants hurriedly composed a story that drew only from evidence that supported their view of what happened. These participants showed a confirmation bias by ignoring evidence that ran counter to their version of events. Be aware of how easy it is for you and your students to become trapped by confirmation bias.

Belief Perseverance Closely related to confirmation bias, **belief perseverance** is the tendency to hold on to a belief in the face of contradictory evidence. People have a difficult time letting go of an idea or a strategy once they have embraced it (Smith, 2005). Consider Madonna. We might have a hard time thinking of her in a maternal role because of the belief perseverance that she is a wild, fun-loving rock star.

Another example of belief perseverance gives some college students trouble. They may have gotten good grades in high school by using the strategy of cramming for tests the night before. The ones who don't adopt a new strategy—spacing their study sessions more evenly through the term—often do poorly in college.

Overconfidence Bias   **Overconfidence bias** is the tendency to have more confidence in judgments and decisions than we should based on probability or past experience. People are overconfident about how long those with a fatal disease will live, which businesses will go bankrupt, whether a defendant is guilty in a court trial, and which students will do well in college (Kahneman & Tversky, 1995). People consistently have more faith in their judgments than predictions based on statistically objective measures indicate they should.

In one study, college students were asked to make predictions about themselves in the coming academic year (Vallone & others, 1990). They were asked to predict whether they would drop any courses, vote in an election, and break up with their girlfriend or boyfriend. At the end of the year, the accuracy of their predictions was examined. The results: They were more likely to drop a class, not vote in an election, and break up with a girlfriend or a boyfriend than they had predicted.

Hindsight Bias   People not only are overconfident about what they predict will happen in the future (overconfidence bias), but also tend to overrate their past performances at prediction (Birch, 2005; Guilbault & others, 2004; Villejoubert, 2005). **Hindsight bias** is our tendency to falsely report, after the fact, that we accurately predicted an event.

As I write this chapter, baseball season is just beginning. Lots of people in different cities are predicting that their teams are going to make it to the World Series. Come October, after almost all of the teams have fallen by the wayside, many of the same people will say, "I told you our team wasn't going to have a good season."

In one study of college students taking introductory psychology, a professor had them make either preverdict predictions regarding the outcome of the O. J. Simpson trial or postverdict predictions about what they would have predicted the outcome to be (Demakis, 1997). Students who estimated their prediction of the trial postverdict were more likely to correctly "predict" the verdict than were students who predicted the outcome preverdict, illustrating the principle of hindsight bias.

Availability Heuristic   A **heuristic** is a rule of thumb that can suggest a solution to a problem but does not ensure it will work. One heuristic that can produce flawed thinking is the **availability heuristic,** a prediction about the probability of an event based on the frequency of the event's past occurrences (Hutchinson & Gigerenzer, 2005; Mazur, 2005). When an event has recently occurred, we especially tend to overestimate its future occurrence (McKelvie & Drumheller, 2001; Redelmeir, 2005; Oppenheimer, 2004).

How likely do you think it is that you will be a victim of a crime, for instance? The fear of crime tends to go up when the media go through a phase of highlighting murder or covering a sensational murder story. Because of the excess information about crime, we are likely to estimate that crime is more prevalent than it really is. The media contribute to this prediction error every time they expose us to a rash of vivid stories about tornadoes, murders, diseases, accidents, or terrorist attacks.

Representativeness Heuristic   The **representativeness heuristic** suggests that we sometimes make faulty decisions based on how well something matches a prototype—that is, the most common or representative example—rather than its relevance to a particular situation (Sheppard & Koch, 2005). Consider this description of an individual's dinner companion: is skilled at carpentry, is proficient at wrestling, owns a pet snake, knows how to repair motorcycles, and has a police record. What is the probability that this person is a male? Most likely the description fits your prototype of a male more than a female, so you might estimate that there is a nine in ten chance the dinner companion is a male.

overconfidence bias The tendency to have more confidence in judgment and decisions than we should based on probability or past experience.

hindsight bias The tendency to falsely report, after the fact, that we accurately predicted an event.

heuristic A strategy or rule of thumb that can suggest a solution to a problem but doesn't ensure it will work.

availability heuristic A prediction about the probability of an event based on the frequency of the event's past occurrences.

representativeness heuristic Making faulty decisions based on how well something matches a prototype—that is, a common or representative example—rather than its relevance to the particular situation.

What characterizes decision making in adolescence?

In this example, your prototype served you well because there are far more men than women in the population who fit the description. Sometimes, however, our prototypes do not take into account the frequency of events in the entire population. For example, would you say that the dinner companion is more likely to be a member of a motorcycle gang or a salesman? You would probably say there is a much greater chance that he is a member of a motorcycle gang, in which case you would be wrong. Why? Although only a very small percentage of the millions of salesmen fit the description of this dinner companion, the total number is greater than the total number of motorcycle gang members who fit the description. Let's assume there are 10,000 members of motorcycle gangs in the world versus 100 million salesmen. Even if 1 of every 100 motorcycle gang members (1 percent) fits our description, there would be only 100 of them. If just 1 of every 100,000 salesmen fits our description (.01 percent), their number would total 1,000, so the probability is 10 times greater that the dinner companion is a salesman than a member of a motorcycle gang.

Our lives involve many such instances in which we judge probabilities based on representativeness and fail to consider the population from which a sample is drawn. If we are to make better decisions, we have to try to avoid this logical error along with the others mentioned here (Todd & Gigerenzer, 2001).

Decision Making in Adolescence Adolescence is a time of increased decision making—about the future, which friends to choose, whether to go to college, which person to date, whether to have sex, whether to buy a car, and so on (Byrnes, 1998, 2001, 2003, 2005; Jacobs & Klaczynski, 2005; Klaczynski, 2005, Kuhn & Franklin, 2006; Reyna & others, 2005; Wigfield, Byrnes, & Eccles, 2006). How competent are adolescents at making decisions?

Older adolescents appear to be more competent decision makers than younger adolescents, who, in turn, are more competent than children (Keating, 1990, 2004). Compared with children, young adolescents are more likely to generate options, to examine the situation from a variety of perspectives, to anticipate the consequences of decisions, and to consider the credibility of sources.

Most individuals make better decisions when they are calm rather than emotionally aroused. That may especially be true for adolescents. Recall from our discussion of brain development in chapter 2 that adolescents have a tendency to be emotionally intense. Thus, the same adolescent who makes a wise decision when calm may make an unwise decision when emotionally aroused (Dahl, 2004). In the heat of the moment, then, adolescents' emotions may especially overwhelm their decision-making ability.

Being able to make competent decisions does not guarantee that one will make them in everyday life, where breadth of experience often comes into play (Jacobs & Klaczynski, 2005; Keating, 1990, 2004). For example, driver-training courses improve adolescents' cognitive and motor skills to levels equal to, or sometimes superior to, those of adults. However, driver training has not reduced adolescents' high rate of traffic accidents (Potvin, Champagne, & Laberge-Nadeau, 1988). An important research agenda is to study the ways adolescents make decisions in actual situations (Fantino & Stolarz-Fantino, 2005).

Creative Thinking

Teresa Amabile remembers that when she was in kindergarten, she rushed into class every day, excited about getting to the easel and playing with all of those bright colors

BEST PRACTICES
Strategies for Making Good Decisions for Yourself and Your Students

1. *Weigh the costs and benefits of various outcomes.* You will encounter many circumstances in which you will benefit from pursuing this strategy. For example, should you spend more time with your friends and family or more time grading students' homework? Will your students benefit from examining a particular topic in a small-group format or a lecture format?

2. *Avoid confirmation bias.* Do you tend to only seek out people to talk with whose views confirm your own? Does a particular student avoid people with dissenting views and, if so, how can you help him or her?

3. *Resist belief perseverance.* Are you holding on to some beliefs that might be outdated and need to be changed? Do students have beliefs based on their past experiences

that they are clinging to which don't fit their current situation? If so, how can you help them?

4. *Don't engage in overconfidence bias.* Do you have more confidence in your decisions than you should based on probability or your past experience? Might one of your future students gloss over the fact that he or she did poorly on the previous test in your class and be overconfident and not put in extra hours of study?

5. *Avoid hindsight bias.* Monitor your tendency and your students' tendencies to be overconfident about circumstances that already have happened.

6. *Be aware of the availability and representativeness heuristics.*

and big paintbrushes. She and her classmates also had free access to a table with all kinds of art materials on it. In Teresa's words, "I remember going home every day after kindergarten and telling my mother I wanted to play with crayons, I wanted to draw, I wanted to paint" (Goleman, Kaufman, & Ray, 1993, p. 60).

Teresa's kindergarten experience, unfortunately, was the peak of her childhood artistic interest. The next year she entered a conventional elementary school and everything became very different. She no longer had free access to art materials every day, and art was now just another subject for her, something she had to do for a short time on Friday afternoon.

All through elementary school her art assignments hardly varied. For Teresa, the art class was restrictive and demoralizing. She recalls being given small reprints of painted masterpieces, a different one each week; one week in second grade, students were presented with pictures of Leonardo da Vinci's *Adoration of the Magi* and told to take out their art materials and try to copy the masterpiece. For Teresa and the other second-grade students, this was very frustrating because they lacked the skill to draw anything that even closely resembled the masterpiece. Needless to say, Teresa's desire to go home and paint after school each day diminished rapidly.

Teresa Amabile eventually obtained her Ph.D. in psychology and went on to become one of the leading researchers in the field of creativity. Today, her hope is that teachers will not crush students' enthusiasm for creativity, as hers did (Goleman, Kaufman, & Ray, 1993).

What Is Creativity?   **Creativity** is the ability to think about something in novel and unusual ways and come up with unique solutions to problems. J. P. Guilford (1967) distinguished between **convergent thinking,** which produces one correct answer and is characteristic of the kind of thinking required on conventional intelligence tests, and **divergent thinking,** which produces many answers to the same question and is more characteristic of creativity (Michael, 1999). For example, a typical convergent item on a conventional intelligence test is "How many quarters will you get in return for 60 dimes?" The question has only one right answer. In contrast, divergent questions have many possible answers. For example, consider these questions: "What image comes to mind when you sit alone in a dark room?" and "What are some unique uses for a paper clip?"

What do you mean, "What is it?" It's the spontaneous, unfettered expression of a young mind not yet bound by the restraints of narrative or pictorial representation.

Sydney Harris. www.ScienceCartoonsPlus.com.

creativity The ability to think about something in novel and unusual ways and come up with unique solutions to problems.

convergent thinking Thinking with the aim of producing one correct answer. This is usually the type of thinking required on conventional intelligence tests.

divergent thinking Thinking with the aim of producing many answers to the same question. This is characteristic of creativity.

What are some good strategies teachers can use to guide children in thinking more creatively?

Are intelligence and creativity related? Although most creative students are quite intelligent (as measured by high scores on conventional intelligence tests), in other respects the reverse is not necessarily true. Many highly intelligent students are not very creative (Sternberg, 2006).

Teachers need to recognize that students will show more creativity in some domains than others (Runco, 2004, 2006). A student who shows creative thinking skills in mathematics may not exhibit these skills in art, for example.

The design of schools and classrooms may influence the creativity of students (Runco, 2004). School environments that encourage independent work, are stimulating but not distracting, and make resources readily available are likely to encourage students' creativity (Hasirci & Demirkan, 2003).

Teaching and Creativity An important teaching goal is to help students become more creative (Baer & Kaufman, 2006; Kaufman & Baer, 2006; Plucker, Beghetto, & Dow, 2004; Runco, 2006). Strategies that can inspire children's creativity include encouraging creative thinking at the group and individual levels, providing students with environments that stimulate creativity, not overcontrolling students, encouraging internal motivation, fostering flexible and playful thinking, and introducing students to creative people.

Encourage Creative Thinking on a Group and Individual Basis *Brainstorming* is a technique in which people are encouraged to come up with creative ideas in a group, play off each other's ideas, and say practically whatever comes to mind that seems relevant to a particular issue (Rickards, 1999; Sternberg & Lubart, 1995). Participants are usually told to hold off from criticizing others' ideas at least until the end of the brainstorming session.

A recent review of research on brainstorming concluded that for many individuals working alone can actually generate more ideas and better ideas than working in groups (Rickards & deCock, 2003). One reason for this is that in groups some individuals loaf, while others do most of the creative thinking. Nonetheless, there may be benefits to brainstorming, such as team building, that support its implementation (Faure, 2004; Runco, 2004, 2006).

Creative people are not afraid of failing or getting something wrong. They might go down twenty dead-end streets before they come up with an innovative idea. They recognize that it's okay to win some and lose some. They are willing to take risks.

Provide Environments That Stimulate Creativity Some classrooms nourish creativity, others inhibit it (Bafumo, 2005; Bereiter & Scardamalia, 2006; Mindham, 2005; Runco, 2006). Teachers who encourage creativity often rely on students' natural curiosity. They provide exercises and activities that stimulate students to find insightful solutions to problems, rather than ask a lot of questions that require rote answers. Teachers also encourage creativity by taking students on field trips to locations where creativity is valued. Howard Gardner (1993) believes that science, discovery, and children's museums offer rich opportunities to stimulate creativity.

THROUGH THE EYES OF STUDENTS

The Eight-Year-Old Filmmaker and Oozy Red Goop

Steven was 8 years old and wanted to get a scout badge in film making. His father bought him a super-8 movie camera. Steven got the inspiration to make a horror movie.

He started imagining what he needed to do to make a movie. Needing some "red, bloody-looking goop to ooze from kitchen cabinets," he got his mother to buy "thirty cans of cherries." Steven dumped the cherries "into the pressure cooker and produced an oozy red goop."

His mother gave him free rein in the house, letting him virtually convert it into a child's movie studio. Steven told his mother he needed to make some costumes, which she obligingly made.

The son's name was Steven Spielberg, whose mother supported his imagination and passion for film making. Of course, Spielberg went on to become one of Hollywood's greatest producers with such films as *E.T.* and *Jurassic Park*. (Source: Goleman, Kaufman, & Ray, 1993, p. 70.)

SELF-ASSESSMENT 9.1

How Good Am I at Thinking Creatively?

Rate each of these activities as they apply to you in terms of how often you engage in them: 1 = never, 2 = rarely, 3 = sometimes, and 4 = a lot.

1	2	3	4

1. I come up with new and unique ideas.

2. I brainstorm with others to creatively find solutions to problems.

3. I am internally motivated.

4. I'm flexible about things and like to play with my thinking.

5. I read about creative projects and creative people.

6. I'm surprised by something and surprise others every day.

7. I wake up in the morning with a mission.

8. I search for alternative solutions to problems rather than giving a pat answer.

9. I spend time around creative people.

10. I spend time in settings and activities that stimulate me to be creative.

Examine your overall pattern of responses. What are your strengths and weaknesses in creativity? Keep practicing your strengths and work on improving your weaknesses to provide students with a creative role model.

Don't Overcontrol Students Teresa Amabile (1993) says that telling students exactly how to do things leaves them feeling that originality is a mistake and exploration is a waste of time. If, instead of dictating which activities they should engage in, you let your students select their interests and you support their inclinations, you will be less likely to destroy their natural curiosity. Amabile also believes that when teachers hover over students all of the time, they make them feel that they are constantly being watched while they are working. When students are under constant surveillance, their creative risk-taking and adventurous spirit diminish. Students' creativity also is diminished when teachers have grandiose expectations for their performance and expect perfection from them, according to Amabile.

Encourage Internal Motivation Excessive use of prizes, such as gold stars, money, or toys, can stifle creativity by undermining the intrinsic pleasure students derive from creative activities. Creative students' motivation is the satisfaction generated by the work itself. Competition for prizes and formal evaluations often undermine intrinsic motivation and creativity (Amabile & Hennesey, 1992). However, this is not to rule out material rewards altogether. We will say more about internal and external motivation in chapter 13, "Motivation, Teaching, and Learning."

Guide Students to Help Them Think in Flexible Ways Creative thinkers are flexible in the way they approach problems in many different ways rather than getting locked into rigid patterns of thought. Give students opportunities to exercise this flexibility in their thinking.

Introduce Students to Creative People A good strategy to identify the most creative people in your community and ask them to come to your class and describe what helps them become creative or to demonstrate their creative skills. A writer, a poet, a craftsperson, a musician, a scientist, and many others can bring their props and productions to your class.

To evaluate how good you are at thinking creatively, complete Self-Assessment 9.1.

Review, Reflect, and Practice

(2) Describe several types of thinking and ways that teachers can foster them.

REVIEW

- What is thinking?
- How do inductive and deductive reasoning differ?
- What is the focus of critical thinking?
- What is decision making? What are some flaws that can hinder effective decision making?
- What is creative thinking? How can teachers foster creative thinking?

REFLECT

- Some experts lament that few schools teach students to think critically. Does your own experience support this view? If you agree with the experts, why is critical thinking not more widely or effectively taught?

PRAXIS™ PRACTICE

1. Ms. McDougal has a pet rabbit in her classroom. One day while Amari is petting the rabbit, it bites her. Amari decides that all rabbits are mean. This is an example of what kind of reasoning?
   a. analogy
   b. critical thinking
   c. deductive
   d. inductive

2. Which teaching strategy is most likely to foster the development of critical thinking skills in social studies?
   a. having students create timelines of important historical dates
   b. presenting students with worksheets that require them to recall the facts presented in their textbooks
   c. presenting students with statements such as "Lincoln was our greatest president" to defend or refute
   d. giving a multiple-choice test

3. Many students enter their educational psychology courses believing that when an authority figure presents an aversive stimulus to a child, and the child's misbehavior diminishes, the authority figure has negatively reinforced the child's behavior. Of course, we know that the authority figure has punished the child's behavior. Many of the students who entered your class with this misconception will get questions that test this idea incorrect on the final exam and will still have this misconception when they leave the class.
   What is the best explanation for this phenomenon?
   a. belief perseverance
   b. confirmation bias
   c. hindsight bias
   d. availability heuristic

4. All fifth-grade classes at Central School have just read the *Jungle Book*. Which assignment is most likely to foster creativity?
   a. The students write a story about how their lives would have been different if they had grown up in the wild like Mogli.
   b. The students complete a story diagram, in which they describe the setting, characters, plot, climax, and theme of the book.

 c. The students create models of the temple where the monkeys lived, following a prototype that the teacher constructed.
 d. The students complete worksheets containing questions about the plot and characters of the book.

Please see the answer key at the end of the book.

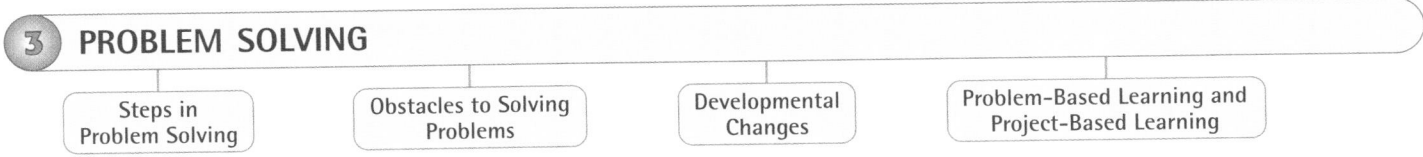

3 **PROBLEM SOLVING**

| Steps in Problem Solving | Obstacles to Solving Problems | Developmental Changes | Problem-Based Learning and Project-Based Learning |

Let's examine problem solving as a cognitive process, including the steps it involves, the obstacles to it, and how best to teach it.

 Problem solving involves finding an appropriate way to attain a goal. Consider these tasks that require students to engage in problem solving: creating a project for a science fair, writing a paper for an English class, getting a community to be more environmentally responsive, and giving a talk on the factors that cause people to be prejudiced. Although they seem quite different, each involves a similar series of steps.

Steps in Problem Solving

Efforts have been made to specify the steps that individuals go through in effectively solving problems (Bransford & Stein, 1993). Following are four such steps.

1. Find and Frame Problems Before you can solve a problem, you must recognize that it exists (Mayer, 2000). In the past, most problem-solving exercises in school involved well-defined problems that lent themselves to specific, systematic operations that produced a well-defined solution. Today, educators increasingly recognize the need to teach students the real-world skill of identifying problems instead of just offering clear-cut problems to be solved.

 Consider a student whose broad goal is to create a science-fair project. What branch of science would it be best for her to present—biology, physics, computer science, psychology? Then, she'll have to narrow the problem even more. For example, which domain within psychology—perception, memory, thinking, personality? Within the domain of memory, she might pose this question: How reliable are people's memories of traumatic events they have experienced? Thus, it may take considerable exploration and refinement for the student to narrow the problem down to a point of generating specific solutions. Exploring such alternatives is an important part of problem solving.

 In sum, an important educational agenda is to give students opportunities to locate and refine problems that need to be solved. The teacher can serve as a guide and a consultant in helping them to frame a meaningful problem and to clearly define it.

2. Develop Good Problem-Solving Strategies Once students find a problem and clearly define it, they need to develop strategies for solving it. Among the effective strategies are setting subgoals, using algorithms, and relying on heuristics.

 Subgoaling involves setting intermediate goals that put students in a better position to reach the final goal or solution. Students might do poorly in solving problems because they don't generate subproblems or subgoals. Let's return to the science-fair

problem solving Finding an appropriate way to attain a goal.

subgoaling The process of setting intermediate goals that place students in a better position to reach the final goal or solution.

project on the reliability of people's memory for traumatic events they have experienced. What might be some subgoaling strategies? One might be locating the right books and research journals on memory; another might be interviewing people who have experienced traumas in which basic facts have been recorded. At the same time as the student is working on this subgoaling strategy, she likely will benefit from establishing further subgoals in terms of what she needs to accomplish along the way to her final goal of a finished science project. If the science project is due in three months, she might set the following subgoals: finishing the first draft of the project two weeks before the project is due; having the research completed a month before the project is due; being halfway through the research two months before the project is due; having three trauma interviews completed two weeks from today; and starting library research tomorrow.

Notice that in establishing the subgoals, we worked backward in time. This is often a good strategy (Reed, 2000). Students first create a subgoal closest to the final goal and then work backward to the subgoal closest to the beginning of the problem-solving effort.

Algorithms are strategies that guarantee a solution to a problem. Algorithms come in different forms, such as formulas, instructions, and tests of all possible solutions (Konidaris & Hayes, 2005; McRae, 2005; Schraw, 2006).

When students solve a multiplication problem by a set procedure, they are using an algorithm. When they follow the directions for diagramming a sentence, they are using an algorithm. Algorithms helpful in solving clear-cut problems. But since many real-world problems aren't so straightforward, looser strategies also are needed.

As we indicated earlier in the chapter in our discussion of decision making, *heuristics* are strategies or rules of thumb that can suggest a solution to a problem but don't ensure it will work. Heuristics help us to narrow down the possible solutions and help us find one that works (Schraw, 2006; Stanovich & West, 2000). Suppose that you go out on a day hike and find yourself lost in the mountains. A common heuristic for getting "unlost" is simply to head downhill and pick up the nearest tiny stream. Small streams lead to larger ones, and large streams often lead to people. Thus, this heuristic usually works, although it could bring you out on a desolate beach.

In the face of a multiple-choice test, several heuristics could be useful. For example, if you are not sure about an answer, you could start by trying to eliminate the answers that look most unlikely and then guess among the remaining ones. Also, for hints about the answer to one question, you could examine the statements or answer choices for other questions on the test.

A **means-end analysis** is a heuristic in which one identifies the goal (end) of a problem, assesses the current situation, and evaluates what needs to be done (means) to decrease the difference between the two conditions. Another name for means-end analysis is difference reduction. Means-end analysis also can involve the use of subgoaling, which we described earlier (Anderson, 1993). Means-end analysis is commonly used in solving problems (Huber, Beckmann, & Herrmann, 2004; Wallis, 2004). Consider a student who wants to do a science-fair project (the end) but has not yet found a topic. Using means-end analysis, she could assess her current situation, in which she is just starting to think about the project. Then she maps out a plan to reduce the difference between her current state and the goal (end). Her "means" might include talking to several scientists in the community about potential projects, going to the library to study the topic she chooses, and exploring the Internet for potential projects and ways to carry them out.

algorithms Strategies that guarantee a solution to a problem.

means-end analysis A heuristic in which one identifies the goal (end) of a problem, assesses the current situation, and evaluates what needs to be done (means) to decrease the difference between the two conditions.

3. Evaluate Solutions   Once we think we have solved a problem, we might not know whether our solution is effective unless we evaluate it. It helps to have in mind a clear criterion for the effectiveness of the solution. For example, what will be the student's criterion for effectively solving the science-fair problem? Will it be simply getting it completed? receiving positive feedback about the project? winning an award? winning first place? gaining the self-satisfaction of having set a goal, planned for it, and reached it?

4. Rethink and Redefine Problems and Solutions Over Time An important final step in problem solving is to continually rethink and redefine problems and solutions over time (Bereiter & Scardamalia, 1993, 2006). People who are good at problem solving are motivated to improve on their past performances and to make original contributions. Thus, the student who completed the science-fair project can look back at the project and think about ways the project can be improved. The student might use feedback from judges or others who attended the fair in order to fine-tune the project for presentation again in some other venue.

Obstacles to Solving Problems

Some common obstacles to solving problems are fixation and a lack of motivation and persistence. We'll also discuss inadequate emotional control, which is another stumbling block to effective problem solving.

Fixation It is easy to fall into the trap of becoming fixated on a particular strategy for solving a problem. **Fixation** involves using a prior strategy and failing to look at a problem from a fresh, new perspective. *Functional fixedness* is a type of fixation in which an individual fails to solve a problem because he or she views the elements involved solely in terms of their usual functions. A student who uses a shoe to hammer a nail has overcome functional fixedness to solve a problem.

A **mental set** is a type of fixation in which an individual tries to solve a problem in a particular way that has worked in the past. I (your author) had a mental set about using a typewriter rather than a computer to write my books. I felt comfortable with a typewriter and had never lost any sections I had written. It took a long time for me to break out of this mental set. Once I did, I found that books are much easier to write using a computer. You might have a similar mental set against using the new computer and video technology available for classroom use. A good strategy is keep an open mind about such changes and monitor whether your mental set is keeping you from trying out new technologies that can make the classroom more exciting and more productive.

Lack of Motivation and Persistence Even if your students already have great problem-solving abilities, that hardly matters if they are not motivated to use them (Perry, Turner, & Meyer, 2006; Sternberg & Spear-Swerling, 1996). It is especially important for students to be internally motivated to tackle a problem and persist at finding a solution. Some students avoid problems or give up too easily.

An important task for teachers is to devise or steer students toward problems that are meaningful to them and to encourage and support them in finding solutions. Students are far more motivated to solve problems that they can relate to their personal lives than textbook problems that have no personal meaning for them. Problem-based learning takes this real-world, personal approach.

Inadequate Emotional Control Emotion can facilitate or restrict problem solving. At the same time that they are highly motivated, good problem solvers are often able to control their emotions and concentrate on a solution to a problem (Barron & Harackiewicz, 2001; Kuhn & Franklin, 2006). Too much anxiety or fear can especially restrict a student's ability to solve a problem. Individuals who are competent at solving problems are usually not afraid of making mistakes.

Developmental Changes

One way that developmental changes in problem solving have been studied is called the *rule-assessment approach*, which focuses on children's increasing ability to effectively use rules to solve problems as they get older (Siegler, 2006; Siegler & Alibali, 2005). Even young children begin to use rules to solve problems. During early childhood, the relatively stimulus-driven toddler is transformed into a child capable of more flexible,

fixation Using a prior strategy and thereby failing to examine a problem from a fresh, new perspective.

mental set A type of fixation in which an individual tries to solve a problem in a particular way that has worked in the past.

What are some developmental changes in problem solving?

goal-directed problem solving (Zelazo & Müller, 2004; Zelazo & others, 2003). Consider a problem in which children must sort stimuli using the rule of *color*. In the course of the color sorting, a child may describe a red rabbit as a *red one* to solve the problem. However, in a subsequent task, the child may need to discover a rule that describes the rabbit as just a *rabbit* to solve the problem. If young children fail to understand that it is possible to provide multiple descriptions of the same stimulus, they persist in describing the stimulus as a red rabbit. Researchers have found that at about 4 years of age, children acquire the concept of perspectives, which allows them to appreciate that a single thing can be described in different ways (Frye, 1999).

Young children, however, have some drawbacks that prevent them from solving many problems effectively. Especially notable is their lack of planning, which improves during the elementary and secondary school years. Among the reasons for the poor planning skills of young children is their tendency to try to solve problems too quickly at the expense of accuracy and their inability to inhibit an activity. Planning often requires inhibiting a current behavior to stop and think; preschool children often have difficulty inhibiting an ongoing behavior, especially if it is enjoyable (Bjorklund, 2005). Another drawback of young children's problem solving ability is that even though they may know a rule they fail to use it.

Other reasons that older children and adolescents become better problem solvers than young children involve *knowledge* and *strategies*. The problems that older children and adolescents must solve are often more complex than those young children face and solving these problems accurately usually requires accumulated knowledge. The more children know about a particular topic, the better they will be able to solve a problem related to the topic. The increase in accumulated knowledge about a topic ties in with our discussion of experts and novices in chapter 8.

Older children and adolescents also are more likely than young children to have effective strategies that help them solve problems (Kuhn & Franklin, 2006; Pressley & Hilden, 2006). Recall our extensive discussion of metacognition and strategies in chapter 8, in which we discussed how children's use of strategies improves as they get older. Especially important in using strategies to solve problems is to have a range of strategies from which to select, and this increases during the elementary and secondary school years. Adolescents have an increased capacity to monitor and manage their resources to effectively meet the demands of a problem solving task (Kuhn & Franklin, 2006). Adolescents also are better than children at screening out information irrelevant to solving a problem (Kail, 2002; Kuhn & Franklin, 2006).

Problem-Based Learning and Project-Based Learning

Now that we have discussed many aspects of problem solving, we turn our attention to two types of learning involving problems. First, we will describe problem-based learning and then explain project-based learning.

Problem-Based Learning **Problem-based learning** emphasizes solving authentic problems like those that occur in daily life (Bereiter & Scardamalia, 2006; Jones, Rasmussen, & Moffit, 1997). Problem-based learning is used in a program called YouthALIVE! at the Children's Museum of Indianapolis (Schauble & others, 1996). There, students solve problems related to conceiving, planning, and installing exhibits; designing videos; creating programs to help visitors understand and interpret museum exhibits; and brainstorming about strategies for reaching the wider community.

The Cognition and Technology Group at Vanderbilt (1997) developed a program of problem-based learning called The Jasper Project. *The Adventures of Jasper Woodbury* consists of twelve videodisc-based adventures designed to improve the mathematical thinking of students in grades 5 and up, as well as to help students make connections with other disciplines, including science, history, and social studies. *Jasper*'s creators argue that too often math and other subjects are taught as isolated skills. One of the *Jasper* adventures, *The Right Angle*, can be used not only in geometry

problem-based learning Learning that emphasizes authentic problems like those that occur in daily life.

classes but also in geography (topography) and history (Native American cultures). The adventures focus on a character named Jasper Woodbury and others, who encounter a number of real-life problems that need to be solved. Figure 9.4 profiles two of the *Jasper* problem-solving adventures.

As we saw earlier, finding and framing a problem is an important aspect of problem solving, and these skills are built into the *Jasper* system. Also, *Jasper* stimulates students to identify a number of subproblems or subgoals on their own. It also encourages collaborative problem solving among students. As students work together over a number of class periods, they have numerous opportunities to communicate about math, share their problem-solving strategies, and get feedback that helps them refine their thinking. Groups of students present their ideas to the class, discussing the strengths and weaknesses of their strategies and solutions. The collaborative aspect of *Jasper* is at the heart of social constructivist approaches to learning, which we will explore in depth in chapter 10.

Each videodisc adventure includes extension problems. This helps students engage in "what-if" thinking by revisiting the original adventures from new points of view. Thus, after finding a way to rescue a wounded eagle in *Rescue at Boone's Meadow* (most students solve the problem with an ultralight airplane that is featured in this adventure), students are presented with a revised problem in which they must rethink how the presence of headwinds or tailwinds might affect their original solution.

The Jasper Project also encourages teachers to develop actual problem-solving projects after students have worked with a *Jasper* adventure. For example, in one school, after creating a business plan for the adventure *The Big Splash,* students were given the opportunity to gather relevant data to create a business plan to present to the principal. In this instance, the creation of a business plan led to a fun fair being held for the entire school. In another school, students who had spent time solving problems in the adventure *Blueprint for Success* were given the opportunity to design a playhouse for preschools. Well-designed playhouses were actually built and donated to the preschools in the students' names.

An optional feature of the *Jasper* series is the video-based SMART Challenge series. Its goal is to connect classes of students to form a community of learners that tries to solve Jasper-related challenges. *SMART* stands for *Special Multimedia Arenas for Refining Thinking.* These arenas use telecommunications, television technology, and Internet technology to give students feedback about the problem-solving efforts of other groups. For example, students who are working on *Blueprint for Success* can see data from sixty other students about the length of legs for A-frame swing sets and the desired height of the swing sets.

In one study, the effects of using *The Adventures of Jasper Woodbury* as part of a constructivist-inspired reform of math curricula in a school district was evaluated in nineteen fifth-grade classrooms (Hickey, Moore, & Pellegrino, 2001). In the ten classrooms in which *Jasper* was implemented, students' overall motivation and academic performance were stronger than in the nine classrooms that did not use *Jasper.*

To obtain more information about the *Jasper*-related projects, contact the Cognition and Technology Group at Vanderbilt University.

Project-Based Learning   In **project-based learning,** students work on real, meaningful problems and create tangible products (Krajcik & Blumenfeld, 2006). Project-based learning and problem-based learning are sometimes treated as synonymous. However, while still emphasizing the process of learning in a constructivist manner, project-based learning gives more attention to the end product than

"Blueprint for Success"

Christina and Marcus, two students from Trenton, visit an architectural firm on Career Day. While learning about the work of architects, Christina and Marcus hear about a vacant lot being donated in their neighborhood for a playground. This is exciting news because there is no place in their downtown neighborhood for children to play. Recently, several students have been hurt playing in the street. The challenge is for students to help Christina and Marcus design a playground and ballfield for the lot.

"The Big Splash"

Jasper's young friend Chris wants to help his school raise money to buy a new camera for the school TV station. His idea is to have a dunking booth in which teachers would be dunked when students hit a target. He must develop a business plan for the school principal in order to obtain a loan for his project. The overall problem centers on developing this business plan, including the use of a statistical survey to help him decide if this idea would be profitable.

FIGURE 9.4 Problem–Solving Adventures in the *Jasper* Series

project-based learning Students work on real, meaningful problems and create tangible products.

BEST PRACTICES
Strategies for Improving Students' Problem Solving

1. *Give students extensive opportunities to solve real-world problems.* Make this a part of your teaching. Develop problems that are relevant to your students' lives. Such real-world problems are often referred to as "authentic," in contrast to textbook problems that too often do not have much meaning for students.

2. *Monitor students' effective and ineffective problem-solving strategies.* Keep the four problem-solving steps in mind when you give students opportunities to solve problems. Also keep in mind such obstacles to good problem solving as becoming fixated, harboring biases, not being motivated, and not persisting. Next, Lawren Giles, who teaches at Baechtel Grove Middle School in Willits, California, describes the different strategies she encourages students to use.

THROUGH THE EYES OF TEACHERS
A Toolbox of Strategies

In teaching math, I use such problem-solving strategies as working backward, making a similar but simpler problem, drawing a diagram, making a table, and looking for patterns. We talk about what strategies make the most sense with different types of problems. When students successfully solve a problem, we look to see what methods were used, often finding more than one. I talk about multiple strategies in terms of carpenters having more than one kind of hammer in their toolboxes.

3. *Involve parents in children's problem solving.* A program of parental involvement has been developed at the University of California at Berkeley (Schauble & others, 1996).

It is called Family Math (Matematica Para la Familia, in Spanish) and helps parents experience math with their children in a positive, supportive way. In the program, Family Math classes are usually taught by grade levels (K–2, 3–5, and 6–8). Many of the math activities require teamwork and communication between parents and children, who come to better understand not only the math but also each other. Family Math programs have served more than 400,000 parents and children in the United States.

4. *Work with children and adolescents to improve their use of rules, knowledge, and strategies in solving problems.* Recognize that young children may know a rule that enables them to solve a problem but not use it, so you may need to encourage them to use the rules they know. Encourage children to build up their knowledge base and to improve their knowledge of effective strategies that will help them solve problems.

5. *Use technology effectively.* Be motivated to incorporate multimedia programs into your classroom. *The Adventures of Jasper Woodbury* contains many of the themes of effective thinking and problem solving that we have described in this chapter. Such programs can significantly improve your students' thinking and problem-solving skills.

Some popular television presentations can be used to foster students' problem-solving and thinking skills (Schauble & others, 1996). For example, *3-2-1 Contact* focuses on 8- to 12-year-olds' appreciation of science; *Square One TV* gives students a better understanding of math and problem solving; and *Ghostwriter* supports the literacy of 7- to 10-year-olds. Kits for these TV programs include videotapes, leader guides, games, puzzles, and magazines.

problem-based learning (Bereiter & Scardamalia, 2006). The types of problems explored in project-based learning are similar to those studied by scientists, mathematicians, historians, writers, and other professionals.

Project-based learning environments are characterized by five main features (Krajcik & Blumenfeld, 2006):

1. *A driving question.* The learning process begins with a key question or problem that needs to be solved.

2. *Authentic, situated inquiry.* As students examine the key question, they learn about the problem-solving process engaged in by experts in the discipline in relevant contexts.

3. *Collaboration.* Students, teachers, and community participants collaborate to find solutions to the problem.

4. *Scaffolding.* Learning technologies are used to challenge students to go beyond what they normally would in a problem-solving context.

5. *End product.* Students create tangible end products that address the key, driving question.

To evaluate your thinking and problem-solving skills, complete Self-Assessment 9.2.

SELF-ASSESSMENT 9.2

How Effective Are My Thinking and Problem-Solving Strategies?

Teachers who practice good thinking and problem-solving strategies themselves are more likely to model and communicate these to their students than teachers who don't use such strategies. Candidly respond to these items about your own thinking and problem-solving strategies. Rate yourself: 1 = very much unlike me, 2 = somewhat unlike me, 3 = somewhat like me, and 4 = very much like me; then total your points.

	1	2	3	4
1. I am aware of effective and ineffective thinking strategies.				
2. I periodically monitor the thinking strategies I use.				
3. I am good at reasoning.				
4. I use good strategies for forming concepts.				
5. I am good at thinking critically and deeply about problems and issues.				
6. I construct my own thinking rather than just passively accept what others think.				
7. I like to use technology as part of my effort to think effectively.				
8. I have good role models for thinking.				
9. I keep up-to-date on the latest educational developments in thinking.				
10. I use a system for solving problems, such as the four-step system described in the text.				
11. I am good at finding and framing problems.				
12. I make good decisions and monitor biases and flaws in my decision making.				
13. When solving problems, I use strategies such as subgoaling and working backward in time.				
14. I don't fall into problem-solving traps such as fixating, lacking motivation and persistence, and not controlling my emotions.				
15. When solving problems, I set criteria for my success and evaluate how well I have met my problem-solving goals.				
16. I make a practice of rethinking and redefining problems over an extended period of time.				
17. I love to work on problem-solving projects.				
18. I am good at creative thinking.				

TOTAL _____

Scoring and Interpretation

If you scored 66–72 points, your thinking strategies likely are very good. If you scored 55–65 points, you likely have moderately good thinking strategies. If you scored below 54 points, you likely would benefit from working on your thinking strategies.

Review, Reflect, and Practice

③ Take a systematic approach to problem solving.

REVIEW

- What is problem solving? What are the main steps in problem solving?
- What are three obstacles to problem solving?
- What are some developmental changes in problem solving?
- What is problem-based learning? What is project-based learning?

REFLECT

- When you tackle a difficult problem, do you follow the four steps we described? What might you do to become a better model of a problem solver for your students?

PRAXIS™ PRACTICE

1. Which of the following is the best example of the use of a heuristic?
   a. Betina needs to compute the average of a series of numbers. First she determines their sum and then dividing the sum by the number in the series.
   b. Anders becomes separated from his mother at the store. He goes to a cashier and tells her that he is lost. The cashier takes him to the service counter and his mother is paged.
   c. Samarie needs to remember all five of the Great Lakes. He uses the acronym HOMES.
   d. Marjorie needs to know how much carpet she needs to cover the floor of her room. She uses the formula for the area of a rectangle and converts square feet to square yards.

2. Which of the following is the best example of functional fixedness?
   a. Zack needs to screw in a screw, but he has no screwdriver. He has some change in his pocket but he does not try to use a dime instead.
   b. Xavier continues to use the strategy of adding a number multiple times rather than learning his multiplication facts.
   c. Maria uses the formula for the area of a rectangle when solving a problem requiring her to find the area of a triangle.
   d. Sol is lost in the woods. He remembers his mother telling him that if he gets lost like this, he should "hug a tree." He stays in one spot and within 30 minutes his family finds him.

3. Jackson is 16 years old and is much better at problem solving than when he was younger. Which of the following is most likely to explain his improved problem solving as a teenager?
   a. His hormones are settling down better since he is no longer in puberty.
   b. He is better at monitoring the demands of a problem-solving task.
   c. He is more stimulus-driven, and that helps him to sort through more stimuli when he is given a problem to solve.
   d. He uses a minimum number of strategies that he knows well.

4. Which of the following is the best example of problem-based learning?
   a. Ms. Christian's science students use a shoebox to protect a raw egg from breaking when dropped off the school roof.
   b. Ms. Kohler's students solve word problems to help them see the application of their math facts to everyday life.
   c. Ms. Kringle's students solve a series of addition and multiplication problems of increasing difficulty.
   d. Ms. Randall's students answer the questions at the end of the chapter in their history book.

Please see the answer key at the end of the book.

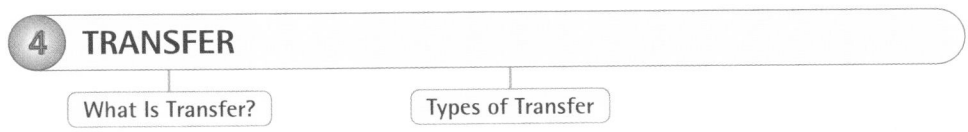

4 TRANSFER

What Is Transfer?   Types of Transfer

An important complex cognitive goal is for students to be able to apply what they learn in one situation to new situations. An important goal of schooling is that students learn things that they can apply outside the classroom. Schools are not functioning effectively if students do well on tests in language arts but can't write a competent letter as part of a job application. Schools also are not effectively educating students if the students do well on math tests in the classroom but can't solve arithmetic problems on a job.

What Is Transfer?

Transfer occurs when a person applies previous experiences and knowledge to learning or problem solving in a new situation (Gentile, 2000; Mayer & Wittrock, 1996). Thus, if a student learns a concept in math and then uses this concept to solve a problem in science, transfer has occurred. It also has occurred if a student reads and studies about the concept of fairness in school and subsequently treats others more fairly outside the classroom. Teaching for transfer helps students make the connection between what they learn in school and how it applies beyond school (Bransford, Darling-Hammond, & LePage, 2005).

Types of Transfer

What are some different types of transfer? Transfer can be characterized as either near or far and as either low-road or high-road (Schunk, 2004).

Near or Far Transfer   **Near transfer** occurs when the classroom learning situation is similar to the one in which the initial learning took place. For example, if a geometry teacher instructs students in how to logically prove a concept, and then tests the students on this logic in the same setting in which they learned the concept, near transfer is involved. Another example of near transfer occurs when students who have learned to type on a typewriter transfer this skill to typing on a computer keyboard.

Far transfer means the transfer of learning to a situation very different from the one in which the initial learning took place. For instance, if a student gets a part-time job in an architect's office and applies what he learned in geometry class to helping the architect analyze a spatial problem different from any problem the student encountered in geometry class, far transfer has occurred.

Low-Road or High-Road Transfer   Gabriel Salomon and David Perkins (1989) distinguished between low-road and high-road transfer. **Low-road transfer** occurs when previous learning automatically, often unconsciously, transfers to another situation. This occurs most often with highly practiced skills in which there is little need for reflective thinking. For example, when competent readers encounter new sentences in their native language, they read them automatically.

By contrast, **high-road transfer** is conscious and effortful. Students consciously establish connections between what they learned in a previous situation and the new situation they now face. High-road transfer is mindful—that is, students have to be aware of what they are doing and think about the connection between contexts. High-road transfer implies abstracting a general rule or principle from previous experience and then applying it to the new problem in the new context. For example, students might learn about the concept of subgoaling (setting intermediate goals) in math class. Several months later, one of the students thinks about how subgoaling might help him complete a lengthy homework assignment in history. This is high-road transfer.

"I don't get it! They make us learn reading, writing and arithmetic to prepare us for a world of videotapes, computer terminals and calculators!"

Harley Schwadron from *Phi Delta Kappan*. Reprinted by permission of Harley Schwadron.

transfer Applying previous experiences and knowledge to learning or problem solving in a new situation.

near transfer The transfer of learning to a situation that is similar to the one in which the initial learning took place.

far transfer The transfer of learning to a situation that is very different from the one in which the initial learning took place.

low-road transfer The automatic, often unconscious, transfer of learning to another situation.

high-road transfer The transfer of learning from one situation to another that is conscious and effortful.

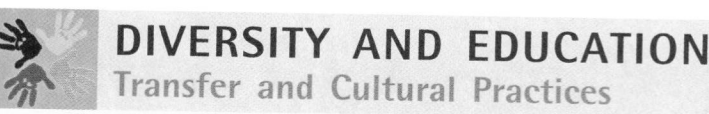

DIVERSITY AND EDUCATION
Transfer and Cultural Practices

Prior knowledge includes the kind of knowledge that learners acquire through cultural experiences, such as those involving ethnicity, socioeconomic status, and gender (National Research Council, 1999). In some cases this cultural knowledge can support children's learning and facilitate transfer, but in others it may interfere (Greenfield & Suzuki, 1998; Greenfield, Suzuki, & Rothstein-Fisch; 2006a; Greenfield & others, 2006b).

For children from some cultural backgrounds, there is a minimal fit or transfer between what they have learned in their home communities and what is required or taught by the school. For example, consider the language skill of storytelling. Euro-American children use a linear style that more closely approximates the linear expository style of writing and speaking taught in most schools (Lee & Slaughter-Defoe, 1995). This may involve recounting a series of events in a rigidly chronological sequence. By contrast, in some ethnic groups—such as Asian Pacific Island or Native American—a nonlinear, holistic/circular style is more common in telling a story, and Euro-American teachers may consider their discourse to be disorganized (Clark, 1993). Also, in African American children, a nonlinear, topic-associative storytelling approach is common (Michaels, 1986).

Methods of argumentation in support of certain beliefs also differ across cultures. Chinese speakers prefer to present supporting evidence first, leading up to a major point or claim (in contrast to a topic sentence followed by supporting details). Non-Chinese listeners sometimes judge this style as "beating around the bush" (Tsang, 1989).

Rather than perceiving such variations in communication styles as being chaotic or as necessarily inferior to Euro-American styles, teachers need to be sensitive to them and aware of cultural differences. This is especially important in the early elementary school grades, when students are making the transition from the home environment to the school environment.

Salomon and Perkins (1989) subdivide high-road transfer into forward-reaching and backward-reaching transfer. **Forward-reaching transfer** occurs when students think about how they can apply what they have learned to new situations (from their current situation, they look "forward" to apply information to a new situation ahead). For forward-reaching transfer to take place, students have to know something about the situations to which they will transfer learning. **Backward-reaching transfer** occurs when students look back to a previous ("old") situation for information that will help them solve a problem in a new context.

To better understand these two types of high-road transfer, imagine a student sitting in English class who has just learned some writing strategies for making sentences and paragraphs come alive and "sing." The student begins to reflect on how she could use those strategies to engage readers next year, when she plans to become a writer for the school newspaper. That is forward-reaching transfer. Now consider a student who is at his first day on the job as editor of the school newspaper. He is trying to figure out how to construct the layout of the pages. He reflects for a few moments and thinks about some geography and geometry classes he has previously taken. He draws on those past experiences for insights into constructing the layout of the student newspaper. That is backward-reaching transfer.

Some experts argue that the best way to ensure transfer is to "teach for it" (Schwartz, Bransford, & Sears, 2006, in press). They stress that transfer problems virtually are eliminated when teaching occurs in contexts where individuals need to perform. By preparing students so that the problems they are likely to encounter in

forward-reaching transfer The transfer of learning that involves thinking about how to apply what has been learned to new situations in the future.

backward-reaching transfer The transfer of learning that involves looking back to a previous ("old") situation for information that might help solve a problem in a new context.

BEST PRACTICES
Strategies for Helping Students Transfer Information

1. *Think about what your students need for success in life.*
We don't want students to finish high school with a huge
data bank of content knowledge but no idea how to apply
it to the real world. One strategy for thinking about what
students need to know is to use the "working-backward"
problem-solving strategy we discussed earlier in this
chapter. For example, what do employers want high
school and college graduates to be able to do? In a
national survey of employers of college students, the
three skills that employers most wanted graduates to
have were (1) oral communication skills, (2) interpersonal skills, and (3) teamwork skills (Collins, 1996). Thus,
the three most desired skills for students to have all
involved communication. The employers also wanted
students to be proficient in their field, have leadership
abilities, have analytical skills, be flexible, and be able
to work with computers. By thinking about and practicing the competencies that your students will need in the
future and working with them to improve these skills,
you will be guiding them for positive transfer.

2. *Give students many opportunities for real-world learning.* Too often, learning in schools has been artificial,
with little consideration for transfer beyond the classroom or textbook. This will be less true for your students
if you give them as many real-world problem-solving and
thinking challenges as possible. In general, the more similar two situations are, the easier it will be for students
to transfer information learned in one to the other. You
can bring the real world into your classroom by inviting
people from varying walks of life to come and talk with
your students. Or you can take your students to the real
world by incorporating visits to museums, businesses,
colleges, and so on in the curriculum. Such learning
opportunities should increase transfer. Next, we describe
how Chris Laster and Myron Blosser, two outstanding
teachers, instruct students in ways that help them transfer
what they learn to the world outside the classroom.

THROUGH THE EYES OF TEACHERS
*Bringing Science Alive and Connecting Students
to the Community*

Chris Laster's students say that he brings science alive.
Among Laster's innovative real-world teaching strategies
that help students transfer their knowledge and understanding beyond the classroom are the following:

1. *Science Blasters.* Students write, direct, and produce
short videos for the school's closed-circuit TV station.

Chris Laster working with a student on the flight deck of
the space shuttle that Laster and other teachers built.

2. *Sci-Tech Safari.* Over the summer, students get hands-
on experience on field trips to intriguing places such
as the Okefenokee Swamp.

3. *Intrepid.* Students engage in vigorous training to prepare for a simulated 27-hour space mission aboard a
realistic-looking space shuttle built by Laster and
other teachers with parts from local businesses and a
nearby air force base (Source: Copeland, 2003).

Myron Blosser is an honors and AP biology teacher at
Harrisonburg High School, in Virginia. He was the leader
in establishing Coast to Coast '98 and 2000, a science
department effort in which students and teachers toured
national parks in a motor coach laboratory, studying the
natural history of water. He coordinates an annual
biotechnology symposium that includes renowned scientists and high school students throughout the Shenandoah Valley region of Virginia. Myron sees his role as
connecting students to the community to give context to
what they are learning.

3. *Root concepts in applications.* The more you attempt to
pour information into students' minds, the less likely it
is that transfer will occur. When you present a concept,
also define it (or get students to help you define it),
and then ask students to generate examples. Challenge
them to apply the concept to their personal lives or to
other contexts.

4. *Teach for depth of understanding and meaning.* Teaching
for understanding and meaning benefits transfers more
than does teaching for the retention of facts. And students'

continued on page 330

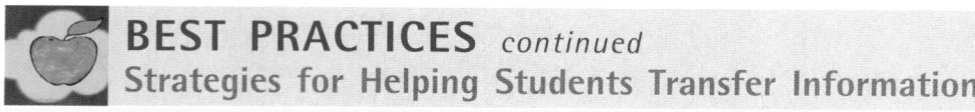

BEST PRACTICES *continued*
Strategies for Helping Students Transfer Information

understanding improves when they actively construct meaning and try to make sense out of material.

5. *Teach strategies that will generalize.* Transfer involves not only skills and knowledge but also strategies (Schunk, 2004). Too often students learn strategies but don't understand how to apply them in other contexts. They might not understand that the strategy is appropriate for other situations, might not know how to modify it for use in another context, or might not have the opportunity to apply it (Pressley, Borkowski, & Schneider, 1989).

One model for teaching strategies that will generalize was developed by Gary Phye (1990; Phye & Sanders, 1994). He described three phases for improving transfer.

In an *initial acquisition* phase, students are given information about the importance of the strategy and how to use as well as opportunities to rehearse and practice using it. In the second phase, called *retention,* students get more practice in using the strategy, and their recall of how to use the strategy is checked out. In the third phase, *transfer,* students are given new problems to solve. These problems require them to use the same strategy, but on the surface the new problems appear to be different. Phye also believes that motivation is an important aspect of transfer. He recommends that teachers increase students' motivation for transfer by showing them examples of how to use knowledge in their real lives.

real life are at worst near-transfer problems, the gap between students' present learning level and learning goals is significantly reduced (Bransford & others, 2005).

Cultural practices may be involved in how easy or difficult transfer is. The Diversity and Education interlude on p. 328 explores this topic.

Review, Reflect and Practice

4 **Define transfer and explain how to enhance it as a teacher.**

REVIEW

- What is transfer? Why should teachers think about it?
- What are some different types of transfer?

REFLECT

- Are there experiences from your own formal education that don't seem to transfer to outside of school? What do you think is going on in such situations?

PRAXIS™ PRACTICE

1. Which of the following is *not* an example of transfer?
   a. Maria reads a novel written in the eighteenth century and uses the information she gleans about marriage customs to answer a question in history class.
   b. Frank studies hard and learns an algorithm in math class.
   c. Danielle learns about endangered amphibians in science class and uses the information to research a science fair project.
   d. Emma learns to use a dictionary in language arts class and uses it to look up a social studies term.

2. Which of the following is the best example of far transfer?
   a. Cory uses the techniques she was taught in statistics class to analyze the data for a research project.
   b. Debbie drives her sister's car with little thought because of her experience driving her own car.
   c. Jason uses the trouble-shooting process that he was taught with regard to computers to successfully diagnose the problem with his car.
   d. Mike is able to read the Spanish word for television (televisión) because it looks like the English word.

Please see the answer key at the end of the book.

CRACK THE CASE
The Case of the Statistics Test

Cassandra has a test in her math class this Friday. She has spent the last several evenings studying the statistical formulas for measures of central tendency and variability, as she knows they will be covered on the test. To do this she has quizzed herself repeatedly. In the beginning, she got them confused, but after repeated tries, she can now recite the formulas for each without fail. She is certain that she will have no problems on the test.

When she receives her test on Friday, the first thing she does is to write down all of the formulas before she can forget them, certain that will be all she will need to do well on the exam. After writing down the formulas, she begins reading the test. The first question gives a list of scores and asks for the mean, median, mode, variance, and standard deviation.

Cassandra anxiously looks at her list of formulas. She knows which formula goes with which measure—for instance, she knows that the formula for the mean is $\sum x/n$. The problem is that she doesn't know what $\sum x$ means. She is reasonably sure that "$/n$" means she is to divide by n, but what is n? When looking at the rest of the formulas, she realizes that she has similar problems. She stares at the test in dismay. After all that studying and careful memorization, she can't complete a single problem on the test.

1. What are the issues in this case?
2. What went wrong for Cassandra?
3. What should she do differently if she wants to do better on her next test?
4. If you were the teacher of Cassandra's class, how would you help your students to prepare for this type of test?
5. Which of the following strategies is most likely to help Cassandra on her next statistics test?
   a. Concentrate on learning only one formula at a time.
   b. Forget about memorizing the formulas.
   c. Learn the definitions of mean, median, and mode, variance, and standard deviation.
   d. Work practice problems of each type.
6. Which of the following teaching strategies would be most likely to help students to do well on this type of test?
   a. Make certain that students understand what the formulas mean by working many example problems in class.
   b. Quiz students on the definitions of mean, median, mode, variance, and standard deviation.
   c. Quiz students on the formulas.
   d. Teach students a mnemonic device to help them remember the formulas.

Reach Your Learning Goals
Complex Cognitive Processes

(1) CONCEPTUAL UNDERSTANDING: Discuss conceptual understanding and strategies for teaching concepts.

What Are Concepts?	Concepts are categories used to group objects, events, and characteristics on the basis of common properties. Concepts are elements of cognition that help to simplify and summarize information. They also improve memory, communication, and time use.
Promoting Concept Formation	In teaching concept formation to children, it is helpful to discuss with them the features of concepts, definitions and examples of concepts (using the rule-example strategy), concept maps and hierarchical organization, hypothesis testing, and prototype matching.

(2) THINKING: Describe several types of thinking and ways that teachers can foster them.

What Is Thinking?	Thinking involves manipulating and transforming information in memory. Types of thinking include forming concepts, reasoning, thinking critically, making decisions, thinking creatively, and solving problems.
Reasoning	Inductive reasoning involves reasoning from the specific to the general. Analogies draw on inductive reasoning. Deductive reasoning is reasoning from the general to the specific. Both inductive and deductive reasoning improve during adolescence.
Critical Thinking	Critical thinking involves thinking reflectively and productively and evaluating evidence. Brooks and Brooks argue that too few schools teach students to think critically and deeply. They stress that too often schools give students a correct answer instead of encouraging them to expand their thinking by coming up with new ideas.
Decision Making	Decision making is thinking that involves evaluating alternatives and making choices among them. One type of decision making involves weighing the costs and benefits of various outcomes. Numerous biases (confirmation bias, belief perseverance, overconfidence bias, and hindsight bias) and the flawed heuristics they use (the availability heuristic and the representativeness heuristic) can interfere with good decision making.
Creative Thinking	Creativity is the ability to think about something in novel and interesting ways and come up with unique solutions to problems. Guilford distinguished between convergent thinking (which produces one correct answer and is characteristic of the type of thinking required on conventional intelligence tests) and divergent thinking (which produces many answers to the same question and is characteristic of creativity). Although most creative students are quite intelligent, the reverse is not necessarily true. Here are some ways teachers can foster creativity in students: encourage creative thinking on a group and individual basis, provide environments that stimulate creativity, don't overcontrol students, encourage internal motivation, foster flexible thinking, and introduce students to creative people.

(3) PROBLEM SOLVING: Take a systematic approach to problem solving.

Steps in Problem Solving	Problem solving involves finding an appropriate way to attain a goal. Four steps in problem solving are (1) finding and framing problems; (2) developing good problem-solving strategies (such as using subgoaling, heuristics, and algorithms); (3) evaluating solutions; and (4) rethinking and redefining problems and solutions over time.

Obstacles to Solving Problems	Obstacles to solving problems include fixedness (functional fixedness and mental set), lack of motivation and persistence, and not controlling one's emotions.
Developmental Changes	Developmental changes in problem solving occur. Even young children begin to use rules to solve problems, including their failure to enact rules they know and their poor planning skills. Accumulated knowledge and effectively using strategies improve older children's and adolescents' problem-solving ability.
Problem-Based Learning and Project-Based Learning	Problem-based learning emphasizes solving authentic problems like those that occur in daily life. *The Adventures of Jasper Woodbury,* a multimedia set of twelve math problem-solving adventures, is an example of problem-based learning. *Jasper*-related projects also can help students with science, history, and social studies. In project-based learning, students work on real meaningful problems and create tangible products.

4 TRANSFER: Define transfer and explain how to enhance it as a teacher.

What Is Transfer?	Transfer occurs when a person applies previous experiences and knowledge to learning or problem solving in a new situation. Students especially benefit when they can apply what they learn in the classroom to situations in their lives outside of the classroom.
Types of Transfer	Types of transfer include near and far and low-road and high-road. Near transfer occurs when situations are similar; far transfer occurs when situations are very different. Low-road transfer occurs when previous learning automatically transfers to another situation. High-road transfer is conscious and effortful. High-road transfer can be subdivided into forward-reaching and backward-reaching.

 KEY TERMS

concepts 302
concept map 304
prototype matching 305
thinking 306
inductive reasoning 307
analogy 307
deductive reasoning 308
critical thinking 308
decision making 309

confirmation bias 312
belief perseverance 312
overconfidence bias 313
hindsight bias 313
heuristic 313
availability heuristic 313
representativeness
   heuristic 313
creativity 315

convergent thinking 315
divergent thinking 315
problem solving 319
subgoaling 319
algorithms 320
means-end analysis 320
fixation 321
mental set 321
problem-based learning 322

project-based learning 323
transfer 327
near transfer 327
far transfer 327
low-road transfer 327
high-road transfer 327
forward-reaching transfer 328
backward-reaching
   transfer 328

 PORTFOLIO ACTIVITIES

Now that you have a good understanding of this chapter, complete these exercises to expand your thinking.

Independent Reflection

Evaluate Your Decision Making Skills. Reflect on the ways that you make decisions. Are you able to make good-quality decisions regardless of opposition from others? Discuss to what extent your decisions are influenced by confirmation bias, belief perseverance, overconfidence bias, and hindsight bias. What can you do to strengthen your decision-making skills? (INTASC: Principles *4, 9*)

Collaborative Work

Create a Problem-Based Learning Project. In the discussion of problem-based learning, the text describes *Jasper* series problem-solving adventures in math. Thinking creatively, get together with three or four other students in the class and devise a problem-solving adventure in a subject area other than math, such as science, social science, or literature. Write it down. (INTASC: Principles *1, 4*)

Research/Field Experience

Creativity Research. Read work by one of the leading researchers in the field of creativity, such as Teresa Amabile or Mark Runco. What are the key findings about creativity discussed in the research? To what extent can this research be implemented in the classroom? (INTASC: Principles *4, 9*)

Go to the Online Learning Center for downloadable portfolio templates.

TAKING IT TO THE NET

- Describe the characteristics of a person who is an effective problem solver. How does open-ended problem solving lead to knowledge and skills that are transferable? Why is the transfer of knowledge so critical to our changing and increasingly complex society? http://www.nwrel.org/msec/nwteacher/spring2000/open.html

- Implementing critical-thinking activities in the classroom can help students take charge of their own learning and take responsibility for their own behavior. Select an online lesson plan (www.lessonplanspage.com), and "remodel" it as a critical thinking activity. Identify elements of the remodeled lesson that will develop and reinforce students' critical-thinking skills. www.criticalthinking.org/resources/articles/#Teaching

- Evaluate an online lesson plan for its creative value. Discuss aspects of the lesson that foster students' creative and divergent thinking. What role would you play in supporting students' creativity? How would your classroom environment support creative thinking? Explain how you think the lesson could be improved to increase its creative value. www.artsedge.kennedy-center.org/teach/les.cfm

Connect to the Online Learning Center to explore possible answers.

 STUDY, PRACTICE, AND SUCCEED

Visit www.mhhe.com/santedu3e to review the chapter with self-grading quizzes and self-assessments, to apply the chapter material to two more Crack the Case studies, and for suggested activities to develop your teaching portfolio.

Social Constructivist Approaches

The human being is by nature a social animal.

—Aristotle
Greek Philosopher, 4th Century B.C.

Chapter Outline

Social Constructivist Approaches to Teaching

Social Constructivism in the Broader Constructivist Context
Situated Cognition

Teachers and Peers as Joint Contributors to Students' Learning

Scaffolding
Cognitive Apprenticeship
Tutoring
Cooperative Learning

Structuring Small-Group Work

Composing the Group
Team-Building Skills
Structuring Group Interaction

Social Consructivist Programs

Fostering a Community of Learners
Schools for Thought
A Collaborative School

Learning Goals

1 Compare the social constructivist approach with other constructivist approaches.

2 Explain how teachers and peers can jointly contribute to children's learning.

3 Make effective decisions in structuring small-group work.

4 Describe three social constructivist programs.

335

TEACHING STORIES   Chuck Rawls

Chuck Rawls teaches language arts at Appling Middle School in Macon, Georgia. He provides this teaching story about peer tutoring, a social constructivist approach to instruction:

I was tricked into trying something different my first year of teaching. It was peer teaching in the guise of a school-wide activity known as "Switch Day." This consists of having selected students switch places with members of the faculty and staff. Each student who wants to switch is required to choose a faculty or staff member and then write an essay explaining why he or she wants to switch with that particular person. To my surprise, Chris wrote a very good essay and was selected to switch with me.

It worked wonderfully. Chris delivered the lesson very professionally, and the students were engaged because it was something new and different. It was a riot to watch because Chris, both intentionally and unintentionally, used many of my pet phrases and mannerisms. He really did know his stuff, though, and demonstrated this as he helped students with their seatwork.

As the saying goes, "I didn't know he had it in him." Chris became my resident expert on subject-verb agreement, as that was the topic of the lesson and the students remembered what he taught them.

I learned two lessons that day: (1) Don't be afraid to try something different. (2) Peer tutoring works. However, it has to be the right student teaching the right material in the right setting.

Preview

Children do some of their thinking by themselves, but because we are social beings, as Chuck Rawls' teaching story indicates, effective learning can also take place when children collaborate. Because of our American emphasis on the individual rather than the group, collaborative thinking only recently emerged as an important theme in American education. This chapter focuses on the collaborative thinking advocated by social constructivist approaches.

 SOCIAL CONSTRUCTIVIST APPROACHES TO TEACHING

> Social Constructivism in the Broader Constructivist Context

> Situated Cognition

The social constructivist approaches involve a number of innovations in classroom learning. Before we study these innovations, let us first consolidate our knowledge about various constructivist perspectives and where the social constructivist approaches fit in the overall constructivist framework.

Social Constructivism in the Broader Constructivist Context

Recall from chapter 1 that *constructivism* emphasizes how individuals actively construct knowledge and understanding. Early in this book (chapter 2, "Cognitive and Language Development"), we described Piaget's and Vygotsky's theories of development, both of which are constructivist. In chapters 8 and 9, our main focus was on the information-processing approaches to learning, which included some ideas about

What is the social constructivist approach to education?

how the individual child uses information-processing skills to think in constructivist ways. According to all of these constructivist approaches, students author their own knowledge.

In general, a **social constructivist approach** emphasizes the social contexts of learning and that knowledge is mutually built and constructed (Horowitz & others, 2005; Rust, O'Donovan, & Price, 2005). Involvement with others creates opportunities for students to evaluate and refine their understanding as they are exposed to the thinking of others and as they participate in creating shared understanding (Gauvain, 2001). In this way, experiences in social contexts provide an important mechanism for the development of students' thinking (Johnson & Johnson, 2005).

Vygotsky's social constructivist theory is especially relevant for the current chapter. Vygotsky's model is a social child embedded in a sociohistorical context. Moving from Piaget to Vygotsky, the conceptual shift is from the individual to collaboration, social interaction, and sociocultural activity (Baroody, Lai, & Mix, 2006; Martin, 2006; Rogoff, 2003). In Piaget's cognitive constructivist approach, students construct knowledge by transforming, organizing, and reorganizing previous knowledge and information. Vygotsky's social constructivist approach emphasizes that students construct knowledge through social interactions with others. The content of this knowledge is influenced by the culture in which the student lives, which includes language, beliefs, and skills (Greenfield, Suzuki, & Rothstein-Fisch, 2006; Greenfield & others, 2006; Shweder & others 2006).

Piaget emphasized that teachers should provide support for students to explore and develop understanding. Vygotsky emphasized that teachers should create many opportunities for students to learn by co-constructing knowledge along with the teacher and with peers (Budrova & Leong, 2001, 2007; Hyson, Copple, & Jones, 2006; Kozulin, 2004; O'Donnell, 2006). In both Piaget's and Vygotsky's models, teachers serve as facilitators and guides rather than directors and molders of children's learning.

Notice that we speak about emphasis rather than a clear-cut distinction. Often there are not clear-cut distinctions between social constructivist and other constructivist approaches (Marshall, 1996). For example, when teachers serve as guides for students in discovering knowledge, there are social dimensions to the construction.

social constructivist approach
Approach that emphasizes the social contexts of learning and that knowledge is mutually built and constructed.

And the same is true for processing information. If a teacher creates a brainstorming session for students to come up with good memory strategies, social interaction is clearly involved.

Some sociocultural approaches, such as Vygotsky's, emphasize the importance of culture in learning; for example, culture can determine what skills are important (such as computer skills, communication skills, teamwork skills) (Martin, 2006; Rowe & Wertsch, 2004). Other approaches focus more exclusively on the immediate social circumstances of the classroom, as when students collaborate to solve a problem.

In one recent study of collaborative learning, pairs of children from two U.S. public schools worked together (Matusov, Bell, & Rogoff, 2001). One member of each pair was from a traditional school that provided only occasional opportunities for children to work together as they learned. The other member of the pair was from a school that emphasized collaboration throughout the school day. The children with the collaborative schooling background more often built on the partner's ideas in a collaborative way than the children with traditional schooling experience. The traditional school children predominately used a "quizzing" form of guidance based on asking known-answer questions and withholding information to test the partner's understanding. Researchers also have found that collaborative learning often works best in classrooms with well-specified learning goals (Gabriele & Montecinos, 2001).

In one analysis of the social constructivist approach, the teacher was described as being drawn to look at learning through the eyes of children (Oldfather & others, 1999). The same analysis also noted these characteristics of social constructivist classrooms (Oldfather & others, 1999):

- An important classroom goal is the construction of collaborative meaning.
- Teachers closely monitor students' perspectives, thinking, and feeling.
- The teacher and the students are learning and teaching.
- Social interaction permeates the classroom.
- The curriculum and the physical contents of the classroom reflect students' interests and are infused with their cultures.

An increasing number of efforts are being made to connect collaborative learning and technology in the classroom (Rummel & Spada, 2005; Schellens & Valcke, 2005; Yang & Liu, 2005). For example, one program, Computer-Supported Collaborative Learning (CSCL), attempts to increase peer interaction and joint construction of knowledge through technology (van Drie & others, 2005).

Situated Cognition

Situated cognition is an important assumption in the social constructivist approaches. It refers to the idea that thinking is located (situated) in social and physical contexts, not within an individual's mind. In other words, knowledge is embedded in, and connected to, the context in which the knowledge developed (Gauvain, 2001; Greeno, 2006; Rowe & Wertsch, 2004). If this is so, it makes sense to create learning situations that are as close to real-world circumstances as possible. For example, to expand students' knowledge and understanding of volcanos, some students are placed in the role of scientists studying an active volcano while other students are given the task of reporting what to expect to an emergency evacuation team (PSU, 2006). Using Internet resources, the "scientist" students examine news stories about active volcanos; the "evacuation team" students search for information about the impact that volcanos have on inhabitants and how they can be removed from the danger of an erupting volcano. Our discussion of problem-based learning and project-based learning in chapter 9 demonstrated a similar emphasis on situated cognition.

situated cognition The idea that thinking is located (situated) in social and physical contexts, not within an individual's mind.

Review, Reflect, and Practice

(1) Compare the social constructivist approach with other constructivist approaches.

REVIEW

- Although they overlap, what is the basic difference between Piaget's and Vygotsky's approach?
- What is situated cognition?

REFLECT

- From what you learned in chapter 2, do you think you would feel more at home with Piaget or Vygotsky? How might that be reflected in your own approach to classroom teaching?

PRAXIS™ PRACTICE

1. Which of the following is an example of a social constructivist approach?
   a. In Mr. Hanratty's class, students work together on social studies projects.
   b. In Ms. Baker's class, students work independently to discover basic principles of science.
   c. In Ms. Rinosa's class, students are assigned one hour of homework a day.
   d. In Mr. Francois' class, students engage in silent reading of their self-chosen books.

2. Which of the following best reflects situated cognition?
   a. Students read a book about the role of a justice of the peace in the legal system.
   b. The teacher arranges for students to visit a local justice of the peace office, talk with the justice of the peace, and observe a justice of the peace session.
   c. Students are given an assignment to collaborate with each other and write a report on the role of the justice of the peace in the legal system.
   d. The teacher assigns students the task of searching for articles about what a justice of the peace does and to do an oral report on what they have found.

Please see the answer key at the end of the book.

(2) TEACHERS AND PEERS AS JOINT CONTRIBUTORS TO STUDENTS' LEARNING

| Scaffolding | Cognitive Apprenticeship | Tutoring | Cooperative Learning |

Social constructivist approaches emphasize that teachers and peers can contribute to students' learning. Four tools for making this happen are scaffolding, cognitive apprenticeship, tutoring, and cooperative learning.

Scaffolding

In chapter 2, we described *scaffolding* as the technique of changing the level of support over the course of a teaching session; a more-skilled person (teacher or more-advanced peer of the child) adjusts the amount of guidance to fit the student's current performance. When the task the student is learning is new, the teacher might use direct instruction. As the student's competence increases, the teacher provides less guidance. Think of scaffolding in learning like the scaffolding used to build a bridge. The scaffolding provides support when needed, but it is gradually removed as the bridge approaches completion. Researchers have found that when teachers and peers

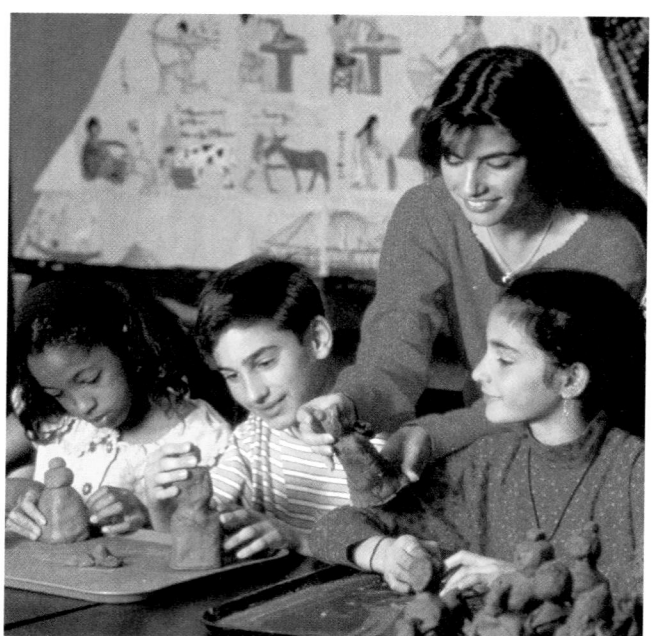

When teachers think of their relationship with students as a cognitive apprenticeship, how is teaching likely to proceed?

use scaffolding in collaborative learning, students' learning benefits (Krajcik & Blumenfeld, 2006; Perry, Turner, & Meyer, 2006; Pressley & others, 2001; Yarrow & Topping, 2001).

Look for situations to use scaffolding in the classroom. For instance, good tutoring involves scaffolding, as we will see shortly. Work on giving just the right amount of assistance. Don't do for students what they can do for themselves. But do monitor their efforts and give them needed support and assistance.

Cognitive Apprenticeship

Developmental psychologist Barbara Rogoff (1990) believes that an important tool of education is **cognitive apprenticeship,** a technique in which an expert stretches and supports a novice's understanding and use of a culture's skills. The term *apprenticeship* underscores the importance of active learning and highlights the situated nature of learning. In a cognitive apprenticeship, teachers often model strategies for students. Then, teachers or skilled peers support students' efforts at doing the task. Finally, they encourage students to continue their work independently.

To illustrate the importance of cognitive apprenticeships in learning, Rogoff (1990) describes the contrasting experiences of students from middle-income and poverty backgrounds. Many middle-income American parents involve their children in cognitive apprenticeships long before they go to kindergarten or elementary school. They read picture books with young children and bathe their children in verbal communication. In contrast, American parents living in poverty are less likely to engage their children in a cognitive apprenticeship that involves books, extensive verbal communication, and scaffolding (Heath, 1989).

Cognitive apprenticeships are important in the classroom (O'Donnell, 2006). Researchers have found that students' learning benefits from teachers who think of their relationship with a student as a cognitive apprenticeship, using scaffolding and guided participation to help the student learn (Englert, Berry, & Dunsmore, 2001; Leonard, Beauvais, & Scholl, 2005; Mathes & others, 2005).

Tutoring

Tutoring is basically a cognitive apprenticeship between an expert and a novice. Tutoring can take place between an adult and a child or between a more-skilled child and a less-skilled child. Individual tutoring is an effective strategy that benefits many students, especially those who are not doing well in a subject (O'Donnell, 2006).

Classroom Aides, Volunteers, and Mentors It is frustrating to find that some students need more individual help than you as their teacher can give them and still meet the needs of the class as a whole. Classroom aides, volunteers, and mentors can help reduce some of this frustration. Monitor and evaluate your class for students you believe could benefit from one-on-one tutoring. Scour the community for individuals with skills in the areas in which these students need more individual attention than you are able to give. Some parents, college students, and retirees might be interested in filling your classroom tutoring needs.

Several individual tutoring programs have been developed. The Reading Recovery program offers daily half-hour one-on-one tutorial sessions for students who are having difficulty learning to read after one year of formal instruction (Sensenbaugh, 1995). Although Reading Recovery is a registered trademark of Ohio State University and authorized programs use creator Marie Clay's (1985) materials, various Reading Recovery programs differ in how they are developed, implemented, and assessed. Evaluations of the Reading Recovery program have

cognitive apprenticeship A relationship in which an expert stretches and supports a novice's understanding and use of a culture's skills.

found that students who participated in the program in the first grade were still performing better in reading in third grade than their counterparts who did not participate (Sensenbaugh, 1995). However, some researchers have found that the key to whether a program like Reading Recovery is effective is the extent to which phonological-processing skills are included (Chapman, Tunmer, & Prochnow, 2001).

Another program that uses tutoring is Success for All (SFA). Developed by Robert Slavin and his colleagues (1996; Slavin, Daniels, & Madden, 2005; Slavin & Madden, 2001), this comprehensive program includes

Participants in the Success for All Middle School program. *What is the nature of the Success for All program?*

- A systematic reading program that emphasizes phonics, vocabulary development, and story telling and retelling in small groups
- A daily 90-minute reading period with students in the first through third grades being regrouped into homogeneous cross-age ability groups
- One-on-one tutoring in reading by specially trained certified teachers who work individually with students who are reading below grade level
- Assessments every 8 weeks to determine students' reading progress, adjust reading group placement, and assign tutoring if needed
- Professional development for teachers and tutors, which includes 3 days of in-service training and guidelines at the beginning of the school year, and follow-up training throughout the year
- A family support team designed to provide parenting education and support family involvement in the school

First implemented during the 1987–1988 school year in five inner-city schools in Baltimore, Maryland, SFA has expanded to over 475 schools in 31 states, now serving more than 250,000 students. Researchers have found that students who have participated in the program have better reading skills and are less likely to be in special education classes than disadvantaged students who have not been involved in the program (Slavin, Daniels, & Madden, 2005; Slavin & Madden, 2001; Weiler, 1998).

Mentors can play an important role in improving some students' learning. Usually viewed as older and wiser, mentors guide, teach, and support younger individuals, who are sometimes called *mentees* or *protégés* (Karcher & others, 2005). "The guidance is accomplished through demonstration, instruction, challenge, and encouragement on a more or less regular basis over an extended period of time. In the course of this process, the mentor and the young person develop a special bond of mutual commitment. In addition, the younger person's relationship to the mentor takes on an emotional character of respect, loyalty, and identification" (Hamilton & Hamilton, 2004, p. 396, based on a personal communication with ecological theorist Urie Bronfenbrenner).

The majority of mentoring programs are outside the school and include such organizations as Big Brothers and Big Sisters, the largest formal mentoring program in the United States, as well as Boys and Girls Clubs of America and YMCA and YWCA. Recently, schools have been the location of an increasing number of mentoring efforts. Mentors come to the school and work with their mentee, in many cases for an hour each week. Schools can be helpful in identifying students who might benefit from mentoring. A good strategy is to select not only high-risk, underachieving students for mentoring, but other students as well (DuBois & Karcher, 2006; Dubois &

others, 2002). Also, some mentoring relationships are more effective than others, and the matching of a student with a mentor requires careful selection and monitoring (Langhout, Rhodes, & Osborne, 2004).

Peer Tutors Fellow students also can be effective tutors (Dufrene & others, 2005; Ginsburg-Block, 2005; Sadler & Graham, 2005). In peer tutoring, one student teaches another. In *cross-age peer tutoring*, the peer is older. In *same-age peer tutoring*, the peer is a classmate. Cross-age peer tutoring usually works better than same-age peer tutoring. An older peer is more likely to be skilled than a same-age peer, and being tutored by a same-age classmate is more likely to embarrass a student and lead to negative social comparison.

Peer tutoring engages students in active learning and allows the classroom teacher to guide and monitor student learning as she or he moves around the classroom (Ginsburg-Block, 2005). Researchers have found that peer tutoring often benefits students' achievement (Mathes & others, 1998; O'Donnell, 2006; McDonnell & others, 2001; Topping & Bryce, 2004; Topping & others, 2004). In some instances, the tutoring benefits the tutor as well as the tutee, especially when the older tutor is a low-achieving student. Teaching something to someone else is one of the best ways to learn.

In a study that won the American Educational Research Association's award for best research study, the effectiveness of a class-wide peer tutoring program in reading was evaluated for three learner types: low-achieving students with and without disabilities and average-achieving students (Fuchs & others, 1997). Twelve elementary and middle schools were randomly assigned to experimental (peer tutoring) and control (no peer tutoring) groups. The peer tutoring program was conducted in 35-minute sessions during regularly scheduled reading instruction 3 days a week. It lasted for 15 weeks. The training of peer tutors emphasized helping students get practice in reading aloud from narrative text, reviewing and sequencing information read, summarizing large amounts of reading material, stating main ideas, predicting and checking story outcomes, and other reading strategies. Pretreatment and posttreatment reading achievement data were collected. Irrespective of the type of learner, students in the peer tutoring classrooms showed greater reading progress over the 15 weeks than their counterparts who did not receive peer tutoring.

The peer tutoring program used in the study just described is called Peer-Assisted Learning Strategies (PALS). PALS was created by the John F. Kennedy Center and the Department of Special Education at Peabody College at Vanderbilt University. In PALS, teachers identify which children require help on specific skills and who the most appropriate children are to help other children learn those skills. Using this information, teachers pair children in the class so that partners work simultaneously and productively on different activities that address the problems they are experiencing. Pairs are changed regularly so that as students work on a variety of skills, all students have the opportunity of being "coaches" and "players."

PALS is a 25- to 35-minute activity that is used two to four times a week. Typically it creates thirteen to fifteen pairs in a classroom. It has been designed for use in the areas of reading and mathematics for kindergarten through sixth grade. It is not designed to replace existing curricula.

In PALS Math, students work on a sheet of problems in a skill area, such as adding, subtracting, number concepts, or charts and graphs. PALS Math involves

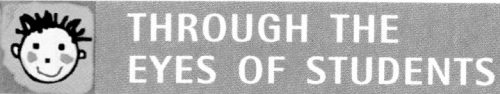

THROUGH THE EYES OF STUDENTS

When I Showed Her How, She Was Spectacular

PALS was a good experience for me. It helped me to cooperate with other students. For example, one of my partners read a four-paragraph page very slowly. I helped him. The next day he read much better. That made me feel really good. Later, another PALS partner I had didn't like to answer the PALS question. When I showed her how, she was spectacular. I loved PALS. I hope to do it again.

Myers
Elementary School Student
Nashville, Tennessee

DIVERSITY AND EDUCATION
The Valued Youth Program

In 24 cities in the United States and Brazil, the Valued Youth program (now jointly sponsored by the Intercultural Development Research Association and Coca-Cola and called the Coca-Cola Valued Youth program) gives secondary school students who are not achieving well or are at risk for school-related problems the responsibility for tutoring elementary school children (Intercultural Development Research Association, 2004; Simons, Finlay, & Yang, 1991). The Valued Youth program began in 1984 and continues to expand today. The hope is that the tutoring experience will improve not only the achievement of the students being tutored but also the achievement of the tutors.

In one school's Valued Youth program, 4 days a week participants walk or ride a bus to tutor for one class period at a nearby elementary school. Each tutor works with three children on subjects such as math or reading, and tutors work with the same children for the entire school year. On the fifth day of the week, the tutors work with their teacher at their own school, discussing tutoring skills, reflecting on how the week has gone, and brushing up on their own literacy skills. For their work, the tutors receive course credit and minimum-wage pay.

One of the Valued Youth program tutors said, "Tutoring makes me want to come to school because I have to come and teach the younger kids." He also said that he did not miss many days of school, as he used to, because when he

The boy on the left is a tutor in the Valued Youth program, which takes at-risk middle and high school students and gives them the responsibility of tutoring elementary school children.

had been absent the elementary school children always ask him where he was and tell him that they missed him. He said that he really liked the kids he taught and that if he had not been a tutor he probably would have dropped out of school already.

In one analysis, fewer than 1% of the Valued Youth program tutors had dropped out of school, compared with a 14% national dropout rate (Intercultural Development Research Association, 1996).

---

pairing students as a coach and a player. The coach uses a sheet with a series of questions designed to guide the player and provides feedback to the player. Students then exchange papers and score each others' practice sheets. Students earn points for cooperating and constructing good explanations during coaching and for doing problems correctly during practice. PALS Math and PALS Reading are effective in developing students' mathematical and reading skills (Fuchs, Fuchs, & Burish, 2000; Mathes, Torgesen, & Allor, 2001).

The PALS program is highly effective with at-risk students, especially students in the early elementary grades, ethnic minority students, students in urban schools, and possibly low-income students (Rohrbeck & others, 2003). In one recent study, the reading comprehension of third- through sixth-grade native Spanish-Speaking English language learners improved more when they were taught in a PALS format than in other reading instruction formats (Saenz, Fuchs, & Fuchs, 2005).

Two other peer tutoring programs are Reciprocal Peer Tutoring (RPT) and Classwide Peer Tutoring (CWPT) (Ginsburg-Block, 2005). RPT was initially developed for use with low-achieving urban elementary school students and provides opportunities for students to alternate in tutor and tutee roles. CWPT includes tutor training, reciprocal teaching, and motivational strategies such as team competition (Greenwood & others, 2002; Struckman, 2005).

The Diversity and Education interlude includes more information about the effectiveness of peer tutoring.

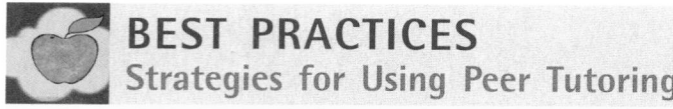

BEST PRACTICES
Strategies for Using Peer Tutoring

Here are some suggestions for how to use peer tutoring (Goodlad & Hirst, 1989; Jenkins & Jenkins, 1987):

1. *Use cross-age tutoring rather than same-age tutoring when possible.* Set aside specific times of the day for peer tutoring and communicate the learning assignment clearly and precisely to the peer tutor—for example, "Today from 9 to 9:30 I would like you to work with Jimmy on the following math problem-solving exercises: _____, _____, and _____."

THROUGH THE EYES OF TEACHERS
Cross-Age Peer Teaching at the Zoo

In Lincoln, Nebraska, several high school science teachers use the Folsum Zoo and Botanical Gardens as a context for guiding students' learning. The science classes are taught in two trailers at the zoo. The teachers emphasize the partnership of students, teachers, zoo, and community. One highlight of the program is the "Bug Bash," when the high school students teach fourth-grade students about insects.

Lincoln zoo crew: clockwise from back left, teachers Beth Briney, Amy Vanderslice, De Tonack, Sara LeRoy-Toren, and James Barstow.

2. *Let students participate in both tutor and tutee roles.* This helps students learn that they can both help and be helped. Pairing of best friends often is not a good strategy because they have trouble staying focused on the learning assignment. Next, you can read about how elementary school teacher Julie Curry in Macon, Georgia, uses cross-age peer interaction in reading instruction.

THROUGH THE EYES OF TEACHERS
Cross-Age Peer Interaction in Reading Instruction

Students with a learning disability in the area of reading often feel a lack of self-worth from years of struggling to read. When remediating a reading disability, it is important to address the emotional as well as the academic deficit. Working with younger peers has proven to be a successful strategy with my students who have a learning disability.

Once my students have mastered a critical skill, I encourage them to create a short student-made book covering the skills mastered (short vowel sounds, for example). Students have created beautiful, informative books related to phonetic awareness skills, reading comprehension, and consonant/vowel blending.

Once students have completed their books, the books are presented to a small group and the project is celebrated. Students then read and discuss their book with a younger child who views them as a hero. It's not embarrassing to make an alphabet book in the fourth grade if your audience is a kindergarten class. Student-made books are then placed on display in the media center.

3. *Don't let tutors give tests to tutees.* This can undermine cooperation between the students.

4. *Spend time training tutors.* For peer tutoring to be successful, you will have to spend some time training the tutors. To get peer tutors started off right, discuss competent peer-tutoring strategies. Demonstrate how scaffolding works. Give the tutors clear, organized instructions and invite them to ask questions about their assignments. Divide the group of peer tutors into pairs and let them practice what you have just demonstrated. Let them alternately be tutor and tutee.

5. *Don't overuse peer tutoring.* It is easy to fall into the trap of using high-achieving students as peer tutors too often. Be sure that these students get ample opportunities to participate in challenging intellectual tasks themselves.

6. *Let parents know that their child will be involved in peer tutoring.* Explain to them the advantages of this learning strategy and invite them to visit the classroom to observe how the peer tutoring works.

Cooperative Learning

Cooperative learning occurs when students work in small groups to help each other learn. Cooperative learning groups vary in size, although four is a typical number of students. In some cases, cooperative learning is done in dyads (two students). When students are assigned to work in a cooperative group, the group usually stays together for weeks or months, but cooperative groups usually occupy only a portion of the student's school day or year (Sherman, 2001). In a cooperative learning group, each student typically learns a part of a larger unit and then teaches that part to the group. When students teach something to others, they tend to learn it more deeply.

Research on Cooperative Learning   Researchers have found that cooperative learning can be an effective strategy for improving achievement, especially when two conditions are met (Slavin, 1995):

- *Group rewards are generated.* Some type of recognition or reward is given to the group so that the group members can sense that it is in their best interest to help each other learn.
- *Individuals are held accountable.* Some method of evaluating a student's individual contribution, such as an individual quiz or report, needs to be used. Without this individual accountability, some students might do some "social loafing" (let other students do their work), and some might be left out because others believe that they have little to contribute. When the conditions of group rewards and individual accountability are met, cooperative learning improves achievement across different grades and in tasks that range from basic skills to problem solving (Johnson & Johnson, 2002, 2005).

Motivation   Increased motivation to learn is common in cooperative groups (Blumenfeld, Kempler, & Krajcik, 2006; Johnson & Johnson, 2002). In one study, fifth- and sixth-grade Israeli students were given a choice of continuing to do schoolwork or going out to play (Sharan & Shaulov, 1990). Only when students were in cooperative groups were they likely to forego going out to play. Positive peer interaction and positive feelings about making their own decisions were motivating factors behind students' choice to participate in the cooperative groups. In another study, high school students made greater gains and expressed more intrinsic motivation to learn algebraic concepts when they were in cooperative rather than individualistic learning contexts (Nichols & Miller, 1994).

Interdependence and Teaching One's Peers   Cooperative learning also promotes increased interdependence and connection with other students (Blumenfeld, Kempler, & Krajcik, 2006; Johnson & Johnson, 2002; Veenman & others, 2005). In one study, fifth-graders were more likely to move to a correct strategy for solving decimal problems if the partners clearly explained their ideas and considered each other's proposals (Ellis, Klahr, & Siegler, 1994).

Cooperative Learning Approaches   A number of cooperative learning approaches have been developed. They include STAD (Student-Teams-Achievement Divisions), the jigsaw classroom, learning together, group investigation, and cooperative scripting. To read about these approaches, see figure 10.1.

Creating a Cooperative Community   The school community is made up of faculty, staff, students, parents, and people in the neighborhood. More broadly, the school community also includes central administrators, college admissions officers, and future employers. To create an effective learning community, David and Roger Johnson (2002, pp. 144–146) believe that cooperation and positive interdependence needs to occur at a number of different levels: the learning group of children within

cooperative learning Learning that occurs when students work in small groups to help each other learn.

STAD (Student-Teams-Achievement Divisions)

STAD involves team recognition and group responsibility for learning in mixed-ability groups (Slavin, 1995). Rewards are given to teams whose members improve the most over their past performances. Students are assigned to teams of four or five members. The teacher presents a lesson, usually over one or two class periods. Next, students study worksheets based on material presented by the teacher. Students monitor their team members' performance to ensure that all members have mastered their material.

Teams practice working on problems together and study together, but the members take quizzes individually. The resulting individual scores contribute to the team's overall score. An individual's

contribution to the team score is based on that individual's improvement, not on an absolute score, which motivates students to work hard because each contribution counts. In some STAD classrooms, a weekly class newsletter is published that recognizes both team and individual performances.

The STAD approach has been used in a variety of subjects (including math, reading, and social studies) and with students at different grade levels. It is most effective for learning situations that involve well-defined objectives or problems with specific answers or solutions. These include math computation, language use, geography skills, and science facts.

The Jigsaw Classroom

In chapter 5, "Sociocultural Diversity," we described the jigsaw classroom, which involves having students from different cultural backgrounds cooperate by doing different parts of a project to reach a common goal. Here we elaborate on the concept.

Developed by Eliot Aronson and his colleagues (1978), *Jigsaw I* is a cooperative learning approach in which six-member teams work on material that has been broken down into parts. Each team member is responsible for a part. Members of different teams who have studied the same part convene, discuss their part, and then return to their teams, where they take turns teaching their part to other team members.

Robert Slavin (1995) created *Jigsaw II*, a modified version of *Jigsaw I*. Whereas *Jigsaw I* consists of teams of six, *Jigsaw II* usually has teams of four or five. All team members study the entire lesson rather than one part, and individual scores are combined to form an overall team score, as in STAD. After they have studied the entire lesson, students become expert on one aspect of the lesson; then students with the same topics meet in expert groups to discuss them. Subsequently, they return to their teams and help other members of the team learn the material.

Learning Together

Created by David and Roger Johnson (1994), this approach has four components: (1) face-to-face interaction, (2) positive interdependence, (3) individual accountability, and (4) development of interpersonal group skills. Thus, in addition to Slavin's interest in achievement, the Johnsons' cooperative learning approach also

focuses on socioemotional development and group interaction. In learning together, students work in four- or five-member heterogeneous groups on tasks with an emphasis on discussion and team building (Johnson & Johnson, 2003).

Group Investigation

Developed by Shlomo Sharan (1990; Sharan & Sharan, 1992), this approach involves a combination of independent learning and group work in two- to six-member groups), as well as a group reward for individual achievement. The teacher chooses a problem for the class to study, but students decide what they want to study in exploring the problem. The work is divided among the

group's members, who work individually. Then the group gets together, integrating, summarizing, and presenting the findings as a group project. The teacher's role is to facilitate investigation and maintain cooperative effort. Students collaborate with the teacher to evaluate their effort. In Sharan's view, this is the way many real-world problems are solved in communities around the world.

Cooperative Scripting

Students work in reciprocal pairs, taking turns summarizing information and orally presenting it to each other (Dansereau, 1988; McDonald and others, 1985). One member of the pair presents the material. The other member listens, monitors the

presentation for any mistakes, and gives feedback. Then the partner becomes the teacher and presents the next set of material while the first member listens and evaluates it.

FIGURE 10.1 Cooperative Learning Approaches

a classroom (which we just discussed), the classroom, between classrooms, school, school-parent, and school-neighborhood:

- *Class cooperation.* There are many ways to create cooperation and inter-dependence for the whole class. Class goals can be generated and class rewards given. This can be accomplished by adding bonus points to all class members' academic scores when all class members attain a goal "or by giving nonacade-mic rewards, such as extra free time, extra recess time, stickers, food, T-shirts, or a class party." Classroom cooperation can be promoted by "putting teams in charge of daily class cleanup, running a class bank or business, or engaging in other activities that benefit the class as a whole. Classroom interdependence may also be structured through dividing resources, such as having the class publish a newsletter in which each cooperative group contributes one article . . . one class was studying geography." The ceiling was turned into a large world map. "The class was divided into eight cooperative groups. Each group was assigned a geographical location on which to do a report. The class then planned an itinerary for a trip to visit all eight places. Yarn was used to mark their journey. As they arrived at each spot, the appropriate group presented its report" about the location.

- *Interclass cooperation.* An interdisciplinary team of teachers may organize their classes into a "neighborhood" or "school within a school" in which classes work together on joint projects.

- *School-wide cooperation.* Cooperation at the level of the entire school can be attained in a number of ways. "The school mission statement may articulate the mutual goals shared by all members of the school and be displayed on the school walls" and highlighted on a school Web page. "Teachers can work in a variety of cooperative teams . . . and faculty/staff can meet weekly in teaching teams and/or study groups. . . . Teachers may be assigned to task forces to plan and implement solutions to school-wide issues. . . . Finally, school interdependence may be highlighted in a variety of school-wide activities, such as the weekly student-produced school news broadcast, . . . all-school projects, and regular school assemblies."

- *School-parent cooperation.* Cooperation is promoted between the school and parents "by involving parents in establishing mutual goals and strategic plans to attain the goals, . . . in sharing resources to help the school achieve its goals," and in creating activities that improve the likelihood that parents will develop a positive attitude toward the school.

- *School-neighborhood cooperation.* If the school is embedded in a neighborhood, a positive interdependence between the school and the neighborhood can ben-efit both. The school's mission "can be supported by neighborhood merchants who provide resources and financing for various events. Classes can perform neighborhood service projects, such as cleaning up a park."

Evaluating Cooperative Learning   Among the positive aspects of cooperative learn-ing are increased interdependence and interaction with other students, enhanced motivation to learn, and improved learning by teaching material to others. The pos-sible drawbacks of cooperative learning are that some students prefer to work alone; low-achieving students may slow down the progress of high-achieving students; a few students may do most or all of the cognitive work while others do little (called "social loafing"; some students may become distracted from the group's task because they enjoy socializing; and many students lack the skills needed to collaborate effectively with others, engage in productive discussions, and explain their ideas or evaluate others' ideas effectively (Blumenfeld, Kempler, & Krajcik, 2006). Teachers who imple-ment cooperative learning in their classroom need to be attentive to these drawbacks and work to reduce them (King & Behnke, 2005).

Review, Reflect, and Practice

(2) **Explain how teachers and peers can jointly contribute to children's learning.**

REVIEW

- What is scaffolding?
- What is a cognitive apprenticeship?
- Is tutoring effective? What are some alternative sources of tutors?
- What is cooperative learning and how might it benefit students? What are some ways to structure it?

REFLECT

- How would you handle the situation if parents became angry that, because of time allotted to cooperative learning, their children were being allowed less time to learn on an individual basis?

PRAXIS™ PRACTICE

1. Which of the following is the best example of scaffolding?
   a. Steve gives his friend Vlade the answers to today's homework.
   b. Steve helps his friend Vlade complete today's homework by giving him the least amount of assistance he needs for each question.
   c. Steve helps his friend Vlade complete today's homework by giving him hints to each answer.
   d. Steve tells his friend Vlade that he has to do his homework on his own.

2. Which of the following is an example of a cognitive apprenticeship?
   a. Ms. Notwitzki asks her students lots of questions. If a student does not know the answer to a question, she moves on to another student because she does not want her students to be embarrassed.
   b. Ms. Edgar pays attention to both the verbal and nonverbal cues her students give her regarding their understanding of her lessons. If she asks a student a question, she can determine if the student is thinking or confused. She often gives her students hints to help them answer.
   c. Ms. Lindell asks her students lots of questions. If a student does not respond immediately to her query, she gives the student the correct answer.
   d. Ms. Samuel lectures her class and they take notes. She answers any questions that they have at the end of the lesson.

3. Which teacher is using peer tutoring in the most positive way for both the tutor and the student?
   a. Ms. Gasol uses sixth-grade students to tutor her third-grade students in math for 30 minutes, four times each week. She gives each tutor explicit instructions.
   b. Ms. Mathews uses the buddy system in her class. Children choose who they would like to tutor them and what they would like to learn. Generally, they pick a close friend.
   c. Ms. Rankowski selects lower-achieving students from the higher grades to come to her class at least once per week to work with her students. She generally has them do things such as administer spelling.
   d. Ms. Taylor likes to use peer tutoring with her students, especially in math. She has found that often other students can explain things to her students more easily than she can. Therefore, she uses more advanced students in her class to teach those who are struggling with math concepts.

4. Mr. Kotter has assigned the students to work cooperatively on a project about the Civil War. He puts the students into heterogeneous groups of four and gives each

group the project guidelines. They are to turn in one project on which they will
receive a group grade. He is surprised when some students contribute little to
their group's effort. What is Mr. Kotter doing *wrong*?
a. Mr. Kotter did not include any individual grades.
b. Mr. Kotter should not give the students a group grade.
c. Mr. Kotter should not have used heterogeneous groups.
d. Mr. Kotter should not use cooperative learning in history.

Please see the answer key at the end of the book.

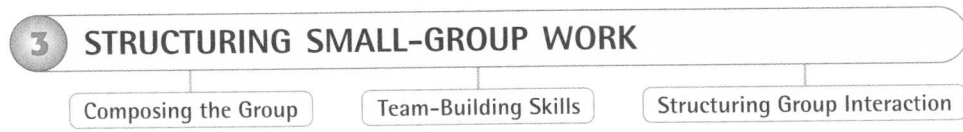

3 STRUCTURING SMALL–GROUP WORK

Composing the Group   **Team–Building Skills**   **Structuring Group Interaction**

We have seen that group work has many benefits for students. It requires careful planning on the teacher's part, however. When you structure students' work in small
groups, you have to make decisions about how to compose the group, build team
skills, and structure group interaction (Webb & Palincsar, 1996).

Composing the Group

Teachers often ask how they should assign students to small groups in their class. The
cooperative learning approaches featured in figure 10.1 generally recommend heterogeneous groups with diversity in ability, ethnic background, socioeconomic status,
and gender (Johnson & Johnson, 2002). The reasoning behind heterogeneous grouping is that it maximizes opportunities for peer tutoring and support, improves cross-
gender and cross-ethnic relations, and ensures that each group has at least one
student who can do the work (Kagan, 1992).

Heterogeneous Ability   One of the main reasons for using heterogeneous ability
groups is that they benefit low-ability students, who can learn from higher-ability
students. However, some critics argue that such heterogeneous groupings hold back
high-ability students. In most studies, though, high-achieving students perform
equally well on achievement tests after working in heterogeneous groups or homogeneous groups (Hooper & others, 1989). In heterogeneous groups, high-ability students often assume the role of "teacher" and explain concepts to other students. In
homogeneous groups, high-ability students are less likely to assume this teaching role.
    One problem with heterogeneous groups is that when high-ability, low-ability, and
medium-ability students are included, the medium-ability students get left out to some
extent; high-ability and low-ability students form teacher-student relationships, exclud-
ing medium-ability students from group interaction. Medium-ability students might
perform better in groups where most or all of the students have medium abilities.

Ethnic, Socioeconomic, and Gender Heterogeneity   Some of the initial reasons
that cooperative learning groups were formed was to improve interpersonal relations
among students from different ethnic and socioeconomic backgrounds. The hope was
that interaction under conditions of equal status in cooperative groups would reduce
prejudice. However, getting students to interact on the basis of equal status has been
more difficult than initially envisioned.
    Some experts recommend that when forming ethnically and socioeconomically het-
erogeneous groups, teachers pay careful attention to a group's composition (Miller &

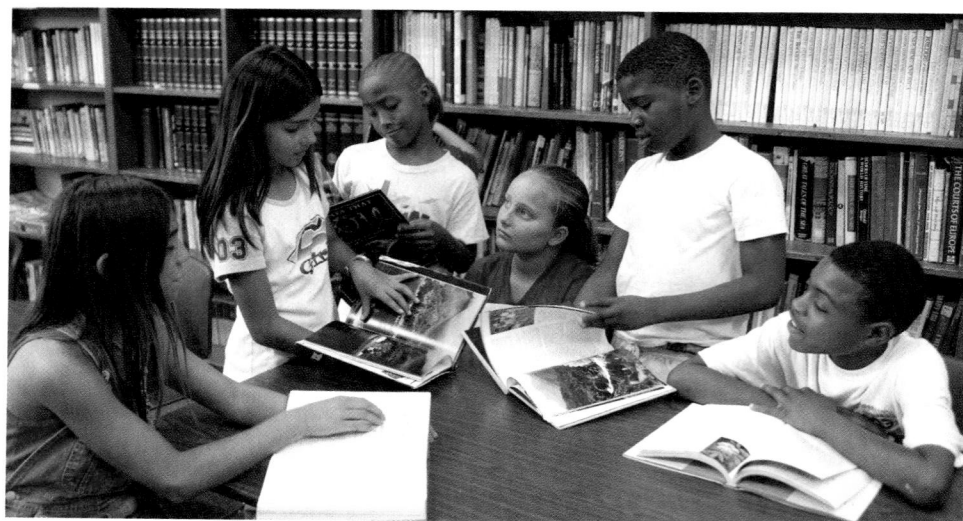

What are some guidelines for forming ethically and socioeconomically heterogeneous groups?

Harrington, 1990). One recommendation is to not make the composition too obvious. Thus, you might vary different social characteristics (ethnicity, socioeconomic status, and gender) simultaneously, such as grouping together a middle-income African American female, a White male from a low-income family, and so on. In this way, for example, the White males would not all be from high-income families. Another recommendation is to avoid forming groups that have only one minority student, if at all possible; this avoids calling attention to the student's "solo status."

In mixed-gender groups, males tend to be more active and dominant (Tannen, 1990). Thus, when mixing females and males, an important task for teachers is to encourage girls to speak up and boys to allow girls to express their opinions and contribute to the group's functioning. A general strategy is to have an equal number of girls and boys. In groups of five or six children in which only one member is a girl, the boys tend to ignore the girl (Webb, 1984).

Team-Building Skills

Good cooperative learning in the classroom requires that time be spent on team-building skills. This involves thinking about how to start team building at the beginning of the school year, helping students become better listeners, giving students practice in contributing to a team product, getting students to discuss the value of a team leader, and working with team leaders to help them deal with problem situations.

Structuring Group Interaction

One way to facilitate students' work in small groups is to assign students different roles. For example, consider these roles that students can assume in a group (Kagan, 1992):

- Encourager—brings out reluctant students and is a motivator
- Gatekeeper—equalizes participation of students in the group
- Coach—helps with academic content
- Checker—makes sure the group understands the material
- Taskmaster—keeps the group on task
- Recorder—writes down ideas and decisions
- Quiet captain—monitors the group's noise level
- Materials monitor—obtains and returns supplies

Such roles help groups to function more smoothly and give all members of the group a sense of importance. Note that although we just described nine different roles that

BEST PRACTICES
Strategies for Developing Students' Team-Building Skills

Here are some guidelines (Aronson & Patnoe, 1997):

1. *Don't begin the year with cooperative learning on a difficult task.* Teachers report that academic cooperative learning often works best when students have previously worked together on team-building exercises. A short period each day for several weeks is usually adequate for this team building.

2. *Do team building at the level of the cooperative group (two to six students) rather than at the level of the entire class.* Some students on the team will be more assertive; others will be more passive. The team-building goal is to give all members some experience in being valuable team members, as well as to get them to learn that being cooperative works more effectively than being competitive.

3. *In team building, work with students to help them become better listeners.* Ask students to introduce themselves by name all at the same time to help them see that they have to take turns and listen to each other instead of hogging a conversation. You also can ask students to come up with behavioral descriptions of how they can show others that they are listening. These might include looking directly at the speaker, rephrasing what she just said, summarizing her statement, and so on.

4. *Give students some practice in contributing to a common product as part of team building.* Ask each student to participate in drawing a group picture by passing paper and pen from student to student. Each student's task is to add something to the picture as it circulates several times through the team. When the picture is finished, discuss each student's contribution to the team. Students will sense that the product is not complete unless each member's contribution is recognized. Next, you can read about how a ninth-grade history teacher uses this strategy effectively.

THROUGH THE EYES OF TEACHERS
An Eye-Level Meeting of the Minds

Jimmy Furlow has groups of students summarize textbook sections and put them on transparencies to help the

Ninth-grade history teacher Jimmy Furlow converses with a student in his class.

entire class prepare for a test. Furlow lost both legs in Vietnam but he rarely stays in one place, moving his wheelchair around the room, communicating with students at eye level. When the class completes their discussion of all the points on the overhead, Furlow edits their work to demonstrate concise, clear writing and help students zero in on an important point (Marklein, 1998).

5. *During team building, you may want to discuss the value of having a group leader.* You can ask students to discuss the specific ways a leader should function to maximize the group's performance. Their brainstorming might come up with such characteristics as "helps get the group organized," "keeps the group on task," "serves as liaison between the teacher and the group," "shows enthusiasm," "is patient and polite," and "helps the group deal with disagreements and conflicts." The teacher may select the group leader or students may be asked to elect one.

6. *Work with team leaders to help them deal with problem situations.* For example, some members might rarely talk, one member might dominate the group, members might call each other names, some members might refuse to work, one member might want to work alone, and everyone might talk at once. You can get group leaders together and get them to role-play such situations and discuss effective strategies for handling the problem situation.

can be played in groups, most experts, as we noted earlier, recommend that groups not exceed five or six members to function effectively. Some members can fill multiple roles, and all roles do not always have to be filled.

Another way roles can be specialized is to designate some students as "summarizers" and others as "listeners." Researchers have consistently found that summarizing benefits learning more than listening, so if these roles are used, all members should get opportunities to be summarizers (Dansereau, 1988).

To evaluate your attitudes toward social constructivist approaches and whether you are likely to use such strategies when you teach, complete Self-Assessment 10.1.

SELF-ASSESSMENT 10.1

Evaluating My Social Constructivist Experiences

What experiences have you already had with social constructivist thinking and learning? You may have had such experiences in school or in other settings. For each of these settings that you have experienced, record at least one instance in which you can look back and see social constructivist principles at work.

1. Your family:

_____

_____

2. A club or program such as the Scouts:

_____

_____

3. Your K–12 school experience:

_____

_____

4. College:

_____

_____

How do those experiences shape your judgment regarding these ideas for classroom teaching?

1. That thinking should be viewed as located (situated) in social and physical contexts, not only within an individual's mind:

_____

_____

2. Vygotsky's sociocultural cognitive theory:

_____

_____

3. Scaffolding:

_____

_____

4. Peer tutoring:

_____

_____

5. Cooperative learning:

_____

_____

6. Small-group work:

_____

_____

Review, Reflect, and Practice

3 Make effective decisions in structuring small-group work.

REVIEW
- What are some important considerations in placing students in small groups?
- What can teachers do to build team skills within groups?
- What types of role assignments can improve a group's structure?

REFLECT
- Suppose you and five other students have decided to form a group to study for a final exam in educational psychology. How would you structure the group? What roles would you want the group to assign?

PRAXIS™ PRACTICE

1. Which of the following represents best practice for forming work groups?
   a. one White, high-achieving girl; three African American, middle-achieving boys
   b. one African American, high-achieving boy; two White, middle-achieving girls; one Asian American, low-achieving boy
   c. two Asian American, high-achieving boys; two White, low-achieving boys
   d. two African American, high-achieving girls; one African American, middle-achieving boy; one African American, low-achieving girl

2. Mr. Fandango decides to work on team building at the beginning of the school year. To this end, he takes his entire class outside and has them create a human knot. They then must work together to untie the "knot." Several students become frustrated and angry during the activity. Mr. Fandango intervenes by encouraging the students to elect a leader and to listen to each other. According to "Best Practices: Strategies for Developing Students' Team-Building Skills," what did Mr. Fandango do *incorrectly*?
   a. He did not emphasize the importance of listening skills.
   b. He did not have enough students in the group.
   c. He did not use heterogeneous grouping.
   d. He started with the whole class and a difficult task.

3. George, John, Paul, Cassie, and Mackenzie are working together on a group project involving the Civil War. George is the resident expert on the Civil War. As they work on the project, he answers the other students' questions. John volunteers to get all the supplies that the group needs. The project goes smoothly and each of the students participates, because Cassie reminds them that everyone's contribution is valuable. During one group work session, the group starts discussing last weekend's football game. Paul says, "Hey guys, we're supposed to be working on this project, you know." After this, the group gets back on task. They become so engrossed in their discussion that they become rather noisy. At this point, Mackenzie reminds her peers to quiet down.
   Which student took the gatekeeper role?
   a. George
   b. John
   c. Mackenzie
   d. Cassie

Please see the answer key at the end of the book.

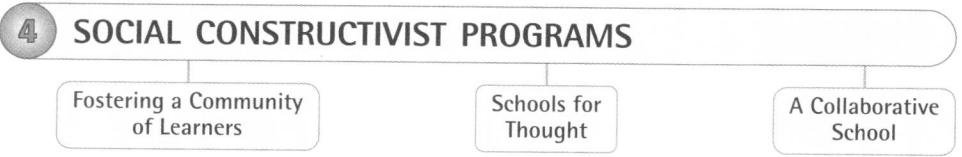

Let's explore several programs that systematically incorporate social constructivist philosophies in their efforts to challenge students to solve real-world problems and develop a deeper understanding of concepts. These programs can show you some ways to successfully use social constructivist ideas and techniques in your classroom.

Fostering a Community of Learners

Ann Brown and Joe Campione (1996; Brown, 1997; Campione, 2001) have developed a program called **Fostering a Community of Learners (FCL),** which focuses on literacy development and biology. As currently established, it is set in inner-city elementary schools and is appropriate for 6- to 12-year-old children. Reflection and discussion are key dimensions of the program. In FCL, constructive commentary, questioning, querying, and criticism are the norm rather than the exception. Many of the class activities occur in small groups in which students talk with, try to convince, and challenge each other. Although teachers guide topic selection, an important goal is to gradually turn over responsibility for learning to students (Lehrer & Schauble, 2006).

The FCL program emphasizes three strategies that encourage reflection and discussion: (1) the use of adults as role models, (2) children teaching children, and (3) online computer consultation.

Adults as Role Models   Visiting experts and classroom teachers introduce the big ideas and difficult principles at the beginning of a unit. The adult demonstrates how to think and self-reflect in the process of identifying topics within a general area of inquiry or reasoning with given information. The adults continually ask students to justify their opinions and then to support them with evidence, to think of counterexamples of rules, and so on.

For example, one area of biological inquiry used in the FCL program is "Changing Populations." Outside experts or teachers introduce this topic and ask students to generate as many questions about it as possible. The teacher and the students categorize the questions into subtopics such as extinct, endangered, artificial, assisted, and urbanized populations. About six students make up a learning group, and each group takes responsibility for one of the subtopics.

Children Teaching Children   Brown (1997) says that children as well as adults enrich the classroom learning experience by contributing their particular expertise. Cross-age teaching, in which older students teach younger students, is used. This occurs both face-to-face and via e-mail. Older students often serve as discussion leaders. Cross-age teaching provides students with invaluable opportunities to talk about learning, gives students responsibility and purpose, and fosters collaboration among peers.

FCL uses **reciprocal teaching,** in which students take turns leading a small-group discussion. Reciprocal teaching requires students to discuss complex passages, collaborate, and share their individual expertise and perspectives on a particular topic. Reciprocal teaching can involve a teacher and a student as well as interaction between students.

A modified version of the jigsaw classroom (which was described in chapter 5 and figure 10.1) also is used. As students create preliminary drafts of reports, they participate in "crosstalk" sessions. These are whole-class activities in which groups

Fostering a Community of Learners (FCL) A social constructivist program that focuses on literacy development and biology. FCL encourages reflection and discussion through the use of adults as role models, children teaching children, and online computer consultation.

reciprocal teaching A learning arrangement in which students take turns leading a small-group discussion.

periodically summarize where they are in their learning activity and get input from the other groups. "Mini-jigsaws" (small groups) also are used. At both the whole-class level and mini-jigsaw level, if group members can't understand what a student is saying or writing about, the student must revise a product and present it again later. Students are then grouped into reciprocal teaching seminars in which each student is an expert on one subtopic, teaches that part to the others, and participates in constructing test questions based on the subunit (Rico & Shulman, 2004).

A Fostering a Community of Learners (FCL) classroom. *What is the nature of this approach to education?*

Online Computer Consultation   As just noted, FCL classrooms also use e-mail to build community and expertise. Through e-mail, experts provide coaching and advice, as well as commentary about what it means to learn and understand. Online experts function as role models of thinking. They wonder, query, and make inferences based on incomplete knowledge.

At the heart of FCL is a culture of learning, negotiating, sharing, and producing work that is displayed to others. Products of students' work are often in the form of text or talk that include posters, presentations, written reports, or teaching ideas for working with younger children (Lehrer & Schauble, 2006). The educational experience involves an interpretive community that encourages active exchange and reciprocity. This approach has much in common with what Jerome Bruner (1996) recommended for improving the culture of education. Research evaluation of the Fostering a Community of Learners approach suggests that it benefits students' understanding and flexible use of content knowledge, resulting in improved achievement in reading, writing, and problem solving. FCL is being increasingly implemented in a number of classrooms (Schoenfeld, 2004; Sherin, Mendez, & Louis, 2004; Shulman & Shulman, 2004; Whitcomb, 2004).

In a recent description, science education experts Richard Lehrer and Laura Schauble (2006) called FCL "a landmark in developmental science education." That said, they also raised several questions about its effectiveness. First, even though many educators might agree that shared discourse is an important aspect of classrooms, it is not clear how to implement this and difficult to know if it is successful or not. Second, in regard to science education, is too much emphasis placed on reading about science, integrating text information, and learning *about* science in FCL and too little emphasis on *doing* science.

Schools for Thought

Schools for Thought (SFT) is another formal program of social constructivist teaching. Too often students emerge from instruction with only a fragile understanding of the material (Segal, 1996). For example, students might be able to repeat various scientific principles they have been taught in science, but they run into difficulties when they have to explain everyday scientific phenomena. Similarly, in math, students might be good at plugging numbers into formulas but when confronted with variations of these problems be unable to solve them. Thus, many students acquire enough information to pass tests in school but gain no deep understanding of concepts.

In one effort, Schools for Thought (Lamon & others, 1996) has combined aspects of The Jasper Project, Fostering a Community of Learners (FCL), and Computer-Supported Intentional Learning Environments (CSILE) in a school learning environment. The project is named after John Bruer's (1993) award-winning book *Schools for Thought*. The Jasper Project, FCL, and CSILE share certain features that allow them to be combined in a school learning environment. We already have described The Jasper Project (chapter 9) and FCL. To learn about CSILE, read the Technology and Education box.

Schools for Thought (SFT) A social constructivist program that combines aspects of The Jasper Project, Fostering a Community of Learners, and CSILE.

TECHNOLOGY AND EDUCATION
Computer–Supported Intentional Learning Environments (Knowledge Forum)

In the early 1990s, researchers at the Centre for Applied Cognitive Science, in the Ontario Institute for Studies in Education, began applying their work on intentional learning to the development of computer applications to support knowledge building communities (Scardamalia & Bereiter, 1994). Their work led to the development of CSILE (Computer-Supported Intentional Learning Environments), an evolving database application that allows students to collaboratively develop a knowledge base, enter their views and questions, compare perspectives, and reflect on their joint understanding of ideas.

CSILE helped students understand how knowledge is socially constructed and gave them opportunities to reflect on, revise, and transform their thinking. In addition students in CSILE classrooms performed better on standardized achievement tests of language and mathematics, gave deeper explanations of concepts, were better problem solvers, and had a more positive attitude toward learning than students in traditional classrooms (Scardamalia, Bereiter, & Lamon, 1994).

More recently, CSILE has morphed into a commercial enterprise known as Knowledge Forum (**www.knowledgeforum.com/**) and expanded from a K–12 focus to incorporate all kinds of education and training (Bruckman, 2006; Scardamalia & Bereiter, 2006). Knowledge Forum includes knowledge building tools for collaboration, constructing, storing, retrieving, referencing, quoting, and tracking notes, identifying gaps or advances in knowledge, building idea networks, and viewing ideas and idea networks from multiple perspectives.

Knowledge Forum is essentially CSILE online. It provides users with structures and tools to create a knowledge building community via a local area network, through Internet communications, or using the World Wide Web. Each community creates its own knowledge base in which it can store notes, connect ideas, and build on previous thinking. Users start with an empty knowledge base to which they submit ideas, share information, reorganize the knowledge, and ultimately build understandings. Knowledge Forum makes information accessible from multiple perspectives and from multiple entry points. With it, any number of individuals and groups can share information, launch collaborative investigations, and build networks of new ideas . . . together.

Curriculum   The three core programs of Schools for Thought stress the importance of getting students to think about real-world problems. Problem-based and project-based activities are at the heart of the curriculum. Extended in-depth inquiry in domains such as science, math, and social studies are emphasized. All three programs also incorporate cross-disciplinary inquiry across traditional boundaries. For example, exploring what it means for an animal to be endangered could involve examining problems related to estimating populations, sampling, and other issues usually restricted to mathematics. In the Schools for Thought project, curricula are being developed that integrate geography, geology, environmental and physical science, ancient and American history, and language arts and reading.

Instruction   All three SFT programs involve a change in the classroom instructional climate. In a traditional classroom, students are receivers of information dispensed by teachers, textbooks, and other media; the teacher's role is to give information and mold students' learning. In many traditional schools, what students mainly do is listen, watch, and mimic what teachers and texts tell them to do (Greeno, 1993, 2006). In contrast, all three SFT programs provide students with many opportunities to plan and organize their own learning and problem solving. They also encourage students to work collaboratively as they learn and think. Students explore ideas, evaluate information, and consider others' ideas in an ongoing reciprocal interchange with peers, teachers, and experts.

The Schools for Thought environments are not simply free-wheeling discovery environments. They involve a considerable amount of structure. Teachers and community experts keep learning focused on key principles in the domains being studied, such as mathematics, science, or social science. They monitor and reframe students' self-generated questions and exploration to keep them within the

A Schools for Thought Science classroom at Compton-Drew School in St. Louis.

perspective of the key principles. In this manner, they guide the direction of students' inquiry so that students discover the deep concepts of the domain. Still, there is considerable flexibility in how this understanding is achieved and the nature of the projects undertaken.

Community   In many schools, classrooms and teachers operate in isolation, not just from each other but from the outside community as well. The Jasper Project, FCL, and CSILE all emphasize the importance of giving students and teachers opportunities to see themselves as part of a team and as members of a larger community. Problems often have a community focus, to encourage students to think about how learning and problem solving can be used to better understand and improve the world in which we live.

Technology   The Jasper Project, FCL, and CSILE all use technology to break the isolation of the traditional classroom. They encourage students to communicate electronically with a community of learners beyond the classroom's walls.

Assessment   The goals in creating The Jasper Project, FCL, and CSILE were not to improve students' achievement test scores. Assessment in the three programs focuses on achieving authentic performances (such as reading for the purpose of answering research questions, writing to build new knowledge), making assessment coordinate smoothly with learning and instruction, and encouraging students to engage in self-assessment.

A Collaborative School

In 1977, a collaborative school was organized as a parent-teacher cooperative and continues today with six classrooms serving kindergarten through sixth grade in Salt Lake City, Utah. It is an optional school serving the whole school district, open to families who choose to have their children educated there. Learning to work effectively in groups is a major emphasis in the curriculum (Rogoff, Turkanis, & Bartlett, 2002). During the school day children usually work in small groups with the teacher

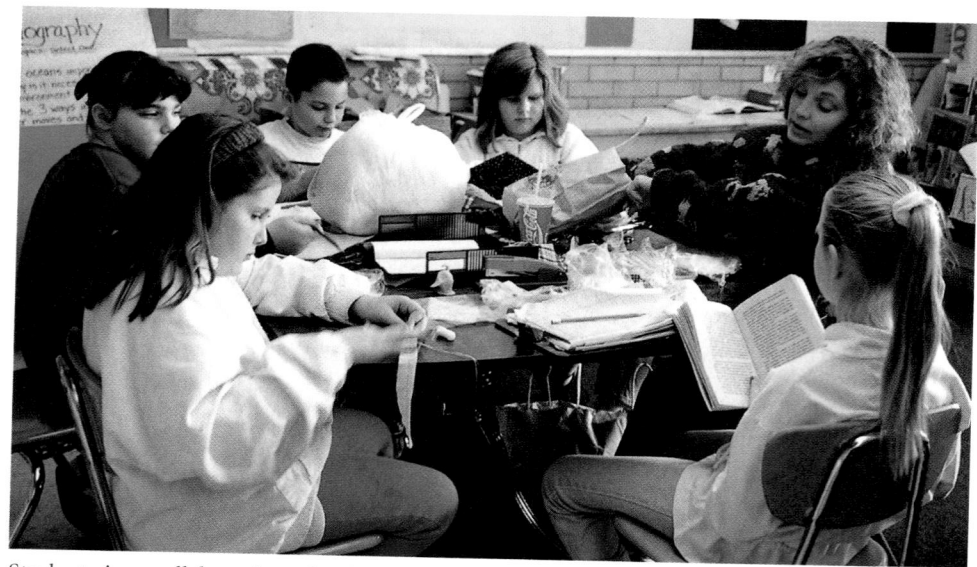

Students in a collaborative school in Salt Lake City. *How might a collaborative school differ from a typical school?*

and/or parent volunteers. In some instances, children work on their own. Children often share decision making on projects with classmates and adults, contribute to adults' guidance by conversing openly with teachers and parent volunteers, as well as with each other, and treat other people as sources of help.

Parents contribute 3 hours of time per week to classroom instruction for each child enrolled in the school. Before the school year begins, parents and the teacher hold a meeting at the family's home to prepare for the upcoming year. Parent meetings are held on a monthly basis to continue planning and discussing what can be done to help in the classroom.

In the collaborative school, teachers, parents, and children help plan and develop a curriculum that includes the following (Turkanis, 2002, pp. 91–92):

- Capturing "the moment to build on interesting ideas that emerge in class discussion"
- "Recognizing that children have their own learning agendas that can provide motivation" and the path to learning in curriculum areas
- "Supporting units of study that often emerge as a group process, as people become interested in others' interests and build on each other's expertise"
- Using extensive and varied resources with little reliance on textbooks
- Focusing in depth on big ideas, concepts, and projects

In one first-/second-grade class, every Monday morning of the whole year was devoted to a project of building a town. Students chose which part of the town they wanted to develop and built storefronts. Students developed their own jobs and a government, named their town by popular election, printed money, and published a newspaper. When a problem arose, students had a town meeting and found a solution for the problem. By the end of the year, they had a smoothly functioning town and invited other classes to patronize their businesses.

The town building project was a comprehensive learning experience. Through this project, students developed a better understanding of interpersonal relationships and problem solving in a business community as well as improved math, reading, and writing skills.

Review, Reflect, and Practice

(4) **Describe three social constructivist programs.**

REVIEW

- What three strategies are embedded in the Fostering a Community of Learners program?
- What programs are combined in Schools for Thought? What do these programs have in common?
- What are some themes of the collaborative school described?

REFLECT

- Which of the three social constructivist programs appeals to you the most? Why?

PRAXIS™ PRACTICE

1. Which of the following is the best example of fostering a community of learners?
   a. Marks Middle School brings students together to work on math projects. They bring in community members to act as mentors to the students and try to make connections between mathematics and the world in which these rural teens live.
   b. Lincoln Elementary School uses small-group discussions in which students challenge each other's perspectives. They bring in community members to act as mentors to the students. When outside mentors lack the expertise needed, students e-mail outside experts. Older students help younger ones.
   c. Johnson High School uses a hands-on approach to teaching biology. Students complete experiments, dissections, and involve themselves in an environmental project. Students work in small groups on these projects under the guidance of an adult role model.
   d. Luther High School uses a flexible, modular approach to teaching science with extensive opportunities for students to engage in projects that they construct themselves. Students are encouraged to engage in self-reflection and cooperative learning.

2. Mr. Patrick, the principal at Johnson High School, wants to implement Schools for Thought. He works with his teachers to integrate various aspects of the curriculum so that students will understand their interdependence. The teachers develop interdisciplinary units that revolve around projects. In addition, the teachers alter the way in which they teach to become facilitators of learning rather than dispensers of knowledge. What aspect of Schools for Thought has Mr. Patrick neglected?
   a. community
   b. curriculum
   c. discipline
   d. instruction

3. If you were to visit a classroom in the collaborative school in Salt Lake City, which of the following would you most likely observe
   a. students working on a project in a small group.
   b. a teacher lecturing to the class.
   c. a teaching controlling a student's behavior.
   d. students working independently at a computer.

CRACK THE CASE
The Case of the Constructivist Classroom

Mariana is a new second-grade teacher and full of enthusiasm about her job. She believes that students should be very active in constructing their own knowledge, and that they should work together in doing this. To that end, she has decided that she wants her classroom to be a social constructivist classroom and has made some decisions about some things she wants to do this year with her students.

First, she knows that she will have to provide students with scaffolding when material is new and gradually adjust the amount of help her students receive. She wants to use peer tutoring for this in her class, because she believes that children can often learn more from each other than they can from an adult. So she sets up a system in which the more-advanced students in her class help those who are less advanced.

Mariana also likes the idea of cooperative learning. She creates student groups so that they are heterogeneous with regard to ability, gender, ethnicity and SES. She then assigns roles to each student in a group. Sometimes these roles are things such as coach, encourager, checker, taskmaster, recorder, and materials monitor. She uses this approach for many content areas. Sometimes she uses a jigsaw approach in which each student is responsible for becoming an expert in a particular area and then sharing that expertise with his or her group members. She uses this approach in science and in social studies.

In math, Mariana feels very fortunate that her school has adopted the Everyday Mathematics curriculum. This program makes connections with the real world that she thinks is so important in math instruction. Group work is also stressed.

Mariana hopes that her students and their parents will share her excitement as they "all learn together." However, she soon becomes disappointed. When she groups students, she hears groans of "Not again." "Why do I have to work with her? She doesn't know anything." "He's too bossy." "I always have to be with him, and then I end up doing everything." "She never lets me do anything but sit there and watch." Parents have gotten in on the act too. She has received calls and letters from parents who don't understand what she's trying to do. They all seem concerned about test scores and grades rather than what their children are learning together. One parent asked that her child no longer be grouped with another child who is "holding back" her child's learning.

1. What are the issues in this case?
2. What do you think Mariana did incorrectly?
3. What should she do now to recover her constructivist classroom?
4. How can she elicit the cooperation of the parents?
5. Which of the following suggestions would you make to Mariana regarding peer tutoring?
   a. Allow children to choose their partners.
   b. Insist that the more advanced students help those who are less advanced, regardless of parental feelings.
   c. Use cross-age peer tutoring rather than same-age peer tutoring.
   d. Use peer tutors who don't like each other so they won't be tempted to goof around instead of working.
6. Which of the following suggestions would you make to Mariana regarding her use of student groups?
   a. Compose gender-segregated groups to make students more comfortable.
   b. Compose racially segregated groups to make students more comfortable.
   c. Give leadership roles to students who are shy to help draw them out.
   d. Mix up the group composition from time to time, so that middle-ability-level students don't get left out.

Reach Your Learning Goals
Social Constructivist Approaches

(1) SOCIAL CONSTRUCTIVIST APPROACHES TO TEACHING: Compare the social constructivist approach with other constructivist approaches.

Social Constructivism in the Broader Constructivist Context

Piaget's and Vygotsky's theories are constructivist. Piaget's theory is a cognitive constructivist theory, whereas Vygotsky's is social constructivist. The implication of Vygotsky's model for teaching is to establish opportunities for students to learn with the teacher and peers in constructing knowledge and understanding. In both Piaget's and Vygotsky's models, teachers are facilitators, not directors. Distinctions between cognitive and social constructivist approaches are not always clear-cut. All social constructivist approaches emphasize that social factors contribute to students' construction of knowledge and understanding.

Situated Cognition

Situated cognition is the idea that thinking is located (situated) in social and physical contexts, not within an individual's mind.

(2) TEACHERS AND PEERS AS JOINT CONTRIBUTORS TO STUDENTS' LEARNING: Explain how teachers and peers can jointly contribute to children's learning.

Scaffolding

Scaffolding is the technique of providing changing levels of support over the course of a teaching session, with a more-skilled individual—a teacher or a more-advanced peer of the child—providing guidance to fit the student's current performance.

Cognitive Apprenticeship

A cognitive apprenticeship involves a novice and an expert, who stretches and supports the novice's understanding of and use of skills.

Tutoring

Tutoring involves a cognitive apprenticeship between an expert and a novice. Tutoring can take place between an adult and a child or a more-skilled child and a less-skilled child. Individual tutoring is effective. Classroom aides, volunteers, and mentors can serve as tutors to support teachers and classroom learning. Reading Recovery and Success for All are examples of effective tutoring programs. In many cases, students benefit more from cross-age tutoring than from same-age tutoring. Tutoring can benefit both the tutee and the tutor.

Cooperative Learning

Cooperative learning occurs when students work in small groups to help each other learn. Researchers have found that cooperative learning can be an effective strategy for improving students' achievement, especially when group goals and individual accountability are instituted. Cooperative learning often improves intrinsic motivation, encourages student interdependence, and promotes deep understanding. Cooperative learning approaches include STAD (Student-Teams-Achievement Divisions), the jigsaw classroom (I and II), learning together, group investigation, and cooperative scripting. Cooperative learning approaches generally recommend heterogeneous groupings with diversity in ability, ethnicity, socioeconomic status, and gender. Creating a cooperative community involves developing positive interdependence at a number of levels: a small group within a classroom, the class as a whole, between classes, the entire school, between parents and the school, and between the school and the neighborhood. Cooperative learning has a number of strengths, but there also are some potential drawbacks to its use.

continued

③ STRUCTURING SMALL-GROUP WORK: Make effective decisions in structuring small-group work.

Composing the Group

Two strategies in composing a small group are to include children with heterogeneous abilities and to have the group membership reflect ethnic, socioeconomic, and gender heterogeneity.

Team-Building Skills

Structuring small-group work also involves attention to team-building skills. A good strategy is to spend several weeks at the beginning of the school year on building team skills. Assigning one student in each small group to be a team leader can help to build the team.

Structuring Group Interaction

A group also can benefit when students are assigned different roles—for example, encourager, gatekeeper, taskmaster, quiet captain, and materials monitor—that are designed to help the group function more smoothly.

④ SOCIAL CONSTRUCTIVIST PROGRAMS: Describe three social constructivist programs.

Fostering a Community of Learners

Fostering a Community of Learners emphasizes (1) using adults as role models, (2) children teaching children, and (3) online computer consultation.

Schools for Thought

Schools for Thought combines activities from three programs: (1) The Jasper Project, (2) Fostering a Community of Learners, and (3) Computer-Supported Intentional Learning Environments. Extended in-depth inquiry is fostered. Teachers guide students in becoming architects of their knowledge.

A Collaborative School

A collaborative school was organized as a parent-teacher cooperative in Salt Lake City, Utah. Children usually work in small groups during the day, share decision making with peers, contribute to adults' guidance, and treat others as sources of help.

 ## KEY TERMS

social constructivist approach 337	cognitive apprenticeship 340	Fostering a Community of Learners (FCL) 354	reciprocal teaching 354
situated cognition 338	cooperative learning 345		Schools for Thought (SFT) 355

 ## PORTFOLIO ACTIVITIES

Now that you have a good understanding of this chapter, complete these exercises to expand your thinking.

Independent Reflection

Evaluating Social Constructivist Experiences. To what extent have you experienced various social constructivist approaches in your education? Think about your different levels of schooling (early childhood, elementary, middle, high school, and college), and evaluate your experience (or lack of experience) with scaffolding, cognitive apprenticeship, tutoring, and cooperative learning. (INTASC: Principles 2, 3, 4, 5, 9)

Collaborative Work

Balancing Individual and Group Activities. With four or five other students in the class, discuss how much of the curriculum should include group activities and how much should involve individual activities at the early childhood, elementary, middle, high school, and college levels. Describe your group's thoughts. Also discuss whether some subject areas might lend themselves better than others to group activities. (INTASC: Principles 1, 3, 4, 5)

Research/Field Experience

Practical Applications of Social Constructivism. Beyond a teacher and a room full of students, what resources do the three social constructivist programs that were described in the chapter require? How practical is it to use these programs on a widespread basis? Write your responses. (INTASC: Principles 4, 5, 7)

Go to the Online Learning Center for downloadable portfolio templates.

TAKING IT TO THE NET

- Imagine that you typically give students frequent opportunities to engage in collaborative group work. What questions should you ask yourself when deciding how to organize the groups and structure the work? Why is collaborative group work an important educational experience for students? **www.netc.org/ classrooms%40work/classrooms/peter/working/grouping. html**

- Multimedia projects offer numerous opportunities for students to engage in social learning. Explore the ThinkQuest Library and evaluate one of the student-created Web projects. In what ways does your selected project employ social constructivist principles of learning? **www.thinkquest.org/library/index.html**

- Work with a partner, and browse the Web to find a high-quality resource that could serve as a "cognitive apprenticeship" for students, and describe its merits as a teaching tool. For example, a student can be an apprentice to astronauts in training by accessing their electronic journals, photos, and interviews. Why is the Web such a powerful tool for implementing social constructivist approaches in the classroom? **www.nasa.gov/audience/foreducators/9-12/features/ F_Astronaut_Journals.html**

Connect to the Online Learning Center to explore possible answers.

STUDY, PRACTICE, AND SUCCEED

Visit **www.mhhe.com/santedu3e** to review the chapter with self-grading quizzes and self-assessments, to apply the chapter material to two more Crack the Case studies, and for suggested activities to develop your teaching portfolio.

CHAPTER 11

Learning and Cognition in the Content Areas

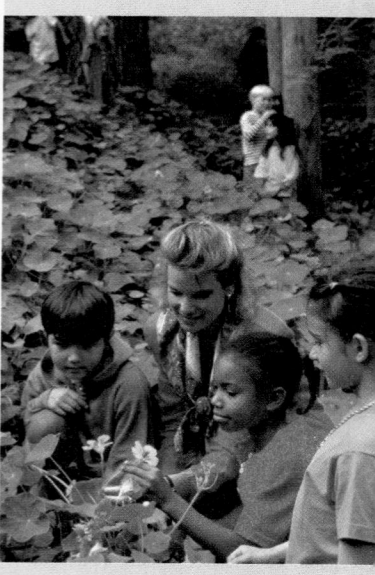

Meaning is not given to us but by us.

—Eleanor Duckworth
Contemporary American Educator

Chapter Outline	Learning Goals
Expert Knowledge and Pedagogical Content Knowledge	**(1)** Distinguish between expert knowledge and pedagogical content knowledge.
Reading A Developmental Model of Reading Language Rule Systems Approaches to Reading Cognitive Approaches Social Constructivist Approaches	**(2)** Explain how reading develops and discuss some useful approaches to teaching reading.
Writing Developmental Changes Cognitive Approaches Social Constructivist Approaches	**(3)** Describe how writing develops and some useful approaches to teaching writing.
Mathematics Developmental Changes Controversy in Math Education Cognitive Processes Some Constructivist Principles Technology and Math Instruction	**(4)** Characterize how mathematical thinking develops and identify some issues related to teaching mathematics.
Science Science Education Constructivist Teaching Strategies	**(5)** Identify some challenges and strategies related to teaching children how to think scientifically.
Social Studies What Is Social Studies? Constructivist Approaches	**(6)** Summarize how learning in social studies is becoming more constructivist.

364

TEACHING STORIES   Wendy Nelson Kauffman

Wendy Nelson Kauffman teaches social studies to tenth- and twelfth-grade students at Bloomfield, Connecticut, high school. Wendy turned to teaching after a career in journalism that left her feeling unfulfilled. Among the many activities she has students do to improve their thinking and writing skills are:

- Writing autobiographies each fall
- Keeping journals all year and writing position papers on historical questions
- Participating in dramatic role-playing
- Carrying out debates and holding "town meetings" to discuss contentious issues such as racial problems
- Interpreting political cartoons and songs
- Making posters

- Engaging in real-world learning experiences. These have included a visit to Ellis Island, after which students acted out immigrant experiences in a school-wide performance, and interviews with retirement home residents about the Great Depression and World War II for an oral history book

In Wendy's words, "Certain skills they have to learn: writing, critical thinking, class participation. If you mix that with something that's fun for them and plays to their strengths, I think it makes it easier for them to do the hard work in class." Wendy also mentors new teachers, about whom she says, "I want them to feel safe, I want them to take risks, I want them to become who they want to be" (Source: From "USA TODAY's 2003 All-USA Teacher Team," *USA TODAY*, October 16, 2003. Reprinted with permission).

Preview

In previous chapters, we described the basic principles of children's learning and cognition. In this chapter, we will apply these principles to learning and cognition in five content areas: reading, writing, mathematics, science, and social studies. We begin the chapter by revisiting the concept of expertise and exploring the distinction between expert knowledge and pedagogical content knowledge, the kind of knowledge that teachers like Wendy Nelson Kauffman use to teach effectively.

1   EXPERT KNOWLEDGE AND PEDAGOGICAL CONTENT KNOWLEDGE

In chapter 8, we discussed the distinction between experts and novices. We saw that sometimes individuals who are experts in the content of a particular area, such as mathematics or biology, aren't good at teaching it in ways that others can effectively learn. These individuals have *expert knowledge* but lack *pedagogical content knowledge*. Let's examine the difference between the two types of knowledge.

Expert knowledge, sometimes referred to as *subject matter knowledge*, means excellent knowledge about the content of a particular discipline. Clearly, expert

expert knowledge Also called *subject matter knowledge*; means excellent knowledge about the content of a particular discipline.

knowledge is important—how can teachers teach students something that they don't understand themselves (Grossman, Schoenfeld, & Lee, 2005)? However, some individuals with expert knowledge about a particular subject area, such as reading, math, or science, have difficulty understanding the subject matter in a way that allows them to teach it effectively to others. The term *expert blind spots* has been used to describe the gap between what an expert knows and what students know (Nathan & Petrosino, 2003). Too often experts (teachers) don't communicate all of the information and steps necessary for students (novices) to learn something (Bransford, Darling-Hammond, & LePage, 2005).

What teachers need in addition to expert knowledge is **pedagogical content knowledge**—knowledge about how to effectively teach a particular discipline (Schoenfeld, 2006). Both expert knowledge and pedagogical content knowledge are required for being an expert teacher. *Expert teachers* know the structure of their disciplines, and this knowledge gives them the ability to create cognitive road maps that guide the assignments they give to students, the assessments they use to evaluate students' progress, and the types of questions and answers they generate in class (National Research Council, 1999, 2005). Being an expert teacher in a particular discipline also involves being aware of which aspects of the discipline are especially difficult or easy for students to learn.

In previous chapters, we explored general teaching strategies that are effective across all disciplines. For example, a good teacher in any discipline asks questions that stimulate students' curiosity, encourages students to go beyond the surface of a topic and gain a depth of understanding about a topic, and pays attention to individual variations in students' learning. However, pedagogical content knowledge about particular disciplines goes beyond these general teaching strategies. We will examine five content areas—reading, writing, mathematics, science, and social studies—and point out effective teaching strategies in each one.

Review, Reflect, and Practice

(1) Distinguish between expert knowledge and pedagogical content knowledge.

REVIEW

- How is expert knowledge different from pedagogical content knowledge?

REFLECT

- Have you ever had a teacher who was clearly an expert in his or her discipline but not a good teacher? What pedagogical content knowledge was missing?

PRAXIS™ PRACTICE

1. Maria is frustrated with her calculus teacher, a former university math professor. He knows his math but has a difficult time communicating his knowledge to his students. In fact, half the time in class, Maria has no idea what he is talking about. When she asks for help, he is willing to meet with her, but his explanations are no clearer than they are in class. Which statement best characterizes Maria's calculus teacher?
   a. He has both expert knowledge in calculus and pedagogical content knowledge.
   b. He has expert knowledge in calculus but lacks pedagogical content knowledge.
   c. He lacks expert knowledge in calculus but has pedagogical content knowledge.
   d. He lacks both expert knowledge in calculus and pedagogical content knowledge.

Please see the answer key at the end of the book.

pedagogical content knowledge
Knowledge about how to effectively teach a particular discipline.

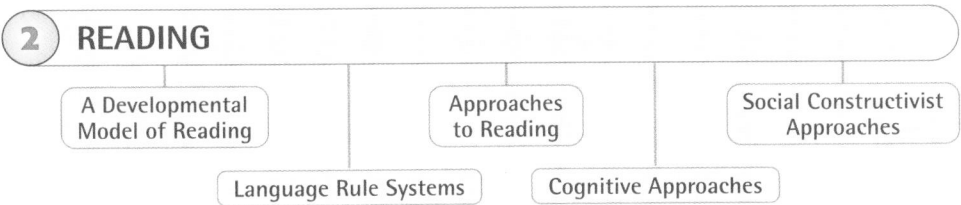

2 READING

A Developmental Model of Reading   Approaches to Reading   Social Constructivist Approaches

Language Rule Systems   Cognitive Approaches

Reading expert Steve Stahl (2002) argues that the three main goals of reading instruction should be to help children (1) automatically recognize words, (2) comprehend text, and (3) become motivated to read and appreciate reading. These goals are interrelated. If children cannot recognize words automatically, their comprehension suffers. If they cannot comprehend the text, they are unlikely to be motivated to read it.

A recent analysis by Rich Mayer (2004) focused on the cognitive processes a child needs to go through in order to read a printed word. In his view, the three processes are:

1. *Being aware of sound units in words,* which consists of "recognizing, producing, and manipulating phonemes"
2. *Decoding words,* which involves converting printed words into sounds
3. *Accessing word meaning,* which consists of "finding a mental representation of the word's meaning in one's memory"

How do children develop the reading skills that Stahl and Mayer describe? What is the best way to teach children to read? How can children construct their reading skills? These are among the main questions that we will examine in our coverage of reading.

A Developmental Model of Reading

In one view, reading skills develop in five stages (Chall, 1979). The age boundaries are approximate and do not apply to every child. For example, some children learn to read before they enter first grade. Nonetheless, Chall's stages convey a general sense of the developmental changes involved in learning to read:

- *Stage 0.* From birth to first grade, children master several prerequisites for reading. Many learn the left-to-right progression and order of reading, how to identify the letters of the alphabet, and how to write their names. Some learn to read words that commonly appear on signs. As a result of watching TV shows such as *Sesame Street* and attending preschool and kindergarten programs, many young children today develop greater knowledge about reading earlier than in the past.

What are some developmental changes in reading?

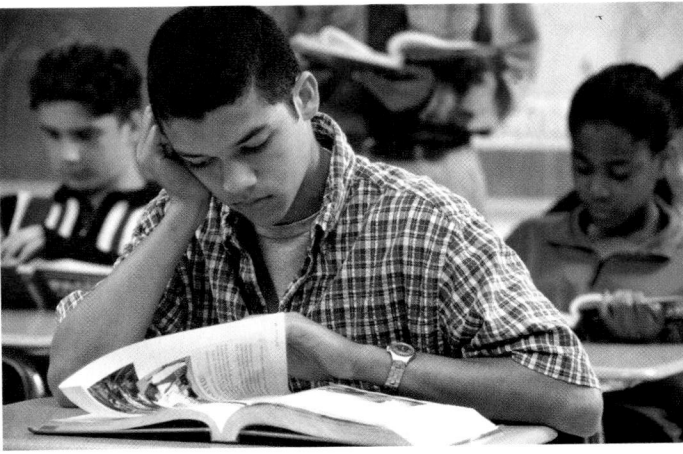

- *Stage 1.* In first and second grade, many children begin to read. They do so by learning to sound out words (that is, translate individual letters or groups of letters into sounds and blend sounds into words). During this stage, they also complete their learning of letter names and sounds.
- *Stage 2.* In second and third grade, children become more fluent at retrieving individual words and other reading skills. However, at this stage, reading is still not used much for learning. The mechanical demands of learning to read are so taxing at this point that children have few resources left over to process the content.
- *Stage 3.* In fourth through eighth grade, children become increasingly able to obtain new information from print. The change from stage 2 to stage 3 involves a shift from "learning to read" to "reading to learn." In stage 3, children still have difficulty understanding information presented from multiple perspectives within the same story. For children who haven't yet learned to read, a downward spiral begins that leads to serious difficulties in many academic subjects.
- *Stage 4.* In the high school years, many students become fully competent readers. They develop the ability to understand material written from many different perspectives. This allows them to engage in sometimes more sophisticated discussions of literature, history, economics, and politics. It is no accident that great novels are not presented to students until high school, because understanding the novels requires advanced reading.

Keep in mind that the age boundaries in Chall's model are approximate and do not apply to every child. However, the stages convey a sense of the developmental changes involved in becoming a competent reader.

Language Rule Systems

As the previous discussion has implied, *reading* is the ability to understand written discourse. Children cannot be said to read if all they can do is respond to flash cards, as in some early child-training programs. Good readers have mastered the basic language rules of phonology, morphology, syntax, and semantics that we discussed in chapter 2, "Cognitive and Language Development."

Phonology *Phonology* is the sound system of a language, including the sounds that are used and how they may be combined. Phonology plays a critical role in the early development of reading skills (Berninger, 2006; Snow & Kang, 2006). Recall Mayer's (2004) conclusion that a child is unlikely to be able to read a printed word if he or she does not become aware of the sound units in words. Providing direct instruction in phonemic awareness improves reading achievement (Ehri & others, 2001). If students don't develop good phonological skills in the first several years of elementary school, they are unlikely to develop automaticity in decoding words, which means they will have to spend more time in decoding, leaving less time for reading comprehension (Stanovich, 1994). A likely outcome of poor phonological skills is a weak vocabulary, which, as we will discuss shortly, is linked to deficiencies in reading comprehension. According to Mayer (2004), as little as 5 to 18 hours of direct instruction in phonological awareness can help put students on the path to becoming proficient readers.

Morphology *Morphology* refers to the units of meaning involved in word formation. Every word in the English language is made up of one or more morphemes. A *morpheme* is a minimal unit of meaning, such as the *-ed* that turns *help* into *helped.* "Morphology is what turns a relatively simple word like *heal* into *health*" (Rutter, 2005, p. 6). Morphology begins to become important in reading around the third and fourth grades when students increasingly encounter words that contain multiple syllables. Readers who are not proficient at morphology often have difficulty recognizing suffixes such as *-tion* and pronouncing words with these suffixes (Rutter, 2005). Many students from the mid-elementary school grades through college who are problem readers do not have good morphological awareness (Berninger, 2006; Mann, 1998; Nagy & others, 2003).

Syntax   *Syntax* involves the way words are combined to form acceptable sentences. Syntax especially focuses on grammar skills. Good grammatical skills play an important role in reading comprehension. A child who has poor grammatical skills for speech and listening and does not understand what is meant by "The car was pushed by a truck" when it is spoken, will not understand its meaning in print either. Likewise, a child who cannot determine what pronouns refer to (as in "John went to the store with his dog. It was closed.") will not do well in reading comprehension.

Semantics   *Semantics* refers to the meaning of words and sentences. Good semantic skills are involved in becoming a proficient reader (McWhorter, 2006; Rubin, 2006). An important aspect of semantics is vocabulary. Recall that in Mayer's definition of reading (2004), accessing word meaning, which involves "finding a mental representation of a word in one's memory," is a key cognitive process in reading. Having a good vocabulary helps readers access word meaning effortlessly, and researchers have found that vocabulary development is an important aspect of reading (Berninger, 2006; Snow & Kang, 2006). For example, a recent study found that a good vocabulary was linked to reading comprehension in second-grade students (Berninger & Abbott, 2005). Other research studies have also found that vocabulary plays an important role in reading comprehension (Paris & Paris, 2006; Snow & Kang, 2006).

Two main ways to increase children's vocabulary involve direct instruction and immersion (Mayer, 2004). Direct instruction involves teaching students the definitions of words. Immersion consists of students engaging in activities such as reading, listening, and producing prose. Some experts on reading argue that students learn most of their vocabulary words through immersion (Nagy & Scott, 2000).

Approaches to Reading

What are some approaches to teaching children how to read? Education and language experts continue to debate how children should be taught to read (May, 2006; Ruddell, 2006; Vacca & others, 2006). Currently, debate focuses on the basic-skills-and-phonics approach versus the whole-language approach.

The **phonics approach** emphasizes that reading instruction should focus on phonics and basic rules for translating written symbols into sounds (Cunningham, 2005; Lane & Pullen, 2004). Early reading instruction should involve simplified materials. Only after they have learned the correspondence rules that relate spoken phonemes to the alphabet letters that represent them should children be given complex reading materials, such as books and poems.

By contrast, the **whole-language approach** stresses that reading instruction should parallel children's natural language learning. Reading materials should be whole and meaningful. That is, children should be given material in its complete form, such as stories and poems, so that they learn to understand language's communicative function. Reading should be connected with listening and writing skills. Although there are variations in whole-language programs, most share the premise that reading should be integrated with other skills and subjects, such as science and social studies, and that it should focus on real-world material. Thus, a class might read newspapers, magazines, or books, and then write about and discuss them. In some whole-language classes, beginning readers are taught to recognize whole words or even entire sentences, and to use the context of what they are reading to guess at unfamiliar words.

Which approach is better? Children can benefit from both approaches, but instruction in phonics needs to be emphasized especially in kindergarten and the first grade (Alvermann, Fitzgerald, & Simpson, 2006; Mayer, 2004; Temple & others, 2005; Tierney & Readence, 2005).

As Mayer (2004) and an increasing number of experts in the field of reading now conclude, direct instruction in phonological training is a key aspect of learning to read. Effective training for phonological awareness includes two main techniques:

- *Blending,* which involves listening to a series of separate spoken sounds and blending them, such as /g/ /o/ = go

phonics approach An approach that emphasizes that reading instruction should teach phonics and its basic rules for translating written symbols into sounds.

whole-language approach An approach that stresses that reading instruction should parallel children's natural language learning. Reading materials should be whole and meaningful.

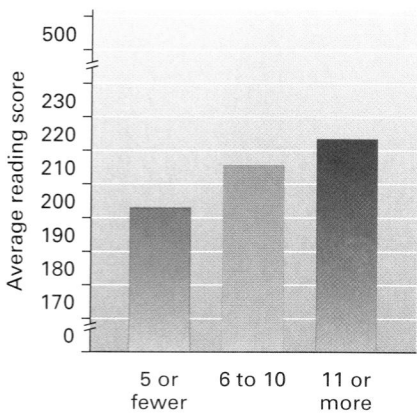

FIGURE 11.1 The Relation of Reading Achievement to Number of Pages Read Daily

In the recent analysis of reading in the fourth grade in the National Assessment of Educational Progress (2000), reading more pages daily in school and as part of homework assignments was related to higher scores on a reading test in which scores ranged from 0 to 500.

• *Segmentation,* which consists of tapping out or counting out the sounds in a word, such as /g/ /o/ = go, which is two sounds

In addition, researchers have found that the best training for phonological awareness has three characteristics: the phonological training is integrated with reading and writing, is simple, and it is conducted in small groups rather than with a whole class (Stahl, 2002).

Conclusions reached by the National Reading Panel (2000) suggest that children benefit from *guided oral* reading—that is, from reading aloud with guidance and feedback. Learning strategies for reading comprehension—such as monitoring one's own reading progress and summarizing—also helps children (Pressley, 2003; Pressley & Harris, 2006; Pressley & Hilden, 2006).

In a recent study, Michael Pressley and his colleagues (2001) examined literacy instruction in five U.S. classrooms. Based on academic and classroom literacy performance of students, the effectiveness of classrooms was analyzed. In the most effective classrooms, teachers exhibited excellent classroom management based on positive reinforcement and cooperation; balanced teaching of skills, literature, and writing; scaffolding and matching of task demands to students' skill level; encouragement of student self-regulation; and strong connections across subject areas. In general, the extensive observations did not support any particular reading approach (such as whole-language or phonics); rather, excellent instruction involved multiple, well-integrated components. An important point in this study is that effective reading instruction involves more than a specific reading approach—it also includes effective classroom management, encouragement of self-regulation, and other components.

Reading, like other important skills, takes time and effort (Graves, Juel, & Graves, 2004). In a national assessment, children in the fourth grade had higher scores on a national reading test when they read 11 or more pages daily for school and homework (National Assessment of Educational Progress, 2000) (see figure 11.1). Teachers who required students to read a great deal on a daily basis had students who were more proficient at reading than teachers who required little reading by their students.

Cognitive Approaches

Cognitive approaches to reading emphasize decoding and comprehending words, constructing meaning, and developing expert reader strategies.

Decoding and Comprehending Words At the beginning of our discussion of reading, we described Mayer's (2004) view that decoding words is a key cognitive process in learning to read. The cognitive approach emphasizes the cognitive processes involved in decoding and comprehending words. Important in this regard are certain metacognitive skills and a general automaticity of information processing.

Metacognition is involved in reading in the sense that good readers develop control of their own reading skills and understand how reading works. For example, good readers know that it is important to comprehend the "gist" of what an author is saying.

Teachers can help students develop good metacognitive strategies for reading by getting them to monitor their own reading, especially when they run into difficulties in their reading. Here are some metacognitive strategies that teachers can help students use to improve their reading (Miholic, 1994; Pressley & Afflerbach, 1995; Pressley & Harris, 2006; Pressley & Hilden, 2006; Singhal, 2001):

• Overview text before reading.
• Look for important information while reading and pay more attention to it than other information; ask yourself questions about the important ideas or relate them to something you already know.

- Attempt to determine the meaning of words not recognized (use the words around a word to figure out its meaning, use a dictionary, or temporarily ignore it and wait for further clarification).
- Monitor text comprehension.
- Understand relationships between parts of text.
- Recognize when you might need to go back and reread a passage (you didn't understand it, to clarify an important idea, it seemed important to remember, or to underline or summarize for study).
- Adjust pace of reading depending on the difficulty of the material.

With regard to automaticity of processing, when word recognition occurs rapidly, meaning also often follows in a rapid fashion (Stanovich, 1994). Many beginning or poor readers do not recognize words automatically. Their processing capacity is consumed by the demands of word recognition, so they have less capacity to devote to comprehension of groupings of words as phrases or sentences.

One factor that limits children's reading comprehension is the amount of information that they can hold in working memory at any one time (Bjorklund, 2005). It is important to retain information in working memory as long as possible so that each newly read word in a passage can be interpreted with the words and concepts that just preceded it. Children who are competent at reading have a larger working memory capacity than children with problems in reading. In one study, 7- to 13-year-old children who either were normal readers or had reading problems were given a series of incomplete sentences such as the following and were asked to supply the final word for each (Siegel & Ryan, 1989): "In the summer it is very _____." "With dinner, we sometimes eat bread and _____." After completing the series, the children were asked to repeat the final word that they had generated for each sentence. As shown in figure 11.2, as children got older, working memory capacity improved for both the normal and problem readers, but the problem readers had lower working memory capacity (shorter memory spans) than the normal readers at each age level.

The cognitive approach also contributed to the discovery that phonemic awareness is present in children who learn to read and absent in those who do not (Hiebert & Raphael, 1996). As we noted earlier, *phonemic awareness* refers to the ability to analyze words into phonemes (basic speech sounds). What makes phonics (the matching of sounds with printed letters and letter groups) work is the cognitive process of phonemic awareness, the ability to manipulate and think about sounds.

Constructing Meaning In the cognitive approach, text has meaning that a reader must construct, not simply decode. Readers actively construct this meaning by using their background knowledge and knowledge of words and how they are linked (Antonaci & O'Callaghan, 2006; Heilman, Blair, & Rupley, 2002). For example, in one study, second-grade students were asked questions about their knowledge of spiders before they read about them (Pearson, Hansen, & Gordon, 1979). The students with more background knowledge about spiders understood the passage about spiders better than the other students did.

Developing Expert Reading Strategies In the cognitive approach, researchers have searched for the underlying cognitive processes that explain reading. This search has led to an interest in strategies, especially the strategies of expert readers compared with those of novice readers (Pressley & Hilden, 2006). Researchers advise teachers to guide students in developing good reading strategies.

Michael Pressley and his colleagues (1992) developed the **transactional strategy instruction approach,** a cognitive approach to reading that emphasizes

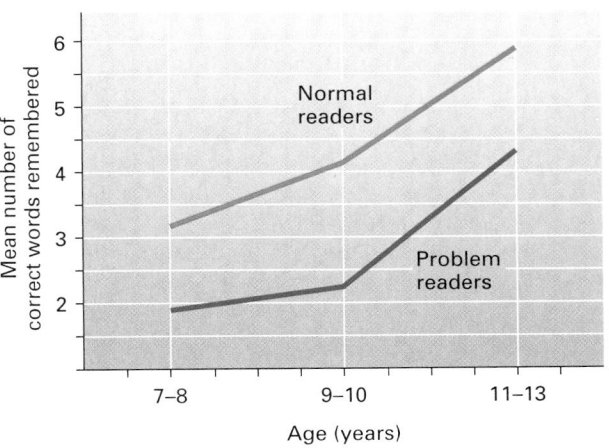

FIGURE 11.2 Working Memory Capacity in Normal and Problem Readers

As both normal readers and problem readers increased in age, their working memory capacity improved (Siegel & Ryan, 1989). However, problem readers had a lower working memory capacity than normal readers at each age level.

transactional strategy instruction approach A cognitive approach to reading that emphasizes instruction in strategies, especially metacognitive strategies.

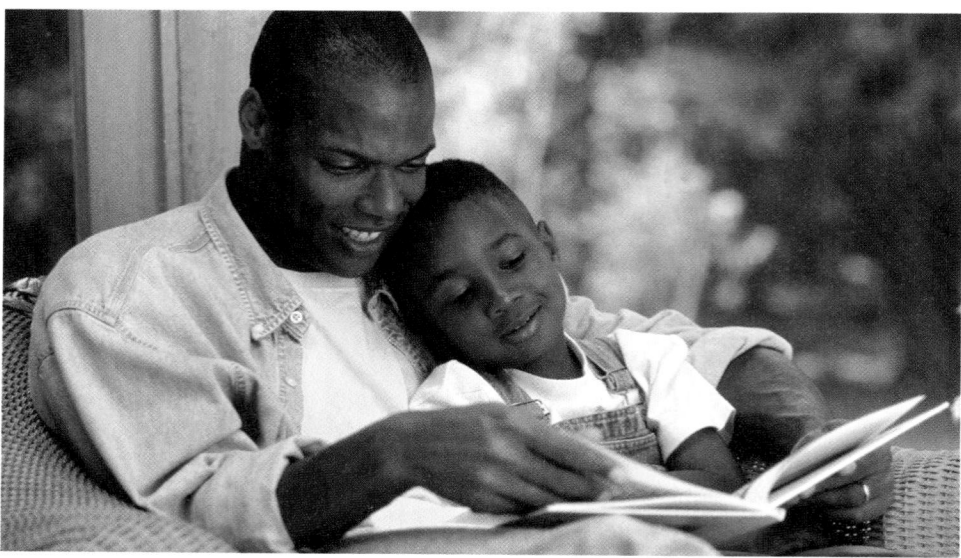

What are some important aspects of social contexts that influence children's reading?

instruction in strategies (especially metacognitive strategies). In their view, strategies control students' abilities to remember what they read. It is especially important to teach students metacognitive strategies to monitor their reading progress. Summarizing is also thought to be an important reading strategy. In the strategy approach, authors of teachers' manuals for subjects other than reading per se are encouraged to include information about the importance of reading strategies, how and when to use particular strategies, and prompts to remind students about using strategies.

Social Constructivist Approaches

The social constructivist approaches bring the social aspects of reading to the forefront (Hiebert & Raphael, 1996; Slavin & Madden, 2001). The contribution of the social context in helping children learn to read includes such factors as how much emphasis the culture places on reading, the extent to which parents have exposed their children to books before they enter formal schooling, the teacher's communication skills, the extent to which teachers give students opportunities to discuss what they have read, and the district-mandated reading curriculum. Whereas cognitive constructivists emphasize the student's construction of meaning, social constructivists stress that meaning is *socially negotiated*. In other words, meaning involves not only the reader's contribution but also the social context and the purpose for reading. Social constructivist approaches emphasize the importance of giving students opportunities for engaging in meaningful dialogue about their reading. One way of doing this is through reciprocal teaching.

Reciprocal Teaching   In our discussion of the Fostering a Community of Learners program in chapter 10, we described **reciprocal teaching** in terms of students taking turns leading a small-group discussion. Reciprocal teaching also can involve a teacher and a student.

In reciprocal teaching, teachers initially explain the strategies and model how to use them to make sense of the text. Then they ask students to demonstrate the strategies, giving them support as they learn them. As in scaffolding, the teacher gradually assumes a less active role, letting the student assume more initiative. For example, Annemarie Palincsar and Ann Brown (1984) used reciprocal teaching to improve students' abilities to enact certain strategies to improve their reading

reciprocal teaching A learning arrangement in which students take turns leading a small-group discussion.

comprehension. In this teacher-scaffolded instruction, teachers worked with students to help them generate questions about the text they had read, clarify what they did not understand, summarize the text, and make predictions.

Research on reciprocal teaching suggests that it is a very effective strategy for improving reading comprehension (Webb & Palincsar, 1996). One study compared four groups of junior high school students with reading problems (Palincsar & Brown, 1984):

1. *Reciprocal teaching group.* Students took turns with the teacher in using four reading comprehension strategies: generating a question about the text, summarizing the text, clarifying any comprehension problems, and making predictions about subsequent text.
2. *Modeling group.* Students observed the teacher as she used each of the four strategies.
3. *Explicit instruction group.* Students listened to the teacher's description of the four strategies and completed paper-and-pencil activities.
4. *Control group.* Students were given no information about the four strategies. As shown in figure 11.3, the reciprocal teaching group had the best gains in reading comprehension.

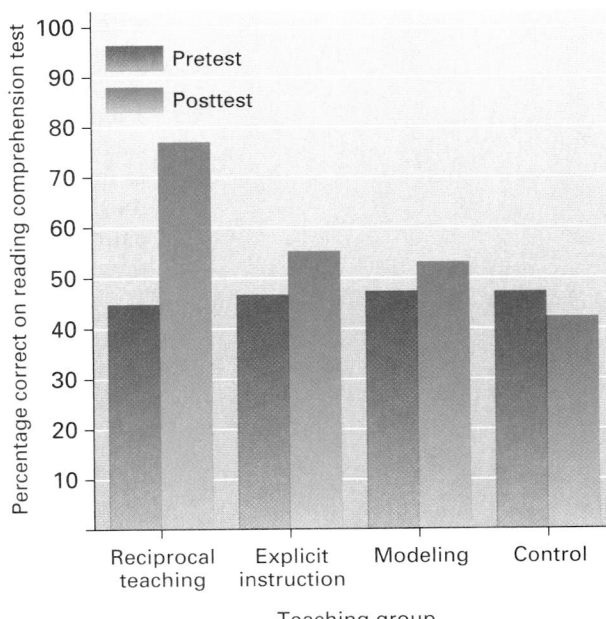

FIGURE 11.3 Reciprocal Teaching and Reading Comprehension

All groups started with approximately 40 percent to 50 percent correct on a reading comprehension pretest. The students were randomly assigned to one of four groups: reciprocal teaching, modeling, explicit teaching, or control. After experiencing these strategies in the classroom, the reciprocal teaching group showed the greatest gains in reading comprehension (posttest).

Book Clubs **Book clubs** involve peer learning and consist of student-led discussions of literature (McMahon, 1994; McMahon, Raphael, & Goatley, 1995). Teachers serve as guides but give students considerable responsibility for leading discussions. Conducted in this manner, book clubs often involve a range of discussions, as children make connections to their own lives, clarify points of confusion in the texts, draw inferences to fill in gaps left by the text, and critique the quality of the texts.

Book clubs reflect the social constructivist principle that meaning is socially negotiated. And book clubs can help fill a void that exists in many classrooms: an absence of talk about text.

School/Family/Community Connections From the social constructivist perspective, schools are not the only sociocultural context that is important in reading. Families and communities are also important (Harris, Kamhi, & Pollock, 2001).

Of special concern are the language experiences of students from low-income families (Garcia & Willis, 2001; Schmidt, 2001). In chapter 5, "Sociocultural Diversity," we discussed research findings that, on average, young children in welfare homes heard about 600 words an hour, whereas young children in professional families heard about 2,100 words an hour (Hart & Risley, 1995). These researchers also found that, on average, children in welfare homes received only half as much language experience in their early years as children in middle-income families. They also revealed that children in high-income families had twice as much language experience as even children in middle-income families. At-risk students who do not read outside of school fall further behind as they go through the elementary school years (Rowe, 1994). Most students who are avid readers report that they have at least one other person to talk with about their reading and about what to read next (Fielding, Wilson, & Anderson, 1986). Many parents of at-risk students have their own reading difficulties, as well as problems in obtaining books (Gunning, 2000).

In one strategy to combat these problems, parents with weak English literacy skills are given literacy training and are guided to introduce books as they interact

book clubs Student-led groups for the discussion of literature. Book clubs are a form of peer learning.

with their children (Edwards, 1989). For instance, in Project Family Literacy in Chicago's Latino community, parents attend twice-weekly English-as-a-second-language (ESL) classes, participate in Parents as Teacher classes twice a month, and attend a summer institute (Shanahan & Rodriguez-Brown, 1993). In the ESL classes, activities include parents making books for their children or sharing books in English. From the larger group, several parent leaders are selected. Twice monthly they hold family literacy seminars at neighborhood schools. The parents' participation in the program over a 3-year period was linked with improved literacy in their children.

Review, Reflect, and Practice

② **Explain how reading develops and discuss some useful approaches to teaching reading.**

REVIEW

- What happens at each stage in Chall's developmental model of reading?
- How are language rule systems involved in reading?
- What are some differences between the whole-language approach and the basic-skills-and-phonics approach to teaching reading? Why is balance needed?
- What are the key ideas in cognitive approaches to reading?
- What are the important features of social constructivist approaches to reading?

REFLECT

- What would be some of the key considerations in a balanced view of teaching reading?

PRAXIS™ PRACTICE

1. Kareem is reading his science text. He is taking notes as he reads to help him remember the information. He has learned much about science from his text this year. For instance, he learned that there are many different kinds of rocks that vary in how they were formed, their hardness, and their color. However, when presented with conflicting views on a scientific matter, Kareem is easily confused. Which of Chall's (1979) developmental stages of reading best characterizes Kareem?
   a. stage 1
   b. stage 2
   c. stage 3
   d. stage 4

2. Which of the following is the best example of a student struggling with phonemic awareness?
   a. Keeshan, who often misorders the words in a sentence
   b. Katrina, who does not recognize that *television* is made up of two units of meaning: *tele,* meaning across, and *vision*
   c. Sam, who struggles to sound out words he doesn't recognize immediately
   d. Tasha, who has a limited vocabulary

3. Which of the following is the best example of the use of the whole-language approach to teaching reading?
   a. Ms. Tillman uses flash cards to help her students develop their sight vocabulary.
   b. Ms. Muhammad's students are immersed in literature. They read various types of literature and write about what they have read.

c. Ms. Orton uses a phonics workbook to help her students develop their decoding skills.

d. Ms. Wade's students use a computer game to practice their reading skills. A character says a word, and the student clicks on the correct printed word.

4. Which of the following is the best example of a teacher using a cognitive approach to teaching reading?

a. Ms. Beckham uses flashcards to help students learn new words and reinforces them with candy for correct responses.

b. Ms. Gomes has her students choose from a variety of books to read. Those students who read a particular book then meet to discuss the book on a regular basis.

c. Ms. Owen emphasizes the importance of using context clues to help determine the meaning of new words.

d. Ms. Ronaldo has her students write each word they miss on a spelling pretest five times to help them remember the word.

5. Which of the following is the best example of a teacher using a social constructivist approach to teaching reading?

a. Ms. Beckham uses flashcards to help students learn new words and reinforces them with candy for correct responses.

b. Ms. Gomes has her students choose from a variety of books to read. Those students who read a particular book then meet to discuss the book on a regular basis.

c. Ms. Owen emphasizes the importance of using context clues to help determine the meaning of new words.

d. Ms. Ronaldo has her students write each word they miss on a spelling pretest five times to help them remember the word.

Please see the answer key at the end of the book.

Next, we turn our attention to writing. In the whole-language approach, writing and reading instruction are often integrated (Ruddell, 2006). Innovations in technology are becoming available that help teachers not only to implement a whole-language approach but also to improve students' decoding skills (Solley, 2000).

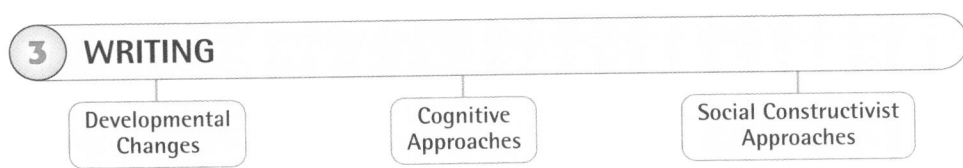

3 WRITING

Developmental Changes | Cognitive Approaches | Social Constructivist Approaches

How do writing skills develop? What are cognitive and social constructivist approaches to writing?

Developmental Changes

Children's writing emerges out of their early scribbles, which appear at around 2 to 3 years of age. In early childhood, children's motor skills usually become well enough developed for them to begin printing letters and their name. In the United States, most 4-year-olds can print their first name. Five-year-olds can reproduce letters and copy several short words. As they develop their printing skills, children

THROUGH THE EYES OF STUDENTS

The Devl and the Babe Goste

Anna Mudd is the 6-year-old author of "The Devl and the Babe Goste." Anna has been writing stories for at least 2 years. Her story includes poetic images, sophisticated syntax, and vocabulary that reflect advances in language development. (Source: From Jean Berko Gleason, The Development of Language, 3/e. Published by Allyn and Bacon, Boston, MA. Copyright © 1993 by Pearson Education. Reprinted by permission of the publisher.)

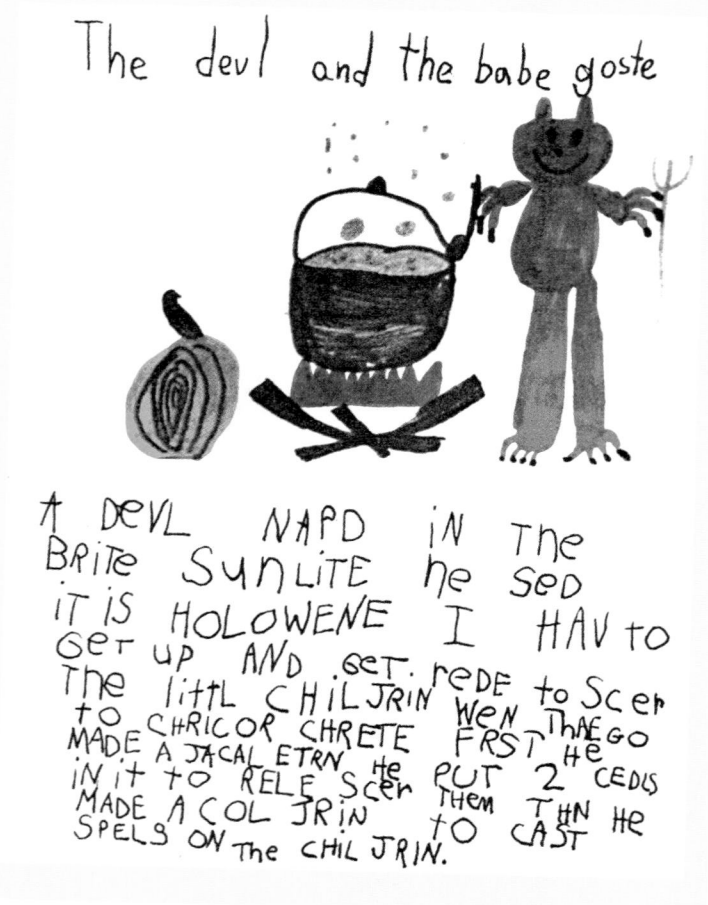

gradually learn to distinguish between the distinctive characteristics of letters, such as whether the lines are curved or straight, open or closed, and so on. Through the early elementary grades, many children still continue to reverse letters such as *b* and *d* and *p* and *q* (Temple & others, 1993). At this point in development, if other aspects of the child's development are normal, these letter reversals are not a predictor of literacy problems.

As they begin to write, children often invent spellings of words (Soderman, Gregory, & O'Neil, 2005). They usually do this by relying on the sounds of words they hear as clues for how to spell. Teachers and parents should encourage children's early writing without being overly concerned about the proper formation of letters or correct conventional spelling. I (your author) once had a conference with my youngest daughter's first-grade teacher after Jennifer brought home a series of papers that the teacher had returned. Jennifer's printing was still a little rough, and the pages were covered with the teacher's corrections and drawings of sad faces. Diplomatically but firmly, I explained to the teacher why I thought this was counterproductive. Fortunately, the teacher agreed to curb her criticism of Jennifer's printing skills. Such printing errors should be viewed as a natural part of the young child's growth, not scrutinized and criticized. Spelling and printing corrections can be made in positive ways and judiciously enough to avoid dampening early enjoyment and spontaneity in writing (Hughey & Slack, 2001; Morrow, 2005).

Like becoming a good reader, becoming a good writer takes many years and lots of practice (Blasingame & Bushman, 2006; Bruning & Horn, 2001; Spandel, 2005). Children should be given many writing opportunities in the elementary and secondary school years (Gunning, 2006). As their language and cognitive skills improve with good instruction, so will their writing skills. For example, developing a more sophisticated understanding of syntax and grammar serves as an underpinning for better writing.

So do such cognitive skills as organization and logical reasoning. Through elementary, middle, and high school, students develop increasingly sophisticated methods of organizing their ideas. In early elementary school, they narrate and describe or write short poems. In late elementary and middle school, they move to projects such as book reports that combine narration with more reflection and analysis. In high school, they become more skilled at forms of exposition that do not depend on narrative structure.

Cognitive Approaches

Cognitive approaches to writing emphasize many of the same themes that we discussed with regard to reading, such as constructing meaning and developing strategies (Pressley & Harris, 2006; Kellogg, 2000; D. Olson, 2001). Planning, problem solving, revising, and metacognitive strategies are thought to be especially important in improving students' writing.

Planning   Planning, which includes outlining and organizing content information, is an important aspect of writing (Graham, 2006; Levy & Randsell, 1996; Mayer, 2004). Teachers should show students how to outline and organize a paper and give feedback about their efforts. One study examined how prewriting activities can affect the quality of students' writing (Kellogg, 1994). As indicated in figure 11.4, outlining was the prewriting activity that helped writers the most. Figure 11.5 provides a model for helping students plan their compositions to meet a deadline.

Problem Solving   Much of the instruction in writing in schools involves teaching students how to write sentences and paragraphs properly. However, there is more to writing than avoiding run-on sentences or making sure that paragraphs support topic sentences (Mayer, 1999, 2004). More fundamentally, writing is a broader sort of problem solving (Mayer & Wittrock, 2006). One psychologist called the problem-solving process in writing "the making of meaning" (Kellogg, 1994).

As problem solvers, writers need to establish goals and work to attain them. It also is helpful to think of writers as constrained by their need for integrated understanding of the subject, knowledge of how the language system works, and the writing problem itself. The writing problem includes the purpose of the paper, the audience, and the role of the writer in the paper to be produced (Flower & Hayes, 1981). A student who is having a problem may be having difficulty with any one of these aspects of writing. Identifying the specific difficulty is the first step in helping the student become a better writer.

Revising   Revising is a major component of successful writing (Mayer, 1999, 2004). Revising involves writing multiple drafts, getting feedback from individuals who are knowledgeable about writing, and learning how to use the critical feedback to improve the writing. It also includes detecting and correcting errors. Researchers have found that older and more-skilled writers are more likely to revise their writing than younger and less-skilled writers (Bartlett, 1982; Hayes & Flower, 1986).

Metacognition   When we emphasize knowledge of writing strategies, we move into the area of metacognition, which we discussed in chapter 8. In one study, students 10 to 14 years of age were asked to write a paper that would be of interest to students in their own age range (Scardamalia, 1981). In carrying out this project, the students were hampered by not planning, not recording ideas in notes for later use, and not monitoring their writing progress by rereading and rewriting. The results are indicative of the fact that many middle school students do not have good knowledge of the planning and organizational strategies required by good writing and need to be taught these skills.

Monitoring one's writing progress is especially important in becoming a good writer (Graham, 2006; Graham & Harris, 2001; Pressley & Harris, 2006). This includes being receptive to feedback and applying what one learns in writing one paper to making the next paper better.

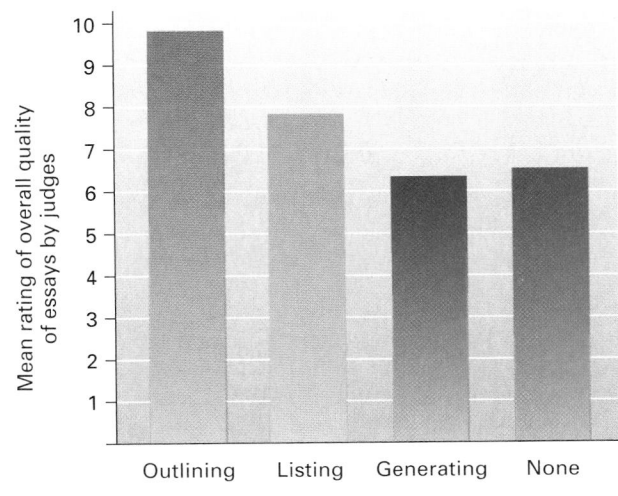

FIGURE 11.4 The Relation of Prewriting Activities to Essay Quality

One study randomly assigned college students to one of four prewriting activity groups: (1) An outlining group produced an outline containing relevant ideas within an hierarchical structure; (2) a listing group generated a list of relevant ideas; (3) a generating group wrote down as many ideas as possible without evaluating or organizing them; and (4) a control group had no prewriting activity. Judges rated the quality of each essay on a 10-point scale from 1 (lowest quality) to 10 (highest quality) (Kellogg, 1994). Organization was the prewriting activity that was most positively related to judges' ratings. When students create an outline, they often use listing and generating strategies as part of the outlining process. Thus, an excellent teaching strategy is to require students to create an outline as a required prewriting activity.

One to two months before the deadline	Select topic. Map ideas. Develop writing plan. Begin to develop a thesis statement. Start research.
Two weeks before the deadline	Develop individual sections of paper. Revise with vigor. Complete research. Finalize thesis statement.
The week before the deadline	Polish the individual sections of the paper. Create an interesting title. Check references for accuracy. Get some feedback.
The night before the deadline	Combine the parts of the paper. Print the final draft. Proofread the paper. Assemble the paper.

FIGURE 11.5 A Sample Timetable for a Writing Deadline

Source: From *Your Guide to College Success: Strategies for Achieving Your Goals*, Media Edition, 2nd edition by Santrock/Halonen. © 2002. Reprinted with permission of Wadsworth, a division of Thomson Learning: www.thomsonrights.com. Fax 800 730-2215.

THROUGH THE EYES OF STUDENTS

Writing Self-Evaluations

San Francisco fifth-grade teacher Keren Abra periodically asks her students to evaluate their writing for their writing portfolios. Here are several of her students' comments toward the end of the school year.

> I am in fifth grade right now and I love writing. Anytime that I get to write I will; as far as I can remember I have loved writing. I feel that my writing has developed since fourth grade and I am pleased with my writing. Some authors might not like their writing unlike me; I have *never* thrown away any of my writing. I love to share my writing and give and get ideas from other writers. . . . If I could describe myself as a writer I would say (not to brag) that I was a descriptive, imaginative, captivating writer.
>
> Michelle

> I think writing a story is easy because there is so much to write about and if I have to write about a certain thing there are also more things to do with the story. . . . If someone read my writing they would think I probably am a happy and energetic kid. They will think this because most of my stories are upbeat.
>
> Sarah

> I feel that when I'm writing I could do better. I could do better especially on spelling. When I was in kindergarten we did not do a lot of writing. When I was in third grade I did not like writing. It was scary learning new things about writing. I'm in fifth grade and I love to write but sometimes it annoys me that I can't spell that well. One thing I like about my writing is the way I put action into all of my work because I love to get excited! I think that if someone were to read my writing uncorrected they would not be able to read it. If it was corrected I think the person would really like my story.
>
> Janet

Social Constructivist Approaches

As in reading, social constructivist approaches emphasize that writing is best understood as being culturally embedded and socially constructed rather than being internally generated (Dauite, 2001; Schultz & Fecho, 2001).

The Social Context of Writing   The social constructivist perspective focuses on the social context in which writing is produced. Students need to participate in a writing community to understand author/reader relationships and learn to recognize how their perspective might differ from that of others (Hiebert & Raphael, 1996).

To see the importance of social context in writing, consider two students. One, Anthony, is a 9-year-old Latino student who has lived in the Manhattan area of New York City his entire life (McCarthey, 1994). He reads and writes extensively, keeps scientific journals, and participated in classrooms with a strong emphasis on writing in his earlier school years. He is enthusiastic about his writing topic, a tribute to his grandmother who has recently died. His teacher encourages Anthony to write about her death, discussing various writing possibilities on this topic with him during their student-teacher writing conference. She and Anthony talk about the best ways to structure and organize the paper. His final writing product is a moving account of his grandmother's life and death. Anthony's teacher believes that writing plays an important role in education, and she communicates this enthusiastically to her students.

Contrast Anthony's writing experience with that of another Latino student, Carlos, whose parents recently immigrated to the Bronx area of New York City. Although his English is good, Carlos has had few classroom experiences in which he has practiced writing about his personal experiences, and he has never done any writing on his own outside the classroom. He feels very uncomfortable when the teacher asks him to write about personal experiences. In the student-teacher writing conference, Carlos is reluctant to discuss his feelings. Carlos' teacher has been mandated by the district to include writing experiences in different subjects. She is not enthusiastic about this and spends little time working with Carlos to improve his writing.

As evidenced by Anthony's and Carlos' situations, the social context plays an important role in writing. Some students bring a rich background of writing experiences and encouragement to write to the classroom; others have little writing experience and have not been encouraged to write extensively. In some classrooms the teacher places a high value on writing; in others the teacher treats writing as being less important.

Meaningful Writing and Student-Teacher Writing Conferences   According to the social constructivist approach, students' writing should include opportunities to create "real" texts, in the sense of writing about personally meaningful situations. For example, Anthony, whose teacher frequently asks students to write about personal experiences, wrote about his grandmother's life and death, and his teacher gave him considerable support for writing about this emotional experience. Student-teacher writing conferences play an important support role in helping students become better writers.

Peer Collaboration   While working in groups, writers experience the processes of inquiry, clarification, and elaboration that are important in good writing (Webb & Palincsar, 1996). Students often bring diverse experiences to bear when they collaborate and coauthor papers. Such rich, shared collaboration can produce new insights into what to write about and how (Graham, 2006).

By contrast, writing simply to meet the teacher's expectations often produces constrained, imitative, and conforming results. In peer writing groups, teacher expectations are often less apparent (Kearney, 1991).

School/Family/Peer Connections   In one project, teachers were encouraged to recognize the existence and richness of the surrounding Latino community and then integrate this into school contexts (Moll, Tapia, & Whitmore, 1993). This included (1) an analysis of how knowledge is transmitted within households in the Latino community; (2) an after-school laboratory in which teachers and students used reading and writing more in line with the way it is used in the students' neighborhoods than the way it is used in their school; and (3) classroom connections that integrated activities from the after-school laboratory. The goal was to integrate these three components. For example, students documented uses and ways of writing in their community, such as letters to relatives in other countries and entries into account books. Then, working with their peers, students created projects on topics that reflected the expertise of members of their communities, such as knowledge about mechanics and repair work. To obtain information for their project, students interviewed members of their communities. The students also communicated through e-mail with students who lived in Latino communities in other parts of the United States.

Involve the writing community in your class. Look around your community and think about expert writers you could invite to your classroom to discuss their work. Most communities have such experts, such as journalists and other authors and editors. One of the four most successful middle schools in the United States identified by Joan Lipsitz (1984) built a special Author's Week into its curriculum. Based on students' interest, availability, and diversity, authors are invited to discuss their craft with students. Students sign up to meet individual authors. Before they meet the author, they are required to read at least one of the author's books. Students prepare questions for their author sessions. In some cases, authors come to the class for several days to work with students on their writing projects.

In the course of our discussion of reading and writing, we have described a number of ideas that can be used in the classroom. To evaluate your reading and writing experiences, complete Self-Assessment 11.1.

PEANUTS © United Features Syndicate, Inc.

SELF-ASSESSMENT 11.1

Evaluating My Reading and Writing Experiences

Regardless of the academic subject or grade you teach, one of your goals should be to help students not only become competent at reading and writing but also enjoy these activities. Think about your own past and current experiences in reading and writing:

1. What made learning to read enjoyable for you?

_____

_____

2. What made learning to read difficult or unenjoyable?

_____

_____

3. How do you feel about reading now?

_____

_____

4. Do you enjoy libraries? Why or why not?

_____

_____

5. Are there reading skills that you still need to improve?

_____

_____

6. What made learning to write enjoyable for you?

_____

_____

7. What made learning to write difficult or unenjoyable?

_____

_____

8. How do you feel about writing now?

_____

_____

9. Are there writing skills that you still need to improve?

_____

_____

Based on your own experience and ideas in this chapter, how could you make learning to read and write more successful and enjoyable for your students?

BEST PRACTICES
Strategies for Incorporating Writing into the Curriculum

You will have many opportunities to incorporate writing into the curriculum. Here are some examples (Bruning & Horn, 2001; Halonen, 2006):

1. *Nurture positive attitudes toward writing.* This can be done by making sure that many writing tasks ensure student success and by displaying the way that teachers write personally. Give students choices about what they will write.

2. *Foster student engagement through authentic writing tasks and contexts.* Encourage students to write about topics of personal interest, have students write for different audiences, and integrate writing into instruction in other disciplines, such as science, mathematics, and social studies.

3. *Provide a supportive context for writing.* Encourage students to set writing goals, plan how to reach the goals, and monitor their progress toward the goals. Assist students in creating goals that are neither too challenging nor too simple. Teach writing strategies and monitor their use by students. Give students feedback on their progress toward their writing goals. Use peers as writing partners in literacy communities.

4. *Have students write to learn.* This can work in any subject area. For example, in biology, after students have studied the adaptation of different species, ask them to write a summary of the main ideas and generate examples not described in class or the text.

5. *Use free-writing assignments.* In free writing, students write whatever they think about a subject. Such assignments are usually unstructured but have time limits. For example, one free-writing assignment in American history might be "Write about the American Revolution for five minutes." Free writing helps students discover new ideas, connections, and questions they might not have generated if they had not had this free-writing opportunity.

6. *Give students creative writing assignments.* These assignments give students opportunities to explore themselves and their world in creative, insightful ways. They might include poetry, short stories, or essays reflecting personal experiences.

THROUGH THE EYES OF TEACHERS
Imagine the Possibilities

Beverly Gallagher, a third-grade teacher at Princeton Day School, in New Jersey, created the Imagine the

Beverly Gallagher, working with students to stimulate their interest in reading and writing.

Possibilities program, which brings nationally known poets and authors to her school. She phones each student's parents periodically to describe their child's progress and new interests. She invites students from higher grades to work with small groups in her class so that she can spend more one-on-one time with students. Beverly also created poetry partnerships between eleventh-graders and her third-graders in which the older and younger students collaborate to create poems. Each of her students keeps a writer's notebook to record thoughts, inspirations, and special words that intrigue them. Students get special opportunities to sit in an author's chair, where they read their writing to the class (Source: *USA Today,* 2000).

7. *Require formal writing assignments.* These involve giving students opportunities to express themselves using an objective point of view, precise writing style, and evidence to support their conclusions. Formal writing helps students learn how to make formal arguments. For example, high school students might construct a major paper on topics such as "Global Warming: Real Fears or Hype?" or "An In-Depth Examination of Faulkner's Writing Style," or "Why People Are Prejudiced." Such writing projects stimulate students to think analytically, learn how to use resources, and cite references. Work with students on generating topics for a paper, structuring the paper, using planning and time management skills for completing the paper in a timely manner, drafting and revising, and overcoming spelling and grammatical errors.

Review, Reflect, and Practice

(3) **Describe how writing develops and some useful approaches to teaching writing.**

REVIEW

- What skills are acquired in writing? At what ages are they commonly acquired?
- What cognitive processes are essential to effective writing?
- What are the key ideas in social constructivist approaches to writing?

REFLECT

- For the age group and subject you plan to teach, in what ways will the writing assignments you give to students likely be highly structured and specific? In what ways might they be flexible and open-ended?

PRAXIS™ PRACTICE

1. Which of the following is the best example of developmentally appropriate writing instruction for first-graders?
   a. Ms. Balboa's students are learning how to spell through the use of drill and practice of specific words.
   b. Ms. Donovan carefully corrects student' grammar and spelling errors on their papers and is critical of their errors.
   c. Ms. Figo's students use invented spelling in their work, and she provides them with correct spelling but she does not criticize their efforts.
   d. Ms. Lalas' students practice writing by copying stories that she has written on the blackboard.

2. Ms. Williams emphasizes the importance of pre-writing activities to her students. Which aspect of the cognitive approach to writing does she emphasize?
   a. metacognitive strategies
   b. planning
   c. problem solving
   d. revising

3. Which of the following is the best example of a social constructivist approach to writing?
   a. Ms. Reddick's students write reports on various subjects, based on research they have completed.
   b. Ms. Duhon's students write about their own personal experiences and meet with her regularly to discuss their work.
   c. Ms. Williams' students write responses to essay questions about material in their social studies text.
   d. Ms. Randolph's students choose the books they want to read and write book reports about each book that they complete.

Please see the answer key at the end of the book.

(4) **MATHEMATICS**

- Developmental Changes
- Cognitive Processes
- Technology and Math Instruction
- Controversy in Math Education
- Some Constructivist Principles

What are some developmental changes in the way children think about mathematics and their math abilities at different grade levels? What is the biggest controversy in mathematics education today?

Developmental Changes

The National Council of Teachers of Mathematics (NCTM, 2000) has described the basic principles and standards for school mathematics at different grade levels. We will survey these for all grade levels, beginning with prekindergarten through grade 2.

Prekindergarten through Grade 2 Children already have a substantial understanding of numbers before they enter first grade (Siegler & Alibali, 2005; Smith, 2006). Most kindergartners from middle-income families can count past 20, and many can count beyond 100; most can accurately count the number of objects in a set, can add and subtract single digits, and know the relative magnitudes of single-digit numbers (for example, that 8 is greater than 6) (Siegler & Robinson, 1982).

Children are likely to enter elementary school with different levels of mathematical understanding (NCTM, 2000; Schoenfeld, 2002). Some children will need additional support for math learning (Van de Walle, 2004). According to the NCTM (2000), early assessments should be used to obtain information for teaching and for potential early interventions rather than for sorting children into tracks.

Understanding basic aspects of number and geometry are critical in kindergarten through the second grade (NCTM, 2000). For example, at these grade levels, children need to learn the base-10 numeration system. They must recognize that the word *ten* may represent a single entity or 10 separate units (10 one's) and that these representations can be interchanged.

When they go to school, children learn many higher numerical skills (Ginsburg, Klein, & Starkey, 1998). It is important to be aware that they are often doing something more than simply learning to calculate in a standard way. In fact, what children learn about mathematics and how to solve mathematical problems often reflects independent thinking as well as what they are being "taught" (Tolchinsky, 2002). This can be true even in the case of learning the basic "facts" of addition and subtraction, which most of us ultimately memorize.

Grades 3 through 5 Three key themes of mathematics in grades 3 through 5 are

- *Multiplicative reasoning.* The emphasis on multiplicative reasoning develops knowledge that children build on as they move to the middle grades, where the focus is on proportional reasoning. In multiplicative reasoning, children need to develop their understanding of fractions as part of a whole and as division.
- *Equivalence.* The concept of *equivalence* helps students to learn different mathematical representations and provides an avenue for exploring algebraic ideas.
- *Computational fluency.* Students need to learn efficient and accurate methods of computing that are based on well-understood properties and number relationships. For example, 298×42 can be thought of as $(300 \times 42) - (2 \times 42)$, or 41×16 is computed by multiplying 41×8 to get 328 and then doubling 328 to obtain 656.

Grades 6 through 8   In middle school, students benefit from a balanced mathematics program that includes algebra and geometry. Teachers can help students understand how algebra and geometry are connected. Middle school mathematics also should prepare students to deal with quantitative solutions in their lives outside of school.

Students develop far more powerful mathematical reasoning when they learn algebra. A single equation can represent an infinite variety of situations. Even many students who get A's and B's in algebra classes, however, do so without understanding what they are learning—they simply memorize the equations. This approach might work well in the classroom, but it limits these students' ability to use algebra in real-world contexts (Heid, 2002).

Grades 9 through 12   The NCTM (2000) recommends that all students study mathematics in each of the four years of high school. Because students' interests may change during and after high school, they will likely benefit from taking a range of math classes. They should experience the interplay of algebra, geometry, statistics, probability, and discrete mathematics (which involves the mathematics of computers). They should become adept at visualizing, describing, and analyzing situations in mathematical terms. They also need to be able to justify and prove mathematically based ideas.

Controversy in Math Education

Educators currently debate whether math should be taught using a cognitive, conceptual, and constructivist approach or a practice, computational approach (Cathcart & others, 2006; Schoenfeld, 2006; Sharp, 2005; Stevenson, 2000). Some proponents of the cognitive approach argue against memorization and practice in teaching mathematics. Instead, they emphasize constructivist mathematical problem solving. Others assume that speed and automaticity are fundamental to effective mathematics achievement and argue that such skills can be acquired only through extensive practice and computation. In recent years, the constructivist approach has become increasingly popular. In this approach, effective instruction focuses on involving children in solving a problem or developing a concept and in exploring the efficiency of alternative solutions (Van de Walle & Lovin, 2006).

A recent study used videotapes of eighth-grade math classrooms to examine how math is taught in different countries (Hiebert & others, 2003). In the two countries in which students had the highest math achievement, different teaching strategies were used: Hong Kong teachers stressed basic skills and formulas; Japanese teachers emphasized how concepts are linked. Thus, at least in this study, a practice, computational approach was successful in one country (Hong Kong), a cognitive approach in another (Japan). The researchers concluded that U.S. math teachers need to develop math activities for both the computational and cognitive aspects of math. In addition, in this study, U.S. teachers were less likely to assign math homework than were teachers in most of the other countries, and Japanese teachers let students spend 15 minutes on average struggling to solve a math problem before offering help, compared with only 5 minutes on average for U.S. teachers.

The NCTM (2000) has developed a number of standards for mathematics education. We have already touched on these standards in describing what should be taught at different grade levels. These standards emphasize that teaching math should involve giving students opportunities to

- Understand numbers and operations.
- Learn the principles of algebra and geometry.
- Collect, organize, analyze, and display data, as well as understand basic concepts of probability.
- Solve problems.

- Organize and consolidate mathematical thinking through communication, including working on problems with classmates.
- Recognize connections among mathematical ideas and apply mathematics in contexts outside of mathematics.

Cognitive Processes

In our discussion of developmental changes and the controversy in math education, we mentioned several cognitive processes that help children learn math, such as problem-solving skills, understanding how math concepts are linked, and exploring alternative solutions. The National Research Council (2005) recently concluded that conceptual understanding, procedural fluency, effective organization of knowledge, and metacognitive strategies are important processes in learning math.

In our discussion of the controversy in math education, we saw that debate flourishes about whether conceptual understanding or procedural competences should be the main focus in math education. The National Research Council's (2005) conclusion is that both are important. Teaching math with only an emphasis on procedural competency results in students having too little conceptual understanding, and when students have too little knowledge of procedures they often do not solve math problems competently.

As students move through elementary and secondary school and take increasingly complex math courses, new knowledge and competencies must build on, and be integrated with, previous knowledge. By the time students begin solving algebra problems, they must have a network of organized knowledge that they can engage to support new algebraic understanding. "The teacher's challenge, then, is to help students build and consolidate prerequisite competencies, understand new concepts in depth, and organize both concepts and competencies in a network of knowledge" (Fuson, Kalchman, & Bransford, 2005, p. 232).

Math instruction that supports students' use of metacognitive strategies also is recommended by the National Research Council (2005). Students can engage in metacognitive self-monitoring to determine their progress in solving individual math problems and their progress in a math course. "Metacognitive functioning is also facilitated by shifting from a focus on answers as just right or wrong to a more detailed focus on 'debugging' a wrong answer, that is, finding where the error is, why it is an error, and correcting it" (Fuson, Kalchman, & Bransford, 2005, p. 239).

Developing some effective general problem solving strategies can also help students' math learning (Fuson, Kalchman, & Bransford, 2005; National Research Council, 2005). Two of these are making a drawing of a situation and asking one's self questions. Students can learn to use these strategies as part of their self-monitoring in math.

Some Constructivist Principles

From a constructivist perspective, the principles discussed next should be followed when teaching math (Middleton & Goepfert, 1996). We will examine strategies for making math realistic and interesting, the need to consider the students' prior knowledge, and how the math curriculum can be socially interactive.

Make Math Realistic and Interesting   Build your teaching of math around realistic and interesting problems. These problems might involve some kind of conflict, suspense, or crisis that motivates students' interest. The math problem-solving activities might center on the student, community issues, scientific discoveries, or

Gary Piercey, who teaches math to high school students in Houston, Texas, makes the classroom an exciting place to be for students. He sometimes dresses up for skits, as in the case shown here in which he plays Freeze, whose evil plans can be foiled only by students being able to successfully solve algebra problems.

historical events. Math games can provide a motivating context for learning math. Questions that teachers can pose during games, such as "What do you need to roll on the dice to move your piece to number 10 on the board?" are more meaningful than decontextualized problems, such as "You have 4; how many more must you add to equal 10?" Math games may also encourage students to discuss math strategies with others, including their peers and parents (Carpenter & others, 1983). Connecting math with other subject areas, such as science, geography, reading, and writing, also is recommended.

Consider the Students' Prior Knowledge In our discussion of cognitive processes, we indicated that building on the student's knowledge is an important aspect of math education (National Research Council, 2005). Evaluate what knowledge the students bring to the unit and the context in which instruction takes place. Make enough information available for students to be able to come up with a method for solving math problems but withhold enough information so that students must stretch their minds to solve the problems.

Make the Math Curriculum Socially Interactive Develop math projects that require students to work together to come up with a solution. Build into the math curriculum opportunities for students to use and improve their communication skills. Generate math projects that engender discussion, argument, and compromise.

Technology and Math Instruction

One issue in math education is how technology intensive it should be (De Corte & Verschafell, 2006; Heid & Blume, 2002). The NCTM's *Curriculum and Evaluation Standards* recommends that calculators be used at all levels of mathematics instruction and that some access to computers is also necessary if students are to be adequately educated for future careers. In many school systems, adequate funds for computers is a major issue.

In contrast to U.S. teachers, Japanese and Chinese teachers do not allow the everyday use of calculators or computers in mathematics classes, because they want the students to understand the concepts and operations required to solve problems. Some critics argue that the American emphasis on the early use of these technology aids prevents students from gaining experience in manipulating concrete objects that they need to learn mathematical concepts (Stevenson, 2001). Only at the high school level, after students have developed a clear understanding of mathematical concepts, are East Asian students allowed to use calculators for solving mathematical problems. In the recent National Assessment of Educational Progress, in the fourth grade, frequent calculator use was associated with lower national achievement test scores in mathematics, while in the eighth and twelfth grades, more frequent use of calculators was linked with higher national test scores (see figure 11.6).

FIGURE 11.6 Frequency of Calculator Use at Different Grade Levels and National Mathematics Achievement Test Scores

Note: Scores on the National Mathematics Achievement Test can range from 0 to 500.

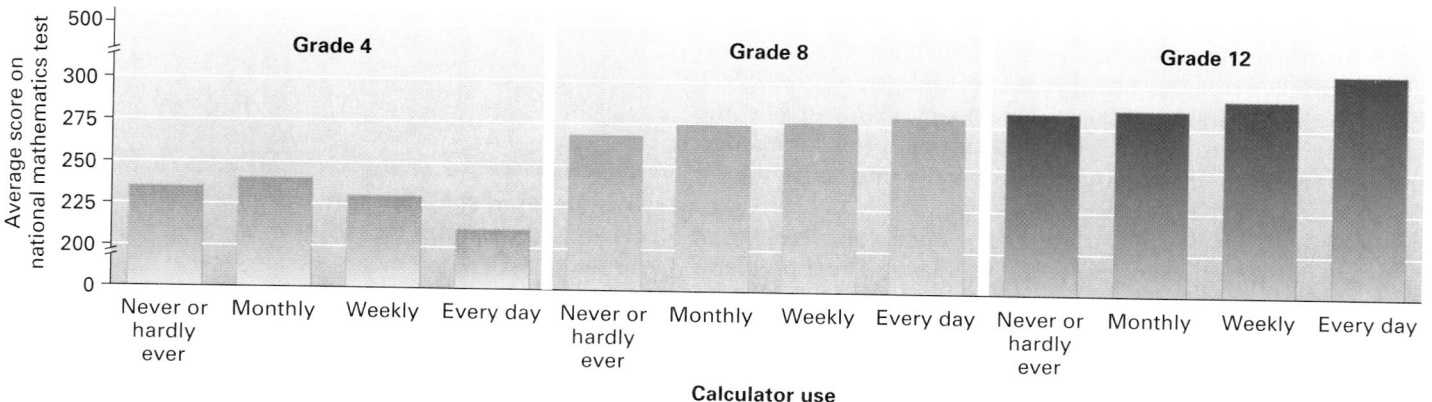

BEST PRACTICES
Strategies for Teaching Mathematics

We have discussed many strategies for teaching mathematics. Here are some of the key ones:

1. *Teach students to become both procedurally and conceptually competent in math.* Students need to develop good computational skills and they also need to understand math concepts.

2. *Help students to develop good math problem-solving skills.*

3. *Encourage students to use metacognitive strategies.* Guide students to monitor their progress in solving math problems and becoming more competent at math.

4. *Make math interesting for students.* For example, using real-world contexts and games can improve many students' motivation for spending more time on math, especially students who are not doing well in math.

THROUGH THE EYES OF TEACHERS

"Never See Failure as Failure"

An at-risk student, Henry Brown's life was turned around by middle school teacher Cora Russell, and the experience inspired him to teach. Brown, a recent Florida Teacher of the Year, teaches math at Hallandale Adult Alternative High School. Half of the students enter this school with math skills below the fifth-grade level.

He believes it is important to teach real-world math skills. In one project, Brown devised a dummy corporation and had students play different roles in it, learning important math skills as they worked and made decisions in the corporation. He also created Helping Hands, which involves senior citizens in the classroom (Source: *USA Today*, 2001).

5. *Use technology effectively.*

6. *Connect with parents.* In chapter 9, we described Family Math, a program that helps parents experience math with their children in a positive, supportive way. In addition to telling parents about Family Math, consider having Family Math nights, especially at the beginning of the school year. Let parents see how the students will be learning math and resolve any of their major concerns. At the Family Math night, offer resources that parents can use at home to help their children learn math more effectively.

7. *If you teach math, one good active step is to join the NCTM and use its resources.* The NCTM has annual conferences, publishes an annual yearbook with stimulating chapters on recent developments in math education, and publishes journals such as *Mathematics Teacher*. For more information about the NCTM, call (703) 620-9840 or go to www.nctm.org/.

Henry Brown.

Review, Reflect, and Practice

④ **Characterize how mathematical thinking develops and identify some issues related to teaching mathematics.**

REVIEW
- What are some developmental changes in mathematical skills?
- What is the main controversy in math education?
- What are some cognitive processes involving math?
- What are some constructivist principles in learning math?
- What role can technology play in math instruction?

continued on page 388

Review, Reflect, and Practice *continued*

REFLECT

- Do you think that teachers in Asia are wise to not allow young students to use calculators? Should the United States follow this example?

PRAXIS™ PRACTICE

1. Ms. Carpenter's students are working on developing an understanding of place value. They are most likely in grade
   a. K–2.
   b. 3–5.
   c. 6–8.
   d. 9–12.

2. Malavi is very fast and accurate at doing multiplication and division. In the controversy on math education, he could be cited as an example of the importance of adopting which of these approaches?
   a. constructivist
   b. practice, computational
   c. conceptual
   d. cognitive

3. Joan is going over her math exam. She is examining her mistakes in an effort to find out what she did wrong. Then she corrects her mistakes and resubmits the exam. Her teacher, Mr. Ewing, allows students to receive credit for going through this process because he believes it helps students to learn from their errors. This is an example of
   a. algebraic reasoning.
   b. algorithms.
   c. debugging.
   d. rote memorization.

4. Which of the following is the best example of application of constructivist principles to math teaching?
   a. Ms. Carmichael's students complete timed tests of basic math facts.
   b. Ms. Dodge's students play store, which allows them to add up their purchases, pay for them, and make change.
   c. Ms. Luker's students solve word problems but do not work on computation.
   d. Mr. Pinks' students complete problems on the board so he can determine if they have grasped the concepts.

5. Based on the results of research on calculator use and math achievement, at which of the following grade levels should Ingrid start using a calculator in doing math?
   a. first
   b. third
   c. fifth
   d. eighth

Please see the answer key at the end of the book.

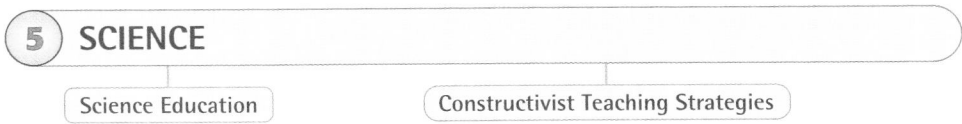

5 **SCIENCE**

[Science Education]   [Constructivist Teaching Strategies]

What are some key ideas in educating students about science? What are some constructivist strategies for teaching science?

Science Education

Scientists typically engage in certain kinds of thinking and behavior. For example, they regularly make careful observations; collect, organize, and analyze data; measure, graph, and understand spatial relations; pay attention to and regulate their own thinking; and know when and how to apply their knowledge to solve problems (Chapman, 2000).

These skills, which are essential to the practice of science, are not routinely taught in schools, especially elementary schools. As a result, many students are not competent at them. Many scientists and educators believe that schools need to increasingly guide students in learning how to use these skills (Chiappetta & Koballa, 2006; Cocking, Mestre, & Brown, 2000; Lehrer & Schauble, 2006; Penner, 2001; Peters & Stout, 2006; Tolman, 2002; Singer, Hilton, & Schweingruber, 2006).

Children have many misconceptions that are incompatible with science and reality (Bransford & Donovan, 2005). They may go through mental gymnastics trying to reconcile seemingly contradictory new information with their new beliefs (Miller, 2000). For example, after learning about the solar system, children sometimes conclude that there are two earths—the seemingly flat world in which they live and the round ball floating in space that their teacher just described.

Good teachers perceive and understand a child's underlying concepts, then use the concepts as a scaffold for learning (Linn & Eylon, 2006; Tippins, Koballa, & Payne, 2002). Effective science teaching helps children distinguish between fruitful errors and misconceptions, and detect plainly wrong ideas that need to be replaced by more accurate conceptions (Bransford & Donovan, 2005).

An effective strategy for helping students to overcome misconceptions is an **interactive demonstration strategy** (Sokoloff & Thornton, 1997). The teacher introduces what the demonstration is about, asks students to discuss the demonstration with their neighbors, tells them to write down a prediction regarding the demonstration, and then performs the demonstration. Consider a physics demonstration involving "a collision between two air carts on an air track, one a stationary light cart, the other a heavy cart moving toward the stationary cart" (National Research Council, 1999, pp. 167–168). "Each cart has an electronic force probe connected to a display." The teacher first asks the students to discuss the situation with their neighbors and then record a prediction about whether one of the carts would exert a bigger force on the other during impact or whether they will exert equal forces. The vast majority of students incorrectly predict that the heavier, moving cart exerts a larger force on the lighter, stationary cart. This prediction seems quite reasonable based on experience students know that a moving Mack truck "inflicts far more damage on a Volkswagen Beetle than vice versa." This is interpreted by students to mean that the Mack truck must have exerted more force on the Volkswagen. However, "notwithstanding the major damage to the Volkswagen, Newton's Third Law of Physics states that two interacting bodies exert equal and opposite forces on each other. After the students make and record their predictions, the instructor performs the demonstration, and the students see on the screen that the force probes record forces of equal magnitude but oppositely directed during the collision."

interactive demonstration strategy
A strategy to help students overcome misconceptions in science in which the teacher introduces the demonstration, asks students to discuss the demonstration with their neighbors and predict its outcome, and then performs the demonstration.

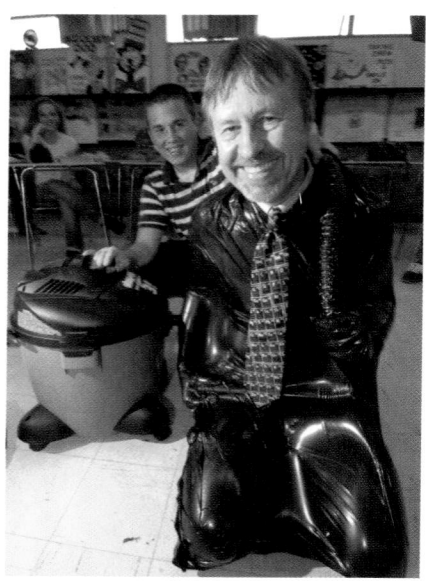

Pete Karpyk, who teaches chemistry in Weirton, West Virginia, uses an extensive array of activities that bring science alive for students. Here he has shrink-wrapped himself to demonstrate the effects of air pressure. He has some students give chemistry demonstrations at elementary schools and has discovered that in some cases students who don't do well on tests excel when they teach children. He also adapts his teaching based on feedback from former students and incorporates questions from their college chemistry tests as bonus questions on the tests he gives his high school students (Source: Briggs, 2005. p. 6D).

Constructivist Teaching Strategies

Many science teachers help their students construct their knowledge of science through discovery and hands-on laboratory investigations (Bransford & Donovan, 2005; Chiappetta & Koballa, 2006; Linn & Eylon, 2006; Martin & others, 2005; Singer, Hilton, & Schweingruber, 2006). Constructivist teaching emphasizes that children have to build their own scientific knowledge and understanding. At each step in science learning, they need to interpret new knowledge in the context of what they already understand. Rather than putting fully formed knowledge into children's minds, in the constructivist approach teachers help children construct scientifically valid interpretations of the world and guide them in altering their scientific misconceptions (Linn & Eylon, 2006; Martin & others, 2005; Peters & Stout, 2006; Songer, 2006).

Some contemporary constructivist approaches to teaching science involve exploring everyday science problems, activities that help students learn how science works, and the social contexts of science (Abruscato, 2004; Linn, Songer, & Eylon, 1996).

Exploring Everyday Science Problems   Most students are far more interested in science that addresses problems relevant to their lives than they are in discussing abstract theories. One elementary school program that reflects this emphasis is the project funded by the National Science Foundation called Science for Life and Living (SLL) (Biological Sciences Curriculum Study, 1989; 2001). The program emphasizes

- *"Science as a way of knowing."* This phrase expresses the idea that science is not just knowledge but a unique way of learning about the world.
- *"Technology as a way of doing."* The focus is not on computers but, rather, on understanding how people use the processes and tools of technology to solve practical problems.
- *"Health as a way of behaving."* The emphasis here is on applying scientific reasoning skills in making decisions about health, focusing on such themes as cause and effect, and understanding how to think critically about information that claims to improve health.

In a study conducted in five North Carolina schools, students who experienced the SLL curriculum scored higher on a standardized test of biology and on other measures that assessed conceptual understanding of biology than did fifth-grade students who were in regular science classes (Maidon & Wheatley, 2001).

Activities That Help Students Learn How Science Works   Some projects help students think about and visualize how scientific principles work. For example, Project STAR (Science Teaching Through Astronomical Roots) uses astronomy as a foundation to teach complex physics principles to high school students (Schneps & Sadler, 1989). Computer simulations can be especially effective in helping students visualize and think about scientific phenomena.

Exploring a Rich Content Domain   Kathleen Metz's (2004) approach to science investigation focuses on introducing students to scientists' methods in the context of extended experience in a limited number of content domains. In her research, fifth-grade students became deeply immersed in one or two areas of science—such as animal behavior—rather than learning a small amount of information about a variety of science areas. In Metz's view, it is unrealistic to think that teachers can get students to engage in deep inquiry if they know only a small amount of information about a field. Thus, from her perspective, effective science education involves depth of inquiry in a limited number of areas, rather than shallow inquiry in many areas. According to Metz (2004), depth of inquiry is more likely to be accomplished when students generate appropriate questions, acquire methods for investigating those questions, and "develop a sense of the forms and qualities of evidence (and counterevidence) that can inform answers. . . . Initial investigations are carefully structured and scaffolded;

subsequent inquiries are planned and conducted by themselves, who are increasingly given independent responsibility for the progress and evaluation of the scientific work" (Lehrer & Schauble, 2006).

The Social Contexts of Science The Fostering a Community of Learners (FCL) project (Brown, 1997; Brown & Campione, 1996), discussed in chapter 10, reflects an emphasis on the social contexts of science. It stresses teacher-student and student-student collaborative interaction. Students investigate environmental science problems, create group or individual reports, and support each other as part of a community of science learners. In FCL, constructive commentary, questioning, querying, and criticism are the norm rather than the exception. Recall that FCL was recently described by two leading educational psychologists as "a landmark in developmental science education" (Lehrer & Schauble, 2006).

An Innovative Middle School Life-Sciences Curriculum In chapter 2, "Cognitive and Language Development," we discussed the need for new middle school curricula. Especially lacking in middle school education have been courses that provide the information, skills, and motivation for young adolescents to learn about themselves and their widening world.

The **Human Biology Middle Grades Curriculum (HumBio)** was developed by Stanford University scientists in collaboration with middle school teachers across the United States (Carnegie Council on Adolescent Development, 1995; Heller, 1993). It integrates the study of ecology, evolution, genetics, physiology, human development, culture, health, and safety. It might seem ironic that we end this section on domain-specific constructivist approaches by emphasizing integration and connection across the school curriculum. However, such cross-curricular integration and connection is an important theme in many disciplines.

HumBio not only is appropriate for teaching science to middle school students with a wide range of abilities, but it simultaneously promotes healthy decision making. HumBio is a 2-year curriculum that consists of 24 units. Schools choose which units they want to teach. Initial units are "The Changing Body, Reproduction, and

In this HumBio classroom, students at Central Park East Secondary School in New York City investigate an important function of the human digestive system by performing the peristalsis activity. The group shown here is moving rice through long, flexible plastic tubing representing the small intestine.

Human Biology Middle Grades Curriculum (HumBio) Developed by Stanford University scientists in collaboration with middle school teachers, this curriculum integrates ecology, evolution, genetics, physiology, human development, culture, health, and safety.

BEST PRACTICES
Strategies for Teaching Science

A summary of important strategies to use when teaching science include:

1. *Helping students learn how to think like scientists.* Create settings in which students are required to make careful observations, work effectively with data, and solve scientific problems.

2. *Monitoring students' misconceptions about science and work with them to develop more accurate conceptions.*

3. *Guiding students in developing inquiry skills.* When teaching inquiry skills, don't leave students completely to their own devices; use guided inquiry.

4. *Teaching science content.* Students not only need to develop inquiry skills, they also need to learn science content.

5. *Making science interesting by giving students opportunities to explore everyday science problems.* Next, you can read about how Peggy Schweiger, a physics teacher at Klein Oak High School in Katy, Texas, does this.

THROUGH THE EYES OF TEACHERS

Dropping an Egg on a Teacher's Head

Peggy Schweiger uses hands-on projects, such as wiring a doll house and making replicas of a boat for a regatta, to improve students' understanding of physics. She especially works hard to create projects that will interest both female and male students. According to former student

Alison Arnett, nineteen, "She taught us how to think and learn, not how to succeed in physics class. We were encouraged to stand on desks, tape things to the ceiling, and even drop an egg on her head to illustrate physics—anything to make us discover that we live with physics every day" (Source: *USA Today*, 2001, p. 6).

Peggy Schweiger with a student who is learning how to think and discover how physics works in people's everyday lives.

Sexuality," "Genetics," "The Nervous System," and "The Life of Cells." Next comes "From Cells to Organisms: Human Development." Finally, "The Circulatory System," "Breathing," and "Digestion and Nutrition" round out the curriculum.

In using HumBio, teachers work cooperatively from the perspectives of their individual disciplines toward imparting a central lesson. For example, a science class discussion of the impact of food and drugs on circulation is coordinated with a physical education class discussion of linkages among food intake, drugs, circulation, and breathing. The study of health includes decisions regarding smoking, analysis of different ways of planning menus, facts behind eating disorders, and ways to reduce stress. One lesson helps students understand how drugs affect their bodies (for example, cocaine increases the production of adrenaline). In the HumBio curriculum at Egan Intermediate School in Los Altos, California, seventh-grade students explore the effects of adrenaline on metabolism by observing brine shrimp through a microscope. Students have an opportunity to discuss the ideas in the demonstration with the teacher and with each other. They ask questions and offer answers.

HumBio has been extensively field-tested at schools selected for their diversity. Training for teaching HumBio is available through summer institutes at Stanford University, and information about HumBio is available from Addison-Wesley Longman Publishers.

Inquiry and Science Content Knowledge   Some critics of constructivist approaches argue that too much attention is given to inquiry skills and not enough is given to discipline-specific information (American Association for the Advancement of Science, 1993). In response, advocates of the constructivist approach to biology argue that it creates more scientifically literate citizens who know how to think in scientific ways rather than just memorize scientific facts (Trowbridge, Bybee, & Powell, 2000).

Keep in mind, though, that it is important that students not be left completely on their own to construct scientific knowledge independent of *science content.* Students' inquiry should be guided (Magnusson & Palinscar, 2005; Minstrell & Kraus, 2005). Teachers to at a minimum should initially scaffold students' science learning, extensively monitor their progress, and ensure that they are learning science content. Thus, in pursuing science investigations, students need to "learn inquiry skills *and* science content" (Lehrer & Schauble, 2006).

Review, Reflect, and Practice

5 **Identify some challenges and strategies related to teaching children how to think scientifically.**

REVIEW
- What are key ideas in science education?
- What are some constructivist approaches to teaching science?

REFLECT
- How effectively did your elementary, middle, and high school teach science to the typical student? If less than perfectly, how could their approach have been improved?

PRAXIS™ PRACTICE
1. Which of the following teachers is most likely to be successful in helping students to overcome scientific misconceptions?
   a. Ms. Coster finds out what her students misconceptions are by carefully asking them questions and then explicitly combats their misconceptions via direct instruction.
   b. Ms. Quigley uses a science text and carefully tests her students over the content in the text.
   c. Mr. Jones sets up situations in which the students explore materials themselves to discover their misconceptions.
   d. Mr. Foster designs experiences that demonstrate to the students that their misconceptions are incorrect and point out the correct principles.
2. Which of the following is the best example of constructivist teaching strategies in science?
   a. Mr. Ricardo's students study the material in their science tests and take quizzes over each chapter.
   b. Mr. Bunker's students have a "science bee" every Friday. He asks questions and the students respond. Students who answer wrong are out of the competition.
   c. Ms. Mertz's students perform carefully designed experiments in a few areas that demonstrate scientific principles, helping them to learn in depth and to learn the process of scientific inquiry.
   d. Ms. O'Connor's students keep science notebooks in which they take notes on her presentations, and she gives periodic tests on the material in the notebooks.

Please see the answer key at the end of the book.

⑥ SOCIAL STUDIES

What Is Social Studies?	Constructivist Approaches

What is the nature of social studies? What key themes characterize teaching and learning in social studies? How can constructivist approaches be applied to social studies?

What Is Social Studies?

In general, the field of **social studies,** also called social sciences, seeks to promote civic competence. The goal is to help students make informed and reasoned decisions for the public good as citizens of a culturally diverse, democratic society in an interdependent world. In schools, social studies draws from disciplines such as anthropology, economics, geography, history, law, philosophy, political science, psychology, religion, and sociology.

Social studies is taught in kindergarten through grade 12 in the United States. In elementary school, children often learn social studies that are integrated across several disciplines (Chapin, 2006). This often takes the form of units constructed around broad themes that are examined in terms of time, continuity, and change (Martorella & Beal, 2002). In middle schools and high schools, courses may be interdisciplinary—such as a history course drawing from geography, economics, and political science—or focused more on a single discipline, such as just history itself (Martorella, 2001; Sunal & Haas, 2005; VanSledright & Limón, 2006).

The National Council for the Social Sciences (2000) proposed ten themes that it believes should be emphasized in courses in the social sciences:

- *Time, continuity, and change.* Students need to understand their historical roots and locate themselves in time. Knowing how to effectively read about and construct the past helps students to explore questions such as "How am I connected to the past?" and "How can my personal experience be viewed as part of the larger human story across time?" This theme typically appears in history courses.

  Many people have had similar experiences in history courses. They learned facts and dates that the teachers and the text presented as important. However, teachers and students who think that history is only about facts and dates miss remarkable opportunities to learn how history is a discipline that involves analyzing events in terms of how they are relevant for people's lives (Fritzer, 2002; National Research Council, 1999). Indeed, experts in history regard evidence in history as far more than a list of facts. And expert history teachers, rather than simply teaching history as lists of facts to be memorized, guide students in analyzing and reflecting about historical events, especially encouraging students to think about possible alternative meanings of events and how they might be interpreted in different ways. A number of expert history teachers also get students to engage in debate about the evidence pertaining to a particular historical circumstance.

- *People, places, and environments.* The study of these topics helps students to develop spatial and geographic perspectives on the world. This helps students make informed and competent decisions about the relationship of humans to their environment. In schools, this theme usually appears in units and courses linked to geography.

- *Individual development and identity.* A student's personal identity is shaped by culture, groups, and institutions. Students can explore such questions as "Who am I?" "How do people learn, think, and develop?" and "How do people meet their needs in a variety of contexts?" In schools, this theme usually appears in units and courses focused on psychology and anthropology.

social studies The field that seeks to promote civic competence with the goal of helping students make informed and reasoned decisions for the public good as citizens of a culturally diverse, democratic society in an interdependent world.

- *Individuals, groups, and institutions.* Students need to learn about the ways in which schools, churches, families, government agencies, and the courts play integral roles in people's lives. Students can explore the roles of various institutions in the United States and other countries. In schools, this theme typically appears in units and courses on sociology, anthropology, psychology, political science, and history.

- *Power, authority, and governance.* Understanding the development of power, authority, and governance in the United States and other parts of the world is essential for developing civic competence. In this theme, students explore such topics as the following: What is power and what forms does it take? How do people gain power, use it, and justify it? How can people keep their government responsive to their needs and interests? How can conflicts within a nation and between nations be resolved? This theme typically appears in units and courses focused on government, political science, history, and other social sciences.

- *Production, distribution, and consumption.* People have needs and desires that sometimes exceed the limited resources that are available to them. As a result, questions such as these are raised: What is to be produced? How is production to be organized? How are goods and services distributed? What is the most effective allocation of production (land, capital, and management)? Increasingly, these questions are global in scope. In schools, this theme typically appears in units and courses focused on economics.

- *Science, technology, and society.* Modern life as we know it would be impossible without technology and the science that supports it. However, technology raises many questions: Is new technology always better? How can people effectively cope with rapid technological advances? How are values related to technology? This theme appears in units and courses involving history, geography, economics, civics, and government. It also draws from such fields as the natural and physical sciences, social sciences, and humanities for specific examples of issues and the knowledge base for considering social issues related to society and technology.

- *Global connections.* The realities of increasing interdependence among nations requires understanding nations and cultures around the world. Conflicts between national and global priorities can involve health care, economic development, environmental quality, universal human rights, and other agendas. Analyzing economic competition, ethnic identities, and political alliances helps students understand why nations develop various policies. This theme typically appears in units and courses involving geography, culture, economics, and other social sciences.

- *Civic ideals and practices.* Understanding civic ideals and the practices of citizenship is important for full participation in society. Students focus on such questions as these: What is civic participation and how can I be involved? What is the balance between individual needs and community responsibilities? In schools, this theme typically appears in units and courses involving history, political science, and anthropology.

- *Culture.* The study of culture prepares students to ask and answer such questions as these: How are cultures similar and different? What is the best way to interact with people who are from cultures that are different from your own? How does religion influence the beliefs of people in different cultures? In schools, the theme of culture typically appears in units and courses that focus on geography, history, and anthropology, as well as multicultural topics that cut across the curriculum.

If a democracy such as the United States is to be secure and stable, each new generation of citizens must believe in the system and believe it works for people like them.

DIVERSITY AND EDUCATION
UN Peacekeeping: A Constructivist Approach

One Canadian middle school social studies teacher developed a project on UN peacekeeping to encourage students to think more deeply and productively about respecting citizens in their own country and about the hardships that people in many countries continue to experience (Welshman, 2000). During the last 50 years, the United Nations has been involved in separating adversaries, maintaining cease-fires, delivering humanitarian relief, helping refugees, and creating conditions that promote democracy. Studying the UN initiatives became a way for students to examine various prosocial values such as kindness, empathy, cooperation, loyalty, equality, and responsibility. In this project, students used a variety of resources, including books and the Internet, over the course of several class periods.

In introducing the UN peacekeeping topic, the teacher asked if any of the students ever had a disagreement with a friend or classmate at school. Students contributed comments and the teacher said that in many instances it takes a third party to sort things out and help solve the problem. The teacher then shifted attention to how such conflicts also characterize world politics between countries and different ethnic groups. Nations, regions, and small groups of people have disagreements, and there is no teacher present to help cool things down. This is where UN peacekeepers often step in to help solve a particular problem.

Then, students brainstormed about UN peacekeeping, during which they recalled any information they had previously learned about the topic and discussed their ideas with each other. The classroom had a world map on which to identify regions of the world where peacekeeping was taking or had taken place.

Next, the students were organized into five small groups of five students each to explore questions they had about UN peacekeeping. The first group of students focused on the history of peacekeeping. Questions explored included where the first peacekeeping mission occurred and how peacekeeping has changed since the end of the Cold War. Group two expressed an interest in the personal side of peacekeeping. Their questions included how much force peacekeepers can use in a mission and some of the dangers they face. The third group wanted to know about the organization of peacekeeping missions and asked questions such as these: Who provides funding for the mission? How are peacekeepers selected? The fourth group was interested in Canada's role in UN peacekeeping, asking these questions: When did Canada get involved in this? Have any Canadians commanded UN peacekeeping missions? The fifth group was intrigued by why peacekeeping occurs and asked questions such as these: What is the decision-making process like in determining when to form a UN peacekeeping mission? How do people decide on which world problems should be dealt with and which should not? After generating these questions, students researched and presented answers.

In addition to the small-group activities, students watched a film, *Caught in the Crossfire,* which portrayed Canadian peacekeepers in the war-torn former Yugoslavia. After viewing this film, the teacher asked students to imagine that they were residents of war-torn Yugoslavia, living in terrible conditions. Then, the students were asked to imagine what life would be like if Canadian peacekeepers were not serving in that part of the world.

Research by Constance Flanagan and her colleagues (Flanagan, 2004; Flanagan & Faison, 2001; Flanagan, Gill, & Gallay, 1998) with American adolescents from different ethnic groups points to the pivotal role of teaching in this regard. They have found that the extent to which teachers ensure that all students are treated equally and listen to and respect each other is related to the students' endorsement of democracy. In the

Diversity and Education interlude, you can read further about teaching culture and cultural diversity in social studies.

Constructivist Approaches

Many social studies classes continue to be taught in a traditional manner of using a single textbook, with the teacher lecturing and controlling question-and-answer strategies. However, some educators believe that learning about social studies would benefit from constructivist strategies, such as using varied sources of information, student-generated questions to guide inquiry, and peer collaboration—the strategy used in the UN peacekeeping unit we just discussed (Gibson & McKay, 2001). In the constructivist view, students should form their own interpretation of evidence and submit it for review. Allowing them to do so should encourage greater reflection and deeper understanding of social issues (Chapin & Messick, 2002; Maxim, 2006; Sunal & Haas, 2005).

Constructivist approaches also emphasize the meaningfulness of social studies (Ellis, 2002; Lee, 2005; Turner, 2004). Students benefit when they find that what they learned in social studies classes is useful both in and outside of school. Meaningful learning often takes place when classroom interaction focuses on sustained examination of a few important topics rather than superficial coverage of many.

Constructivist approaches to social studies also stress the importance of thinking critically about values. Ethical dimensions of topics and controversial issues provide an arena for reflective thinking and understanding. Effective teachers recognize opposing points of view, respect for well-supported positions, sensitivity to cultural similarities and differences, and a commitment to social responsibility. From the constructivist perspective, teachers guide students to consider ethical dimensions of topics and address controversial issues rather than directly telling students what is ethical.

One constructivist approach to teaching social studies created by the Teacher's Curriculum Institute (2001) uses these teaching strategies to help students "experience" history:

- *Interactive slide lecture.* This strategy turns what is typically a passive, teacher-centered activity into a participative experience for students. Students view, touch, interpret, and act out images projected on slides. As the teacher asks a series of questions, students take notes.

In the History Alive! Program of the Teacher's Curriculum Institute, students work in cooperative groups of four to prepare one student to be the actor in a lively panel debate.

- *Social studies skill builders.* Students sit in pairs to complete skill-oriented tasks such as mapping geographic features, analyzing political cartoons, and graphing economic trends.
- *Writing for understanding.* Students are challenged to write for a purpose.
- *Response groups.* This exercise creates rich classroom discussions of controversial topics. Students sit in small groups to view slides depicting historical events and respond to critical thinking questions related to each slide.

To close our discussion of social studies education, the following comments of former high school history teacher Robert Bain (2005, p. 209) capture many of themes we have emphasized in this chapter, not only about social science education but also about education in other content areas:

> When my high school students began to study history, they tended to view the subject as a fixed entity, a body of facts that historians retrieved and placed in textbooks (or in the minds of history teachers) for students to memorize. The purpose of history, if it had one, was to somehow inoculate students from repeating past errors. The process of learning history was straightforward and, while not always exciting, relatively simple. Ironically, when I first entered a school to become a history teacher over 30 years ago, I held a similar view, often supported by my education and history courses . . . I no longer hold such innocent and naïve views of learning or teaching history, and I try to disabuse my students of these views as well. Indeed, our experiences in my history courses have taught us that, to paraphrase Yogi Berra, it's not what we know that's the issue, it's what we know for sure that isn't so. . . . Learning and teaching history demands complex thinking by both teachers and students. It centers around interesting, generative, and organizing problems; critical weighing of evidence and accounts; suspension of our views to understand those of others; use of facts, concepts, and interpretations to make judgments; and later, if the evidence persuades, to changes in our views and judgments.

In this chapter, we have explored effective strategies for educating students in a number of content areas. To read about some of the best ways to use technology in these and other content areas, see the Technology and Education box.

Review, Reflect, and Practice

(6) Summarize how learning in social studies is becoming more constructivist.

REVIEW

- What does social studies instruction aim to accomplish?
- What are some constructivist approaches to teaching social studies?

REFLECT

- Think about a specific community in which you might teach one day. How might you tailor social studies instructions specifically for those children? How could you make it constructivist?

PRAXIS™ PRACTICE

1. Mr. Chen wants his students to understand that not all people live in the same way that they do. His students study the ways of life of different people around the world. Which theme of social studies does Mr. Chen emphasize?
   a. culture
   b. civic ideals and practice
   c. power, authority, and governance
   d. production, distribution, and consumption

TECHNOLOGY AND EDUCATION
Content Area–Specific Technology Applications

There are a wealth of content specific technology resources available for teachers, some of which are commercial products, some of which free.

In English language arts, there are many good programs for beginning readers, such as the *Reader Rabbit* or *Living Books* series. The latter provides software versions of children's literature classics with which young students can read along and interact. For older students. The Gutenberg Project (**www.gutenberg.org**) gives the full texts of thousands of books whose copyright has expired. Many children's authors have Web sites that provide supplementary information about the authors and their books (see for example, **www.judyblume. com**). There are good supports for writing in most word processors, as well as programs that read written text back to students, such as *Write OutLoud!,* and so help improve their writing.

There are many commercial programs for giving students practice in arithmetic and algebra as well as interesting applications that support geometry explorations, such as the *Geometric Supposer.* Symbol manipulation programs, like Mathematica (**www.wolfram.com/products/mathematica/index. html**) or Maple (**www.maplesoft.com/**), allow students to explore algebra and calculus in multiple representations. There are also large repositories of mathematics learning objects (see **www.walterfendt.de/ml4e/** or **www.merlot.org/ artifact/BrowseArtifacts.po?catcode=223&browsecat=223& sort=rating**) for supporting the learning of specific mathematical concepts. The National Council for Teachers of Mathematics (**www.ntm.org**) provides a variety of digital objects for illustrating mathematical concepts for its members called *Illuminations.*

Technology support for inquiry-based science includes the use of science probes, online access to science expeditions, online interactive activities for students (for example, www.exploratorium.edu/), and virtual science laboratories. Vernier (**www.vernier.com**) and Pasco (**www.pasco.com**) offer a wide variety of hardware and software for supporting hands-on science activities. There are also good online repositories of learning objects for teaching science including the National Science Foundation's *Digital Library* (**http://nsdl.org/**) and the National Science Teachers Association's *SciLinks* (**www.nsta.org/scilinks**).

In social studies, Tom Snyder Productions (**www.tomsnyder. com**) offers a variety of role-playing simulations that introduce students to decision making among competing stakeholders as do *SimCity* and *Civilization* from Aspyr (**www.aspyr. com/**) on a grander and more complex scale. There are also incredible sources of original documents (for example, see the Library of Congress *American Memory Collection* (**http:// memory.loc.gov/ammem/**) or the *Congressional Record,* (**www. gpoaccess.gov/crecord/**), virtual tours of cities all over the world, world newspapers, and collections of maps including Google Earth (**http://earth.google.com/**).

There are also good resources for specialized content areas. For example the *WebMuseum* is a good source of reproductions for teaching art history, especially the Impressionists. Indeed, museums around the world have good reproductions available. The *Afropop Worldwide* site has a wealth of information about African and world music including music downloads.

And there is much, much more available over the Internet. For example, the WebQuests created by teachers available at **http://webquest.org/** can be sorted by topic as can the digital objects available in the MERLOT (**www.merlot.org**) library. In addition, many publishers provide CD-ROMs and online sites for teachers using their texts. A good source for selected commercial software is KidsClick (**www.Kidsclick.com**).

2. Which is the best example of a constructivist approach to social studies?
   a. Mr. Ewing's students listen to his lectures and take notes on the content covered.
   b. Ms. Drexler's students color and label detailed maps to help them learn geography.
   c. Ms. Byrd's students learn the material in their textbooks and take tests covering the content on a regular basis.
   d. Mr. Jordan presents his students with a controversial issue, which they discuss and debate.

Please see the answer key at the end of the book.

CRACK THE CASE
The Case of the Constructivist Math Curriculum

Connie teaches fourth grade in a middle-SES school district. Her district has adopted a new K–6 math curriculum for this year, based on constructivist principles. In attending the in-service devoted to training teachers in implementing the new curriculum, Connie discovers that many differences exist between what she has been teaching for the past 20 years and this new curriculum. The new curriculum focuses on the use of math in "real life." Instead of endless speed drills, the problems ask the students to think and make connections between their lives at home and what they are doing in math. What drill and practice there is takes place in the context of various games the children play together. Students are allowed, and even taught, to approach problems in a variety of ways rather than focusing on a single algorithm for a particular type of problem. Many of these approaches are completely alien to Connie and, she guesses, to other teachers and parents. "This is going to be a lot of work," she thinks. "I'm going to have to relearn math myself in order to teach this way."

As the school year begins, other teachers begin expressing their concerns over the new curriculum. It is just so different from anything they have ever done in the past. Most of the teachers are managing to stay just a lesson or two ahead of the students. The children in first and second grade seem to love the new math program. They are actively involved during math period, and many of them have said that math is fun. The students in fourth through sixth grade don't appear to be as enthusiastic about the new curriculum, however. Many of them are unable to complete their homework. They can't seem to grasp how to complete problems using the techniques taught in the new curriculum. They constantly fall back on the old algorithms they were taught when they were younger. This is frustrating Connie and her colleagues, as they have worked very hard to master the alternate ways of approaching problems themselves.

To make matters worse, parents are complaining. They can't help their children with their homework because they don't know how to use the new approaches, either. This has caused many parents to become angry. Several have threatened to remove their children from the school and take them "somewhere where they teach normal math." A group of parents will be addressing the board of education regarding this at their next meeting.

Adding fuel to the fire is one of the middle school math teachers, who insists that this new curriculum won't give the students the foundation they need for algebra. "They need to develop automaticity with their math facts. That just isn't going to happen with this program. It takes them in too many directions. They'll never make it back to normal in time for algebra."

Proponents answer the middle school teacher by indicating that the new curriculum will actually better prepare the students for higher math because they will have a better conceptual understanding of *why* they are doing things and how the traditional algorithms work. Connie feels caught in the middle. She understands what the curriculum is supposed to do. She even believes it might actually benefit the students in the long run. However, every day she has students in tears in her class because they don't understand what she is asking them to do. She has fielded her share of phone calls from angry parents as well.

1. What are the issues in this case?
2. The students in first and second grade seem to be flourishing in this curriculum, while the older students are struggling. Why might this be? Tie your answer to a constructivist principle.
3. How should the teachers address parental concerns regarding the new curriculum?
4. How should they address the concerns of the algebra teacher?
5. What can the teachers do to help their students at this point?

Reach Your Learning Goals

Learning and Cognition in the Content Areas

(1) EXPERT KNOWLEDGE AND PEDAGOGICAL CONTENT KNOWLEDGE: Distinguish between expert knowledge and pedagogical content knowledge.

Expert knowledge, also called *subject matter knowledge,* involves being an expert regarding the content of a discipline. Pedagogical content knowledge involves knowledge of how to effectively teach a particular discipline. Both are required for being an expert teacher.

(2) READING: Explain how reading develops and discuss some useful approaches to teaching reading.

A Developmental Model of Reading

Chall's model proposes five stages in reading development: (0) From birth to first grade, identify letters of the alphabet and learn to write one's name. (1) In first and second grade, learn to sound out words and complete learning of letter names and sounds. (2) In second and third grade, learn to retrieve individual words and complete learning of names and sounds. (3) In fourth through eighth grade, increasingly obtain new information from print. (4) In high school, become a fully competent reader and understand material from different perspectives.

Language Rule Systems

The language rules systems of phonology, morphology, syntax, and semantics play important roles in reading. Phonological awareness, which involves becoming aware of the sound units in words, is especially important in early reading development. Morphological awareness begins to become important in the middle of elementary school when students increasingly encounter multisyllabic words. Syntax is involved in reading because students who have poor grammar skills have difficulty detecting the way words are combined in sentences. Good semantic skills are involved in becoming a proficient reader because a good vocabulary helps readers to access word meaning effortlessly and is linked to reading comprehension.

Approaches to Reading

Current debate focuses on the phonics approach versus the whole-language approach. The phonics approach advocates providing phonetics instruction and giving children simplified materials. The whole-language approach stresses that reading instruction should parallel children's natural language learning and give children whole-language materials, such as books and poems. Although both approaches can benefit children, the phonics approach needs to be emphasized. Research indicates that phonological awareness instruction is especially effective when it is combined with letter training and as part of a total literacy program. Effective phonological awareness training mainly involves two skills: blending and segmentation. Children's reading also benefits from guided oral reading and instruction in reading strategies.

Cognitive Approaches

Cognitive approaches to reading emphasize decoding and comprehending words, constructing meaning, and developing expert reading strategies. Text has meaning that the reader must actively construct. Metacognitive strategies and automatic processes are involved in decoding and comprehending words. The ability to manipulate and think about sounds also is important. Transactional strategy instruction is one approach to helping students learn to read.

Social Constructivist Approaches

Social constructivist approaches to reading stress that (1) the social context plays an important part in reading and (2) knowledgeable readers in the culture teach less-knowledgeable ones. Meaning is socially negotiated. Reciprocal teaching is a valuable technique in helping students improve their reading. Book clubs and school/family/community connections also reflect the social constructivist perspective.

continued

Developmental Changes	Children's writing follows a developmental timetable, emerging out of scribbling. Most 4-year-olds can print their name. Most 5-year-olds can reproduce letters and copy several short words. Advances in children's language and cognitive development provide the foundation for improved writing.
Cognitive Approaches	Cognitive approaches to writing emphasize many of the same themes as for reading, such as constructing meaning and developing strategies. Planning, problem solving, revising, and metacognitive strategies are thought to be especially important.
Social Constructivist Approaches	Social constructivist approaches to writing focus on the social context in which writing is produced. This social context includes the importance of students participating in a writing community to understand author/reader relationships and taking perspectives of others. Social constructivist approaches to writing include writing of "real texts" about meaningful experiences, teacher-student writing conferences, peer collaboration in writing, and school/family/community connections.

Developmental Changes	Children have a substantial understanding of numerical concepts before they enter first grade. When they go to school, children learn many more advanced kinds of numerical skills. The National Council of Teachers of Mathematics has developed standards for learning mathematics at these grade levels: prekindergarten through grade 2 (base-10 numeration system, for example), grades 3 through 5 (multiplicative reasoning, equivalence and computational fluency), grades 6 through 8 (mathematical reasoning—algebra and geometry), and grades 9 through 12 (interplay of algebra, geometry, statistics, and discrete mathematics).
Controversy in Math Education	Currently, there is controversy in math education about whether math should be taught using a cognitive, conceptual, and constructivist approach, or a practice, computational approach. Students need to develop both a conceptual understanding of math and procedural competency in math.
Cognitive Processes	Among the cognitive processes involved in math are conceptual understanding, knowledge of math procedures, effective organization of knowledge, and metacognitive strategies.
Some Constructivist Principles	Reforms focus on making math education more meaningful, making connections to prior knowledge, and discussing math concepts with others.
Technology and Math Instruction	The NTCM's *Curriculum and Evaluation Standards* recommends that calculators be used at all levels of mathematical instruction. However, some education experts argue that, as in East Asia, calculators should not be used prior to high school to improve students' ability to learn math concepts.

Science Education	Too often, the skills scientists use, such as careful observation, graphing, self-regulatory thinking, and knowing when and how to apply one's knowledge to solve problems, are not routinely taught in schools. Children have many concepts that are incompatible with science and reality. Good teachers perceive and understand a child's underlying scientific concepts, then use the concepts as a scaffold for learning.

| Constructivist Teaching Strategies |

Constructivist teaching strategies include an emphasis on discovery learning and hands-on laboratory investigation. Other strategies include exploring everyday science problems, using activities that help students learn how science works, examining a limited number of science areas in depth, and considering the social contexts of science. The Human Biology Middle Grades Curriculum (HumBio) integrates the study of ecology, evolution, genetics, physiology, health, safety, culture, and human development. Inquiry should not be emphasized alone, and when used it should be guided inquiry. Effective science education emphasizes inquiry and science content knowledge.

(6) SOCIAL STUDIES: Summarize how learning in social studies is becoming more constructivist.

| What Is Social Studies? |

The field of social studies seeks to promote civic competence. In schools, social studies draws from disciplines such as anthropology, economics, geography, history, law, philosophy, political science, psychology, religion, and sociology. Ten themes are recommended to be used for units and courses in social studies by the National Council for the Social Sciences: time, continuity, and change; people, places, and environment; individual development and identity; individuals, groups, and institutions; power, authority, and governance; production, distribution, and consumption; science, technology, and society; global connections; civic ideals and practices; and culture.

| Constructivist Approaches |

Many social studies classes continue to be taught in a traditional lecture format, but there is increasing interest in teaching these classes from a constructivist perspective. This perspective emphasizes the importance of greater reflection, understanding, meaning, critical thinking about values, and sustained examination of a few important topics rather than superficial coverage of many topics.

 KEY TERMS

expert knowledge 365
pedagogical content
   knowledge 366
phonics approach 369

whole-language approach 369
transactional strategy
   instruction approach 371
reciprocal teaching 372

book clubs 373
interactive demonstration
   strategy 389

Human Biology Middle Grades
   Curriculum (HumBio) 391
social studies 394

 PORTFOLIO ACTIVITIES

Now that you have a good understanding of this chapter, complete these exercises to expand your thinking.

Independent Reflection

The Cognitive and Socially Constructive Classroom. For the grade level you plan to teach, create a summary of good ideas for making learning both cognitive and socially constructive. Draw ideas from this and other chapters. Add further ideas of your own. (INTASC: Principles *4, 5*)

Collaborative Work

Taking a Stand in the Math Controversy. There is controversy in math education about whether math should be taught in a constructivist manner or in a more traditional manner. There is also controversy about whether calculators and computers should be used in math instruction in the elementary school years. Get together with several students and evaluate these controversies. Summarize your discussion. (INTASC: Principles *1, 2, 4*)

Research/Field Experience

Researching the Nuts and Bolts of Reading. Read about current trends in teaching children to read. Evaluate these trends based on what you've learned in this chapter. Compare current trends with how you were taught to read. Which method do you think is most effective? Why? What do you think accounts for persistent low reading scores on nationwide standardized tests? (INTASC: Principles *1, 7*)

Go to the Online Learning Center for downloadable portfolio templates.

TAKING IT TO THE NET

- The social constructivist approach to writing emphasizes students' participation in a writing community. Explore an educational, electronic pen pals Web site, and develop an action plan for integrating this resource into your content area. Describe the kinds of opportunities students will have to write "real" texts, collaborate with peers, and share diverse perspectives. **www.epals.com/**

- Online exhibits designed by science museums such as The Exploratorium (**www.exploratorium.edu**) and The Franklin Institute of Science (**www.fi.edu**) offer a gold mine of hands-on science projects that emphasize discovery and exploration. Visit a science museum online and discuss how its resources can enrich science learning in the classroom. **www.exploratorium. edu/sports/index.html**

- Evaluate a Web site that could be used in a social studies classroom. Illustrate how the resource could help you portray events from several different perspectives. Describe historical documents and artifacts provided by the resource. How could you use this information to challenge students to think critically about past events or current social issues? Develop a lesson or project using this resource. **http://memory.loc.gov/**

Connect to the Online Learning Center to explore possible answers.

 STUDY, PRACTICE, AND SUCCEED

Visit **www.mhhe.com/santedu3e** to review the chapter with self-grading quizzes and self-assessments, to apply the chapter material to two more Crack the Case studies, and for suggested activities to develop your teaching portfolio.

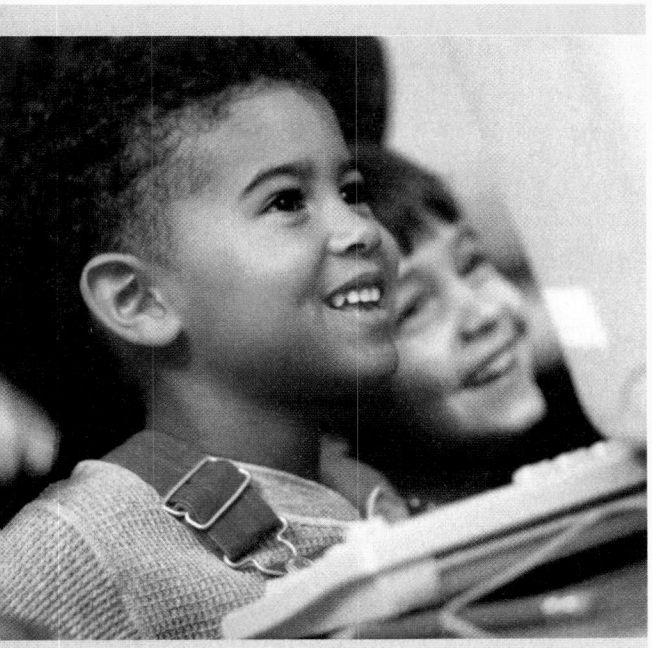

CHAPTER 12

Planning, Instruction, and Technology

Education is the transmission of civilization.

—Ariel and Will Durant
American Authors and Philosophers,
20th Century

Learning Goals

1 Explain what is involved in classroom planning.

2 Identify important forms of teacher-centered instruction.

3 Discuss important forms of learner-centered instruction.

4 Summarize how to effectively use technology to help children learn

TEACHING STORIES   Lois Guest and Kevin Groves

In Lois Guest's fifth-grade classroom at Hesperian Elementary School in San Lorenzo, California, 30 students are working on their new laptop computers provided by the school district. A month after the computers arrived, outdated encyclopedias sit on shelves, and students no longer have to compete for time in the school's computer lab.

The new laptops mark a monumental shift in Guest's career. She has taught for 35 years at Hesperian Elementary and remembers when slide projectors were the height of high tech. Now, she is building a Web site for her class and learning how to use a digital camera and an optical scanner. Guest says that she is learning a lot about technology and that her students are also teaching her how to do things on the computer. Ten-year-old Bianca Guitierrez said that she enjoys working on her new laptop computer so much that it makes her look forward to coming to school.

When Kevin Groves took his fifth-grade class on a field trip to a botanical garden, his students insisted that they be allowed to bring their laptops. One of his students, Salvador Mata, spread out on the grass with his mother and explained to her how to make a PowerPoint presentation. His mother is pleased about Salvador learning how to use a computer at such an early age, believing that it will help him get a good job later in his life. Groves commented that he researches every link he puts on his Web site to make sure it is educational and won't lead to something bad for his students (Source: May, 2001, pp. A1, A24).

Preview

This chapter builds on the learning and cognitive processes we discussed in chapters 7 through 11 and addresses instructional planning at the level of the overall lesson plan or unit. We explore teacher-centered lesson planning, building on the behavioral principles covered in chapter 7, and learner-centered planning, building on material covered in chapters 8 through 11. Finally, we explore important classroom applications of technology, such as use of the Internet.

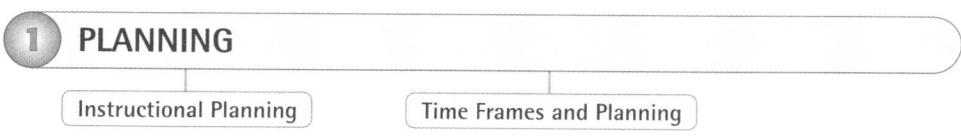

It has been said that when people fail to plan, they plan to fail. Many successful people attribute their accomplishments to effective planning. For example, Lee Iacocca (1984), former chairman of Chrysler Corporation, credits his success to his weekly planner. Our introduction to planning describes what instructional planning is and the different time frames of planning.

Instructional Planning

Planning is a critical aspect of being a competent teacher. **Instructional planning** involves developing a systematic, organized strategy for lessons. Teachers need to decide what and how they are going to teach before they do it. Although some wonderful instructional moments are spontaneous, lessons still should be carefully planned.

It might seem tedious to spend so much time writing out lesson plans. However, they will give you confidence, guide you in covering the most important topics, and keep you from wasting precious class time.

instructional planning A systematic, organized strategy for planning lessons.

FRANK AND ERNEST © Thaves/Dist. by Newspaper Enterprise Association Inc.

Instructional planning might be mandated by the school in which you teach. Many principals and instructional supervisors require teachers to keep written plans, and you may be asked to submit lesson plans several weeks in advance. When observing classroom teachers, supervisors check to see if the teacher is following the plan. If a teacher is absent, a substitute teacher can follow the plan.

Expectations for teacher planning have increased with the promulgation of state learning standards that specify what students need to know and be able to do (Darling-Hammond & others, 2005). However, these standards usually do not state what the teacher should do in the classroom to reach these standards. When standards are in place, teachers must figure out how to plan and organize their curriculum around the most important dimensions implied by the standards and create a "sequence and set of learning activities for the particular students they teach" (Darling-Hammond & others, 2005, p. 184).

Many planning strategies are organized around four elements: "the nature of the subject matter, the learners, the context, and the teacher's role" (Darling-Hammond & others, 2005, p. 184). One effective planning strategy that many teachers use is *mapping backward* from "goals to desired performances to activities and elements of scaffolding needed to support student progress." Indeed, a good strategy is to begin your planning by thinking about what goals you want your students to reach by the end of the school year and then map backward from that point. In a recent analysis, many experienced teachers described how in the early years of their teaching they lacked a long-term vision in their curriculum planning and strongly urged beginning teachers to think more about the big picture—the key things they want their students to learn this year—and how they can guide their students to get there (Kunzmann, 2003).

Linda Darling-Hammond and her colleagues (2005, pp. 185–186) recently described how planning learning experiences to reach goals

> . . . requires attention to selection and organization of content and activities—what is often called 'scope and sequence.' Teachers must decide what is important to include, given their goals, and know how to make it accessible to a particular group of students. This requires thinking about how to give students a schema or conceptual map of the domain to be studied (National Research Council, 2000) as well as planning specific activities in light of students' levels of readiness for various kinds of learning experiences. It also requires consideration of the kinds of information, demonstrations, models, inquiry opportunities, discussion, and practice students need over time to understand particular concepts and develop particular skills. . . .

In sum, teachers need to "figure out which things students should do when, in what order, and how" to implement the big picture of their curricular vision.

Time Frames and Planning

As we just indicated, developing systematic time plans involves knowing what needs to be done and when to do it, or focusing on "task" and "time." Here is one helpful six-part task and time plan (Douglass & Douglass, 1993):

What Needs to Be Done

1. *Set instructional goals.* (What do I expect to accomplish?)
2. *Plan activities.* (What do I have to do to reach the goals?)
3. *Set priorities.* (Which tasks are more important than others?)

The Time to Do It

4. *Make time estimates.* (How much time will each activity take?)
5. *Create schedules.* (When will we do each activity?)
6. *Be flexible.* (How will I handle unexpected occurrences?)

You will need to plan for different time spans, ranging from yearly to daily planning (Arends, 2004). If school-wide planning or your own career planning is involved, the time frame likely will be a number of years.

Robert Yinger (1980) identified five time spans of teacher planning: yearly planning, term planning, unit planning, weekly planning, and daily planning. Figure 12.1 illustrates these time frames and shows planning for them. Yinger also recommends that teachers attend to four areas when planning: goals, sources of information, the form of the plan, and criteria for the effectiveness of the planning. Figure 12.2 shows what is involved in these areas across the five different time frames.

Although planning is a key dimension of successful teaching, don't overplan to the point of becoming an automaton. Develop organized plans and try to carry them out, but be flexible; as a year, month, week, or day unfolds, adapt to changing circumstances. A controversial current event or necessary topic might emerge that you did not originally include. Monitor and rework your plans as the school year goes by to suit these changing circumstances.

If you plan effectively, you won't have to keep all of the details of a lesson in mind all of the time (Middleton & Goepfert, 1996). Your plan lets you focus on the immediate dialogue you are having with students and guides the interactive aspect of your instruction.

Many teachers rely heavily on published teachers' guides or textbook structures to direct their instructional planning. This can have positive benefits because, with activities or lessons developed for the entire time, you can focus more on the day-to-day aspects of teaching. However, you might go into greater depth about some topics and develop larger projects for the entire term than are included in the teachers' guides.

A final comment needs to be made about planning. It is increasingly understood that teachers need to monitor and evaluate their curriculum planning in terms of

FIGURE 12.1 Five Time Spans of Teacher Planning and Their Occurrence over the School Year

Source: From R. J. Yinger, "A Study of Teaching Planning," *The Elementary School Journal*, Vol. 80, No. 3 (Jan. 1980), p. 113. Copyright © 1980 by The University of Chicago. Reprinted by permission of the University of Chicago Press.

	Goals of planning	Sources of information	Form of the plan	Criteria for judging the effectiveness of planning
Yearly planning	1. Establishing general content (fairly general and framed by district curriculum objectives) 2. Establishing basic curriculum sequence 3. Ordering and reserving materials	1. Students (general information about numbers and returning students) 2. Resources available 3. Curriculum guidelines (district objectives) 4. Experience with specific curricula and materials	General outlines listing basic content and possible ideas in each subject matter area (spiral notebook used for each subject)	1. Comprehensiveness of plans 2. Fit with own goals and district objectives
Term planning	1. Detailing of content to be covered in next 3 months 2. Establishing a weekly schedule for term that conforms to teacher's goals and emphases for the term	1. Direct contact with students 2. Time constraints set by school schedule 3. Resources available	1. Elaboration of outlines constructed for yearly planning 2. A weekly schedule outline specifying activities and times	1. Outlines— comprehensiveness, completeness, and specificity of elaborations 2. Schedule— comprehensiveness and fit with goals for term, balance 3. Fit with goals for term
Unit planning	1. Developing a sequence of well-organized learning experiences 2. Presenting comprehensive, integrated, and meaningful content at an appropriate level	1. Students' abilities, interests, etc. 2. Materials, length of lessons, set-up time, demand, format 3. District objectives 4. Facilities available for activities	1. Lists of outlines of activities and content 2. Lists of sequenced activities 3. Notes in plan book	1. Organization, sequence, balance, and flow of outlines 2. Fit with yearly and term goals 3. Fit with anticipated student interest and involvement
Weekly planning	1. Laying out the week's activities within the framework of the weekly schedule 2. Adjusting schedule for interruptions and special needs 3. Maintaining continuity and regularity of activities	1. Students' performance in preceding days and weeks 2. Scheduled school interruptions (for example, assemblies, holidays) 3. Materials, aides, and other resources	1. Names and times of activities in plan book 2. Day divided into four instructional blocks punctuated by morning recess, lunch, and afternoon recess	1. Completeness of plans 2. Degree to which weekly schedule had been followed 3. Flexibility of plans to allow for special time constraints or interruptions 4. Fit with goals
Daily planning	1. Setting up and arranging classroom for next day 2. Specifying activity components not yet decided upon 3. Fitting daily schedule to last-minute intrusions 4. Preparing students for day's activities	1. Instructions in materials to be used 2. Set-up time required for activities 3. Assessment of class "disposition" at start of day 4. Continued interest, involvement, and enthusiasm	1. Schedule for day written on the chalkboard and discussed with students 2. Preparation and arrangement of materials and facilities in the room	1. Completion of last-minute preparations and decisions about content, materials, etc. 2. Involvement, enthusiasm, and interest communicated by students

FIGURE 12.2 Five Time Spans of Teacher Planning and the Activities Involved

Source: From R. J. Yinger, "A Study of Teaching Planning," *The Elementary School Journal*, Vol. 80, No. 3 (Jan. 1980), pp. 114–115. Copyright © 1980 by The University of Chicago. Reprinted by permission of the University of Chicago Press.

how well students are making progress toward learning goals as they go through the term (Darling-Hammond & others, 2005). Thus, time for assessment and feedback to students needs to be built into the planning process. We will explore different types of assessment in chapters 15 and 16.

Review, Reflect, and Practice

(1) Explain what is involved in classroom planning.

REVIEW

- Why does instruction need to be planned?
- What planning needs to be done related to the use of time?

REFLECT

- In your own K–12 experiences, did you ever have a teacher who did not put enough effort into planning? What was that like for students?

PRAXIS™ PRACTICE

1. Ms. Swenson is planning for the school year. Which of the following strategies should she follow?
   a. Plan forward, starting with plans for the first week of school.
   b. Map backward, determining the goals she wants her students to reach by the end of the school year.
   c. Not spend too much time in planning but rather get a sense of where her students are in the first month of school.
   d. Engage in circular planning.

2. In planning, Mr. Tomasello considers the objectives established by the district and state mandated standards and aligns his curriculum to them. After doing this, he considers what he wants to teach when, based on the sequence that makes the most sense. Finally, he reserves the necessary equipment and requests the appropriate materials to carry out his plans. At what level of planning is Mr. Tomasello most likely to be engaging?
   a. daily
   b. weekly
   c. term
   d. yearly

Please see the answer key at the end of the book.

(2) TEACHER-CENTERED LESSON PLANNING AND INSTRUCTION

| Teacher-Centered Lesson Planning | Direct Instruction | Teacher-Centered Instructional Strategies | Evaluating Teacher-Centered Instruction |

Traditionally, the focus in schools has been on teacher-centered lesson planning and instruction. In this approach, planning and instruction are highly structured and the teacher directs students' learning.

Teacher-Centered Lesson Planning

Three general tools are especially useful in teacher-centered planning. These are behavioral objectives, task analysis, and instructional taxonomies (classifications), which we explore next.

behavioral objectives Statements that communicate proposed changes in students' behavior to reach desired levels of performance.

Behavioral Objectives **Behavioral objectives** are statements about changes that the teacher wishes to see in students' performance. In Robert Mager's (1962) view, behavioral objectives should be very specific. Mager believes that behavioral objectives should have three parts:

- *Student's behavior.* Focus on what the student will learn or do.
- *Conditions under which the behavior will occur.* State how the behavior will be evaluated or tested.
- *Performance criteria.* Determine what level of performance will be acceptable.

For example, a teacher might develop a behavioral objective around the idea that the student will describe five causes of the decline of the British Empire (student's behavior). The teacher plans to give the student an essay test on this topic (conditions under which the behavior will occur). And the teacher decides that explaining four or five causes will be acceptable performance (performance criterion).

Task Analysis Another tool of teacher-centered planning is **task analysis,** which focuses on breaking down a complex task that students are to learn into its component parts (Alberto & Troutman, 2006; Miller, 2006). The analysis can proceed in three basic steps (Moyer & Dardig, 1978):

1. Determine what skills or concepts the student needs to have to learn the task.
2. List any materials that will be required in order to perform the task, such as paper, pencil, and calculator.
3. List all of the components of the task in the order in which they must be performed.

Instructional Taxonomies Instructional taxonomies also aid teacher-centered approaches. A **taxonomy** is a classification system. **Bloom's taxonomy** was developed by Benjamin Bloom and his colleagues (1956). It classifies educational objectives into three domains: cognitive, affective, and psychomotor. Bloom's taxonomy has been used by many teachers in their lesson planning to create goals and objectives.

The Cognitive Domain Bloom's cognitive taxonomy has six objectives (Bloom & others, 1956):

- *Knowledge.* Students have the ability to remember information. For example, an objective might be to list or describe four main advantages of using a computer for word processing.
- *Comprehension.* Students understand the information and can explain it in their own words. For example, an objective might be to explain or discuss how a computer can effectively be used for word processing.
- *Application.* Students use knowledge to solve real-life problems. For example, an objective might be to apply what has been learned about using a computer for word processing to how this could be used in various careers.
- *Analysis.* Students break down complex information into smaller parts and relate information to other information. For example, an objective might be to compare one type of word-processing program with another for doing term papers.
- *Synthesis.* Students combine elements and create new information. For example, an objective might be to organize all that has been learned about the use of computers for writing.)
- *Evaluation.* Students make good judgments and decisions. For example, an objective might be to critique different word-processing programs or to judge the strengths and weaknesses of a particular word-processing program.

When Bloom originally presented his taxonomy, he described these six cognitive objectives as hierarchically arranged from *lower level* (knowledge, comprehension) to *higher level* (application, analysis, synthesis, evaluation), with higher-level objectives

task analysis Breaking down a complex task that students are to learn into its component parts.

taxonomy A classification system.

Bloom's taxonomy Developed by Benjamin Bloom and colleagues; consists of educational objectives in three domains—cognitive, affective, and psychomotor.

building on the lower ones. However, educators often strip the objectives of their level and simply use them as a comprehensive way of considering different cognitive goals.

Bloom's cognitive objectives can be used when planning assessment. True/false, matching, multiple-choice, and short-answer items are often used to assess knowledge and comprehension. Essay questions, class discussions, projects, and portfolios are especially good for assessing application, analysis, synthesis, and evaluation.

The Affective Domain The affective taxonomy consists of five objectives related to emotional responses to tasks (Krathwohl, Bloom, & Masia, 1964). Each of the following five objectives requires the student to show some degree of commitment or emotional intensity:

- *Receiving*. Students become aware of or attend to something in the environment. For example, a guest comes to class to talk with students about reading. An objective might be for students to listen carefully to the speaker.
- *Responding*. Students become motivated to learn and display a new behavior as a result of an experience. An objective might be for students to become motivated to become better readers as a result of the guest speaker's appearance.
- *Valuing*. Students become involved in, or committed to, some experience. An objective might be for students to value reading as an important skill.
- *Organizing*. Students integrate a new value into an already existing set of values and give it proper priority. An objective might be to have students participate in a book club.
- *Value characterizing*. Students act in accordance with the value and are firmly committed to it. An objective might be that over the course of the school year, students increasingly value reading.

The Psychomotor Domain Most of us link motor activity with physical education and athletics, but many other subjects, such as handwriting and word processing, also involve movement. In the sciences, students have to manipulate complex equipment; the visual and manual arts require good hand-eye coordination. Bloom's psychomotor objectives include these:

- *Reflex movements*. Students respond involuntarily without conscious thought to a stimulus—for example blinking when an object unexpectedly hurtles their way.
- *Basic fundamentals*. Students make basic voluntary movements that are directed toward a particular purpose, such as grasping a microscope knob and correctly turning it.

- *Perceptual abilities*. Students use their senses, such as seeing, hearing, or touching, to guide their skill efforts, such as watching how to hold an instrument in science, like a microscope, and listening to instructions on how to use it.
- *Physical abilities*. Students develop general skills of endurance, strength, flexibility, and agility, such as running long distances or hitting a softball.
- *Skilled movements*. Students perform complex physical skills with some degree of proficiency, such as effectively sketching a drawing.
- *Nondiscussive behaviors*. Students communicate feelings and emotions through bodily actions, such as doing pantomimes or dancing to communicate a musical piece.

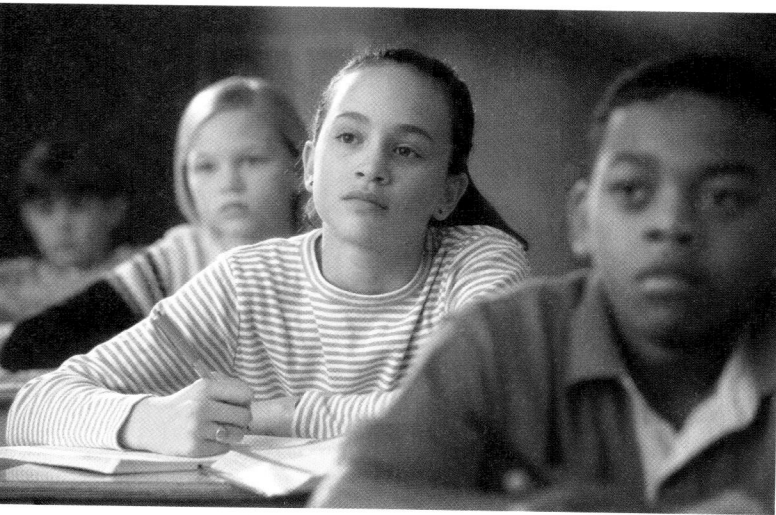

What are some objectives in Bloom's original cognitive taxonomy? How have these been modified in the update of Bloom's taxonomy?

Teachers can use Bloom's taxonomies for the cognitive, affective, and psychomotor domains to

Category	Associated verbs
Cognitive domain	
Knowledge	List, read, identify, define, indicate, describe, name, quote, underline
Comprehension	Translate, transform, summarize, paraphrase, illustrate, interpret, estimate, interpolate, extrapolate, classify, categorize, reorganize, explain, predict
Application	Apply, generalize, relate, use, employ, transfer, graph, exemplify, illustrate, tabulate, calculate, compute, derive, calibrate
Analysis	Analyze, contrast, compare, distinguish, detect, edit, discriminate
Synthesis	Produce, constitute, modify, originate, propose, plan, design, combine, organize, synthesize, develop, formulate
Evaluation	Judge, argue, validate, predict, assess, decide, appraise, conclude, evaluate, explain, criticize
Affective domain	
Receiving	Accept, differentiate, listen, separate, select, share, agree
Responding	Approve, applaud, comply, follow, discuss, volunteer, practice, spend time with, paraphrase
Valuing	Argue, debate, deny, help, support, protest, participate, subsidize, praise
Organizing	Discuss, compare, balance, define, abstract, formulate, theorize, organize
Value characterizing	Change, avoid, complete, manage, resolve, revise, resist, require
Psychomotor domain	
Reflex movements	Blink, stretch, relax, jerk, straighten up
Basic fundamentals	Walk, run, jump, push, pull, manipulate, catch, grasp, stand
Perceptual abilities	Follow, dodge, maintain, identify, read, write, list, balance, trace, brush, print, pronounce
Physical abilities	Hop, skip, jump, run, touch, lift, push, pull, tap, float, hit, throw, toss, strum
Skilled movements	Draw, dance, ski, skate, paint, build, volley, race, whistle, march, somersault, hammer, sculpt, sketch
Nondiscussive behaviors	Pantomime, mimic, direct, perform, communicate, gesture, use body movement

FIGURE 12.3 Action Verbs for Writing Objectives in the Cognitive, Affective, and Psychomotor Domains

plan instruction. In the past, instructional planning has generally focused on cognitive or behavioral objectives. Bloom's taxonomy provides for a more expansive consideration of skills by also including affective and psychomotor domains. Figure 12.3 presents Bloom's domains and lists associated action verbs you can use for creating objectives during instructional planning.

A group of educational psychologists updated Bloom's knowledge and cognitive process dimensions in light of recent theory and research (Anderson & Krathwohl,

2001). In the update, the knowledge dimension has four categories, which lie along a continuum from concrete (factual) to abstract (metacognition):

- *Factual:* the basic elements students must know to be acquainted with a discipline or solve problems in it (technical vocabulary, sources of information)
- *Conceptual:* the interrelationships among the basic elements within a larger structure that allows them to function together (periods of geological time, forms of business ownership)
- *Procedural:* how to do something, methods of inquiry, and criteria for using skills (skills used in painting with watercolors, interviewing techniques)
- *Metacognitive:* knowledge of cognition and awareness of one's own cognition (knowledge of outlining and strategies for remembering)

In the update of the cognitive process dimension, six categories lie along a continuum from less complex (remember) to more complex (create):

- *Remember.* Retrieve relevant knowledge from long-term memory. (Recognize the dates of important events in U.S. history.)
- *Understand.* Construct meaning from instruction that includes interpreting, exemplifying, classifying, summarizing, inferring, comparing, and explaining. (Explain the causes of important eighteenth-century events in France.)
- *Apply.* Carry out or use a procedure in a given situation. (Use a law in physics in situations in which it is appropriate.)
- *Analyze.* Break material into its component parts and determine how the parts relate to each other and to overall structure or purpose. (Distinguish between relevant and irrelevant numbers in a math word problem.)
- *Evaluate.* Make judgments based on criteria and standards. (Detect inconsistencies or fallacies in a product.)
- *Create.* Put elements together to form a coherent or functional whole; reorganize elements into a new pattern or structure. (Generate hypotheses to account for an observed phenomenon.)

Direct Instruction

As we indicated in chapter 1, **direct instruction** is a structured, teacher-centered approach that is characterized by teacher direction and control, high teacher expectations for students' progress, maximum time spent by students on academic tasks, and efforts by the teacher to keep negative affect to a minimum. The focus of direct instruction is academic activity; nonacademic materials (such as toys, games, and puzzles) tend not to be used; also deemphasized is nonacademically oriented teacher-student interaction (such as conversations about self or personal concerns).

Teacher direction and control take place when the teacher chooses students' learning tasks, directs students' learning of the tasks, and minimizes the amount of nonacademic talk (Marchand-Martella, Slocum, & Martella, 2004). The teacher sets high standards for performance and expects students to reach these levels of excellence.

An important goal in the direct-instruction approach is maximizing student learning time (Stevenson, 2000). Time spent by students on academic tasks in the classroom is called *academic learning time.* Learning takes time. The more academic learning time students experience, the more likely they are to learn the material and achieve high standards. The premise of direct instruction is that the best way to maximize time on academic tasks is to create a highly structured, academically oriented learning environment. The Diversity and Education interlude describes cross-cultural research about the amount of time students spend on math in different countries, as well as other comparisons across countries.

Yet another emphasis in the direct-instruction approach is keeping negative affect to a minimum. Researchers have found that negative affect interferes with learning (Rosenshine, 1971). Advocates of direct instruction underscore the importance of keeping an academic focus and avoiding negative affect, such as the negative feelings that can often arise in both the teacher and students when a teacher overcriticizes.

direct instruction A structured, teacher-centered approach that is characterized by teacher direction and control, high teacher expectations for students' progress, maximum time spent by students on academic tasks, and efforts by the teacher to keep negative affect to a minimum.

DIVERSITY AND EDUCATION
Cross-Cultural Comparisons in Math Education

The University of Michigan's Harold Stevenson is one of the leading experts on children's learning and has been conducting research on this topic for five decades. In the 1980s and 1990s, he turned his attention to discovering ways to improve children's learning by conducting cross-cultural comparisons of children in the United States with children in Asian countries, especially Japan, China, and Taiwan (Stevenson, 1992, 1995, 2000; Stevenson & Hofer, 1999; Stevenson & others, 1990). In Stevenson's research, Asian students consistently outperformed American students in mathematics. Also, the longer students are in school, the wider the gap became—the lowest difference was in first grade, the highest in eleventh grade (the highest grade studied).

To learn more about the reasons for these cross-cultural differences, Stevenson and his colleagues spent thousands of hours observing in classrooms, as well as interviewing and surveying teachers, students, and parents. They found that Asian teachers spent more of their time teaching math than American teachers did. For example, in Japan more than one-fourth of the total classroom time in first grade was spent on math instruction, compared with only one-tenth of the time in U.S. first-grade classrooms. Also, Asian students were in school an average of 240 days a year, compared with 178 days in the United States.

In addition to the substantially greater time spent on math instruction in Asian schools than in American schools, differences were found between Asian and American parents. American parents had much lower expectations for their children's education and achievement than Asian parents did. Also, American parents were more likely to believe that their children's math ability is due to innate ability, whereas Asian parents were more likely to say that their children's math achievement was the consequence of effort and training (see figure 12.4) (Stevenson, Lee, & Stigler, 1986). Asian students were more likely than American students to do math homework, and Asian parents were far more likely to help their children with their math homework than American parents were (Chen & Stevenson, 1989).

In another cross-cultural comparison of math education, videotapes of eighth-grade teachers' instruction in the United States, Japan, and Germany were analyzed (Stigler & Hiebert, 1997, 1999). Differences among the countries included (1) Japanese students spent less time solving routine math problems and more time inventing, analyzing, and proving than American or German students did; (2) Japanese teachers engaged in more direct lecturing than American or German teachers did; and (3) Japanese teachers were more likely to emphasize math thinking, whereas American and German teachers were more likely to stress math skills (solving a specific problem or using a specific formula). Also noticeable was how much emphasis there was on collaborative planning with other teachers in Japanese math education.

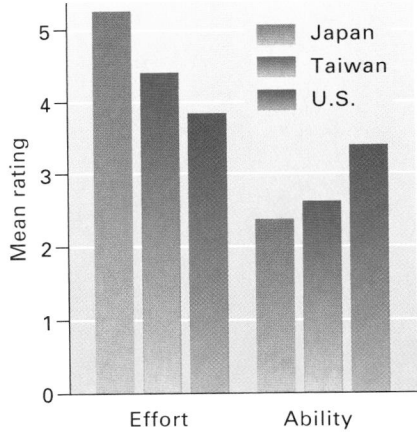

FIGURE 12.4 Mothers' Beliefs about the Factors Responsible for Children's Math Achievement in Three Countries

In one study, mothers in Japan and Taiwan were more likely to believe that their children's math achievement was due to effort rather than innate ability, while U.S. mothers were more likely to believe their children's math achievement was due to innate ability (Stevenson, Lee, & Stigler, 1986). If parents believe that their children's math achievement is due to innate ability and their children are not doing well in math, the implication is that they are less likely to think their children will benefit from putting forth more effort.

Source: Reprinted with permission from *Science*, Vol. 231 (1986), pp. 693–699, Figure 6. H. W. Stevenson, S. Lee, and J. W. Stigler, "Mathematics Achievement of Chinese, Japanese, and American Children." Copyright 1986 AAAS.

In Stevenson's research, Asian students scored considerably higher than U.S. students on math achievement tests. *What are some possible explanations for these findings?*

Teacher–Centered Instructional Strategies

Many teacher-centered strategies reflect direct instruction. Here we will talk about orienting students to new material; lecturing, explaining, and demonstrating; questioning and discussing; mastery learning; seatwork; and homework.

Orienting Before presenting and explaining new material, establish a framework for the lesson and orient students to the new material (Joyce, Weil, & Calhoun, 2004): (1) review the previous day's activities; (2) discuss the lesson's objective; (3) provide clear, explicit instructions about the work to be done; and (4) give an overview of today's lesson. Such orientation and structuring at the beginning of a lesson are linked with improved student achievement (Fisher & others, 1980).

Advance organizers are teaching activities and techniques that establish a framework and orient students to material before it is presented (Ausubel, 1960). You can use advance organizers when you begin a lesson to help students see the "big picture" of what is to come and how information is meaningfully connected.

Advance organizers come in two forms: expository and comparative. **Expository advance organizers** provide students with new knowledge that will orient them to the upcoming lesson. The chapter-opening outline and learning goals in each chapter of this book are expository advance organizers. Another way to provide an expository advance organizer is to describe the lesson's theme and why it is important to study this topic. For example, in orienting students to the topic of exploring the Aztec civilization in a history class, the teacher says that they are going to study the Spanish invasion of Mexico and describes who the Aztecs were, what their lives were like, and their artifacts. To heighten student interest, she also says that they will study worlds in collision as Spain's conquistadors were filled with awe at sights of a spectacular Western civilization. There are Mexican American students in her class, and the teacher emphasizes how this information can help everyone in the class understand these students' personal and cultural identity.

Comparative advance organizers introduce new material by connecting it with what students already know. For example, in the history class just mentioned, the teacher says that the Spanish invasion of Mexico continues the transatlantic traffic that changed two worlds: Europe and the Americas. She asks students to think about how this discussion of the Aztecs connects with Columbus' journey, which they examined last week.

Lecturing, Explaining, and Demonstrating Lecturing, explaining, and demonstrating are common teacher activities in the direct-instruction approach. Researchers have found that effective teachers spend more time explaining and demonstrating new material than their less-effective counterparts do (Rosenshine, 1986). In chapter 11, we described the process of interactive demonstration strategy, an effective strategy for teaching concepts in science.

On some occasions we sit through boring lectures, yet on other occasions we have been captivated by a lecturer and learned a great deal from the presentation. Let's explore some guidelines for when lecturing is a good choice and some strategies for delivering an effective lecture. Here are some goals that lecturing can accomplish (Henson, 1988):

1. Presenting information and motivating students' interest in a subject
2. Introducing a topic before students read about it on their own, or giving instructions on how to perform a task
3. Summarizing or synthesizing information after a discussion or inquiry
4. Providing alternative points of view or clarifying issues in preparation for discussion
5. Explaining materials that students are having difficulty learning on their own

Questioning and Discussing It is necessary but challenging to integrate questions and discussion in teacher-centered instruction (Weinstein, 2003). Teachers should respond to each student's learning needs while maintaining the group's interest and attention. It also is important to distribute participation widely while also retaining

advance organizers Teaching activities and techniques that establish a framework and orient students to material before it is presented.

expository advance organizers Organizers that provide students with new knowledge that will orient them to the upcoming lesson.

comparative advance organizers Connections with prior knowledge that help to introduce new material.

BEST PRACTICES
Strategies for Lecturing

These are some good strategies to use when lecturing:

1. *Be prepared.* Don't just "wing" a lecture. Spend time preparing and organizing what you will present.

2. *Keep lectures short and intersperse them with questions and activities.* For example, lecture for 10 or 15 minutes to provide the background information and framework for a topic, then place students in small discussion groups.

3. *Make the lecture interesting and exciting.* Think about what you can say that will motivate students' interest in a topic. Vary the pace of the lecture by interlacing it with related video clips, demonstrations, handouts, and/or activities for students.

4. *Follow a designated sequence and include certain key components:*
   - Begin with advance organizers or previews of the topic.
   - Verbally and visually highlight any key concepts or new ideas (like the boldfaced key terms in this book). Use the blackboard, an overhead projector, or another large-display device.
   - Present new information in relation to what students already know about the topic.
   - Periodically elicit student responses to ensure that they understand the information up to that point and to encourage active learning.
   - At the end of the lecture, provide a summary or an overview of the main ideas.
   - Make connections to future lectures or activities.

the enthusiasm of eager volunteers. An additional challenge is allowing students to contribute while still maintaining the focus on the lesson.

A special concern is that male students are more likely than female students to dominate the discussion. In one study of ten high school geometry classes, males called out answers to the teacher twice as frequently as females did (Becker, 1981). Similar results were found in a study of sixty physical science and chemistry classes (Jones & Wheatley, 1990). Be sensitive to gender patterns and ensure that girls get equal discussion time.

Mastery Learning　**Mastery learning** involves learning one concept or topic thoroughly before moving on to a more difficult one. A successful mastery learning approach involves these procedures (Bloom, 1971; Carroll, 1963):

- Specify the learning task or lesson. Develop precise instructional objectives. Establish mastery standards (this typically is where *A* students perform).
- Break the course into learning units that are aligned with instructional objectives.
- Plan instructional procedures to include corrective feedback to students if they fail to master the material at an acceptable level, such as 90 percent correct. The corrective feedback might take place through supplemental materials, tutoring, or small-group instruction.
- Give an end-of-unit or end-of-course test that evaluates whether the student has mastered all of the material at an acceptable level.

Mastery learning gets mixed reviews. Some researchers indicate that mastery learning is effective in increasing the time that students spend on learning tasks (Kulik, Kulik, & Bangert-Drowns, 1990), but others find less support for mastery learning (Bangert, Kulik, & Kulik, 1983). Outcomes of mastery learning depend on the teacher's skill in planning and executing the strategy. One context in which mastery learning might be especially beneficial is remedial reading (Schunk, 2004). A well-organized mastery learning program for remedial reading allows students to progress at their own rates based on their skills, their motivation, and the time they have to learn.

Seatwork　*Seatwork* refers to the practice of having all or a majority of students work independently at their seats. Teachers vary in how much they use seatwork as part of their instruction (Weinstein, 2003). Some teachers use it every day; others rarely use it. Figure 12.5 summarizes the challenges of seatwork for the teacher and the student.

FIGURE 12.5 Challenges of Seatwork for Teachers and Students

For the teacher
1. Keeping track of what the rest of the class is doing
2. Keeping students on-task
3. Dealing with the varying paces at which students work ("ragged" endings)
4. Selecting or creating seatwork that is clear and meaningful
5. Matching seatwork to students' varying levels of achievement
6. Collecting, correcting, recording, and returning seatwork assignments

For the student
1. Completing assigned work on their own
2. Understanding how and when to obtain the teacher's help
3. Understanding the norms for assisting peers
4. Learning how to be effective in obtaining help from peers

mastery learning Learning one concept or topic thoroughly before moving on to a more difficult one.

BEST PRACTICES
Strategies for the Effective Use of Questions

Let's examine some effective strategies for using questions in the classroom:

1. *Use fact-based questions as entrees into thinking-based questions.* For example, in teaching a lesson on environmental pollution, the teacher might ask the fact-based question: "What are three types of environmental pollution?" Then she could follow with this thinking-based question: "What strategies can you think of for reducing one of these types of environmental pollution?" Don't overuse fact-based questions, because they tend to produce rote learning rather than learning for understanding.

2. *Avoid yes/no and leading questions.* Yes/no questions should be used only as a segue into more probing questions. For example, avoid questions like "Was environmental pollution responsible for the dead fish in the lake?" Keep these questions to a minimum, only occasionally using them as a warm-up for questions such as these: "How did the pollution kill the fish?" "Why do you think companies polluted the lake?" "What can be done to clean up environmental pollution?"

   Also avoid asking leading questions such as "Don't you agree?" or other rhetorical questions such as "You do want to read more about environmental pollution, don't you?" These types of questions don't produce meaningful responses and simply hand the initiative back to the teacher.

4. *Leave enough time for students to think about answers.* Too often when teachers ask questions, they don't give students enough time to think. In one study, teachers waited less than one second, on the average, before calling on a student to respond (Rowe, 1986)! In the same study, teachers waited only about one second, on the average, for the student to respond before supplying the answer themselves. Such intrusions don't give students adequate time to construct answers. In the study just mentioned, teachers were subsequently instructed to wait three to five seconds to allow students to respond to questions. The increased wait time led to considerable improvements in responses, including better inferences about the

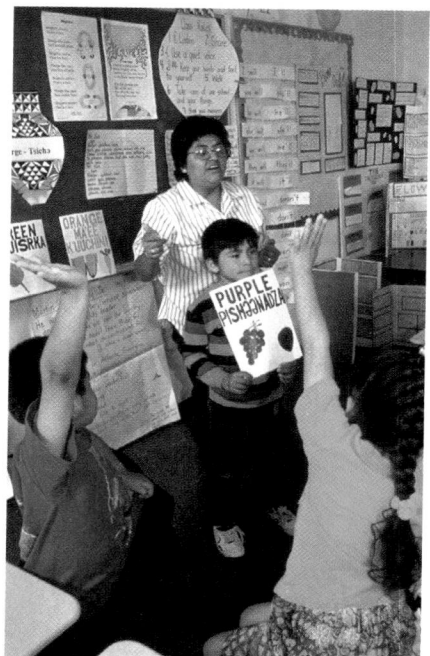

What are some good teaching strategies for the effective use of questions?

materials and more student-initiated questions. Waiting three to five seconds or more for students to respond is not as easy as it might seem; it takes practice. But your students will benefit considerably from having to think and construct responses. Next, Kathy Fuchser, a high school English and journalism teacher, describes her thoughts about the importance of silence.

THROUGH THE EYES OF TEACHERS
Examine Your Silence

Become comfortable with silence, for it offers opportunity to think through responses intellectually *and* emotionally instead of reacting emotionally to what's been said.

5. *Ask clear, purposeful, brief, and sequenced questions.* Avoid being vague. Focus the questions on the lesson at hand. Plan ahead so that your questions are meaningfully tied to the topic. If your questions are long-winded, you run the risk that they will not be understood, so briefer is better. Also plan questions so that they follow a logical sequence, integrating them with previously discussed material before moving to the next topic (Grossier, 1964).

6. *Monitor how you respond to students' answers.* What should you do next after a student responds to your question? Many teachers just say "Okay" or "Uh-huh" (Sadker & Sadker, 2005). Usually it is wise to do more. You can use the student's response as a basis for follow-up questions and engage the student or other students in a dialogue. Provide feedback that is tailored to the student's existing level of knowledge and understanding.

7. *Be aware of when it is best to pose a question to the entire class or to a particular student.* Asking the entire class a question makes all students in the class responsible for responding. Asking a specific student a question can make other students less likely to answer it. Some reasons to ask a question to a particular student are (Grossier, 1964) (a) to draw an inattentive student into the

lesson, (b) to ask a follow-up question of someone who has just responded, and (c) to call on someone who rarely responds when questions are asked to the class as a whole. Don't let a small group of assertive students dominate the responses. Talk with them independently about continuing their positive responses without monopolizing class time. One strategy for giving students an equal chance to respond is to pull names from a cookie jar or check names off a class list as students respond (Weinstein & Mignano, 2003).

8. *Encourage students to ask questions.* Praise them for good questions. Ask them "How?" and "Why?" and encourage them to ask "How?" and "Why?"

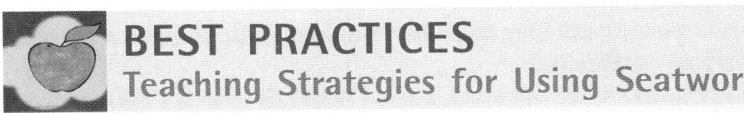

BEST PRACTICES
Teaching Strategies for Using Seatwork

Here are some good guidelines for minimizing the problems that seatwork poses (Weinstein & Mignano, 1997, pp. 177–192):

1. *"Check students' seatwork for clarity, meaningfulness, and appropriateness."* Seatwork often involves worksheets. Their layout should be attractive and functional. At least some of the worksheets should be fun to do.

2. *Clearly describe seatwork assignments.* Give students an introductory explanation of the seatwork and describe its purpose.

3. *Monitor students' behavior and comprehension.* Students can become bored and easily distracted during seatwork, especially if it goes on too long. Thus, monitoring behavior during seatwork is crucial to its learning contribution. And it's not just enough for students to be busy and on-task; they also need to be actively engaged in learning something. One strategy "is to spend the first five minutes of seatwork circulating around the room." Once you feel confident that students understand what to do, establish the first small group. Then, after spending time with that group, circulate again, form a second group if desired, and so on.

4. *Teach students what to do if they get stuck.* Students need to know how and when they can ask for your help. Effective teachers often tell students not to disrupt them while they are working with a small group but, rather, to ask for help while the teacher circulates between small-group sessions. Some teachers develop special systems for help, such as a small red flag for students to keep on their desk and raise if they need assistance. You can tell students to skip the tasks that are troublesome and work on other tasks until you are available. You also need to make it clear to students whether it is okay to ask peers for assistance. Many teachers not only allow peer help but actively encourage it.

5. *Tell students what to do when they are finished.* Provide enjoyable educational activities for students to engage in if they finish before the time allotted for seatwork is up. These activities might include working on a computer, doing free reading or journal writing, solving brainteasers and puzzles, or resuming work on long-term, ongoing projects.

6. *Search for alternatives to workbook pages.* Relying too much on commercially prepared workbook pages can induce boredom and off-task behavior. Spend some time creating seatwork that challenges your students to think reflectively, deeply, and creatively; don't bore them with trivial tasks. Alternatives to such common worksheet activities (such as fill-in-the-blanks) include reading, writing, doing ongoing projects, spending time in learning centers, working on a computer, and doing cross-age tutoring.

Science

- Simple experiments with lab sheets
- Observations over time with recording forms
- Exploring properties of objects and classifying them

Social studies

- Recreating items used by different civilizations
- Creating charts or graphs of population trends
- Map making

Mathematics

- Math "challenges" and puzzles
- Manipulative activities

Art

- Holiday or thematic projects
- Crafts related to curriculum studies (quilting, quilling, origami, etc.)

Writing

- Class story writing (e.g., add-on stories)
- Rewrites of literature
- Writing plays or puppet shows

Computer

- Content-related programs
- Simulations
- Story writing

FIGURE 12.6 Suggestions for Learning Centers

Learning centers are especially good alternatives to paper-and-pencil seatwork. Figure 12.6 provides some suggestions for learning centers. A computer station can be an excellent learning center.

Homework   Another important instructional decision involves how much and what type of homework to give students. In the cross-cultural research discussed earlier that focused on Asian and American students, the time spent on homework was assessed (Chen & Stevenson, 1989). Asian students spent more time doing homework than American students did. For example, on weekends Japanese first-graders did an average of 66 minutes of homework, and American first-graders did only 18 minutes. Also, Asian students had a much more positive attitude about homework than American students did. And Asian parents were far more likely to help their children with their homework than American parents were.

Harris Cooper (1998; Cooper & Valentine, 2001; Cooper & others, 1998) analyzed more than 100 research studies on homework in American schools and concluded that for elementary school students, the effects of homework on achievement are trivial, if they exist at all. In a recent study, Cooper (1998) collected data on 709 students in grades 2 through 4 and 6 through 12. In the lower grades, there was a significant negative relation between the amount of homework assigned and students' attitudes, suggesting that elementary school children resent having to do homework. But in grades 6 and higher, the more homework students completed, the higher their achievement. It is not clear which was the cause and which the effect, though. Were really good students finishing more assignments because they were motivated and competent in academic subjects, or was completing homework assignments causing students to achieve more?

A key aspect of the debate about whether elementary school children should be assigned homework is the type of homework assigned (Begley, 1998). What is good homework? Especially for younger children, the emphasis should be on homework that fosters a love of learning and hones study skills. Short assignments that can be quickly completed should be the goal. With young children, long assignments that go uncompleted or completed assignments that bring a great deal of stress, tears, and tantrums should be avoided. Too often teachers assign homework that duplicates without reinforcing material that is covered in class. Homework should be an opportunity for students to engage in creative, exploratory activities, such as doing an oral history of one's family or determining the ecological effects of neighborhood business. Instead of memorizing names, dates, and battles of the Civil War as a homework assignment, students might write fictional letters from Northerners to Southerners, expressing their feelings about the issues dividing the nation. The homework assignments should be linked to the next day's class activities to emphasize to students that homework has meaning and is not just a plot to make them miserable. Homework also should have a focus. Don't ask students to write an open-ended theme from a novel the class is reading. Rather, ask them to select a character and explain why he or she behaved in a particular way.

In Cooper's analysis of more than 100 studies of homework, in middle school homework began to have a payoff. How can homework have little or no effect in elementary school yet be so beneficial in middle and high school? In the higher grades, it is easier to assign focused, substantive homework that requires students to integrate and apply knowledge—the type of homework that promotes learning (Corno, 1998). Also, by high school, students have resigned themselves to the routine of homework. Working hard after school and having good study skills are more accepted by middle and high school students.

Some educational psychologists argue that the main reason homework has not been effective in elementary school is that it has focused too much on subject matter and not enough on developing attitudes toward school, persistence, and responsible completion of assignments (Corno, 1998). They stress that it is not homework per se that benefits students but, rather, the opportunities it provides for the student to take responsibility. They think that teachers need to inform parents about guiding their children in these aspects of doing their homework: setting goals, managing their time, controlling their emotions, and checking their work, rather than playing avoidance games or leaving hard work for last. Teachers and parents can use homework in the early grades to help children wrestle with goal setting and follow-through.

Cooper (1989; Cooper & Valentine, 2001) also has found that

- Homework has more positive effects when it is distributed over a period of time rather than done all at once. For example, doing 10 math problems each night for five nights is better than doing 50 over the weekend.
- Homework effects are greater for math, reading, and English than for science and social studies.
- For middle school students, 1 or 2 hours of homework a night is optimal. High school students benefit from even more hours of homework, but it is unclear what a maximum number of hours ought to be.

Homework can be a valuable tool for increasing learning, especially in middle and high school (Cooper & Valentine, 2001). However, it is important to make homework meaningful, monitor it and give students feedback about it, and involve parents in helping their child with it. Many parents wish they knew more about teachers' learning goals for homework and teachers' suggestions for involvement strategies that will help their children learn and succeed (Hoover-Demsey & others, 2001). Also, a recent study found that mothers' positive affect played an important role in students' motivation to do homework (Pomerantz, Wang, & Ng, 2005).

In chapter 3, "Social Contexts and Socioemotional Development," we described the importance of students doing "interactive homework" (Epstein, 1996)—homework that requires students to go to their parents for help. In one elementary school, a weekly teacher's letter informs parents about the objectives of each homework assignment, gives them directions, and asks for comments. Think about setting up tutoring sessions for parents to help them interact effectively with their children in homework sessions.

Evaluating Teacher–Centered Instruction

Research on teacher-centered instruction has contributed many valuable suggestions for teaching, including these:

- Be an organized planner, create instructional objectives, and spend initial time orienting students to a lesson.
- Have high expectations for students' progress and ensure that students have adequate academic learning time.
- Use lecturing, explaining, and demonstrating to benefit certain aspects of students' learning.
- Engage students in learning by developing good question-asking skills and getting them involved in class discussion.
- Have students do meaningful seatwork or alternative work to allow individualized instruction with a particular student or a small group.
- Give students meaningful homework to increase their academic learning time and involve parents in students' learning.

Advocates of the teacher-centered approach especially believe that it is the best strategy for teaching basic skills, which involve clearly structured knowledge and skills (such as those needed in English, reading, math, and science). Thus, in teaching basic skills, the teacher-centered approach might consist of a teacher explicitly or directly teaching grammar rules, reading vocabulary, math computations, and science facts (Rosenshine, 1986).

Teacher-centered instruction has not been without criticism. Critics say that teacher-centered instruction often leads to passive, rote learning and inadequate

"I don't have my homework because my little brother put a Pop-Tart® in my disk drive!"

Art Bouthillier, from *Phi Delta Kappan* (February 1997). Reprinted by permission of Art Bouthillier.

What are some guidelines for assigning homework to students?

opportunities to construct knowledge and understanding. They also criticize teacher-centered instruction as producing overly structured and rigid classrooms, inadequate attention to students' socioemotional development, external rather than internal motivation to learn, too much reliance on paper-and-pencil tasks, few opportunities for real-world learning, and too little collaborative learning in small groups. Such criticisms often are leveled by advocates of learner-centered planning and instruction, which we will turn to next.

Review, Reflect, and Practice

(2) Identify important forms of teacher-centered instruction.

REVIEW

- How are creating behavioral objectives, task analysis, and instructional taxonomies tools for teacher-centered lesson planning?
- What is direct instruction?
- What are some good teacher-centered instructional strategies?
- What are some pros and cons of teacher-centered instruction?

REFLECT

- As a student, have you ever wished that a teacher used more (or less) teacher-centered instruction? What lessons can you draw from this for your own work as a teacher?

PRAXIS™ PRACTICE

1. Mr. McGregor has assigned his students to write an essay explaining the impact of the use of the atomic bomb during World War II. Which cognitive level of Bloom's taxonomy is best illustrated by this assignment?
   a. analysis
   b. application
   c. comprehension
   d. knowledge

2. A math teacher works with students to solve higher-level problems. The teacher engages the students in discussions of various approaches to solving the problems. The emphasis is on understanding the processes of solving the problems, rather than on getting the correct answer. This math class is most typical of instructional methods in
   a. United States
   b. France
   c. Japan
   d. Germany

3. Ms. Davidson is giving a lecture to introduce her students to a unit on the American Revolution. She begins with a little-known fact to pique her students' interest. She then distributes a brief outline of what her lesson will cover. She lectures from carefully prepared notes, using visual aids to help her students understand the material and keep their interest. Periodically, during the lecture, she asks questions to make sure her students are attending to, and understanding, the material. She calls on the first person to raise her hand to answer the question. If this person does not answer immediately, she supplies the answer herself, so the students do not become confused, and the lesson does not drag on. What should Ms. Davidson do differently?
   a. Allow her students more time to answer questions.
   b. Avoid asking questions during the lecture.

   c. Be more spontaneous in her class presentations.
   d. Avoid using distracting visual aids.
4. Ms. Bancroft likes to lecture most of the time, make sure that her students stay on task when they are in the classroom, and has students do meaningful seat-work. Ms. Bancroft is following which of these approaches?
   a. cognitive constructivist
   b. social constructivist
   c. direct instruction
   d. individualized

Please see the answer key at the end of the book.

3 LEARNER-CENTERED LESSON PLANNING AND INSTRUCTION

| Learner-Centered Principles | Some Learner-Centered Instructional Strategies | Evaluating Learner-Centered Instruction |

Just as the behavioral approaches described in chapter 7 provide the conceptual underpinnings for teacher-centered lesson planning and instruction, the information-processing and constructivist approaches discussed in chapters 2, 8, 9, 10, and 11 form the theoretical backdrop for learner-centered lesson planning and instruction. In this section, we will explore the principles and strategies used in learner-centered instruction.

Learner-Centered Principles

Learner-centered lesson planning and instruction move the focus away from the teacher and toward the student (Silberman, 2006). In one large-scale study, students' perceptions of a positive learning environment and interpersonal relationship with the teacher, factors associated with learner-centered instruction, were important in enhancing students' motivation and achievement (McCombs, 2001; McCombs & Quiat, 2001).

Increased interest in learner-centered principles of lesson planning and instruction has resulted in a set of guidelines called *Learner-Centered Psychological Principles: A Framework for School Reform and Redesign* (Presidential Task Force on Psychology and in Education, 1992; Work Group of the American Psychological Association Board of Educational Affairs, 1995, 1997). The guidelines were constructed and are now periodically revised by a prestigious group of scientists and educators from a wide range of disciplines and interests. These principles have important implications for the way teachers plan and instruct, as they are based on research on the most effective ways children learn.

The Work Group of the American Psychological Association Board of Educational Affairs (1997) stresses that research in psychology relevant to education has been especially informative, including advances in our understanding of cognitive, motivational, and contextual aspects of learning. The work group states that the learner-centered psychological principles it has proposed are widely supported and are being increasingly adopted in many classrooms. The principles emphasize the active, reflective nature of learning and learners. According to the work group, education will benefit when the primary focus is on the learner.

The fourteen learner-centered principles can be classified in terms of four main sets of factors: cognitive and metacognitive, motivational and emotional, developmental and social, and individual differences (Work Group of the American Psychological Association Board of Educational Affairs, 1997, pp. 2–4).

Cognitive and Metacognitive Factors

1. *Nature of the learning process.* The learning of complex subject matter is most effective when it is an intentional process of constructing meaning from information and experience.

Learning in schools emphasizes the use of intentional processes that students can use to construct meaning from information, experiences, and their own thoughts and beliefs. Successful learners are active, goal directed, self-regulating, and assume personal responsibility for contributing to their own learning.

2. *Goals of the learning process.* The successful learner, over time and with support and instructional guidance, can create meaningful, coherent representations of knowledge.

The strategic nature of learning requires students to be goal directed. To construct useful representations of knowledge and to acquire the thinking and learning strategies necessary for continued learning success across the life span, students must generate and pursue personally relevant goals. Initially, students' short-term goals and learning may be sketchy in an area, but over time their understanding can be refined by filling gaps, resolving inconsistencies, and deepening their understanding of the subject matter so that they can reach longer-term goals. Educators can assist learners in creating meaningful learning goals that are consistent with both personal and educational aspirations and interests.

3. *Construction of knowledge.* The successful learner can link new information with existing knowledge in meaningful ways.

Knowledge widens and deepens as students continue to build links between new information and experiences and their existing knowledge base. The nature of these links can take a variety of forms, such as adding to, modifying, or reorganizing existing knowledge or skills. Educators can assist learners in acquiring and integrating knowledge by a number of strategies, such as concept mapping and thematic organization or categorizing.

John Mahoney teaches high school math in Washington, D.C. One of his students, Nicole Williams, says, "He's not going to tell you the answer. He's going to make you think" (Briggs, 2004, p. 6D). *What are some important cognitive and metacognitive factors in learner-centered instruction?*

4. *Strategic thinking.* The successful learner can create and use a repertoire of thinking and reasoning strategies to achieve complex learning goals.

Successful learners use strategic thinking in their approach to learning, reasoning, problem solving, and concept learning. They understand and can use a variety of strategies to help them reach learning and performance goals, and to apply their knowledge in novel situations. They also continue to expand their repertoire of strategies by reflecting on the methods they use to see which work well for them, by receiving guided instruction and feedback, and by observing or interacting with appropriate models. Learning outcomes can be enhanced if educators assist learners in developing, applying, and assessing their strategic learning skills.

5. *Thinking about thinking.* Higher-order strategies for selecting and monitoring mental operations facilitate creative and critical thinking.

Successful learners can reflect on how they think and learn, set reasonable learning or performance goals, select potentially appropriate learning strategies or methods, and monitor their progress toward these goals. In addition, successful learners know what to do if a problem occurs or if they are not making sufficient or timely progress toward a goal. They can generate alternative methods to reach their goal (or reassess the appropriateness and utility of the goal). Instructional methods that focus on helping learners develop these higher-order (metacognitive) strategies can enhance student learning and personal responsibility for learning.

6. *Context of learning.* Learning is influenced by environmental factors, including culture, technology, and instructional practices.

Learning does not occur in a vacuum. Teachers play a major interactive role with both the learner and the learning environment. Cultural or group influences on students can impact many educationally relevant variables, such as motivation, orientation toward learning, and ways of thinking. Technologies and instructional practices must be appropriate for learners' level of prior knowledge, cognitive abilities, and their learning and thinking strategies.

Motivational and Affective Factors

1. *Motivational and emotional influences on learning.* What and how much is learned is influenced by the learner's motivation. Motivation to learn, in turn, is influenced by the individual's emotional states, beliefs, interests and goals, and habits of thinking.

The rich internal world of thoughts, beliefs, goals, and expectations for success or failure can enhance or interfere with the learner's quality of thinking and information processing. Students' beliefs about themselves as learners and the nature of learning have a marked influence on motivation. Motivational and emotional factors also influence both the quality of thinking and information processing as well as an individual's motivation to learn. Positive emotions, such as curiosity, generally enhance motivation and facilitate learning and performance. Mild anxiety can also enhance learning and performance by focusing the learner's attention on a particular task. However, intense negative emotions (for example, anxiety, panic, rage, insecurity) and related thoughts (for example, worrying about competence, ruminating about failure, fearing punishment, ridicule, or stigmatizing labels) generally detract from motivation, interfere with learning, and contribute to low performance.

2. *Intrinsic motivation to learn.* The learner's creativity, higher-order thinking, and natural curiosity all contribute to motivation to learn. Intrinsic motivation is stimulated by tasks of optimal novelty and difficulty, relevant to personal interests, and providing for personal choice and control.

Curiosity, flexible and insightful thinking, and creativity are major indicators of the learners' intrinsic motivation to learn, which is in large part a function of meeting basic

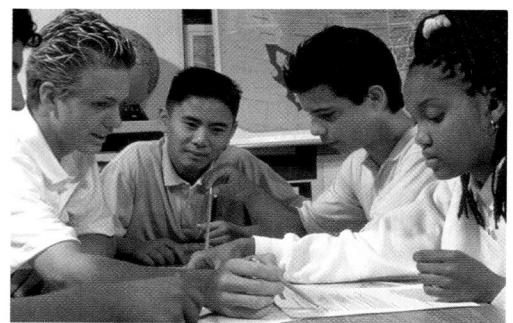

What are some learner-centered psychological principles?

needs to be competent and to exercise personal control. Intrinsic motivation is facilitated on tasks that learners perceive as interesting and personally relevant and meaningful, appropriate in complexity and difficulty to the learners' abilities, and on which they believe they can succeed. Intrinsic motivation is also facilitated on tasks that are comparable to real-world situations and meet needs for choice and control.

3. *Effects of motivation on effort.* Acquisition of complex knowledge and skills requires extended learner effort and guided practice. Without learners' motivation to learn, the willingness to exert this effort is unlikely without coercion.

Effort is another major indicator of motivation to learn. The acquisition of complex knowledge and skills demands the investment of considerable learner energy and strategic effort, along with persistence over time. Educators need to be concerned with facilitating motivation by strategies that enhance learner effort and commitment to learning and to achieving high standards of comprehension and understanding. Effective strategies include purposeful learning activities, guided by practices that enhance positive emotions and intrinsic motivation to learn, and methods that increase learners' perceptions that a task is interesting and personally relevant.

Developmental and Social Factors

1. *Developmental influences on learning.* As individuals develop, there are different opportunities and constraints for learning. Learning is most effective when differential development within and across physical, intellectual, emotional, and social domains is taken into account.

Individuals learn best when material is appropriate to their developmental level and is presented in an enjoyable and interesting way. Because individual development varies across intellectual, social, emotional, and physical domains, achievement in different instructional domains may also vary. Overemphasis on one type of developmental readiness—such as reading readiness, for example—may preclude learners from demonstrating that they are more capable in other areas of performance. The cognitive, emotional, and social development of individual learners and how they interpret life experiences are affected by prior schooling, home, culture, and community factors. Early and continuing parental involvement in schooling, and the quality of language interactions and two-way communications between adults and children can influence these developmental areas. Awareness and understanding of developmental differences among children with and without emotional, physical, or intellectual disabilities, can facilitate the creation of optimal learning contexts.

2. *Social influences on learning.* Learning is influenced by social interactions, interpersonal relations, and communication with others.

Learning can be enhanced when the learner has an opportunity to interact and to collaborate with others on instructional tasks. Learning settings that allow for social interactions, and that respect diversity, encourage flexible thinking and social competence. In interactive and collaborative instructional contexts, individuals have an opportunity for perspective taking and reflective thinking that may lead to higher levels of cognitive, social, and moral development, as well as self-esteem. Quality personal relationships that provide stability, trust, and caring can increase learners' sense of belonging, self-respect and self-acceptance, and provide a positive climate for learning. Family influences, positive interpersonal support, and instruction in self-motivation strategies can offset factors that interfere with optimal learning such as negative beliefs about competence in a particular subject, high levels of test anxiety, negative sex role expectations, and undue pressure to perform well. Positive learning climates can also help to establish the context for healthier levels of thinking, feeling, and behaving. Such contexts help learners feel safe to share ideas, actively participate in the learning process, and create a learning community.

1. *Individual differences in learning.* Learners have different strategies, approaches, and capabilities for learning that are a function of prior experience and heredity. Individuals are born with and develop their own capabilities and talents. In addition, through learning and social acculturation, they have acquired their own preferences for how they like to learn and the pace at which they learn.

However, these preferences are not always useful in helping learners reach their learning goals. Educators need to help students examine their learning preferences and expand or modify them, if necessary. The interaction between learner differences and curricular and environmental conditions is another key factor affecting learning outcomes. Educators need to be sensitive to individual differences, in general. They also need to attend to learner perceptions of the degree to which these differences are accepted and adapted to by varying instructional methods and materials.

2. *Learning and diversity.* Learning is most effective when differences in learners' linguistic, cultural, and social backgrounds are taken into account.

The same basic principles of learning, motivation, and effective instruction apply to all learners. However, language, ethnicity, race, beliefs, and socioeconomic status all can influence learning. When learners perceive that their individual differences in abilities, backgrounds, cultures, and experiences are valued, respected, and accommodated in learning tasks and contexts, levels of motivation and achievement are enhanced.

3. *Standards and assessments.* Setting appropriately high and challenging standards and assessing the learner as well as learning progress—including diagnostic, process, and outcome assessment—are integral parts of the learning process.

Assessment provides important information to both the learner and teacher at all stages of the learning process. Effective learning takes place when learners feel challenged to work toward appropriately high goals; therefore, appraisal of the learner's cognitive strengths and weaknesses, as well as current knowledge and skills, is important for the selection of instructional materials of an optimal degree of difficulty. Ongoing assessment of the learner's understanding of the curricular material can provide valuable feedback to both learners and teachers about progress toward the learning goals. Standardized assessment of learner progress and outcomes assessment provides one type of information about achievement levels both within and across individuals that can inform various types of programmatic decisions. Performance assessments can provide other sources of information about the attainment of learning outcomes. Self-assessments of learning progress can also improve students self appraisal skills and enhance motivation and self-directed learning.

Some Learner-Centered Instructional Strategies

We have already discussed a number of strategies that teachers can consider in developing learner-centered lesson plans. These especially include the teaching strategies based on the theories of Piaget and Vygotsky (chapter 2), constructivist aspects of thinking (chapters 8 and 9), social constructivist aspects of thinking (chapter 10), and learning in content areas (chapter 11). To provide you with a further sense of learner-centered strategies that you can incorporate into your lesson planning, we will elaborate here on the topic of problem-based learning (which was initially described in chapter 9) and examine two other strategies: essential questions and discovery learning.

Problem-Based Learning   *Problem-based learning* emphasizes real-life problem solving. A problem-based curriculum exposes students to authentic problems like those that crop up in everyday life (Jones, Rasmussen, & Moffitt, 1997).

Problem-based learning is a learner-centered approach that focuses on a problem to be solved through small-group efforts. Students identify problems or issues that they wish to explore, then locate materials and resources they need to address the issues or solve the problems. Teachers act as guides, helping students to monitor their own problem-solving efforts.

One problem-based learning project has been developed by Delamie Thompson, Paul Gilvary, and Mary Moffitt of Gladstone Elementary School, an inner-city school in Chicago (Jones, Rasmussen, & Moffitt, 1997, pp. 113–117). The project involves sixth-grade students in exploring an authentic health problem in the local community: the causes, incidence, and treatment of asthma and its related conditions. Students learn how environmental conditions affect their health and share this understanding with others. The project integrates information from many subject areas, including health, science, math, and the social sciences.

The students use a simple syringe air pump to assess air quality and determine its link to the incidence of asthma. The air pump was developed by Technical Education Research Centers (TERC), which also provides Gladstone students with shared databases of information gathered by students around the world. "Gladstone students learn to (a) think like scientists by working with data and addressing substantive problems, (b) collaborate as scientists by working with peers and mentors to plan and carry out an investigation, (c) communicate and debate their findings, and (d) evaluate their own work and the work of others."

The project's flow is "organized around a number of student research groups, each group focusing on a separate problem related to the question, 'Why there is so much asthma in our community and what can we do about it?'" All groups use the scientific method in their research.

Essential Questions **Essential questions** are questions that reflect the heart of the curriculum, the most important things that students should explore and learn (Jacobs, 1997). For example, in one lesson the initial essential question was "What flies?" Students explored the question by examining everything from birds, bees, fish, and space shuttles to the notion that time flies and ideas fly. The initial question was followed by other questions, such as "How and why do things fly in nature?" "How does flight affect humans?" and "What is the future of flight?"

Essential questions like these perplex students, cause them to think, and motivate their curiosity. Essential questions are creative choices. With just a slight change, a lackluster question such as "What was the effect of the Civil War?" can become the thought-provoking question "Is the Civil War still going on?"

Advocates of using essential questions argue that too often lesson planning and instruction become rigid and stiff. For example, a history teacher in high school might come up with this as one of the objectives for a year-long course on Western civilization: "Students will recognize personal responsibility to the community." Consider how much more enthusiastic students might be about studying Western civilization if they are asked instead to consider "How does my community affect my life?"

In sixth-grade teacher Barb Johnson's class, students generate the essential questions to be explored (National Research Council, 1999, pp. 144–145). In the first week of school, she presents two questions to her class: "What questions do you have about yourself?" and "What questions do you have about the world?" In response, students begin asking questions themselves. One student asks, "Can they be about silly, little things?" She tells the student that if they are questions that they really want answered, they are not silly and they are not little. After the students state their questions, Barb breaks out the students "into small groups where they share lists and search for questions they have in common. After much discussion each group comes up with a priority list of questions, rank-ordering the questions about themselves and those about the world."

Back together in a whole-class format, a representative of each group informs the class of his or her group's list of questions. "These questions will become the

essential questions Questions that reflect the heart of the curriculum, the most important things that students should explore and learn.

basis for guiding the curriculum in Barb's class. One question, 'Will I live to be 100 years old?' spawned educational investigations into genetics, family and oral history, science, statistics and probability, heart disease, cancer, and hypertension. The students had the opportunity to seek out information from family members, friends, experts in various fields, on-line computer services, websites, and books, as well as from the teacher. She describes what they had to do as becoming part of a learning community," much as described in Fostering a Community of Learners in chapter 10.

At the end of exploring a topic, Barb "works with students to help them see how their investigation relates to conventional subject areas. They create a chart on which they tally experiences in language and literacy, mathematics, science, social studies, and history, music, and art. Students often are surprised at how much and how varied their learning is." One student said, "I just thought we were having fun. I didn't realize that we were learning too."

Barb Johnson's teaching requires a wide range of disciplinary knowledge because she begins with students' questions rather than a fixed curriculum. Because of her extensive knowledge, she can map students' questions onto important concepts in relevant disciplines.

Discovery Learning   **Discovery learning** is learning in which students construct an understanding on their own. Discovery learning stands in contrast to the direct-instruction approach discussed earlier, in which the teacher directly explains information to students. In discovery learning, students have to figure out things for themselves. Discovery learning meshes with the ideas of Piaget, who once commented that every time you teach a child something you keep the child from learning.

Educator John Dewey (1933) and cognitive psychologist Jerome Bruner (1966) promoted the concept of discovery learning by encouraging teachers to give students more opportunities to learn on their own. In their view, discovery learning encourages students to think for themselves and discover how knowledge is constructed. It also feeds their natural curiosity and inquiry.

Teachers facilitate discovery learning by providing students with stimulating activities that activate their natural curiosity (de Jong & others, 2005). After you present such activities, your role becomes one of answering student-generated questions. You also promote discovery learning on the part of students by being naturally curious yourself and having a strong interest in uncovering solutions to problems.

Discovery learning is especially effective in science classes. Researchers have found that students in activity-based, discovery-learning science classes score higher on science achievement tests than students in traditional direct-instruction science classes (Glasson, 1989). These findings hold at the elementary, middle school, and secondary school levels.

However, most discovery-learning approaches used in schools today do not involve "pure" discovery learning. In "pure" discovery learning, students are encouraged to learn on their own and instruction is minimal to nonexistent. Working completely on their own doesn't benefit many students. For example, given materials and left to their own devices to learn, some students end up with the wrong solutions and use inefficient strategies to discover information. Others never discover what it is they are trying to find out or why. And in many cases, such as initially learning how to add and subtract, direct instruction can get the job done much more quickly (van Lehn, 1990).

As teachers began to use discovery learning, they soon found that for it to be effective as a systematic instruction approach it needed to be modified. This led to the development of **guided discovery learning,** in which students are still encouraged to construct their understanding, but with the assistance of teacher-guided questions and directions (Minstrell & Kraus, 2005).

A recent review of research indicated that guided discovery learning was superior to pure discovery learning in every case (Mayer, 2004). In this review, it also was

discovery learning Learning in which students construct an understanding on their own.

guided discovery learning Learning in which students are encouraged to construct their understanding with the assistance of teacher-guided questions and directions.

What is guided discovery learning?

concluded that constructivist learning is best supported by curricular focus rather than pure discovery.

Evaluating Learner-Centered Instruction

The learner-centered approach to lesson planning and instruction is positive in many ways. The fourteen learner-centered principles developed by the American Psychological Association task force can be very helpful in guiding students' learning. The principles encourage teachers to help students actively construct their understanding, set goals and plan, think deeply and creatively, monitor their learning, solve real-world problems, develop more positive self-esteem and control their emotions, be internally motivated, learn in a developmentally appropriate way, collaborate effectively with others (including diverse others), evaluate their learner preferences, and meet challenging standards.

Critics of learner-centered instruction argue that it gives too much attention to the process of learning (such as learning creatively and collaboratively) and not enough to academic content (such as the facts of history) (Hirsch, 1996). Some critics stress that learner-centered instruction works better in some subjects than in others (Feng, 1996). They say that in areas with many ill-defined problems, such as the social sciences and humanities, learner-centered instruction can be effective. However, they believe that in well-structured knowledge domains such as math and science, teacher-centered structure works better. Critics also say that learner-centered instruction is less effective at the beginning level of instruction in a field because students do not have the knowledge to make decisions about what and how they should learn. And critics stress that there is a gap between the theoretical level of student-centered learning and its actual application (Airasian & Walsh, 1997). The consequences of implementing learner-centered strategies in the classroom are often more challenging than anticipated.

Although we have presented teacher-centered and learner-centered planning and instruction in separate sections, don't think of them as always being either/or approaches (Schuh, 2001). Many effective teachers use some of both in making the classroom a positive learning experience for children. Research on the choice and sequencing of learning activities in the classroom indicates that the use of constructivist and

BEST PRACTICES
Strategies for Using Learner-Centered Instruction

1. *Become familiar with the learner-centered psychological principles and incorporate them in your lesson planning and teaching.*

2. *Focus on the whole child.* Pay attention to motivational and affective factors, and developmental and social factors, in addition to cognitive factors.

THROUGH THE EYES OF TEACHERS
Fostering Learning, Unity, and Civic Pride

Luis Recalde, a fourth- and fifth-grade science teacher at Vincent E. Mauro Elementary School, in New Haven, Connecticut, uses every opportunity to make science fascinating and motivating for students to learn. Recalde infuses hands-on science experiences with energy and enthusiasm. To help students get a better sense of what it is like to be a scientist, he brings lab coats to the classroom for students to wear. He holds science fair workshops for teachers and often gives up his vacation time to help students with science projects. He started soccer teams and gardens to foster unity and civic pride among African American and Latino students. An immigrant

himself, he knows the importance of fostering positive relations among students from different ethnic groups.

3. *Use problem-based learning, essential questions, and guided discovery learning in your teaching.*

THROUGH THE EYES OF TEACHERS
Guiding Students to Discover

Mary Lynn Peacher, a fourth-grade teacher at East Elementary School, in Oklahoma, emphasizes a learner-centered, guided discovery approach. Students' desks are clustered together for cooperative learning. In social science, she guides students in developing a mini-society with its own government and economy—"senators" draft and chart rules, listing rights and responsibilities. She also oversees a classroom free-enterprise system with student companies, assembly lines, bank accounts, and credit. In teaching science, Peacher tells her students they are scientists and ask them to describe what they see as they carry out various exercises (Source: *USA Today,* 2001).

Elementary school science teacher, Luis Recalde, holds up a seaweed specimen in one of the hands-on, high interest learning contexts he creates for students.

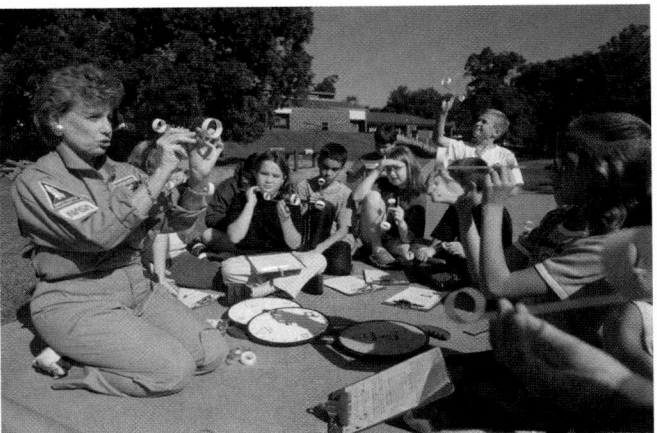

Mary Lynn Peacher demonstrates airfoil "charks" to students.

direct instruction approaches are often more effective than when either approach is used alone (Darling-Hammond & others, 2005; Schwartz & others, 1999).

Consider high school history teacher Robert Bain's (2005) description of how students initially spent time in learner-centered instruction working on constructing accounts of Columbus' voyage to America and struggled with the question of how the anniversaries of the voyage were celebrated. So Bain then used teacher-centered direct instruction by lecturing about leading historians' current thinking about the topic. Leading experts on how students learn often conclude that "how the balance is struck in creating a classroom that functions as a learning community attentive to learner's needs, the knowledge to be mastered, and assessments that guide and support instruction will certainly vary from one teacher and classroom to the next" (Donovan & Bransford, 2005, p. 588).

Review, Reflect, and Practice

(3) Discuss important forms of learner-centered instruction.

REVIEW
- Summarize the APA's fourteen learner-centered principles.
- How do problem-based learning, essential questions, and discovery learning each embody learner-centered principles?
- What are some pros and cons of learner-centered instruction?

REFLECT
- As a student, have you ever wished that a teacher would use more (or less) learner-centered instruction? What lessons can you draw from this for your own work as a teacher?

PRAXIS™ PRACTICE

1. Joan just received a *D* on her science exam. "I knew it," she states, "I've never been any good at science." Which set of factors of the APA's learner-centered principles is best exemplified by Joan's statement?
   a. cognitive and metacognitive
   b. developmental and social
   c. individual differences
   d. motivational and emotional

2. Mr. Williams wants his third-grade students to understand the purpose of blubber in marine mammals. He sets up an experiment for his students using ice water, latex gloves, and lard. First, students put their gloved hands in ice water until they cannot keep them there any longer. Other students time how long they keep their hands submerged. Then, students put their gloved hands in bags of lard and submerge their hands again. Again, other students time how long they keep their hands submerged. All of the students are able to keep their hands in the ice water longer with their hands in the lard than they can when their hands are merely gloved.

   What learner-centered instructional strategy has Mr. Williams used?
   a. discovery learning
   b. essential questions
   c. guided discovery
   d. problem-based learning

3. Ms. Flanagan, who takes a teacher-centered approach, just observed Mr. Houston's constructivist teaching in his seventh-grade math class. Ms. Flanagan is likely to be most critical of which of the following she observed?
   a. Mr. Houston assigning students homework
   b. Mr. Houston encouraging students to construct their own math problem-solving strategies
   c. Mr. Houston having high expectations for student learning
   d. Mr. Houston using technology to help students learn

Please see the answer key at the end of the book.

4 TECHNOLOGY AND EDUCATION

The Technology Revolution and the Internet	Teaching, Learning, and Technology	The Future of Technology in Schools

Standards for Technology-Literate Students	Technology and Sociocultural Diversity

So far in this chapter we have described many aspects of planning and instruction. In contemporary society, technology plays important roles in planning and instruction. Three important ways that technology affects curriculum planning are: (1) as a learning goal for students to develop certain technology competencies; (2) as a resource for curriculum planning through the extensive materials that are available on the Internet; and (3) as tools that improve students' ability to learn through techniques such as simulation and visualization in science and text analysis in literature, as well as software that encourages reflection and provides models of good performances (Darling-Hammond & others, 2005).

Technology is such an important theme in education that it is woven throughout this book. In each chapter you read a Technology and Education box related to the chapter's contents. For example, you already have studied such topics as "Technology and Children's Vocabulary Development" (chapter 2), "Technology Connections with Students Around the World" (chapter 5), and "Computer-Supported Intentional Learning Environments" (chapter 10). Here we will explore the technology revolution and the Internet, standards for technology-literate students, teaching and learning with technology, technology and sociocultural diversity, and the future of technology in schools.

The Technology Revolution and the Internet

Students today are growing up in a world that is far different technologically from the world in which their parents and grandparents were students. If students are to be adequately prepared for tomorrow's jobs, technology must become an integral part of schools and classrooms (Bitter & Legacy, 2006; Hoffner, 2007; Lajoie & Azevedo, 2006; Stahl, Koschmann, & Suthers, 2006; Thorsen, 2006).

The technology revolution is part of the information society in which we now live. People are using computers to communicate today the way people used to use pens, postage stamps, and telephones. The new information society still relies on some basic nontechnological competencies: good communication skills, the ability to solve problems, deep thinking, creative thinking, and positive attitudes. However, in today's technology-oriented world, how people pursue these competencies is being challenged and extended in ways and at a speed that few people had to cope with in previous eras (Bitter & Pierson, 2005; Reisser & Dempsey, 2007).

Technology has been a part of schooling for many decades, but until recently the technologies were rather simple and changed slowly. To underscore how technology in schools has changed dramatically, consider the fact that in 1983 there were fewer than 50,000 computers in America's schools. In 2002, there were more than 6 million! Hardly a school in America today is without at least one computer. However, in that same year, 42 percent of teachers reported that their students used computers less than 15 minutes per week, and 65 percent said that their students accessed the Internet less than 15 minutes per week (Norris, Soloway, & Sullivan, 2002).

The **Internet** is a system of computer networks that operates worldwide. As the core of computer-mediated communication, the Internet is playing an important role in the technology revolution, especially in schools. In many cases, the Internet has more current, up-to-date information than textbooks. By 2003, nearly 100 percent of

A student creating a multimedia program in the Research Center for Educational Technology's AT&T classroom at Kent State University.

Internet The core of computer-mediated communication; a system of computer networks that operates worldwide.

"I see what's wrong with your calculator—it's the remote control to your TV."

John R. Shanks, from *Phi Delta Kappan* (June 1997). Reprinted by permission of John R. Shanks.

public schools in the United States were connected to the Internet, and 93 percent of instructional classrooms had Internet-connected computers (National Center for Education Statistics, 2005).

However, the Internet did not become the common portal it is today until the introduction of the World Wide Web (the Web). The **Web** is a system for browsing Internet sites. It is named the Web because it is made of many sites linked together. The Web presents the user with documents, called web pages, full of links to other documents or information systems. Selecting one of these links, the user can access more information about a particular topic. Web pages include text as well as multimedia (images, video, animation, and sound—all of which can be accessed by students with a click on words or images presented on a computer screen). Web indexes and search engines such as Google and Yahoo can help students find the information they are seeking by examining and collating a variety of sources.

By going to the McGraw-Hill Santrock *Educational Psychology* Web site (www.mhhe.com/santedu3e), you can immediately connect with the associated Web sites by scrolling to the appropriate chapter and label. Also in the section on general Internet resources on the Santrock Educational Psychology Web site, there are links to a number of Web sites with information about integrating technology into the classroom that you can access.

The Internet can be an important learning tool in many classroom contexts (Bruckman, 2006; Cunningham & Bilingsley, 2006; Hiltz & Goldman, 2005; Provenzo, 2005). For example, consider a technology-rich project called Cooperative Networked Educational Community of Tomorrow (Co-NECT) (Jones, Rasmussen, & Moffitt, 1997). Some Co-NECT schools become immersed in learning about worldwide scientific expeditions such as Earthwatch's Mystery of the Pipe Wreck project in the Caribbean. In such investigations, students and teachers can download data from project sites, conduct data analysis, and communicate electronically with project participants and staff (Bolt, Baraneck, & Newman, 1993). A Co-NECT student e-mailed a lawyer in Northern Ireland to request information about this question: "Can there be lasting peace in Northern Ireland?" The lawyer responded with a two-page e-mail that included current news and perspectives on the topic.

The Internet can be a valuable tool for helping students learn (Berson & others, 2007; Koedinger & Corbett, 2006; Scardamalia & Bereiter, 2006). However, it has some potential drawbacks (Schofeld, 2006). To use it effectively with your students, you will have to know how to use it and feel comfortable with it, as well as have up-to-date equipment and software. In addition, concerns have been raised about students accessing pornographic material and biased Web sites, as well as the accuracy of information gleaned from the Internet. Many of these problems are solved by installing firewalls or blocking software on school servers.

When used effectively, however, the Internet expands access to a world of knowledge and people that students cannot experience in any other way (Cruz & Duplass, 2007). Some good ideas for using the Internet with your students can be found in the Technology and Education box in this chapter.

The growth of the Internet has also led to a new phenomenon in distance learning, the virtual school (Simonson & others, 2006; Wang & Gearhart, 2006). *Virtual schools* are "educational organizations that offer K–12 courses through the Internet or Web-based methods" (Clark, 2001, p. 1). Recent surveys show that virtual schools are rapidly growing in enrollments, with an estimated half million K–12 students enrolled in online courses in 2005 (Smith, Clark, & Bloymeyer, 2005). Indeed, the U.S. Department of Education (2004) has made the "support of e-learning and virtual schools" one of their top priorities in the technology area.

Standards for Technology–Literate Students

Students today are growing up in a world that is far different technologically from the world in which their parents and grandparents were students. If students are to

Web A system for browsing Internet sites that refers to the World Wide Web; named the Web because it is comprised of many sites that are linked together.

TECHNOLOGY AND EDUCATION

Using the Internet in the Classroom

Here are some effective ways that the Internet can be used in classrooms:

- *Navigating and integrating knowledge.* The Internet has huge databases of information on a vast array of topics that are organized in different ways. As students explore Internet resources, they can work on projects that integrate information from various sources that they could not otherwise access. One way to support such work is through WebQuests (**http://webquest.sdsu.edu/**). A WebQuest is an inquiry-oriented activity designed by teachers that maximizes student learning time, emphasizes using information rather than looking for it, and stimulates thinking. WebQuests focus student efforts on doable tasks, provide a set of information resources and guidance for completing those tasks, and frame the work in an integrative context. They help introduce students to Internet searching in meaningful ways.

- *Collaborative learning.* One of the most effective ways to use the Internet in your classroom is through project-centered activities (Bruckman, 2006). Indeed, many WebQuests are designed to be collaborative, with roles and tasks assigned to different members of each group. Another collaborative use of the Internet is to have a group of students conduct a survey on a topic (Maddux, Johnson, & Willis, 1997). Students can construct a survey on their topic, put it out on the Internet, and expect to get responses back from many parts of the world. They can organize, analyze, and summarize the data they receive, and then share them with other classes around the world. Another type of collaborative learning project involves sending groups of students on Internet "scavenger hunts" to find information and/or solve a problem.

- *Computer-mediated communications (CMC).* An increasing number of innovative educational projects include the use of computer-mediated communications. For example, there are many online sites (such as **www.studentsoftheworld.info/**, **www.tesol.net/teslpnpl.html**) set up for teachers and students to correspond with "pen pals" around the world. Some of these even provide safe access to more innovative CMC forms such as chats and blogs (such as **www.studentsoftheworld.info/**). In chapter 10, we examined Ann Brown and Joe Campione's (1996) program, Fostering a Community of Learners, in which students communicate with experts via e-mail, giving them access to a wider circle of knowledgeable people. In the Global Lab project (**http://globallab.terc.edu/**), a year-long, interdisciplinary science curriculum for middle school students, students conduct science investigations at their own local "study sites" and then share their findings with students around the country through an Internet discussion board.

- *Improving teachers' knowledge and understanding.* Two excellent Internet resources for teachers are the Educational Resources Information Center (ERIC at **www.eric.ed.gov/**) and the Educators' Reference Desk (**www.eduref.org/**), which provide free information about a wide range of educational topics. The ERIC database gives abstracts of more than 1 million journal and nonjournal educational papers going back to 1966 and the full text of over 100,000 papers from educational conferences. The Educators' Reference Desk gives easy access to over 2,000 lesson plans and over 3,000 links to online education information. Other excellent Internet resources for teachers include TappedIn (**http://tappedin.org/tappedin/**), an online site that brings educators together in learning communities to discuss educational issues and work on collaborative projects, and the PBS TeacherLine (**http://teacherline.pbs.org/teacherline/**), which provides both links to teaching resources and online professional development courses for teachers.

be adequately prepared for tomorrow's jobs, schools must take an active role in ensuring students become technologically literate. Most national standards recognize this. For example, the National Council of Teachers of English/International Reading Association Standards for the English Language Arts (NCTE/IRA, 1996) include the following "Students use a variety of technological and information resources (such as libraries, databases, computer networks, and video) to gather and synthesize information and to create and communicate knowledge," and a major theme in the National Council for the Social Studies, Curriculum Standards for the Social Studies (NCSS, 1994) is "Science, Technology, and Society."

The International Society for Technology in Education (ISTE, 2000), in collaboration with the U.S. Department of Education, has developed six technology standards for students to achieve technology literacy. The standards describe technology skills students should acquire in four functional areas—productivity, communications, research, and problem solving—as well as an understanding of basic concepts and social and ethical issues relating to technology. These are as follows:

1. *Basic operations and concepts*
   - Students demonstrate a sound understanding of the nature and operation of technology systems.
   - Students are proficient in the use of technology.
2. *Social, ethical, and human issues*
   - Students understand the ethical, cultural, and societal issues related to technology.
   - Students practice responsible use of technology systems, information, and software.
   - Students develop positive attitudes toward technology uses that support life-long learning, collaboration, personal pursuits, and productivity.
3. *Technology productivity tools*
   - Students use technology tools to enhance learning, increase productivity, and promote creativity.
   - Students use productivity tools to collaborate in constructing technology-enhanced models, prepare publications, and produce other creative works.
4. *Technology communications tools*
   - Students use telecommunications to collaborate, publish, and interact with peers, experts, and other audiences.
   - Students use a variety of media and formats to communicate information and ideas effectively to multiple audiences.
5. *Technology research tools*
   - Students use technology to locate, evaluate, and collect information from a variety of sources.
   - Students use technology tools to process data and report results.
   - Students evaluate and select new information resources and technological innovations based on the appropriateness for specific tasks.
6. *Technology problem-solving and decision-making tools*
   - Students use technology resources for solving problems and making informed decisions.
   - Students employ technology in the development of strategies for solving problems in the real world.

In addition, ISTE provides performance indicators for achieving these standards at four levels: prekindergarten through second grade, grades 3 through 5, grades 6 through 8, and grades 9 through 12. ISTE also includes examples and scenarios to illustrate how technology literacy can be integrated across the curriculum at each of these levels.

For example, a curriculum example that effectively uses technology at the first level focuses on animals and their sounds. In Sharon Fontenot's class at Prien Lake Elementary School, students learn to identify polar bears, lions, and other wild animals through images, video clips, and sounds on the *World of Animals* CD-ROM. The teacher models the effective use of technology by creating a tape recording based on information from the CD-ROM and incorporating her own voice to fit the needs of the class. Students practice reading and listening skills by answering questions that encourage them to think about both the science and social living issues related to these animals. Students create their own stories about what they learned using *Kid Pix*, a software program that lets them make their own pictures of the animals, turn them into slide shows, and print out their own books to share with family and friends.

At the second level (grades 3 through 5), a teacher might make extensive use of Internet resources. She could use the *Exploring the Environment* Web site (www.cotf.edu/ete/) to access class-tested problem-based learning modules or the

Global Learning and Observations for a Better Environment (GLOBE) Web site (www.globe.gov/) to engage students in making environmental observations around the school, reporting the data to a processing facility through GLOBE, and using global images created from their data to examine local environmental issues.

Population growth and urban planning are the focus of a social studies technology-based learning activity in grades 9 through 12. The activity challenges students to find sources online and elsewhere that describe real-world population dilemmas. The activity can be altered to address different cities and regions worldwide. In small groups in class, students can discuss problems that may occur as a result of a city being heavily populated. They can be asked to project what problems a city such as Tokyo is likely to face in terms of population growth in the year 2050.

These scenarios capture most aspects of the ways in which the Partnership for 21st Century Skills (2003) suggests technology can help teachers and schools look beyond the requirements of the No Child Left Behind legislation to help students develop the knowledge, skills and attitudes they will need in the coming era. They advocate emphasizing core subjects and learning skills, using twenty-first-century tools to develop learning skills, teaching and learning twenty-first-century content in a twenty-first-century context, and using twenty-first-century assessments that measure twenty-first-century skills.

Teaching, Learning, and Technology

A special concern is how technology can be used to improve teaching and learning (Jonassen, 2006; Lajoie & Azevedo, 2006; Spector & others, 2005). Over the last two decades at the Educational Technology Center at Harvard University, a number of educators have worked on ways to use technology to improve students' understanding. Martha Stone Wiske has especially been instrumental in creating ways to incorporate technology into classroom context that transform student learning. Stone Wiske and her colleagues (2005) recently described how to more effectively use technology to teach for understanding by considering (1) the topics that are worth understanding, (2) what students should understand about such topics, (3) how students develop and demonstrate understanding, (4) how students and teachers assess understanding, and (5) how students and teachers learn together. These five aspects of understanding are based on ideas developed at Harvard by David Perkins, Howard Gardner, and Vito Perrone. Following are Stone Wiske and her colleagues' (2005) views of how to use technology for understanding:

1. *Evaluate which topics are worth understanding.* Technology is especially appropriate for generating appropriate and interesting learning topics. The Internet provides a wealth of information about virtually every topic imaginable that can be mined to generate new topics or expand what students are studying as part of the curriculum. (Bruckman, 2006; Cunningham & Billingsley, 2006). The wide range of information provided by the Internet allows students to learn more about their own interests and ideas and carve a unique pathway in learning about a topic, instead of following cookie-cutter steps in a traditional textbook or workbook (Roblyer, 2006).

   Wiske and her colleagues (2005) also recommend that technology can often be used effectively to teach where problem spots emerge every year. "Examples include heat and temperature or weight and density in science, ratios in mathematics, and stereotypes in history and social studies classes" (p. 28). These topics, which many students struggle to understand, are central to the subject matter and are frequently more easily understood through the use of technology.

2. *Think about what students should understand about a topic.* When teachers consider using technology in the classroom, it is important for them to think about the learning goals they have for their students. Goals might include learning a new concept or applying a key concept to relevant situations. A

goal related to technology might be to understand how to find and critically examine information on the Internet that is relevant to a classroom topic. Generating goals in this manner remind the teacher that "surfing the Web" is "not an end in itself" but rather a way to use "technology to accomplish meaningful work" (Wiske, Franz, & Breit, 2005, p. 44).

3. *Pay attention to how students develop and demonstrate understanding.* Use technology to help students "stretch their minds" and understand something in ways that they never did before. In improving students' understanding, Stone Wiske and her colleagues (2005) recommend that teachers use technology when it can "enhance and enrich their performances of understanding. . . . Word processors, digital audio and video technologies, and tolls for creating Web sites allow students to express their understanding in a rich variety of media. These technologies also capture student work in forms that can be easily revised, combined, and distributed" (Wiske, Franz, & Breit, 2005, pp. 65–66).

4. *Consider how students and teachers assess learning.* Use ongoing assessment instead of only using a final assessment (Means, 2006). During ongoing assessment, you might guide students in understanding what quality work involves or use peer collaboration to help students analyze and improve their work. A helpful strategy is to also encourage students to assess their own learning progress and to monitor how effectively they are learning. Technology can be used in several ways to effectively assess learning.

> "Digital technologies, including audio and video recorders and computers, can capture student work in forms that are easy to review. Interactive workspaces and software with multiple windows can help to keep assessment guidelines in view and even offer prompts and reminders as work. . . . Using networked technologies, students may post their work online where it can be reallly reviewed and annotated by multiple advisors, including distant teachers and peers who cannot meet face-to-face. Technologies also provide easy means of preserving digital archives of student work. These may allow teachers and students to create individual portfolios to demonstrate and evaluate a student's work over time" (Wiske, Franz, & Breit, 2005, pp. 84–85).

We will have much more to say about technology and ongoing assessment in chapter 16, "Classroom Assessment."

5. *Reflect on how students and teachers can learn together.* "Networked technologies provide multiple advantages for connecting learners with reflective, collaborative communities. . . ." For example,

> "E-mail permits users to send and receive many-to-many messages and to do quickly. Students can share information and work with many other students all over the world, exchanging multiple rounds of reflective dialogue. The Web, with digital images, video and audio recordings, and videoconferencing, also allows students and their teachers to publish and collaborate on work, opening up the possibility of communicating with a wide range of audiences outside the classroom" (Wiske, Franz, & Breit, 2005, pp. 100, 102).

To evaluate your technology skills and attitudes, complete Self-Assessment 12.1.

Technology and Sociocultural Diversity

Technology brings with it certain social issues (Comstock & Scharrer, 2006). For example, will schools' increased use of technology, especially computers, widen the learning gap between rich and poor students or between male and female students?

In fact, there is still a gap between rich and poor schools in computer and Internet availability and use. In 2003, for example, 96 percent of schools with the lowest poverty concentration had a school Web site, while only 72 percent of schools with the highest poverty concentration had a school Web site (National Center for

SELF-ASSESSMENT 12.1

Evaluating My Technology Skills and Attitudes

How good are your technology skills? How positive are your attitudes about using technology and incorporating it into your classroom? For these items, consider the grade and subject(s) you are most likely to teach. Rate yourself from 1 to 5, with 1 = Not like me at all and 5 = Very much like me.

	1	2	3	4	5

1. I'm reasonably proficient at using a computer and installing and uninstalling software.

2. I have become comfortable with using a word-processing program.

3. I know when and how to use technology to improve students' understanding.

4. I have ideas for using word processing together with other language learning resources in the classroom.

5. I know how to search efficiently and thoroughly for information that interests me on the Internet.

6. I have ideas about how to use the Internet in my classroom.

7. I'm proficient at using e-mail.

8. I know how to use PowerPoint.

9. I have been part of collaborative learning exercises that involve technology.

10. I can see how collaborative learning can be used with technology in my classroom.

11. I am aware of the sociocultural issues involved in technology and education.

12. I know some good Web sites, journals, and software catalogs that can help me learn how to use technology more effectively in the classroom.

Scoring and Interpretation

Look at your scores for each item and evaluate your technology strengths and weaknesses. By the time you step into your classroom for your first day of teaching, make it a goal to be able to confidently rate yourself on each of these items at the level of 4 or 5. On items on which you rated yourself 1, 2, and 3, try to take technology courses at your local college that will improve your knowledge and skills in those areas.

Education Statistics, 2005). The problem of computer access and use also is compounded by the far greater presence of computers in the homes of middle- and upper-income families. There are gaps in computer availability across ethnic groups as well (Gorski, 2005). A recent study found that while 80 percent of non-Latino White children have Internet access at home, only 67 percent of Latino children and 61 percent of African American children do (Rideout, Roberts, & Foehr, 2005).

In addition, computers are often used for different activities in different sociocultural groups. Schools with high percentages of low-income ethnic minority students tend to use computers for drill and practice exercises (Maddux, Johnson, & Willis, 1997). In contrast, schools with high percentages of White middle- and upper-income students are more likely to use computers for more creative, constructivist learning activities. Boys are more likely to use computers for math and science applications, girls for word processing (Beal, 1994).

To put these findings in context, a recent study revealed that access to, and use of, a home computer, presence of a computer area in classrooms, lower child/

What are some important concerns about sociocultural diversity and technology?

computer ratios in school, and frequent use of software for literacy and math were linked to higher academic achievement in African American kindergarten and first-grade students (Judge, 2005).

Here are some recommendations for preventing or reducing inequity in computer access and use (Gipson, 1997; Sheffield, 1997):

- Screen technology materials for ethnic, cultural, and gender bias.
- Use technology as a tool for providing active, constructive learning opportunities for all students, regardless of their cultural, ethnic, or gender background.
- Provide students with information about experts from diverse ethnic and gender backgrounds who use technology effectively in their work and lives. For example, invite an African American female computer analyst to come to your classroom and talk with your students. Take your students on a field trip to an engineering firm and request that at least one of the available engineers be a female. Request that she demonstrate how she uses computer technology in her work.
- Talk with parents about providing their children with appropriate computer-based learning activities at home. Look for ways that government and community agencies may be able to help fund the purchase of a computer by low-income families with students in your classroom. Encourage parents to give their daughters positive feedback for using computers.

Another way to address inequities in computer access, and perhaps more importantly knowledge and skills in the use of computers, is to develop and support community organizations with that focus. A good example of such an organization is the Center for Urban Youth and Technology (www.albany.edu/cuyt/) in Albany, New York, which provides a range of initiatives in this area including after-school and summer programs for local minority students.

The Future of Technology in Schools

In *The Educator's Manifesto* (1999), Robbie McClintock argues that the innovations in communications and digital technologies have the potential to dramatically change teaching and learning. He identifies three areas where technological innovations have already changed what is educationally possible. First, the growth of the Internet and broadband, wireless communications have the potential to change schools and classrooms from isolated places with relatively scarce access to information to ones with rich connections to the world and its ideas. Second, emerging technologies "make it increasingly evident that the work of thinking can take place through many forms—verbal, visual, auditory, kinetic, and blends of all and each" (p. 13). Basic educational strategies must accordingly be broadened to include the presentation, manipulation, evaluation, creation and communication of knowledge in a variety of media forms. Third, digital tools, such as calculators, word processors, databases, spreadsheets, and graphical organizers, help to automate lower-level intellectual skills, thus allowing users to concentrate more on higher-level thinking. According to McClintock, the basic curricular question is "What knowledge is of most worth?" and it must accordingly be rethought as digital technologies change what is educationally possible.

Of course, McClintock's educational technology vision has yet to be realized. Although in the world outside the classroom people commonly use a variety of digital devices, such as cell phones, to access information in a variety of formats, and a variety of digital tools, such as calculators and iPods, to organize and manipulate that information wherever and whenever they need it, most classrooms today are not significantly different from classrooms of 50 years ago. However, some new developments that can be generally characterized as *ubiquitous computing* initiatives have the potential to dramatically transform classrooms.

The term "ubiquitous computing" was introduced by Mark Weiser (2001) of Xerox PARC, who wrote, "The most profound technologies are those that disappear. They weave themselves into the fabric of everyday life until they are indistinguishable from it." Weiser envisions ubiquitous computers as embedded in the environments we inhabit; others see them as devices we carry through those environments (Kay, 2005). Some experts maintain that what is most important about ubiquitous computing in schools is the provision of one computing device for every student (Papert, 2002; Silvernail & Lane, 2004).

In general, most contemporary educators view ubiquitous computing as encompassing all three of these notions, as well as the importance of Internet connectivity. Ubiquitous computing refers to learning environments in which all students have access to a variety of digital devices, including computers connected to the Internet and mobile computing devices, whenever and wherever they need them. This concept of ubiquitous computing is centered on the notion of portable and virtual technologies that are always available but not themselves the focus of learning. An important goal is for students and teachers to make informed choices about which technologies to use for particular tasks (Swan & others, 2006).

Pioneering educators are embracing the idea of ubiquitous computing. For example, Apple's Classrooms of Tomorrow (ACOT) program explored teaching and learning in technology-rich environments in the 1990s (Apple Computer, 1995). The Palm Education Pioneers (PEP) project studied what students and teachers could do when everyone had handheld computers (Vahey & Crawford, 2002). And in the state of Maine, every middle school student is being provided with a laptop computer (Silvernail & Lane, 2004). Researchers are documenting changes in ubiquitous computing classroom that suggest what the future of technology in schools may hold.

Across implementations of ubiquitous computing, researchers have found much greater use of Internet resources (Zucker & McGhee, 2005; Swan & others, 2006) and more presentations that communicate findings (Hill & others, 2002). They have discovered a much greater variety of representations being used to explore, create, and communicate knowledge including the use of a much wider variety of visual representations, spreadsheets and databases, simulations, and exploratory environments (Honey & Henriquez, 2000; Roschell, 2003; Swan & others, 2006). Such findings suggest that McClintock's (1999) possibilities are becoming reality in some classrooms.

Possibly as a result of the presence of ubiquitous computing, researchers are also documenting changes in interactions among students and between students and

THROUGH THE EYES OF STUDENTS

Future Technology Chat

The Threshold/ISTE Youth Forum (2004, pp. 26–30) recently asked 11 students from around the world to talk about technology and learning and what they think the future is likely to bring. Following are some of their responses to why they think technology is so essential today:

> Sharn B: All jobs that we may get have to do with tech
> Jon V: I personally go to a school where it is super important . . . it's life essential.
> Blake P: Abstract concepts are often easier to grasp when technology is used effectively as a teaching tool.
> Elena M: Yeah, some students at my school who weren't great students are better ones now thanks to computers.
> Sundip P: Technology allows us to learn as much as we want about virtually any topic. There are a ton of tutorials and explanations on things from improving test scores to videoediting and graphic design.

In response to how they are using technology outside of school that would make learning easier in school, they commented:

> Blake P: My powerbook never leaves a 6 foot radius of me.
> Sundip P: Sometimes if a teacher's explanation doesn't make sense to me, I search for it on the Net and see if I can get a feel for the topic using another approach.
> Mick S: Using instant messenger at home is something that could be very useful at school to communicate.

In response to what they see as hot technology trends, one student said:

> Blake P: Wi-Fi (a way of using the Internet wirelessly) . . . We already have a schoolwide wireless network, and it is great . . . could be faster.

In response to how they think schools will be different 15 years from now, they predicted:

> Mick S: I think schools will be more tech savvy, but around here, funding is a huge problem.
> Sharn B: The computers will be much smaller. . . they'll be able to fit into your palm.

In response to whether people will be able to learn more because of technology, they said:

> Sundip P: I think people will evolve to multitask better, as well as learn more rapidly. Technology is responsible for that.
> Sharn B: I think technology is speeding up our thinking process.

teachers (Swan & others, 2006). They find that learning is becoming more efficient and that students are becoming "experts" on particular topics (Hill & others, 2002). In addition, researchers note significant increases in collaboration among students and between students in teachers in ubiquitous computing classes (Swan & others, 2006).

These changed learning environments also bring about changes in teaching. In ubiquitious computing classrooms, teachers become more student-centered, constructivist, and flexible (Swan & others, 2006; Zucker & McGhee, 2005). They also develop lessons that are more project-oriented and more inquiry-based, and possibly as a result give assignments that involve collaboration with other students (Honey & Rodriquez, 2000; Swan & others, 2006).

Researchers are documenting positive effects of ubiquitous computing on students that include improved motivation, more engagement in learning, fewer behavior problems, improved school attendance, better organizational skills, and more independent learning (Apple Computer, 1995; Silvernail & Lane, 2004; Stevenson, 1998; Swan & others, 2006; van't Hooft, Díaz, & Swan, 2004; Zucker & McGhee, 2005). Ubiquitous access to computing devices can affect student learning. Researchers have documented increased media literacy, improved writing, and in some cases, higher scores on standardized tests (Hill & others, 2002; Rockman, 2003; Vahey & Crawford, 2002; Swan & others, 2006). In addition, some experts argue that ubiquitous computing "levels the playing field" for special needs and lower-ability students (Hill & others, 2002; Swan & others, 2006).

These early findings suggest that ubiquitous computing can produce significant changes in teaching and learning. Consider, for example, the following circumstance that actually took place at the Research Center for Educational Technology's ubiquitous computing classroom at Kent State University. It provides a glimpse of what may be possible in tomorrow's classrooms.

> It's an ordinary school day, as a group of kindergarten students gets off the bus. Suddenly, one of them spots an unusual bird high up in a tree. Running inside, they tell their teacher in excited voices that there is an owl in the tree. Armed with cameras they run back outside with their teacher, who identifies the bird as a red-tailed hawk as students capture it digitally. Discussing the bird on their way back to the classroom, one student asks, "Can I google 'red-tailed hawk'?" He does so, sharing his findings with his classmates via large screen projection. Using multimedia software, each student creates a small piece of illustrated writing about the hawk, some e-mailing what they have created to their parents. At the students' request, the teacher organizes the class to create a torn-paper collage of the red-tailed hawk which is framed and displayed prominently in the classroom.

BEST PRACTICES
Strategies for Choosing and Using Technology in the Classroom

Technology will be a part of your classroom. Here are some guidelines for choosing and using it:

1. *Choose technology with an eye toward how it can help students actively explore construct, and restructure information.* Look for software that lets students directly manipulate the information. One review found that students' learning improved when information was presented in a multimedia fashion that stimulated them to actively select, organize, and integrate visual and verbal information (Mayer, 1997). You might want to consult with a school or district media specialist for the software that best reflects these characteristics. Two excellent technology resources for teachers that emphasize the use of technology to improve students' learning and understanding are the Education with New Technologies (ENT) Web site **http://learnweb.harvard.edu/ent/home/index. cfm** and the International Society for Technology in Education (ISTE) Web site (**www.iste.org**). The ENT Web site is especially designed to help you integrate technology into your own classroom. Software catalogs and journals also are good sources.

2. *Look for ways to use technology as part of collaborative and real-world learning.* In Ann Brown and Joe Campione's (1996) words, education should be about "fostering a community of learners." Students often learn better when they work together to solve challenging problems and construct innovative projects (Hiltz & Goldman, 2005; Wiske, Franz, & Breit, 2005). Think of technologies such as the Web and e-mail as tools for providing students with opportunities to engage in collaborative learning, reaching outside the classroom to include the real world and the entire world and communicating with people in locations that otherwise would be inaccessible to them.

3. *Choose technology that presents positive models for students.* When you invite someone from the community to talk with your class, you likely will consider the person's values and the type of role model that he or she presents. Keep in mind our earlier comments about monitoring technology for equity in ethnicity and culture. Be sure that the models that students associate with technology are diverse individuals who serve as positive role models.

4. *Your teaching skills are critical, regardless of the technology you use.* You don't have to worry that technology will replace you as a teacher. Technology becomes effective in the classroom only when you know how to use it, demonstrate it, guide and monitor its use, and incorporate it into a larger effort to develop students who are motivated to learn, actively learn, and communicate effectively. Even the most sophisticated hypermedia will not benefit students much unless you appropriately orient students to it, ask them good questions about the material, orchestrate its use, and tailor it to their needs.

5. *Continue to learn about technology yourself and increase your technological competence.* Digital technology is still changing at an amazing pace. Make it a personal goal to be open to new technology, keep up with technological advances by reading educational journals, and take courses in educational computing to increase your skills. You will be an important model for your students in terms of your attitude toward technology, your ability to use it effectively yourself, and your ability to communicate how to use it effectively to your students. In a study of computers and education in many countries, the main determinants of effective use of information technology in classrooms were the teacher's competence in using technology and the teacher's positive attitude toward technology (Collis & others, 1996).

Review, Reflect, and Practice

(4) **Summarize how to effectively use technology to help children learn.**

REVIEW

- What characterizes the technology revolution and the Internet?
- What are some standards for technology-literate students?
- What are five things that teachers need to ask when considering the use of technology in the classroom to improve students' understanding?
- What are some current sociocultural inequities regarding educational technology?
- What might the future bring to technology in the classroom?

REFLECT

- Would one or more of the ways that computers can be used to support learning and instruction be useful to the subject and grade level you plan to teach? How?

PRAXIS™ PRACTICE

1. Ms. Carlson has her students enrolled in an online history course. This type of distance learning is referred to as
   a. e-mail.
   b. virtual school.
   c. tutorial.
   d. web enhancement.

2. Mr. Gonzales has students frequently use the Internet in his classroom. Which of the following situations in which he allows students to use the Internet should he likely eliminate?
   a. e-mail
   b. learning how to create a Web site
   c. being part of a worldwide science project
   d. accessing personal Web sites with little monitoring

3. Ms. Hamilton uses computers in her classroom for active, constructivist activities. The background of most students in her classroom is most likely to be
   a. low-income African American.
   b. low-income Latino.
   c. middle-income White.
   d. middle-income Native American.

4. Mrs. Hanratty has received awards for her effective use of computers in her classroom for improving student understanding. Which of the following computer activities is she *least* likely to have her students engage in?
   a. using the Internet to create a unique pathway of learning
   b. using word processors to express their understanding
   c. using computers to connect students with reflective, collaborative communities
   d. drill and practice with math formulas

5. Which of the following is the best example of ubiquitous computing?
   a. John is using a handheld computer to collect and store data for his science research project.
   b. Juan is immersed in a computer simulation of the desert ecosystem.
   c. Maria is communicating via an instant messaging system with a friend in another country.
   d. Patricia is using her computer to write a paper for her English class.

Please see the answer key at the end of the book.

CRACK THE CASE
The Case of the Big Debate

Mrs. Rumer was new to teaching third grade at Hillside Elementary School. Before the school year began, she met with other new teachers and their mentors for planning sessions. The administration appeared to be aware of just how much planning was necessary for successful teaching. Mrs. Rumer openly shared her ideas with her mentor, Mrs. Humbolt, and the rest of the group.

"I really want to have a learner-centered classroom," she said. "I'd like to use aspects of problem-based learning, essential questions, and guided discovery. I think the students will learn so much more that way than if I use teacher-centered instruction."

Mrs. Humbolt smiled and said, "Well, they'd probably have more fun, but I doubt that their test scores would reflect much learning at all. We really need to prepare our students to meet state standards, Mrs. Rumer. To do that, you'd better throw in some good old-fashioned direct instruction." Several other teachers readily agreed. One commented, "That constructivist stuff is too much fluff; I want my students to be serious and learn what I teach them." Another said, "I use the computers in the classroom for drilling students to memorize material for the state tests they have to take, sort of like giving them electronic flash cards. I guess that wouldn't fit your scheme."

The other teachers' comments surprised Mrs. Rumer. She had learned in her education courses that learner-centered instruction is supposed to be the best way to teach children. She wanted her students to actively construct their knowledge, not merely have her pour information into their minds. The principal assured her that if she wanted to use a learner-centered approach, she would have that freedom.

With this assurance, Mrs. Rumer began making lists of everything she would have to plan for in order to have an effective learner-centered classroom. She began by going through the district's curriculum guide for third grade. She made lists of all the objectives. Then she went through the learner-centered psychological principles from the APA. After doing this, she realized her job was going to be a daunting one.

1. What are the issues in this case?
2. Where should Mrs. Rumer go from here?
3. How can she take a curriculum that has been taught in a teacher-centered manner and convert it to a learner-centered curriculum? Should she? Why or why not?
4. How can she incorporate technology into the curriculum so that the computers don't become mere electronic flash-cards?
5. Which of the following is an activity that would most likely appeal to Mrs. Rumer?
   a. The students will master their basic multiplication facts by completing a worksheet covering them each day.
   b. The students will master their basic multiplication facts by playing multiplication baseball.
   c. The students will master their basic multiplication facts by taking daily timed tests covering them.
   d. The students will master their basic multiplication facts by writing out their multiplication tables repeatedly.
6. Which of the following is an activity that would most likely appeal to Mrs. Rumer's colleagues?
   a. The students will learn the scientific process by completing several experiments.
   b. The students will learn the scientific process by focusing on essential questions in science.
   c. The students will learn the scientific process by reading about it in their science texts and listening to lectures.
   d. The students will learn the scientific process by testing the water in a nearby creek.

Reach Your Learning Goals

Planning, Instruction, and Technology

1 **PLANNING:** Explain what is involved in classroom planning.

Instructional Planning

Instructional planning involves developing a systematic, organized strategy of instruction that benefits students' learning.

Time Frames and Planning

Good planning addresses both task (setting instructional goals, planning activities, and setting priorities) and time (making time estimates, creating schedules, and being flexible). You will need to make plans for different time frames, ranging from yearly planning to daily planning.

2 **TEACHER-CENTERED LESSON PLANNING AND INSTRUCTION:** Identify important forms of teacher-centered instruction.

Teacher-Centered Lesson Planning

Teacher-centered lesson planning includes creating behavioral objectives, analyzing tasks, and developing instructional taxonomies (classifications). Behavioral objectives are statements that propose changes in students' behavior to reach desired performance levels. Task analysis focuses on breaking down a complex task into its component parts. Bloom's taxonomy consists of cognitive, affective, and psychomotor domains and is used by many teachers to create goals and objectives in lesson planning.

Direct Instruction

Direct instruction is a structured, teacher-centered approach that involves teacher direction and control, high expectations for students' progress, maximum time spent by students on academic tasks, and efforts by the teacher to keep negative affect to a minimum. The use of nonacademic materials is deemphasized, as is nonacademically oriented teacher-student interaction.

Teacher-Centered Instructional Strategies

Teacher-centered instructional strategies include orienting students; lecturing, explaining, and demonstrating; questioning and discussion; mastery learning; seatwork; and homework.

Evaluating Teacher-Centered Instruction

Teacher-centered instruction includes useful techniques and its advocates especially believe it is effective in improving children's basic skills. Critics of teacher-centered instruction say that by itself it tends to lead to passive rote learning, overly rigid and structured classrooms, inadequate attention to socioemotional development, external motivation, excess use of paper-and-pencil tasks, too few opportunities for real-world learning, and too little collaborative learning in small groups.

3 **LEARNER-CENTERED LESSON PLANNING AND INSTRUCTION:** Discuss important forms of learner-centered instruction.

Learner-Centered Principles

Learner-centered planning and instruction moves the focus away from the teacher and toward the student. The APA's learner-centered psychological principles involve cognitive and metacognitive factors (the nature of the learning process, goals of the learning process, the construction of knowledge, strategic thinking, thinking about thinking, and the context of learning), motivational and affective factors (motivational and emotional influences on learning, intrinsic motivation to learn, and effects of motivation on effort), developmental and social factors (developmental influences on learning and social influences on learning), and individual difference factors (individual differences in learning, learning and diversity, and standards and assessments).

Some Learner-Centered Instructional Strategies

Problem-based learning emphasizes real-world learning. A problem-based curriculum exposes students to authentic problems. Problem-based learning focuses on small-group discussion rather than lecture. Students identify issues they wish to explore, and teachers act as guides, helping students monitor their problem-solving efforts. Essential questions are questions that engagingly reflect the heart of the curriculum. Discovery learning is learning in which students construct an understanding on their own. Discovery learning is designed to get students to think for themselves, to discover how knowledge is constructed, to stimulate their curiosity, and to motivate their inquiry. Most discovery-learning approaches today involve guided discovery, in which students are encouraged to construct their understanding with the assistance of teacher-guided questions and directions.

Evaluating Learner-Centered Instruction

The learner-centered model of planning and instruction has many positive features. The fourteen APA learner-centered principles are guidelines that can help teachers develop strategies that benefit student learning (such as encouraging students to actively construct knowledge, think deeply and creatively, be internally motivated, solve real-world problems, and collaboratively learn). Critics argue that learner-centered planning and instruction focuses too much on process and not enough on content, is more appropriate for social sciences and humanities than science and math, is not appropriate for beginning instruction when students have little or no knowledge about the topic, and is more challenging to implement than most teachers envision. Keep in mind that although we presented teacher-centered and learner-centered approaches separately, many teachers use aspects of both approaches.

④ TECHNOLOGY: Summarize how to effectively use technology to help children learn.

The Technology Revolution and the Internet

The technology revolution is part of the information society in which we now live, and students will increasingly need to have technological skills. Today's technologies can be remarkable tools for motivating students and guiding their learning. The Internet is the core of computer-mediated communication. The Web is a system for browsing Internet sites. The Internet can be an important learning tool in many classrooms. The growth of the Internet has led to a new phenomenon in distance learning, the virtual school. Cautions about Internet use need to be observed.

Standards for Technology-Literate Students

The International Society for Technology in Education has established technology standards for students that involve basic operations and concepts; social, ethical, and human issues; technology productivity tools; technology communication needs; technology research tools; and technology problem-solving and decision-making tools. In addition, ISTE provides performance indicators for achieving these standards at different grade levels.

Teaching, Learning, and Technology

Five things teachers need to ask regarding using technology more effectively in the classroom to improve students' learning include considering (1) which topics are worth understanding, (2) what students should understand about such topics, (3) how students develop and demonstrate understanding, (4) how students and teachers assess understanding, and (5) how students and teachers learn together.

Technology and Sociocultural Diversity

A special concern is that students from low-income, ethnic backgrounds, as well as schools in low-income areas, are underserved. Females also might have less access and be technologically underserved.

The Future of Technology in Schools

Schools are likely to see increased ubiquitous computing, including portable and virtual technologies. Early research on ubiquitous computing indicates positive results for teaching and learning.

KEY TERMS

instructional planning 406
behavioral objectives 410
task analysis 411
taxonomy 411
Bloom's taxonomy 411

direct instruction 414
advance organizers 416
expository advance
    organizers 416

comparative advance
    organizers 416
mastery learning 417
essential questions 428
discovery learning 429

guided discovery
    learning 429
Internet 433
Web 434

 PORTFOLIO ACTIVITIES

Now that you have a good understanding of this chapter, complete these exercises to expand your thinking.

Independent Reflection

Developing a Classroom Technology Plan. Create a written plan for how you might use computers for the subject(s) and grade level you plan to teach. How will you adapt your plan for students with little or no experience with computers? How can your classroom benefit from students with advanced technology skills? (INTASC: Principles *1, 2, 4*)

Collaborative Work

Evaluating Teacher-Centered and Learner-Centered Classrooms. With three other students in the class, divide up the work of observing an early childhood, an elementary, a middle school, and a high school classroom. Reconvene after each of you has observed a classroom, and discuss the aspects of teacher-centered and learner-centered approaches the teachers were using. Evaluate how effective the approaches were. Write a comparative analysis. (INTASC: Principles *1, 2, 3, 4, 5, 6, 7, 8, 9*)

Research/Field Experience

Instructional Planning in Action. Ask a teacher at the grade level you plan to teach to show you the materials he or she uses in planning lessons, units, the term, and the yearly curriculum for one or more subjects. Create samples for your own later use based on what the teacher shows you. Discuss the importance of planning at each of these levels. (INTASC: Principles *7, 9*)

Go to the Online Learning Center for downloadable portfolio templates.

 TAKING IT TO THE NET

- List the primary components of a good lesson plan. Dissect an online lesson plan and assess its component parts. Describe the quality of your chosen lesson and how you think it could be improved. Why is it so critical to develop clear objectives? Why is it good practice to think about your method of assessment prior to conducting the lesson? **www.eduref.org/Virtual/Lessons/index.shtml**

- Using the selected Web site on the Online Learning Center or a site of your own choice, review an exemplary model of educational technology in action. Why is your selected program or project so successful? Reflect on your own technology skills, and note your strengths and weaknesses. Develop a professional development action plan to enhance your educational technology skills. **www.ncrel.org/sdrs/areas/issues/methods/technlgy/te800.htm**

- Evaluate an online, interactive activity, such as a WebQuest. How does it measure up in these areas: academic rigor, student interest and motivation, user interface and navigability, relevance to real-world issues, and accessibility to students/teachers? **http://webquest.sdsu.edu/**

Connect to the Online Learning Center to explore possible answers.

 STUDY, PRACTICE, AND SUCCEED

Visit **www.mhhe.com/santedu3e** to review the chapter with self-grading quizzes and self-assessments, to apply the chapter material to two more Crack the Case studies, and for suggested activities to develop your teaching portfolio.

CHAPTER 13

Motivation, Teaching, and Learning

The art of teaching is the art of awakening
the curiosity of young minds.

—Anatole France
French Novelist and Poet, 20th Century

TEACHING STORIES   Jaime Escalante

In the 1970s, an immigrant from Bolivia named Jaime Escalante became a math teacher at Garfield High School in East Los Angeles, a school largely populated by Latino students from low-income families. When he began teaching at Garfield, many of the students had little confidence in their math abilities, and most of the teachers had low expectations for the students' success. Escalante took it as a special challenge to improve the students' math skills, even enable them to perform well on the Educational Testing Service Advanced Placement calculus exam.

The first year was difficult. Escalante's calculus class began at 8 A.M. He told the students the doors would be open at 7 A.M. and that instruction would begin at 7:30 A.M. He also worked with them after school and on weekends. He put together lots of handouts, told the students to take extensive notes, and required them to keep a folder. He gave them a five-minute quiz each morning and a test every Friday. He started with fourteen students, but in two weeks the number was cut in half. Only five students lasted through the spring. One of the boys who quit said, "I don't want to come at 7 o'clock. Why should I?"

When Escalante was teaching, on the 5-point AP calculus test (with 5 highest, 1 lowest), a 3 or better meant that a student is performing at a college level and would receive credit for the course at most major universities. The AP calculus scores for Escalante's first five students were two 4's, two 2's, and one 1. This was better than the school had done in the past, but Escalante resolved to do better.

Three years later, the AP calculus test scores for Escalante's class of 15 students were one 5, four 4's, nine 3's, and one 2. Ten years after Escalante's first class, 151 students were taking calculus in the East Los Angeles high school.

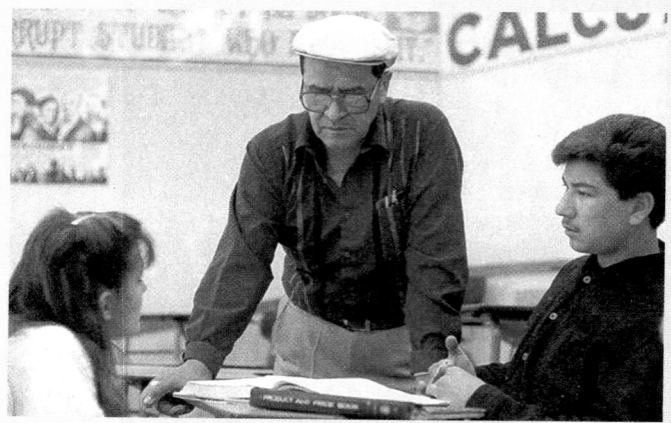

Jaime Escalante in a classroom teaching math.

Escalante's persistent, challenging, and inspiring teaching raised Garfield High, a school plagued by poor funding, violence, and inferior working conditions, to seventh place among U.S. schools in calculus. Escalante's commitment and motivation were transferred to his students, many of whom no one had believed in before Escalante came along. Escalante's contributions were portrayed in the film *Stand and Deliver*. Escalante, his students, and celebrity guests also introduce basic math concepts for sixth- to twelfth-grade students on *Futures 1 and 2 with Jaime Escalante*, a PBS series. Escalante has now retired from teaching but continues to work in a consulting role to help improve students' motivation to do well in math and improve their math skills. Escalante's story is testimony to how one teacher can make a major difference in students' motivation and achievement.

Preview

In chapter 12, you learned that motivation is a key component of the American Psychological Association's learner-centered psychological principles. Indeed, motivation is a critical aspect of teaching and learning. Unmotivated students won't expend the necessary effort to learn. As Jaime Escalante's Teaching Story shows, highly motivated students are eager to come to school and are absorbed in the learning process.

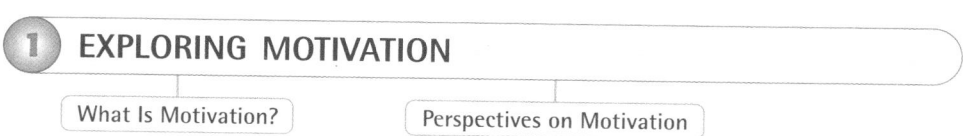

1   EXPLORING MOTIVATION

What Is Motivation?   Perspectives on Motivation

A young Canadian, Terry Fox, completed one of the great long-distance runs in history (McNally, 1990). Averaging a marathon (26.2 miles) a day for 5 months, he ran

3,359 miles across Canada. What makes his grueling feat truly remarkable is that Terry Fox had lost a leg to cancer before the run, so he was running with the aid of a prosthetic limb. Terry Fox clearly was a motivated person, but exactly what does it mean to be motivated?

What Is Motivation?

Motivation involves the processes that energize, direct, and sustain behavior. That is, motivated behavior is behavior that is energized, directed, and sustained. Why did Terry Fox complete his run? When Terry was hospitalized with cancer, he told himself that if he survived he would do something to help fund cancer research. Thus, the motivation for his run was to give purpose to his life by helping other people with cancer.

Terry Fox's behavior was energized, directed, and sustained. Running across Canada, he encountered unforeseen hurdles: severe headwinds, heavy rain, snow, and icy roads. Because of these conditions, he averaged only 8 miles a day after the first month, far below what he had planned. But he kept going and picked up the pace in the second month until he was back on track to reach his goal. His example stands as a testimonial to how motivation can help each of us prevail.

Lance Armstrong after winning his seventh Tour de France in a row.

Terry Fox's story is portrayed in a good classroom film, *The Power of Purpose.* One sixth-grade teacher showed the film to her class and then asked her students to write down what they learned from it. One student wrote, "I learned that even if something bad happens to you, you have to keep going, keep trying. Even if your body gets hurt, it can't take away your spirit."

Let's look at another example of motivation. Lance Armstrong was an accomplished cyclist when he was diagnosed with testicular cancer in 1996. Chances of his recovery were estimated at less than 50 percent when he began chemotherapy. However, Lance did recover from the cancer and set a goal of winning the 3-week, 2,000-plus-mile Tour de France, the world's premier bicycle race and one of the great tests of human motivation in sports. Day after day, Lance trained intensely, keeping the goal of winning the Tour de France in mind. Lance won the Tour de France not once but 7 years in a row from 1999 through 2005.

As with Terry Fox's marathon run and Lance Armstrong's winning of the Tour de France, motivation in the classroom involves why students are behaving in a particular way and the extent to which their behavior is energized, directed, and sustained. If students don't complete an assignment because they are bored, lack of motivation is involved. If students encounter challenges in researching and writing a paper, but persist and overcome hurdles, motivation is involved.

Perspectives on Motivation

Different psychological perspectives explain motivation in different ways. Let's explore four of these perspectives: behavioral, humanistic, cognitive, and social.

The Behavioral Perspective   The behavioral perspective emphasizes external rewards and punishments as keys in determining a student's motivation. **Incentives** are positive or negative stimuli or events that can motivate a student's behavior. Advocates of the use of incentives emphasize that they add interest or excitement to the class and direct attention toward appropriate behavior and away from inappropriate behavior (Emmer, Evertson, & Worsham, 2006).

Incentives that classroom teachers use include numerical scores and letter grades, which provide feedback about the quality of the student's work, and checkmarks or stars for competently completing work. Other incentives include giving students recognition—for example, by displaying their work, giving them a certificate of achievement, placing them on the honor roll, and verbally mentioning their accomplishments. Another type of incentive focuses on allowing students to do something special—such as playing computer games or going on a field trip—as a reward for good work. Shortly, in our discussion of intrinsic and extrinsic motivation, we will

motivation The processes that energize, direct, and sustain behavior.

incentives Positive or negative stimuli or events that can motivate a student's behavior.

FIGURE 13.1 Maslow's Hierarchy of Needs

Abraham Maslow developed the hierarchy of human needs to show how we have to satisfy certain basic needs before we can satisfy higher needs. In the diagram, lower-level needs are shown toward the base of the pyramid, higher-level needs toward the peak.

humanistic perspective A view that stresses students' capacity for personal growth, freedom to choose their destiny, and positive qualities.

hierarchy of needs Maslow's concept that individual needs must be satisfied in this sequence: physiological, safety, love and belongingness, esteem, and self-actualization.

self-actualization The highest and most elusive of Maslow's needs; the motivation to develop one's full potential as a human being.

look more closely at the issue of whether incentives are a good idea.

The Humanistic Perspective The **humanistic perspective** stresses students' capacity for personal growth, freedom to choose their destiny, and positive qualities (such as being sensitive to others). This perspective is closely associated with Abraham Maslow's (1954, 1971) belief that certain basic needs must be met before higher needs can be satisfied. According to Maslow's **hierarchy of needs,** individuals' needs must be satisfied in this sequence (see figure 13.1):

- *Physiological:* hunger, thirst, sleep
- *Safety:* ensuring survival, such as protection from war and crime
- *Love and belongingness:* security, affection, and attention from others
- *Esteem:* feeling good about oneself
- *Self-actualization:* realization of one's potential

Thus, In Maslow's view, students must satisfy their need for food before they can achieve. His view also provides an explanation of why children who come from poor or abusive homes are less likely to achieve in school than children whose basic needs are met.

Self-actualization, the highest and most elusive of Maslow's needs, is the motivation to develop one's full potential as a human being. In Maslow's view, self-actualization is possible only after the lower needs have been met. Maslow cautions that most people stop maturing after they have developed a high level of esteem and therefore never become self-actualized. Some characteristics of self-actualized individuals include being spontaneous, problem-centered rather than self-centered, and creative.

The idea that human needs are hierarchically arranged is appealing. However, not everyone agrees with Maslow's ordering of motives. For example, for some students cognitive needs might be more fundamental than esteem needs. Other students might meet their cognitive needs even though they have not experienced love and belongingness.

The Cognitive Perspective According to the cognitive perspective on motivation, students' thoughts guide their motivation. In recent years there has been a tremendous surge of interest in the cognitive perspective on motivation (Meece, Anderman, & Anderman, 2006; Oka, 2005; Pintrich & Schunk, 2002; Weiner, 2005; Wigfield, Byrnes, & Eccles, 2006). This interest focuses on such ideas as students' internal motivation to achieve, their attributions (perceptions about the causes of success or failure, especially the perception that effort is an important factor in achievement), and their beliefs that they can effectively control their environment. The cognitive perspective also stresses the importance of goal setting, planning, and monitoring progress toward a goal (Lepper, Corpus, & Iyengar, 2005; Schunk & Zimmerman, 2006).

Thus, whereas the behavioral perspective sees the student's motivation as a consequence of external incentives, the cognitive perspective argues that external pressures should be deemphasized. The cognitive perspective recommends that students should be given more opportunities and responsibility for controlling their own achievement outcomes (Perry, Turner, & Meyer, 2006).

The cognitive perspective on motivation fits with the ideas of R. W. White (1959), who proposed the concept of **competence motivation,** the idea that people are motivated to deal effectively with their environment, to master their world, and to process information efficiently. White said that people do these things because they are internally motivated to interact effectively with the environment. The concept of competence motivation explains why humans are motivated to achieve scientific and technological innovation.

The Social Perspective   Are you the kind of person who is motivated to be around people a lot? Or would you rather stay home and read a book? The **need for affiliation or relatedness** is the motive to be securely connected with other people. This involves establishing, maintaining, and restoring warm, close personal relationships. Students' need for affiliation or relatedness is reflected in their motivation to spend time with peers, their close friendships, their attachment to their parents, and their desire to have a positive relationship with their teachers.

Students in schools with caring and supportive interpersonal relationships have more positive academic attitudes and values and are more satisfied with school (Baker, 1999; Stipek, 2002). One of the most important factors in students' motivation and achievement was their perception of whether they had a positive relationship with the teacher (McCombs, 2001; McCombs & Quiat, 2001). The value that middle school students assigned to math increased when they had a teacher whom they perceived to be high in support (Eccles, 1993).

Review, Reflect, and Practice

(1) Define motivation and compare the behavioral, humanistic, cognitive, and social perspectives on motivation.

REVIEW
- What is motivated behavior?
- How would you briefly summarize the four main perspectives on motivation?

REFLECT
- Recall a situation in which you were highly motivated to accomplish something. How would you describe your motivation in terms of each of the four perspectives?

PRAXIS™ PRACTICE
1. Which of the following best exemplifies what motivation is?
   a. Robbie is emotional about the upcoming school year and wants to do well.
   b. Sherrie is energized, sets a high goal for doing well in her English class, persists with considerable effort, and makes an *A* in the class.
   c. Carmello is good at directing his attention to what he wants to accomplish.
   d. Latisha works hard, experiences positive feelings about her academic work, and enjoys working with others.
2. Which of the following best exemplifies the cognitive perspective of motivation?
   a. Mr. Davidson gives his students tickets when he "catches them being good" so that they will continue to behave appropriately.
   b. Mr. McRoberts wants his students to believe they can be successful in anything if they try, so he ensures success for those students who work hard.
   c. Ms. Boeteng believes that her students will be more motivated in school if they establish good relationships with both her and with their classmates, so she provides emotional support.
   d. Ms. Pocius keeps a supply of cereal in her desk drawer so that if one of her students is hungry, she can provide food.

Please see the answer key at the end of the book.

competence motivation The idea that people are motivated to deal effectively with their environment, to master their world, and to process information efficiently.

need for affiliation or relatedness The motive to be securely connected with other people.

2 ACHIEVEMENT PROCESSES

```
Extrinsic and
Intrinsic Motivation          Mastery          Goal Setting, Planning,
                              Motivation        and Self-Monitoring

        Attribution          Self-Efficacy                    Expectations
```

The current interest in motivation in school has been fueled by the cognitive perspective and an emphasis on discovering the most important processes involved in students' achievement. In this section, we will study a number of effective cognitive strategies for improving students' motivation to achieve. We'll begin by exploring a crucial distinction between extrinsic (external) and intrinsic (internal) motivation. That will lead us to examine several other important cognitive insights about motivation. Then, we will study the role of teachers' expectations in students' motivation.

Extrinsic and Intrinsic Motivation

Extrinsic motivation involves doing something to obtain something else (a means to an end). Extrinsic motivation is often influenced by external incentives such as rewards and punishments. For example, a student may study hard for a test in order to obtain a good grade in the course.

These students were given an opportunity to write and perform their own play. These kinds of self-determining opportunities can enhance students' motivation to achieve.

While the behavioral perspective emphasizes the importance of extrinsic motivation in achievement, the humanistic and cognitive approaches stress the importance of intrinsic motivation in achievement. **Intrinsic motivation** involves the internal motivation to do something for its own sake (an end in itself). For example, a student may study hard for a test because he or she enjoys the content of the course.

Current evidence strongly favors establishing a classroom climate in which students are intrinsically motivated to learn (Hennesey & Amabile, 1998; Lepper, Corpus, & Iyengar, 2005; Wigfield, Byrnes, & Eccles, 2006; Wigfield & others, 2006). For example, one recent study of third- to eighth-grade students found that intrinsic motivation was positively linked with grades and standardized test scores, while extrinsic motivation was negatively related to achievement outcomes (Lepper, Corpus, & Iyengar, 2005).

Students are more motivated to learn when they are given choices, become absorbed in challenges that match their skills, and receive rewards that have informational value but are not used for control. Praise also can enhance students' intrinsic motivation. To see why these things are so, let's first explore four types of intrinsic motivation: (1) self-determination and personal choice, (2) optimal experience and flow, (3) interest, and (4) cognitive engagement and self-responsibility. Then we'll discuss how external rewards can either enhance or undermine intrinsic motivation. Next we will identify some developmental changes in intrinsic and extrinsic motivation as students move up the educational ladder. Finally, we will offer some concluding thoughts about intrinsic and extrinsic motivation.

Self-Determination and Personal Choice   One view of intrinsic motivation emphasizes self-determination (Deci, Koestner, & Ryan, 2001; Deci & Ryan, 1994; Ryan & Deci, 2000). In this view, students want to believe that they are doing something because of their own will, not because of external success or rewards.

Researchers have found that students' internal motivation and intrinsic interest in school tasks increase when students have some choice and some opportunities to take personal responsibility for their learning (Grolnick & others, 2002; Stipek, 2002). For example, in one study, high school science students who were encouraged to organize their own experiments demonstrated more care and interest in laboratory work than did their counterparts who had to follow detailed instructions and directions (Rainey, 1965).

In another study, which included mainly African American students from low-income backgrounds, teachers were encouraged to give the students more responsibility

extrinsic motivation The external motivation to do something to obtain something else (a means to an end).

intrinsic motivation The internal motivation to do something for its own sake (an end in itself).

BEST PRACTICES
Strategies for Student Self-Determination and Choice

Here are some ways you can promote self-determination and choice in your class-room (Brophy, 2004; Deci & Ryan, 1994):

1. *Take the time* to talk with students and explain why a learning activity is important.

2. *Be attentive* to students' feelings when they are being asked to do something they don't want to do.

3. *Manage the classroom effectively,* in a way that lets students make personal choices. Let students select topics for book reports, writing assignments, and research projects and decide how they want to report their work (for instance, to you or to the class as a whole, individually or with a partner).

4. *Establish learning centers* where students can work individually or collaboratively with other students on different projects and can select their activities from a menu that you have developed.

5. *Create self-selected interest groups* and let students work on relevant research projects.

for their school programs (deCharms, 1984)—in particular, opportunities to set their own goals, plan how to reach the goals, and monitor their progress toward the goals. Students were given some choice in the activities they wanted to engage in and when they would do them. They also were encouraged to take personal responsibility for their behavior, including reaching the goals that they had set. Compared with a control group, students in this intrinsic motivation/self-determination group had higher achievement gains and were more likely to graduate from high school.

Optimal Experiences and Flow   Mihaly Csikszentmihalyi (1990, 1993, 2000; Nakamura & Csikszentmihalyi, 2002; Rathunde & Csikszentmihalyi, 2006) also has developed ideas that are relevant to understanding intrinsic motivation. He has studied the optimal experiences of people for more than two decades. People report that these optimal experiences involve feelings of deep enjoyment and happiness. Csikszentmihalyi uses the term *flow* to describe optimal experiences in life. He has found that flow occurs most often when people develop a sense of mastery and are absorbed in a state of concentration while they engage in an activity. He argues that flow occurs when individuals are engaged in challenges they find neither too difficult nor too easy.

Perceived levels of challenge and skill can result in different outcomes (see figure 13.2) (Brophy, 1998). Flow is most likely to occur in areas in which students are challenged and perceive themselves as having a high degree of skill. When students' skills are high but the activity provides little challenge, the result is boredom. When both the challenge and skill levels are low, students feel apathy. And when students face a challenging task that they don't believe they have adequate skills to master, they experience anxiety.

Interest   Educational psychologists also have examined the concept of *interest,* which has been proposed as more specific than intrinsic motivation (Blumenfeld, Kempler, & Krajcik, 2006; Wigfield & others, 2006). A distinction has been made between individual interest, which is thought to be relative stable, and situational interest, which is believed to be generated by specific aspects of a task activity. Research on interest has focused mainly on how interest is related to learning.

FIGURE 13.2 Outcomes of Perceived Levels of Challenge and Skill

BEST PRACTICES
Strategies for Helping Students Achieve Flow

How can you encourage students to achieve flow? Here are some strategies (Csikszentmihalyi, Rathunde, & Whalen, 1993):

1. *Be competent and motivated.* Become an expert about the subject matter, show enthusiasm when you teach, and present yourself as a model who is intrinsically motivated.

THROUGH THE EYES OF TEACHERS
Turning the Classroom into an Egyptian Tomb, New York City, and Mount Olympus

Rhonda Nachamkin, who teaches first grade at River Eves Elementary School in Roswell, Georgia, has a high-energy style and approaches each unit as if it were a Hollywood production. She turns the classroom into an Egyptian tomb, New York City, and Mount Olympus. She sends parents scurrying to learn who Anubis (Egyptian god) and Prometheus (Greek Titan who stole fire) were so they can converse about these topics with their 6-year-olds. Rhonda likes to use multiple versions of fairy tales to teach reading, spelling, and analytical concepts (Source: *USA Today,* 1999).

Rhonda Nachamkin helps one of her students, Patrick Drones, with his work.

2. *Create an optimal match.* A good strategy is to develop and maintain an optimal match between what you challenge students to do and what their skills are. That is, encourage students to achieve challenging but reasonable goals.

3. *Raise confidence.* Provide students with both instructional and emotional support that encourages them to tackle learning with confidence and a minimum of anxiety. As you will see next, Alan Haskitz, a middle school social studies teacher, describes how he does this by finding a topic that students find intrinsically interesting.

THROUGH THE EYES OF TEACHERS
Achieving Flow in a Math Class by Appraising Car Values

Most middle and high school students like cars, so I use the National Automobile Dealers Association (NADA) appraisal guides that provide an estimated value for new and used vehicles to make math more interesting for students. NADA makes the guides available without charge (www.nada.com). The students are exposed to the basic math concepts from lecture and using the textbook. However, that does not achieve flow. To acquire that level of motivation, the students design their own lessons to teach others the concepts using the NADA guidebooks for the values they are going to use in their work. I teach them how to write a multiple-choice question with stems and distracters and then stand back and watch the flow start. I hear students shuffling through the books shouting out figures, vehicle names, and "I want this car," and "Look at how much this costs." They see the lesson as important to them because they want to own a car—but more importantly, they want to be a knowledgeable buyer. They use the data to apply real-world statistics to creating problems that teach such fundamental, and sometimes difficult to grasp, concepts as percentages, depreciation, and graphing. Using these books is especially a powerful tool for remediation as it appeals to those students with difficulty graphing abstract reasoning.

Interest is especially linked to measures of deep learning, such as recall of main ideas and responses to more difficult comprehension questions, than to surface learning, such as responses to simple questions and verbatim recall of text (Schiefele, 1996; Wigfield & others, 2006). To read further about ways to stimulate students' interest, see the Technology and Education Box.

Cognitive Engagement and Self-Responsibility Phyllis Blumenfeld and her colleagues (2006) have proposed another variation on intrinsic motivation. They emphasize the importance of creating learning environments that encourage students to become cognitively engaged and take responsibility for their learning. The goal is to get students to become motivated to expend the effort to persist and master ideas rather than simply doing enough work to just get by and make passing grades. Especially important is to embed subject matter content and skills learning within meaningful contexts, especially real-world situations that mesh with students' interests (Perry, Turner, & Meyer, 2006).

TECHNOLOGY AND EDUCATION

Technology Integration, Authentic Tasks, Curiosity, and Interest

Authentic tasks approximate the real world or real life as closely as possible, and they can spark students' interest and curiosity. Students often perceive technology-based learning experiences as real-world activities (Cognition and Technology Group at Vanderbilt, 1997).

Integrating technology into the classroom has clearly been found to increase students' motivation to learn and engagement in learning, especially when it is used to foster authentic learning. For example, researchers have documented improved motivation (Zucker & McGhee, 2005; Swan & others, 2005), engagement (Silvernail & Lane, 2004; Zucker & McGhee, 2005), behavior (Apple Computer, 1995), and school attendance (Apple Computer, 1995) among students involved in technology-rich initiatives. In addition, research indicates that such students are better organized and more independent learners (Zucker & McGhee, 2005). Also, research reveals that special

Second-grade students in the Research Center for Educational Technology's AT&T classroom at Kent State University engaged in writing activities on mobile computers they can take with them and work on anywhere and anytime.

needs students can achieve at the same levels as regular students in some situations when using technology (Hill & others, 2002; Swan & others, 2006).

One example of technology-based authentic learning is the use of a commercial movie, *Young Sherlock Holmes,* for social studies and humanities classes. Researchers have found that even when authentic technology tasks require considerable work, students often rise to the task in pursuing solutions to the problems they pose (Goldman & others, 1996).

Technology applications aimed at stimulating students' interest, curiosity, and creativity are likely to increase their motivation far more than technology that involves drill and practice. For example, an increasing number of computer simulations, such as *SimCity, SimTown,* and *SimEarth,* stir students' curiosity by letting

them create and manage environments (Maddux, Johnson, & Willis, 1997).

Extrinsic Rewards and Intrinsic Motivation Now that we have discussed a number of views of intrinsic motivation, let's examine whether classroom rewards might be useful in some situations and whether certain types of rewards might actually increase intrinsic motivation. As we saw in chapter 7, external rewards can be useful in changing behavior. However, in some situations rewards can undermine learning. In one study, students who already had a strong interest in art and did not expect a reward spent more time drawing than did students who also had a strong interest in art but knew they would be rewarded for drawing (Lepper, Greene, & Nisbett, 1973).

However, classroom rewards can be useful (Cameron, 2001; Reeve, 2006). Two uses are (1) as an incentive to engage in tasks, in which case the goal is to control the student's behavior; and (2) to convey information about mastery (Bandura, 1982; Deci, 1975). When rewards are offered that convey information about mastery, students' feelings of competence are likely to be enhanced. It is not the reward itself that causes the effect but, rather, the offer or expectation of the reward (Schunk, 2001). Rewards used as incentives lead to perceptions that the student's behavior was caused by the external reward, and not by the student's own motivation to be competent.

To better understand the difference between using rewards to control students' behavior and using them to provide information about mastery, consider this example (Schunk, 2004): A teacher puts a reward system in place in which the more work students accomplish, the more points they will earn. Students will be motivated to work to earn points because they are told that the points can be exchanged for privileges. However, the points also provide information about their capabilities. That is, the more points students earn, the more work they have accomplished. As they accumulate points, students are more likely to feel competent. In contrast, if points are provided simply for spending time on a task, the task might be perceived as a means to an end. In this case, because the points don't convey anything about capabilities, students are likely to perceive the rewards as controlling their behavior.

Thus, rewards that convey information about students' mastery can increase intrinsic motivation by increasing their sense of competence (Reeve, 2006). However, negative feedback, such as criticism, that carries information that students are incompetent can undermine intrinsic motivation, especially if students doubt their ability to become competent (Stipek, 2002).

Judy Cameron (2001; Cameron & Pierce, 1996) argues that rewards do not always decrease a student's intrinsic motivation. In her analysis of approximately a hundred studies, she found that verbal rewards (praise and positive feedback) can be used to enhance students' intrinsic motivation. She also concluded that when tangible rewards (such as gold stars and money) were offered contingent on task performance or given unexpectedly, intrinsic motivation was maintained. Some critics argue that Cameron's analysis is flawed—for instance, that it does not adequately detect some of the negative effects of rewards on motivation (Deci, Koestner, & Ryan, 2001; Kohn, 1996).

In summary, it is important to examine what rewards convey about competence (Reeve, 2006). When rewards are tied to competence, they tend to promote motivation and interest. When they are not, they are unlikely to raise motivation or may diminish it once the rewards are withdrawn (Schunk, 2004).

Developmental Shifts in Intrinsic and Extrinsic Motivation   Many psychologists and educators stress that it is important for children to develop greater internalization and intrinsic motivation as they grow older (Wigfield, Byrnes, & Eccles, 2006; Wigfield & others, 2006). However, researchers have found that as students move from the early elementary school years to the high school years, their intrinsic motivation decreases (Harter, 1996). In one research study, the biggest drop in intrinsic motivation and increase in extrinsic motivation occurred between sixth grade and seventh grade (Harter, 1981). In another study, as students moved from sixth through eighth grade, they increasingly said school was boring and irrelevant (Harter, 1996). In this study, however, students who were intrinsically motivated did much better academically than those who were extrinsically motivated.

Why the shift toward extrinsic motivation as children move to higher grades? One explanation is that school grading practices reinforce an external motivation orientation. That is, as students get older, they lock into the increasing emphasis on grades, and their internal motivation drops.

Jacquelynne Eccles and her colleagues (Eccles, 2004; Eccles & Midgley, 1989; Eccles & Wigfield, 2002; Wigfield, Byrnes, & Eccles, 2006; Wigfield, Eccles, & Pintrich, 1996; Wigfield & others, 2006) identified some specific changes in the school context that help to explain the decline in intrinsic motivation. Middle and junior high

According to Jacquelynne Eccles and her colleagues, too many middle and junior high schools do not reflect an adequate person-environment fit. *What do they mean by that concept?*

schools are more impersonal, more formal, more evaluative, and more competitive than elementary schools. Students compare themselves more with other students because they increasingly are graded in terms of their relative performance on assignments and standardized tests.

Proposing the concept of *person-environment fit,* Eccles and her colleagues (1993; Wigfield, Byrnes, & Eccles, 2006; Wigfield & others, 2006) argue that a lack of fit between the middle school/junior high environment and the needs of young adolescents produces increasingly negative self-evaluations and attitudes toward school. Their study of more than 1,500 students found that teachers became more controlling just at the time when adolescents were seeking more autonomy, and the teacher-student relationship became more impersonal at a time when students were seeking more independence from their parents and needed more support from other adults. At a time when adolescents were becoming more self-conscious, an increased emphasis on grades and other competitive comparisons only made things worse.

Although there is less research on the transition to high school, the existing research suggests that, like the transition to middle school, it can produce similar problems (Eccles, Wigfield, & Schiefele, 1998; Wehlage, 1989). High schools often are even larger and more bureaucratic than middle schools. In such schools, a sense of community usually is undermined, with little opportunity for students and teachers to get to know each other (Bryk, Lee, & Smith, 1989). As a consequence, distrust between students and teachers develops easily and there is little communication about students' goals and values. Such contexts can especially harm the motivation of students who are not doing well academically.

What lessons can be drawn from this discussion? Perhaps the single most important lesson is that middle school and junior high school students benefit when teachers think of ways to make their school settings more personal, less formal, and more intrinsically challenging.

Some Final Thoughts about Intrinsic and Extrinsic Motivation   An overwhelming conclusion of motivation research is that teachers should encourage students to become intrinsically motivated. Similarly, teachers should create learning environments that promote students' cognitive engagement and self-responsibility for learning (Blumenfeld, Krajcik, & Kempler, 2006). That said, the real world includes both intrinsic and extrinsic motivation, and too often intrinsic and extrinsic motivation have been pitted against each other as polar opposites. In many aspects of students' lives, both intrinsic and extrinsic motivation are at work (Wigfield & others, 2006). Keep in mind, though, that many educational psychologists recommend that extrinsic motivation by itself is not a good strategy.

Our discussion of extrinsic and intrinsic motivation sets the stage for introducing other cognitive processes involved in motivating students to learn. As we explore five additional cognitive processes, notice how intrinsic and extrinsic motivation continue to be important. The five processes are (1) attribution; (2) mastery motivation; (3) self-efficacy; (4) goal setting, planning, and self-monitoring; and (5) expectations.

Attribution

Attribution theory states that individuals are motivated to discover the underlying causes of their own performance and behavior. Attributions are perceived causes of outcomes. In a way, attribution theorists say, students are like intuitive scientists, seeking to explain the cause behind what happens (Weary, 2000; Weiner, 2000, 2005). For example, a secondary school student asks, "Why am I not doing well in this class?" or "Did I get a good grade because I studied hard or the teacher made up an easy test, or both?" The search for a cause or explanation is most likely to be initiated when unexpected and important events end in failure, such as when a good student gets a low grade (Graham & Weiner, 1996). Some of the most frequently inferred causes of success and failure are ability, effort, task ease or difficulty, luck, mood, and help or hindrance from others.

attribution theory The theory that in their effort to make sense of their own behavior or performance, individuals are motivated to discover its underlying causes.

Bernard Weiner (1986, 1992) identified three dimensions of causal attributions: (1) *locus*, whether the cause is internal or external to the actor; (2) *stability*, the extent to which the cause remains the same or changes; and (3) *controllability*, the extent to which the individual can control the cause. For example, a student might perceive his aptitude as located internally, stable, and uncontrollable. The student also might perceive chance or luck as external to himself, variable, and uncontrollable. Figure 13.3 lists eight possible combinations of locus, stability, and controllability and how they match up with various common explanations of failure.

- *Locus.* A student's perception of success or failure as due to internal or external factors influences the student's self-esteem. Students who perceive their success as being due to internal reasons, such as effort, are more likely to have higher self-esteem following success than students who believe that their success was due to external reasons, such as luck. In the aftermath of failure, internal attributions lead to decreased self-esteem.
- *Stability.* A student's perception of the stability of a cause influences her expectation of success. If she ascribes a positive outcome to a stable cause, such as aptitude, she expects future success. Similarly, if she attributes a negative outcome to a stable cause, she expects future failure. When students attribute failure to unstable causes, such as bad luck or lack of effort, they might develop expectations that they will be able to succeed in the future, because they perceive the cause of their failure as changeable.
- *Controllability.* A student's perception of the controllability of a cause is related to a number of emotional outcomes such as anger, guilt, pity, and shame (Graham & Weiner, 1996). When students perceive that they are prevented from succeeding because of external factors that other people could have controlled, such as noise or bias, they often become angry. When students perceive that they have not done well because of internally controllable causes, such as not making enough effort or being negligent, they often feel guilty. When students perceive that others do not achieve their goals because of uncontrollable causes, such as lack of ability or a physical handicap, they feel pity or sympathy. And when students fail because of internally uncontrollable factors, such as low ability, they feel shame, humiliation, and embarrassment.

Combination of causal attributions	Reason students give for failure
Internal-stable-uncontrollable	Low aptitude
Internal-stable-controllable	Never study
Internal-unstable-uncontrollable	Sick the day of the test
Internal-unstable-controllable	Did not study for this particular test
External-stable-uncontrollable	School has tough requirements
External-stable-controllable	The instructor is biased
External-unstable-uncontrollable	Bad luck
External-unstable-controllable	Friends failed to help

FIGURE 13.3 Combinations of Causal Attributions and Explanations for Failure
When students fail or do poorly on a test or an assignment, they attribute the outcome to certain causes. The explanation reflects eight combinations of Weiner's three main categories of attributions: locus (internal-external), stability (stable-unstable), and controllability (controllable-uncontrollable).

What are the best strategies for teachers to use in helping students improve how they deal with their attributions? Educational psychologists often recommend providing students with a planned series of achievement experiences in which modeling, information about strategies, practice, and feedback are used to help them (1) concentrate on the task at hand rather than worrying about failing; (2) cope with failures by retracing their steps to discover their mistake or by analyzing the problem to discover another approach; and (3) attribute their failures to a lack of effort rather than lack of ability (Boekaerts, 2006; Brophy, 2004; Dweck & Elliott, 1983).

The current strategy is not to expose students to models who handle tasks with ease and demonstrate success—but, rather, to expose them to models who struggle to overcome mistakes before finally succeeding (Brophy, 2004). In this way, students learn how to deal with frustration, persist in the face of difficulties, and constructively cope with failure.

Mastery Motivation

Closely related to ideas about intrinsic motivation and attribution is the concept of mastery motivation (Jennings & Dietz, 2002). Researchers have identified mastery as one of three types of achievement orientation: mastery, helpless, and performance.

Carol Dweck and her colleagues (Dweck, 2002; Dweck & Leggett, 1988; Dweck, Mangels, & Good, 2004; Henderson & Dweck, 1990) have found that children show two distinct responses to challenging or difficult circumstances: a mastery orientation or a helpless orientation. Children with a **mastery orientation** focus on the task rather than on their ability, have positive affect (suggesting they enjoy the challenge), and generate solution-oriented strategies that improve their performance. Mastery-oriented students often instruct themselves to pay attention, to think carefully, and to remember strategies that worked for them in the past (Anderman, Maehr, & Midgley, 1996). In contrast, children with a **helpless orientation** focus on their personal inadequacies, often attribute their difficulty to a lack of ability, and display negative affect (including boredom and anxiety). This orientation undermines their performance. Figure 13.4 describes some behaviors that might reflect learned helplessness.

Mastery- and helpless-oriented students do not differ in general ability. However, they have different theories about their abilities. Mastery-oriented students believe their ability can be changed and improved. They agree with statements such as "Smartness is something you can increase as much as you want to." In contrast, helpless-oriented students believe that ability is basically fixed and cannot be changed. They agree with statements such as "You can learn new things, but how smart you are pretty much stays the same." The mastery orientation is much like the attributional combination of internal-unstable-controllable. The helpless orientation is much like the attributional combination of internal-stable-uncontrollable.

A mastery orientation also can be contrasted with a **performance orientation,** which involves being concerned with outcome rather than with process. For

The student

- Says, "I can't"
- Doesn't pay attention to teacher's instructions
- Doesn't ask for help, even when it is needed
- Does nothing (for example, stares out the window)
- Guesses or answers randomly without really trying
- Is unresponsive to teacher's exhortations to try
- Is easily discouraged
- Doesn't volunteer answers to teacher's questions
- Maneuvers to get out of or to avoid work (for example, has to go to the nurse's office)

FIGURE 13.4 Behaviors That Suggest Learned Helplessness

Source: From Deborah Stipek, *Motivation to Learn: Integrating Theory and Practice*, 4e. Published by Allyn and Bacon, Boston, MA. Copyright © 2002 by Pearson Education. Reprinted by permission of the publisher.

mastery orientation A personal stance that involves mastery of the task, positive affect, and solution-oriented strategies.

helpless orientation A personal stance that focuses on personal inadequacies, attribution of difficulty to a lack of ability, and negative affect.

performance orientation A personal stance of concern with the outcome rather than the process; for performance-oriented individuals, winning is what matters and happiness is believed to result from winning.

performance-oriented students, winning is what matters and happiness is thought to be a result of winning. Researchers have found that a performance orientation in classrooms is related to self-reported cheating and disruptive behavior (teasing and talking out of turn, for example) (Meece, Anderman, & Anderman, 2006). For mastery-oriented students, what matters is the sense that they are effectively interacting with their environment. Mastery-oriented students do like to win, but winning isn't as important to them as it is to performance-oriented students. Developing their skills is more important (Wolters, 2004).

Mastery motivation has much in common with Csikszentmihalyi's concept of flow—being absorbed in a state of concentration during an activity. Mastery-oriented students immerse themselves in a task and focus their concentration on developing their skills rather than worrying about whether they are going to outperform others. In a state of flow, students become so attuned to what they are doing that they are oblivious to distractions.

Performance-oriented students who are not confident of their success face a special problem (Stipek, 2002). If they try and fail, they often take their failure as evidence of low ability. By not trying at all, they can maintain an alternative, personally more acceptable explanation for their failure. This dilemma leads some students to engage in behavior that protects them from an image of incompetence in the short run but interferes with their learning and achievement in the long run (Covington & Dray, 2002; Urdan, 2004). To avoid the attribution of low ability, some of these students simply don't try, or they cheat; others might resort to more subtle image-protecting strategies such as procrastinating, making excuses, working halfheartedly, or setting unrealistic goals.

Recall that the No Child Left Behind Act (NCLB) emphasizes testing and accountability. Although NCLB may motivate some teachers and students to work harder, motivation experts worry that it encourages a performance rather than a mastery motivational orientation on the part of students (Meece, Anderman, & Anderman, 2006).

Self-Efficacy

In chapter 7, "Behavioral and Social Cognitive Approaches," we introduced Albert Bandura's concept of **self-efficacy,** the belief that one can master a situation and produce positive outcomes. Bandura (1997, 2001, 2004) believes that self-efficacy is a critical factor in whether or not students achieve. Self-efficacy has much in common with mastery motivation and intrinsic motivation. Self-efficacy is the belief that "I can"; helplessness is the belief that "I cannot" (Maddux, 2002; Lodewyk & Winne, 2005; Stipek, 2002). Students with high self-efficacy agree with such statements as "I know that I will be able to learn the material in this class" and "I expect to be able to do well at this activity."

Dale Schunk (1991, 1999, 2001, 2004) has applied the concept of self-efficacy to many aspects of students' achievement. In his view, self-efficacy influences a student's choice of activities. Students with low self-efficacy for learning might avoid many learning tasks, especially those that are challenging, whereas students with high self-efficacy eagerly approach these learning tasks. Students with high self-efficacy are more likely to persist with effort at a learning task than are students with low self-efficacy.

Your self-efficacy as a teacher will have a major impact on the quality of learning that your students experience. Students learn much more from teachers with a sense of efficacy than from those beset by self-doubts. Teachers with low self-efficacy often become mired in classroom problems and are inclined to say that low student ability is the reason their students are not learning. Low-self-efficacy teachers don't have confidence in their ability to manage their classrooms, become stressed and angered at students' misbehavior, are pessimistic about students' ability to improve, take a custodial view of their job, often resort to restrictive and punitive modes of discipline, and say that if they had it to do all over again they would not choose teaching as a profession (Melby, 1995).

self-efficacy The belief that one can master a situation and produce positive outcomes.

BEST PRACTICES
Strategies for Improving Students' Self-Efficacy

Here are some good strategies for improving students' self-efficacy (Stipek, 1996, 2002):

1. *Teach specific strategies.* Teach students specific strategies, such as outlining and summarizing, that can improve their ability to focus on their tasks.

2. *Guide students in setting goals.* Help them create short-term goals after they have made long-term goals. Short-term goals especially help students to judge their progress.

3. *Consider mastery.* Give students performance-contingent rewards, which are more likely to signal mastery, rather than rewards for merely engaging in a task.

4. *Combine strategy training with goals.* Schunk and his colleagues (Schunk, 2001; Schunk & Rice, 1989; Schunk & Swartz, 1993) have found that a combination of strategy training and goal setting can enhance students' self-efficacy and skill development. Give feedback to students on how their learning strategies relate to their performance.

5. *Provide students with support.* Positive support can come from teachers, parents, and peers. Sometimes a teacher just needs to tell a student, "You can do this."

    Next, Joanna Smith, a high school English teacher, describes how she helps students who struggle with "failure syndrome."

THROUGH THE EYES OF TEACHERS

Helping Students Who Feel Like Failures Gain Confidence

I believe that encouragement can help students overcome "failure syndrome." Students with failure syndrome give up immediately when they sense any difficulty whatsoever. It is easy to feel frustrated when facing these students, but I have found success when I truly reach them. The only way for me to reach individual students is to get to know them and their families by giving journal assignments, choices about books they read, opportunities to tell me about themselves, and by opening myself up to them. These students also need a lot of encouragement. They need to know that you have noticed and are not happy with their failure, and then they need to know you believe in them. Only then will students with failure syndrome perform.

6. *Make sure that students are not overly aroused and anxious.* When students overly worry and agonize about their achievement, their self-efficacy diminishes.

7. *Provide students with positive adult and peer models.* Certain characteristics of these models can help students develop their self-efficacy. For example, students who observe teachers and peers cope effectively and master challenges often adopt the models' behaviors. Modeling is especially effective in promoting self-efficacy when students observe success by peers who are similar in ability to themselves. One positive way for teachers to use peer modeling to improve students' self-efficacy is to have each student work on some aspect of a task and then have the students explain their part to other group members after they have mastered it (Zimmerman & Schunk, 2001). This type of peer modeling, discussed in chapter 10 as collaborative and cooperative learning, teaches skills and raises others' self-efficacy.

The ability to transmit subject matter is one aspect of instructional self-efficacy, but instructional self-efficacy also includes the belief that one can maintain an orderly classroom that is an exciting place to learn and the belief that it is possible to enlist resources and get parents positively involved in children's learning (Bandura, 1997).

Bandura (1997) also addressed the characteristics of efficacious schools. School leaders seek ways to improve instruction. They figure out ways to work around stifling policies and regulations that impede academic innovations. Masterful academic leadership by the principal builds teachers' sense of instructional efficacy; in low-achieving schools, principals function more as administrators and disciplinarians (Coladarci, 1992).

Efficacious schools are pervaded by high expectations and standards for achievement. Teachers regard their students as capable of high academic achievement, set challenging academic standards for them, and provide support to help them reach these high standards. In contrast, in low-achieving schools not much is expected academically of students, teachers spend less time actively teaching and monitoring students' academic progress, and tend to write off a high percentage of students as unteachable (Brookover & others, 1979). Not surprisingly, students in such schools have low self-efficacy and a sense of academic futility.

Goal Setting, Planning, and Self-Monitoring

Researchers have found that self-efficacy and achievement improve when students set goals that are specific, proximal, and challenging (Bandura, 1997; Lapierre, 2005; Schunk, 2004; Schunk & Zimmerman, 2006; Zimmerman & Schunk, 2004). A nonspecific, fuzzy goal is "I want to be successful." A more concrete, specific goal is "I want to make the honor roll by the end of the semester."

Students can set both long-term (distal) and short-term (proximal) goals. It is okay to let students set some long-term goals, such as "I want to graduate from high school" or "I want to go to college," but if you do, make sure that they also create short-term goals as steps along the way. "Getting an *A* on the next math test" is an example of a short-term, proximal goal. So is "Doing all of my homework by 4 P.M. Sunday." As mentioned earlier, attention should focus mainly on short-term goals, which help students judge their progress better than do long-term goals. David McNally (1990), author of *Even Eagles Need a Push,* advises that when students set goals and plan, they should be reminded to live their lives one day at a time. Have them make their commitments in bite-size chunks. As McNally says, a house is built one brick at a time, a cathedral one stone at a time. The artist paints one stroke at a time. The student should also work in small increments.

Another good strategy is to encourage students to set challenging goals. A challenging goal is a commitment to self-improvement. Strong interest and involvement in activities is sparked by challenges. Goals that are easy to reach generate little interest or effort. However, goals should be optimally matched to the student's skill level. If goals are unrealistically high, the result will be repeated failures that lower the student's self-efficacy.

Carol Dweck (1996; Dweck & Leggett, 1988; Dweck, Mangels, & Good, 2004), John Nicholls (1979; Nicholls & others, 1990), and their colleagues define goals in terms of the type of achievement the goal represents and the definition of success. For example, Nicholls distinguishes among ego-involved goals, task-involved goals, and work-avoidant goals. Students who have ego-involved goals strive to maximize favorable evaluations and minimize unfavorable ones. Thus, ego-involved students might focus on how smart they will look and how effectively they can outperform other students. In contrast, students who have task-involved goals focus on mastering tasks. They concentrate on how they can do the task and what they will learn. Students with work-avoidant goals try to exert as little effort as possible on a task. Encourage students to develop task-involved mastery goals rather than ego-involved or work-avoidant goals.

Unfortunately, many of the changes involved in the transition to middle schools are likely to increase students' motivation to achieve performance goals rather than mastery goals (Eccles, 2004; Midgley, 2001; Wigfield, Byrnes, & Eccles, 2006; Wigfield & others, 2006). Consider that these often include a drop in grades, a lack of support for autonomy, whole-class task organization and between-class ability groupings that likely increase social comparison, concerns about evaluation, and competitiveness.

In one research study, both teachers and students reported that performance-focused goals were more common and task-focused goals less common in middle school than in elementary school classrooms (Midgley, Anderman, & Hicks, 1995). In addition, the elementary school teachers reported using task-focused goals more than middle school teachers did. At both grades, the extent to which the teachers were task-focused was linked with the students' and the teachers' sense of personal efficacy. Not unexpectedly, personal efficacy was lower for the middle school than elementary school participants. Thus, middle school teachers especially need to increasingly include task-focused goals in their instruction (Anderman, Austin, & Johnson, 2002).

In chapter 12, we described the importance of planning for teachers. Planning is also important for students. It is not enough just to get students to set goals. It also is important to encourage them to plan how they will reach their goals (Elliot &

Thrash, 2001; Maehr, 2001; Randi & Corno, 2000). Being a good planner means managing time effectively, setting priorities, and being organized. Give students, especially at the middle school and high school levels, practice at managing their time, setting priorities, and being organized.

You might start by giving them a calendar for the term on which they can write down their important exam dates, the due dates for papers, homework assignments, and the dates when other tasks and activities are going to occur. Ask them to think about how many days or weeks they will need to study for major exams and write major papers. Have them mark the necessary days or weeks in which these tasks will be their main priorities. Tell them that their term calendar is not etched in stone. Encourage them to monitor it regularly and modify it when needed. For example, you might add another assignment or two, change a test date, and so on. Students might find that they need more study time than they originally predicted for a particular course.

After they have made out their term calendar, photocopy a blank weekly plan form and give it to your students. The form should have the days of the week across the top, with headings of "Planned" and "Actual" under each day. The 24 hours of the day should be listed vertically on the left side of the paper in a column. Have students fill in their class hours, leisure activities (such as sports, music practice, TV), and other routine activities such as sleeping and eating. A good strategy is to have students create this plan at the end of the preceding week. Then have them monitor it the next week to see how effectively they carried out their plan.

After students have created term and weekly plans, give them practice in setting priorities for the next day. A critical skill for a good time manager is figuring out what the most important things are to get done and when to do them—in other words, setting priorities. An effective way to get students to do this is to have them create manageable daily to-do lists. Their goal should be to make up the list in the evening and then complete all of the items on the list the next day. Get them to identify the top-priority tasks on the list and make sure that those get done. Have them examine their to-do list toward the end of the day and evaluate what they have accomplished. Encourage students to challenge themselves to finish the few remaining tasks.

You might be surprised at what students discover from their time use plans. Some students will be totally unaware of how much time they've been wasting, underestimate how much time they need to study, and be far less effective at using time than they imagined. Other students will learn that proper time management requires planning, organization, and self-discipline but that the results are worth it.

Most successful adults are good time managers, yet schools have not given students adequate opportunities to practice time management skills. If you are going to be a middle school or secondary teacher, make a commitment to working with students to help them improve their time management skills. This strategy not only should improve their achievement in your class but also should help them develop critical skills for success in work and life beyond school.

Older students should not only plan their next week's activities but also monitor how well they are sticking to their plan. Once students engage in a task, they need to monitor their progress, judge how well they are doing on the task, and evaluate the outcomes to regulate what they do in the future (Wigfield, Byrnes, & Eccles, 2006; Wigfield & others, 2006). Researchers have found that high-achieving students often are self-regulatory learners (Boekaerts, 2006; Pressley & Harris, 2006; Pressley & Hilden, 2006; Schunk & Zimmerman, 2006). For example, high-achieving students self-monitor their learning more and systematically evaluate their progress toward a goal more than low-achieving students do. Encouraging students to self-monitor their learning conveys the message that students are responsible for their own behavior and that learning requires the students' active, dedicated participation (Boekaerts, 2006).

Expectations

Expectations can exert a powerful influence on students' motivation. Let's examine student expectations and teacher expectations.

BEST PRACTICES
Strategies for Helping Students Manage Their Time

Here are some good tips that teachers can give to students to help them manage their time more effectively and increase their achievement (Zimmerman, Bonner, & Kovach, 1996, p. 33):

1. *Be proactive, not reactive.* Students rarely plan or manage their available time for studying; instead, most tend to complete their assignments on a reactive basis at the last moment. Encourage them to be more proactive and develop term plans, weekly plans, and daily to-do lists from the middle school grades on.

2. *Set regular study times.*

3. *Use a regular study area that is well lighted and free from noise.*

4. *Learn to say "no" to distractions.* When peers try to talk them out of studying, help them resist the pressure.

5. *Reward yourself for your success.* Encourage students to delay desirable activities and use them as rewards for completing their studying. This can include getting food treats, watching TV, or spending time with friends.

Students' Expectations How hard students will work can depend on how much they expect to accomplish. If they expect to succeed, they are more likely to work hard to reach a goal than if they expect to fail. Jacquelynne Eccles (1987, 1993) defined expectations for students' success as "beliefs about how well they will do on upcoming tasks, either in the immediate or long-term future" (Wigfield & others, 2006). Three aspects of ability beliefs, according to Eccles, are students' beliefs about how good they are at a particular activity, how good they are in comparison to other individuals, and how good they are in relation to their performance in other activities.

How hard students work also depends on the value they place on the goal. Indeed, the combination of expectancy and value has been the focus of a number of efforts to better understand students' achievement motivation across the last six decades (Atkinson, 1957; Eccles, 1987, 1993; Feather, 1966; Wigfield & Eccles, 2002). In Jacquelynne Eccles's (1987, 1993) model, "expectancies and values are assumed to directly influence performance, persistence, and task choice. Expectancies and values are . . . influenced by perceptions of competence, perceptions of the difficulty of different tasks, and individuals' goals (Wigfield & others, 2006, pp. 938–939). In Eccles's model, the culture's achievement orientation also plays a role in influencing students' expectations.

Teachers' Expectations Teachers' expectations influence students' motivation and performance (Alderman, 2004; National Research Council, 2004). "When teachers hold high generalized expectations for student achievement and students perceive these expectations, students achieve more, experience a greater sense of self-esteem and competence as learners, and resist involvement in problem behaviors both during childhood and adolescence" (Wigfield & others, 2006, p. 976).

Teachers often have more positive expectations for high-ability than for low-ability students, and these expectations are likely to influence their behavior toward them. For example, teachers require high-ability students to work harder, wait longer for them to respond to questions, respond to them with more information and in a more elaborate fashion, criticize them less often, praise them more often, are more friendly to them, call on them more often, seat them closer to the teachers' desks, and are more likely to give them the benefit of the doubt on close calls in grading than they are for students with low ability (Brophy, 2004; Brophy & Good, 1974). An important teaching strategy is to monitor your expectations and be sure to have positive expectations for students with low abilities. Fortunately, researchers have found that with support teachers can adapt and raise their expectations for students with low abilities (Weinstein, Madison, & Kuklinski, 1995).

Review, Reflect, and Practice

(2) Discuss the important processes in motivation to achieve.

REVIEW

- What are extrinsic and intrinsic motivation? How are they involved in students' achievement?
- What is attribution theory? What are Weiner's three dimensions of causal attributions?
- How does a mastery orientation compare with a helpless orientation and a performance orientation?
- What is self-efficacy? What types of instructional strategies benefit students' self-efficacy?
- How are goal setting, planning, and self-monitoring important in improving students' motivation to achieve?
- How can students' and teachers' expectations affect students' motivation?

REFLECT

- Sean and Dave both get cut from the basketball team. The next year, Sean tries out again but Dave does not. What causal attributions (and their effects) could explain the behaviors of these two students?

PRAXIS™ PRACTICE

1. Which of the following is the best example of someone who is intrinsically motivated?
   a. Eric is reading the latest Harry Potter book because he wants to become a better reader.
   b. Jordan is reading the latest Harry Potter book because he can't wait to see what happens to Harry and his friends.
   c. Josh is reading the latest Harry Potter book so that he will have read enough pages to qualify for the class pizza party at the end of the month.
   d. Martynas is reading the latest Harry Potter book because his teacher assigned it and he wants to please his teacher.

2. Joan just failed a science test. "I knew it," she says, "I have never been any good at science, and I never will be." Which of the following best characterizes Joan's attribution for her failure?
   a. external-stable-controllable
   b. external-unstable-uncontrollable
   c. internal-stable-controllable
   d. internal-stable-uncontrollable

3. Which of the following is the best example of a performance goal orientation?
   a. Alicia competes with her best friend to see who can get the higher grade on every test, taking delight in receiving the high score.
   b. Cassandra hates math, does not believe that she can be successful, and gives up at the first sign of struggling.

continued on page 468

Review, Reflect, and Practice *continued*

    c. Ed struggles in math, but wants very much to learn the material, so when he gets stuck on a problem, he asks for help.

    d. Martin does his work as requested and does a fair job on it, but he doesn't really care about his grades or about how much he learns.

4. Jacob is struggling in algebra and as a result is experiencing low self-efficacy. Which of the following students would provide the best role model?

    a. David, a local engineer, who tells the class how useful math will be in their futures

    b. Jamal, a fellow student, who has also struggled in the course but is now grasping the concepts

    c. Mrs. Jackson, Jacob's algebra teacher, who has always loved math

    d. Suzanne, a fellow student, who is getting an *A* with minimal effort

5. Which student has a work-avoidant goal?

    a. As Mark is choosing courses for his senior year in high school, he decides to take the more challenging of the two courses his counselor suggested to him.

    b. Sam is taking geometry in his senior year of high school, because he has always struggled in math.

    c. Sylvia decides to take advanced placement calculus in her senior year, although she knows it is a difficult course.

    d. Zelda is a capable math student, but she chooses an easy math course in which she is almost certain to get an *A*.

6. Ms. Martin teaches eighth-grade history to an academically diverse class. DeMarcus is a gifted student who has always earned high marks. Joe has a learning disability. Ms. Martin does not believe it would be fair to expect the same performance from Joe as from DeMarcus. However, she knows that Joe can learn the material with proper scaffolding. Because of this, she seats Joe near her desk, praises him when he does something well, and gives him constructive criticism when needed.

    How are her expectations and behavior likely to affect the achievement of these students?

    a. Her expectations are likely to result in similar achievement from both students.

    b. Her expectations are likely to result in high achievement from DeMarcus and fairly high achievement from Joe.

    c. Her expectations are likely to result in high achievement from Joe and low achievement from DeMarcus.

    d. Her expectations are likely to result in low achievement from both students.

Please see the answer key at the end of the book.

③ MOTIVATION, RELATIONSHIPS, AND SOCIOCULTURAL CONTEXTS

Social Motives	Social Relationships	Sociocultural Contexts

Motivation has a social component. In addition to achievement motives, students also have social motives. Our coverage of the social dimensions of motivation focuses on students' social motives, relationships, and sociocultural contexts.

Social Motives

Childrens' social concerns influence their lives at school (Anderman & Wolters, 2006; Wentzel, 2006). Every school day, students work at establishing and maintaining social relationships. Researchers have found that students who display socially competent behavior are more likely to excel academically than those who do not (Wentzel, 1996). Overall, though, researchers have given too little attention to how students' social worlds are related to their motivation in the classroom.

Social motives are needs and desires that are learned through experiences with the social world. Interest in social motives stems from Henry Murray's (1938) long catalog of needs (or motives), including the *need for affiliation or relatedness,* which is the motive to be securely connected to other people. This involves establishing, maintaining, and restoring warm, close, personal relationships. Students' social needs are reflected in their desires to be popular with peers and have close friends and the powerful attraction they feel to someone they love. Though each student has a need for affiliation or relatedness, some students have a stronger need than others (O'Conner & Rosenblood, 1996). Some students like to be surrounded by lots of friends. In middle and high school, some students feel something is drastically missing from their lives if they don't have a girlfriend or boyfriend to date regularly. Others don't have such strong needs for affiliation. They don't fall apart if they don't have several close friends around all day and don't sit in class in an anxious state if they don't have a romantic partner.

Both teacher approval and peer approval are important social motives for most students. In the elementary school years, students are motivated to please their parents more than their peers (Berndt, 1979). By the end of elementary school, parent approval and peer approval are about equal in most students' motive systems. By eighth or ninth grade, peer conformity outstrips conformity to parents. By twelfth grade, conformity to peers drops off somewhat as students become more autonomous and make more decisions on their own.

Adolescence can be an especially important juncture in achievement motivation and social motivation (Henderson & Dweck, 1990). New academic and social pressures force adolescents toward new roles that involve more responsibility. As adolescents experience more intense achievement demands, their social interests might cut into the time they need for academic matters. Or ambitions in one area can undermine the attainment of goals in another area, as when academic achievement leads to social disapproval. In early adolescence, students face a choice between whether they will spend more of their time pursuing social goals or academic goals. The results of this decision have long-term consequences in terms of how far adolescents will go in their education and the careers they will pursue.

Social Relationships

Students' relationships with parents, peers, and friends have a tremendous impact on their lives. Their interactions with teachers, mentors, and others also can profoundly affect their achievement and social motivation.

Parents   Research has been done on links between parenting and students' motivation. Studies have examined family demographic characteristics, child-rearing practices, and provision of specific experiences at home (Eccles, Wigfield, & Schiefele, 1998).

Demographic Characteristics   Parents with more education are more likely than less-educated parents to believe that their involvement in their child's education is important, to be active participants in their child's education, and to have intellectually stimulating materials at home (Schneider & Coleman, 1993). When parents' time and energy are largely consumed by other concerns or people other than the child, the child's motivation can suffer. Living in a single-parent family, having parents who are consumed by their work, and living in a large family can undercut children's achievement.

Child-Rearing Practices   Even though demographic factors can affect students' motivation, more important are the parents' child-rearing practices (Wigfield &

social motives Needs and desires that are learned through experiences with the social world.

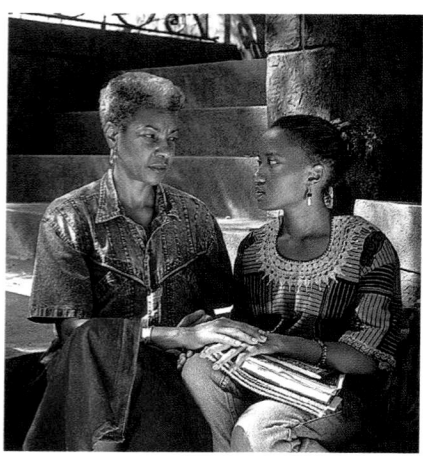

What are some good strategies parents can adopt to guide students' achievement?

others, 2006). Here are some positive parenting practices that result in improved motivation and achievement:

- Knowing enough about the child to provide the right amount of challenge and the right amount of support
- Providing a positive emotional climate, which motivates children to internalize their parents' values and goals
- Modeling motivated achievement behavior: working hard and persisting with effort at challenging tasks

Provision of Specific Experiences at Home In addition to general child-rearing practices, parents provide various activities or resources at home that may influence students' interest and motivation to pursue various activities over time (Wigfield & others, 2006). For example, reading to one's preschool children and providing reading materials in the home are positively related to students' later reading achievement and motivation (Wigfield & Asher, 1984). Indeed, researchers have found that children's skills and work habits when they enter kindergarten are among the best predictors of academic motivation and performance in both elementary and secondary school (Entwisle & Alexander, 1993). The extent to which parents emphasize academic achievement or sports and provide opportunities and resources for their children to participate in these activities in the elementary school years influence whether the children are likely to continue to choose course work and extracurricular activities consistent with these activities in adolescence (Simpkins & others, 2004).

Peers Peers can affect a student's motivation through social comparison, social competence and motivation, peer co-learning, and peer-group influences (Wigfield & others, 2006).

Students compare themselves with their peers on where they stand academically and socially (Ruble, 1983). Adolescents are more likely than younger children to engage in social comparison, although adolescents are prone to deny that they ever compare themselves with others (Harter, 1990, 2006). Positive social comparisons usually result in higher self-esteem, negative comparisons in lower self-esteem. Students are most likely to compare themselves with others who are most similar to them in age, ability, and interests.

Students who are more accepted by their peers and who have good social skills often do better in school and have positive academic achievement motivation (Asher & Coie, 1990; Rubin, Bukowski, & Parker, 2006; Wentzel, 1996, 2006). In contrast, rejected students, especially those who are highly aggressive, are at risk for a number of achievement problems, including getting low grades and dropping out of school (Dodge, Coie, & Lynam, 2006).

In chapter 10, "Social Constructivist Approaches," we highlighted the role of peers in collaborative and cooperative learning, as well as peer tutoring. Peers can help each other learn material through discussion in small groups. Peer tutoring often brings achievement gains to the tutor as well as to the student being tutored.

Early work on the role of the peer group in students' achievement focused on its negative role in distracting adolescents from a commitment to academic learning (Goodlad, 1984). More recently, the peer group has been viewed as a positive or negative influence, depending on its motivational orientation. If the peer group has high achievement standards, it will support the student's academic achievement. But if a low-achieving student joins a low-achieving peer group or clique, the student's academic work can deteriorate even further (Kinderman, McCollam, & Gibson, 1996).

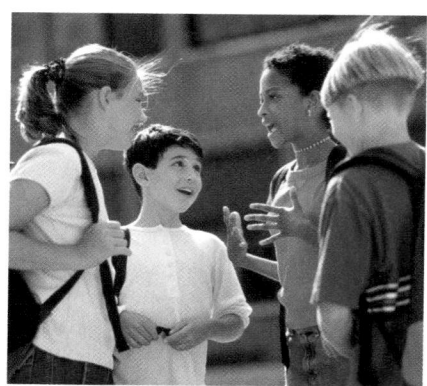

How might peer relations contribute to students' achievement?

Teachers Many children who do not do well in school consistently have negative interactions with their teachers (Stipek, 2002). They are frequently in trouble for not

	Teachers who care	Teachers who do not care
Teaching behaviors	Makes an effort to make class interesting; teaches in a special way	Teaches in a boring way, gets off-task, teaches while students aren't paying attention
Communication style	Talks to me, pays attention, asks questions, listens	Ignores, interrupts, screams, yells
Equitable treatment and respect	Is honest and fair, keeps promises, trusts me, tells the truth	Embarrasses, insults
Concern about individuals	Asks what's wrong, talks to me about my problems, acts as a friend, asks when I need help, takes time to make sure I understand, calls on me	Forgets name, does nothing when I do something wrong, doesn't explain things or answer questions, doesn't try to help me

FIGURE 13.5 Students' Descriptions of Teachers Who Care

completing assignments, not paying attention, goofing off, or acting out. In many cases, they deserve to be criticized and disciplined, but too often the classroom becomes a highly unpleasant place for them.

Nel Noddings (1992, 1998, 2001) stresses that students are most likely to develop into competent human beings when they feel cared for. This requires teachers to get to know students fairly well. She says that this is difficult in large schools with large numbers of students in each class. She would have teachers remain with the same students for 2 to 3 years (voluntarily on the part of the teacher and the pupil) so that teachers would be better positioned to attend to the interests and capacities of each student (Thornton, 2001).

Researchers have found that students who feel they have supportive, caring teachers are more strongly motivated to engage in academic work than students with unsupportive, uncaring teachers (McCombs, 2001; Newman, 2002; Perry, Turner, & Meyer, 2006; Ryan & Deci, 2000; Theobold, 2005). One researcher examined students' views of the qualities of good relationships with a teacher by asking middle school students questions such as how they knew a teacher cared about them (Wentzel, 1997). As shown in figure 13.5, students had favorable impressions of teachers who were attentive to them as human beings. Interestingly, students also considered teachers' instructional behaviors in evaluating how much their teachers cared about them. The students said that teachers convey that they care about their students when they make serious efforts to promote learning and have appropriately high standards.

Students' motivation is optimized when teachers provide them with challenging tasks in a mastery-oriented environment that includes good emotional and cognitive support, meaningful and interesting material to learn and master, and sufficient support for autonomy and initiative (Blumenfeld, Kempler, & Krajcik, 2006; Covington & Dray, 2002; Eccles, Wigfield, & Schiefele, 1998; Graham & Taylor, 2002; Wigfield & others, 2006). Many researchers conclude that when academic work is meaningful, it sustains students' attention and interest, engages them in learning, and reduces the likelihood that students will feel alienated from school (Blumenfeld, Krajcik, & Kempler, 2006; National Research Council, 2004). Also, as we saw in our earlier discussion of

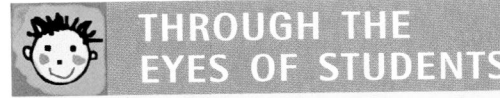

THROUGH THE EYES OF STUDENTS

"You Always Manage to Cheer Us Up"

I know our science class sometimes is obnoxious and negative but we really appreciate you. You always manage to cheer us up and treat us like your kids. That shows how much you care about us. If you hadn't been there for me like you were, I probably wouldn't be where I am now. Good luck with all of your other students and I hope they learn as much as I have. I'll miss you next year. Hope to see you around.

Letter from Jennifer to William Williford, Her Middle School Science Teacher, Perry, Georgia

Bandura's ideas on self-efficacy (chapter 7), the motivation and achievement climate of the entire school affects students' motivation. Schools with high expectations and academic standards, as well as academic and emotional support for students, often have students who are motivated to achieve.

Teachers and Parents In the past, schools have given little attention to how teachers can enlist parents as partners with them in providing opportunities for students to achieve. Currently there is considerable interest in how to accomplish this partnership. When teachers systematically and frequently inform parents of their children's progress and get involved in their children's learning, children often reach higher levels of academic achievement (Epstein, 1996).

Sociocultural Contexts

In this section we will focus on how socioeconomic status, ethnicity, and gender can influence motivation and achievement. A special focus is diversity.

Socioeconomic Status and Ethnicity The diversity within ethnic minority groups that we discussed in chapter 5 also is evident in their achievement. For example, many Asian American students have a strong academic achievement orientation, but some do not.

In addition to recognizing the diversity that exists within every cultural group in terms of their achievement, it also is important to distinguish between difference and deficiency. Too often, the achievements of ethnic minority students—especially African American, Latino, and Native American—have been interpreted in terms of middle-socioeconomic-status White standards as deficits when these students simply are culturally different and distinct.

However, achievement differences are more closely related to socioeconomic status than to ethnicity. Many studies have found that socioeconomic status predicts achievement better than ethnicity. Regardless of their ethnic background, students from middle- and upper-income families fare better than their counterparts from low-income backgrounds in a host of achievement situations—expectations for success, achievement aspirations, and recognition of the importance of effort, for example (Gibbs, 1989).

Sandra Graham (1986, 1990) has conducted a number of studies that reveal not only a stronger role of socioeconomic status than of ethnicity in achievement but also the importance of studying ethnic minority student motivation in the context of general motivational theory. Her inquiries fall within the framework of attribution theory and focus on the causes African American students identify for their achievement orientation, such as why they succeed or fail. Graham has found that middle-income African American students, like their White middle-income counterparts, have high achievement expectations and understand that failure is usually due to a lack of effort rather than bad luck. In one recent study in which the participants were mainly ethnic minority students from low-income families, a mastery motivation classroom that provided considerable positive support was linked with students' motivation to learn and to resist distractions of emotional distress (Strobel, 2001).

A special challenge for many ethnic minority students, especially those living in poverty, is dealing with racial prejudice, conflict between the values of their group and the majority group, and a lack of high-achieving adults in their cultural group who can serve as positive role models (McLoyd, 2000; Spencer,

UCLA educational psychologist Sandra Graham is shown talking with adolescent boys about motivation. She has conducted a number of studies which reveal that middle-socioeconomic-status African American students—like their White counterparts—have high achievement expectations and attribute success to internal factors such as effort rather than external factors such as luck.

DIVERSITY AND EDUCATION
Henry Gaskins

A special concern among educators is to find ways to support the achievement efforts of ethnic minority students, many of whom come from low-income backgrounds. In the Teaching Stories segment that opened this chapter, you read about Jaime Escalante, who made a major difference in the motivation of Latino students to learn and excel at math in East Los Angeles. Another individual has been exceptional in supporting the motivation of African American students in Washington, D.C.

Henry Gaskins, a physician, began an after-school tutoring program for ethnic minority students. For 4 hours every weeknight and all day on Saturdays, 80 students receive study assistance from Gaskins, his wife, two adult volunteers, and academically talented peers. Those who can afford it contribute $5 to cover the cost of school supplies. In addition to tutoring them in various school subjects, Gaskins helps the tutees learn how to set academic goals and plan how to achieve these goals. Gaskins also encourages students to self-monitor their progress toward the goals. Many of the students being tutored have parents who are high school dropouts and either can't or aren't motivated to help their sons and daughters achieve.

Every community has people like Henry Gaskins who can help provide much-needed mentoring and tutoring for students from low socioeconomic backgrounds whose parents cannot help them achieve academically. Many of these potential mentors and tutors from the community have not been contacted by school personnel. If the need exists among your students, make a commitment to scour the community for talented, motivated, and concerned adults like Gaskins, who might only need to be asked to provide mentoring and tutoring support for disadvantaged students.

Dr. Henry Gaskins, here talking with three high school students, began an after-school tutorial program for ethnic minority students in 1983 in Washington, D.C. Volunteers like Dr. Gaskins can be especially helpful in developing a stronger sense of the importance of education in ethnic minority adolescents.

2006; Spencer & Markstrom-Adams, 1990). The lack of high-achieving role models relates to the discussion in chapter 7, "Behavioral and Social Cognitive Approaches," in which we described the importance of increasing the number of mentors in these students' lives.

It also is important to consider the nature of the schools that primarily serve ethnic minority students (Eccles, Wigfield, & Schiefele, 1998; Wigfield & others, 2006). More than one-third of African American and almost one-third of Latino students attend schools in the 47 largest city school districts in the United States, compared with only 5 percent of White and 22 percent of Asian American students. Many of these ethnic minority students come from low-income families (more than half are eligible for free or reduced-cost lunches). These inner-city schools are less likely than other schools to serve more-advantaged populations or to offer high-quality academic support services, advanced courses, and courses that challenge students' active thinking skills. Even students who are motivated to learn and achieve can find it difficult to perform effectively in such contexts. The Diversity and Education interlude focuses on one individual who has become an important role model for African American students.

Gender Our discussion of gender and motivation focuses on how males and females differ in their beliefs and values. Female and male students' competence-related beliefs vary by achievement context. For example, boys have higher competence beliefs than girls for math and sports, and girls have higher competence beliefs for English, reading, and social activities. These differences increase after puberty (Eccles & others, 1993). Thus, how competently female and male students expect to perform is consistent with gender-role stereotypes (Wigfield & others, 2006).

With regard to achievement values, beginning in high school, girls do not value math achievement as highly as boys do (Eccles & others, 1993). Gifted girls often experience conflicts between gender roles and achievement. One study of gifted girls showed that they felt caught between achieving and appearing either feminine or caring (Bell, 1989).

In chapter 5, "Sociocultural Diversity," we charted many other aspects of gender and school, such as gender differences in teacher-student interaction, curriculum, and content; sexual harassment; and gender-bias reduction. Because those differences are so important in students' achievement, we briefly summarize them here: Girls are more compliant, boys more rambunctious. Teachers give boys more attention and instruction than girls, yet boys get lower grades than girls. By middle school, girls have lower self-esteem. Boys list more career options than girls do.

Schools have made considerable progress in reducing sexism and sex stereotyping in books and curriculum materials, but sexism still exists. Sexual harassment is a special concern in schools and is more pervasive than once thought. Every student deserves an education free from gender bias. You might want to return to chapter 5 and again read the section on gender and schools, thinking about how such gender differences might affect students' motivation and achievement.

Review, Reflect, and Practice

③ Explain how relationships and sociocultural contexts can support or undercut motivation.

REVIEW
- What are social motives and the need for affiliation?
- In what ways are students' school performances linked to relationships with parents, peers, friends, and teachers?
- How do ethnicity and socioeconomic status influence motivation to achieve at school? What are some gender differences in motivation?

REFLECT
- Suppose a boy in your kindergarten class appears to have a strong social motivation. How might this become an asset or a liability in his future academic performance?

PRAXIS™ PRACTICE
1. Which of the following students is most likely to conform to peer expectations for academic achievement?
   a. Patrick, who is in second grade
   b. Ross, who is in fifth grade
   c. Sheldon, who is in eighth grade
   d. Ross, who is a senior in high school
2. Which classroom is likely to have the most positive impact on student motivation?
   a. Ms. Davidson is only concerned about her students' academic performance, not their personal lives. Her class is very challenging, though not terribly interesting.

b. Mr. Nelson works hard to get to know his students on a personal as well as an academic basis. Because he cares so much for them, he makes sure that his class is easy enough for all of his students to do well.

c. Ms. Pagliuca works hard to get to know her students on a personal as well as an academic basis. She gives her students work that is challenging and interesting.

d. Mr. Williams' class is very challenging and competitive. His students compete on a daily basis for points.

3. Which of the following students is *least* likely to have a strong achievement motivation?

a. Lee, an African American student from a middle-income family
b. Pedro, a Latino student from a middle-income family
c. Ross, an African-American student from an affluent family
d. Sean, a White student from a low-income family

Please see the answer key at the end of the book.

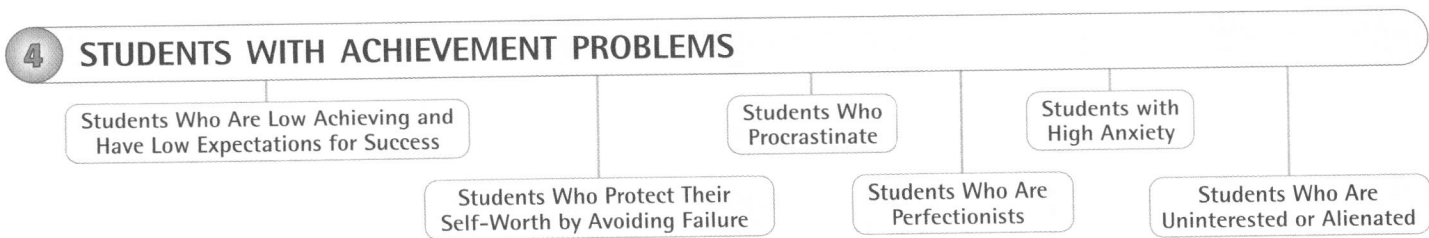

4   STUDENTS WITH ACHIEVEMENT PROBLEMS

Students Who Are Low Achieving and Have Low Expectations for Success

Students Who Protect Their Self-Worth by Avoiding Failure

Students Who Procrastinate

Students Who Are Perfectionists

Students with High Anxiety

Students Who Are Uninterested or Alienated

Achievement problems can surface when students don't set goals, don't plan how to reach them, and don't adequately monitor their progress toward the goals. They also can arise when students are low achievers and have low expectations for success, try to protect their self-worth by avoiding failure, procrastinate, are perfectionists, become overwhelmed by anxiety, or become uninterested or alienated from school. Many of these obstacles to achievement surface during elementary school and then become more pronounced during middle school or high school. We will discuss a number of strategies that teachers, counselors, mentors, and parents can use to help students overcome obstacles to their achievement.

Students Who Are Low Achieving and Have Low Expectations for Success

Jere Brophy (1998) provided the following description of low-achieving students with low expectations for success: These students need to be consistently reassured that they can meet the goals and challenges you have set for them and that you will give them the help and support they need to succeed. However, they need to be reminded that you will accept their progress only as long as they make a real effort. They might require individualized instructional materials or activities to provide an optimal challenge for their skill level. Help them set learning goals and give them support for reaching these goals. Require these students to put forth considerable effort and make progress, even though they might not have the ability to perform at the level of the class as a whole.

Failure syndrome refers to having low expectations for success and giving up at the first sign of difficulty. Failure syndrome students are different from low-achieving

failure syndrome Having low expectations for success and giving up at the first sign of difficulty.

Training method	Primary emphasis	Main goals
Efficacy training	Improve students' self-efficacy perceptions	Teach students to set and strive to reach specific, proximal, and challenging goals. Monitor students' progress and frequently support students by saying things like "I know you can do it." Use adult and peer modeling effectively. Individualize instruction and tailor it to the student's knowledge and skills. Keep social comparison to a minimum. Be an efficacious teacher and have confidence in your abilities. View students with a failure syndrome as challenges rather than losers.
Attribution and achievement orientation retraining	Change students' attributions and achievement orientation	Teach students to attribute failures to factors that can be changed, such as insufficient knowledge or effort and ineffective strategies. Work with students to develop a mastery orientation rather than a performance orientation by helping them focus on the achievement process (learning the task) rather than the achievement product (winning or losing).
Strategy training	Improve students' domain- and task-specific skills and strategies	Help students to acquire and self-regulate their use of effective learning and problem-solving strategies. Teach students what to do, how to do it, and when and why to do it.

FIGURE 13.6 Cognitive Retraining Methods for Increasing the Motivation of Students Who Display Failure Syndrome

students, who fail despite putting forth their best effort. Failure syndrome students don't put forth enough effort, often beginning tasks in a halfhearted manner and giving up quickly at the first hint of a challenge. Failure syndrome students often have low self-efficacy or attribution problems, ascribing their failures to internal, stable, and uncontrollable causes, such as low ability.

A number of strategies can be used to increase the motivation of students who display failure syndrome. Especially beneficial are cognitive retraining methods, such as efficacy retraining, attribution retraining, and strategy training, which are described in figure 13.6.

Students Who Protect Their Self-Worth by Avoiding Failure

Some individuals are so interested in protecting their self-worth and avoiding failure that they become distracted from pursuing goals and engage in ineffective strategies. These strategies include (Covington & Dray, 2002; Covington & Teel, 1996):

- *Nonperformance.* The most obvious strategy for avoiding failure is to not try. In the classroom, nonperformance tactics include appearing eager to answer a teacher's question but hoping the teacher will call on another student, sliding down in the seat to avoid being seen by the teacher, and avoiding eye contact. These can seem like minor deceptions, but they might portend other, more chronic forms of noninvolvement such as dropping out and excessive absences.

- *Procrastination.* Individuals who postpone studying for a test until the last minute can blame failure on poor time management, thus deflecting attention away from the possibility that they are incompetent. A variation on this theme is to take on so many responsibilities that you have an excuse for not doing any one of them in a highly competent manner.

- *Setting unreachable goals.* By setting goals so high that success is virtually impossible, individuals can avoid the implication that they are incompetent, because virtually anyone would fail to reach this goal.

Efforts to avoid failure often involve *self-handicapping strategies* (Urdan & Midgley, 2001). That is, some individuals deliberately handicap themselves by not making an effort, by putting off a project until the last minute, by fooling around the night before a test, and so on so that if their subsequent performance is at a low level, these circumstances, rather than lack of ability, will be seen as the cause.

Here are a few strategies to help students reduce preoccupation with protecting self-worth and avoiding failure (Covington & Dray, 2002; Covington & Teel, 2002):

- Guide students in setting challenging but realistic goals.
- Help students strengthen the link between their effort and self-worth. Tell them to take pride in their effort and minimize social comparison.
- Encourage students to have positive beliefs about their abilities.

Students Who Procrastinate

In our discussion of protecting self-worth by avoiding failure, we indicated that procrastination is one of the ineffective strategies that students use. Let's further examine procrastination. Why do students procrastinate? The reasons include (University of Buffalo Counseling Services, 2005) poor time management, difficulty concentrating, fear and anxiety (being overwhelmed by the task and afraid of getting a bad grade, for example), negative beliefs ("I can never succeed at anything," for example), personal problems (financial problems, problems with a boyfriend or girlfriend, and so on), boredom, unrealistic expectations and perfectionism (believing you must read everything written on a subject before you begin to write a paper, for example), and fear of failure (thinking that if you don't get an *A*, you are a failure, for example).

Procrastination can take many forms, including these (University of Illinois Counseling Center, 1996):

- Ignoring the task with the hope that it will go away
- Underestimating the work involved in the task or overestimating one's abilities and resources
- Spending endless hours on computer games and surfing the Internet
- Deceiving oneself that a mediocre or poor performance is acceptable
- Substituting a worthy but lower-priority activity, such as cleaning one's room instead of studying
- Believing that repeated minor delays won't hurt
- Dramatizing a commitment to a task rather than doing it—for example, taking books along for a weekend trip but never opening them
- Persevering on only part of the task, such as writing and rewriting the first paragraph of a paper but never getting to the body of it
- Becoming paralyzed when having to choose between two alternatives—for example, agonizing over doing biology homework or English homework first with the outcome that neither is done

Students Who Are Perfectionists

As mentioned earlier in this chapter, perfectionism is sometimes the underlying reason for procrastinating. Perfectionists think that mistakes are never acceptable, that the highest standards of performance always have to be achieved. As indicated in figure 13.7, healthy achievement and perfectionism differ in a number of ways. Perfectionists are vulnerable to decreased productivity, impaired health, relationship problems, and low self-esteem (Haring, Hewitt, & Flett, 2003). Depression, anxiety, and eating disorders are common outcomes of perfectionism (Sherry & others, 2003, 2004).

BEST PRACTICES
Strategies for Helping Students Conquer Procrastination

Here are some good strategies for helping students reduce or eliminate procrastination:

1. *Get them to acknowledge that procrastinaton is a problem.* Too often, procrastinators don't face up to their problem. When students admit that they procrastinate, this can sometimes get them to begin thinking about how to solve the problem.

2. *Encourage them to identify their values and goals.* Get them to think about how procrastination can undermine their values and goals.

3. *Help them manage their time more effectively.* Have student make yearly (or term), monthly, weekly, and daily plans. Then help them monitor how they use their time and find ways to use it more wisely.

4. *Have them divide the task into smaller parts.* Sometimes students procrastinate because they view the task as so large and overwhelming that they will never be able to finish it. When this is the case, get them to divide the task into smaller units and set subgoals for completing one unit at a time. This strategy can often make what seems to be a completely unmanageable task manageable.

5. *Teach them to use behavioral strategies.* Have them identify the diversions that might be keeping them from focusing on the most important tasks and activities. Get them to note when and where they engage in these diversions. Then have them plan how to diminish and control their use. Another behavioral strategy is to have students make a contract with you, their parents, or a mentor. Yet another behavioral strategy is to have students build in a reward for themselves, which gives them an incentive to complete all or part of the task. For example, students might say to themselves that if they get all of their math problems completed, they will treat themselves to a movie when they finish them.

6. *Help them learn how to use cognitive strategies.* Encourage students to watch for mental self-seductions that can lead to behavioral diversions, such as "I'll do it tomorrow," "What's the problem with watching an hour of TV now?" and "I can't do it." Help them learn how to dispute mental diversions. For example, get them to tell themselves, "I really don't have much time left and other things are sure to come up later," "If I get this done, I'll be able to better enjoy my time," or "Maybe if I just go ahead and get going on this, it won't be so bad."

FIGURE 13.7 Differences between Perfectionists and Healthy Strivers

Perfectionist	Healthy striver
Sets standards beyond reach and reason	Sets high standards, but just beyond reach
Is never satisfied by anything less than perfection	Enjoys process as well as outcome
Becomes dysfunctionally depressed when experiences failure and disappointment	Bounces back from failure and disappointment quickly and with energy
Is preoccupied with fear of failure and disapproval—this can deplete energy levels	Keeps normal anxiety and fear of failure and disapproval within bounds—uses them to create energy
Sees mistakes as evidence of unworthiness	Sees mistakes as opportunities for growth and learning
Becomes overly defensive when criticized	Reacts positively to helpful criticism

Students with High Anxiety

Anxiety is a vague, highly unpleasant feeling of fear and apprehension. It is normal for students to be concerned or worried when they face school challenges, such as doing well on a test. Indeed, researchers have found that many successful students have

BEST PRACTICES
Strategies for Reducing Perfectionist Tendencies

Here are some good strategies for helping students to reduce or eliminate perfectionist tendencies (University of Texas at Austin Counseling and Mental Health
Center, 1999):

1. *Have students list the advantages and disadvantages of trying to be perfect.*
   When students do this, they may discover that the cost of trying to be perfect
   is too great. They may find out that problems with relationships, feeling anxious, feeling inadequate, being depressed, and so on actually outweigh whatever advantages perfectionism brings them.

2. *Guide students in becoming more aware of the self-critical nature of all-or-
   none thinking.* Help students learn how to substitute more realistic, reasonable thoughts for their habitually critical ones. When students berate a less
   than perfect performance, tell them to acknowledge the good aspects of their
   performance. Then encourage them to ask themselves questions, such as "Is it
   really as bad as I make it out to be?"

3. *Help students to become realistic about what they can achieve.* By getting students to set more realistic goals, they will gradually see that "imperfect" outcomes don't lead to the negative consequences they expect and fear.

4. *Encourage students to set strict time limits on each of their projects. When
   the time is up, they need to move on and engage in another activity.* This
   strategy often reduces the procrastination that may result from perfectionist
   tendencies.

5. *Talk with students about learning how to accept criticism.* Perfectionists frequently view criticism as a personal attack and respond to it defensively. Guide
   students to become more objective about the criticism and about themselves.
   Encourage them to look at criticism as something from which to learn and
   grow rather than something to be avoided at all costs.

moderate levels of anxiety (Bandura, 1997). However, some students have high levels
of anxiety and worry constantly, which can significantly impair their ability to achieve.

Some students' high anxiety levels are the result of parents' unrealistic achievement
expectations and pressure (Wigfield & others, 2006). For many students, anxiety
increases across the school years as they "face more frequent evaluation, social comparison, and (for some) experiences of failure" (Eccles, Wigfield, & Schiefele, 1998,
p. 1043). When schools create such circumstances, they likely increase students' anxiety.

A number of intervention programs have been created to reduce high anxiety
levels (Wigfield & others, 2006). Some intervention programs emphasize relaxation
techniques. These programs often are effective at reducing anxiety but do not always
lead to improved achievement. Anxiety intervention programs linked to worrying
emphasize modifying the negative, self-damaging thoughts of anxious students by
getting them to engage in more positive, task-focused thoughts (Meichenbaum &
Butler, 1980). These programs have been more effective than the relaxation programs
in improving students' achievement (Wigfield & others, 2006).

Students Who Are Uninterested or Alienated

Brophy (1998) argues that the most difficult motivation problem involves students
who are apathetic, uninterested in learning, or alienated from school learning.

BEST PRACTICES
Strategies to Reach the Uninterested or Alienated

Here are some ways you might be able to reach students who are uninterested or alienated (Brophy, 1998):

1. *Work on developing a positive relationship with the student.* If the uninterested or alienated student doesn't like you, it is hard to get the student to work toward any achievement goals. Show patience, but be determined to help the student and push for steady progress in spite of setbacks or resistance.

2. *Make school more intrinsically interesting.* To make school more intrinsically interesting for this type of student, find out the student's interests and if possible include those interests in assignments that you make.

3. *Teach strategies for making academic work more enjoyable.* Help students understand that they are causing their own problems, and find ways to guide them in taking pride in their work.

4. *Consider a mentor.* Think about enlisting the aid of a mentor in the community or an older student whom you believe the uninterested or alienated student will respect.

Achieving in school is not an important value for them. To reach apathetic students requires sustained efforts to resocialize their attitudes toward school achievement (Murdock, 1999).

This chapter has focused on student motivation. It also is important for you to be motivated as a teacher as well. To evaluate your motivation, complete Self-Assessment 13.1 on p. 482.

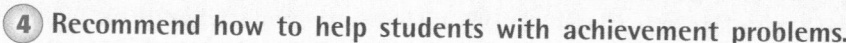

Review, Reflect, and Practice

④ Recommend how to help students with achievement problems.

REVIEW
- How can low-achieving students with low achievement expectations be described and how can teachers help them?
- What are some strategies students use to protect their self-worth to avoid failure? How can these students be helped?
- What characterizes students who procrastinate and what are some strategies to help them?
- What characterizes students who are perfectionists and how can teachers help students with these tendencies?
- What is anxiety, how does high anxiety interfere with achievement, and what type of programs can benefit students with high anxiety?
- How can teachers help students who are uninterested or alienated?

REFLECT
- Think about several of your own past schoolmates who showed low motivation in school. Why do you think they behaved the way they did? What teaching strategies might have helped them?

Review, Reflect, and Practice *continued*

PRAXIS™ PRACTICE

1. Which of the following students is the best example of failure syndrome?
   a. Andrea, who does not do well in school and rarely tries anymore
   b. Marcy, who works very hard and manages to earn C's
   c. Samantha, who does very well in school but does not try very hard
   d. Vivi, who is never satisfied with her own performance

2. Scott slides down in his seat to avoid being called on by the teacher. His behavior reflects which of the following in an effort to protect his self-worth by avoiding failure?
   a. failure syndrome
   b. nonperformance
   c. procrastination
   d. setting unreachable goals

3. Which teaching strategy is most likely to help students overcome procrastination?
   a. assigning a large project to be done in parts, with each part due at a different time
   b. assigning many large projects in a semester to ensure that students will have to learn to manage their time
   c. assigning no work that must be done outside of class
   d. assigning students to list all of the things they would rather do than their homework

4. Becky gets very upset when she does not receive full credit on an assignment. She takes particular offense at any critical remarks that are made of her work. Which of the following strategies is most likely to help Becky overcome her perfectionism?
   a. Give Becky lots of constructive feedback, both positive and negative, and allow her to revise her work.
   b. Make sure that Becky is capable of earning full credit on every assignment you give her.
   c. Make sure that Becky is not capable of earning full credit on any assignments you give her so she will get used to it.
   d. Never give Becky any kind of feedback other than a grade, so you don't upset her.

5. Carmella has a great deal of anxiety about school, and it is interfering with her ability to concentrate in school. Which of the following is most likely to help her reduce her anxiety?
   a. helping her to replace her negative, self-damaging thoughts with more positive, task-focused thoughts
   b. encouraging her to set higher goals
   c. guiding her to reduce procrastination
   d. getting her to face the reality of concentrating better

6. Which of the following is most likely to help a teacher get an uninterested or alienated student to become more motivated to do well in school?
   a. Stress how important going to college is.
   b. Find out the student's interests and include those in the student's assignments.
   c. Compare the student with other students who are more motivated.
   d. Describe some strategies for reducing perfectionism.

Please see the answer key at the end of the book.

SELF-ASSESSMENT 13.1

Evaluating My Motivation

Here are 18 statements you can use to analyze your motivational makeup. Rate yourself from 1 (not like me at all) to 5 (very much like me) on each of the statements.

	1	2	3	4	5

1. I am aware of the hierarchy of motives in my life and which ones are the most important for me.

2. I am intrinsically motivated.

3. I have high expectations and standards for success.

4. My life has many moments of flow.

5. I am aware of the people in my life who have motivated me the most and what it is they did that motivated me.

6. I make achievement-related attributions that emphasize effort.

7. I have a mastery motivation orientation rather than a helpless or performance orientation.

8. I am motivated to learn and succeed because of my success aspirations, not because I want to protect my self-worth or avoid failure.

9. I have high self-efficacy in general.

10. I have high instructional self-efficacy in terms of my ability as a teacher and in terms of managing my classroom effectively.

11. I regularly set goals, plan how to reach those goals, and systematically monitor my progress toward the goals.

12. I set specific, proximal, and challenging goals.

13. I am a good time manager, regularly doing weekly plans, monitoring my use of time, and making to-do lists.

14. I am good at learning from my mistakes to improve my future success.

15. I don't let anxiety or other emotions get in the way of my motivation.

16. I have a good support system for my motivation and have positive, close relationships with people who can help me sustain my motivation.

17. I do tasks in a timely manner and I don't procrastinate.

18. I'm not a perfectionist.

Scoring and Interpretation

Examine the pattern of your responses. If you rated yourself 4 or 5 on each of the items, you likely are getting your motivation to work to your advantage, and you likely will be a positive motivational model for your students. However, for any items on which you rated yourself 3 or below, spend some time thinking about how you can improve those aspects of your motivational life.

CRACK THE CASE
The Case of the Reading Incentive Program

Catherine teaches second grade in an economically disadvantaged elementary school. Many of her students read below grade level. Some of her students have had little exposure to reading outside of school, and most do not choose to read during their free time at school. Knowing that reading skills are important to future success in school, Catherine is justifiably concerned.

In an effort to entice her students to read more, Catherine develops a reading incentive program. She places a large chart on the classroom wall to track student progress. Each time a student completes a book, he or she tells Catherine, who then places a star next to the student's name on the chart. Each student who reads five books per month receives a small prize from the class prize box. The student who reads the most books in any given month receives a larger prize. When Catherine tells her students about the new incentive program, they are very excited.

"This is great!" says Joey. "I'm gonna get the most stars!"

"No, you won't," says Peter. "Sami will. She's always got her nose stuck in a book. She's the best reader in the class."

Sami is a very good reader. She is reading well above grade level and generally favors novels from the young adult section of the library. These books are rather lengthy and take her quite some time to finish. However, she really enjoys them. Catherine has brought her several from her own collection as well, since none of her classroom books seem to interest Sami.

The first week of the program is quite exciting. Every day students tell Catherine about the books they have read. The chart begins to fill with stars. By the end of the week, all the students have at least one star next to their name except Sami. During the last week of the month many students choose reading as a free-time activity. The students are anxious to ensure that they will earn at least one prize, and many are devouring books in anticipation of being the month's "top reader." At the end of the month, 23 of Catherine's 25 students have 5 stars on the chart. The only exceptions are Sami, who has only 1 star, and Michael, who had chicken pox during the month. True to his word, Joey receives the most stars—15. The students excitedly choose their prizes.

The following month, the reading frenzy continues. This time Sami joins her classmates in their accumulation of stars and receives 30, making her the top reader. Joey is right behind her with 25. Every student in the class earns at least 5 stars, entitling all to a prize. Because they are all reading so much, Catherine gives them a Friday afternoon party, at which they watch an animated movie and eat popcorn.

A similar pattern is repeated over the next several months. The star chart fills quickly. Catherine believes that the students are reading enough that they will do quite well on the annual state achievement test. She is thrilled with their progress. She decides that after the test, she will drop the incentive program and just quietly keep track of how much her students read. After doing this, she notices that once again very few students are reading during their free time. Even Sami is no longer reading when she is finished with her other work. Now she draws instead.

1. What are the issues in this case?
2. Analyze the case from the perspective of extrinsic and intrinsic motivation.
3. Analyze the case from a goal orientation perspective.
4. Why do you think Sami went from receiving 1 star the first month to receiving 30 stars the next? Why does she no longer read in her free time at school?
5. What are the problems with this type of incentive program? How might an incentive program be developed that does not undermine students' motivation to read?

Reach Your Learning Goals
Motivation, Teaching, and Learning

(1) EXPLORING MOTIVATION: Define motivation and compare the behavioral, humanistic, cognitive, and social perspectives on motivation.

What Is Motivation?

The study of motivation focuses on the processes that energize, direct, and sustain behavior.

Perspectives on Motivation

The behavioral perspective on motivation emphasizes that external rewards and punishments are the key factors that determine a student's motivation. Incentives are positive or negative stimuli or events that can motivate a student's behavior. The humanistic perspective stresses our capacity for personal growth, freedom to choose our own destiny, and our positive qualities. According to Maslow's humanistic perspective, there is a hierarchy of motives, and students' needs must be satisfied in a particular sequence. Self-actualization, the highest and most elusive of the needs Maslow describes, involves the motivation to develop one's full potential as a human being. In the cognitive perspective on motivation, students' thoughts guide their motivation. The cognitive perspective focuses on the internal motivation to achieve, attributions, students' beliefs that they can effectively control their environment, and goal setting, planning, and monitoring progress toward a goal. The cognitive perspective meshes with R. W. White's concept of competence motivation. The social perspective emphasizes the need for affiliation.

(2) ACHIEVEMENT PROCESSES: Discuss the important processes in motivation to achieve.

Extrinsic and Intrinsic Motivation

Extrinsic motivation involves doing something to obtain something else (a means to an end). Intrinsic motivation involves the internal motivation of doing something for its own sake (an end in itself). Overall, most experts recommend that teachers create a classroom atmosphere in which students are intrinsically motivated to learn. One view of intrinsic motivation emphasizes its self-determining characteristics. Giving students some choice and providing opportunities for personal responsibility increase intrinsic motivation. Csikszentmihalyi uses the term *flow* to describe life's optimal experiences, which involve a sense of mastery and absorbed concentration in an activity. Flow is most likely to occur in areas in which students are challenged and perceive themselves as having a high degree of skill. Interest is conceptualized as more specific than intrinsic motivation and interest is positively linked to learning. It is important for teachers to create learning environments that encourage students to become cognitively engaged and develop a responsibility for their learning. In some situations, rewards can actually undermine performance. When rewards are used, they should convey information about task mastery rather than external control. Researchers have found that as students move from the early elementary school years to high school, their intrinsic motivation drops, especially during the middle school years. The concept of person-environment fit calls attention to the lack of fit between adolescents' increasing interest in autonomy and schools' increasing control, which results in students' negative self-evaluations and attitudes toward school. Overall, the overwhelming conclusion is that it is a wise strategy to create learning environments that encourage students to become intrinsically motivated. However, in many real world situations, both intrinsic and extrinsic motivation are involved and too often intrinsic and extrinsic motivation have been pitted against each other as polar opposites.

Attribution

Attribution theory states that individuals are motivated to discover the underlying causes of behavior in an effort to make sense of the behavior. Weiner identified three dimensions of causal attributions: (1) locus, (2) stability, and (3) controllability. Combinations of these dimensions produce different explanations of failure and success.

| Mastery Motivation |

A mastery orientation focuses on the task rather than ability, involves positive affect, and includes solution-oriented strategies. A helpless orientation focuses on personal inadequacies, attributing difficulty to lack of ability, and displaying negative affect (such as boredom or anxiety). A performance orientation involves being concerned with the achievement outcome rather than the achievement process.

| Self-Efficacy |

Self-efficacy is the belief that one can master a situation and produce positive outcomes. Bandura stresses that self-efficacy is a critical factor in whether students will achieve. Schunk argues that self-efficacy influences a student's choice of tasks and that low-self-efficacy students avoid many learning tasks, especially those that are challenging. Instructional strategies that emphasize "I can do it" benefit students. Low-self-efficacy teachers become mired in classroom problems. Setting specific, proximal (short-term), and challenging goals benefits students' self-efficacy and achievement.

| Goal Setting, Planning, and Self-Monitoring |

Dweck and Nicholls define goals in terms of immediate achievement-related focus and definition of success. Being a good planner helps students manage time effectively, set priorities, and be organized. Giving students opportunities to develop their time management skills likely will benefit their learning and achievement. Self-monitoring is a key aspect of learning and achievement.

| Expectations |

Students' expectations for success and the value they place on what they want to achieve influence their motivation. The combination of expectancy and value have been the focus of a number of models of achievement motivation. Teachers' expectations can have a powerful influence on students' motivation and achievement. Teachers often have higher expectations for high-ability students than low-ability students. It is important for teachers to monitor their expectations and to have high expectations for all students.

③ MOTIVATION, RELATIONSHIPS, AND SOCIOCULTURAL CONTEXTS: Explain how relationships and sociocultural contexts can support or undercut motivation.

| Social Motives |

Social motives are needs and desires that are learned through experience with the social world. The need for affiliation or relatedness involves the motive to be securely connected with people, which consists of establishing, maintaining, and restoring warm, close personal relationships.

| Social Relationships |

In terms of social approval, both teacher and peer approval are important. Peer conformity peaks in early adolescence, a time of important decisions about whether to pursue academic or social motives. Understanding the parent's role in students' motivation focuses on demographic characteristics (such as education level, time spent at work, and family structure), child-rearing practices (such as providing the right amount of challenge and support), and provision of specific experiences at home (such as providing reading materials). Peers can affect students' motivation through social comparison, social competence, peer learning, and peer-group influences. Research shows that a teacher's support and caring can play a powerful role in students' motivation. A teacher's instructional and managerial style also can play a role in a student's achievement. An important aspect of student motivation is enlisting parents as partners with you in educating the student.

| Sociocultural Contexts |

Teachers should recognize and value diversity within any cultural group and should be careful to distinguish the influences of socioeconomic status from those of ethnicity. Differences in achievement are more closely linked to socioeconomic status than to ethnicity. The quality of schools for many socioeconomically impoverished students is lower than for their middle-income counterparts. Gender differences in achievement involve beliefs and values—for example, girls have higher competence beliefs for English and reading, and boys have higher competence beliefs for math and sports. Special concerns are gender differences in teacher-student interaction, curriculum and content, sexual harassment, and gender bias.

485

STUDENTS WITH ACHIEVEMENT PROBLEMS: Recommend how to help students with achievement problems.

Students Who Are Low Achieving and Have Low Expectations for Success

A student with low ability and low expectations for success who often needs reassurance and support but also needs to be reminded that progress will be acceptable only when considerable effort is put forth. A student with failure syndrome (who has low expectations for success and gives up easily) likely will benefit from cognitive retraining methods such as efficacy training, attribution retraining, and strategy training.

Students Who Protect Their Self-Worth by Avoiding Failure

Students motivated to protect self-worth and avoid failure often engage in one or more of these ineffective strategies: nonperformance, procrastination, or setting unreachable goals. These students likely need guidance in setting challenging but realistic goals, need the link between their effort and self-worth strengthened, and benefit from developing positive beliefs about their abilities.

Students Who Procrastinate

Procrastination can take many forms including ignoring a task with the hope it will go away, underestimating the amount of work a task requires, spending endless hours on distracting activities, substituting worth but lower-priority activities, and others. Strategies for helping students overcome procrastination include acknowledging they have a procrastination problem, encouraging them to identify their values and goals, helping them mange time more effectively, having them divide the task into smaller parts, and teaching them to use behavioral and cognitive strategies.

Students Who Are Perfectionists

Perfectionists think that mistakes are never acceptable and that the highest standards of performance always have to be achieved. Perfectionists are vulnerable to a number of physical and mental health problems. Teachers can help students with perfectionist tendencies by having them list the advantages and disadvantages of trying to be perfect, guiding students to become more aware of the self-critical nature of their all-or-none thinking, helping them become more realistic about what they can achieve, encouraging them to set time limits on their projects, and helping them learn how to accept criticism.

Students with High Anxiety

Anxiety is a vague, highly unpleasant feeling of fear and apprehension. High anxiety can result from unrealistic parental expectations. Students' anxiety increases as they get older and face more evaluation, social comparison, and failure (for some students). Cognitive programs that replace students' self-damaging thoughts with positive, constructive thoughts have been more effective than relaxation programs in benefiting student achievement.

Students Who Are Uninterested or Alienated

Strategies for helping an uninterested or alienated student include establishing a positive relationship with the student, making school more intrinsically interesting, using teaching strategies for making academic work more enjoyable, and considering a mentor in the community or an older student as a support person for the student.

 KEY TERMS

motivation 451
incentives 451
humanistic perspective 452
hierarchy of needs 452
self-actualization 452

competence motivation 453
need for affiliation or
 relatedness 453
extrinsic motivation 454
intrinsic motivation 454

attribution theory 459
mastery orientation 461
helpless orientation 461
performance orientation 461
self-efficacy 462

social motives 469
failure syndrome 475

PORTFOLIO ACTIVITIES

Now that you have a good understanding of this chapter, complete these exercises to expand your thinking.

Independent Reflection

Motivate, Invigorate, and Innovate Your Students. Design a motivationally rich classroom. What materials would be available? Describe your classroom walls and learning centers. How would teaching proceed? What types of activities would students participate in? Write up your classroom design. (INTASC: Principle 5)

Collaborative Work

Case Studies in Motivation. With three other students in the class, create a plan to improve the motivation of these students: (1) 7-year-old Tanya, who has low ability and low expectations for success; (2) 10-year-old Samuel, who works overtime to keep his self-worth at a high level but has a strong fear of failure; (3) 13-year-old Sandra, who is quiet in the classroom and underestimates her skills; and (4) 16-year-old Robert, who shows little interest in school and currently lives with his aunt (you have been unable to contact his parents). (INTASC: Principles 2, 3, 5)

Research/Field Experience

The Face of Student Motivation. Observe a teacher at the grade level you plan to teach and note the strategies he or she uses to motivate the students. Which strategies are most effective? Least effective? Why do you think this is so? Which students seem particularly difficult to motivate? Why do you think this is so? What would you do differently to foster student motivation in the classroom? (INTASC: Principles 5, 7, 9)

Go to the Online Learning Center for downloadable portfolio templates.

 TAKING IT TO THE NET

- A student tells you that she lacks the ability to succeed in class. How do you respond? How would you describe your student's locus of control and attribution style? Take an online self-assessment to discover your own locus of control and attribution style. How could your style affect the way you teach and interact with students? **http://discoveryhealth.queendom.com/lc_short_access.html**

- Reflect on your teaching goals and what you hope to accomplish in the classroom. Take yourself through the online process of setting a goal. Design a goal-setting activity that you could integrate into your regular curriculum. Why are goals an important element of a student's learning experience? **www.mygoals.com/**

- At-risk students are typically characterized as unmotivated and underachieving and often are placed in classes that emphasize remediation. What are some successful alternatives? Find an exemplary model for teaching at-risk students on the Web, and summarize its program components. Illustrate why students in the program become motivated to achieve at higher levels than their counterparts in remedial programs. **www.ncrel.org/sdrs/areas/issues/students/atrisk/at700.htm**

Connect to the Online Learning Center to explore possible answers.

 STUDY, PRACTICE, AND SUCCEED

Visit **www.mhhe.com/santedu3e** to review the chapter with self-grading quizzes and self-assessments, to apply the chapter material to two more Crack the Case studies, and for suggested activities to develop your teaching portfolio.

CHAPTER 14

Managing the Classroom

Precision in communication is more important than ever in our era of hair-trigger balances, when a false or misunderstood word may create as much disaster as a sudden thoughtless act.

—James Thurber
American Essayist and Humorist, 20th Century

Learning Goals

1 Explain why classroom management is both challenging and necessary.

2 Describe the positive design of the classroom's physical environment.

3 Discuss how to create a positive classroom environment.

4 Identify some good approaches to communication for both students and teachers.

5 Formulate some effective approaches that teachers can use to deal with problem behaviors.

TEACHING STORIES   Adriane Lonzarich

Adriane Lonzarich owns and operates Heartwood, a small preschool in San Mateo, California. In the afternoons, she also holds art classes for 5- to 12-year-old children. She talks about her ideas for managing the classroom:

> The most valuable advice I ever received for managing the classroom is to approach a problem or area of difficulty with three questions in this order: (1) Is it the environment? (2) Is it the teacher? (3) Is it the child? For example, if the issue of concern is unfocused energy of the group, I would first ask myself, Is it the environment? Is it overstimulating? Is there not enough to do? Do I need to rearrange the classroom and create more intimate spaces for quiet activity, or do I need to let them have more time outside, and so on? In many cases, I don't need to go on to the next two questions.
>
> Is it the teacher? Am I tired? nervous? uninspiring? Have I not taken the time to demonstrate the activities? Have I not been consistent in presenting, monitoring, and enforcing basic classroom rules? Have I not paid enough attention to their needs that day?
>
> Is it the child? If I've addressed all the other possibilities and I'm convinced that the problem is the child's problem, not the environment's or the teacher's, I explore what might be going on. Is anything happening in the child's home that might be causing his or her problems? Is it time for a parent conference? Does the child need help in bonding with a friend? Is the child afraid of failure and avoiding meaningful learning for that reason?
>
> This approach is empowering because it is much easier to change the environment or oneself than to change someone else's behavior. It also is effective because it does not zero in on the problem as the child's until all other avenues have been explored.

Preview

In educational circles, it is commonly said that no one pays any attention to good classroom management until it is missing. When classrooms are effectively managed, they run smoothly and students are actively engaged in learning. When they are poorly managed, they can become chaotic settings in which learning is a foreign activity. Our coverage begins by examining why classrooms need to be managed effectively, followed by strategies for designing the classroom's physical environment. Then we discuss the importance of creating a positive environment for learning and ways to be an effective communicator. The chapter concludes with information about what to do when students engage in problem behavior.

(1) WHY CLASSROOMS NEED TO BE MANAGED EFFECTIVELY

| Management Issues in Elementary and Secondary School Classrooms | The Crowded, Complex, and Potentially Chaotic Classroom | Getting Off to the Right Start | Emphasizing Instruction and Positive Classroom Climate | Management Goals and Strategies |

Effective classroom management maximizes children's learning opportunities (Evertson, Emmer, & Worsham, 2006; Evertson & Weinstein, 2006; Larrivee, 2005; Weinstein & Mignano, 2007). Experts in classroom management report that there has been a change

Carmella Williams Scott, a middle school English and law teacher at Fairmont Alternative School in Newman, Georgia, created Juvenile Video Court TV, a student-run judicial system, so that students could experience the "other side of the bench" as a judge, lawyer, bailiff, and camera operator. She especially targeted gang leaders for inclusion in the system because they ran the school. Carmella likes to use meaningful questions to guide students' critical thinking. She believes that mutual respect is a key factor in her success as a teacher and the lack of discipline problems she has in her classes (Briggs, 1999).

in thinking about the best way to manage classrooms. The older view emphasized creating and applying rules to control students' behavior. The newer view focuses more on students' needs for nurturing relationships and opportunities for self-regulation (Bear, 2005a, b; Pianta, 2006; Watson & Battistich, 2006). Classroom management that orients students toward passivity and compliance with rigid rules can undermine their engagement in active learning, higher-order thinking, and the social construction of knowledge (Charles & Senter, 2005; Jones & Jones, 2004). The new trend in classroom management places more emphasis on guiding students toward self-discipline and less on externally controlling the student (Bear, 2005a, b). Historically in classroom management, the teacher was thought of as a director. In the current learner-centered trend in classroom management, the teacher is more of a guide, coordinator, and facilitator (Kauffman & others, 2006; Larivee, 2005). The new classroom management model does not mean slipping into a permissive mode. Emphasizing caring and students' self-regulation does not mean that the teacher abdicates responsibility for what happens in the classroom (Emmer & Stough, 2001).

As you explore various aspects of managing the classroom, realize the importance of consulting and working with other staff members on management issues (Evertson & Harris, 1999). Also recognize that your class is part of the broader context of school culture and that in such areas as discipline and conflict management your policies will need to reflect and be consistent with the policies of the school and other teachers in the school. We will begin our tour of effective classroom management by exploring how management issues sometimes differ in elementary and secondary classrooms.

Management Issues in Elementary and Secondary School Classrooms

Elementary and secondary school classrooms have many similar management issues. At all levels of education, good managers design classrooms for optimal learning, create positive environments for learning, establish and maintain rules, get students to cooperate, effectively deal with problems, and use good communication strategies.

However, the same classroom management principles sometimes are applied differently in elementary and secondary schools because these two types of schools are structured differently (Brophy, 2006; Emmer & Gerwels, 2006; Evertson, Emmer, & Worsham, 2006; Weinstein, 2007). In many elementary schools, teachers face the challenge of managing the same 20 to 25 children for the entire day. In middle and high schools, teachers face the challenge of managing five or six different groups of 20 to 25 adolescents for about 50 minutes each day. Compared with secondary school students, elementary school students spend much more time with the same students in the small space of a single classroom, and having to interact with the same people all day can breed feelings of confinement and boredom and other problems. However, with 100 to 150 students, secondary school teachers are more likely to be confronted with a wider range of problems than elementary school teachers. Also, because secondary school teachers spend less time seeing students in the classroom, it can be more difficult for them to establish personal relationships with students. And secondary school teachers have to get the classroom lesson moving quickly and manage time effectively, because class periods are so short.

Secondary school students' problems can be more long-standing and more deeply ingrained, and therefore more difficult to modify, than those of elementary school students. Also in secondary schools, discipline problems are frequently more severe, the students being potentially more unruly and even dangerous. Because most secondary school students have more advanced reasoning skills than elementary school students, they might demand more elaborate and logical explanations of rules and discipline. And in secondary schools, hallway socializing can carry into the

What are some different management issues in teaching elementary and secondary school students?

classroom. Every hour there is another "settling down" process. Keep in mind these differences between elementary and secondary schools as we further explore how to effectively manage the classroom. As we see next, at both elementary and secondary school levels, classrooms can be crowded, complex, and potentially chaotic.

The Crowded, Complex, and Potentially Chaotic Classroom

Carol Weinstein and Andrew Mignano (1997) used the title of this section, "The crowded, complex, and potentially chaotic classroom," as an alert for potential problems and highlighted Walter Doyle's (1986, 2006) six characteristics that reflect a classroom's complexity and potential for problems:

- *Classrooms are multidimensional.* Classrooms are the setting for many activities, ranging from academic activities, such as reading, writing, and math, to social activities, such as playing games, communicating with friends, and arguing. Teachers have to keep records and keep students on a schedule. Work has to be assigned, monitored, collected, and evaluated. Students have individual needs that are more likely to be met when the teacher takes them into account.
- *Activities occur simultaneously.* Many classroom activities occur simultaneously. One cluster of students might be writing at their desks, another might be discussing a story with the teacher, one student might be picking on another, others might be talking about what they are going to do after school, and so on.
- *Things happen quickly.* Events often occur rapidly in classrooms and frequently require an immediate response. For example, two students suddenly argue about the ownership of a notebook, a student complains that another student is copying her answers, a student speaks out of turn, a student marks on another student's arm with a felt-tip pen, two students abruptly start bullying another student, or a student is rude to you.
- *Events are often unpredictable.* Even though you might carefully plan the day's activities and be highly organized, events will occur that you never expect: A fire alarm goes off; a student gets sick; two students get into a fight; a computer won't work; a previously unannounced assembly takes place; the heat goes off in the middle of the winter; and so on.
- *There is little privacy.* Classrooms are public places where students observe how the teacher handles discipline problems, unexpected events, and frustrating circumstances. Some teachers report that they feel like they are in a "fishbowl," or constantly onstage. Much of what happens to one student is observed by other

students, and students make attributions about what is occurring. In one case, they might perceive that the teacher is being unfair in the way she disciplines a student. In another, they might appreciate her sensitivity to a student's feelings.

- *Classrooms have histories.* Students have memories of what happened earlier in their classroom. They remember how the teacher handled a discipline problem earlier in the year, which students have gotten more privileges than others, and whether the teacher abides by her promises. Because the past affects the future, it is important for teachers to manage the classroom today in a way that will support rather than undermine learning tomorrow. This means that the first several weeks of the school year are critical for establishing effective management principles.

The crowded, complex nature of the classroom can lead to problems if the classroom is not managed effectively. Indeed, such problems are a major public concern about schools. Year after year, the Gallup Poll has asked the public what they perceive to be the main problems schools face. In the 2004 poll (Gallup Organization, 2004), lack of discipline was rated as the second most important problem, after lack of financial support.

Getting Off to the Right Start

One key to managing the complexity of the classroom is to make careful use of the first few days and weeks of school. You will want to use this time to (1) communicate your rules and procedures to the class and get student cooperation in following them and (2) get students to engage effectively in all learning activities.

Taking the time in the first week of school to establish these expectations, rules, and routines will help your class run smoothly and set the tone for developing a positive classroom environment.

Emphasizing Instruction and a Positive Classroom Climate

Despite the public's belief that a lack of discipline is the number one problem in schools, educational psychology emphasizes ways to develop and maintain a positive classroom environment that supports learning (Evertson, Emmer, & Worsham, 2006; Larrivee, 2005). This involves using preventive, proactive strategies rather than becoming immersed in reactive disciplinary tactics.

In a classic study, Jacob Kounin (1970) was interested in discovering how teachers responded to student misbehaviors. Kounin was surprised to find that effective and ineffective classroom managers responded in very similar ways to the misbehaviors. What the effective managers did far better than the ineffective managers was manage the group's activities. Researchers in educational psychology consistently find that teachers who competently guide and structure classroom activities are more effective than teachers who emphasize their disciplinary role (Brophy, 1996).

Throughout this book we emphasize a vision of students as active learners engaged in meaningful tasks, who think reflectively and critically and often interact with other students in collaborative learning experiences. Historically, the effectively managed classroom has been described as a "well-oiled machine," but a more appropriate metaphor for today's effectively managed classroom is "beehive of activity" (see figure 14.1) (Randolph & Evertson, 1995). This does not imply that classrooms should be wildly noisy and chaotic. Rather, students should be actively learning

THROUGH THE EYES OF STUDENTS

First Week of School

Sept. 8:   Well, now that I know what my teacher is like, I
(First   wish I didn't. My best friend Annie, got the good
Day of   teacher, Ms. Hartwell. I got the witch, Ms. Birdsong.
Class)   The first thing she did was to read all of her rules
           to us. It must have taken half an hour. We will never
           get to do anything fun. Fifth grade is ruined.

Sept. 12: Ms. Birdsong is still strict but I'm starting to like her
           better. And she even is beginning to be a little funny
           sometimes. I guess she's just serious about wanting
           us to learn.

Brooke
Fifth-Grade Student
St. Louis, Missouri

BEST PRACTICES
Strategies for a Good Beginning of the School Year

Here are some good teaching strategies for the beginning of the school year (Emmer, Evertson, & Worsham, 2006):

1. *Establish expectations for behavior and resolve student uncertainties.* At the beginning of the school year, students will not be sure what to expect in your classroom. They might have expectations, based on their experiences with other teachers, that are different from what your classroom will be like. In the first few days of school, lay out your expectations for students' work and behavior. Don't focus just on course content in the first few days and weeks of school. Be sure to take the time to clearly and concretely spell out class rules, procedures, and requirements so that students know what to expect in your class. Next, middle school history teacher Chuck Rawls describes what he does at the beginning of the school year.

THROUGH THE EYES OF TEACHERS
Establish Yourself in a Positive Manner

My first few days and weeks are highly structured—desks in straight rows, and daily assignments starting with Day One. I try to make the initial environment as businesslike, straightforward, and structured as I possibly can. The games and easy give-and-take come later, after it is firmly established who is in charge of the class, and also if the kids are capable of doing that. Sometimes they aren't.

I'm not saying to scare the kids—they still need to feel safe and comfortable. The main thing is to establish yourself, at least in the minds of the kids, as an organized, confident, firm but fair subject matter expert.

Someone said the lasting impression is made in the first 15 or 45 seconds of the first introduction. This is true.

2. *Make sure that students experience success.* In the first week of school, content activities and assignments should be designed to ensure that students succeed. This helps students develop a positive attitude and provides them with confidence to tackle more difficult tasks later.

3. *Be available and visible.* Show your students that they can approach you when they need information. During seatwork or group work, make yourself available instead of going to your desk and completing paperwork. Move around the room, monitor students' progress, and provide assistance when needed.

4. *Be in charge.* Even if you have stated your class rules and expectations clearly, some students will forget and others will test you to see if you are willing to enforce the rules, especially in the first several weeks of school. Continue to consistently establish the boundaries between what is acceptable and what is not acceptable in your classroom.

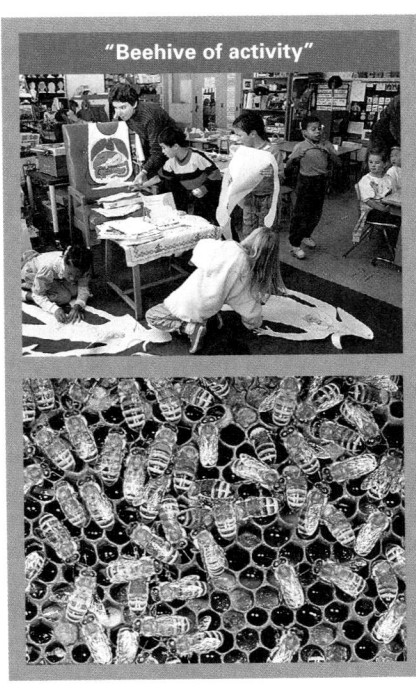

FIGURE 14.1 The Effectively Managed Classroom

"Well-oiled machine" or "beehive of activity"?

BEST PRACTICES
Strategies for Increasing Academic Learning Time

Strategies for increasing academic learning time include maintaining activity flow, minimizing transition time, and holding students accountable (Weinstein, 2003):

1. *Maintain activity flow.* In an analysis of classrooms, Jacob Kounin (1970) studied teachers' ability to initiate and maintain the flow of activity. Then he searched for links between activity flow and students' engagement and misbehavior. He found that some ineffective managers engaged in "flip-flopping"—terminating an activity, starting another, and then returning to the first one. Other ineffective managers were distracted from an ongoing activity by a small event that really did not need attention. For example, in one situation a teacher who was explaining a math problem at the board noticed a student leaning on his left elbow while working on the problem. The teacher went over to the student and told him to sit up straight, interrupting the flow of the class. Some ineffective managers "overdwell" on something that students already understand or go on at length about appropriate behavior. All of these situations—flip-flopping, responding to distractions, and overdwelling—can interrupt the classroom's flow.

2. *Minimize transition time.* In transitions from one activity to another, there is more room for disruptive behavior to occur. In one study of 50 classes, disruptions such as hitting, yelling, and using obscene gestures occurred twice as often during transitions between activities than during activities (Arlin, 1979). Teachers can decrease the potential for disruption during transitions by preparing students for forthcoming transitions, establishing transition routines, and clearly defining the boundaries of lessons.

3. *Hold students accountable.* If students know they will be held accountable for their work, they are more likely to make good use of class time. Clearly communicating assignments and requirements encourages student accountability. Explain to students what they will be doing and why, how long they will be working on the activity, how to obtain help if they need it, and what to do when they are finished. Helping students establish goals, plan, and monitor their progress also increases students' accountability. And maintaining good records can help you hold students accountable for their performance.

and busily engaged in tasks that they are motivated to do rather than quietly and passively sitting in their seats. Often they will be interacting with each other and the teacher as they construct their knowledge and understanding.

Management Goals and Strategies

Effective classroom management has two main goals: to help students spend more time on learning and less time on non-goal-directed activity, and to prevent students from developing academic and emotional problems.

Help Students Spend More Time on Learning and Less Time on Non-Goal-Directed Behavior In chapters 12 and 13, we discussed the importance, for both teachers and students, of being a good time manager. Effective classroom management will help you maximize your instructional time and your students' learning time. Carol Weinstein (2003) described the amount of time available for various classroom activities in a typical 42-minute secondary school class over the course of a school year. Actual yearly learning time is only about 62 hours, which is approximately half of the mandated school time for a typical class. Although her time figures are only estimates, they suggest that the hours available for learning are far less than would appear. And as we underscored in chapter 12, "Planning, Instruction, and Technology," learning takes time.

Prevent Students from Developing Problems A well-managed classroom not only fosters meaningful learning but also helps prevent academic and emotional problems from developing. Well-managed classrooms keep students busy with active, appropriately challenging tasks, have activities in which students become absorbed and motivated to learn, and establish clear rules and regulations students must abide by. In such

TECHNOLOGY AND EDUCATION

Automating Classroom Management with Student Response Systems

Classroom management involves not only managing student behaviors but also managing instruction. Ideally, the two go hand in hand—students who are engaged in learning tasks are less likely to become behavior problems. Another aspect of classroom is record keeping. A new, relatively simple and inexpensive technology can help in all three areas.

Recent years have seen a rise in popularity of classroom response systems. These systems traditionally consist of each of the following: a set of networked, low-cost handheld devices (which may be as simple as a keypad), a computer that is used as a central hub to aggregate student responses, and a whole-class display that shows questions posed to the class and the aggregation of student responses. Each of these components has a key role as teachers pose questions to students, who indicate an answer on their own devices. All answers then appear on the whole-class display in aggregated form, typically as a histogram.

Using student response systems, teachers have the ability to pose questions and give practice to whole classes of students, and to gather instant data on all of their students, which can be used to quickly assess comprehension. This true, formative assessment enables the teacher to identify students' misconceptions and errors and then correct them immediately. In addition, it encourages active student participation and helps students explore what they know and don't know—and hence take control of their own learning. Most student response systems also produce records of student responses, which can be automatically entered as grades.

Numerous studies show that these relatively simple systems can be effective classroom management tools (Burnstein & Lederman, 2001; Swan, Kratcoski, & Miller, 2006; Vahey, Roschell, & Tatar, 2006). Common outcomes include increases in student engagement, teacher awareness of student knowledge, and student understanding of content matter.

A number of companies offer student response systems. Some of the more popular ones are InterWrite's Personal Response System (www.gtcocalcomp.com/interwriteprs.htm), TurningPoint's Audience Response System (www.turning technologies.com/highereducation.htm), and Quizdom's Student Response System (www.qwizdom.com/education_solutions_applications.htm).

classrooms, students are less likely to develop academic and emotional problems. By contrast, in poorly managed classrooms, students' academic and emotional problems are more likely to fester. The academically unmotivated student becomes even less motivated. The shy student becomes more reclusive. The bully becomes meaner.

Technology is increasingly being used in classroom management. To read about automating classroom management, see the Technology and Education box.

Review, Reflect, and Practice

(1) **Explain why classroom management is both challenging and necessary.**

REVIEW

- Why must management principles be applied differently to elementary and secondary school classrooms?
- What are six reasons that classrooms are crowded, complex, and potentially chaotic?
- What strategies are most likely to get a school year off to the right start for a teacher?
- What do experts say should be the basic approach to classroom management? What did Kounin find that effective teachers did differently than ineffective teachers did in managing the classroom?
- What are the two main goals of effective classroom management?

REFLECT

- Which would probably be easier for you to manage—an elementary school classroom or a high school classroom? Why?

continued on page 496

Review, Reflect, and Practice *continued*

PRAXIS™ PRACTICE

1. Which characteristic of classrooms is best exemplified in the following scenario? Holly and Alex are having a conflict. Holly takes a black, permanent marker and makes a large mark on Alex's shirt. Mr. Bronson witnesses the incident and does nothing. Two weeks later, during another conflict, Alex makes a mark on the back of Holly's shirt with a pen. This time Mr. Bronson gives Alex a detention. Alex becomes upset at what he perceives as unfair treatment.
   a. Classrooms are multidimensional.
   b. Classrooms have histories.
   c. There is little privacy.
   d. Things happen quickly.

2. Mr. McClure wants to be certain that his students understand that he has high expectations for them. Therefore, he gives a very difficult exam during the first week of school. Which principle of getting off to the right start did Mr. McClure ignore?
   a. Be available and visible.
   b. Be in charge.
   c. Establish expectations for behavior and resolve student uncertainties.
   d. Make sure that students experience success.

3. Which teacher is most likely to have classroom management problems?
   a. Mr. Knight, who, in an effort to keep students from being bored, has numerous activities during the period, all of which require transitional time
   b. Mr. Quinn, whose students know that they have to accomplish a significant amount of work during the period, which will be collected at the end
   c. Ms. Leifeit, whose students are always actively engaged in activities that require students to work together
   d. Ms. Jefferson, who establishes rules and procedures early in the school year and consistently enforces them

Please see the answer key at the end of the book.

(2) DESIGNING THE PHYSICAL ENVIRONMENT OF THE CLASSROOM

| Principles of Classroom Arrangement | Arrangement Style |

When thinking about effectively managing the classroom, inexperienced teachers sometimes overlook the physical environment. As you will see in this section, designing the physical environment of the classroom involves far more than arranging a few items on a bulletin board.

Principles of Classroom Arrangement

Here are four basic principles that you can use when arranging your classroom (Evertson, Emmer, & Worsham, 2006):

- *Reduce congestion in high-traffic areas.* Distraction and disruption can often occur in high-traffic areas. These include group work areas, students' desks, the teacher's desk, the pencil sharpener, bookshelves, computer stations, and storage locations. Separate these areas from each other as much as possible and make sure they are easily accessible.

- *Make sure that you can easily see all students.* An important management task is to carefully monitor students. To do this, you will need to be able to see all students at all times. Make sure there is a clear line of sight between your desk, instructional locations, students' desks, and all student work areas. Stand in different parts of the room to check for blind spots.
- *Make often-used teaching materials and student supplies easily accessible.* This minimizes preparation and cleanup time, as well as slowdowns and breaks in activity flow.
- *Make sure that students can easily observe whole-class presentations.* Establish where you and your students will be located when whole-class presentations take place. For these activities, students should not have to move their chairs or stretch their necks. To find out how well your students can see from their locations, sit in their seats in different parts of the room.

Arrangement Style

In thinking about how you will organize the classroom's physical space, you should ask yourself what type of instructional activity students will mainly be engaged in (whole-class, small-group, individual assignments, and so on). Consider the physical arrangements that will best support that type of activity (Crane, 2001; Fickes, 2001; Weinstein, 2007).

Standard Classroom Arrangements　Figure 14.2 shows a number of classroom arrangement styles: auditorium, face-to-face, off-set, seminar, and cluster (Renne, 1997). In traditional **auditorium style,** all students sit facing the teacher (see figure 14.2A). This arrangement inhibits face-to-face student contacts, and the teacher is free to move anywhere in the room. Auditorium style often is used when the teacher lectures or someone is making a presentation to the entire class.

In **face-to-face style,** students sit facing each other (see figure 14.2B). Distraction from other students is higher in this arrangement than in the auditorium style.

In **off-set style,** small numbers of students (usually three or four) sit at tables but do not sit directly across from one another (see figure 14.2C). This produces less distraction than face-to-face style and can be effective for cooperative learning activities.

In **seminar style,** larger numbers of students (ten or more) sit in circular, square, or U-shaped arrangements (see figure 14.2D). This is especially effective when you want students to talk with each other or to converse with you.

In **cluster style,** small numbers of students (usually four to eight) work in small, closely bunched groups (see figure 14.2E). This arrangement is especially effective for collaborative learning activities.

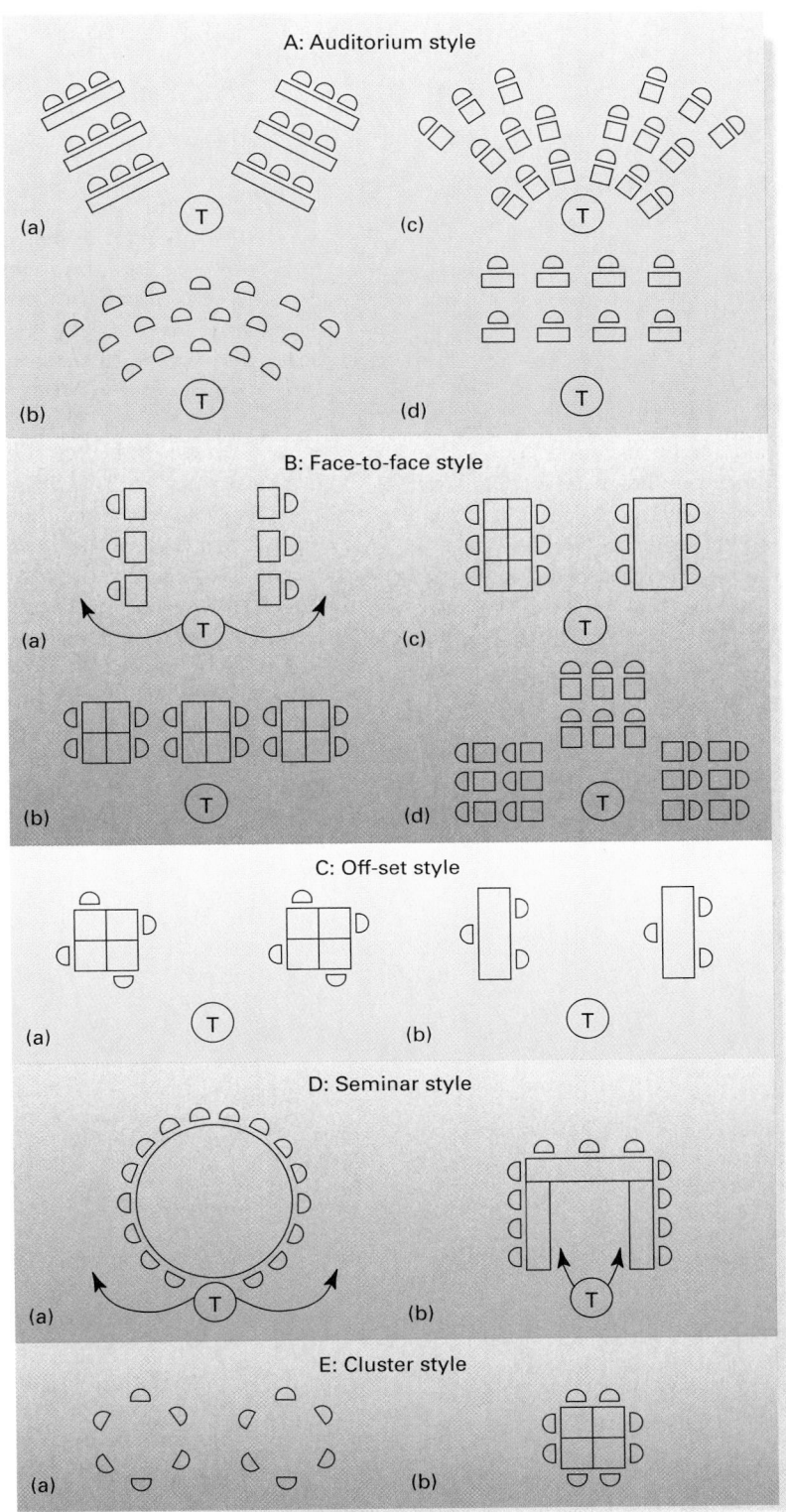

FIGURE 14.2 Variations of Classroom Seating Arrangements

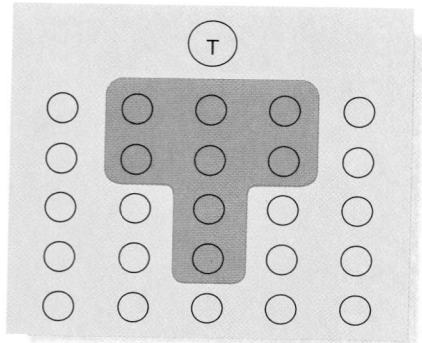

FIGURE 14.3 The Action Zone

"Action zone" refers to the seats in the front and center of row arrangement. Students in these seats are more likely to interact with the teacher, ask questions, and initiate discussion than students seated in more peripheral locations.

Source: From *Excellent Classroom Management* 1st edition by Rinne. © 1997. Reprinted with permission of Wadsworth, a division of Thomson Learning: www.thomsonrights.com. Fax 800 730-2215.

Clustering desks encourages social interaction among students. In contrast, rows of desks reduce social interaction among students and direct students' attention toward the teacher. Arranging desks in rows can benefit students when they are working on individual assignments, whereas clustered desks facilitate cooperative learning. In classrooms in which seats are organized in rows, the teacher is most likely to interact with students seated in the front and center of the classroom (Adams & Biddle, 1970) (see figure 14.3). This area has been called the "action zone" because students in the front and center locations interact the most with the teacher. For example, they most often ask questions and are most likely to initiate discussion. If you use a row arrangement, move around the room when possible, establish eye contact with students seated outside the "action zone," direct comments to students in the peripheral seats, and periodically have students change seats so that all students have an equal opportunity of being in the front and center seats.

Personalizing the Classroom According to classroom management experts Carol Weinstein and Andrew Mignano (2007), classrooms too often resemble motel rooms—pleasant but impersonal, revealing nothing about the people who use the space. Such anonymity is especially true of secondary school classrooms, where six or seven different classes might use the space in a single day. To personalize classrooms, post students' photographs, artwork, written projects, charts that list birthdays (of early childhood and elementary school students), and other positive expressions of students' identities. A bulletin board can be set aside for the "student of the week" or be used to display each student's best work of the week, personally chosen by each student.

None of the classrooms we have described will exactly match yours. However, keeping in mind the basic principles we have described should help you create an optimal classroom arrangement for learning.

Review, Reflect, and Practice

2 Describe the positive design of the classroom's physical environment.

REVIEW

- What are some basic principles of classroom design and arrangement?
- What are some standard styles of arrangement?

REFLECT

- How would you design and arrange your ideal classroom? How would you personalize it?

PRAXIS™ PRACTICE

1. Ms. Craig likes her students to work in small groups. Therefore, she arranges her students' desks in small circles or clusters. What is the problem with this arrangement for whole-class presentations?
   a. Ms. Craig will be unable to see all of her students.
   b. Some students will have to turn their chairs to see.
   c. The classroom will be too congested.
   d. There will be blind spots.
2. Mr. James wants his students to be able to talk to each other as well as to him. What type of classroom arrangement is best suited to his needs?
   a. auditorium style
   b. cluster style
   c. offset style
   d. seminar style

Please see the answer key at the end of the book.

auditorium style A classroom arrangement style in which all students sit facing the teacher.

face-to-face style A classroom arrangement style in which students sit facing each other.

off-set style A classroom arrangement style in which small numbers of students (usually three or four) sit at tables but do not sit directly across from one another.

seminar style A classroom arrangement style in which large numbers of students (ten or more) sit in circular, square, or U-shaped arrangements.

cluster style A classroom arrangement style in which small numbers of students (usually four to eight) work in small, closely bunched groups.

BEST PRACTICES
Strategies for Designing a Classroom Arrangement

Follow these steps in designing a classroom arrangement (Weinstein, 2007; Weinstein & Mignano, 2007):

1. *Consider what activities students will be engaging in.* If you will be teaching kindergarten or elementary school students, you might need to create settings for reading aloud, small-group reading instruction, sharing time, group math instruction, and arts and crafts. A secondary school science teacher might have to accommodate whole-group instruction, "hands-on" lab activities, and media presentations. On the left side of a sheet of paper, list the activities your students will perform. Next to each activity, list any special arrangements that need to be taken into account; for instance, art and science areas need to be near a sink, and computers need to be near an electrical outlet. Next, William Williford, who teaches science at Perry Middle School in Perry, Georgia, provides a recommendation for classroom arrangement.

THROUGH THE EYES OF TEACHERS
Hissing Cockroaches and Mini-Cams

My classroom is set up with tables with about four students per table. This allows for individual or group activities without a lot of transition time or movement. Since my current subject is science, there is an aquarium with fish, a terrarium with a lizard or praying mantis, and a cage with Madagascar hissing cockroaches. There is a table with gadgets and mini-experiments. A mini-cam may be focused on an earthworm or a spider with the image on the TV as students enter the classroom. The idea is to arrange the classroom so that it promotes inquiry, questioning, and thinking about science.

2. *Draw up a floor plan.* Before you actually move any furniture, draw several floor plans and then choose the one that you think will work the best.

3. *Involve students in planning the classroom layout.* You can do most of your environmental planning before school starts, but once it begins, ask students how they like your arrangement. If they suggest improvements that are reasonable, try them out. Students often report that they want adequate room and a place of their own where they can keep their things.

4. *Try out the arrangement and be flexible in redesigning it.* Several weeks into the school year, evaluate how effective your arrangement is. Be alert for problems that the arrangement might be generating. For example, one study found that when kindergarten students crowded around a teacher who was reading a story to them, they often misbehaved (Krantz & Risley, 1972). Just spreading the children apart in a semicircle significantly decreased the misbehaviors.

THROUGH THE EYES OF TEACHERS
Classroom Arrangement Tips

Here are some additional tips from teachers:

- Make areas of the classroom well defined.
- Arrange good traffic flow and storage.
- Safe, clean furniture is a must.
- It can be refreshing to rearrange the classroom during the year. Looking at the environment from a different angle puts a new perspective on people and things.
- Materials should be kept in the same places throughout the school year.
- A classroom should be bright and colorful with lots of materials and school memorabilia for students to read and look at.
- "My desk is always at the rear of the classroom. I keep a podium in one corner of the front and teach from there most of the time." (High school teacher)
- "My desk is in an open space that is easily accessible to students." (Middle school teacher)
- "I never stand in front of the classroom and speak. I constantly walk around the class, making contact with each and every student. I always make sure I am on the child's eye level when asking a question. Sometimes we sit in a circle so that I can be on their level." (Early childhood teacher)
- "I have one area where everyone can sit in one group for class lessons. I also like smaller areas where small groups can meet. Having students move about from one area to another gives students a chance to stretch. Small areas can also be set up to encourage learning about a specific subject area." (Special education high school teacher)
- See what other teachers do.
- Locate computers where they will not distract other students.

(3) CREATING A POSITIVE ENVIRONMENT FOR LEARNING

| General Strategies | Creating, Teaching, and Maintaining Rules and Procedures | Getting Students to Cooperate |

Students need a positive environment for learning. We will discuss some general classroom management strategies for providing this environment, ways to effectively establish and maintain rules, and positive strategies for getting students to cooperate.

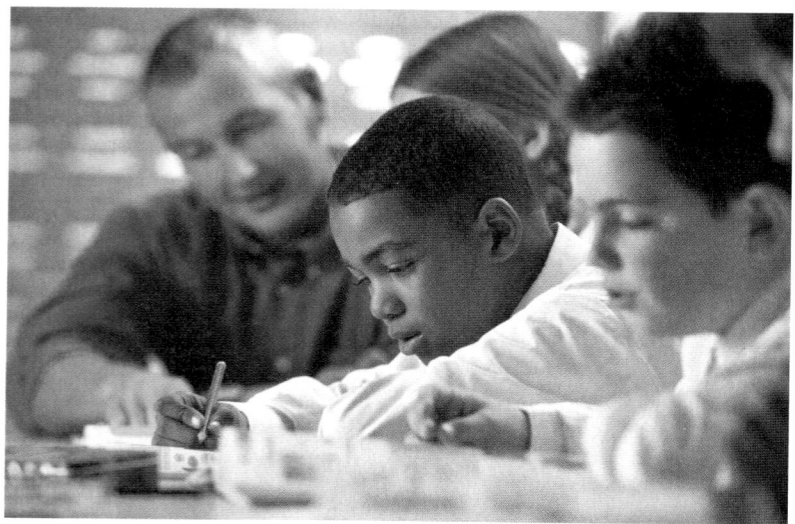

What characterizes an authoritative teaching style?

General Strategies

General strategies include using an authoritative style and effectively managing classroom activities.

The **authoritative classroom management style** is derived from Diana Baumrind's (1971, 1996) parenting styles, which were discussed in chapter 3, "Social Contexts and Socioemotional Development." Like authoritative parents, authoritative teachers have students who tend to be self-reliant, delay gratification, get along well with their peers, and show high self-esteem. An authoritative strategy of classroom management encourages students to be independent thinkers and doers but still involves effective monitoring. Authoritative teachers engage students in considerable verbal give-and-take and show a caring attitude toward them. However, they still declare limits when necessary. Authoritative teachers clarify rules and regulations, establishing these standards with input from students.

The authoritative style contrasts with two ineffective strategies: authoritarian and permissive. The **authoritarian classroom management style** is restrictive and punitive. The focus is mainly on keeping order in the classroom rather than on instruction and learning. Authoritarian teachers place firm limits and controls on students and have little verbal exchange with them. Students in authoritarian classrooms tend to be passive learners, fail to initiate activities, express anxiety about social comparison, and have poor communication skills. The **permissive classroom management style** offers students considerable autonomy but provides them with little support for developing learning skills or managing their behavior. Not surprisingly, students in permissive classrooms tend to have inadequate academic skills and low self-control.

Overall, an authoritative style will benefit your students more than authoritarian or permissive styles. An authoritative style will help your students become active, self-regulated learners.

We described some aspects of Jacob Kounin's (1970) work on classroom management earlier in the chapter. Kounin concluded that effective teachers differ from ineffective teachers not in the way they respond to students' misbehaviors but, instead, in how competently they manage the group's activities. Next we focus on some of the differences between effective and ineffective classroom group managers.

Creating, Teaching, and Maintaining Rules and Procedures

To function smoothly, classrooms need clearly defined rules and procedures. Students need to know specifically how you want them to behave. Without clearly defined classroom rules and procedures, the inevitable misunderstandings can breed chaos. For example, consider these procedures or routines: When students enter the classroom, are they supposed to go directly to their seats or may they socialize for a few minutes

authoritative classroom management style A management style that encourages students to be independent thinkers and doers but still provides effective monitoring. Authoritative teachers engage students in considerable verbal give-and-take and show a caring attitude toward them. However, they still set limits when necessary.

authoritarian classroom management style A management style that is restrictive and punitive, with the focus mainly on keeping order in the classroom rather than instruction or learning.

permissive classroom management style A management style that allows students considerable autonomy but provides them with little support for developing learning skills or managing their behavior.

BEST PRACTICES
Strategies for Being an Effective Classroom Manager

Effective classroom managers:

1. *Show how they are "with it."* Kounin used the term **withitness** to describe a management strategy in which teachers show students that they are aware of what is happening. These teachers closely monitor students on a regular basis. This allows them to detect inappropriate behavior early before it gets out of hand. Teachers who are not "with it" are likely to not notice such misbehaviors until they gain momentum and spread.

2. *Cope effectively with overlapping situations.* Kounin observed that some teachers seem to have one-track minds, dealing with only one thing at a time. This ineffective strategy often led to frequent interruptions in the flow of the class. For example, one teacher was working with a reading group when she observed two boys on the other side of the room hitting each other. She immediately got up, went over to the other side of the room, harshly criticized them, and then returned to the reading group. However, by the time she returned to the reading group, the students in the reading group had become bored and were starting to misbehave themselves. In contrast, effective managers were able to deal with overlapping situations in less disruptive ways. For example, in the reading group situation, they quickly responded to students from outside the group who came to ask questions but not in a way that significantly altered the flow of the reading group's activity. When moving around the room and checking each student's seatwork, they kept a roving eye on the rest of the class.

3. *Maintain smoothness and continuity in lessons.* Effective managers keep the flow of a lesson moving smoothly, maintaining students' interest and not giving them opportunities to be easily distracted. Earlier in the chapter, we mentioned some ineffective practices of teachers that can disrupt the flow of a lesson, including flip-flopping and overdwelling. Another teacher action that disrupts the lesson's flow is called "fragmentation," in which the teacher breaks an activity into components even though the activity could be performed as an entire unit. For example, a teacher might individually ask six students to do something, such as get out their art supplies, when all six could be asked to do this as a group.

4. *Engage students in a variety of challenging activities.* Kounin also found that effective classroom managers engage students in a variety of challenging but not overly hard activities. The students frequently worked independently rather than being directly supervised by a teacher who hovered over them. Next, Mark Fodness, an award-wining seventh-grade social studies teacher in Bemidji, Minnesota, gives this advice on managing the classroom.

THROUGH THE EYES OF TEACHERS
Great Teachers Have Few Discipline Problems

The single best method of decreasing undesirable behaviors among students is by increasing the effectiveness of teaching methods. The best teachers have very few discipline problems, not because they are great disciplinarians, but because they are great teachers. To emphasize this point with one of my student teachers, I had her follow our class out the door and into their next classes. She later returned, amazed at what she had seen. Students who she had thought were very well behaved had been off-task or disruptive in other classrooms. In one room, where a substitute teacher was doing his best to fill in, she described students' behavior as "shocking." Yet in another class, where the teacher was presenting a riveting lesson on a novel, the same students once again were well behaved even though the teacher did not seem to be using any specific discipline strategy.

Many first-year teachers, and veterans alike, identify discipline as their number one teaching challenge. However, the best solution is to use exemplary teaching strategies. I asked my seventh-grade students to identify the characteristics of teachers who had well-behaved classes. Here is a sample of their responses: well-prepared, interesting, funny, organized, fair, caring, nice, and energetic.

until you tell them to be seated? When students want to go to the library, do they need a pass? When students are working at their seats, may they help each other or are they required to work individually?

Both rules and procedures are stated expectations about behavior (Evertson, Emmer, & Worsham, 2006). *Rules* focus on general or specific expectations or standards for behavior. An example of a general rule is "Respect other persons." An example of a more specific rule is "Cell phones must always be turned off when you are in this classroom." *Procedures,* or routines, also communicate expectations about behavior, but they usually are applied to a specific activity, and "they are directed at

withitness A management style described by Kounin in which teachers show students that they are aware of what is happening. Such teachers closely monitor students on a regular basis and detect inappropriate behavior early before it gets out of hand.

accomplishing something rather than prohibiting some behavior or defining a general standard" (Evertson, Emmer, & Worsham, 2006, p. 22). You might establish procedures for collecting homework assignments, turning in work late, using the pencil sharpener, or using equipment. You can develop procedures for beginning the day (for example, a procedure for "settling in" to the classroom—maybe a social item such as a riddle or brief note about school events), leaving the room (for example, to go to the bathroom), returning to the room (such as after lunchtime), and ending the day (for example, clearing off desks and leaving on time).

Rules tend not to change because they address fundamental ways we deal with others, ourselves, and our work, such as having respect for others and their property, and keeping our hands and our feet to ourselves. On the other hand, procedures may change because routines and activities in classrooms change.

Teaching Rules and Procedures What is the best way to get students to learn about rules and procedures? Should the teacher make the rules and procedures, then inform the class about them? Should students be allowed to participate in generating rules and procedures?

Some teachers like to include students in setting rules in the hope that this will encourage them to take more responsibility for their own behavior (Emmer, Evertson, & Worsham, 2006). Student involvement can take many different forms, including a discussion of the reason for having rules and the meaning of particular rules. The teacher might begin by having students discuss why rules are needed and then move on to a number of individual rules. The teacher can clarify the rule by describing, or asking students to describe, the general area of behavior it involves. Students usually can contribute concrete examples of the rule.

Some teachers start off with a whole-class discussion of classroom rules. During the discussion, the teacher and the students suggest possible rules for the classroom and the teacher records these on an overhead projector, a chalk-board, or a large piece of chart paper. Then, the teacher and students arrange them into broad categories and develop titles for the categories. In some classrooms, this activity is followed by having students role-play each of the rules.

What are some good strategies for establishing rules and procedures?

BEST PRACTICES
Strategies for Establishing Classroom Rules and Procedures

Here are four principles to keep in mind when you establish rules and procedures for your classroom (Weinstein, 2003, pp. 53–56):

1. *Rules and procedures should be reasonable and necessary.* Ask yourself if the rules and procedures you are establishing are appropriate for this grade level. Also ask yourself if there is a good reason for the rule or procedure. For example, one secondary school teacher has a rule that students must come to class on time. Students are clearly told that if they are late, they will get a detention even on the first violation. She explains the rule to the students at the beginning of the school year and tells them the reason for the rule: If they are late, they might miss important material.

2. *Rules and procedures should be clear and comprehensible.* If you have general rules, make sure that you clearly specify what they mean. For example, one teacher has the rule "Be prepared." Instead of leaving the rule at this general level, the teacher specifies what it means to be prepared and describes specific procedures involving the rule: having your homework, notebook, pen or pencil, and textbook with you every day.

   As mentioned earlier, one issue that crops up when establishing classroom rules is whether to let students participate in making them. Involving students in generating classroom rules can increase students' sense of responsibility to abide by them, especially in secondary schools. Some students will suggest ridiculous rules, which you can simply veto. Some teachers will establish general rules and then ask students to generate specific examples of the rules.

3. *Rules and procedures should be consistent with instructional and learning goals.* Make sure that rules and procedures do not interfere with learning. Some teachers become so concerned about having an orderly, quiet classroom that they restrict students from interacting with each other and from engaging in collaborative learning activities.

4. *Classroom rules should be consistent with school rules.* Know what the school's rules are, such as whether particular behaviors are required in the halls, in the cafeteria, and so on. Many schools have a handbook that spells out what is acceptable and what is not. Familiarize yourself with the handbook. Some teachers go over the handbook with students at the beginning of the school year so that students clearly understand the school's rules regarding absenteeism, truancy, fighting, smoking, substance abuse, abusive language, and so on.

In some schools, students are allowed to participate in setting rules for the entire school. In some cases, student representatives from each room or grade level participate in generating school-wide rules with guidance from teachers and school administrators. However, within individual classrooms, especially in elementary schools, it is uncommon for students to participate in creating rules. Most teachers prefer to create and present their rules, although as indicated earlier, they may encourage discussion of the rules. In secondary schools, especially high schools, greater student contribution to rule setting is possible because of their more-advanced cognitive and socioemotional knowledge and skills.

Many effective classroom teachers clearly present their rules to students and give explanations and examples of them. Teachers who set reasonable rules, provide understandable rationales for them, and enforce them consistently usually find that the majority of the class will abide by them.

Getting Students to Cooperate

You want your students to cooperate with you and abide by classroom rules without always having to resort to discipline to maintain order. How can you get your students to cooperate? There are three main strategies: Develop a positive relationship with students, get students to share and assume responsibility, and reward appropriate behavior.

Develop a Positive Relationship with Students   When most of us think of our favorite teacher, we think of someone who cared about whether or not we learned. Showing that you genuinely care about students as individuals apart from their academic work helps to gain their cooperation (Pianta, 2006). It is easy to get caught up in the pressing demands of academic achievement and classroom business and ignore the socioemotional needs of students.

One study found that in addition to having effective rules and procedures, successful classroom managers also showed a caring attitude toward students (Emmer, Evertson, & Anderson, 1980). This caring was evidenced in part by a classroom environment in which students felt safe and secure and were treated fairly. The teachers were sensitive to their needs and anxieties (for example, they created enjoyable activities the first several days of the school year rather than giving them diagnostic tests) and had good communication skills (including listening skills), and they effectively expressed their feelings to students. The classroom atmosphere was relaxed and pleasant. For example, the focus was on academic work but teachers gave students breaks and allowed them free time to read, use the computer, or draw.

The Child Development Project (CDP) is a comprehensive elementary school program in which teachers and administrators build supportive relationships with students and encourage students to develop similarly warm relationships with each other (Battistich & Solomon, 1995). Five instructional practices form the core of this project: (1) cooperative learning activities that facilitate teamwork; (2) a literature-based, values-rich, multicultural language arts program that encourages students to think critically about relevant social and ethical issues; (3) classroom management techniques that emphasize prevention and responsibility; (4) classroom and school-wide community-building projects that involve students, teachers, parents, and extended family members; and (5) "homeside" activities that improve communication between students and parents, build bridges between schools and families, and encourage students' understanding of their family's heritage. Research evaluations of CDP in a large number of geographically diverse elementary schools revealed that students who participated in the project were more cooperative, had better social understanding, possessed more positive values, were more likely to help others, and had better conflict resolution skills than their counterparts who did not participate in the project (Battistich & others, 1989). Figure 14.4 presents some teaching guidelines for developing a positive relationship with students.

Get Students to Share and Assume Responsibility Earlier in this chapter, we discussed the importance of developing an authoritative atmosphere in the classroom and the issue of whether students should be allowed to participate in establishing class rules. Some experts on classroom management argue that sharing responsibility with students for making classroom decisions increases the students' commitment to the decisions (Blumenfeld, Kempler & Krajcik, 2006; Eggleton, 2001; Lewis, 2001; Risley & Walther, 1995).

Reward Appropriate Behavior We have discussed rewards extensively in chapter 7, "Behavioral and Social Cognitive Approaches." You might want to read the discussion of rewards in that chapter again, especially the section "Applied Behavior Analysis in Education," and think about how rewards can be used in effectively managing the classroom. The discussion of rewards in chapter 13, "Motivation, Teaching, and Learning," also is relevant to classroom management, especially the information about rewards and intrinsic motivation. Following are some guidelines for using rewards in managing the classroom.

1. Give a student a friendly "hello" at the door.
2. Have a brief one-on-one conversation about things that are happening in the student's life.
3. Write a brief note of encouragement to the student.
4. Use students' names in class more.
5. Show enthusiasm about being with students (even late in the day, week, or year).
6. Risk more personal self-disclosures, which help students see you as a real person. However, don't cross the line and go too far. Always take into account children's level of understanding and emotional vulnerability in disclosing information about yourself to them.
7. Be an active listener who carefully attends to what the student is saying, even if it is something trivial.
8. Let students know that you are there to support and help them.
9. Keep in mind that developing positive, trusting relationships takes time. This especially is the case for students from high-risk environments who might not initially trust your motives.

FIGURE 14.4 Guidelines for Establishing Positive Relationships with Students

BEST PRACTICES
Strategies for Guiding Students to Share and Assume Responsibility

Here are some guidelines for getting students to share and assume responsibility in the classroom (Fitzpatrick, 1993):

1. *Involve students in the planning and implementation of school and classroom initiatives.* This participation helps to satisfy students' needs for self-confidence and belonging.

2. *Encourage students to judge their own behavior.* Rather than pass judgment on students' behavior, ask questions that motivate students to evaluate their own behavior. For example, you might ask, "Does your behavior reflect the class rules?" or "What's the rule?" Such questions place responsibility on the student. Initially, some students try to blame others or change the subject. In such situations, stay focused and guide the student toward accepting responsibility.

3. *Don't accept excuses.* Excuses just pass on or avoid responsibility. Don't even entertain a discussion about excuses. Rather, ask students what they can do the next time a similar situation develops.

4. *Give the self-responsibility strategy time to work.* Students don't develop responsibility overnight. Many student misbehaviors are ingrained habits that take a long time to break. One strategy is to be patient one more time than the student expects—difficult to do, but good advice.

5. *Let students participate in decision making by holding class meetings.* In his book *Schools Without Failure,* William Glasser (1969) argued that class meetings can be used to deal with student behavior problems or virtually any issue that is of concern to teachers and students.

Choose Effective Reinforcers Find out which reinforcers work best with which students and individualize reinforcement. For one student, the most effective reward might be praise; for another, it might be getting to do a favorite activity. Remember that pleasurable activities often are especially valuable in gaining students' cooperation. You might tell a student, "When you complete your math problems, you can go to the media area and play a computer game."

Use Prompts and Shaping Effectively Remember that if you wait for students to perform perfectly, they might never do so. A good strategy is to use prompts and

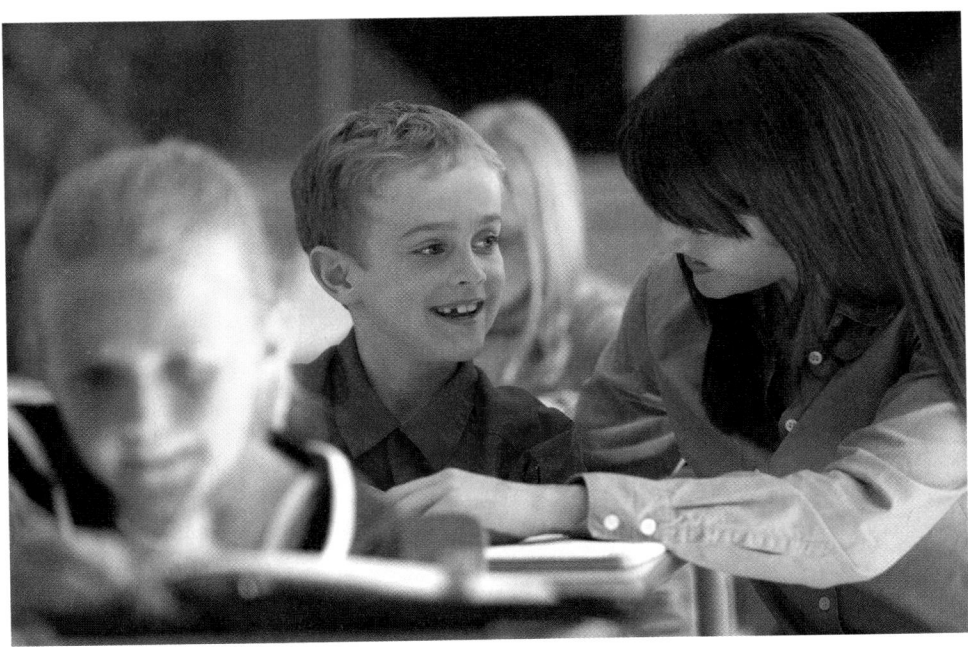

What are some guidelines for the effective use of rewards in the classroom?

shape students' behavior by rewarding improvement. Some prompts come in the form of hints or reminders, such as "Remember the rule about lining up." Recall from chapter 7 that shaping involves rewarding a student for successive approximations to a specified target behavior. Thus, you might initially reward a student for getting 60 percent of her math problems right, then for 70 percent the next time, and so on.

Use Rewards to Provide Information about Mastery, Not to Control Students' Behavior Rewards that impart information about students' mastery can increase their intrinsic motivation and sense of responsibility. However, rewards that are used to control students' behavior are less likely to promote self-regulation and responsibility. For example, a student's learning might benefit from the student being selected as student of the week because the student engaged in a number of highly productive, competent activities. However, the student likely will not benefit from being given a reward for sitting still at a desk; such a reward is an effort by the teacher to control the student, and students in heavily controlled learning environments tend to act like "pawns."

Review, Reflect, and Practice

③ Discuss how to create a positive classroom environment.

REVIEW

- What are some general strategies for creating a positive environment for learning?
- What are some hallmarks of good classroom rules?
- What are the best approaches in getting students to cooperate?

REFLECT

- In your classroom, what standards of "good" behavior would be nonnegotiable? Would you be flexible about some things? Explain.

PRAXIS™ PRACTICE

1. Ms. Rockefeller has high expectations for her students' behavior. She is rather harsh with punishments when they do not live up to these expectations and accepts no explanations for noncompliance. Her standard response to excuses is, "I don't want to hear it. You broke the rules. You know the consequences." Which management style does Ms. Rockefeller exemplify?
   a. authoritative
   b. authoritarian
   c. permissive
   d. neglectful

2. Which of the following is the best example of a clearly stated classroom procedure?
   a. Keep your hands to yourself.
   b. Put all homework in the homework folder when you come in.
   c. Respect other people's property.
   d. Stay in your seat unless you have permission to get up.

3. Which teacher is most likely to gain the cooperation of students in following classroom rules and procedures?
   a. Ms. Benes and her students developed a list of rules and procedures at the beginning of the school year; however, she does not enforce the rules and procedures she has established. There are no reinforcements for proper behavior and no consequences for inappropriate behavior.

    b. Ms. Costanza wants her classroom to be very orderly. As a result, she punishes students for the slightest infractions.

    c. Ms. Kramer's students participated in the development of classroom rules. They all agreed that each rule was necessary and that the procedures would make things run more smoothly. When students disobey a rule, she asks them if their behavior is appropriate.

    d. Ms. Peterman has a long list of rules and procedures for students to follow. For instance, when they come in the classroom, they are to first put their homework in the proper folder, then change into their P.E. shoes. If students do these things in the opposite order, they are reprimanded.

Please see the answer key at the end of the book.

Managing classrooms and constructively resolving conflicts require good communication skills. Three key aspects of communication are speaking skills, listening skills, and nonverbal communication.

Speaking Skills

You and your students will benefit considerably if you have effective speaking skills and you work with your students on developing their speaking skills. Let's first explore some strategies for speaking with your class.

Speaking with the Class and Students   In speaking with your class and students, one of the most important things to keep in mind is to clearly communicate information (Brydon & Scott, 2006; Gregory, 2005; Sellnow, 2005). *Clarity* in speaking is essential to good teaching.

    Some good strategies for speaking clearly with your class include (Florez, 1999):

1. Using grammar correctly
2. Selecting vocabulary that is understandable and appropriate for the level of your students
3. Applying strategies to improve students' ability to understand what you are saying, such as emphasizing key words, rephrasing, or monitoring students' comprehension
4. Speaking at an appropriate pace, neither too rapidly nor too slowly
5. Being precise in your communication and avoiding being vague
6. Using good planning and logical thinking skills as underpinnings of speaking clearly with your class

"You" and "I" Messages   Let's examine another aspect of verbal communication. How often have you been involved in a conversation in which someone says something like this: "Why are you being so negative?" or "You did not do what you said you were going to do," or "You are not very considerate." These are examples of what communication experts call using **"you" messages,** an undesirable style in which speakers appear to judge people and place them in a defensive position. "You" communication does not always literally include the word *you*. "You" is implied when someone says, "That was a really stupid thing to say" (which means "What you said was really stupid") or "Stay out of my life" (which means "You are intruding in my life").

It is easy for you and your students to fall into the trap of using too many "you" messages and not enough "I" messages, which are less provocative. **"I" messages** reflect the speaker's true feelings better than judgmental "you" statements.

Communication experts recommend replacing "you" messages with "I" messages: "I'm angry that this has gotten so negative," or "I don't like it when promises get broken," or "I'm hurt when my feelings aren't taken into account."

"You" messages bog down conversation with judgments of the other person (Stewart, 2006; Wood, 2006). "I" messages help to move the conversation in a more constructive direction by expressing your feelings without judging the other person. Monitor your own conversation from time to time to make sure you are using "I" messages rather than "you" messages. Also monitor your students' conversations and guide them toward using more "I" messages.

Being Assertive Another aspect of verbal communication involves how people deal with conflict, which can be done in four styles: aggressive, manipulative, passive, or assertive. People who use an **aggressive style** run roughshod over others. They demand, are abrasive, and act in hostile ways. Aggressive individuals are often insensitive to others' rights and feelings. People who use a **manipulative style** try to get what they want by making people feel guilty or sorry for them. Rather than take responsibility for meeting their own needs, they play the role of the victim or the martyr to get people to do things for them. People who use a **passive style** are nonassertive and submissive. They let others run roughshod over them. Passive individuals don't express their feelings and don't let others know what they want.

In contrast, people with an **assertive style** express their feelings, ask for what they want, and say "no" to things they don't want. When people act assertively, they act in their own best interests. They stand up for their legitimate rights and express their views openly. Assertive individuals insist that misbehavior be corrected, and they resist being coerced or manipulated (Dobkin & Pace, 2006; Evertson, Emmer, & Worsham, 2006; Lumsden & Lumsden, 2006). In the view of assertiveness experts Robert Alberti and Michael Emmons (2001), assertiveness builds positive, constructive relationships.

Of the four styles of dealing with conflict, acting assertively is by far the best choice. Here are some strategies for becoming a more assertive individual (Bourne, 1995):

- *Evaluate your rights.* Determine your rights in the situation at hand. For example, you have the right to make mistakes and to change your mind.
- *State the problem to the person involved in terms of its consequences for you.* Clearly outline your point of view, even if it seems obvious to you. This allows the other person to get a better sense of your position. Describe the problem as objectively as you can without blaming or judging. For example, you might tell a student, "I'm having a problem with your humming in class. It is bothering me, so please don't do it anymore." "When you come in late, it disrupts the class and you miss important information." "Saying that to another student hurts his feelings."
- *Express your feelings about the particular situation.* When you express your feelings, even others who completely disagree with you can tell how strongly you feel about the situation. Remember to use "I" messages rather than "you" messages.
- *Make your request.* This is an important aspect of being assertive. Simply ask for what you want (or don't want) in a straightforward manner.

Here are some guidelines for making assertive requests:

- *Use assertive nonverbal behavior.* For example, establish eye contact, square your shoulders, remain calm, and be self-confident.

"you" messages Undesirable messages in which speakers appear to judge people and place them in a defensive position.

"I" messages Desirable messages that reflect the speaker's true feelings better than judgmental "you" messages.

aggressive style A way of dealing with conflict in which people run roughshod over others in demanding, abrasive, and hostile ways.

manipulative style A way of dealing with conflict in which people try to get what they want by making others feel guilty or sorry for them.

passive style A way of dealing with conflict in which people are nonassertive and submissive and don't let others know what they want.

assertive style A way of dealing with conflict in which people express their feelings, ask for what they want, say "no" to things they don't want, and act in their own best interests.

- *Keep your request simple.* One or two easy-to-understand sentences is adequate. For example, you might tell a student, "We need to go to the principal to get this straightened out."
- *Avoid asking for more than one thing at a time.* For example, don't ask the principal for a new computer and a new projector.
- *Don't apologize for your request.* Request directly, as in "I want you to . . ." Don't say "I know this is an imposition on you, but . . ." What if the other person responds with criticism, tries to make you feel guilty, or makes sarcastic remarks? Simply repeat your assertive request directly, strongly, and confidently.
- *Describe the benefits of your request.* Describing the benefits of cooperating with the request can be an honest offer of mutual give-and-take rather than manipulation. If you feel that you are too aggressive, manipulative, or passive, work on being more assertive. An excellent book to read that can help you become more assertive is *Your Perfect Right,* by Robert Alberti and Michal Emmons (2001). When you are assertive and you help your students become more assertive rather than aggressive, manipulative, or passive, your class will run more smoothly.

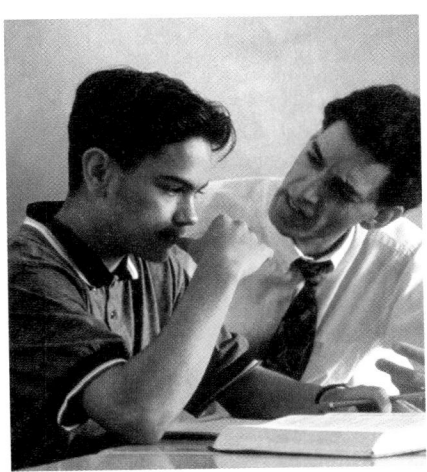

What are some barriers to effective verbal communication?

Barriers to Effective Verbal Communication   Barriers to effective verbal communication include (Gordon, 1970):

- *Criticizing.* Harsh, negative evaluations of another person generally reduce communication. An example of criticizing is telling a student, "It's your fault you flunked the test; you should have studied." Instead of criticizing, you can ask students to evaluate why they did not do well on a test and try to get them to arrive at an attribution that reflects lack of effort as the reason for the poor grade.
- *Name-calling and labeling.* These are ways of putting down the other person. Students engage in a lot of name-calling and labeling. They might say to another student, "You are a loser," or "You are stupid." Monitor students' use of such name-calling and labeling. When you hear this type of statement, intervene and talk with them about considering other students' feelings.
- *Advising.* Advising is talking down to others while giving them a solution to a problem. For example, a teacher might say, "That's so easy to solve. I can't understand why . . ."
- *Ordering.* Commanding another person to do what you want is often not effective because it creates resistance. For example, a teacher might yell at a student, "Clean up this space, right now!" Instead, a calm, firm reminder such as "Remember the rule of cleaning things up when we are finished" works better.
- *Threatening.* Threats are intended to control the other person by verbal force. For example, a teacher might say, "If you don't listen to me, I'm going to make your life miserable here." A better strategy is to approach the student more calmly and talk with the student about listening better.
- *Moralizing.* This means preaching to the other person about what he or she should do. For example, a teacher might say, "You know you should have turned your homework in on time. You ought to feel bad about this." Moralizing increases students' guilt and anxiety. A better strategy in this case is not to use words such as *should* and *ought* but, instead, to talk with the student in a less condemning way about why the homework was not turned in on time.

Giving an Effective Speech   Not only will you be speaking in your class every day to your students in both formal and informal ways, but you also will have opportunities to give talks at educational and community meetings. Knowing some good strategies for giving a speech can significantly reduce your anxiety and help you deliver an effective speech (Verderber & Verderber, 2006).

Also, as most of us reflect on our experiences as students, we can remember few opportunities to give talks in class unless we took a specific class in speech. But not

THROUGH THE EYES OF STUDENTS

Forensics Teacher Tommie Lindsey's Students

Tommie Lindsey teaches competitive forensics (public speaking and debate) at Logan High School in Union City, California. Forensics classes in most U.S. schools are mainly in affluent areas, but most of Lindsey's students come from impoverished or at-risk backgrounds. His students have won many public speaking honors.

The following comments by his students reflect Lindsey's outstanding teaching skills:

> He's one of the few teachers I know who cares so much. . . . He spends hours and hours, evenings, and weekends, working with us.
>
> —Justin Hinojoza, 17

> I was going through a tough time. . . . Mr. Lindsey helped me out. I asked how I could pay back and and he said, "Just help someone the way I helped you."
>
> —Robert Hawkins, 21

> This amazing opportunity is here for us students and it wouldn't be if Mr. Lindsey didn't create it.
>
> —Michael Joshi, 17

As a ninth-grade student, Tommie Lindsey became a public speaker. He says that his English teacher doubted his ability, and he wanted to show her how good he could be at public speaking, preparing a speech that received a standing ovation. Lindsey remembers, "She was expecting me to fail, and I turned the tables on her. . . . And we do that with our forensic program. When we started, a lot of people didn't believe our kids could do the things they do."

For his outstanding teaching efforts, Tommie Lindsey was awarded a prestigious McArthur Fellowship in 2005. (Source: Seligson, 2005.)

Tommie Lindsey, working with his students on improving their public speaking and debate skills.

only can students be given speaking opportunities through formal presentations, but they also can participate in panel discussions and debates. All these activities give students opportunities to improve their speaking, organizational, and thinking skills.

Here are some guidelines for delivering a speech, which can benefit students as well as teachers (Alverno College, 1995):

- *Connect with the audience.* Talk directly to the audience; don't just read your notes or recite a memorized script.
- *State your purpose.* Keep this focus throughout the talk.
- *Effectively deliver the speech.* Use eye contact, supportive gestures, and effective voice control.
- *Follow appropriate conventions.* This includes using correct grammar.
- *Effectively organize the speech.* Include an introduction, a main body, and a conclusion.
- *Include evidence that supports and develops your ideas.*
- *Use media effectively.* This can help the audience grasp key ideas and varies the pace of the talk.

People often list fear of public speaking as their single greatest fear. If we give students more opportunities to practice public speaking, this fear likely would diminish. To help your students overcome this fear, give them plenty of opportunities to talk in front of a group and provide them with supportive advice (Santrock & Halonen, 2006). When they prepare for their talk, get them to rehearse the talk a number of times until they are confident they know the material. Tell them that most people fear talking in front of groups but that once they do it, their fear subsides. And get them to imagine how successful their talks are going to be.

Working with students on their speaking skills provides an excellent opportunity to invite someone from the community to come talk with your class. If a local college or university has a communications department, contact the department and ask one of the faculty to talk with your students about speaking skills or other aspects of communication. You also might have heard someone give a speech that you thought was outstanding; you might invite the speaker to come to your class and give students tips on how to give a great talk.

Listening Skills

Effectively managing your classroom will be easier if you and your students have good listening skills. Listening is a critical skill for making and keeping relationships (Pearson & others, 2006; Tubbs & Moss, 2006). If you are a good listener, students, parents, other teachers, and administrators will be drawn to you. If your students are good listeners, they will benefit more from your instruction and will have better social relationships. Poor listeners "hog" conversations. They talk "to" rather than "with" someone. Good listeners actively listen. They don't just passively absorb information. **Active listening** means giving full attention to the speaker, focusing on both the intellectual and the emotional content of the message.

The following are some good strategies for developing active listening skills (Santrock & Halonen, 2006). Incorporate these skills into your style of interacting with students and work with students to help them develop these skills:

- *Pay careful attention to the person who is talking.* This shows the person that you are interested in what he or she is saying. Maintain good eye contact and lean forward slightly when another person is speaking to you.

- *Paraphrase.* State in your own words what the other person has just said. You can start your paraphrase with words such as "Let me see, what I hear you saying is . . ." or "Do you mean . . . ?" Use paraphrasing when someone says something that is important.

- *Synthesize themes and patterns.* The conversation landscape can become strewn with bits and pieces of information that are not tied together in meaningful ways. A good active listener puts together a summary of the main themes and feelings the speaker has expressed over a reasonably long conversation. These sentence stems can help you and your students get started in synthesizing the themes of a conversation: "One theme you keep coming back to is . . ." and "Let's go over what we have been covering so far. . . ."

- *Give feedback in a competent manner.* Verbal or nonverbal feedback gives the speaker an idea of how much progress the speaker is making in getting a point across. Good listeners give feedback quickly, honestly, clearly, and informatively.

Giving students opportunities to practice their speaking skills is a vastly underutilized aspect of elementary and secondary education. Fear of speaking in front of a group is consistently listed as the number one fear of adults. *How do you think you can help your students become more effective speakers?*

Nonverbal Communication

In addition to what you say, you also communicate by how you fold your arms, cast your eyes, move your mouth, cross your legs, or touch another person. Here are some examples of some common behaviors by which individuals communicate nonverbally:

- Lift an eyebrow in disbelief.
- Clasp their arms to isolate or protect themselves.
- Shrug their shoulders when they are indifferent.
- Wink one eye to show warmth and approval.
- Tap their fingers when they are impatient.
- Slap their forehead when they forget something.

Indeed, many communication experts maintain that most interpersonal communication is nonverbal. Even a person sitting in a corner, silently reading, is nonverbally

active listening A listening style that gives full attention to the speaker and notes both the intellectual and emotional content of the message.

PEANUTS © United Features Syndicates, Inc.

communicating something, perhaps that he or she wants to be left alone. And when you notice your students blankly staring out the window, it likely indicates that they are bored. It is hard to mask nonverbal communication. Recognize that it can tell you how you and others really feel.

Facial Expressions and Eye Communication People's faces disclose emotions and telegraph what really matters to them (Lumsden & Lumsden, 2006; Pearson & others, 2006). A smile, a frown, a puzzled look all communicate. Most Americans use more eye contact the more they like the other person. They avoid eye contact with people they dislike. However, ethnic variations in eye contact exist, with African Americans, Latinos, and Native Americans avoiding eye contact more than Anglo-Americans. In general, smiling and maintaining eye contact with your students indicates that you like them.

Touch Touch can be a powerful form of communication. Touch especially can be used when consoling someone who has undergone a stressful or unfortunate experience. For example, if a student's parent has become seriously ill or died, a student's parents have recently divorced, or a student has lost a pet, gently touching the student's hand while consoling the student can add warmth to the communication. Because of concerns about sexual harassment and potential lawsuits, many teachers have refrained from touching students at all. Tiffany Field (1995), director of the Touch Research Institute at the University of Miami in Florida, and a leading expert in developmental psychology, believes that teachers should use touch appropriately and courteously in their interaction with students.

Space Each of us has a personal space that at times we don't want others to invade. Not surprisingly, given the crowdedness of the classroom, students report that having their own space where they can put their materials and belongings is important to them. Make sure that all students have their own desks or spaces. Tell students that they are entitled to have this individual space, and that they should courteously respect other students' space.

Silence In our fast-paced, modern culture we often act as if there is something wrong with anyone who remains silent for more than a second or two after something is said to them. In chapter 10, we indicated that after asking a question of students,

How would you describe the nonverbal behaviors of the teachers and the students in these two photographs?

SELF-ASSESSMENT 14.1

Evaluating My Communication Skills

Good communication skills are critical for effectively managing a classroom. Read each of the statements and rate them on a scale from 1 (very much unlike me) to 5 (very much like me).

1. I know the characteristics of being a good speaker in class and with students.
2. I am good at public speaking.
3. I do not tend to dominate conversations.
4. I talk "with" people, not "to" people.
5. I don't criticize people very much.
6. I don't talk down to people or put them down.
7. I don't moralize when I talk with people.
8. I use "I" messages rather than "you" messages.
9. I do not have an aggressive style.
10. I do not have a manipulative style.
11. I do not have a passive style.
12. I do have an assertive style.
13. I'm good at giving my full attention to someone when they are talking with me.
14. I maintain eye contact when I talk with people.
15. I smile a lot when I interact with people.
16. I know the value of silence in communication and how to practice it effectively.

1	2	3	4	5

Scoring and Interpretation

Look over your self-ratings. For any items on which you did not give yourself a 4 or 5, work on improving these aspects of your communication skills. Both you and your students will benefit.

many teachers rarely remain silent long enough for students to think reflectively before giving an answer.

By being silent, a good listener can

- Observe the speaker's eyes, facial expressions, posture, and gestures for communication.
- Think about what the other person is communicating.
- Wonder what the other person is feeling.
- Consider what the most appropriate response is.

Of course, silence can be overdone and is sometimes inappropriate. It is rarely wise to listen for an excessive length of time without making some verbal response. Interpersonal communication should be a dialogue, not a monologue.

We have discussed a number of communication skills that will help you manage your classroom effectively. To evaluate your communication skills, complete Self-Assessment 14.1.

Review, Reflect, and Practice

④ Identify some good approaches to communication for both students and teachers.

REVIEW

- What are some barriers to effective speech? What are some principles of good speech?
- What is active listening and what can teachers and students do to develop active listening skills?
- What are some important aspects of nonverbal communication for teachers to understand?

REFLECT

- What are your own communication strengths and weaknesses? What might you do to improve them?

PRAXIS™ PRACTICE

1. Ms. Carmichael is upset with Zack, one of her fifth-grade students, because he has not turned in his homework for the third time in the past week. She is discussing the situation with him, trying to express the importance of turning in assignments on time. Which of the following is an assertive response to the situation?
   a. "Okay, Zack, you may turn it in tomorrow."
   b. "What is wrong with you, Zack? This is the third time in a week! I know you can do the work. Are you just plain lazy? Is that it? This is getting ridiculous. Do you want to fail?"
   c. "Zack, I know you can do the work. Are you trying to make things more difficult for me by not turning it in?"
   d. "Zack, I can't possibly assess your understanding of the material when you don't turn in your work. This can't continue. Please get it to me by the end of the day, and no more late work."

2. Edward and James are having a discussion about the best way to engage their students' interest in American history. Which of the following best exemplifies active listening?
   a. As Edward speaks about the importance of integrating electronic media into their courses, James interrupts with an argument that primary sources are much more useful and accurate.
   b. As Edward speaks about the importance of integrating electronic media into their courses, James makes a rude noise and tells him that is a bunch of nonsense.
   c. As Edward speaks, James maintains eye contact and nods occasionally. However, James is really planning how he will counter Edward's assertion that electronic media will engage the students.
   d. As Edward speaks, James maintains eye contact, nods his head occasionally, and leans forward. When Edward has finished, James says, "So what you're saying is that if we used more electronic media, the kids would be more interested, right?"

3. As Edward is speaking about the importance of integrating electronic media into their American history courses, James checks his watch, looks toward the door, and drums his fingers on the desk. What message is James communicating?
   a. interest
   b. disdain
   c. anxiety
   d. boredom

Please see the answer key at the end of the book.

5 DEALING WITH PROBLEM BEHAVIORS

| Management Strategies | Dealing with Aggression | Classroom and School-Based Programs |

"How come when you say we have a problem, I'm always the one who has the problem?"

George Abbott from *Phi Delta Kappan*, vol. 74, no. 2 (October 1992), p. 171. Reprinted by permission of George Abbott.

No matter how well you have planned and created a positive classroom environment, problem behaviors will emerge. It is important that you deal with them in a timely, effective manner.

Management Strategies

Classroom management expert Carolyn Evertson and her colleagues (Evertson, Emmer, & Worsham, 2006) distinguish between minor and moderate interventions for problem behaviors. The following discussion describes their approach.

Minor Interventions   Some problems require only minor interventions. These problems involve behaviors that, if infrequent, usually don't disrupt class activities and learning. For example, students might call out to the teacher out of turn, leave their seats without permission, engage in social talk when it is not allowed, or eat candy in class. When only minor interventions are needed for problem behaviors, these strategies can be effective (Evertson, Emmer, & Worsham, 2006, pp. 175–176):

- "*Use nonverbal cues.* Make eye contact with the student and give a signal such as a finger to the lips, a head shake, or a hand signal to issue a desist."
- *Keep the activity moving.* Sometimes transitions between activities take too long, or a break in activity occurs when students have nothing to do. In these situations, students might leave their seats, socialize, crack jokes, and begin to get out of control. A good strategy is not to correct students' minor misbehaviors in these situations but, rather, start the next activity in a more timely fashion. By effectively planning the day, you should be able to eliminate these long transitions and gaps in activity.
- *Move closer to students.* When a student starts misbehaving, simply moving near the student will often cause the misbehavior to stop.
- "*Redirect the behavior.*" If students get off-task, let them know what they are supposed to be doing. You might say, "Okay, remember, everybody is supposed to be working on math problems."
- "*Provide needed instruction.*" Sometimes students engage in minor misbehaviors when they haven't understood how to do the task they have been assigned. Unable to effectively do the activity, they fill the time by misbehaving. Solving this problem involves carefully monitoring students' work and providing guidance when needed.
- *Directly and assertively tell the student to stop.* Establish direct eye contact with the student, be assertive, and tell the student to stop the behavior. "Keep your comments brief and monitor the situation until the student complies. Combine this strategy with redirection to encourage desirable behavior."
- "*Give the student a choice.*" Place responsibility in the student's hands by saying that he or she has a choice of either behaving appropriately or receiving a negative consequence. Be sure to tell the student what the appropriate behavior is and what the consequence is for not performing it.

Moderate Interventions   Some misbehaviors require a stronger intervention than those just described—for example, when students abuse privileges, disrupt an activity, goof off, or interfere with your instruction or other students' work. Here are some moderate interventions for dealing with these types of problems (Evertson, Emmer, & Worsham, 2006, pp. 177–178):

- *"Withhold a privilege or a desired activity."* Inevitably, you will have students who abuse privileges they have been given, such as being able to move around the classroom or to work on a project with friends. In these cases, you can revoke the privilege.
- *"Isolate or remove students."* In chapter 7, we also discussed the time-out, which involves removing a student from positive reinforcement. If you choose to use a time-out, you have several options. You can (1) keep the student in the classroom, but deny the student access to positive reinforcement; (2) take the student outside the activity area or out of the classroom; or (3) place the student in a time-out room designated by the school. If you use a time-out, be sure to clearly identify the student's behavior that resulted in the time-out, such as "You are being placed in time-out for 30 minutes because you punched Derrick." If the misbehavior occurs again, reidentify it and place the student in time-out again. After the time-out, don't comment on how well the student behaved during the time-out; just return the student to the activity that was interrupted.
- *Impose a penalty.* A small amount of repetitious work can be used as a penalty for misbehavior. In writing, a student might have to write an extra page; in math, a student might have to do extra problems; in physical education, a student might have to run an extra lap. The problem with penalties is that they can harm the student's attitude toward the subject matter.

Students also can be made to serve a detention for their misbehaviors, at lunch, during recess, before school, or after school. Teachers commonly assign detentions for goofing off, wasting time, repeating rule violations, not completing assignments, and disrupting the class. Some detentions are served in the classroom; some schools have a detention hall where students can be sent. If the detention occurs in your classroom, you will have to supervise it. The length of the detention should initially be short, on the order of 10 to 15 minutes, if the misbehavior is not severe. As when using the time-out, you will need to keep a record of the detention.

Using Others as Resources Among the people who can help you get students to engage in more-appropriate behavior are peers, parents, the principal or counselor, and mentors.

Peer Mediation Peers sometimes can be very effective at getting students to behave more appropriately. Peer mediators can be trained to help students resolve quarrels and change undesirable behaviors. For example, if two students have started to argue with each other, an assigned peer mediator can help to mediate the dispute, as described later in the chapter when we discuss conflict resolution.

Parent-Teacher Conference You can telephone the student's parents or confer with them in a face-to-face conference. Just informing them can sometimes get the student to improve behavior. Don't put the parents on the defensive or suggest that you are blaming them for their child's misbehavior in school. Just briefly describe the problem and say that you would appreciate any support that they can give you.

Enlist the Help of the Principal or Counselor Many schools have prescribed consequences for particular problem behaviors. If you have tried unsuccessfully to deal with the behavior, consider asking the school's administration for help. This might involve referring the student to the principal or a counselor, which may result in a detention or warning to the student, as well as a parent conference with the principal. Letting the principal or counselor handle the problem can save you time. However, such help is not always practical on a regular basis in many schools.

Find a Mentor   Earlier we underscored the importance of students having at least one person in their life who cares about them and supports their development. Some students, especially those from high-risk impoverished backgrounds, do not have that one person. A mentor can provide such students with the guidance they need to reduce problem behaviors. Look around the community for potential mentors for students in high-risk, low-income circumstances.

Dealing with Aggression

Violence in schools is a major, escalating concern. In many schools, it now is common for students to fight, bully other students, or threaten each other and teachers verbally or with a weapon. These behaviors can arouse your anxiety and anger, but it is important to be prepared for their occurrence and handle them calmly. Avoiding an argument or emotional confrontation will help you to solve the conflict.

Fighting   Classroom management expert Carolyn Evertson and her colleagues (Evertson, Emmer, & Worsham, 2006) give the following recommendations for dealing with students who are fighting. In elementary school, you can usually stop a fight without risking injury to yourself. If for some reason you cannot intervene, immediately get help from other teachers or administrators. When you intervene, give a loud verbal command: "Stop!" Separate the fighters, and as you keep them separated, tell other students to leave or return to what they are doing. If you intervene in a fight that involves secondary school students, you will probably need the help of one or two other adults. Your school likely will have a policy regarding fighting. If so, you should carry it out and involve the principal and/or parents if necessary.

Generally, it is best to let the fighters have a cooling-off period so that they will calm down. Then meet with the fighters and get their points of view on what precipitated the fight. Question witnesses if necessary. Have a conference with the fighters, emphasizing the inappropriateness of fighting, the importance of taking each other's perspective, and the importance of cooperation.

Bullying   Significant numbers of students are victimized by bullies (Dao & others, 2006; Hyman & others, 2006; Milsom & Gallo, 2006; Robinson, 2006; Snell & Hirschstein, 2005). In one national survey of more than 15,000 sixth- through tenth-grade U.S. students, nearly 1 of every 3 students said that they had experienced occasional or frequent involvement as a victim or perpetrator in bullying (Nansel & others, 2001). In this study, bullying was defined as verbal or physical behavior intended to disturb someone less powerful. Boys and younger middle school students were most likely to be affected. As shown in figure 14.5, being belittled about looks or speech was the most frequent type of bullying. Children who said they were bullied reported more loneliness and difficulty in making friends, whereas those who did the bullying were more likely to have low grades and to smoke and drink alcohol. In another recent study of more than 4,000 middle schoool students in Maryland, 31 percent reported being victimized three or more times in the past year (Haynie & others, 2001). Also, children with disabilities may be at risk for being bullied more than other children (Rigby, 2002, 2004).

Victims of bullying have been found to have certain characteristics (Dill, Vernberg, & Fonagy, 2004; Eslea & others, 2004; Hannish & Guerra, 2004). One recent study found that victims of bullies had parents who were intrusive, demanding, and unresponsive with their children (Ladd & Kochenderfer-Ladd, 2002). Also in this study, parent-child relationships characterized by intense closeness were linked with higher levels of peer victimization in boys. Such intense closeness promotes self-doubts and worries, which are perceived as weaknesses when expressed in male peer groups. Another study found that for both bullies and victims, the parenting they experienced was linked with their peer interaction (Olweus, 1980). Bullies' parents were more likely to be rejecting, authoritarian, or permissive about their sons' aggression, whereas victims' parents were more likely to be anxious and overprotective.

"*. . . and suddenly there were teachers all over the place!*"

From *Classroom Chuckles* by Bill Knowlton. Copyright © 1968 by Bill Knowlton. Reprinted by permission of Scholastic Inc.

FIGURE 14.5 Bullying Behaviors among U.S. Youth

This graph shows the types of bullying most often experienced by U.S. youth. The percentages reflect the extent to which bullied students said that they had experienced a particular type of bullying. In terms of gender, note that when they were bullied, boys were more likely to be hit, slapped, or pushed than girls were.

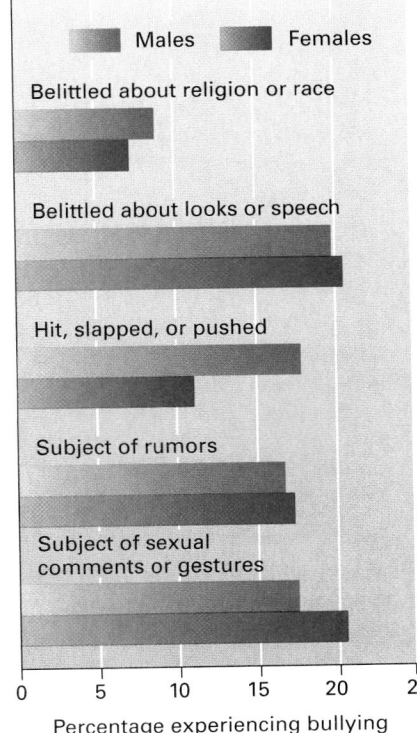

Victims of bullies can suffer both short-term and long-term effects (Fekkes & others, 2006; Milsom & Gallo, 2006; Roberts, 2005). Short-term, they can become depressed, lose interest in schoolwork, or even avoid going to school. A recent study of 9- to 12-year-old children in the Netherlands found that the victims of bullies had a much higher incidence of headaches, sleeping problems, abdominal pain, feeling tired, and depression than children not involved in bullying behavior (Fekkes, Pijpers, & Verloove-Vanhorick, 2004). The effects of bullying can persist into adulthood. One longitudinal study of male victims who were bullied during childhood found that in their twenties they were more depressed and had lower self-esteem than their counterparts who had not been bullied in childhood (Olweus, 1994). A recent study revealed that adults who had been bullied as children had high levels of anxiety (Gladstone, Parker, & Malhi, 2006). Bullying also can indicate a serious problem for the bully as well as the victim (Milsom & Gallo, 2006). In the study just mentioned, about 60 percent of the boys who were identified as bullies in middle school had at least one criminal conviction (and about one-third had three or more convictions) in their twenties, rates that are far higher than the rates for nonbullies.

Some children are both bullies and victims. A study of U.S. sixth-grade students examined three groups: bullies, victims, and those who were both bullies and victims (Juvonen, Graham, & Schuster, 2003). Bully-victims were the most troubled group, displaying the highest level of conduct, school, and relationship problems. Despite increased conduct problems, bullies enjoyed the highest standing of the three groups among their classmates.

School climate may play a role in bullying, although few research studies have been conducted on this topic (Espelage & Swearer, 2003). A school climate in which adults and peers accept bullying fosters bullying. One study revealed that schools with high academic standards, high parental involvement, and effective discipline had less bullying (Ma, 2002).

An increasing number of prevention/intervention programs have been developed to reduce bullying (Fekkes, Pijpers, & Verloove-Vanhorick, 2006; Mytton & others, 2006). Following are three of the most promising programs and where you can obtain information about them:

- *Olweus Bullying Prevention.* Created by Dan Olweus, this program focuses on 6- to 15-year-olds, with the goal of decreasing opportunities and rewards for bullying. School staff are instructed in ways to improve peer relations and make schools safer. A large study with 2,500 students in 42 schools in Norway found that the Olweus program was effective in reducing bullying (Olweus, 1994). Information on how to implement the program can be obtained from the Center for the Prevention of Violence at the University of Colorado (www.colorado.edu/cspv/blueprints).

- *Bully-Proofing Your School.* This program is tailored for students in kindergarten through the eighth grade and offers a school-wide approach and a teacher curriculum for reducing bullying. It emphasizes how to recognize bullying behavior and quickly respond to it and how to develop students' communication skills in conflict situations. Intervention methods are provided, school posters related to bullying are available, and a parent's guide helps involve parents in effective ways to reduce bullying. Recent research indicates that this program is effective in reducing bullying (Beran & Tutty, 2002; Plog, Epstein, & Porter, 2004). Information about the Bully-Proofing Your School program is available at www.sopriswest.com.

- *Steps to Respect.* This bullying program consists of three steps: (1) establishing a school-wide approach, such as creating antibullying policies and determining consequences for bullying, (2) training staff and parents to deal with bullying, and (3) teaching students to recognize, not tolerate, and handle bullying. In this third step, teachers provide skills training, such as how to be assertive, and information about bullying to students in grades 3 through 6. The skills training

BEST PRACTICES
Strategies for Reducing Bullying

Here are some suggestions for how teachers and schools can reduce bullying (Cohn & Canter, 2003; Hyman & others, 2006; Limber, 1997, 2004; Milsom & Gallo, 2006):

1. *Get older peers to serve as monitors for bullying and intervene when they see it taking place.*

2. *Develop school-wide rules and sanctions against bullying and post them throughout the school.*

3. *Form friendship groups for adolescents who are regularly bullied by peers.*

4. *Be aware that bullying often occurs outside the classroom, so you may not actually see it taking place. Also, many victims of bullying don't report the bullying to adults.* Unsupervised areas such as the playground, bus, and school corridors are common places where students are bullied.

5. *If you observe bullying in your classroom or in other locations, you will need to make a decision about whether it is serious enough to report to school authorities or parents.*

6. *Incorporate the message of the antibullying program into places of worship, school, and other community activities where adolescents are involved.*

7. *Encourage parents to reinforce their children's positive behaviors and model appropriate interpersonal interactions.*

8. *Identify bullies and victims early and use social skills training to improve their behavior.* Teaching empathy, especially perspective taking, promoting self-control, and training social skills have been found to reduce the negative behavior of bullies (Macklem, 2003). Researchers have also found that when victims of bullying develop assertiveness skills, bullying is reduced (Kaiser & Raminsky, 2003; Macklem, 2003). They also have documented that improving students' social skills, including friendship skills and how to approach people, can reduce a victim's chances of being bullied (Rigby, 2002).

by teachers occurs over a 12- to 14-week period. A recent study found that Steps to Respect was successful in reducing bullying and argumentativeness in third- through sixth-grade students (Frey & others, 2005). For more information about Steps to Respect, call 1-800-634-4449, ext. 6223, or consult this Web site: www.cfchildren.org/.

Defiance or Hostility toward the Teacher Edmund Emmer and his colleagues (Emmer, Evertson, & Worsham, 2006) discussed the following strategies for dealing with students who defy you or are hostile toward you. If students get away with this type of behavior, it likely will continue and even spread. Therefore, try to defuse the event by keeping it private and handling the student individually, if possible. If the defiance or hostility is not extreme and occurs during a lesson, try to depersonalize it and say that you will deal with it in a few minutes to avoid a power struggle. At an appropriate later time, meet with the student and spell out any consequence the misbehavior might merit.

In extreme and rare cases, students will be completely uncooperative, in which case you should send another student to the office for help. In most instances, though, if you stay calm and don't get into a power struggle with the student, the student will calm down, and you can talk with the student about the problem.

Classroom and School-Based Programs

A number of classroom and school-based programs for dealing with problem behaviors involve social competence enhancement and conflict resolution (Coie & Dodge, 1998; Dodge, Coie, & Lynam, 2006).

Social Competence Enhancement Programs Some educational experts argue that coordinated school-based planning, high-quality curriculum and instruction, and a supportive school environment might be needed to deal with students' problem behaviors (Weissberg & Greenberg, 1998). These types of programs often try to improve the student's social competence by enhancing life skills, providing health education, and developing socioemotional skills.

Researchers have found that information-only or knowledge-only programs have minimal effects on decreasing students' problem behaviors (Kirby, 1992). In contrast, programs that teach broadly applicable personal and social competencies have been found to reduce students' aggressive behavior and improve their adjustment (Greenberg, 1996; Weissburg & others, 1981). Such competency programs deal with subjects such as self-control, stress management, problem solving, decision making, communication, peer resistance, and assertiveness. Following are some examples of effective social competence enhancement programs.

The Improving Social Awareness–Social Problem Solving Project This program is designed for elementary school students (Elias & Schwab, 2006; Elias & others, 1991). During the instructional phase, teachers use scripted lessons to introduce classroom activities. The lessons follow this format: (1) group sharing of interpersonal successes, problem situations, and feelings that students wish to share with the teacher and other students; (2) a brief overview of cognitive, emotional, or behavioral skills to be taught during the lesson; (3) written and video presentations of situations that call for and model skill application; (4) discussion of the situations and ways to use the new skills; (5) role-playing that encourages behavioral rehearsal of skills; and (6) summary and review. Teachers also integrate problem-solving and social-awareness activities into the regular classroom routine and their daily instruction. Evaluations indicate that the program has been positive in helping students cope with everyday problem situations and reduce their violent behaviors (Elias & Schwab, 2006; Elias & others, 1986).

The Social Competence Program for Young Adolescents This 45-session program for middle school students provides classroom-based instruction and establishes environmental supports designed to (1) promote social competence by increasing self-control, managing stress, engaging in responsible decision making, solving social problems, and improving communication skills; (2) improve communication between school personnel and students; and (3) prevent antisocial and aggressive behavior, substance abuse, and high-risk sexual behaviors (Weissberg & Caplan, 1994). Evaluations of the social competence program have been positive. Students involved in the program show fewer aggressive behaviors, more consideration of alternative solutions to problems, improved stress management strategies, and more prosocial values than control groups (Weissberg, Barton, & Shriver, 1997). Teachers who have participated in the program indicate that it addresses important issues that are important for their students and helps them communicate better with students. A program that emphasizes cultural sensitivity as part of social competence enhancement is described in the Diversity and Education interlude.

DIVERSITY AND EDUCATION
Cultural Sensitivity, Social Development, and Collaboration with the Community

In an ideal world, the combined efforts of responsible parents, quality child care, health-care services, and family-centered communities would provide the necessary foundations for children to come to school ready to learn (Weissberg & Greenberg, 1998). But in the real world of your classroom, children will bring varying propensities to learn. Some will be highly motivated, others listless. Some will require little management; others will test your patience and coping skills.

The growing diversity of students makes classroom management more challenging. You must be prepared to know and demonstrate sensitivity to the cultural and socioeconomic variations in your students (Gay, 2006; McLoyd, 1998). It is equally important to recognize the existence of differences within groups of students from ethnic minority and impoverished backgrounds. Without this knowledge and sensitivity, a trusting and mutually respectful relationship is difficult to establish.

An increasing number of programs reveal that showing greater cultural sensitivity to socioculturally diverse students benefits these students when they are at risk for academic and emotional problems (Weissberg & Greenberg, 1998). One type of successful intervention program for at-risk youth from poor rural or inner-city minority settings involves ethnically and culturally compatible adults from the community who develop culturally relevant activities for students that include ethnically relevant theater, music, and dance productions (Botvin, Schinke, & Orlandi, 1995; Hudley & Graham, 1995).

Effectively intervening in the lives of high-risk students often consists of providing not only individualized attention but also community-wide collaboration for support and guidance. One program that focuses on community-wide collaboration was described by Roger Weissberg and Mark Greenberg (1998, pp. 920–921). It is called the New Haven Social Development Project and involves a high percentage of students from low-income, ethnic minority backgrounds (Kasprow & others, 1993; Schwab-Stone & others, 1995). Problem behaviors such as drug use, poor sexual decision making, delinquency, and truancy harm students' academic performance, health, and future. Many of the "problem behaviors had common roots, such as poor problem-solving and communication skills . . . and a lack of monitoring and guidance by positive adult role models."

The superintendent and board of education for the New Haven schools established a comprehensive K–12 social development curriculum. The project's mission was to help students

(a) develop a sense of self-worth and feel effective as they deal with daily responsibilities and challenges; (b) engage in positive, safe, health-protective behavior practices; (c) become socially skilled and have positive relationships with peers and adults; (d) feel motivated to contribute responsibly to their peer group, family, school, and community; and (e) acquire a set of basic skills, work habits, and values as a foundation for a lifetime of meaningful work.

The program consists of 25 to 50 hours of classroom-based instruction at each grade level. "The curriculum emphasized self-monitoring, problem solving, conflict resolution, and communication skills; values such as personal responsibility and respect for self and others; and content about health, culture, interpersonal relationships, and careers." The program also involves "educational, recreational, and health-promotion opportunities at the school and community levels to reinforce classroom-based instruction. These included programs such as mentoring, peer mediation, leadership groups, an Extended Day Academy with after-school clubs, health center services, and an outdoor adventure class." In addition, a school-based mental health planning team focuses attention on developing a positive climate for learning in the school. Teachers reported that the program improved the social skills and frustration tolerance of more than 80 percent of the students in grades K–3. Also, secondary school students decreased their participation in fights, felt safer at school and in the neighborhood, and felt more positive about the future as the program progressed.

The Three C's of School and Classroom Management   David and Roger Johnson (1999) created a classroom management program to deal with problems that cause disruptions and undermine learning. Their program emphasizes the importance of guiding students in learning how to regulate their own behavior. These are the three *C*'s:

- *Cooperative community.* Learning communities benefit when the participants have a positive interdependence on each other. They work toward attaining mutual goals by engaging in cooperatively structured learning activities.

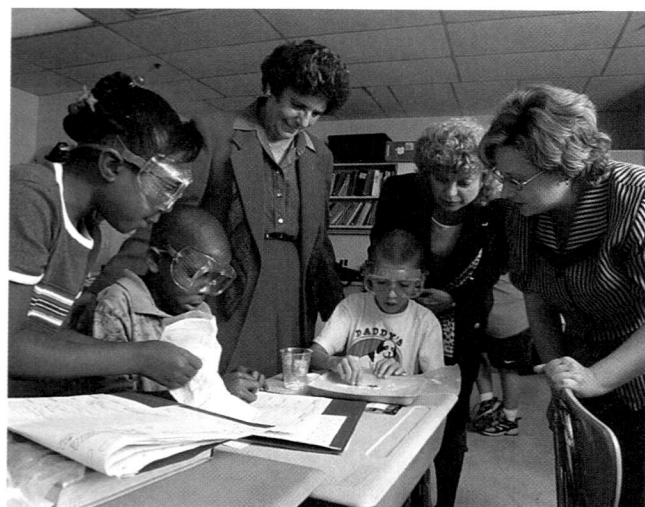

Carolyn Evertson (*center in red*) in a COMP classroom with Arlene Harris. They created a classroom management framework that emphasizes problem prevention. *What are other features of COMP classrooms?*

- *Constructive conflict resolution.* When conflicts arise, they can be resolved constructively through conflict resolution training for all participants in the learning community.
- *Civic values.* There can be cooperative communities and constructive conflict resolution only if the learning community shares common civic values, values that guide decision making. These values include believing that success depends on joint efforts to achieve mutual goals and valuing others.

Support for Managing Learning-Centered Classrooms: The Classroom Organization and Management Program (COMP)
The COMP program, developed by Carolyn Evertson, advocates a classroom management framework that emphasizes supporting students' learning and that guides students in taking responsibility for their own decisions, behavior, and learning. COMP emphasizes problem prevention, management and instruction integration, student involvement, and professional collaboration among teachers. The program is implemented through training workshops, classroom application, and collaborative reflection. Research has revealed that COMP results in positive changes in teacher and student behavior (Evertson & Harris, 1999).

Skills for Life This program seeks to improve students' self-control, responsibility, and ability to solve social problems and improve conflict reduction skills. It targets students from kindergarten through fifth grade. Classroom teachers are trained to help students develop these skills through the use of activities, class discussions, and workbooks. A parent workshop is also available. One research study with more than 1,800 students in K–5 found that based on teacher ratings the program was effective in improving a number of student behaviors, including keeping their hands to themselves, not teasing or calling other students names, and reducing fighting and bullying (Manning, Mohole, & the Goodman Research Group, 2002). Information about the Skills for Life program is available at www. lessonone.org.

Good Behavior Game The Good Behavior Game (GBG) is a classroom-based behavior management program that is designed to decrease students' disruptive behavior and increase their positive behaviors through a team-based approach (Barrish, Saunders, & Wolfe, 1969; Dolan & others, 1989). In GBG, teachers discuss with their students the importance of creating class rules and with student input establishing class rules. The rules are placed on a poster board accompanied with pictograms depicting the rules. Then teachers assign students to one of three or four teams that consist of an equal number of disruptive and nondisruptive students. Students are instructed to manage their own and their teammates' behavior and given strategies for doing so. Each team gets an equal number of cards, and teams are rewarded when at least one card remains on their desk at the end of a 15- to 60-minute period. Teachers take a card when a student violates a rule. Teams are rewarded for good behavior with compliments by the teacher and tangible rewards (stickers) after each game, at the end of a week, and at the end of a month. Researchers have found that the GBG is effective in reducing disruptive student behavior and increasing positive behavior in the classroom (Ialongo & others, 2001; Van Lier & others, 2004). One recent study found that the positive results of the GBG program lasted 2 years, and that the program was effective even for the most disruptive students (Van Lier & others, 2004).

BEST PRACTICES
Strategies for Conflict Resolution

Here are some good strategies for conflict resolution in the classroom (Johnson & Johnson, 1995, pp. 64–66):

1. *"Don't attempt to eliminate all conflicts."* Eliminating all violence does not mean getting rid of all conflict. For example, moderate conflicts can sometimes increase students' achievement, motivation to learn, and ability to solve problems. What is important is not eliminating conflict but helping students to learn how to manage it more effectively.

2. *Develop a supportive context.* The most effective conflict resolution programs attempt to do more than just change individual students. Rather, the goal is to change the school environment into a learning setting in which students live in accord with a standard of nonviolence. Creating a supportive context involves placing students in situations in which they are more likely to cooperate than to compete. In a cooperative context, conflicts tend to be resolved in constructive rather than destructive ways. Students are more likely to communicate effectively with each other, trust each other, and define conflicts as mutual rather than individual problems.

3. *Decrease in-school risk factors.* Factors that place students at risk for violent behavior include academic failure and alienation from classmates. Thus, aspects of the school that can support students' academic success and sense of belongingness should be monitored and improved in an effort to reduce violence.

4. *"Teach all students how to resolve conflicts constructively."* Two types of conflict resolution programs are the cadre approach and the total student body approach. "In the *cadre approach,* a small number of students are trained to serve as peer mediators for the entire school." Johnson and Johnson (1995) believe this approach is not as effective as the *total student body approach,* in which "every student learns how to manage conflicts constructively by negotiating agreements and mediating schoolmates' conflicts." A disadvantage of the total student body approach is the time and commitment required from school personnel. However, the more students who are trained in conflict resolution, the more constructively conflicts will be managed.

    One example of the total student body approach was developed by Johnson and Johnson (1991). Their Teaching Students to Be Peacemakers program involves both negotiation and mediation strategies. Students learn these negotiation steps: (a) Define what they want, (b) describe their feelings, (c) explain the reasons underlying the wants and feelings, (d) take the perspective of the other student to see the conflict from both sides, (e) generate at least three optional agreements that benefit both parties, and (f) come to an agreement about the best course of action.

    Students learn these mediation steps: (a) Stop the hostilities, (b) ensure that the disputants are committed to the mediation, (c) facilitate negotiations between the disputants, and (d) formalize the agreement.

    When students have completed negotiation and mediation training, the school or teacher implements the Peacemakers program by choosing two student mediators for each day. Being a mediator helps students learn how to negotiate and resolve conflicts. Evaluations of the Peacemakers program have been positive, with participants showing more constructive conflict resolution than nonparticipants (Johnson & Johnson, 1994).

Review, Reflect, and Practice

(5) **Formulate some effective approaches that teachers can use to deal with problem behaviors.**

REVIEW

- What are some minor and moderate interventions? Who else can help?
- What can the teacher do about fighting, bullying, and defiance?
- What are some effective classroom and school-based programs for dealing with problem behavior?

REFLECT

- How worried are you about problem behaviors among the students you plan to teach? In view of your own current skills, personality, and values, what steps could you begin to take to prepare yourself for dealing with them?

PRAXIS™ PRACTICE

1. Mr. Martin is telling his students how to complete their assignment for tomorrow. While he talks, Sally and Shelly are discussing their after-school plans. Mr. Martin should
   a. interrupt his instruction to say, "Listen up, girls or you'll be spending your after school hours with me."
   b. interrupt his instructions to ask, "Is there something that you would like to share with the class, girls?"
   c. keep talking, but look directly at Sally and Shelly; if that doesn't work, slowly approach them.
   d. stop his instructions and wait silently for the girls to stop talking, while looking directly at them, then say, "Thank you, ladies."

2. Ken is a fifth-grade student who is not well liked by his peers. They tease him about the way he looks, the way he dresses, his lack of coordination, and his lack of emotional self-regulation. The bulk of this takes place on the playground during recess. The teasing often reduces Ken to tears, which seems to add fuel to the fire. Which of the following is most likely to reduce this bullying behavior?
   a. in-school suspensions for the bullies
   b. isolating Ken from his peers so he does not have to deal with the bullying
   c. removing the bullies' recess privileges
   d. social skills training for both the bullies and Ken

3. Which of the following strategies is most likely to be effective in reducing aggression?
   a. Have the students sign a contract promising that they will not engage in bullying.
   b. Institute severe sanctions for verbal aggression.
   c. Intervene in all conflicts so that they cannot escalate.
   d. Teach students to resolve conflicts peacefully, regulate their emotional responses, and communicate assertively.

Please see the answer key at the end of the book.

CRACK THE CASE
The Case of the Chatty Student

Mrs. Welch was a new middle school language arts teacher. Prior to beginning her new position, she developed a classroom management plan that mirrored the code of conduct for the school. She expected the students to behave respectfully toward her and toward their classmates. She also expected them to respect school property and the learning environment. In addition, she expected them to keep their hands, feet, and possessions to themselves. Minor behavioral infractions were to result in a verbal warning. Further infractions would net more severe consequences in steps: a detention, a referral to the office, and a call to the students' parents. Mrs. Welch was pleased with her management plan. She distributed it to students on the first day of class. She also distributed it to parents at the annual Back-to-School Night during the first week of school.

Darius, a student in one of Mrs. Welch's seventh-grade classes, was what Mrs. Welch termed "chatty." He was very social and spent much of his class time talking to other students rather than working. Mrs. Welch tried moving him to different parts of the room and tried seating him next to students to whom she had never seen him talk, neither of which decreased his chattiness. He simply made new friends and continued chatting, sometimes disrupting the class in the process. She tried seating him next to girls, and this even seemed to make things even worse.

Darius was very bright in addition to being very social. Although he was only in seventh grade, he was taking algebra with a group of mathematically advanced eighth-grade students. This was something of an anomaly in this school; in fact, it had never been done previously. The algebra teacher, Mrs. Zaccinelli, and Darius had a good relationship. He *never* disrupted her class or misbehaved in any way in her class. Mrs. Zaccinelli was amazed to hear that Darius did not always behave appropriately in his other classes.

Mrs. Zaccinelli served as Mrs. Welch's mentor. She had helped Mrs. Welch to write her classroom management plan and served as a sounding board when she had difficulties. At one point when Mrs. Welch was discussing her eighth-grade classes, Mrs. Zaccinelli referred to inclusion in the eighth-grade algebra class as "a privilege, not a right." She further told Mrs. Welch that she expected her students to behave appropriately at all times.

The next day, Darius was especially talkative in class. Mrs. Welch asked him to stop talking. He did, but he resumed his chatter within 5 minutes. When he began talking again, Mrs. Welch took him aside and told him loudly, "That's it, Darius. I'm going to have you removed from algebra class. You know taking that class is a privilege, not a right."

Darius was stunned. He sat quietly for the rest of the period but did not participate. He made no eye contact with Mrs. Welch or any other students. The rest of the day was something of a blur to him. He had no idea how he would explain this to his parents.

When Darius told his mother he was going to be removed from algebra for his behavior in language arts, she immediately went to see Mrs. Welch. She tried to tell Mrs. Welch that to remove Darius from algebra would be to deny him the free and appropriate public education to which he (and all other students) was entitled. Mrs. Welch held her ground and insisted that she could and would have his placement altered.

1. What are the issues in this case?

2. Is removal from algebra class an appropriate consequence for Darius? Why or why not?

3. Do you think removal from algebra class would have a positive effect on Darius' behavior? Why or why not?

4. What impact do you think this would have on his motivation in school?

5. How do you think this situation will impact the relationship between Mrs. Welch and Darius?

6. What do you think Darius' mother will do now?

7. How do you think Mrs. Zaccinelli will react when she hears about the situation?

8. How do you think the principal will react?

9. What should Mrs. Welch do?

10. How would Mrs. Welch's strategy of moving Darius to quiet him be characterized?
    a. This is an example of a minor intervention.
    b. This is an example of a moderate intervention.
    c. This is an example of a severe intervention.
    d. This is an example of an effective intervention.

11. Which of the following is likely to be the most effective way for Mrs. Welch to deal with Darius' chatty behavior?
    a. Make Darius write out a page of the dictionary.
    b. Put tape over Darius' mouth.
    c. Isolate Darius from his peers for the remainder of the period.
    d. Send Darius to the office for the principal to discipline.

Reach Your Learning Goals
Managing the Classroom

① WHY CLASSROOMS NEED TO BE MANAGED EFFECTIVELY: Explain why classroom management is both challenging and necessary.

Management Issues in Elementary and Secondary School Classrooms

Many management issues are similar across elementary and secondary school classrooms. However, these differences in elementary and secondary classrooms have meaning for the way classrooms need to be managed: Elementary school teachers often see the same 20 to 25 students all day long; secondary school teachers see 100 to 150 students about 50 minutes a day. Confinement, boredom, and interaction with the same people all day in elementary school can create problems. Secondary school teachers have to get the lesson moving quickly. They also might see a greater range of problems, and their students can have more long-standing problems that are more difficult to modify. These problems can be more severe than those of elementary school students. Secondary school students might demand more elaborate and logical explanations of rules and discipline.

The Crowded, Complex, and Potentially Chaotic Classroom

Doyle described six characteristics that reflect the classroom's complexity and potential for problems: (1) multidimensionality, (2) simultaneous activities going on, (3) events occurring at a rapid pace, (4) often unpredictable events, (5) lack of privacy, and (6) classroom histories.

Getting Off to the Right Start

Good strategies for getting off to the right start are to (1) establish expectations for behavior and resolve student uncertainties, (2) make sure that students experience success, (3) be available and visible, and (4) be in charge.

Emphasizing Instruction and Positive Classroom Climate

The focus in educational psychology used to be on discipline. Today it is on developing and maintaining a positive classroom environment that supports learning. This involves using proactive management strategies rather than being immersed in reactive discipline tactics. Historically, the well-managed classroom was conceptualized as a "well-oiled machine," but today it is more often viewed as a "beehive of activity." Kounin found that good classroom managers effectively manage the group's activities.

Management Goals and Strategies

Goals and strategies include (1) helping students spend more time on learning and less time on non-goal-directed activity (maintain activity flow, minimize transition times, and hold students accountable) and (2) preventing students from developing problems.

② DESIGNING THE PHYSICAL ENVIRONMENT OF THE CLASSROOM: Describe the positive design of the classroom's physical environment.

Principles of Classroom Arrangement

Basic principles of effective design of the classroom's physical environment include (1) reducing congestion in high-traffic areas, (2) making sure that you can easily see all students, (3) making often-used teaching materials and student supplies easily accessible, and (4) making sure that all students can see whole-class presentations.

Arrangement Style

Classroom arrangement styles include auditorium, face-to-face, off-set, seminar, and cluster. It is important to personalize the classroom and become an environmental designer who considers what activities students will be engaging in, draw up a floor plan, involve students in classroom design, and try out the arrangement and be flexible in redesigning it.

3 **CREATING A POSITIVE ENVIRONMENT FOR LEARNING:** Discuss how to create a positive classroom environment.

General Strategies

Use an authoritative style of classroom management rather than an authoritarian or permissive style. The authoritative style involves considerable verbal give-and-take with students, a caring attitude toward students, and limits on student behavior when necessary. Authoritative teaching is linked with competent student behavior. Kounin's work revealed other characteristics that were associated with effective classroom management: exhibiting withitness, coping with overlapping situations, maintaining smoothness and continuity in lessons, and engaging students in a variety of challenging activities.

Creating, Teaching, and Maintaining Rules and Procedures

Distinguish between rules and procedures and consider the appropriateness of including students in the discussion and generation of rules. Classroom rules should be (1) reasonable and necessary, (2) clear and comprehensible, (3) consistent with instructional and learning goals, and (4) compatible with school rules.

Getting Students to Cooperate

Getting students to cooperate involves (1) developing a positive relationship with students; (2) getting students to share and assume responsibility (involve students in the planning and implementation of school and classroom initiatives, encourage students to judge their own behavior, don't accept excuses, and give the self-responsibility strategy time to work); and (3) rewarding appropriate behavior (choose effective reinforcers, use prompts and shaping effectively, and use rewards to provide information about mastery).

4 **BEING A GOOD COMMUNICATOR:** Identify some good approaches to communication for both students and teachers.

Speaking Skills

Some barriers to effective speech include poor grammar, using vocabulary inappropriate for the students' level, and speaking too quickly or too slowly. You and your students will benefit considerably if you have effective speaking skills and you work with your students on developing their speaking skills. Speaking effectively with the class and students involves being a clear communicator, using "I" messages, being assertive, and avoiding barriers to verbal communication. Both teachers and students can benefit from knowing how to give speeches effectively.

Listening Skills

Active listening occurs when a person gives full attention to the speaker, focusing on both the intellectual and the emotional content of the message. Some good active listening strategies are to (1) pay careful attention to the person who is talking, including maintaining eye contact; (2) paraphrase; (3) synthesize themes and patterns; and (4) give feedback in a competent manner.

Nonverbal Communication

A number of communication experts stress that the majority of communication is nonverbal rather than verbal. It is hard to mask nonverbal communication, so a good strategy is to recognize that nonverbal communication usually reflects how a person really feels. Nonverbal communication involves facial expressions and eye communication, touch, space, and silence.

5 **DEALING WITH PROBLEM BEHAVIORS:** Formulate some effective approaches that teachers can use to deal with problem behaviors.

Management Strategies

Interventions can be characterized as minor or moderate. Minor interventions involve using nonverbal cues, keeping the activity moving, moving closer to students, redirecting the

continued

behavior, giving needed instruction, directly and assertively telling the student to stop the behavior, and giving the student a choice. Moderate interventions include withholding a privilege or a desired activity, isolating or removing students, and imposing a penalty or detention. A good management strategy is to have supportive resources. These include using peers as mediators, calling on parents for support, enlisting the help of a principal or counselor, and finding a mentor for the student.

Dealing with Aggression

Violence is a major, escalating concern in schools. Be prepared for aggressive actions on the part of students so that you can calmly cope with them. Try to avoid an argument or emotional confrontation. Helpful guidelines for dealing with fighting, bullying, and defiance or hostility toward the teacher include developing and posting school-wide rules and sanctions against bullying, defusing the hostile event by keeping it private and handling the student individually, and if needed sending another student to the office for help.

Classroom and School-Based Programs

Effective programs for managing classroom behavior include social competence enhancement programs, the three *C*'s of school and classroom management, support for managing learner-centered classrooms (the Classroom Organization and Management Program [COMP]), Skills for Life, and the Good Behavior Game (GBG).

 ## KEY TERMS

auditorium style 498	authoritative classroom	permissive classroom	aggressive style 508
face-to-face style 498	management style 500	management style 500	manipulative style 508
off-set style 498	authoritarian classroom	withitness 501	passive style 508
seminar style 498	management style 500	"you" messages 508	assertive style 508
cluster style 498		"I" messages 508	active listening 511

 ## PORTFOLIO ACTIVITIES

Now that you have a good understanding of this chapter, complete these exercises to expand your thinking.

Independent Reflection

Cultivating Respectful Student-Teacher Relationships. How self-disclosing and open should teachers be with students? It is important for teachers to develop positive relationships with students, but is there a point at which teachers become too close with their students? Write a personal reflection on this issue, incorporating thoughts about how it might relate to your future work as a teacher. (INTASC: Principle 6)

Collaborative Work

Creating Classroom Rules. List the rules you feel your students must follow. Describe how you might react when students break

these rules. Then get together with three or four of your classmates and discuss each other's lists. Revise your rules based on their feedback. (INTASC: Principle 5)

Research/Field Experience

Researching School Discipline Policies. Interview school counselors at an elementary, a middle, or a high school. Ask them to describe the discipline policies at their schools and to evaluate how well they work. Also ask them to describe the most difficult student problem they have ever dealt with. Write up that problem as a case study. (INTASC: Principles 5, 9)

Go to the Online Learning Center for downloadable portfolio templates.

TAKING IT TO THE NET

- A classroom's organization, physical space, and design highly influence the overall learning environment. List several descriptors that depict your ideal classroom environment. Anticipate challenges, and discuss how you could compensate for a classroom lacking storage space, natural light, or special areas for computer or group work. **www.teachervision.com/lesson-plans/lesson-5803.html**

- Make a list of rules for your classroom. Review the list and think about these questions: Are the rules worded in a positive manner? Are they appropriate and understandable for your target grade level? Did you consider involving your students in creating the rules? Design a class project for developing rules together as a collaborative group. **www.educationworld.com/a_lesson/lesson/lesson274.shtml**

- A student continually is disruptive in your class and has difficulty staying on task. You have lost your temper occasionally and have also sent the student to the office, all with no effect on the student's behavior. Develop a new discipline strategy for this student. What do you think the student needs in order to successfully participate in class? **www.honorlevel.com/**

Connect to the Online Learning Center to explore possible answers.

STUDY, PRACTICE, AND SUCCEED

Visit **www.mhhe.com/santedu3e** to review the chapter with self-grading quizzes and self-assessments, to apply the chapter material to two more Crack the Case studies, and for suggested activities to develop your teaching portfolio.

CHAPTER 15

Standardized Tests and Teaching

People do not have equal talents.
But all individuals should have an equal
opportunity to develop their talents.

—John F. Kennedy
U.S. President, 20th Century

Chapter Outline	Learning Goals

The Nature of Standardized Tests

Standardized Tests and Their Purposes
Criteria for Evaluating Standardized Tests

(1) Discuss the nature and purpose of standardized tests, as well as the criteria for evaluating them.

Aptitude and Achievement Tests

Comparing Aptitude and Achievement Tests
Types of Standardized Achievement Tests
High-Stakes State Standards-Based Tests
District and National Tests
Standardized Tests of Teacher Candidates

(2) Compare aptitude and achievement testing and describe current uses of achievement tests.

The Teacher's Roles

Preparing Students to Take Standardized Tests
Administering Standardized Tests
Understanding and Interpreting Test Results
Using Standardized Test Scores to Plan and Improve Instruction

(3) Identify the teacher's roles in standardized testing.

Issues in Standardized Tests

Standardized Tests, Alternative Assessments, and High-Stakes Testing
Diversity and Standardized Testing

(4) Evaluate some key issues in standardized testing.

TEACHING STORIES   Barbara Berry

Barbara Berry teaches French and humanities at Ypsilanti High School in Ypsilanti, Michigan, where she also is chairperson of the foreign languages department. She offers this story related to standardized tests:

> I had a fourth-year French student who was a wonderful student and clearly had a gift for languages. A minority student, she had been recruited by a major state university and offered a "full-ride" scholarship, provided she met certain requirements on the Scholastic Assessment Test (SAT). She took the test and did well on the verbal part but not well enough on the math part to meet the scholarship requirements. She was taking her fourth year of math classes and receiving above-average grades but said she just didn't like math and didn't understand it.
>
> Although I was teaching French at the time, I knew that I enjoyed math and had done well in school and on standardized tests. I knew that the SAT math section includes a lot of algebra. I offered to tutor her before she retook the SAT. She accepted the offer. I obtained some algebra materials from the math department to help work with her. Mostly, though, she worked on her own, reading the book and doing problems, only coming to me when she encountered problems. We met about once a week. About six weeks later, she retook the test and improved her math SAT score by 110 points. She got the scholarship.
>
> I did not teach this student much math, although I did help her work through some of the more difficult problems. What I did most to help her were two things: (1) I communicated my own enthusiasm for math and expressed confidence in her ability to do it, and (2) I focused her efforts on the material that the test assesses. Since we related so well with each other in my French class, I felt that I could help her feel better about her ability to do math.

Preview

As Barbara Berry's story shows, standardized tests can have a major impact on students' lives. They are widely used to evaluate students' learning and achievement. Although they are increasingly used to compare students' performance in different schools, districts, states, and countries, they are not without controversy. We begin our discussion in this chapter by examining some basic ideas about standardized tests and then distinguish aptitude and achievement tests. Then we explore what your role as a teacher is likely to be in regard to standardized testing and conclude the chapter by describing several important issues in standardized testing.

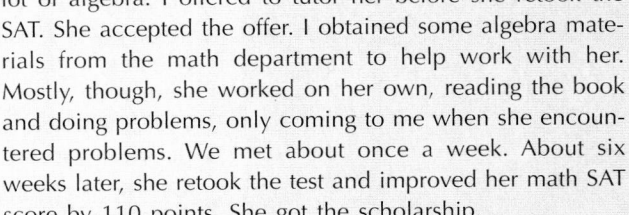

① THE NATURE OF STANDARDIZED TESTS

- Standardized Tests and Their Purposes
- Criteria for Evaluating Standardized Tests

Chances are, you have taken a number of standardized tests. In kindergarten, you may have taken a school readiness test, in elementary school some basic skills or achievement tests, and in high school the SAT or ACT test for college admission. But what does it mean to say that a test is "standardized"? And what purpose is served by standardized testing?

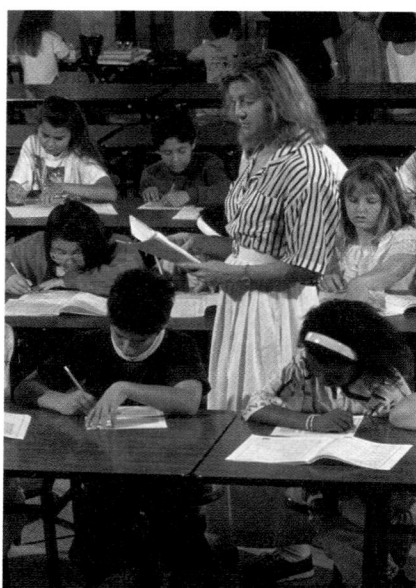

What are some of the most important purposes of standardized tests?

Standardized Tests and Their Purposes

Standardized tests have uniform procedures for administration and scoring and often allow a student's performance to be compared with the performance of other students at the same age or grade level on a national basis. Standardized tests attempt to include material that is common across most classrooms (Airasian, 2005; Chatterji, 2003), whereas teacher-made tests tend to focus on instructional objectives for a particular classroom. Some other ways standardized tests differ from teacher-made tests are that many standardized tests have norms, and most have been evaluated extensively for their validity and reliability. We will discuss validity and reliability shortly, but first let's examine the purposes of standardized tests.

Standardized tests can serve a number of purposes:

- *Provide information about students' progress.* Standardized tests are a source of information about how well students are performing. Students in one class might get *A*'s but perform at a mediocre level on a nationally standardized test, and students in another class might get *B*'s and do extremely well on the same nationally standardized test. Without an external, objective marker such as a standardized test, individual classroom teachers have difficulty knowing how well their students are performing compared with students elsewhere in the state or nation.

- *Diagnose students' strengths and weaknesses.* Standardized tests also can provide information about a student's learning strengths or weaknesses (Popham, 2005). For example, a student who is not doing well in reading might be given one or more standardized tests to pinpoint the student's learning weaknesses. When standardized tests are given for diagnostic purposes, they usually are given individually rather than to a group of students.

  In a national survey, teachers said that they often use standardized test results to help diagnose what individuals need in the way of instruction (Quality Counts, 2001). However, less than 20 percent of the teachers said that they have had adequate training in interpreting test scores for appropriate diagnosis of students.

- *Provide evidence for placement of students in specific programs.* Standardized tests can be used to make decisions about whether a student should be allowed to enter a specific program. In elementary school, a standardized test might be used to provide information for placing students in different reading groups. In high school, a standardized test might be used to determine which math classes a student should take. In some cases, standardized tests are used along with other information to evaluate whether a student might be allowed to skip a grade or to graduate. Students also might take standardized tests to determine their suitability for particular careers.

- *Provide information for planning and improving instruction.* In conjunction with other information about students, scores from standardized tests can be used by teachers in making decisions about instruction. For example, students' scores on a standardized test of reading skills administered at the start of the school year can help teachers determine the level at which they need to gear their reading instruction. Students' scores on a standardized test at the end of the year might inform teachers about how effective their reading instruction has been, information that could be used to continue similar instruction or modify it accordingly.

- *Help administrators evaluate programs.* If a school changes to a new educational program, the school administration will want to know how effective the new program is. One way to determine this is to give students relevant standardized tests to see how they are performing under the new program. For example, a school might change from a basic-skills-and-phonetics approach to a combined basic-skills-and-phonetics and whole-language approach in teaching reading. Students' scores on a relevant standardized test of reading skills can be used along with other evidence to determine the effectiveness of the change.

standardized tests Tests that have uniform procedures for administration and scoring. They assess students' performance in different domains and allow a student's performance to be compared with the performance of other students at the same age or grade on a national basis.

- *Contribute to accountability.* Schools and teachers are increasingly being held accountable for students' learning. Although this is controversial, standardized tests are being used to determine how effectively schools are using tax dollars. In Texas, principals can lose their jobs if their school's standardized test scores don't measure up. In Maryland, schools that don't do well forfeit thousands of dollars in reward money. Interest in accountability has led to the creation of **standards-based tests,** which assess skills that students are expected to have mastered before they can be promoted to the next grade or permitted to graduate. Schools that use standards-based tests often require students who do not pass the tests to attend special programs in the summer that will help them reach the minimum level of competency required by the school system. **High-stakes testing** is using tests in a way that will have important consequences for the student, affecting decisions such as whether the student will be promoted to the next grade or be allowed to graduate. Later in the chapter we will discuss state-mandated tests, which are increasingly being used to make such "high-stakes" decisions.

For now, though, note that an important theme throughout this chapter is that a standardized test should not be the only method for evaluating a student's learning. Nor should standardized tests by themselves be considered sufficient information in holding schools accountable for students' learning (Popham, 2005; Taylor & Nolen, 2005).

Criteria for Evaluating Standardized Tests

Among the most important criteria for evaluating standardized tests are norms, validity, reliability, and fairness. Let's begin our discussion by comparing national norms, special group norms, and local norms.

Norms   To understand an individual student's performance on a test, it needs to be compared with the performance of the **norm group,** a group of similar individuals who previously were given the test by the test maker. The test is said to be based on *national norms* when the norm group consists of a nationally representative group of students. For example, a standardized test for fourth-grade science knowledge and skills might be given to a national sample of fourth-grade students. The scores of the representative sample of thousands of fourth-grade students become the basis for comparison. This norm group should include students from urban, suburban, and rural areas; different geographical regions; private and public schools; boys and girls; and different ethnic groups. Based on an individual student's score on the standardized science test, the teacher can determine whether a student is performing above, on a level with, or below a national norm (Freeland, 2005; Gregory, 2007). The teacher also can see how the class as a whole is performing in relation to the general population of students.

In addition to national norms, standardized tests also can have special group norms and local norms. *Special group norms* consist of test scores for subgroups from the national sample. For example, special group norms might be available for students from low, middle, and high socioeconomic groups; for inner-city, suburban, and rural schools; for public and private schools; for female and male students; and for students from different ethnic groups. *Local norms* are sometimes available for standardized tests. These allow comparison of a student's performance with that of students in the same class, school, or district. Thus, evaluations of a student's test performance might differ, depending on what norm group is used.

Validity   Traditionally, validity has been defined as the extent to which a test measures what it is intended to measure. However, an increasing number of assessment experts in education argue that not just the characteristics of the test itself are valid or invalid—rather, it also is important to consider the inferences are made about the test scores (American Educational Research Association, 1999; McMillan, 2002). Thus, **validity** involves the extent to which a test measures what it is intended to measure and whether inferences about test scores are accurate.

standards-based tests Tests that assess skills that students are expected to have mastered before they can be promoted to the next grade or permitted to graduate.

high-stakes testing Using tests in a way that will have important consequences for the student, affecting such decisions as whether the student will be promoted or be allowed to graduate.

norm group A group of similar individuals who previously were given the test by the test maker.

validity The extent to which a test measures what it is intended to measure and whether inferences about the test scores are accurate.

In terms of the test characteristics themselves—the substance of the test—three types of validity can be described: content validity, criterion validity, and construct validity. A valid standardized test should have good **content validity,** which is the test's ability to sample the content that is to be measured. This concept is similar to "content-related evidence." For example, if a standardized fourth-grade science test purports to assess both content information and problem-solving skills, then the test should include items that measure content information about science and items that measure problem-solving skills.

Another form of validity is **criterion validity,** which is the test's ability to predict a student's performance as measured by other assessments or criteria. How might criterion validity be assessed for the standardized science test? One method is to get a representative sample of fourth-grade teachers to evaluate the competence of the students in their science classes and then compare those competence ratings with the students' scores on the standardized tests. Another method is to compare the scores of students on the standardized test with the scores of the same students on a different test that was designed to test the same material.

Criterion validity can be either concurrent or predictive (Osterlind, 2006). **Concurrent validity** is the relation between the test's scores and other criteria that are currently (concurrently) available. For example, does the standardized fourth-grade science test correspond to students' grades in science this semester? If it does, we say that test has high concurrent validity. **Predictive validity** is the relation between test scores and the student's future performance. For example, scores on the fourth-grade science test might be used to predict how many science classes different students will take in high school, whether middle school girls are interested in pursuing a science career, or whether students will win an award in science at some point in the future. Another example of predictive validity is how accurately students' scores on the SAT test predict their later grades in college and occupational success thereafter.

A third type of validity is **construct validity.** A *construct* is an unobservable trait or characteristic of a person, such as intelligence, creativity, learning style, personality, or anxiety. Construct validity is the extent to which there is evidence that a test measures a particular construct. Construct validity is the broadest of the types of validity we have discussed and can include evidence from concurrent and predictive validity (Gronlund, 2006). Judgments about construct validity might also rely on a description of the development of the test, the pattern of the relations between the test and other significant factors (such as high correlations with similar tests and low correlations with tests measuring different constructs), and any other type of evidence that contributes to understanding the meaning of test scores. Because a construct typically is abstract, a variety of evidence may be needed to determine whether a test validly measures a particular construct.

Earlier we indicated that we should consider not only the substance of the test in determining validity but also whether inferences about the test scores are accurate (McMillan, 2002). Let's look at an example of how this might work. A school superintendent decides to use test scores from a standardized test given to students each spring as an indicator of teacher competence. In other words, the test scores are being used to *infer* whether teachers are competent. These are the validity questions in this situation: How reasonable is it to use standardized test scores to measure teacher competence? Is it actually true (accurate) that teachers whose students score high are more competent than teachers whose students score low?

Reliability **Reliability** is the extent to which a test produces a consistent, reproducible score. To be called reliable, scores must be stable, dependable, and relatively free from errors of measurement (Gronlund, 2006; Popham, 2006). Reliability can be measured in several ways, including test-retest reliability, alternate forms reliability, and split-half reliability.

Test-retest reliability is the extent to which a test yields the same performance when a student is given the same test on two occasions. Thus, if the standardized

content validity A test's ability to sample the content that is to be measured.

criterion validity A test's ability to predict a student's performance as measured by other assessments or criteria.

concurrent validity The relation between a test's scores and other criteria that are currently (concurrently) available.

predictive validity The relation between test scores and the student's future performance.

construct validity The extent to which there is evidence that a test measures a particular construct. A construct is an unobservable trait or characteristic of a person, such as intelligence, learning style, personality, or anxiety.

reliability The extent to which a test produces a consistent, reproducible score.

test-retest reliability The extent to which a test yields the same performance when a student is given the same test on two occasions.

fourth-grade science test is given to a group of students today and then given to them again a month later, the test would be considered reliable if the students' scores were consistent across the two testings. There are two negative features of test-retest reliability: Students sometimes do better the second time they take the test because of their familiarity with it, and some students may have learned information in the time between the first test and the second test that changes their performance.

Alternate-forms reliability is determined by giving different forms of the same test on two different occasions to the same group of students and observing how consistent the scores are. The test items on the two forms are similar but not identical. This strategy eliminates the likelihood that students will perform better on the second test administration due to their familiarity with the items, but it does not eliminate a student's increase in knowledge and increased familiarity with the testing procedures and strategies.

Split-half reliability involves dividing the test items into two halves, such as the odd-numbered and even-numbered items. The scores on the two sets of items are compared to determine how consistently the students performed across each set. When split-half reliability is high, we say that the test is *internally consistent*. For example, on the standardized fourth-grade science test, the students' scores on the odd-numbered and even-numbered items could be compared. If they scored similarly on the two sets of items, we could conclude that the science test had high split-half reliability.

Reliability is influenced by a number of errors in measurement. A student can have adequate knowledge and skill, yet still not perform consistently across several tests because of a number of internal and external factors. Internal factors include health, motivation, and anxiety. External factors include inadequate directions given by the examiner, ambiguously created items, poor sampling of information, and inefficient scoring. When students perform inconsistently across the same or similar tests of their knowledge and skill, careful analysis should be made of internal and external factors that may have contributed to the inconsistency.

Validity and reliability are related (Gregory, 2007). A test that is valid is reliable, but a test that is reliable is not necessarily valid. People can respond consistently on a test, but the test might not be measuring what it purports to measure. To understand this, imagine that you have three darts to throw. If all three fall close together, you have reliability. However, you have validity only if all three hit the bull's-eye.

Fairness and Bias Fair tests are unbiased and nondiscriminatory (McMillan, 2004). They are not influenced by factors such as gender, ethnicity, or subjective factors such as the bias of a scorer. When tests are fair, students have the opportunity to demonstrate their learning so that their performance is not affected by their gender, ethnicity, disability, or other factors unrelated to the purpose of the test.

An unfair test is a test that puts a particular group of students at a disadvantage (Popham, 2006; Reynolds, Livingston, & Willson, 2006). This often occurs when there is something about the test that makes it more difficult for students with certain characteristics. For instance, suppose a test that is supposed to assess writing skills asks students to write a short story about a boy who practices very hard to be good in football and makes the team. Clearly, this type of item will be easier for boys than girls because boys are generally more familiar with football, so the test will be unfair to girls as an assessment of their writing stills. Consider also an item that might be used to assess reading comprehension. The reading passage is about a sailing experience. Thus, students who have had experience in sailing are likely to have an easier time reading and understanding the passage than those who have not. It is impossible to completely eliminate all unfair aspects of a test for every student, but test-makers can do much to create tests that are as fair as possible.

For students with disabilities, fairness often requires adaptations in administering the test. Many of the adaptations depend on the particular disability. The goal is to lessen the negative influence of the disability on the trait being tested. For example, for students with a hearing disability, be sure that the directions are written; for students with a visual problem, be sure that directions are given orally.

alternate-forms reliability Reliability judged by giving different forms of the same test on two different occasions to the same group of students to determine how consistent their scores are.

split-half reliability Reliability judged by dividing the test items into two halves, such as the odd-numbered and even-numbered items. The scores on the two sets of items are compared to determine how consistently the students performed across each set.

Review, Reflect, and Practice

(1) **Discuss the nature and purpose of standardized tests, as well as the criteria for evaluating them.**

REVIEW

- What is meant by *standardized test?* What are the uses of standardized tests?
- What do norms, validity, reliability, and fairness have to do with judging the quality of a standardized test?

REFLECT

- Can a test be valid but not reliable? reliable but not valid? Explain in your own words.

PRAXIS™ PRACTICE

1. Which of the following is an example of using the results of a standardized test to aid in program evaluation?
   a. At Lincoln Elementary School, students take a standardized achievement test each year to help determine who is in need of specialized services.
   b. Jefferson Elementary School purchased a new math curriculum. They are tracking the results of the math portion of the state-mandated standardized test and comparing the school's mean performance before and after the implementation of the new curriculum.
   c. Mr. Whitney uses the results of the social studies portion of the state-mandated standardized achievement test to help him to see how well his instruction is working to help his students meet state standards in history.
   d. Ms. Walker uses the results of a standardized reading test to place her students into small instructional reading groups. She gives the same test several times throughout the school year to gauge progress and regroup students.

2. Sidney is in third grade. He scores well above the national norm in the mathematics portion of a third-grade standardized achievement test. What does this mean?
   a. Sidney has an above-average IQ.
   b. Sidney is performing above the national average for third-graders in math.
   c. Sidney is performing below the national average for third-graders in math.
   d. Sidney should be placed in a fourth-grade math class.

Please see the answer key at the end of the book.

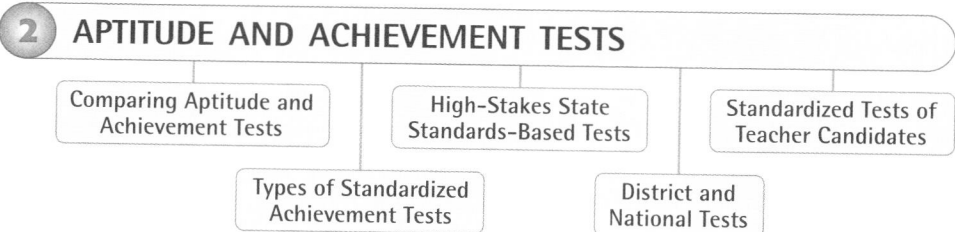

(2) APTITUDE AND ACHIEVEMENT TESTS

| Comparing Aptitude and Achievement Tests | High-Stakes State Standards–Based Tests | Standardized Tests of Teacher Candidates |

| Types of Standardized Achievement Tests | District and National Tests |

There are two main types of standardized tests: aptitude tests and achievement tests. First, we will define and compare these types of tests. Then, we'll discuss some different types of achievement tests and their use for state, district, and national purposes.

Comparing Aptitude and Achievement Tests

An **aptitude test** is designed to predict a student's ability to learn a skill or accomplish something with further education and training. Aptitude tests include general mental ability tests such as the intelligence tests (Stanford-Binet, Wechsler scales, and so on) that we described in chapter 4, "Individual Variations" (Kaufman & Lictenberger, 2002). They also include tests used to predict success in specific academic subjects or occupational areas (Thorndike, 2005). For example, one aptitude test might be given to students to predict their future success in math, while another might be given to predict whether an individual is likely to do well in sales or medicine.

An **achievement test** is intended to measure what the student has learned or what skills the student has mastered (Aiken & Groth-Marnat, 2006; Gronlund, 2006). However, the distinction between aptitude and achievement tests is sometimes blurred. Both types of tests assess a student's current status, the questions they use are often quite similar, and usually the results of the two kinds of tests are highly correlated.

The SAT that you may have taken as part of your admission to college is usually described as an aptitude test, but the SAT can be an aptitude test or an achievement test, depending on the purpose for which it is used. If it is used to predict your success in college, it is an aptitude test. If it is used to determine what you have learned (such as vocabulary, reading comprehension, and math skills), it is an achievement test.

Types of Standardized Achievement Tests

There are numerous types of standardized achievement tests. One common way to classify them is as survey batteries, specific subject tests, or diagnostic tests (Payne, 1997).

Survey Batteries A *survey battery* is a group of individual subject matter tests that is designed for a particular level of students. Survey batteries are the most widely used national norm-referenced standardized tests (McMillan, 2004). Some common batteries are the California Achievement tests, *Terra Nova* Comprehensive Tests for Basic Skills, Iowa Tests of Basic Skills, Metropolitan Achievement Tests, and Stanford Achievement Test Series.

The Stanford Achievement Test Series has tests for three different levels: kindergarten to grade 1.5, grades 1.5 to 9.9, and grades 9 to 13.0. The battery can be customized to fit the needs of a particular district or school. The Stanford battery includes a number of subject matter tests at each level. For example, at the sixth-grade level, there are subject matter tests for reading, mathematics, language, listening, spelling, study skills, science, social studies, information use, and thinking skills.

Many survey batteries also contain a number of subtests within a subject area. For example, the Metropolitan Achievement Tests include reading as one of the subject areas at each level. The reading subtests on the Metropolitan Tests include vocabulary, word recognition, and reading comprehension.

In their early years, survey batteries consisted of multiple-choice items to assess the student's content knowledge. However, recent editions have increasingly included more open-ended items that evaluate the student's thinking and reasoning skills.

Tests for Specific Subjects Some standardized achievement tests assess skills in a particular area such as reading or mathematics. Because they focus on a specific area, they usually assess the skill in a more detailed, extensive way than a survey battery. Two examples of specific area tests that involve reading are the Woodcock Reading Mastery Tests and the Gates-McKillop-Horowitz Reading Diagnostic Test (Mather & Gregg, 2001). Some standardized subject-area tests cover topics, such as chemistry, psychology, or computer science, that are not included in survey batteries.

Diagnostic Tests As we said earlier, diagnosis is an important function of standardized testing. *Diagnostic testing* consists of a relatively in-depth evaluation of a

aptitude test A type of test that is used to predict a student's ability to learn a skill or accomplish something with further education and training.

achievement test A test that measures what the student has learned or what skills the student has mastered.

specific area of learning. Its purpose is to determine the specific learning needs of a student so that those needs can be met through regular or remedial instruction. Reading and mathematics are the two areas in which standardized tests are most often used for diagnosis (Berninger & others, 2001).

In many cases, diagnostic testing is done after considerable instruction already has taken place. An achievement test is sometimes used for diagnostic purposes (such as one of the reading tests just mentioned). In many circumstances, though, both observations and achievement tests will be used to make a diagnosis. A typical diagnostic sequence might involve (Payne, 1997) (1) informal observations by the teacher, (2) a survey battery, (3) a group diagnostic test, and (4) an individual diagnostic test. Note that in this sequence, diagnostic tests can often be given in a group format or an individual format.

Test publishers of all national norm-referenced standardized achievement tests claim that their tests can be used for diagnosis (McMillan, 2004). However, for a test to be effective in diagnosis it should have several test items for each skill or objective that is measured, and many of these national tests fall short in this regard.

High-Stakes State Standards-Based Tests

As the public and government have demanded increased accountability of how effectively schools are educating our nation's children, state standards-based tests have taken on a more powerful role (Marzano & Kendall, 2006; Popham, 2005, 2006; Shaftel, 2005; Shepard & others, 2005).

States have mandated tests for many years but their emphasis has recently changed (Airasian, 2005). Prior to the 1990s, their content was not closely linked with what was actually taught and learned in the classroom. The early state-mandated assessments simply provided an overall view of how students in a state were performing in certain subject areas, especially reading and mathematics.

In the 1990s, efforts began to connect state-mandated testing to state-endorsed instructional objectives. Most states already have identified or are in the process of identifying objectives that every student in the state is expected to achieve. These objectives form the basis not only for these mandated standards-based tests but also for such activities as teacher education and curriculum decisions (Whitford & Jones, 2000). Teachers are strongly encouraged to incorporate these objectives into their classroom planning and instruction. In many states, the objectives are reflected in the achievement tests that are given to every student in the state.

The Format of State Standards-Based Tests From a constructivist point of view, state standards-based tests have the wrong format, consisting mainly of multiple-choice items. Only seven states currently use essay or performance assessments (Quality Counts, 2001). When construction-based assessments are included, they typically involve short-answer items or writing prompts. Very few states include a portfolio as part of their assessment.

Almost all states use criterion-referenced scoring, which means that the student's score is evaluated against predetermined standards. Most states have a cutoff score (such as correct answers to 70 percent of the items) that the student has to reach to pass the test. Such tests also provide comparative scores.

Possible Advantages and Uses of High-Stakes Testing A number of policy-makers argue that high-stakes state standards-based testing will have a number of positive effects:

- Improved student performance
- More time teaching the subjects tested
- High expectations for all students
- Identification of poorly performing schools, teachers, and administrators
- Improved confidence in schools as test scores increase

The widest uses of these tests for guiding the progress of individual students have to do with decisions regarding remediation, promotion, and graduation. Remediation consists of assigning students who do not do well on the tests to special classes. Such remediation usually occurs after school, on Saturday, or during the summer. Currently, thirteen states require and fund remediation strategies to help low-performing students reach state standards.

Many endorsers of state standards-based tests argue that students should not be promoted to the next grade without reaching a certain standard of performance on the tests. In this regard, the goal is to end social promotion (promotion based on the idea that students should not be left behind their age-mates). Currently, test-based promotion policies have been instituted in nine states.

State standards-based tests are also being used to determine whether a student should be allowed to graduate from high school in twenty-four states. Such a decision can have a major impact on a youth's future.

In addition, state standards-based tests are used to make decisions about school and staff accountability. Holding schools accountable means using test scores to place the schools in designated categories, such as watch/warning (which is publicly reported and implies that improvement is expected), probation (which usually requires the school to submit a comprehensive reform plan), failing/in crisis (which requires serious outside assistance in developing an improvement plan), accredited, accredited with warning, and nonaccredited.

Criticism of State Standards-Based Tests   Critics of the state standards-based tests argue that state-mandated tests lead to these negative consequences (McMillan, 2002):

- *Dumbing down of the curriculum with greater emphasis on rote memorization than on problem-solving and critical thinking skills.* In one analysis, most state tests focused on less-demanding knowledge and skills rather than more-complex cognitive skills (Quality Counts, 2001). This narrows the curriculum and focuses it more on lower-order cognitive skills (Linn, 2000). Adhering to a test-driven curriculum often means superficial coverage of topics (Shepard & others, 2005).

- *Teaching to the test.* Teachers increasingly teach knowledge and skills that are to be covered on the state tests (Bransford & others, 2005; Gallagher, 2000). They spend inordinate amounts of time on testlike activities and practice tests, with less time for actual teaching of important content and skills. In a recent survey, more than six of ten public school teachers said that state standards-based testing has led to teaching that focuses too much on state tests (Quality Counts, 2001). About two-thirds indicated that state standards-based testing was forcing them to concentrate too much on information that would be tested, to the detriment of other important areas.

- *Discrimination against low-socioeconomic-status (SES) and ethnic minority children.* This results when disproportionate percentages of these children do not meet the state standards, while higher-SES and non-Latino White students do. Researchers have found that students who are placed in the lowest tracks or remedial programs—disproportionately low-income and minority students—are most likely to experience subsequent inferior teaching and reduced achievement (Cooper & Sherk, 1989;

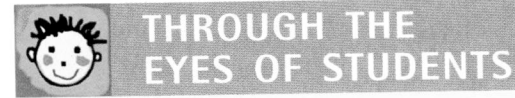

THROUGH THE EYES OF STUDENTS

"It's as If a Test Score Is All There Is to a Person"

"Spend enough time in school and you start to think that standardized tests are the only things that matter in life. My standardized test scores are disappointing but I take pride in being in the top four percent of my class. I have a 4.0 GPA. If I can pull off those kinds of grades in tough classes—including three Advanced Placement courses—I'm forced to wonder, what do these tests really prove?

"It's as if a test score is all there is to a person. I enjoy all kinds of creative writing, and I spend long nights trying to *understand* school subjects, rather than just memorize formulas. But none of this matters for standardized tests" (Garcia, 2001).

Tania Garcia
Twelfth-Grade Student
Oakland High School
Oakland, California

Oakes, 1990). There is evidence that high-stakes state standards-based testing that rewards or sanctions schools based on average student scores can create incentives for pushing low-scorers into special education, holding them back a grade, and encouraging them to drop out of school so that the schools' average scores will look better (Darling-Hammond, 2001; Haney, 2000).

For these reasons and others, the American Psychological Association, the American Educational Research Association, and the National Council on Measurement in Education have issued standards for the use of tests, noting that test scores are too limited and unstable to be used as the sole source of information for any major decision about student placement or promotion. Test scores should always be used in combination with other sources of information about student achievement when making important decisions about students (National Research Council, 2001).

Because high-stakes state standards-based testing is relatively new, there is little systematic research on its consequences (McMillan, 2002). However, there are some serious concerns about the way high-stakes testing currently is structured. One concern involves the validity of the inferences that can be drawn from the results (National Research Council, 2001). Just documenting higher test scores does not mean that education has improved. Indeed, if the tests are assessing the wrong skills or are flawed, it could mean just the opposite. As yet, we do not know if the high-stakes testing is causing students to be better prepared for college and the workplace.

Yet another concern is the extent to which high-stakes testing is useful for improving teaching and learning—the ultimate goal of educational reforms (National Research Council, 2001). Most current high-stakes tests provide very limited information for teachers and administrators about why students do not perform well or how they can modify instruction to improve student achievement. Most of the high-stakes tests provide only general information about where a student stands relative to peers (such as scoring at the 63rd percentile) or whether the students have not performed well in certain domains (such as performing below the basic level in mathematics). Such tests do not provide information about whether students are using misguided strategies to solve problems or which concepts in a domain students do not understand. In sum, most current high-stakes tests do not provide information about the types of interventions that would improve students' performance or even yield information about their strengths and weaknesses.

We also know that it is not a good strategy to rely solely on a single test when making important decisions about students or evaluating schools. Multiple indicators, including grades, attendance, performance assessments, and percentage of students who go to college, also need to be considered. We also know that if state standards-based tests continue to be used, they need to be changed to better reflect higher-order thinking skills, not encourage teachers to teach to the test and not penalize students from low-income and minority backgrounds (Stansfield & Rivera, 2002). Later in the chapter, we will further discuss problems with the formats of high-stakes testing.

District and National Tests

In addition to state standards-based tests, a particular district might mandate standardized tests. Students also might take national tests.

District-Mandated Tests In Spencerport, New York, the school district collects information about student performance with the following tests: the Stanford Achievement Test in Reading (grades 2–8) and Math (grades 1–8); the New York State Pupil Evaluation Test in Reading (grades 3–6), Written Expression (grade 5), and Mathematics (grades 3 and 6); the New York State Program Evaluation Test, which assesses programs in science and social studies; the New York Preliminary

Competency Test, which is used to predict future success in reading, writing, and math (given in any grade); the New York State Regents Competency Test, which assesses competency in math, science, global studies, and U.S. history and government (given in high school to students who do not take the Regents Test); the Scholastic Assessment Test (SAT) and American College Test (ACT), given to students who plan to apply to college; and Advanced Placement tests in U.S. history, biology, chemistry, English literature and composition, French, Spanish, calculus, and music theory, which can be taken by students to place out of certain classes because of the knowledge and skill levels they have attained. In 1999, Spencerport also began assessing students' ability to apply knowledge and problem-solving skills in a number of subject areas.

Types of standardized tests vary across school districts. However, as in Spencerport, the overall number is typically large.

No Child Left Behind   In chapter 1, we described the No Child Left Behind (NCLB) Act, the federal government's legislation that was signed into law in 2002. NCLB is the U.S. government's effort to hold schools and school districts accountable for the success or failure of their students. The legislation shifts responsibility to the states, with states being required to create their own standards for students' achievement in mathematics, English/language arts, and science. In the 2005–2006 school year, states began giving all students annual tests in grades 3 through 8. States are required to create an accountability system that ensures students are making adequate annual progress in the subject areas mentioned above. Although all students must show adequate progress, separate objectives are to be proposed for students who are economically disadvantaged, students from ethnic minority groups, students with disabilities, and students with limited English proficiency.

Schools that fail to make *adequate yearly progress (AYP)* for two consecutive years are labeled "underperforming." Underperforming schools are to be given special help, but they must give parents the option of moving their children to a better-performing school (Duke, 2006). If underperforming schools don't improve after 4 years, states are required to implement major staff and curriculum changes in the schools, and if progress is not made after 5 years, states must close the schools (Kubick & Mcloughin, 2005).

Also as part of the No Child Left Behind legislation, states and districts are required to provide report cards that show a school's performance level, so that the public is aware of which schools are underperforming. Another aspect of the No Child Left Behind legislation is that all teachers hired by June 30, 2006, were required to be "highly qualified," which means being licensed and having an academic major in the field in which they are teaching. Schools are required to notify parents if a teacher is not "highly qualified."

A number of criticisms of No Child Left Behind have been made. Some critics argue that the NCLB legislation will do more harm than good (Booher-Jennings, 2006; Lederman & Burnstein, 2006; Lewis, 2006; Neil, 2006). One widely adopted criticism stresses that using a single score from a test as the sole indicator of students' and teachers' progress and competence represents a very narrow aspect of students' and teachers' skills. This criticism is similar to the one leveled at IQ testing, described in chapter 4. To more accurately assess student progress and achievement, many psychologists and educators argue that a number of measures should be used, including tests, quizzes, projects, portfolios, and classroom observations—rather than a single score on a single test. Also, the tests schools are using to assess achievement and progress as part of NCLB don't measure such important skills as creativity, motivation, persistence, flexible thinking, and social skills (Droege, 2004; Goldberg, 2005). Critics point out that teachers and schools are spending far too much class time "teaching to the test" by drilling students and having them memorize isolated facts at the expense of more student-centered constructivist teaching that focuses on higher-level thinking skills, which students need for success in life (Posner, 2004; Neil, 2006).

TECHNOLOGY AND EDUCATION
Standardized Testing, Data-Driven Decision Making, and Handheld Computers

The growing emphasis on accountability and data-driven decision making occasioned by the No Child Left Behind legislation has prompted educators to think differently about how standardized assessments and resulting data can inform classroom instruction, and, ultimately, affect student achievement. Educators across the country, therefore, are working hard to develop strategies that provide standardized test data to stakeholders at all levels of the educational system and offer teachers technical assistance to administer assessments and use results effectively. Increasingly, districts and schools are turning to technology-based applications.

A good example is the state of New Mexico's early literacy program. A recipient of a federal Department of Education *Reading First* grant, the state recognized that Reading First offered them not only a unique opportunity to support literacy instruction, but also a way to collect and use data in a standardized fashion. State education officials contracted with Wireless Generation, a company that provides mobile software for early literacy assessments and that allows teachers to use handheld computers to administer assessments, record student data, and then upload that assessment data to a desktop computer and to a Web site where it is immediately made available in graphic form. This lets teachers view a student's assessment results, as well as individual students' data in relation to previous assessments or assessment data from other students in the same classroom. While several assessments reside on the handhelds,

the state required that the participating teachers administer the Dynamic Indicators of Basic Early Literacy Skills, also known as the DIBELS (Good & Kaminski, 2003) to all of their students during three assessment windows throughout the school year—fall, winter, and spring.

Researchers found many benefits for the handheld computers in the program (Hupert & Heinze, 2006, in press). Teachers reported that the use of handhelds was much more efficient. They said it was much easier to bring the handheld around with them to administer the DIBELS. Also the results were instantly uploaded in contrast to having to reenter pencil and paper data. This led to a second benefit, instantaneous feedback—teachers immediately saw results in a variety of formats for both individual students and their entire class. These first two benefits, in turn, led to several others, including shaping professional development opportunities to address perceived problems, strengthening home-school communications in that teachers could immediately report on student achievement, and enhancing the use of data to drive instruction.

The success of New Mexico's Reading First project has led several other states (Florida, Oklahoma, and Ohio), the Bureau of Indian Affairs, and school districts, such as those of Chicago and New York City, to contract with Wireless Generation to supply participating teachers with handhelds to administer the DIBELS.

Another criticism is that the increased cost of carrying out standardized testing on a statewide basis, including creating tests, administering them, scoring them, and reporting their results to the federal government come at a time when most states are facing budget crunches (Lewis, 2005). Having to spend so much more money on testing means that some existing resources and programs in other areas will have to be trimmed or eliminated (Kubick & Mcloughlin, 2005).

Despite such criticisms, the U.S. Department of Education is committed to implementing No Child Left Behind, and schools are making accommodations to meet the requirement of this law. Indeed, most educators support the importance of high expectations and high standards of excellence for students and teachers (Houston, 2005; Revelle, 2004). At issue, however, is whether the tests and procedures mandated by NCLB are the best ones for achieving these high standards.

Educators are increasingly interested in ways that technology can be used effectively in conjunction with standardized tests, such as those required by No Child Left Behind. To read about how this was accomplished in an early literacy program in New Mexico, see the Technology and Education box.

National Assessment of Students and World-Class Standards   The federal
government also is involved in standardized testing of students through the
National Assessment of Educational Progress (NAEP). States are not required
to participate in the national assessment, although many do (for example,
more than forty states have their students take the reading portion of the test).
The NAEP is a censuslike examination of young Americans' knowledge, skills,
understanding, and attitudes. The subject areas include reading, writing, literature, mathematics, science, social studies, art, citizenship, and career and
occupational development. NAEP assessments began in 1969 for science, writing, and citizenship. Care is taken not to identify any student, school, city, or
state, although states can choose to have scores identified by state. Any student
who takes the NAEP responds only to a portion of the entire assessment.

Recent findings from the NAEP (2000, 2005) show these trends:

- *Reading.* From 1992 through 2005, slight improvements occurred for
  fourth- and eighth-graders.
- *Mathematics.* Scores improved from 1990 through 2005 for fourth-
  and eighth-graders but showed a decline in 2000 for twelfth-graders
  (see figure 15.1).
- *Science.* No change in scores occurred from 1996 through 2000 for fourth- and
  eighth-graders but scores of twelfth-graders declined in this time frame.

The federal government has proposed a voluntary national test of fourth- and
eighth-grade students' reading (Applebome, 1997). The hope is that it will become
so widely used that it will become America's first truly national assessment of students' achievement. The national test would be similar to the NAEP reading and math
tests and the math component of the Third International Mathematics and Science
Study. However, currently tests are given only to a sample of students to compute
national averages. The new tests would assess a much larger number of students and
evaluate individual students.

National assessment of students is part of an effort to get American students to
measure up to, and eventually set the standard for, world-class achievement in education. In an analysis of national testing in 12 major countries, the United States
and Canada were the only countries without a standardized national test (for example, most Asian countries, such as Japan, Thailand, and Singapore, have national
tests) (Haynes & Chalker, 1997). In reading, American students do well against
students from other countries during the elementary school years, but by the end of
high school they have fallen behind students in many other countries. In recent comparisons of U.S. students with students from 24 other countries in math, U.S.
students exceeded the international average but students in 11 of the 25 countries
outperformed U.S. students in the fourth grade (Asian countries took the top four
positions—Singapore, Hong Kong, Japan, and Chinese Taipei) and students in 9 of
the 34 countries outperformed U.S. students in the eighth grade (Asian students also
scored the highest in the eighth grade) (Gonzales & others, 2004). U.S. fourth-grade
students fared better in science, being outperformed only by students from Chinese
Taipei, Japan, and Singapore, but in the eighth grade, students in seven countries
(Singapore, Chinese Taipei, Korea, and Hong Kong were the highest) fared better than
U.S. students.

In comparisons with previous assessments, no changes occurred from 1995 to
2003 in the average scores for U.S. fourth-graders in math and science, but U.S.
eighth-graders slightly improved their average math and science scores across this
time frame. In comparison to the 14 other countries that were included in both the
1995 and 2003 assessments, the performance of U.S. fourth-graders was lower in 2003
than in 1995. Among the reasons given for the weaker performance of U.S. students in
comparison to the top countries in reading, math, and science are inadequate time spent
on academic schoolwork, expectations for achievement that are too low, larger class

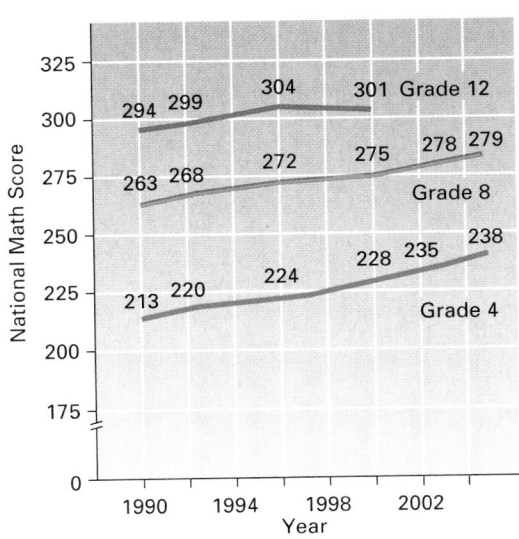

FIGURE 15.1 **Trends in Mathematics
Scores in the National Assessment of
Educational Progress**

Note: Scores could range from 0 to 500.
Data for grade 12 were not reported in
2003 and 2005.

Japanese secondary school students. *How do U.S. students fare on international comparisons with Japanese students and students in other countries?*

sizes, too much time spent on television and nonacademic media, too little time spent doing homework, and inadequate spending on education (Ravitch, 1995).

Critics of the cross-national comparisons argue that in many comparisons virtually all U.S. children are being compared with a "select" group of children from other countries, especially in the secondary school comparisons. Therefore, they conclude, it is no wonder that American students don't fare so well. That criticism holds for some international comparisons. However, even when the top 25 percent of students in different countries were more recently compared, U.S. students did not rank much higher (Mullis, 1999). For example, in a recent comparison of the top 25 percent of high school seniors (in terms of math and science knowledge and skills) in different countries, Sweden, the Netherlands, Norway, and Switzerland ranked highest. The United States was still below the international average in math and science knowledge and skills, even when their best students were compared with other countries' best students.

An analysis of national standardized tests found that, compared with American standardized tests, other countries' tests (1) included more short-answer, open-ended, and essay questions and (2) were more closely linked with the curriculum and textbooks so that foreign students knew what they needed to study (Jacobson, 1996). Recently, publishers of commercial standardized tests in America have begun to include more constructed-item and performance assessments in their tests.

One of the dilemmas in pursuing internationally competitive standards involves deciding what they should be and who should set them (Tanner, 1997). Should they be based on the standards of the countries whose students achieve the highest scores on tests? What roles do the federal and state governments play in developing these standards? Which educators should participate in their creation? Should instruction be tied to the standards? Consensus on these questions has not yet been reached.

Standardized Tests of Teacher Candidates

Not only do students have to take standardized tests, but as you are likely aware, so do teacher candidates (Darling-Hammond, 2006; Pecheone & Chung, 2006). Many teacher candidates are required to take some version of the PRAXIS™ tests or a test created by an individual state.

The Praxis™ Tests and State Tests for Teachers   Most states now require teacher candidates to take a licensing exam. In some cases, this involves one or more PRAXIS™ tests published by Educational Testing Service or a test that is used only by a particular state. The tests used by states for licensing of teacher candidates assess (1) basic skills or general academic ability, (2) subject matter knowledge (such as math, English, science, or social studies), and/or (3) pedagogical knowledge. In many cases, there is little consistency across states in which specific tests are used.

The PRAXIS™ tests consist of PRAXIS I™, PRAXIS II™, and PRAXIS III™. The PRAXIS I™ test is a preliminary screening of basic skills that is often taken early in an undergraduate program or before a student is formally admitted to a teacher certification program.

PRAXIS II™ tests are essentially exit exams that typically are taken in the junior or senior year of undergraduate school to ensure that students know their specialty content areas and/or effective pedagogy before being awarded a preliminary teaching certificate. The PRAXIS II™ tests cover four main categories: organizing content knowledge for student learning, creating an environment for student learning, teaching for student learning, and teacher professionalism. They use a case-study approach to measure students' pedagogical knowledge. The PRAXIS II™ tests are oriented toward specific age groups (elementary school—K–6; middle school—grades 5–9; and secondary school—grades 7–12).

PRAXIS III™ tests are assessments of classroom teaching performance. They are typically administered during the first year of teaching and can be used as part of a licensing decision. PRAXIS III™ tests include essays, oral response tests, listening tasks, portfolio reviews, video stimuli, and in-class observation.

Criticisms of the current PRAXIS™ and state licensure tests for teacher candidates have been made. Three such criticisms are (Darling-Hammond & Baratz-Snowden, 2005, pp. 61–62):

* *Tests assess "low-level or marginally relevant knowledge and skills" rather than "deep knowledge of subject matter and actual teaching skills."*
* *The cutoff scores for the tests sometimes are low or not enforced.* If states are experiencing a shortage of teachers, "they often waive the testing requirement" and hire individuals who have failed the test.
* *There is a lack of consistency across states that has restricted teacher mobility.* This is especially a problem because some states have teacher surpluses, others teacher shortages.

The Call for a National Test for Teacher Candidates   Currently, no national test is required for teacher candidates, but recently the call for one was made (Keller, 2005; Wineburg, 2006). The National Academy of Education, which is made up of a distinguished group of educators, prepared *A Good Teacher in Every Classroom* (Darling-Hammond & Baratz-Snowden, 2005). The report states that the national test should assess a common core of knowledge for professional preparation, including how to create learning opportunities that make subjects accessible to all students. The National Academy of Education also recommended that the test results should be incorporated into state licensing requirements:

> Such a test, like those used to certify doctors, lawyers, and architects, should demonstrate not only what teachers *know* about their subjects and how to teach them but also what they can *do* in the classroom; for example, whether they can plan and implement lessons to teach standards, evaluate students' needs and design instruction to meet them, use a variety of teaching strategies, and maintain a purposeful, productive classroom. Fortunately, assessments that use videotapes of teaching and teachers' and students' work samples to evaluate what teachers actually do in the classroom have been developed by the National Board for Professional Teaching Standards (for use in certifying veteran accomplished teachers) and by states such as Connecticut for use in licensing beginning teachers (Darling-Hammond & Baratz-Snowden, 2005, pp. 62–63).

Review, Reflect, and Practice

(2) **Compare aptitude and achievement testing and describe current uses of achievement tests.**

REVIEW

- How clearly do aptitude and achievement tests differ in purpose? in form?
- What are *survey batteries, specific subject tests,* and *diagnostic tests*?
- What are some possible advantages to high-stakes state standards-based testing and what are some ways their results are being used? What are some criticisms of high-stakes state standards-based testing?
- What is the argument for national standardized testing? Why is it resisted?
- How can standardized tests of teachers be characterized?

REFLECT

- What value do you see in the idea of international standards for what students learn in school? What problems?

PRAXIS™ PRACTICE

1. Which of the following is an appropriate use of an aptitude test?
   a. Josh takes a standardized test to help determine whether he is likely to succeed in medical school.
   b. Ike takes a standardized test to help determine what he has learned in his teacher preparation program.
   c. Stan takes a standardized test to determine to what degree he has met state mathematics standards.
   d. Penelope takes a standardized test to determine if she can graduate from high school.

2. Ms. Jerovitz is reviewing the results of a standardized achievement test her students have taken. She carefully examines and charts the scores on each of the subtests included in the test. She has scores in mathematical reasoning, computation, vocabulary, reading comprehension, spelling, science, and social studies. What type of test did her students most likely take?
   a. diagnostic test
   b. aptitude test
   c. intelligence test
   d. survey battery

3. Ms. Comer is frustrated by the state standards-based tests she must give to her third-grade students. State funding for the district is now tied to performance on these tests. As a result, Ms. Comer and other teachers are under pressure from the administration and board of education to ensure that all students meet state standards. Which of the following is the most likely outcome of this scenario?
   a. Ms. Comer and other teachers will become better teachers so that their students will achieve at higher levels.
   b. Ms. Comer and other teachers will begin to teach only the things that will be covered on the state standards-based test, thus narrowing the curriculum and student learning opportunities.
   c. Ms. Comer and other teachers will ignore the pressure from administrators and the board of education, continue to teach as they always have, and hope for the best.
   d. Ms. Comer and other teachers will spend more time enriching their curriculum so that students will achieve at higher levels.

4. Mr. Carlson, a fifth-grade teacher, described what he thinks are four provisions of the No Child Left Behind legislation to his colleagues. The four provisions he described follow. Which one did he describe inaccurately?

   a. In 2005–2006, states began giving annual tests to all students in grades 1 through 12.
   b. Schools that fail to make adequate yearly progress for two consecutive years are labeled "underperforming."
   c. States and districts are required to provide report cards that show a school's performance level.
   d. Although all students must show adequate progress, separate objectives are to be proposed for students who are economically disadvantaged.

5. Sally is nervous about the test she will be taking as part of the teacher certification process. The test will cover information regarding educational psychology and child development. Which test is Sally most likely taking?
   a. PRAXIS I™
   b. PRAXIS II™
   c. PRAXIS III™
   d. National Teacher Certification Test

Please see the answer key at the end of the book.

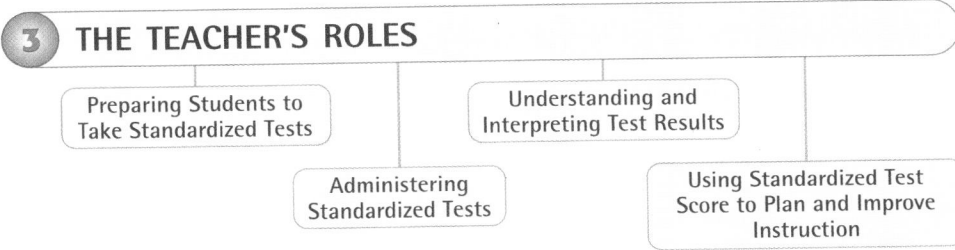

The teacher's roles in standardized testing include preparing students for the test, administering the test, understanding and interpreting test results, and communicating test results to parents. Teachers also use test scores to plan and improve instruction.

Preparing Students to Take Standardized Tests

All students need the opportunity to do their best. One way to do this is to make sure that students have good test-taking skills (McMillan, 2004). You should communicate a positive attitude about the test to students. Explain the test's nature and purpose and describe it as an opportunity and a challenge rather than an ordeal. Avoid saying anything that can cause students to get nervous about the test. If you observe that anxiety in some students may hinder their performance, consider having a counselor talk with them about ways to reduce their test anxiety.

   In this era of high-stakes testing in which scores on standardized tests can have serious consequences for students, teachers, and schools, many schools are establishing programs designed to improve students' test-taking skills (Payne, 1997). However, researchers have found that "coaching" or training students to do well on a test, such as the SAT, gives only a slight boost to scores. For example, 20-hour coaching classes increase math and verbal scores on the SAT by only about 15 and 10 points, respectively, on the 200- to 800-point scale, contrary to the exaggerated claims made by SAT coaching programs (Bond, 1989; Educational Testing Service, 1994). The Educational Testing Service (ETS), which publishes the SAT, says that the best way for students to do well on the SAT is to take rigorous courses, work hard in them, brush

BEST PRACTICES
Strategies for Improving Students' Test-Taking Skills

Here are some important test-taking skills that you might want to discuss with your students (Linn & Gronlund, 2000):

1. *Read the instructions carefully.*

2. *Read the items carefully.*

3. *Keep track of the time and work quickly enough to finish the test.*

4. *Skip difficult items and return to them later.*

5. *Make informed guesses instead of omitting items, if scoring favors doing so.*

6. *Eliminate as many items as possible on multiple-choice items.*

7. *Follow directions carefully in marking the answer (such as darkening the entire space).* Make sure students know how to do this. Next, Marlene Wendler, a fourth-grade teacher in New Ulm, Minnesota, describes her experiences with standardized tests that her students take.

THROUGH THE EYES OF TEACHERS
Make Sure You Evaluate Your Students on More than Just Tests

Standardized tests are just one very small, isolated picture of a child. A much fuller "video" comes from daily observations. Do not unfairly label a child based on a test.

Rarely or never during the school year do my students encounter fill-in-the-oval items like those on standardized tests. Therefore, to be fair, before standardized testing I give them examples similar to the format of the test. If adults take a test with a special format, they prepare themselves by practicing in that format. Why should it be any different for children?

8. *Check to be sure that the appropriate response was marked on the answer sheet.*

9. *Go back and check answers if time permits.*

up on their algebra and geometry, familiarize themselves with the test, and get a good night's sleep the night before the test. Taking a practice test or two is wise in preparing for any standardized test.

Some don'ts regarding teachers preparing students for standardized tests include (McMillan, 2002): don't teach to the test, don't use the standardized test format for classroom tests, don't describe tests as a burden, don't tell students that important decisions will be made solely on the results of a single test, don't use previous forms of the same test to prepare students, and don't convey a negative attitude about the test.

Administering Standardized Tests

Most standardized tests spell out in considerable detail how the test should be administered (Airasian, 2005). This includes how to set up the testing room, what to do when students take the test, how to distribute the test and answer sheets, and how to time the tests.

The physical testing environment should be well lighted and well ventilated. Students should have adequate work space. Seat students in a manner that will avoid distractions or cheating. Hang a sign on the door to the room that says something like "Testing in Progress—Do Not Disturb" (McMillan, 2004).

In administering the test, the teacher should follow word for word the script that is included in the test manual, to ensure that the test is being given under standardized conditions (Gay & Airasian, 2000). If this script is not followed exactly, comparisons of the students' performance with the population of students on which the norms for the test were established could be invalid (Airasian, 2005). Be sure to write the start and finish times for the test on the chalkboard. At start time, tell students clearly to begin. Make sure students stop when the time has expired.

After your students have completed the test, count the booklets and answer sheets. Also record any incidents that you observed that might invalidate students' scores.

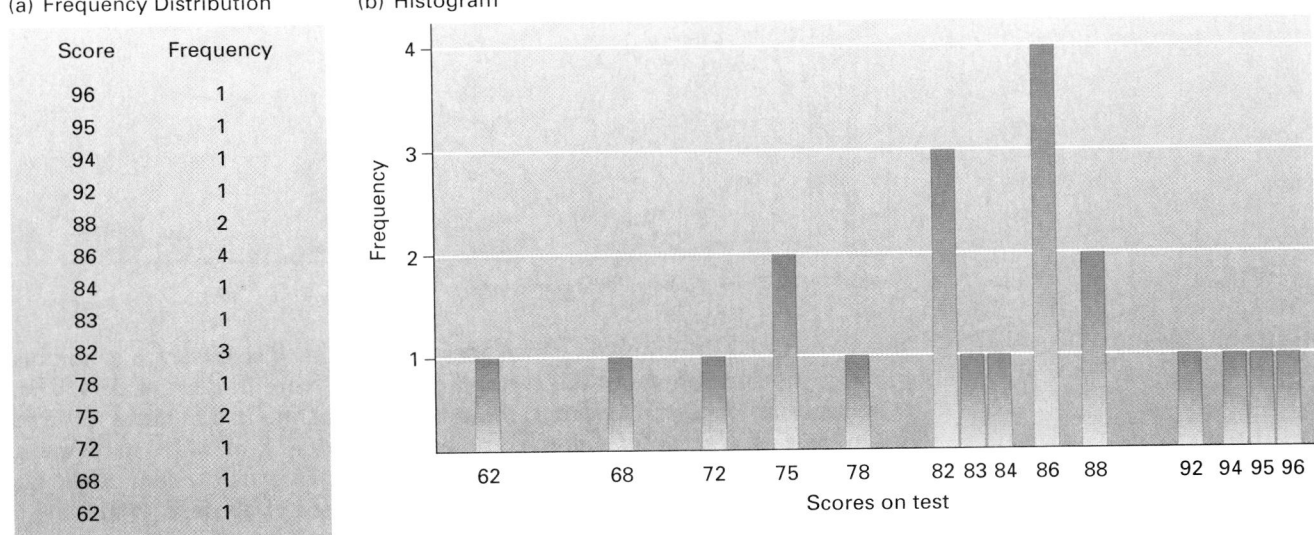

<table>
<tr><td colspan="2">(a) Frequency Distribution</td></tr>
</table>

Score	Frequency
96	1
95	1
94	1
92	1
88	2
86	4
84	1
83	1
82	3
78	1
75	2
72	1
68	1
62	1

FIGURE 15.2 A Frequency Distribution and Histogram

Understanding and Interpreting Test Results

Knowledge of some basic descriptive statistics will help you interpret standardized tests. Your ability to understand and interpret standardized tests will come in handy when you have parent-teacher conferences regarding children in your class. We will discuss these basic statistics as well as some ways that test results are commonly reported.

Understanding Descriptive Statistics   Although we are discussing statistics here to help you understand standardized tests, the information about statistics also can help you with many other aspects of classroom assessment, such as interpreting a student's scores on tests you have created and administered, as well as calculating a student's grade point average (Best & Kahn, 2003; Hurlburt, 2006; Jackson, 2005). Our primary focus here is on **descriptive statistics,** which are mathematical procedures used to describe and summarize data (information) in a meaningful way (Kiess, 2002). We will study frequency distributions, measures of central tendency, measures of variability, and the normal distribution.

Frequency Distributions   The first step in organizing data involves creating a **frequency distribution,** a listing of scores, usually from highest to lowest, along with the number of times each score appears. Imagine that a test was given and 21 students received the following scores on the test: 96, 95, 94, 92, 88, 88, 86, 86, 86, 86, 84, 83, 82, 82, 82, 78, 75, 75, 72, 68, and 62. Figure 15.2a shows a frequency distribution for these scores. Frequency distributions often are presented graphically. For example, a **histogram** is a frequency distribution in the form of a graph. Vertical bars represent the frequency of scores per category. Figure 15.2b shows a histogram for the 21 scores. A histogram often is called a *bar graph.* Notice in the histogram that the horizontal axis (the *x*-axis) indicates the obtained scores and the vertical axis (the *y*-axis) indicates how often each score occurs.

Although representing a group of scores graphically can provide insight about students' performance, so can some statistical techniques that represent scores numerically. These techniques involve the concepts of central tendency and variability, each of which we will discuss.

"Tonight, we're going to let the statistics speak for themselves."

descriptive statistics Mathematical procedures that are used to describe and summarize data (information) in a meaningful way.

frequency distribution A listing of scores, usually from highest to lowest, along with the number of times each score appears.

histogram A frequency distribution in the form of a graph.

MISS PEACH. By permission of Mell Lazarus and Creators Syndicate, Inc.

Measures of Central Tendency A measure of **central tendency** is a number that provides information about the average, or typical, score in a set of data. There are three measures of central tendency: mean, median, and mode. The **mean** is the numerical average of a group of scores, commonly labeled as X or M by statisticians. The mean is computed by adding all the scores and then dividing the sum by the number of scores. Thus, the mean for the 21 students' test scores above is $1740/21 = 82.86$. The mean often is a good indicator of the central tendency of a group of scores.

The **median** is the score that falls exactly in the middle of a distribution of scores after they have been arranged (or ranked) from highest to lowest. In our example of 21 test scores, the median is the 11th ranked score (10 above, 10 below it), so the median is 84.

The **mode** is the score that occurs most often. The mode can be determined easily by looking at the frequency distribution or histogram. In our example of 21 scores, the mode is 86 (the score occurring most often—four times). The mode is most revealing when its value is much more frequent than the other values or scores. For example, in the 21 scores in our example, if 15 of the 21 scores had been the same, then the mode probably would be the best measure of central tendency for the data. In this case, the mean and median would be less meaningful.

A set of scores may have more than one mode. For example, in our example of 21 students taking a test, if four students had scored 86 and four students had scored 75, then the set of scores would have two modes (86 and 75). A set of scores with two modes is called a *bimodal distribution*. It is possible for a set of scores to have more than two modes, in which case it is called a *multimodal distribution*.

Measures of Variability In addition to obtaining information about the central tendency of a set of scores, it also is important to know about their variability (Abrami, Cholmsky, & Gordon, 2001). **Measures of variability** tell us how much the scores vary from one another. Two measures of variability are range and standard deviation.

The **range** is the distance between the highest and lowest scores. The range of the 21 students' test scores in our example is 34 points ($96 - 62 = 34$). The range is a rather simple measure of variability and it is not used often. The most commonly used measure of variability is the standard deviation.

The **standard deviation** is a measure of how much a set of scores varies on the average around the mean of the scores. In other words, it reveals how closely scores cluster around the mean (Frey, 2005). The smaller the standard deviation, the less the scores tend to vary from the mean. The greater the standard deviation, the more the scores tend to spread out from the mean. Calculating a standard deviation is not very difficult, especially if you have a calculator that computes square roots. To calculate a standard deviation, follow these four steps:

1. Find the mean of the scores.
2. From each score, subtract the mean and then square the difference between the score and the mean. (Squaring the scores will eliminate any minus signs that result from subtracting the mean.)
3. Add the squares and then divide that sum by the number of scores.

central tendency A statistic that provides information about the average, or typical, score in a set of data.

mean The numerical average of a group of scores.

median The score that falls exactly in the middle of a distribution of scores after they have been arranged (or ranked) from highest to lowest.

mode The score that occurs most often.

measures of variability Measures that tell how much scores vary from one another.

range The distance between the highest and lowest scores.

standard deviation A measure of how much a set of scores varies on the average around the mean of the scores.

SELF-ASSESSMENT 15.1

Evaluating My Knowledge of and Skills in Computing Measures of Central Tendency and Variability

Examine each of these statements and place a checkmark next to the statement if you feel confident of your knowledge of the concept and your skill in computing the measure or using the instrument.

_____ I know what a frequency distribution is.

_____ I can describe what a histogram is and know how to create one.

_____ I understand what a mean is and know how to compute it.

_____ I understand what a median is and know how to calculate it.

_____ I know what a mode is and am aware of how to compute it.

_____ I know what a range is and how to arrive at it.

_____ I can discuss what a standard deviation is and know how to compute it.

_____ I have a good calculator and know how to use it to compute basic descriptive statistics.

For any items that you did not check off, go back and study the concept again. If you are still not confident about computing the various measures, seek additional help from a college instructor, a math skills tutor (many colleges have these available for students), or a capable friend. Practice the calculations in order to absorb the concepts.

4. Compute the square root of the value obtained in step 3. This is the standard deviation.

The formula for these four steps is

$$\sqrt{\frac{\Sigma(\chi - \overline{\chi})^2}{N}}$$

where χ = the individual score and $\overline{\chi}$ = the mean, N = the number of scores, and Σ means "the sum of."

Applying this formula to the test scores of the 21 students,

1. We already computed the mean of the scores and found that it was 82.86.
2. Subtract 82.86 from the first score: $96 - 82.86 = 13.14$. Square 13.14 to get 172.66. Save the value and go on to do the same for the second score, the third score, and so on.
3. Add the 21 scores to get 1543.28. Divide the sum by 21: $1543.28/21 = 73.49$.
4. Find the square root of 73.49. The result is 8.57, the standard deviation.

Calculators are very helpful in computing a standard deviation. To evaluate your knowledge of and skills in computing the various measures of central tendency and variability we have described, complete Self-Assessment 15.1. Mastering these kinds of descriptive statistics is useful not only for classroom work but also for understanding research results. The standard deviation is a better measure of variability than the range because the range represents information about only two bits of data (the highest and lowest scores), whereas the standard deviation represents combined information about all the data. It also usually is more helpful to know how much test scores are spread out or clustered together than to know the highest and lowest scores. If a teacher gives a test and the standard deviation turns out to be very low, it means the scores tend to cluster around the same value. That could mean that everyone in the class learned the material equally well, but it more likely suggests that the test

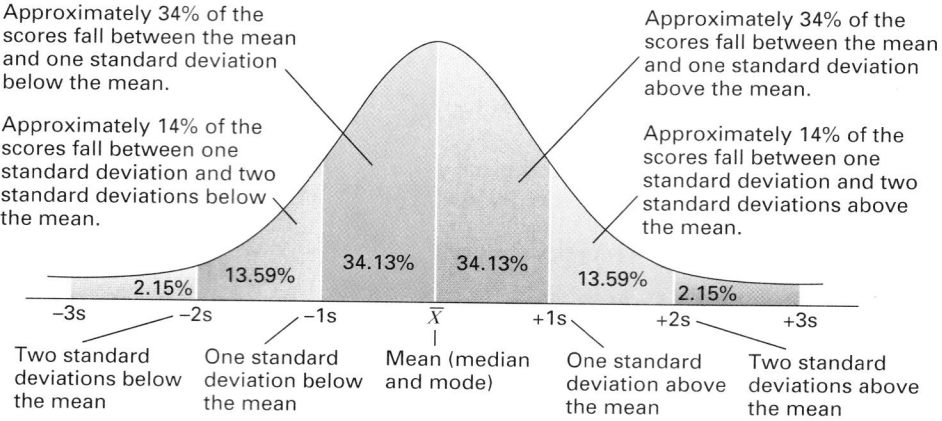

Approximately 34% of the scores fall between the mean and one standard deviation below the mean.

Approximately 14% of the scores fall between one standard deviation and two standard deviations below the mean.

Approximately 34% of the scores fall between the mean and one standard deviation above the mean.

Approximately 14% of the scores fall between one standard deviation and two standard deviations above the mean.

2.15% 13.59% 34.13% 34.13% 13.59% 2.15%

−3s −2s −1s $\overline{X}$ +1s +2s +3s

Two standard deviations below the mean

One standard deviation below the mean

Mean (median and mode)

One standard deviation above the mean

Two standard deviations above the mean

FIGURE 15.3 The Normal Distribution

was too easy and is not discriminating very effectively between students who mastered the material and those who did not.

The Normal Distribution In a **normal distribution**, most of the scores cluster around the mean. The farther above or below the mean we travel, the less frequently each score occurs. A normal distribution also is called a *normal curve, bell-shaped curve,* or *bell curve.* Many characteristics, such as human intelligence measured by intelligence tests, athletic ability, weight, and height, follow or approximate a normal distribution. Normal distributions are useful to know about because when testing a large number of students with a good standardized test, the graph of resulting scores will tend to resemble a normal curve (Lowe, 2005). We presented the normal distribution for standardized testing of intelligence in chapter 4, "Individual Variations." Figure 15.3 illustrates what a normal distribution, or "bell-shaped curve," looks like and describes its statistical properties.

Figure 15.3 illustrates several important characteristics of a normal distribution. First, it is symmetrical. Because of this symmetry, the mean, median, and mode are identical in a normal distribution. Second, its bell shape shows that the most common scores are near the middle. The scores become less frequent the farther away from the middle they appear (that is, as they become more extreme). Third, the normal distribution incorporates information about both the mean and the standard deviation, as indicated in figure 15.3. The area on the normal curve that is 1 standard deviation above the mean and 1 standard deviation below it represents 68.26 percent of the scores. At 2 standard deviations above and below the mean, 95.42 percent of the scores are represented. Finally, at 3 standard deviations above and below the mean, 99.74 percent of the scores are included. If we apply this information to the normal distribution of IQ scores in the population, 68 percent of the population has an IQ between 85 and 115, 95 percent an IQ between 70 and 130, and 99 percent between 55 and 145.

Interpreting Test Results Understanding descriptive statistics provides the foundation for effectively interpreting test results (Aiken & Groth-Marnat, 2006). About four to eight weeks after a standardized test has been administered, test results are returned to the school. A **raw score** is the number of items the student answered correctly on the test. Raw scores, by themselves, are not very useful because they don't provide information about how easy or difficult the test was or how the student fared compared with other students. Test publishers usually provide teachers with many different kinds of scores that go beyond raw scores. These include percentile-rank scores, stanine scores, grade-equivalent scores, and standard scores.

Percentile-Rank Scores A **percentile-rank score** reveals the percentage of the distribution that lies at or below the score. It also provides information about the score's position in relation to the rest of the scores. Percentile ranks range from 1 to 99.

normal distribution A "bell-shaped curve" in which most of the scores are clustered around the mean; the farther above or below the mean that we travel, the less frequently each score occurs.

raw score The number of items the student answered correctly on the test.

percentile-rank score The percentage of a distribution that lies at or below the score.

If a student has a percentile rank of 81 on a test, it means that the student performed as well as or higher on the test than 81 percent of the sample who made up the norm group. Note that percentiles do not refer to percentages of items answered correctly on the test. Percentile rank for standardized tests is determined by comparison with the norm group distribution (Tollefson, 2005a). Different comparison groups may be used in computing percentile ranks, such as urban norms or suburban norms.

Stanine Scores   A **stanine score** describes a student's test performance on a 9-point scale ranging from 1 to 9. Scores of 1, 2, and 3 are usually considered to be below average; 4, 5, and 6 average; and 7, 8, and 9 above average (Tollefson, 2005b). As in the case of a student's percentile rank score, a stanine score in one subject area (such as science) can be compared with the student's stanine score in other areas (such as math, reading, and social studies).

A stanine refers to a specific percentage of the normal curve's area. The correspondence between a stanine score and a percentile rank is shown in figure 15.4. A stanine score provides a more general index of a student's performance, while a percentile rank score yields a more precise estimation.

Grade-Equivalent Scores   A **grade-equivalent score** indicates a student's performance in relation to grade level and months of the school year, assuming a 10-month school year (Tollefson, 2005c). Thus, a grade-equivalent score of 4.5 refers to fourth grade, fifth month in school. A grade equivalent of 6.0 stands for the beginning of the sixth grade. In some test reports, a decimal is omitted so that 45 is the same as 4.5 and 60 is the same as 6.0.

Grade-equivalent scores should be used only to interpret a student's progress, not for grade placement. Many educators believe that because grade-equivalent scores are often misleading and misinterpreted, other types of scores, such as standard scores, are more appropriate to use.

Standard Scores   A **standard score** is expressed as a deviation from the mean, which involves the concept of standard deviation that we discussed earlier. The term *standard* as used in *standard score* does not refer to a specific level of performance or expectation but, rather, to the standard normal curve (McMillan, 2002). Scores on state standards-based tests that we discussed earlier in our coverage of high-stakes testing are standard scores derived from raw score distributions and they are unique to each state. For example, in Virginia, the standard score ranges from 0 to 600 with a score of 400 designated as "proficient."

Actually, the stanine scores and grade-equivalent scores we already have profiled are standard scores. Two additional standard scores we will evaluate here are *z*-scores and *T*-scores (Peyton, 2005).

A **z-score** provides information about how many standard deviations a raw score is above or below the mean. Calculation of a *z*-score is done using this formula:

$$z\text{-score} = \frac{X - \overline{X}}{SD}$$

where X = any raw score, $\overline{X}$ = mean of the raw scores, and SD equals the standard deviation of the raw score distribution.

Consider again our example of 21 students taking a test. What would a student's *z*-score be if the student's raw score were 86? Using the formula just shown it would be

$$\frac{86 - 82.6}{8.57} = .37$$

Thus, the raw score of 86 is .37 of a standard deviation above the mean. The *z*-score mean is 0 and the standard deviation is 1.

Stanine Score	Percentile Rank Score
9	96 or Higher
8	89–95
7	77–88
6	60–76
5	40–59
4	23–39
3	11–22
2	4–10
1	Below 4

FIGURE 15.4 The Relation between Stanine Score and Percentile Rank Score

stanine score A 9-point scale that describes a student's performance.

grade–equivalent score A score that indicates students' performance in relation to grade level and months of the school year, assuming a 10-month school year.

standard score A score expressed as a deviation from the mean; involves the standard deviation.

***z*-score** A score that provides information about how many standard deviations a raw score is above or below the mean.

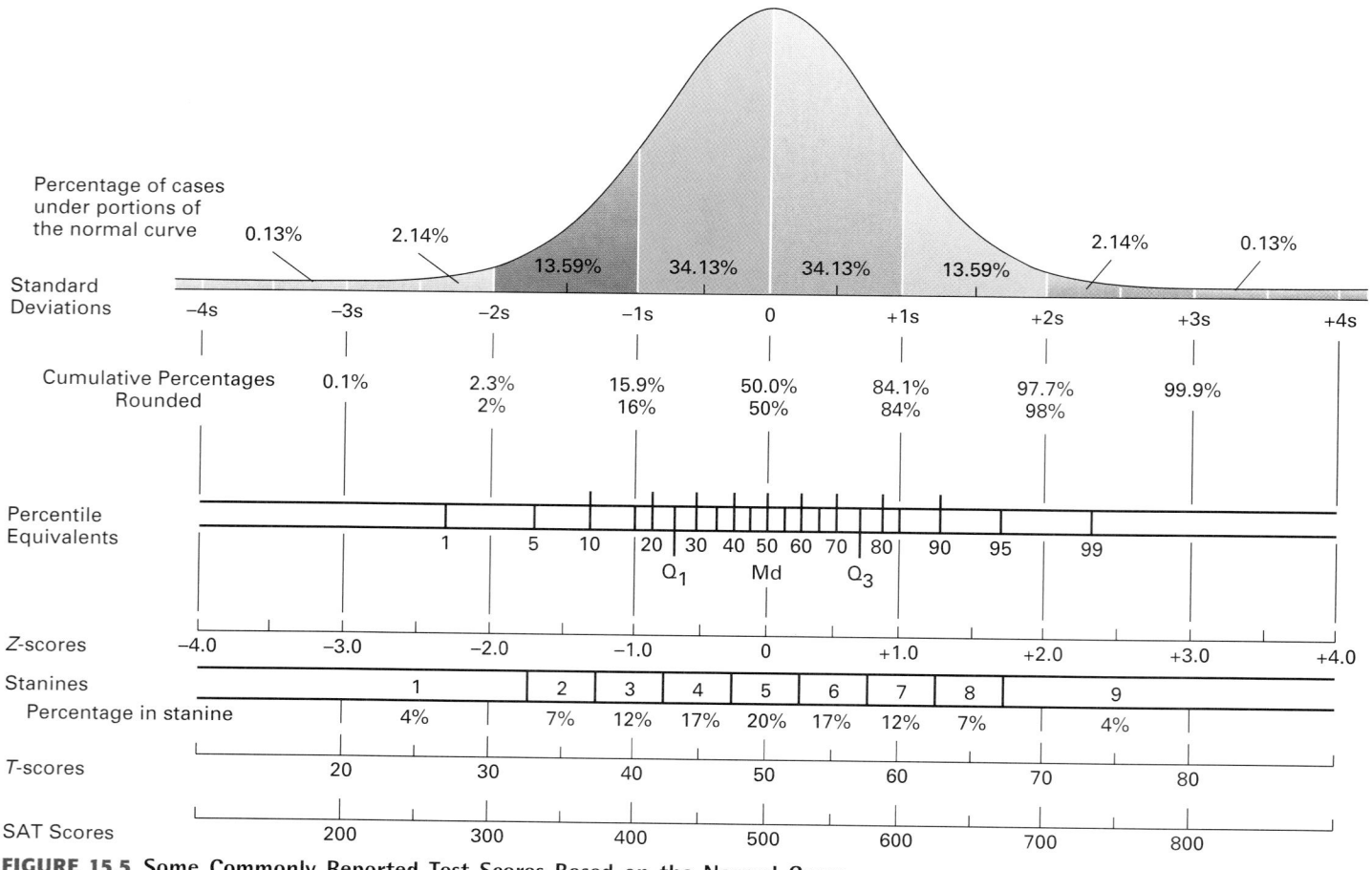

FIGURE 15.5 Some Commonly Reported Test Scores Based on the Normal Curve

A **T-score** is a standard score in which the mean is set at 50 and the standard deviation is set at 10. This formula can be used to compute a *T*-score:

$$T\text{-score} = 50 + 10(z)$$

For example, a *T*-score of 70 is the same as a *z*-score of 2, and a *T*-score of 40 is the same as a *z*-score of -1. For the raw score of 86, the corresponding *T*-score is, therefore, 54.

The college entrance SAT is based on a similar scoring strategy. Its mean is 500 and its standard deviation is 100. The lowest possible score of 200 on the SAT is calibrated to occur at 3 standard deviations below the mean, and the maximum score of 800 is designated to occur at 3 standard deviations above the mean. Thus, only a very small percentage of students (about .10 percent) score at these extremes.

Figure 15.5 presents an overall comparison of many of the types of standardized scores you will see on test reports. Most raw standardized test scores are forced into a normal curve representation.

In addition to showing a student's relative placement on a test, standard scores also allow for comparisons across different types of tests (Powell, 2002). For example, a student may score one standard deviation above the mean on a math test and one standard deviation below the mean on a reading test. Comparisons of raw scores don't always allow for such comparisons.

Don't Overinterpret Test Results Use caution in interpreting small differences in test scores, especially percentile rank and grade-equivalent test scores (Airasian, 2005). All tests have some degree of error.

T-score A standard score in which the mean is set at 50 and the standard deviation is set at 10.

BEST PRACTICES
Strategies for Communicating Test Results to Parents

Here are some good strategies for communicating test results to parents (McMillan, 1997):

1. *Don't report the test scores in isolation.* Report the scores in the context of the student's overall work and performance on other classroom assessments. This will help keep parents from placing too much importance on a score from a single standardized test.

2. *Try to use easy-to-understand language when you describe the students' test results to parents.* Don't get caught up in using obscure test language. Be able to report the information in your own words.

3. *Let parents know that the scores are approximate rather than absolute.* You might say something about how various internal and external factors can affect students' test scores.

4. *Recognize that percentile scores or bands are the easiest set of scores for parents to understand.*

5. *Prior to the conference, spend some time familiarizing yourself with the student's test report.* Make sure you know how to interpret each score you report to parents.

It is not a good idea just to show parents the numbers on a test report. You will need to summarize what the scores mean.

6. *Be ready to answer questions that parents might have about their child's strengths weaknesses, and progress.*

7. *Rather than talking "to" or lecturing parents, talk "with" them in a discussion format.* After you have described a test result, invite them to ask questions that will help you to further clarify for them what the test results mean.

THROUGH THE EYES OF TEACHERS

Vicky Stone, a middle school language arts teacher in Huntington, West Virginia, says that parental support is also vital to the success of her strategy. She holds parent conferences to inform and enable parents to be partners in the student's educational program for the year. They discuss the student's strengths and weaknesses. Based on the SAT (Stanford Achievement Test) and the parental input, her lesson plans take into account the students' weaknesses, including outcome for correction.

A good strategy is to think of a score not as a single number but as a location in a band or general range. Small differences in test scores are usually not meaningful.

Some test reports include percentile bands, a range of scores (rather than a single score) expressed in percentiles, such as 75th to 85th percentile. The Metropolitan Achievement Tests use percentile bands in reporting scores. A percentile rank of 6 to 8 points or a two- to five-month grade-equivalence difference between two students rarely indicates any meaningful difference in achievement.

When considering information from a standardized test, don't evaluate it in isolation (Kaplan & Saccuzzo, 2005; Neukrug & Fawcett, 2006). Evaluate it in conjunction with other information you know about the student and your classroom instruction (Airasian, 2005). Most manuals that accompany standardized tests warn against overinterpretation.

Using Standardized Test Scores to Plan and Improve Instruction

Teachers can use standardized test scores from the end of the previous year in planning their instruction for the next year and as a way to evaluate the effectiveness of instruction after content and skills have been taught (McMillan, 2002). Any use of standardized test results should be made in conjunction with information from other sources.

Prior to instruction, standardized test results may provide an indication of the general ability of the students in the class. This can help the teacher select the appropriate level of instruction and materials to begin the school year. A standardized test should not be used to develop a very low or very high expectation for a student or the entire class. Expectations should be appropriate and reasonable. If the results of a reading readiness test suggest that the class overall lacks appropriate reading skills, the teacher needs to carefully select reading materials that the students will be able to understand.

Standardized tests are sometimes used in grouping students. In cooperative learning, it is common to group students so that a wide range of abilities is reflected in the group. However, a single test score or single test should not be used by itself for any instructional purpose. It always should be used in conjunction with other information.

The subscales of tests (such as in reading and math) can be used to pinpoint strengths and weaknesses of incoming students in particular subject areas. This can help teachers to determine the amount of instruction to give in different areas. If students' achievement is considerably lower than what is expected on the basis of ability testing, they may need further testing, special attention, or counseling.

Standardized tests administered after instruction can be used to evaluate the effectiveness of instruction and the curriculum. Students should score well in the areas that have been emphasized in instruction. If they do not, then both the test itself and the instruction need to be analyzed to determine why this is the case.

In using standardized tests to plan and improve instruction, we underscore again, it is important not to use a single test or test score to make decisions. This is especially relevant in placement decisions, which should be made on the basis of information from multiple sources, including prior teachers' comments, grades, systematic observations, and further assessments. It also is very important to guard against using a single test to develop an expectation for a student's ability and to make sure that the student's test scores reflect a fair assessment.

Review, Reflect, and Practice

③ Identify the teacher's roles in standardized testing.

REVIEW

- What are effective ways to prepare students for standardized tests?
- What steps should teachers take in administering standardized tests?
- What roles do frequency distributions, measures of central tendency and variability, and normal distributions play in describing standardized test results? What are some different types of scores?
- How can standardized tests be used in planning and improving instruction?

REFLECT

- Considering the grade level and subject(s) that you plan to teach, how might standardized test results be useful to you in your instructional planning?

PRAXIS™ PRACTICE

1. Mark, Jenny, Nicole, and Chris are all taking the SAT this year. Which student is preparing the most wisely?
   a. Chris, who has taken a test-taking skills test every year throughout high school.
   b. Jenny, who has consistently taken relatively easy high school courses, and has gotten straight *A*'s.
   c. Mark, who has enrolled in a specialized, expensive SAT preparation program.
   d. Nicole, who has taken a rigorous high school program of studies, and has reviewed some of the math she took in her early high school years.

2. Ms. Koehler's first-grade students will be taking their first high-stakes state standards-based test this week. Because she wants the students to do well, she is careful not to create any anxiety. She avoids using the word *test* and tells her students simply to do their best. She hangs a sign on her door warning others that testing is in progress and that the class is not to be disturbed. As she reads the instructions to the students, she notices that the vocabulary in the

instructions may be a bit complex for some of her students, so she simplifies it. To eliminate distractions, she plays soft music as the students take the test. As they are taking the test, one student asks Ms. Koehler a question. She responds, "I'm sorry, Bill, but I can't answer that for you." What did Ms. Koehler do wrong?

   a. Ms. Koehler deviated from the standard testing procedure.
   b. Ms. Koehler did not answer Bill's question.
   c. Ms. Koehler did not tell the students how important their performance on the test was.
   d. Ms. Koehler did not explain the reason for high-stakes state standards-based testing.

3. Ms. Scott has just received the standardized test scores for her class. As she reviews each of them, she notices that Pete scored at the 98th percentile on the reading portion of this nationally normed test. What does this mean?

   a. Pete did better than all but 2 percent of the norm group on the test.
   b. Pete's score is one standard deviation above the mean score of the norm group.
   c. Pete got 98 percent of the answers correct on the reading portion of the test.
   d. Pete's score is three standard deviations above the mean score of the norm group.

4. Which of the following is an example of best practices in using the results of standardized tests to plan and improve instruction?

   a. Ms. Carter uses her students' standardized test scores to determine their placement in her class.
   b. Mr. Peabody decides that the standardized test scores are invalid when his students do not do well in an area he emphasized in class.
   c. Mr. Lemhert looks at the standardized test scores of each student and uses the information to help him identify relative strengths and weaknesses.
   d. Ms. Ziegler uses her students' standardized test scores to explain their classroom performance to their parents.

Please see the answer key at the end of the book.

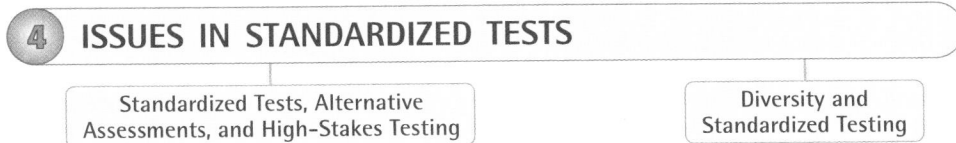

4 ISSUES IN STANDARDIZED TESTS

| Standardized Tests, Alternative Assessments, and High-Stakes Testing | Diversity and Standardized Testing |

As we have already mentioned, standardized testing is controversial. One debate concerns how standardized tests stack up against alternative methods of assessment, especially in high-stakes state standards-based testing. Another is about whether standardized tests discriminate against ethnic minority students and students from low-income backgrounds.

Standardized Tests, Alternative Assessments, and High-Stakes Testing

As we will explain in greater detail in chapter 16, alternative assessments include assessments of student performance, such as assessments of oral presentations, real-world problems, projects, and portfolios (systematic and organized collections of the student's work that demonstrate the student's skills and accomplishments) (Knotek, 2005; Powers, 2005). Which is the best way to assess student performance—standardized tests that mainly rely on multiple-choice questions, or alternative assessments?

DIVERSITY AND EDUCATION
Mirror, Mirror on the Wall, Which Is the Fairest Test of All?

The title above was used to introduce a discussion of whether portfolio assessment is more equitable than standardized tests for ethnic minority students, students from impoverished backgrounds, and females (Supovitz & Brennan, 1997). The researchers compared the traditional standardized test results and portfolio assessment performance of first- and second-grade students in a medium-size urban setting. They analyzed the relative contribution of students' background characteristics to their performance. If the portfolio assessments are more equitable than standardized tests, the gap in scores between high-income non-Latino White students and low-income minority students should be reduced.

At both grade levels, the gap in performance between African American and non-Latino White students was reduced by about half in portfolio assessment when compared with scores on standardized tests. Thus, portfolio assessment significantly reduced the gap between African American and non-Latino White students' performance but did not eliminate it. Interestingly, a gender gap appeared, with girls outperforming boys by a larger margin on portfolio assessment than on assessment with standardized tests. Portfolio assessment had no detectable impact, on the average, on the relative performance of students from low-income backgrounds or students in the English language learning program. These students performed consistently worse than their counterparts on both portfolio assessment and standardized tests.

In sum, portfolio assessment holds considerable promise by focusing instruction on higher-level thinking skills, providing useful feedback to teachers about students' thinking skills, and emphasizing real-world problem solving. However, in this study, portfolio assessment had mixed effects on equalizing the differences in performance of students with different backgrounds and experience.

Assessment expert Grant Wiggins (1992) argued that performance tests should be used, either instead of standardized tests that mainly include multiple-choice questions or at least as part of the student's total assessment. He concluded that performance assessment is more meaningful, involves higher-level thinking skills, and fits better with current educational reform that emphasizes constructivist and social constructivist learning. In Kentucky and Vermont, the inclusion of problem solving in mathematics and the written communication of mathematical ideas on state-mandated tests led teachers to work more on these areas in their math instruction (Olson, 2001).

Some states—such as Arizona, California, Kentucky, and Wisconsin—have pulled back from earlier, more ambitious efforts to include alternative assessments in state-mandated tests. In part, that was because early studies indicated that the alternative assessments did not yield results that were as consistent as multiple-choice tests. Also, the alternative assessments were more time consuming and costly than off-the-shelf, norm-referenced tests.

Blaine Worthen and Vicki Spandel (1991) argued that when used correctly, standardized tests do have value. However, they provide only partial assessment and, thus, have limits. Worthen and Spandel stress that standardized tests are especially helpful in providing information about comparability from a "big picture" perspective. Comparing their class with the one down the hall won't give teachers the information they need about where their students stand compared with the broader population of students. Standardized tests can provide better information about "big picture" questions: Are my fourth-grade students learning basic math? Can my seventh-grade students read at a predefined level of competency?

At the same time, Worthen and Spandel urge teachers to scrupulously avoid any misuses of tests or test results and to educate themselves about tests so that they understand their capabilities and limitations, not asking tests to do more than they can or are intended to do. They also say a standardized test should be only one of a number of assessments used to evaluate students.

Ronald Hambleton (1996) concluded that multiple-choice standardized testing is not likely to be completely abandoned in the foreseeable future, but he predicts that we will see more of a balance in assessment with inclusion of writing tasks, performance tests, computer simulation exercises, hands-on projects, and portfolios of work.

Diversity and Standardized Testing

Earlier in the chapter we raised the issue of fairness in standardized testing. And in chapter 4, "Individual Variations," we discussed issues related to diversity and assessment. For example, we indicated that African American and Latino students score, on the average, about 15 points below non-Latino White students on standardized intelligence tests. This gap was attributed to environmental rather than hereditary factors. In addition, African American, Latino, and Native American students show the lowest proficiency levels, on the average, of all ethnic groups on mathematics, science, reading, writing, history, geography, and literature, according to "report cards" from the National Assessment of Educational Progress (Riley, 1997).

A special concern is cultural bias in tests and the importance of creating culturally responsive tests for diagnostic and instructional purposes (Bigelow, 1999; Gay, 1997; Sandoval & others, 1999). Because of the potential for cultural bias in standardized tests, it is important to assess students using a variety of methods. As indicated earlier, many assessment experts consider that performance and portfolio assessments reduce some of the inequity that characterizes standardized tests for ethnic minority students and students from low-income backgrounds. To read further about whether portfolio assessment is more equitable for students from ethnic minority and other backgrounds, read the Diversity and Education interlude.

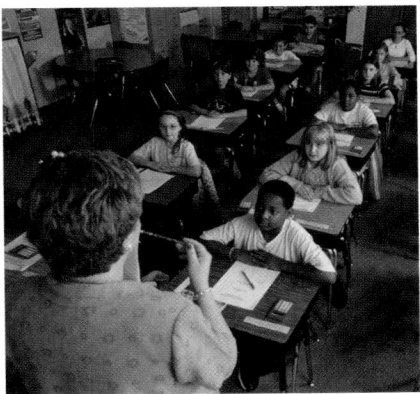

How might standardized tests discriminate against ethnic minority students?

Review, Reflect, and Practice

4 Evaluate some key issues in standardized testing.

REVIEW
- Why is it argued that performance assessments should accompany standardized tests in high-stakes testing?
- What has changed when different ethnic groups have been compared using performance assessments instead of standardized tests?

REFLECT
- In what situations would you rather be tested with standardized testing? with performance assessments? Why?

PRAXIS™ PRACTICE
1. Which of the following is the best example of a performance test used to issue a driver's license?
   a. a road test
   b. a written test covering the rules of the road
   c. a vision test
   d. a computerized test covering the meaning of road signs
2. What is a good test strategy to avoid cultural bias?
   a. Use a single, good standardized test to control for extraneous influences.
   b. Assess students using a variety of methods.
   c. Assume that ethnic differences are due to heredity.
   d. Avoid using portfolios for assessment purposes.

Please see the answer key at the end of the book.

CRACK THE CASE
The Case of the Standardized Tests

Ms. Carter is a third-grade teacher in a district that uses more than one standardized test to measure student achievement and ability. It uses the test required by its state to assess the degree to which students have met or exceeded state standards in math, science, reading, writing, and social sciences. This test yields individual, school, and district scores, and compares these to state averages. In addition, the district uses a nationally normed test to assess both achievement and cognitive ability. The achievement test yields individual scores as they relate to national norms. These scores are reported as percentile rank scores and grade-equivalent scores. The cognitive ability test yields percentile rank scores and IQ-type scores. In addition, the testing service provides a narrative that discusses and compares the achievement and cognitive ability scores for each student.

Ms. Carter is not thrilled about giving her students so many standardized tests. She says, "Sometimes it seems all we do is prepare for these tests and take them." She makes sure she has taught her students appropriate test-taking strategies. She also tries to give her students some experiences that mirror the standardized tests—such as filling in bubbles on answer sheets, and having limited time in which to complete tests. She also sends notes home to parents asking them to ensure that their children get adequate sleep and eat breakfast during testing weeks.

During testing, she always hangs a sign on the door communicating that she does not wish to be disturbed. She reads the instructions verbatim and asks her students if they have any questions prior to beginning the test. She tries to keep the testing situation as low-key as possible for her students. To this end, she generally plays music quietly while the students are taking the tests.

Test results are routinely distributed to parents with student report cards. Parent-teacher conferences are conducted in the week following distribution. Parents inevitably have many questions about standardized test scores, such as:

- "Ms. Carter, what does this grade equivalent mean? It says here that Emily has a grade equivalent of 4.3. Does that mean we should ask to have her placed in fourth grade?"
- "Ms. Carter, John scored at the 90th percentile on language, but he's getting C's in your class. I just don't understand."
- "Ms. Carter, how can it be that my daughter scored in the 60th percentile on the ability test, the 70th on the achievement test, and doesn't meet state standards in math?"
- "Ms. Carter, how can my son score at the 40th percentile on the ability test and the 80th percentile on the achievement test? That just doesn't make any sense!"

1. What are the issues regarding standardized tests in this case study?

2. Examine Ms. Carter's testing procedures. What does she do incorrectly? How might this reduce the validity of the students' scores?

3. How would you answer each of the parents' questions?

4. What does scoring at the 90th percentile on the language portion of the standardized test mean?
   a. The student got 90 percent of the items correct.
   b. The student scored as well or better than 90 percent of the students in the norm group.
   c. The student scored as well as or worse than 90 percent of the students in the norm group.
   d. The student scored as well or better than 90 percent of the students in his class.

5. If a student scored at the 70th percentile on the math portion of an achievement test, and doesn't meet state standards in math, which of the following would be true?
   a. The achievement test has poor predictive validity for performance on the state math test.
   b. The achievement test has good predictive validity for performance on the state math test.
   c. The achievement test is unreliable.
   d. The state math test is easier than the achievement test.

Reach Your Learning Goals
Standardized Tests and Teaching

(1) THE NATURE OF STANDARDIZED TESTS: Discuss the nature and purpose of standardized tests, as well as the criteria for evaluating them.

| Standardized Tests and Their Purposes | Standardized tests are prepared by test specialists to assess performance under uniform conditions. Many standardized tests allow a student's performance to be compared with the performance of other students at the same age or grade level on a national basis. The purposes of standardized tests include providing information about students' progress, diagnosing students' strengths and weaknesses, providing evidence for placement of students in specific programs, helping administrators evaluate programs, providing information for planning and improving instruction, and contributing to accountability. Interest in accountability has led to the creation of standards-based tests and high-stakes testing. Important decisions about students should be made not on the basis of a single standardized test but, rather, on the basis of information from a variety of assessments. |

| Criteria for Evaluating Standardized Tests | Among the most important criteria for evaluating standardized tests are norms, validity, reliability, and fairness. To understand an individual's performance on a test, it needs to be compared with the performance of a group of individuals who previously were given the test by the test maker. This is the norm group. National norms are based on a nationally representative group of students. Standardized tests also can have special group and local norms. Validity is the extent to which a test measures what it is intended to measure and the extent to which inferences about test scores are accurate. Three important types of validity are content validity, criterion validity (which can be either concurrent or predictive), and construct validity. Reliability is the extent to which a test produces a consistent, reproducible measure of performance. Reliable measures are stable, dependable, and relatively free from errors of measurement. Reliability can be measured in several ways, including test-retest reliability, alternate-forms reliability, and split-half reliability. Fair tests are unbiased and nondiscriminatory, uninfluenced by irrelevant factors such as gender, ethnicity, or bias on the part of the scorer. |

(2) APTITUDE AND ACHIEVEMENT TESTS: Compare aptitude and achievement testing and describe current uses of achievement tests.

| Comparing Aptitude and Achievement Tests | An aptitude test predicts a student's ability to learn, or what the student can accomplish with further education and training. An achievement test measures what the student has learned, or the skills the student has mastered. Aptitude tests include general ability tests, such as intelligence tests, and specific aptitude tests used to predict success in an academic subject or occupational area. The SAT test is typically used as an aptitude test, although it can be used as an achievement test. The distinction between aptitude and achievement tests sometimes is blurred. |

| Types of Standardized Achievement Tests | Standardized achievement tests include survey batteries (individual subject matter tests that are designed for a particular level of students), tests for specific subjects (assess a skill in a more detailed, extensive way than a survey battery), and diagnostic tests (given to students to pinpoint weaknesses, often after instruction has taken place). |

| High-Stakes State Standards-Based Tests | Some possible advantages of high-stakes state standards-based testing: improved student performance; more time teaching subjects being tested; high expectations for all students; identification of poorly performing schools, teachers, and administrators; and improved |

continued

confidence in schools as test scores improve. High-stakes state standards-based tests are being used in decisions about remediation, promotion, and graduation. High-stakes state standards-based tests are criticized for dumbing down the curriculum, promoting rote memorization, encouraging teachers to teach to the test, and discriminating against students from low-income and minority backgrounds.

District and National Tests

A major issue in education today is whether the No Child Left Behind legislation is the best way to raise educational standards. The NAEP is the federal government's national examination of young Americans' knowledge, skills, understanding, and attitudes. National testing also can show which schools are underperforming. On many comparisons with students in other countries, American students do not fare well. Many issues are involved in the concept of world-class standards. National testing is being resisted because, for example, it does not measure important skills such as creativity, motivation, persistence, and social skills, and educators are concerned whether the NCLB tests and procedures are the best ones for achieving high standards.

Standardized Tests of Teacher Candidates

Most teacher candidates have to take one or more standardized tests as part of licensure to teach in a particular state. Many states use one or more of the PRAXIS™ tests created by Educational Testing Service, although some states create their own test. Criticisms of the current tests of teacher candidates have been made, and a call for a national test of teacher candidates has been made.

(3) THE TEACHER'S ROLE: Identify the teacher's roles in standardized testing.

Preparing Students to Take Standardized Tests

Make sure that students have good test-taking skills. Also communicate a positive attitude about the test to students. Coaching programs to improve students' test scores have had minimal effects.

Administering Standardized Tests

Most standardized testing manuals spell out how to set up the testing room, what to do when students take the test, how to distribute the test and answer sheets, and how to time the tests. In administering the test, it is important to follow the script word for word.

Understanding and Interpreting Test Results

Descriptive statistics are math procedures used to describe and summarize data in a meaningful way. A frequency distribution is a listing of scores from highest to lowest along with the number of times each score appears. A histogram is one way that frequency distribution information can be presented. Measures of central tendency include the mean, median, and mode. Measures of variability include the range and standard deviation. The normal curve is a bell-shaped curve in which most scores cluster around the mean. A normal curve is symmetrical and incorporates information about both the mean and the standard deviation. A raw score is the number of items a student gets right on a test, which typically is not as useful as many other types of scores. Percentile-rank scores reveal the percentage of the distribution that lies at or below the particular score. Stanine scores describe a student's performance on a 9-point scale ranging from 1 to 9. Grade-equivalent scores are expressed in terms of the grade level of students who perform at that level. Standard scores are expressed as a deviation from the mean and involve the concept of standard deviation (z-scores and T-scores are examples of standard scores). Avoid overinterpreting test results. A good strategy is to think of a score not as a single score but as being located in a band or general range. Don't evaluate standardized test results in isolation from other information about the student, such as classroom performance and the nature of instruction.

Using Standardized Test Scores to Plan and Improve Instruction

Standardized test scores can be used to plan and improve instruction. This can be done prior to instruction or after instruction. Standardized tests sometimes are used in grouping students, but it is important to guard against unrealistic expectations for students based on test scores. The subscales of tests can be used to pinpoint students' strengths and weaknesses in particular subject areas, which can help teachers determine the amount of instruction to give in different areas. Standardized tests should always be used in conjunction with other information about students and the appropriateness and fairness of the tests evaluated.

4 ISSUES IN STANDARDIZED TESTS: Evaluate some key issues in standardized testing

Standardized Tests, Alternative Assessments, and High-Stakes Testing

There is disagreement about the value of standardized tests versus alternative assessments such as performance and portfolio assessments. When used correctly, standardized tests have value but provide only part of the assessment picture and do have limits. Some assessment experts and teachers believe that high-stakes state standards-based testing should include more alternative assessments.

Diversity and Standardized Testing

African American, Latino, and Native American students perform more poorly than non-Latino White students on many standardized tests. Cultural bias is of special concern in standardized testing. Some assessment experts believe that performance assessments have the potential to reduce bias in testing.

KEY TERMS

standardized tests 532
standards-based tests 533
high-stakes testing 533
norm group 533
validity 533
content validity 534
criterion validity 534
concurrent validity 534
predictive validity 534

construct validity 534
reliability 534
test-retest reliability 534
alternate-forms reliability 535
split-half reliability 535
aptitude test 537
achievement test 537
descriptive statistics 549
frequency distribution 549

histogram 549
central tendency 550
mean 550
median 550
mode 550
measures of variability 550
range 550
standard deviation 550
normal distribution 552

raw score 552
percentile-rank score 552
stanine score 553
grade-equivalent score 553
standard score 553
z-score 553
T-score 554

PORTFOLIO ACTIVITIES

Now that you have a good understanding of this chapter, complete these exercises to expand your thinking.

Independent Reflection

Find a Frequency Distribution. Create a frequency distribution and histogram for the following scores: 98, 96, 94, 94, 92, 90, 90, 88, 86, 86, 86, 82, 80, 80, 80, 80, 80, 78, 76, 72, 70, 68, 64. (INTASC: Principle 8)

Collaborative Work

Calculate and Interpret Test Results. With a partner in your class, calculate the mean, median, and mode of the 23 scores listed above. Compute the range and standard deviation for these scores. What do these figures mean? (INTASC: Principle 8)

Research/Field Experience

What Do the Critics Say about Standardized Testing? In a short essay, evaluate each of the following criticisms of standardized tests. State whether you agree with the criticism and then explain your reasoning. (1) High-stakes multiple-choice tests will lead to a "dumbing-down" of teaching and learning. (2) Establishing national tests will undermine new educational programs at the state and local levels. (INTASC: Principle 8)

Go to the Online Learning Center for downloadable portfolio templates.

TAKING IT TO THE NET

- A current trend in assessment is returning to traditional testing formats, such as true/false and multiple-choice. Discuss how these items can be written so that students' higher-level, critical thinking skills are evaluated. Provide several examples of multiple-choice items that utilize students' analytical skills rather than recognition and recall. //cit.necc.mass.edu/atlt/TestCritThink.htm

- Standardized tests that were designed to measure student achievement are now being used to assess the quality of a student's education, including the teacher, principal, school, and school system. Is this use of standardized achievement test scores valid? Why or why not? //familyeducation.com/article/0, 1120,1-6219,00.html

- One criticism of high-stakes standardized testing is that teachers spend too much time "teaching to the test." Examine this criticism and brainstorm ways that teachers can implement a standards-based curriculum without sacrificing creativity and differentiated instruction. www.ascd.org/ed_topics/el200009_tomlinson.html

Connect to the Online Learning Center to explore possible answers.

 ## STUDY, PRACTICE, AND SUCCEED

Visit **www.mhhe.com/santedu3e** to review the chapter with self-grading quizzes and self-assessments, to apply the chapter material to two more Crack the Case studies, and for suggested activities to develop your teaching portfolio.

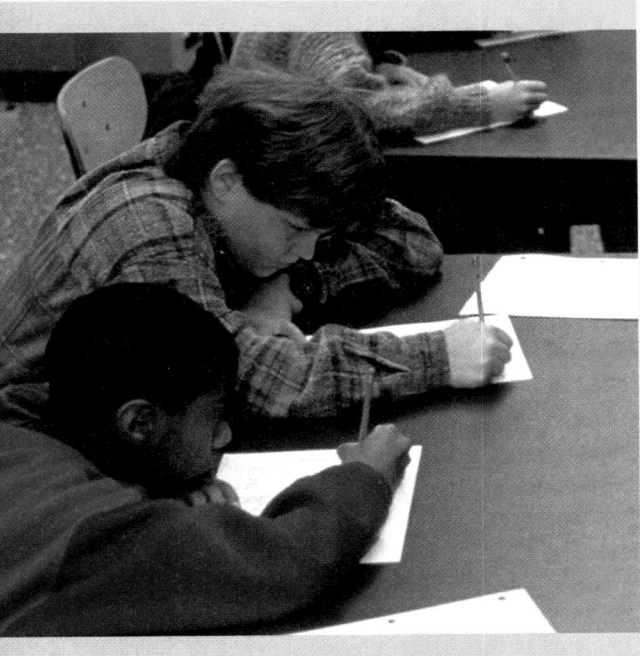

CHAPTER 16

Classroom Assessment

*I call my tests "opportunities" to give students
a different way of thinking about them.*

—Bert Moore
Contemporary American Psychologist

Learning Goals

1 Discuss the classroom as an
assessment context.

2 Provide some guidelines for
constructing traditional tests.

3 Describe some types of
alternative assessments.

4 Construct a sound approach
to grading.

4 Identify some uses of computers
in assessment.

TEACHING STORIES   Vicky Farrow

Vicky Farrow is a former high school teacher who currently teaches educational psychology at Lamar University in Beaumont, Texas. She reflects on the ongoing process of assessment in the classroom and what to do and what not to do in constructing tests:

> Assessment is an ongoing process. It is more than giving tests or assigning grades. It is everything a teacher does to determine if his or her students are learning. It may be asking students questions, monitoring their understanding as you circulate through the room during an activity, and noticing the frown on the face of a student who is confused or the smile of a student who has grasped the concept. Without this ongoing assessment, a teacher can never know if instruction is effective or needs to be modified. Done effectively, assessment provides a teacher with valuable information for providing an optimal learning experience for every child.
>
> When you do give tests, every item on a test should relate back to the objectives. This helps the teacher avoid "gotcha" questions—those questions that may be trivial or unimportant to the intended learning outcomes. If it is not

> important enough to spend valuable class time on, it probably is not important enough to test the student over.
>
> Be careful that test items are written at an appropriate level. The test should be testing students' understanding of the unit content, not their reading skills (unless, of course, it is reading skills that are being tested). I remember as a student taking an analogies test that was intended to assess my ability to identify relationships between concepts. However, the vocabulary was so difficult that I missed some items because the words were too difficult for that level of schooling.
>
> If an essay question is on an examination, write a model answer *before* grading the exam. Would you make your answer key for a multiple-choice test from a student's paper, wrong answers and all? Of course not! It does not make any more sense to do that with an essay item. If an essay item is well written and a model answer is constructed in advance, the grade a student receives will more accurately reflect the level of that student's understanding of the material being tested.

Preview

Assessment of students' learning has recently generated considerable interest in educational circles. This interest has focused on such issues as the extent to which teachers should incorporate state standards into their teaching and assessment, as well as the degree to which teachers should use traditional tests or alternative assessments. Our coverage of classroom assessments begins with an examination of the varied features of the classroom as an assessment context. Then we contrast traditional tests and alternative assessments, followed by discussion of the role of grading in education. We conclude the chapter by exploring the use of computers in assessment.

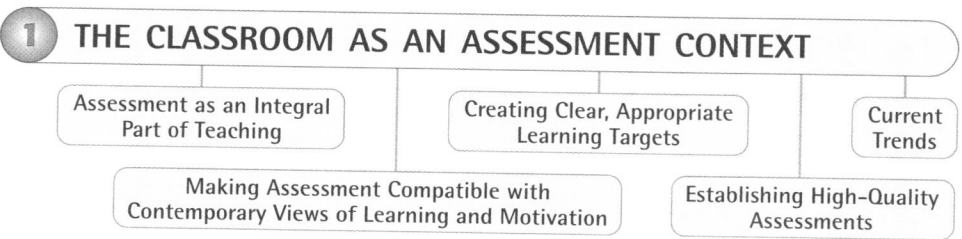

① THE CLASSROOM AS AN ASSESSMENT CONTEXT

Assessment as an Integral Part of Teaching

Creating Clear, Appropriate Learning Targets

Current Trends

Making Assessment Compatible with Contemporary Views of Learning and Motivation

Establishing High–Quality Assessments

When you think of assessment, what comes to mind? Probably tests. However, as we discuss the classroom as a context for assessment, you will discover that contemporary assessment strategies involve far more than testing.

Assessment as an Integral Part of Teaching

Teachers spend more time in assessment than you might imagine. In one analysis, they spent 20 percent to 30 percent of their professional time dealing with assessment matters (Stiggins, 2001). With so much time spent on assessment, it should be done well (Gardner, 2006; Popham, 2005, 2006). Assessment expert James McMillan (2007) stresses that competent teachers frequently evaluate their students in relation to learning goals and adapt their instruction accordingly. Assessment not only documents what students know and can do but also affects their learning and motivation. These ideas represent a change in the way assessment is viewed, away from the concept that assessment is an isolated outcome done only after instruction is finished and toward the concept of integrating assessment with instruction (Otero, 2006).

Think of integrating instruction and assessment in terms of three time frames: preinstruction, during instruction, and postinstruction. The Standards for Teacher Competence in Educational Assessment, developed jointly in the early 1990s by the American Federation of Teachers, National Council on Measurement in Education, and National Education Association, describe the teacher's responsibility for student assessment in these three time frames (see figure 16.1).

Preinstruction Assessment   Imagine that you want to know how well your students can solve a certain level of math problem before you begin formal instruction on a more advanced level. You might look at your students' prior grades and their scores on standardized math tests, as well as observe your students for several days to see how well they perform. These assessments are designed to answer this question: What math skills are my students able to demonstrate? If the results of your assessment indicate that students lack prerequisite knowledge and skills, you will decide to begin with materials that are less difficult for them. If they do extremely well on your preinstruction assessment, you will move your level of instruction to a higher plane. Without this preinstructional assessment, you run the risk of having a class that is overwhelmed (if your instruction level is too advanced) or bored (if your instruction level is too low).

Much of preinstructional assessment is informal observation (Taylor & Nolen, 2005). In the first several weeks of school, you will have numerous opportunities to

Pre-instruction	During instruction	Post-instruction
Do my students have the prerequisite knowledge and skills to be successful?	Are students paying attention to me?	How much have my students learned?
What will interest my students?	Are students understanding the material?	What should I do next?
What will motivate my students?	To which students should I direct questions?	Do I need to review anything the class didn't understand?
How long should I plan to cover each unit?	What type of questions should I ask?	What grades should I give?
What teaching strategies should I use?	How should I respond to student questions?	What should I tell my students?
How should I grade students?	When should I stop lecturing?	How should I change my instruction next time?
What type of group learning should I use?	Which students need extra help?	Do the test scores really reflect what my students know and can do?
What are my learning objectives or targets?	Which students should be left alone?	Is there anything that students misunderstood?

FIGURE 16.1 Teacher Decision Making Before, During, and After Instruction

These are questions a teacher can answer to improve assessment before, during, and after instruction.

observe students' characteristics and behavior. Be sensitive to whether a student is shy or outgoing, has a good or weak vocabulary, speaks and listens effectively, is considerate of others or is egocentric, engages in appropriate or inappropriate behavior, and so on. Also focus on the student's nonverbal behavior for cues that might reveal nervousness, boredom, frustration, or a lack of understanding.

In preinstructional assessments, guard against developing expectations that will distort your perception of a student. It is virtually impossible not to have expectations about students. Because teacher expectations are potentially powerful influences on student learning, some teachers don't even want to look at a student's prior grades or standardized test scores. Whether you do or do not examine such assessment information, work on making your expectations realistic. If you err, err in the direction of having overly positive expectations for students.

A good strategy is to treat your initial impressions of students as hypotheses to be confirmed or modified by subsequent observation and information. Some of your initial observations will be accurate; others will need to be revised. As you try to get a sense of what your students are like, refrain from believing hearsay information, from making enduring judgments based on only one or two observations, and from labeling the student (Airasian, 2005).

Some teachers also administer diagnostic pretests in subject areas to examine a student's level of knowledge and skill. And many schools are increasingly collecting samples of students' work in portfolios, which can accompany a student from grade to grade. The portfolios provide teachers with a far more concrete, less-biased set of information to evaluate than other teachers' hearsay comments. We will describe portfolios in much greater depth later in the chapter.

Assessment during Instruction An increasing trend is the use of **formative assessment,** which is assessment during the course of instruction rather than after it is completed. Formative assessment has become a buzzword with its emphasis on assessment *for* learning rather than assessment *of* learning (Ainsworth & Viegut, 2006; Black & William, 2006; Stiggins, 2006). An important aspect of being an effective teacher is assessing students' understanding—formative assessment is extremely important in this regard. Your ongoing observation and monitoring of students' learning while you teach informs you about what to do next. Assessment during instruction helps you set your teaching at a level that challenges students and stretches

What is formative assessment? Why is it such as important aspect of assessment?

formative assessment Assessment during the course of instruction rather than after it is completed.

their thinking. It also helps you to detect which students need your individual attention (Stobart, 2006).

Assessment during instruction takes place at the same time as you make many other decisions about what to do, say, or ask next to keep the classroom running smoothly and help students actively learn (Airasian, 2005). It requires listening to student answers, observing other students for indications of understanding or confusion, framing the next question, and looking around the class for misbehavior (Doyle, 1986, 2006). Simultaneously, the teacher needs to monitor the pace of the activity, which students to call on, answer quality, and the sequence of content. With small groups, the teacher might need to be aware of several different activities simultaneously.

Oral questions are an especially important aspect of assessment during instruction. Some teachers ask as many as 300 to 400 questions a day, not only to stimulate students' thinking and inquiry but also to assess their knowledge and skill level (Morgan & Saxton, 1991).

When you ask questions, remember to avoid overly broad, general questions; involve the whole class in questioning instead of calling on the same students all of the time; allow sufficient "wait time" after asking a question; probe students' responses with follow-up questions; and highly value students' own questions (Airasian, 2005).

Feedback is an important aspect of formative assessment. The idea is to not only continually assess students as they learn but to provide informative feedback so that students' focus is appropriate. Figure 16.2 describes some do's and don'ts in giving praise as a part of feedback.

Postinstruction Assessment   **Summative assessment** (or formal assessment) is assessment after instruction is finished with the purpose of documenting student performance. Assessment after instruction provides information about how well your students have mastered the material, whether students are ready for the next unit, what grades they should be given, what comments you should make to parents, and how you should adapt your instruction (McMillan, 2007).

Making Assessment Compatible with Contemporary Views of Learning and Motivation

Throughout this book, we have encouraged you to view students as active learners who discover and construct meaning; set goals, plan, and reach goals; associate and link new information with existing knowledge in meaningful ways; think reflectively, critically, and creatively; develop self-monitoring skills; have positive expectations for learning and confidence in their skills; are enthusiastically and internally motivated to learn; apply what they learn to real-world situations; and communicate effectively.

Assessment plays an important role in effort, engagement, and performance (Earl, 2006; Harlen, 2006). Your informal observations can provide information about how motivated students are to study a subject. If you have a good relationship with the student, direct oral questioning in a private conversation can often produce valuable insight about the student's motivation. In thinking about how assessment and motivation are linked, ask yourself if your assessments will encourage students to become more meaningfully involved in the subject matter and more intrinsically motivated to study the topic (Butler & McMunn, 2006). Assessments that are challenging but fair should increase students' enthusiasm for learning. Assessments that are too difficult will lower students' self-esteem and self-efficacy, as well as raise their anxiety. Assessing students with measures that are too easy will bore them and not motivate them to study hard enough.

Susan Brookhart (1997, 2002, 2004) developed a model of how classroom assessment helps motivate students. She argues that every classroom environment hosts a series of repeated assessment events. In each assessment event, the teacher communicates with the students through assignments, activities, and feedback about performance. Students respond according to their perceptions of these learning opportunities

Do
Focus on specific accomplishments.
Attribute success to effort and ability.
Praise spontaneously.
Refer to prior achievement.
Individualize and use variety.
Give praise immediately.
Praise correct strategies leading to success.
Praise accurately with credibility.
Praise privately.
Focus on progress.

Don't
Focus on general or global achievement.
Attribute success to luck or other's help.
Praise predictably.
Ignore prior achievement.
Give the same praise to all students.
Give praise much later.
Ignore strategies and focus only on outcomes.
Praise for undeserving performance.
Praise publicly.
Focus solely on current performance.

FIGURE 16.2 Do's and Dont's of Using Praise When Giving Feedback during Formative Assessment

Source: From McMillan, J. H., *Classroom Assessment: Principles and Practice for Effective Standards-Based Instruction*, 4e. Published by Allyn and Bacon, Boston, MA. Copyright © 2007 by Pearson Education. Reprinted by permission of the publisher.

summative assessment Assessment after instruction is finished; also called formal assessment.

and how well they think they will be able to perform. Brookhart argues that this view of classroom assessment suggests that teachers should evaluate students using a variety of performances, especially performances that are meaningful to students.

Similarly, many other classroom assessment experts argue that if you think motivated, active learning is an important goal of instruction, you should create alternative assessments that are quite different from traditional tests, which don't evaluate how students construct knowledge and understanding, set and reach goals, and think critically and creatively (Brookhart, 2004; McMillan, 2007; Stiggins, 2005). Later in the chapter we will explore how alternative assessments can be used to examine these aspects of students' learning and motivation.

Creating Clear, Appropriate Learning Targets

Tying assessment to current views on learning and motivation also involves developing clear, appropriate learning goals, or targets (Butler & McMunn, 2006). A *learning target* consists of what students should know and be able to do. You should establish criteria for judging whether students have attained the learning target (McMillan, 2007). Figure 16.3 provides some examples of unit learning targets.

Among the types of learning targets that you can weave through instruction and assessment are these (Stiggins & Conklin, 1992):

- *Knowledge.* This involves what students need to know to solve problems and perform skills. Knowledge gives students the ability to master substantive subject matter.
- *Reasoning/thinking.* An important learning goal is for students not just to acquire knowledge but also to be able to think about the knowledge using problem solving, inductive and deductive reasoning, strategies, and critical thinking.
- *Products.* Products are samples of students' work. Essays, term papers, oral reports, and science reports reflect students' ability to use knowledge and reasoning.

FIGURE 16.3 Examples of Unit Learning Targets

Students will be able to explain how various cultures are different and how cultures influence people's beliefs and lives by answering orally a comprehensive set of questions about cultural differences and their effects.

Students will demonstrate their knowledge of the parts of a plant by filling in words or a diagram for all parts studied.

Students will demonstrate their understanding of citizenship by correctly identifying whether previously unread statements about citizenship are true or false. A large number of items is used to sample most of the content learned.

Students will be able to explain why the American Constitution is important by writing an essay that indicates what would happen if we abolished our Constitution. The papers would be graded holistically, looking for evidence of reasons, knowledge of the Constitution, and organization.

Students will show that they know the difference between components of sentences by correctly identifying verbs, adverbs, adjectives, nouns, and pronouns in seven of eight long, complex sentences.

Students will be able to multiply fractions by correctly computing eight of ten fraction problems. The problems are new to the students; some are similar to "challenge" questions in the book.

Students will be able to use their knowledge of addition, subtraction, division, and multiplication to solve word problems that are similar to those used in the sixth-grade standardized test.

Students will demonstrate their understanding of how visual art conveys ideas and feelings by correctly indicating, orally, how examples of art communicate ideas and feelings.

- *Affect.* Affective targets are students' emotions, feelings, and values. Help students develop emotional self-awareness (such as understanding the causes of their feelings), manage emotions (such as managing anger), read emotions (such as being good at listening to what other people say), and handle relationships (such as being competent at solving relationship problems). However, including affective goals in assessment is controversial.

Establishing High-Quality Assessments

Another important goal for the classroom as an assessment context is achieving high-quality assessment. Assessment reaches a high level of quality when it yields reliable and valid information about students' performance. High-quality assessments also are fair (McMillan, 2007). Validity and reliability are concerned with the consistency and accuracy of the inferences teachers make about students from assessment information.

Validity *Validity* refers to the extent to which assessment measures what it is intended to measure. In the context of classroom assessment, *validity* also includes how accurate and useful a teacher's inferences are about the assessment. *Inferences* are conclusions that individuals draw from information.

You can't obtain information about everything a student learns. Thus, your assessment of a student will necessarily be a sample of the student's learning. The most important source of information for validity in your classroom will be *content-related evidence,* the extent to which the assessment reflects what you have been teaching (McMillan, 2007).

Adequately sampling content is clearly an important goal of valid assessment (Weller, 2001). Use your best professional judgment when sampling content. Thus, you wouldn't want to use just one multiple-choice question to assess a student's knowledge of a chapter on geography. An increasing trend is to use multiple methods of assessment, which can provide a more comprehensive sampling of content. Thus, the teacher might assess students' knowledge of the geography chapter with some multiple-choice questions, several essay questions, and a project to complete. Always ask yourself whether your assessments of students are adequate samples of their performance. For example, is the completed science project all that you will use to grade the student, or will you include information about the student's mastery of the general course content, the student's effort, and his or her class participation in your grading?

Linking instruction and assessment in the classroom leads to the concept of **instructional validity:** the extent to which the assessment is a reasonable sample of what actually went on in the classroom (McMillan, 2007). For example, a classroom assessment should reflect both what the teacher taught and students' opportunity to learn the material. Consider a math class in which the teacher gives students a test on their ability to solve multiplication problems. For instructional validity, it is important that the teacher competently instructed students in how to solve the problems and gave students adequate opportunities to practice this skill.

An important strategy for validity in classroom assessment is to systematically link learning targets, content, instruction, and assessment (McMillan, 2007). Imagine that you are a science teacher and that one of your learning targets is to get students to think more critically and creatively in designing science projects. Ask yourself what content is important to achieve this learning target. For instance, will it help students to read biographies of famous scientists that include information about how they came up with their ideas? Also ask yourself what learning targets you will emphasize in instruction. For your target regarding students' science projects, it will be important for you to carry through in your instruction on the theme of helping students to think critically and creatively about science.

instructional validity The extent to which the assessment is a reasonable sample of what went on in the classroom.

Reliability *Reliability* is the extent to which a test produces consistent, reproducible scores. Reliable scores are stable, dependable, and relatively free from errors of measurement. Consistency depends on circumstances involved in taking the test and student factors that vary from one test to another (McMillan, 2007).

Reliability is not about the appropriateness of the assessment information but is about determining how consistently an assessment measures what it is measuring (Parkes & Giron, 2006). If a teacher gives students the same test in a math class on two occasions and the students perform in a consistent manner on the tests, this indicates that the test was reliable. However, the consistency in students' performance (with high scorers being high both times the test was given, middle scorers performing similarly across the two assessments, and low scorers doing poorly on both assessments) says nothing about whether the test actually measured what it was designed to measure (for example, being an accurate, representative sample of questions that measured the math content that had been taught). Thus, reliable assessments are not necessarily valid.

Reliability is reduced by errors in measurement. A student can have adequate knowledge and skill and still not perform consistently across several tests because of a number of factors. Internal factors can include health, motivation, and anxiety. External factors can include inadequate directions given by the teacher, ambiguously created items, poor sampling of information, and inefficient scoring of the student's responses. For example, a student might perform extremely well on the first test a teacher gives to assess the student's reading comprehension but considerably lower on the second test in this domain. The student's lack of knowledge and skill could be the reason for the low reliability across the two assessments, but the low reliability also could be due to any number of measurement errors.

Fairness High-quality classroom assessment is not only valid and reliable but also fair (McMillan, 2007; National Research Council, 2001; Popham, 2006; Reynolds, Livingston, & Willson, 2006). Assessment is fair when all students have an equal opportunity to learn and demonstrate their knowledge and skill (Yung, 2001). Assessment is fair when teachers have developed appropriate learning targets, provided competent content and instruction to match those targets, and chosen assessments that reflect the targets, content, and instruction.

Assessment bias includes offensiveness and unfair penalization (Popham, 2005). An assessment is biased if it is offensive to a subgroup of students. This occurs when negative stereotypes of particular subgroups are included in the test. For example, consider a test in which the items portray males in high-paying and prestigious jobs (doctors and business executives) and females in low-paying and less-prestigious jobs (clerks and secretaries). Because some females taking the test likely will be offended by this gender inequality, and appropriately so, the stress this creates may produce a less-successful outcome for females on the test.

An assessment also may be biased if it unfairly penalizes a student based on the student's group membership, such as ethnicity, socioeconomic status, gender, religion, and disability (Hargis, 2006). For example, consider an assessment that focuses on information that students from affluent families are far more likely to be familiar with than students from low-income families (Popham, 2005). A teacher decides to see how well students can collaboratively solve problems in groups. The content of the problem to be discussed is a series of locally presented operas and symphonies likely to have been attended only by those who can afford the high ticket prices. Even if the affluent students didn't attend these musical events themselves, they may have heard their parents talk about them. Thus, students from low-income families might perform less effectively on the collaborative problem-solving exercise pertaining to musical events not because they are less skilled at such problem solving but because they are unfamiliar with the events.

Some assessment experts believe it is important to create a philosophy of *pluralistic assessment,* which includes being responsive to cultural diversity in the

DIVERSITY AND EDUCATION
Culturally Responsive Strategies for Assessing Students

Geneva Gay (1997, pp. 215–216, 218) evaluated the role of ethnicity and culture in assessment and recommended a number of culturally responsive strategies in assessing students. She advocates modifying (1) the Eurocentric nature of current U.S. instruction and achievement assessments, (2) use of a wider variety of assessment methods that take into account the cultural styles of students of color, (3) evaluation of students against their own records, and (4) assessment of students in ways that serve culturally appropriate diagnostic and developmental functions.

Achievement assessments "are designed to determine what students know. Presumably they reflect what has been taught in schools." Gay believes that "although progress has been made in the last three decades to make school curricula more inclusive of ethnic and cultural diversity, most of the knowledge taught, and consequently the achievement tests, continue to be Eurocentric." She points out that even mastery of skills tends to be "transmitted through Eurocentric contexts. For instance, achievement tests may embed skills in scenarios that are not relevant to the cultural backgrounds and life experiences of students of color," as when a teacher asks "immigrant students from the Caribbean who have never experienced snow to engage in problem solving" by evaluating the challenges and dilemmas presented by a blizzard—the students might have the problem-solving skill to respond to this request, but their unfamiliarity with cold winters can inter-

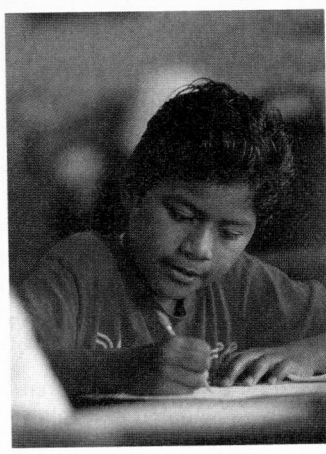

What are some culturally responsive strategies for assessing students?

fere with their ability to perform the task effectively.

This does not mean that students of color should not be assessed or that they should not be expected to meet high achievement standards. They should. However, "to avoid perpetuating educational inequality through assessment procedures, these students should not always be expected to demonstrate" knowledge and skills in terms of contexts with which they are not familiar. A good strategy is to use a variety of assessment methods to ensure that no single method gives an advantage to one ethnic group or another. These methods should include socioemotional measures as well as measures of academic content. Teachers also should carefully observe and monitor students' performance for verbal and nonverbal information in the assessment context.

Gay further argues that norm-referenced traditional assessments should be used only in conjunction with performance assessments. More emphasis should be given to evaluating students against their own records, with the focus being on improvement, rather than on comparisons with other students.

Gay also believes that assessment should always "serve diagnostic and developmental functions and be culturally responsible. . . . Narrative reports, developmental profiles, student-teacher-parent conferences, and anecdotal records should always be included in reporting students' progress."

classroom and at school (Payne, 1997). This usually includes performance assessments during instruction and after instruction. Performance assessments that can be used as part of pluralistic assessment include portfolios, projects, demonstrations, interviews, and oral presentations. This does not mean abandoning objective measurement in the form of multiple-choice exams and essay questions but, rather, making sure that a variety of methods are used, including at least some performance assessments. To learn more about culturally responsive strategies in assessing students, read the Diversity and Education interlude.

Current Trends

Here are some current trends in classroom assessment (Hambleton, 1996; McMillan, 2007; National Research Council, 2001):

- *Using at least some performance-based assessment.* Historically, classroom assessment has emphasized the use of **objective tests**, such as multiple-choice, which

objective tests Tests that have relatively clear, unambiguous scoring criteria, usually multiple-choice tests.

have relatively clear, unambiguous scoring criteria. In contrast, **performance assessments** require students to create answers or products that demonstrate their knowledge or skill. Examples of performance assessment include writing an essay, conducting an experiment, carrying out a project, solving a real-world problem, and creating a portfolio.

- *Examining higher-level cognitive skills.* Rather than assess only content knowledge, as many objective tests do, a current trend is to evaluate a student's higher-level cognitive skills, such as problem solving, critical thinking, decision making, drawing of inferences, and strategic thinking.

- *Using multiple assessment methods.* In the past, assessment meant using a test—often a multiple-choice test—as the sole means of assessing a student. A current trend is to use multiple methods to assess students. Thus, a teacher might use any number of these methods: a multiple-choice test, an essay, an interview, a project, a portfolio, and student evaluations of themselves. Multiple assessments provide a broader view of the child's learning and achievement than a single measure.

- *Using more multiple-choice items to prepare students for taking high stakes state standards-based tests.* Just when a trend in assessment that was more compatible with cognitive, constructivist, and motivational approaches (performance assessment, use of portfolios, and student self-assessment) had developed, teachers returned to using objective formats for assessment, in many cases more than before.

- *Having high performance standards.* Another trend is the demand for high performance standards, even world-class performance standards, for interpreting educational results. Some experts say that world-class performance standards are driving contemporary classroom assessment by providing goals, or targets, to attain (Taylor, 1994). However, questions arise about who should set these standards and whether they should be set at all.

- *Using computers as part of assessment.* Traditionally, computers have been used to score tests, analyze test results, and report scores. Today, computers increasingly are being used to construct and administer tests, as well as to present different assessment formats to students in a multimedia environment. With coming advances in technology, assessment practices are likely to be very different from traditional paper-and-pencil tests (van der Linden, 1995).

Trends in assessment also include emphasizing integrated rather than isolated skills, giving students more feedback, and making standards and criteria public rather than private and secretive. We will revisit many of these current trends later in this chapter.

Review, Reflect, and Practice

1 **Discuss the classroom as an assessment context.**

REVIEW

- Describe assessment before, after, and during instruction.
- How can assessment be brought into line with contemporary views of learning and motivation?
- What are some useful types of learning targets?
- What standards can be used to judge the quality of classroom assessments?
- What are some current trends in assessing students' learning?

performance assessment Assessment that requires creating answers or products that demonstrate knowledge and skill; examples include writing an essay, and conducting an experiment, carrying out a project, solving a real-world problem, and creating a portfolio.

REFLECT

- Think of one of the better teachers that you had as a K–12 student. In retrospect, how would you describe the teacher's classroom as an "assessment context"?

PRAXIS™ PRACTICE

1. Which of the following is the best example of formative assessment?
   a. Mr. Harrison's students write a paper at the conclusion of a unit of instruction. This allows him to assess to what degree his students understand the content of the unit.
   b. Mr. Shockey asks his students open-ended questions during instruction. This way he can determine to what degree his students understand the content of his lesson.
   c. Ms. Manning plays a game of *Jeopardy* at the end of her unit of instruction to assess student understanding of the content of the unit.
   d. Ms. Walker gives her students a brief assessment prior to beginning a unit of instruction, so she knows what her students are already capable of doing. This allows her to gear her instruction to her students' zones of proximal development.

2. Which of the following assessments will most likely enhance student motivation to study and learn?
   a. Mr. Ditka assigns his students a project that requires knowledge from the unit of instruction to complete successfully.
   b. Mr. Payton gives periodic tests that are easy enough for all of his students to earn high scores if they have attended class.
   c. Mr. Rivera puts two or three tricky questions in each test so he can determine which of his students read the items carefully before responding.
   d. Mr. Singletary constructs very challenging exams to ensure that only those students who have studied the material carefully will be successful.

3. Ms. Ramirez has assigned her students to analyze the water in a nearby stream, determine the level of pollution in the stream, and develop a solution to the pollution problem. What type of learning target has she created?
   a. affect
   b. knowledge
   c. product
   d. reasoning

4. Ms. Vick has created an assessment to measure the degree to which her students have mastered the content of her unit on the U.S. Constitution. Included in the test are items about the Bill of Rights, other Constitutional amendments, the American Revolution, and World War II. What is the best description of this assessment?
   a. It is likely to yield both valid and reliable scores.
   b. The scores are unlikely to be valid or reliable.
   c. While the scores may be reliable, they will not be valid.
   d. While the scores may be valid, they will not be reliable.

5. Ms. Krzyzewski is teaching a science unit on anatomy. Students have been studying the anatomy of various animals. Which of the following is the best example of a performance assessment of this material?
   a. Students answer oral questions regarding the structures present in different animals.
   b. Students write an essay comparing and contrasting the anatomy of frogs and pigs.
   c. Students dissect animals and identify their anatomical parts.
   d. Students take a multiple-choice test covering the material in the unit.

Please see the answer key at the end of the book.

② TRADITIONAL TESTS

| Selected-Response Items | Constructed-Response Items |

Traditional tests are typically paper-and-pencil tests in which students select from choices, calculate numbers, construct short responses, or write essays. Our coverage of traditional tests focuses on two main types of item formats in assessment: (1) selected-response items and (2) constructed-response items.

Selected-Response Items

Selected-response items have an objective format that allows students' responses to be scored quickly. A scoring key for correct responses is created and can be applied by an examiner or by a computer. True/false, multiple-choice, and matching items are the most widely used types of items in selected-response tests (Reynolds, Livingston, & Willson, 2006). We also will describe several other recently developed objective-item formats.

True/False Items A true/false item asks a student to mark whether a statement is true or false—for example:

> Montpelier is the capital of Vermont.   True   False

The ease with which true/false items can be constructed has a potential drawback. Teachers sometimes take statements directly from a text or modify them slightly when making up true/false items. Avoid this practice, because it tends to encourage rote memorization with little understanding of the material.

The strengths and limitations of true/false items are described in figure 16.4.

Multiple-Choice Items A **multiple-choice item** consists of two parts: the stem plus a set of possible responses. The stem is a question or statement. Incorrect alternatives

selected-response items Test items with an objective format in which responses can be scored on quick inspection. A scoring guide for correct responses is created and can be used by an examiner or a computer.

multiple-choice item An objective test item consisting of two parts: a stem plus a set of possible responses.

Strengths

1. The item is useful for outcomes where there are only two possible alternatives (for example, fact or opinion, valid or invalid).
2. Less demand is placed on reading ability than in multiple-choice items.
3. A relatively large number of items can be answered in a typical testing period.
4. Scoring is easy, objective, and reliable.

Limitations

1. It is difficult to write items at a high level of knowledge and thinking that are free from ambiguity.
2. When a statement indicates correctly that a statement is false, that response provides no evidence that the student knows what is correct.
3. No diagnostic information is provided by the incorrect answers.
4. Scores are more influenced by guessing than with any other item type.

FIGURE 16.4 Strengths and Limitations of True/False Items

Source: From Norman E. Gronlund, *Assessment of Student Achievement,* 6/e. Published by Allyn and Bacon, Boston, MA. Copyright © 1998 by Pearson Education. Reprinted by permission of the publisher.

BEST PRACTICES
Strategies for Writing True/False Items

Some good strategies for writing true/false items are (Gronlund, 2003, pp. 78–84)

1. *Use only one key idea in each statement.* Including several ideas in a true/false statement usually should be avoided because it tends to confuse the student and the answer is likely to be influenced more by reading ability than learning.

    Example: The first item is better than the second.
    Montpelier is the capital of Vermont.
    Montpelier is the capital of Vermont, which is a New England state, and has fewer than 50,000 inhabitants.

2. *"Keep the statement short, and use simple vocabulary and sentence structure"* (p. 80).

    Example: The first item is better than the second.
    Montpelier is the capital of Vermont.
    The capital city of the state of Vermont is a small metropolis known as Montpelier.

3. *Use words so precisely that the statement can clearly be judged as true or false.* True statements should be true under all circumstances and yet free of qualifiers, such as *might* and *possible.* Vague terms such as *seldom, frequently,* and *often* should be avoided.

    Example: The first item is better than the second.
    Polls at the end of 2004 showed that a majority of Americans supported higher standards for students.
    A lot of people believe that higher standards for students might be justified.

4. *"Use negatives sparingly and avoid double negatives"* (p. 81).

    Example: The first item is better than the second.
    In the presence of high heat, oxygen bonds readily with hydrogen.
    In the presence of high heat, oxygen is not unlikely to bond with hydrogen.

5. *"Avoid extraneous clues to the answer.* Statements that include absolutes such as always, never, all, none, and only tend to be false. Statements with qualifiers such as usually, might, and sometimes tend to be true" (pp. 83–84). Either eliminate these verbal clues to correct answers or balance them between true and false items.

    Example: The first item is better than the second.
    Martin Luther King made important civil rights speeches.
    Martin Luther King never made an unimportant speech.

are called *distractors.* The student's task is to select the correct choice from among the distractors—for example:

What is the capital of Vermont? (Stem)
  a. Portland (Distractor)
  b. Montpelier (Answer)
  c. Boston (Distractor)
  d. Weston (Distractor)

BEST PRACTICES
Strategies for Writing Multiple-Choice Items

Some good strategies for writing high-quality multiple-choice items include (Gronlund, 2006; Haladyna, 1997, 2002; Linden, 1996; McMillan, 2007; Sax, 1997):

1. *Write the stem as a question.*

2. *Give three or four possible alternatives from which to choose.*

3. *State items and options positively when possible.* Elementary school students especially find negatives confusing. If you use the word *not* in the stem, *italicize* or <u>underline</u> it—for example:

    Which of the following cities is *not* in New England?
    a. Boston
    b. Chicago
    c. Montpelier
    d. Providence

4. *Include as much of the item as possible in the stem, thus making the stem relatively long and the alternatives relatively short*—for example:

    Which U.S. president wrote the Gettysburg Address?
    a. Thomas Jefferson
    b. Abraham Lincoln
    c. James Madison
    d. Woodrow Wilson

5. *Alternatives should grammatically match the stem so that no answers are grammatically wrong.* For example, the first item is better than the second:

    Orville and Wilbur Wright became famous because of which type of transportation?
    a. airplane
    b. automobile
    c. boat
    d. train

    Orville and Wilbur Wright became famous because of an
    a. airplane
    b. automobile
    c. boat
    d. train

6. *Write items that have a clearly defensible correct or best option.* Unless you give alternative directions, students will assume that there is only one correct or best answer to an item.

7. *Vary the placement of the correct option.* Students who are unsure of an answer tend to select the middle options and avoid the extreme options. Alphabetizing response choices (by the first letters in the response) will help to vary the placement of the correct option.

8. *Beware of cues in the length of the options.* Correct answers tend to be longer than incorrect ones because of the need to include specifications and qualifications that make it true. Lengthen the distractors (incorrect responses) to approximately the same length as the correct answer.

9. *Don't expect students to make narrow distinctions among answer choices.* For example, the first item is better than the second:

    The freezing point of water is
    a. 25°F
    b. 32°F
    c. 39°F
    d. 46°F

    The freezing point of water is
    a. 30°F
    b. 31°F
    c. 32°F
    d. 33°F

10. *Do not overuse "None of the above" and "All of the above."* Also avoid using variations of "a and b" or "c and d but not a."

11. *Don't use the exact wording in a textbook when writing a question.* Weak students might recognize the correct answer but not really understand its meaning.

12. *Write at least some items that encourage students to engage in higher-level thinking.* As we indicated earlier in the chapter, a current trend is to use more multiple-choice items in classroom assessment because of the demands imposed on teachers by high-stakes state standards-based tests. An important issue in the return to using more multiple-choice items is the cognitive level demanded by the items. Many teachers report using "higher-level" test items, but in reality they mainly are lower-level recall and recognition items (McMillan, 2007).

Here are some recommendations for writing higher-level thinking multiple-choice items (Center for Instructional Technology, 2006):

• Don't write more than three or four items a day that involve higher-level thinking because they are more difficult to write and take more time than more simple, straightforward items.

- Write one or two items after a class (a good idea for writing any test items) and then simply assemble them at a later time when making up a test.
- Use some analogy-based items. An example of a multiple-choice item using an analogy is:

  Bandura is to social cognitive theory as _____ is to social constructivist theory:
  - a. Piaget
  - b. Siegler
  - c. Vygotsky
  - d. Skinner

- Write some case study items. You already have encountered many of these in this textbook. Many of the Praxis™ Practice at the end of main sections in a chapter and all of the Crack the Case multiple-choice items at the end of chapters involve case studies.
- Write items in which students have to select what is missing or needs to be changed in a scenario you provide.

Students below the fourth grade probably should answer questions on the test page rather than on a separate answer sheet. Young elementary school students tend to respond slowly and lose their place easily when they have to use a separate answer sheet (Sax, 1997). Using a separate answer sheet with older students often reduces scoring time because the answers usually can fit on only one page.

For most classroom requirements, simply count the number of answers marked correctly. Some teachers penalize students for guessing by deducting for wrong answers, but assessment experts say that this probably is not worth the extra bother and frequently leads to mistakes in scoring (Sax, 1997).

Strengths and limitations of multiple-choice items are listed in figure 16.5.

Matching Items   Used by many teachers with younger students, matching requires students to connect one group of stimuli correctly with a second group of stimuli (Hambleton, 1996). Matching is especially well suited for assessing associations or links between two sets of information. In a typical matching format, a teacher places a list of terms on the left side of the page and a description or definition of the terms on the right side of the page. The student's task is to draw lines between the columns that correctly link terms with their definitions or descriptions. In another format, a space is left blank next to each term, in which the student writes the correct number or letter of the description/definition. When using matching, limit the number of items to be matched to no more than eight or ten. Many experts recommend using no more than five or six items per set (Linden, 1996).

Matching tests are convenient for teachers in that (Popham, 2005) (1) their compact form requires little space, thus making it easy to assess quite a lot of information efficiently, and (2) they can be easily scored by using a correct-answer template.

But matching tests may tend to ask students to connect trivial information. Also, most matching tasks require students to connect information they have simply memorized, although items can be constructed that measure more complex cognitive skills (Sax, 1997).

Other Objective Assessment Formats   Other objective or selected-response tests make use of audiovisuals and problem sets (Hambleton, 1996). The audiovisual format takes advantage of the ease with which we now can create and show slides and videotapes. Students are presented with a problem in an audiovisual format and asked to make decisions about what is going on or how to solve the problem. The student selects answers from sets of options, just as in a paper-and-pencil multiple-choice test. The main advantages of this audiovisual format are that it can depict the real world and can be used to evaluate higher-level cognitive skills. The main drawbacks are the costs in time and money.

FIGURE 16.5 Strengths and Limitations of Multiple-Choice Items

Source: From Norman E. Gronlund, *Assessment of Student Achievement*, 6/e. Published by Allyn and Bacon, Boston, MA. Copyright © 1998 by Pearson Education. Reprinted by permission of the publisher.

Strengths

1. Both simple and complex learning outcomes can be measured.
2. The task is highly structured and clear.
3. A broad sample of achievement can be measured.
4. Incorrect alternatives provide diagnostic information.
5. Scores are less influenced by guessing than true/false items.
6. Scoring is easy, objective, and reliable.

Limitations

1. Constructing good items is time consuming.
2. It is frequently difficult to find plausible distractors.
3. The multiple-choice format is ineffective for measuring some types of problem solving and the ability to organize and express ideas.
4. Score can be influenced by reading ability.

Problem sets involve presenting two or more multiple-choice or objective short-answer items in reference to a single stimulus, "such as an illustration, a graph, or a passage" (Hambleton, 1996, p. 910). For example, in math class, a graph might be displayed together with a series of multiple-choice items. In history or social studies, a map might be the stimulus for half a dozen questions. Some students report that the problem-set format seems more realistic than a set of discrete, independent items.

How Good Are Your Test Items? One way to evaluate the quality of your test items is to conduct an item analysis of them. One method for doing this involves computing the difficulty level of the items. Another method involves determining how well the items discriminate among students who scored high and those who scored low on the entire test (Gronlund, 2006; Linden, 1996; Reynolds, Livingston, & Willson, 2006).

The **item difficulty index** is the percentage of students who obtain the correct answer on an item. To compute the difficulty index for each item, go through these steps:

1. Rank-order the scores on the test from highest to lowest.
2. Identify the high-scoring group and the low-scoring group. With 30 students you might choose the 10 students who scored the highest on the test and the 10 students who scored the lowest. A good strategy is to select the top-scoring one-third of students and the bottom-scoring one-third of students.
3. Determine the percentage of high scorers and low scorers passing an item by adding a zero. In one example, 8 of 10 students in the high-scoring group correctly answered the item, which equals 80 percent; 4 of 10 students in the low-scoring group answered it correctly, which equals 40 percent.
4. To obtain the item difficulty index, add the percentage correct in the high and low groups and then divide by 2. Add a percent sign to the answer. Thus, in our example,

$$\frac{80 + 40}{2} = 60\%$$

When the item difficulty index is 75 percent or higher, the item is usually interpreted as easy in terms of difficulty level; when the index is 25 percent or less, the item is usually interpreted as hard in difficulty level. Thus, the higher the item difficulty index, the easier the item is. Any items with a difficulty index between 25 percent and 75 percent—including the item in our example—are usually interpreted as average in difficulty level.

Assessment experts recommend that most of the items on a test be in the 40 percent to 60 percent range, with only a few hard items (0 percent to 25 percent) or easy items (75 percent to 100 percent).

The **item discrimination index** reflects the item's ability to discriminate between individuals who scored high and those who scored low on the entire test. Obtain the item discrimination index by subtracting the percentage correct in the low-scoring group from the percentage correct in the high-scoring group. Then, add a decimal point to the answer. Thus, in our example,

$$80 - 40 = .40$$

This item discrimination index has a decimal point, and its value ranges from 0 to 1.00. If the index is 0 to .19, there was little or no difference between the high- and low-scoring groups on the item; if the index is .20 to .39, the item discriminated moderately well between the high- and low-scoring groups; if the index is .40 or greater, the item strongly discriminated between the high- and low-scoring groups (which was the case for the item in our example: .40). If the item discrimination index is below .20, you likely will want to improve the item or eliminate it; if it is

problem sets Groups of two or more multiple-choice or objective short-answer items that are related to the same stimulus, such as an illustration, a graph, or a passage.

item difficulty index The percentage of students who obtain the correct answer on an item.

item discrimination index An index that reflects the item's ability to discriminate between individuals who scored high and those who scored low on the entire test.

.20 to .39, you might want to keep the item but improve it; and if the index is .40 or above, you likely will want to keep the item as it is.

Constructed-Response Items

Constructed-response items require students to write out information rather than select a response from a menu. Short-answer and essay items are the most commonly used forms of constructed-response items. In scoring, many constructed-response items require judgment on the part of the examiner (Reynolds, Livingston, & Willson, 2006).

Short-Answer Items A **short-answer item** is a constructed-response format in which students are required to write a word, a short phrase, or several sentences in response to a task. For example, a student might be asked, "Who discovered penicillin?" The short-answer format allows recall and could provide a problem-solving assessment of a wide range of material. The disadvantages of short-answer questions are that they can require judgment to be scored and typically measure rote learning.

Sentence completion is a variation of the short-answer item, in which students express their knowledge and skill by completing a sentence. For example, a student might be asked to complete this sentence stem: The name of the person who discovered penicillin is _____.

Essays **Essay items** allow students more freedom of response to questions but require more writing than other formats. Essay items are especially good for assessing students' understanding of material, higher-level thinking skills, ability to organize information, and writing skills. Here are some examples of high school essay questions:

What are the strengths and weaknesses of a democratic approach to government?

Describe the main themes of the novel you just read.

Argue that the United States is a gender-biased nation.

Essay items can require students to write anything from a few sentences to several pages. In some cases, teachers ask all students to answer the same essay question(s). In others, teachers let students select from a group of items the item(s) they want to write about, a strategy that makes it more difficult to compare different students' responses.

Suggestions for writing good essay items include these (Sax, 1997):

- *Specify limitations.* Be sure to specify the length of the desired answer and the weight that will be given to each item in determining scores or judgments.
- *Structure and clarify the task.* Make clear what they are supposed to write about. A poorly worded item is "Who was George Washington?" This could be answered in six words: "First president of the United States." In cases like this, ask yourself what more you want the student to tell. These more-structured essay items would require more thinking on the part of the student:

    Discuss several events in the life of George Washington that confirm or disprove the claim that "he never told a lie." Use the events to support a claim of your own about how truthful Washington was.

- *Ask questions in a direct way.* Don't get too tricky.

You might hear the term *rubric* used in regard to scoring students' responses on essays and other tests. In this context, *rubric* simply means a scoring system. Figure 16.6 lists some strengths and limitations of essay questions.

Strengths

1. The highest level of learning outcomes (analysis, synthesis, evaluation) can be measured.
2. The integration and application of ideas can be emphasized.
3. Preparation time is usually less than for selection-type formats.

Limitations

1. Achievement may not be adequately sampled due to the time needed to answer each question.
2. It can be difficult to relate essay responses to intended learning outcomes because of freedom to select, organize, and express ideas.
3. Scores are raised by writing skill and bluffing, and lowered by poor handwriting, misspelling, and grammatical errors.
4. Scoring is time consuming, subjective, and possibly unreliable.

FIGURE 16.6 Strengths and Limitations of Essay Questions

Source: From Norman E. Gronlund, *Assessment of Student Achievement*, 6/e. Published by Allyn and Bacon, Boston, MA. Copyright © 1998 by Pearson Education. Reprinted by permission of the publisher.

constructed-response items Items that require students to write out information rather than select a response from a menu.

short-answer item A constructed-response format in which students are required to write a word, a short phrase, or several sentences in response to a task.

essay items Items that require a lengthy written answer; they allow more freedom of response to questions but require more writing than other formats.

BEST PRACTICES
Strategies for Scoring Essay Questions

Here are some good strategies for scoring essays (Sax, 1997):

1. *Outline a plan for what constitutes a good or acceptable answer prior to administering or scoring students' responses* (McMillan, 2007). Essays can be scored holistically or analytically. *Holistic scoring* means making an overall judgment about the student's answer and giving it a single number or letter. You might make this judgment based on your overall impression of the essay or base it on several criteria that you have generated. Holistic scoring is often used when essays are long. *Analytic scoring* means scoring various criteria separately, then adding up the points to produce an overall score for the essay. Analytic scoring can be time consuming, so avoid having more than three or four criteria for an essay.

2. *Devise a method by which you can score the essays without knowing which students wrote them.* You might do this by having students write their name beside a number on a separate sheet, then write only their number on the essay. When you record the grade, you can match up the student's number and name. This reduces the chance that your positive or negative expectations for the student will enter into your evaluation of the responses.

3. *Evaluate all answers to the same questions together.* Read and score all students' responses to one item before moving on to the next item. It is easier for you to remember the criteria for evaluating an answer to a single essay item than to remember the criteria for all essay items. Also, if you read all of one student's responses together, your evaluation of the first few items will tend to influence your evaluation of the remaining items.

4. *Decide on a policy for handling irrelevant or incorrect responses.* Some students try to bluff their way through essays. Other students write everything they know about a topic without taking the time to zero in on what the item is asking for. Still other students might use poor grammar, misspell words, or write illegibly. Decide ahead of time whether and how much you will penalize such responses.

5. *If possible, reread papers before handing them back to students.* This helps you guard against any flaws or oversights in your scoring.

6. *Write comments on the paper.* An essay, especially a long one, with only a number or letter grade on it does not give adequate feedback to a student. And if you only circle or correct spelling errors and grammar, you are not giving students insight about the content of their essay responses. A good strategy is to write a number of brief comments at appropriate places throughout the essay, such as "Expand this idea more," "Unclear," or "Needs an example," in addition to making overall comments about the essay at its beginning or end. It is better to write comments throughout the essay than to make one or two minor comments in one part of the essay.

Review, Reflect, and Practice

(2) Provide some guidelines for constructing traditional tests.

REVIEW

- What are some important ideas to remember when creating true/false, multiple-choice, and matching items? What are some basic tools for evaluating item quality?
- What are constructed-response items and how do short-answer items differ from essay items?

REFLECT

- Why do you think traditional testing has survived so long in K–12 classrooms?

PRAXIS™ PRACTICE

1. Mr. Brown, a college instructor, includes the following item in a test about the impact of the family on children: What parenting style does Homer Simpson exhibit? Mr. Brown's possible answers are: authoritative, authoritarian, neglectful, and permissive. Which of the following is the most appropriate criticism of Mr. Brown's question and answers?
   a. It is too easy to eliminate options because they are not all parenting styles.
   b. Parenting style has nothing to do with the impact of family on children.

    c. The question is biased in favor of people who watch *The Simpsons*.

    d. There is more than one clearly correct response.

2. Mr. Dent has just returned Marcia's graded essay to her. Notations of spelling and grammar errors, and the grade, 42/50—B, are all he has written on the test. What is the most appropriate criticism of this assessment?

    a. An essay should never be worth this many points on a test.

    b. Essays should not be graded numerically.

    c. There is no indication of why she lost points.

    d. Spelling and grammar errors should not be marked on an essay.

Please see the answer key at the end of the book.

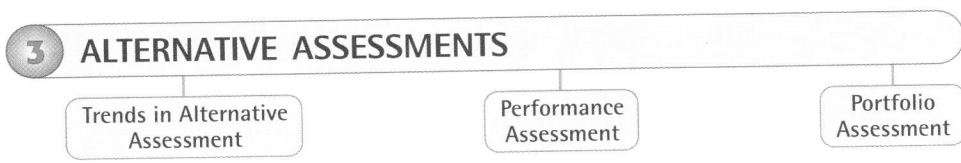

3 ALTERNATIVE ASSESSMENTS

| Trends in Alternative Assessment | Performance Assessment | Portfolio Assessment |

There are alternatives to the traditional assessments that we just discussed (Linn & Miller, 2005; McMillan, 2007; Popham, 2005; Stiggins, 2005). Let's examine some trends in this regard.

Trends in Alternative Assessment

One current trend is to require students to solve some type of authentic problem or to perform in terms of completing a project or demonstrating other skills outside the context of a test or an essay (Banks, 2005). Another trend is to have students create a learning portfolio to demonstrate what they have learned (Klenowski, Askew, & Carnell, 2006; Stiggins, 2005). Such alternative assessments are needed to make instruction compatible with contemporary views of learning and motivation.

    Alternative assessments offer students more choices than they would have in taking a test or writing an essay (Powers, 2005). Consider several alternative assessments that a middle school language arts teacher devised (Combs, 1997). She gave students a menu of options to choose from that included book reports, artwork, videos, and models. For example, in a unit on mystery, students might choose to write a report on an author of mystery stories, write an original mystery, make a children's mystery book, or conduct an interview with a private investigator. Each of these options came with a detailed set of instructions and a scoring guide for quality control. Figure 16.7 shows the directions and scoring guide for alternative assessments that focus on the Middle Ages and family history.

    Authentic assessment means evaluating a student's knowledge or skill in a context that approximates the real world or real life as closely as possible (Pokey & Siders, 2001; Powers, 2005). Traditional assessment has involved the use of paper-and-pencil tests that are often far removed from real-world contexts. An increasing trend is to assess students with items that more closely reflect reality (Palomba & Banta, 1999). In some circles, the terms *performance assessment* and *authentic assessment* have been used interchangeably. However, not all performance assessments are authentic (McMillan, 2002).

    Critics of authentic assessment argue that such assessments are not necessarily superior to more conventional assessments, such as multiple-choice and essay tests (Terwilliger, 1997). They say that the proponents of authentic assessment rarely present data in support of the validity of authentic assessments (Braden, 2005). They also believe that authentic assessments don't adequately examine knowledge and basic skills.

FIGURE 16.7 Examples of Alternative Assessment in a Middle School Language Arts Class

Middle ages option model

Directions:

Make a model of a creature or character from the Middle Ages. Write a one-half to one page description of your character (tell who or what it is and its importance in the Middle Ages). Your model must portray the creature or character through the use of appropriate costume, props, or other attributes.

Scoring Guide

25   Model portrays the character or creature and time period through the use of attire, props, and other attributes

10   Artistic quality

15   The model shows evidence of effort

50   A ½ to 1 page written description of the character is included

Family history option: family tree poster

Directions:

Make a poster of your family tree, going back at least three generations. Provide as much information about the family members as possible, including, but not limited to, birthdate, death date (if not living), occupation, place of birth, accomplishments, etc. In addition, provide at least two anecdotes about your family's history (how they came to live in our town, special notoriety, honors, awards, medals, etc.). You must *write out* your family tree! (You may not make a copy of a commercially prepared family tree and paste it on the poster.) Make your poster attractive and neat!

Scoring Guide

25   Family tree includes at least three generations prior to you

25   In addition to names, most entries include information such as birth, death, and place of birth

25   Poster includes at least two anecdotes about interesting or well-known family members

15   Poster is neatly and attractively typed or written by you

10   Mechanics, spelling, usage

Performance Assessment

Moving from traditional assessment with objective tests to performance assessment has been described as going from "knowing" to "showing" (Burz & Marshall, 1996). Performance assessments include what is commonly thought of as students' actual performances (such as in dance, music, art, and physical education), as well as papers, projects, oral presentations, experiments, and portfolios (Gronlund, 2006). Figure 16.8 shows an example of a performance assessment in science (Solano-Flores & Shavelson, 1997). We will cover the main features of performance assessments, guidelines for using them, and their strengths and weaknesses.

Some disciplines, such as art, music, and physical education, have been using performance assessments for many years. The major change in performance assessment has involved introducing these forms of assessment into the traditional "academic areas."

Features of Performance Assessment Performance assessments often include an emphasis on "doing" open-ended activities for which there is no correct, objective answer and that may assess higher-level thinking. Performance assessment tasks sometimes also are realistic. Evaluating performance often includes direct methods of evaluation, self-assessment, assessment of group performance as well as individual performance, and an extended period of time for assessment (Hambleton, 1996).

Traditional tests emphasize what students know. Performance assessments are designed to evaluate what students know and can do (Maki, 2001). In many cases, there is no correct, objective answer. For example, there is no one "correct answer" when a student gives a talk in class, creates a painting, performs a gymnastic routine, or designs a science project. Many performance assessments give students considerable freedom to construct their own responses rather than narrowing their range of

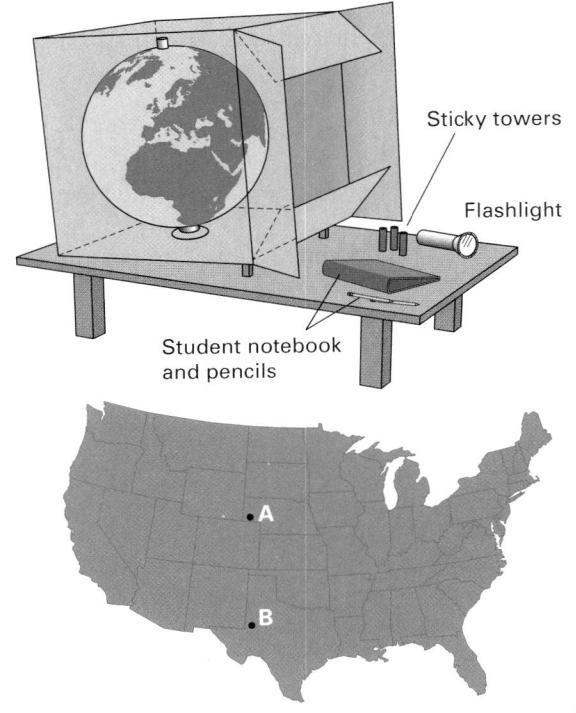

(a) The equipment consists of a spinning Earth globe inside a carton box, three sticky towers, and a flashlight; the students stick Towers A and B at two specific U.S. locations on the globe and are told what Tower C's shadow looks like when it is noon for Towers A and B. They have to find out where in the U.S. Tower C is. The solution requires modeling the sunlight by using the flashlight to project the towers' shadows onto the globe.

Sticky towers

Flashlight

Student notebook and pencils

A

B

(b) Draw a dot on this map to show where you think Tower C is. How did you figure out where Tower C is?

(c)

Observation/results	score
Tower C is in eastern United States	1
Tower C is in northeastern United States	1
Tower C is somewhere between Pennsylvania and Maine	1

Data gathering/modeling		score
Flashlight Position	Point flashlight at Equator	2
Flashlight Motion	Moves flashlight from E to W	2
Globe Rotation	Rotates globe Rotates globe from W to E	1 2
Towers	Moves Tower C around on the map/globe until shadow is matched	1
	Moves Tower C around on the map/globe in the E/NE region until shadow is matched	2
Shadows	Uses shadows of Towers A and B as reference	1

(b) The response format involves having students record in notebooks their solutions, the actions they carried out, and the reasoning behind their actions.

(c) Students' performances are scored for the accuracy of their results and the accuracy of their modeling, reasoning, and observations.

FIGURE 16.8 A Performance–Based Assessment in Science: Daytime Astronomy

answers. Although this makes scoring more difficult, it provides a context for evaluating students' higher-level thinking skills, such as the ability to think deeply about an issue or a topic (Wiggins, 1993).

Performance assessments use direct methods of evaluation, such as evaluating writing samples to assess writing skills and oral presentations to assess speaking and judging oral presentations to assess speaking skills (Banks, 2005). Observing a student give an oral presentation is a more direct assessment than asking the student a series of questions about speaking skills on a paper-and-pencil test.

Some performance assessments also involve having students evaluate their own performance. This emphasis shifts responsibility away from teachers and places it more squarely on the student's shoulders. Rubrics are useful aids to students in conducting self-assessments. For example, students might be required to evaluate a scrapbook that they have created (Goodrich, 1997). One criterion for evaluation might be "Gives enough details?" with the following possible responses: excellent ("Yes, I put enough details to give the reader a sense of time, place, and events"), good ("Yes, I put in some details, but some key details are missing"), minimal ("No, I did not put in enough details but did include a few"), and inadequate ("No, I had almost no details").

Some performance assessments evaluate how effectively a group of students perform, not just how the students perform individually. Thus, a group of students might be assigned to create a science project rather than having each student do a project individually. Evaluation of the student can include both the individual's contribution and the group's product. Group projects are often complex and allow for the assessment of cooperative skills, communication skills, and leadership skills.

Finally, as we noted, performance assessments may take place over an extended period of time. In traditional assessment, assessment occurs in a single time frame. For example, a teacher gives a multiple-choice test and students are allowed an hour to take it. By contrast, it is not unusual for performance assessments to involve sustained work over days, weeks, and even months. For example, a student might be evaluated once a month on the progress the student is making on a science project, then receive a final evaluation when the project is completed.

Guidelines for Performance Assessment   Guidelines for using performance assessments cover four general issues (Airasian, 2005): (1) establishing a clear purpose, (2) identifying observable criteria, (3) providing an appropriate setting, and (4) judging or scoring the performance.

Make sure that any performance assessment has a clear purpose and that a clear decision can be made from the assessment (McKinley, Boulet, & Hambleton, 2000). The purposes can be diverse: to assign a grade, to evaluate a student's progress, to recognize the important steps in a performance, to generate products to be included in a learning portfolio, to provide concrete examples of students' work for admission to college or other programs, and so forth.

Performance criteria are specific behaviors that students need to perform effectively as part of the assessment. Establishing performance criteria helps the teacher to go beyond general descriptions (such as "Do an oral presentation" or "Complete a science project") in specifying what the student needs to do. Performance criteria help you make your observations more systematic and focused. As guidelines, they direct your observations. Without such criteria, your observations can be unsystematic and haphazard. Communicating these performance criteria to students at the beginning of instruction lets students know how to focus their learning.

Once you have clearly outlined the performance criteria, it is important to specify the setting in which you will observe the performance or product. You may want to observe behaviors directly in the regular flow of classroom activity, in a special context you create in the classroom, or in a context outside the classroom. As a rule of thumb it is a good idea to observe the student on more than one occasion, because a single performance might not fairly represent the student's knowledge or skill.

Finally, you will need to score or rate the performance. Scoring rubrics involve the criteria that are used to judge performance, what the range in the quality of the performance should look like, what score should be given and what that score means, and how the different levels of quality should be described and differentiated from one another (Meir, Rich, & Cady, 2006).

In preparing a rubric, you may want to (Re: Learning by Design, 2000)

1. *Include a scale of possible points to be assigned in scoring work.* High numbers usually are assigned to the best work. Scales typically use 4, 5, or 6 as the highest score, down to 1 or 0 for the lowest score.

2. *Provide descriptors for each performance criteria to increase reliability and avoid biased scoring.*

3. *Decide whether the rubric will be generic, genre-specific, or task-specific.* If generic, the rubric can be used to judge a broad performance, such as communication or problem solving. If genre-specific, the rubric applies to a more specific type of performance, such as an essay, a speech, or a narrative as a form of communication; open-ended or closed-end problems as kinds of problems solved. A task-specific rubric is unique to a single task, such as a single math problem or a speech on a specific topic.

4. *Decide whether the rubric should be longitudinal.* This type of rubric assesses progress over time toward mastery of educational objectives. One strategy for developing rubrics is to work backward from *exemplars*—examples of student

performance criteria Specific behaviors that need to be performed effectively as part of an assessment.

Criteria	Quality			
Purposes	The report explains the key purposes of the invention and also points out less obvious ones.	The report explains all of the key purposes of the invention.	The report explains some of the purposes of the invention but misses key purposes.	The report does not refer to the purposes of the invention.
Features	The report details both key and hidden features of the invention and explains how they serve several purposes.	The report details the key features of the invention and explains the purposes they serve.	The report neglects some of the features of the invention or the purposes they serve.	The report does not detail the features of the invention or the purposes they serve.
Critique	The report discusses the strengths and weaknesses of the invention, and suggests ways that it can be improved.	The report discusses the strengths and weaknesses of the invention.	The report discusses either the strengths or weaknesses of the invention, but not both.	The report does not mention the strengths or weaknesses of the invention.
Connections	The report makes appropriate connections between the purposes and features of the invention and many different kinds of phenomena.	The report makes appropriate connections between the purposes and features of the invention and one or two phenomena.	The report makes unclear or inappropriate connections between the invention and other phenomena.	The report makes no connections between the invention and other things.

FIGURE 16.9 Scoring Rubric for a Report on an Invention

Note: A teacher might assign each of the columns a score and/or label, such as column 1: 4 (Excellent), column 2: 3 (Good), column 3: 2 (Minimal), and column 4: 1 (Inadequate).

work (McMillan, 1997, p. 218). "These exemplars can be analyzed to determine what descriptors distinguish them. The examples can also be used as *anchor* papers for making judgments, and can be given to students to illustrate the dimensions." An *anchor* is a sample of work or performance used to set the specific performance standard for a rubric level. Thus, attached to a paragraph describing a six-level performance in writing might be two or three samples of writing to illustrate several levels (Re: Learning by Design, 2000). Figure 16.9 shows a scoring rubric for scoring a report on an invention. Figure 16.10 indicates the importance of clarity in creating rubrics.

Evaluating Performance Assessment   Many educational psychologists support the increased use of performance-based assessment (Eisner, 1999; Stiggins, 2005). They contend that performance assessments involve students more in their learning, encourage higher-level thinking skills, can measure what is really important in the curriculum, and can tie assessment more to real-world, real-life experiences.

However, "although support for performance-based assessment is high in many parts of the United States and Canada, effective implementation" faces several hurdles (Hambleton, 1996, p. 903). Performance assessments often "take considerably more time to construct, administer, and score than objective tests." Also, many performance tests do not meet the standards of validity and reliability outlined by

Criterion: gains audience's attention

Quality

(a)	Creative beginning	Boring beginning	No beginning
(b)	Gives details or an amusing fact, a series of questions, a short demonstration, a colorful visual or a personal reason for why they picked the topic	Gives a one- or two-sentence introduction, then starts the speech	Does not attempt to gain the audience's attention, just starts the speech

FIGURE 16.10 Creating Clarity in a Rubric for One Dimension of an Oral Presentation

The descriptions in (a) are rather vague and do not clearly specify what students need to do to be evaluated very positively on the criterion. The descriptions in (b) provide more detailed specifications of how the criterion will be rated, a recommended strategy.

BEST PRACTICES
Strategies for Developing Scoring Rubrics

Here are some good strategies for incorporating scoring rubrics in performance assessment (Goodrich, 1997; McMillan, 2007; Re: Learning by Design, 2000):

1. *Match the type of rating with the purpose of the assessment.* If your purpose is global and you need a general judgment, use a holistic scale. If your purpose is to provide specific feedback on different aspects of a performance, use a more analytical approach.

2. *Share the criteria with students prior to instruction.* This encourages students to incorporate the descriptions as standards to guide their work.

3. *Build your rubrics from the top, starting from a description of an exemplary performance.* Even if no student can perform at an exemplary level, the rubric should be built from a picture of excellence to establish an anchor for scoring. A good strategy is to use two or three examples of excellence rather than a single example so that students are not limited in their thinking about what an excellent performance is. After you have described the best level of quality, describe the worst; then fill in the middle levels.

4. *Carefully construct the rubric language for each criterion or score.* Use words such as *excellent* and *good,* and carefully describe what each term means. Typically, you will have a paragraph for each criterion or score that includes concrete indicators of when the criterion or score has been met.

5. *Make rubrics more authentic.* Criteria should validly, not arbitrarily, distinguish different degrees of performance. Here are some criteria that are often used in assessing writing in large-scale performance tests: organization, usage/word choice, focus, sentence construction, mechanics, and voice. However, the following criteria are more authentic in that they relate more clearly to the impact of the writing (and they include the previously mentioned criteria without restricting the writer to conventions and rules): clarity, memorability, persuasiveness, and enticingness.

6. *Show students models.* Let students examine examples of good and not-so-good work. Identify what's good or bad about the models.

7. *Take appropriate steps to minimize scoring error.* A scoring system should be objective and consistent. Some types of errors, in particular, should be avoided in scoring rubrics. The most common errors involve personal bias and halo effects of the person making the judgment. *Personal bias* occurs when teachers tend to give students higher scores (such as mostly 5 and 6 on a 1- to 6-point scale), lower scores (give mostly 1 or 2), or scores in the middle (give mostly 3 or 4). A *halo effect* occurs when a teacher's general impression of the student influences the score given on a particular performance.

such education groups as the American Educational Research Association, the American Psychological Association, and the National Council on Measurement in Education. Moreover, the research base for performance tests is not well established.

Still, even the strongest supporters of traditional tests acknowledge that traditional tests do not measure all of what schools expect students to learn (Hambleton, 1996). Although planning, constructing, and scoring performance tests is challenging, teachers should make every effort to include performance assessments as an important aspect of their teaching (Mabry, 1999).

Portfolio Assessment

Interest in portfolio assessment has increased dramatically in recent years (Burke, 2006; Butler & McMunn, 2006). Portfolios represent a significant departure from traditional tests of learning. Figure 16.11 summarizes the contrast between portfolios and traditional testing.

A **portfolio** consists of a systematic and organized collection of a student's work that demonstrates the student's skills and accomplishments. A portfolio is a purposeful collection of work that tells the story of the student's progress and achievements (Gronlund, 2006; Knotek, 2005). It is much more than a compilation of student papers stuffed into a manila folder or a collection of memorabilia pasted into a scrapbook (Hatch, 2000). To qualify for inclusion in a portfolio, each piece of work should be created and organized in a way that demonstrates progress and purpose. Portfolios can include many different types of work, such as writing samples, journal

portfolio A systematic and organized collection of a student's work that demonstrates the student's skills and accomplishments.

Traditional tests	Portfolios
• Separate learning, testing, and teaching	• Link assessment and teaching to learning
• Fail to assess the impact of prior knowledge on learning by using short passages that are often isolated and unfamiliar	• Address the importance of the student's prior knowledge as a critical determinant to learning by using authentic assessment activities
• Rely on materials requesting only literal information	• Provide opportunities to demonstrate inferential and critical thinking that are essential for constructing meaning
• Prohibit collaboration during the assessment process	
• Often treat skills in isolated contexts to determine achievement for reporting purposes	• Represent a collaborative approach to assessment involving both students and teachers
• Assess students across a limited range of assignments that may not match what students do in classrooms	• Use multifaceted activities while recognizing that learning requires integration and coordination of communication skills
• Assess students in a predetermined situation where the content is fixed	• Represent the full range of instructional activities that students are doing in their classrooms
• Assess all students on the same dimensions	• Can measure the student's ability to perform appropriately in unanticipated situations
• Address only achievement	• Measure each student's achievements while allowing individual differences
• Seldom provide vehicles for assessing students' abilities to monitor their own learning	• Address improvement, effort, and achievement
• Are mechanically scored or scored by teachers who have little input into the assessment	• Implement self-assessment by having students monitor their learning
• Rarely include items that assess emotional responses to learning	• Engage students in assessing their progress and/or accomplishments and establishing on-going learning goals
	• Provide opportunities to reflect upon feelings about learning

FIGURE 16.11 Contrasting Traditional Tests and Portfolios

entries, videotapes, art, teacher comments, posters, interviews, poetry, test results, problem solutions, recordings of foreign language communication, self-assessments, and any other expression of the student that the teacher believes demonstrates the student's skills and accomplishments (Knotek, 2005). Portfolios can be collected on paper, in photographs, and on audio-tape, videotape, computer disk, or CD-ROM. Assessment expert Joan Herman (1996) says that portfolio assessment has become increasingly popular because it is a natural way to integrate instruction and assessment.

Four classes of evidence that can be placed in students' portfolios are artifacts, reproductions, attestations, and productions (Barton & Collins, 1997). *Artifacts* are documents or products, such as student papers and homework, that are produced during normal academic work in the classroom. *Reproductions* consist of documentation of a student's work outside the classroom, such as special projects and interviews. For example, a student's description of an interview with a local scientist in the community about the scientist's work is a reproduction. *Attestations* represent the teacher's or other responsible persons' documentation of the student's progress. For example, a teacher might write evaluative notes about a student's oral presentation and place them in the student's portfolio. *Productions* are documents the student prepares especially for the portfolio. Productions consist of three types of materials: goal statements, reflections, and captions. Students generate goal statements about what they want to accomplish with their portfolio, write down their reflections about their work and describe their progress, and create captions that describe each piece of work in the portfolio and its importance.

Using Portfolios Effectively Effective use of portfolios for assessment requires (1) establishing the portfolio's purpose, (2) involving the student in decisions about it, (3) reviewing the portfolio with the student, (4) setting criteria for evaluation, and (5) scoring and judging the portfolio.

Establishing Purpose Portfolios can be used for different purposes (Lyons, 1999). Two broad types of purpose are to document growth and to show best work. A **growth portfolio** consists of the student's work over an extended time frame (throughout the school year or even longer) to reveal the student's progress in meeting learning targets. Growth portfolios also are sometimes referred to as "developmental portfolios." Growth portfolios are especially helpful in providing concrete evidence of how much a student has changed or learned over time. As students examine their portfolios, they can see for themselves how much they have improved. One example of a growth portfolio is the Integrated Language Arts Portfolio used in the elementary school grades in Juneau, Alaska (Arter, 1995). It is designed to replace report cards and grades as a way to demonstrate growth and accomplishments. Growth is tracked along a developmental continuum for levels of skills in reading, writing, speaking, and listening. A student's status on the continuum is marked at several designated times during the year. Samples of the student's work are used as the basis for judgments about the student's developmental level.

A **best-work portfolio** showcases the student's most outstanding work. Sometimes it even is called a "showcase portfolio." Best-work portfolios are more selective than developmental portfolios and often include the student's latest product. Best-work portfolios are especially useful for parent-teacher conferences, students' future teachers, and admission to higher education levels.

"Passportfolios," or "proficiency portfolios," are sometimes used to demonstrate competence and readiness to move on to a new level of work (Arter, 1995; Lankes, 1995). For example, the Science Portfolio is an optional aspect of the Golden State Evaluation in California (California State Department of Education, 1994). It is produced during a year of science and contains a problem-solving investigation, a creative expression (presenting a scientific idea in a unique and original manner), a "growth through writing" section that demonstrates progress over time in understanding a concept, and self-reflection. The Central Park East Secondary School in New York City uses portfolios to determine graduation eligibility. Students are required to complete fourteen portfolios that demonstrate their competence in areas such as science and technology, ethics and social issues, community service, and history (Gold & Lanzoni, 1993).

Involving Students in Selecting Portfolio Materials Many teachers let students make at least some of the decisions about the portfolio's contents (Weasmer & Woods, 2001). Throughout Vermont, students in the fourth through eighth grades select five to seven items to be placed in their portfolio to demonstrate their competence in math problem solving. Student-led parent conferences allow students to demonstrate to parents what they have learned (Borba & Olvera, 2001). When students are allowed to choose the contents for their own portfolios, a good strategy is to encourage self-reflection by having them write a brief description of why they chose each piece of work (Airasian, 2005).

Reviewing with Students Explain to students at the beginning of the year what portfolios are and how they will be used. You also should have a number of student-teacher conferences throughout the year to review the student's progress and help the student to plan future work for the portfolio (McMillan, 2007; Weldin & Tumarkin, 1999).

Setting Criteria for Evaluation Clear and systematic performance criteria are essential for effectively using portfolios (Burke, 2006; Gronlund, 2006; Reynolds, Livingston, & Willson, 2006). Clear learning targets for students make developing performance criteria much easier. Ask yourself what knowledge and skills you want your students to have. This should be the focus of your teaching and your performance criteria.

Scoring and Judging It takes considerable time to score and judge portfolios (Airasian, 2005). Teachers must evaluate not only each individual item but also the portfolio as a whole. When the portfolio's purpose is to provide descriptive information about the student for the teacher at the next grade level, no scoring or summarizing of the portfolio might be necessary. However, when its purpose is to

growth portfolio A portfolio of work over an extended time frame (throughout the school year or longer) to reveal the student's progress in meeting learning targets.

best-work portfolio A portfolio that showcases the student's most outstanding work.

diagnose, reflect improvement, provide evidence for effective instruction, motivate students to reflect on their work, or give grades to students, summary scoring and judgments are needed. Checklists and rating scales are commonly used for this purpose. As with other aspects of portfolio assessment, some teachers give students the opportunity to evaluate and critique their own work.

Evaluating the Role of Portfolios in Assessment   Learning portfolios have several strengths: Their comprehensive nature captures the complexity and completeness of the student's work and accomplishments. They provide opportunities for encouraging student decision making and self-reflection. They motivate students to think critically and deeply. And they provide an excellent mechanism for evaluating student progress and improvement (Berryman & Russell, 2001; Richard, 2001).

Learning portfolios also have several weaknesses: They take considerable time to coordinate and evaluate. Their complexity and uniqueness make them difficult to evaluate, and their reliability is often much lower than that of traditional tests. And their use in large-scale assessments (such as statewide evaluation) is expensive. However, even with these weaknesses in mind, most educational psychology experts and educational organizations, such as the National Education Association, support the use of portfolios (Coffin, 1996).

Now that you've read about many types of assessment, this is a good time to think about what your classroom assessment philosophy will be. Self-Assessment 16.1 on p. 592 gives you this opportunity.

Review, Reflect, and Practice

(3) **Describe some types of alternative assessments.**

REVIEW
- What makes an assessment "authentic"? What are some criticisms of authentic assessments?
- What are some of the features of performance assessment? What are some guidelines for using them?
- How can portfolios be used in assessment? What are some strengths and weaknesses of portfolios?

REFLECT
- Suppose that you were teaching this course in educational psychology. How would you go about creating rubrics for assessing answers to the preceding three items?

PRAXIS™ PRACTICE
1. Nicole has just been told that as part of her teacher certification process, there will be a performance assessment. Which of the following is the best performance assessment of Nicole's teaching skills?
   a. a multiple-choice exam
   b. an essay exam
   c. an exam based on case studies
   d. direct observation of classroom teaching
2. Kyle is working on his portfolio for journalism class. Included in the portfolio are his teacher's evaluation notes regarding articles he has written for the school newspaper. These notes are examples of which of the following:
   a. artifacts
   b. attestations
   c. productions
   d. reproductions

Please see the answer key at the end of the book.

SELF-ASSESSMENT 16.1

Planning My Classroom Assessment Philosophy

With the subject matter and grade level at which you plan to teach in mind, examine the following list of assessments that we have discussed in this chapter. Rate each of the assessments on this scale: 1 = I don't plan to use this at all, 2 = I plan to use this occasionally, 3 = I plan to use this moderately, 4 = I plan to use this often, and 5 = This will be one of the most important assessments I will use.

1	2	3	4	5

1. Informal observations in preinstructional assessment

2. Structured exercises in preinstructional assessment

3. Observation during instruction

4. Questions during instruction

5. Assessments of students' affect

6. True/false items

7. Multiple-choice items

8. Matching

9. Audiovisual context setting

10. Problem sets

11. Figural responses

12. Short-answer items

13. Essays

14. Authentic assessment

15. Experiments

16. Projects

17. Oral presentations

18. Interviews

19. Performances

20. Exhibitions

21. Portfolios

Look back through your responses and then use this information to help you formulate your classroom assessment philosophy here. If you need more space, do this outside the book or on the student website.

_____

_____

_____

_____

④ GRADING AND REPORTING PERFORMANCE

| The Purposes of Grading | The Components of a Grading System | Reporting Students' Progress and Grades to Parents | Some Issues in Grading |

"Your grading curve and my learning curve don't intersect."

Dave Carpenter from *Phi Delta Kappan* (1997). Reprinted with permission of Dave Carpenter.

Grading means translating descriptive assessment information into letters, numbers, or other marks that indicate the quality of a student's learning or performance.

The Purposes of Grading

Grading is carried out to communicate meaningful information about a student's learning and achievement (Butler & McMunn, 2006; Taylor & Nolen, 2005). In this process, grades serve four basic purposes (Airasian, 2005):

- *Administrative.* Grades help determine students' class rank, credits for graduation, and whether a student should be promoted to the next grade.
- *Informational.* Grades can be used to communicate with students, parents, and others (such as admissions officers for subsequent schooling) about a student's work. A grade represents the teacher's overall conclusion about how well a student has met instructional objectives and learning targets.
- *Motivational.* Many students work harder because they are extrinsically motivated by a desire for high grades and a fear of low grades.
- *Guidance.* Grades help students, parents, and counselors to select appropriate courses and levels of work for students. They provide information about which students might require special services and what levels of future education students will likely be able to handle.

The Components of a Grading System

Grades reflect teachers' judgments. Three main types of teacher judgments underlie a teacher's grading system (Airasian, 2005): (1) What standard of comparison will I use for grading? (2) What aspects of students' performance will I use to establish grades? and (3) How will I weight different kinds of evidence in giving grades?

Standards of Comparison A student's performance can be graded by comparing it with the performance of other students or to predefined standards of performance.

Comparing Performance across Students **Norm-referenced grading** is a grading system based on comparison of a student's performance with that of other students in the class or of other classes and other students. In such a system, students get high grades for performing better than most of their classmates, and students get low grades for performing worse. Norm-referenced grading is commonly referred to as *grading on the curve.* In norm-referenced grading, the grading scale determines what percentages of students get particular grades. In most instances, the scale is created so that the largest percentage of students get *C*'s.

This is a typical breakdown of grades: 15 percent *A*'s, 25 percent *B*'s, 40 percent *C*'s, 15 percent *D*'s, and 5 percent *F*'s. In assigning grades, instructors often look for gaps in the range of scores. If 6 students score 92 to 100 and 10 students score 81 to 88, and there are no scores between 88 and 92, the teacher would assign a grade of *A* to the 92 to 100 scores and a *B* to the 81 to 88 scores. Norm-referenced grading has been criticized for reducing students' motivation, increasing their anxiety, increasing negative interactions among students, and hindering learning.

Comparing Performance with a Predetermined Standard **Criterion-referenced grading** is being used when students receive a certain grade for a certain level of

grading Translating descriptive assessment information into letters, numbers, or other marks that indicate the quality of a student's learning or performance.

norm-referenced grading A grading system based on a comparison of a student's performance with that of other students in the class or of other classes and other students.

criterion-referenced grading A grading system based on comparison with predetermined standards.

performance, regardless of any comparison with the work of other students. Sometimes criterion-referenced grading is called *absolute grading*. Typically, criterion-referenced grading is based on the proportion of points attained on a test or the level of mastery reached in a performance skill, such as giving an oral presentation and meeting all the predetermined criteria. Criterion-referenced grading is recommended over norm-referenced grading.

In theory, the standard established is supposed to be absolute, but in practice it doesn't always work out that way (McMillan, 2007). For example, a school system often develops a grading system that goes something like this: *A* 94 percent to 100 percent correct, *B* 87 percent to 93 percent, *C* 77 percent to 86 percent, *D* 70 percent to 76 percent, *F* below 70 percent. Although this system is absolute in the sense that every student must get 94 points to get an *A* and every student who does not get at least 70 points gets an *F*, teachers and classrooms vary enormously in what constitutes mastery of material to get a 94, an 87, a 77, or a 70. One teacher might give very hard tests, another very easy tests.

Many teachers use different cutoff scores than the ones just mentioned. Some teachers argue that low grades discourage student motivation and refuse to give *D*'s or *F*'s; others won't fail students unless their scores fall below 50.

Standards-based grading is a recent development based on criterion-referenced grading. It involves basing grading on standards that students are expected to achieve in a course. In some cases, national associations, such as the National Council of Teachers of Mathematics (NCTM), have developed standards that students should achieve. Thus, in one form of standards-based grading, a mathematics teacher might tie students' grades to how well they meet these national standards.

Aspects of Performance   Over the course of a grading period, students will likely have created many products that can be evaluated and used as a basis for grading. These can include test and quiz results, as well as various alternative assessments such as oral reports, projects, interviews, and homework. Increasingly, portfolios are used as the complete collection of materials to be graded or a portion of the work on which an overall grade is based. Some educators believe that grades should be based only on academic performance. In the view of other educators, grades should be based mainly on academic performance, but teacher ratings of motivation and effort can be factored in as well.

Many teachers use tests as the main, or even sole, basis for assigning grades. However, many assessment experts recommend basing an overall grade on a series of tests and other types of assessments (McMillan, 2007). Thus, a semester grade in geography might be based on two major tests and a final, eight quizzes, homework, two oral reports, and a project. Basing a grade on a series of tests and different types of assessment helps to balance out students' strengths and weaknesses, as well as compensate for a poor performance or two because of internal and external sources of measurement error.

Some educators advocate factoring affective characteristics such as motivation and effort into grades, especially by giving borderline students a plus or minus. Thus, a teacher might convert a student's *B* to a *B*+ if the student was highly motivated, put forth considerable effort, and actively participated in the class—or to a *B*−, if the student was poorly motivated, made little effort, and did not actively participate. However, some educators believe that grades should be based only on academic performance. One of the problems with including factors such as effort in grades is the difficulty in determining the reliability and validity of effort. Measures of effort or improvement can be made more systematic and reliable by developing scoring rubrics and examples (McMillan, 2004).

Weighting Different Kinds of Evidence   You will need to determine how much weight to give the different components of a student's

THROUGH THE EYES OF STUDENTS

Accepting Responsibility

Our teacher tells us that our grades are our responsibility. Nobody else's. "Don't blame anybody else but yourself if you don't make good grades," she says. At the beginning of the year, she said she would help us every way she could to help us make good grades and she has been good about that.

Cassandra
Middle School Student
Atlanta, Georgia

grade. For example, the teacher might arrive at a weighting system that looks something like this:

Major tests (2) 20 percent

Final test 25 percent

Quizzes 20 percent

Homework 5 percent

Oral report 10 percent

Project 20 percent

Many teachers don't use homework as a component for a grade. One reason for this is that when a student's grade depends on homework or other work done outside class, parents might be tempted to do their child's work to ensure a high grade. Another reason is that including homework as a component of grading favors students from better home environments. As with other aspects of classroom assessment, your judgment is involved in how you synthesize information to arrive at a student's grade. If a student fails to turn in a certain number of homework assignments, some teachers lower the student's grade.

Reporting Students' Progress and Grades to Parents

Grades are the most common method of informing parents about a child's progress and performance in the classroom (Airasian, 2005). However, grades by themselves provide limited information, are usually given infrequently, communicate little in the way of specific information about how the student is learning, and rarely include information about the student's motivation, cooperation, and classroom behavior. Because of these limitations, more than grades are needed to give parents a full portrait of the student (Durham, 2006).

The Report Card   The report card is a standard method of reporting students' progress and grades to parents. The form of judgments on report cards varies from one school system to another, and, in many cases, from one grade level to another. Some report cards convey letter grades (typically *A, B, C, D,* and *F,* sometimes also allowing pluses and minuses). Some report cards convey numerical scores (such as 91 in math, 85 in English, and so on). Other report cards have a pass/fail category in one or more subjects. Yet other report cards have checklists indicating skills or objectives the student has attained. Some report cards have categories for affective characteristics, such as effort, cooperation, and other appropriate and inappropriate behaviors.

Checklists of skills and objectives are mainly used in elementary schools or kindergartens. In the higher elementary school grade levels and secondary schools, letter grades are mainly used, although these might be accompanied by other information such as written comments.

Written Progress Reports   Another reporting strategy is to provide parents with a weekly, biweekly, or monthly report of the student's progress and achievement (McMillan, 2007). These written reports can include the student's performance on tests and quizzes, projects, oral reports, and so on. They also can include information about the student's motivation, cooperation, and behavior, as well as suggestions for how parents can help students improve their performance.

Parent–Teacher Conferences   Parent-teacher conferences are another way to communicate information about grades and assessment. Such conferences are both a responsibility and an opportunity (Durham, 2006). Parents have a right to know how their child is doing in school and how their child might improve. Conferences provide an opportunity for giving parents helpful information about how they can be partners with you in helping the child learn more effectively.

"How much to shred a report card?"

© Martha F. Campbell from *Phi Delta Kappan* (1996). Reprinted by permission of Martha F. Campbell.

"I don't know why you're so surprised by his poor grades. Every day you asked him what he did at school, and every day he answered, 'Nothing.'"

© Art Bouthiller. Reprinted with permission.

BEST PRACTICES
Strategies for Parent-Teacher Conferences Related to Grades and Assessment

Here are some good strategies for meeting with parents about their child's progress and grades (Payne, 1997):

1. *Be prepared.* Review the student's performance prior to the meeting with parents. Think about what you are going to say to the parents.

2. *Be positive.* Even if the student has performed poorly, try to find at least some areas to discuss in which the student has performed well. This does not mean glossing over and ignoring a student's lack of achievement; it means including positive areas in addition to the negative ones.

3. *Be objective.* Even though you want to look for positive aspects of the student's record to communicate to parents, be objective and honest. Don't give parents false hopes if the student has low ability in a particular subject area.

4. *Practice good communication skills.* Good communication means being an active listener and giving parents adequate opportunities to contribute to the conversation. Make sure that parents and students understand your grading criteria. Next, Lynn Ayres, an English teacher at

East Middle School, Ypsilanti, Michigan, provides her thoughts about this topic.

THROUGH THE EYES OF TEACHERS
Some Grading Strategies

I think it is extremely important that parents and students clearly know what is expected of students if they are to succeed in my class. I try to help students understand that they are in control of the grade they get. If students think a grading system is capricious or unknowable, it creates frustration, anxiety, and is of little use in motivating students. By getting them to see that their grades are in their own hands, I move to the position of "facilitator" in the classroom. The students see me as someone who is there to *help* them achieve rather than someone who sits in judgment of their work and gives them a grade.

---

5. *Don't talk about other students.* The focus of the parent-teacher conference should be on the parent's child. Don't compare the child with other students.

Some Issues in Grading

Should a zero be given to a missed assignment or paper? Should teachers go strictly by the numbers when assigning a grade? Should grading be abolished? Is there too much grade inflation? These are important issues that concern many educators today.

Should a Missed Assignment or Paper Receive a Zero? One grading issue is whether a student should be given a zero or at least some points for a missed assignment or paper. Including a zero with other scores badly skews the mean of the scores. Many experts on assessment recommend not using a zero in this manner because it weights the assignment or paper more than what was intended because the interval between 0 and 65 or 70 is more than the intervals between the scores for other grades (McMillan, 2007). Using a score of 60 for a missed assignment or paper is considered more reasonable.

Should Teachers Go Strictly by the Numbers in Grading? A concern in making out grades is that too many teachers engage in "mindless" number crunching, which is now more likely to occur with grading software available. No matter how objective the process is for averaging scores and grades, grading is a matter of professional judgment (Durham, 2006). Going strictly by the numbers can result in a grade that is not consistent with the actual knowledge and skill of the student, especially if pulled down by minor assignments and homework, or a later paper. In the end, it is important for teachers to be confident that the grade they give reflects what the student knows, understands, and is able to do in relation to standards of performance (McMillan, 2007).

Should Grading Be Abolished? Occasionally there are calls to abandon grades, usually based on the belief that evaluation of students is necessary but that competitive

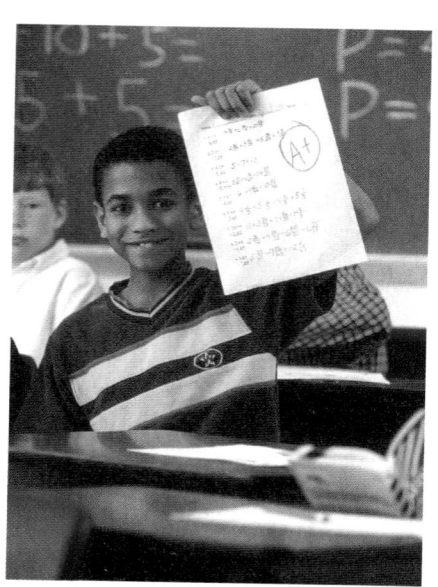

What are some issues in grading?

grading deemphasizes learning in favor of judging. Critics argue that grading discourages the vast majority of students, especially those who receive below-average grades. The critics often call for more constructive evaluation that encourages students to engage in maximum effort by underscoring their strengths, identifying concrete ways to improve, and providing positive feedback (Culbertson & Jalongo, 1999). Critics also point out that grading often motivates students to study only the material that will be on the test.

As classroom assessment expert Peter Airasian (2005) concluded, grades are powerful symbols in our society that are taken seriously by students, teachers, and the public. Regardless of whether you like the way grading is currently conducted or think it should be drastically changed, in the foreseeable future it is important for you to take grading your students seriously and do it in a way that is fair to your students. Never use grades to reward or punish students because you like them or don't like them. Always base students' grades on how well they have learned the subject matter, based on objective evidence of learning (Colby, 1999).

Is There Too Much Grade Inflation? Some teachers do not like to give low grades because they believe they diminish the student's motivation to learn. However, some critics argue that grade inflation, especially in the form of giving high grades for mediocre performance, provides students a false belief that they are learning and achieving more than they actually are. The result is that many students discover that they can perform well below their ability and still achieve high grades (Guskey, 2001). A rising tide of grade inflation has occurred (Sraiheen & Lesisko, 2006). In 2003, 42 percent of U.S. college-bound seniors had an *A* average compared to 28 percent in 1989, but the average scores of the students on college admissions tests in 2003 were lower than in 1989 (College Board, 2004).

Review, Reflect, and Practice

4 Construct a sound approach to grading.

REVIEW
- What are the purposes of grading?
- What types of judgments underlie a teacher's grading system? Comment about each type.
- What are some choices in reporting students' progress to parents?
- What are some issues in grading?

REFLECT
- What criteria would you adopt for deciding whether a teacher is doing an excellent job in grading?

PRAXIS™ PRACTICE
1. Amaal brings home her school report card. On the card are letter grades indicating that Amaal has earned an *A* in math, reading, and social studies, and a *B* in science and P.E. Her parents look over her grades, sign the card, and return it to the school. What purpose did these grades serve?
   a. administrative
   b. guidance
   c. informational
   d. motivational

continued on page 598

Review, Reflect, and Practice *continued*

2. Mr. Walker teaches algebra. On the first day of class, he tells students that of the 25 students in the class, 5 would receive *A*'s, 6 would receive *B*'s, 7 would receive *C*'s, 4 would receive *D*'s, and 3 would receive *F*'s. What type of grading system is Mr. Walker using?
   a. criterion referenced
   b. norm referenced
   c. standards based
   d. weighted

3. Isabella brings home her quarterly school report card. On the card are letter grades indicating that Isabella has earned an *A* in math, language arts, and social studies, and a *B* in science and P.E. Which of the following is a valid criticism of such a grading system?
   a. It gives parents too much information about the student's performance.
   b. It is too specific.
   c. Letter grades are unfair.
   d. It does not provide enough information to allow parents to evaluate the child's performance.

4. Ms. Gregory and Ms. Templeton are discussing grading issues. Which of the following comments made by Ms. Gregory and Ms. Templeton is the *least* likely to be supported by educational psychologists?
   a. Many students are being rewarded with high grades for mediocre performance.
   b. In the last several decades, grades have been increasing, while SAT scores have been going down.
   c. Some teachers don't like to give low grades because they believe the low grades decreased students' motivation.
   d. Grades should be abolished.

Please see the answer key at the end of the book.

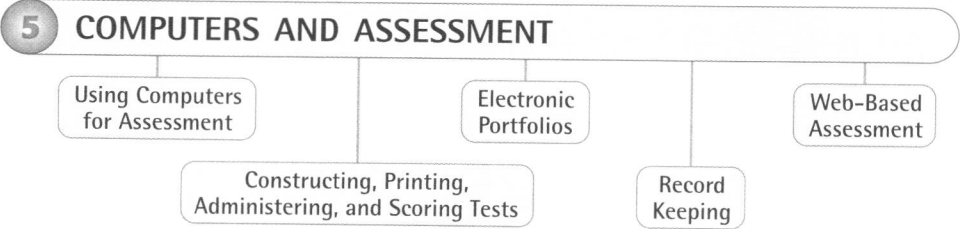

5   COMPUTERS AND ASSESSMENT

Earlier in the chapter we described the use of audiovisuals for creating realistic contexts for assessment. Here we continue our exploration of the use of computers in assessment.

Using Computers for Assessment

Computers can be used to construct, print, administer, and score tests; provide a medium for portfolios; and maintain student records (Bitter & Legacy, 2006; Britten & Cassidy, 2006; Gronlund, 2006; Newby & others, 2006). Concerns about the validity and reliability of assessment using a computer are no different than for paper-and-pencil measures. Just because validity and reliability have been established for a paper-and-pencil assessment, this does not mean that the validity and reliability will automatically hold when the student is assessed with the same measure on a computer.

Although the assessment data can be analyzed by a computer, computers are not capable of using common sense, intuition, or judgment in their analysis. Decisions based on computerized scores still rely on the teacher's interpretation and judgment, just as with paper-and-pencil measures (Fulda, 2006; Morrison & Lowther, 2005).

Constructing, Printing, Administering, and Scoring Tests

One way computers can aid test construction is through item banking. This consists of maintaining test item files that can be retrieved for preparing a test. Items typically are coded by subject area, instructional level, instructional objective measured, and item difficulty.

Computers can be used to print tests from the item bank. The coded information about each item makes it possible to create different forms of tests, such as a test arranged by instructional objective or increasing difficulty.

Computers also can be used directly in the administration of tests. The student is presented with test items on a computer screen and answers the items accordingly.

After the test is administered, the computer can be used to score the test and arrange the scores in different ways. Computer scoring especially can be helpful in relieving teachers from the time-consuming task of scoring test item responses.

Electronic Portfolios

As we saw earlier in the chapter, portfolio assessment is increasingly common. The terms *electronic portfolio, computer-based portfolio,* and *digital portfolio* are used to describe portfolio work that is saved in an electronic format (Hardy, 2001; Hartnell-Young & Morriss, 2006). The record can include text, graphics, sound, and video. Thus, students can save writing samples, math solutions, samples of artwork, depictions of science projects, and multimedia presentations in an electronic portfolio (Inkrott, 2001). A single computer with a large storage capacity can store portfolios for all the students in a class. If a number of students store multimedia material, a floppy or hard disk might not have sufficient storage. An alternative is to store students' portfolios on a "rewritable" compact disc (CD-RW, a compact disc that stores text, sound, graphics, and video). A computer-based portfolio allows for easy transfer of information from teacher to teacher or school to school.

Several electronic portfolio programs are available. The most widely used is *Aurbach's Grady Profile,* in which both teachers and students can enter work samples. The electronic portfolio programs can include writing samples, standardized test scores, oral communication skills, and math assessments. Other software programs (such as *Hyper-Studio* by Roger Wagner [1993] and *FileMaker Pro* by Claris) let teachers create their own template for portfolio assessment. Teachers can adapt these programs to the needs of their classes. For example, one high school English portfolio might consist of the outlines and drafts for each writing assignment; another might include only the finished product along with the student's reflections and self-evaluation of the product. Figure 16.12 shows a computer screen of a lab report that was included in one student's portfolio.

One school that uses electronic portfolios is East Syracuse–Minoa High School in Syracuse, New York. Its students create electronic portfolios that can be sent to colleges as part of an admissions application and to potential employers as part of their job application. The electronic portfolios are created using *HyperStudio* software. They contain information about the student (such as transcripts, letters of recommendation, and work history) and student-selected work (such as writing samples, multimedia projects, artwork, and video clips from a school play). The students are responsible for updating and selecting the work samples in their portfolios. Students begin creating these portfolios in their sophomore year and continue updating and revising them through their senior year. The portfolios can be distributed in computer disc, CD-RW, videotape, or print versions.

FIGURE 16.12 Computer Screen of One Student's Lab Report in an Electronic Portfolio

Electronic portfolios are mandated by the 1996 Jobs Through Education Act, which is intended to get public schools to focus more on preparing students for the workplace (Kabler, 1997). The vision is that student transcripts will eventually be replaced with electronic portfolios that include a full history of the student's classroom performances, work samples, and activities. To read further about electronic portfolios, see the Technology and Education box.

Record Keeping

Record keeping is a burden for many teachers, and assessment information represents a considerable chunk of this record keeping. Fortunately, the burden can be reduced by computer technology (Maddux, Johnson, & Willis, 1997). For example, electronic grade books can keep track of students' grades in a course. Excelsior's *Grade 2* program can store many types of student information, including test scores, project grades, homework assignments, semester averages, and teacher judgments. Each component of your assessment system can be weighted, and the program will compute the student's overall performance based on the formula you create. This can take less time than tediously computing grades by hand. Some electronic grade book programs have parent access options. Parents or students who have an appropriate computer and modem can connect with the school computer, enter a personal identification number, and access the student's grades and teacher's comments.

Many teachers use computers to maintain and compute grades and to keep students and parents informed of their progress. Lynn Ayres, a middle-school English teacher in Michigan, uses a computer in grading. In her words:

> I now use the computer in grading and use it to generate an individual report on each student. I print these reports every two weeks. I give a copy to each student so that he or she is clear about a particular grade and what can be done about it. I also make sure these grades get home to parents. I also print out a copy of what I call a "grade sheet" for long assignments, which indicates how I intend to grade the assignments. I give it to my students before they do the assignment and then use it to score the assignment when it is submitted.

TECHNOLOGY AND EDUCATION
The Features of an Electronic Portfolio

David Niguidula (1997) designs and customizes computer software that includes electronic portfolios. He believes it is important to integrate the following considerations into any plan for student electronic portfolios.

Vision

The main menu of an electronic portfolio should contain a set of goals that reflect the vision of what the student should know and be able to do. For example, at one high school, the domains students are expected to master include communicating, crafting, reflecting, knowing, respecting oneself, and respecting others. At others, they might include such goals as content knowledge about subject matter, ability to think critically, effective communication, and cooperative skills. As students and teachers enter work into their portfolios, they consider how the activities in the classroom correspond to the learning goals.

Assessment

Assessment involves answering such questions as "How can students demonstrate that they have reached the learning goals?" "How will the portfolio be evaluated and scored?" and "What audiences are the portfolios intended for?"

Technology

Technology involves making decisions about what hardware, software, and networking will be required. At one school "where students and teachers spend most of their day together as a team (consisting of about 80 students and 3 teachers), each team shared a set of six computers, at least one of which had multimedia input capabilities, a scanner, and a laser printer. In other schools, 5 to 15 computers were designated as digital portfolio stations" (Niguidula, 1997, p. 28). Ideally, a school will have a technical coordinator who can help teachers set up electronic portfolios. At one high school, the school's technical coordinator helps a class to become the electronic portfolio support team for the rest of the school.

Logistics

Decisions need to be made about when the information will be placed in the electronic portfolios, who will do it, who will select the work, and who will reflect on the work. Two middle school teachers at Pierre van Cortlandt Middle School in Croton-Harmon, New York, described the logistics of electronic portfolios as collecting, selecting, reflecting, and presenting. "Students need to think about what entries they will *collect*, how to *select* the ones that best convey their abilities, how to *reflect* on what their portfolio means, and how to *present* what they have learned" (Niguidula, 1997, p. 28). Teachers also need to be involved in these steps as well.

The School's Culture

The school's culture is an important aspect of whether electronic portfolios will become innovative, meaningful aspects of a student's learning or merely a technological version of a file cabinet. Several school administrators and teachers that Niguidula worked with presented their vision statement to others to get feedback, which helped them fine-tune their learning goals. When the school community encourages teachers, students, and others to reflect on their learning goals and effectively integrate technology in the classroom, electronic portfolios can become far more than file cabinets. They can represent an important, meaningful dimension of a student's learning.

Web-Based Assessment

Many school systems are turning to *Web-based assessment*—assessment available on the Internet—because of its potential for greater accuracy and cost reduction. A number of testing firms, including Educational Testing Service, are developing tests to be administered on computers in the classroom, school, or district, but those are not Web-based assessments. If an assessment is Web-based, students use a computer and the assessment takes place on the Internet.

Some of the best Web-based assessments can be easily adapted to the curriculum you use in your classroom. Some of the assessments focus on recording and evaluating student behavior, some involve academic progress, and others include all of these areas. The best Web-based assessments let teachers "develop their own tests or forms and usually include a databank of questions or other assessment tools. Most are aligned with various state and national standards," or No Child Left Behind (Doe, 2004).

The following are three examples of Web-based assessments, each of which has appropriate security included (Doe, 2004):

S–BIP Online   This Web-based student-intervention planner can be used to record many aspects of student behavior as observed by teachers and other school personnel. Various report forms can be generated, and some of these can be used to plan for special education IEPs. You can read more about this assessment at www. curricassoc.com/SBIP.

Assessa Server   This Web-based assessment provides a number of data management services to help you create your own tests, track students' progress, and create reports. You can learn more about this assessment at www.eyecues.com.

Plato EduTest Assessment   This Web-based assessment can be used to describe students' progress throughout the school year and to document students' strengths and needs. The assessment generates student reports, including progress charts, which you can use when you communicate with student's parents. You can obtain more information about the Plato assessment at www.edutest.com/.

Review, Reflect, and Practice

(5) Identify some uses of computers in assessment.

REVIEW

- In what ways is computer assessment much like paper-and-pencil assessment?
- How can computers help in constructing, printing, administering, and scoring tests?
- What can be done with electronic portfolios?
- How can computers be used for record keeping?
- What characterizes Web-based assessment?

REFLECT

- How close do you think you are right now to being able to use computers for assessment? What do you need to learn?

PRAXIS™ PRACTICE

1. Mr. Tomlinson is preparing a presentation to give at a parents' meeting about the use of computers for assessment. Which of the following statements should he not include in his presentation?
   a. Just because validity and reliability have been established for paper-and-pencil assessments doesn't mean this transfers to computer assessments.
   b. Computers can provide a medium for students' portfolios.
   c. Computers are capable of intuition in their assessment.
   d. Decisions about computerized assessment scores still rely on teachers' interpretation and judgment.
2. A new teacher, Ms. Banks, wants to use computers in her assessment of students. Which of the following would you recommend that she not do?
   a. Print items from the test bank.
   b. Use computers to administer tests.
   c. Use computers for scoring test item responses.
   d. Use the computer for drill and practice.

Please see the answer key at the end of the book.

CRACK THE CASE
The Case of the Project

Mr. Andrews generally was using traditional, multiple-choice tests in his sixth-grade class on ancient history, but the students seemed bored with studying for these tests and with his lectures. Therefore, for the unit on ancient Mesopotamia, he decided to allow the students to complete a project instead of taking a test. He gave these choices:

- Construct a test covering the chapter on Mesopotamia.
- Create a game about Mesopotamia.
- Create a diorama about Mesopotamia.
- Write a play about life in Mesopotamia.
- Create artifacts from Mesopotamia that an archaeologist might find.

Mr. Andrews' co-teacher, Ms. Benjamin, told the children that they could not use a computer to complete their projects.

Sally decided to write a test for her project. She carefully read the chapter and constructed questions as she went along. She used short-answer questions because she was worried about constructing good multiple-choice questions. It had been her experience that the distractors used in these questions were often confusing. She felt the same way about true/false questions. She wanted to make her questions as clear as possible because she didn't want her classmates mad at her when they took her test.

Sally carefully printed each question because of the ban on using a computer. She then created a key, which she intended to use to grade her classmates' tests. The final product consisted of 25 short-answer questions. She was very proud of her work the day she turned it in.

Mr. Andrews looked at her test and told her, "This isn't acceptable. Why didn't you type it?"

"Ms. Benjamin told us we couldn't use computers."

"That isn't what she meant. She meant you couldn't use the Internet," responded Mr. Andrews. "Take it home and type it. Turn it in tomorrow."

Sally left the room, very upset. She took her test home and carefully typed both the test and the key. She turned them in the next day. Three days later, Sally received these marks:

Content: **B** Did not include a question on religion (actually Sally did have a question regarding polytheism). Should have included a variety of question types, such as multiple-choice, matching, and T/F.

Mechanics: **A** Nicely typed. Correct spelling used.

Accuracy: **B**

Effort: **C**

Overall Grade C

Sally was upset with her grade. "A *C* for effort?! I worked really hard on this! I even had to do it twice, 'cause of stupid Ms. Benjamin!" She took her grade sheet and test home and showed it to her mother. Sally's mother was equally upset, particularly about the low grade for effort. She called Mr. Andrews, asking to see the guidelines for the project and the grading rubric. Mr. Andrews was unable to provide either. She asked him the difference between content and accuracy. He could not tell her. She also asked him how he had measured effort, to which he responded, "I consider what I expect from students and then what they give me."

"So you're telling me that you graded content three times. Once you gave her a *B*, once a *B*, and once a *C*, right?"

Mr. Andrews did not know how to respond to her question.

1. What are the issues involved in this situation?
2. What did Mr. Andrews do wrong?
3. How should he have gone about developing his alternative assessments?
4. How should he have developed his grading guide?
5. What do you think of the practice of including an effort grade on students' projects? Why?

Reach Your Learning Goals
Classroom Assessments

① THE CLASSROOM AS AN ASSESSMENT CONTEXT: Discuss the classroom as an assessment context.

Assessment as an Integral Part of Teaching

Preinstruction assessment, assessment during instruction, and postinstruction assessment should be integral to teaching. Much of preinstruction assessment involves informal observations, which require interpretation. In informal observations, watch for nonverbal cues that give insights about the student. Structured exercises also can be used in preinstruction assessment. Guard against expectations that will distort your perception of a student. Treat your initial perceptions as hypotheses to be confirmed or modified by subsequent observation and information. Some teachers also administer pretests in subject areas. An increasing trend is to examine students' learning portfolios from previous grades. Formative assessment is the fast-paced observation and monitoring that go on during instruction. Summative assessment, or formal assessment, is assessment after instruction is finished. This usually involves more formal types of assessment, such as tests.

Making Assessment Compatible with Contemporary Views of Learning and Motivation

To bring assessment into line with contemporary views of motivation and learning, it is important to focus on the following: active learning and constructing meaning; the use of planning and goal setting; reflective, critical, and creative thinking; positive student expectations for learning and confidence in skills; degree of motivation; the ability to apply what is learned to real-world situations; and effective communication. Consider the role that assessment (especially alternative assessment) plays in effort, engagement, and performance.

Creating Clear, Appropriate Learning Targets

A learning target, much like an instructional objective, consists of what students should know and be able to do. Learning targets might focus on knowledge, reasoning/thinking, products, or affect.

Establishing High-Quality Assessments

High-quality assessments are valid, reliable, and fair. Validity is the extent to which an assessment measures what it is intended to measure, as well as how accurate and useful a teacher's inferences are. Reliability is the extent to which assessments produce consistent, reproducible scores. Assessment is fair when all students have an equal opportunity to learn and demonstrate their knowledge and skills. A pluralistic assessment philosophy also contributes to fairness.

Current Trends

Current trends in assessment include using at least some performance-based assessments, examining higher-level skills, using multiple assessment methods, having high performance standards, and using computers as a part of assessment. Other trends focus on assessing an integration of skills, giving students considerable feedback, and making standards and criteria public.

② TRADITIONAL TESTS: Provide some guidelines for constructing traditional tests.

Selected-Response Items

True/false items can seem easy to construct but can encourage mere memorization. A multiple-choice item has two parts: a stem and a number of options or alternatives. Incorrect alternatives are called distractors. Matching items often are used with younger students. Two tools for computing the quality of test items are the item difficulty index, which describes the percentage of students who obtain the correct answer, and the item discrimination index, which reflects the item's ability to discriminate between students who scored high or low on the entire test.

| Constructed-Response Items |

Constructed-response items require students to write out information rather than select it from a menu. Short-answer and essay items are the most commonly used constructed-response items. Short-answer items require students to write a word, a short phrase, or several sentences in response to a task and often encourage rote memorization. Essay questions allow students more freedom of response than the other item formats. Essay questions are especially good for assessing students' understanding, higher-level thinking skills, organizational skills, and writing skills.

(3) ALTERNATIVE ASSESSMENTS: Describe some types of alternative assessments.

| Trends in Alternative Assessment |

Authentic assessment is evaluating a student's knowledge or skill in a context that approximates the real world or real life as closely as possible. Critics argue that authentic assessments are not necessarily better than more conventional assessments, that there are few data to support their validity, and that they don't adequately examine knowledge and basic skills.

| Performance Assessment |

Performance assessments of higher-level thinking often emphasize "doing," open-ended activities for which there is no one correct answer. The tasks are sometimes realistic, and many, but not all, performance assessments are authentic. Evaluating performance often includes direct methods of evaluation, self-assessment, assessment of group performance as well as individual performance, and an extended period of time. There are four main guidelines in using performance assessments: (1) establishing a clear purpose, (2) identifying observable criteria, (3) providing an appropriate setting, and (4) judging or scoring the performance.

| Portfolio Assessment |

A portfolio is a systematic and organized collection of a student's work to demonstrate skills and accomplishments. Four classes of evidence can be included: artifacts, reproductions, attestations, and productions. Using portfolios requires (1) establishing the portfolio's purpose, (2) involving students in decisions about it, (3) reviewing the portfolio with students, (4) setting criteria for evaluation, and (5) scoring and judging the portfolio. Two broad types of purposes of portfolios are to document growth through a growth portfolio and to showcase the student's most outstanding work through a best-work portfolio. Learning portfolios have strengths—such as capturing the complexity and completeness of the student's work and accomplishments, as well as encouraging student decision making and self-reflection—and weaknesses—such as the time required to coordinate and evaluate them and the difficulty in evaluating them.

(4) GRADING AND REPORTING PERFORMANCE: Construct a sound approach to grading.

| The Purposes of Grading |

Grading purposes include administrative (help determine students' class rank, credits), informational (communicate with parents, teachers, students), motivational (students' desire for higher grades), and guidance (select appropriate courses and levels for students).

| The Components of a Grading System |

Three main types of teacher judgments underlie a grading system: (1) standard of comparison to use for grading (norm-referenced or criterion-referenced); (2) aspects of performance (a good strategy is to base an overall grade on a series of assessments, including tests and other assessments); and (3) weighting of different kinds of evidence (judgment is involved in how teachers synthesize information to arrive at a student's grade).

| Reporting Students' Progress and Grades to Parents |

Report cards are the standard method of reporting. Checklists of skills and objectives are sometimes used in kindergarten and elementary school. Letter grades are standard in the higher elementary grades and secondary schools. Reporting also includes written progress reports and parent-teacher conferences.

continued

| Some Issues in Grading | Issues in grading include (1) whether teachers should assign a zero for a missed assignment or paper, (2) whether teachers should go strictly by the numbers in grading, (3) whether grading should be abolished (although the form of grading might change in the future, judgments about students' performance will still be made and communicated to students, parents, and others), and (4) whether grade inflation is a problem. |

⑤ COMPUTERS AND ASSESMENT: Identify some uses of computers in assessment.

| Using Computers for Assessment | The same concerns arise about validity and reliability for electronic assessment as for paper-and-pencil assessment. |

| Constructing, Printing, Administering, and Scoring Tests | Computers can be used for test constructing through item banking, printing tests from the item bank, administering through presenting items on a computer screen, and scoring test item responses. |

| Electronic Portfolios | The terms *electronic portfolio* and *computer-based portfolio* describe portfolios that are saved in an electronic format. Several electronic portfolio programs are available. Electronic portfolios can be sent to admissions departments at colleges and to potential employers. |

| Record Keeping | Computer technology can help to reduce the burden of record keeping for teachers. For example, electronic grade books can keep track of a student's grades in a course and allow parents or students to access grades and teacher comments. |

| Web-Based Assessment | Web-based assessment, which means that assessment takes place on the Internet, is increasingly being used to record and evaluate student behavior and/or chart academic progress. |

 KEY TERMS

formative assessment 568
summative assessment 569
instructional validity 571
objective tests 573
performance assessment 574
selected-response items 576

multiple-choice item 576
problem sets 580
item difficulty index 580
item discrimination index 580
constructed-response
  items 581

short-answer item 581
essay items 581
performance criteria 586
portfolio 588
growth portfolio 590
best-work portfolio 590

grading 593
norm-referenced
  grading 593
criterion-referenced
  grading 593

 PORTFOLIO ACTIVITIES

Now that you have a good understanding of this chapter, complete these exercises to expand your thinking.

Independent Reflection

State Your Views on Assessment. Think about the following statements and decide whether you agree or disagree with each. (1) Multiple-choice tests should not be used to assess students' learning. (2) A teacher should never use a single measure to assess learning. (3) Performance-based assessment is too subjective. (INTASC: Principle 8). Explain your position.

Collaborative Work

Develop an Assessment Plan. Get together with a classmate who plans to teach the same subject(s) and grade level. Select a subject and construct a plan for assessment throughout the course. (INTASC: Principles *1, 8*)

Research/Field Experience

Balancing Traditional and Alternative Assessments. Consider a course you took in grade school or high school in which your performance was assessed using traditional methods. In a brief position statement, explain how students could have been evaluated using alternative assessments or some combination of traditional and alternative assessments. What would have been gained (or lost) by using alternative assessments? (INTASC: Principle *8*)

Go to the Online Learning Center for downloadable portfolio templates.

TAKING IT TO THE NET

- The Coalition of Essential Schools (CES) is a national network of schools that uses alternative assessments and culminating exhibitions to evaluate their students. Read one or more CES articles. What is your analysis? Discuss the effectiveness of CES assessment strategies. To what degree do you believe the CES approach is replicable across schools? www.essentialschools.org/cs/resources/view/ces_res/223

- Your fifth-grade science students are engaged in a one-week collaborative project. They are constructing models of world habitats and will conduct oral presentations of their finished projects. Design a scoring rubric and outline the criteria you will use to measure student performance. Will students be graded as a group, independently, or both? Will they conduct self- or peer-assessments? //school.discovery.com/schrockguide/assess.html

- Browse the Web to locate examples of K–12 electronic student portfolios. What are typically the main components of a digital portfolio? Discuss the benefits of using electronic portfolios to showcase and archive student work. Include benefits to students, families, teachers, and schools in your response. www.education-world.com/a_tech/tech111.shtml

Connect to the Online Learning Center to explore possible answers.

 ## STUDY, PRACTICE, AND SUCCEED

Visit www.mhhe.com/santedu3e to review the chapter with self-grading quizzes and self-assessments, to apply the chapter material to two more Crack the Case studies, and for suggested activities to develop your teaching portfolio.

PRAXIS™ Answer Key

CHAPTER 1

Historical Background
1. b
2. c

Effective Teaching
1. d
2. b

Research in Educational Psychology
1. a
2. d
3. c

CHAPTER 2

An Overview of Child Development
1. d   3. a
2. c   4. d

Cognitive Development
1. b
2. d
3. c

Language Development
1. a
2. b
3. b

CHAPTER 3

Contemporary Theories
1. b
2. c

Social Contexts of Development
1. b
2. d
3. a

Socioemotional Development
1. c
2. b

CHAPTER 4

Intelligence
1. d   3. d
2. b   4. b

Learning and Thinking Styles
1. a
2. d

Personality and Temperament
1. b
2. b

CHAPTER 5

Culture and Ethnicity
1. c   3. a
2. c   4. c

Multicultural Education
1. d   3. a
2. d   4. b

Gender
1. c   4. a
2. c   5. a
3. b

CHAPTER 6

Who Are Children with Disabilities?
1. c   4. b   7. b
2. b   5. c   8. d
3. a   6. b

Educational Issues Involving Children with Disabilities
1. b
2. c
3. c

Children Who Are Gifted
1. a
2. a
3. b

CHAPTER 7

What Is Learning?
1. b
2. b

Behavioral Approaches to Learning
1. d
2. b

Applied Behavior Analysis in Education
1. a   3. d
2. a   4. d

Social Cognitive Approaches to Learning
1. b   3. a
2. a   4. d

CHAPTER 8

The Nature of the Information-Processing Approach
1. b
2. a
3. a

Attention
1. a
2. a

Memory
1. a   3. a
2. b   4. d

Expertise
1. b
2. a
3. b

Metacognition
1. d
2. c
3. a

CHAPTER 9

Conceptual Understanding
1. b
2. c

Thinking
1. d   3. a
2. c   4. a

Problem Solving
1. b   3. b
2. a   4. a

Transfer
1. b
2. c

CHAPTER 10

Social Constructivist Approaches to Teaching
1. a
2. b

Teachers and Peers as Joint Contributors to Students' Learning
1. b   3. a
2. b   4. a

Structuring Small-Group Work
1. b
2. d
3. d

Social Constructivist Programs
1. b
2. a
3. a

CHAPTER 11

Expert Knowledge and Pedagogical Content Knowledge
1. b

Reading
1. c   4. c
2. c   5. b
3. b

Writing
1. c
2. b
3. b

Mathematics
1. a   4. b
2. b   5. d
3. c

Science
1. d
2. c

Social Studies
1. a
2. d

CHAPTER 12

Planning
1. b
2. d

Teacher-Centered Lesson Planning and Instruction
1. a   3. a
2. c   4. c

Learner-Centered Lesson Planning and Instruction
1. d
2. c
3. b

Technology and Education
1. b   4. d
2. d   5. a
3. c

CHAPTER 13

Exploring Motivation
1. b
2. b

Achievement Processes
1. b   4. b
2. d   5. d
3. a   6. b

Motivation, Relationships, and Sociocultural Contexts
1. c
2. c
3. d

Students with Achievement Problems
1. a   4. a
2. b   5. a
3. a   6. b

CHAPTER 14

Why Classrooms Need to Be Managed Effectively
1. b
2. d
3. a

Designing the Physical Environment of the Classroom
1. b
2. d

Creating a Positive Environment for Learning
1. b
2. b
3. c

Being a Good Communicator
1. d
2. d
3. d

Dealing with Problem Behaviors
1. c
2. d
3. d

CHAPTER 15

The Nature of Standardized Tests
1. b
2. b

Aptitude and Achievement Tests
1. a   4. a
2. d   5. b
3. b

The Teacher's Roles
1. d   3. a
2. a   4. c

Issues in Standardized Tests
1. a
2. b

CHAPTER 16

The Classroom as an Assessment Context
1. b   4. c
2. a   5. c
3. d

Traditional Tests
1. c
2. c

Alternative Assessments
1. d
2. b

Grading and Reporting Performance
1. c   3. d
2. b   4. d

Computers and Assessment
1. c
2. d

Glossary

A

accommodation Piagetian concept of adjusting schemes to fit new information and experiences. 37

achievement test A test that measures what the student has learned or what skills the student has mastered. 537

action research Research used to solve a specific classroom or school problem, improve teaching and other educational strategies, or make a decision at a specific level. 20

active listening A listening style that gives full attention to the speaker and notes both the intellectual and emotional content of the message. 511

advance organizers Teaching activities and techniques that establish a framework and orient students to material before it is presented. 416

aggressive style A way of dealing with conflict in which people run roughshod over others in demanding, abrasive, and hostile ways. 508

algorithms Strategies that guarantee a solution to a problem. 320

alternate-forms reliability Reliability judged by giving different forms of the same test on two different occasions to the same group of students to determine how consistent their scores are. 535

analogy A correspondence in some respects between otherwise dissimilar things. 307

androgyny The presence of desirable masculine and feminine characteristics in the same individual. 171

applied behavior analysis Application of the principles of operant conditioning to change human behavior. 235

aptitude test A type of test that is used to predict a student's ability to learn a skill or accomplish something with further education and training. 537

articulation disorders Problems in pronouncing sounds correctly. 197

Asperger syndrome A relatively mild autism spectrum disorder in which the child has relatively good language, milder nonverbal language problems, a restricted range of interests and relationships, and often engages in repetitive routines. 199

assertive style A way of dealing with conflict in which people express their feelings, ask for what they want, say "no" to things they don't want, and act in their own best interests. 508

assimilation Piagetian concept of the incorporation of new information into existing knowledge (schemas). 37

associative learning Learning that two events are connected (associated). 227

Atkinson-Shiffrin model A model of memory that involves a sequence of three stages: sensory memory, short-term memory, and long-term memory. 275

attention Concentrating and focusing mental resources. 267

attention deficit hyperactivity disorder (ADHD) A disability in which children consistently show one or more of the following characteristics over a period of time: (1) inattention, (2) hyperactivity, and (3) impulsivity. 188

attribution theory The theory that in their effort to make sense of their own behavior or performance, individuals are motivated to discover its underlying causes. 459

auditorium style A classroom arrangement style in which all students sit facing the teacher. 498

authoritarian classroom management style A management style that is restrictive and punitive, with the focus mainly on keeping order in the classroom rather than instruction or learning. 500

authoritarian parenting A restrictive and punitive parenting style in which there is little verbal exchange between parents and children; associated with children's social incompetence. 76

authoritative classroom management style A management style that encourages students to be independent thinkers and doers but still provides effective monitoring. Authoritative teachers engage students in considerable verbal give-and-take and show a caring attitude toward them. However, they still set limits when necessary. 500

authoritative parenting A positive parenting style that encourages children to be independent but still places limits and controls on their actions; extensive verbal give-and-take is allowed; associated with children's social competence. 76

autism spectrum disorders (ASD) Also called pervasive developmental disorders, they range from the severe disorder labeled autistic disorder to the milder disorder called Asperger syndrome. Children with these disorders are characterized by problems in social interaction, verbal and nonverbal communication, and repetitive behaviors. 199

autistic disorder A severe developmental autism spectrum disorder that has its onset in the first 3 years of life and includes deficiencies in social relationships, abnormalities in communication, and restricted, repetitive, and stereotyped patterns of behavior. 199

automaticity The ability to process information with little or no effort. 265

autonomous morality In Piaget's theory, the second stage of moral development (entered at about 10 years of age), in which children become aware that rules and laws are created by people and that in judging action, the actor's intentions as well as consequences need to be considered. 102

availability heuristic A prediction about the probability of an event based on the frequency of the event's past occurrences. 313

B

backward-reaching transfer The transfer of learning that involves looking back to a previous ("old") situation for information that might help solve a problem in a new context. 328

behavioral objectives Statements that communicate proposed changes in students' behavior to reach desired levels of performance. 410

behaviorism The view that behavior should be explained by observable experiences. 227

belief perseverance The tendency to hold on to a belief in the face of contradictory evidence. 312

best-work portfolio A portfolio that showcases the student's most outstanding work. 590

between-class ability grouping (tracking) Grouping students based on their ability or achievement. 129

"big five" factors of personality Emotional stability, extraversion, openness to experience, agreeableness, and conscientiousness. 135

bilingual education Teaching academic subjects to immigrant children in their native language while slowly teaching English 153

Bloom's taxonomy Developed by Benjamin Bloom and colleagues; consists of educational objectives in three domains—cognitive, affective, and psychomotor. 411

book clubs Student-led groups for the discussion of literature. Book clubs are a form of peer learning. 373

C

care perspective A moral perspective that focuses on connectedness and relationships among people; Gilligan's approach reflects a care perspective. 104

case study An in-depth look at an individual. 17

central tendency A statistic that provides information about the average, or typical, score in a set of data. 550

centration Focusing, or centering, attention on one characteristic to the exclusion of all others; characteristic of preoperational thinking. 41

cerebral palsy A disorder that involves a lack of muscle coordination, shaking, or unclear speech. 195

character education A direct approach to moral education that involves teaching students basic moral literacy to prevent them from engaging in immoral behavior and doing harm to themselves or others. 105

children who are gifted Children with above-average intelligence (usually defined as an IQ of 130 or higher) and/or superior talent in some domain such as art, music, or mathematics. 215

chunking Grouping, or "packing," information into "higher-order" units that can be remembered as single units. 273

classical conditioning A form of associative learning in which a neutral stimulus becomes associated with a meaningful stimulus and acquires the capacity to elicit a similar response. 229

cluster style A classroom arrangement style in which small numbers of students (usually four to eight) work in small, closely bunched groups. 498

cognitive apprenticeship A relationship in which an expert stretches and supports a novice's understanding and use of a culture's skills. 340

cognitive behavior approaches Changing behavior by getting individuals to monitor, manage, and regulate their own behavior rather than letting it be controlled by external factors. 249

cognitive moral education An approach to moral education based on the belief that students should value things such as democracy and justice as their moral reasoning develops; Kohlberg's theory has served as the foundation for many cognitive moral education efforts. 106

collectivism A set of values that support the group. 145

comparative advance organizers Connections with prior knowledge that help to introduce new material. 416

competence motivation The idea that people are motivated to deal effectively with their environment, to master their world, and to process information efficiently. 453

concept map A visual presentation of a concept's connections and hierarchical organization. 304

concepts Categories used to group objects, events, and characteristics on the basis of common properties. 302

concrete operational stage Piaget's third cognitive developmental stage, occurring between about 7 to 11 years of age. At this stage, the child thinks operationally and logical reasoning replaces intuitive thought but only in concrete situations; classification skills are present but abstract problems present difficulties. 42

concurrent validity The relation between a test's scores and other criteria that are currently (concurrently) available. 534

confirmation bias The tendency to search for and use information that supports our ideas rather than refutes them. 312

conservation The idea that some characteristic of an object stays the same even though the object might change in appearance; a cognitive ability that develops in the concrete operational stage, according to Piaget. 41

construct validity The extent to which there is evidence that a test measures a particular construct. A construct is an unobservable trait or characteristic of a person, such as intelligence, learning style, personality, or anxiety. 534

constructed-response items Items that require students to write out information rather than select a response from a menu. 581

constructivist approach A learner-centered approach to learning that emphasizes the importance of individuals actively constructing knowledge and understanding with guidance from the teacher. 6

content validity A test's ability to sample the content that is to be measured. 534

continuity-discontinuity issue The issue regarding whether development involves gradual, cumulative change (continuity) or distinct stages (discontinuity). 30

contracting Putting reinforcement contingencies into writing. 237

control group In an experiment, a group whose experience is treated in every way like the experimental group except for the manipulated factor. 19

conventional reasoning In Kohlberg's theory, the middle level of moral development; at this level, internalization is intermediate in the sense that individuals abide by certain standards (internal) but these essentially are the standards of others (external). 103

convergent thinking Thinking with the aim of producing one correct answer. This is usually the type of thinking required on conventional intelligence tests. 315

cooperative learning Learning that occurs when students work in small groups to help each other learn. 345

correlational research Research that describes the strength of the relation between two or more events or characteristics. 18

creativity The ability to think about something in novel and unusual ways and come up with unique solutions to problems. 315

criterion validity A test's ability to predict a student's performance as measured by other assessments or criteria. 534

criterion-referenced grading A grading system based on comparison with predetermined standards. 593

critical thinking Thinking reflectively and productively and evaluating the evidence. 308

cross-cultural studies Studies that compare what happens in one culture with what happens in one or more other cultures; they provide information about the degree to which people are similar and to what degree behaviors are specific to certain cultures. 145

cue-dependent forgetting Retrieval failure caused by a lack of effective retrieval cues. 279

culture The behavior patterns, beliefs, and all other products of a particular group of people that are passed on from generation to generation. 145

culture-fair tests Tests of intelligence that are intended to be free of cultural bias. 128

D

decay theory The theory that new learning involves the creation of a neurochemical "memory trace," which will eventually disintegrate. Thus, decay theory suggests that the passage of time is responsible for forgetting. 279

decision making Evaluating alternatives and making choices among them. 309

declarative memory The conscious recollection of information, such as specific facts or events that can be verbally communicated. 276

deductive reasoning Reasoning from the general to the specific. 308

deep/surface styles Involve the extent to which students approach learning materials in a way that helps them understand the meaning of the materials (deep style) or as simply what needs to be learned (surface style). 133

dependent variable The factor that is measured in an experiment. 19

descriptive statistics Mathematical procedures that are used to describe and summarize data (information) in a meaningful way. 549

development The pattern of biological, cognitive, and socioemotional processes that begins at conception and continues through the life span. Most development involves growth, although it also eventually involves decay (dying). 28

developmentally appropriate education Education based on knowledge of the typical development of children within an age span (age appropriateness) as well as the uniqueness of the child (individual appropriateness). 88

differentiated instruction Involves recognizing individual variations in students' knowledge, readiness, interests, and other characteristics, and taking these differences into account when planning curriculum and engaging in instruction. 8

difficult child A temperament style in which the child tends to react negatively, has aggressive tendencies, lacks self-control, and is slow to accept new experiences. 136

direct instruction approach A structured, teacher-centered approach characterized by teacher direction and control, high teacher expectations for students' progress, maximum time spent by students on academic tasks, and efforts by the teacher to keep negative affect to a minimum. 6, 414

disability A personal limitation that restricts an individual's functioning. 185

discovery learning Learning in which students construct an understanding on their own. 429

divergent thinking Thinking with the aim of producing many answers to the same question. This is characteristic of creativity. 315

divided attention Concentrating on more than one activity at a time. 267

Down syndrome A genetically transmitted form of mental retardation due to an extra (47th) chromosome. 193

dyscalculia Also known as developmental arithmetic disorder, this learning disability involves difficulty in math computation. 187

dysgraphia A learning disability that involves difficulty in expressing thoughts in writing composition. In general, the term dysgraphia is used to describe extremely poor handwriting. 187

dyslexia A severe impairment in the ability to read and spell. 187

E

early-later experience issue The issue of the degree to which early experiences (especially infancy) or later experiences are the key determinants of the child's development. 31

easy child A temperament style in which the child is generally in a positive mood, quickly establishes regular routines, and easily adapts to new experiences. 136

ecological theory Bronfenbrenner's theory that consists of five environmental systems: microsystem, mesosystem, exosystem, macrosystem, and chronosystem. 71

educational psychology The branch of psychology that specializes in understanding teaching and learning in educational settings. 2

elaboration The extensiveness of information processing involved in encoding. 271

emotional and behavioral disorders Serious, persistent problems that involve relationships, aggression, depression, fears associated with personal or school matters, and other inappropriate socioemotional characteristics. 200

emotional intelligence The ability to monitor one's own and others' emotions and feelings, to discriminate among them, and to use this information to guide one's thinking and action. 121

empowerment Providing people with intellectual and coping skills to succeed and make this a more just world. 157

encoding The mechanism by which information gets into memory. 265

encoding specificity principle The principle that associations formed at the time of encoding or learning tend to be effective retrieval cues. 279

epilepsy A neurological disorder characterized by recurring sensorimotor attacks or movement convulsions. 195

episodic memory The retention of information about the where and when of life's happenings. 277

equilibration A mechanism that Piaget proposed to explain how children shift from one stage of thought to the next. The shift occurs as children experience cognitive conflict or disequilibrium in trying to understand the world. Eventually, they resolve the conflict and reach a balance or equilibrium of thought. 38

essay items Items that require a lengthy written answer; they allow more freedom of response to questions but require more writing than other formats. 581

essential questions Questions that reflect the heart of the curriculum, the most important things that students should explore and learn. 428

ethnicity A shared pattern of characteristics such as cultural heritage, nationality, race, religion, and language. 150

ethnographic study In-depth description and interpretation of behavior in an ethnic or a cultural group that includes direct involvement with the participants. 18

experimental group The group whose experience is manipulated in an experiment. 19

experimental research Research that allows the determination of the causes of behavior; involves conducting an experiment, which is a carefully regulated procedure in which one or more of the factors believed to influence the behavior being studied is manipulated and all others are held constant. 18

expert knowledge Also called *subject matter knowledge;* means excellent knowledge about the content of a particular discipline. 365

expository advance organizers Organizers that provide students with new knowledge that will orient them to the upcoming lesson. 416

expressive language The ability to use language to express one's thoughts and communicate with others. 198

extrinsic motivation The external motivation to do something to obtain something else (a means to an end). 454

F

face-to-face style A classroom arrangement style in which students sit facing each other. 498

failure syndrome Having low expectations for success and giving up at the first sign of difficulty. 475

far transfer The transfer of learning to a situation that is very different from the one in which the initial learning took place. 327

fetal alcohol syndrome (FAS) A cluster of abnormalities, including mental retardation and facial abnormalities, that appear in the offspring of mothers who drink alcohol heavily during pregnancy. 194

fixation Using a prior strategy and thereby failing to examine a problem from a fresh, new perspective. 321

fluency disorders Disorders that often involve what is commonly referred to as "stuttering." 198

formal operational stage Piaget's fourth cognitive developmental stage, which emerges between about 11 and 15 years of age; thought is more abstract, idealistic, and logical in this stage. 44

formative assessment Assessment during the course of instruction rather than after it is completed. 568

forward-reaching transfer The transfer of learning that involves thinking about how to apply what has been learned to new situations in the future. 328

Fostering a Community of Learners (FCL) A social constructivist program that focuses on literacy development and biology. FCL encourages reflection and discussion through the use of adults as role models, children teaching children, and online computer consultation. 354

fragile X syndrome A genetically transmitted form of mental retardation due to an abnormality on the X chromosome. 194

frequency distribution A listing of scores, usually from highest to lowest, along with the number of times each score appears. 549

fuzzy trace theory States that memory is best understood by considering two types of memory representations: (1) verbatim memory trace and (2) gist. In this theory, older children's better memory is attributed to the fuzzy traces created by extracting the gist of information. 278

G

gender The sociocultural and psychological dimensions of gender. 165

gender roles The social expectations that prescribe how males and females should think, act, and feel. 165

gender schema theory States that gender typing emerges as children gradually develop gender schemas of what is gender-appropriate and gender-inappropriate in their culture. 166

gender stereotypes Broad categories that reflect impressions and beliefs about what behavior is appropriate for females and males. 167

gender-role transcendence View that people's competence should be conceptualized in terms of them as persons rather than in terms of whether they are masculine, feminine, or androgynous. 173

grade-equivalent score A score that indicates students' performance in relation to grade level and months of the school year, assuming a 10-month school year. 553

grading Translating descriptive assessment information into letters, numbers, or other marks that indicate the quality of a student's learning or performance. 593

growth portfolio A portfolio of work over an extended time frame (throughout the school year or longer) to reveal the student's progress in meeting learning targets. 590

guided discovery learning Learning in which students are encouraged to construct their understanding with the assistance of teacher-guided questions and directions. 429

H

handicap A condition imposed on a person who has a disability. 185

helpless orientation A personal stance that focuses on personal inadequacies, attribution of difficulty to a lack of ability, and negative affect. 461

heteronomous morality In Piaget's theory, the first stage of moral development (about 4 to 7 years of age), in which justice and rules are conceived of as unchangeable properties of the world, beyond the control of people. 102

heuristic A strategy or rule of thumb that can suggest a solution to a problem but doesn't ensure it will work. 313

hidden curriculum Dewey's concept that every school has a pervasive moral atmosphere even if it does not have a program of moral education. 105

hierarchy of needs Maslow's concept that individual needs must be satisfied in this

sequence: physiological, safety, love and belongingness, esteem, and self-actualization. 452

high-road transfer The transfer of learning from one situation to another that is conscious and effortful. 327

high-stakes testing Using tests in a way that will have important consequences for the student, affecting such decisions as whether the student will be promoted or be allowed to graduate. 533

hindsight bias The tendency to falsely report, after the fact, that we accurately predicted an event. 313

histogram A frequency distribution in the form of a graph. 549

hostile environment sexual harassment Subjection of students to unwelcome sexual conduct that is so severe, persistent, or pervasive that it limits the students' ability to benefit from their education. 175

Human Biology Middle Grades Curriculum (HumBio) Developed by Stanford University scientists in collaboration with middle school teachers, this curriculum integrates ecology, evolution, genetics, physiology, human development, culture, health, and safety. 391

humanistic perspective A view that stresses students' capacity for personal growth, freedom to choose their destiny, and positive qualities. 452

hypothetical-deductive reasoning Piaget's formal operational concept that adolescents can develop hypotheses to solve problems and systematically reach (deduce) a conclusion. 44

I

"I" messages Desirable messages that reflect the speaker's true feelings better than judgmental "you" messages. 508

identity achievement The identity status in which individuals have explored meaningful alternatives and made a commitment. 100

identity diffusion The identity status in which individuals have neither explored meaningful alternatives nor made a commitment. 99

identity foreclosure The identity status in which individuals have made a commitment but have not explored meaningful alternatives. 99

identity moratorium The identity status in which individuals are in the midst of exploring alternatives but have not yet made a commitment. 99

impulsive/reflective styles Also referred to as conceptual tempo, they involve a student's tendency either to act quickly and impulsively or to take more time to respond and reflect on the accuracy of the answer. 133

incentives Positive or negative stimuli or events that can motivate a student's behavior. 451

inclusion Educating children with special education needs full-time in the regular classroom. 206

independent variable The manipulated, influential, experimental factor in an experiment. 19

individualism A set of values that give priority to personal rather than to group goals. 145

individualized education plan (IEP) A written statement that spells out a program specifically tailored for the student with a disability. 205

Individuals with Disabilities Education Act (IDEA) This act spells out broad mandates for services to all children with disabilities, including evaluation and determination of eligibility, appropriate education and an individualized education plan (IEP), and education in the least restrictive environment (LRE). 205

inductive reasoning Reasoning from the specific to the general. 307

indulgent parenting A parenting style of involvement but few limits or restrictions on children's behavior; linked with children's social incompetence. 77

information-processing approach A cognitive approach in which children manipulate information, monitor it, and strategize about it. Central to this approach are the cognitive processes of memory and thinking. 264

instructional planning A systematic, organized strategy for planning lessons. 406

instructional validity The extent to which the assessment is a reasonable sample of what went on in the classroom. 571

intelligence Problem-solving skills and the ability to adapt to and learn from life's everyday experiences. 115

intelligence quotient (IQ) A person's mental age (MA) divided by chronological age (CA), multiplied by 100. 115

interactive demonstration strategy A strategy to help students overcome misconceptions in science in which the teacher introduces the demonstration, asks students to discuss the demonstration with their neighbors and predict its outcome, and then performs the demonstration. 389

interference theory The theory that we forget not because we actually lose memories from storage but because other information gets in the way of what we are trying to remember. 279

Internet The core of computer-mediated communication; a system of computer networks that operates worldwide. 433

intrinsic motivation The internal motivation to do something for its own sake (an end in itself). 454

intuitive thought substage The second substage of preoperational thought, lasting from about 4 to 7 years of age. Children begin to use primitive reasoning and want to know the answer to all sorts of questions. They seem so sure about their knowledge in this substage but are unaware of how they know what they know. 40

item difficulty index The percentage of students who obtain the correct answer on an item. 580

item discrimination index An index that reflects the item's ability to discriminate between individuals who scored high and those who scored low on the entire test. 580

J

jigsaw classroom A classroom in which students from different cultural backgrounds cooperate by doing different parts of a project to reach a common goal. 159

Joplin plan A standard nongraded program for instruction in reading. 130

justice perspective A moral perspective that focuses on the rights of the individual; Kohlberg's theory is a justice perspective. 104

L

laboratory A controlled setting from which many of the complex factors of the real world have been removed. 16

language A form of communication, whether spoken, written, or signed, that is based on a system of symbols. 54

language disorders Significant impairments in a child's receptive or expressive language. 198

lateralization The specialization of functions in each hemisphere of the brain. 36

law of effect The principle that behaviors followed by positive outcomes are strengthened and that behaviors followed by negative outcomes are weakened. 232

learning A relatively permanent influence on behavior, knowledge, and thinking skills, which comes about through experience. 227

learning and thinking styles Individuals' preferences in how they use their abilities. 132

learning disability A disability in which children (1) have an IQ above the retarded

range; (2) have significant difficulty in an academic area; and (3) have no other diagnosed problem or disorder, such as sensory disabilities or severe emotional disorders causing the difficulty. 185

least restrictive environment (LRE) A setting that is as similar as possible to the one in which children who do not have a disability are educated. 206

levels of processing theory The theory that processing of memory occurs on a continuum from shallow to deep, with deeper processing producing better memory. 271

long-term memory A type of memory that holds enormous amounts of information for a long period of time in a relatively permanent fashion. 275

low-road transfer The automatic, often unconscious, transfer of learning to another situation. 327

M

manipulative style A way of dealing with conflict in which people try to get what they want by making others feel guilty or sorry for them. 508

mastery learning Learning one concept or topic thoroughly before moving on to a more difficult one. 417

mastery orientation A personal stance that involves mastery of the task, positive affect, and solution-oriented strategies. 461

mean The numerical average of a group of scores. 550

means-end analysis A heuristic in which one identifies the goal (end) of a problem, assesses the current situation, and evaluates what needs to be done (means) to decrease the difference between the two conditions. 320

measures of variability Measures that tell how much scores vary from one another. 550

median The score that falls exactly in the middle of a distribution of scores after they have been arranged (or ranked) from highest to lowest. 550

memory The retention of information over time, which involves encoding, storage, and retrieval. 270

memory span The number of digits an individual can report back without error in a single presentation. 273

mental age (MA) An individual's level of mental development relative to others. 115

mental processes Thoughts, feelings, and motives that cannot be observed by others. 227

mental retardation A condition with an onset before age 18 that involves low intelligence (usually below 70 on a traditional individually administered intelligence test) and difficulty in adapting to everyday life. 192

mental set A type of fixation in which an individual tries to solve a problem in a particular way that has worked in the past. 321

metacognition Cognition about cognition, or "knowing about knowing." 265

metalinguistic awareness Knowledge of language. 61

mode The score that occurs most often. 550

moral development Development with respect to the rules and conventions of just interactios between people. 102

morphology Refers to the units of meaning involved in word formation. 55

motivation The processes that energize, direct, and sustain behavior. 451

multicultural education Education that values diversity and includes the perspectives of a variety of cultural groups on a regular basis. 157

multiple-choice item An objective test item consisting of two parts: a stem plus a set of possible responses. 576

N

naturalistic observation Observation outside of a laboratory in the real world. 16

nature-nurture issue *Nature* refers to an organism's biological inheritance, *nurture* to environmental influences. The "nature" proponents claim biological inheritance is the most important influence on development; the "nurture" proponents claim environmental experiences are the most important. 30, 125

near transfer The transfer of learning to a situation that is similar to the one in which the initial learning took place. 327

need for affiliation or relatedness The motive to be securely connected with other people. 453

negative reinforcement Reinforcement based on the principle that the frequency of a response increases because an aversive (unpleasant) stimulus is removed. 232

neglectful parenting A parenting style of uninvolvement in which parents spend little time with their children; associated with children's social incompetence. 77

neo-Piagetians Developmental psychologists who believe that Piaget got some things right but that his theory needs considerable revision; emphasize how to process information through attention, memory, and strategies. 47

network theories Theories that describe how information in memory is organized and connected; they emphasize nodes in the memory network. 277

nongraded (cross-age) program A variation of between-class ability grouping in which students are grouped by their ability in particular subjects, regardless of their age or grade level. 130

norm group A group of similar individuals who previously were given the test by the test maker. 533

norm-referenced grading A grading system based on a comparison of a student's performance with that of other students in the class or of other classes and other students. 593

normal distribution A "bell-shaped curve" in which most of the scores are clustered around the mean; the farther above or below the mean that we travel, the less frequently each score occurs. 115

normal distribution A symmetrical distribution, with a majority of scores falling in the middle of the possible range of scores and few scores appearing toward the extremes of the range. 552

O

objective tests Tests that have relatively clear, unambiguous scoring criteria, usually multiple-choice tests. 573

observational learning Learning that involves acquiring skills, strategies, and beliefs by observing others. 244

off-set style A classroom arrangement style in which small numbers of students (usually three or four) sit at tables but do not sit directly across from one another. 498

operant conditioning Also called instrumental conditioning, this is a form of learning in which the consequences of behavior produce changes in the probability that the behavior will occur. 232

organization Piaget's concept of grouping isolated behaviors into a higher-order, more smoothly functioning cognitive system; the grouping or arranging of items into categories. 38

orthopedic impairments Restricted movements or lack of control of movements, due to muscle, bone, or joint problems. 195

overconfidence bias The tendency to have more confidence in judgment and decisions than we should based on probability or past experience. 313

P

participant observation Observation conducted at the same time the teacher-researcher is actively involved as a participant in the activity or setting. 16

passive style A way of dealing with conflict in which people are nonassertive and submissive and don't let others know what they want. 508

pedagogical content knowledge Knowledge about how to effectively teach a particular discipline. 366

percentile-rank score The percentage of a distribution that lies at or below the score. 552

performance assessment Assessment that requires creating answers or products that demonstrate knowledge and skill; examples include writing an essay, and conducting an experiment, carrying out a project, solving a real-world problem, and creating a portfolio. 574

performance criteria Specific behaviors that need to be performed effectively as part of an assessment. 586

performance orientation A personal stance of concern with the outcome rather than the process; for performance-oriented individuals, winning is what matters and happiness is believed to result from winning. 461

permissive classroom management style A management style that allows students considerable autonomy but provides them with little support for developing learning skills or managing their behavior. 500

person-situation interaction The view that the best way to conceptualize personality is not in terms of personal traits or characteristics alone but also in terms of the situation involved. 135

personality Distinctive thoughts, emotions, and behaviors that characterize the way an individual adapts to the world. 135

phonics approach An approach that emphasizes that reading instruction should teach phonics and its basic rules for translating written symbols into sounds. 369

phonology A language's sound system. 55

portfolio A systematic and organized collection of a student's work that demonstrates the student's skills and accomplishments. 588

positive reinforcement Reinforcement based on the principle that the frequency of a response increases because it is followed by a rewarding stimulus. 232

postconventional reasoning In Kohlberg's theory, the highest level of moral development; at this level, moral development is internalized and moral reasoning is self-generated. 103

pragmatics The use of appropriate use of language in different contexts. 56

preconventional reasoning In Kohlberg's theory, the lowest level of moral development; at this level, the child shows no internalization of moral values and moral reasoning is controlled by external rewards and punishments. 103

predictive validity The relation between test scores and the student's future performance. 534

prejudice An unjustified negative attitude toward an individual because of the individual's membership in a group. 152

Premack principle The principle that a high-probability activity can serve as a reinforcer for a low-probability activity. 235

preoperational stage The second Piagetian stage, lasting from about 2 to 7 years of age; symbolic thought increases but operational thought is not yet present. 39

problem sets Groups of two or more multiple-choice or objective short-answer items that are related to the same stimulus, such as an illustration, a graph, or a passage. 580

problem solving Finding an appropriate way to attain a goal. 319

problem-based learning Learning that emphasizes authentic problems like those that occur in daily life. 322

procedural memory Knowledge in the form of skills and cognitive operations. Procedural memory cannot be consciously recollected, at least not in the form of specific events or facts. 276

program evaluation research Research designed to make decisions about the effectiveness of a particular program. 20

project-based learning Students work on real, meaningful problems and create tangible products. 323

prompt An added stimulus or cue that is given just before a response and increases the likelihood the response will occur. 237

prototype matching A process in which individuals decide whether an item is a member of a category by comparing it with the most typical item(s) of the category. 305

psychoanalytic theory of gender A theory that stems from Freud's view that the preschool child develops a sexual attraction to the opposite-sex parent, then by about five or six years of age renounces the attraction because of anxious feelings. Subsequently, the child identifies with the same-sex parent, unconsciously adopting the same-sex parent's characteristics. 165

Public Law 94-142 The Education for All Handicapped Children Act, which required that all students with disabilities be given a free, appropriate public education and which provided the funding to help implement this education. 205

punishment A consequence that decreases the probability that a behavior will occur. 232

Q

quid pro quo sexual harassment Threats by a school employee to base an educational decision (such as a grade) on a student's submission to unwelcome sexual conduct. 175

R

random assignment In experimental research, the assignment of participants to experimental and control groups by chance. 19

range The distance between the highest and lowest scores. 550

rapport talk The language of conversation and a way of establishing connections and negotiating relationships; more characteristic of females than males. 169

raw score The number of items the student answered correctly on the test. 552

receptive language The reception and understanding of language. 198

reciprocal teaching A learning arrangement in which students take turns leading a small-group discussion. 354, 372

rehearsal The conscious repetition of information over time to increase the length of time information stays in memory. 270

reinforcement (reward) A consequence that increases the probability that a behavior will occur. 232

reliability The extent to which a test produces a consistent, reproducible score. 534

report talk Talk that gives information; more characteristic of males than females. 169

representativeness heuristic Making faulty decisions based on how well something matches a prototype—that is, a common or representative example—rather than its relevance to the particular situation. 313

response cost Taking a positive reinforcer away from an individual. 240

S

scaffolding A technique that involves changing the level of support for learning. A teacher or more-advanced peer adjusts the amount of guidance to fit the student's current performance. 49

schedules of reinforcement Partial reinforcement timetables that determine when a response will be reinforced. 236

schema Information—concepts, knowledge, information about events—that already exists in a person's mind. 277

schema theories Theories that when we construct information, we fit it into information that already exists in our mind. 277

schemas In Piaget's theory, actions or mental representations that organize knowledge. 37

Schools for Thought (SFT) A social constructivist program that combines aspects of The Jasper Project, Fostering a Community of Learners, and CSILE. 355

script A schema for an event. 278

selected-response items Test items with an objective format in which responses can be scored on quick inspection. A scoring guide for correct responses is created and can be used by an examiner or a computer. 576

selective attention Focusing on a specific aspect of experience that is relevant while ignoring others that are irrelevant. 267

self-actualization The highest and most elusive of Maslow's needs; the motivation to develop one's full potential as a human being. 452

self-efficacy The belief that one can master a situation and produce positive outcomes. 244, 462

self-esteem Also called self-image and self-worth, the individual's overall conception of himself or herself. 97

self-instructional methods Cognitive behavior techniques aimed at teaching individuals to modify their own behavior. 251

self-regulatory learning The self-generation and self-monitoring of thoughts, feelings, and behaviors in order to reach a goal. 251

semantic memory A student's general knowledge about the world. 277

semantics The meaning of words and sentences. 56

seminar style A classroom arrangement style in which large numbers of students (ten or more) sit in circular, square, or U-shaped arrangements. 498

sensorimotor stage The first Piagetian stage, lasting from birth to about 2 years of age, in which infants construct an understanding of the world by coordinating sensory experiences with motor actions. 38

sensory memory Memory that holds information from the world in its original form for only an instant. 273

serial position effect The principle that recall is better for items at the beginning and the end of a list than for items in the middle. 278

seriation A concrete operation that involves ordering stimuli along some quantitative dimension. 43

service learning A form of education that promotes social responsibility and service to the community. 106

sexism Prejudice and discrimination against an individual because of the person's sex; of being female or male. 168

shaping Teaching new behaviors by reinforcing successive approximations to a specified target behavior. 238

short-answer item A constructed-response format in which students are required to write a word, a short phrase, or several sentences in response to a task. 581

short-term memory A limited-capacity memory system in which information is retained for as long as 30 seconds, unless the information is rehearsed, in which case it can be retained longer. 273

situated cognition The idea that thinking is located (situated) in social and physical contexts, not within an individual's mind. 338

slow-to-warm-up child A temperament style in which the child has a low activity level, is somewhat negative, shows low adaptability, and displays a low intensity of mood. 136

social cognitive theory of gender A theory that children's gender development occurs through observation and imitation of gender behavior, as well as reinforcement and punishment of gender behavior. 166

social cognitive theory Bandura's theory that social and cognitive factors, as well as behavior, play important roles in learning. 243

social constructivist approach Approach that emphasizes the social contexts of learning and that knowledge is mutually built and constructed. 133

social constructivist approach Emphasizes the social contexts of learning and that knowledge is mutually built and constructed; Vygotsky's theory exemplifies this approach. 50

social motives Needs and desires that are learned through experiences with the social world. 469

social studies The field that seeks to promote civic competence with the goal of helping students make informed and reasoned decisions for the public good as citizens of a culturally diverse, democratic society in an interdependent world. 394

socioeconomic status (SES) The categorization of people according to their economic, educational, and occupational characteristics. 147

specific language impairment (SLI) Involves problems in language development that are not accompanied by other obvious physical, sensory, or emotional problems; in some cases, the disorder is called developmental language disorder. 198

speech and language disorders A number of speech problems (such as articulation disorders, voice disorders, and fluency disorders) and language problems (difficulties in receiving information and expressing language). 197

splintered development The circumstances in which development is uneven across domains. 32

split-half reliability Reliability judged by dividing the test items into two halves, such as the odd-numbered and even-numbered items. The scores on the two sets of items are compared to determine how consistently the students performed across each set. 535

standard deviation A measure of how much a set of scores varies on the average around the mean of the scores. 550

standard score A score expressed as a deviation from the mean; involves the standard deviation. 553

standardized tests Tests with uniform procedures for administration and scoring. They assess students' performance in different domains and allow a student's performance to be compared with the performance of other students at the same age or grade level on a national basis. 17, 532

standards-based tests Tests that assess skills that students are expected to have mastered before they can be promoted to the next grade or permitted to graduate. 533

stanine score A 9-point scale that describes a student's performance. 553

stereotype threat The anxiety that one's behavior might confirm a negative stereotype about one's group. 128

strategy construction Discovering a new procedure for processing information. 265

subgoaling The process of setting intermediate goals that place students in a better position to reach the final goal or solution. 319

summative assessment Assessment after instruction is finished; also called formal assessment. 569

sustained attention The ability to maintain attention to a selected stimulus for a prolonged period of time; also called vigilance. 267

symbolic function substage The first substage of preoperational thought, occurring between about 2 to 4 years of age; the ability to represent an object not present develops and symbolic thinking increases; egocentrism and animism occur. 39

syntax The ways that words must be combined to form acceptable phrases and sentences. 55

systematic desensitization A method based on classical conditioning that reduces anxiety by getting the individual to associate deep relaxation with successive visualizations of increasingly anxiety-provoking situations. 231

T

T-score A standard score in which the mean is set at 50 and the standard deviation is set at 10. 554

task analysis Breaking down a complex task that students are to learn into its component parts. 411

taxonomy A classification system. 411

teacher-as-researcher Also called teacher-researcher, this concept involves classroom teachers conducting their own studies to improve their teaching practice. 20

temperament A person's behavioral style and characteristic ways of responding. 136

test-retest reliability The extent to which a test yields the same performance when a student is given the same test on two occasions. 534

theory of mind Awareness of one's own mental processes and the mental processes of others. 292

thinking Manipulating and transforming information in memory, which often is done to form concepts, reason, think critically, make decisions, think creatively, and solve problems. 306

time-out Removing an individual from positive reinforcement. 240

transactional strategy instruction approach A cognitive approach to reading that emphasizes instruction in strategies, especially metacognitive strategies. 371

transfer Applying previous experiences and knowledge to learning or problem solving in a new situation. 327

transitivity The ability to reason and logically combine relationships. 43

triarchic theory of intelligence Sternberg's view that intelligence comes in three main forms: analytical, creative, and practical. 118

V

validity The extent to which a test measures what it is intended to measure and whether inferences about the test scores are accurate. 533

values clarification An approach to moral education that emphasizes helping people clarify what their lives are for and what is worth working for; students are encouraged to define their own values and understand the values of others. 105

voice disorders Disorders producing speech that is hoarse, harsh, too loud, too high-pitched, or too low-pitched. 198

Web A system for browsing Internet sites that refers to the World Wide Web; named the Web because it is comprised of many sites that are linked together. 434

whole-language approach An approach that stresses that reading instruction should parallel children's natural language learning.

Reading materials should be whole and meaningful. 369

within-class ability grouping Placing students in two or three groups within a class to take into account differences in students' abilities. 131

withitness A management style described by Kounin in which teachers show students that they are aware of what is happening. Such teachers closely monitor students on a regular basis and detect inappropriate behavior early before it gets out of hand. 501

working memory A kind of "mental work-bench" that lets individuals manipulate, assemble, and construct information when they make decisions, solve problems, and comprehend written and spoken language. 273

"you" messages Undesirable messages in which speakers appear to judge people and place them in a defensive position. 508

zone of proximal development (ZPD) Vygotsky's term for the range of tasks that are too difficult for children to master alone but that can be mastered with guidance and assistance from adults or more-skilled children. 49

z-score A score that provides information about how many standard deviations a raw score is above or below the mean. 553

References

A

Abrami, P. C., Cholmsky, P., & Gordon, R. (2001). *Statistical analysis for the social sciences.* Boston: Allyn & Bacon.

Abruscato, J. (2004). *Teaching children science* (2nd ed.). Boston: Allyn & Bacon.

Academic Software. (1996). *Adaptive Device Locator System* [computer program]. Lexington, KY: Author.

Achenbach, T. M., Howell, C. T., Quay, H. C., & Conners, C. K. (1991). National survey of problems and competencies among four- to sixteen-year-olds. *Monographs of the Society for Research in Child Development,* Serial No. 225 (Vol. 56, No. 3).

Adams, A., Carnine, D., & Gersten, R. (1982). Instructional strategies for studying content area texts in the intermediate grades. *Reading Research Quarterly, 18,* 27–53.

Adams, R., & Biddle, B. (1970). *Realities of teaching.* New York: Holt, Rinehart & Winston.

Aiken, L. R. (2003). *Psychological testing and assessment* (11th ed.). Boston: Allyn & Bacon.

Aiken, L. R., & Groth-Marnat, G. (2006). *Psychological testing and assessment* (12th ed.). Boston: Allyn & Bacon.

Ainsworth, L. B., & Viegut, D. J. (2006). *Common formative assessments.* Thousand Oaks, CA: Corwin.

Airasian, P. (2005). *Classroom assessment* (5th ed.). New York: McGraw-Hill.

Airasian, P., & Walsh, M. E. (1997, February). Constructivist cautions. *Phi Delta Kappan,* pp. 444–450.

Alberti, R. E., & Emmons, M. L. (2001). *Your perfect right* (8th ed.). San Luis Obispo, CA: Impact.

Alberto, P. A., & Troutman, A. C. (2006). *Applied analysis for teachers* (7th ed.). Upper Saddle River, NJ: Prentice Hall.

Alderman, M. K. (2004). *Motivation for achievement.* Mahwah, NJ: Erlbaum.

Aldridge, J., & Goldman, R. (2007). *Current issues and trends in education* (2nd ed.). Boston: Allyn & Bacon.

Alexander, P. A. (2003). The development of expertise. *Educational Researcher, 32,* (8), 10–14.

Alexander, P. A. (2006). *Psychology in learning and instruction.* Upper Saddle River, NJ: Pearson Merrill Prentice Hall.

All Kinds of Minds. (2005). *Learning Base: Self-regulating and learning.* Retrieved October 15, 2005, from http://www.allkindsofminds.org/learning

Allan, K., Wolf, H. A., Rosenthal, C. R., & Rugg, M. D. (2001). The effects of retrieval cues on post-retrieval monitoring in episodic memory: An electrophysiological study. *Brain Research, 12,* 289–299.

Alvermann, D. E., Fitzgerald, J., & Simpson, M. (2006). Teaching and learning in reading. In P. A. Alexander & P. H. Winne (Eds.), *Handbook of educational psychology* (2nd ed.). Mahwah. NJ: Erlbaum.

Alverno College. (1995). *Writing and speaking criteria.* Milwaukee, WI: Alverno Productions.

Amabile, T. (1993). (Commentary). In D. Goleman, P. Kafman, & M. Ray, (Eds.), *The creative spirit.* New York: Plume.

Amabile, T. M., & Hennesey, B. A. (1992). The motivation for creativity in children. In A. K. Boggiano & T. S. Pittman (Eds.), *Achievement and motivation.* New York: Cambridge University Press.

American Association for the Advancement of Science. (1993). *Benchmarks for science literacy: Project 2061.* New York: Oxford University Press.

American Association of University Women. (1993). *Hostile hallways.* Washington, DC: Author.

American Association of University Women. (2003). Isi puede! Yes, we can: Latinas in school by Angela Ginorio and Michelle Huston (2002). Available at www.aaww.org/research/latina.cfm

American Association on Mental Retardation, Ad Hoc Committee on Terminology and Classification. (1992). *Mental retardation* (9th ed.). Washington, DC: Author.

American Educational Research Association. (1999). *Standards for educational and psychological testing.* Washington, DC: Author.

Anastasi, A., & Urbina, S. (1997). *Psychological testing* (11th ed.). Upper Saddle River, NJ: Prentice Hall.

Anderman, E. M., Austin, C. C., & Johnson, D. M. (2002). The development of goal orientation. In A. Wigfield & J. S. Eccles (Eds.), *Development of achievement motivation.* San Diego: Academic Press.

Anderman, E. M., Maehr, M. L., & Midgley, C. (1996). *Declining motivation after the transition to middle school: Schools can make a difference.* Unpublished manuscript, University of Kentucky, Lexington.

Anderman, E. M., & Wolters, C. A. (2006). Goals, values, and affect: Influences on student motivation. In P. A. Alexander & P. H. Winne (Eds.), *Handbook of educational psychology* (2nd ed.). Mahwah, NJ: Erlbaum.

Anderson, D. R., Lorch, E. P., Field, D. E., Collins, P. A., & Nathan, J. G. (1985, April). *Television viewing at home: Age trends in visual attention and time with TV.* Paper presented at the biennial meeting of the Society for Research in Child Development, Toronto.

Anderson, J., Moffatt, L., & Shapiro, J. (2006). Reconceptualizing language education in early childhood: Socio-cultural perspectives. In B. Spodek & O. N. Saracho (Eds.), *Handbook of research on the education of young children.* Mahwah, NJ: Erlbaum.

Anderson, J. R. (1993). Problem solving and learning. *American Psychologist, 48,* 35–44.

Anderson, J. R. (2005). *Cognitive psychology and its implications* (6th ed.). New York: Worth.

Anderson, L. M., Shinn, C., Fullilove, M. T., Serimshaw, S. C., Fielding, J. E., Normand, J., & Carande-Kulis, V. G. (2003). The effectiveness of early childhood programs: A systematic review. *American Journal of Preventive Medicine, 24* (3 Suppl.), 32–46.

Anderson, L. W., & Krathwohl, D. R. (Eds.). (2001). *A taxonomy for learning, teaching, and assessing.* New York: Longman.

Anderson, N., & Shames, G. H. (2006). *Human communication disorders* (7th ed.). Allyn & Bacon.

Andriessen, J. (2006). Arguing to learn. In R. K. Sawyer (Ed.), *The Cambridge handbook of learning sciences.* Mahwah, NJ: Erlbaum.

Anguiano, R. P. V. (2004). Families and schools: The effect of parental involvement on high school completion. *Journal of Family Issues, 25,* 61–85.

Ansari, D. (2005). Paving the way towards meaningful interactions between neuroscience and education. *Developmental Science, 8,* 466–467.

Antonaci, P. A. P., & O'Callaghan, C. (2006). *A handbook for literacy instructional and assessment strategies: K–8.* Boston: Allyn & Bacon.

Apple Computer. (1995). Changing the conversation about teaching, learning and technology: A report on 10 years of ACOT research. Retrieved April 8, 2005, from http://images.apple.com/education/k12/leadership/acot/pdf/10yr.pdf

Applebome, P. (1997, September 3). Students' test scores show slow but steady gains at nation's schools. *New York Times,* Section B, p. 8.

Arends, R. I. (2004). *Learning to teach.* (6th ed.). New York: McGraw-Hill.

Ariza, E. N. W. (2006). *Not for ESOL teachers: What every classroom teacher needs to know about the linguistically, culturally, and ethnically diverse student.* Boston: Allyn & Bacon.

Arlin, M. (1979). Teacher transitions can disrupt time flow in classrooms. *American Educational Research Journal, 16,* 42–56.

Arndt, J., & Goldenberg, J. L. (2002). From threat to sweat: The role of physiological arousal in the motivation to maintain self-esteem. In A. Tesser, D. A. Stapel, & J. V. Wood (Eds.), *Self and motivation: Emerging psychological perspectives.* Washington, DC: American Psychological Association.

Aronson, E. E. (1986, August). *Teaching students things they think they already know about: The case of prejudice and desegregation.* Paper presented at the meeting of the American Psychological Association, Washington, DC.

Aronson, E. E., Blaney, N., Sephan, C., Sikes, J., & Snapp, M. (1978). *The jigsaw classroom.* Beverly Hills, CA: Sage.

Aronson, E. E., & Patnoe, S. (1997). *The jigsaw classroom* (2nd ed.). Boston: Addison-Wesley.

Aronson, J. (2002). Stereotype threat: Contending and coping with Unnerving Expectations. *Improving academic achievement.* San Diego: Academic Press.

Arter, J. (1995). *Portfolios for assessment and instruction.* ERIC Document Reproduction Service No. ED388890.

Arter, J., & McTighe, J. (2001). *Scoring rubrics in the classroom.* Thousand Oaks, CA: Corwin Press.

Artiles, A. J., Rueda, R., Salazar, J. J., & Higareda, I. (2005). Within-group diversity in minority disproportionate representation: English language learners in urban school districts. *Exceptional Children, 71,* 283–300.

Ashcraft, M. H., & Kirk, E. P. (2001). The relationships among working memory, math anxiety, and performance. *Journal of Experimental Psychology: General, 130,* 224–237.

Asher, J., & Garcia, R. (1969). The optimal age to learn a foreign language. *Modern Language Journal, 53,* 334–341.

Asher, S. R., & Cole, J. D. (Eds.). (1990). *Peer rejection in childhood.* New York: Cambridge University Press.

Ashton, P. T., & Webb, R. B. (1986). *Making a difference: Teachers' sense of efficacy and student achievement.* White Plains, NY: Longman.

Ateah, C. A. (2005). Maternal use of physical punishment in response to child misbehavior: Implications for child abuse prevention. *Child Abuse and Neglect, 29,* 169–185.

Atkinson, J. W. (1957). Motivational determinants of risk-taking behavior. *Psychological Review, 64,* 359–372.

Atkinson, R. C., & Shiffrin, R. M. (1968). Human memory: A proposed system and its control processes. In K. W. Spence & J. T. Spence (Eds.), *The psychology of learning and motivation* (Vol. 2). San Diego: Academic Press.

August, P. (2002, September 26). They all look alike. *San Francisco Chronicle,* p. A29.

Ausubel, D. P. (1960). The use of advance organizers in the learning and retention of meaningful verbal material. *Journal of Educational Psychology, 51,* 267–272.

B

Baddeley, A. (1993). Working memory and conscious awareness. In A. F. Collins, S. E. Gatherhole, M. A. Conway, & P. E. Morris (Eds.), *Theories of memory.* Mahwah, NJ: Erlbaum.

Baddeley, A. (1998). *Human memory* (rev. ed.). Boston: Allyn & Bacon.

Baddeley, A. (2000). Short-term and working memory. In E. Tulving & F. I. M. Craik (Eds.), *The Oxford handbook of memory.* New York: Oxford University Press.

Baddeley, A. (2001). *Is working memory still working?* Paper presented at the meeting of the American Psychological Association, San Francisco.

Baer, J., & Kaufman, J. C. (2006). Creativity research in English-speaking countries. In J. C. Kaufman & R. J. Sternberg (Eds.), *The International handbook of creativity.* New York: Cambridge University Press.

Bafumo, M. E. (2005). The arts in your classroom. *Teaching PreK–8, 35,* 8–9.

Bailey, B. N., Delaney-Black, V., Covington, C. Y., Ager, J., Janisse, J., Hannigan, J. H., & Sokol, R. J. (2004). Prenatal exposure to binge drinking and cognitive and behavioral outcomes at age 7 years. *American Journal of Obstetrics and Gynecology, 191,* 1037–1043.

Bain, R. B. (2005). "They thought the world was flat?": Applying the principles of *How people learn* in teaching high school history. In *How students learn.* Washington, DC: National Academies Press.

Baker, J. (1999). Teacher-student interaction in urban at-risk classrooms: Differential behavior, relationship quality, and student satisfaction with school. *The Elementary School Journal, 100,* 57–70.

Baltes, P. B. (2003). On the incomplete architecture of human ontogeny: Selection, optimization, and compensation as foundation for developmental theory. In U. M. Staudinger & U. Lindenberger (Eds.), *Understanding human development.* Boston: Kluwer.

Baltes, P. B., Lindenberger, U., & Staudinger, U. (2006). Life span theory in developmental psychology. In W. Damon & R. Lerner (Eds.), *Handbook of child psychology* (6th ed.). New York: Wiley.

Bandura, A. (1965). Influence of models' reinforcement contingencies on the acquisition of imitative responses. *Journal of Personality and Social Psychology, 1,* 589–596.

Bandura, A. (1982). Self-efficacy mechanism in human agency. *American Psychologist, 37,* 122–147.

Bandura, A. (1986). *Social foundations of thought and action.* Englewood Cliffs, NJ: Prentice Hall.

Bandura, A. (1997). *Self-efficacy: The exercise of control.* New York: W. H. Freeman.

Bandura, A. (2001). Social cognitive theory. *Annual Review of Psychology,* Palo Alto, CA: Annual Reviews.

Bandura, A. (2004, May). *Toward a psychology of human agency.* Paper presented at the meeting of the American Psychological Society, Chicago.

Bandura, A. (2005). The primacy of self-efficacy in health promotion. *Applied Psychology: An International Review, 54,* 245–254.

Bandura, A. (2006). Going global with social cognitive theory: From prospect to pay dirt. In S. I. Donaldson, D. E. Berger, & K. Pezdek (Eds.), *The Rise of Applied Psychology.* Mahwah, NJ: Erlbaum.

Bandura, A., & Locke, E. A. (2003). Negative self-efficacy and goals revisited. *Journal of Applied Psychology, 88,* 87–99.

Bangert, K., Kulik, J., & Kulik, C. (1983). Individualized systems of instruction in secondary schools. *Review of Educational Research, 53,* 143–158.

Banks, J. A. (1995). *Multicultural education: Its effects on students racial and gender role attitudes.* In J. A. Banks & C. A. M. Banks (Eds.), *Handbook of research on multicultural education.* New York: Macmillan.

Banks, J. A. (1997). *Teaching strategies for ethnic studies* (6th ed.). Boston: Allyn & Bacon.

Banks, J. A. (2001). Multicultural education. In J. A. Banks & C. A. M. Banks (Eds.), *Multicultural education: Issues and perspectives.* New York: Wiley.

Banks, J. A. (2003). *Teaching strategies for ethnic studies* (7th ed.). Boston: Allyn & Bacon.

Banks, J. A. (2006). *Cultural diversity and education* (5th ed.). Boston: Allyn & Bacon.

Banks, J. A., Cochran-Smith, M., Moll, L., Richert, A., Zeichner, K., LePage, P., Darling-Hammond, L., Duffy, H., & McDonald, M. (2005). Teaching diverse learners. In L. Darling-Hammond & J. Bransford (Eds.), *Preparing teachers for a changing world.* San Francisco: Jossey-Bass.

Banks, S. A. (2005). *Classroom assessment: Issues and practices.* Boston: Allyn & Bacon.

Barbaresi, W. J., Katusic, S. K., Colligan, R. C., Weaver, A. L., Leibson, C. L., & Jacobsen, S. J. (2006). Long-term stimulant medication treatment of attention-deficit/hyperactivity disorder: Results from a population-based study. *Journal of Developmental and Behavioral Pediatrics, 27,* 1–10.

Barber, B. L., Eccles, J. S., & Stone, M. R. (2001, April). *Whatever happened to the jock, the brain, and the princess? Young adult pathways linked to adolescent activity involvement and identity.* Paper presented at the meeting of the Society for Research in Child Development, Minneapolis.

Barnett, R. C., & Gareis, K. (2006). Parental after-school stress and psychological well-being. *Journal of Marriage and the Family, 68,* 101–108.

Baron-Cohen, S. (2004). Autism: Research into causes and intervention. *Pediatric Rehabilitation, 7,* 73–78.

Baroody, A. J., Lai, M., & Mix. K. S. (2006). The development of young children's early number and operation sense and its implication for early childhood education. In B. Spodak & O. N. Saracho (Eds.), *Handbook of research on the education of young children.* Mahwah, NJ: Erlbaum.

Barr, W. B. (2000). Epilepsy. In A. Kazdin (Ed.), *Encyclopedia of psychology.* Washington, DC, and New York: American Psychological Association and Oxford University Press.

Barrish, H. H., Saunders, M., & Wolfe, M. D. (1969). Good Behavior Game: Effects of individual contingencies for group consequences and disruptive behavior in the classroom. *Journal of Applied Behavior Analyses, 2,* 119–124.

Barron, K. E., & Harackiewicz, J. M. (2001). Achievement goals and optimal motivation: Testing multiple goal models. *Journal of Personality and Social Psychology, 80,* 706–722.

Barsalou, L. W. (2000). Concepts: Structure. In A. Kazdin (Ed.), *Encyclopedia of psychology.* Washington, DC, and New York: American Psychological Association and Oxford University Press.

Bartlett, E. J. (1982). Learning to revise: Some component processes. In M. Nystrand (Ed.), *What writers know.* New York: Academic Press.

Bartlett, F. C. (1932). *Remembering.* Cambridge, England: Cambridge University Press.

Bartlett, J. (2005, April). *Personal conversation.* Richardson, TX: Department of Psychology, University of Texas at Dallas.

Barton, J., & Collins, A. (1997). Starting Out: Designing your portfolio. In J. Barton & A. Collins (Eds.), *Portfolio assessment: A handbook for educators.* Boston: Addison-Wesley.

Battistich, V., & Solomon, D. (1995, April). *Linking teacher change to student change.* Paper presented at the meeting of the American Educational Research Association, San Francisco.

Battistich, V., Solomon, D., Watson, M., Solomon, J., & Schaps, E. (1989). Effects of an elementary school program to enhance prosocial behavior on children's cognitive social-problem solving skills and strategies. *Journal of Applied Developmental Psychology, 10,* 147–169.

Bauer, P. J. (2006). Event memory. In W. Damon & R. Lerner (Eds.), *Handbook of child psychology* (6th ed.). New York: Wiley.

Baumeister, R. F., Campbell, J. D., Krueger, J. I., & Vohs, K. D. (2003). Does high self-esteem cause better performance, interpersonal success, happiness, or healthier lifestyles? *Psychological Science in the Public Interest, 4* (No. 1), 1–44.

Baumrind, D. (1971). Current patterns of parental authority. *Developmental Psychology Monographs, 4* (1, Part 2).

Baumrind, D. (1996, April). Unpublished review of J. W. Santrock's *Children,* 5th ed. (New York: McGraw-Hill).

Baumrind, D., Larzelere, R. E., & Cowan, P. A. (2002). Ordinary physical punishment: Is it harmful? Comment on Gershoff (2002). *Psychological Bulletin, 128,* 590–595.

Beal, C. (1994). *Boys and girls: The development of gender roles.* New York: McGraw-Hill.

Bear, G. G. (2005a). *Developing self-discipline and preventing and correcting misbehavior.* Boston: Allyn & Bacon.

Bear, G. G. (2005b). Discipline. In S. W. Lee (Ed.), *Encyclopedia of school psychology.* Thousand Oaks, CA: Sage.

Beatty, B. (1998). From laws of learning to a science of values: Efficiency and morality in Thorndike's educational psychology. *American Psychologist, 53,* 1145–1152.

Beck, I. L., McKeown, G. M., Sinatra, K. B., & Loxterman, J. A. (1991). Revising social studies texts from a text-processing perspective: Evidence of improved comprehensibility. *Reading Research Quarterly, 26,* 251–276.

Becker, J. R. (1981). Differential treatment of females and males in mathematics classes. *Journal for Research in Mathematics Education, 12,* 40–53.

Beckham, E. E. (2000). Depression. In A. Kazdin (Ed.), *Encyclopedia of psychology.* Washington, DC, and New York: American Psychological Association and Oxford University Press.

Bednar, R. L., Wells, M. G., & Peterson, S. R. (1995). *Self-esteem* (2nd ed.). Washington, DC: American Psychological Association.

Begley, S. (1998, March 30). Homework doesn't help. *Newsweek,* pp. 30–31.

Beins, B. (2004). *Research methods.* Boston: Allyn & Bacon.

Beirne-Smith, M., Patton, J. R., & Kim, S. H. (2006). *Mental retardation* (7th ed.). Upper Saddle River, NJ: Prentice Hall.

Bell, L. A. (1989). Something's wrong here and its not me: Challenging the dilemmas that block girls' success. *Journal for the Education of the Gifted, 12,* 118–130.

Bem, S. L. (1977). On the utility of alternative procedures for assessing psychological androgyny. *Journal of Consulting and Clinical Psychology, 45,* 196–205.

Bennett, C. I. (2007). *Comprehensive multicultural education* (6th ed.). Boston: Allyn & Bacon.

Bennett, W. (1993). *The book of virtues.* New York: Simon & Schuster.

Benson, P. L., Scales, P. C., Hamilton, S. F., & Sesma, A. (2006). Positive youth development. In W. Damon & R. Lerner (Eds.), *Handbook of child psychology* (6th ed.). New York: Wiley.

Benveniste, L., Carnoy, M., & Rothstein, R. (2003). *All else equal.* New York: Routledge-Farmer.

Beran, T. N., & Tutty, L. (2002) *An evaluation of the Bully Proofing Your School, School Program.* Unpublished manuscript, Calgary: RESOLVE, Alberta, CAN.

Bereiter, C., & Scardamalia, M. (2006a). Education for the knowledge age: Design-centered models of teaching and instruction. In P. A. Alexander & P. H. Winne (Eds.), *Handbook of educational psychology* (2nd ed.). Mahwah, NJ: Erlbaum.

Bereiter, C., & Scardamalia, M. (2006b). Knowledge building: Theory, pedagogy, and technology. In R. K. Sawyer (Ed.), *The Cambridge handbook of the learning sciences.* New York: Cambridge University Press.

Berg, B. L. (2007). *Qualitative methods for the social sciences* (6th Ed.). Boston: Allyn & Bacon.

Berk, L. E. (1994). Why children talk to themselves. *Scientific American, 271* (5), 78–83.

Berk, L. E., & Spuhl, S. T. (1995). Maternal interaction, private speech, and task performance in preschool children. *Early Childhood Research Quarterly, 10,* 145–169.

Berko Gleason, J. (2004). Unpublished review of J. W. Santrock's *Life-span development,* 9th ed. (New York: McGraw-Hill).

Berko Gleason, J. (2005). The development of language. In J. Berko Gleason (Ed.), *The development of language* (6th ed.). Boston: Allyn & Bacon.

Berko, J. (1958). The child's learning of English morphology. *Word, 14,* 150–177.

Berliner, D. (2006). Educational psychology: Searching for essence throughout a century of influence. In P. A. Alexander & P. H. Winne (Eds.), *Handbook of educational psychology* (2nd ed.). Mahwah, NJ: Erlbaum.

Berndt, T. J. (1979). Developmental changes in conformity to peers and parents. *Developmental Psychology, 15,* 608–616.

Berndt, T. J. (1999). Friend's influence on children's adjustment. In W. A. Collins & B. Laursen (Eds.), *Relationships as developmental contexts.* Mahwah, NJ: Erlbaum.

Berninger, V. W. (2006). A developmental approach to learning disabilities. In W. Damon & R. Lerner (Eds.), *Handbook of child psychology* (6th ed.). New York: Wiley.

Berninger, V. W., & Abbott, R. (2005, April). *Paths leading to reading comprehension in at-risk and normally developing second-grade readers.* Paper presented at the meet-ing of the Society for Research in Child Development, Atlanta.

Berninger, V. W., Stage, S. A., Smith, D. R., & Hildebrand, D. (2001). Assessment for reading and writing intervention. In J. J. W. Andrews, D. H. Saklofske, & D. Hildebrand (Eds.), *Handbook of psychoeducational assessment.* San Diego: Academic Press.

Berry, J. W., Phinney, J. S., Sam, D. L., & Vedder, P. (2006). *Immigrant Youth in Cultural Transition: Acculturation, Identity and Adaptation Across National Contexts.* Mahwah, NJ: Erlbaum.

Berryman, L., & Russell, D. R. (2001). Portfolios across the curriculum: Whole school assessment in Kentucky. *English Journal, 90,* 76–83.

Berson, M. J., Cruz, B. C., Duplass, J. A., & Johnston, J. H. (2007). *Social studies on the internet* (3rd ed.). Upper Saddle River, NJ: Prentice Hall.

Best, D. (2001). Cross-cultural gender roles. In J. Worell (Ed.), *Encyclopedia of women and gender.* San Diego: Academic Press.

Best, J. W., & Kahn, J. V. (2003). *Research in education* (9th ed.). Boston: Allyn & Bacon.

Best, J. W., & Kahn, J. V. (2006). *Research in education* (10th ed.). Boston: Allyn & Bacon.

Best, S. J., Heller, K. W., & Bigge, J. L. (2005). *Teaching individuals with physical and multiple abilities* (5th ed.). Upper Saddle River, NJ: Prentice Hall.

Betch, T., Haberstroh, S., Glockner, A., Haar, T., & Fiedler, K. (2001). The effects of routine strength on adaptation and information search in recurrent decision making. *Organizational Behavior and Human Decision Processes, 84,* 23–53.

Bialystok, E. (1997). Effects of bilingualism and biliteracy on children's emerging concepts of print. *Developmental Psychology, 33,* 429–440.

Bialystok, E. (1999). Cognitive complexity and attentional control in the bilingual mind. *Child Development, 70,* 537–804.

Bialystok, E. (2001). Metalinguistic aspects of bilingual processing. *Annual Review of Applied Linguistics, 21,* 169–181.

Biederman, J., & Faraone, S. V. (2003). Current concepts on the neurobiology of attention-deficit/hyperactivity disorder. *Journal of Attention Disorders, 6* (Suppl. 1). S7–S16.

Bigelow, B. (1999, April). Why standardized tests threaten multiculturalism. *Educational Leadership, 56,* 37–40.

Biological Sciences Curriculum Study. (1989). *Science for life and living.* Colorado Springs: Author.

Biological Sciences Curriculum Study. (2001). *Science for life and living.* Colorado Springs: Author.

Birch, S. A. J. (2005). When knowledge is a curse. *Current Directions in Psychological Science, 14,* 25–29.

Birney, D. P., Citron-Pusty, J. H., Lutz, D. J., & Sternberg, R. J. (2005). The development of cognitive and intellectual abilities. In M. H. Bornstein & M. E. Lamb (Eds.), *Developmental psychology* (5th ed.). Mahwah, NJ: Erlbaum.

Bitter, G. G., & Pierson, M. E. (2005). *Using technology in the classroom* (6th ed.). Boston: Allyn & Bacon.

Bitter, G. G., & Legacy, J. M. (2006). *Using technology in the classroom* (Brief version). Boston: Allyn & Bacon.

Bjorklund, D. F. (2005). *Children's thinking* (4th ed.), Belmont, CA: Wadsworth.

Bjorklund, D. F. (2006). Mother knows best: Epigenetic inheritance, maternal effects, and the evolution of human intelligence. *Developmental Review, 26,* 213–242.

Bjorklund, D. F., & Rosenbaum, K. (2000). Middle childhood: Cognitive development. In A. Kazdin (Ed.), *Encyclopedia of psychology.* Washington, DC, & New York: American Psychological Association and Oxford University Press.

Blachman, B. A., Ball, E., Black, R., & Tangel, D. (1994). Kindergarten teachers develop phoneme awareness in low-income inner-city classrooms: Does it make a difference? In B. A. Blachman (Ed.), *Reading and writing.* Mahwah, NJ: Erlbaum.

Black, P., & William, D. (2006). Developing a theory of formative assessment. In J. Gardner (Ed.), *Assessment and learning.* London: Paul Chapman.

Black, S. (2004). Teaching students to think critically. *American School Board Journal, 191,* 52–54.

Blackhurst, A. E. (1997, May/June). Perspectives on technology in special education. *Teaching Exceptional Children,* pp. 41–47.

Blakemore, J. E. O., Berenbaum, S. A., & Liben, L. S. (2005 in preparation). *Gender development.* Mahwah, NJ: Erlbaum.

Blakemore, S-J., & Choudhury, S. (2006). Brain development during puberty: State of the science. *Developmental Science, 9,* 11–14.

Blasi, A. (2005). Moral character: A psychological approach. In D. K. Lapsley & F. C. Power (Eds.), *Character psychology and character education.* Notre Dame: University of Notre Dame Press.

Blasingame, J., & Bushman, J. H. (2005). *Teaching writing in middle and secondary schools.* Upper Saddle River, NJ: Prentice Hall.

Block, J. H., & Block, J. (1980). The role of ego-control and ego-resiliency in the organization of behavior. In W. A. Collins (Ed.), *Minnesota symposium on child psychology* (Vol. 13). Minneapolis: University of Minnesota Press.

Bloom, B. S. (1971). Mastering learning. In J. H. Block (Ed.), *Mastery learning.* New York: Holt, Rinehart & Winston.

Bloom, B. S. (Ed.). (1985). *Developing talent in young people.* New York: Ballantine.

Bloom, B. S., & Dey, A. N. (2006). Summary health statistics for U.S. children: National Health Interview Survey, 2004. *Vital Health Statistics, 227,* 1–85.

Bloom, B. S., & Krathwohl, D. (Eds.). (1956). *Taxonomy of education objectives: Handbook 1. Cognitive domain.* New York: Longman, Green.

Bloom, B. S., Engelhart, M. D., Frost, E. J., Hill, W. H., & Krathwohl, D. R. (1956). *Taxonomy of educational objectives.* New York: David McKay.

Bloom, L. (1998). Language acquisition in its developmental context. In W. Damon (Ed.), *Handbook of child psychology* (5th ed., Vol. 2). New York: Wiley.

Blumenfeld, P. C., Kempler, T. M., & Krajcik, J. S. (2006). Motivation and cognitive engagement in learning environments. In R. K. Sawyer (Ed.). *Cambridge handbook of learning sciences.* New York: Cambridge University Press.

Blumenfeld, P. C., Pintrich, P. R., Wessles, K., & Meece, J. (1981, April). *Age and sex differences in the impact of classroom experiences on self-perceptions.* Paper presented at the biennial meeting of the Society for Research in Child Development, Boston.

Blumenfeld, P. C., Marx, R., & Harris, C. J. (2006). Learning environments. In W. Damon & R. Lerner (Eds.), *Handbook of child psychology* (6th ed.). New York: Wiley.

Blumenfeld, P. C., Modell, J., Bartko, T., Secade, J., Fredricks, J., Friedel, J., & Paris, A. (2005). School engagement of inner city students during middle childhood. In C. R. Cooper, Coll, C. T. G., Bartko, W. T. Davis, H. M., & Chatman, C. (Eds.). *Developmental pathways through middle childhood.* Mahwah, NJ: Erlbaum.

Bo, I. (1994). The sociocultural environment as a source of support. In F. Nestmann & K. Hurrelmann (Eds.), *Social networks and social support in childhood and adolescence.* New York: Walter de Gruyter.

Bodes, J. S., & Midgley, C. (1989). Stage-environment fit: Developmentally appropriate classrooms for young adolescents. In C. Ames & R. Ames (Eds.), *Research on motivation in education* (Vol. 3). Orlando: Academic Press.

Bodrova, E., & Leong, D. J. (2001). *Tools of the mind.* Geneva: International Bureau of Education, UNESCO.

Bodrova, E., & Leong, D. J. (2007). *Tools of the mind* (2nd ed.). Geneva: International Bureau of Education, UNESCO.

Boekaerts, M., & Corno, L. (2005). Self-regulation in the classroom: A perspective on assessment and intervention. *Applied Psychology: An International Review, 54,* 199–232.

Boekaerts, M. (2006). Self-regulation and effort investment. In W. Damon & R. Lerner (Eds.), *Handbook of child psychology* (6th ed.). New York: Wiley.

Bogdan, R., & Biklin, S. K. (2007). *Qualitative research for education* (5th ed.). Boston: Allyn & Bacon.

Bolt, Beraneck, & Newman, Inc. (1993). *The Co-NECT school: Design for a new generation of American schools.* Cambridge, MA: Author.

Bond, L. (1989). The effects of special preparation measures of scholastic ability. In R. Linn (Ed.), *Educational measurement* (3rd ed.). New York: Macmillan.

Booher-Jennings, J. (2006). Rationing education in an era of accountability. *Phi Delta Kappan, 87,* 756–761.

Bookstein, F. L., Streissguth, A. P., Sampson, P. D., Connor, P. D., & Barr, H. M. (2002). Corpus callosum shape and neuropsychological deficits in adult males with heavy fetal alcohol exposure. *Neuroimage, 15,* 233–251.

Borba, J. A., & Olvera, C. M. (2001). Student-led parent-teacher conferences. *The Clearing House, 74,* 333–336.

Borden, L. M., Donnermeyer, J. F., & Scheer, S. D. (2001). The influence of extracurricular activities and peer influence on substance abuse. *Adolescent & Family Health, 2,* 12–19.

Bornstein, M. H., Arterberry, M. E., & Mash, C. (2005). Perceptual development. In M. H. Bornstein & M. E. Lamb (Eds.), *Developmental psychology* (5th ed.). Mahwah, NJ: Erlbaum.

Bost, C. S., & Vaughn, S. (2002). *Strategies for teaching students with learning and behavioral problems* (5th ed.). Boston: Allyn & Bacon.

Botvin, G. J., Schinke, S., & Orlandi, M. A. (1995). School-based health promotion: Substance abuse and sexual behavior. *Applied and Preventive Psychology, 4,* 167–184.

Bourne, E. J. (1995). *The anxiety and phobia workbook.* Oakland, CA: New Harbinger.

Bowles, T. (1999). Focusing on time orientation to explain adolescent self concept and academic achievement: Part II. Testing a model. *Journal of Applied Health Behaviour, 1,* 1–8.

Boyd-Batsone, P. (2006). *Differentiated early literacy for English language learners: Practical strategies.* Boston: Allyn & Bacon.

Boyles, N. S., & Contadino, D. (1997). *The learning differences sourcebook.* Los Angeles: Lowell House.

Braden, J. P. (2005). Performance-based assessment. In S. W. Lee (Ed.), *Encyclopedia of school psychology.* Thousand Oaks, CA: Sage.

Bradley, R. H., Corwyn, R. F., McAdoo, H., & Coll, C. (2001). The home environments of children in the United States: Part I. Variations by age, ethnicity, and poverty status. *Child Development, 72,* 1844–1867.

Brainerd, C. J., & Gordon, L. L. (1994). Development of verbatim and gist memory for numbers. *Developmental Psychology, 30,* 163–177.

Brainerd, C. J., & Reyna, V. F. (2004). Fuzzy-trace theory and memory development. *Developmental Review, 24,* 396–439.

Branch, M. N. (2000). Punishment. In A. Kazdin (Ed.), *Encyclopedia of psychology.* Washington, DC, & New York: American Psychological Association and Oxford University Press.

Bransford, J. (2006). Learning theories and education: Toward a decade of synergy. In P. A. Alexander & P. H. Winne (Eds.), *Handbook of educational psychology* (2nd ed.). Mahwah, NJ: Erlbaum.

Bransford, J., Barron, B., Pea, R., Meltzoff, A., Kuhl, P., Bell, P., Stevens, R., Schwartz, D., Vye, N., Reeves, B., Roschelle, J., & Sabelli, N. (2006). Foundations and opportunities for an interdisciplinary science. In R. K. Sawyer (Ed.), *The Cambridge handbook of the learning sciences.* New York: Cambridge University Press.

Bransford, J., Darling-Hammond, L., & LePage, P. (2005). Introduction. In L. Darling-Hammond & J. Bransford (Eds.), *Preparing teachers for a changing world.* New York: Jossey-Bass.

Bransford, J., Derry, S., Berliner, D., Hammerness, K., & Beckett, K. L. (2005). Theories of learning and their role in teaching. In L. Darling-Hammond & J. Bransford (Eds.), *Preparing teachers for a changing world.* San Francisco: Jossey-Bass.

Bransford, J., Stevens, R., Schwartz, D., Meltzoff, A., Pea, R., Roschelle, J., Vye, N., Kuhl, P., Bell, P., Barron, B., Reeves, B., & Sabelli, N. (2006). Learning theories and education: Toward a decade of synergy. In P. A. Alexander & P. H. Winne (Eds.), *Handbook of educational psychology* (2nd ed.). Mahwah, NJ: Erlbaum.

Bransford, J. D., & Donovan, M. S. (2005). Scientific inquiry and *How people learn.* In M. S. Donovan & J. D. Bransford (Eds.), *How students learn.* Washington, DC: National Academies Press.

Bransford, J. D., & Stein, B. S. (1993). *The IDEAL problem solver.* New York: W. H. Freeman.

Bredekamp, S., & Copple, C. (Eds.). (1997). *Developmentally appropriate practice in early childhood programs* (rev. ed.). Washington, DC: National Association for the Education of Young Children.

Breivik, K., & Olweus, D. (2006). Children of divorce in a Scandinavian welfare state. *Scandinavian Journal of Psychology, 47,* 61–74.

Breur, J. T. **(1999).** In search of . . . brain-based education. *Phi Delta Kappan, 80,* 648–655.

Brewer, D. J., Rees, D. I., & Argys, L. M. (1995). Detracking America's schools. *Phi Delta Kappan, 77,* 210–215.

Brewer, M. B., & Campbell, D. I. (1976). *Ethnocentrism and intergroup attitudes.* New York: Wiley.

Briggs, T. W. (1999, October 14). Honorees find keys to unlock kids' minds. *USA Today,* Section D.

Briggs, T. W. (1999, October 14). Honorees find keys to unlocking kids' minds. Retrieved July 22, 2004, from www.usatoday.com/education/1999

Briggs, T. W. (1999, October 14). Honorees find keys to unlocking kids' minds. Retrieved March 10, 2000, from www.usatoday.com/education

Briggs, T. W. (2004, October 14). Students embrace vitality of USA Today's top 20 teachers. *USA Today,* p. 7D.

Briggs, T. W. (2004, October 14). USA TODAY's 2004 all-USA teacher team. *USA TODAY,* p. 6D.

Briggs, T. W. (2005). Math teacher resets the learning curve. Retrieved from http://www.usatoday.com/news/education/2005-04-05-math-teacher_x.htm

Briggs, T. W. (2005, October 13). *USA Today's* 2005 all-USA teacher team. *USA Today,* p. 6D.

Britten, J. S., & Cassidy, J. C. (2006). The technology integration assessment instrument: Understanding planned use of technology by classroom teachers. *Computers in Schools, 22*(No. 3–4), 49–61.

Brodkin, A., & Coleman, M. (1995, January/February). Children of divorce. *Instructor, 32,* 30.

Brody, G. H., Ge, X., Conger, R. D., Gibbons, F., Murry, V., Gerrard, M., & Simons, R. (2001). The influence of neighborhood disadvantage, collective socialization, and parenting on African American children's affiliation with deviant peers. *Child Development, 72,* 1231–1246.

Brody, N. (2000). Intelligence. In A. Kazdin (Ed.), *Encyclopedia of psychology.* Washington, DC, & New York: American Psychological Association and Oxford University Press.

Brody, N. (2006). Does education influence intelligence? In P. C. Kyllonen, R. D. Roberts, & L. Stankov (Eds.), *Extending intelligence.* Mahwah, NJ: Erlbaum.

Bronfenbrenner, U. (1995). Developmental ecology through space and time: A future perspective. In P. Moen, G. H. Elder, & K. Luscher (Eds.), *Examining lives in context.* Washington, DC: American Psychological Association.

Bronfenbrenner, U. (2000). Ecological theory. In A. Kazdin (Ed.), *Encyclopedia of psychology.* Washington, DC, & New York: American Psychological Association and Oxford University Press.

Bronfenbrenner, U. (2004). *Making human beings human.* Thousand Oaks, CA: Sage.

Bronfenbrenner, U., & Morris, M. A. (1998). The ecology of developmental processes. In W. Damon (Ed.), *Handbook of child psychology* (5th ed., Vol. 1). New York: Wiley.

Bronfenbrenner, U., & Morris, M. A. (2006). The ecology of developmental processes. In W. Damon & R. Lerner (Eds.), *Handbook of child psychology* (6th ed.). New York: Wiley.

Bronstein, W. P. (2006). The family environment: where gender socialization begins. In J. Worell & C. D. Goodheart (Eds.), *Handbook of girls' and women's psychological health.* New York: Oxford University Press.

Brookhart, S. M. (1997). A theoretical framework for the role of classroom assessment in motivating student effort and achievement. *Applied Measurement in Education, 10,* 161–180.

Brookhart, S. M. (2002). What will teachers know about assessment, and how will that improve instruction? In R. W. Kissitz & W. D. Schafer (Eds.), *Assessment in educational reform: Both means and ends.* Boston: Allyn & Bacon.

Brookhart, S. M. (2004). *Grading.* Upper Saddle River, NJ: Prentice Hall.

Brookover, W. B., Beady, C., Flood, P., Schweitzer, U., & Wisenbaker, J. (1979). *School social systems and student achievement: Schools make a difference.* New York: Praeger.

Brooks, J. G., & Brooks, M. G. (1993). *The case for constructivist classrooms.* Alexandria, VA: Association for Supervision and Curriculum Development.

Brooks, J. G., & Brooks, M. G. (2001). *In search of understanding: The case for constructivist classrooms.* Upper Saddle River, NJ: Merrill.

Brooks-Gunn, J., Currie, J., Emde, R. E., & Zigler, E. (2003). Do you believe in magic? What we can expect from early childhood intervention programs. *SRCD Social Policy Report, 17*(1), 3–15.

Brophy, J. (1998). *Motivating students to learn.* New York: McGraw-Hill.

Brophy, J. (2004). *Motivating students to learn* (2nd ed.). Mahwah, NJ: Erlbaum.

Brophy, J. (2006). History of research on classroom management. In C. M. Evertson & C. S. Weinstein (Eds.), *Handbook of classroom management.* Mahwah, NJ: Erlbaum.

Brophy, J. (2006). Observational research on generic aspects of classroom teaching. In P. A. Alexander & P. H. Winne (Eds.), *Handbook of educational psychology* (2nd ed.). Mahwah, NJ: Erlbaum.

Brophy, J., & Good, T. (1974). *Teacher-student relationships: Causes and consequences.* New York: Holt, Rinehart & Winston.

Brown, A. L. (1997). Transforming schools into communities of thinking and learning about serious matters. *American Psychologist, 52,* 399–413.

Brown, A. L., & Campione, J. C. (1996). Psychological learning theory and the design of innovative environments. In L. Schuable & R. Glaser (Eds.), *Contributions of instructional innovation to understanding learning.* Mahwah, NJ: Erlbaum.

Brown, B. B. (2004). Adolescents' relationships with peers. In R. Lerner & L. Steinberg (Eds.), *Handbook of adolescent psychology* (2nd ed.). New York: Wiley.

Brown, L., & Brown, M. (1988). *Dinosaurs divorce.* Boston: Little, Brown.

Brown, R. (1973). *A first language: The early stages.* Cambridge, MA: Harvard University Press.

Brown, R. P., & Day, E. A. (2006). The difference isn't black and white: stereotype threat and the race gap on Ravens Advanced Progressive Matrices. *Journal of Applied Psychology, 91,* 979–985.

Brown, S., & Kysilka, M. (2002). *Applying multicultural and global concepts in the classroom and beyond.* Boston: Allyn & Bacon.

Bruckman, A. (2006). Learning in online communities. In R. K. Sawyer (Ed.), *The*

Cambridge handbook of the learning sciences. New York: Cambridge University Press.

Bruer, J. (1993) *Schools for Thought.* Cambridge, MA: MIT University Press.

Bruner, J. (1996). *Toward a theory of instruction.* Cambridge, MA: Harvard University Press.

Bruning, R., & Horn, C. (2001). Developing motivation to write. *Educational Psychologist, 35,* 25–37.

Bryant, D. P., & Bryant, B. R. (1998). Using assistive technology adaptations to include students with learning disabilities in cooperative learning activities. *Journal of Learning Disabilities, 31,* 41–54.

Bryant, J. A. (Ed.) (2006). *The children's television community.* Mahwah, NJ: Erlbaum.

Bryant, J. B. (2005). Language in social contexts: Communicative competence in the preschool years. In J. Berko Gleason (Ed.), *The development of language* (6th ed.). Boston: Allyn & Bacon.

Brydon, S. R., & Scott, M. D. (2006). *Between one and many* (5th ed.). New York: McGraw-Hill.

Bryk, A. S., Lee, V. E., & Smith, J. B. (1989, May). *High school organization and its effects on teachers and students: An interpretive summary of the research.* Paper presented at the conference on Choice and Control in American Education, University of Wisconsin, Madison.

Buck, J. B. (2002). Re-segregating America's public schools. In C. C. Yeakey & R. D. Henderson (Eds.), *Surmounting the odds: Equalizing educational opportunity in the new millennium.* Greenwich, CT: IAP.

Buhrmester, D., & Furman, W. (1987). The development of companionship and intimacy. *Child Development, 58,* 1101–1113.

Bukowski, W. M., & Adams, R. (2005). Peer relationships and psychopathology. *Journal of Clinical Child and Adolescent Psychology, 34,* 3–10.

Burke, K. (2006). *From standards to rubrics in six steps.* Thousand Oaks, CA: Corwin.

Burkham, D. T., Lee, V. E., & Smerdon, B. A. (1997). Gender and science learning early in high school: Subject matter and laboratory experiences. *American Educational Research Journal, 34,* 297–331.

Burnette, J. (1998). Reducing the disproportionate representation of minority students in special education. *ERIC/OSEP Digest, No. E566.*

Burnstein, R., & Lederman, L. M. (2001). Using wireless keypads in lecture classes. *Physics Teacher, 39* (8), 8–11.

Burton, L. A., Rabin, L., Vardy, S. B., Frohlich, J., Wyatt, G., Dimitri, D., Constante, S., & Guterman, E. (2004). Gender differences in implicit and explicit memory for explicit passages. *Brain and Cognition, 54,* 218–224.

Burz, H. L., & Marshall, K. (1996). *Performance-based curriculum for mathematics: From knowing to showing.* ERIC Document Reproduction Service No. ED400194.

Buss, D. M. (2004). *Evolutionary psychology* (2nd ed.). Boston: Allyn & Bacon.

Butler, S. M., & McMunn, N. D. (2006). *A teacher's guide to classroom assessment.* Thousand Oaks, CA: Corwin.

Byrnes, J. P. (1998). *The nature and development of decision making.* Mahwah, NJ: Erlbaum.

Byrnes, J. P. (2001). *Cognitive development and learning in instructional contexts* (2nd ed.). Boston: Allyn & Bacon.

Byrnes, J. P. (2003). Cognitive development during adolescence. In G. Adams & M. Berzonsky (Eds.), *Blackwell handbook of adolescence.* Malden, MA: Blackwell.

Byrnes, J. P. (2005). The development of regulated decision making. In J. E. Jacobs & P. A. Klaczynski (Eds.), *The development of judgment and decision making in children and adolescents.* Mahwah, NJ: Erlbaum.

C

Cahill, L., Haier, R. J., White, N. S., Fallon, J., Kilparaick, L., Lawrence, C., Potkin, S. G., & Alkire, M. T. (2001). Sex-related differences in amygdala activity during emotionally influenced memory storage. *Neurobiology of Learning and Memory, 75,* 1–9.

Calabrese, R. L., & Schumer, H. (1986). The effects of service activities on adolescent alienation. *Adolescence, 21,* 675–687.

California State Department of Education. (1994). *Golden State examination science portfolio.* Sacramento: California State Department of Education.

Callan, J. E. (2001). Gender development: Psychoanalytic perspectives. In J. Worrel (Ed.), *Encyclopedia of women and gender.* San Diego: Academic Press.

Cameron, J. R. (2001). Negative effects of reward on intrinsic motivation—A limited phenomenon. *Review of Educational Research, 71,* 29–42.

Cameron, J. R., & Pierce, W. D. (1996). The debate about rewards and intrinsic motiva-

tion. *Review of Educational Research, 66,* 39–62.

Cameron, J. R., Hansen, R., & Rosen, D. (1989). Preventing behavioral problems in infancy through temperament assessment and parental support programs. In W. B. Carey & S. C. McDevitt (Eds.), *Clinical and educational applications of temperament research.* Amsterdam: Sets & Zeitlinger.

Camilleri, B. (2005). Dynamic assessment and intervention: Improving children's narrative abilities. *International Journal of Language & Communication Disorders, 40,* 240–242.

Campbell, C. Y. (1988, August 24). Group raps depiction of teenagers. *Boston Globe,* p. 44.

Campbell, D. T., & LeVine, D. T. (1968). Ethnocentrism and intergroup relations. In R. Abelson & others (Eds.), *Theories of cognitive consistency.* Chicago: Rand McNally.

Campbell, F. A. (2006). The malleability of the cognitive development of children of low-income African-American families: Intellectual test performance over twenty-one years. In P. C. Kyllonen, R. D. Roberts, & L. Stankov (Eds.), *Extending intelligence.* Mahwah, NJ: Erlbaum.

Campbell, F. A., Pungello, E. P., Miller-Johnson, S., Burchinal, M., & Ramey, C. T. (2001). The development of cognitive and academic abilities: Growth curves from an early childhood educational experiment. *Developmental Psychology, 37,* 231–243.

Campbell, F. A., & Ramey, C. T. (1994). Effects of early intervention on intellectual and academic achievement: A follow-up study of children from low-income families. *Child Development, 65,* 684–698.

Campbell, L., Campbell, B., & Dickinson, D. (2004). *Teaching and learning through multiple intelligence* (3rd ed.). Boston: Allyn & Bacon.

Campione, J. (2001, April). *Fostering a Community of Learners.* Paper presented at the meeting of the American Educational Research Association, Seattle.

Cardelle-Elawar, M. (1992). Effects of teaching metacognitive skills to students with low mathematics ability. *Teaching and Teacher Education, 8,* 109–121.

Carlson, E. A., Sroufe, L. A., & Egeland, B. (2004). The construction of experience: A longitudinal study of representation and behavior. *Child Development, 75,* 66–83.

Carnegie Corporation. (1996). *Report on education for children 3–10 years of age.* New York: Carnegie Foundation.

Carnegie Council on Adolescent Development. (1995). *Great transitions.* New York: Carnegie Foundation.

Carnegie Foundation. (1989). *Turning points: Preparing youth for the 21st century.* New York: Author.

Carpendale, J. I., & Chandler, M. J. (1996). On the distinction between false belief understanding and subscribing to an interpretive theory of mind. *Child Development, 67,* 1686–1706.

Carpenter, T. P., Lindquist, M. M., Matthews, W., & Silver, E. A. (1983). Results of the Third NAEP Mathematics Assessment: Secondary school. *Mathematics Teachers, 76* (9), 652–659.

Carpenter-Aeby, T., & Aeby, V. G. (2001). Family-school-community interventions for chronically disruptive students: An evaluation of outcomes in an alternative school. *School Community Journal, 11*(2), 75–92.

Carroll, J. (1993). *Human cognitive abilities.* Cambridge: Cambridge University Press.

Carroll, J. B. (1963). A model of school learning. *Teachers College Record, 64,* 723–733.

Carver, S. M., & Klahr, D. (Eds.). (2001). *Cognition and instruction.* Mahwah, NJ: Erlbaum.

Casbergue, R. M., & Harris, K. (1996). Listening and literacy: Audiobooks in the reading program. *Reading Horizons, 37,* 48–59.

Case, R. (2000). Conceptual structures. In M. Bennett (Ed.), *Developmental psychology.* Philadelphia: Psychology Press.

Caspi, A., Henry, B., McGee, R. O., Moffitt, T. E., & Silva, P. A. (1995). Temperamental origins of child and adolescent behavior problems: From age three to age fifteen. *Child Development, 66,* 55–68.

Castellano, J. A., & Diaz, E. (Eds.), (2002). *Reaching new horizons: Gifted and talented education for culturally and linguistically diverse students.* Boston: Allyn & Bacon.

Cathcart, G. G., Pothier, Y. M., Vance, J. H., & Bezuk, N. S. (2006). *Learning math in elementary and middle school & IMAP package* (4th ed.). Upper Saddle River, NJ: Prentice Hall.

Cave, R. K. (2002, August). *Early adolescent language: A content analysis of child development and educational psychology textbooks.* Unpublished doctoral dissertation, University of Nevada–Reno, Reno.

Ceci, S. J., & Gilstrap, L. L. (2000). Determinants of intelligence: Schooling and intelligence. In A. Kazdin (Ed.), *Encyclopedia of psychology.* Washington, DC, & New York: American Psychological Association and Oxford University Press.

Ceci, S. J., & Williams, W. M. (1997). Schooling, intelligence, and income. *American Psychologist, 52,* 1051–1058.

Center for Instructional Technology. (2006). Writing multiple-choice questions that demand critical thinking. Retrieved January 12, 2006, from http://cit.necc.mass.edu/atlt/TestCritThink.htm

Chall, J. S. (1979). The great debate: Ten years later with a modest proposal for reading stages. In L. B. Resnick & P. A. Weaver (Eds.), *Theory and practice of early reading.* Mahwah, NJ: Erlbaum.

Chan, W. S. (1963). *A source book in Chinese philosophy.* Princeton, NJ: Princeton University Press.

Chance, P. (2006). *Learning and behavior: Active Learning Edition.* Belmont, CA: Wadsworth.

Chandler, L. K., & Dahlquist, C. (2006). *Functional assessment to prevent and remediate challenging behavior in school settings* (2nd ed.). Upper Saddle River, NJ: Prentice Hall.

Chang, F., Dell, G. S., & Bock, K. (2006). Becoming syntactic. *Psychological Review, 113,* 234–272.

Chao, R. K. (2001). Extending research on the consequences of parenting style for Chinese Americans and European Americans. *Child Development, 72,* 1832–1843.

Chao, R. K. (2005, April). *The importance of guan in describing the parental control of immigrant Chinese.* Paper presented at the meeting of the Society for Research in Child Development, Atlanta.

Chao, R. K., & Tseng, V. (2002). Parenting of Asians. In M. H. Bornstein (Series Ed.), *Handbook of parenting: Vol. 4. Social conditions and applied parenting* (2nd ed.). Mahwah, NJ: Erlbaum.

Chapin, J. R. (2006). *Elementary social studies* (6th ed.). Boston: Allyn & Bacon.

Chapin, J. R., & Messick, R. G. (2002). *Elementary social studies* (5th ed.). Boston: Allyn & Bacon.

Chapman, J. W., Tunmer, W. E., & Prochnow, J. E. (2001). Does success in the Reading Recovery program depend on developing proficiency in phonological-processing skills? A longitudinal study in the whole language instructional context. *Scientific Studies of Reading, 15,* 141–176.

Chapman, O. L. (2000). Learning science involves language, experience, and modeling. *Journal of Applied Developmental Psychology, 21,* 97–108.

Charles, C. M. (2005). *Building classroom discipline* (8th ed.). Boston: Allyn & Bacon.

Charles, C. M., & Sentar, G. W. (2005). *Elementary classroom management* (4th ed.). Boston: Allyn & Bacon.

Charney, R. S. (2005). *Exploring the first "R": To reinforce.* Retrieved November, 15, 2005, from http://www.nea.org/classmanagement/ifc050201.html

Chatterji, M. (2003). *Designing and using tools for educational assessment.* Boston: Allyn & Bacon.

Chen, C., & Stevenson, H. W. (1989). Homework: A cross-cultural comparison. *Child Development, 60,* 551–561.

Chen, Z., & Mo, L. (2004). Schema induction in problem solving: A multidimensional analysis. *Journal of Experimental Psychology: Learning, Memory, and Cognition, 30,* 583–600.

Chess, S., & Thomas, A. (1977). Temperamental individuality from childhood to adolescence. *Journal of Child Psychiatry, 16,* 218–226.

Chi, M. T. H. (1978). Knowledge structures and memory development. In R. S. Siegler (Ed.), *Children's thinking.* Mahwah, NJ: Erlbaum.

Chiappe, D., & MacDonald, K. (2005). The evolution of domain-general mechanisms in intelligence and learning. *Journal of General Psychology, 132,* 5–40.

Chiappetta, E. L., & Koballa, T. R. (2006). *Science instruction in the middle and secondary schools* (6th ed.). Upper Saddle River, NJ: Prentice Hall.

Child Trends. (2006). *Dropout rates.* Retrieved April 30, 2006, from http://www.childtrendsdatabank.org/indicators/1HighSchoolDropout.cfm

Children's Defense Fund. (1992). *The state of America's children.* Washington, DC: Author.

Chira, S. (1993, June 23). What do teachers want most? Help from parents. *New York Times,* sec. 1, p. 7.

Choi, N. (2004). Sex role group differences in specific, academic, and general self-efficacy. *Journal of Psychology, 138,* 149–159.

Choi, N. (2005). Self-efficacy and self-concept as predictors of college students' academic performance. *Psychology in the Schools, 42,* 197–205.

Chomsky, N. (1957). *Syntactic structures.* The Hague: Mouton.

Christenson, S. L., & Thurlow, M. L. (2004). School dropouts: Prevention considerations, interventions, and challenges. *Current Directions in Psychological Science, 13,* 36–39.

Christian, K., Bachnan, H. J., & Morrison, F. J. (2001). Schooling and cognitive development. In R. J. Sternberg & E. L.

Grigorenko (Eds.), *Environmental effects on cognitive abilities.* Mahwah, NJ: Erlbaum.

Chronis, A. M., Chacko, A., Fabiano, G. A., Wymbs, B. T., & Pelham, W. E. (2004). Enhancements to the behavioral parent training paradigm for families of children with ADHD: Review and future directions. *Clinical Child and Family Psychology Review, 7,* 1–27.

Chun, K. M., Organista, P. B., & Marin, G. (Eds.). (2002). *Acculturation.* Washington, DC: American Psychological Association.

Clark, K. B., & Clark, M. P. (1939). The development of the self and the emergence of racial identification in Negro preschool children. *Journal of Social Psychology, 10,* 591–599.

Clark, L. (Ed.). (1993). *Faculty and student challenges in facing cultural and linguistic diversity.* Springfield, IL: Charles C Thomas.

Clark, T. (2001). *Virtual schools: Status and trends.* Phoenix, AZ: West Ed.

Clay, M. M. (1985). *The early detection of reading difficulties* (3rd ed.). Portsmouth, NH: Heinemann.

Coben, S. S., Thomas, C. C., Sattler, R. O., & Morsink, C. V. (1997). Meeting the challenge of consultation and collaboration: Developing interactive teams. *Journal of Learning Disabilities, 30,* 427–432.

Cochran, M., Larner, M., Riley, D., Gunnarson, L., & Henderson, C. (1990). *Extending families: The social networks of parents and their children.* New York: Cambridge University Press.

Cochran-Smith, M. (1995). Color blindness and basket making are not the answers: Confronting the dilemmas of race, culture, and language diversity in teacher education. *American Educational Research Journal, 32,* 493–522.

Cocking, R. R., Mestre, J. P., & Brown, A. L. (2000). New developments in the use of science learning: Using research to help students learn science and mathematics. *Journal of Applied Developmental Psychology, 21,* 1–11.

Coffin, L. (1996). Commentary in "The latest on student portfolios." *NEA Today, 17,* 18.

Cognition and Technology Group at Vanderbilt. (1997). *The Jasper Project.* Mahwah, NJ: Erlbaum.

Cohen, D., & others. (2005). Specific gene disorders and autism. *Journal of Autism and Developmental Disorders, 35,* 103–116.

Cohen, G. L., & Sherman, D. K. (2005). Stereotype threat and the social and scientific contexts of the race achievement gap. *American Psychologist, 60,* 270–271.

Cohen, L. B., & Cashon, C. H. (2006). Infant cognition. In W. Damon & R. Lerner (Eds.), *Handbook of child psychology* (6th ed.). New York: Wiley.

Cohn, A., & Canter, A. (2003). *Bullying: Facts for schools and parents.* Washington, DC: National Association of School Psychologists.

Coie, J. D., & Dodge, K. A. (1998). Aggression and antisocial behavior. In W. Damon (Ed.), *Handbook of child psychology* (Vol. 3). New York: Wiley.

Coladarci, T. (1992). Teachers' sense of efficacy and commitment to teaching. *Journal of Experimental Education, 60,* 323–337.

Colangelo, N., & Davis, G. A. (2003). *Handbook of gifted education* (3rd ed.). Boston: Allyn & Bacon.

Colangelo, N. C., Assouline, S. G., & Gross, M. U. M. (2004). *A nation deceived: How schools hold back America's brightest students.* Retrieved February 12, 2005, from http://nationdeceived.org/

Colby, A., Kohlberg, L., Gibbs, J., & Lieberman, M. (1983). A longitudinal study of moral judgment. *Monographs of the Society for Research in Child Development, 48* (21, Serial No. 201).

Colby, S. A. (1999, March). Grading in a standard-based system. *Educational Leadership, 56,* 52–55.

Cole, C. F., Arafat, C., Tidhar, C., Tafesh, W. Z., Fox, N. A., Killen, M., Ardila-Rey, A. Leavitt, L. A., Lesser, G., Richman, B. A., & Yung, F. (2003). The educational impact of Rechov Sumsum/Shar's Simsim: A *Sesame Street* television series to promote respect and understanding among children living in Israel, the West Bank, and Gaza. *International Journal of Behavioural Development, 27,* 409–423.

Cole, C. M., Waldron, N., & Majid, M. (2004). Academic progress of students across inclusive and traditional settings. *Mental Retardation, 42,* 136–144.

Cole, M. (2005). Culture in development. In M. H. Bornstein & M. E. Lamb (Eds.), *Developmental science* (5th ed.). Mahwah, NJ: Erlbaum.

Cole, M. (2006). Culture and cognitive development in phylogenetic, historical, and ontogenetic perspective. In W. Damon & R. Lerner (Eds.), *Handbook of child psychology* (6th ed.). New York: Wiley.

Cole, M., Cole, S. R., & Lightfoot, C. (2005). *The development of children* (5th ed.). New York: Worth.

Coleman, M. C., & Webber, J. (2002). *Emotional and behavioral disorders* (4th ed.). Boston: Allyn & Bacon.

Coley, R. (2001). *Differences in the gender gap: Comparisons across/racial/ethnic groups in the United States.* Princeton, NJ: Educational Testing Service.

Coley, R. L., Morris, J. E., & Hernandez, D. (2004). Out-of-school care and problem behavior trajectories among low-income adolescents: Individual, family, and neighborhood characteristics as added risks. *Child Development, 75,* 948–965.

College Board. (2004). *2003 college-bound seniors tables and related items.* Princeton, NJ: College Board.

Collins, A. (2006). Cognitive apprenticeship. In R. K. Sawyer (Ed.), *The Cambridge handbook of the learning sciences.* New York: Cambridge University Press.

Collins, M. (1996, Winter). The job outlook for '96 grads. *Journal of Career Planning,* pp. 51–54.

Collins, W. A., & Steinberg, L. (2006). Adolescent development in interpersonal context. In W. Damon & R. Lerner (Eds.), *Handbook of child psychology* (6th ed.). New York: Wiley.

Collis, B. A., Knezek, G. A., Lai, K. W., Miyashita, K. T., Pelgrum, W. J., Plomp, T., & Sakamoto, T. (1996). *Children and computers in school.* Mahwah, NJ: Erlbaum.

Combs, D. (1997, September). Using alternative assessment to provide options for student success. *Middle School Journal,* pp. 3–8.

Comer, J. P. (1988). Educating poor minority children. *Scientific American, 259,* 42–48.

Comer, J. P. (2004). *Leave no child behind.* New Haven, CT: Yale University Press.

Comer, J. P. (2005). Child and adolescent development: The critical missing focus in school reform. *Phi Delta Kappan, 86,* 757–763.

Comer, J. P. (2006). Child development: The under-weighted aspect of intelligence. In P. C. Kyllonen, R. D. Roberts, & L. Stankov (Eds.), *Extending intelligence.* Mahwah, NJ: Erlbaum.

Comer, J. P., Haynes, N. M., Joyner, E. T., & Ben-Avie, M. (1996). *Rallying the whole village: The Comer process for reforming urban education.* New York: Teachers College Press.

Comstock, G., & Scharrer, E. (2006). Media and popular culture. In W. Damon & R. Lerner (Eds.), *Handbook of child psychology* (6th ed.). New York: Wiley.

Connors, L. J., & Epstein, J. L. (1995). Parent and school partnerships. In M. Bornstein (Ed.), *Handbook of parenting* (Vol. 2). Mahwah, NJ: Erlbaum.

Conti, R. (2001). Motivational change and transition in the transition from primary school to secondary school. In C. Y. Chiu, F. Salilli, & Y. Hong (Eds.), *Multiple competencies and self-regulated learning.* Greenwich, CT: IAP.

Cooper, C. R. (1995, March). *Multiple selves, multiple worlds.* Paper presented at the meeting of the Society for Research in Child Development, Indianapolis.

Cooper, E., & Sherk, J. (1989). Addressing urban school reform: Issues and alliances, *Journal of Negro Education, 58,* 315–331.

Cooper, H. (1998, April). *Family, student, and assignment characteristics of positive homework experiences.* Paper presented at the meeting of the American Educational Research Association, San Diego.

Cooper, H. (1989). Synthesis of research on homework. *Educational Leadership, 47*(3), 85–91.

Cooper, H., Lindsay, J. J., Nye, B., & Greathouse, S. (1998). Relationships among attitudes about homework, amount of homework assigned and completed, and student achievement. *Journal of Educational Psychology, 90,* 70–83.

Cooper, H., & Valentine, J. C. (2001). Using research to answer practical questions about homework. *Educational Psychologist, 36,* 143–153.

Cooper, J. E., Horn, S., & Strahan, D. B. (2005). "If only they would do their homework": Promoting self-regulation in high school English classes. *High School Journal, 88,* 10–25.

Copeland, L. (2003, December). Science teacher just wanted to do some good, and he has. *USA Today.* Retrieved from www.usatoday.com/news/education/2003-12-30-laster-usal_x.htm

Corno, L. (1998, March 30). Commentary. *Newsweek,* p. 51.

Cote, J. E. (2006). Emerging adulthood as an institutional moratorium: Risks and benefits to identity formation. In J. J. Arnett & J. L. Tanner (Eds.), *Emerging adults in America.* Washington, DC: American Psychological Association.

Council for Exceptional Children. (1998). *CECs comments on the proposed IDEA regulations.* Washington, DC: Author.

Council of Chief State School Officers. (2005). *Marilyn Jachetti Whirry.* Retrieved November 12, 2005, from http://www.ccsso.org/

Covington, M. V., & Dray, E. (2002). The development course of achievement motivation: A need-based approach. In A. Wigfield & J. S. Eccles (Eds.), *Development of achievement motivation.* San Diego: Academic Press.

Covington, M. V., & Teel, K. T. (1996). *Overcoming student failure.* Washington, DC: American Psychological Association.

Craik, F. I. M., & Lockhart, R. S. (1972). Levels of processing: A framework for memory research. *Journal of Verbal Learning and Verbal Behavior, 11,* 671–684.

Crane, C. (2001). General classroom space. *School Planning and Management, 40,* 54–55.

Crawford, M., & Unger, R. (2004). *Women and gender* (3rd ed.) New York: McGraw-Hill.

Cress, S. W. (2004). Assessing standards in the "real" kindergarten classroom. *Early Childhood Education Journal, 32,* 95–99.

Creswell, J. (2005). *Educational research* (2nd ed.). Boston: Pearson Education.

Crick, N. R., Ostrov, J. M., & Werner, N. E. (2006, in press). A longitudinal study of relational aggression, physical aggression, and children's social-psychological adjustment. *Journal of Abnormal Child Psychology.*

Crowley, K., Callahan, M. A., Tenenbaum, H. R., & Allen, E. (2001). Parents explain more to boys than to girls during shared scientific thinking. *Psychological Science, 12,* 258–261.

Cruz, B. C., & Duplass, J. A. (2007). *The elementary teacher's guide to the best Internet resources.* Upper Saddle River, NJ: Prentice Hall.

Csikszentmihalyi, M. (1990). *Flow.* New York: Harper & Row.

Csikszentmihalyi, M. (1993). *The evolving self.* New York: HarperCollins.

Csikszentmihalyi, M. (2000). Creativity: An overview. In A. Kazdin (Ed.), *Encyclopedia of psychology.* Washington, DC, & New York: American Psychological Association and Oxford University Press.

Csikszentmihalyi, M., Rathunde, K., & Whalen, S. (1993). *Talented teenagers: The roots of success and failure.* Cambridge, UK: Cambridge University Press.

Culbertson, F. M. (1997). Depression and gender. *American Psychologist, 52,* 25–31.

Culbertson, L. D., & Jalongo, M. R. (1999). "But what's wrong with letter grades?" Responding to parents questions about alternative assessments. *Childhood Education, 75,* 130–135.

Cullen, M. J., Hardison, C. M., & Sackett, P. R. (2004). Using SAT-grade and ability-job performance relationships to test predictions derived from stereotype threat theory. *Journal of Applied Psychology, 89,* 220–230.

Cunningham, C. A., & Billingsley, M. (2006). *Curriculum webs* (2nd ed.). Boston: Allyn & Bacon.

Cunningham, P. M. (2005). *Phonics they use* (4th ed.). Boston: Allyn & Bacon.

Curran, K., DuCette, J., Eisenstein, J., & Hyman, I. A. (2001, August). *Statistical analysis of the cross-cultural data: The third year.* Paper presented at the meeting of the American Psychological Association, San Francisco.

Curtis, M. E., & Longo, A. M. (2001, November). Teaching vocabulary development to adolescents to improve comprehension. Retrieved April 26, 2006, from http://www.readingonline.org/articles/curtis/

Cushner, K. H. (2006). *Human diversity in action* (3rd ed.). New York: McGraw-Hill.

D

Dahl, R. E. (2004). Adolescent brain development: A period of vulnerabilities and opportunities. *Annals of the New York Academy of Sciences, 1021,* 1–22.

Daley, D. (2006). Attention deficit hyperactivity disorder: A review of the essential facts. *Child: Care, Health, and Development, 32,* 193–204.

Damon, W. (1995). *Greater expectations.* New York: Free Press.

Dansereau, D. F. (1988). Cooperative learning strategies, In C. E. Weinstein, E. T. Goetz, & P. A. Alexander (Eds.), *Learning and study strategies.* Orlando, FL: Academic Press.

Dao, T. K., Kerbs, J. J., Rollin, S. A., Potts, I., Gutierrez, R., Choi, K., Creason, A. H., Wolf, A., & Prevatt, F. (2006). The association of bullying dynamics and psychological distress. *Journal of Adolescent Health, 39,* 277–282.

Darling-Hammond, L. (2001, August). *What's at stake in high-stakes testing?* Paper presented at the meeting of the American Psychological Association, San Francisco.

Darling-Hammond, L. (2006). Assessing teacher education. *Journal of Teacher Education, 57,* 120–138.

Darling-Hammond, L., Banks, J., Zumwalt, K., Gomez, L., Sherin, M. G., Griesdorn, J., & Finn, L-E. (2005). Educational goals and purposes: Developing a curricular vision for education. In L. Darling-Hammond & J. Bransford (Eds.), *Preparing teachers for a changing world.* San Francisco: Jossey-Bass.

Darling-Hammond, L., & Baratz-Snowden, J. (Eds.). (2005). *A good teacher in every classroom: Preparing the highly qualified teachers our children deserve.* San Francisco: Jossey-Bass.

Darling-Hammond, L., & Bransford, J. (Eds.). (2005). *Preparing teachers for a changing world.* San Francisco: Jossey-Bass.

Das, J. P. (2000). Mental retardation. In A. Kazdin (Ed.), *Encyclopedia of psychology.*

Washington, DC, & New York: American Psychological Association and Oxford University Press.

Dauite, C. (2001). Social relational knowing in writing development. In J. Byrnes & E. Amsel (Eds.), *Language, literacy, and cognitive development.* Mahwah, NJ: Erlbaum.

Davidson, D. (1996). The effects of decision characteristics on children's selective search of predecisional information. *Acta Psychologica, 92,* 263–281.

Davidson, J. (2000). Giftedness. In A. Kazdin (Ed.), *Encyclopedia of psychology.* Washington, DC, & New York: American Psychological Association and Oxford University Press.

Davidson, G. C., & Neale, J. M. (2007). *Abnormal psychology* (10th ed.). New York: Wiley.

Davidson, J., & Davidson, B. (2004). *Genius denied: How to stop wasting our brightest young minds.* New York: Simon & Schuster.

Davies, J., & Brember, I. (1999). Reading and mathematics attainments and self-esteem in years 2 and 6—an eight-year cross-sectional study. *Educational Studies, 25,* 145–157.

Davis, A. E., Hyatt, G., & Arrasmith, D. (1998, February). "I Have a Dream" program. *Class One Evaluation Report.* Portland, OR: Northwest Regional Education Laboratory.

Davis, G. A., & Rimm, S. B. (2004). *Education of the gifted and talented* (6th ed.). Boston: Allyn & Bacon.

De Corte, E., & Verschaffel, L. (2006). Mathematical thinking and learning. In W. Damon & R. Lerner (Eds.), *Handbook of child psychology* (6th ed.). New York: Wiley.

de Jong, T., Beishuizen, J., Hulshof, C., Prins, F., van Rijn, H., van Someren, M., Veenman, M., & Wilhelm, P. (2005). Determinants of discovery learning in a complex simulation learning environment. In P. Gardenfors & P. Johansson (Eds.), *Cognition, education, and communication technology.* Mahwah, NJ: Erlbaum.

De Raad, B. (2005). The trait-coverage of emotional intelligence. *Personality & Individual Differences, 38,* 673–687.

de Vries, P. (2005). Lessons from home: Scaffolding vocal improvisation and song acquisition in a 2-year-old. *Early Childhood Education Journal, 32,* 307–312.

deCharms, R. (1984). Motivation enhancement in educational settings. In R. Ames & C. Ames (Eds.), *Research on motivation in education* (Vol. 1). Orlando: Academic Press.

Deci, E. L. (1975). *Intrinsic motivation.* New York: Plenum.

Deci, E. L., Koestner, R., & Ryan, R. M. (2001). Extrinsic rewards and intrinsic motivation in education: Reconsidered once again. *Review of Educational Research, 71,* 1–28.

Deci, E. L., & Ryan, R. (1994). Promoting self-determined education. *Scandinavian Journal of Educational Research, 38,* 3–14.

Delisle, J. R. (1987). *Gifted kids speak out.* Minneapolis: Free Spirit Publishing.

Demaree, H. A., Everhart, D. E., Youngstrom, E. A., & Harrison, D. W. (2005). Brain lateralization of emotional processing: Historical roots and a future incorporating dominance. *Behavioral and Cognitive Neuroscience Reviews, 4,* 3–20.

DeMirjyn, M. (2006, April). *Surviving the system: Narratives of Chicana/Latina undergraduates.* Paper presented at the meeting of the American Educational Research Association, San Francisco.

Dempster, F. N. (1981). Memory span: Sources of individual and developmental differences. *Psychological Bulletin, 89,* 63–100.

Denny, C. B. (2001). Stimulant effects in attention deficit hyperactivity disorder. *Journal of Clinical Child Psychology, 30,* 98–109.

DeRaad, B. (2005). The trait-coverage of emotional intelligence. *Personality & Individual Differences, 38,* 673–687.

Derman-Sparks, L., & the Anti-Bias Curriculum Task Force. (1989). *Anti-bias curriculum.* Washington, DC: National Association for the Education of Young Children.

DeRosier, M. E., & Marcus, S. R. (2005). Building friendships and combating bullying: Effectiveness of S. S. GRIN at one-year follow-up. *Journal of Clinical Child and Adolescent Psychology, 34,* 140–150.

Desberg, P., & Fisher, F. (2001). *Teaching with technology* (3rd ed.). Boston: Allyn & Bacon.

Detterman, D. K. (2000). Determinants of intelligence: Heritability of intelligence. In A. Kazdin (Ed.), *Encyclopedia of psychology.* Washington, DC, & New York: American Psychological Association and Oxford University Press.

Dettmer, P., Dyck, N., & Thurston, L. P. (2002). *Consultation, collaboration, and teamwork for students with special needs* (4th ed.). Boston: Allyn & Bacon.

Dewey, J. (1933). *How we think.* Lexington, MA: D. C. Heath.

DeZolt, D. M., & Hull, S. H. (2001). Classroom and school climate. In J. Worell (Ed.), *Encyclopedia of women and gender.* San Diego: Academic Press.

Diaz, C. (1997). Unpublished review of J. W. Santrock's *Educational psychology.* New York: McGraw-Hill.

Diaz, C. (2001). *Multicultural education in the 21st century.* Boston: Allyn & Bacon.

Diaz, C. (2005). Unpublished review of J. W. Santrock's *Educational psychology* (3rd ed.). New York: McGraw-Hill.

Diaz, C. F., Pelletier, C. M., & Provenzo, E. F. (2006). *Touch the future . . . teach!* Boston: Allyn & Bacon.

Dick, F., Dronkers, N. F., Pizzamiglio, L., Saygin, A. P., Small, S. L., & Wilson, S. (2005). Language and the brain. In M. Tomasello & D. A. Slobin (Eds.), Beyond nature-nurture. Mahwah, NJ: Erlbaum.

Dick, F., Leech, R., Moses, P., & Saccuman, M. C. (2006). The interplay of learning and development in shaping neural organization. *Developmental Science, 9,* 14–16.

Dick, W. O., Carey, L., & Carey, J. O. (2005). *The systematic design of instruction* (6th ed.). Boston: Allyn & Bacon.

Dickinson, D. (1998). *How technology enhances Howard Gardners eight intelligences.* Available at www.america-tomorrow.com/ati/nhl80402.htm

Diener, E., & Diener, M. (1995). Cross-cultural and self-esteem. *Journal of Personality and* 663.

Dill, E. J., Vernberg, E. M., & Fonagy, P. (2004). Negative affect in victimized children. *Journal of Abnormal Psychology, 32,* 159–173.

Dobkin, B. A., & Pace, R. (2006). *Communication in a changing world.* New York: McGraw-Hill.

Dodge, K. A., Coie, J. D., & Lynam, D. R. (2006). Aggression and antisocial behavior in youth. In W. Damon & R. Lerner (Eds.), *Handbook of child psychology* (6th ed.). New York: Wiley.

Doe, C. G. (2004). A look at . . . Web-based assessment. *Multimedia Schools, 11*(2), 1–6.

Dolan, L. J., Jaylan, T., Werthamer, L., & Kellam, S. (1989). *The good behavior game manual.* Baltimore: The Johns Hopkins Prevention Research Center.

Domino, G. (2000). *Psychological testing.* Upper Saddle River, NJ: Prentice Hall.

Domjan, M. (2006). *The principles of learning and behavior* (5th ed.). Belmont, CA: Wadsworth.

Donovan, M. S., & Bransford, J. D. (2005). Introduction. In M. S. Donovan & J. D. Bransford (Eds.), *How students learn.* Washington, DC: National Academies Press.

Doseis, S., Zito, J. M., Safer, D. J., Soeken, K. L., Mitchell, J. W., Ellwood, L. C. (2003).

Parental perceptions and satisfaction with stimulant medication for attention deficit hyperactivity disorder. *Journal of Developmental and Behavioral Pediatrics, 24,* 155–162.

Douglass, M. E., & Douglass, D. N. (1993). *Manage your work yourself* (updated ed.). New York: American Management Association.

Doyle, W. (1986). Classroom organization and management. In M. C. Wittrock (Ed.), *Handbook of research on teaching* (3rd ed.). New York: Macmillan.

Doyle, W. (2006). Ecological approaches to classroom management. In C. M. Evertson & C. S. Weinstein (Eds.), *Handbook of classroom management.* Mahwah, NJ: Erlbaum.

Droege, K. L. (2004). Turning accountability on its head. *Phi Delta Kappan, 85,* 610–612.

Drummond, R. J. (2000). *Appraisal procedures for counselors and helping professionals* (4th ed.). Upper Saddle River, NJ: Merrill.

Dubois, D. L., Holloway, B. E., Valentine, J. C., & Cooper, H. (2002). Effectiveness of mentoring programs for youth: A meta-analytical review. In S. W. Lee (Ed.), *Encyclopedia of school psychology.* Thousand Oaks, CA: Sage.

Dubois, D. L., & Karcher, M. J, (Eds.). (2006). *Handbook of youth mentoring.* Thousand Oaks, CA: Sage.

Dufrene, B. A., Noell, G. H., Gilbertson, D. N., & Duhon, G. J. (2005). Monitoring implementation of reciprocal peer tutoring: Identifying and intervening with students who do not maintain accurate implementation. *School Psychology Review, 34,* 74–86.

Duke, D. L. (2006). What we know and don't know about improving low-performance schools. *Phi Delta Kappan, 87,* 729–734.

Dunn, L., & Kontos, S. (1997). What have we learned about developmentally appropriate practice? *Young Children, 52* (2), 4–13.

Durham, Q. (2006). *The realities of classroom testing and grading.* Lanham, MD: Rowman & Littlefield.

Dweck, C. S. (1996). Social motivation: Goals and social-cognitive processes. In J. Juvonen & K. R. Wentzel (Eds.), *Social motivation.* New York: Cambridge University Press.

Dweck, C. S. (2002). The development of ability conceptions. In A. Wigfield & J. S. Eccles (Eds.), *Development of achievement motivation.* San Diego: Academic Press.

Dweck, C. S., & Elliott, E. (1983). Achievement motivation. In P. Mussen (Ed.), *Handbook of child psychology* (4th ed., Vol. 4). New York: Wiley.

Dweck, C. S., & Leggett, E. (1988). A social cognitive approach to motivation and personality. *Psychological Review, 95,* 256–273.

Dweck, C. S., Mangels, J. A., & Good, C. (2004). Motivational effects on attention, cognition, and performance. In D. Yun Dai & R. J. Sternberg (Eds.), *Motivation, emotion, and cognition.* Mahwah, NJ: Erlbaum.

E

Eagly, A. H. (2001). Social role theory of sex differences and similarities. In J. Worell (Ed.), *Encyclopedia of women and gender.* San Diego: Academic Press.

Eagly, A. H., & Crowley, M. (1986). Gender and helping behavior: A meta-analytic review of the social psychological literature. *Psychological Bulletin, 100,* 283–308.

Eagly, A. H. & Diekman, A. B. (2003). The malleability of sex differences in response to social roles. In L. G. Aspinwall & V. M. Staudinger (Eds.), *A psychology of human strengths.* Washington, DC: American Psychological Association.

Eagly, A. H., & Steffen, V. J. (1986). Gender and aggressive behavior: A meta-analytic review of the social psychological literature. *Psychological Bulletin, 100,* 309–330.

Eamon, M. K. (2002). Effects of poverty on mathematics and reading achievement of young adolescents. *Journal of Early Adolescence, 22,* 49–74.

Earl, E. A. (2006). Assessment as learning. In W. D. Hawley (Ed.), *Educational reform as continuous improvement.* Thousand Oaks, CA: Corwin.

Eby, J. W., Herrell, A., & Jordan, M. L. (2006). *Teaching K–12 schools: A reflective action approach* (4th ed.). Upper Saddle River, NJ: Prentice Hall.

Eccles, J. S. (1987). Gender roles and womens achievement-related decisions. *Psychology of Women Quarterly, 11,* 135–172.

Eccles, J. S. (1993). School and family effects on the ontogeny of children's interests, self-perceptions, and activity choice. In J. Jacobs (Ed.), *Nebraska symposium on motivation.* Lincoln: University of Nebraska Press.

Eccles, J. S. (2004). Schools, academic motivation, and stage-environment fit. In R. Lerner & L. Steinberg (Eds.), *Handbook of adolescent psychology,* (2nd ed.). New York: Wiley.

Eccles, J. S., Jacobs, J., Harold, R., Yoon, K., Aberbach, A., & Dolan, C. F. (1991, August).

Expectancy effects are alive and well on the home front. Paper presented at the meeting of the American Psychological Association, San Francisco.

Eccles, J. S., Lord, S., & Buchanan, C. M. (1996). School transitions in early adolescence: What are we doing to our young people? In J. A. Graeber, J. Brooks-Gunn, & A. C. Petersen (Eds.), *Transitions in adolescence.* Mahwah, NJ: Erlbaum.

Eccles, J. S., & Wigfield, A. (2002). Motivational beliefs, values, and goals. *Annual Review of Psychology* (Vol. 53). Palo Alto, CA: Annual Reviews.

Eccles, J. S., Wigfield, A., Harold, R., & Blumenfeld, P. B. (1993). Age and gender differences in children's self- and task-perceptions during elementary school. *Child Development, 64,* 830–847.

Eccles, J. S., Wigfield, A., & Schiefele, U. (1998). Motivation to succeed. In W. Damon (Ed.), *Handbook of child psychology* (5th ed., Vol. 3). New York: Wiley.

Echevarria, J., & Graves, A. (2007). *Sheltered content instruction* (3rd ed.). Boston: Allyn & Bacon.

Educational Cyber Playground. (2006). *Ringleader Alan Haskvitz.* Retrieved July 1, 2006, from http://www.edu-cyberpg.com/ringleaders/al.html

Educational Testing Service. (1994). *Taking the SAT I reasoning test.* Princeton, NJ: College Board SAT Program.

Educational Testing Service. (2002). *Differences in the gender gap.* Princeton: Author.

Edwards, P. A. (1989). Supporting lower SES mothers' attempts to provide scaffolding for book reading. In J. Allen & J. M. Mason (Eds.), *Risk makers, risk takers: Reducing the risks for young literacy learners.* Portsmouth, NH: Heinemann Educational Books.

Edwards, P. A. (2004). *Children's literacy development.* Boston: Allyn & Bacon.

Edwards, R., & Hamilton, M. A. (2004). You need to understand my gender role: An empirical test of Tannen's model of gender and communication. *Sex Roles, 50,* 491–504.

Eggleton, T. (2001). Discipline in the schools. *ERIC Digest,* ED451554.

Ehri, L., Nunes, S., Stahl. S., & Willows. D. (2001). Systematic phonics instruction helps students learn to read: Evidence from the National Reading Panel's meta-analysis. *Review of Educational Research, 71,* 393–447.

Eisenberg, N. (1986). *Altruistic emotion, cognition, and behavior.* Hillsdale, N.J: Erlbaum.

Eisenberg, N., & Fabes, R. A. (1998). Prosocial development. In N. Eisenberg (Ed.), *Handbook of child psychology* (5th ed., Vol. 3). New York: Wiley.

Eisenberg, N., Fabes, R. A., & Spinrad, T. L. (2006). Prosocial development. In W. Damon & R. Lerner (Eds.), *Handbook of child psychology* (6th ed.). New York: Wiley.

Eisenberg, N., Guthrie, I. K., Fabes, R. A., Shepard, S., Losoya, S., Murphy, B. C., & others. (2000). Prediction of elementary school children's externalizing problem behaviors from attentional and behavioral regulation and negative emotionality. *Child Development, 71*, 1367–1382.

Eisenberg, N., Martin, C. L., & Fabes, R. A. (1996). Gender development and gender effects. In D. C. Berliner & R. C. Calfee (Eds.), *Handbook of educational psychology,* New York: Macmillan.

Eisenberg, N., & Morris, A. S. (2004). Moral cognitions and prosocial responding in adolescence. In R. Lerner & L. Steinberg (Eds.), *Handbook of adolescent psychology* (2nd ed.). New York: Wiley.

Eisenberg, N., Spinrad, T. L., & Smith, C. L. (2004). Emotion-related regulation: Its conceptualization, relations to social functioning, and socialization. In P. Philippot & R. S. Feldman (Eds.), *The regulation of emotion.* Mahwah, NJ: Erlbaum.

Eisner, E. W. (1999, May). The uses and limits of performance assessment. *Phi Delta Kappan, 80*, 658–661.

Elder, G. H., & Shanahan, M. J. (2006). The life course and human development. In W. Damon & R. Lerner (Eds.), *Handbook of child psychology* (6th ed.). New York: Wiley.

Elias, M. J., & Schwab, Y. (2006). From compliance to responsibility: Social and emotional learning and classroom management. In C. Evertson & C. Weinstein (Eds.) *Handbook of classroom management: Research, practice, and contemporary issues.* Mahwah, NJ: Erlbaum.

Elias, M. J., Gara, M. A., Schuyler, T. F., Branden-Muller, L. R., & Sayette, M. A. (1991). The promotion of social competence: Longitudinal study of a preventive school-based program. *American Journal of Orthopsychiatry, 61*, 409–417.

Elias, M. J., Gara, M., Ubriaco, M., Rothbaum, P. A., Clabby, J. P., & Schuyler, T. (1986). The impact of a preventive social problem-solving intervention on children's coping with middle-school stressors. *American Journal of Community Psychology, 14*, 259–275.

Elkind, D. (1976). *Child development and education: A Piagetian perspective.* New York: Oxford University Press.

Elkind, D. (1978). Understanding the young adolescent. *Adolescence, 13*, 127–134.

Elkind, D. (2004). Vygotsky's educational theory in cultural context. *Bulletin of the Menninger Clinic, 68*, 352–353.

Ellis, A. (2007). *Teaching and learning elementary social studies* (8th ed.). Boston: Allyn & Bacon.

Elliot, A. J., & Thrash, T. M. (2001). Achievement goals and the hierarchical model of achievement motivation. *Educational Psychology Review, 13*, 139–156.

Ellis, A. K. (2002). *Teaching and learning elementary social studies* (7th ed.). Boston: Allyn & Bacon.

Ellis, H. C. (1987). Recent developments in human memory. In V. P. Makosky (Ed.), *The G. Stanley Hall Lecture Series.* Washington, DC: American Psychological Association.

Ellis, S., Klahr, D., & Siegler, R. S. (1994, April). *The birth, life, and sometimes death of good ideas in collaborative problem-solving.* Paper presented at the meeting of the American Educational Research Association, New Orleans.

Ely, R. (2005). Language and literacy in the school years. In J. Berko Gleason (Ed.), *The development of language* (6th ed.). Boston: Allyn & Bacon.

Emery, R. E., & Laumann-Billings, L. (1998). An overview of the nature, causes, and consequences of abusive family relationships. *American Psychologist, 53*, 121–135.

Emmer, E. T., Evertson, C. M., & Anderson, L. M. (1980). Effective classroom management at the beginning of the school year. *Elementary School Journal, 80*, 219–231.

Emmer, E. T., Evertson, C. M., & Worsham, M. E. (2006). *Classroom management for middle and high school teachers* (7th ed.). Boston: Allyn & Bacon.

Emmer, E. T., & Gerwels, M. C. (2006). Classroom management in middle and high school classrooms. In C. M. Evertson & C. S. Weinstein (Eds.), *Handbook of classroom management.* Mahwah, NJ: Erlbaum.

Emmer, E. T., & Stough, L. M. (2001). Classroom management: A critical part of educational psychology, with implications for teacher education. *Educational Psychologist, 36*, 103–112.

Englert, C. S., Berry, R., & Dunsmore, K. (2001). A case study of the apprenticeship process. *Journal of Learning Disabilities, 34*, 152–171.

Entwisle, D. R., & Alexander, K. L. (1993). Entry into the school: The beginning school transition and educational stratification in the United States. *Annual Review of Sociology, 19*, 401–423.

Epstein, J. L. (1983). Longitudinal effects of family-school-person interactions on student outcomes. *Research in Sociology and Education and Socialization, 4*, 101–127.

Epstein, J. L. (1996). Perspectives and previews on research and policy for school, family, and community partnerships. In A. Booth & J. F. Dunn (Eds.), *Family-school links.* Mahwah, NJ: Erlbaum.

Epstein, J. L. (1998, April). *Interactive homework: Effective strategies to connect home and school.* Paper presented at the meeting of the American Educational Research Association, San Diego.

Epstein, J. L. (2001). *School, family, and community partnerships.* Boulder, CO: Westview Press.

Epstein, J. L. (2005). Results of the Partnership Schools-CSR model for student achievement over three years. *Elementary School Journal, 106*, 151–170.

Epstein, J. L., & Sanders, M. G. (2002). Family, schools, and community partnerships. In M. H. Bornstein (Ed.), *Handbook of parenting* (2nd ed.). Mahwah, NJ: Erlbaum.

Epstein, J. L., Sanders, M. G., Salinas, K. C., Simon, B. S., Jansorn, N. R., & Van Voorhis, F. L. (2002). *School, family, and community partnerships* (2nd ed.). Thousand Oaks, CA: Corwin Press.

Epstein, J. L., & Sheldon, S. B. (2006). Moving forward: Ideas for research on school, family, and community partnerships. In C. F. Conrad & R. Serlin (Eds.), *Sage handbook for research in education.* Thousand Oaks, CA: Sage.

Ercikan, K. (2006). Development in the assessment of student learning. In P. A. Alexander & P. H. Winne (Eds.), *Handbook of educational psychology* (2nd ed.). Mahwah, NJ: Erlbaum.

Ericsson, K. A. (Ed.). (1996). *The road to excellence.* Mahwah, NJ: Erlbaum.

Ericsson, K. A. (2006). The influence of experience and deliberate practice on the development of superior expert performance. In K. A. Ericsson, N. Charness, P. J. Feltovich, & R. R. Hoffman (Eds.), *The Cambridge handbook of expertise and expert performance.* New York: Cambridge University Press.

Ericsson, K. A., Charness, N., Feltovich, P. J., & Hoffman, R. R. (Eds.). (2006). *The Cambridge handbook of expertise and expert performance.* New York: Cambridge University Press.

Ericsson, K. A., Krampe, R. T., & Tesch-Romer, C. (1993). The role of deliberate practice in the acquisition of expert performance. *Psychological Review, 100*, 363–406.

Erikson, E. H. (1968). *Identity: Youth and crisis.* New York: W. W. Norton.

Eslea, M., Menesini, E., Monta, Y., OMoor, M., More-Merchen, J. A., Pereira, B., & Smith, P. K. (2004). Friendship and loneliness among bullies and victims: Data from seven countries. *Aggressive Behavior, 30,* 71–83.

Essex, N. L. (2006). *What every teacher should know about No Child Left Behind.* Boston: Allyn & Bacon.

Evans, G. W. (2004). The environment of childhood poverty. *American Psychologist, 59,* 77–92.

Evertson, C. M., Emmer, E. T., & Worsham, M. E. (2006). *Classroom management for elementary teachers* (7th ed.). Boston: Allyn & Bacon.

Evertson, C. M., & Harris, A. H. (1999). Support for managing learning-centered classrooms: The classroom organization and management program. In H. J. Freiberg (Ed.), *Beyond behaviorism: Changing the classroom management paradigm.* Boston: Allyn & Bacon.

Evertson, C. M., & Weinstein, C. S. (2006). Classroom management as a field of inquiry. In C. M. Evertson & C. S. Weinstein (Eds.), *Handbook of classroom management.* Mahwah, NJ: Erlbaum.

F

Fantino, E., & Stolarz-Fantino, S. (2005). Decision-making: Context matters. *Behavioural Processes, 69,* 165–171.

Faraone, S. V., Biederman, J., & Mick, E. (2006). The age-dependent decline of attention deficit hyperactivity disorder: A meta-analysis of follow-up studies. *Psychological Medicine, 36,* 159–165.

Farkas, G. (2001). *Poverty and children's vocabulary development.* Unpublished manuscript, Pennsylvania State University.

Farr, M. (Ed.). (2005). *Latino language and literacy in ethnolinguistic Chicago.* Mahwah, NJ: Erlbaum.

Faure, C. (2004). Beyond brainstorming: Effects of different group procedures on selection of ideas and satisfaction with the process. *Journal of Creative Behavior, 38,* 13–34.

Feather, N. T. (1966). Effects of prior success and failure on expectations of success and subsequent performance. *Journal of Personality and Social Psychology, 3,* 287–298.

Feist, J., & Feist, G. J. (2006). *Theories of personality* (6th ed.). New York: McGraw-Hill.

Fekkes, M., Pijpers, F. I., Fedriks, A. M., Vogels, T., & Verloove-Vanhorick, S. P. (2006). Do bullied children get ill, or do ill children get bullied? A prospective cohort study on the relationship between bullying and health-related symptoms. *Pediatrics, 117,* 1568–1576.

Fekkes, M., Pijpers, F. I., & Verloove-Vanhorick, S. P. (2004). Bullying behavior and associations with psychosomatic complaints and depression in victims. *Journal of Pediatrics, 144,* 17–22.

Fekkes, M., Pijpers, F. I., & Verloove-Vanhorick, S. P. (2006). Effects of antibullying school program on bullying and health complaints. *Archives of Pediatric and Adolescent Medicine, 160,* 638–644.

Felner, R. (2006). School and program evaluation. In P. A. Alexander & P. H. Winne (Eds.), *Handbook of educational psychology* (2nd ed.). Mahwah, NJ: Erlbaum.

Feng, Y. (1996). Some thoughts about applying constructivist theories to guide instruction. *Computers in the Schools, 12,* 71–84.

Fenzel, L. M. (1994, February). *A prospective study of the effects of chronic strains on early adolescent self-worth and school adjustment.* Paper presented at the meeting of the Society for Research on Adolescence, San Diego.

Fenzel, L. M., Blyth, D. A., & Simmons, R. G. (1991). School transitions, secondary. In R. M. Lerner, A. C. Petersen, & J. Brooks-Gunn (Eds.). *Encyclopedia of Adolescence* (Vol. 2). New York: Garland.

Ferrando-Lucas, M. T. (2006). Attention deficit hyperactivity disorder: Its aetiological factors and endophenotypes. *Revista de Neurologia* (Spanish), *42,* (Suppl.) S9–S11.

Fickes, M. (2001). The furniture of science. *School Planning and Management, 50,* 71–73.

Fidalgo, Z., & Pereira, F. (2005). Sociocultural differences and the adjustment of mothers' speech to their children's cognitive and language comprehension skills. *Learning & Instruction, 15,* 1–21.

Field, T. (Ed.). (1995). *Touch in early development.* Mahwah, NJ: Erlbaum.

Fielding, L. G., Wilson, P. T., & Anderson, R. C. (1986). A new focus on free reading: The role of tradebooks in reading instruction. In T. Raphael (Ed.), *The contexts of school-based literacy.* New York: Random House.

Fiese, B. H., Eckert, T., & Spagnola, M. (2006). Family context in early childhood: A look at practices and beliefs that promote early learning. In B. Spodak & O. N. Sarancho (Eds.), *Handbook of research on the education of young children* (2nd ed.). Mahwah, NJ: Erlbaum.

Firlik, R. (1996). Can we adapt the philosophies and practices of Reggio Emilia, Italy, for use in American schools? *Young Children, 51,* 217–220.

Fisch, S. M. (2004). *Children's learning from educational television.* Mahwah, NJ: Erlbaum.

Fisch, S. M. (2006). Peeking behind the screen: Varied approaches to the production of children's television. In J. A. Bryant (ed.), *The children's television community.* Mahwah, NJ: Erlbaum.

Fisher, C. W., Berliner, D. C., Filby, N. N., Marliave, R., Ghen, L. S., & Dishaw, M. M. (1980). Teaching behaviors, academic learning time, and student achievement: An overview. In C. Denham & A. Lieberman (Eds.), *Time to learn.* Washington, DC: National Institute of Education.

Fitzgerald, L., Collinsworth, L. L., & Harned, M. S. (2001). Sexual harassment. In J. Worell (Ed.), *Encyclopedia of women and gender.* San Diego: Academic Press.

Fitzpatrick, J. (1993). *Developing responsible behavior in schools.* South Burlington, VT: Fitzpatrick Associates.

Fitzpatrick, J. L., Sanders, J. R. & Worthen, B. R. (2004). *Program evaluation* (3rd ed.). Boston: Allyn & Bacon.

Flake, C., Kuhs, T., Donnelly, A., & Ebert, C. (1995). Teacher as researcher: Reinventing the role of teacher. *Phi Delta Kappan, 76,* 405–407.

Flanagan, C. (2004). Volunteerism. In R. Lerner & L. Steinberg (Eds.), *Handbook of adolescent psychology.* New York: Wiley.

Flanagan, C., & Faison, N. (2001). Youth civic development: Implications of research for social policy and programs. *SRCD Social Policy Report, XV* (No. 1), 1–14.

Flanagan, C., Gill, S., & Gallay, L. (1998, November). *Intergroup understanding, social justice, and the "social contract" in diverse communities of youth.* Project report prepared for the workshop on research to improve intergroup relations among youth. Forum on Adolescence, National Research Council, Washington, DC.

Flavell, J. H. (1999). Cognitive development. *Annual Review of Psychology* (Vol. 50). Palo Alto, CA: Annual Reviews.

Flavell, J. H. (2004). Theory-of-mind development: Retrospect and prospect. *Merrill-Palmer Quarterly, 50,* 274–290.

Flavell, J. H., Friedrichs, A., & Hoyt, J. (1970). Developmental changes in memorization processes. *Cognitive Psychology, 1,* 324–340.

Flavell, J. H., Green, F. L., & Flavell, E. R. (1998). The mind has a mind of its own: Developing knowledge about mental uncontrollability. *Cognitive Development, 13,* 127–138.

Flavell, J. H., Miller, P. H., & Miller, S. A. (2002). *Cognitive development* (4th ed.). Upper Saddle River, NJ: Prentice Hall.

Floel, A., Poeppel, D., Buffalo, E. A., Braun, A., Wu, C. W., Seo, H. J. Knecht, S. & Cohen, L. G. (2004). Prefrontal cortex asymmetry for memory encoding of words and abstract shapes. *Cerebral Cortex, 14,* 404–409.

Florez, M. A. C. (1999). Improving adult English language learners' speaking skills. *ERIC Digest,* EDO-LE-99-01, 1–5.

Flower, L. S., & Hayes, J. R. (1981). Problem-solving and the cognitive processes in writing. In C. Frederiksen & J. F. Dominic (Eds.), *Writing: The nature, development, and teaching of written communication.* Mahwah, NJ: Erlbaum.

Flynn, J. R. (1999). Searching for justice: The discovery of IQ gains over time. *American Psychologist, 54,* 5–20.

Flynn, J. R. (2006). The history of the American mind in the 20th century: A scenario to explain gains over time and a case for the irrelevance of *g.* In P. C. Kyllonen, R. D. Roberts, & L. Stankov (Eds.), *Extending intelligence.* Mahwah, NJ: Erlbaum.

Fogarty, R. (Ed.). (1993). *The multiage classroom.* Palatine, IL: IRI/Skylight.

Forehand, R., Ragosta, J., & Rock, D. (1976). *Conditions and processes of effective school desegregation.* Princeton, NJ: Educational Testing Service.

Fox, P. G., Burns, K. R., Popovich, J. M., Belknap, R. A., & Frank-Stromberg, M. (2004). Southeast Asia refugee children: Self-esteem as a predictor of depression and Scholastic achievement in the U.S. *International Journal of Nursing Research, 9,* 1063–1072.

Fraenkel, J. R., & Wallen, N. E. (2006). *How to design and evaluate research in education* (6th ed.). New York: McGraw-Hill.

Francis, D. J., Fletcher, J. M., Stuebing, K. K., Lyon, G. R., Shaywitz, B. A., & Shaywitz, S. E. (2005). Psychometric approaches to the identification of LD: IQ and achievement scores are not sufficient. *Journal of Learning Disabilities, 38,* 98–108.

Frede, E. C. (1995). The role of program quality in producing early childhood program benefits. *The Future of Children.* (Vol. 5, No. 3), 115–132.

Frederikse, M., Lu, A., Aylward, E., Barta, P., Sharma, T., & Pearlson, G. (2000). Sex differences in inferior lobule volume in schizophrenia. *American Journal of Psychiatry, 157,* 422–427.

Freeland, J. T. (2005). Norm-referenced tests. In S. W. Lee (Ed.), *Encyclopedia of school psychology.* Thousand Oaks, CA: Sage.

Frey, B. (2005). Standard deviation. In S. W. Lee (Ed.), *Encyclopedia of school psychology.* Thousand Oaks, CA: Sage.

Frey, K. S., Hirschstein, M. K., Snell, J. L., Edstrom, L. V. S., & Broderick, C. J. (2005). Reducing playground bullying and supporting beliefs: An experimental trial of the Steps to Respect program. *Developmental Psychology, 41,* 479–490.

Frieman, J. L. (2002). *Learning and adaptive behavior.* Belmont, CA: Wadsworth.

Friend, M. (2006). *Special education (IDEA 2004, Update ed.).* Boston: Allyn & Bacon.

Friend, M., & Bursuck, W. (2006). *Including students with special needs* (4th ed.). Boston: Allyn & Bacon.

Fritzer, P. J. (2002). *Social studies content in elementary and middle school.* Boston: Allyn & Bacon.

Frye, D. (1999). Development of intention: The relation of executive function to theory of mind. In P. D. Zelazo, J. W. Astington, & D. R. Olson (Eds.), *Developing theories of intention: Social understanding and self-control.* Mahwah, NJ: Erlbaum.

Frye, D. (2004). Unpublished review of J. W. Santrock's *Child development* (11th ed.). New York: McGraw-Hill.

Fuchs, D., Fuchs, L. S., & Burish, P. (2000). Peer-assisted strategies: An empirically-supported practice to promote reading. *Learning Disabilities Research and Practice, 9,* 203–212.

Fuchs, D., Fuchs, L. S., Mathes, P. G., & Simmons, D. C. (1997). Peer-assisted learning strategies: Making classrooms more responsive to diversity. *American Educational Research Journal, 34,* 174–206.

Fuchs, D., Mock, D., Morgan, P. L., & Young, C. L. (2003). Responsiveness-to-intervention: Definitions, evidence, and implications for the learning disabilities construct. *Learning Disabilities Research & Practice, 18,* 157–171.

Fulda, J. S. (2006). The ethical limitations of online grading systems. *British Journal of Educational Technology, 36,* 559–561.

Fuligni, A. J., Witkow, M., & Garcia, C. (2005, April). *Ethnic identity and the academic adjustment of adolescents from Mexican, Chinese, and European backgrounds.* Paper presented at the meeting of the Society for Research in Child Development, Atlanta.

Furman, W., & Buhrmester, D. (1992). Age and sex differences in perceptions of networks of personal relationships. *Child Development, 63,* 103–115.

Furth, H. G., & Wachs, H. (1975). *Thinking goes to school.* New York: Oxford University Press.

Fuson, K. C., Kalchman, M., & Bransford, J. D. (2005). Mathematical understanding: An introduction. In *How students learn.* Washington, DC: National Academies Press.

G

Gabriele, A. J., & Montecinos, C. (2001). Collaborating with a skilled peer: The influence of achievement goals and perceptions of partners' competence on the participation and learning of low-achieving students. *Journal of Experimental Education, 69,* 152–178.

Gage, N. L. (1978). *The scientific basis of the art of teaching.* New York: Teachers College Press.

Galambos, N. L. (2004). Gender and gender role development in adolescence. In R. Lerner & L. Steinberg (Eds.), *Handbook of adolescence.* New York: Wiley.

Galambos, N. L., Barker, E. T. & Krahn, H. J. (2006). Depression, self-esteem, and anger in emerging adulthood: Seven-year trajectories. *Developmental Psychology, 42,* 350–365.

Gall, M. D., Gall, J. P., & Borg, W. R. (2007). *Educational research* (8th ed.). Boston: Allyn & Bacon.

Gallagher, C. (2000). A seat at the table: Teachers reclaiming assessment through rethinking accountability. *Phi Delta Kappan, 81,* 502–507.

Gallup Organization. (2004). *Gallup Poll: The public's attitudes toward schools.* Princeton, NJ: Author.

Gamaron, A. (1990, April). *The consequences of track-related instructional differences for student achievement.* Paper presented at the meeting of American Educational Research Association, Boston.

Gandara, P. (2002). *Peer group influence and academic aspirations across cultural/ethnic groups of high school students.* Santa Cruz, University of California, Center for Research on Education, Diversity & Excellence.

Garcia, G. E., & Willis, A. I. (2001). Frameworks for understanding multicultural literacies. In P. R. Schmidt & P. B. Mosenthal (Eds.), *Reconceptualizing literacy in the new age of multiculturalism and pluralism.* Greenwich, CT: IAP.

Gardner, H. (1983). *Frames of mind.* New York: Basic Books.

Gardner, H. (1985). *The mind's new science.* New York: Basic Books.

Gardner, H. (1993). *Multiple intelligences.* New York: Basic Books.

Gardner, H. (1998). Multiple intelligences: Myths and messages. In A. Woolfolk (Ed.), *Readings in educational psychology* (2nd ed.). Boston: Allyn & Bacon.

Gardner, H. (2002). The pursuit of excellence through education. In M. Ferrari (Ed.), *Learning from extraordinary minds.* Mahwah, NJ: Erlbaum.

Gardner, H., Feldman, D. H., & Krechevsky, M. (Eds.). (1998). *Project Spectrum.* New York: Teachers College Press.

Gardner, J. (2006). Assessment for learning: A compelling conceptualization. In J. Gardner (Ed.), *Assessment and learning.* London: Paul Chapman.

Gardner, R. (1985). *The boys' and girls' book about divorce.* New York: Bantam.

Garmon, A., Nystrand, M., Berends, M., & LePore, P. C. (1995). An organizational analysis of the effects of ability grouping. *American Educational Research Journal, 32,* 687–715.

Garrod, A., Smulyan, L., Powers, S. I., & Kilenny, R. (1992). *Adolescent portraits.* Boston: Allyn & Bacon.

Garton, A. F. (2004). *Exploring cognitive development: The child as a problem solver.* Malden, MA: Blackwell.

Gauvain, M. (2001). *The social context of cognitive development.* New York: Guilford.

Gavetti, G., & Rivkin, J. W. (2005). How strategists really think: Tapping the power of analogy. *Harvard Business Review, 83,* 54–63.

Gay, G. (1997). Educational equality for students of color. In J. A. Banks & C. M. Banks (Eds.), *Multicultural Education* (3rd ed.). Boston: Allyn & Bacon.

Gay, G. (2006). Connections between classroom management and culturally responsive teaching. In C. M. Evertson & C. S. Weinstein (Eds.), *Handbook of classroom management.* Mahwah, NJ: Erlbaum.

Gay, L. R., & Airasian, P. (2000). *Educational research* (6th ed.). Upper Saddle River, NJ: Merrill.

Gegeshidze, K., & Tsagareli, M. G. (2004). Influence of emotional words on human visual recognition and brain asymmetry. *World Journal of Biological Psychiatry, 5,* 26–32.

Gelman, R. (1969). Conservation acquisition: A problem of learning to attend to relevant attributes. *Journal of Experimental Child Psychology, 7,* 67–87.

Gelman, R., & Williams, E. M. (1998). Enabling constraints for cognitive development and learning. In W. Damon (Ed.), *Handbook of child psychology* (5th ed., Vol. 4). New York: Wiley.

Gelman, S. A., & Opfer, J. E. (2004). Development of the animate-inanimate distinction. In U. Goswami (Ed.), *Blackwell handbook of childhood cognitive development.* Malden, MA: Blackwell.

Gentile, J. R. (2000). Learning, transfer of. In A. Kazdin (Ed.), *Encyclopedia of psychology.* Washington, DC, & New York: American Psychological Association and Oxford University Press.

Gest, S. D., Graham-Bermann, S. A., & Hartup, W. W. (2001). Peer experience: Common and unique features of number of friendships, social network centrality, and sociometric status. *Social Development 10,* 23–40.

Giavecchio, L. (2001, April). *Sustained attention and receptive language in preschool Head Start story time.* Paper presented at the meeting of the Society for Research in Child Development, Minneapolis.

Gibbs, J. C. (2003). *Moral development & reality.* Thousand Oaks, CA: Sage.

Gibbs, J. T. (1989). Black American adolescents. In J. T. Gibbs & L. N. Huang (Eds.), *Children of color.* San Francisco: Jossey-Bass.

Gibson, S., & McKay, R. (2001). *What constructivist theory and brain research may offer social studies.* School of Education, University of Alberta, Canada.

Giedd, J. N. (2004). Structural magnetic resonance imaging of the adolescent brain. *Annals of the New York Academy of Sciences, 1021,* 77–85.

Giedd, J. N., & others. (2006). Puberty-related influences on brain development. *Molecular and Cellular Endocrinology, 25,* 154–162.

Gigerenzer, G., & Selten, R. (Eds.). (2001). *Bounded rationality.* Cambridge, MA: MIT Press.

Gill, J. (1997, July). Personal conversation. Richardson: University of Texas at Dallas.

Gill, D. L. (2001). Sports and athletics. In J. Worell (Ed.), *Encyclopedia of women and gender.* San Diego: Academic Press.

Gillberg, C., & Cederlund, M. (2005). Asperger syndrome: Familial and prenatal factors. *Journal of Autism and Developmental Disorders, 35,* 159–166.

Gilligan, C. (1982). *In a different voice.* Cambridge, MA: Harvard University Press.

Gilligan, C. (1996). The centrality of relationships in psychological development: A puzzle, some evidence, and a theory. In G. G. Noam & K. W. Fischer (Eds.), *Development and vulnerability in close relationships.* Hillsdale, NJ: Erlbaum.

Gilligan, C. (1998). *Minding women: Reshaping the education realm.* Cambridge, MA: Harvard University Press.

Ginorio, A., & Huston, M. (2000). *Si Puede! Yes, we can: Latinas in school.* Washington, DC: American Association of University Women.

Ginsburg, H. P., Klein, A., & Starkey, P. (1998). The development of children's mathematical thinking. In I. E. Sigel & K. A. Renninger (Eds.), *Handbook of child psychology* (5th ed., Vol. 4). New York: Wiley.

Ginsburg-Block, M. (2005). Peer tutoring. In S. W. Lee (Ed.), *Encyclopedia of school psychology.* Thousand Oaks, CA: Sage.

Gipson, J. (1997, March/April). Girls and computer technology: Barrier or key? *Educational Technology,* pp. 41–43.

Gladstone, G. L., Parker, G. B., & Malhi, G. S. (2006). Do bullied children become anxious and depressed adults? A cross-sectional investigation of the correlates of bullying and anxious depression. *Journal of Nervous and Mental Disorders, 194,* 201–208.

Glasser, W. (1969). *Schools without failure.* New York: Harper & Row.

Glassman, M. (2001). Dewey and Vygotsky: Society, experience, and inquiry in educational practice. *Educational Researcher, 30* (4), 3–14.

Glasson, G. E. (1989). The effects of hands-on and teacher demonstration laboratory methods on science achievement in relation to reasoning ability and prior knowledge. *Journal of Research in Science Teaching, 26,* 121–131.

Glesne, C. (2007). *Becoming qualitative researchers* (3rd ed.). Boston: Allyn & Bacon.

Gold, J., & Lanzoni, M. (Eds.). (1993). [Video] *Graduation by portfolio—Central Park East Secondary School.* New York: Post Production, 29th St. Video, Inc.

Goldberg, M. (2005, January). Test mess 2: Are we doing better a year later? *Phi Delta Kappan,* 389–395.

Goldberg, L., & Richburg, C. M. (2004). Minimal hearing impairment. *Communication Disorders Quarterly, 25,* 152–160.

Goldman, S. (1998, October). Unpublished review of J. W. Santrocks *Educational psychology.* (New York: McGraw-Hill).

Goldman, S. R., Petrosino, A., Sherwood, R. D., Garrison, S., Hickey, D., Bransford, J. D., & Pellegrino, J. (1996). Anchoring science instruction in multimedia learning environments. In S. Vosniadou, E. De Corte, R. Glaser, & H. Mandl (Eds.), *International perspectives on the design of technology-*

supported learning environments. Hillsdale, NJ: Erlbaum.

Goldman-Rakic, P. (1996). *Bridging the gap.* Presentation at the workshop sponsored by the Education Commission of the States and the Charles A. Dana Foundation, Denver.

Goldstein, E. B. (2006). *Cognitive psychology.* Belmont, CA: Wadsworth.

Goleman, D., Kaufman, P., & Ray, M. (1993). *The creative spirit.* New York: Plume.

Goleman, D. (1995). *Emotional intelligence.* New York: Basic Books.

Gonzales, N. A., Knight, G. P., Birman, D., & Sirolli, A. A. (2004). Acculturation and enculturation among Latino youths. In K. L. Maton, C. J. Schellenbach, B. J. Leadbetter, & A. L. Solarz (Eds.), *Investing in children, youth, families, and communities.* Mahwah, NJ: Erlbaum.

Gonzáles, P., Guzman, J. C., Partelow, L., Pahlke, E., Jocelyn, L., Kastberg, D., & Williams, T. (2004). *Highlights from the Trends in International Mathematics and Science Study (TIMSS) 2003.* Washington, DC: U.S. Government Printing Office.

González, N., & Moll, L. C., & Amanti, C. (Eds.). (2005). *Funds of knowledge: Theorizing practices in households, communities, and classrooms.* Mahwah, NJ: Erlbaum.

González, V., Yawkey, T. D., & Minaya-Rowe, L. (2006). *English-as-a-second-language (ESL) teaching and learning.* Boston: Allyn & Bacon.

Good, R. H., & Kaminski, R. A. (2003). *Dynamic indicators of basic early literacy skills* (6th ed.). Longmont, CO: Sopris West Educational Services.

Goodlad, J. I. (1984). *A place called school.* New York: McGraw-Hill.

Goodlad, S., & Hirst, B. (1989). *Peer R-17 tutoring: A guide to learning by teaching.* New York: Nichols.

Goodrich, H. (1997). Understanding rubrics. *Educational Leadership, 54,* 14–17.

Goorhuis-Brouwer, S., Coster, H., Nakken, H., & Spelberg, H. L. (2004). Environmental factors in developmental language disorders. In L. Verhoeven & H. Van Balkom (Eds.), *The classification of language disorders.* Mahwah, NJ: Erlbaum.

Goos, M. (2004). Learning mathematics in a classroom community of inquiry. *Journal for Research in Mathematics Education, 35,* 258–291.

Gordon, T. (1970). *Parent effectiveness training.* New York: McGraw-Hill.

Gorski, P. (2005). *Multicultural education and the internet* (2nd ed.). New York: McGraw-Hill.

Goswami, U. (2004). Inductive and deductive reasoning. In U. Goswami (Ed.), *Blackwell handbook of childhood cognitive development.* Malden, MA: Blackwell.

Goswami, U. (2005). The brain in the classroom? The state of the art. *Developmental Science, 8,* 467–469.

Gottlieb, G., Wahlsten, D., & Lickliter, R. (2006). The significance of biology for human development: A developmental psychobiological systems view. In W. Damon & R. Lerner (Eds.), *Handbook of child psychology* (6th ed.). New York: Wiley.

Gottman, J. M. (1996). *What predicts divorce.* New York: Milton H. Erickson Foundation.

Graham, S. (1986, August). *Can attribution theory tell us something about motivation in Blacks?* Paper presented at the meeting of the American Psychological Association, Washington, DC.

Graham, S. (1990). Motivation in African Americans. In G. L. Berry & J. K. Asamen (Eds.), *Black students.* Newbury Park, CA: Sage.

Graham, S. (2005, February 16). Commentary in *USA Today,* p. 2D.

Graham, S. (2006). Strategy instruction and the teaching of writing: A meta-analysis. In C. A. MacArthur, S. Graham, & J. Fitzgerald (Eds.), *Handbook of writing research.* Mahwah, NJ: Erlbaum.

Graham, S. (2006). Writing. In P. A. Alexander & P. H. Winne (Eds.), *Handbook of educational psychology* (2nd ed.). Mahwah, NJ: Erlbaum.

Graham, S., & Harris, K. R. (2001). The role of self-regulation and transcription skills in writing and writing development. *Educational Psychologist, 35,* 3–12.

Graham, S., & Taylor, A. Z. (2002). Ethnicity, gender, and the development of achievement values. In A. Wigfield & J. S. Eccles (Eds.), *Development of achievement motivation.* San Diego: Academic Press.

Graham, S., & Weiner, B. (1996). Theories and principles of motivation. In D. C. Berliner & R. C. Calfee (Eds.), *Handbook of educational psychology.* New York: Macmillan.

Gratz, R. R., & Bouton, P. J. (1996). Erikson and early childhood educators. *Young Children, 51,* 74–78.

Graves, M. F., Juel, C., & Graves, B. B. (2004). *Teaching reading in the 21st century.* Boston: Allyn & Bacon.

Gray, J. (1992). *Men are from Mars, women are from Venus.* New York: HarperCollins.

Gray, J. R. (2001). Emotional modulation of cognitive control: Approach-withdrawal states of double-dissociate spatial from verbal two-back task performance. *Journal of Experimental Psychology: General, 130,* 436–452.

Gray, J. R., & Kagan J. (2000). The challenge of determining which children with attention deficit hyperactivity disorder will respond positively to methylphenidate. *Journal of Applied Developmental Psychology, 21,* 471–489.

Gray, P., & Feldman, J. (2004). Playing in the zone of proximal development: Qualities of self-directed age-mixing between adolescents and young children at a democratic school. *American Journal of Education, 110,* 108–143.

Greenberg, M. T. (1996). *The PATHS project.* Seattle: University of Washington.

Greenberger, E., & Steinberg, L. (1986). *When teenagers work. The psychological and social costs of adolescent employment.* New York: Basic Books.

Greenfield, P. M., & Suzuki, L. K. (1998). Culture and human development. In W. Damon (Ed.), *Handbook of child psychology* (Vol. 4). New York: Wiley.

Greenfield, P. M., Suzuki, L. K., & Rothstein-Fisch, C. (2006a). Cultural pathways through human development. In W. Damon & R. Lerner (Eds.), *Handbook of child psychology* (6th ed.). New York: Wiley.

Greenfield. P. M., Trumbull, E., Keller, H., Rothstein-Fisch, Suzuki, L., & Quiroz, B. (2006b). Cultural conceptions of learning and development. In P. A. Alexander & P. H. Winne (Eds.), *Handbook of educational psychology* (2nd ed.). Mahwah, NJ: Erlbaum.

Greeno, J. G. (1993). For research to reform education and cognitive science. In L. A. Penner, G. M. Batche, H. M. Knoff, & D. L. Nelson (Eds.). *The challenge in mathematics and science education: Psychology's response.* Washington, DC: American Psychological Association.

Greeno, J. G. (2006). Learning in activity. In R. K. Sawyer (Ed.), *The Cambridge handbook of learning sciences.* New York: Oxford University Press.

Greenough, W. T. (1997, April 21). Commentary in article, "Politics of biology." *U.S. News & World Report,* p. 79.

Greenough, W. T. (2000). Brain development. In A. Kazdin (Ed.), *Encyclopedia of psychology.* Washington, DC, & New York: American Psychological Association and Oxford University Press.

Greenwood, C. R., Maheady, L., & Delquadri, J. (2002). Classwide Peer Tutoring Programs. In M. R. Shinn, H. M., Walker, & G. Stoner (Eds.), *Interventions for academic and behavior problems II.* Bethesda, MD: National Association of School Psychologists.

Gregory, H. (2005). *Public speaking for college and career* (7th ed.). New York: McGraw-Hill.

Gregory, R. J. (2007). *Psychological testing* (5th ed.). Boston: Allyn & Bacon.

Grigg, W. S., Lauko, M. A., and Brockway, D. M. (2006). *The nation's report card: Science 2005* (NCES 2006–466). U.S. Department of Education, National Center for Education Statistics. Washington, DC: U.S. Government Printing Office.

Grolnick, W. S., Gurland, S. T., Jacob, K. F., & Decourcey, W. (2002). The development of self-determination in middle childhood and adolescence. In A. Wigfield & J. S. Eccles (Eds.), *Development of achievement motivation*. San Diego: Academic Press.

Gronlund, N. E. (2006). *Assessment of student achievement* (8th ed.). Boston: Allyn & Bacon.

Grossier, P. (1964). *How to use the fine art of questioning*. New York: Teachers' Practical Press.

Grossman, P., Schoenfeld, A., & Lee, C. (2005). Teaching subject matter. In L. Darling-Hammond & J. Bransford (Eds.), *Preparing teachers for a changing world*. New York: Jossey-Bass.

Guilbault, R., Bryant, F. B., Brockway, J. H., & Posavac, E. J. (2004). A meta-analysis of research on hindsight bias. *Basic & Applied Social Psychology, 26*, 103–117.

Guilford, J. P. (1967). *The structure of intellect*. New York: McGraw-Hill.

Gunning, T. G. (2000). *Creating literacy instruction for all children* (3rd ed.). Boston: Allyn & Bacon.

Gunning, T. G. (2006). *Closing the literacy gap*. Boston: Allyn & Bacon.

Gur, R. C., Mozley, L. H., Mozley, P. D., Resnick, S. M., Karp, J. S., Alavi, A., Arnold, S. E., & Gur, R. E. (1995). Sex differences in regional cerebral glucose metabolism during a resting state. *Science, 267*, 528–531.

Guskey, T. R. (2001). Fixing grading policies that undermine standards. *The Education Digest, 66*(7),16–21.

Gustafsson, J-E. (2006). Schooling and intelligence: Effects of track of study on level and profile of cognitive abilities. In P. C. Kyllonen, R. D. Roberts, & L. Stankov (Eds.), *Extending intelligence*. Mahwah, NJ: Erlbaum.

Guthrie, J. T., Wigfield, A., Barbosa, P., Perencevich, K. C., Taboada, A., Davis, M. H., Scafiddi, N., & Tonks, S. (2004). Increasing reading comprehension and engagement through Concept Oriented Reading Instruction. *Journal of Educational Psychology, 96*, 403–423.

Guthrie, J. T., Wigfield, A., & Perencevich, K. (Eds.). (2004). *Motivating reading comprehension: Concept Oriented Reading Instruction*. Mahwah, NJ: Lawrence Erlbaum Associates.

Guttentag, M., & Bray, H. (1976). *Undoing sex stereotypes: Research and resources for educators*. New York: McGraw-Hill.

H

Haager, D., & Klinger, J. K. (2005). *Differentiating instruction in inclusive classrooms*. Boston: Allyn & Bacon.

Hahn, U., & Ramscar, M. (Eds.). (2001). *Similarity and categorization*. New York: Oxford University Press.

Haith, M. M., & Benson, J. B. (1998). Infant cognition. In W. Damon (Ed.), *Handbook of child psychology* (5th ed., Vol. 2). New York: Wiley.

Hakuta, K. (2000). Bilingualism. In A. Kazdin (Ed.). *Encyclopedia of psychology*. Washington, DC, and New York: American Psychological Association and Oxford University Press.

Hakuta, K. (2001, April 5). *Key policy milestones and directions in the education of English language learners*. Paper prepared for the Rockefeller Foundation Symposium, Leveraging change: An emerging framework for educational equity, Washington, DC.

Hakuta, K. (2005, April). *Bilingualism at the intersection of research and public policy*. Paper presented at the meeting of the Society for Research in Child Development, Atlanta.

Hakuta, K., Butler, Y. G., & Witt, D. (2000). *How long does it take English learners to attain proficiency?* Berkeley, CA: The University of California Linguistic Minority Research Institute Policy Report 2000–1.

Haladyna, T. M. (1997). *Writing test items to evaluate higher-order thinking*. Boston: Allyn & Bacon.

Haladyna, T. M. (2002). *Essentials of standardized achievement testing: Validity and accountability*. Boston: Allyn & Bacon.

Hale, S. (1990). A global developmental trend in cognitive processing speed. *Child Development, 61*, 653–663.

Hale-Benson, J. E. (1982). *Black children: Their roots, culture, and learning styles*. Baltimore: The Johns Hopkins University Press.

Halford, G. S. (2004). Information-processing models of cognitive development. In U. Goswami (Ed.), *Blackwell handbook of childhood cognitive development*. Malden, MA: Blackwell.

Hallahan, D. P., & Kauffman, J. M. (2006). *Exceptional learners* (10th ed.). Boston: Allyn & Bacon.

Hallahan, D. P., Lloyd, J. W., Kauffman, J. M., Weiss, M. P., & Martinez, E. A. (2005). *Learning disabilities* (3rd ed.). Boston: Allyn & Bacon.

Hallinan, M. (2003). Ability grouping and student learning. In D. Ravitch (Ed.), *Brookings' papers on educational policy, 2003*. Washington, DC: Brookings Institution.

Halonen, J. (2006). Refine your expression. In J. W. Santrock & J. Halonen, *Your guide to college success* (4th ed.). Belmont, CA: Wadsworth.

Halpern, D. F. (2006). Assessing gender gaps in learning. In P. A. Alexander & P. H. Winne (Eds.), *Handbook of educational psychology* (2nd ed.). Mahwah, NJ: Erlbaum.

Halpern, D. F. (2007). The nature and nurture of critical thinking. In R. J. Sternberg, H. Roediger, & D. Halpern (Eds.), *Critical thinking in psychology*. New York: Cambridge University Press.

Hambleton, R. K. (1996). Advances in assessment models, methods, and practices. In D. C. Berliner & R. C. Calfee (Eds.), *Handbook of educational psychology*. New York: Macmillan.

Hamburg, D. A. (1997). Meeting the essential requirements for healthy adolescent development in a transforming world. In R. Takanishi & D. Hamburg (Eds.), *Preparing adolescents for the 21st century*. New York: Cambridge University Press.

Hamilton, M. A., & Hamilton, S. F. (2004). Designing work and service for learning. In S. F. Hamilton & M. A. Hamilton (Eds.), *The youth development handbook*. Thousand Oaks, CA: Sage.

Hamilton, S. F., & Hamilton, M. A. (2004). Contexts for mentoring: adolescent-adult relationships in workplaces and communities. In R. Lerner & L. Steinberg (Eds.), *Handbook of adolescent psychology* (2nd ed.). New York: Wiley.

Hammerness, K., Darling-Hammond, L., Grossman, P., Rust, F., & Shulman, L. (2005). How teachers learn and develop. In L. Darling-Hammond & J. Bransford (Eds.), *Preparing teachers for a changing world*. San Francisco: Jossey-Bass.

Hammill, D. D. (2004). What we know about correlates of reading. *Exceptional Children, 70*, 453–468.

Haney, W. (2000). The myth of the Texas miracle in education. *Education Policy Analysis Archives, 8*(41). Retrieved March 10, 2004, from http://epaa.asu.edu/epaa/ v8n41/

Hannish, L. D., & Guerra, N. G. (2004). Aggressive victims, passive victims, and bullies: Development continuity or developmental change? *Merrill-Palmer Quarterly, 50,* 17–38.

Hansford, B. C., & Hattie, J. A. (1982). The relationship between self and achievement/performance measures. *Review of Educational Research, 52,* 123–142.

Hardman, M. L., Drew, C. J., & Egan, M. W. (2006). *Human exceptionality* (8th ed., Update). Boston: Allyn & Bacon.

Hardy, L. (2001). High tech high. *The American School Board Journal, 188,* 12–15.

Hargis, C. H. (2006). *Teaching low achieving and disadvantaged students* (3rd ed.). Springfield, IL: Charles C Thomas.

Hargrove, K. (2005). What makes a "good" teacher "great"? *Gifted Child Today, 28,* 30–31.

Haring, M., Hewitt, P. L., & Flett, G. L. (2003). Perfectionism and quality of intimate relationships. *Journal of Marriage and the Family, 65,* 143–158.

Harlen, W. (2006). Role of assessment in developing motivation for learning. In J. Gardner (Ed.), *Assessment and learning.* London: Paul Chapman.

Harris, J. L., Kamhi, A. G., & Pollock, K. E. (2001). *Literacy in African American communities.* Mahwah, NJ: Erlbaum.

Harrison-Hale, A. O., McLoyd, V. C., & Smedley, B. (2004). Racial and ethnic status: Risk and protective processes among African-American families. In K. L. Maton, C. J. Schellenbach, B. J. Leadbetter, & A. L. Solarz (Eds.), *Investing in children, youth, families, and communities.* Washington, DC: American Psychological Association.

Hart, B., & Risley, T. R. (1995). *Meaningful differences.* Baltimore: Paul H. Brookes.

Hart, C. H., Charlesworth, R., Durland, M. A., Burts, D. C., DeWolf, M., & Fleege, P. O. (1996). *Developmentally appropriate practice in preschool classrooms.* Unpublished manuscript, Brigham Young University, Provo, Utah.

Hart, C. H., Yang, C., Charlesworth, R., & Burts, D. C. (2003, April). *Early childhood teachers' curriculum beliefs, classroom practices, and childrens' outcomes: What are the connections?* Paper presented at the biennial meeting of the Society for Research in Child Development, Tampa, FL.

Hart, D. (2006). Service commitment and care exemplars. In M. Killien & J. G. Smetana (Eds.), *Handbook of moral development.* Mahwah, NJ: Erlbaum.

Harter, S. (1981). A new self-report scale of intrinsic versus extrinsic orientation in the classroom: Motivational and informational components. *Developmental Psychology, 17,* 300–312.

Harter, S. (1989). *Self-perception profile for adolescents.* Denver: University of Denver, Department of Psychology.

Harter, S. (1990). Self and identity development. In S. S. Feldman & G. R. Elliott (Eds.), *At the threshold: The developing adolescent.* Cambridge, MA: Harvard University Press.

Harter, S. (1996). Teacher and classmate influences on scholastic motivation, self-esteem, and level of voice in adolescents. In J. Juvonen & K. R. Wentzel (Eds.), *Social motivation.* New York: Cambridge University Press.

Harter, S. (1999). *The construction of the self.* New York: Guilford.

Harter, S. (2006). The self. In W. Damon & R. Lerner (Eds.), *Handbook of child psychology* (6th ed.). New York: Wiley.

Hartnell-Young, E., & Morriss, M. P. (2006). *Digital portfolios* (2nd ed.). Thousand Oaks, CA: Corwin.

Hartup, W. W. (1983). Peer relations. In P. H. Mussen (Ed.), *Handbook of child psychology* (4th ed., Vol. 4). New York: Wiley.

Harwood, R., Lyendecker, B., Carlson, V., Ascencio, M., & Miller, A. (2002). Parenting among Latino families in the U.S. In M. H. Bornstein (Ed.), *Handbook of parenting* (2nd ed.). Mahwah, NJ: Erlbaum.

Hasirci, D., & Demirkan, H. (2003). Creativity in learning environments: The case of two sixth grade art rooms. *Journal of Creative Behavior, 37,* 17–41.

Hatano, G. (1990). The nature of everyday science. *British Journal of Educational Developmental Psychology, 8,* 245–250.

Hatano, G., & Oura, Y. (2003). Commentary: Reconceptualizing school learning using insight from expertise research. *Educational Researcher, 32,* 26–29.

Hatch, T. (2000, April). *Portfolios and the scholarship of teaching.* Paper presented at the meeting of the American Educational Research Association, New Orleans.

Hayes, J. R., & Flower, L. S. (1986). Writing research and the writer. *American Psychologist, 41,* 1106–1113.

Haynes, R. M., & Chalker, D. M. (1997, May). World class schools. *American School Board Journal,* pp. 20–25.

Haynie, D. L., Nansel, T., Eitel, P., Crump, A. D., Saylor, K., Yu, K., & Simons-Morton, B. (2001). Bullies, victims, and bully/victims: Distinct groups of at-risk youth. *Journal of Early Adolescence, 21,* 29–49.

Hazel, C., & Gredler, G. R. (2005). Building positive behavior support systems in schools: Functional behavioral assessment. *Psychology in the Schools, 42,* 217–218.

Heath, S. B. (1989). Oral and literate traditions among Black Americans living in poverty. *American Psychologist, 44,* 367–373.

Heath, S. B., & McLaughlin, M. W. (Eds.). (1993). *Identity and inner-city youth: Beyond ethnicity and gender.* New York: Teachers College Press.

Heid, M. K. (2002). Algebra and function development. In M. K. Heid & G. W. Blume (Eds.), *Mathematics learning, teaching, and policy.* Greenwich, CT: IAP.

Heid, M. K., & Blume, G. W. (Eds.). (2002). *Mathematics curriculum development and tool development.* Greenwich, CT: IAP.

Heilman, A. W., Blair, T. R., & Rupley, W. H. (2002). *Principles and practices of teaching reading* (10th ed.). Upper Saddle River, NJ: Merrill.

Heiser, P. Friedel, S., Dempfile, A., Kongrad, K., Smidt, J., Grabarkiewicz, J., Herpertz-Dahlann, B., Remschmidt, H., & Hebebrand, J. (2004). Molecular genetic aspects of attention deficit/hyperactivity disorder. *Neuroscience and Biobehavioral Reviews, 28,* 625–641.

Heller, H. C. (1993). The need for a core, interdisciplinary, life-sciences curriculum in the middle grades. In R. Takanishi (Ed.), *Adolescence in the 1990s.* New York: Teachers College Press.

Heller, H. C., & Hawkins, J. (1994, Spring). Teaching tolerance. *Teachers College Record,* p. 2.

Helms, J. E. (2005). Stereotype threat might explain the black-white test-score difference. *American Psychologist, 60,* 269–270.

Henderson, V. L., & Dweck, C. S. (1990). Motivation and achievement. In S. S. Feldman & G. R. Elliott (Eds.), *At the threshold: The developing adolescent.* Cambridge, MA: Harvard University Press.

Hendricks, C. C. (2006). *Improving schools through action research.* Boston: Allyn & Bacon.

Hennessey, B. A., & Amabile, T. M. (1998). Reward, intrinsic motivation, and creativity. *American Psychologist, 53,* 674–675.

Henson, K. (1988). *Methods and strategies for teaching in secondary and middle schools.* New York: Longman.

Henson, K. (2004). *Constructivist teaching strategies for diverse middle school classrooms.* Boston: Allyn & Bacon.

Hergenhahn, B. R., & Olson, M. H. (2001). *An introduction to theories of learning* (6th ed.). Upper Saddle River, NJ: Prentice Hall.

Herman, J. (1996). Commentary in "The latest on student portfolios." *NEA Today, 15*(4), 17.

Herrera, S. G., & Murry, K. G. (2005). *Mastering ESL and bilingual methods.* Boston: Allyn & Bacon.

Herrnstein, R. J., & Murray, C. (1994). *The bell curve: Intelligence and class structure in modern life.* New York: Free Press.

Hertzog, N. B. (1998, January/February). Gifted education specialist. *Teaching Exceptional Children*, pp. 39–43.

Hetherington, E. M. (1995, March). *The changing American family and the well-being of others.* Paper presented at the meeting of the Society for Research in Child Development, Indianapolis.

Hetherington, E. M. (2000). Divorce. In A. Kazdin (Ed.), *Encyclopedia of psychology.* Washington, DC, & New York: American Psychological Association and Oxford University Press.

Hetherington, E. M. (2005). Divorce and the adjustment of children. *Pediatrics in Review, 26*, 163–169.

Hetherington, E. M., & Kelly, J. (2002). *For better or for worse: Divorce reconsidered.* New York: W. W. Norton.

Hetherington, E. M., & Stanley-Hagan, M. (2002). Parenting in divorced and remarried families. In M. H. Bornstein (Ed.), *Handbook of parenting* (2nd ed.). Mahwah, NJ: Erlbaum.

Hetzroni, O. E., & Shrieber, B. (2004). Word processing as an assertive technology tool for enhancing academic outcomes of students with writing disabilities in the regular classroom. *Journal of Learning Disabilities, 37*, 143–154.

Heward, W. L. (2006). *Exceptional children* (8th ed.). Upper Saddle River, NJ: Prentice Hall.

Heward, W. L., Heron, T. E., Neef, N. A., Peterson, S. M., Sainato, D. M., Cartledge, G., Gardner, R., Peterson, L. D., Hersh, S. B., & Dardig, J. C. (2005). *Focus on behavior analysis in education.* Boston: Allyn & Bacon.

Hiatt-Michael, D. (Ed.). (2001). *Promising practices in family involvement.* Greenwich, CT: IAP.

Hickey, D. T., Moore, A. L., & Pellegrino, J. W. (2001). The motivational and academic consequences of elementary mathematics environments: Do constructivist innovations and reforms make a difference? *American Educational Research Journal, 38*, 611–652.

Hiebert, E. H., & Kamil, M. L. (Eds.). (2005). *Teaching and learning vocabulary.* Mahwah, NJ: Erlbaum.

Hiebert, E. H., & Raphael, T. E. (1996). Psychological perspectives on literacy and extensions to educational practice. In D. C. Berliner & R. C. Calfee (Eds.), *Handbook of educational psychology.* New York: Macmillan.

Hiebert, J., Gallimore, R., Garnier, H., Givvin, K. B., Hollingsworth, H., Jacobs, J., Chui, A. M. Y., Wearne, D., Smith, M., Kersting, N., Manaster, A., Tseng, E., Etterbeek, W., Manaster, C., Gonzales, P., & Stigler, J. W. (2003). *Teaching mathematics in seven countries: Results from the TIMSS 1999 video study* (NCES 2003-013). Washington, DC: U.S. Department of Education.

Higgins, A., Power, C., & Kohlberg, L. (1983, April). *Moral atmosphere and moral judgment.* Paper presented at the biennial meeting of the Society for Research in Child Development, Detroit.

Hightower, E. (1990). Adolescent interpersonal and familial precursors of positive mental health at midlife. *Journal of Youth and Adolescence, 19*, 257–275.

Hildebrand, V., Phenice, A., & Hines, R. P. (2000). *Knowing and serving diverse families.* Columbus, OH: Merrill.

Hilgard, E. R. (1996). History of educational psychology. In D. C. Berliner & R. C. Calfee (Eds.), *Handbook of educational psychology.* New York: Macmillan.

Hill, J. R., Reeves, T. C., Grant, M. M., Wang, S-K. & Han, S. (2002). The impact of portable technologies on teaching and learning: Year three report. Retrieved April 8, 2005, from http://lpsl.coe.uga.edu/Projects/aalaptop/pdf/aa3rd/Year3ReportFinalVersion.pdf

Hiltz, S. R., & Goldman, R. (Eds.). (2005). *Learning together online.* Mahwah, NJ: Erlbaum.

Hirsch, E. D. (1987). *Cultural literacy.* New York: Random House.

Hirsch, E. D. (1996). *The schools we need: And why we don't have them.* New York: Doubleday.

Hirsh, R. (2004). *Early childhood curriculum: Incorporating multiple intelligences, developmentally appropriate practices, and play.* Boston: Allyn & Bacon.

Hitch, G. H. (2006). Working memory in children. In E. Bialystok & F. I. M. Craik (Eds.), *Lifespan cognition.* New York: Oxford University Press.

Hock, R. R. (2007). *Human sexuality.* Upper Saddle River, NJ: Prentice Hall.

Hocutt, A. M. (1996). Effectiveness of special education: Is placement the critical factor? *Future of Children, 6*(1), 77–102.

Hodapp, R. M., & Dykens, E. M. (2006). Mental retardation. In W. Damon & R. Lerner (Eds.), *Handbook of child psychology* (6th ed.). New York: Wiley.

Hoff, E., Laursen, B., & Tardif, T. (2002). Socioeconomic status and parenting. In M. H. Bornstein (Ed.), *Handbook of parenting* (2nd ed.). Mahwah, NJ: Erlbaum.

Hoff, E. (2006). How social contexts support and shape language development. *Developmental Review, 26*, 55–88.

Hoffner, H. (2007). *The elementary teacher's digital toolbox.* Upper Saddle River, NJ: Prentice Hall.

Hollingworth, L. S. (1916). Sex differences in mental tests. *Psychological Bulletin, 13*, 377–383.

Holzberg, C. (1995). Technology in special education. *Technology and Learning, 14*, 18–21.

Honey, M., & Henriquez, A. (2000). More things that do make a difference for youth. Union City School District, NJ. Retrieved April 8, 2005, from http://www.aypf.org/compendium/C2s18.pdf

Hooper, S., Ward, T. J., Hannafin, M. J., & Clark, H. T. (1989). The effects of aptitude composition on achievement during small group learning. *Journal of Computer-Based Instruction, 16*, 102–109.

Hoover-Dempsey, K. V., Battiato, C., Walker, J. M. T., Reed, R. P., Dejong, J. M., & Jones, K. P. (2001). Parental involvement in homework. *Educational Psychologist, 36*, 195–209.

Horn, J. (2006). Spearman, g, expertise, and the nature of human cognitive capacity. In P. C. Kyllonen. R. D. Roberts, & L. Stankov (Eds.), *Extending intelligence.* Mahwah, NJ: Erlbaum.

Horowitz, F. D., Darling-Hammond, L., Bransford, J., Comer, J., Rosebrock, K., Austin, K., & Rust, F. (2005). Educating teachers for developmentally appropriate practice. In L. Darling-Hammond & J. Bransford (Eds.), *Preparing teachers for a changing world.* San Francisco: Jossey-Bass.

Houston, P. D. (2005, February). NCLB: Dreams and nightmares. *Phi Delta Kappan*, 469–470.

Howard-Jones, P. (2005). An invaluable foundation for better bridges. *Developmental Science, 8*, 469–471.

Howe, M. J. A., Davidson, J. W., Moore, D. G., & Sloboda, J. A. (1995). Are there early childhood signs of musical ability? *Psychology of Music, 23*, 162–176.

Howes, C., & Tonyan, H. (2000). Peer relations. In L. Balter & C. S. Tamis-LeMonda (Eds.), *Child psychology: A handbook of contemporary issues.* Philadelphia: Psychology Press.

Huber, F., Beckmann, S. C., & Herrmann, A. (2004). Means-end analysis: Does the affective state influence information processing style. *Psychology & Marketing, 21,* 715–737.

Hudley, C., & Graham, S. (1995). School-based interventions for aggressive African-American boys. *Applied and Preventive Psychology, 4,* 185–195.

Huerta, M., Cortina, L. M., Pang, J. S., Torges, C. M., & Magley, V. J. (2006). Sex and power in the academy: modeling sexual harassment in the lives of college women. *Personality and Social Psychology Bulletin, 32,* 616–628.

Hulit, L. M., & Howard, M. R. (2006). *Born to talk: An introduction to speech and language development* (4th ed.). Boston: Allyn & Bacon.

Hunt, E. (2006). Expertise, talent, and social encouragement. In K. A. Ericsson, N. Charness, P. J. Feltovich, & R. R. Hoffman (Eds.), *The Cambridge handbook of expertise and expert performance.* New York: Cambridge University Press.

Hunt, E. B. (1995). *Will we be smart enough? A cognitive analysis of the coming work force.* New York: Russell Sage.

Hunt, R. R., & Ellis, H. C. (2004). *Fundamentals of cognitive psychology* (7th ed.). New York: McGraw-Hill.

Hunt, R. R., & Kelly, R. E. S. (1996). Accessing the particular from the general: The power of distinctiveness in the context of organization. *Memory and Cognition, 24,* 217–225.

Hupert, N., & Heinze, J. (2006). Results in the Palms of their hands: Using handheld computers for data-driven decision making in the classroom. In M. van't Hooft & K. Swan (Eds.), *Ubiquitous computing in education: Invisible technology, visible results.* Mahwah, NJ: Erlbaum.

Hurlburt, R. T. (2006). *Comprehending behavioral statistics* (4th ed.). Belmont, CA: Wadsworth.

Hutchinson, J. M., & Gigerenzer, G. (2005). Simple heuristics and rules of thumb. *Behavioural Processes, 69,* 97–124.

Huttenlocher, J., Haight, W., Bruk, A., Seltzer, M., & Lyons, T. (1991). Early vocabulary growth: Relation to language input and gender. *Developmental Psychology, 27,* 236–248.

Huttenlocher, P. R., & Dabholkar, A. S. (1997). Regional differences in synaptogenesis in human cerebral cortex. *Journal of Comparative Neurology, 37(2),* 167–178.

Huurre, T., Junkkari, H., & Aro, H. (2006). Long-term psychological effects of parental divorce: A follow-up study from adolescence to adulthood. *European Archives of Psychiatry and Clinical Neuroscience, 256,* 256–263.

Hyde, J. S. (2005). The gender similarities hypothesis. *American Psychologist, 60,* 581–592.

Hyde, J. S. (2007). *Half the human experience* (7th ed.). Boston: Houghton Mifflin.

Hyde, J. S., & Plant, E. A. (1995). Magnitude of psychological gender differences: Another side of the story. *American Psychologist, 50,* 159–161.

Hyman, I. (1997). *The case against spanking: How to discipline your child without hitting.* San Francisco: Jossey-Bass.

Hyman, I., Eisenstein, J., Amidon, A., & Kay, B. (2001, August 28). An update on the cross-cultural study of corporal punishment and abuse. In F. Farley (Chair), *Cross cultural aspects of corporal punishment and abuse: A research update.* Symposium presented at the 2001 Annual Convention of the American Psychological Association, San Francisco.

Hyman, I., Kay, B., Tabori, A., Weber, M., Mahon, M., & Cohen, I. (2006). Bullying: Theory, research, and interventions. In C. M. Evertson & C. S. Weinstein (Eds.), *Handbook of classroom management: Research, practice, and contemporary issues.* Mahwah, NJ: Erlbaum.

Hyman, I. & Snook, P. (1999). *Dangerous schools: What we can do about the physical and emotional abuse of our children.* San Francisco: Jossey-Bass.

Hyson, M. C., Copple, C., & Jones, J. (2006). Early childhood development and education. In W. Damon & R. Lerner (Eds.), *Handbook of child psychology* (6th ed.). New York: Wiley.

I

"I Have a Dream" Foundation. (2005). *About us.* Retrieved April 30, 2006 from http://www.ihad.org

Iacocca, L. (1984). *Iacocca: An autobiography.* New York: Bantam.

Ialongo, N., Poduska, J., Werthamer, L., & Kellam, S. (2001). The distal impact of two first-grade preventive interventions on conduct problems and disorder in early adolescence. *Journal of Emotional and Behavioral*

IBM. (2006). Valuing diversity. Retrieved January 15, 2006, from http://www.306.ibm.com/employment/us/diverse/camps

Ickes, W., Snyder, M., & Garcia, S. (1997). Personality influences or the choice of situations. In R. Hogan, J. Johnson, & S. Briggs (Eds.), *Handbook of personality psychology.* San Diego: Academic Press.

Idol, L., Nevin, A., & Paolucci-Whitcomb, P. (1994). *Collaborative consultation.* Austin, TX: PRO-ED.

Indiana University High School Survey of Student Engagement. (2004). Bloomington, IN: School of Education, University of Indiana.

Inkrott, C. (2001). Beyond drill and practice: Managing courseware and electronic portfolios. *Multimedia Schools, 8,* 44–47.

Intercultural Development Research Association. (1996). *More at-risk students to tutor others.* Unpublished manuscript, Intercultural Development Research Association, San Antonio.

Intercultural Development Research Association. (2004). *Coca-Cola Valued Youth program.* Retrieved November 15, 2005, from http://www.idra.org/ccvyp/

International Society for Technology in Education. (2000). *National educational technology standards for students: Connecting curriculum and technology.* Eugene, OR: Author.

International Society for Technology in Education (ISTE). (2001). *National educational technology standards for teachers—Preparing teachers to use technology.* Eugene, OR: Author.

Irvine, J. J. (1990). *Black students and school failure.* New York: Greenwood Press.

J

Jabbour, R. A., Hempel, A., Gates, J. R., Zhang, W., & Risse, G. L. (2005). Right hemisphere language mapping in patients with bilateral language. *Epilepsy & Behavior, 6,* 587–592.

Jackson, A. W., & Davis, G. A. (2000). *Turning points 2000.* New York: Teachers College Press.

Jackson, J. F. (1997, April). *Primary grade public schooling: A risk factor for African American children?* Paper presented at the meeting of the Society for Research in Child Development, Washington, DC.

Jackson, S. L. (2005). *Statistics plain and simple.* Belmont, CA: Wadsworth.

Jacobs, H. H. (1997). *Mapping the big picture: Integrating curriculum and assessment K–12.* Alexandria, VA: Association for Supervision and Curriculum Development.

Jacobs, J., & Klaczynski, P. (Eds.). (2005). *The development of judgment and decision*

making in children and adolescents. Mahwah, NJ: Erlbaum.

Jacobson, L. (1996, January). First in the world? *American School Board Journal,* pp. 21–23.

Jacobson, L. (2004). Pre–K standards said to slight social, emotional skills. *Education Week, 23, Issue 42,* 13–14.

Jaffee, S., & Hyde, J. S. (2000). Gender differences in moral orientation: A meta-analysis. *Psychological Bulletin, 126,* 703–726.

James, W. (1890). *Principles of psychology.* New York: Dover.

James, W. (1899/1993). *Talks to teachers.* New York: W. W. Norton.

Jenkins, J., & Jenkins, L. (1987). Making peer tutoring work. *Educational Leadership, 44,* 64–68.

Jenkins, J. M., & Astington, J. W. (1996). Cognitive factors and family structure associated with theory of mind development in young children. *Developmental Psychology, 32,* 70–78.

Jennings, K. D., & Deitz, L. J. (2002). Mastery motivation. In M. H. Bornstein, L. Davidson, C. L. M. Keyes, & K. Moore (Eds.). *Well-being.* Mahwah, NJ: Erlbaum.

Jensen, A. R. (1969). How much can we boost IQ and academic achievement? *Harvard Educational Review, 39,* 1–123.

Jensen, M. M. (2005). *Introduction to emotional and behavioral disorders.* Upper Saddle River, NJ: Prentice Hall.

Jeynes, W. H. (2003). A meta-analysis: The effects of parental involvement on minority children's academic achievement. *Education and Urban Society, 35,* 202–218.

Johnsen, S. (2005). Within-class acceleration. *Gifted Child Today, 28,* 5.

Johnson, D. W., & Johnson, R. T. (1991). *Teaching students to be peacemakers.* Edina, MN: Interaction.

Johnson, D. W., & Johnson, R. T. (1994). *Learning together and alone* (4th ed.). Boston: Allyn & Bacon.

Johnson, D. W., & Johnson, R. T. (1995, February). Why violence prevention programs don't work—and what does. *Educational Leadership,* pp. 63–68.

Johnson, D. W., & Johnson, R. T. (1999). The three Cs of school and classroom management. In H. J. Frieberg (Ed.), *Beyond behaviorism: Changing the classroom management paradigm.* Boston: Allyn & Bacon.

Johnson, D. W., & Johnson, R. T. (2003). *Joining together: Group theory and group skills* (7th ed.). Boston: Allyn & Bacon.

Johnson, D. W., & Johnson, R. T. (2002). *Multi-cultural and human relations.* Allyn & Bacon.

Johnson, D. W., & Johnson, R. T. (2005). Cooperative learning. In S. W. Lee (Ed.), *Encyclopedia of school psychology.* Thousand Oaks, CA: Sage.

Johnson, J. S., & Newport, E. L. (1991). Critical period effects on universal properties of language: The status of subjacency in the acquisition of a second language. *Cognition, 39,* 215–258.

Johnson, M. K., Beebe, T., Mortimer, J. T., & Snyder, M. (1998). Volunteerism in adolescence: A process perspective. *Journal of Research on Adolescence, 8,* 309–332.

Johnson, V. R. (1994). *Parent centers in urban schools.* (Center Report no. 23). Baltimore: Johns Hopkins University, Center on Families, Communities, Schools, and Children's Learning.

Johnson, W. B., Bouchard, T. J., Krueger, R. F., McGue, M., & Gottesman, I. I. (2004). Just one *g*: Consistent results from three test batteries. *Intelligence, 32,* 95–107.

Johnson, W. B. (2006). *On being a mentor.* Mahwah, NJ: Erlbaum.

Johnson-Laird, P. (2000). Reasoning. In A. Kazdin (Ed.), *Encyclopedia of psychology.* Washington, DC, & New York: American Psychological Association and Oxford University Press.

John-Steiner, V., & Mahn, H. (2003). Sociocultural contexts for teaching and learning. In I. B. Weiner (Ed.), *Handbook of psychology* (Vol. VII). New York: Wiley.

Jonassen, D. H. (1996). *Computers in the classroom: Mindtools for critical thinking.* Columbus, OH: Merrill/Prentice Hall.

Jonassen, D. H. (2006). *Modeling with technology* (3rd ed.). Upper Saddle River, NJ: Prentice Hall.

Jonassen, D. H., & Grabowski, B. L. (1993). *Handbook of individual differences, learning, and instruction.* Mahwah, NJ: Erlbaum.

Jones, B. F., Rasmussen, C. M., & Moffitt, M. C. (1997). *Real-life problem solving.* Washington, DC: American Psychological Association.

Jones, J. M. (1994). The African American: A duality dilemma? In W. J. Lonner & R. Malpass (Eds.), *Psychology and culture.* Boston: Allyn & Bacon.

Jones, J. M. (1997). *Prejudice and racism* (2nd ed.). New York: McGraw-Hill.

Jones, M. G., & Wheatley, J. (1990). Gender differences in teacher-student interactions in science classrooms. *Journal of Research in Science Teaching, 27,* 861–874.

Jones, V., & Jones, L. (2004). *Comprehensive classroom management* (7th ed.). Boston: Allyn & Bacon.

Joyce, B., Weil, M., & Calhoun, E. (2004). *Models of teaching* (7th ed.). Boston: McGraw-Hill.

Judge, S. (2005, April). *Impact of computer technology on the academic achievement of young African American children.* Paper presented at the meeting of the Society for Research in Child Development, Atlanta.

Justice, L. M. (2006). *Communication sciences and disorders* (5th ed.). Upper Saddle River, NJ: Prentice Hall.

Juvonen, J., Graham, S., & Schuster, M. A. (2003). Bullying among young adolescents: The strong, the weak, and the troubled. *Pediatrics, 112,* 1231–1237.

K

Kabler, P. (1997, November 14). School officials work bugs out of computer act. *Charleston Gazette,* p. C1.

Kafai, Y. B. (2006). Constructivism. In R. K. Sawyer (Ed.), *Cambridge handbook of the learning sciences.* New York: Cambridge University Press.

Kagan, J. (1965). Reflection-impulsivity and reading development in primary grade children. *Child Development, 36,* 609–628.

Kagan, J. (1992). Yesterday's promises, tomorrow's promises. *Developmental Psychology, 28,* 990–997.

Kagan, J. (2002). Behavioral inhibition as a temperamental category. In R. J. Davidson, K. R. Scherer, & H. H. Goldsmith (Eds.), *Handbook of affective sciences.* New York: Oxford University Press.

Kagan, J. (2003). Biology, context, and developmental inquiry. *Annual Review of Psychology* (Vol. 54). Palo Alto, CA: Annual Reviews.

Kagan, J., & Fox, N. A. (2006). Biology, culture, and temperamental biases. In W. Damon & R. Lerner (Eds.), *Handbook of child psychology* (6th ed.). New York: Wiley.

Kagan, J., & Snidman, N. (1991). Infant predictors of inhibited and uninhibited behavioral profiles. *Psychological Science, 2,* 40–44.

Kagan, S. (1992). *Cooperative learning.* San Juan Capistrano, CA: Resources for Teachers.

Kagan, S. L., & Scott-Little, C. (2004). Early learning standards. *Phi Delta Kappan, 82,* 388–395.

Kagiticibasi, C. (1996). *Human development across cultures.* Mahwah, NJ: Erlbaum.

Kahneman, D., & Tversky, A. (1995). Conflict resolution: A cognitive perspective.

In K. Arrow, R. H. Mnookin, L. Ross, A. Tversky, & R. Wilson (Eds.), *Barriers to conflict resolution.* New York: Norton.

Kail, R. (2000). Speed of information processing: Developmental change and links to intelligence. *Journal of School Psychology, 38,* 51–62.

Kail, R. (2002). Developmental change in proactive interference. *Child Development, 73*(6), 1703–1714.

Kalter, N. (1990). *Growing up with divorce.* New York: Free Press.

Kamii, C. (1985). *Young children reinvent arithmetic: Implications of Piaget's theory.* New York: Teachers College Press.

Kamii, C. (1989). *Young children continue to reinvent arithmetic.* New York: Teachers College Press.

Kammrath, L. K., Mendonza-Denton, R., & Mischel, W. (2005). Incoporating if . . . then . . . personality signatures in person perception: Beyond the person-situation dichotomy. *Journal of Personality and Social Psychology, 88,* 605–618.

Kane, M. J., Hambrick, D. Z., Tuholski, S. W., Wilhelm, O., Payne, T. W., & Engle, R. W. (2004). The generality of working memory capacity: A latent-variable approach to verbal and visuospatial memory span and reasoning. *Journal of Experimental Psychology: General, 133,* 189–217.

Kaplan, R. M., & Saccuzzo, D. P. (2005). *Psychological testing* (6th ed.). Belmont, CA: Wadsworth.

Karcher, M. J., Roy-Carolson, L., Allen, C., & Gil-Hernandez, D. (2005). Mentoring. In S. W. Lee (Ed.), *Encyclopedia of school psychology.* Thousand Oaks, CA: Sage.

Kasprow, W. J., & others. (1993). *New Haven Schools Social Development Project: 1992.* New Haven, CT: New Haven Public Schools.

Katz, L. (1999). Curriculum disputes in early childhood education. *ERIC Clearinghouse on Elementary and Early Childhood Education.* Document EDO-PS-99-13.

Katz, L., & Chard, S. (1989). *Engaging the minds of young children: The project approach.* Norwood, NJ: Ablex.

Kaufman, A. S., & Lictenberger, E. O. (2002). *Assessing adolescent and adult intelligence* (2nd ed.). Boston: Allyn & Bacon.

Kaufman, J. C. (Ed.) (2006). *Creative and reason in development.* New York: Cambridge University Press.

Kaufmann, L. (2003). More evidence for the role of the central executive in retrieving arithmetic facts—a case study of severe developmental dyscalculia. *Journal of Clinical and Experimental Neuropsychology, 24,* 302–310.

Kaufman, P. (2001). Dropping out of school: Detours in the life course. In T. Urdan & F. Pajares (Eds.), *Adolescence and education.* Greenwich, CT: IAP.

Kauffman, J. M. (2005). *Characteristics of emotional and behavioral disorders of children and youth* (8th ed.). Upper Saddle River, NJ: Prentice Hall.

Kauffman, J. M., & Hallahan, D. P. (2005). *Special education.* Boston: Allyn & Bacon.

Kauffman, J. M., McGee, K., & Brigham, M. (2004). Enabling or disabling? Observations on changes in special education. *Phi Delta Kappan, 85,* 613–620.

Kauffman, J. M., Mostert, M. P., Trent, S. C., & Pullen, P. L. (2006). *Managing classroom behavior* (4th ed.). Boston: Allyn & Bacon.

Kavale, K. A., Holdnack, J. A., & Mostert, M. P. (2005). Responsiveness to intervention and the identification of specific learning disability: A critique and alternative proposal. *Learning Disability Quarterly, 28,* 2–16.

Kay, A. (2005). The Dynabook revisited: A conversation with Alan Kay. *The Book and the Computer: Exploring the Future of the Printed Word in the Digital Age.* Retrieved May 26, 2005, from http://www.honco.net/os/kay.html

Kazdin, A. E. (2001). *Behavior modification in applied settings* (6th ed.). Belmont, CA: Wadsworth.

Kearney, B. A. (1991, April). *The teacher as absent presence.* Paper presented at the meeting of the American Educational Research Association, Chicago.

Keating, D. P. (1990). Adolescent thinking. In S.S. Feldman & G. R. Elliott (Eds.), *At the threshold: The developing adolescent.* Cambridge, MA: Harvard University Press.

Keating, D. P. (2004). Cognitive and brain development. In R. Lerner & L. Steinberg (Ed.), *Handbook of adolescent psychology* (2nd ed.). New York: Wiley.

Keenan, K., Hipwell, A., Duax, J., Stouthamer-Loeber, M., & Lober, R. (2004). Phenomenology of depression in young girls. *Journal of the Academy of Child and Adolescent Psychiatry, 43,* 1098–1106.

Keil, F. (2006). Cognitive science and cognitive development. In W. Damon & R. Lerner (Eds.), *Handbook of child psychology* (6th ed.). New York: Wiley.

Keller, B. (2005, May 25). Panel urges new testing for teachers. *Education Week, 24* (No. 38), 1–2.

Keller, H. (2007). *Cultures of infancy.* Mahwah, NJ: Erlbaum.

Kellogg, R. T. (1994). *The psychology of writing.* New York: Oxford University Press.

Kellogg, R. T. (2000). Writing. In A. Kazdin (Ed.), *Encyclopedia of psychology.* Washington, DC, & New York: American Psychological Association and Oxford University Press.

Keogh, B. K. (2003). *Temperament in the classroom.* Baltimore: Brookes.

Kerr, M. M., & Nelson, C. M. (2006). *Strategies for assessing behavior problems in the classroom* (5th ed.). Upper Saddle River, NJ: Prentice Hall.

Kiess, H. O. (2002). *Statistical concepts for the behavioral sciences* (3rd ed.). Boston: Allyn & Bacon.

Kinchin, I. M., Hay, D. B., & Adams, A. (2000). How a qualitative approach to concept map analysis can be used to aid learning by illustrating patterns of conceptual development. *Educational Research, 42*(1), 43–57.

Kinderman, T. A., McCollam, T. L., & Gibson, E. (1996). Peer networks and students' classroom engagement during childhood and adolescence. In J. Juvonen & K. R. Wentzel (Eds.), *Social motivation.* New York: Cambridge University Press.

King, P. E., & Behnke, R. R. (2005). Problems associated with evaluating student performance in groups. *College Teaching, 53,* 57–61.

Kinginger, C. (2002). Defining the zone of proximal development in U. S. foreign language education. *Applied Linguistics, 23,* 240–261.

Kirby, D. (1992). School-based programs to reduce sexual risk-taking behaviors. *Journal of School Health, 62,* 280–287.

Kirsh, S. J. (2006). *Children, adolescents, and media violence.* Mahwah. NJ: Erlbaum.

Kite, M. (2001). Gender stereotypes. In J. Worell (Ed.), *Encyclopedia of women and gender.* San Diego: Academic Press.

Kivel, P. (1995). *Uprooting racism: How White people can work for racial justice.* Philadelphia: New Society.

Klaczynski, P. (2005). Metacognition and cognitive variability: A two-process model of decision making and its development. In J. Jacobs & P. Klaczynski (Eds.), *The development of decision making: Cognitive. sociocultural, and legal perspectives.* Mahwah NJ: Erlbaum.

Klaczynski, P. A., & Narasimham, G. (1998). Development of scientific reasoning biases: Cognitive versus ego-protective explanations. *Developmental Psychology, 34,* 175–187.

Klausmeier, H. J. (2004). Conceptual learning and development. In W. E. Craighead

& C. B. Nemeroff (Eds.), *The concise Corsini encyclopedia of psychology and behavioral sciences.* New York: Wiley.

Klein, K., & Boals, A. (2001). Expressive writing can increase working memory capacity. *Journal of Experimental Psychology: General, 130,* 520–533.

Klenowski, V., Askew, S., & Carnell, E. (2006). Portfolios for learning, assessment, and professional development in higher education. *Assessment and Evaluation in Higher Education, 31,* 267–286.

Kling, K. C., Hyde, J. S., Showers, C. J., & Buswell, B. N. (1999). Gender differences in self-esteem: A meta-analysis. *Psychological Bulletin, 125,* 470–500.

Knecht, S., Draeger, B., Floel, A., Lohmann, H., Breitenstein, C., Henningson, H., & Ringelstein, E. (2001). Behavioral relevance of atypical language lateralization in healthy subjects. *Brain, 124,* 1657–1665.

Knotek, S. (2005). Portfolio assessment. In S. W. Lee (Ed.), *Encyclopedia of school psychology.* Thousand Oaks, CA: Sage.

Koedinger, K. R., & Corbett. A. (2006). Cognitive tutors: Technology bringing learning sciences to the classroom. In R. K. Sawyer (Ed.), *The Cambridge handbook of learning sciences.* New York: Cambridge University Press.

Kohlberg, L. (1966). A cognitive-developmental analysis of children's sex-role concepts and attitudes. In E. E. Maccoby (Ed.), *The development of sex differences.* Palo Alto, CA: Stanford University Press.

Kohlberg, L. (1976). Moral stages and moralization: The cognitive-developmental approach. In T. Lickona (Ed.), *Moral development and behavior.* New York: Holt, Rinehart & Winston.

Kohlberg, L. (1986). A current statement of some theoretical issues. In S. Modgil & C. Modgil (Eds.), *Lawrence Kohlberg.* Philadelphia: Falmer.

Kohn, A. (1996). By all available means: Cameron and Pierce's defense of extrinsic motivators. *Review of Educational Research, 66,* 5–32.

Konidaris, G. D., & Hayes, G. M. (2005). An architecture for behavior-based reinforcement. *Adaptive Behavior, 13,* 5–32.

Kornhaber, M., Fierros, E., & Veenema, S. (2005). *Multiple intelligences: Best ideas from research and practice.* Boston: Allyn & Bacon.

Kounin, J. S. (1970). *Discipline and management in classrooms.* New York: Holt, Rinehart & Winston.

Kozol, J. (1991). *Savage inequalities.* New York: Crown.

Kozol, J. (2005). *The shame of a nation.* New York: Crown.

Kozulin, A. (2004). Vygotsky's theory in the classroom: Introduction. *European Journal of Psychology of Education, 19,* 3–7.

Krajcik, J. S., & Blumenfeld, P. C. (2006). Project-based learning. In R. K. Sawyer (Ed.), *The Cambridge Handbook of learning sciences.* New York: Oxford University Press.

Krantz, P. J., & Risley, T. R. (1972, September). *The organization of group care environments: Behavioral ecology in the classroom.* Paper presented at the meeting of the American Psychological Association, Honolulu.

Krathwohl, D. R., Bloom, B. S., & Masia, B. B. (1964). *Taxonomy of educational objectives. Handbook II: Affective domain.* New York: David McKay.

Kress, J. S., & Elias, M. J. (2006). School-based social and emotional learning. In W. Damon & R. Lerner (Eds.), *Handbook of child psychology* (6th ed.). New York: Wiley.

Kreutzer, L. C., & Flavell, J. H. (1975). An interview study of childrens knowledge about memory. *Monographs of the Society for Research in Child Development, 40* (1, Serial No. 159).

Kroger, J. (2007). *Identity development* (2nd ed.). Thousand Oaks, CA: Sage.

Kubick, R. J., & McLoughlin, C. S. (2005). No Child Left Behind Act of 2001. In S. W. Lee (Ed.), *Encyclopedia of school psychology.* Thousand Oaks, CA: Sage.

Kuhn, D. (1999). Metacognitive development. In L. Balter & S. Tamis-Lemonda (Eds.), *Child psychology: A handbook of contemporary issues.* Philadelphia: Psychology Press.

Kuhn, D. (2006, in press). *Education for thinking.* Cambridge: Harvard University Press.

Kuhn, D., & Franklin, S. (2006). The second decade: What develops (and how)? In W. Damon & R. Lerner (Eds.), *Handbook of child psychology* (6th ed.). New York: Wiley.

Kuhn, D., Garcia-Mila, M., Zohar, Z., & Anderson, C. (1995). Strategies for knowledge acquisition. *Monographs of the Society for Research in Child Development, 60* (4, Serial No. 245), 1–127.

Kuhn, D., Katz, J., & Dean, D. (2004). Developing reason. *Thinking & Reasoning, 10*(2), 197–219.

Kuhn, D., Weinstock, M., & Flaton, R. (1994). How well do jurors reason? Competence dimensions of individual variation in a juror reasoning task. *Psychological Science, 5,* 289–296.

Kulczewski, P. (2005). Vygotsky and the three bears. *Teaching children mathematics, 11,* 246–248.

Kulik, C. L., Kulik, J. A., & Bangert-Drowns, R. L. (1990). Effectiveness of mastery learning programs: A meta-analysis. *Review of Educational Research, 60,* 265–299.

Kulik, J. A. (1992). An analysis of the research on ability grouping. *Monograph of the National Research Center on the Gifted and Talented* (No. 9204). Storrs: University of Connecticut.

Kunzmann, R. (2003). From teacher to student: The value of teacher education for experienced teachers. *Journal of Teacher Education, 54,* 241–253.

Kupersmidt, J. B., & Coie, J. D. (1990). Preadolescent peer status, aggression, and school adjustment as predictors of externalizing problems in adolescence. *Child Development, 61,* 1350–1363.

L

Lacey, P. (2001). The role of learning support assistants in inclusive learning of pupils with severe and profound learning difficulties. *Educational Review, 53,* 157–167.

Ladd, G., Buhs, E., & Troop, W. (2004). School adjustment and social skills training. In P. K. Smith & C. H. Hart (Eds.), *Blackwell handbook of childhood social development.* Malden, MA: Blackwell.

Ladd, G. W., Herald, S. L., & Andrews, R. K. (2006). Young children's peer relations and social competence. In B. Spodak & O. N. Sarancho (Eds.), *Handbook of research on the education of young children* (2nd ed.). Mahwah, NJ: Erlbaum.

Ladd, G. W., & Kochenderfer-Ladd, B. (2002). Identifying victims of peer aggression from early to middle childhood: Analysis of cross-informant data for concordance, incidence of victimization, characteristics of identified victims, and estimation of relational adjustment. *Psychological Assessment, 14,* 74–96.

Lainhart, J. E. (2006). Advances in autism neuroimaging research for the clinician and geneticist. *American Journal of Medical Genetics, C: Seminars in Medical Genetics, 142,* 33–39.

Lajoie, S. P., & Azevedo, R. (2006). Teaching and learning in technology-rich environments. In P. A. Alexander & P. H. Winne (Eds.), *Handbook of educational psychology* (2nd ed.). Mahwah, NJ: Erlbaum.

Lamb, M. E., & Sternberg, K. J. (1992). Sociocultural perspectives in nonparental childcare. In M. E. Lamb, K. J. Sternberg, C. Hwang, & A. G. Broberg (Eds.), *Child care in context.* Hillsdale, NJ: Erlbaum.

Lamb, M. E., Bornstein, M., & Teti, D. (2002). *Development in infancy* (4th ed.). Mahwah, NJ: Erlbaum.

Lammers, W. J., & Badia, P. (2005). *Fundamentals of behavioral research.* Belmont, CA: Wadsworth.

Lamon, M., Secules, T., Petrosino, A. J., Hackett, R., Bransford, J. D., & Goldman, S. R. (1996). Schools for thought. In L. Schauble & R. Glaser (Eds.), *Innovations in learning.* Mahwah, NJ: Erlbaum.

Landa, S. (2000, Fall). If you can't make waves, make ripples. *Intelligence Connections Newsletter of the ASCD, X* (No. 1), 6–8.

Lane, H. B., & Pullen, P. C. (2004). *Phonological awareness assessment and instruction.* Boston: Allyn & Bacon.

Lane, K. L., Greshman, F. M., & O'Shaughnessy, T. E. (2002). *Interventions for children with or at-risk for emotional and behavioral disorders.* Boston: Allyn & Bacon.

Langhout, R. D., Rhodes, J. E., & Osborne, L. N. (2004). An exploratory study of youth mentoring in an urban context: Adolescents' perceptions of relationship styles. *Journal of Youth and Adolescence, 33,* 293–306.

Lankes, A. M. D. (1995). *Electronic portfolios: A new idea in assessment.* ERIC Document Reproduction Service No. ED390377.

Lansford, J. E., Malone, P. S., Castellino, D. R., Dodge, K. A., Pettit, G. S., & Bates, J. E. (2006). Trajectories of internalizing, externalizing, and grades for children who have and have not experienced their parents' divorce or separation. *Journal of Family Psychology, 20,* 292–301.

Lapierre, C. (2005). Goal-attainment scaling. In S. W. Lee (Ed.), *Encyclopedia of school psychology.* Thousand Oaks, CA: Sage.

Lapsley, D. K. (2005). Moral stage theory. In M. Killen & J. Smetana (Eds.), *Handbook of moral development.* Mahwah, NJ: Erlbaum.

Lapsley, D. K., & Narvaez, D. (2006). Character education. In W. Damon & R. Lerner (Eds.), *Handbook of child psychology* (6th ed.). New York: Wiley.

Lara, L. E. (2006, April). *Young Latinas and their relation to the new technologies.* Paper presented at the meeting of the American Educational Research Association, San Francisco.

Larrivee, B. (2005). *Authentic classroom management* (2nd ed.). Boston: Allyn & Bacon.

Larson, R. W. (2001). How U.S. children and adolescents spend their time: What it does (and doesn't) tell us about their development: *Current Directions in Psychological Science, 10,* 160–164.

Larson, R. W., & Verma, S. (1999). How children and adolescents spend time across the world: Work, play, and developmental opportunities. *Psychological Bulletin, 125,* 701–736.

Larson, R. W., & Wilson, S. (2004), Adolescence across place and time: Globalization and the changing pathways to adulthood. In R. Lerner & L. Steinberg (Eds.), *Handbook of adolescent psychology.* New York: Wiley.

Lazar, L., & others. (1982). Lasting effects of early education. *Monographs of the Society for Research in Child Development, 47.*

Leaper, C., & Smith, T. E. (2004). A meta-analytic review of gender variations in children's language use: Talkativeness, affiliative speech, and assertive speech. *Developmental Psychology, 40,* 993–1027.

Leary, M. R. (2004). *Introduction to behavioral research methods* (4th ed.). Boston: Allyn & Bacon.

Lederman, L. M., & Burnstein, R. A. (2006). Alternative approaches to high-stakes testing. *Phi Delta Kappan, 87,* 429–432.

LeDoux, J. E. (1996). *The emotional brain.* New York: Simon & Schuster.

LeDoux, J. E. (2002). *The synaptic self.* New York: Viking.

Lee, C. D., & Slaughter-Defoe, D. (1995). Historical and sociocultural influences of African American education. In J. A. Banks, & C. M. Banks (Eds.), *Handbook of research on multicultural education.* New York: Macmillan.

Lee, K., Ashton, M. C., & Shin, K-H. (2005). Personality correlates of workplace anti-social behavior. *Applied Psychology: An International Review, 54,* 81–97.

Lee, P. J. (2005). Putting principles into practice: Understanding history. *How students learn.* Washington, DC: National Academies Press.

Lee, R. M. (2005). Resilience against discrimination: Ethnic identity and other-group orientation as protective factors for Korean Americans. *Journal of Counseling Psychology, 52,* 36–44.

Lehr, C. A., Hanson, A., Sinclair, M. F., & Christenson, S. L. (2003). Moving beyond dropout prevention towards school completion: An integrative review of data-based interventions. *School Psychology Review, 32,* 342–364.

Lehrer, R., & Schauble, L. (2006). Scientific thinking and science literature: Supporting development in learning contexts. In W. Damon & R. Lerner (Eds.), *Handbook of child psychology* (6th ed.). New York: Wiley.

Leonard, N. H., Beauvais, L. L., & Scholl, R. W. (2005). A multi-level model of group cognitive style in strategic decision making. *Journal of Managerial Issues, 17,* 119–138.

Lepper, M. R., Corpus, J. H., & Iyengar, S. S. (2005). Intrinsic and extrinsic orientations in the classroom: Age differences and academic correlates. *Journal of Educational Psychology, 97,* 184–196.

Lepper, M. R., Greene, D., & Nisbett, R. (1973). Undermining children's intrinsic interest with intrinsic rewards: A test of the overjustification hypothesis. *Journal of Personality and Social Psychology, 28,* 129–137.

Lesaux, N., & Siegel, L. (2003). The development of reading in children who speak English as a second language. *Developmental Psychology, 39,* 1005–1019.

Lesser, G. (1972). Learning, teaching, and television production for children: The experience of *Sesame Street. Harvard Educational Review, 42,* 232–272.

Lesser, G. (1989, November 15). *Television and reading: Can they still be friends?* Paper presented at the Library of Congress, Washington, DC.

Lessow-Hurley, J. (2005). *Foundations of dual language instruction* (4th ed.). Boston: Allyn & Bacon.

Levin, J. (1980). *The mnemonics '80s: Keywords in the classroom.* Theoretical paper No. 86. Wisconsin Research and Development Center for Individualized Schooling, Madison.

Levy, C. M., & Randsell, S. (Eds.). (1996). *The science of writing.* Mahwah, NJ: Erlbaum.

Lewis, A. C. (2005, January). States feel the crunch of NCLB. *Phi Delta Kappan,* 339–340.

Lewis, A. C. (2006). Clean up the test mess. *Phi Delta Kappan, 87,* 643–644.

Lewis, R. (2001). Classroom discipline and student responsibility: The students' view. *Teaching and Teacher Education, 17,* 307–319.

Lewis, R. B., & Doorlag, D. (2006). *Teaching special students in general education classrooms* (7th ed.). Upper Saddle River, NJ: Prentice Hall.

Lewis, V. (2002). *Development and disability* (2nd ed.). Malden, MA: Blackwell.

Liben, L. S. (1995). Psychology meets geography: Exploring the gender gap on the national geography bee. *Psychological Science Agenda, 8,* 8–9.

Liben, L. S., & Bigler, R. S. (2002). The developmental course of gender differentiation. *Monographs of the Society for Research in Child Development 67*(2), 1–147.

Liederman, J., Kantrowitz, L., & Flannery, K. (2005). Male vulnerability to reading disability is not likely to be a myth: A call for new data. *Journal of Learning Disabilities, 38,* 109–129.

Limber, S. P. (1997). Preventing violence among school children. *Family Futures, 1,* 27–28.

Limber, S. P. (2004). Implementation of the Olweus Bullying Prevention Program in American schools: Lessons learned from the field. In D. L. Espelage & S. M. Swearer (Eds.), *Bullying in American schools.* Mahwah, NJ: Erlbaum.

Linden, K. W. (1996). *Cooperative learning and problem solving.* Prospect Heights, IL: Waveland Press.

Linebarger, D. L., & Walker, D. (2005). Infants' and toddlers' television viewing and language outcomes. *American Behavioral Scientist, 48,* 624–645.

Linn, R. L. (2000). Assessments and accountability. *Educational Research, 29,* 4–15.

Linn, M. C., & Eylon, B-S. (2006). Science education: Integrating views of learning and instruction. In P. A. Alexander & P. H. Winne (Eds.), *Handbook of educational psychology* (2nd ed.). Mahwah, NJ: Erlbaum.

Linn, M. C., & Hyde, J. S. (1989). Gender, mathematics, and science. *Educational Researcher, 18,* 17–27.

Linn, M. C., Songer, N. B., & Eylon, B. (1996). Shifts and convergences in science learning and instruction. In D. C. Berliner & R. C. Calfee (Eds.), *Handbook of educational psychology.* New York: Macmillan.

Linn, R. L., & Miller, M. D. (2005). *Measurement and assessment in teaching* (9th ed.). Upper Saddle River, NJ: Prentice Hall.

Linn, R. L., & Gronlund, N. E. (2000). *Measurement and assessment in teaching* (8th ed.). Upper Saddle River, NJ: Prentice Hall.

Lippa, R. A. (2005). *Gender, nature, and nurture* (2nd ed.). Mahwah, NJ: Erlbaum.

Lipsitz, J. (1984). *Successful schools for young adolescents.* New Brunswick, NJ: Transaction Books.

Litt, J., Taylor, H. G., Klein, N., & Hack, M. (2005). Learning disabilities in children with very low birthweight: Prevalence, neuropsychological correlates, and educational interventions. *Journal of Learning Disabilities, 38,* 130–141.

Litton, E. F. (1999). Learning in America: The Filipino-American sociocultural perspective. In C. Park & M. M. Chi (Eds.), *Asian-American education: Prospects and challenges.* Westport, CT: Bergin & Garvey.

Local Initiatives Support Corp. (LISC). (2005, August). LISC/NEF and One Economy launch $1 billion initiative to bridge the digital divide. Retrieved January 10, 2006, from http://www.lisc.org/whatsnew/press/releases/2005.08.08.0.shtml

Lodewyk, K. R., & Winne, P. H. (2005). Relations among the structure of learning tasks, achievement, and changes in self-efficacy in secondary students. *Journal of Educational Psychology, 97,* 3–12.

Logan, J. (1997). *Teaching stories.* New York: Kodansha International.

Lohmann, H., Drager, B., Muller-Ehrenberg, S., Deppe, M., & Knecht, S. (2005). Language lateralization in young children assessed by functional transcranial Doppler sonography. *Neuroimage, 24,* 780–790.

LoLordo, V. M. (2000). Classical conditioning. In A. Kazdin (Ed.), *Encyclopedia of psychology.* Washington, DC, New York: American Psychological Association and Oxford University Press.

Lott, B., & Maluso, D. (2001). Gender development: Social learning. In J. Worell (Ed.), *Encyclopedia of women and gender.* San Diego: Academic Press.

Lowe, P. A. (2005). Normal distribution. In S. W. Lee (Ed.), *Encyclopedia of school psychology.* Thousand Oaks, CA: Sage.

Lubinski, D. (2000). Measures of intelligence: Intelligence tests. In A. Kazdin (Ed.), *Encyclopedia of psychology.* Washington, DC, & New York: American Psychological Association and Oxford University Press.

Lumsden, G., & Lumsden, D. (2006). *Communicating with credibility and confidence* (3rd ed.). Belmont, CA: Thompson.

Luna, B., Garver, K., Urban, T., Lazar, N., & Sweeney, J. (2004). Maturation of cognitive processes from late childhood to adulthood. *Child Development, 75*(5), 1357–1372.

Luria, A., & Herzog, E. (1985, April). *Gender segregation across and within settings.* Paper presented at the biennial meeting of the Society for Research in Child Development, Toronto.

Luster, T., & Okaghi, L. (Eds.). (2005). *Parenting: An ecological perspective* (2nd ed.). Mahwah, NJ: Erlbaum.

Lutzker, J. R., & Whitaker, D. J. (2005). The expanding role of behavior analysis and support: Current status and future directions. *Behavior Modification, 29,* 575–594.

Lynn, R. (1996). Racial and ethnic differences in intelligence in the U.S. on the Differential Ability Scale. *Personality and Individual Differences, 26,* 271–273.

Lyon, G. R. (1996). Learning disabilities. *Future of Children, 6*(1), 54–76.

Lyon, T. D., & Flavell, J. H. (1993). Young children's understanding of forgetting over time. *Child Development, 64,* 789–800.

Lyons, N. (1999, May). How portfolios can shape emerging practice. *Educational Leadership, 56,* 63–67.

M

Ma, X. (2002). Bullying in middle school: Individual and school characteristics of victims and offenders. *School Effectiveness and School Improvement, 13,* 63–89.

Maag, J. W. (2001). Rewarded by punishment: Reflections on the disuse of positive reinforcement in schools. *Exceptional Children, 67,* 173–186.

Mabry, L. (1999, May). Writing to the rubric: Lingering effects of traditional standardized testing on direct writing assessment. *Phi Delta Kappan, 80,* 673–679.

Maccoby, E. E. (1998). *The two sexes: Growing up apart, coming together.* Cambridge, MA: Harvard University Press.

Maccoby, E. E. (2002). Gender and group processes: A developmental perspective. *Current Directions in Psychological Science, 11,* 54–58.

Maccoby, E. E., & Jacklin, C. N. (1974). *The psychology of sex differences.* Palo Alto, CA: Stanford University Press.

MacGeorge, E. L. (2004). The myth of gender cultures: Similarities outweigh differences in men's and women's provisions of and responses to supportive communication. *Sex Roles, 50,* 143–175.

Macklem, G. (2003). Bullying and teasing: Social power in children's groups. New York: Kluwer Academic.

MacLean, W. E. (2000). Down syndrome. In A. Kazdin (Ed.), *Encyclopedia of psychology.* Washington, DC, & New York: American Psychological Association and Oxford University Press.

Maddi, S. R. (2005). On hardiness and other pathways to resilience. *American Psychologist, 60,* 261–262.

Maddux, C. D., Johnson, D. L., & Willis, J. W. (1997). *Educational computing* (2nd ed.). Boston: Allyn & Bacon.

Maddux, J. (2002). The power of believing you can. In C. R. Snyder & S. J. Lopez (Eds.), *Handbook of positive psychology.* New York: Oxford University Press.

Maehr, M. L. (2001). Goal theory is *not* dead—not yet, anyway: A reflection on the special issue. *Educational Psychology Review, 13*, 177–188.

Mael, F. A. (1998). Single-sex and coeducational schooling: Relationships to socioemotional and academic development. *Review of Educational Research, 68*(2), 101–129.

Mager, R. (1962). *Preparing instructional objectives* (2nd ed.). Palo Alto, CA: Fearon.

Maggio, R. (1987). *The non-sexist word finder: A dictionary of gender-free usage.* Phoenix: Oryx Press.

Magnusson, D. (1988). *Individual development from an interactional perspective: A longitudinal study.* Hillsdale, NJ: Erlbaum.

Magnusson, S. J., & Palinscar, A. S. (2005). Teaching to promote the development of scientific knowledge and reasoning about light at the elementary school level. In *How people learn.* Washington, DC: National Academies Press.

Maidon, C. H., & Wheatley, J. H. (2001, July). *Outcomes for students using a model science curriculum.* Paper presented at the meeting of the National Association of Research in Science Teaching, St. Louis.

Major, B., Barr, L., Zubek, J., & Babey, S. H. (1999). Gender and self-esteem: A meta-analysis. In W. Swann & J. Langlois (Eds.), *Sexism and stereotypes in modern society: The gender science of Janet Taylor Spence.* Washington, DC: American Psychological Association.

Maki, P. L. (2001). From standardized tests to alternative methods. *Change, 33*(2), 28–31.

Malik, N. M., & Furman, W. (1993). Practitioner review: Problems in children's peer relations: What can the clinician do? *Journal of Child Psychology and Psychiatry, 34*, 1303–1326.

Mandler, G. (1980). Recognizing: The judgment of previous occurrence. *Psychological Review, 87*, 252–271.

Mandler, J. M. (2004). *The origins of mind.* New York: Oxford University Press.

Manis, F. R., Keating, D. P., & Morrison, F. J. (1980). Developmental differences in the allocation of processing capacity. *Journal of Experimental Child Psychology, 29*, 156–169.

Mann, V. (1998). Language problems: A key to early reading problems. In B. Y. L. Wong (Ed.), *Learning about learning disabilities* (2nd ed.). San Diego: Academic Press.

Manning, C. F., Mohole, K., & the Goodman Research Group. (2002). *The Lesson One program results of a controlled pre and post study.* Unpublished manuscript, Lesson One Foundation, Boston, MA.

Marchand-Martella, N. E., Slocum, T. A., & Martella, R. C. (2004). *Introduction to direct instruction.* Boston: Allyn & Bacon.

Marchman, V., & Thal, D. (2005). Words and grammar. In M. Tomasello & D. I. Slobin (Eds.), *Beyond nature-nurture.* Mahwah, NJ: Erlbaum.

Marcia, J. E. (1980). Identity in adolescence. In J. Adelson (Ed.), *Handbook of adolescent psychology.* New York: Wiley.

Marcia, J. E. (1998). Optimal development from an Eriksonian perspective. In H. S. Friedman (Ed.), *Encyclopedia of mental health* (Vol. 2). San Diego: Academic Press.

Marcovitch, H. (2004). Use of stimulants for attention deficit hyperactivity disorder: AGAINST. *British Medical Journal, 329*, 908–909.

Marklein, M. B. (1998, November 24). An eye-level meeting of the minds. *USA Today*, p. 9D.

Markman, A., & Gentner, D. (2001). Learning and reasoning. *Annual Review of Psychology* (Vol. 51). Palo Alto, CA: Annual Reviews.

Marshall, H. H. (1996). Implications of differentiating and understanding constructivist approaches. *Educational Psychologist, 31*, 240–243.

Martin, J. (2006). Social cultural perspectives in educational psychology. In P. A. Alexander & P. H. Winne (Eds.), *Handbook of educational psychology* (2nd ed.). Mahwah, NJ: Erlbaum.

Martin, C. L., & Dinella, L. (2001). Gender development: Gender schema theory. In J. Worell (Ed.), *Encyclopedia of women and gender.* San Diego: Academic Press.

Martin, C. L., & Halverson, C. F. (1981). A schematic processing model of sex typing and stereotyping in children. *Child Development, 52*, 1119–1134.

Martin, C. L., Ruble, D. N., & Szkrybalo, J. (2002). Cognitive theories of early gender development. *Psychological Bulletin, 128*, 903–933.

Martin, G., & Pear, J. (2002). *Behavior modification* (7th ed.). Upper Saddle River, NJ: Prentice Hall.

Martin, G. L., & Pear, J. (2007). *Behavior modification* (8th ed.). Upper Saddle River, NJ: Prentice Hall.

Martin, R., Sexton, C., Franklin, T., & Gerlovich, J. (2005). *Teaching science for all children* (5th ed.). Boston: Allyn & Bacon.

Marton, F., Hounsell, D. J., & Entwistle, N. J. (1984). *The experience of learning.* Edinburgh: Scottish Academic Press.

Martorella, P. (2001). *Teaching social studies in middle and secondary schools* (3rd ed.). Upper Saddle River, NJ: Merrill.

Marx, D. M., & Stapel, D. A. (2006). Distinguishing stereotype threat from priming effects: on the role of the social self and threat-based concerns. *Journal of Personality and Social Psychology, 91*, 243–254.

Marzano, R. J., & Kendall, J. S. (2006). *The new taxonomy of educational objectives* (2nd ed.). Thousand Oaks, CA: Corwin Press.

Maslow, A. H. (1954). *Motivation and personality.* New York: Harper & Row.

Maslow, A. H. (1971). *The farther reaches of human nature.* New York: Viking Press.

Masten, A. S. (2005). Peer relationships and psychopathology in developmental perspective: Reflections on progress and promise. *Journal of Clinical Child and Adolescent Psychology, 34*, 87–92.

Mastropieri, M. A., & Scruggs, T. E. (2007). *Inclusive classroom* (3rd ed.). Upper Saddle River, NJ: Prentice Hall.

Mather, N., & Gregg, N. (2001). Assessment and the Woodcock-Johnson III. In J. W. Andrews, D. H. Saklofske, & H. L. Janzen (Eds.), *Handbook of psychoeducational assessment.* San Diego: Academic Press.

Mathes, P. G., Denton, C. A., Fletcher, J. M., Anthony, J. L., Francis, D. J., & Schatschneider, C. (2005). The effects of theoretically different instruction and student characteristics on the skills of struggling readers. *Reading Research Quarterly, 40*, 148–182.

Mathes, P. G., Howard, J. K., Allen, S. H., & Fuchs, D. (1998). Peer-assisted learning strategies for first-grade readers: Responding to the needs of diverse learners. *Reading Research Quarterly, 33*, 62–94.

Mathes, P. G., Torgesen, J. K., & Allor, J. H. (2001). The effects of peer-assisted literacy strategies for first-grade readers with and without additional computer-assisted instruction in phonological awareness. *American Educational Research Journal, 38*, 371–410.

Matlin, M. (2005). *Cognition* (6th ed.). New York: Wiley.

Matsumoto, D. (2004). *Culture and psychology* (3rd ed.). Belmont, CA: Wadsworth.

Matthews, G., Zeidner, M., & Roberts, R. D. (2006). Models of personality and affect for education: A review and synthesis. In P. A. Alexander & P. H. Wynne (Eds.), *Handbook of educational psychology* (2nd ed.). Mahwah, NJ: Erlbaum.

Matusov, E., Bell, N., & Rogoff, B. (2001). *Schooling as a cultural process: Working together and guidance by children from schools differing in collaborative practices.* Unpublished manuscript, Department of Psychology, University of California at Santa Cruz.

Maxim, G. W. (2006). *Dynamic social studies for constructivist classrooms* (8th ed.). Upper Saddle River, NJ: Prentice Hall.

May, F. B. (2006). *Teaching reading creatively: Reading and writing as communication* (7th ed.). Upper Saddle River, NJ: Prentice Hall.

May, M. (2001, November 21). San Leandro kids lap up their lessons. *San Francisco Chronicle*, pp. A1, 24.

Mayer, J. D., Salovey, P. R., & Caruso, D. R. (2002). *Mayer–Salovey–Caruso Emotional Intelligence Test (MSCEIT): User's Manual.* Toronto, Ontario, Canada: Multi-Health Systems.

Mayer, J. D., Salovey, P., & Caruso, D. R. (2004). Emotional intelligence: Theory, findings, and implications. *Psychological Inquiry, 15,* 197–215.

Mayer, J. D., Salovey, P. R., & Caruso, D. R. (2006). What is emotional intelligence and what does it predict? In P. C. Kyllonen, R. D. Roberts, & L. Stankov (Eds.), *Extending intelligence.* Mahwah, NJ: Erlbaum.

Mayer, R. E. (1997). Multimedia learning: Are we asking the right questions? *Educational Psychologist, 32,* 1–19.

Mayer, R. E. (1999). *The promise of educational psychology.* Upper Saddle River, NJ: Prentice Hall.

Mayer, R. E. (2000). Problem solving. In M. A. Runco & S. Pritzker (Eds.), *Encyclopedia of psychology.* San Diego: Academic Press.

Mayer, R. E. (2002). *The promise of educational psychology: Teaching for meaningful learning* (Vol. 2). Upper Saddle River, NJ: Prentice Hall.

Mayer, R. E. (2004). Should there be a three-strike rule against pure discovery learning? *American Psychologist, 59,* 14–19.

Mayer, R. E. (2004). Teaching of subject matter. *Annual Review of Psychology, 55.* Palo Alto, CA: Annual Reviews.

Mayer, R. E., & Wittrock, M. C. (1996). Problem-solving transfer. In D. C. Berliner & R. C. Calfee (Eds.), *Handbook of educational psychology.* New York: Macmillan.

Mayer, R. E., & Wittrock, M. C. (2006). Problem solving. In P. A. Alexander & P. H. Winne (Eds.), *Handbook of educational psychology* (2nd ed.). Mahwah, NJ: Erlbaum.

Mazur, J. E. (2002). *Learning and behavior* (5th ed.). Upper Saddle River, NJ: Prentice Hall.

Mazur, J. E. (2005). Heuristics and general principles of learning. *Behavioural Processes, 69,* 137–138.

Mazurek, K., Winzer, M. A., & Majorek, C. (2000). *Education in a global society.* Boston: Allyn & Bacon.

McAdoo, H. P. (2002). African-American parenting. In M. H. Bornstein (Ed.), *Handbook of parenting* (2nd ed.). Mahwah, NJ: Erlbaum.

McBurney, D. H., & White, T. L. (2007). *Research methods* (7th Ed.). Belmont, CA: Wadsworth.

McCarthey, S. (1994). Opportunities and risks of writing from personal experience. *Language Arts, 71,* 182–191.

McCarty, F., Abbott-Shim, M., & Lambert, R. (2001). The relationship between teacher beliefs and practices and Head Start classroom quality. *Early Education & Development, 12,* 225–238.

McClintock, R. (1999). *The Educator's Manifesto: Renewing the Progressive Bond with Posterity through the Social Construction of Digital Learning Communities.* New York: Institute For Learning Technologies, Teachers College, Columbia University. Retrieved March 21, 2005, from http://www.ilt.columbia.edu/publications/manifesto/contents.html

McCombs, B. L. (2001, April). *What do we know about learners and learning? The learner-centered framework.* Paper presented at the meeting of the American Educational Research Association, Seattle.

McCombs, B. L., & Quiat, M. A. (2001). *Development and validation of norms and rubrics for the Grades K–5 assessment of learner-centered principles (ALCP) surveys.* Unpublished manuscript, University of Denver Research Institute, Denver.

McCormick, C. B., & Pressley, M. (1997). *Educational psychology.* New York: Longman.

McCrae, R. R., & Costa, P. T. (2003). *Personality in adulthood* (2nd ed.). New York: Guilford.

McCrae, R. R., & Costa, P. T. (2006). Cross-cultural perspectives on adult personality trait development. In D. K. Mroczek & T. D. Little (Eds.), *Handbook of personality development.* Mahwah, NJ: Erlbaum.

McCrory, E. J., Mechelli, A., Frith, U., & Price, C. J. (2005). More than words: A common neural basis for reading and naming deficits in developmental dyslexia. *Brain, 128,* 261–267.

McDonald, B. A., Larson, C. D., Dansereau, D. I., & Spurlin, J. E. (1985). Cooperative dyads: Impact on text learning and transfer. *Contemporary Educational Psychology, 10,* 369–377.

McDonnell, J. M., Mathot-Buckner, C., Thorson, N., & Fiter, S. (2001). Supporting the inclusion of students with moderate and severe learning disabilities in junior high general education classes. *Education and Treatment of Children, 24,* 141–160.

McKelvie, S. J., & Drumheller, A. (2001). The availability heuristic with famous names: A replication. *Perceptual and Motor Skills, 92,* 507–516.

McKinley, D. W., Boulet, J. R., & Hambleton, R. K. (2000, August). *Standard-setting for performance-based assessment.* Paper presented at the meeting of the American Educational Research Association, New Orleans.

McLaren, P. (2007). *Life in schools* (5th ed.). Boston: Allyn & Bacon.

McLoyd, V. C. (1998). Children in poverty: Development, public policy, and practice. In W. Damon (Ed.), *Handbook of child psychology* (5th ed., Vol. 4). New York: Wiley.

McLoyd, V. C. (2000). Poverty. In A. Kazdin (Ed.), *Encyclopedia of psychology.* Washington, DC, & New York: American Psychological Association and Oxford University Press.

McLoyd, V. C. (2005). Pathways to academic achievement among children from immigrant families: a commentary. In C. R. Cooper, C. T. G. Coll, W. T. Bartko, H. M. Davis, & C. Chatman (Eds.), *Developmental pathways through middle childhood.* Mahwah, NJ: Erlbaum.

McLoyd, V. C., Aikens, N. L., & Burton, L. M. (2006). Childhood poverty, policy, and practice. In W. Damon & R. Lerner (Eds.), *Handbook of child psychology* (6th ed.). New York: Wiley.

McLoyd, V. C., & Smith, J. (2002). Physical discipline and behavior problems in African American, European American, and Hispanic children: Emotional support as a moderator. *Journal of Marriage and the Family, 64,* 40–53.

McMahon, S. I. (1994). Student-led book clubs: Traversing a river of interpretation. *New Advocate, 7,* 109–125.

McMahon, S. I., Raphael, T. E., & Goatley, V. J. (1995). Changing the context for classroom reading instruction: The Book Club project. In J. Brophy (Ed.), *Advances in research on teaching.* Greenwich, CT: JAI Press.

McMillan, J. H. (1997). *Classroom assessment.* Boston: Allyn & Bacon.

McMillan, J. H. (2002). *Essential assessment concepts for teachers and administrators.* Thousand Oaks, CA: Corwin Press.

McMillan, J. H. (2004). *Educational research* (4th ed.). Boston: Allyn & Bacon.

McMillan, J. H. (2007). *Classroom assessment* (4th ed.). Boston: Allyn & Bacon.

McMillan, J. H., & Schumacher, S. (2006). *Research in education: Evidence based inquiry* (6th ed.). Boston: Allyn & Bacon.

McMillan, J. H., & Wergin, J. F. (2002). *Understanding and evaluating educational research* (2nd ed.). Upper Saddle River, NJ: Prentice Hall.

McNally, D. (1990). *Even eagles need a push.* New York: Dell.

McNeil, D. (2000). Systematic desensitization. In A. Kazdin (Ed.), *Encyclopedia of psychology.* Washington, DC, & New York: American Psychological Association and Oxford University Press.

McNergney, R. F., & McNergney, J. M. (2007). *Education: The practice and profession of teaching* (5th Ed.). Boston: Allyn & Bacon.

McRae, S. J. (2005). The diagnostic evaluation of pulmonary embolism. *American Heart Hospital Journal, 3,* 14–20.

McWhorter, K. T. (2006). *Vocabulary simplified* (2nd ed.). Boston: Allyn & Bacon.

Means, B. (2006). Prospects for transforming schools with technology-supported assessment. In R. K. Sawyer (Ed.), *The Cambridge handbook of the learning sciences.* New York: Cambridge University Press.

Meberg, A., & Broch, H. (2004). Etiology of cerebral palsy. *Journal of Perinatal Medicine, 32,* 434–439.

Meece, J. L., Anderman, E. M., & Anderman, L. H. (2006). Classroom goal structures, student motivation, and academic achievement. *Annual Review of Psychology, 57.* Palo Alto, CA: Annual Reviews.

Meece, J. L., & Kurtz-Costes, B. (2001). Introduction: The schooling of ethnic minority children. *Educational Psychologist, 36,* 57–66.

Meece, J. L., & Scantlebury, K. (2006). Gender and schooling: Progress and persistent barriers. In J. Worell & C. D. Goodheart (Eds.), *Handbook of girls and womens psychological health.* New York: Oxford University Press.

Meichenbaum, D. (1993). Cognitive behavior modification. In F. H. Kanfer & A. P. Goldstein (Eds.), *Helping people change: A handbook of methods.* New York: Pergamon.

Meichenbaum, D., & Butler, L. (1980). Toward a conceptual model of the treatment of test anxiety: Implications for research and treatment. In I. G. Sarason (Ed.), *Test anxiety.* Mahwah, NJ: Erlbaum.

Meichenbaum, D., Turk, D., & Burstein, S. (1975). The nature of coping with stress. In I. Sarason & C. Spielberger (Eds.), *Stress and anxiety.* Washington, DC: Hemisphere.

Meier, S. L., Rich, B. S., & Cady, J. A. (2006). Teachers' use of rubrics to score nontraditional tasks: Factors related to discrepancies in scoring. *Assessment in Education, 13,* 69–95.

Meijer, J., & Elshout, J. J. (2001). The predictive and discriminant validity of the zone of proximal development. *British Journal of Educational Psychology, 71,* 93–113.

Melby, L. C. (1995). *Teacher efficacy and classroom management: A study of teacher cognition, emotion, and strategy usage associated with externalizing student behavior.* Ph.D. dissertation, University of California at Los Angeles.

Menn, L., & Stoel-Gammon, C. (2005). Phonological development: Learning sounds and sound patterns. In J. Berko Gleason (Ed.), *The development of language* (6th ed.). Boston: Allyn & Bacon.

Mercer, C. D., & Pullen, P. C. (2005). *Students with learning disabilities* (6th ed.). Upper Saddle River, NJ: Prentice Hall.

Merenda, P. (2004). Cross-cultural adaptation of educational and psychological testing. In R. K. Hambleton, P. F. Merenda, & C. D. Spielberger (Eds.), *Adapting educational and psychological tests for cross-cultural assessment.* Mahwah, NJ: Erlbaum.

Mertler, C. A., & Charles, C. M. (2005). *Introduction to educational research* (5th ed.). Boston: Allyn & Bacon.

Metz, E. C., & Youniss, J. (2005). Longitudinal gains in civic development through school-based required service. *Political Psychology, 26,* 413–437.

Metz, K. E. (2004). Children's understanding of scientific inquiry: Their conceptualization of uncertainty in investigations of their own design. *Cognition and Instruction, 22*(2), 219–290.

Metzger, M. (1996, January). Maintaining a life. *Phi Delta Kappan, 77,* 346–351.

Mezzacappa, E. (2004). Alerting, orienting, and executive attention: Developmental properties and socioeconomic correlates in an epidemiological sample of young, urban children. *Child Development, 75,* 1373–1386.

Michael, W. (1999). Guilford's view. In M. A. Runco & S. Pritzker (Eds.), *Encyclopedia of creativity.* San Diego: Academic Press.

Michaels, S. (1986). Narrative presentations: An oral preparation for literacy with first graders. In J. Cook-Gumperz (Ed.), *The social construction of literacy.* New York: Cambridge University Press.

Middleton, J., & Goepfert, P. (1996). *Inventive strategies for teaching mathematics.* Washington, DC: American Psychological Association.

Midgley, C. (2001). A goal theory perspective on the current status of middle level schools. In T. Urdan & F. Pajares (Eds.), *Is adolescence here to stay?* Greenwich, CT: IAP.

Midgley, C., Anderman, E., & Hicks, L. (1995). Differences between elementary school and middle school teachers and students: A goal theory approach. *Journal of Early Adolescence, 15,* 90–113.

Miholic, V. (1994). An inventory to pique students' metacognitive awareness of reading strategies. *Journal of Reading, 38,* 84–86.

Miller, C. F., & Ruble, D. N. (2005). *Developmental changes in the accessibility of gender stereotypes.* Unpublished manuscript, Department of Psychology, New York University.

Miller, G. A. (1956). The magical number seven, plus or minus two: Some limits on our capacity for information processing. *Psychological Review, 48,* 337–442.

Miller, J. W. (2001). *Using educational technologies to promote vocabulary development among heterogeneously-grouped fifth graders.* Unpublished manuscript, Harvard University, Boston.

Miller, K. F. (2000). Representational tools and conceptual change: The young scientist's tool kit. *Journal of Applied Developmental Psychology, 21,* 21–25.

Miller, L. K. (2006). *Principles of everyday behavior analysis* (4th ed.). Belmont, CA: Wadsworth.

Miller, N., & Harrington, H. J. (1990). A situational identity perspective on cultural diversity and teamwork in the classroom. In S. Sharan (Ed.), *Cooperative learning: Theory and research.* New York: Praeger.

Miller, P. H. (2000). How best to utilize a deficiency: A commentary on Water's "Memory strategy development." *Child Development,* 71, 1013–1017.

Miller-Jones, D. (1989). Culture and testing. *American Psychologist, 44,* 360–366.

Milsom, A., & Gallo, L. L. (2006). Bullying in middle schools: Prevention and intervention. *Middle School Journal, 37,* 12–19.

Mindham, C. (2005). Creativity and the young child. *Early Years: Journal of International Research & Development, 25,* 81–84.

Minstrell, J., & Kraus, P. (2005). Guided inquiry in the science classroom. In M. S. Donovan & J. D. Bransford (Eds.), *How students learn.* Washington, DC: National Research Council.

Minuchin, P. P., & Shapiro, E. K. (1983). The school as a context for social development. In P. H. Mussen (Ed.), *Handbook of child psychology* (4th ed., Vol. 4). New York: Wiley.

Mitchell, M. L., & Jolley, J. M. (2007). *Research designs explained* (6th Ed.). Belmont, CA: Wadsworth.

Miyake, A. (2001, September). Commentary in S. Carpenter. A new reason for keeping a diary. *Monitor on Psychology, 32*, 68–70.

Moats, L. (2004). Relevance of neuroscience to effective education for students with reading and other learning disabilities. *Journal of Child Neurology, 19*, 840–845.

Molina, I. A., Dulmus, C. N., & Sowers, K. M. (2005). Secondary prevention for youth violence: A review of selected school-based programs. *Brief Treatment and Crisis Intervention, 5*, 1–3.

Moll, L. C., & González, N. (2004). Engaging life: A funds of knowledge approach to multicultural education. In J. A. Banks & C. A. M. Banks (Eds.), *Handbook of research on multicultural education* (2nd ed.). San Francisco: Jossey-Bass.

Moll, L. C., Tapia, J., & Whitmore, K. (1993). Living knowledge: The social distribution of cultural resources for thinking. In G. Salomon (Ed.), *Distributed cognitions: Psychological and educational considerations.* Cambridge: Cambridge University Press.

Monteith, M. (2000). Prejudice. In A. Kazdin (Ed.), *Encyclopedia of psychology.* Washington, DC, & New York: American Psychological Association and Oxford University Press.

Monuteaux, M. C., Faraone, S. V., Herzig, K., Navsaria, N., & Biederman, J. (2005). ADHD and dyscalculia: Evidence for independent familial transmission. *Journal of Learning Disabilities, 38*, 86–93.

Moore, K. D. (1998). *Classroom teaching skills* (4th ed.). New York: McGraw-Hill.

Moran, S., & Gardner, H. (2006). Extraordinary achievements. In W. Damon & R. Lerner (Eds.), *Handbook of child psychology* (6th ed.). New York: Wiley.

Morgan, N., & Saxton, J. (1991). *Teaching, questioning, and learning.* New York: Routledge.

Morris, P., & Kalil, A. (2006). Out-of-school time use during middle childhood in a low-income sample: do combinations of activities affect achievement and behavior? In A. C. Huston & M. N. Ripke (Eds.), *Developmental contexts in middle childhood.* New York: Cambridge University Press.

Morrison, G. (2006). *Teaching in America* (4th ed.). Boston: Allyn & Bacon.

Morrison, G. R., & Lowther, D. L. (2005). *Integrating computer technology into the class-room* (3rd ed.). Upper Saddle River, NJ: Prentice Hall.

Morrow, L. (2005). *Literacy development in the early years* (5th ed.). Boston: Allyn & Bacon.

Moseley, D., Baumfield, V., Elliott, J., Higgins, S., Miller, J., Newton, D. P., & Gregson, M. (2006). *Frameworks for thinking.* New York: Cambridge University Press.

Moyer, J. R., & Dardig, J. C. (1978). Practical task analysis for teachers. *Teaching Exceptional Children, 11*, 16–18.

Mroczek, D. K., & Little, T. D. (Eds.). (2006). *Handbook of personality development.* Mahwah, NJ: Erlbaum.

Mule, M. (2003). *Technology for inclusion* (4th ed.). Boston: Allyn & Bacon.

Mullis, I. V. S. (1999, April). *Using TIMSS to gain new perspectives about different school organizations and policies.* Paper presented at the meeting of the American Educational Research Association, Montreal.

Munakata, Y. (2006). Information processing approaches to development. In W. Damon & R. Lerner (Eds.), *Handbook of child psychology* (6th ed.). New York: Wiley.

Murdock, T. B. (1999). The social context of risk: Status and motivational predictors of alienation in middle school. *Journal of Educational Psychology, 91*, 62–75.

Murnane, R. J., & Levy, F. (1996). *Teaching the new basic skills.* New York: Free Press.

Murphy, K., & Schneider, B. (1994). Coaching socially rejected adolescents regarding behaviors used by peers to infer liking: A dyad-specific intervention, *Journal of Early Adolescence, 14*, 83–95.

Murphy, P. K., & Mason, L. (2006). Changing knowledge and beliefs. In P. A. Alexander & P. H. Winne (Eds.), *Handbook of educational psychology* (2nd ed.). Mahwah, NJ: Erlbaum.

Murphy, R. A., Baker, A. G., & Fouguet, N. (2001). Relative validity effects with either one or two more valid cues in Pavlovian and instrumental conditioning. *Journal of Experimental Psychology: Animal Processes, 27*, 59–67.

Murray, H. A. (1938). *Explorations in personality.* Cambridge, MA: Harvard University Press.

Murrell, A. J. (2000). Discrimination. In A. Kazdin (Ed.), *Encyclopedia of psychology.* Washington, DC, & New York: American Psychological Association and Oxford University Press.

Myers, D., Baer, W., & Choi, S. (1996). The changing problem of overcrowded housing. *Journal of the American Planning Association, 62*, 66–84.

Myerson, J., Rank, M. R., Raines, F. Q., & Schnitzler, M. A. (1998). Race and general cognitive ability: The myth of diminishing returns in education. *Psychological Science, 9*, 139–142.

Myers-Walls, J. A., & Frias, L. (2007). Family, school, and community: Finding green lights at the intersection. In B. S. Trask & R. R. Harmon (Eds.), *Cultural diversity and families.* Thousand Oaks, CA: Sage.

Mytton, J., Diguiseppi, C., Gough, D., Taylor, R., & Logan, S. (2006). School-based secondary programs for preventing violence. *Cochrane Database System Review, 3*, CD004606.

N

NAASP. (1997, May/June). Students say: What makes a good teacher? *Schools in the Middle*, pp. 15–17.

NAEYC. (2002). *Early learning standards: Creating the conditions for success.* Washington, DC: National Association for the Education of Young Children.

Nagy, W. (2005). Why vocabulary development needs to be long-term and comprehensive. In E. H. Hiebert & M. L. Kamil (Eds.), *Teaching and learning vocabulary.* Mahwah, NJ: Erlbaum.

Nagy, W., Berninger, V., Abbott, R., Vaughan, K., & Vermeulin. K. (2003). Relationship of morphology and other language skills to literacy skills in at-risk second graders and at-risk fourth grade writers. *Journal of Educational Psychology, 95*, 730–742.

Nagy, W. E., & Scott, J. A. (2000). Vocabulary processes. In M. L. Kamil, P. B. Mosenthal, P. D. Pearson, & R. Barr (Eds.), *Handbook of reading research* (Vol. 3). Mahwah, NJ: Erlbaum.

Nakamura, J., & Csikszentmihalyi, M. (2002). The concept of flow. In C. R. Snyder & S. J. Lopez (Eds.), *Handbook of positive psychology.* New York: Oxford University Press.

Nansel, T. R., Overpeck, M., Pilla, R. S., Ruan, W. J., Simons-Morton, B., & Scheidt, P. (2001). Bullying behaviors among U.S. youth: Prevalence and association with psychosocial adjustment. *Journal of the American Medical Association, 285*, 2094–2100.

Nardi, P. M. (2006). *Doing survey research* (2nd ed.). Boston: Allyn & Bacon.

Nash, J. M. (1997, February 3). Fertile minds. *Time*, pp. 50–54.

Nasir, N. S., Rosebery, A. S., Warren. B., & Lee, C. D. (2006). Learning as a cultural process: Achieving equity through diversity. In R. K. Sawyer (Ed.), *The Cambridge* *handbook of learning sciences.* New York: Cambridge University Press.

Nathan, M. J., & Petrosino, A. J. (2003). Expert blind spot among preservice teachers. *American Educational Research Journal, 40*(4), 905–928.

National Assessment of Educational Progress. (1998). *National report: 1998.* Washington, DC: National Center for Educational Statistics.

National Assessment of Educational Progress. (2000). *The nations report card.* Washington, DC: National Center for Educational Statistics.

National Assessment of Educational Progress. (2001). *The nation's report card. National report: 2001.* Washington, DC: National Center for Educational Statistics.

National Assessment of Educational Progress. (2002). *The nations report card.* Washington, DC: National Center for Education Statistics.

National Assessment of Educational Progress. (2005). *The nation's report card: 2005.* Washington, DC: National Center for Educational Statistics.

National Association for the Education of Young Children. (1996). NAEYC position statement: Responding to linguistic and cultural diversity—Recommendations for effective early childhood education. *Young Children, 51,* 4–12.

National Center for Education Statistics. (1997). School-family linkages. Washington, DC: U.S. Department of Education.

National Center for Education Statistics. (2001). *Dropout rates in the United States: 2000.* Washington, DC: U.S. Department of Education.

National Center for Education Statistics. (2002). *Digest of Education Statistics 2002.* Washington, DC: Author.

National Center for Education Statistics. (2003). *Digest of Education Statistics, Table 52.* Washington, DC: Author.

National Center for Education Statistics. (2005). *Contexts of elementary and secondary education.* Washington, DC: Author.

National Center for Education Statistics. (2005). *Internet access in U.S. public schools.* Washington, DC: U.S. Department of Education.

National Center for Education Statistics. (2006). *Children with disabilities in public schools.* Washington, DC: U.S. Department of Education.

National Center for Learning Disabilities. (2006). *Learning disabilities.* Retrieved March 6, 2006, from http://www.ncld.org/

National Commission on the High School Senior Year. (2001). *Youth at the crossroads: Facing high school and beyond.* Washington, DC: The Education Trust.

National Council for the Social Studies (NCSS). (1994). *Expectations of excellence: Curriculum standards for social studies.* Waldorf, MD: NCSS.

National Council for the Social Sciences (NCSS). (2000). *National standards for social studies teachers.* Baltimore: NCSS.

National Council of Teachers of English/ International Reading Association (NCTE/IRA). (1996). *Standards for the English Language Arts.* Urbana, IL: National Council of Teachers of English.

National Council of Teachers of Mathematics. (2000). *Principles and standards for school mathematics.* Reston, VA: Author.

National Institute of Mental Health. (2006). *Autism spectrum disorders (pervasive developmental disorders).* Retrieved April 8, 2006, from http://www.nimh.nih.gov/publicat/autism.com

National Reading Panel. (2000). *Teaching children to read.* Washington, DC: National Institute of Child Health and Human Development.

National Research Council. (1999). *How people learn.* Washington, DC: National Academic Press.

National Research Council. (2001). *Knowing what students know.* Washington, DC: National Academic Press.

National Research Council. (2004). *Engaging schools: Fostering high school students' motivation to learn.* Washington, DC: National Academic Press.

National Research Council. (2005). *How students learn.* Washington, DC: National Academic Press.

Neil, M. (2006). Preparing teachers to beat the agonies of NCLB. Retrieved August 3, 2006, from www.eddigest.com

Neisser, U., Boodoo, G., Bouchard, T. J., Boykin, A. W., Brody, N., Ceci, S. J., Halpern, D. F., Loehlin, J. C., Perloff, R., Sternberg, R. J., & Urbina, S. (1996). Intelligence: Knowns and unknowns. *American Psychologist, 51,* 77–101.

Nelson, C. A., Thomas, K. M., & de Haan, M. (2006). Neural bases of cognitive development. In W. Damon & R. Lerner (Eds.), *Handbook of child psychology* (6th ed.). New York: Wiley.

Nelson, K. (2006). Development of representation in childhood. In E. Bialystok & F. I. M. Craik (Eds.), *Lifespan cognition.* New York: Oxford University Press.

Nesbit, J. C., & Hadwin, A. F. (2006). Methodological issues in educational psychology. In P. A. Alexander & P. H. Winne (Eds.), *Handbook of educational psychology* (2nd ed.). Mahwah, NJ: Erlbaum.

Neugarten, B. L. (1988, August). *Policy issues for an aging society.* Paper presented at the meeting of the American Psychological Association, Atlanta.

Neukrug, E. S., & Fawcett, C. (2006). *Essentials of testing and assessment.* Belmont, CA: Wadsworth.

Newby, T. J., Stepich, D., Lehman, J., & Russell, J. D. (2006). *Educational technology for teaching and learning* (3rd ed.). Upper Saddle River, NJ: Erlbaum.

Newman, R. S. (2002). What do I need to succeed? . . . When I don't understand what I'm doing!?: Developmental influences on students' adaptive help seeking. In A. Wigfield & J. S. Eccles (Eds.), *Development of achievement motivation.* San Diego: Academic Press.

NICHD Early Child Care Research Network. (2003). Do children's attention processes mediate the link between family predictors and school readiness. *Developmental Psychology, 39,* 581–593.

NICHD Early Child Care Research Network. (2004). Are child developmental outcomes related to before- and after-school care arrangement? *Child Development, 75,* 280–295.

Nicholls, J. G. (1979). Development of perception of own attainment and causal attribution for success and failure in reading. *Journal of Educational Psychology, 71,* 94–99.

Nicholls, J. G., Cobb, P., Wood, T., Yackel, E., & Pataschnick, M. (1990). Assessing students' theories of success in mathematics: Individual and classroom differences. *Journal for Research in Mathematics Education, 21,* 109–122.

Nichols, J. D., & Miller, R. B. (1994). Cooperative learning and student motivation. *Contemporary Educational Psychology, 19,* 167–178.

Nicoll, G. (2001). A three-tier system for assessing concept map links: A methodological study. *International Journal of Science Education 23*(8), 863–875.

Nieto, S. (1992). *Affirming diversity: The sociopolitical context of multicultural education.* White Plains, NY: Longman.

Nieto, S. (2003). *Affirming diversity* (4th ed.). Boston: Allyn & Bacon.

Nieto, S. (2004). *Affirming diversity* (4th ed.). Boston: Allyn & Bacon.

Nieto, S. (2005). *Why we teach.* New York: Teachers College Press.

Niguidula, D. (1997, November). Picturing performance with digital portfolios. *Educational Leadership*, pp. 26–29.

Nikola-Lisa, W., & Burnaford, G. E. (1994). A mosaic: Contemporary schoolchildren's images of teachers. In P. B. Joseph & G. E. Burnaford (Eds.), *Image of schoolteachers in twentieth century America*. New York: St. Martin's Press.

Nisbett, R. E., & Ross, L. (1980). *Human inference*. Upper Saddle River, NJ: Prentice Hall.

Nitko, A. J., & Brookhart, S. M. (2007). *Educational assessment of students* (5th Ed.). Upper Saddle River, NJ: Prentice Hall.

Noddings, N. (1992). *The challenge to care in schools*. New York: Teachers College Press.

Noddings, N. (1992). Teaching themes of care. *Phi Delta Kappan, 76*, 675–679.

Noddings, N. (1998). *Teaching for continuous learning*. Paper presented at the meeting of the American Educational Research Association, San Diego.

Noddings, N. (2001). The care tradition: Beyond "add women and stir." *Theory into Practice, 40*, 29–34.

Nokelainen, P., & Flint, J. (2002). Genetic effects on human cognition: Lessons from the study of mental retardation syndromes. *Journal of Neurology, Neurosurgery, and Psychiatry, 43*, 287–296.

Nolen-Hoeksema, S. (2007). *Abnormal psychology* (4th ed.). New York: McGraw-Hill.

Norcross, J. C., Santrock, J. W., Campbell, L. F., Smith, T. P., Sommer, R., & Zuckerman, E. L. (2003). *Authoritative guide to self-help resources in mental health* (Revised ed.) New York: Guilford.

Norris, C., Soloway, E., & Sullivan T. (2002). Examining 25 years of technology in U.S. education. *Communications of the ACM, 45*(8), 15–18.

Nucci, L. P. (2004). The development of moral reasoning. In P. Smith & C. Hart (Eds.), *Blackwell handbook of cognitive development*. Malden, MA: Blackwell.

O

O'Conner, S. C., & Rosenblood, L. K. (1996). Affiliation motivation in everyday experience: A theoretical comparison. *Journal of Personality and Social Psychology, 70*, 513–522.

O'Donnell, A. M., & Levin, J. R. (2001). Educational psychology's healthy growing pains. *Educational Psychologist, 36*, 73–82.

O'Donnell, A. M. (2006). The role of peers and group learning. In P. A. Alexander &

P. H. Winne (Eds.), *Handbook of educational psychology* (2nd ed.). Mahwah, NJ: Erlbaum.

O'Leary, C. (2004). Fetal alcohol syndrome. *Journal of Pediatric Child Health, 40*, 2–7.

O'Toole, A. (2005, April). Personal communication. Richardson, TX: Department of Psychology, University of Texas at Dallas.

Oakes, J., & Saunders, M. (2002). *Access to textbooks, instructional materials, equipment, and technology: Inadequacy of California's schools*. Los Angeles: Department of Education, UCLA.

Oakes, J. (1990). *Multiplying inequalities: The effects of race, social class, and tracking on opportunities to learn mathematics and science*. Santa Monica: The RAND Corporation.

Oakes, J., & Lipton, M. (2007). *Teaching to change the world* (3rd ed.). New York: McGraw-Hill.

Oates, J., & Grayson, A. (Eds.). (2004). *Cognitive and language development in children*. Malden, MA: Blackwell.

OBLEMA. (2000). *Survey of states limited English proficient students and available educational programs and services: 1997–1998*. Washington, DC: U.S. Department of Education.

Ogbu, J., & Stern, P. (2001). Caste status and intellectual development. In R. J. Sternberg & E. L. Grigorenko (Eds.), *Environmental effects on cognitive abilities*. Mahwah, NJ: Erlbaum.

Ogbu, J. U. (1989, April). *Academic socialization of Black children: An inoculation against future failure?* Paper presented at the meeting of the Society for Research in Child Development, Kansas City.

Oka, E. R. (2005). Motivation. In S. W. Lee (Ed.), *Encyclopedia of school psychology*. Thousand Oaks, CA: Sage.

Okagaki, L. (2006). Ethnicity, learning. In P. A. Alexander & P. H. Winne (Eds.), *Handbook of educational psychology* (2nd ed.). Mahwah, NJ: Erlbaum.

Oldfather, P., West, J., White, J., & Wilmarth, J. (1999). *Learning through childrens eyes: Social constructivism and the desire to learn*. Washington, DC: American Psychological Association.

Olson, D. (2001). *What writing does to the mind*. In J. Byrnes & E. Amsel (Eds.), *Language, literacy, and cognitive development*. Mahwah, NJ: Erlbaum.

Olson, L. (2001). Overboard on testing? *Editorial Projects in Education, 20* (No. 17), 23–30.

Olweus, D. (1980). Bullying among school boys. In R. Barnen (Ed.), *Children and violence*. Stockholm: Academic Literature.

Olweus, D. (1994). Bullying at school: Basic facts and effects of a school based intervention program. *Journal of Child Psychology and Psychiatry, 33*(7), 1171–1190.

Onwuegbuzi, A. J., & Daley, C. E. (2001). Racial differences in IQ revisited: A synthesis of nearly a century of research. *Journal of Black Psychology, 27*, 209–220.

Oppenheimer, D. M. (2004). Spontaneous discounting of availability in frequency judgment tasks. *Psychological Science, 15*, 100–115.

Ornstein, A. C., Lasley, T., & Mindes, G. (2005). *Secondary and middle school methods*. Boston: Allyn & Bacon.

Ornstein, P. A., Haden, C. A., & Elischberger, H. B. (2006). Children's memory development. In E. Bialystok & F. I. M. Craik (Eds.), *Lifespan cognition*. New York: Oxford University Press.

Osterlind, S. J. (2006). *Modern measurement theory*. Upper Saddle River, NJ: Prentice Hall.

Ostrov, J. M., Keating, C. F., & Ostrov, J. M. (2004). Gender differences in preschool aggression during free play and structured interactions: An observational study. *Social Development, 13*, 255–277.

Osvath, P., Voros, V., & Fekete, S. (2004). Life events and psychopathology in a group of suicide attempters. *Psychopathology, 37*, 36–40.

Otero, V. K. (2006). Moving beyond the "get it or don't" conception of formative assessment. *Journal of Teacher Education, 57*, 247–255.

Otten, L. J., Henson, R. N., & Rugg, M. D. (2001). Depth of processing effects on neural correlates of memory encoding. *Brain, 124*, 399–412.

Owen, R. E. (2005). *Language development* (6th ed.). Boston: Allyn & Bacon.

P

Pacheco, S., & Hurtado, S. (2001). Media stereotypes. In J. Worell (Ed.), *Encyclopedia of women and gender*. San Diego: Academic Press.

Padilla, A. M. (2006). Second language learning issues in research and teaching. In P. A. Alexander & P. H. Winne (Eds.), *Handbook of educational psychology* (2nd ed.). Mahwah, NJ: Erlbaum.

Paivio, A. (1971). *Imagery and verbal processes*. Fort Worth, TX: Harcourt Brace.

Paivio, A. (1986). *Mental representations: A dual coding approach*. New York: Oxford University Press.

Palincsar, A. S. (1986). The role of dialogue in providing scaffolded instruction. *Educational Psychologist, 21*, 73–98.

Palincsar, A. S., & Brown, A. L. (1984). Reciprocal teaching of comprehension-fostering and comprehension-monitoring activities. *Cognition and Instruction, 1*, 117–175.

Palomba, C., & Banta, T. W. (1999). *Assessment essentials.* San Francisco: Jossey-Bass.

Pals, J. L. (2006). Constructing the "springboard effect": Causal connections, self-making, and growth within the life story. In D. P. McAdams, R. Josselson, & A. Lieblich (Eds.), *Identity and story.* Washington, DC: American Psychological Association.

Paludi, M. A. (2002). *Psychology of women* (2nd ed.) Upper Saddle River, NJ: Prentice Hall.

Pan, B. (2005). Semantic development: Learning the meaning of words. In J. Berko Gleason (Ed.), *The development of language* (6th ed.). Boston: Allyn & Bacon.

Pang, V. O. (2005). *Multicultural education.* (3rd ed.). New York: McGraw-Hill.

Papert, S. (2002). Learners, laptops, and powerful ideas. *Scholastic Administrator,* Fall 2002. Retrieved May 26, 2005, from http://www.learningbarn.org

Paris, S. G., & Paris, A. H. (2006). Assessments of early reading. In W. Damon & R. Lerner (Eds.), *Handbook of child psychology* (6th ed.). New York: Wiley.

Park, C. (1997). Learning style preferences of Asian American (Chinese, Filipino, Korean, and Vietnamese) students in secondary schools. *Equity & Excellence in Education, 30*(2), 68–77.

Parke, R. D., & Buriel, R. (2006). Socialization in the family. In W. Damon & R. Lerner (Eds.), *Handbook of child psychology* (6th ed.). New York: Wiley.

Parker, J. G., & Asher, S. R. (1987). Peer relations and later personal adjustment: Are low accepted children at risk? *Psychological Bulletin, 102*, 357–389.

Parkes, J., & Giron, T. (2006, April). *Reliability arguments in the classroom.* Paper presented at the meeting of the National Council on Measurement in Education, San Francisco.

Partnership for 21st Century Skills. (2003). Learning for the 21st century, Washington. DC: Author. Retrieved January 30, 2006, from http://www.21stcenturyskills.org/images/stories/otherdocs/P21_Report.pdf

Pataraia, E., Billingsley-Marshall, R. L., Castillo, E. M., Breier, J. I., Simos, P. G., Sarkari, S., Fitzgerald, M., Clear, T., &

Papanicolaou, A. C. (2005). Organization of receptive language-specific cortex before and after left temporal lobectomy. *Neurology, 64,* 481–487.

Pavlov, I. P. (1927). *Conditioned reflexes.* New York: Dover.

Payne, D. A. (1997). *Applied educational assessment.* Belmont, CA: Wadsworth.

Pea, R. D., & Maldonado, H. (2006). WILD for learning: Interacting through new computing devices anytime, anywhere. In D. K. Sawyer (Ed.), *The Cambridge handbook of the learning sciences.* New York: Cambridge University Press.

Pearson, J. C., Nelson, P. E., Titsworth, S., & Harter, L. (2006). *Human communication with learning tools suite* (2nd ed.). New York: McGraw-Hill.

Pearson, P. D., Hansen, J., & Gordon, C. (1979). The effect of background knowledge on young children's comprehension of explicit and implicit information. *Journal of Reading Behavior, 11*, 201–210.

Pecheone, R. L., & Chung, R. R. (2006). Evidence in teacher education. *Journal of Teacher Education, 57*, 22–36.

Penn, H. E. (2006). Neurobiological correlates of autism: A review of recent research. *Child Neuropsychopathology, 12*, 57–79.

Penner, D. (2001). Complexity, emergence, and synthetic models in science education. In K. Crowley, C. Schunn, & T. Okada (Eds.), *Designing for science.* Mahwah, NJ: Erlbaum.

Pérez, B. (2004). Language, literacy, and biliteracy. In B. Pérez, T. L. McCarty, L. J. Watahomigie, M. E. Torres-Guzman, T. Dien, J. Chang, H. L. Smith, A. Davila de Silva, & A. Norlander (Eds.), *Sociocultural contexts of language and literacy.* Mahwah, NJ: Erlbaum.

Pérez, B., McCarty, T. L., Watahomigie, L. J., Torres-Guzman, M. E., Dien, T., Chang, J., Smith, H. L., Davila de Silva, A., & Norlander, A. (Eds.). (2004). *Sociocultural contexts of language and literacy.* Mahwah, NJ: Erlbaum.

Perry, N. E., Turner, J. C., & Meyer, D. K. (2006). Classrooms as contexts for motivating learning. In P. A. Alexander & P. H. Winne (Eds.), *Handbook of educational psychology* (2nd ed.). Mahwah, NJ: Erlbaum.

Peters, J. M., & Stout, D. L. (2007). *Concepts and inquiries for teaching elementary school science* (5th ed.). Upper Saddle River, NJ: Prentice Hall.

Peterson, K. S. (1998, July 14). Teens learn "I do" can last forever, *USA Today,* pp. D1, D2.

Petosa, R. L., Hortz, B. V., Cardinia, C. E., & Suminski, R. R. (2005). Social cognitive the-

ory variables associated with physical activity among high school students. *International Journal of Sports Medicine, 26,* 158–163.

Petrill, S. A., Deater-Deckhard, K., Thompson, L. A., Dethorne, L. S., & Schatschneider, C. (2006). Reading skills in early readers: genetic and shared environmental influences. *Journal of Learning Disabilities, 39*, 48–55.

Pettit, G. S., Bates, J. E., Dodge, K. A., & Meece, D. W. (1999). The impact of after-school peer contact on early adolescent externalizing problems is moderated by parental monitoring, perceived neighborhood safety, and prior adjustment. *Child Development, 70*, 768–778.

Pettito, L. A., Kovelman, I., & Harasymowycz, U. (2003, April). *Bilingual language development: Does learning the new damage the old?* Paper presented at the meeting of the Society for Research in Child Development, Tampa.

Peyton, V. (2005). Standard score. In S. W. Lee (Ed.), *Encyclopedia of school psychology.* Thousand Oaks, CA: Sage.

Phinney, J. S. (1996). When we talk about American ethnic groups, what do we mean? *American Psychologist, 51*, 918–927.

Phinney, J. S. (2003). Identity and acculturation. In K. M. Chun, P. B. Organista, & G. Marin (Eds.), *Acculturation.* Washington, DC: American Psychological Association.

Phinney, J. S. (2006, April). *Acculturation and adaptation of immigrant youth in thirteen countries.* Paper presented at the meeting of the Society for Research on Adolescence, San Francisco.

Phinney, J., Berry, J., Sam, D., & Vedder, S. (2006). Understanding immigrant youth: Conclusions and implications. In J. Berry, J. Phinney, D. Sam, & P. Vedder (Eds.), *Immigrant youth in cultural transition.* Mahwah, NJ: Erlbaum.

Phye, G. D. (1990). Inductive problem solving: Schema inducement and memory-based transfer. *Journal of Educational Psychology, 82*, 826–831.

Phye, G. D., & Sanders, C. E. (1994). Advice and feedback: Elements of practice for problem solving. *Contemporary Educational Psychology, 19*, 286–301.

Piaget, J. (1932). *The moral judgment of the child.* New York: Harcourt Brace Jovanovich.

Piaget, J. (1954). *The construction of reality in the child.* New York: Basic Books.

Piaget, J., & Inhelder, B. (1969). *The child's conception of space.* New York: Norton.

Pianta, R. C. (2006). Classroom management and relationships between children and teachers: Implications for practice. In C. M. Evertson & C. S. Weinstein (Eds.), *Handbook of classroom management.* Mahwah, NJ: Erlbaum.

Pintrich, P. R. (2000). The role of goal orientation in self-regulated learning. In M. Boekaerts, P. R. Pintrich, & M. Zeidner (Eds.), *Handbook of self-regulation.* San Diego: Academic Press.

Pleck, J. H. (1983). The theory of male sex role identity: Its rise and fall, 1936–present. In M. Levin (Ed.), *In the shadow of the past: Psychology portrays the sexes.* New York: Columbia University Press.

Pleck, J. H. (1995). The gender-role strain paradigm. In R. F. Levant & W. S. Pollack (Eds.), *A new psychology of men.* New York: Basic Books.

Pleiss, M. K., & Feldhusen, J. F. (1995). Mentors, role models, and heroes in the lives of gifted children. *Educational Psychologist 30,* 159–169.

Plog, A., Epstein, L., & Porter, W. (2004, April). *Implementation fidelity: Lessons learned from the Bully-Proofing Your School Program.* Paper presented at the meeting of the National School Psychologists Association, Dallas, TX.

Plomin, R. (1997). Identifying genes for cognitive abilities and disabilities. In R. J. Sternberg & E. Grigorenko (Eds.), *Intelligence, heredity, and environment.* New York: Cambridge University Press.

Plucker, J. A., Beghetto, R. A., & Dow, G. T. (2004). Why isn't creativity more important to educational psychologists? Potentials, pitfalls, and future directions in creativity research. *Educational Psychologist, 39,* 83–96.

Pokey, S., & Siders, J. A. (2001). Authentic assessment for intervention. *Intervention in School and Clinic, 36,* 163–167.

Polson, D. (2001). Helping children learn to make responsible choices. In B. Rogoff, C. G. Turkanis & L. Bartlett (Eds.), *Learning together: Children and adults in a school community.* New York: Oxford University Press.

Pomerantz, E. M., Wang, Q., & Ng, F. (2005). Mothers' affect in the homework context: The importance of staying positive. *Developmental Psychology, 41,* 414–427.

Popham, W. J. (2005). *Classroom assessment* (4th ed.). Boston: Allyn & Bacon.

Popham, W. J. (2006). *Assessment for educational leaders.* Boston: Allyn & Bacon.

Posner, D. (2004). Whats wrong with teaching to the test? *Phi Delta Kappan, 85,* 749–751.

Posner, G. J., & Rudnitsky, A. N. (2006). *Course design: A guide to curriculum development for teachers* (7th ed.). Boston: Allyn & Bacon.

Potvin, L., Champagne, F., & Laberge-Nadeau, C. (1988). Mandatory driver training and road safety: The Quebec experience. *American Journal of Public Health, 78,* 1206–1212.

Powell, B. (2002). Unpublished review of J. W. Santrock's *Educational psychology* (2nd ed.) New York: McGraw-Hill.

Powell, R. A., & Symbaluk, D. G. (2002). *Introduction to learning and behavior.* Belmont, CA: Wadsworth.

Powell, R. G., & Caseau, D. (2004). *Classroom communication and diversity.* Mahwah, NJ: Erlbaum.

Powers, K. (2005). Authentic assessment. In S. W. Lee (Ed.), *Encyclopedia of school psychology.* Thousand Oaks, CA: Sage.

Presidential Task Force on Psychology and Education. (1992). *Learner-centered psychological principles: Guidelines for school redesign and reform* (Draft). Washington, DC: American Psychological Association.

Pressley, M. (1983). Making meaningful materials easier to learn. In M. Pressley & J. R. Levin (Eds.), *Cognitive strategy research: Educational applications.* New York: Springer-Verlag.

Pressley, M. (2003). Psychology of literacy and literacy instruction. In I. B. Weiner (Ed.), *Handbook of psychology* (Vol. 7). New York: Wiley.

Pressley, M., & Afflerbach, P. (1995). *Verbal protocols of reading.* Mahwah, NJ: Erlbaum.

Pressley, M., Allington, R., Wharton-McDonald, R., Block, C. C., & Morrow, L. M. (2001). *Learning to read: Lessons from exemplary first grades.* New York: Guilford.

Pressley, M., Borkowski, J. G., & Schneider, W. (1989). Good information processing: What it is and what education can do to promote it. *International Journal of Educational Research, 13,* 857–867.

Pressley, M., Cariliga-Bull, T., Deane, S., & Schneider, W. (1987). Short-term memory, verbal competence, and age as predictors of imagery instructional effectiveness. *Journal of Experimental Child Psychology, 43,* 194–211.

Pressley, M., Dolezal, S. E., Raphael, L. M., Welsh, L. M. Bogner, K., & Roehrig, A. D. (2003). *Motivating primary-grades teachers.* New York: Guilford.

Pressley, M., & Harris, K. (2006). Cognitive strategies instruction. In P. A. Alexander &

P. H. Winne (Eds.), *Handbook of educational psychology* (2nd ed.). Mahwah, NJ: Erlbaum.

Pressley, M., & Hilden, K. (2006). Cognitive strategies. In W. Damon & R. Lerner (Eds.), *Handbook of child psychology* (6th ed.). New York: Wiley.

Pressley, M., Levin, J. R., & McCormick, C. B. (1980). Young children's learning of a foreign language vocabulary: A sentence variation of the keyword. *Contemporary Educational Psychology, 5,* 22–29.

Pressley, M., & McCormick, C. (1995). Cognition, teaching and assessment. New York: HarperCollins.

Pressley, M., Raphael, L. Gallagher, D., & DiBella, J. (2004). Providence–St. Mel School: How a school that works for African-American students works. *Journal of Educational Psychology, 96,* 216–235.

Pressley, M., Schuder T., SAIL Faculty and Administration, German, J., & El-Dinary, P. B. (1992). A researcher-educator collaborative interview study of transactional comprehension strategies instruction. *Journal of Educational Psychology, 84,* 231–246.

Pressley, M., Wharto-McDonald, R., Allington, R., Block, C. C., Morrow, H. L., Tracey, D., Baker, K., Brooks, G., Cronin, J., Nelson, E., & Woo, D. (2001). A study of effective first grade literacy instruction. *Scientific Studies of Reading, 15,* 35–58.

Price, L. F. (2005). The biology of risk-taking. *Educational Leadership, 62* (No. 7), 22–26.

Pritchard, F. F., & Whitehead, G. I. (2004). *Serve and learn.* Mahwah, NJ: Erlbaum.

Provenzo, E. F. (2005). *The Internet and online research for teachers* (3rd ed.). Boston: Allyn & Bacon.

Pryor, J. H., Hurtado, S., Saenz, V. B., Lindholm, J. A., Korn, W. S, & Mahoney, K. M. (2005). *The American freshman: National norms for 2005.* Los Angeles: Higher Education Research Institute, UCLA.

PSU. (2006). Anchored instruction. Retrieved January 6, 2006, from http://www.ed.psu.edu/nasa/achrtxt.html

Pueschel, S. M., Scola, P. S., Weidenman, L. E., & Bernier, J. C. (1995). *The special child.* Baltimore: Paul H. Brookes.

Purcell-Gates, V. (1997, June 18). Commentary in "Diagnosing learning problems can be difficult for parents and teachers." *USA Today,* p. D8.

Purdy, J. E., Markham, M., Schwartz, B. & Gordon, W. M. (2001). *Learning and memory* (2nd ed.). Belmont, CA: Wadsworth.

Q

Quality Counts. (2001). *A better balance: Standards, tests, and the tools to succeed.* Bethesda, MD: Education Week on the Web.

Quintana, C., Shin, N., Norris, C., & Soloway, E. (2006). Learner-centered design. In R. K. Sawyer (Ed.). *The Cambridge handbook of the learning sciences.* New York: Cambridge University Press.

R

Raffaelli, M., & Ontai, L. L. (2004). Gender socialization in Latino/a families: Results from two retrospective studies. *Sex Roles, 50,* 287–299.

Rainey, R. (1965). The effects of directed vs. nondirected laboratory work on high school chemistry achievement. *Journal of Research in Science Teaching, 3,* 286–292.

Ramey, C. T., Bryant, D. M., Campbell, F. A., Sparling, J. J., & Wasik, B. H. (1988). Early intervention for high-risk children. The Carolina Early Intervention Program. In R. H. Price, E. L. Cowen, R. P. Lorion, & J. Ramos-McKay (Eds.), *14 ounces of prevention.* Washington, DC: American Psychological Association.

Ramey, C. T., Ramey, S. L., & Lanzi, R. G. (2001). Intelligence and experience. In R. J. Sternberg & E. L. Grigorenko (Eds.), *Environmental effects on cognitive abilities.* Mahwah, NJ: Erlbaum.

Ramey, C. T., Ramey, S. L., & Lanzi, R. G. (2006), Children's health and education. In W. Damon & R. Lerner (Eds.), *Handbook of child psychology* (6th ed.). New York: Wiley.

Ramphal, C. (1962). *A study of three current problems in education.* Unpublished doctoral dissertation, University of Natal, India.

Ramsay, P. G. (2006). Early childhood multicultural education. In B. Spodak & O. N. Sarancho (Eds.), *Handbook of research on the education of young children* (2nd ed.). Mahwah, NJ: Erlbaum.

Ramus, F. (2004). Neurobiology of dyslexia: A reinterpretation of the data. *Trends in Neuroscience, 27,* 720–726.

Randi, J., & Corno, L. (2000). Teacher innovations in self-regulated learning. In M. Boekaerts, P. R. Pintrich, & M. Zeidner (Eds.), *Handbook of self-regulation.* San Diego: Academic Press.

Randolph, C. H., & Evertson, C. M. (1995). Managing for learning: Rules, roles, and meanings in a writing class. *Journal of Classroom Interaction, 30,* 17–25.

Raphaelson, M. (2004). Stimulants and attention-deficit/hyperactivity disorder. *Journal of the American Medical Association, 292.* 2214.

Raschke, D. (1981). Designing reinforcement surveys: Let the student choose the reward. *Teaching Exceptional Children, 14,* 92–96.

Ratey, J. (2006, March 27). Commentary in L. Szabo, "ADHD treatment is getting a workout." *USA Today,* p. 6D.

Rathunde, K., & Csikszentmihalyi, M. (2006). The developing person: An experiential perspective. In W. Damon & R. Lerner (Eds.), *Handbook of child psychology* (6th ed.). New York: Wiley.

Ratner, N. B. (2005). Atypical language development. In J. B. Gleason (Ed.), *The development of language.* Boston: Allyn & Bacon.

Raver, C. C., & Zigler, E. F. (1997). Social competence: An untapped dimension in evaluating Head Start's success. *Early Childhood Research Quarterly, 13,* 365–385.

Ravitch, D. (1995). *National standards in American education: A citizen's guide.* Washington, DC: Brookings Institution.

Re: Learning by Design. (2000). *Design resource center.* Re: Learning by Design. Retrieved June 15, 2004, from http://www. relearning.org

Rea, P. J., McLaughlin, V. L., & Walther-Thomas, C. (2002). Outcomes of students with learning disabilities in inclusive and pullout programs. *Exceptional Children, 68,* 203–222.

Rebollo, M. A., & Montiel, S. (2006). Attention and the executive functions. *Revista de Neurologia* (Spanish), *42,* (Suppl.) S3–S7.

Redelmeier, D. A. (2005). Improving patient care: The cognitive psychology of missed diagnoses. *Annals of Internal Medicine, 142,* 115–120.

Redman, G. L. (2007). *Casebook for exploring diversity* (3rd ed.). Upper Saddle River, NJ: Prentice Hall.

Reed, A. J. S., Bergemann, V. E., & Olson, M. W. (2001). *A guide to observation and participation in the classroom.* New York: McGraw-Hill.

Reed, S. (2000). Problem solving. In A. Kazdin (Ed.), *Encyclopedia of psychology.* Washington, DC, & New York: American Psychological Association and Oxford University Press.

Reed, V. A. (2005). *Introduction to children with language disorders* (3rd ed.). Boston: Allyn & Bacon.

Reeve, J. (2006). Extrinsic rewards and inner motivation. In C. M. Evertson & C. S.

Weinstein (Eds.), *Handbook of classroom management.* Mahwah, NJ: Erlbaum.

Reeves, G., & Schweitzer, J. (2004). Pharmacological management of attention deficit hyperactivity disorder. *Expert Opinions in Pharmacotherapy, 5,* 1313–1320.

Regalado, M., Sareen, H., Inkelas, M., Wissow, L. S., & Halfon, N. (2004). Parents' discipline of young children: Results from the National Survey of Early Childhood Health. *Pediatrics, Supplement, 113,* 1952–1958.

Reinders, H., & Youniss, J. (2006). Community service and civic development in adolescence: theoretical considerations and empirical evidence. In A. Sliwka, M. Dietrich, & M. Hofer (Eds.), *Citizenship education.* Munster, GER: Waxmann.

Reiser, R., & Dempsey, J. V. (Eds.). (2007). *Trends and issues in instructional design* (2nd ed.). Upper Saddle River, NJ: Prentice Hall.

Renne, C. H. (1997). *Excellent classroom management.* Belmont, CA: Wadsworth.

Renzulli, J. S. (1998). A rising tide lifts all ships: Developing the gifts and talents of all students. *Phi Delta Kappan, 80,* 1–15.

Renzulli, J. S., & Reis, S. M. (1997). The schoolwide enrichment model. In N. Colangelo & G. A. Davis (Eds.), *Handbook of gifted education.* Boston: Allyn & Bacon.

Reschly, D. (1996). Identification and assessment of students with disabilities. *Future of Children, 6*(1), 40–53.

Revelle, S. P. (2004). High standards + high stakes = high achievement in Massachusetts. *Phi Delta Kappan, 85,* 591–597.

Reyna, V. F. (2004). How people make decisions that involve risk: A dual-process approach. *Current Directions in Psychological Science, 13,* 60–66.

Reyna, V. F., Adam, M. B., Walsk, M. E., LeCroy, C. W., Muller, K., & Brainerd, C. J. (2005). The development of judgment and decision making from childhood to adolescence. In J. E. Jacobs & P. A. Klaczynski (Eds.), *The development of judgment and decision making in children and adolescents.* Mahwah, NJ: Erlbaum.

Reyna, V. F., & Brainerd, C. J. (1995). Fuzzy-trace theory: An interim synthesis. *Learning and Individual Differences, 7,* 1–75.

Reynolds, C. R., Livingston, R., & Willson, V. (2006). *Measurement and assessment in education.* Boston: Allyn & Bacon.

Richard, A. (2001). Rural schools trying out portfolio assessment. *Education Week, 21,* 5.

Richards, T., Aylward, E., Raskind, W., Abbott, R., Field, K., Parsons, A., Richards, A., Nagy, W., Eckert, M., Leonard, C., &

Berninger, V. (2006, in press). Converging evidence for triple word form theory in child dyslexics. *Developmental Neuropsychology.*

Rickards, T. (1999). Brainstorming. In M. A. Runco & S. Pritzker (Eds.), *Encyclopedia of creativity.* San Diego: Academic Press.

Rickards, T., & deCock, C. (2003). Understanding organizational creativity: Toward a paradigmatic approach. In M.A. Runco (Ed.), *Creativity Research Handbook.* Cresskill, NJ: Hampton.

Rico, S. A., & Shulman, J. H. (2004). Invertebrates and organ systems: Science instruction. "Fostering a Community of Learners." *Journal of Curriculum Studies, 36,* 159–182.

Rideout, V., Roberts, D. F., & Foehr, U. G. (2005). *Generation M.* Menlo Park, CA: Kaiser Family Foundation.

Rieckmann, T. R., Wadsworth, M. E., & Deyhle, D. (2004). Cultural identity, explanatory style, and depression in Navajo adolescents. *Cultural Diversity & Ethnic Minority Psychology, 10,* 365–382.

Rigby, K. (2002). *New perspectives on bullying.* London: Jessica Kingsley.

Rigby, K. (2004). Bullying in childhood. In P. K. Smith & C. H. Hart (Eds.), *Blackwell handbook of childhood social development.* Malden, MA: Blackwell.

Riley, R. W. (1997, August 31). Long-term trend assessment of American students finds significant progress in science and mathematics. *New York Times,* Section 1, p. 18.

Risley, D. S., & Walther, B. (1995). *Creating responsible learners.* Washington, DC: American Psychological Association.

Roberts, D. F., Henriksen, L., & Foehr, V. G. (2004). Adolescents and the media. In R. Lerner & L. Steinberg (Eds.), *Handbook of adolescent psychology.* New York: Wiley.

Roberts, J. E., Schaaf, J. M., Skinner, M., Wheeler, A., Hooper, S., Hatton, D., & Bailey, D. B. (2005). Academic skills of boys with fragile X syndrome: Profiles and predictors. *American Journal of Mental Retardation, 110,* 107–120.

Roberts, W. B. (2005). *Bullying from both sides.* Thousand Oaks, CA: Sage.

Robins, R. W. (2005). Do people know how their personality has changed? Correlates of perceived and actual personality change in young adulthood. *Journal of Personality, 73,* 489–522.

Robins, R. W., Trzesniewski, K. H., Tracey, J. L., Potter, J., & Gosling, S. D. (2002). Age differences in self-esteem from age 9 to 90. *Psychology and Aging, 17,* 423–434.

Robinson, N. S. (1995). Evaluating the nature of perceived support and its relation to perceived self-worth in adolescents. *Journal of Research on Adolescence, 5,* 253–280.

Robinson, S. (2006). Victimization of obese adolescents. *Journal of School Nursing, 22,* 201–206.

Roblyer, M. D. (2006). *Integrating educational technology into teaching* (4th ed.). Upper Saddle River, NJ: Prentice Hall.

Roblyer, M. D., Edwards, J., & Havriluk, M. A. (1997). *Integrating educational technology into education.* Upper Saddle River, NJ: Merrill/Prentice Hall.

Rock, M. L. (2005). Use of strategic monitoring to enhance academic engagement, productivity, and accuracy of students with and without exceptionalities. *Journal of Positive Behavior Interventions, 7,* 3–17.

Rockman, S. (2003). Learning from laptops. *Threshold 1(1),* 24–28.

Rockman, S., & Mayer, K. (1994). The Buddy System, 1988–1993: A synthesis of research findings and recommendations for future research and action. San Francisco: Rockman et al. Retrieved January 10, 2006, from http://rockman.com/projects/buddy/budsyn93.pdf

Rodriquez-Galindo, C. A. (2006, April). *What's left behind: Home and school understandings of literacy.* Paper presented at the meeting of the American Educational Research Association, San Francisco.

Roff, M., Sells, S. B., & Golden, M. W. (1972). *Social adjustment and personality development in children.* Minneapolis: University of Minnesota Press.

Rogan, P., Luecking, R., & Held, R. G. (2001). Career development: Helping youth with mild cognitive limitations achieve successful careers. In A. J. Tymchuk (Ed.), *The forgotten generation.* Baltimore: Paul H. Brookes.

Rogers, C. R. (1961). *On becoming a person.* Boston: Houghton Mifflin.

Rogoff, B. (1990). *Apprenticeship in thinking.* New York: Oxford University Press.

Rogoff, B. (2003). *The cultural nature of human development.* New York: Oxford University Press.

Rogoff, B., Turkanis, C. G., & Barlett, L. (Eds.). (2001). *Learning together. Children and adults in a school community.* New York: Oxford University Press.

Rohrbeck, C. A., Ginsburg-Block, M. D., Fantuzzo, J. W., & Miller, T. R. (2003). Peer-assisted learning interventions with elementary school students: A meta-analytic review. *Journal of Educational Psychology, 95,* 240–257.

Roopnarine, J. L., & Metindogan, A. (2006). Early childhood education research in cross-national perspective. In B. Spodek & O. N. Saracho (Eds.), *Handbook of research on the education of young children.* Mahwah, NJ: Erlbaum.

Rosch, E. H. (1973). On the internal structure of perceptual and semantic categories. In T. E. Moore (Ed.), *Cognition and the acquisition of language.* New York: Academic Press.

Roschelle, J. (2003). Unlocking the value of wireless mobile devices. *Journal of Computer Assisted Learning 19,* 260–272.

Rosenshine, B. (1971). *Teaching behaviors and student achievement.* London: National Foundation for Educational Research.

Rosenshine, B. (1986). Synthesis of research on explicit teaching. *Educational Leadership, 43,* 60–69.

Rosenthal, D. M., & Sawyers, J. Y. (1997). Building successful home/school partnerships. *Young Children, 52,* 194–200.

Rosenthal, H. E., & Crisp, R. J. (2006). Reducing stereotype threat by blurring intergroup boundaries. *Personality and Social Psychology Bulletin, 32,* 501–511.

Rosenzweig, M. R. (1969). Effects of heredity and environment on brain chemistry, brain anatomy, and learning ability in the rat. In M. Monosevitz, G. Lindzey, & D. D. Thiessen (Eds.), *Behavioral genetics.* New York: Appleton-Century-Crofts.

Rosnow, R. L., & Rosenthal, R. L. (2005). *Beginning behavioral research* (5th ed.). Upper Saddle River, NJ: Prentice Hall.

Rosselli, H. C. (1996, February/March). Gifted students. *National Association for Secondary School Principals,* pp. 12–17.

Rothbart, M. K. (2004). Temperament and the pursuit of an integrated developmental psychology. *Merrill-Palmer Quarterly, 50,* 492–505.

Rothbart, M. K., & Bates, J. E. (1998). Temperament. In W. Damon (Ed.), *Handbook of child psychology* (5th ed., Vol. 3). New York: Wiley.

Rothbart, M. K., & Bates, J. E. (2006). Temperament. In W. Damon & R. Lerner (Eds.), *Handbook of child psychology* (6th ed.). New York: Wiley.

Rowe, M. (1986). Wait time: Slowing down may be a way of speeding up! *Journal of Teacher Education, 37,* 43–50.

Rowe, R. J. (Ed.). (1994). *Preschoolers as authors: Literacy learning in the social world of the classroom.* Cresskill, NJ: Hampton Press.

Rowe, S. M., & Wertsch, J. V. (2004). Vygotsky's model of cognitive development. In U. Goswami (Ed.), *Blackwell handbook of childhood cognitive development.* Malden, MA: Blackwell.

Rubin, D. (2006). *Gaining word power* (7th ed.). Boston: Allyn & Bacon.

Rubin, K. H., Bukowski, W., & Parker, J. G. (2006). Peer interactions, relationships, and groups. In W. Damon & R. Lerner (Eds.), *Handbook of child psychology* (6th ed.). New York: Wiley.

Ruble, D. (1983). The development of social comparison processes and their role in achievement-related self-socialization. In E. T. Higgins, D. N. Ruble, & W. W. Hartup (Eds.), *Social cognition and development.* New York: Cambridge University Press.

Ruble, D. N., Martin, C. L., & Berenbaum, S. A. (2006). Gender development. In W. Damon & R. Lerner (Eds.), *Handbook of child psychology* (6th ed.). New York: Wiley.

Ruddell, R. B. (2006). *Teaching children to read and write* (4th ed.). Boston: Allyn & Bacon.

Rueda, R., & Yaden, D. B. (2006). The literacy education of linguistically and culturally diverse young children: An overview of outcomes, assessment, and large-scale interventions. In B. Spodek & O. N. Saracho (Eds.), *Handbook of research on the education of young children.* Mahwah, NJ: Erlbaum.

Ruff, H. A., & Capozzoli, M. C. (2003). Development of attention and distractibility in the first 4 years of life. *Developmental Psychology, 39,* 877–890.

Ruff, H. A., & Rothbart, M. K. (1996). *Attention in early development.* New York: Oxford University Press.

Rumberger, R. W. (1995). Dropping out of middle school: A multilevel analysis of students and schools. *American Education Research Journal, 3,* 583–625.

Rummell, N., & Spada, H. (2005). Learning to collaborate: An instructional approach to promoting collaborative problem solving in computer-mediated settings. *Journal of Learning Sciences, 14,* 201–241.

Runco, M. A. (2004). Creativity. *Annual Review of Psychology, 55.* Palo Alto, CA: Annual Reviews.

Runco, M. A. (2006). The development of children's creativity. In B. Spodek & O. N. Saracho (Eds.). *Handbook of research on the education of young children* (2nd ed.). Mahwah, NJ: Erlbaum.

Russman, B. S., & Ashwal, S. (2004). Evaluation of the child with cerebral palsy. *Seminars in Pediatric Neurology, 11,* 47–57.

Rust, C., O'Donovan, B., & Price, M. (2005). A social constructivist assessment process model: How the research literature shows us this could be best practice. *Assessment & Evaluation in Higher Education, 30,* 231–240.

Rutter, M., & Schopler, E. (1987). Autism and pervasive developmental disorders: Concepts and diagnostic issues. *Journal of Autism and Pervasive Developmental Disorders, 17,* 154–186.

Rutter, T. (2005). *What separates problem readers from proficient ones? Virginia Mann focuses on three elements.* Retrieved June 6, 2005, from www.brainconnection.com/

Ryan, R. & Deci, E. (2000). Self-determination theory and the facilitation of intrinsic motivation, social development, and well-being. *American Psychologist, 55,* 68–78.

Ryan, R. M., Fauth, R. C, & Brooks-Gunn, J. (2006). Childhood poverty: Implications for school readiness and early childhood education. In B. Spodak & O. N. Saracho (Eds.), *Handbook of research on the education of young children* (2nd ed.). Mahwah, NJ: Erlbaum.

S

Sabers, D. S., Cushing, K. S., & Berliner, D. C. (1991). Differences among teachers in a task characterized by simultaneity, multidimensionality, and immediacy. *American Educational Research Journal 28,* 63–88.

Sackett, P. R., Hardison, C. M., & Cullen, M. J. (2004). On interpreting stereotype threat as accounting for African-American White differences in cognitive tests. *American Psychologist, 59,* 7–13.

Sackett, P. R., Hardison, C. M., & Cullen, M. J. (2005). On interpreting research on stereotype threat and test performance. *American Psychologist, 60,* 271–272.

Saddler, B., & Graham, B. (2005). The effects of peer-assisted sentence-combining instruction on the writing performance of more and less skilled young writers. *Journal of Educational Psychology, 97,* 43–54.

Sadker, D. M. P., & Sadker, D. M. (2005). *Teachers, schools, and society* (7th ed.). New York: McGraw-Hill.

Sadker, M. P., & Sadker, D. M. (1994). *Failing at fairness: How Americas schools cheat girls.* New York: Scribners.

Saenz, L. M., Fuchs, L. S., & Fuchs, D. (2005). Peer-assisted learning strategies for English language learners with learning disabilities. *Exceptional Children, 71,* 231–247.

Sailor, W., & Roger, B. (2005). Rethinking inclusion: Schoolwide applications. *Phi Delta Kappan, 86,* 503–509.

Salomon, G., & Perkins, D. (1989). Rocky roads to transfer: Rethinking mechanisms of a neglected phenomenon. *Educational Psychologist, 24,* 113–142.

Salovey, P., & Mayer, J. D. (1990). Emotional intelligence. *Imagination, Cognition, and Personality, 9,* 185–211.

Salovey, P., & Pizarro, D. A. (2003). The value of emotional intelligence. In R. J. Sternberg, J. Lautrey, & T. I. Lubert (Eds.), *Models of intelligence: International perspectives.* Washington, DC: American Psychological Association.

Sam, D. L., & Berry, J. W. (Eds) (2006). *Cambridge handbook of acculturation psychology.* New York: Cambridge University Press.

Sampson, R., Raudenbush, S., & Earls, F. (1997). Neighborhoods and violent crime: A multilevel study of collective efficacy. *Science, 277,* 918–924.

Sandoval, J., Scheuneman, J. D., Ramos-Grenier, J., Geisinger, K. F., & Frisby, C. (Eds.). (1999). *Test interpretation and diversity: Achieving equity in assessment.* Washington, DC: American Psychological Association.

Sanson, A. V., & Rothbart, M. K. (1995). Child temperament and parenting. In M. H. Bornstein (Ed.), *Handbook of parenting* (Vol. 4). Hillsdale, NJ: Erlbaum.

Sanson, A. V., & Rothbart, M. K. (2002). Child temperament and parenting. In M. H. Bornstein (Ed.), *Handbook of parenting.* Mahwah, NJ: Erlbaum.

Santiago-Delefosse, M. J., & Delefosse, J. M. O. (2002). Three positions on child thought and language. *Theory and Psychology, 12,* 723–747.

Santrock, J. W., & Halonen, J. S. (2006). *Your guide to college success* (4th ed.). Belmont, CA: Wadsworth.

Saucier, G., & Simonds, J. (2006). The structure of personality and temperament. In D. K. Mroczek & T. D. Little (Eds.), *Handbook of personality development.* Mahwah, NJ: Erlbaum.

Sawyer, D. K. (Ed.) (2006). Conclusion: The schools of the future. In D. K. Sawyer (Ed.), *The Cambridge handbook of the learning sciences.* New York: Cambridge University Press.

Sawyer, R. K. (2006). Introduction: The new science of learning. In R. K. Sawyer (Ed.), *The Cambridge handbook of the learning sciences.* New York: Cambridge University Press.

Sax, G. (1997). *Principles of educational and psychological measurement and evaluation* (4th ed.). Belmont, CA: Wadsworth.

Scardamalia, M. (1981). How children cope with the cognitive demands of writing. In C. Frederiksen & J. F. Dominic (Eds.). *Writing: The nature, development, and teaching of* *written communication.* Mahwah, NJ: Erlbaum.

Scardamalia, M., & Bereiter, C. (1994). Computer support for knowledge-building communities. *Journal of the Learning Sciences, 3*(3), 265–283.

Scardamalia, M., & Bereiter, C. (2006). Knowledge building: Theory, pedagogy, and technology. In R. K. Sawyer (Ed.), *Cambridge handbook of learning sciences.* New York: Oxford University Press.

Scardamalia, M., Bereiter, C., & Lamon, M. (1994). The CSILE Project: Trying to bring the classroom into the world. In K. McGilly (Ed.), *Classroom lessons.* Cambridge, MA: MIT Press.

Scarr, S., & Weinberg, R. A. (1983). The Minnesota Adoption Studies: Genetic differences and malleability. *Child Development, 54,* 253–259.

Schacter, D. L. (2000). Memory systems. In A. Kazdin (Ed.), *Encyclopedia of psychology.* Washington, DC, & New York: American Psychological Association and Oxford University Press.

Schacter, D. L. (2001). *The seven deadly sins of memory.* Boston: Houghton Mifflin.

Schauble, L., Beane, D. B., Coates, G. D., Martin, L. M. W., & Sterling, P. V. (1996). Outside classroom walls: Learning in informal environments. In L. Schauble & R. Glaser (Eds.), *Innovations in learning.* Mahwah, NJ: Erlbaum.

Schellens, T., & Valcke, M. (2005). Collaborative learning in asynchronous discussion groups: What about the impact of cognitive processing? *Computers in Human Behavior, 21,* 957–975.

Schiefele, U. (1996). Topic interest, text representation, and quality of experience. *Contemporary Educational Psychology, 21,* 3–18.

Schlesinger, A. M. (1991). *The disuniting of America.* Knoxville, TN: Whittle Direct Books.

Schmidt, R. (2001). The power to empower. In P. R. Schmidt & P. B. Mosenthal (Eds.), *Reconceptualizing literacy in the new age of multiculturalism and pluralism.* Greenwich, CT: IAP.

Schneider, B., & Coleman, J. S. (1993). *Parents, their children, and schools.* Boulder, CO: Westview Press.

Schneider, W. (2004). Memory development in childhood. In U. Goswami (Ed.), *Blackwell handbook of childhood cognitive development.* Malden, MA: Blackwell.

Schneider, W., & Bjorklund, D. F. (1998). Memory. In W. Damon (Ed.), *Handbook of child psychology* (5th ed., Vol. 2). New York: Wiley.

Schneider, W., & Pressley, M. (1997). *Memory development between 2 and 20* (2nd ed.). Mahwah, NJ: Erlbaum.

Schneps, M. H., & Sadler, P. M. (1989). [Video.] *A private universe.* Cambridge, MA: Harvard-Smithsonian Center for Astrophysics.

Schoenfeld, A. H. (2002). Making mathematics work for all children: Issues of standards, testing, and equity. *Educational Researcher, 31,* 13–25.

Schoenfeld, A. H. (2004). Multiple learning communities: Students, teachers, instructional designers, and researchers. *Journal of Curriculum Studies, 36,* 237–255.

Schoenfeld, A. H. (2006). Mathematics teaching and learning. In P. A. Alexander and P. H. Winne (Eds.), *Handbook of educational psychology* (2nd ed.). Mahwah, NJ: Erlbaum.

Schofield, J. W. (2006). Internet use in the schools: Promise and problems. In R. K. Sawyer (Ed.), *The Cambridge handbook of the learning sciences.* New York: Cambridge University Press.

Schofield, W. (2003). The colorblind perspective in school: Causes and consequences. In J. A. Banks & C. A. M. Banks (Eds.), *Multicultural education* (updated 4th ed.). New York: Wiley.

Schoon, I., Parsons, S., & Sacker, A. (2004). Socioeconomic adversity, educational resilience, and subsequent levels of adult adaptation. *Journal of Adoelescent Research, 19,* 383–404.

Schraw, G. (2006). Knowledge structures and processes. In P. A. Alexander & P. H. Winne (Eds.), *Handbook of educational psychology* (2nd ed.). Mahwah, NJ: Erlbaum.

Schrum, L., & Berenfeld, B. (1997). *Teaching and learning in the information age: A guide to telecommunications.* Boston: Allyn & Bacon.

Schuh, K. (2001, April). *Teacher-centered and learner-centered: What's the relationship?* Paper presented at the meeting of the American Educational Research Association, Seattle.

Schultz, K., & Fecho, B. (2001). Society's child: Social context and writing development. *Educational Psychologist, 35,* 51–62.

Schunk, D. H. (1991). Self-efficacy and academic motivation. *Educational Psychologist, 25,* 71–86.

Schunk, D. H. (1999, August). *Social-self interaction and achievement behavior.* Presidential address, Division 15, presented at the meeting of the American Psychological Association, Boston.

Schunk, D. H. (2001). Social cognitive theory and self-regulated learning. In B. J.

Zimmerman & D. H. Schunk (Eds.), *Self-regulated learning and achievement* (2nd ed.). Mahwah, NJ: Erlbaum.

Schunk, D. H. (2004). *Learning theories: An educational perspective* (4th ed.). Upper Saddle River, NJ: Prentice Hall.

Schunk, D. H., & Meece, J. L. (2006). Self-efficacy in adolescence. In F. J. Pajares & T. Urdan (Eds.), *Adolescence and education.* Greenwich, GT: Information Age Publishing.

Schunk, D. H., & Rice, J. M. (1989). Learning goals and children's reading comprehension. *Journal of Reading Behavior, 23,* 351–364.

Schunk, D. H., & Swartz, C. W. (1993). Goals and progressive feedback: Effects on self-efficacy and writing achievement. *Contemporary Educational Psychology, 18,* 337–354.

Schunk, D. H., & Zimmerman, B. J. (2006). Competence and control beliefs: Distinguishing the means and ends. In P. A. Alexander & P. H. Winne: (Eds.), *Handbook of educational psychology* (2nd ed.). Mahwah, NJ: Erlbaum.

Schwab-Stone, M., & others. (1995). *New Haven Public Schools Social Development Project: 1994.* New Haven, CT: New Haven Public Schools.

Schwartz, D. L., Bransford, J. D., & Sears, D. (2006, in press). Efficiency and innovation in transfer. In J. Mestre (Ed.), *Transfer of learning: Research and perspectives.* Greenwich, CT: Information Age Publishing.

Schwartz, D. L., Lin, X., Brophy, J., & Bransford, J. D. (1999). Toward the development of flexibly adaptive instructional designs. In C. M. Reigelut (Ed.), *Instructional design theories and models* (Vol. II). Mahwah, NJ: Erlbaum.

Schweinhart, L. J. (1999, April). *Generalizing from High/Scope longitudinal studies.* Paper presented at the meeting of the Society for Research in Child Development, Albuquerque.

Search Institute. (1995). *Barriers to participation in youth programs.* Unpublished manuscript, the Search Institute, Minneapolis.

Sears, H. A., Byers, E. S., Whelan, J. J., & Saint-Pierre, M. (2006). "If it hurts you, then it is not a joke": adolescents' ideas about girls' and boys' use and experience of abusive behavior in dating relationships. *Journal of Interpersonal Violence, 21,* 1191–1207.

Segal, J. W. (1996). Foreword. In L. Schauble & R. Glaser (Eds.), *Innovations in learning.* Mahwah, NJ: Erlbaum.

Seidman, L. J. (2006, in press). Neuropsychological functioning in people with

ADHD across the lifespan. *Clinical Psychology Review*.

Seligson, T. (2005, February 20). They speak for success. *Parade Magazine*.

Sellnow, D. D. (2005). *Confident public speaking* (2nd ed.). Belmont, CA: Wadsworth.

Sensenbaugh, R. (1995). Reading Recovery. *ERIC Clearinghouse on Reading, English, and Communication Digest, No. 106*.

Sergerie, K., Lepage, M., & Armony, J. L. (2005). A face to remember: Emotional expression modulates prefrontal activity during memory formation. *Neuroimage, 24*, 580–585.

Shaftel, J. (2005). Statewide tests. In S. W. Lee (Ed.), *Encyclopedia of school psychology*. Thousand Oaks, CA: Sage.

Shalev, R. S. (2004). Developmental dyscalculia. *Journal of Child Neurology, 19*, 765–771.

Shalev, R. S., Manor, O., & Gross-Tsur, V. (2005). Developmental dyscalculia: A prospective six-year follow-up. *Developmental Medicine and Child Neurology, 47*, 121–125.

Shanahan, T., & Rodriguez-Brown, F. V. (1993, April). *Project FLAME: The theory and structure of a family literacy program for the Latino community*. Paper presented at the meeting of the American Educational Research Association, Atlanta.

Sharan, S. (1990). Cooperative learning and helping behavior in the multi-ethnic classroom. In H. C. Foot, M. J. Morgan, & R. H. Shute (Eds.), *Children helping children*. New York: Wiley.

Sharan, S., & Sharan, S. (1992). *Expanding cooperative learning through group investigation*. New York: Teachers College Press.

Sharan, S., & Shaulov, A. (1990). Cooperative learning, motivation to learn, and academic achievement. In S. Sharan (Ed.), *Cooperative learning*. New York: Praeger.

Sharp, J. M. (2005). *Learning and teaching K–8 mathematics*. Boston: Allyn & Bacon.

Sheets, R. H. (2005). *Diversity pedagogy*. Boston: Allyn & Bacon.

Sheffield, C. J. (1997, March/April). Instructional technology for teachers: Preparation for classroom diversity. *Educational Technology*, pp. 16–18.

Sheldon, S. B., & Epstein, J. L. (2005). School programs of family and community involvement to support children's reading and literacy involvement across the grades. In J. Flood & P. Anders (Eds.), *Literacy development of students in urban schools*. Newark, DE: International Reading Association.

Shepard, L., Hammerness, K., Darling-Hammond, L., Rust, F., Snowden, Baratz-Snowden, J., Gordon, E., Cutierrez, C., & Pacheco, A. (2005). Assessment. In L. Darling-Hammond & J. Bransford (Eds.), *Preparing teachers for a changing world*. San Francisco: Jossey-Bass.

Sheppard, J. A., & Koch, E. J. (2005). Pitfalls in teaching judgment heuristics. *Teaching of Psychology, 32*, 43–46.

Sherin, M. G., Mendez, E. P., & Louis, D. A. (2004). A discipline apart: The challenges of Fostering a Community of Learners in a mathematics classroom. *Journal of Curriculum Studies, 36*, 207–232.

Sherman, C. W., & Mueller, D. P. (1996, June). *Developmentally appropriate practice and student achievement in inner-city elementary schools*. Paper presented at Head Start's Third National Research Conference, Washington, DC.

Sherman, L. W. (2001). Cooperative learning and computer-supported intentional learning experiences. In C. R. Wolfe (Ed.), *Learning and teaching on the World Wide Web*. San Diego: Academic Press.

Sherry, S. B., Hewitt, P. L., Besser, A., McGee, B. J., & Flett, G. L. (2004). Self-oriented and socially prescribed perfectionism in the Eating Disorder Inventory perfectionism subscale. *International Journal of Eating Disorders, 22*(1), 39–57.

Sherry, S. B., Hewitt, P. L., Flett, G. L., & Harvey, M. (2003). Perfectionism dimensions, perfectionistic dysfunctional attitudes, need for approval, and depression symptoms in adult psychiatric patients and young adults. *Journal of Counseling Psychology, 50*, 373–386.

Shields, P. M. & others. (2001). *The status of the teaching profession 2001*. Santa Cruz, CA: The Center for the Future of Teaching and Learning.

Shields, S. A. (1991). Gender in the psychology of emotion: A selective research review. In K. T. Strongman (Ed.), *International review of studies on emotion* (Vol. I). New York: Wiley.

Shiffrin, R. M. (1996). Laboratory experimentation on the genesis of expertise. In K. A. Ericsson (Ed.), *The road to excellence*. Mahwah, NJ: Erlbaum.

Shiner, R. L. (2006). Temperament and personality in childhood. In D. K. Mrocezek & T. D. Little (Eds.), *Handbook of personality development*. Mahwah, NJ: Erlbaum.

Shiraev, E., & Levy, D. (2007). *Cross-cultural psychology: Critical thinking and critical applications* (3rd ed.). Belmont, CA: Wadsworth.

Shirts, R. G. (1997). *BAFA, BAFA, a cross-cultural simulation*. Del Mar, CA: SIMILE II.

Shonkoff, J. (1996). Mental retardation. In R. Behrman, R. Kliegman, & A. Arvin (Eds.), *Nelson textbook of pediatrics* (15th ed.). Philadelphia: W. B. Saunders.

Shulman, L. S. (1987). Knowledge and teaching: Foundations of the new reform. *Harvard Educational Review, 57*, 1–22.

Shulman, L. S., & Shulman, J. H. (2004). How and what teachers learn: A shifting perspective. *Journal of Curriculum Studies, 36*, 257–274.

Shweder, R., Goodnow, J., Hatano, G., LeVine, R. A., Markus, H., & Miller, P. (2006). The cultural psychology of development. In W. Damon & R. Lerner (Eds.), *Handbook of child psychology* (6th ed.). New York: Wiley.

Siegel, L. S. (2003). Learning disabilities. In I. B. Weiner (Ed.), *Handbook of psychology* (Vol. 7). New York: Wiley.

Siegel, L. S., & Ryan, E. B. (1989). The development of working memory in normally achieving and subtypes of learning disabled children. *Child Development, 60*, 973–980.

Siegler, R. S. (1998). *Children's thinking* (3rd ed.). Upper Saddle River, NJ: Erlbaum.

Siegler, R. S. (2004). Learning about learning. *Merrill-Palmer Quarterly, 50*, 353–368.

Siegler, R. S. (2006). Microgenetic analysis of learning. In W. Damon & R. Lerner (Eds.), *Handbook of child psychology* (6th ed.). New York: Wiley.

Siegler, R. S., & Alibali, M. W. (2005). *Children's thinking* (4th ed.). Upper Saddle River, NJ: Prentice Hall.

Siegler, R. S., & Robinson, M. (1982). The development of numerical understandings. In H. W. Reese & L. P. Litsitt (Eds.), *Advances in child development and behavior* (Vol. 12). New York: Academic Press.

Sigman, M., & McGovern, C. W. (2005). Improvement in cognitive and language skills from preschool to adolescence. *Journal of Autism and Developmental Disorders, 35*, 15–23.

Silberman, M. (2006). *Teaching actively*. Boston: Allyn & Bacon.

Silverman, L. K. (1993). A developmental model for counseling the gifted. In L. K. Silverman (Ed.), *Counseling the gifted and the talented*. Denver: Love.

Silvernail, D. L., & Lane, D. M. M. (2004). *The impact of Maine's one-to-one laptop program on middle school teachers and students*. (Report #1). Gorham, ME: Maine Education Policy Research Institute, University of Southern Maine Office.

Sim, T. N., & Ong, L. P. (2005). Parent punishment and child aggression in a Singapore Chinese preschool sample. *Journal of Marriage and the Family, 67,* 85–99.

Simon, B. S. (2001). Family involvement in high school: Predictors and effects. *NASSP Bulletin, 85*(2), 8–19.

Simon, B. S. (2004). High school outreach and family involvement. *School Psychology of Education, 7,* 185–209.

Simon, H. (2001). Learning to research about learning. In S. M. Carver & D. Klahr (Eds.), *Cognition and instruction.* Mahwah, NJ: Erlbaum.

Simons, J., Finlay, B., & Yang, A. (1991). *The adolescent and young adult fact book.* Washington, DC: Children's Defense Fund.

Simonson, M., Smaldino, S. E., Albright., M. J., & Zvacek, S. (2006). *Teaching and learning at a distance* (3rd ed.). Upper Saddle River, NJ: Prentice Hall.

Simpkins, S. D., Fredricks, J. A., Davis-Kean, P. E., & Eccles, J. S. (2004). Healthy mind, healthy habits: The influence of activity involvement in middle childhood. In A. C. Huston & M. N. Ripke (Eds.), *Middle childhood: Contexts of development.* New York: Cambridge University Press.

Simpson, J., & Rice, M. L. (2005). *Specific language impairment.* Retrieved April 8, 2006, from http://www.speech-express.com/diagnosis-destinations/

Singer, D. G., & Singer, J. L. (1987). Practical suggestions for controlling television. *Journal of Early Adolescence, 7,* 365–369.

Singer, S. R., Hilton, M. L., & Schweingruber, H. A. (Eds.). (2006). *America's lab report: Investigations in high school science.* Washington, DC: National Academic Press.

Singhal, M. (2001). Reading proficiency, reading strategies, metacognitive awareness, and L2 readers. *Reading Matrix, 1,* 1–6.

Skinner, B. F. (1938). *The behavior of organisms.* New York: Appleton-Century-Crofts.

Skinner, B. F. (1954). The science of learning and the art of teaching. *Harvard Educational Review, 24,* 86–97.

Skinner, B. F. (1957). *Verbal behavior.* New York: Appleton-Century-Crofts.

Skinner, B. F. (1958). Teaching machines. *Science, 128,* 969–977.

Slade, E. P., & Wissow, L. S. (2004). Spanking in early childhood and later behavior problems: A prospective study. *Pediatrics, 113,* 1321–1330.

Slavin, R. E. (1990). Achievement effects of ability grouping in secondary schools: A best-evidence synthesis. *Review of Educational Research, 60,* 471–500.

Slavin, R. E. (1995). *Cooperative learning: Theory, research, and practice* (2nd ed.). Boston: Allyn & Bacon.

Slavin, R. E., Daniels, C., & Madden, N. A. (2005). "Success for All" middle schools add content to middle grades reform. *Middle School Journal, 36*(5), 1–8.

Slavin, R. E., & Madden N. A. (Eds.). (2001). *Success for all.* Mahwah, NJ: Erlbaum.

Slavin, R. E., Madden, N. A., Dolan, L. J., & Wasik, B. A. (1996). *Every child, every school: Success for all.* Newbury Park, CA: Corwin Press.

Slentz, K. L., & Krogh, S. L. (2001). *Teaching young children.* Mahwah, NJ: Erlbaum.

Smith, B. (2007). *The psychology of sex and gender.* Boston: Allyn & Bacon.

Smith, D. D. (2007). *Introduction to special education* (6th ed.). Boston: Allyn & Bacon.

Smith, L. (2004). Piaget's model. In U. Goswami (Ed.), *Blackwell handbook of childhood cognitive development.* Malden, MA: Blackwell.

Smith, R., Clark, T., & Bloymeyer, R. L. (2005). *A synthesis of new research on K–12 online learning.* Naperville, IL: Learning Point Associates. Retrieved January 30, 2006, from http://www.ncrel.org/tech/synthesis/synthesis.pdf

Smith, R. A. (2005). The classroom as a social psychology laboratory. *Journal of Social & Clinical Psychology, 24,* 62–71.

Smith, S. D., & Bulman-Fleming, M. B. (2005). An examination of the right-hemisphere hypothesis of the lateralization of emotion. *Brain and Cognition, 57,* 210–213.

Smith, S. S. (2006). *Early childhood mathematics* (3rd ed.). Boston: Allyn & Bacon.

Smith, T. E. C., Polloay, E. A., Patton, J. R., & Dowdy, C. A. (2006). *Teaching students with special needs in inclusive settings* (4th ed., Update). Boston: Allyn & Bacon.

Smith-Maddox, R., & Wheelock, A. (1995). Untracking and student's futures. *Phi Delta Kappan, 77,* 222–228.

Smoll, F. L., & Schutz, R. W. (1990). Quantifying gender differences in physical performance: A developmental perspective. *Developmental Psychology, 26,* 360–369.

Smyth, M. M., Collins, A. F., Morris, P. E., & Levy, P. (1994). *Cognition in action* (2nd ed.). Hove, UK: Erlbaum.

Snell, J. L., & Hirschstein, M. (2005). Bullying and victimization. In S. W. Lee (Ed.), *Encyclopedia of school psychology.* Thousand Oaks, CA: Sage.

Snow, C. E., & Kang, J. Y. (2006). Becoming bilingual, biliterate, and bicultural. In

W. Damon & R. Lerner (Eds.), *Handbook of child psychology* (6th ed.). New York: Wiley.

Snow, R. E., Como, L., & Jackson, D. (1996). Individual differences in affective and conative functions. In D. C. Berliner & R. C. Calfee (Eds.), *Handbook of educational psychology.* New York: Macmillan.

Soderman, A. K., Gregory, K. M., & O'Neill, L. T. (2005). *Scaffolding emerging literacy* (2nd ed.). Boston: Allyn & Bacon.

Sokoloff, D. R., & Thornton, R. K. (1997). Using interactive lecture demonstration to create an active learning environment. *American Journal of Physics, 64,* 338–352.

Solano-Flores, G., & Shavelson, R. J. (1997, Fall). Development of performance assessments in science: Conceptual, practical, and logistical issues. *Educational Measurement,* pp. 16–24.

Solley, B. A. (2000). *Writer's workshop: Reflections of elementary and middle school teachers.* Boston: Allyn & Bacon.

Soltero, S. W. (2004). *Dual language: Teaching and learning in two languages.* Boston: Allyn & Bacon.

Songer, N. B. (2006). BioKIDS. In R. K. Sawyer (Ed.), *The Cambridge handbook of learning sciences.* New York: Cambridge University Press.

Sousa, D. A. (1995). *How the brain learns: A classroom teacher's guide.* Reston, VA: National Association of Secondary School Principals.

South, M., Ozonoff, S., & McMahon, W. M. (2005). Repetitive behavior profiles in Asperger syndrome and high-functioning autism. *Journal of Autism and Developmental Disorders, 35,* 145–158.

Spafford, C. S., Grosser, G. S., & Daurich, B. (2005). *Dyslexia and reading difficulties* (2nd ed.). Boston: Allyn & Bacon.

Spandel, V. (2005). *Creating writers through writing assessment and instruction* (4th ed.). Boston: Allyn & Bacon.

Spearman, C. E. (1927). *The abilities of man.* New York: Macmillan.

Spector, J. M., Ohrazda, C., Van Schaack, A., & Wiley D. A. (Eds.). (2005). *Innovations in instructional technology.* Mahwah, NJ: Erlbaum.

Spence, J. T., & Helmreich, R. (1978). *Masculinity and femininity: Their psychological dimensions.* Austin: University of Texas Press.

Spencer, M. B. (2000). Ethnocentrism. In A. Kazdin (Ed.), *Encyclopedia of psychology.* New York and Washington, DC: Oxford University Press and the American Psychological Association.

Spencer, M. B. (2006). Phenomenology and ecological systems theory. In W. Damon &

R. Lerner (Eds.), *Handbook of child psychology* (6th ed.). New York: Wiley.

Spencer, M. B., & Dornbusch, S. M. (1990). Challenges in studying minority youth. In S. S. Feldman & G. R. Elliott (Eds.), *At the threshold: The developing adolescent.* Cambridge, MA: Harvard University Press.

Spencer, M. B., & Markstrom-Adams, C. (1990). Identity processes among racial and ethnic minority children in America. *Child Development, 61,* 290–310.

Spencer, M. B., Noll, E., Stoltzfuz, J., & Harpolani, V. (2001). Identity and school adjustment: Revisiting the "acting white" assumption. *Educational Psychologist, 36,* 21–30.

Spring, J. (2006). *American education* (12th ed.). New York: McGraw-Hill.

Spring, J. (2007). *Deculturalization and the struggle for equality* (5th ed.). New York: McGraw-Hill.

Sprinthall, R. C. (2007). *Basic statistical analysis* (8th ed.). Boston: Allyn & Bacon.

Squire, L. (1987). *Memory and brain.* New York: Oxford University Press.

Sraiheen, A., & Lesisko, L. J. (2006). Grade inflation: An elementary and secondary perspective. *ERIC Documents,* ED490038.

Sroufe, L. A., Cooper, R. G., DeHart, G., and Bronfenbrenner, U. (1992). *Child development: Its nature and course* (2nd ed.). New York: McGraw-Hill.

Sroufe, L. A., Egeland, B., Carlson, E. A., & Collins, W. A. (2005a). The place of early attachment in developmental context. In K. E. Grossman, K. Krossman, & E. Waters (Eds.), *The power of longitudinal attachment research: From infancy and childhood to adulthood.* New York: Guilford Press.

Sroufe, L. A., Egeland, B., Carlson, E. A., & Collins, W. A. (2005b). *The development of the person.* New York: Oxford University Press.

St. Pierre, R., Layzer, J., & Barnes, H. (1996). *Regenerating two-generation programs.* Cambridge, MA: Abt Associates.

Stahl, G., Koschmann, T., & Suthers, D. (2006). Computer-based collaborative learning. In R. K. Sawyer (Ed.). *The Cambridge Handbook of the learning sciences.* New York: Cambridge University Press.

Stahl, S. (2002, January). *Effective reading instruction in the first grade.* Paper presented at the Michigan Reading Recovery conference, Dearborn, MI.

Stanovich, K. E. (1994). Romance and reality. *Reading Teacher, 47,* 280–291.

Stanovich, K. E. (2004). *How to think straight about psychology* (7th ed.). Boston: Allyn & Bacon.

Stanovich, K. E., & West, R. E. (2000). Individual differences in reasoning: Implications for the rationality debate? *Behavior and Brain Sciences, 23,* 646–665.

Stansfield, C. W., & Rivera, C. (2002). 2nd language testing: How will English language learners be accommodated? In R. W. Lissitz & W. D. Schafer (Eds.), *Assessment in educational reform: Both means and ends.* Boston: Allyn & Bacon.

Starko, A. J. (2005). *Creativity in the classroom.* Mahwah, NJ: Erlbaum.

Steele, C. M., & Aronson, J. (1995). Stereotype threat and the intellectual test performance of African-Americans. *Journal of Personality and Social Psychology, 69,* 797–811.

Steele, C. M., & Aronson, J. A. (2004). Stereotype threat does not live by Steele and Aronson (1995) alone. *American Psychologist, 59,* 47–48.

Stegelin, D. A. (2003). Application of Reggio Emilia approach to early childhood science curriculum. *Early Childhood Education Journal, 30,* 163–169.

Stein, M. T. (2004). ADHD: The diagnostic process from different perspectives. *Journal of Developmental and Behavioral Pediatrics. 25* (5 Suppl.), S54–S58.

Stein, M. T., & Perrin, J. M. (2003). Diagnosis and treatment of ADHD in school-age children in primary care settings: A synopsis of the AAP practice guidelines. *Pediatric Review, 24,* 92–98.

Steinberg, L. (2004). Risk taking in adolescence: What changes, and why? *Annals of the New York Academy of Sciences, 1021,* 51–58.

Steinberg, L. (2005). Cognitive and affective development in adolescence. *Trends in cognitive sciences, 9,* 69–74.

Steinberg, L. (2006, April). *A new approach to the study of adolescent cognitive development.* Paper presented at the meeting of the Society for Research on Adolescent Development, San Francisco.

Steinberg, L., Blatt-Eisengart, I., & Cauffman, E. (2006). Patterns of competence and adjustment among adolescents from authoritative, authoritarian, indulgent, and neglectful homes: A replication in a sample of juvenile defenders. *Journal of Research on Adolescent Development, 16,* 47–58.

Sternberg, R. J. (1986). *Intelligence applied.* Fort Worth, TX: Harcourt Brace.

Sternberg, R. J. (1993). *Sternberg Triarchic Abilities Test (STAT).* Unpublished test, Department of Psychology, Yale University, New Haven, Ct.

Sternberg, R. J. (1997). *Thinking styles.* New York: Cambridge University Press.

Sternberg, R. J. (2002). Intelligence: The triarchic theory of intelligence. In J. W. Gutherie (Ed.), *Encyclopedia of education* (2nd ed.). New York: Macmillan.

Sternberg, R. J. (2004). Individual differences in cognitive development. In P. Smith & C. Hart (Eds.), *Blackwell handbook of cognitive development.* Malden, MA: Blackwell.

Sternberg, R. J. (2006). *Cognitive psychology* (4th ed.). Belmont, CA: Wadsworth.

Sternberg, R. J. (2007). Critical thinking in psychology: It really is critical. In R. J. Sternberg, H. Roediger, & D. Halpern (Eds.), *Critical thinking in psychology.* New York: Cambridge University Press.

Sternberg, R. J., & Ben-Zeev, T. (2001). *Complex cognitive processes.* New York: Oxford University Press.

Sternberg, R. J., Castejøn, J. L., Prieto, M. D., Hautamäki, J., & Grigorenko, E. L. (2001). Confirmatory factory analysis of the Sternberg triarchic abilities test in three international samples: An empirical test of the triarchic theory of intelligence. *European Journal of Psychological Assessment, 17*(1), 1–16.

Sternberg, R. J., & Clinkenbeard, P. R. (1995, May/June). The triarchic model applied to identifying, teaching, and assessing gifted children. *Roeper Review,* 255–260.

Sternberg, R. J., & Grigorenko, E. L. (Eds.). (2004). *Culture and competence.* Washington, DC: American Psychological Association.

Sternberg, R. J., Grigorenko, E. L., & Kidd, K. K. (2005). Intelligence, race, and genetics. *American Psychologist, 60,* 46–59.

Sternberg, R. J., & Lubart, T. I. (1995). *Defying the crowd: Cultivating creativity in a culture of conformity.* New York: Free Press.

Sternberg, R. J., Roediger, H., & Halpern, D. (Eds.) (2007). *Critical thinking in psychology.* New York: Cambridge University Press.

Sternberg, R. J., & Spear-Swerling, P. (1996). *Teaching for thinking.* Washington, DC: American Psychological Association.

Stetsenko, A., & Arievitch, I. M. (2004). The self in cultural-historical activity theory: Reclaiming the unity of social and individual dimensions of human development. *Theory and Psychology, 14,* 475–503.

Stettler, D. D., Yamahachi, H., Li, W., Denk, W., & Gilbert, C. D. (2006). Axons and synaptic buttons are highly dynamic in adult visual cortex. *Neuron, 49,* 877–887.

Stevenson, H. W. (1992, December). Learning from Asian schools. *Scientific American,* pp. 6, 70–76.

Stevenson, H. W. (1995). Mathematics achievement of American students: First in the world by 2000? In C. A. Nelson (Ed.), *Basic and applied perspectives in learning, cognition, and development.* Minneapolis: University of Minnesota Press.

Stevenson, H. W. (2000). Middle childhood: Education and schooling. In A. Kazdin (Ed.), *Encyclopedia of psychology.* Washington, DC & New York: American Psychological Association and Oxford University Press.

Stevenson, H. W. (2001). *Commentary on NCTM standards.* Department of Psychology, University of Michigan, Ann Arbor.

Stevenson, H. W., & Hofer, B. K. (1999). Education policy in the United States and abroad: What we can learn from each other. In G. J. Cizek (Ed.), *Handbook of educational policy.* San Diego: Academic Press.

Stevenson, H. W., Lee, S., Chen, C., Stigler, J. W., Hsu, C., & Kitamura, S. (1990). Contexts of achievement. *Monographs of the Society for Research in Development, 55* (Serial No. 221).

Stevenson, H. W., Lee, S., & Stigler, J. W. (1986). Mathematics achievement of Chinese, Japanese, and American children. *Science, 231,* 693–699.

Stevenson, H. W., & Zusho, A. (2002). Adolescence in China and Japan: Adapting to a changing environment. In B. B. Brown, R. W. Larson, & T. S. Saraswathi (Eds.), *The world's youth.* New York: Cambridge University Press.

Stevenson, K. R. (1998). Evaluation report: Year 2: Schoolbook laptop project. Retrieved April 8, 2005, from http://www.beaufort.k12.sc.us/district/Itopeval.html

Stewart, J. (2006). *Bridges not walls* (9th ed.). New York: McGraw-Hill.

Stiggins, R. (2006, July 9). *Understanding the basics of assessment for learning.* Pre-conference session at the Assessment Training Institute Conference, Portland, OR.

Stiggins, R. J. (2001). *Student-involved classroom assessment* (3rd ed.). Upper Saddle River, NJ: Prentice Hall.

Stiggins, R. J. (2005). *Student-involved assessment for learning* (4th ed.). Upper Saddle River, NJ: Prentice Hall.

Stiggins, R. J., & Conklin, N. F. (1992). *In teacher's hands: Investigating the practices of classroom assessment.* Albany: State University of New York Press.

Stigler, J. W., & Hiebert, J. (1997, September). Understanding and improving classroom mathematics instruction. *Phi Delta Kappan, 79,* 14–21.

Stigler, J. W., & Hiebert, J. (1999). *The teaching gap.* New York: Free Press.

Stipek, D. J. (1996). Motivation and instruction. In D. C. Berliner & R. C. Calfee (Eds.), *Handbook of educational psychology.* New York: Macmillan.

Stipek, D. J. (2002). *Motivation to learn* (4th ed.). Boston: Allyn & Bacon.

Stipek, D. J. (2005, February 16). Commentary in *USA Today,* p. ID.

Stipek, D. J., Feiler, R., Daniels, D., & Milburn, S. (1995). Effects of different instructional approaches on young children's achievement and motivation. *Child Development, 66,* 209–223.

Stobart, G. (2006). The validity of formative assessment. In J. Gardner (Ed.), *Assessment and learning.* London: Paul Chapman.

Straus, M. A. (1991). Discipline and deviance: Physical punishment of children and violence and other crimes in adulthood. *Social Problems, 38,* 133–154.

Strichart, S. S., & Mangrum, C. T. (2002). *Teaching study skills and strategies to students with learning disabilities, attention deficit disorders, or special needs* (3rd ed.). Boston: Allyn & Bacon.

Strobel, K. R. (2001, April). *Successful outcomes for at-risk youth.* Paper presented at the meeting of the American Educational Research Association, Seattle.

Struckman, A. (2005). Classwide peer tutoring. In S. W. Lee (Ed.), *Encyclopedia of school psychology.* Thousand Oaks, CA: Sage.

Suarez-Orozco, C. (2002). Afterword: Understanding and serving the children of immigrants. *Harvard Educational Review, 71,* 579–589.

Sullivan, H. S. (1953). *The interpersonal theory of psychiatry.* New York: W. W. Norton.

Sunal, C. S., & Haas, M. E. (2005). *Social studies for the elementary and middle grades* (2nd ed.). Boston: Allyn & Bacon.

Supovitz, J. A., & Brennan, R. T. (1997, Fall). Mirror, mirror on the wall, which is the fairest test of all? An examination of the equality of portfolio assessment relative to standardized tests. *Harvard Educational Review, 67*(3), 472–501.

Suthers, D., Weiner, A., Connelly, J., & Paolucci, M. (1995, August). *Engaging students in critical discussion of science and public policy issues.* Paper presented at the 7th World Conference on Artificial Intelligence, Washington, DC.

Swan, K., Cook, D., Kratcoski, A., Lin, Y., Schenker, J., & van't Hooft, M. (2006). Ubiquitous computing: Rethinking teaching, learning and technology integration. In S. Tettegah & R. Hunter (Eds.), *Educational and technology: Issues and applications, policy, and administration,* pp. 231–252. New York: Elsevier.

Swan, K., Kratcoski, A. & Miller, D. (2006). Technology support for whole group engagement. Paper presented at the annual meeting of the American Educational Research Association, San Francisco, CA.

Swan, K., van't Hooft, M., Kratcoski, A., & Unger, D. (2005). Uses and effects of mobile computing devices in K–8 classrooms: a preliminary study. *Journal of Research on Technology and Education, 38*(1), 99–112.

Swanson, H. L. (1999). What develops in working memory? A life-span perspective. *Developmental Psychology, 35,* 986–1000.

Sykes, C. J. (1995). *Dumbing down our kids: Why American children feel good about themselves but can't read, write, or add.* New York: St. Martin's Press.

T

Tager-Flusberg, H. (2005). Putting words together: morphology and syntax. In J. Berko Gleason (Ed.), *The development of language* (6th ed.). Boston: Allyn & Bacon.

Tamis-LeMonda, C. S., Bornstein, M. H., & Baumwell, L. (2001). Maternal responsiveness and children's achievement of language milestones. *Child Development, 72,* 748–767.

Tannen, D. (1990). *You just don't understand!* New York: Ballantine.

Tanner, D. E. (1997, Spring). Standards. *Educational Horizons,* pp. 115–120.

Tanner, J. M. (1978). *Fetus into man.* Cambridge, MA: Harvard University Press.

Tantillo, M., Kesick, C. M., Hynd, G. W., & Dishman, R. K. (2002). The effects of exercise on children with attention-deficit hyperactivity disorder. *Medical Science and Sports Exercise, 34,* 203–212.

Tappan, M. B. (1998). Sociocultural psychology and caring psychology: Exploring Vygotsky's "hidden curriculum." *Educational Psychologist, 33,* 23–33.

Tassell-Baska, J., & Stambaugh, T. (2006). *Comprehensive curriculum for gifted learners* (3rd ed.). Boston: Allyn & Bacon.

Taylor, C. (1994). Assessment of measurement or standards: The peril and the promise of large-scale assessment reform. *American Educational Research Journal, 32,* 231–262.

Taylor, C. S., & Nolen, S. B. (2005). *Classroom assessment.* Upper Saddle River, NJ: Prentice Hall.

Taylor, R. D. (1996). Kinship support, family management, and adolescent adjustment and competence in African American families. *Developmental Psychology, 32*, 687–695.

Taylor, R. D., & Lopez, E. I. (2005). Family management practice, school achievement, and problem behavior in African American adolescents: Mediating processes. *Applied Developmental Psychology, 26*, 39–49.

Taylor, R. L., Brady, M., & Richards, S. B. (2005). *Mental retardation.* Boston: Allyn & Bacon.

Teacher's Curriculum Institute. (2001). *Social studies alive!* Rancho Cordovo, CA: Author.

Temple, C., Nathan, R., Temple, F., & Burris, N. A. (1993). *The beginnings of writing* (3rd ed.). Boston: Allyn & Bacon.

Temple, C. A., Ogle, D., Crawford, A. N., & Freppon, P. (2005). *All children read.* Boston: Allyn & Bacon.

Tenenbaum, H. R., Callahan, M., Alba-Speyer, C., & Sandoval, L. (2002). Parent-child science conversations in Mexican descent families: Educational background, activity, and past experience as moderators. *Hispanic Journal of Behavioral Science, 24*, 225–248.

Tennyson, R., & Cocchiarella, M. (1986). An empirically based instructional design theory for teaching concepts. *Review of Educational Research, 56*, 40–71.

Terman, D. L., Larner, M. B., Stevenson, C. S., & Behrman, R. E. (1996). Special education for students with disabilities: Analysis and recommendations. *Future of Children, 6*(1), 4–24.

Terry, W. S. (2006). *Learning and memory* (3rd ed.). Boston: Allyn & Bacon.

Terwilliger, J. (1997). Semantics, psychometrics, and assessment reform: A close look at "authentic" assessments. *Educational Researcher, 26*, 24–27.

The Nation's Report Card. (2005). *National Assessment of Educational Progress: 2005.* Washington, DC: U.S. Department of Education.

The Wallace Foundation. (2004). *Out-of-School learning: All work and no play.* New York City: Wallace Foundation.

Thelen, E., & Smith, L. B. (2006). Dynamics systems theories. In W. Damon & R. Lerner (Eds.), *Handbook of child psychology* (6th ed.). New York: Wiley.

Theobold, M. A. (2005). *Increasing student motivation.* Thousand Oaks, CA: Sage.

Thomas, A., & Chess, S. (1991). Temperament in adolescence and its functional significance. In R. M. Lerner, A. C. Petersen, & J. Brooks-Gunn (Eds.), *Encyclopedia of adolescence* (Vol. 2). New York: Garland.

Thomas, C. C., Correa, V. I., & Morsink, C. V. (1995). *Interactive teaming:*

Consultation and collaboration in special programs (2nd ed.). Upper Saddle River, NJ: Merrill/Prentice Hall.

Thomas, J. R., & Thomas, K. T. (1988). Developmental gender differences in physical activity. *Quest, 40*, 219–229.

Thomas, R. M. (2005). *Teachers doing research.* Boston: Allyn & Bacon.

Thompson, P. M., Giedd, J. N., Woods, R. P., MacDonald, D., Evans, A. C., & Toga, A. W. (2000). Growth patterns in the developing brain detected by using continuum mechanical tensor maps. *Nature, 404*, 190–193.

Thompson, R. A. (2006). The development of the person. In W. Damon & R. Lerner (Eds.), *Handbook of child psychology* (6th ed.). New York: Wiley.

Thorndike, E. L. (1906). *Principles of teaching.* New York: Seiler.

Thorndike, R. M. (2005). *Measurement and evaluation in psychology and education* (7th ed.). Upper Saddle River, NJ: Prentice Hall.

Thornton, C. D., & Goldstein, L. S. (2006). Feminist issues in early childhood scholarship. In B. Spodek & O. N. Saracho (Eds.), *Handbook of research on the education of young children.* Mahwah, NJ: Erlbaum.

Thornton, S. J. (2001, April). *Caring and competence: Nel Noddings' curriculum thought.* Paper presented at the meeting of the American Educational Research Association, Seattle.

Thorsen, C. (2006). *Tech tactics* (2nd ed.). Boston: Allyn & Bacon.

Threshold/ISTE Youth Forum. (2004). Summer future chat. *Threshold, 26–30.* Retrieved December 15, 2004, from www.conline.org

Thurgood, S. (2001). Inside home visits: Response from the Early Head Start program director. *Early Childhood Research Quarterly, 16*, 73–75.

Thurstone, L. L. (1938). *Primary mental abilities.* Chicago: University of Chicago Press.

Tierney, R. J., & Readence, J. E. (2005). *Reading strategies and practice* (6th ed.). Boston: Allyn & Bacon.

Tippins, D. J., Koballa, T. R., & Payne, B. D. (2002). *Elementary science teaching.* Boston: Allyn & Bacon.

Tittle, C. (2006). Assessment of teacher learning and development. In P. A. Alexander & P. H. Winne (Eds.), *Handbook of educational psychology* (2nd ed.). Mahwah, NJ: Erlbaum.

Todd, G. S., & Gigerenzer, G. (2001). Precis of simple heuristics that make us smart. *Behavior and Brain Sciences, 23*, 727–741.

Toga, A. W., Thompson, P. M., & Sowell, E. R. (2006). Mapping brain maturation. *Trends in Neuroscience, 29*, 148–159.

Tolchinsky, L. (2002). *The child's path to writing and numbers.* Mahwah, NJ: Erlbaum.

Tollefson, N. (2005a). Percentile ranks. In S. W. Lee (Ed.), *Encyclopedia of school psychology.* Thousand Oaks, CA: Sage.

Tollefson, N. (2005b). Stanines. In S. W. Lee (Ed.), *Encyclopedia of school psychology.* Thousand Oaks, CA: Sage.

Tolman, M. N. (2002). *Discovering elementary science* (3rd ed.). Boston: Allyn & Bacon.

Tomasello, M. (2006). Acquiring linguistic constructions. In W. Damon & R. Lerner (Eds.), *Handbook of child psychology* (6th ed.). New York: Wiley.

Tomblin, B. (1996). *The big picture of SLI: Results of an epidemiological study of SLI among kindergarten children.* Paper presented at the Symposium on Research in Child Language Disorders, University of Wisconsin, Madison.

Tomlinson, C. A. (2001). *How to differentiate instruction in mixed-ability classrooms* (2nd ed.). Alexandria, VA: ASCD.

Topping, K. J., & Bryce, A. (2004). Cross-age peer tutoring of reading and thinking: Influence on thinking skills. *Educational Psychology, 24*, 595–616.

Topping, K. J., Peter, C., Stephan, P., & Whale, M. (2004). Cross-age peer tutoring of science in the primary school: Influence of scientific language and thinking. *Educational Psychology, 24*, 57–75.

Torgesen, J. D. (1995, December). *Prevention and remediation of reading disabilities.* Progress Report (NICHD Grant HD 30988). Bethesda, MD: National Institute of Child Health and Human Development.

Trask, B. S., & Hamon, R. R. (Eds.). (2007). *Cultural diversity and families.* Thousand Oaks, CA: Sage.

Trautner, H. M., Ruble, D. N., Cyphers, L. Kirsten, B., Behrendt, R., & Hartmann, P. (2005). Rigidity and flexibility of gender stereotypes in children: Developmental or differential? *Infant and Child Development, 14*, 365–381.

Triandis, H. C. (2001). Individualism and collectivism. In D. Matsumoto (Ed.), *The handbook of culture and psychology.* New York: Oxford University Press.

Triandis, H. C., Brislin, R., & Hui, C. H. (1988). Cross-cultural training across the individualism divide. *International Journal of Intercultural Relations, 12*, 269–288.

Trinidad, D. R., & Johnson, C. A. (2002). The association between emotional intelligence and early adolescent tobacco and alcohol use. *Personality and Individual Differences, 32,* 95–105.

Trowbridge, L. W., Bybee, R. W., & Powell, J. C. (2000). *Teaching secondary school science* (7th ed.). Upper Saddle River, NJ: Merrill.

Truglio, R., & Kotler, J. (2006). The role of basic and formative research in creating children's television programming. In J. A. Bryant (ed.), *The children's television community.* Mahwah, NJ: Erlbaum.

Trzesniewski, K. H., Donnellan, M. B., Moffit, T. E., Robins, R. W., Poulton, R., & Caspi, A. (2006). Low self-esteem during adolescence predicts poor health, criminal behavior, and limited income prospects during adulthood. *Developmental Psychology, 42,* 381–390.

Tsal, Y., Shalev, L., & Mevorach, C. (2005). The diversity of attention deficits in ADHD. *Journal of Learning Disabilties, 38,* 142–157.

Tsang, C. L. (1989). Bilingual minorities and language issues in writing. *Written Communication, 9*(1), 1–15.

Tubbs, S. L., & Moss, S. (2006). *Human communication* (10th ed.). New York: McGraw-Hill.

Tubman, J. G., & Windle, M. (1995). Continuity of difficult temperament in adolescence: Relations with depression, life events, family support, and substance abuse across a one-year period. *Journal of Youth and Adolescence, 24,* 133–152.

Tucha, O., Prell, S., Meclinger, L., Bormann-Kischkel, C., Kubber, S., Linder, M., Walitza, S., & Lange, K. W. (2006). Effects of methylphenidate on multiple components of attention in children with attention deficit hyperactivity disorder. *Psychopharmacology 185,* 315–326.

Tucker, M. B., Subramanian, S.K., & James, A. (2004). Diversity in African American families. In M. Coleman & L. Ganong (Eds.), *Handbook of contemporary families.* Thousand Oaks, CA: Sage.

Tulving, E. (1972). Episodic and semantic memory. In E. Tulving & W. Donaldson (Eds.), *Origins of memory.* San Diego: Academic Press.

Tulving, E. (2000). Concepts of memory. In E. Tulving & F. I. M. Craik (Eds.), *The Oxford handbook of memory.* New York: Oxford University Press.

Turiel, E. (2006). The development of morality. In W. Damon & R. Lerner (Eds.), *Handbook of child psychology* (6th ed.). New York: Wiley.

Turkanis, C. G. (2002). Creating curriculum with children. In B. Rogoff, C. G. Turkanis, &

L. Bartlett (Eds.), *Learning together.* New York: Oxford University Press.

Turnbull, A., Turnbull, H. R., & Tompkins, J. R. (2007). *Exceptional lives* (5th ed.). Upper Saddle River, NJ: Prentice-Hall.

Turner, T. N. (2004). *Essentials of elementary social studies* (3rd ed.). Boston: Allyn & Bacon.

Tversky, A., & Fox, C. R. (1995). Weighing risk and uncertainty. *Psychological Review, 102,* 269–283.

U.S. Census Bureau. (2005). *Poverty: 2004 highlights.* Washington, DC: U.S. Census Bureau, Housing and Household Economics Statistics Division.

U.S. Department of Education. (1996). *Number and disabilities of children and youth served under IDEA.* Washington, DC: Office of Special Education Programs, Data Analysis System.

U.S. Department of Education. (2000). *To assure a free and appropriate public education of all children with disabilities.* Washington, DC: U.S. Office of Education.

U.S. Department of Education. (2004). *Golden age in American education: How the Internet, the law and today's students are revolutionizing expectations.* Retrieved January 30, 2006, from http://www. nationaledtechplan.org/docs_and_pdf/ National_Education_Technology_Plan_ 2004.pdf

U.S. Department of Education. (2006). *Teaching our youngest.* Washington, DC: U.S. Department of Education.

U.S. Department of Health and Human Services. (1999). *Trends in the well being of America's children and youth 1999.* Washington, DC: U.S. Government Printing Office.

U.S. Office of Education. (1998). *The Benchmark Study.* Washington, DC: Office of Education & Minority Affairs.

U.S. Office of Education. (1999). *Elementary and secondary school compliance reports.* Washington, DC: U.S. Government Printing Office.

Ullman, J. G. (2005). *Making technology work for learners with special needs.* Boston: Allyn & Bacon.

Umana-Taylor, A. J. (2004). Ethnic identity and self-esteem: Examining the role of social contexts. *Journal of Adolescence, 27,* 139–146.

Umana-Taylor, A. J. (2006, March). *Ethnic identity.* Paper presented at the meeting of the Society for Research on Adolescence, San Francisco.

Umbreit, J., Ferro, J., Liaupsin, C. J., & Lane, K. L. (2007). *Functional behavioral assessment and function-based intervention.* Upper Saddle River, NJ: Prentice Hall.

University of Buffalo Counseling Services. (2005). *Procrastination.* Buffalo, NY: Author.

University of Illinois Counseling Center. (1996). *Overcoming procrastination.* Urbana-Champaign, IL: Department of Student Affairs.

University of Texas at Austin Counseling and Mental Health Center. (1999). *Coping with perfectionism.* Austin, TX: Author.

Upfront. (2001, January 1). Cheating hall of shame (Vol. 133, No. 9), 12–14.

Urdan, T. (2004). Predictors of academic self-handicapping and achievement: Examining achievement goals, classroom goal structures, and culture. *Journal of Educational Psychology, 96,* 251–264.

Urdan, T., & Midgley, C. (2001). Academic self-handicapping: What we know, what more there is to learn. *Educational Psychology Review, 13,* 115–138.

USA Today. (1999). All-USA TODAY Teacher Team. Retrieved January 15, 2004, from www.usatoday.com/news/ education/1999

USA Today. (2000, October 10). All-USA first teacher team. Retrieved November 15, 2004, from http://www.usatoday.com/ life/teacher/teach/htm.

USA Today. (2001, October 10). All-USA first teacher team. Retrieved November 20, 2004, from http://www.usatoday.com/ news/education2001

Vacca, J. A. L., Vacca, R. T., Gove, M. K., Burkey, L. C., Lenhart, L. A., & McKeon, C. A. (2006). *Reading and learning to read* (6th ed.). Boston: Allyn & Bacon.

Vahey, P., & Crawford, V. (2002). Palm education pioneers program: Final evaluation report. Menlo Park, CA: SRI International. Retrieved April 8, 2005, from http://www.palmgrants.sri.com/ PEP_Final_Report.pdf

Vahey, P., Roschelle, J., & Tatar, D. (2006, in press). Moving between the private and the public in the mathematics classroom with handheld technology. In M. van't Hooft & K. Swan (Eds.), *Ubiquitous computing: Invisible technology, visible impact.* Mahwah, NJ: Erlbaum.

Vallone, R. P., Griffin, D. W., Lin, S., & Ross, L. (1990). Overconfident prediction of future actions and outcomes by self and others. *Journal of Personality and Social Psychology, 58,* 582–592.

van't Hooft, M., Diaz, S. & Swan, K. (2004). Examining the potential of the handheld computers: Findings from the Ohio PEP project. *Journal of Educational Computing Research, 30* (4).

Van Buren, E., & Graham, S. (2003). *Redefining ethnic identity: Its relationship to positive and negative school adjustment outcomes for minority youth.* Paper presented at the meeting of the Society for Research in Child Development, Tampa.

Van de Walle, J. A. (2004). *Elementary and middle school mathematics* (5th ed.). Boston: Allyn & Bacon.

Van de Walle, J. A. (2007). *Elementary and middle school mathematics* (6th ed.). Boston: Allyn & Bacon.

Van de Walle, J. A., & Lovin, L. A. H. (2006). *Teaching student-centered mathematics: Grades 3–5.* Boston: Allyn & Bacon.

van der Linden, W. J. (1995). Advances in computer applications. In T. Oakland & R. K. Hambleton (Eds.), *International perspectives on academic assessment.* Boston: Kluwer Academic.

van Drie, J., van Boxtel, C., Jasper, J., & Kanselar, G. (2005). Effects of representational guidance on domain specific reasoning in CSCL. *Computers in Human Behavior, 21,* 575–602.

Van Gelder, T. (2005). Teaching critical thinking. *College Teaching, 53,* 41–46.

Van Houten, R., Nau, P., Mackenzie-Keating, S., Sameoto, D., & Colavecchia, B. (1982). An analysis of some variables influencing the effectiveness of reprimands. *Journal of Applied Behavior Analysis, 15,* 65–83.

van Lehn, K. (1990). *Mind bugs.* Cambridge, MA: MIT Press.

Van Lier, P. A. C., Muthen, B. O., van der Sar, R. M., & Crijen, A. A. M. (2004). Preventing disruptive behavior in elementary school-children: Impact of a universal classroom-based intervention. *Journal of Consulting and Clinical Psychology, 72,* 467–478.

Vandell, D. L., & Pierce, K. M. (2002). After-school programs and structured activities that support children's development. In R. Garner (Ed.), *Hanging out: Community-based after-school programs for children.* Westport CT: Greenwood.

VanSledright, B., & Limón, M. (2006). Learning and teaching social studies: A review of cognitive research in history and geography. In P. A. Alexander & P. H. Winne (Eds.), *Handbook of educational psychology* (2nd ed.). Mahwah, NJ: Erlbaum.

Vaughn, S. S., Bos, C. S., & Schumm, J. S. (2007). *Teaching students who are exceptional, diverse, and at risk in the general education classroom* (4th ed.). Boston: Allyn & Bacon.

Veenman, S., Denessen, E., & van den Akker, A. (2005). Effects of cooperative learning program on the elaborations of students during help seeking and help giving. *American Educational Research Journal, 42,* 115–151.

Vellutino, F., Fletcher, J. M., Snowling, M. J., & Scanlon, D. M. (2004). Specific reading disability (dyslexia): What have we learned in the past four decades? *Journal of Child Psychology and Psychiatry and Allied Disciplines, 45,* 2–40.

Verderber, R. F., & Verderber, K. S. (2006). *The challenge of effective speaking* (13th ed.). Belmont, CA: Wadsworth.

Vidal, F. (2000). Piaget, Jean. In A. Kazdin (Ed.), *Encyclopedia of psychology.* Washington, DC, & New York: American Psychological Association and Oxford University Press.

Villejoubert, G. (2005). Could they have known better? *Applied Cognitive Psychology, 19,* 140–143.

Vinckenbosch, E., Robichon, F., & Eliez, S. (2005). Gray matter alteration in dyslexia: Converging evidence from volumetric and voxel-by-voxel MRI analyses. *Neuropsychologia, 43,* 324–331.

Vogt, W. P. (2007). *Quantitative research methods for professionals in education and other fields.* Boston: Allyn & Bacon.

Volkmar, F. R., Lord, C., Bailey, A., Schultz, R. T., & Klin, A. (2004). Autism and pervasive developmental disorders. *Journal of Child Psychology and Psychiatry, 45,* 135–170.

Voss, J. F., Greene, T. A., Post, B. C., & Penner, J. (1984). Problem solving skills in the social sciences. In G. H. Bower (Ed.), *The psychology of learning and motivation.* San Diego: Academic Press.

Vukovic, R. K., & Siegel, L. S. (2006). The double-deficit hypothesis: A comprehensive analysis of the evidence. *Journal of Learning Disabilities, 39,* 25–47.

Vygotsky, L. S. (1962). *Thought and language.* Cambridge, MA: MIT Press.

Wagner, M. (1995). Outcomes for youths with serious emotional disturbance in secondary school and early adulthood. *Future of Children 5*(2), 90–112.

Wagner, M. W., & Blackorby, J. (1996). Transition from high school to work or college: How special education students fare. *Future of Children, 6*(1), 103–120.

Wagner, R. (1993). *HyperStudio.* El Cajon, CA: Roger Wagner.

Wagner, R. K. (1997). Intelligence, training, and employment. *American Psychologist, 52,* 1059–1069.

Wagner, R. K., & Sternberg, R. J. (1986). Tacit knowledge and intelligence in the everyday world. In R. J. Sternberg & R. K. Wagner (Eds.), *Practical intelligence.* Cambridge, UK: Cambridge University Press.

Wake, M., & Poulakis, Z. (2004). Slight and mild hearing loss in primary school children. *Journal of Pediatrics and Child Health, 40,* 11–13.

Waldman, I. D., & Gizer, I. R. (2006, in press). The genetics of attention deficit hyperactivity disorder. *Clinical Psychology Review.*

Walker, L. (2006). Gender and morality. In M. Killien & J. G. Smetana (Eds.), *Handbook of moral development.* Mahwah, NJ: Erlbaum.

Walker, L. J. (2002). Moral Exemplarity. In W. Damon (Ed.), *Bringing in a new era of character.* Stanford, CA: Hoover Press.

Wallis, P. (2004). Intention without representation. *Philosophical Psychology, 17,* 209–224.

Wang, H., & Gearhart, D. L. (2006). *Designing and developing web-based instruction.* Upper Saddle River, NJ: Prentice Hall.

Ward, L. M. (2003). Understanding the role of entertainment media in the sexual socialization of American youth: A review of empirical research. *Developmental Review, 23,* 347–388.

Warrington, M., & Younger, M. (2003). "We decided to give it a twirl": Single-sex teaching in English comprehensive schools. *Gender and Education, 15,* 339–350.

Watson, D. L., & Tharp, R. G. (2007). *Self-directed behavior* (9th ed.). Belmont, CA: Wadsworth.

Watson, M., & Battistich, V. (2006). Building and sustaining caring communities. In C. M. Evertson & C. S. Weinstein (Eds.), *Handbook of classroom management.* Mahwah, NJ: Erlbaum.

Waxman, S. R., & Lidz, J. L. (2006). Early word learning. In W. Damon & R. Lerner (Eds.), *Handbook of child psychology* (6th ed.). New York: Wiley.

Weary, G. (2000). Attribution theories. In A. Kazdin (Ed.), *Encyclopedia of psychology.* Washington, DC, & New York: American Psychological Association and Oxford University Press.

Weasmer, J., & Woods, A. (2001). Encouraging student decision making. *Kappa Delta Pi Record, 38,* 40–42.

Webb, N. M. (1984). Sex differences in interaction and achievement in cooperative small groups. *Journal of Educational Psychology, 76,* 33–34.

Webb, N. M., & Palincsar, A. S. (1996). Group processes in the classroom. In D. C. Berliner & R. C. Calfee (Eds.), *Handbook of educational psychology.* New York: Macmillan.

Weber, E. (2005). *MI strategies in the classroom and beyond.* Boston: Allyn & Bacon.

Wehlage, G. (1989). Dropping out: Can schools be expected to prevent it? In L. Weis, E. Farrar, & H. Petrie (Eds.), *Dropouts from school.* Albany: State University of New York Press.

Weiler, J. (1998). Success for All. *ERIC/CUE Digest, No. 139.*

Weiner, B. (1986). *An attributional theory of motivation and emotion.* New York: Springer.

Weiner, B. (1992). *Human motivation: Metaphors, theories, and research.* Newbury Park, CA: Sage.

Weiner, B. (2000). Motivation: An overview. In A. Kazdin (Ed.), *Encyclopedia of psychology.* Washington, DC, & New York: American Psychological Association and Oxford University Press.

Weiner, B. (2005). *Social motivation, justice, and the moral emotions.* Mahwah, NJ: Erlbaum.

Weinstein, C. S. (2003). *Secondary classroom management.* (2nd ed). New York: McGraw-Hill.

Weinstein, C. S. (2007). *Middle and secondary management: Lessons from research and practice* (3rd ed.). New York: McGraw-Hill.

Weinstein, R. S., Madison, S. M., & Kuklinski, M. R. (1995). Raising expectations in schooling: Obstacles and opportunities for change. *American Educational Research Journal, 32*(1), 121–159.

Weinstein, C. S., & Mignano, A. J., Jr. (1997). *Elementary classroom management.* New York: McGraw-Hill.

Weinstein, C. S., & Mignano, A. J., Jr. (2003). *Elementary classroom management* (2nd ed.). New York: McGraw-Hill.

Weinstein, C. S., & Mignano, A. J., Jr. (2007). *Elementary classroom management* (4th ed.). New York: McGraw-Hill.

Weiser, M. (2001, September). *Ubiquitous computing and communications.* Paper presented at the PACT international conference, Barcelona, Spain.

Weissberg, R. P., Barton, H. A., & Shriver, T. P. (1997). The Social-Competence Promotion Program for young adolescents. In G. W. Albee & T. P. Gullotta (Eds.), *Primary prevention exemplars: The Lela Rowland Awards.* Thousand Oaks, CA: Sage.

Weissberg, R. P., & Caplan, M. (1994). *Promoting social competence and preventing antisocial behavior in young urban adolescents.* Unpublished manuscript, University of Illinois, Chicago.

Weissberg, R. P., Gesten, E. L., Rapkin, B. D., Cowen, E. L., Davidson, E., Flores de Apodaca, R., & McKim, B. J. (1981). The evaluation of a social problem-solving training program for suburban and inner-city third grade children. *Journal of Consulting and Clinical Psychology, 49,* 251–261.

Weissberg, R. P., & Greenberg, M. T. (1998). School and community competence-enhancement prevention programs. In W. Damon (Ed.), *Handbook of child psychology* (Vol. 4). New York: Wiley.

Weldin, D. J., & Tumarkin, S. R. (1999). Parent involvement: More power in the portfolio process. *Childhood Education, 75,* 90–96.

Weller, L. D. (2001). Building validity and reliability into classroom tests. *NASSP Bulletin, 85,* 32–37.

Wellhousen, K. (1996, Fall). Do's and dont's for eliminating hidden bias. *Childhood Education,* pp. 36–39.

Wellman, H. M. (1997, April). *Ten years of theory of mind: Telling the story backwards.* Paper presented at the meeting of the Society for Research in Child Development, Washington, DC.

Wellman, H. M. (2000). Early childhood. In A. Kazdin (Ed.), *Encyclopedia of psychology.* Washington, DC, & New York: American Psychological Association and Oxford University Press.

Wellman, H. M. (2004). Understanding the psychological world: Developing a theory of mind. In U. Goswami (Ed.), *Blackwell handbook of childhood cognitive development.* Maiden, MA: Blackwell.

Wellman, H. M., Cross, D., & Watson, J. (2001). Meta-analysis of theory-of-mind development: The truth about false belief. *Child Development, 72,* 655–684.

Welshman, D. (2000). *Social studies resources.* St. Johns, Newfoundland: Leary Brooks Jr. High School.

Wenglinsky, H. (2002). The link between teacher classroom practices and student academic performance. *Education Policy Analysis Archives, 10,* 12.

Wentzel, K. R. (1996). Social goals and social relationships as motivators of school

adjustment. In J. Juvonen & R. Wentzel (Eds.), *Social motivation.* New York: Cambridge University Press.

Wentzel, K. R. (1997). Student motivation in middle school: The role of perceived pedagogical caring. *Journal of Educational Psychology, 89,* 411–419.

Wentzel, K. R. (2006). A social motivation perspective for classroom management. In C. M. Evertson & C. S. Weinstein (Eds.), *Handbook of classroom management.* Mahwah, NJ: Erlbaum.

Wentzel, K. R., & Battle, A. (2001). Social relationships and school adjustment. In T. Urdan & F. Pajares (Eds.), *Adolescence and education.* Greenwich, CT: IAP.

Wentzel, K. R., Barry, C. M., & Caldwell, K. A. (2004). Friendships in middle school: Influences on motivation and school adjustment. *Journal of Educational Psychology, 96,* 195–203.

Wentzel, K. R., & Erdley, C. A. (1993). Strategies for making friends: Relations to social behavior and peer acceptance in early adolescence. *Developmental Psychology, 29,* 819–826.

Wertheimer, M. (1945). *Productive thinking.* New York: Harper.

Werts, M. G., Culatta, R. A., & Tompkins, J. R. (2007). *Fundamentals of special education* (3rd ed.). Upper Saddle River, NJ: Prentice Hall.

Westling, D. L., & Fox, L. (2000). *Teaching students with severe disabilities* (2nd ed.). Upper Saddle River, NJ: Prentice Hall.

Wheeler, J. J., & Richey, D. (2005). *Behavior management: Principles and practices of positive behavior supports.* Upper Saddle River, NJ: Prentice Hall.

Wheelock, A. (1992). *Crossing the tracks: How "untracking" can save America's schools.* New York: New Press.

Whitcomb, J. A. (2004). Dilemmas of design and predicaments of practice: Adapting the 'Fostering a Community of Learners' model in secondary school English language arts. *Journal of Curriculum Studies, 36,* 183–206.

White, J. W., & Frabutt, J. M. (2006). Violence against girls and women. In J. Worell & C. D. Goodheart (Eds.), *Handbook of girls' and women's psychological health.* New York: Oxford University Press.

White, R. W. (1959). Motivation reconsidered: The concept of confidence. *Psychological Review, 66,* 297–333.

Whitford, B. L., & Jones, K. (Eds.). (2000). *Accountability, assessment, and teacher commitment.* Albany: State University of New York Press.

Whitford, T. J., Rennie, C. J., Grieve, S. M., Clark, C. R., Gordon, E., & Williams, L. M. (2006, in press). Brain maturation in adolescence. *Human Brain Mapping.*

Wiese, A-M., & Garcia, E. E. (2006). Educational policy in the United States regarding bilinguals in early childhood education. In B. Spodek & O. N. Saracho (Eds.), *Handbook of research on the education of young children.* Mahwah, NJ: Erlbaum.

Wigfield, A., & Asher, S. R. (1984). Social and motivational influences on reading. In P. D. Pearson, R. Barr, M. L. Kamil, & P. Mosenthal (Eds.), *Handbook of reading research.* New York: Longman.

Wigfield, A., & Eccles, J. S. (Eds.). (2002). *Development of achievement motivation.* San Diego: Academic Press.

Wigfield, A., Byrnes, J. P., & Eccles, J. S. (2006). Developing during early adolescence. In P. A. Alexander & P. H. Winne (Eds.), *Handbook of educational psychology* (2nd ed.). Mahwah, NJ: Erlbaum.

Wigfield, A., Eccles, J. S., & Pintrich, P. R. (1996). Development between the ages of 11 and 25. In D. C. Berliner & R. C. Calfee (Eds.), *Handbook of educational psychology.* New York: Macmillan.

Wigfield, A., Eccles, J. S., Schiefele, U., Roeser, R., & Davis-Kean, P. (2006). Development of achievement motivation. In W. Damon & R. Lerner (Eds.), *Handbook of child psychology* (6th ed.). New York: Wiley.

Wiggins, G. (1992, May). Creating tests worth taking. *Educational Leadership,* pp. 26–33.

Wiggins, G. (1993, November). Assessment: Authenticity, context, and validity. *Phi Delta Kappan,* pp. 200–214.

Wilke, M., Lidzba, K., Staudt, M., Buchenau, K., Grodd, W., & Krageloh-Mann, I. (2005). Comprehensive language mapping in children, using functional magnetic resonance imaging: Whats missing counts. *Neuroreport, 16,* 915–919.

Wineburg, M. S. (2006). Evidence in teacher preparation. *Journal of Teacher Education, 57,* 51–64.

Winne, P. H. (1995). Inherent details in self-regulated learning. *Educational Psychologist, 30,* 173–187.

Winne, P. H. (1997). Experimenting to bootstrap self-regulated learning. *Journal of Educational Psychology, 89,* 397–410.

Winne, P. H. (2001). Self-regulated learning viewed from models of information processing. In B. J. Zimmerman & D. H. Schunk (Eds.), *Self-regulated learning and academic achievement.* Mahwah, NJ: Erlbaum.

Winne, P. H. (2005). Key issues in modeling and applying research on self-regulated learning. *Applied Psychology: An International Review, 54,* 232–238.

Winner, E. (1986, August). Where pelicans kiss seals. *Psychology Today,* pp. 24–35.

Winner, E. (1996). *Gifted children: Myths and realities.* New York: Basic Books.

Winner, E. (1997). Exceptionally high intelligence and schooling. *American Psychologist, 52,* 1070–1081.

Winner, E. (2000). The origins and ends of giftedness. *American Psychologist, 55,* 159–169.

Winner, E. (2006). Development in the arts. In W. Damon & R. Lerner (Eds.), *Handbook of child psychology* (6th ed.). New York: Wiley.

Winsler, A., Carlton, M. P., & Barry, M. J. (2000). Age-related changes in preschool children's systematic use of private speech in a natural setting. *Journal of Child Language, 27,* 665–687.

Winsler, A., Caverly, S. L, Willson-Quayle, A., Carlton, M. P., & Howell, C. (2002). The social and behavioral ecology of mixed-age and same-age preschool classrooms: A natural experiment. *Journal of Applied Developmental Psychology, 23,* 305–330.

Winsler, A., Diaz, R. M., & Montero, I. (1997). The role of private speech in the transition from collaborative to independent task performance in young children. *Early Childhood Research Quarterly, 12,* 59–79.

Wiske, S., Franz, K. R., & Breit, L. (2005). *Teaching for understanding with technology.* New York: Wiley.

Wittmer, D. S., & Honig, A. S. (1994). Encouraging positive social development in young children. *Young Children, 49,* 4–12.

Wittrock, M. C., & Lumsdaine, A. A. (1977). Instructional psychology. *Annual Review of Psychology, 28,* 417–459.

Wolters, C. A. (2004). Advancing achievement goal theory: Using goal structures and goal orientations to predict students' motivation, cognition, and achievement. *Journal of Educational Psychology, 96,* 236–250.

Wong, T. B. (2004, October 14). *USA Today's* 2004 all-USA team. *USA Today,* p. 6D.

Wood, J. (2001). Can software support children's vocabulary development? *Language Learning & Technology, 5,* 166–201.

Wood, J., & Duke, N. K. (1997). Inside "Reading Rainbow": A spectrum of strategies for promoting literacy. *Language Arts, 74,* 95–106.

Wood, J. T. (2006). *Introduction to human communication* (4th ed.). Belmont, CA: Wadsworth.

Wood, J. W. (2006). *Teaching students in inclusive settings* (5th ed.). Upper Saddle River, NJ: Prentice Hall.

Woodhill, B. M., & Samuels, C. A. (2004). Desirable and undesirable androgyny: A prescription for the twenty-first century. *Journal of Gender Studies, 13,* 15–28.

Woolger, C. (2001). Wechsler Intelligence Scale for Children–Third Edition (WISC-III). In W. Dorfman & M. Hersen (Eds.), *Understanding psychological assessment.* New York: Plenum.

Work Group of the American Psychological Association Board of Educational Affairs. (1995). *Learner-centered psychological principles: A framework for school redesign and reform* (Draft). Washington, DC: American Psychological Association.

Work Group of the American Psychological Association Board of Educational Affairs. (1997). *Learner-centered psychological principles: A framework for school reform and redesign.* Washington, DC: American Psychological Association.

Workman, S. H., & Gage, J. A. (1997). Family-school partnerships: A family strengths approach. *Young Children, 52,* 10–14.

Worthen, B. R., & Spandel, V. (1991, February). Putting the standardized test debate in perspective. *Educational Leadership,* pp. 65–69.

Y

Yang, S. C., & Liu, S. F. (2005). The study of interactions and attitudes of third-grade students' learning information technology via a cooperative approach. *Computers in Human Behavior, 21,* 45–72.

Yarrow, F., & Topping, K. J. (2001). Collaborative writing. *British Journal of Educational Psychology, 7,* 261–282.

Yates, M. (1995, March). *Community service and political-moral discussions among Black urban adolescents.* Paper presented at the meeting of the Society for Research in Child Development, Indianapolis.

Yeakey, C. C., & Henderson, R. D. (Eds.). (2002). *Surmounting the odds: Equalizing educational opportunity in the new millennium.* Greenwich, CT: IAP.

Yinger, R. J. (1980). Study of teacher planning. *Elementary School Journal, 80,* 107–127.

Young, E. L., Boye, A. E., & Nelson, D. A. (2006). Relational aggression: Understanding, identifying, and responding in schools. *Psychology in the Schools, 43,* 297–312.

Youniss, J. (2006). Forming a political-moral identity through service. In A. Sliwka, M. Diedrich, & M. Hofer (Eds.), *Citizenship education.* Munster, GER: Waxmann.

Yung, B. H. W. (2001). Three views of fairness in a school-based assessment scheme of practical work in biology. *International Journal of Science Education, 23,* 985–1005.

Z

Zelazo, P. D., & Müller, U. (2004). Executive function in typical and atypical development. In U. Goswami (Ed.), *Blackwell handbook of cognitive development.* Malden, MA: Blackwell.

Zelazo, P. D., Müller, U., Frye, D., & Marcovitch, S. (2003). The development of executive function in early childhood. *Monographs of the Society for Research in Child Development, 68* (3, Serial No. 274).

Zentall, S. S. (2006). *ADHD and education.* Upper Saddle River, NJ: Prentice Hall.

Zigler, E. F. (2002). Looking back 40 years and seeing the person with mental retardation as a whole person. In H. N. Switzky (Ed.), *Personality and motivational differences in persons with mental retardation.* Mahwah, NJ: Erlbaum.

Zigler, E. F., & Finn-Stevenson, M. (1999). Applied developmental psychology. In M. H. Bornstein & M. E. Lamb (Eds.), *Developmental psychology* (4th ed.). Mahwah, NJ: Erlbaum.

Zigler, E. F., & Styco, S. (2004). Moving Head Start to the states: One experiment too many. *Journal of Applied Developmental Science, 8,* 51–55.

Zimmerman, B. J., Bonner, S., & Kovach, R. (1996). *Developing self-regulated learners.* Washington, DC: American Psychological Association.

Zimmerman, B. J., & Schunk, D. H. (Eds.). (2001). *Self-regulated learning and academic achievement.* Mahwah, NJ: Erlbaum.

Zimmerman, B. J., & Schunk, D. H. (2004). Self-regulating intellectual processes and outcomes: A social cognitive perspective. In D. Y. Dai & R. J. Sternberg (Eds.), *Motivation, emotion, and cognition.* Mahwah, NJ: Erlbaum.

Zirpoli, T. J. (2005). *Behavior management: Applications for teachers* (4th ed.). Upper Saddle River, NJ: Prentice Hall.

Zucker, A. A., & McGhee, R. (2005). A study of one-to-one computer use in mathematics and science instruction at the secondary level in Henrico County Public Schools. Washington, DC: SRI International.

Credits

of Supports. Copyright 1992 by American Association on Mental Retardation (AAMR). Reproduced with permission of American Association on Mental Retardation (AAMR) via Copyright Clearance Center.

Chapter 7

p. 226 From Ruth Sidney Charney, "Using Language to Encourage and Empower Children, Part 2: Exploring the First 'R': To Reinforce," *Education World* (2005), http://www.educationworld.com/ a_curr/columnists/charney/charney 004b.shtml. Reprinted with permission of Ruth S. Charney and EducationWorld.com. **Figure 7.5:** From John W. Santrock, *Psychology,* 7th ed., Figure 7.9. Copyright © 2003 by The McGraw-Hill Companies, Inc. Reprinted with permission from The McGraw-Hill Companies. **Figure 7.6:** After Irwin Hyman, *Statistical Analysis of the Cross-Cultural Data: The Third Year.* Paper presented at the meeting of the American Psychological Association, San Francisco, 2001. Reprinted by permission of Irwin Hyman. **Figure 7.7:** From John W. Santrock, *Psychology,* 7th ed., Figure 12.6, p. 487. Copyright © 2003 by The McGraw-Hill Companies, Inc. Reprinted with permission. **p. 252,** S-A 7.2: From Zimmerman, B. J., Bonner, S., & Kovach, R. (1996). *Developing self-regulated learners: Beyond achievement to self-efficacy.* Washington, DC: American Psychological Association (Exhibit 1, p. 28). Copyright © 1996 by the American Psychological Association. Reprinted with permission. **Figure 7.11:** From Zimmerman, B. J., Bonner, S., & Kovach, R. (1996). *Developing self-regulated learners: Beyond achievement to self-efficacy.* Washington, DC: American Psychological Association (Figure 1, p. 11). Copyright © 1996 by the American Psychological Association. Adapted with permission.

Chapter 8

Figure 8.1: From John W. Santrock, *Psychology,* 7th ed. Copyright © 2003 by The McGraw-Hill Companies, Inc. Reprinted with permission from The McGraw-Hill Companies. **Figure 8.2:** Reprinted from *Contemporary Educational Psychology,* vol. 5 (1980), M. Pressley, J. R. Levin, and C. B. McCormick, "Young Children's

Learning of a Foreign Language Vocabulary: A Sentence Variation of the Keyword Method," pp. 22–29, Copyright 1980, with permission from Elsevier. **Figure 8.3:** Reprinted from *Journal of Experimental Child Psychology,* vol. 43 (1987), M. Pressley, T. Cariligia-Bull, S. Deane, and W. Schneider, "Short-Term Memory, Verbal Competence, and Age as Predictors of Imagery Instructional Effectiveness," pp. 194–211, Copyright 1987, with permission from Elsevier. **Figure 8.5:** From John W. Santrock, *Psychology,* 7th ed., Figure 8.8, p. 314. Copyright © 2003 by The McGraw-Hill Companies, Inc. Reprinted with permission from The McGraw-Hill Companies. **Figure 8.6:** From Swanson, H. L. (1999). What develops in working memory? A life span perspective. *Developmental Psychology,* 35, 986–1000 (Table 1, p. 990). Copyright © 1999 by the American Psychological Association. Adapted with permission. **Figure 8.7:** From John W. Santrock, *Psychology,* 7th ed., Figure 8.5, p. 312. Copyright © 2003 by The McGraw-Hill Companies, Inc. Reprinted with permission from The McGraw-Hill Companies. **Figure 8.8:** From John W. Santrock, *Psychology,* 7th ed., Figure 8.9, p. 316. Copyright © 2003 by The McGraw-Hill Companies, Inc. Reprinted with permission from The McGraw-Hill Companies. **Figure 8.9:** Adapted from Bennet B. Murdock, Jr., *Human Memory: Theory and Data.* Potomac, MD: Lawrence Erlbaum Associates, 1974. **Figure 8.10:** From John W. Santrock, *Life-Span Development,* 6th ed. Copyright © 1997 by The McGraw-Hill Companies, Inc. Reprinted with permission from The McGraw-Hill Companies. **Figure 8.11** After Chi, M. T. H. (1978). Knowledge structures and memory development. In R. S. Siegler (Ed.), *Children's Thinking.* Hillsdale, NJ: Lawrence Erlbaum. Reprinted by permission of Lawrence Erlbaum Associates, Publishers, and the author. **Figure 8.12:** From Frederick Reif, "Cognitive Mechanisms Facilitating Human Problem Solving in a Realistic Domain: The Example of Physics," printed at the University of California at Berkeley, October 19, 1979. Reprinted by permission of the author. **Figure 8.13:** From John W. Santrock, *Life-Span Development,* 10th ed., Figure 8.15, p. 244.

Copyright © 2006 by The McGraw-Hill Companies, Inc. Reprinted with permission from The McGraw-Hill Companies.

Chapter 9

p. 302 Council of Chief State School Officers. (2000). Description of 2000 National Teacher of the Year Marilyn Jachetti Whirry. Washington, DC: Author. http:// www.ccsso.org/Projects/national_ teacher_of_the_year/national_ teachers/156.cfm. Used by permission of the Council of Chief State School Officers. **Figure 9.2:** From John W. Santrock, *Psychology,* 5th ed. Copyright © 1997 by The McGraw-Hill Companies, Inc. Reprinted with permission from The McGraw-Hill Companies.

Chapter 11

Figure 11.3: After Palincsar, A. S. and Brown, A. L. (1984). Reciprocal teaching of comprehension-fostering and comprehension-monitoring activities. *Cognition and Instruction,* 1, 117–175. Reprinted by permission of Lawrence Erlbaum Associates, Publishers, and Annemarie S. Palincsar. **Figure 11.4:** Data from Ronald T. Kellogg, "Observations on the Psychology of Thinking and Writing," *Composition Studies,* vol. 21 (1993), pp. 3–41. **pp. 394–395** From National Council for the Social Sciences, *National Standards for Social Studies Teachers* (2000). © National Council for the Social Studies. Reprinted by permission.

Chapter 12

Figure 12.3: From Kathryn W. Linden, *Cooperative Learning and Problem-Solving,* 2nd ed. Waveland Press, 1996, pp. 143–144 (This figure was originally adapted from Norman E. Gronlund, *Assessment of Student Achievement,* 6th ed., 1988). Reprinted by permission of Kathryn W. Linden. **Figure 12.5:** From Carol Simon Weinstein and Andrew J. Mignano, Jr., *Elementary Classroom Management,* 2nd ed. Copyright © 1997 by The McGraw-Hill Companies, Inc. Reprinted with permission. **Figure 12.6:** From Carol Simon Weinstein and Andrew J. Mignano, Jr., *Elementary Classroom Management,* 2nd ed. Copyright © 1997 by The McGraw-Hill Companies, Inc. Reprinted with permission. **pp. 424–427** Adapted

from Work Group of The American Psychological Association Board of Educational Affairs, *Learner-Centered Psychology Principles: A Framework for School Redesign and Reform,* November 1997, pp. 2–4. www.apa.org/ed/lcp.html. Used by permission from Barbara L. McCombs, Ph.D. **pp. 428–429** From National Research Council, *How People Learn: Brain, Mind, Experience, and School,* ed. John D. Bransford, Ann L. Brown, and Rodney R. Cocking. Washington, DC: National Academy Press, 1999, pp. 144–145. Used by permission of the publisher. **pp. 434–436** Reprinted with permission from *National Educational Technology Standards for Students: Connecting Curriculum and Technology,* © 2000, ISTE ® (International Society for Technology in Education), iste@iste.org, www.iste.org. All rights reserved. Permission does not constitute an endorsement by ISTE. **pp. 437–438** From Martha Stone Wiske, with Kristi Rennebohm Franz and Lisa Breit, *Teaching for Understanding with Technology.* Copyright © 2005 by John Wiley & Sons, Inc. Reprinted with permission of John Wiley & Sons, Inc. **p. 442** Excerpts from "Future Chat," *Threshold,* Summer 2004, pp. 26–30. Reprinted by permission of CCI Crosby Publishing, Allston, MA.

Chapter 13

Figure 13.2: From J. Brophy, *Motivating Students to Learn.* Copyright © 1998 by The McGraw-Hill Companies, Inc. Reprinted with permission. **Figure 13.3:** From Bernard Weiner, *Human Motivation: Metaphors, Theories, and Research,* Table 6.4, p. 253. Copyright 1992 by Sage Publications, Inc. Reprinted by permission of Sage Publications, Inc. **p. 460** From S. Graham and B. Weiner, "Theories and Principles of Motivation," in *Handbook of Educational Psychology,* ed. David Berliner and R. C. Calfee. New York: Macmillan Library Reference, 1996, p. 72. **Figure 13.6:** From Jere Brophy, *Motivating Students to Learn.* Copyright © 1998 by The McGraw-Hill Companies, Inc. Reprinted with permission. **Figure 13.7:** Based on "Perfectionism: A Double-Edged Sword" by the University of Texas at Austin, Counseling and Mental Health Center, 1999.

Chapter 14

Figure 14.4: From Carol Simon Weinstein, *Secondary Classroom Management.* Copyright © 1996 by The McGraw-Hill Companies, Inc. Reprinted with permission. **Figure 14.5:** From Tonja R. Nansel et al., "Bullying Behaviors among U.S. Youths: Prevalence and Association with Psychosocial Adjustment," *Journal of the American Medical Association,* Vol. 285 (2001), pp. 2094–2100.

Chapter 15

Figure 15.3: From John W. Santrock, *Psychology,* 5th ed., p. 624. Copyright © 1997 by The McGraw-Hill Companies, Inc. Reprinted with permission from The McGraw-Hill Companies.

Chapter 16

Figure 16.1: From James H. McMillan, *Essential Assessment Concepts for Teachers and Administrators,* Figure 1.1, p. 3, copyright 2001 by Corwin Press, Inc. Reprinted by permission of Corwin Press, Inc. **Figure 16.7:** From Dorie Combs, "Using Alternative Assessment to Provide Options for Student Success," *Middle School Journal,* September 1997, Figure 1, p. 5. Reprinted with permission from National Middle School Association. **Figure 16.8:** From G. Solano-Flores and R. J. Shavelson, "Development of Performance Assessments in Science," *Educational Measurement,* September 1997, Figure 1, p. 17. Reprinted by permission of the National Council on Measurement in Education. **Figure 16.9:** From Heidi Goodrich, "Understanding Rubrics," *Educational Leadership,* Vol. 54, No. 4 (1997), Figure 1. Reprinted by permission of the author. **Figure 16.10:** From Heidi Goodrich, "Understanding Rubrics," *Educational Leadership,* Vol. 54, No. 4 (1997), Figure 3. Reprinted by per-mission of the author. **Figure 16.11:** From Nancy Jean Johnson and Leonie Marie Rose, *Portfolios.* Lanham, MD: Rowman & Littlefield Education, 1997. Reprinted by permission of the publisher.

PHOTOS

Chapter 1

Opener: © LWA-Dann Tardif/CORBIS; **p. 3** (top): © Brown Brothers; **p. 5** (middle): Columbia University Archives, Columbia University in the City of New York; **p. 3** (bottom): Archives of the History of American Psychology-The University of Akron; **p. 4** (left): Prints and Photographs Collection CN10383, Center for American History, University of Texas at Austin.; **p. 4** (middle): Courtesy of Kenneth Clark; **p. 4** (right): © Archives of the History of American Psychology, University of Akron; **p. 7:** © Ariel Skelley/CORBIS; **p. 9** (left): © PunchStock; **p. 9** (right): © Ariel Skelley/CORBIS; **p. 11** (top): Courtesy Donald L. Mccoy, Program Manager, IBM Multicultural People in Technology; **p. 11** (bottom): © LWA-JDC/CORBIS; **p. 14:** © Alan Marler; **p. 17:** Courtesy of Steven and Cindi Binder; **p. 20:** © Gabe Palmer/CORBIS

Chapter 2

Opener: © Jose Luis Pelaez/CORBIS; 2.1 (Infancy): John Santrock; 2.1 (Early childhood): © Joe Sohm/The Image Works; 2.1 (Middle childhood): © CORBIS website; 2.1 (Adolescence): © James L. Shaffer; 2.1 (Early adulthood): © Vol. 155/CORBIS; **p. 31** (left): © David Young-Wolff/Photo Edit; **p. 31** (right): © Jose Luis Pelaez/-CORBIS; 2.6: © A. Glaubman/Photo Researchers; **p. 45** (top): © David Young-Wolff/Photo Edit; **p. 45** (bottom): © Stewart Cohen/Stone/Getty Images; **p. 47** (top): © Archives Jean Piaget, Universite De Geneve, Switzerland; **p. 47** (bottom): © M & E Bernheim/Woodfin Camp; **p. 48:** © Billy Calzada; 2.14: © Elizabeth Crews/The Image Works; **p. 51:** © 2005, USA Today. Reprinted with permission; 2.15 (left): A.R. Lauria/Dr. Michael Cole, Laboratory of Human Cognition, University of California, San Diego; 2.15 (right): © 1999 Yves deBraine/Black Star; **p. 57:** © Anne Rippy/The Image Bank/Getty Images; **p. 61:** Reading Rainbo © GPN/University of Nebraska

Chapter 3

Opener: © SuperStock; **p. 71:** Courtesy of Urie Bronfenbrenner; **p. 75:** © Sarah Putnam/Index Stock; **p. 77:** © Michael Newman//Photo Edit; **p. 80:** © Michael Newman/Photo Edit; **p. 84:** © Elizabeth Crews; **p. 85:** © Eric Anderson/Stock Boston; **p. 91:** © Ronnie Kaufman/The Stock Market/CORBIS; **p. 94:** Courtesy of "I Have a Dream", Houston, TX; **p. 100:** © USA Today Library, photo by Robert Deutsch; **p. 103:**; **p. 104:** © Keith Carter; **p. 106:** © Anthony Verde Photography

Chapter 4

Opener: © Will Hart/Photo Edit; **p. 118:** Courtesy of Robert Sternberg; **p. 120:** © Jay Gardner, 1998; **p. 121:** © Joe McNally

Chapter 5

Opener: © David Young-Wolff/Stone/Getty Images; **p. 145:** © Charles Gupton/CORBIS; **p. 149:** © Lonnie Harp; **p. 150:** © 2004, USA Today. Reprinted with permission; **p. 152:** "Bookjacket", from THE SHAME OF THE NATION by Jonathan Kozol, copyright © 2005 by Jonathan Kozol. Used by permission of Crown Publishers, a division of Random House, Inc.; **p. 153:** © Elizabeth Crews; **p. 160:** © Ellis Herwig/Stock Boston; **p. 161:** Courtesy Rod Chlysta, Research Center for Educational Technology, Kent State University; **p. 162:** © John S. Abbott; **p. 167:** © O'Brien Productions/CORBIS; **p. 174:** © Jim Cummins/CORBIS; **p. 176:** © Judy Logan

Chapter 6

Opener: © Tony Freeman/Photo Edit; **p. 190:** © Spencer Tirey; **p. 191:** © David Young-Wolff/Photo Edit; **p. 193:** © Jill Cannefax/EKM Nepenthe; **p. 195:** Courtesy of Angie Erickson; **p. 201** (left): © PunchStock; **p. 201** (right): © LWA-Dann Tardif/CORBIS; **p. 206:** © Richard Hutchings/Photo Researchers; **p. 213** (left): Bob Daemmrich/Stock Boston; **p. 213** (right): Used by permission of Don Johnston Inc.; **p. 215:** © Koichi Kamoshida/Newsmakers/Getty Images

Chapter 7

Opener: © Tony Freeman/Photo Edit; **p. 229:** © Sovfoto; 7.3: © Elizabeth Crews; **p. 232:** Nina Leen, Life Magazine. © Time, Inc.; 7.4 (top): © Bob Daemmrich/Stock Boston; 7.4 (middle): © Michael Newman/Photo Edit; 7.4 (bottom): © David Young-Wolff/Photo Edit; **p. 240:** © B. Daemmrich/The Image Works; **p. 243:** Courtesy of Albert Bandura; 7.8 (top & bottom): Courtesy of Albert Bandura; 7.9: © Jeffry W. Myers/Corbis; **p. 247:** © Irwin Thompson/The Dallas Morning News; **p. 249:** © 2000 Sesame Workshop. Photograph by Richard Termine.

Chapter 8

Opener: © Photophile/Tom Tracy; **p. 265:** © LWA-JDC/CORBIS; **p. 267:** © Michael Prince/CORBIS; **p. 269:** © Paul Conklin/Photo Edit; **p. 281:** © David Butow/CORBIS/SABA; **p. 285:** © Gill Ross/CORBIS; **p. 286:** Color Day Productions/The Image Bank/Getty Images; **p. 289:** © Yellow Dog Productions/The Image Bank/Getty Images; **p. 293:** © Royalty-Free/CORBIS

Chapter 9

Opener: © Ellen Senis/The Image Works; **p. 309:** © Elizabeth Crews; **p. 310** (left & right): Courtesy Rod Chlysta, Research Center for Educational Technology, Kent State University; **p. 311:** © Copyright 1999, USA TODAY. Reprinted with permission; **p. 314:** © Aristide Economopoulos/Star Ledger/CORBIS; **p. 316:** © Francisco Cruz/SuperStock; **p. 321:** © Gabe Palmer/CORBIS; 9.4 (top & bottom): © Cognition & Technology Group, LTC, Peabody College, Vanderbilt University; **p. 329:** USA TODAY. Copyright © December 30, 2003. Reprinted with permission

Chapter 10

Opener: Courtesy of Compton-Drew Investigative Learning Center Middle School, St. Louis, MO; **p. 337:** © Spencer Grant/Photo Edit; **p. 340:** © David Young-Wolff/Photo Edit; **p. 341:** Courtesy Robert Slavin, Success For All; **p. 343:** Courtesy of Coca-Cola Valued Youth Program; **p. 344:** © S.E. McKee/AP/Wide World; **p. 350:** © Tony Freeman/Photo Edit; **p. 351:** © Todd Hampton Lillard; **p. 355:** Courtesy of Joe Campione, University of Berkeley, School of Education.; **p. 357:** Courtesy of Compton-Drew Investigative Learning Center Middle School, St. Louis, MO; **p. 358:** Copyright © 1993 OC Program, Salt Lake City

Chapter 11

Opener: © David Young-Wolff/Photo Edit; **p. 367** (left): © Tom & Dee Ann McCarthy/CORBIS; **p. 367** (right): © Gabe Palmer/CORBIS; **p. 372:** © Michael Keller/CORBIS; **p. 381:** © Jim Graham; **p. 385:** © Paul S. Howell; **p. 387:** © Andrew Itkoff; **p. 390:** © Dale Sparks; **p. 391:** Courtesy of The Middle Grades Life Science Project, Program in Human Biology, Stanford University; **p. 392:** © Patty Wood; **p. 397:** © Teacher's Curriculum Institute

Chapter 12

Opener: © SuperStock; **p. 412:** © John Henley/CORBIS; **p. 415:** © Robert Isaacs/Photo Researchers; **p. 418:** © Bob Daemmrich/The Image Works; **p. 421:** © Anna Palma; **p. 424:** © 2004, USA Today. Reprinted with permission; **p. 426:** © William Hart/Photo Edit; **p. 430:** © Tom & Dee Ann McCarthy/CORBIS; **p. 431** (left): © Stan Godlewski Photography; **p. 431** (right): © Sherry Brown; **p. 433:** Courtesy Rod Chlysta, Research Center for Educational Technology, Kent State University; **p. 440:** © Ariel Skelley/CORBIS

Chapter 13

Opener: © Cleve Bryant/Photo Edit; **p. 450:** © Michael Tweed/AP/Wide World Photos; **p. 451:** © Oliver Hoslet/CORBIS; 13.1 (family): ©

Lawrence Migdale; 13.1 (crossing): © David Young-Wolff/Stone/Getty Images; 13.1 (teens): © Tessa Codrington/Stone/Getty Images; 13.1 (mirror): © Rhoda Sidney; 13.1 (flute): © Lonnie Duka/Stone/Getty Images; **p. 455:** © Elizabeth Crews/The Image Works; **p. 456:** © Michael A. Schwarz Photography, Inc.; **p. 457:** Courtesy Rod Chlysta, Research Center for Educational Technology, Kent State University; **p. 458:** © M. Antman/The Image Works; **p. 469:** © Bill Stanton; **p. 470:** © Michael Keller/CORBIS; **p. 472:** Courtesy of Sandra Graham; **p. 473:** © Joan Marcus

Chapter 14

Opener: © Todd Pearson/CORBIS; **p. 490:** © Michael A. Schwarz Photography, Inc.; **p. 491** (left): ©

PunchStock; **p. 491** (right): © Royalty-Free/CORBIS; 14.1 (top left): © Spencer Grant/Photo Edit; 14.1 (bot left): © David Young-Wolff/Photo Edit; 14.1 (top right): © Elizabeth Crews; 14.1 (bot right): © Rick Raymond/Stone/Getty Images; **p. 500:** © Royalty-Free/CORBIS; **p. 502:** © O'Brien Productions/CORBIS; **p. 505:** © LWA-Dann Tardif/zefa/CORBIS; **p. 509:** © Gabe Palmer/CORBIS; **p. 510:** © Tommie Lindsey; **p. 511:** © Tom Stewart/CORBIS; **p. 512** (left): © Royalty-Free/CORBIS; **p. 512** (right): © Gabe Palmer/CORBIS; **p. 522:** Courtesy of Department of Teaching and Learning, Peabody College, Vanderbilt University

Chapter 15

Opener: © Bill Aron/Photo Edit; **p. 532:** © Bob Daemmrich/The Image Works; **p. 542:** Photos courtesy Martha McArthur, Reading First Program, NM; **p. 544:** © Charles Gupton/Stone/Getty Images; **p. 559:** © Will & Deni McIntyre/CORBIS

Chapter 16

Opener: © David Young-Wolff/Photo Edit; **p. 568:** © First Light/CORBIS; **p. 573:** © Will & Deni McIntyre/CORBIS; **p. 596:** © Gabe Palmer/CORBIS; **p. 600:** © Asymetric ToolBook II Assistant by Asymetric Learning Systems

Name Index

A

Abbott, R.D., 62, 369
Abbott-Shim, M., 91
Abra, K., 70, 378
Abrami, P.C., 550
Abruscato, J., 390
Academic Software, 212
Achenbach, T.M., 200
Adams, A., 287, 304
Adams, R., 85, 498
Aeby, V.G., 81
Aiken, L.R., 116, 537, 552
Aikens, N.L., 71, 78, 79, 147, 148, 149,
    151, 152
Ainsworth, L.B., 568
Airasian, P., 430, 532, 538, 548, 554,
    555, 568, 569, 586, 590, 593,
    595, 597
Alberti, R.E., 8, 508, 509
Alberto, P.A., 194, 200, 206, 235, 237,
    238, 239, 411
Alderman, M.K., 466
Aldridge, J., 157
Alexander, K.L., 470
Alexander, P.A., 251, 254, 286
Alibali, M.W., 52, 265, 295, 321, 383
All Kinds of Minds, 254
Allan, K., 279
Allor, J.H., 343
Alvermann, D.E., 369
Alverno College, 510
Amabile, T., 314, 315, 317
Amabile, T.M., 317, 454
Amanti, C., 158
American Association for the
    Advancement of Science, 393
American Association of University
    Women, 175
American Association on Mental
    Retardation, 193
American Educational Research
    Association, 533
Anastasi, A., 118, 128
Anderman, E., 464
Anderman, E.M., 7, 452, 461, 462,
    464, 468
Anderman, L.H., 7, 452, 462
Anderson, D.R., 267
Anderson, J., 57, 264
Anderson, J.R., 320
Anderson, L., 91, 153
Anderson, L.M., 504
Anderson, L.W., 413
Anderson, N., 197, 198
Anderson, R.C., 373

Andrews, R.K., 85
Andriessen, J., 309
Anguiano, R.P.V., 81
Ansari, D., 37
Anti-Bias Curriculum Task Force,
    160, 176
Antonaci, P.A.P., 371
Apple Computer, 441, 442, 457
Applebome, P., 543
Arends, R.I., 408
Argys, L.M., 130
Arievitch, I.M., 47, 50
Ariza, E.N.W., 155
Arlin, M., 494
Armony, J.L., 36
Armstrong, L., 451
Arndt, J., 98
Arnoux, D., 154
Aro, H., 78
Aronson, E.E., 159, 346, 351
Aronson, J.A., 128
Arrasmith, D., 94
Arter, J., 590
Arterberry, M.E., 46
Ashcraft, M.H., 274
Asher, S.R., 86, 470
Ashton, M.C., 135
Ashwal, S., 195
Askew, S., 583
Assouline, S.G., 216, 217
Astington, J.W., 292
Ateah, C.A., 241
Atkinson, J.W., 466
Atkinson, R.C., 275, 276
August, P., 14
Austin, C.C., 464
Ausubel, D.P., 416
Ayres, L., 268, 596
Azevedo, R., 433, 437

B

Bachnan, H.J., 126
Baddeley, A., 273, 274, 275
Badia, P., 16
Baer, J., 316
Baer, W., 148
Bafumo, M.E., 316
Bailey, B.N., 195
Bain, R.B., 398, 431
Baker, J., 453
Baltes, P.B., 31
Bandura, A., 227, 243–245, 254, 457,
    462, 463, 464, 472, 479
Bangert, K., 417

Bangert-Drowns, R.L., 417
Banks, J., 152, 157
Banks, J.A., 3, 9, 129, 130, 145, 151,
    153, 157, 158, 163, 174
Banks, S.A., 148, 583, 585
Banta, T.W., 583
Baratz-Snowden, J., 545
Barbaresi, W.J., 191
Barber, B.L., 85
Barden, J.P., 583
Barker, E.T., 97
Barnes, H., 149
Barnett, R.C., 85
Baron-Cohen, S., 200
Baroody, A.J., 337
Barrish, H.H., 522
Barron, K.E., 321
Barry, C.M., 86
Barry, M.J., 50
Barsalou, L.W., 303
Bartlett, E.J., 377
Bartlett, J., 275, 276
Bartlett, L., 27, 357
Barton, H.A., 520
Barton, J., 589
Bates, J.E., 137
Battistich, V., 490, 504
Battle, A., 85
Bauer, P.J., 47
Baumeister, R.F., 98
Baumrind, D., 76, 241, 500
Baumwell, L., 57
Beal, C., 394, 439
Bear, G.G., 490
Beatty, B., 3
Beauvais, L.L., 340
Beck, I.L., 285
Becker, J.R., 417
Beckham, E.E., 201
Beckmann, S.C., 320
Bednar, R.L., 99
Beghetto, R.A., 316
Begley, S., 420
Behnke, R.R., 347
Beins, B., 16
Beirne-Smith, M., 195
Bell, L.A., 474
Bell, N., 338
Bem, J.S., 171
Bennett, C.I., 8, 157
Bennett, W., 105
Benson, J.B., 45
Benson, P.L., 28, 106, 108
Benveniste, L., 148
Ben-Zeev, T., 288, 289
Beran, T.N., 518

Bereiter, C., 10, 316, 321, 322, 324,
    356, 434
Berenbaum, S.A., 167, 168, 169, 170,
    171, 172, 174, 175
Berenfeld, B., 161
Berg, B.L., 18
Bergemann, V.E., 21
Berk, L.E., 50
Berko, J., 59
Berko Gleason, J., 55, 57, 60, 61,
    63, 198
Berliner, D., 3
Berliner, D.C., 284
Berndt, T.J., 86, 469
Berninger, V.W., 7, 62, 186, 187, 188,
    368, 369, 538
Berry, B., 531
Berry, J.W., 145
Berry, L., 247
Berry, R., 340
Berryman, L., 591
Berson, M.J., 10, 434
Best, D., 172
Best, J.W., 19, 549
Best, S.J., 195
Betch, T., 312
Betti, U., 97
Bialystok, E., 153
Bickford, L., 263
Biddle, B., 498
Biederman, J., 191
Bigelow, B., 559
Bigge, J.L., 195
Bigler, R.S., 167
Biklin, S.K., 20
Billingsley, M., 434, 437
Binder, B., 17
Binet, A., 115–116
Biological Sciences Curriculum
    Study, 390
Birch, S.A.J., 313
Birney, D.P., 114, 125
Bitter, G.G., 10, 433, 598
Bjorklund, D.F., 30, 47, 265, 281, 292,
    295, 322, 371
Blachman, B.A., 188
Black, P., 568
Black, S., 309
Blackhurst, A.E., 212
Blackorby, J., 186
Blair, T.R., 371
Blakemore, J.E.O., 168
Blakemore, S.J., 35
Blankenship, K., 189
Blasi, A., 104
Blasingame, J., 376

Herrera, S.G., 155
Herrmann, A., 320
Herrnstein, R.J., 125
Hertzog, N.B., 216
Herzog, E., 87, 166, 217
Hesirci, D., 316
Hetherington, E.M., 78, 79
Hetzroni, O.E., 213
Heward, W.L., 205, 206, 235
Hewitt, P.L., 477
Hiatt-Michael, D., 81
Hickey, D.T., 323
Hicks, L., 464
Hiebert, E.H., 58, 60, 371, 372,
    378, 384
Hiebert, J., 415
Higgins, A., 106
Hightower, E., 85
Hildebrand, V., 91
Hilden, K., 4, 265, 286, 293, 294, 295,
    322, 370, 371, 465
Hilgard, E.R., 4
Hill, J.R., 441, 442, 457
Hilton, M.L., 389, 390
Hiltz, S.R., 434, 443
Hines, R.P., 91
Hirsch, E.D., 162, 430
Hirschstein, M., 517
Hirsh, R., 123
Hirst, B., 344
Hitch, G.H., 274
Hitler, A., 311
Hock, R.R., 175
Hocutt, A.M., 186, 207
Hodapp, R.M., 192, 194
Hofer, B.K., 145, 415
Hoff, E., 57, 79
Hoffner, H., 433
Holdnack, J.A., 186
Hollingsworth, L., 3, 4
Holmes, Z., 247
Holzberg, C., 213
Honey, M., 441, 442
Honig, A.S., 107
Hooper, S., 349
Hoover-Dempsey, K.V., 421
Horn, C., 376
Horn, J., 125
Horn, S., 251, 254, 381
Horowitz, F.D., 7, 32, 42, 47, 49, 50,
    98, 337
Hounsell, D.J., 133
Houston, P.D., 542
Howard, M.R., 197, 198
Howard-Jones, P., 37
Howe, M.J.A., 215
Howes, C., 85
Hoyt, J., 292
Huber, F., 320
Hudley, C., 521
Huerta, M., 175
Hui, C.H., 146
Hulit, L.M., 197, 198
Hull, S.H., 169, 174
Hunt, E., 289
Hunt, E.B., 125
Hunt, R.R., 271

Hupert, N., 542
Hurlburt, R.T., 549
Hurtado, S., 166
Huston, M., 80
Hutchinson, J.M., 313
Huttenlocher, J., 34
Huttenlocher, P.R., 34
Huurre, T., 78
Huxley, A., 114
Hyatt, G., 94
Hyde, J.S., 75, 104, 168, 171, 281
Hyman, I., 240, 241, 517, 519
Hyson, M., 6, 32, 47, 51
Hyson, M.C., 337

I

"I Have a Dream" Foundation, 94
Iacocca, L., 406
Ialongo, N., 522
IBM, 11
Ickes, W., 135
Idol, L., 212
Indiana University High School Survey
    of Student Engagement, 95
Inhelder, B., 40
Inkrott, C., 599
Intercultural Development Research
    Association, 343
International Society for Technology
    in Education, 10, 11, 435, 436
Irvine, J.J., 158
Iyengar, S.S., 452, 454

J

Jabbour, R.A., 36
Jacklin, C.N., 169
Jackson, A.W., 93
Jackson, D., 133
Jackson, J.F., 152
Jackson, S.L., 549
Jacobs, H.H., 428
Jacobs, J., 314
Jacobson, L., 91, 544
Jaffee, S., 104
Jalongo, M.R., 597
James, A., 79
James, W., 2–3, 6, 45
Jenkins, J., 344
Jenkins, J.M., 292
Jenkins, L., 344
Jennings, K.D., 461
Jensen, A.R., 125
Jensen, M.M., 201
Jeynes, W.H., 81
Johnson, C.A., 122
Johnson, D.L., 435, 439, 457, 600
Johnson, D.M., 464
Johnson, D.W., 337, 345, 346, 349,
    521, 523
Johnson, J.S., 153
Johnson, M.K., 107
Johnson, R.T., 337, 345, 346, 349,
    521, 523

Johnson, V.R., 83
Johnson, W., 125
Johnson-Laird, P., 307
John-Steiner, V., 49, 51
Johnston, J.H., 10
Jolley, J.M., 19
Jonassen, D.H., 133, 310, 437
Jones, B.F., 322, 427, 428, 434
Jones, J., 6, 32, 51, 151, 337
Jones, K., 538
Jones, L., 490
Jones, M.G., 417
Jones, V., 490
Jordan, M.L., 6
Joyce, B., 416
Judge, S., 440
Juel, C., 370
Junkkari, H., 78
Justice, L.M., 197
Juvonen, J., 518

K

Kabler, P., 600
Kafai, Y.B., 6
Kagan, J., 31, 133, 136–137, 191,
    349, 350
Kagan, S.L., 91
Kagiticibasi, C., 145
Kahn, J.V., 19, 549
Kahneman, D., 313
Kail, R., 265, 322
Kalchman, M., 385
Kalil, A., 85
Kamhi, A.G., 373
Kamil, M.L., 58, 60
Kaminski, R.A., 542
Kammrath, L.K., 136
Kane, M.J., 274
Kang, J.Y., 57, 62, 154, 155,
    368, 369
Kantrowitz, L., 186
Kaplan, R.M., 555
Karcher, M.J., 341
Karr, M.M., 235
Kasprow, W.J., 521
Katz, J., 307
Katz, L., 91, 92
Kauffman, J.M., 7, 8, 186, 197, 200,
    201, 205, 207, 208, 212, 241, 490
Kauffman, P., 316
Kauffman, W.N., 365
Kaufman, A.S., 93, 537
Kaufman, J.C., 316
Kaufman, P., 121, 315
Kaufmann, L., 187
Kavale, K.A., 186
Kay, A., 441
Kazdin, A.E., 241
Keating, C.F., 170
Keating, D.P., 35, 47, 268, 292,
    309, 314
Keenan, K., 200
Keil, F., 264, 283
Keller, B., 545
Keller, H., 31

Kellogg, R.T., 376, 377
Kelly, J., 78, 79
Kelly, R.E.S., 271
Kempler, T., 254
Kempler, T.M., 7, 8, 345, 347, 455, 459,
    471, 504
Kendall, J.S., 538
Kennedy, J., 157
Keogh, B.K., 137
Kidd, K.K., 125
Kiess, H.O., 549
Kim, S.H., 195
Kinchin, I.M., 304
Kinderman, T.A., 470
King, M.L., Jr., 157
King, P.E., 347
Kinginger, C., 49
Kirby, D., 520
Kirk, E.P., 274
Kirton, J., 72, 83
Kite, M., 167
Kivel, P., 163
Klaczynski, P., 314
Klaczynski, P.A., 309
Klahr, D., 283, 345
Klausmeier, H.J., 302
Klein, A., 383
Klein, K., 274
Klenowski, V., 583
Kling, K.C., 97
Knecht, S., 36
Knotek, S., 557, 588, 589
Koballa, T.R., 389, 390
Koch, E.J., 313
Kochenderfer-Ladd, B., 517
Koedinger, K.R., 434
Koestner, R., 454, 458
Kohlberg, L., 102, 103, 104, 106
Kohn, A., 458
Konidaris, G.D., 320
Kontos, S., 89
Kornhaber, M., 122, 123
Korniaris, A., 2
Koschmann, T., 433
Kotler, J., 249
Kounin, J.S., 492, 494, 500
Kovach, R., 251, 255, 466
Kozol, J., 148, 149, 152
Kozulin, A., 337
Krahn, H.J., 97
Krajcek, J.S., 504
Krajcik, J.S., 7, 8, 254, 323, 324, 340,
    345, 347, 455, 459, 471
Krampe, R.T., 216, 288
Krantz, P.J., 499
Kratcoski, A., 495
Krathwohl, D., 4
Krathwohl, D.R., 412, 413
Kraus, P., 393, 429
Krechevsky, M., 120
Kress, J.S., 4
Kreutzer, L.C., 291
Kroger, J., 75, 98
Krogh, S.L., 88
Kubick, R.J., 541, 542
Kuhn, D., 35, 47, 264, 265, 291, 292,
    293, 307, 308, 312, 314, 321, 322

Subject Index

Performance assessments, 574, 583
    developing scoring rubrics, 588
    evaluating, 587–588
    features of, 584–586
    guidelines, 586–587
Performance criteria, 586
Performance orientation, 461–462
Permissive classroom management
    style, 500
Persistence, 321
Personality, 135–136
Person-environment fit, 459
Person-situation interaction, 135–136
Perspective taking, 160
Phonological awareness
    blending, 369
    segmentation, 370
Phonological loop, 274
Phonology, 55, 368. See also language;
    reading
Physical disorders, 195
    cerebral palsy, 195
    orthopedic impairments, 195
    seizure disorders, 196
Piaget's Theory, 37
    animism, 40
    applying to children's education, 48
    assimilation and accommodation,
        37–38
    centration, 41
    compared to Vygotsky's Theory, 53
    concrete operational stage, 42–44
    conservation, 41–42
    contributions, 45–46
    criticisms, 46–47
    egocentrism, 40, 45
    equilibration, 38
    formal operational stage, 44–45, 46
    hypothetical-deductive reasoning,
        44–45
    intuitive thought substage, 40–41
    and moral development, 102
    neo-Piagetians, 47
    operations, 42
    organization, 38
    preoperational stage, 39–42, 43
    schemes, 37
    sensorimotor stage, 38–39
    seriation, 43
    symbolic function substage, 39–40
    transitivity, 43–44
Planning
    behavioral objectives, 410–411
    instructional, 406–407
    instructional taxonomies, 411–414
    learner-centered lesson planning,
        423–432
    mapping backward, 407
    and motivation, 464–465
    task analysis, 411
    teacher-centered lesson planning,
        410–414
    time frames and, 407–409
    using standardized test scores to
        plan instruction, 555–556
Plasticity, 34, 36–37
Plato EduTest Assessment, 602

Pluralistic assessments, 572–573
Portfolio assessments, 588–591
    artifacts, 589
    attestations, 589
    best-work portfolios, 590
    growth portfolios, 590
    productions, 589
    reproductions, 589
    vs. traditional testing, 589
Positive environment for learning
    authoritarian classroom
        management style, 500
    authoritative classroom
        management style, 500
    Child Development Project
        (CDP), 504
    getting students to cooperate,
        503–506
    permissive classroom management
        style, 500
    rules and procedures, 500–503
    withitness, 501
Positive reinforcement, 232–233
Postconventional reasoning, 103
Postinstruction assessment, 569. See
    also classroom assessment
Poverty, 147–150
Practice, 288–289
Pragmatics, 56. See also language
PRAXIS tests, 544–545
Preconventional reasoning, 103
Predictive validity, 534
Preinstruction assessment, 567–569.
    See also classroom assessment
Prejudice, 152. See also ethnicity
    reduction, 157
Premack principle, 235–236
Principals, enlisting help from
    regarding problem
    behaviors, 516
Private speech, 50
Problem behaviors. See also aggression
    bullying, 517–519
    Classroom Organization
        Management Program
        (COMP), 522
    conflict resolution, 523
    defiance or hostility toward the
        teacher, 519–520
    enlisting help from principals and
        counselors, 516
    fighting, 517
    finding a mentor, 517
    Good Behavior Game, 522
    Improving Social Awareness-Social
        Problem Solving Project, 520
    minor interventions, 515
    moderate interventions, 515–516
    parent-teacher conferences, 516
    peer mediation, 516
    Skills for Life, 522
    social competence enhancement
        programs, 520–522
    Social Competence Program for
        Young Adolescents, 520
    Three C's of School and Classroom
        Management, 521–522

Problem sets, 580
Problem solving
    algorithms, 320
    defined, 319
    developmental changes, 321–322
    improving students' problem
        solving, 324
    means-end analysis, 320
    obstacles to, 321
    rule-assessment approach,
        321–322
    steps, 319–321
    subgoaling, 319–320
    and writing, 377
Problem-based learning, 322–323,
    427–428
Procedural memory, 276
Procedures and rules,
    500–503
Procrastination, 476, 477
    helping students conquer, 478
Program evaluation research, 20
Programmed learning, 4
Progress reports, 595
Project Spectrum, 120–121
Project STAR, 390
Project-based learning, 323–324
Prompts, 237–238, 505–506
Prosocial behavior
    and gender, 170
    improving, 107
Prototype matching, 305
Psychoanalytic theory of gender,
    165–166
Public Law 94-142, 205
Punishment, 232–233,
    240–241

Q

Quantum Opportunities Program,
    149
Questioning, 416–417, 418–419
    essential questions, 428–429
Questionnaires, 17
Quid pro quo sexual harassment, 175

R

Race. See ethnicity
Random assignment, 19
Range, 550
Rapport talk, 169
Reaction-time tasks, 265
Reading
    book clubs, 373
    cognitive processes in, 367
    constructing meaning, 371
    decoding and comprehending
        words, 370–371
    developmental model of, 368
    and metacognition, 370–371
    morphology, 368
    phonics approach, 369–370

phonology, 368
    reciprocal teaching, 372–373
    school/family/community
        connections, 373–374
    semantics, 369
    syntax, 369
    transactional strategy instruction
        approach, 371–372
    whole language approach, 369
Reasoning
    analogies, 307–308
    critical thinking, 308–309
    decision making, 309–312
    deductive, 308
    defined, 307
    inductive, 307–308
    multiplicative reasoning, 383
Recall, 279. See also memory
Receptive language, 198, 199
Reciprocal Peer Tutoring (RPT), 343
Reciprocal teaching, 354, 372–373
Recognition, 279. See also memory
Record keeping, 600
Referral bias, 186. See also learning
    disabilities
Rehearsal, 270
Reinforcement, 232–233, 235–237. See
    also negative reinforcement
    differential reinforcement, 238–239
    schedules of, 236–237
    terminating, 239–240
Reinforcers, 505
Relational aggression, 170
Reliability
    of classroom assessments, 572
    of standardized tests, 534–535
Report cards, 595
Report talk, 169
Representativeness heuristic,
    313–314
Research
    action, 20
    case studies, 17–18
    correlational, 18
    descriptive, 16
    ethnographic studies, 18
    experimental, 18–19
    importance of, 15–16
    interviews and questionnaires, 17
    methods, 16–19
    observation, 16–17
    program evaluation, 20
    standardized tests, 17
    teacher-as-researcher, 20, 21
Research Center for Educational
    Technology (RCET), 161
Response cost, 240
Response-to-intervention, 186
Responsibility, getting students to
    share and assume, 504, 505
Rewards, 504, 506
Role models
    adults as, 354
    male and minority, 247
Rule-assessment approach,
    321–322
Rules and procedures, 500–503

S

S-BIP online, 602
Scaffolding, 49–50, 339–340
Schedules of reinforcement, 236–237
Schemas, 277
Schemes, 37
Schools
  changing social contexts, 88
  collaborative, 357–358
  and communities, 11, 162
  developmentally appropriate
    education, 88–91
  early childhood education, 88–92
  effective schools for young
    adolescents, 93
  and ethnicity, 151–152
  family-school linkages, 80–82
  improving high schools, 93–95
  school-family-community
    connections, 81–82, 83–84
  transition to elementary schools, 92
  transition to middle or junior high
    schools, 92–93
Schools for Thought (SFT), 355–357
Schoolwide Enrichment Model
  (SEM), 217
Science education, 389
  constructivist teaching strategies,
    390–393
  Fostering a Community of Learners
    (FCL), 391
  Human Biology Middle Grades
    Curriculum (HumBio),
    391–392
  Project STAR, 390
  science content, 393
  social contexts of science, 391
  strategies for teaching, 392
Scripts, 278
Seatwork, 417, 419, 420
Segmentation, 370
Seizure disorders, 196. See also
  learning disabilities; physical
  disorders
Selective attention, 267
Self, the, 97–102
Self-actualization, 452
Self-determination, 454–455
Self-efficacy, 244, 254, 462–464
Self-esteem, 97–98
  improving, 99
Self-handicapping strategies, 476–477
Self-instructional methods, 250
Self-modification, 265
Self-monitoring, 464–465
Self-regulatory learning, 250–255
Self-responsibility, 456
Semantic memory, 277
Semantic organization tools, 310
Semantics, 56, 369. See also language;
  reading
Sensory disorders
  hearing impairments, 197
  visual impairments, 196
Sensory memory, 273

Serial position effect, 278
Seriation, 43
Service learning, 106–108
Sesame Street, 249
Sexism, 168. See also gender
Sexual harassment, 175. See also
  gender
Shaping, 238, 505–506
Short-answer items, 581
Short-term memory, 273–275
Silence, 512–513. See also
  communication skills
Situated cognition, 338
Skills for Life, 522
Slow-to-warm-up child, 136
Small-group work. See group
  interaction
Social cognitive approach to learning,
  227, 228, 255
  Bandura's social cognitive theory,
    243–244
Social cognitive theory, 243–244
Social cognitive theory of gender, 166
Social Competence Program for Young
  Adolescents, 520
Social constructivist approach, 50, 227,
  228. See also Piaget's Theory;
  Vygotsky's Theory
  in the broader constructivist
    context, 336–338
  cognitive apprenticeship, 340
  collaborative school, 357–358
  Computer-Supported Intentional
    Learning Environments
    (CSILE), 356
  cooperative learning, 345–347
  Fostering a Community of Learners
    (FCL), 354–355
  to reading, 372–374
  scaffolding, 339–340
  Schools for Thought (SFT),
    355–357
  situated cognition, 338
  small-group work, 349–351
  teachers and peers as joint
    contributors to learning,
    339–347
  tutoring, 340–344
  to writing, 378–379
Social contexts of development
  families, 76–85
  peers, 85–88
  schools, 88–95
Social development, 521
Social motives, 468–469. See also
  motivation
Social relationships. See also
  motivation
  with parents, 469–470
  with peers, 470
  with teachers, 470–472
Social skills, strategies for
  improving, 87
Social studies
  constructivist approaches, 397–398
  defined, 394–397
Sociocultural contexts, 472–474

Sociocultural diversity, and
  technology, 438–440
Socioeconomic status, 147
  educating students from low-SES
    backgrounds, 147–150
  and motivation, 472–474
  poverty in America, 147
Socioeconomic variations in families,
  79–80
Socioemotional development
  Bronfenbrenner's ecological theory,
    71–72
  Erikson's life-span development
    theory, 72–75
  moral development, 102–108
  the self, 97–102
Socioemotional processes, 28
Software
  electronic portfolio, 599–600
  electronic portfolios, 601
Space, 512. See also communication
  skills
Speaking skills, 507–510
Special education, 184–185. See also
  learning disabilities
  disproportionate representation of
    minorities in, 208
  individualized education plans
    (IEPs), 205, 209
  Individuals with Disabilities
    Education Act (IDEA),
    205–206
  interactive teaming, 212
  Least Restrictive Environment
    (LRE), 206–208
  legal aspects, 205–208
  parents as educational partners, 212
  placements, 208
  Public Law 94-142, 205
  services, 210–212
  technology, 212–213
Specific language impairment (SLI),
  198–199
Speech and language disorders, 197
  articulation disorders, 197–198
  fluency disorders, 198
  language disorders, 198
  specific language impairment (SLI),
    198–199
  voice disorders, 198
Speeches, 509–510
Splintered development, 32
Split-half reliability, 535
Standard deviation, 550–552
Standardized tests, 17
  achievement tests, 537–538
  administering, 548
  alternative assessments, 557–559
  aptitude tests, 537
  bimodal distribution, 550
  communicating test results to
    parents, 555
  defined, 532
  descriptive statistics, 549
  diagnostic tests, 537–538
  district-mandated tests, 540–541
  and diversity, 559

  and ethnic minority groups, 558
  evaluating, 533–535
  fairness and bias, 535
  frequency distributions, 549
  grade-equivalent scores, 553
  high-stakes testing, 533, 538–540,
    557–559
  histograms, 549
  improving students' test-taking
    skills, 548
  interpreting test scores, 552–555
  mean, 550
  measures of central tendency, 550
  measures of variability, 550–552
  median, 550
  mode, 550
  multimodal distribution, 550
  No Child Left Behind, 541–544
  normal distribution, 552
  norms, 533
  percentile-rank scores, 552–553
  PRAXIS tests, 544–545
  preparing students to take, 547–548
  purposes of, 532–533
  range, 550
  raw score, 552
  reliability, 534–535
  for specific subjects, 537
  standard deviation, 550–552
  standard scores, 553–554
  standards-based tests, 533
  stanine scores, 553
  state standards-based tests, 538–540
  survey batteries, 537
  of teacher candidates, 544–545
  and technology, 542
  test results, 549–555
  T-scores, 554
  using to plan and improve
    instruction, 555–556
  validity, 533–534
  z-scores, 553
Standards-based instruction, 10. See
  also No Child Left Behind
  (NCLB) legislation
  standards-based tests, 533
  state standards-based tests, 538–540
Stanford-Binet tests, 115–116
State standards-based tests, 538–540
Statuses, 85–86
Stereotypes, gender, 167–168
Sternberg Triarchic Abilities Test
  (STAT), 119
Storage
  declarative memory, 276
  episodic memory, 277
  fuzzy trace theory, 278
  long-term memory, 275
  model of memory stores, 275–276
  network theories, 277
  procedural memory, 276
  schema theories, 277–278
  semantic memory, 277
  sensory memory, 273
  short-term memory, 273–275
Strategy construction, 265
Student response systems, 495